THE ART OF
COMPUTER PROGRAMMING

SECOND EDITION

DONALD E. KNUTH *Stanford University*

▲
▼▼ ADDISON–WESLEY
An Imprint of Addison Wesley Longman, Inc.

Volume 3 / **Sorting and Searching**

THE ART OF
COMPUTER PROGRAMMING

SECOND EDITION

Reading, Massachusetts · Harlow, England · Menlo Park, California
Berkeley, California · Don Mills, Ontario · Sydney
Bonn · Amsterdam · Tokyo · Mexico City

TEX is a trademark of the American Mathematical Society

METAFONT is a trademark of Addison–Wesley

Library of Congress Cataloging-in-Publication Data

Knuth, Donald Ervin, 1938-
   The art of computer programming / Donald Ervin Knuth. -- 2nd ed.
   xiv,780 p. 24 cm.
   Includes bibliographical references and index.
   Contents: v. 1. Fundamental algorithms. -- v. 2. Seminumerical
algorithms. -- v. 3. Sorting and Searching.
   ISBN 0-201-03809-9 (v. 1)
   ISBN 0-201-03822-6 (v. 2)
   ISBN 0-201-89685-0 (v. 3)
   1. Electronic digital computers--Programming. I. Title.
QA76.6.K64 1997   001.6'42   73-1830
                                         CIP

Internet page `http://www-cs-faculty.stanford.edu/~knuth/taocp.html` contains current information about this book and related books.

Copyright © 1998 by Addison Wesley Longman

ISBN 0-201-89685-0
Text printed on acid-free paper
1 2 3 4 5 6 7 8 9 MA 0201009998
First printing, March 1998

PREFACE

THIS BOOK forms a natural sequel to the material on information structures in Chapter 2 of Volume 1, because it adds the concept of linearly ordered data to the other basic structural ideas.

The title "Sorting and Searching" may sound as if this book is only for those systems programmers who are concerned with the preparation of general-purpose sorting routines or applications to information retrieval. But in fact the area of sorting and searching provides an ideal framework for discussing a wide variety of important general issues:

- How are good algorithms discovered?
- How can given algorithms and programs be improved?
- How can the efficiency of algorithms be analyzed mathematically?
- How can a person choose rationally between different algorithms for the same task?
- In what senses can algorithms be proved "best possible"?
- How does the theory of computing interact with practical considerations?
- How can external memories like tapes, drums, or disks be used efficiently with large databases?

Indeed, I believe that virtually *every* important aspect of programming arises somewhere in the context of sorting or searching!

This volume comprises Chapters 5 and 6 of the complete series. Chapter 5 is concerned with sorting into order; this is a large subject that has been divided chiefly into two parts, internal sorting and external sorting. There also are supplementary sections, which develop auxiliary theories about permutations (Section 5.1) and about optimum techniques for sorting (Section 5.3). Chapter 6 deals with the problem of searching for specified items in tables or files; this is subdivided into methods that search sequentially, or by comparison of keys, or by digital properties, or by hashing, and then the more difficult problem of secondary key retrieval is considered. There is a surprising amount of interplay between both chapters, with strong analogies tying the topics together. Two important varieties of information structures are also discussed, in addition to those considered in Chapter 2, namely priority queues (Section 5.2.3) and linear lists represented as balanced trees (Section 6.2.3).

Like Volumes 1 and 2, this book includes a lot of material that does not appear in other publications. Many people have kindly written to me about their ideas, or spoken to me about them, and I hope that I have not distorted the material too badly when I have presented it in my own words.

I have not had time to search the patent literature systematically; indeed, I decry the current tendency to seek patents on algorithms (see Section 5.4.5). If somebody sends me a copy of a relevant patent not presently cited in this book, I will dutifully refer to it in future editions. However, I want to encourage people to continue the centuries-old mathematical tradition of putting newly discovered algorithms into the public domain. There are better ways to earn a living than to prevent other people from making use of one's contributions to computer science.

Before I retired from teaching, I used this book as a text for a student's second course in data structures, at the junior-to-graduate level, omitting most of the mathematical material. I also used the mathematical portions of this book as the basis for graduate-level courses in the analysis of algorithms, emphasizing especially Sections 5.1, 5.2.2, 6.3, and 6.4. A graduate-level course on concrete computational complexity could also be based on Sections 5.3, and 5.4.4, together with Sections 4.3.3, 4.6.3, and 4.6.4 of Volume 2.

For the most part this book is self-contained, except for occasional discussions relating to the MIX computer explained in Volume 1. Appendix B contains a summary of the mathematical notations used, some of which are a little different from those found in traditional mathematics books.

Preface to the Second Edition

This new edition matches the third editions of Volumes 1 and 2, in which I have been able to celebrate the completion of TEX and METAFONT by applying those systems to the publications they were designed for.

The conversion to electronic format has given me the opportunity to go over every word of the text and every punctuation mark. I've tried to retain the youthful exuberance of my original sentences while perhaps adding some more mature judgment. Dozens of new exercises have been added; dozens of old exercises have been given new and improved answers. Changes appear everywhere, but most significantly in Sections 5.1.4 (about permutations and tableaux), 5.3 (about optimum sorting), 5.4.9 (about disk sorting), 6.2.2 (about entropy), 6.4 (about universal hashing), and 6.5 (about multidimensional trees and tries).

The Art of Computer Programming is, however, still a work in progress. Research on sorting and searching continues to grow at a phenomenal rate. Therefore some parts of this book are headed by an "under construction" icon, to apologize for the fact that the material is not up-to-date. For example, if I were teaching an undergraduate class on data structures today, I would surely discuss randomized structures such as treaps at some length; but at present, I am only able to cite the principal papers on the subject, and to announce plans for a future Section 6.2.5 (see page 478). My files are bursting with important material that I plan to include in the final, glorious, third edition of Volume 3, perhaps 17 years from now. But I must finish Volumes 4 and 5 first, and I do not want to delay their publication any more than absolutely necessary.

I am enormously grateful to the many hundreds of people who have helped me to gather and refine this material during the past 35 years. Most of the hard work of preparing the new edition was accomplished by Phyllis Winkler (who put the text of the first edition into TEX form), by Silvio Levy (who edited it extensively and helped to prepare several dozen illustrations), and by Jeffrey Oldham (who converted more than 250 of the original illustrations to METAPOST format). The production staff at Addison–Wesley has also been extremely helpful, as usual.

I have corrected every error that alert readers detected in the first edition — as well as some mistakes that, alas, nobody noticed — and I have tried to avoid introducing new errors in the new material. However, I suppose some defects still remain, and I want to fix them as soon as possible. Therefore I will cheerfully pay $2.56 to the first finder of each technical, typographical, or historical error. The webpage cited on page iv contains a current listing of all corrections that have been reported to me.

Stanford, California   D. E. K.
February 1998

> There are certain common Privileges of a Writer,
> the Benefit whereof, I hope, there will be no Reason to doubt;
> Particularly, that where I am not understood, it shall be concluded,
> that something very useful and profound is coucht underneath.
> — JONATHAN SWIFT, *Tale of a Tub*, Preface (1704)

NOTES ON THE EXERCISES

THE EXERCISES in this set of books have been designed for self-study as well as classroom study. It is difficult, if not impossible, for anyone to learn a subject purely by reading about it, without applying the information to specific problems and thereby being encouraged to think about what has been read. Furthermore, we all learn best the things that we have discovered for ourselves. Therefore the exercises form a major part of this work; a definite attempt has been made to keep them as informative as possible and to select problems that are enjoyable as well as instructive.

In many books, easy exercises are found mixed randomly among extremely difficult ones. This is sometimes unfortunate because readers like to know in advance how long a problem ought to take — otherwise they may just skip over all the problems. A classic example of such a situation is the book *Dynamic Programming* by Richard Bellman; this is an important, pioneering work in which a group of problems is collected together at the end of some chapters under the heading "Exercises and Research Problems," with extremely trivial questions appearing in the midst of deep, unsolved problems. It is rumored that someone once asked Dr. Bellman how to tell the exercises apart from the research problems, and he replied, "If you can solve it, it is an exercise; otherwise it's a research problem."

Good arguments can be made for including both research problems and very easy exercises in a book of this kind; therefore, to save the reader from the possible dilemma of determining which are which, *rating numbers* have been provided to indicate the level of difficulty. These numbers have the following general significance:

Rating   Interpretation

00 An extremely easy exercise that can be answered immediately if the material of the text has been understood; such an exercise can almost always be worked "in your head."

10 A simple problem that makes you think over the material just read, but is by no means difficult. You should be able to do this in one minute at most; pencil and paper may be useful in obtaining the solution.

20 An average problem that tests basic understanding of the text material, but you may need about fifteen or twenty minutes to answer it completely.

    30 A problem of moderate difficulty and/or complexity; this one may involve more than two hours' work to solve satisfactorily, or even more if the TV is on.

    40 Quite a difficult or lengthy problem that would be suitable for a term project in classroom situations. A student should be able to solve the problem in a reasonable amount of time, but the solution is not trivial.

    50 A research problem that has not yet been solved satisfactorily, as far as the author knew at the time of writing, although many people have tried. If you have found an answer to such a problem, you ought to write it up for publication; furthermore, the author of this book would appreciate hearing about the solution as soon as possible (provided that it is correct).

By interpolation in this "logarithmic" scale, the significance of other rating numbers becomes clear. For example, a rating of *17* would indicate an exercise that is a bit simpler than average. Problems with a rating of *50* that are subsequently solved by some reader may appear with a *45* rating in later editions of the book, and in the errata posted on the Internet (see page iv).

The remainder of the rating number divided by 5 indicates the amount of detailed work required. Thus, an exercise rated *24* may take longer to solve than an exercise that is rated *25*, but the latter will require more creativity.

The author has tried earnestly to assign accurate rating numbers, but it is difficult for the person who makes up a problem to know just how formidable it will be for someone else to find a solution; and everyone has more aptitude for certain types of problems than for others. It is hoped that the rating numbers represent a good guess at the level of difficulty, but they should be taken as general guidelines, not as absolute indicators.

This book has been written for readers with varying degrees of mathematical training and sophistication; as a result, some of the exercises are intended only for the use of more mathematically inclined readers. The rating is preceded by an *M* if the exercise involves mathematical concepts or motivation to a greater extent than necessary for someone who is primarily interested only in programming the algorithms themselves. An exercise is marked with the letters "*HM*" if its solution necessarily involves a knowledge of calculus or other higher mathematics not developed in this book. An "*HM*" designation does *not* necessarily imply difficulty.

Some exercises are preceded by an arrowhead, "▶"; this designates problems that are especially instructive and especially recommended. Of course, no reader/student is expected to work *all* of the exercises, so those that seem to be the most valuable have been singled out. (This is not meant to detract from the other exercises!) Each reader should at least make an attempt to solve all of the problems whose rating is *10* or less; and the arrows may help to indicate which of the problems with a higher rating should be given priority.

Solutions to most of the exercises appear in the answer section. Please use them wisely; do not turn to the answer until you have made a genuine effort to solve the problem by yourself, or unless you absolutely do not have time to work this particular problem. *After* getting your own solution or giving the problem a decent try, you may find the answer instructive and helpful. The solution given will often be quite short, and it will sketch the details under the assumption that you have earnestly tried to solve it by your own means first. Sometimes the solution gives less information than was asked; often it gives more. It is quite possible that you may have a better answer than the one published here, or you may have found an error in the published solution; in such a case, the author will be pleased to know the details. Later editions of this book will give the improved solutions together with the solver's name where appropriate.

When working an exercise you may generally use the answers to previous exercises, unless specifically forbidden from doing so. The rating numbers have been assigned with this in mind; thus it is possible for exercise $n + 1$ to have a lower rating than exercise n, even though it includes the result of exercise n as a special case.

Summary of codes:		*00*	Immediate
		10	Simple (one minute)
		20	Medium (quarter hour)
▸	Recommended	*30*	Moderately hard
M	Mathematically oriented	*40*	Term project
HM	Requiring "higher math"	*50*	Research problem

EXERCISES

▸ **1.** [*00*] What does the rating "*M20*" mean?

2. [*10*] Of what value can the exercises in a textbook be to the reader?

3. [*HM45*] Prove that when n is an integer, $n > 2$, the equation $x^n + y^n = z^n$ has no solution in positive integers x, y, z.

> *Two hours' daily exercise ... will be enough*
> *to keep a hack fit for his work.*
> — M. H. MAHON, *The Handy Horse Book* (1865)

CONTENTS

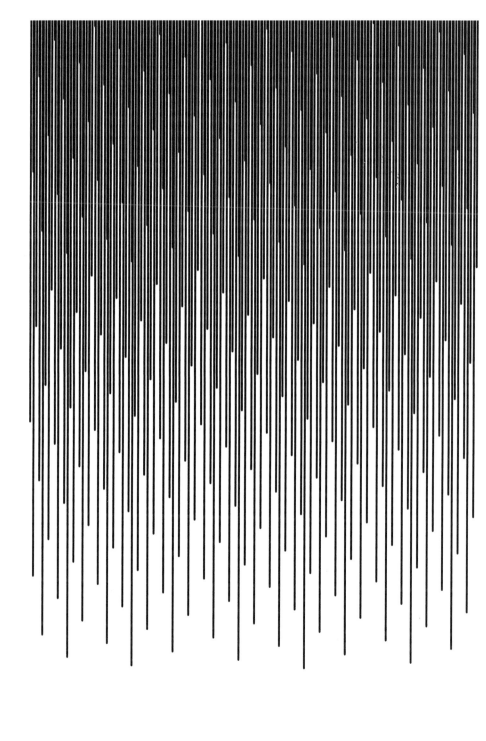

CHAPTER FIVE

SORTING

> *There is nothing more difficult to take in hand,*
> *more perilous to conduct, or more uncertain in its success,*
> *than to take the lead in the introduction of*
> *a new order of things.*
> — NICCOLÒ MACHIAVELLI, *The Prince* (1951)

> *"But you can't look up all those license*
> *numbers in time," Drake objected.*
> *"We don't have to, Paul. We merely arrange a list*
> *and look for duplications."*
> — PERRY MASON, in *The Case of the Angry Mourner* (1951)

> *"Treesort" Computer — With this new 'computer-approach'*
> *to nature study you can quickly identify over 260*
> *different trees of U.S., Alaska, and Canada,*
> *even palms, desert trees, and other exotics.*
> *To sort, you simply insert the needle.*
> — Catalog of Edmund Scientific Company (1964)

IN THIS CHAPTER we shall study a topic that arises frequently in programming: the rearrangement of items into ascending or descending order. Imagine how hard it would be to use a dictionary if its words were not alphabetized! We will see that, in a similar way, the order in which items are stored in computer memory often has a profound influence on the speed and simplicity of algorithms that manipulate those items.

Although dictionaries of the English language define "sorting" as the process of separating or arranging things according to class or kind, computer programmers traditionally use the word in the much more special sense of marshaling things into ascending or descending order. The process should perhaps be called *ordering*, not sorting; but anyone who tries to call it "ordering" is soon led into confusion because of the many different meanings attached to that word. Consider the following sentence, for example: "Since only two of our tape drives were in working order, I was ordered to order more tape units in short order, in order to order the data several orders of magnitude faster." Mathematical terminology abounds with still more senses of order (the order of a group, the order of a permutation, the order of a branch point, relations of order, etc., etc.). Thus we find that the word "order" can lead to chaos.

Some people have suggested that "sequencing" would be the best name for the process of sorting into order; but this word often seems to lack the right

1

connotation, especially when equal elements are present, and it occasionally conflicts with other terminology. It is quite true that "sorting" is itself an overused word ("I was sort of out of sorts after sorting that sort of data"), but it has become firmly established in computing parlance. Therefore we shall use the word "sorting" chiefly in the strict sense of sorting into order, without further apologies.

Some of the most important applications of sorting are:

a) *Solving the "togetherness" problem*, in which all items with the same identi- fication are brought together. Suppose that we have 10000 items in arbitrary order, many of which have equal values; and suppose that we want to rearrange the data so that all items with equal values appear in consecutive positions. This is essentially the problem of sorting in the older sense of the word; and it can be solved easily by sorting the file in the new sense of the word, so that the values are in ascending order, $v_1 \leq v_2 \leq \cdots \leq v_{10000}$. The efficiency achievable in this procedure explains why the original meaning of "sorting" has changed.

b) *Matching items in two or more files.* If several files have been sorted into the same order, it is possible to find all of the matching entries in one sequential pass through them, without backing up. This is the principle that Perry Mason used to help solve a murder case (see the quotation at the beginning of this chapter). We can usually process a list of information most quickly by traversing it in sequence from beginning to end, instead of skipping around at random in the list, unless the entire list is small enough to fit in a high-speed random-access memory. Sorting makes it possible to use sequential accessing on large files, as a feasible substitute for direct addressing.

c) *Searching for information by key values.* Sorting is also an aid to searching, as we shall see in Chapter 6, hence it helps us make computer output more suitable for human consumption. In fact, a listing that has been sorted into alphabetic order often looks quite authoritative even when the associated nu- merical information has been incorrectly computed.

Although sorting has traditionally been used mostly for business data pro- cessing, it is actually a basic tool that every programmer should keep in mind for use in a wide variety of situations. We have discussed its use for simplify- ing algebraic formulas, in exercise 2.3.2–17. The exercises below illustrate the diversity of typical applications.

One of the first large-scale software systems to demonstrate the versatility of sorting was the LARC Scientific Compiler developed by J. Erdwinn, D. E. Ferguson, and their associates at Computer Sciences Corporation in 1960. This optimizing compiler for an extended FORTRAN language made heavy use of sorting so that the various compilation algorithms were presented with relevant parts of the source program in a convenient sequence. The first pass was a lexical scan that divided the FORTRAN source code into individual tokens, each representing an identifier or a constant or an operator, etc. Each token was assigned several sequence numbers; when sorted on the name and an appropriate sequence number, all the uses of a given identifier were brought together. The "defining entries" by which a user would specify whether an identifier stood for a function name, a parameter, or a dimensioned variable were given low sequence numbers, so that they would appear first among the tokens having a given identifier; this made it easy to check for conflicting usage and to allocate storage with respect to `EQUIVALENCE` declarations. The information thus gathered about each identifier was now attached to each token; in this way no "symbol table" of identifiers needed to be maintained in the high-speed memory. The updated tokens were then sorted on another sequence number, which essentially brought the source program back into its original order except that the numbering scheme was cleverly designed to put arithmetic expressions into a more convenient "Polish prefix" form. Sorting was also used in later phases of compilation, to facilitate loop optimization, to merge error messages into the listing, etc. In short, the compiler was designed so that virtually all the processing could be done sequentially from files that were stored in an auxiliary drum memory, since appropriate sequence numbers were attached to the data in such a way that it could be sorted into various convenient arrangements.

Computer manufacturers of the 1960s estimated that more than 25 percent of the running time on their computers was spent on sorting, when all their customers were taken into account. In fact, there were many installations in which the task of sorting was responsible for more than half of the computing time. From these statistics we may conclude that either (i) there are many important applications of sorting, or (ii) many people sort when they shouldn't, or (iii) inefficient sorting algorithms have been in common use. The real truth probably involves all three of these possibilities, but in any event we can see that sorting is worthy of serious study, as a practical matter.

Even if sorting were almost useless, there would be plenty of rewarding reasons for studying it anyway! The ingenious algorithms that have been discovered show that sorting is an extremely interesting topic to explore in its own right. Many fascinating unsolved problems remain in this area, as well as quite a few solved ones.

From a broader perspective we will find also that sorting algorithms make a valuable *case study* of how to attack computer programming problems in general. Many important principles of data structure manipulation will be illustrated in this chapter. We will be examining the evolution of various sorting techniques in an attempt to indicate how the ideas were discovered in the first place. By extrapolating this case study we can learn a good deal about strategies that help us design good algorithms for other computer problems.

Sorting techniques also provide excellent illustrations of the general ideas involved in the *analysis of algorithms*—the ideas used to determine performance characteristics of algorithms so that an intelligent choice can be made between competing methods. Readers who are mathematically inclined will find quite a few instructive techniques in this chapter for estimating the speed of computer algorithms and for solving complicated recurrence relations. On the other hand, the material has been arranged so that readers without a mathematical bent can safely skip over these calculations.

Before going on, we ought to define our problem a little more clearly, and introduce some terminology. We are given N items

$$R_1, R_2, \ldots, R_N$$

to be sorted; we shall call them *records*, and the entire collection of N records will be called a *file*. Each record R_j has a *key*, K_j, which governs the sorting process. Additional data, besides the key, is usually also present; this extra "satellite information" has no effect on sorting except that it must be carried along as part of each record.

An ordering relation "$<$" is specified on the keys so that the following conditions are satisfied for any key values a, b, c:

i) Exactly one of the possibilities $a < b$, $a = b$, $b < a$ is true. (This is called the law of trichotomy.)

ii) If $a < b$ and $b < c$, then $a < c$. (This is the familiar law of transitivity.)

Properties (i) and (ii) characterize the mathematical concept of *linear ordering*, also called *total ordering*. Any relationship "$<$" satisfying these two properties can be sorted by most of the methods to be mentioned in this chapter, although some sorting techniques are designed to work only with numerical or alphabetic keys that have the usual ordering.

The goal of sorting is to determine a permutation $p(1)\, p(2) \ldots p(N)$ of the indices $\{1, 2, \ldots, N\}$ that will put the keys into nondecreasing order:

$$K_{p(1)} \leq K_{p(2)} \leq \cdots \leq K_{p(N)}. \tag{1}$$

The sorting is called *stable* if we make the further requirement that records with equal keys should retain their original relative order. In other words, stable sorting has the additional property that

$$p(i) < p(j) \qquad \text{whenever} \quad K_{p(i)} = K_{p(j)} \quad \text{and} \quad i < j. \tag{2}$$

In some cases we will want the records to be physically rearranged in storage so that their keys are in order. But in other cases it will be sufficient merely to have an auxiliary table that specifies the permutation in some way, so that the records can be accessed in order of their keys.

A few of the sorting methods in this chapter assume the existence of either or both of the values "∞" and "$-\infty$", which are defined to be greater than or less than all keys, respectively:

$$-\infty < K_j < \infty, \qquad \text{for } 1 \leq j \leq N. \tag{3}$$

Such extreme values are occasionally used as artificial keys or as sentinel indicators. The case of equality is excluded in (3); if equality can occur, the algorithms can be modified so that they will still work, but usually at the expense of some elegance and efficiency.

Sorting can be classified generally into *internal sorting*, in which the records are kept entirely in the computer's high-speed random-access memory, and *external sorting*, when more records are present than can be held comfortably in memory at once. Internal sorting allows more flexibility in the structuring and accessing of the data, while external sorting shows us how to live with rather stringent accessing constraints.

The time required to sort N records, using a decent general-purpose sorting algorithm, is roughly proportional to $N \log N$; we make about $\log N$ "passes" over the data. This is the minimum possible time, as we shall see in Section 5.3.1, if the records are in random order and if sorting is done by pairwise comparisons of keys. Thus if we double the number of records, it will take a little more than twice as long to sort them, all other things being equal. (Actually, as N approaches infinity, a better indication of the time needed to sort is $N(\log N)^2$, if the keys are distinct, since the size of the keys must grow at least as fast as $\log N$; but for practical purposes, N never really approaches infinity.)

On the other hand, if the keys are known to be randomly distributed with respect to some continuous numerical distribution, we will see that sorting can be accomplished in $O(N)$ steps on the average.

EXERCISES — First Set

1. [M20] Prove, from the laws of trichotomy and transitivity, that the permutation $p(1)\,p(2)\dots p(N)$ is *uniquely* determined when the sorting is assumed to be stable.

2. [21] Assume that each record R_j in a certain file contains *two* keys, a "major key" K_j and a "minor key" k_j, with a linear ordering $<$ defined on each of the sets of keys. Then we can define *lexicographic order* between pairs of keys (K, k) in the usual way:

$$(K_i, k_i) < (K_j, k_j) \quad \text{if} \quad K_i < K_j \quad \text{or if} \quad K_i = K_j \quad \text{and} \quad k_i < k_j.$$

Alice took this file and sorted it first on the major keys, obtaining n groups of records with equal major keys in each group,

$$K_{p(1)} = \cdots = K_{p(i_1)} < K_{p(i_1+1)} = \cdots = K_{p(i_2)} < \cdots < K_{p(i_{n-1}+1)} = \cdots = K_{p(i_n)},$$

where $i_n = N$. Then she sorted each of the n groups $R_{p(i_{j-1}+1)}, \dots, R_{p(i_j)}$ on their minor keys.

Bill took the same original file and sorted it first on the minor keys; then he took the resulting file, and sorted it on the major keys.

Chris took the same original file and did a single sorting operation on it, using lexicographic order on the major and minor keys (K_j, k_j).

Did everyone obtain the same result?

3. [M25] Let $<$ be a relation on $K_1, \dots, K_N$ that satisfies the law of trichotomy but *not* the transitive law. Prove that even without the transitive law it is possible to sort the records in a stable manner, meeting conditions (1) and (2); in fact, there are at least three arrangements that satisfy the conditions!

▶ **4.** [21] Lexicographers don't actually use strict lexicographic order in dictionaries, because uppercase and lowercase letters must be interfiled. Thus they want an ordering such as this:

$$\text{a} < \text{A} < \text{aa} < \text{AA} < \text{AAA} < \text{Aachen} < \text{aah} < \cdots < \text{zzz} < \text{ZZZ}.$$

Explain how to implement dictionary order.

▶ **5.** [*M28*] Design a binary code for all nonnegative integers so that if n is encoded as the string $\rho(n)$ we have $m < n$ if and only if $\rho(m)$ is lexicographically less than $\rho(n)$. Moreover, $\rho(m)$ should not be a prefix of $\rho(n)$ for any $m \neq n$. If possible, the length of $\rho(n)$ should be at most $\lg n + O(\log \log n)$ for all large n. (Such a code is useful if we want to sort texts that mix words and numbers, or if we want to map arbitrarily large alphabets into binary strings.)

6. [*15*] Mr. B. C. Dull (a MIX programmer) wanted to know if the number stored in location A is greater than, less than, or equal to the number stored in location B. So he wrote "LDA A; SUB B" and tested whether register A was positive, negative, or zero. What serious mistake did he make, and what should he have done instead?

7. [*17*] Write a MIX subroutine for multiprecision comparison of keys, having the following specifications:

Calling sequence: JMP COMPARE

Entry conditions: rI1 $= n$; CONTENTS$(A+k) = a_k$ and CONTENTS$(B+k) = b_k$, for $1 \leq k \leq n$; assume that $n \geq 1$.

Exit conditions: CI = GREATER, if $(a_n, \ldots, a_1) > (b_n, \ldots, b_1)$;
                      CI = EQUAL,   if $(a_n, \ldots, a_1) = (b_n, \ldots, b_1)$;
                      CI = LESS,   if $(a_n, \ldots, a_1) < (b_n, \ldots, b_1)$;
                      rX and rI1 are possibly affected.

Here the relation $(a_n, \ldots, a_1) < (b_n, \ldots, b_1)$ denotes lexicographic ordering from left to right; that is, there is an index j such that $a_k = b_k$ for $n \geq k > j$, but $a_j < b_j$.

▶ **8.** [*30*] Locations A and B contain two numbers a and b, respectively. Show that it is possible to write a MIX program that computes and stores $\min(a, b)$ in location C, *without using any jump operators*. (Caution: Since you will not be able to test whether or not arithmetic overflow has occurred, it is wise to guarantee that overflow is impossible regardless of the values of a and b.)

9. [*M27*] After n independent, uniformly distributed random variables between 0 and 1 have been sorted into nondecreasing order, what is the probability that the rth smallest of these numbers is $\leq x$?

EXERCISES — Second Set

Each of the following exercises states a problem that a computer programmer might have had to solve in the old days when computers didn't have much random-access memory. Suggest a "good" way to solve the problem, *assuming that only a few thousand words of internal memory are available*, supplemented by about half a dozen tape units (enough tape units for sorting). Algorithms that work well under such limitations also prove to be efficient on modern machines.

10. [*15*] You are given a tape containing one million words of data. How do you determine how many distinct words are present on the tape?

11. [*18*] You are the U. S. Internal Revenue Service; you receive millions of "information" forms from organizations telling how much income they have paid to people, and millions of "tax" forms from people telling how much income they have been paid. How do you catch people who don't report all of their income?

12. [*M25*] (*Transposing a matrix.*) You are given a magnetic tape containing one million words, representing the elements of a 1000×1000 matrix stored in order by rows: $a_{1,1} \, a_{1,2} \ldots a_{1,1000} \, a_{2,1} \ldots a_{2,1000} \ldots a_{1000,1000}$. How do you create a tape in which the elements are stored by columns $a_{1,1} a_{2,1} \ldots a_{1000,1} a_{1,2} \ldots a_{1000,2} \ldots a_{1000,1000}$ instead? (Try to make at most ten passes over the data.)

13. [*M26*] How could you "shuffle" a large file of N words into a random rearrangement?

14. [*20*] You are working with two computer systems that have different conventions for the "collating sequence" that defines the ordering of alphameric characters. How do you make one computer sort alphameric files in the order used by the other computer?

15. [*18*] You are given a list of the names of a fairly large number of people born in the U.S.A., together with the name of the state where they were born. How do you count the number of people born in each state? (Assume that nobody appears in the list more than once.)

16. [*20*] In order to make it easier to make changes to large FORTRAN programs, you want to design a "cross-reference" routine; such a routine takes FORTRAN programs as input and prints them together with an index that shows each use of each identifier (that is, each name) in the program. How should such a routine be designed?

▶ **17.** [*33*] (*Library card sorting.*) Before the days of computerized databases, every library maintained a catalog of cards so that users could find the books they wanted. But the task of putting catalog cards into an order convenient for human use turned out to be quite complicated as library collections grew. The following "alphabetical" listing indicates many of the procedures recommended in the *American Library Association Rules for Filing Catalog Cards* (Chicago: 1942):

Text of card	*Remarks*
R. Accademia nazionale dei Lincei, Rome	Ignore foreign royalty (except British)
1812; ein historischer Roman.	Achtzehnhundert zwölf
Bibliothèque d'histoire révolutionnaire.	Treat apostrophe as space in French
Bibliothèque des curiosités.	Ignore accents on letters
Brown, Mrs. J. Crosby	Ignore designation of rank
Brown, John	Names with dates follow those without
Brown, John, mathematician	... and the latter are subarranged
Brown, John, of Boston	by descriptive words
Brown, John, 1715–1766	Arrange identical names by birthdate
BROWN, JOHN, 1715–1766	Works "about" follow works "by"
Brown, John, d. 1811	Sometimes birthdate must be estimated
Brown, Dr. John, 1810–1882	Ignore designation of rank
Brown-Williams, Reginald Makepeace	Treat hyphen as space
Brown America.	Book titles follow compound names
Brown & Dallison's Nevada directory.	& in English becomes "and"
Brownjohn, Alan	
Den', Vladimir Éduardovich, 1867–	Ignore apostrophe in names
The den.	Ignore an initial article
Den lieben süssen Mädeln.	... provided it's in nominative case
Dix, Morgan, 1827–1908	Names precede words
1812 ouverture.	Dix-huit cent douze
Le XIXe siècle français.	Dix-neuvième
The 1847 issue of U. S. stamps.	Eighteen forty-seven
1812 overture.	Eighteen twelve
I am a mathematician.	(a book by Norbert Wiener)

Text of card	*Remarks*
IBM journal of research and development.	Initials are like one-letter words
ha-I ha-ehad.	Ignore initial article
Ia; a love story.	Ignore punctuation in titles
International Business Machines Corporation	
al-Khuwārizmī, Muḥammad ibn Mūsā,	
fl. 813–846	Ignore initial "al-" in Arabic names
Labour. A magazine for all workers.	Respell it "Labor"
Labor research association	
Labour, *see* Labor	Cross-reference card
McCall's cookbook	Ignore apostrophe in English
McCarthy, John, 1927–	Mc = Mac
Machine-independent computer	
programming.	Treat hyphen as space
MacMahon, Maj. Percy Alexander,	
1854–1929	Ignore designation of rank
Mrs. Dalloway.	"Mrs." = "Mistress"
Mistress of mistresses.	
Royal society of London	Don't ignore British royalty
St. Petersburger Zeitung.	"St." = "Saint", even in German
Saint-Saëns, Camille, 1835–1921	Treat hyphen as space
Ste-Marie, Gaston P	Sainte
Seminumerical algorithms.	(a book by Donald Ervin Knuth)
Uncle Tom's cabin.	(a book by Harriet Beecher Stowe)
U. S. bureau of the census.	"U. S." = "United States"
Vandermonde, Alexandre Théophile,	
1735–1796	
Van Valkenburg, Mac Elwyn, 1921–	Ignore space after prefix in surnames
Von Neumann, John, 1903–1957	
The whole art of legerdemain.	Ignore initial article
Who's afraid of Virginia Woolf?	Ignore apostrophe in English
Wijngaarden, Adriaan van, 1916–	Surname begins with upper case letter

(Most of these rules are subject to certain exceptions, and there are many other rules not illustrated here.)

   If you were given the job of sorting large quantities of catalog cards by computer, and eventually maintaining a very large file of such cards, and if you had no chance to change these long-standing policies of card filing, how would you arrange the data in such a way that the sorting and merging operations are facilitated?

18. [*M25*] (E. T. Parker.) Leonhard Euler once conjectured [*Nova Acta Acad. Sci. Petropolitanæ* **13** (1795), 45–63, §3; written in 1778] that there are no solutions to the equation

$$u^6 + v^6 + w^6 + x^6 + y^6 = z^6$$

in positive integers u, v, w, x, y, z. At the same time he conjectured that

$$x_1^n + \cdots + x_{n-1}^n = x_n^n$$

would have no positive integer solutions, for all $n \geq 3$, but this more general conjecture was disproved by the computer-discovered identity $27^5 + 84^5 + 110^5 + 133^5 = 144^5$; see L. J. Lander, T. R. Parkin, and J. L. Selfridge, *Math. Comp.* **21** (1967), 446–459.

Infinitely many counterexamples when $n = 4$ were subsequently found by Noam Elkies [*Math. Comp.* **51** (1988), 825–835]. Can you think of a way in which sorting would help in the search for counterexamples to Euler's conjecture when $n = 6$?

▶ **19.** [*24*] Given a file containing a million or so distinct 30-bit binary words $x_1, \ldots, x_N$, what is a good way to find all *complementary* pairs $\{x_i, x_j\}$ that are present? (Two words are complementary when one has 0 wherever the other has 1, and conversely; thus they are complementary if and only if their sum is $(11\ldots1)_2$, when they are treated as binary numbers.)

▶ **20.** [*25*] Given a file containing 1000 30-bit words $x_1, \ldots, x_{1000}$, how would you prepare a list of all pairs (x_i, x_j) such that $x_i = x_j$ except in at most two bit positions?

21. [*22*] How would you go about looking for five-letter anagrams such as CARET, CARTE, CATER, CRATE, REACT, RECTA, TRACE; CRUEL, LUCRE, ULCER; DOWRY, ROWDY, WORDY? [One might wish to know whether there are any sets of ten or more five-letter English anagrams besides the remarkable set

APERS, ASPER, PARES, PARSE, PEARS, PRASE, PRESA, RAPES, REAPS, SPAER, SPARE, SPEAR,

to which we might add the French word APRÈS.]

22. [*M28*] Given the specifications of a fairly large number of directed graphs, what approach will be useful for grouping the *isomorphic* ones together? (Directed graphs are isomorphic if there is a one-to-one correspondence between their vertices and a one-to-one correspondence between their arcs, where the correspondences preserve incidence between vertices and arcs.)

23. [*30*] In a certain group of 4096 people, everyone has about 100 acquaintances. A file has been prepared listing all pairs of people who are acquaintances. (The relation is symmetric: If x is acquainted with y, then y is acquainted with x. Therefore the file contains roughly 200,000 entries.) How would you design an algorithm to list all the k-person *cliques* in this group of people, given k? (A clique is an instance of mutual acquaintances: Everyone in the clique is acquainted with everyone else.) Assume that there are no cliques of size 25, so the total number of cliques cannot be enormous.

▶ **24.** [*30*] Three million men with distinct names were laid end-to-end, reaching from New York to California. Each participant was given a slip of paper on which he wrote down his own name and the name of the person immediately west of him in the line. The man at the extreme western end didn't understand what to do, so he threw his paper away; the remaining 2,999,999 slips of paper were put into a huge basket and taken to the National Archives in Washington, D.C. Here the contents of the basket were shuffled completely and transferred to magnetic tapes.

At this point an information scientist observed that there was enough information on the tapes to reconstruct the list of people in their original order. And a computer scientist discovered a way to do the reconstruction with fewer than 1000 passes through the data tapes, using only sequential accessing of tape files and a small amount of random-access memory. How was that possible?

[In other words, given the pairs (x_i, x_{i+1}), for $1 \le i < N$, in random order, where the x_i are distinct, how can the sequence $x_1 x_2 \ldots x_N$ be obtained, restricting all operations to serial techniques suitable for use with magnetic tapes? This is the problem of sorting into order when there is no easy way to tell which of two given keys precedes the other; we have already raised this question as part of exercise 2.2.3–25.]

25. [*M21*] (*Discrete logarithms.*) You know that p is a (rather large) prime number, and that a is a primitive root modulo p. Therefore, for all b in the range $1 \le b < p$, there is a unique n such that $a^n \bmod p = b$, $1 \le n < p$. (This n is called the index of b modulo p, with respect to a.) Explain how to find n, given b, without needing $\Omega(n)$ steps. [*Hint:* Let $m = \lceil \sqrt{p} \, \rceil$ and try to solve $a^{mn_1} \equiv ba^{-n_2}$ (modulo p) for $0 \le n_1, n_2 < m$.]

*5.1. COMBINATORIAL PROPERTIES OF PERMUTATIONS

A PERMUTATION of a finite set is an arrangement of its elements into a row. Permutations are of special importance in the study of sorting algorithms, since they represent the unsorted input data. In order to study the efficiency of different sorting methods, we will want to be able to count the number of permutations that cause a certain step of a sorting procedure to be executed a certain number of times.

We have, of course, met permutations frequently in previous chapters. For example, in Section 1.2.5 we discussed two basic theoretical methods of constructing the $n!$ permutations of n objects; in Section 1.3.3 we analyzed some algorithms dealing with the cycle structure and multiplicative properties of permutations; in Section 3.3.2 we studied their "runs up" and "runs down." The purpose of the present section is to study several other properties of permutations, and to consider the general case where equal elements are allowed to appear. In the course of this study we will learn a good deal about combinatorial mathematics.

The properties of permutations are sufficiently pleasing to be interesting in their own right, and it is convenient to develop them systematically in one place instead of scattering the material throughout this chapter. But readers who are not mathematically inclined and readers who are anxious to dive right into sorting techniques are advised to go on to Section 5.2 immediately, since the present section actually has little *direct* connection to sorting.

*5.1.1. Inversions

Let $a_1 a_2 \ldots a_n$ be a permutation of the set $\{1, 2, \ldots, n\}$. If $i < j$ and $a_i > a_j$, the pair (a_i, a_j) is called an *inversion* of the permutation; for example, the permutation $3\,1\,4\,2$ has three inversions: $(3,1)$, $(3,2)$, and $(4,2)$. Each inversion is a pair of elements that is out of sort, so the only permutation with no inversions is the sorted permutation $1\,2\ldots n$. This connection with sorting is the chief reason why we will be so interested in inversions, although we have already used the concept to analyze a dynamic storage allocation algorithm (see exercise 2.2.2–9).

The concept of inversions was introduced by G. Cramer in 1750 [*Intr. à l'Analyse des Lignes Courbes Algébriques* (Geneva: 1750), 657–659; see Thomas Muir, *Theory of Determinants* **1** (1906), 11–14], in connection with his famous rule for solving linear equations. In essence, Cramer defined the determinant of an $n \times n$ matrix in the following way:

$$\det \begin{pmatrix} x_{11} & x_{12} & \cdots & x_{1n} \\ \vdots & \vdots & & \vdots \\ x_{n1} & x_{n2} & \cdots & x_{nn} \end{pmatrix} = \sum (-1)^{\mathrm{inv}(a_1 a_2 \ldots a_n)} x_{1a_1} x_{2a_2} \cdots x_{na_n},$$

summed over all permutations $a_1 a_2 \ldots a_n$ of $\{1, 2, \ldots, n\}$, where $\mathrm{inv}(a_1 a_2 \ldots a_n)$ is the number of inversions of the permutation.

The *inversion table* $b_1 b_2 \ldots b_n$ of the permutation $a_1 a_2 \ldots a_n$ is obtained by letting b_j be the number of elements to the left of j that are greater than j.

In other words, b_j is the number of inversions whose second component is j. It follows, for example, that the permutation

$$5\ 9\ 1\ 8\ 2\ 6\ 4\ 7\ 3 \tag{1}$$

has the inversion table

$$2\ 3\ 6\ 4\ 0\ 2\ 2\ 1\ 0, \tag{2}$$

since 5 and 9 are to the left of 1; 5, 9, 8 are to the left of 2; etc. This permutation has 20 inversions in all. By definition the numbers b_j will always satisfy

$$0 \le b_1 \le n-1, \quad 0 \le b_2 \le n-2, \quad \ldots, \quad 0 \le b_{n-1} \le 1, \quad b_n = 0. \tag{3}$$

Perhaps the most important fact about inversions is Marshall Hall's observation that *an inversion table uniquely determines the corresponding permutation.* [See *Proc. Symp. Applied Math.* **6** (American Math. Society, 1956), 203.] We can go back from any inversion table $b_1 b_2 \ldots b_n$ satisfying (3) to the unique permutation that produces it, by successively determining the relative placement of the elements $n, n-1, \ldots, 1$ (in this order). For example, we can construct the permutation corresponding to (2) as follows: Write down the number 9; then place 8 after 9, since $b_8 = 1$. Similarly, put 7 after both 8 and 9, since $b_7 = 2$. Then 6 must follow two of the numbers already written down, because $b_6 = 2$; the partial result so far is therefore

$$9\ 8\ 6\ 7.$$

Continue by placing 5 at the left, since $b_5 = 0$; put 4 after four of the numbers; and put 3 after six numbers (namely at the extreme right), giving

$$5\ 9\ 8\ 6\ 4\ 7\ 3.$$

The insertion of 2 and 1 in an analogous way yields (1).

This correspondence is important because we can often translate a problem stated in terms of permutations into an equivalent problem stated in terms of inversion tables, and the latter problem may be easier to solve. For example, consider the simplest question of all: How many permutations of $\{1, 2, \ldots, n\}$ are possible? The answer must be the number of possible inversion tables, and they are easily enumerated since there are n choices for b_1, independently $n-1$ choices for b_2, ..., 1 choice for b_n, making $n(n-1)\ldots 1 = n!$ choices in all. Inversions are easy to count, because the b's are completely independent of each other, while the a's must be mutually distinct.

In Section 1.2.10 we analyzed the number of local maxima that occur when a permutation is read from right to left; in other words, we counted how many elements are larger than any of their successors. (The right-to-left maxima in (1), for example, are 3, 7, 8, and 9.) This is the number of j such that b_j has its maximum value, $n - j$. Since b_1 will equal $n - 1$ with probability $1/n$, and (independently) b_2 will be equal to $n - 2$ with probability $1/(n - 1)$, etc., it is clear by consideration of the inversions that the average number of right-to-left

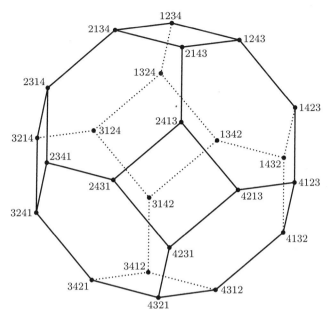

Fig. 1. The truncated octahedron, which shows the change in inversions when adjacent elements of a permutation are interchanged.

maxima is

$$\frac{1}{n} + \frac{1}{n-1} + \cdots + \frac{1}{1} = H_n.$$

The corresponding generating function is also easily derived in a similar way.

If we interchange two *adjacent* elements of a permutation, it is easy to see that the total number of inversions will increase or decrease by unity. Figure 1 shows the 24 permutations of $\{1, 2, 3, 4\}$, with lines joining permutations that differ by an interchange of adjacent elements; following any line downward inverts exactly one new pair. Hence the number of inversions of a permutation π is the length of a downward path from 1234 to π in Fig. 1; all such paths must have the same length.

Incidentally, the diagram in Fig. 1 may be viewed as a three-dimensional solid, the "truncated octahedron," which has 8 hexagonal faces and 6 square faces. This is one of the classical uniform polyhedra attributed to Archimedes (see exercise 10).

The reader should not confuse inversions of a permutation with the *inverse* of a permutation. Recall that we can write a permutation in two-line form

$$\begin{pmatrix} 1 & 2 & 3 & \ldots & n \\ a_1 & a_2 & a_3 & \ldots & a_n \end{pmatrix} ; \tag{4}$$

the inverse $a_1' \, a_2' \, a_3' \ldots a_n'$ of this permutation is the permutation obtained by interchanging the two rows and then sorting the columns into increasing order of the new top row:

$$\begin{pmatrix} a_1 & a_2 & a_3 & \dots & a_n \\ 1 & 2 & 3 & \dots & n \end{pmatrix} = \begin{pmatrix} 1 & 2 & 3 & \dots & n \\ a_1' & a_2' & a_3' & \dots & a_n' \end{pmatrix}. \tag{5}$$

For example, the inverse of 591826473 is 359716842, since

$$\begin{pmatrix} 5 \ 9 \ 1 \ 8 \ 2 \ 6 \ 4 \ 7 \ 3 \\ 1 \ 2 \ 3 \ 4 \ 5 \ 6 \ 7 \ 8 \ 9 \end{pmatrix} = \begin{pmatrix} 1 \ 2 \ 3 \ 4 \ 5 \ 6 \ 7 \ 8 \ 9 \\ 3 \ 5 \ 9 \ 7 \ 1 \ 6 \ 8 \ 4 \ 2 \end{pmatrix}.$$

Another way to define the inverse is to say that $a_j' = k$ if and only if $a_k = j$.

The inverse of a permutation was first defined by H. A. Rothe [in *Samm-lung combinatorisch-analytischer Abhandlungen*, edited by K. F. Hindenburg, **2** (Leipzig: 1800), 263–305], who noticed an interesting connection between inverses and inversions: *The inverse of a permutation has exactly as many inversions as the permutation itself.* Rothe's proof of this fact was not the simplest possible one, but it is instructive and quite pretty nevertheless. We construct an $n \times n$ chessboard having a dot in column j of row i whenever $a_i = j$. Then we put $\times$'s in all squares that have dots lying both below (in the same column) and to their right (in the same row). For example, the diagram for 591826473 is

The number of $\times$'s is the number of inversions, since it is easy to see that b_j is the number of $\times$'s in column j. Now if we transpose the diagram — interchanging rows and columns — we get the diagram corresponding to the inverse of the original permutation. Hence the number of $\times$'s (the number of inversions) is the same in both cases. Rothe used this fact to prove that the determinant of a matrix is unchanged when the matrix is transposed.

The analysis of several sorting algorithms involves the knowledge of how many permutations of n elements have exactly k inversions. Let us denote that number by $I_n(k)$; Table 1 lists the first few values of this function.

By considering the inversion table $b_1 b_2 \dots b_n$, it is obvious that $I_n(0) = 1$, $I_n(1) = n - 1$, and there is a symmetry property

$$I_n\left(\binom{n}{2} - k\right) = I_n(k). \tag{6}$$

Table 1

PERMUTATIONS WITH k INVERSIONS

n	$I_n(0)$	$I_n(1)$	$I_n(2)$	$I_n(3)$	$I_n(4)$	$I_n(5)$	$I_n(6)$	$I_n(7)$	$I_n(8)$	$I_n(9)$	$I_n(10)$	$I_n(11)$
1	1	0	0	0	0	0	0	0	0	0	0	0
2	1	1	0	0	0	0	0	0	0	0	0	0
3	1	2	2	1	0	0	0	0	0	0	0	0
4	1	3	5	6	5	3	1	0	0	0	0	0
5	1	4	9	15	20	22	20	15	9	4	1	0
6	1	5	14	29	49	71	90	101	101	90	71	49

Furthermore, since each of the b's can be chosen independently of the others, it is not difficult to see that the generating function

$$G_n(z) = I_n(0) + I_n(1)z + I_n(2)z^2 + \cdots \qquad (7)$$

satisfies $G_n(z) = (1 + z + \cdots + z^{n-1})G_{n-1}(z)$; hence it has the comparatively simple form noticed by O. Rodriguez [J. de Math. **4** (1839), 236–240]:

$$(1 + z + \cdots + z^{n-1})\ldots(1 + z)(1) = (1 - z^n)\ldots(1 - z^2)(1 - z)/(1 - z)^n. \qquad (8)$$

From this generating function, we can easily extend Table 1, and we can verify that the numbers below the zigzag line in that table satisfy

$$I_n(k) = I_n(k - 1) + I_{n-1}(k), \quad \text{for} \quad k < n. \qquad (9)$$

(This relation does *not* hold *above* the zigzag line.) A more complicated argument (see exercise 14) shows that, in fact, we have the formulas

$$I_n(2) = \binom{n}{2} - 1, \qquad\qquad n \geq 2;$$

$$I_n(3) = \binom{n+1}{3} - \binom{n}{1}, \qquad\qquad n \geq 3;$$

$$I_n(4) = \binom{n+2}{4} - \binom{n+1}{2}, \qquad\qquad n \geq 4;$$

$$I_n(5) = \binom{n+3}{5} - \binom{n+2}{3} + 1, \qquad n \geq 5;$$

in general, the formula for $I_n(k)$ contains about $1.6\sqrt{k}$ terms:

$$I_n(k) = \binom{n+k-2}{k} - \binom{n+k-3}{k-2} + \binom{n+k-6}{k-5} + \binom{n+k-8}{k-7} - \cdots$$

$$+ (-1)^j\left(\binom{n+k-u_j-1}{k-u_j} + \binom{n+k-u_j-j-1}{k-u_j-j}\right) + \cdots, \quad n \geq k, \qquad (10)$$

where $u_j = (3j^2 - j)/2$ is a so-called "pentagonal number."

If we divide $G_n(z)$ by $n!$ we get the generating function $g_n(z)$ for the probability distribution of the number of inversions in a random permutation of n elements. This is the product

$$g_n(z) = h_1(z)h_2(z)\ldots h_n(z),\tag{11}$$

where $h_k(z) = (1 + z + \cdots + z^{k-1})/k$ is the generating function for the uniform distribution of a random nonnegative integer less than k. It follows that

$$\mathrm{mean}(g_n) = \mathrm{mean}(h_1) + \mathrm{mean}(h_2) + \cdots + \mathrm{mean}(h_n)$$

$$= \quad 0 \quad + \quad \frac{1}{2} \quad + \cdots + \quad \frac{n-1}{2} \quad = \frac{n(n-1)}{4};\tag{12}$$

$$\mathrm{var}(g_n) = \mathrm{var}(h_1) + \mathrm{var}(h_2) + \cdots + \mathrm{var}(h_n)$$

$$= \quad 0 \quad + \quad \frac{1}{4} \quad + \cdots + \quad \frac{n^2-1}{12} \quad = \frac{n(2n+5)(n-1)}{72}.\tag{13}$$

So the average number of inversions is rather large, about $\frac{1}{4}n^2$; the standard deviation is also rather large, about $\frac{1}{6}n^{3/2}$.

A remarkable discovery about the distribution of inversions was made by P. A. MacMahon [*Amer. J. Math.* **35** (1913), 281–322]. Let us define the *index* of the permutation $a_1 a_2 \ldots a_n$ as the sum of all subscripts j such that $a_j > a_{j+1}$, $1 \le j < n$. For example, the index of $5\,9\,1\,8\,2\,6\,4\,7\,3$ is $2 + 4 + 6 + 8 = 20$. By coincidence the index is the same as the number of inversions in this case. If we list the 24 permutations of $\{1, 2, 3, 4\}$, namely

Permutation	Index	Inversions	Permutation	Index	Inversions
1 2 3 4	0	0	3|1 2 4	1	2
1 2 4|3	3	1	3|1 4|2	4	3
1 3|2 4	2	1	3|2|1 4	3	3
1 3 4|2	3	2	3|2 4|1	4	4
1 4|2 3	2	2	3 4|1 2	2	4
1 4|3|2	5	3	3 4|2|1	5	5
2|1 3 4	1	1	4|1 2 3	1	3
2|1 4|3	4	2	4|1 3|2	4	4
2 3|1 4	2	2	4|2|1 3	3	4
2 3 4|1	3	3	4|2 3|1	4	5
2 4|1 3	2	3	4|3|1 2	3	5
2 4|3|1	5	4	4|3|2|1	6	6

we see that *the number of permutations having a given index, k, is the same as the number having k inversions.*

At first this fact might appear to be almost obvious, but further scrutiny makes it very mysterious. MacMahon gave an ingenious indirect proof, as follows: Let $\mathrm{ind}(a_1 a_2 \ldots a_n)$ be the index of the permutation $a_1 a_2 \ldots a_n$, and let

$$H_n(z) = \sum z^{\mathrm{ind}(a_1 a_2 \ldots a_n)}\tag{14}$$

be the corresponding generating function; the sum in (14) is over all permutations of $\{1, 2, \ldots, n\}$. We wish to show that $H_n(z) = G_n(z)$. For this purpose we will define a one-to-one correspondence between arbitrary n-tuples $(q_1, q_2, \ldots, q_n)$ of nonnegative integers, on the one hand, and ordered pairs of n-tuples

$$((a_1\, a_2 \ldots a_n),\ (p_1, p_2, \ldots, p_n))$$

on the other hand, where $a_1\, a_2 \ldots a_n$ is a permutation of the indices $\{1, 2, \ldots, n\}$ and $p_1 \geq p_2 \geq \cdots \geq p_n \geq 0$. This correspondence will satisfy the condition

$$q_1 + q_2 + \cdots + q_n = \text{ind}(a_1, a_2, \ldots, a_n) + (p_1 + p_2 + \cdots + p_n). \qquad (15)$$

The generating function $\sum z^{q_1+q_2+\cdots+q_n}$, summed over all n-tuples of nonnegative integers $(q_1, q_2, \ldots, q_n)$, is $Q_n(z) = 1/(1-z)^n$; and the generating function $\sum z^{p_1+p_2+\cdots+p_n}$, summed over all n-tuples of integers $(p_1, p_2, \ldots, p_n)$ such that $p_1 \geq p_2 \geq \cdots \geq p_n \geq 0$, is

$$P_n(z) = 1/(1-z)(1-z^2)\ldots(1-z^n), \qquad (16)$$

as shown in exercise 15. In view of (15), the one-to-one correspondence we are about to establish will prove that $Q_n(z) = H_n(z)P_n(z)$, that is,

$$H_n(z) = Q_n(z)/P_n(z). \qquad (17)$$

But $Q_n(z)/P_n(z)$ is $G_n(z)$, by (8).

The desired correspondence is defined by a simple sorting procedure: Any n-tuple $(q_1, q_2, \ldots, q_n)$ can be rearranged into nonincreasing order $q_{a_1} \geq q_{a_2} \geq \cdots \geq q_{a_n}$ in a stable manner, where $a_1\, a_2 \ldots a_n$ is a permutation such that $q_{a_j} = q_{a_{j+1}}$ implies $a_j < a_{j+1}$. We set $(p_1, p_2, \ldots, p_n) = (q_{a_1}, q_{a_2}, \ldots, q_{a_n})$ and then, for $1 \leq j < n$, subtract 1 from each of $p_1, \ldots, p_j$ for each j such that $a_j > a_{j+1}$. We still have $p_1 \geq p_2 \geq \cdots \geq p_n$, because p_j was strictly greater than p_{j+1} whenever $a_j > a_{j+1}$. The resulting pair $((a_1, a_2, \ldots, a_n), (p_1, p_2, \ldots, p_n))$ satisfies (15), because the total reduction of the p's is $\text{ind}(a_1\, a_2 \ldots a_n)$. For example, if $n = 9$ and $(q_1, \ldots, q_9) = (3, 1, 4, 1, 5, 9, 2, 6, 5)$, we find $a_1 \ldots a_9 = 6\,8\,5\,9\,3\,1\,7\,2\,4$ and $(p_1, \ldots, p_9) = (5, 2, 2, 2, 2, 2, 1, 1, 1)$.

Conversely, we can easily go back to $(q_1, q_2, \ldots, q_n)$ when $a_1\, a_2 \ldots a_n$ and $(p_1, p_2, \ldots, p_n)$ are given. (See exercise 17.) So the desired correspondence has been established, and MacMahon's index theorem has been proved.

D. Foata and M. P. Schützenberger discovered a surprising extension of MacMahon's theorem, about 65 years after MacMahon's original publication: *The number of permutations of n elements that have k inversions and index l is the same as the number that have l inversions and index k.* In fact, Foata and Schützenberger found a simple one-to-one correspondence between permutations of the first kind and permutations of the second (see exercise 25).

EXERCISES

1. [*10*] What is the inversion table for the permutation $2\,7\,1\,8\,4\,5\,9\,3\,6$? What permutation has the inversion table $5\,0\,1\,2\,1\,2\,0\,0$?

2. [*M20*] In the classical problem of Josephus (exercise 1.3.2–22), n men are initially arranged in a circle; the mth man is executed, the circle closes, and every mth man is repeatedly eliminated until all are dead. The resulting execution order is a permutation of $\{1, 2, \ldots, n\}$. For example, when $n = 8$ and $m = 4$ the order is $5\,4\,6\,1\,3\,8\,7\,2$; the inversion table corresponding to this permutation is $3\,6\,3\,1\,0\,0\,1\,0$.

Give a simple recurrence relation for the elements $b_1\, b_2 \ldots b_n$ of the inversion table in the general Josephus problem for n men, when every mth man is executed.

3. [*18*] If the permutation $a_1\, a_2 \ldots a_n$ corresponds to the inversion table $b_1\, b_2 \ldots b_n$, what is the permutation $\bar{a}_1\, \bar{a}_2 \ldots \bar{a}_n$ that corresponds to the inversion table

$$(n - 1 - b_1)(n - 2 - b_2) \ldots (0 - b_n)?$$

▶ **4.** [*20*] Design an algorithm suitable for computer implementation that constructs the permutation $a_1\, a_2 \ldots a_n$ corresponding to a given inversion table $b_1\, b_2 \ldots b_n$ satisfying (3). [*Hint:* Consider a linked-memory technique.]

5. [*35*] The algorithm of exercise 4 requires an execution time roughly proportional to $n + b_1 + \cdots + b_n$ on typical computers, and this is $\Theta(n^2)$ on the average. Is there an algorithm whose worst-case running time is substantially better than order n^2?

▶ **6.** [*26*] Design an algorithm that computes the inversion table $b_1\, b_2 \ldots b_n$ corresponding to a given permutation $a_1\, a_2 \ldots a_n$ of $\{1, 2, \ldots, n\}$, where the running time is essentially proportional to $n \log n$ on typical computers.

7. [*20*] Several other kinds of inversion tables can be defined, corresponding to a given permutation $a_1\, a_2 \ldots a_n$ of $\{1, 2, \ldots, n\}$, besides the particular table $b_1\, b_2 \ldots b_n$ defined in the text; in this exercise we will consider three other types of inversion tables that arise in applications.

Let c_j be the number of inversions whose *first* component is j, that is, the number of elements to the *right* of j that are less than j. [Corresponding to (1) we have the table $0\,0\,0\,1\,4\,2\,1\,5\,7$; clearly $0 \le c_j < j$.] Let $B_j = b_{a_j}$ and $C_j = c_{a_j}$.

Show that $0 \le B_j < j$ and $0 \le C_j \le n - j$, for $1 \le j \le n$; furthermore show that the permutation $a_1\, a_2 \ldots a_n$ can be determined uniquely when either $c_1\, c_2 \ldots c_n$ or $B_1\, B_2 \ldots B_n$ or $C_1\, C_2 \ldots C_n$ is given.

8. [*M24*] Continuing the notation of exercise 7, let $a'_1\, a'_2 \ldots a'_n$ be the inverse of the permutation $a_1\, a_2 \ldots a_n$, and let the corresponding inversion tables be $b'_1\, b'_2 \ldots b'_n$, $c'_1\, c'_2 \ldots c'_n$, $B'_1\, B'_2 \ldots B'_n$, and $C'_1\, C'_2 \ldots C'_n$. Find as many interesting relations as you can between the numbers a_j, b_j, c_j, B_j, C_j, a'_j, b'_j, c'_j, B'_j, C'_j.

▶ **9.** [*M21*] Prove that, in the notation of exercise 7, the permutation $a_1\, a_2 \ldots a_n$ is an involution (that is, its own inverse) if and only if $b_j = C_j$ for $1 \le j \le n$.

10. [*HM20*] Consider Fig. 1 as a polyhedron in three dimensions. What is the diameter of the truncated octahedron (the distance between vertex 1234 and vertex 4321), if all of its edges have unit length?

11. [*M25*] If $\pi = a_1\, a_2 \ldots a_n$ is a permutation of $\{1, 2, \ldots, n\}$, let

$$E(\pi) = \{(a_i, a_j) \mid i < j,\ a_i > a_j\}$$

be the set of its inversions, and let

$$\bar{E}(\pi) = \{(a_i, a_j) \mid i > j,\ a_i > a_j\}$$

be the non-inversions.

a) Prove that $E(\pi)$ and $\bar{E}(\pi)$ are transitive. (A set S of ordered pairs is called *transitive* if (a, c) is in S whenever both (a, b) and (b, c) are in S.)

b) Conversely, let E be any transitive subset of $T = \{(x, y) \mid 1 \le y < x \le n\}$ whose complement $\bar{E} = T \setminus E$ is also transitive. Prove that there exists a permutation π such that $E(\pi) = E$.

12. [*M28*] Continuing the notation of the previous exercise, prove that if π_1 and π_2 are permutations and if E is the smallest transitive set containing $E(\pi_1) \cup E(\pi_2)$, then $\bar{E}$ is transitive. [Hence, if we say π_1 is "above" π_2 whenever $E(\pi_1) \subseteq E(\pi_2)$, a *lattice* of permutations is defined; there is a unique "lowest" permutation "above" two given permutations. Figure 1 is the lattice diagram when $n = 4$.]

13. [*M23*] It is well known that half of the terms in the expansion of a determinant have a plus sign, and half have a minus sign. In other words, there are just as many permutations with an *even* number of inversions as with an *odd* number, when $n \ge 2$. Show that, in general, the number of permutations having a number of inversions congruent to t modulo m is $n!/m$, regardless of the integer t, whenever $n \ge m$.

14. [*M24*] (F. Franklin.) A partition of n into k distinct parts is a representation $n = p_1 + p_2 + \cdots + p_k$, where $p_1 > p_2 > \cdots > p_k > 0$. For example, the partitions of 7 into distinct parts are 7, $6 + 1$, $5 + 2$, $4 + 3$, $4 + 2 + 1$. Let $f_k(n)$ be the number of partitions of n into k distinct parts; prove that $\sum_k (-1)^k f_k(n) = 0$, unless n has the form $(3j^2 \pm j)/2$, for some nonnegative integer j; in the latter case the sum is $(-1)^j$. For example, when $n = 7$ the sum is $-1 + 3 - 1 = 1$, and $7 = (3 \cdot 2^2 + 2)/2$. [*Hint:* Represent a partition as an array of dots, putting p_i dots in the ith row, for $1 \le i \le k$. Find the smallest j such that $p_{j+1} < p_j - 1$, and encircle the rightmost dots in the first j rows. If $j < p_k$, these j dots can usually be removed, tilted 45°, and placed as a new $(k{+}1)$st row. On the other hand if $j \ge p_k$, the kth row of dots can usually be removed, tilted 45°, and placed to the right of the circled dots. (See Fig. 2.) This process pairs off partitions having an odd number of rows with partitions having an even number of rows, in most cases, so only unpaired partitions must be considered in the sum.]

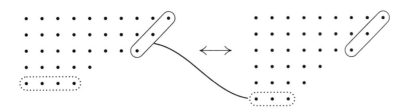

Fig. 2. Franklin's correspondence between partitions with distinct parts.

Note: As a consequence, we obtain Euler's formula

$$(1 - z)(1 - z^2)(1 - z^3)\ldots = 1 - z - z^2 + z^5 + z^7 - z^{12} - z^{15} + \cdots$$

$$= \sum_{-\infty < j < \infty} (-1)^j z^{(3j^2 + j)/2}.$$

The generating function for ordinary partitions (whose parts are not necessarily distinct) is $\sum p(n) z^n = 1/(1 - z)(1 - z^2)(1 - z^3)\ldots$; hence we obtain a nonobvious recurrence relation for the partition numbers,

$$p(n) = p(n - 1) + p(n - 2) - p(n - 5) - p(n - 7) + p(n - 12) + p(n - 15) - \cdots.$$

15. [*M23*] Prove that (16) is the generating function for partitions into at most n parts; that is, prove that the coefficient of z^m in $1/(1-z)(1-z^2)\dots(1-z^n)$ is the number of ways to write $m = p_1 + p_2 + \dots + p_n$ with $p_1 \geq p_2 \geq \dots \geq p_n \geq 0$. [*Hint:* Drawing dots as in exercise 14, show that there is a one-to-one correspondence between n-tuples $(p_1, p_2, \dots, p_n)$ such that $p_1 \geq p_2 \geq \dots \geq p_n \geq 0$ and sequences $(P_1, P_2, P_3, \dots)$ such that $n \geq P_1 \geq P_2 \geq P_3 \geq \dots \geq 0$, with the property that $p_1 + p_2 + \dots + p_n = P_1 + P_2 + P_3 + \dots$. In other words, partitions into at most n parts correspond to partitions into parts not exceeding n.]

16. [*M25*] (L. Euler.) Prove the following identities by interpreting both sides of the equations in terms of partitions:

$$\prod_{k\geq 0} \frac{1}{(1-q^k z)} = \frac{1}{(1-z)(1-qz)(1-q^2 z)\dots}$$

$$= 1 + \frac{z}{1-q} + \frac{z^2}{(1-q)(1-q^2)} + \dots = \sum_{n\geq 0} z^n \Big/ \prod_{1\leq k\leq n}(1-q^k).$$

$$\prod_{k\geq 0}(1+q^k z) = (1+z)(1+qz)(1+q^2 z)\dots$$

$$= 1 + \frac{z}{1-q} + \frac{z^2 q}{(1-q)(1-q^2)} + \dots = \sum_{n\geq 0} z^n q^{n(n-1)/2} \Big/ \prod_{1\leq k\leq n}(1-q^k).$$

17. [*20*] In MacMahon's correspondence defined at the end of this section, what are the 24 quadruples (q_1, q_2, q_3, q_4) for which $(p_1, p_2, p_3, p_4) = (0,0,0,0)$?

18. [*M30*] (T. Hibbard, *CACM* **6** (1963), 210.) Let $n > 0$, and assume that a sequence of 2^n n-bit integers $X_0, \dots, X_{2^n-1}$ has been generated at random, where each bit of each number is independently equal to 1 with probability p. Consider the sequence $X_0 \oplus 0$, $X_1 \oplus 1$, $\dots$, $X_{2^n-1} \oplus (2^n - 1)$, where $\oplus$ denotes the "exclusive or" operation on the binary representations. Thus if $p = 0$, the sequence is $0, 1, \dots, 2^n - 1$, and if $p = 1$ it is $2^n - 1, \dots, 1, 0$; and when $p = \frac{1}{2}$, each element of the sequence is a random integer between 0 and $2^n - 1$. For general p this is a useful way to generate a sequence of random integers with a biased number of inversions, although the distribution of the elements of the sequence taken as a whole is uniform in the sense that each n-bit integer has the same distribution. What is the average number of inversions in such a sequence, as a function of the probability p?

19. [*M28*] (C. Meyer.) When m is relatively prime to n, we know that the sequence $(m \bmod n)(2m \bmod n)\dots((n-1)m \bmod m)$ is a permutation of $\{1, 2, \dots, n-1\}$. Show that the number of inversions of this permutation can be expressed in terms of Dedekind sums (see Section 3.3.3).

20. [*M43*] The following famous identity due to Jacobi [*Fundamenta Nova Theoriæ Functionum Ellipticarum* (1829), §64] is the basis of many remarkable relationships involving elliptic functions:

$$\prod_{k\geq 1}(1-u^k v^{k-1})(1-u^{k-1}v^k)(1-u^k v^k)$$

$$= (1-u)(1-v)(1-uv)(1-u^2 v)(1-uv^2)(1-u^2 v^2)\dots$$

$$= 1 - (u+v) + (u^3 v + uv^3) - (u^6 v^3 + u^3 v^6) + \dots$$

$$= \sum_{-\infty < j < +\infty}(-1)^j u^{\binom{j}{2}} v^{\binom{j+1}{2}}.$$

For example, if we set $u = z$, $v = z^2$, we obtain Euler's formula of exercise 14. If we set $z = \sqrt{u/v}$, $q = \sqrt{uv}$, we obtain

$$\prod_{k \geq 1}(1 - q^{2k-1}z)(1 - q^{2k-1}z^{-1})(1 - q^{2k}) = \sum_{-\infty < n < \infty}(-1)^n z^n q^{n^2}.$$

Is there a combinatorial proof of Jacobi's identity, analogous to Franklin's proof of the special case in exercise 14? (Thus we want to consider "complex partitions"

$$m + ni = (p_1 + q_1 i) + (p_2 + q_2 i) + \cdots + (p_k + q_k i)$$

where the $p_j + q_j i$ are distinct nonzero complex numbers, p_j and q_j being nonnegative integers with $|p_j - q_j| \leq 1$. Jacobi's identity says that the number of such representations with k even is the same as the number with k odd, except when m and n are consecutive triangular numbers.) What other remarkable properties do complex partitions have?

▶ **21.** [*M25*] (G. D. Knott.) Show that the permutation $a_1 \ldots a_n$ is obtainable with a stack, in the sense of exercise 2.2.1–5 or 2.3.1–6, if and only if $C_j \leq C_{j+1} + 1$ for $1 \leq j < n$ in the notation of exercise 7.

22. [*M26*] Given a permutation $a_1 a_2 \ldots a_n$ of $\{1, 2, \ldots, n\}$, let h_j be the number of indices $i < j$ such that $a_i \in \{a_j+1, a_j+2, \ldots, a_{j+1}\}$. (If $a_{j+1} < a_j$, the elements of this set "wrap around" from n to 1. When $j = n$ we use the set $\{a_n+1, a_n+2, \ldots, n\}$.) For example, the permutation $5\,9\,1\,8\,2\,6\,4\,7\,3$ leads to $h_1 \ldots h_9 = 0\,0\,1\,2\,1\,4\,2\,4\,6$.

a) Prove that $a_1 a_2 \ldots a_n$ can be reconstructed from the numbers $h_1 h_2 \ldots h_n$.

b) Prove that $h_1 + h_2 + \cdots + h_n$ is the index of $a_1 a_2 \ldots a_n$.

▶ **23.** [*M27*] (*Russian roulette.*) A group of n condemned men who prefer probability theory to number theory might choose to commit suicide by sitting in a circle and modifying Josephus's method (exercise 2) as follows: The first prisoner holds a gun and aims it at his head; with probability p he dies and leaves the circle. Then the second man takes the gun and proceeds in the same way. Play continues cyclically, with constant probability $p > 0$, until everyone is dead.

Let $a_j = k$ if man k is the jth to die. Prove that the death order $a_1 a_2 \ldots a_n$ occurs with a probability that is a function only of n, p, and the index of the dual permutation $(n+1-a_n) \ldots (n+1-a_2)(n+1-a_1)$. What death order is least likely?

24. [*M26*] Given integers $t(1)\,t(2) \ldots t(n)$ with $t(j) \geq j$, the *generalized index* of a permutation $a_1 a_2 \ldots a_n$ is the sum of all subscripts j such that $a_j > t(a_{j+1})$, plus the total number of inversions such that $i < j$ and $t(a_j) \geq a_i > a_j$. Thus when $t(j) = j$ for all j, the generalized index is the same as the index; but when $t(j) \geq n$ for all j it is the number of inversions. Prove that the number of permutations whose generalized index equals k is the same as the number of permutations having k inversions. [*Hint:* Show that, if we take any permutation $a_1 \ldots a_{n-1}$ of $\{1, \ldots, n-1\}$ and insert the number n in all possible places, we increase the generalized index by the numbers $\{0, 1, \ldots, n-1\}$ in some order.]

▶ **25.** [*M30*] (Foata and Schützenberger.) If $\alpha = a_1 \ldots a_n$ is a permutation, let $\text{ind}(\alpha)$ be its index, and let $\text{inv}(\alpha)$ count its inversions.

a) Define a one-to-one correspondence that takes each permutation α of $\{1, \ldots, n\}$ to a permutation $f(\alpha)$ that has the following two properties: (i) $\text{ind}(f(\alpha)) = \text{inv}(\alpha)$; (ii) for $1 \leq j < n$, the number j appears to the left of $j + 1$ in $f(\alpha)$ if and only if it appears to the left of $j + 1$ in α. What permutation does your construction assign to $f(\alpha)$ when $\alpha = 1\,9\,8\,2\,6\,3\,7\,4\,5$? For what permutation α is $f(\alpha) = 1\,9\,8\,2\,6\,3\,7\,4\,5$? [*Hint:* If $n > 1$, write $\alpha = x_1\alpha_1x_2\alpha_2\ldots x_k\alpha_ka_n$, where $x_1, \ldots, x_k$ are all the elements $< a_n$ if $a_1 < a_n$, otherwise $x_1, \ldots, x_k$ are all the elements $> a_n$; the other elements appear in (possibly empty) strings $\alpha_1, \ldots, \alpha_k$. Compare the number of inversions of $h(\alpha) = \alpha_1x_1\alpha_2x_2\ldots\alpha_kx_k$ to inv(α); in this construction the number a_n does not appear in $h(\alpha)$.]

b) Use f to define another one-to-one correspondence g having the following two properties: (i) ind$(g(\alpha)) = $ inv(α); (ii) inv$(g(\alpha)) = $ ind(α). [*Hint:* Consider inverse permutations.]

26. [*M25*] What is the statistical correlation coefficient between the number of inversions and the index of a random permutation? (See Eq. 3.3.2–(24).)

27. [*M37*] Prove that, in addition to (15), there is a simple relationship between inv$(a_1\,a_2\ldots a_n)$ and the n-tuple $(q_1, q_2, \ldots, q_n)$. Use this fact to generalize the derivation of (17), obtaining an algebraic characterization of the bivariate generating function

$$H_n(w, z) = \sum w^{\text{inv}(a_1\,a_2\ldots a_n)}\,z^{\text{ind}(a_1\,a_2\ldots a_n)},$$

where the sum is over all $n!$ permutations $a_1\,a_2\ldots a_n$.

▶ **28.** [*25*] (R. W. Floyd, 1983.) If $a_1\,a_2\,\ldots\,a_n$ is a permutation of $\{1, 2, \ldots, n\}$, its *total displacement* is defined to be $\sum_{j=1}^{n}|a_j - j|$. Find upper and lower bounds for total displacement in terms of the number of inversions.

29. [*28*] If $\pi = a_1\,a_2\,\ldots\,a_n$ and $\pi' = a_1'\,a_2'\,\ldots\,a_n'$ are permutations of $\{1, 2, \ldots, n\}$, their product $\pi\pi'$ is $a_{a_1'}'\,a_{a_2'}'\,\ldots\,a_{a_n'}'$. Let inv$(\pi)$ denote the number of inversions, as in exercise 25. Show that inv$(\pi\pi') \le $ inv$(\pi) + $ inv(π'), and that equality holds if and only if $\pi\pi'$ is "below" π' in the sense of exercise 12.

*5.1.2. Permutations of a Multiset

So far we have been discussing permutations of a *set* of elements; this is just a special case of the concept of permutations of a *multiset*. (A multiset is like a set except that it can have repetitions of identical elements. Some basic properties of multisets have been discussed in exercise 4.6.3–19.)

For example, consider the multiset

$$M = \{a, a, a, b, b, c, d, d, d, d\}, \tag{1}$$

which contains 3 a's, 2 b's, 1 c, and 4 d's. We may also indicate the multiplicities of elements in another way, namely

$$M = \{3 \cdot a, \, 2 \cdot b, \, c, \, 4 \cdot d\}. \tag{2}$$

A permutation* of M is an arrangement of its elements into a row; for example,

$$c \ a \ b \ d \ d \ a \ b \ d \ a \ d.$$

From another point of view we would call this a string of letters, containing 3 a's, 2 b's, 1 c, and 4 d's.

How many permutations of M are possible? If we regarded the elements of M as distinct, by subscripting them a_1, a_2, a_3, b_1, b_2, c_1, d_1, d_2, d_3, d_4,

---

* Sometimes called a "permatution."

we would have $10! = 3{,}628{,}800$ permutations, but many of those permutations would actually be the same when we removed the subscripts. In fact, each permutation of M would occur exactly $3! \, 2! \, 1! \, 4! = 288$ times, since we can start with any permutation of M and put subscripts on the a's in 3! ways, on the b's (independently) in 2! ways, on the c in 1 way, and on the d's in 4! ways. Therefore the true number of permutations of M is

$$\frac{10!}{3! \, 2! \, 1! \, 4!} = 12{,}600.$$

In general, we can see by this same argument that the number of permutations of any multiset is the multinomial coefficient

$$\binom{n}{n_1, n_2, \ldots} = \frac{n!}{n_1! \, n_2! \ldots}, \tag{3}$$

where n_1 is the number of elements of one kind, n_2 is the number of another kind, etc., and $n = n_1 + n_2 + \cdots$ is the total number of elements.

The number of permutations of a set has been known for more than 1500 years. The Hebrew *Book of Creation* (c. A.D. 400), which was the earliest literary product of Jewish philosophical mysticism, gives the correct values of the first seven factorials, after which it says "Go on and compute what the mouth cannot express and the ear cannot hear." [*Sefer Yetzirah*, end of Chapter 4. See Solomon Gandz, *Studies in Hebrew Astronomy and Mathematics* (New York: Ktav, 1970), 494–496; Aryeh Kaplan, *Sefer Yetzirah* (York Beach, Maine: Samuel Weiser, 1993).] This is the first known enumeration of permutations in history. The second occurs in the Indian classic *Anuyogadvāra-sutra* (c. 500), rule 97, which gives the formula

$$6 \times 5 \times 4 \times 3 \times 2 \times 1 - 2$$

for the number of permutations of six elements that are neither in ascending nor descending order. [See G. Chakravarti, *Bull. Calcutta Math. Soc.* **24** (1932), 79–88. The *Anuyogadvāra-sutra* is one of the books in the canon of Jainism, a religious sect that flourishes in India.]

The corresponding formula for permutations of multisets seems to have appeared first in the *Lílávatí* of Bháscara Áchárya (c. 1150), sections 270–271. Bháscara stated the rule rather tersely, and illustrated it only with two simple examples $\{2, 2, 1, 1\}$ and $\{4, 8, 5, 5, 5\}$. Consequently the English translations of his work do not all state the rule correctly, although there is little doubt that Bháscara knew what he was talking about. He went on to give the interesting formula

$$\frac{(4 + 8 + 5 + 5 + 5) \times 120 \times 11111}{5 \times 6}$$

for the sum of the 20 numbers $48555 + 45855 + \cdots$.

The correct rule for counting permutations when there is only one repeated element was found independently by the German Jesuit scholar Athanasius Kircher in his voluminous treatise on music [*Musurgia Universalis* **2** (Rome: 1650), 5–7.] Kircher was interested in the number of tunes that could be made from a given collection of notes, so he devised what he called "musarithmetic." On pages 18–21 of his treatise he correctly gave the number of permutations of the multiset $\{m \cdot C, n \cdot D\}$ for several values of m and n, although he didn't reveal his method of calculation except when $n = 1$.

The general rule (3) then appeared in Jean Prestet's *Elémens de Mathématiques* (Paris: 1675), 351–352, one of the very first expositions of combinatorial mathematics to be written in the Western world. Prestet stated the rule correctly for a general multiset, but illustrated it only in the simple case $\{a, a, b, b, c, c\}$. He specifically pointed out that division by the *sum* of the factorials, which he considered to be the natural generalization of Kircher's rule, did not work properly. A few years later, John Wallis's *Discourse of Combinations* (Oxford: 1685), Chapter 2 (published with his *Treatise of Algebra*) gave a clearer and somewhat more detailed discussion of the rule.

In 1965, Dominique Foata introduced an ingenious idea called the "intercalation product," which makes it possible to extend many of the known results about ordinary permutations to the general case of multiset permutations. [See *Publ. Inst. Statistique*, Univ. Paris, **14** (1965), 81–241; also *Lecture Notes in Math.* **85** (Springer, 1969).] Assuming that the elements of a multiset have been linearly ordered in some way, we may consider a *two-line notation* such as

$$\begin{pmatrix} a & a & a & b & b & c & d & d & d & d \\ c & a & b & d & d & a & b & d & a & d \end{pmatrix},$$ (4)

where the top line contains the elements of M sorted into nondecreasing order and the bottom line is the permutation itself. The *intercalation product* $\alpha \top \beta$ of two multiset permutations α and β is obtained by (a) expressing α and β in the two-line notation, (b) juxtaposing these two-line representations, and (c) sorting the columns into nondecreasing order of the top line. The sorting is supposed to be stable, in the sense that left-to-right order of elements in the bottom line is preserved when the corresponding top line elements are equal. For example, $c\ a\ d\ a\ b \top b\ d\ d\ a\ d = c\ a\ b\ d\ d\ a\ b\ d\ a\ d$, since

$$\begin{pmatrix} a & a & b & c & d \\ c & a & d & a & b \end{pmatrix} \top \begin{pmatrix} a & b & d & d & d \\ b & d & d & a & d \end{pmatrix} = \begin{pmatrix} a & a & a & b & b & c & d & d & d & d \\ c & a & b & d & d & a & b & d & a & d \end{pmatrix}.$$ (5)

It is easy to see that the intercalation product is associative:

$$(\alpha \top \beta) \top \gamma = \alpha \top (\beta \top \gamma);$$ (6)

it also satisfies two cancellation laws:

$$\begin{array}{lll} \pi \top \alpha = \pi \top \beta & \text{implies} & \alpha = \beta, \\ \alpha \top \pi = \beta \top \pi & \text{implies} & \alpha = \beta. \end{array}$$ (7)

There is an identity element,

$$\alpha \top \epsilon = \epsilon \top \alpha = \alpha,$$ (8)

where ϵ is the null permutation, the "arrangement" of the empty set. Although the commutative law is not valid in general (see exercise 2), we do have

$$\alpha \top \beta = \beta \top \alpha \qquad \text{if } \alpha \text{ and } \beta \text{ have no letters in common.} \tag{9}$$

In an analogous fashion we can extend the concept of *cycles* in permutations to cases where elements are repeated; we let

$$(x_1 \quad x_2 \quad \dots \quad x_n) \tag{10}$$

stand for the permutation obtained in two-line form by sorting the columns of

$$\begin{pmatrix} x_1 & x_2 & \dots & x_n \\ x_2 & x_3 & \dots & x_1 \end{pmatrix} \tag{11}$$

by their top elements in a stable manner. For example, we have

$$(d\ b\ d\ d\ a\ c\ a\ a\ b\ d) = \begin{pmatrix} d & b & d & d & a & c & a & a & b & d \\ b & d & d & a & c & a & a & b & d & d \end{pmatrix} = \begin{pmatrix} a & a & a & b & b & c & d & d & d & d \\ c & a & b & d & d & a & b & d & a & d \end{pmatrix},$$

so the permutation (4) is actually a cycle. We might render this cycle in words by saying something like "d goes to b goes to d goes to d goes $\dots$ goes to d goes back." Note that these general cycles do not share all of the properties of ordinary cycles; $(x_1\ x_2 \dots x_n)$ is not always the same as $(x_2 \dots x_n\ x_1)$.

We observed in Section 1.3.3 that every permutation of a set has a unique representation (up to order) as a product of disjoint cycles, where the "product" of permutations is defined by a law of composition. It is easy to see that *the product of disjoint cycles is exactly the same as their intercalation*; this suggests that we might be able to generalize the previous results, obtaining a unique representation (in some sense) for any permutation of a multiset, as the intercalation of cycles. In fact there are at least two natural ways to do this, each of which has important applications.

Equation (5) shows one way to factor $c\ a\ b\ d\ d\ a\ b\ d\ a\ d$ as the intercalation of shorter permutations; let us consider the general problem of finding all factorizations $\pi = \alpha \top \beta$ of a given permutation π. It will be helpful to consider a particular permutation, such as

$$\pi = \begin{pmatrix} a & a & b & b & b & b & b & c & c & c & d & d & d & d & d \\ d & b & c & b & c & a & c & d & a & d & d & b & b & b & d \end{pmatrix}, \tag{12}$$

as we investigate the factorization problem.

If we can write this permutation π in the form $\alpha \top \beta$, where α contains the letter a at least once, then the leftmost a in the top line of the two-line notation for α must appear over the letter d, so α must also contain at least one occurrence of the letter d. If we now look at the leftmost d in the top line of α, we see in the same way that it must appear over the letter d, so α must contain at least two d's. Looking at the second d, we see that α also contains at least one b. We have deduced the partial result

$$\alpha = \begin{pmatrix} a & & b & & d & d & \\ d & \dots & & \dots & d & b & \dots \end{pmatrix} \tag{13}$$

on the sole assumption that α is a left factor of π containing the letter a. Proceeding in the same manner, we find that the b in the top line of (13) must appear over the letter c, etc. Eventually this process will reach the letter a again, and we can identify this a with the first a if we choose to do so. The argument we have just made essentially proves that any left factor α of (12) that contains the letter a has the form $(d\ d\ b\ c\ d\ b\ b\ c\ a)_\top \alpha'$, for some permutation α'. (It is convenient to write the a last in the cycle, instead of first; this is permissible since there is only one a.) Similarly, if we had assumed that α contains the letter b, we would have deduced that $\alpha = (c\ d\ d\ b)_\top \alpha''$ for some α''.

In general, this argument shows that, *if we have any factorization $\alpha_\top \beta = \pi$, where α contains a given letter y, exactly one cycle of the form*

$$(x_1\ \ldots\ x_n\ y), \qquad n \geq 0, \qquad x_1, \ldots, x_n \neq y, \tag{14}$$

is a left factor of α. This cycle is easily determined when π and y are given; it is the shortest left factor of π that contains the letter y. One of the consequences of this observation is the following theorem:

Theorem A. *Let the elements of the multiset M be linearly ordered by the relation "$<$". Every permutation π of M has a unique representation as the intercalation*

$$\pi = (x_{11}\ldots x_{1n_1}y_1)_\top (x_{21}\ldots x_{2n_2}y_2)_\top \cdots_\top (x_{t1}\ldots x_{tn_t}y_t), \quad t \geq 0, \tag{15}$$

where the following two conditions are satisfied:

$$y_1 \leq y_2 \leq \cdots \leq y_t \qquad \text{and} \qquad y_i < x_{ij} \quad \text{for } 1 \leq j \leq n_i,\ 1 \leq i \leq t. \tag{16}$$

(*In other words, the last element in each cycle is smaller than every other element, and the sequence of last elements is in nondecreasing order.*)

Proof. If $\pi = \epsilon$, we obtain such a factorization by letting $t = 0$. Otherwise we let y_1 be the smallest element permuted; and we determine $(x_{11}\ldots x_{1n_1}y_1)$, the shortest left factor of π containing y_1, as in the example above. Now $\pi = (x_{11}\ \ldots\ x_{1n_1}\ y_1)_\top \rho$ for some permutation ρ; by induction on the length, we can write

$$\rho = (x_{21}\ \ldots\ x_{2n_2}\ y_2)_\top \cdots_\top (x_{t1}\ \ldots\ x_{tn_t}\ y_t), \quad t \geq 1,$$

where (16) is satisfied. This proves the existence of such a factorization.

Conversely, to prove that the representation (15) satisfying (16) is unique, clearly $t = 0$ if and only if π is the null permutation ϵ. When $t > 0$, (16) implies that y_1 is the smallest element permuted, and that $(x_{11}\ \ldots\ x_{1n_1}\ y_1)$ is the shortest left factor containing y_1. Therefore $(x_{11}\ \ldots\ x_{1n_1}\ y_1)$ is uniquely determined; by the cancellation law (7) and induction, the representation is unique. ∎

For example, the "canonical" factorization of (12), satisfying the given conditions, is

$$(d\ d\ b\ c\ d\ b\ b\ c\ a)_\top (b\ a)_\top (c\ d\ b)_\top (d), \tag{17}$$

if $a < b < c < d$.

It is important to note that we can actually drop the parentheses and the $_T$'s in this representation, without ambiguity! Each cycle ends just after the first appearance of the smallest remaining element. So this construction associates the permutation

$$\pi' = d\ d\ b\ c\ d\ b\ b\ c\ a\ b\ a\ c\ d\ b\ d$$

with the original permutation

$$\pi = d\ b\ c\ b\ c\ a\ c\ d\ a\ d\ d\ b\ b\ b\ d.$$

Whenever the two-line representation of π had a column of the form $\frac{y}{x}$, where $x < y$, the associated permutation π' has a corresponding pair of adjacent elements $\ldots y\,x\ldots$. Thus our example permutation π has three columns of the form $\frac{d}{b}$, and π' has three occurrences of the pair $d\,b$. In general this construction establishes the following remarkable theorem:

Theorem B. *Let M be a multiset. There is a one-to-one correspondence between the permutations of M such that, if π corresponds to π', the following conditions hold:*

a) *The leftmost element of π' equals the leftmost element of π.*

b) *For all pairs of permuted elements (x, y) with $x < y$, the number of occurrences of the column $\frac{y}{x}$ in the two-line notation of π is equal to the number of times x is immediately preceded by y in π'.* ∎

When M is a set, this is essentially the same as the "unusual correspondence" we discussed near the end of Section 1.3.3, with unimportant changes. The more general result in Theorem B is quite useful for enumerating special kinds of permutations, since we can often solve a problem based on a two-line constraint more easily than the equivalent problem based on an adjacent-pair constraint.

P. A. MacMahon considered problems of this type in his extraordinary book *Combinatory Analysis* **1** (Cambridge Univ. Press, 1915), 168–186. He gave a constructive proof of Theorem B in the special case that M contains only two different kinds of elements, say a and b; his construction for this case is essentially the same as that given here, although he expressed it quite differently. For the case of three different elements a, b, c, MacMahon gave a complicated nonconstructive proof of Theorem B; the general case was first proved constructively by Foata [*Comptes Rendus Acad. Sci. Paris* **258** (1964), 1672–1675].

As a nontrivial example of Theorem B, let us find the number of strings of letters a, b, c containing exactly

A occurrences of the letter a;
B occurrences of the letter b;
C occurrences of the letter c;
k occurrences of the adjacent pair of letters ca;
l occurrences of the adjacent pair of letters cb;
m occurrences of the adjacent pair of letters ba.   (18)

The theorem tells us that this is the same as the number of two-line arrays of the form

$$
\begin{array}{ccc}
A & B & C
\end{array}
$$

$$
\left(
\begin{array}{cccccccccccc}
\overbrace{a & \cdots & a} & \overbrace{b & \cdots & b} & \overbrace{c & \cdots & c} \\
\underbrace{\sqcup & \cdots & \sqcup} & \underbrace{\sqcup & \cdots & \sqcup} & \underbrace{\sqcup & \cdots & \sqcup}
\end{array}
\right)
$$

$$
\begin{array}{ccc}
A-k-m \text{ } a\text{'s} & m \text{ } a\text{'s} & k \text{ } a\text{'s}
\end{array}
$$
$$
\begin{array}{cc}
B-l \text{ } b\text{'s} & l \text{ } b\text{'s}
\end{array}
$$
$$
C \text{ } c\text{'s}
$$

(19)

The a's can be placed in the second line in

$$
\binom{A}{A-k-m}\binom{B}{m}\binom{C}{k} \qquad \text{ways;}
$$

then the b's can be placed in the remaining positions in

$$
\binom{B+k}{B-l}\binom{C-k}{l} \qquad \text{ways.}
$$

The positions that are still vacant must be filled by c's; hence the desired number is

$$
\binom{A}{A-k-m}\binom{B}{m}\binom{C}{k}\binom{B+k}{B-l}\binom{C-k}{l}.
$$

(20)

Let us return to the question of finding all factorizations of a given permutation. Is there such a thing as a "prime" permutation, one that has no intercalation factors except itself and ϵ? The discussion preceding Theorem A leads us quickly to conclude that *a permutation is prime if and only if it is a cycle with no repeated elements.* For if it is such a cycle, our argument proves that there are no left factors except ϵ and the cycle itself. And if a permutation contains a repeated element y, it has a nontrivial cyclic left factor in which y appears only once.

A nonprime permutation can be factored into smaller and smaller pieces until it has been expressed as a product of primes. Furthermore we can show that the factorization is unique, if we neglect the order of factors that commute:

Theorem C. *Every permutation of a multiset can be written as a product*

$$
\sigma_1 \top \sigma_2 \top \cdots \top \sigma_t, \qquad t \geq 0,
$$

(21)

where each σ_j is a cycle having no repeated elements. This representation is unique, in the sense that any two such representations of the same permutation may be transformed into each other by successively interchanging pairs of adjacent disjoint cycles.

The term "disjoint cycles" means cycles having no elements in common. As an example of this theorem, we can verify that the permutation

$$\begin{pmatrix} a & a & b & b & c & c & d \\ b & a & a & c & d & b & c \end{pmatrix}$$

has exactly five factorizations into primes, namely

$$(a\ b)\ {\top}\ (a)\ {\top}\ (c\ d)\ {\top}\ (b\ c) = (a\ b)\ {\top}\ (c\ d)\ {\top}\ (a)\ {\top}\ (b\ c)$$
$$= (a\ b)\ {\top}\ (c\ d)\ {\top}\ (b\ c)\ {\top}\ (a)$$
$$= (c\ d)\ {\top}\ (a\ b)\ {\top}\ (b\ c)\ {\top}\ (a)$$
$$= (c\ d)\ {\top}\ (a\ b)\ {\top}\ (a)\ {\top}\ (b\ c). \tag{22}$$

Proof. We must show that the stated uniqueness property holds. By induction on the length of the permutation, it suffices to prove that if ρ and σ are unequal cycles having no repeated elements, and if

$$\rho\ {\top}\ \alpha = \sigma\ {\top}\ \beta,$$

then ρ and σ are disjoint, and

$$\alpha = \sigma\ {\top}\ \theta, \qquad \beta = \rho\ {\top}\ \theta,$$

for some permutation θ.

If y is any element of the cycle ρ, then any left factor of $\sigma\ {\top}\ \beta$ containing the element y must have ρ as a left factor. So if ρ and σ have an element in common, σ is a multiple of ρ; hence $\sigma = \rho$ (since they are primes), contradicting our assumption. Therefore the cycle containing y, having no elements in common with σ, must be a left factor of β. The proof is completed by using the cancellation law (7). ∎

As an example of Theorem C, let us consider permutations of the multiset $M = \{A \cdot a,\ B \cdot b,\ C \cdot c\}$ consisting of A a's, B b's, and C c's. Let $N(A, B, C, m)$ be the number of permutations of M whose two-line representation contains *no* columns of the forms $\frac{a}{a}$, $\frac{b}{b}$, $\frac{c}{c}$, and exactly m columns of the form $\frac{a}{b}$. It follows that there are exactly $A - m$ columns of the form $\frac{a}{c}$, $B - m$ of the form $\frac{c}{b}$, $C - B + m$ of the form $\frac{c}{a}$, $C - A + m$ of the form $\frac{b}{c}$, and $A + B - C - m$ of the form $\frac{b}{a}$. Hence

$$N(A, B, C, m) = \binom{A}{m} \binom{B}{C - A + m} \binom{C}{B - m}. \tag{23}$$

Theorem C tells us that we can count these permutations in another way: Since columns of the form $\frac{a}{a}$, $\frac{b}{b}$, $\frac{c}{c}$ are excluded, the only possible prime factors of the permutation are

$$(a\ b), \qquad (a\ c), \qquad (b\ c), \qquad (a\ b\ c), \qquad (a\ c\ b). \tag{24}$$

Each pair of these cycles has at least one letter in common, so the factorization into primes is completely unique. If the cycle $(a\ b\ c)$ occurs k times in the factorization, our previous assumptions imply that $(a\ b)$ occurs $m - k$ times,

$(b\ c)$ occurs $C - A + m - k$ times, $(a\ c)$ occurs $C - B + m - k$ times, and $(a\ c\ b)$ occurs $A + B - C - 2m + k$ times. Hence $N(A, B, C, m)$ is the number of permutations of these cycles (a multinomial coefficient), summed over k:

$$N(A, B, C, m)$$

$$= \sum_k \frac{(C+m-k)!}{(m-k)!\,(C-A+m-k)!\,(C-B+m-k)!\,k!\,(A+B-C-2m+k)!}$$

$$= \sum_k \binom{m}{k} \binom{A}{m} \binom{A-m}{C-B+m-k} \binom{C+m-k}{A}. \tag{25}$$

Comparing this with (23), we find that the following identity must be valid:

$$\sum_k \binom{m}{k} \binom{A-m}{C-B+m-k} \binom{C+m-k}{A} = \binom{B}{C-A+m} \binom{C}{B-m}. \tag{26}$$

This turns out to be the identity we met in exercise 1.2.6–31, namely

$$\sum_j \binom{M-R+S}{j} \binom{N+R-S}{N-j} \binom{R+j}{M+N} = \binom{R}{M} \binom{S}{N}, \tag{27}$$

with $M = A+B-C-m$, $N = C-B+m$, $R = B$, $S = C$, and $j = C-B+m-k$.

Similarly we can count the number of permutations of $\{A\cdot a,\ B\cdot b,\ C\cdot c,\ D\cdot d\}$ such that the number of columns of various types is specified as follows:

Column type:	$\begin{matrix}a\\d\end{matrix}$	$\begin{matrix}a\\b\end{matrix}$	$\begin{matrix}b\\a\end{matrix}$	$\begin{matrix}b\\c\end{matrix}$	$\begin{matrix}c\\b\end{matrix}$	$\begin{matrix}c\\d\end{matrix}$	$\begin{matrix}d\\a\end{matrix}$	$\begin{matrix}d\\c\end{matrix}$	
Frequency:	r	$A-r$	q	$B-q$	$B-A+r$	$D-r$	$A-q$	$D-A+q$	(28)

(Here $A + C = B + D$.) The possible cycles occurring in a prime factorization of such permutations are then

Cycle:	$(a\ b)$	$(b\ c)$	$(c\ d)$	$(d\ a)$	$(a\ b\ c\ d)$	$(d\ c\ b\ a)$	
Frequency:	$A-r-s$	$B-q-s$	$D-r-s$	$A-q-s$	s	$q-A+r+s$	(29)

for some s (see exercise 12). In this case the cycles $(a\ b)$ and $(c\ d)$ commute with each other, and so do $(b\ c)$ and $(d\ a)$, so we must count the number of distinct prime factorizations. It turns out (see exercise 10) that there is always a unique factorization such that no $(c\ d)$ is immediately followed by $(a\ b)$, and no $(d\ a)$ is immediately followed by $(b\ c)$. Hence by the result of exercise 13, we have

$$\sum_{s,t} \binom{B}{t} \binom{A-q-s}{A-r-s-t} \binom{B+D-r-s-t}{B-q-s}$$

$$\times \frac{D!}{(D-r-s)!\,(A-q-s)!\,s!\,(q-A+r+s)!}$$

$$= \binom{A}{r} \binom{B+D-A}{D-r} \binom{B}{q} \binom{D}{A-q}.$$

Taking out the factor $\binom{D}{A-q}$ from both sides and simplifying the factorials slightly leaves us with the complicated-looking five-parameter identity

$$\sum_{s,t}\binom{B}{t}\binom{A-r-t}{s}\binom{B+D-r-s-t}{D+q-r-t}\binom{D-A+q}{D-r-s}\binom{A-q}{r+t-q}$$

$$=\binom{A}{r}\binom{B+D-A}{D-r}\binom{B}{q}. \quad (30)$$

The sum on s can be performed using (27), and the resulting sum on t is easily evaluated; so, after all this work, we were not fortunate enough to discover any identities that we didn't already know how to derive. But at least we have learned how to count certain kinds of permutations, in two different ways, and these counting techniques are good training for the problems that lie ahead.

EXERCISES

1. [M05] *True or false:* Let M_1 and M_2 be multisets. If α is a permutation of M_1 and β is a permutation of M_2, then $\alpha \top \beta$ is a permutation of $M_1 \cup M_2$.

2. [10] The intercalation of $c\ a\ d\ a\ b$ and $b\ d\ d\ a\ d$ is computed in (5); find the intercalation $b\ d\ d\ a\ d \top c\ a\ d\ a\ b$ that is obtained when the factors are interchanged.

3. [M13] Is the converse of (9) valid? In other words, if α and β commute under intercalation, must they have no letters in common?

4. [M11] The canonical factorization of (12), in the sense of Theorem A, is given in (17) when $a < b < c < d$. Find the corresponding canonical factorization when $d < c < b < a$.

5. [M23] Condition (b) of Theorem B requires $x < y$; what would happen if we weakened the relation to $x \leq y$?

6. [M15] How many strings are there that contain exactly m a's, n b's, and no other letters, with exactly k of the a's preceded immediately by a b?

7. [M21] How many strings on the letters a, b, c satisfying conditions (18) begin with the letter a? with the letter b? with c?

▸ **8.** [20] Find all factorizations of (12) into two factors $\alpha \top \beta$.

9. [33] Write computer programs that perform the factorizations of a given multiset permutation into the forms mentioned in Theorems A and C.

▸ **10.** [M30] *True or false:* Although the factorization into primes isn't quite unique, according to Theorem C, we can insure uniqueness in the following way: "There is a linear ordering $\prec$ of the set of primes such that every permutation of a multiset has a unique factorization $\sigma_1 \top \sigma_2 \top \cdots \top \sigma_n$ into primes subject to the condition that $\sigma_i \preceq \sigma_{i+1}$ whenever σ_i commutes with σ_{i+1}, for $1 \leq i < n$."

▸ **11.** [M26] Let $\sigma_1, \sigma_2, \ldots, \sigma_t$ be cycles without repeated elements. Define a partial ordering $\prec$ on the t objects $\{x_1, \ldots, x_t\}$ by saying that $x_i \prec x_j$ if $i < j$ and σ_i has at least one letter in common with σ_j. Prove the following connection between Theorem C and the notion of (Section 2.2.3): *The number of distinct prime factorizations of $\sigma_1 \top \sigma_2 \top \cdots \top \sigma_t$ is the number of ways to sort the given partial ordering topologically.* (For example, corresponding to (22) we find that there are five ways to sort the ordering $x_1 \prec x_2$, $x_3 \prec x_4$, $x_1 \prec x_4$ topologically.) Conversely, given any partial ordering on t elements, there is a set of cycles $\{\sigma_1, \sigma_2, \ldots, \sigma_t\}$ that defines it in the stated way.

12. [*M16*] Show that (29) is a consequence of the assumptions of (28).

13. [*M21*] Prove that the number of permutations of the multiset

$$\{A \cdot a, B \cdot b, C \cdot c, D \cdot d, E \cdot e, F \cdot f\}$$

containing no occurrences of the adjacent pairs of letters *ca* and *db* is

$$\sum_t \binom{D}{A-t}\binom{A+B+E+F}{t}\binom{A+B+C+E+F-t}{B}\binom{C+D+E+F}{C,D,E,F}.$$

14. [*M30*] One way to define the inverse π^- of a general permutation π, suggested by other definitions in this section, is to interchange the lines of the two-line representation of π and then to do a stable sort of the columns in order to bring the top row into nondecreasing order. For example, if $a < b < c < d$, this definition implies that the inverse of $c\ a\ b\ d\ d\ a\ b\ d\ a\ d$ is $a\ c\ d\ a\ d\ a\ b\ b\ d\ d$.

Explore properties of this inversion operation; for example, does it have any simple relation with intercalation products? Can we count the number of permutations such that $\pi = \pi^-$?

▸ **15.** [*M25*] Prove that the permutation $a_1 \ldots a_n$ of the multiset

$$\{n_1 \cdot x_1, n_2 \cdot x_2, \ldots, n_m \cdot x_m\},$$

where $x_1 < x_2 < \cdots < x_n$ and $n_1 + n_2 + \cdots + n_m = m$, is a cycle if and only if the directed graph with vertices $\{x_1, x_2, \ldots, x_m\}$ and arcs from x_j to $a_{n_1 + \cdots + n_j}$ contains precisely one oriented cycle. In the latter case, the number of ways to represent the permutation in cycle form is the length of the oriented cycle. For example, the directed graph corresponding to

$$\begin{pmatrix} a\ a\ a\ b\ b\ c\ c\ c\ d\ d \\ d\ c\ b\ a\ c\ a\ a\ b\ d\ c \end{pmatrix} \qquad \text{is}$$

and the two ways to represent the permutation as a cycle are $(b\ a\ d\ d\ c\ a\ c\ a\ b\ c)$ and $(c\ a\ d\ d\ c\ a\ c\ b\ a\ b)$.

16. [*M35*] We found the generating function for *inversions* of permutations in the previous section, Eq. 5.1.1–(8), in the special case that a set was being permuted. Show that, in general, if a *multiset* is permuted, the generating function for inversions of $\{n_1 \cdot x_1, n_2 \cdot x_2, \ldots\}$ is the "z-multinomial coefficient"

$$\binom{n}{n_1, n_2, \ldots}_z = \frac{n!_z}{n_1!_z\, n_2!_z \cdots}, \qquad \text{where} \quad m!_z = \prod_{k=1}^m (1 + z + \cdots + z^{k-1}).$$

[Compare with (3) and with the definition of z-nomial coefficients in Eq. 1.2.6–(40).]

17. [*M24*] Find the average and standard deviation of the number of inversions in a random permutation of a given multiset, using the generating function found in exercise 16.

18. [*M30*] (P. A. MacMahon.) The *index* of a permutation $a_1 a_2 \ldots a_n$ was defined in the previous section; and we proved that the number of permutations of a given set that have a given index k is the same as the number of permutations that have k inversions. Does the same result hold for permutations of a given multiset?

19. [*HM28*] Define the *Möbius function* $\mu(\pi)$ of a permutation π to be 0 if π contains repeated elements, otherwise $(-1)^k$ if π is the product of k primes. (Compare with the definition of the ordinary Möbius function, exercise 4.5.2–10.)

  a) Prove that if $\pi \neq \epsilon$, we have

$$\sum \mu(\lambda) = 0,$$

  summed over all permutations λ that are left factors of π (namely all λ such that $\pi = \lambda_T \rho$ for some ρ).

  b) Given that $x_1 < x_2 < \cdots < x_m$ and $\pi = x_{j_1} x_{j_2} \ldots x_{j_n}$, where $1 \le j_k \le m$ for $1 \le k \le n$, prove that

$$\mu(\pi) = (-1)^n \epsilon(i_1 i_2 \ldots i_n), \quad \text{where} \quad \epsilon(i_1 i_2 \ldots i_n) = \text{sign} \prod_{1 \le j < k \le n} (i_k - i_j).$$

▶ **20.** [*HM33*] (D. Foata.) Let (a_{ij}) be any matrix of real numbers. In the notation of exercise 19(b), define $\nu(\pi) = a_{i_1 j_1} \ldots a_{i_n j_n}$, where the two-line notation for π is

$$\begin{pmatrix} x_{i_1} & x_{i_2} & \cdots & x_{i_n} \\ x_{j_1} & x_{j_2} & \cdots & x_{j_n} \end{pmatrix}.$$

This function is useful in the computation of generating functions for permutations of a multiset, because $\sum \nu(\pi)$, summed over all permutations π of the multiset

$$\{n_1 \cdot x_1, \ldots, n_m \cdot x_m\},$$

will be the generating function for the number of permutations satisfying certain restrictions. For example, if we take $a_{ij} = z$ for $i = j$, and $a_{ij} = 1$ for $i \neq j$, then $\sum \nu(\pi)$ is the generating function for the number of "fixed points" (columns in which the top and bottom entries are equal). In order to study $\sum \nu(\pi)$ for all multisets simultaneously, we consider the function

$$G = \sum \pi \nu(\pi)$$

summed over all π in the set $\{x_1, \ldots, x_m\}^*$ of all permutations of multisets involving the elements $x_1, \ldots, x_m$, and we look at the coefficient of $x_1^{n_1} \ldots x_m^{n_m}$ in G.

In this formula for G we are treating π as the product of the x's. For example, when $m = 2$ we have

$$G = 1 + x_1\nu(x_1) + x_2\nu(x_2) + x_1 x_1\nu(x_1 x_1) + x_1 x_2\nu(x_1 x_2) + x_2 x_1\nu(x_2 x_1) + x_2 x_2\nu(x_2 x_2) + \cdots$$

$$= 1 + x_1 a_{11} + x_2 a_{22} + x_1^2 a_{11}^2 + x_1 x_2 a_{11} a_{22} + x_1 x_2 a_{21} a_{12} + x_2^2 a_{22}^2 + \cdots.$$

Thus the coefficient of $x_1^{n_1} \ldots x_m^{n_m}$ in G is $\sum \nu(\pi)$ summed over all permutations π of $\{n_1 \cdot x_1, \ldots, n_m \cdot x_m\}$. It is not hard to see that this coefficient is also the coefficient of $x_1^{n_1} \ldots x_m^{n_m}$ in the expression

$$(a_{11}x_1 + \cdots + a_{1m}x_m)^{n_1} (a_{21}x_1 + \cdots + a_{2m}x_m)^{n_2} \ldots (a_{m1}x_1 + \cdots + a_{mm}x_m)^{n_m}.$$

The purpose of this exercise is to prove what P. A. MacMahon called a "Master Theorem" in his *Combinatorial Analysis* **1** (1915), Section 3, namely the formula

$$G = 1/D, \quad \text{where} \quad D = \det \begin{pmatrix} 1 - a_{11}x_1 & -a_{12}x_2 & \cdots & -a_{1m}x_m \\ -a_{21}x_1 & 1 - a_{22}x_2 & & -a_{2m}x_m \\ \vdots & & & \vdots \\ -a_{m1}x_1 & -a_{m2}x_2 & \cdots & 1 - a_{mm}x_m \end{pmatrix}.$$

For example, if $a_{ij} = 1$ for all i and j, this formula gives

$$G = 1/(1 - (x_1 + x_2 + \cdots + x_m)),$$

and the coefficient of $x_1^{n_1} \ldots x_m^{n_m}$ turns out to be $(n_1 + \cdots + n_m)!/n_1! \ldots n_m!$, as it should. To prove the Master Theorem, show that

a) $\nu(\pi \top \rho) = \nu(\pi)\nu(\rho)$;

b) $D = \sum \pi \mu(\pi)\nu(\pi)$, in the notation of exercise 19, summed over all permutations π in $\{x_1, \ldots, x_m\}^*$;

c) therefore $D \cdot G = 1$.

21. [*M21*] Given $n_1, \ldots, n_m$, and $d \geq 0$, how many permutations $a_1 a_2 \ldots a_n$ of the multiset $\{n_1 \cdot 1, \ldots, n_m \cdot m\}$ satisfy $a_{j+1} \geq a_j - d$ for $1 \leq j < n = n_1 + \cdots + n_m$?

22. [*M30*] Let $P(x_1^{n_1} \ldots x_m^{n_m})$ denote the set of all possible permutations of the multiset $\{n_1 \cdot x_1, \ldots, n_m \cdot x_m\}$, and let $P_0(x_0^{n_0} x_1^{n_1} \ldots x_m^{n_m})$ be the subset of $P(x_0^{n_0} x_1^{n_1} \ldots x_m^{n_m})$ in which the first n_0 elements are $\neq x_0$.

a) Given a number t with $1 \leq t < m$, find a one-to-one correspondence between $P(1^{n_1} \ldots m^{n_m})$ and the set of all ordered pairs of permutations that belong respectively to $P_0(0^k 1^{n_1} \ldots t^{n_t})$ and $P_0(0^k (t+1)^{n_{t+1}} \ldots m^{n_m})$, for some $k \geq 0$. [*Hint:* For each $\pi = a_1 \ldots a_n \in P(1^{n_1} \ldots m^{n_m})$, let $l(\pi)$ be the permutation obtained by replacing $t+1, \ldots, m$ by 0 and erasing all 0s in the last $n_{t+1} + \cdots + n_m$ positions; similarly, let $r(\pi)$ be the permutation obtained by replacing $1, \ldots, t$ by 0 and erasing all 0s in the first $n_1 + \cdots + n_t$ positions.]

b) Prove that the number of permutations of $P_0(0^{n_0} 1^{n_1} \ldots m^{n_m})$ whose two-line form has p_j columns $\genfrac{}{}{0pt}{}{0}{j}$ and q_j columns $\genfrac{}{}{0pt}{}{j}{0}$ is

$$\frac{|P(x_1^{p_1} \ldots x_m^{p_m} y_1^{n_1 - p_1} \ldots y_m^{n_m - p_m})| \, |P(x_1^{q_1} \ldots x_m^{q_m} y_1^{n_1 - q_1} \ldots y_m^{n_m - q_m})|}{|P_0(0^{n_0} 1^{n_1} \ldots m^{n_m})|}.$$

c) Let $w_1, \ldots, w_m, z_1, \ldots, z_m$ be complex numbers on the unit circle. Define the weight $w(\pi)$ of a permutation $\pi \in P(1^{n_1} \ldots m^{n_m})$ as the product of the weights of its columns in two-line form, where the weight of $\genfrac{}{}{0pt}{}{j}{k}$ is w_j/w_k if j and k are both $\leq t$ or both $> t$, otherwise it is z_j/z_k. Prove that the sum of $w(\pi)$ over all $\pi \in P(1^{n_1} \ldots m^{n_m})$ is

$$\sum_{k \geq 0} \frac{k!^2 (n_{\leq t} - k)! (n_{>t} - k)!}{n_1! \ldots n_m!} \left| \sum \binom{n_1}{p_1} \cdots \binom{n_m}{p_m} \left(\frac{w_1}{z_1}\right)^{p_1} \cdots \left(\frac{w_m}{z_m}\right)^{p_m} \right|^2,$$

where $n_{\leq t}$ is $n_1 + \cdots + n_t$, $n_{>t}$ is $n_{t+1} + \cdots + n_m$, and the inner sum is over all $(p_1, \ldots, p_m)$ such that $p_{\leq t} = p_{>t} = k$.

23. [*M23*] A strand of DNA can be thought of as a word on a four-letter alphabet. Suppose we copy a strand of DNA and break it completely into one-letter bases, then recombine those bases at random. If the resulting strand is placed next to the original, prove that the number of places in which they differ is more likely to be even than odd. [*Hint:* Apply the previous exercise.]

24. [*27*] Consider any relation R that might hold between two unordered pairs of letters; if $\{w, x\} R \{y, z\}$ we say $\{w, x\}$ *preserves* $\{y, z\}$, otherwise $\{w, x\}$ *moves* $\{y, z\}$.

The operation of *transposing* $\genfrac{}{}{0pt}{}{w\ x}{y\ z}$ with respect to R replaces $\genfrac{}{}{0pt}{}{w\ x}{y\ z}$ by $\genfrac{}{}{0pt}{}{x\ w}{y\ z}$ or $\genfrac{}{}{0pt}{}{x\ w}{z\ y}$, according as the pair $\{w, x\}$ preserves or moves the pair $\{y, z\}$, assuming that $w \neq x$ and $y \neq z$; if $w = x$ or $y = z$ the transposition always produces $\genfrac{}{}{0pt}{}{x\ w}{z\ y}$.

The operation of *sorting* a two-line array $\left(\begin{smallmatrix} x_1 & \cdots & x_n \\ y_1 & \cdots & y_n \end{smallmatrix}\right)$ with respect to R repeatedly finds the largest x_j such that $x_j > x_{j+1}$ and transposes columns j and $j+1$, until eventually $x_1 \leq \cdots \leq x_n$. (We do not require $y_1 \ldots y_n$ to be a permutation of $x_1 \ldots x_n$.)

a) Given $\left(\begin{smallmatrix} x_1 & \cdots & x_n \\ y_1 & \cdots & y_n \end{smallmatrix}\right)$, prove that for every $x \in \{x_1, \ldots, x_n\}$ there is a unique $y \in \{y_1, \ldots, y_n\}$ such that $\text{sort}\left(\begin{smallmatrix} x_1 & \cdots & x_n \\ y_1 & \cdots & y_n \end{smallmatrix}\right) = \text{sort}\left(\begin{smallmatrix} x & x_2' & \cdots & x_n' \\ y & y_2' & \cdots & y_n' \end{smallmatrix}\right)$ for some $x_2', y_2', \ldots, x_n', y_n'$.

b) Let $\left(\begin{smallmatrix} w_1 & \cdots & w_k \\ y_1 & \cdots & y_k \end{smallmatrix}\right) \circledR \left(\begin{smallmatrix} x_1 & \cdots & x_l \\ z_1 & \cdots & z_l \end{smallmatrix}\right)$ denote the result of sorting $\left(\begin{smallmatrix} w_1 & \cdots & w_k & x_1 & \cdots & x_l \\ y_1 & \cdots & y_k & z_1 & \cdots & z_l \end{smallmatrix}\right)$ with respect to R. For example, if R is always true, $\circledR$ is simply juxtaposition; if R is always false, $\circledR$ is the intercalation product $\top$. Generalize Theorem A by proving that every permutation π of a multiset M has a unique representation of the form

$$\pi = (x_{11} \ldots x_{1n_1} \, y_1) \circledR \left((x_{21} \ldots x_{2n_2} \, y_2) \circledR \cdots \circledR (x_{t1} \ldots x_{tn_t} \, y_t) \right)$$

satisfying (16), if we redefine cycle notation by letting (11) stand for $(x_2 \ldots x_n \, x_1)$ instead of $(x_1 \, x_2 \ldots x_n)$. For example, suppose $\{w, x\} R \{y, z\}$ means that w, x, y, and z are distinct; then it turns out that the factorization of (12) analogous to (17) is

$$(d\,d\,b\,c\,a) \circledR \left((c\,b\,b\,a) \circledR \left((c\,d\,b) \circledR \left((d\,b) \circledR (d) \right) \right) \right).$$

(The operation $\circledR$ does not always obey the associative law; parentheses in the generalized factorization should be nested from right to left.)

*5.1.3. Runs

In Chapter 3 we analyzed the lengths of upward runs in permutations, as a way to test the randomness of a sequence. If we place a vertical line at both ends of a permutation $a_1 a_2 \ldots a_n$ and also between a_j and a_{j+1} whenever $a_j > a_{j+1}$, the *runs* are the segments between pairs of lines. For example, the permutation

$$|\,3\ 5\ 7\,|\,1\ 6\ 8\ 9\,|\,4\,|\,2\,|$$

has four runs. The theory developed in Section 3.3.2G determines the average number of runs of length k in a random permutation of $\{1, 2, \ldots, n\}$, as well as the covariance of the numbers of runs of lengths j and k. Runs are important in the study of sorting algorithms, because they represent sorted segments of the data, so we will now take up the subject of runs once again.

Let us use the notation

$$\left\langle \begin{matrix} n \\ k \end{matrix} \right\rangle \tag{1}$$

to stand for the number of permutations of $\{1, 2, \ldots, n\}$ that have exactly k "descents" $a_j > a_{j+1}$, thus exactly $k+1$ ascending runs. These numbers $\left\langle \begin{smallmatrix} n \\ k \end{smallmatrix} \right\rangle$ arise in several contexts, and they are usually called *Eulerian numbers* since Euler discussed them in his famous book *Institutiones Calculi Differentialis* (St. Petersburg: 1755), 485–487, after having introduced them several years earlier in a technical paper [*Comment. Acad. Sci. Imp. Petrop.* **8** (1736), 147–158, §13]; they should not be confused with the *Euler numbers* E_n discussed in exercise 5.1.4–23. The angle brackets in $\left\langle \begin{smallmatrix} n \\ k \end{smallmatrix} \right\rangle$ remind us of the ">" sign in the definition of a descent. Of course $\left\langle \begin{smallmatrix} n \\ k \end{smallmatrix} \right\rangle$ is also the number of permutations that have k "ascents" $a_j < a_{j+1}$.

We can use any given permutation of $\{1, \ldots, n-1\}$ to form n new permutations, by inserting the element n in all possible places. If the original permutation has k descents, exactly $k+1$ of these new permutations will have k descents; the remaining $n-1-k$ will have $k+1$, since we increase the number of descents unless we place the element n at the end of an existing run. For example, the six permutations formed from $3\,1\,2\,4\,5$ are

$$6\,3\,1\,2\,4\,5, \qquad 3\,6\,1\,2\,4\,5, \qquad 3\,1\,6\,2\,4\,5,$$
$$3\,1\,2\,6\,4\,5, \qquad 3\,1\,2\,4\,6\,5, \qquad 3\,1\,2\,4\,5\,6;$$

all but the second and last of these have two descents instead of one. Therefore we have the recurrence relation

$$\left\langle {n \atop k} \right\rangle = (k+1) \left\langle {n-1 \atop k} \right\rangle + (n-k) \left\langle {n-1 \atop k-1} \right\rangle, \quad \text{integer } n > 0, \text{ integer } k. \quad (2)$$

By convention we set

$$\left\langle {0 \atop k} \right\rangle = \delta_{k0}, \quad (3)$$

saying that the null permutation has no descents. The reader may find it interesting to compare (2) with the recurrence relations for Stirling numbers in Eqs. 1.2.6–(46). Table 1 lists the Eulerian numbers for small n.

Several patterns can be observed in Table 1. By definition, we have

$$\left\langle {n \atop 0} \right\rangle + \left\langle {n \atop 1} \right\rangle + \cdots + \left\langle {n \atop n} \right\rangle = n!; \quad (4)$$

$$\left\langle {n \atop 0} \right\rangle = 1; \quad (5)$$

$$\left\langle {n \atop n-1} \right\rangle = 1, \qquad \left\langle {n \atop n} \right\rangle = 0, \qquad \text{for } n \geq 1. \quad (6)$$

Eq. (6) follows from (5) because of a general rule of symmetry,

$$\left\langle {n \atop k} \right\rangle = \left\langle {n \atop n-1-k} \right\rangle, \qquad \text{for } n \geq 1, \quad (7)$$

which comes from the fact that each nonnull permutation $a_1 a_2 \ldots a_n$ having k descents has $n-1-k$ ascents.

Another important property of the Eulerian numbers is the formula

$$\sum_k \left\langle {n \atop k} \right\rangle \binom{m+k}{n} = m^n, \qquad n \geq 0, \quad (8)$$

which was discovered by the Chinese mathematician Li Shan-Lan and published in 1867. [See J.-C. Martzloff, *A History of Chinese Mathematics* (Berlin: Springer, 1997), 346–348; special cases for $n \leq 5$ had already been known to Yoshisuke Matsunaga in Japan, who died in 1744.] Li Shan-Lan's identity follows from the properties of sorting: Consider the m^n sequences $a_1 a_2 \ldots a_n$ such that $1 \leq a_i \leq m$. We can sort any such sequence into nondecreasing order in a stable manner, obtaining

$$a_{i_1} \leq a_{i_2} \leq \cdots \leq a_{i_n} \quad (9)$$

Table 1

EULERIAN NUMBERS

n	$\left\langle{n\atop0}\right\rangle$	$\left\langle{n\atop1}\right\rangle$	$\left\langle{n\atop2}\right\rangle$	$\left\langle{n\atop3}\right\rangle$	$\left\langle{n\atop4}\right\rangle$	$\left\langle{n\atop5}\right\rangle$	$\left\langle{n\atop6}\right\rangle$	$\left\langle{n\atop7}\right\rangle$	$\left\langle{n\atop8}\right\rangle$
0	1	0	0	0	0	0	0	0	0
1	1	0	0	0	0	0	0	0	0
2	1	1	0	0	0	0	0	0	0
3	1	4	1	0	0	0	0	0	0
4	1	11	11	1	0	0	0	0	0
5	1	26	66	26	1	0	0	0	0
6	1	57	302	302	57	1	0	0	0
7	1	120	1191	2416	1191	120	1	0	0
8	1	247	4293	15619	15619	4293	247	1	0
9	1	502	14608	88234	156190	88234	14608	502	1

where $i_1\,i_2\ldots i_n$ is a uniquely determined permutation of $\{1,2,\ldots,n\}$ such that $a_{i_j}=a_{i_{j+1}}$ implies $i_j<i_{j+1}$; in other words, $i_j>i_{j+1}$ implies that $a_{i_j}<a_{i_{j+1}}$. If the permutation $i_1\,i_2\ldots i_n$ has k runs, we will show that the number of corresponding sequences $a_1\,a_2\ldots a_n$ is $\binom{m+n-k}{n}$. This will prove (8) if we replace k by $n-k$ and use (7), because $\left\langle{n\atop k}\right\rangle$ permutations have $n-k$ runs.

For example, if $n=9$ and $i_1\,i_2\ldots i_n=3\,5\,7\,1\,6\,8\,9\,4\,2$, we want to count the number of sequences $a_1\,a_2\ldots a_n$ such that

$$1\le a_3\le a_5\le a_7<a_1\le a_6\le a_8\le a_9<a_4<a_2\le m;\qquad(10)$$

this is the number of sequences $b_1\,b_2\ldots b_9$ such that

$$1\le b_1<b_2<b_3<b_4<b_5<b_6<b_7<b_8<b_9\le m+5,$$

since we can let $b_1=a_3$, $b_2=a_5+1$, $b_3=a_7+2$, $b_4=a_1+2$, $b_5=a_6+3$, etc. The number of choices of the b's is simply the number of ways of choosing 9 things out of $m+5$, namely $\binom{m+5}{9}$; a similar proof works for general n and k, and for any permutation $i_1\,i_2\ldots i_n$ with k runs.

Since both sides of (8) are polynomials in m, we may replace m by any real number x, and we obtain an interesting representation of powers in terms of consecutive binomial coefficients:

$$x^n=\left\langle{n\atop0}\right\rangle\binom{x}{n}+\left\langle{n\atop1}\right\rangle\binom{x+1}{n}+\cdots+\left\langle{n\atop n-1}\right\rangle\binom{x+n-1}{n},\quad n\ge1.\quad(11)$$

For example,

$$x^3=\binom{x}{3}+4\binom{x+1}{3}+\binom{x+2}{3}.$$

This is the key property of Eulerian numbers that makes them useful in the study of discrete mathematics.

Setting $x=1$ in (11) proves again that $\left\langle{n\atop n-1}\right\rangle=1$, since the binomial coefficients vanish in all but the last term. Setting $x=2$ yields

$$\left\langle{n\atop n-2}\right\rangle=\left\langle{n\atop1}\right\rangle=2^n-n-1,\qquad n\ge1.\quad(12)$$

Setting $x = 3, 4, \ldots$ shows that relation (11) completely defines the numbers $\left\langle {n \atop k} \right\rangle$, and leads to a formula originally given by Euler:

$$\left\langle {n \atop k} \right\rangle = (k+1)^n - k^n \binom{n+1}{1} + (k-1)^n \binom{n+1}{2} - \cdots + (-1)^k 1^n \binom{n+1}{k}$$

$$= \sum_{j=0}^{k} (-1)^j \binom{n+1}{j}(k+1-j)^n, \qquad n \geq 0, \; k \geq 0. \tag{13}$$

Now let us study the generating function for runs. If we set

$$g_n(z) = \sum_k \left\langle {n \atop k-1} \right\rangle \frac{z^k}{n!}, \tag{14}$$

the coefficient of z^k is the probability that a random permutation of $\{1, 2, \ldots, n\}$ has exactly k runs. Since k runs are just as likely as $n+1-k$, the average number of runs must be $\frac{1}{2}(n+1)$, hence $g_n'(1) = \frac{1}{2}(n+1)$. Exercise 2(b) shows that there is a simple formula for all the derivatives of $g_n(z)$ at the point $z = 1$:

$$g_n^{(m)}(1) = \left\{ {n+1 \atop n+1-m} \right\} \Big/ \binom{n}{m}, \qquad n \geq m. \tag{15}$$

Thus in particular the variance $g_n''(1) + g_n'(1) - g_n'(1)^2$ comes to $(n+1)/12$, for $n \geq 2$, indicating a rather stable distribution about the mean. (We found this same quantity in Eq. 3.3.2–(18), where it was called $\text{covar}(R_1', R_1')$.) Since $g_n(z)$ is a polynomial, we can use formula (15) to deduce the Taylor series expansions

$$g_n(z) = \frac{1}{n!} \sum_{k=0}^{n} (z-1)^{n-k} k! \left\{ {n+1 \atop k+1} \right\} = \frac{1}{n!} \sum_{k=0}^{n} z^{k+1} (1-z)^{n-k} k! \left\{ {n+1 \atop k+1} \right\}. \tag{16}$$

The second of these equations follows from the first, since

$$g_n(z) = z^{n+1} g_n(1/z), \qquad n \geq 1, \tag{17}$$

by the symmetry condition (7). The Stirling number recurrence

$$\left\{ {n+1 \atop k+1} \right\} = (k+1) \left\{ {n \atop k+1} \right\} + \left\{ {n \atop k} \right\}$$

gives two slightly simpler representations,

$$g_n(z) = \frac{1}{n!} \sum_{k=0}^{n} z(z-1)^{n-k} k! \left\{ {n \atop k} \right\} = \frac{1}{n!} \sum_{k=0}^{n} z^k (1-z)^{n-k} k! \left\{ {n \atop k} \right\}, \tag{18}$$

when $n \geq 1$. The super generating function

$$g(z, x) = \sum_{n \geq 0} \frac{g_n(z) x^n}{z} = \sum_{k, n \geq 0} \left\langle {n \atop k} \right\rangle \frac{z^k x^n}{n!} \tag{19}$$

is therefore equal to

$$\sum_{k,n\geq 0}\frac{((z-1)x)^n}{(z-1)^k}\left\{{n\atop k}\right\}\frac{k!}{n!}=\sum_{k\geq 0}\left(\frac{e^{(z-1)x}-1}{z-1}\right)^k=\frac{(1-z)}{e^{(z-1)x}-z};\qquad(20)$$

this is another relation discussed by Euler.

Further properties of the Eulerian numbers may be found in a survey paper by L. Carlitz [*Math. Magazine* **33** (1959), 247–260]. See also J. Riordan, *Introduction to Combinatorial Analysis* (New York: Wiley, 1958), 38–39, 214–219, 234–237; D. Foata and M. P. Schützenberger, *Lecture Notes in Math.* **138** (Berlin: Springer, 1970).

Let us now consider the length of runs; how long will a run be, on the average? We have already studied the expected number of runs having a given length, in Section 3.3.2; the average run length is approximately 2, in agreement with the fact that about $\frac{1}{2}(n+1)$ runs appear in a random permutation of length n. For applications to sorting algorithms, a slightly different viewpoint is useful; we will consider the length of the kth run of the permutation from left to right, for $k=1,2,\ldots$.

For example, how long is the first (leftmost) run of a random permutation $a_1 a_2 \ldots a_n$? Its length is always ≥ 1, and its length is ≥ 2 exactly one-half the time (namely when $a_1 < a_2$). Its length is ≥ 3 exactly one-sixth of the time (when $a_1 < a_2 < a_3$), and, in general, its length is $\geq m$ with probability $q_m = 1/m!$, for $1 \leq m \leq n$. The probability that its length is exactly equal to m is therefore

$$p_m = q_m - q_{m+1} = 1/m! - 1/(m+1)!, \qquad \text{for } 1 \leq m < n;$$
$$p_n = 1/n!. \qquad(21)$$

The average length of the first run therefore equals

$$p_1 + 2p_2 + \cdots + np_n = (q_1 - q_2) + 2(q_2 - q_3) + \cdots + (n-1)(q_{n-1} - q_n) + nq_n$$
$$= q_1 + q_2 + \cdots + q_n = \frac{1}{1!} + \frac{1}{2!} + \cdots + \frac{1}{n!}. \qquad(22)$$

If we let $n \to \infty$, the limit is $e - 1 = 1.71828\ldots$, and for finite n the value is $e - 1 - \delta_n$ where δ_n is quite small;

$$\delta_n = \frac{1}{(n+1)!}\left(1 + \frac{1}{n+2} + \frac{1}{(n+2)(n+3)} + \cdots\right) \leq \frac{e-1}{(n+1)!}.$$

For practical purposes it is therefore convenient to study runs in a random *infinite* sequence of distinct numbers

$$a_1, a_2, a_3, \ldots;$$

by "random" we mean in this case that each of the $n!$ possible relative orderings of the first n elements in the sequence is equally likely. The average length of the first run in a random infinite sequence is exactly $e - 1$.

By slightly sharpening our analysis of the first run, we can ascertain the average length of the kth run in a random sequence. Let q_{km} be the probability that the first k runs have total length $\geq m$; then q_{km} is $1/m!$ times the number of permutations of $\{1, 2, \ldots, m\}$ that have $\leq k$ runs,

$$q_{km} = \left(\left\langle {m \atop 0} \right\rangle + \cdots + \left\langle {m \atop k-1} \right\rangle \right) \Big/ m!. \tag{23}$$

The probability that the first k runs have total length m is $q_{km} - q_{k(m+1)}$. Therefore if L_k denotes the average length of the kth run, we find that

$$L_1 + \cdots + L_k = \text{average total length of first } k \text{ runs}$$
$$= (q_{k1} - q_{k2}) + 2(q_{k2} - q_{k3}) + 3(q_{k3} - q_{k4}) + \cdots$$
$$= q_{k1} + q_{k2} + q_{k3} + \cdots.$$

Subtracting $L_1 + \cdots + L_{k-1}$ and using the value of q_{km} in (23) yields the desired formula

$$L_k = \frac{1}{1!} \left\langle {1 \atop k-1} \right\rangle + \frac{1}{2!} \left\langle {2 \atop k-1} \right\rangle + \frac{1}{3!} \left\langle {3 \atop k-1} \right\rangle + \cdots = \sum_{m \geq 1} \left\langle {m \atop k-1} \right\rangle \frac{1}{m!}. \tag{24}$$

Since $\left\langle {0 \atop k-1} \right\rangle = 0$ except when $k = 1$, L_k turns out to be the coefficient of z^{k-1} in the generating function $g(z, 1) - 1$ (see Eq. (19)), so we have

$$L(z) = \sum_{k \geq 0} L_k z^k = \frac{z(1-z)}{e^{z-1} - z} - z. \tag{25}$$

From Euler's formula (13) we obtain a representation of L_k as a polynomial in e:

$$L_k = \sum_{m \geq 0} \sum_{j=0}^{k} (-1)^{k-j} \binom{m+1}{k-j} \frac{j^m}{m!}$$

$$= \sum_{j=0}^{k} (-1)^{k-j} \sum_{m \geq 0} \binom{m}{k-j} \frac{j^m}{m!} + \sum_{j=0}^{k} (-1)^{k-j} \sum_{m \geq 0} \binom{m}{k-j-1} \frac{j^m}{m!}$$

$$= \sum_{j=0}^{k} \frac{(-1)^{k-j} j^{k-j}}{(k-j)!} \sum_{n \geq 0} \frac{j^n}{n!} + \sum_{j=0}^{k} \frac{(-1)^{k-j} j^{k-j-1}}{(k-j-1)!} \sum_{n \geq 0} \frac{j^n}{n!}$$

$$= k \sum_{j=0}^{k} \frac{(-1)^{k-j} j^{k-j-1}}{(k-j)!} e^j. \tag{26}$$

This formula for L_k was first obtained by B. J. Gassner [see *CACM* **10** (1967), 89–93]. In particular, we have

$$L_1 = e - 1 \qquad\qquad \approx 1.71828\ldots;$$
$$L_2 = e^2 - 2e \qquad\quad \approx 1.95249\ldots;$$
$$L_3 = e^3 - 3e^2 + \tfrac{3}{2}e \approx 1.99579\ldots.$$

The second run is expected to be longer than the first, and the third run will be longer yet, on the average. This may seem surprising at first glance, but a moment's reflection shows that the first element of the second run tends to be

Table 2

AVERAGE LENGTH OF THE kTH RUN

k	L_k	k	L_k
1	1.71828 18284 59045+	10	2.00000 00012 05997+
2	1.95249 24420 12560−	11	2.00000 00001 93672+
3	1.99579 13690 84285−	12	1.99999 99999 99909+
4	2.00003 88504 76806−	13	1.99999 99999 97022−
5	2.00005 75785 89716+	14	1.99999 99999 99719+
6	2.00000 50727 55710−	15	2.00000 00000 00019+
7	1.99999 96401 44022+	16	2.00000 00000 00006+
8	1.99999 98889 04744+	17	2.00000 00000 00000+
9	1.99999 99948 43434−	18	2.00000 00000 00000−

small (it caused the first run to terminate); hence there is a better chance for the second run to go on longer. The first element of the third run will tend to be even smaller than that of the second.

The numbers L_k are important in the theory of replacement-selection sorting (Section 5.4.1), so it is interesting to study their values in detail. Table 2 shows the first 18 values of L_k to 15 decimal places. Our discussion in the preceding paragraph might lead us to suspect at first that $L_{k+1} > L_k$, but in fact the values oscillate back and forth. Notice that L_k rapidly approaches the limiting value 2; it is quite remarkable to see these monic polynomials in the transcendental number e converging to the rational number 2 so quickly! The polynomials (26) are also somewhat interesting from the standpoint of numerical analysis, since they provide an excellent example of the loss of significant figures when nearly equal numbers are subtracted; using 19-digit floating point arithmetic, Gassner concluded incorrectly that $L_{12} > 2$, and John W. Wrench, Jr., has remarked that 42-digit floating point arithmetic gives L_{28} correct to only 29 significant digits.

The asymptotic behavior of L_k can be determined by using simple principles of complex variable theory. The denominator of (25) is zero only when $e^{z-1} = z$, namely when

$$ e^{x-1} \cos y = x \qquad \text{and} \qquad e^{x-1} \sin y = y, \tag{27} $$

if we write $z = x + iy$. Figure 3 shows the superimposed graphs of these two equations, and we note that they intersect at the points $z = z_0, z_1, \bar{z}_1, z_2, \bar{z}_2, \ldots$, where $z_0 = 1$,

$$ z_1 = (3.08884\ 30156\ 13044-) + (7.46148\ 92856\ 54255-)\,i, \tag{28} $$

and the imaginary part $\Im(z_{k+1})$ is roughly equal to $\Im(z_k) + 2\pi$ for large k. Since

$$ \lim_{z \to z_k} \left(\frac{1-z}{e^{z-1} - z} \right) (z - z_k) = -1, \qquad \text{for } k > 0, $$

and since the limit is -2 for $k = 0$, the function

$$ R_m(z) = L(z) + \frac{2}{z - z_0} + \frac{z_1}{z - z_1} + \frac{\bar{z}_1}{z - \bar{z}_1} + \frac{z_2}{z - z_2} + \frac{\bar{z}_2}{z - \bar{z}_2} + \cdots + \frac{z_m}{z - z_m} + \frac{\bar{z}_m}{z - \bar{z}_m} $$

has no singularities in the complex plane for $|z| < |z_{m+1}|$. Hence $R_m(z)$ has a power series expansion $\sum_k \rho_k z^k$ that converges absolutely when $|z| < |z_{m+1}|$; it follows that $\rho_k M^k \to 0$ as $k \to \infty$, where $M = |z_{m+1}| - \epsilon$. The coefficients of $L(z)$ are the coefficients of

$$\frac{2}{1-z} + \frac{1}{1-z/z_1} + \frac{1}{1-z/\bar{z}_1} + \cdots + \frac{1}{1-z/z_m} + \frac{1}{1-z/\bar{z}_m} + R_m(z),$$

namely,

$$L_n = 2 + 2r_1^{-n}\cos n\theta_1 + 2r_2^{-n}\cos n\theta_2 + \cdots + 2r_m^{-n}\cos n\theta_m + O(r_{m+1}^{-n}), \quad (29)$$

if we let

$$z_k = r_k e^{i\theta_k}. \quad (30)$$

This shows the asymptotic behavior of L_n. We have

$$r_1 = 8.07556\ 64528\ 89526-, \qquad \theta_1 = 1.17830\ 39784\ 74668+;$$
$$r_2 = 14.35456\ 68997\ 62106-, \qquad \theta_2 = 1.31268\ 53883\ 87636+;$$
$$r_3 = 20.62073\ 15381\ 80628-, \qquad \theta_3 = 1.37427\ 90757\ 91688-;$$
$$r_4 = 26.88795\ 29424\ 54546-, \qquad \theta_4 = 1.41049\ 72786\ 51865-; \quad (31)$$

so the main contribution to $L_n - 2$ is due to r_1 and θ_1, and convergence of (29) is quite rapid. Further analysis [W. W. Hooker, *CACM* **12** (1969), 411–413] shows that $R_m(z) \to -z$ as $m \to \infty$; hence the series $2\sum_{k\geq 0} r_k^{-n}\cos n\theta_k$ actually *converges* to L_n when $n > 1$.

A more careful examination of probabilities can be carried out to determine the complete probability distribution for the length of the kth run and for the total length of the first k runs (see exercises 9, 10, 11). The sum $L_1 + \cdots + L_k$ turns out to be asymptotically $2k - \frac{1}{3} + O(8^{-k})$.

Let us conclude this section by considering the properties of runs when equal elements are allowed to appear in the permutations. The famous nineteenth-century American astronomer Simon Newcomb amused himself by playing a game of solitaire related to this question. He would deal a deck of cards into a pile, so long as the face values were in nondecreasing order; but whenever the next card to be dealt had a face value lower than its predecessor, he would start a new pile. He wanted to know the probability that a given number of piles would be formed after the entire deck had been dealt out in this manner.

Simon Newcomb's problem therefore consists of finding the probability distribution of runs in a random permutation of a multiset. The general answer is rather complicated (see exercise 12), although we have already seen how to solve the special case when all cards have a distinct face value. We will content ourselves here with a derivation of the *average* number of piles that appear in the game.

Suppose first that there are m different types of cards, each occurring exactly p times. An ordinary bridge deck, for example, has $m = 13$ and $p = 4$ if suits are disregarded. A remarkable symmetry applying to this case was discovered

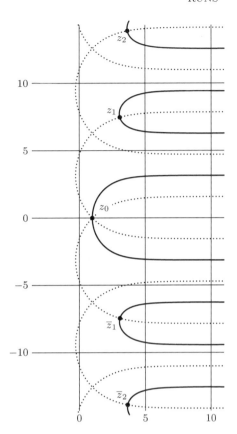

$e^{x-1} \sin y = y$ ———

$e^{x-1} \cos y = x$ ··········

Fig. 3. Roots of $e^{z-1} = z$.

by P. A. MacMahon [*Combinatory Analysis* **1** (Cambridge, 1915), 212–213]:
The number of permutations with $k + 1$ runs is the same as the number with
$mp - p - k + 1$ runs. When $p = 1$, this relation is Eq. (7), but for $p > 1$ it is
quite surprising.

We can prove the symmetry by setting up a one-to-one correspondence
between the permutations in such a way that each permutation with $k + 1$ runs
corresponds to another having $mp - p - k + 1$ runs. The reader is urged to try
discovering such a correspondence before reading further.

No very simple correspondence is evident; MacMahon's proof was based
on generating functions instead of a combinatorial construction. But Foata's
correspondence (Theorem 5.1.2B) provides a useful simplification, because it
tells us that there is a one-to-one correspondence between multiset permutations
with $k + 1$ runs and permutations whose two-line notation contains exactly k
columns $\frac{y}{x}$ with $x < y$.

Suppose the given multiset is $\{p \cdot 1, p \cdot 2, \ldots, p \cdot m\}$, and consider the
permutation whose two-line notation is

$$
\begin{pmatrix}
1 & \cdots & 1 & 2 & \cdots & 2 & \cdots & m & \cdots & m \\
x_{11} & \cdots & x_{1p} & x_{21} & \cdots & x_{2p} & \cdots & x_{m1} & \cdots & x_{mp}
\end{pmatrix}.
\tag{32}
$$

We can associate this permutation with another one,

$$\begin{pmatrix} 1 & \cdots & 1 & 2 & \cdots & 2 & \cdots & m & \cdots & m \\ x'_{11} & \cdots & x'_{1p} & x'_{m1} & \cdots & x'_{mp} & \cdots & x'_{21} & \cdots & x'_{2p} \end{pmatrix}, \qquad (33)$$

where $x' = m+1-x$. If (32) contains k columns of the form $\frac{y}{x}$ with $x < y$, then (33) contains $(m-1)p-k$ such columns; for we need only consider the case $y > 1$, and $x < y$ is equivalent to $x' \geq m+2-y$. Now (32) corresponds to a permutation with $k+1$ runs, and (33) corresponds to a permutation with $mp - p - k + 1$ runs, and the transformation that takes (32) into (33) is reversible — it takes (33) back into (32). Therefore MacMahon's symmetry condition has been established. See exercise 14 for an example of this construction.

Because of the symmetry property, the average number of runs in a random permutation must be $\frac{1}{2}\big((k+1) + (mp-p-k+1)\big) = 1 + \frac{1}{2}p(m-1)$. For example, the average number of piles resulting from Simon Newcomb's solitaire game using a standard deck will be 25 (so it doesn't appear to be a very exciting way to play solitaire).

We can actually determine the average number of runs in general, using a fairly simple argument, given *any* multiset $\{n_1 \cdot x_1, n_2 \cdot x_2, \ldots, n_m \cdot x_m\}$ where the x's are distinct. Let $n = n_1 + n_2 + \cdots + n_m$, and imagine that all of the permutations $a_1 a_2 \ldots a_n$ of this multiset have been written down; we will count how often a_i is greater than a_{i+1}, for each fixed value of i, $1 \leq i < n$. The number of times $a_i > a_{i+1}$ is just half of the number of times $a_i \neq a_{i+1}$; and it is not difficult to see that $a_i = a_{i+1} = x_j$ exactly $Nn_j(n_j - 1)/n(n - 1)$ times, where N is the total number of permutations. Hence $a_i = a_{i+1}$ exactly

$$\frac{N}{n(n-1)}\big(n_1(n_1 - 1) + \cdots + n_m(n_m - 1)\big) = \frac{N}{n(n-1)}(n_1^2 + \cdots + n_m^2 - n)$$

times, and $a_i > a_{i+1}$ exactly

$$\frac{N}{2n(n-1)}\big(n^2 - (n_1^2 + \cdots + n_m^2)\big)$$

times. Summing over i and adding N, since a run ends at a_n in each permutation, we obtain the total number of runs among all N permutations:

$$N\left(\frac{n}{2} - \frac{1}{2n}(n_1^2 + \cdots + n_m^2) + 1\right). \qquad (34)$$

Dividing by N gives the desired average number of runs.

Since runs are important in the study of "order statistics," there is a fairly large literature dealing with them, including several other types of runs not considered here. For additional information, see the book *Combinatorial Chance* by F. N. David and D. E. Barton (London: Griffin, 1962), Chapter 10; and the survey paper by D. E. Barton and C. L. Mallows, *Annals of Math. Statistics* **36** (1965), 236–260.

EXERCISES

1. [*M26*] Derive Euler's formula (13).

▶ **2.** [*M22*] (a) Extend the idea used in the text to prove (8), considering those sequences $a_1 a_2 \ldots a_n$ that contain exactly q distinct elements, in order to prove that

$$\sum_k \left\langle {n \atop k} \right\rangle \binom{k}{n-q} = \left\{ {n \atop q} \right\} q!.$$

(b) Use this identity to prove that

$$\sum_k \left\langle {n \atop k} \right\rangle \binom{k+1}{m} = \left\{ {n+1 \atop n+1-m} \right\} (n-m)!, \qquad \text{for } n \geq m.$$

3. [*HM25*] Evaluate the sum $\sum_k \left\langle {n \atop k} \right\rangle (-1)^k$.

4. [*M21*] What is the value of $\sum_k (-1)^k \left\{ {n \atop k} \right\} k! \binom{n-k}{m}$?

5. [*M20*] Deduce the value of $\left\langle {p \atop k} \right\rangle \bmod p$ when p is prime.

▶ **6.** [*M21*] Mr. B. C. Dull noticed that, by Eqs. (4) and (13),

$$n! = \sum_{k \geq 0} \left\langle {n \atop k} \right\rangle = \sum_{k \geq 0} \sum_{j \geq 0} (-1)^{k-j} \binom{n+1}{k-j} (j+1)^n.$$

Carrying out the sum on k first, he found that $\sum_{k \geq 0} (-1)^{k-j} \binom{n+1}{k-j} = 0$ for all $j \geq 0$; hence $n! = 0$ for all $n \geq 0$. Did he make a mistake?

7. [*HM40*] Is the probability distribution of runs, given by (14), asymptotically normal? (See exercise 1.2.10–13.)

8. [*M24*] (P. A. MacMahon.) Show that the probability that the first run of a sufficiently long permutation has length l_1, the second has length l_2, ..., and the kth has length $\geq l_k$, is

$$\det \begin{pmatrix} 1/l_1! & 1/(l_1+l_2)! & 1/(l_1+l_2+l_3)! & \cdots & 1/(l_1+l_2+l_3+\cdots+l_k)! \\ 1 & 1/l_2! & 1/(l_2+l_3)! & \cdots & 1/(l_2+l_3+\cdots+l_k)! \\ 0 & 1 & 1/l_3! & \cdots & 1/(l_3+\cdots+l_k)! \\ \vdots & & & & \vdots \\ 0 & 0 & \cdots & 1 & 1/l_k! \end{pmatrix}.$$

9. [*M30*] Let $h_k(z) = \sum p_{km} z^m$, where p_{km} is the probability that m is the total length of the first k runs in a random (infinite) sequence. Find "simple" expressions for $h_1(z)$, $h_2(z)$, and the super generating function $h(z,x) = \sum_k h_k(z) x^k$.

10. [*HM30*] Find the asymptotic behavior of the mean and variance of the distributions $h_k(z)$ in the preceding exercise, for large k.

11. [*M40*] Let $H_k(z) = \sum P_{km} z^m$, where P_{km} is the probability that m is the length of the kth run in a random (infinite) sequence. Express $H_1(z)$, $H_2(z)$, and the super generating function $H(z,x) = \sum_k H_k(z) x^k$ in terms of familiar functions.

12. [*M33*] (P. A. MacMahon.) Generalize Eq. (13) to permutations of a multiset, by proving that the number of permutations of $\{n_1 \cdot 1, n_2 \cdot 2, \ldots, n_m \cdot m\}$ having exactly k runs is

$$\sum_{j=0}^k (-1)^j \binom{n+1}{j} \binom{n_1 - 1 + k - j}{n_1} \binom{n_2 - 1 + k - j}{n_2} \cdots \binom{n_m - 1 + k - j}{n_m},$$

where $n = n_1 + n_2 + \cdots + n_m$.

13. [*05*] If Simon Newcomb's solitaire game is played with a standard bridge deck, ignoring face value but treating clubs < diamonds < hearts < spades, what is the average number of piles?

14. [*M18*] The permutation 3 1 1 1 2 3 1 4 2 3 3 4 2 2 4 4 has 5 runs; find the corresponding permutation with 9 runs, according to the text's construction for MacMahon's symmetry condition.

▶ **15.** [*M21*] (*Alternating runs.*) The classical nineteenth-century literature of combinatorial analysis did not treat the topic of runs in permutations, as we have considered them, but several authors studied "runs" that are alternatively ascending and descending. Thus 5 3 2 4 7 6 1 8 was considered to have 4 runs: 5 3 2, 2 4 7, 7 6 1, and 1 8. (The first run would be ascending or descending, according as $a_1 < a_2$ or $a_1 > a_2$; thus $a_1 a_2 \ldots a_n$ and $a_n \ldots a_2 a_1$ and $(n + 1 - a_1)(n + 1 - a_2) \ldots (n + 1 - a_n)$ all have the same number of alternating runs.) When n elements are being permuted, the maximum number of runs of this kind is $n - 1$.

Find the average number of alternating runs in a random permutation of the set $\{1, 2, \ldots, n\}$. [*Hint:* Consider the proof of (34).]

16. [*M30*] Continuing the previous exercise, let $\left|{n \atop k}\right|$ be the number of permutations of $\{1, 2, \ldots, n\}$ that have exactly k alternating runs. Find a recurrence relation, by means of which a table of $\left|{n \atop k}\right|$ can be computed; and find the corresponding recurrence relation for the generating function $G_n(z) = \sum_k \left|{n \atop k}\right| z^k / n!$. Use the latter recurrence to discover a simple formula for the *variance* of the number of alternating runs in a random permutation of $\{1, 2, \ldots, n\}$.

17. [*M25*] Among all 2^n sequences $a_1 a_2 \ldots a_n$, where each a_j is either 0 or 1, how many have exactly k runs (that is, $k - 1$ occurrences of $a_j > a_{j+1}$)?

18. [*M28*] Among all $n!$ sequences $b_1 b_2 \ldots b_n$ such that each b_j is an integer in the range $0 \le b_j \le n - j$, how many have (a) exactly k descents (that is, k occurrences of $b_j > b_{j+1}$)? (b) exactly k distinct elements?

Fig. 4. Nonattacking rooks on a chessboard, with $k = 3$ rooks below the main diagonal.

▶ **19.** [*M26*] (J. Riordan.) (a) In how many ways can n nonattacking rooks — no two in the same row or column — be placed on an $n \times n$ chessboard, so that exactly k lie below the main diagonal? (b) In how many ways can k nonattacking rooks be placed below the main diagonal of an $n \times n$ chessboard?

For example, Fig. 4 shows one of the 15619 ways to put eight nonattacking rooks on a standard chessboard with exactly three rooks in the unshaded portion below the main diagonal, together with one of the 1050 ways to put three nonattacking rooks on a triangular board.

▶ **20.** [*M21*] A permutation is said to require k *readings* if we must scan it k times from left to right in order to read off its elements in nondecreasing order. For example, the permutation $4\,9\,1\,8\,2\,5\,3\,6\,7$ requires four readings: On the first we obtain 1, 2, 3; on the second we get 4, 5, 6, 7; then 8; then 9. Find a connection between runs and readings.

21. [*M22*] If the permutation $a_1\,a_2\ldots a_n$ of $\{1,2,\ldots,n\}$ has k runs and requires j readings, in the sense of exercise 20, what can be said about $a_n\ldots a_2\,a_1$?

22. [*M26*] (L. Carlitz, D. P. Roselle, and R. A. Scoville.) Show that there is no permutation of $\{1,2,\ldots,n\}$ with $n+1-r$ runs, and requiring s readings, if $rs < n$; but such permutations do exist if $n \geq n+1-r \geq s \geq 1$ and $rs \geq n$.

23. [*HM42*] (Walter Weissblum.) The "long runs" of a permutation $a_1\,a_2\ldots a_n$ are obtained by placing vertical lines just before a segment fails to be monotonic; long runs are either increasing or decreasing, depending on the order of their first two elements, so the length of each long run (except possibly the last) is ≥ 2. For example, $7\,5\,\mid\,6\,2\,\mid\,3\,8\,9\,\mid\,1\,4$ has four long runs. Find the average length of the first two long runs of an infinite permutation, and prove that the limiting long-run length is

$$(1 + \cot \tfrac{1}{2})/(3 - \cot \tfrac{1}{2}) \approx 2.4202.$$

24. [*M30*] What is the average number of runs in sequences generated as in exercise 5.1.1–18, as a function of p?

25. [*M25*] Let $U_1,\ldots,U_n$ be independent uniform random numbers in $[0\,..\,1)$. What is the probability that $\lfloor U_1 + \cdots + U_n \rfloor = k$?

26. [*M20*] Let ϑ be the operation $z\frac{d}{dz}$, which multiplies the coefficient of z^n in a generating function by n. Show that the result of applying ϑ to $1/(1-z)$ repeatedly, m times, can be expressed in terms of Eulerian numbers.

▶ **27.** [*M21*] An *increasing forest* is a forest in which the nodes are labeled $\{1,2,\ldots,n\}$ in such a way that parents have smaller numbers than their children. Show that $\left\langle {n \atop k} \right\rangle$ is the number of n-node increasing forests with $k+1$ leaves.

*5.1.4. Tableaux and Involutions

To complete our survey of the combinatorial properties of permutations, we will discuss some remarkable relations that connect permutations with arrays of integers called tableaux. A *Young tableau of shape* $(n_1, n_2, \ldots, n_m)$, where $n_1 \geq n_2 \geq \cdots \geq n_m > 0$, is an arrangement of $n_1 + n_2 + \cdots + n_m$ distinct integers in an array of left-justified rows, with n_i elements in row i, such that the entries of each row are in increasing order from left to right, and the entries of each column are increasing from top to bottom. For example,

$$
\begin{array}{|c|c|c|c|c|c|}
\hline
1 & 2 & 5 & 9 & 10 & 15 \\
\hline
\end{array}
$$

1	2	5	9	10	15
3	6	7	13		
4	8	12	14		
11					

(1)

is a Young tableau of shape (6, 4, 4, 1). Such arrangements were introduced by
Alfred Young as an aid to the study of matrix representations of permutations
[see *Proc. London Math. Soc.* (2) **28** (1928), 255–292; Bruce E. Sagan, *The
Symmetric Group* (Pacific Grove, Calif.: Wadsworth & Brooks/Cole, 1991)]. For
simplicity, we will simply say "tableau" instead of "Young tableau."

An *involution* is a permutation that is its own inverse. For example, there
are ten involutions of $\{1, 2, 3, 4\}$,

$$\begin{pmatrix}1\ 2\ 3\ 4\\1\ 2\ 3\ 4\end{pmatrix}\begin{pmatrix}1\ 2\ 3\ 4\\2\ 1\ 3\ 4\end{pmatrix}\begin{pmatrix}1\ 2\ 3\ 4\\3\ 2\ 1\ 4\end{pmatrix}\begin{pmatrix}1\ 2\ 3\ 4\\4\ 2\ 3\ 1\end{pmatrix}\begin{pmatrix}1\ 2\ 3\ 4\\1\ 3\ 2\ 4\end{pmatrix}$$

$$\begin{pmatrix}1\ 2\ 3\ 4\\1\ 4\ 3\ 2\end{pmatrix}\begin{pmatrix}1\ 2\ 3\ 4\\1\ 2\ 4\ 3\end{pmatrix}\begin{pmatrix}1\ 2\ 3\ 4\\2\ 1\ 4\ 3\end{pmatrix}\begin{pmatrix}1\ 2\ 3\ 4\\3\ 4\ 1\ 2\end{pmatrix}\begin{pmatrix}1\ 2\ 3\ 4\\4\ 3\ 2\ 1\end{pmatrix}$$

$$(2)$$

The term "involution" originated in classical geometry problems; involutions in
the general sense considered here were first studied by H. A. Rothe when he
introduced the concept of inverses (see Section 5.1.1).

It may appear strange that we should be discussing both tableaux and
involutions at the same time, but there is an extraordinary connection between these two apparently unrelated concepts: *The number of involutions of
$\{1, 2, \ldots, n\}$ is the same as the number of tableaux that can be formed from the
elements $\{1, 2, \ldots, n\}$.* For example, exactly ten tableaux can be formed from
$\{1, 2, 3, 4\}$, namely,

$$(3)$$

corresponding respectively to the ten involutions (2).

This connection between involutions and tableaux is by no means obvious,
and there is probably no very simple way to prove it. The proof we will discuss
involves an interesting tableau-construction algorithm that has several other
surprising properties. It is based on a special procedure that inserts new elements
into a tableau.

For example, suppose that we want to insert the element 8 into the tableau

$$(4)$$

The method we will use starts by placing the 8 into row 1, in the spot previously occupied by 9, since 9 is the least element greater than 8 in that row. Element 9 is "bumped down" into row 2, where it displaces the 10. The 10 then "bumps" the 13 from row 3 to row 4; and since row 4 contains no element greater than 13, the process terminates by inserting 13 at the right end of row 4. Thus, tableau (4) has been transformed into

$$
\begin{array}{|c|c|c|c|c|c|}
\hline
1 & 3 & 5 & 8 & 12 & 16 \\
\hline
\end{array}
$$

1	3	5	8	12	16
2	6	9	15		
4	10	14			
11	13				
17					

(5)

A precise description of this process, together with a proof that it always preserves the tableau properties, appears in Algorithm I.

Algorithm I (*Insertion into a tableau*). Let $P = (P_{ij})$ be a tableau of positive integers, and let x be a positive integer not in P. This algorithm transforms P into another tableau that contains x in addition to its original elements. The new tableau has the same shape as the old, except for the addition of a new position in row s, column t, where s and t are quantities determined by the algorithm.

(Parenthesized remarks in this algorithm serve to prove its validity, since it is easy to verify inductively that the remarks are valid and that the array P remains a tableau throughout the process. For convenience we will assume that the tableau has been bordered by zeros at the top and left and with ∞'s to the right and below, so that P_{ij} is defined for all $i, j \geq 0$. If we define the relation

$$a \lesssim b \qquad \text{if and only if} \qquad a < b \quad \text{or} \quad a = b = 0 \quad \text{or} \quad a = b = \infty, \qquad (6)$$

the tableau inequalities can be expressed in the convenient form

$$
\begin{aligned}
P_{ij} = 0 \qquad &\text{if and only if} \qquad i = 0 \quad \text{or} \quad j = 0; \\
P_{ij} \lesssim P_{i(j+1)} \quad &\text{and} \quad P_{ij} \lesssim P_{(i+1)j}, \qquad \text{for all } i, j \geq 0.
\end{aligned} \qquad (7)
$$

The statement "$x \notin P$" means that either $x = \infty$ or $x \neq P_{ij}$ for all $i, j \geq 0$.)

I1. [Input x.] Set $i \leftarrow 1$, set $x_1 \leftarrow x$, and set j to the smallest value such that $P_{1j} = \infty$.

I2. [Find x_{i+1}.] (At this point $P_{(i-1)j} < x_i < P_{ij}$ and $x_i \notin P$.) If $x_i < P_{i(j-1)}$, decrease j by 1 and repeat this step. Otherwise set $x_{i+1} \leftarrow P_{ij}$ and set $r_i \leftarrow j$.

I3. [Replace by x_i.] (Now $P_{i(j-1)} < x_i < x_{i+1} = P_{ij} \lesssim P_{i(j+1)}$, $P_{(i-1)j} < x_i < x_{i+1} = P_{ij} \lesssim P_{(i+1)j}$, and $r_i = j$.) Set $P_{ij} \leftarrow x_i$.

I4. [Is $x_{i+1} = \infty$?] (Now $P_{i(j-1)} < P_{ij} = x_i < x_{i+1} \lesssim P_{i(j+1)}$, $P_{(i-1)j} < P_{ij} = x_i < x_{i+1} \lesssim P_{(i+1)j}$, $r_i = j$, and $x_{i+1} \notin P$.) If $x_{i+1} \neq \infty$, increase i by 1 and return to step I2.

I5. [Determine s, t.] Set $s \leftarrow i$, $t \leftarrow j$, and terminate the algorithm. (At this point the conditions

$$P_{st} \neq \infty \quad \text{and} \quad P_{(s+1)t} = P_{s(t+1)} = \infty \qquad (8)$$

are satisfied.) ∎

Algorithm I defines a "bumping sequence"

$$x = x_1 < x_2 < \cdots < x_s < x_{s+1} = \infty, \qquad (9)$$

as well as an auxiliary sequence of column indices

$$r_1 \geq r_2 \geq \cdots \geq r_s = t; \qquad (10)$$

element P_{ir_i} has been changed from x_{i+1} to x_i, for $1 \leq i \leq s$. For example, when we inserted 8 into (4), the bumping sequence was 8, 9, 10, 13, ∞, and the auxiliary sequence was 4, 3, 2, 2. We could have reformulated the algorithm so that it used much less temporary storage; only the current values of j, x_i, and x_{i+1} need to be remembered. But sequences (9) and (10) have been introduced so that we can prove interesting things about the algorithm.

The key fact we will use about Algorithm I is that it can be run backwards: Given the values of s and t determined in step I5, we can transform P back into its original form again, determining and removing the element x that was inserted. For example, consider (5) and suppose we are told that element 13 is in the position that used to be blank. Then 13 must have been bumped down from row 3 by the 10, since 10 is the greatest element less than 13 in that row; similarly the 10 must have been bumped from row 2 by the 9, and the 9 must have been bumped from row 1 by the 8. Thus we can go from (5) back to (4). The following algorithm specifies this process in detail:

Algorithm D (*Deletion from a tableau*).   Given a tableau P and positive integers s, t satisfying (8), this algorithm transforms P into another tableau, having almost the same shape, but with ∞ in column t of row s. An element x, determined by the algorithm, is deleted from P.

(As in Algorithm I, parenthesized assertions are included here to facilitate a proof that P remains a tableau throughout the process.)

D1. [Input s, t.] Set $j \leftarrow t$, $i \leftarrow s$, $x_{s+1} \leftarrow \infty$.

D2. [Find x_i.] (At this point $P_{ij} < x_{i+1} \lesssim P_{(i+1)j}$ and $x_{i+1} \notin P$.) If $P_{i(j+1)} < x_{i+1}$, increase j by 1 and repeat this step. Otherwise set $x_i \leftarrow P_{ij}$ and $r_i \leftarrow j$.

D3. [Replace by x_{i+1}.] (Now $P_{i(j-1)} < P_{ij} = x_i < x_{i+1} \lesssim P_{i(j+1)}$, $P_{(i-1)j} < P_{ij} = x_i < x_{i+1} \lesssim P_{(i+1)j}$, and $r_i = j$.) Set $P_{ij} \leftarrow x_{i+1}$.

D4. [Is $i = 1$?] (Now $P_{i(j-1)} < x_i < x_{i+1} = P_{ij} \lesssim P_{i(j+1)}$, $P_{(i-1)j} < x_i < x_{i+1} = P_{ij} \lesssim P_{(i+1)j}$, and $r_i = j$.) If $i > 1$, decrease i by 1 and return to step D2.

D5. [Determine x.] Set $x \leftarrow x_1$; the algorithm terminates. (Now $0 < x < \infty$.) ∎

The parenthesized assertions appearing in Algorithms I and D are not only a useful way to prove that the algorithms preserve the tableau structure; they also serve to verify that *Algorithms I and D are perfect inverses of each other.* If we perform Algorithm I first, given some tableau P and some positive integer $x \notin P$, it will insert x and determine positive integers s, t satisfying (8); Algorithm D applied to the result will recompute x and will restore P. Conversely, if we perform Algorithm D first, given some tableau P and some positive integers s, t satisfying (8), it will modify P, deleting some positive integer x; Algorithm I applied to the result will recompute s, t and will restore P. The reason is that the parenthesized assertions of steps I3 and D4 are identical, as are the assertions of steps I4 and D3, and these assertions characterize the value of j uniquely. Hence the auxiliary sequences (9), (10) are the same in each case.

Now we are ready to prove a basic property of tableaux:

Theorem A. *There is a one-to-one correspondence between the set of all permutations of $\{1, 2, \ldots, n\}$ and the set of ordered pairs (P, Q) of tableaux formed from $\{1, 2, \ldots, n\}$, where P and Q have the same shape.*

(An example of this theorem appears within the proof that follows.)

Proof. It is convenient to prove a slightly more general result. Given any two-line array

$$\begin{pmatrix} q_1 & q_2 & \cdots & q_n \\ p_1 & p_2 & \cdots & p_n \end{pmatrix}, \qquad \begin{matrix} q_1 < q_2 < \cdots < q_n, \\ p_1, p_2, \ldots, p_n \text{ distinct}, \end{matrix} \qquad (11)$$

we will construct two corresponding tableaux P and Q, where the elements of P are $\{p_1, \ldots, p_n\}$ and the elements of Q are $\{q_1, \ldots, q_n\}$ and the shape of P is the shape of Q.

Let P and Q be empty initially. Then, for $i = 1, 2, \ldots, n$ (in this order), do the following operation: Insert p_i into tableau P using Algorithm I; then set $Q_{st} \leftarrow q_i$, where s and t specify the newly filled position of P.

For example, if the given permutation is $\begin{pmatrix} 1 & 3 & 5 & 6 & 8 \\ 7 & 2 & 9 & 5 & 3 \end{pmatrix}$, we obtain

$$\begin{array}{ccc} & P & Q \end{array}$$

Insert 7:
$$\boxed{7} \qquad \boxed{1}$$

Insert 2:
$$\begin{matrix} \boxed{2} \\ \boxed{7} \end{matrix} \qquad \begin{matrix} \boxed{1} \\ \boxed{3} \end{matrix}$$

Insert 9:
$$\begin{matrix} \boxed{2}\,\boxed{9} \\ \boxed{7} \end{matrix} \qquad \begin{matrix} \boxed{1}\,\boxed{5} \\ \boxed{3} \end{matrix} \qquad (12)$$

Insert 5:
$$\begin{matrix} \boxed{2}\,\boxed{5} \\ \boxed{7}\,\boxed{9} \end{matrix} \qquad \begin{matrix} \boxed{1}\,\boxed{5} \\ \boxed{3}\,\boxed{6} \end{matrix}$$

Insert 3:
$$\begin{matrix} \boxed{2}\,\boxed{3} \\ \boxed{5}\,\boxed{9} \\ \boxed{7} \end{matrix} \qquad \begin{matrix} \boxed{1}\,\boxed{5} \\ \boxed{3}\,\boxed{6} \\ \boxed{8} \end{matrix}$$

so the tableaux (P, Q) corresponding to $\left(\begin{smallmatrix} 1 & 3 & 5 & 6 & 8 \\ 7 & 2 & 9 & 5 & 3 \end{smallmatrix}\right)$ are

$$
P = \begin{array}{|c|c|} \hline 2 & 3 \\ \hline 5 & 9 \\ \hline 7 \\ \cline{1-1} \end{array} , \qquad
Q = \begin{array}{|c|c|} \hline 1 & 5 \\ \hline 3 & 6 \\ \hline 8 \\ \cline{1-1} \end{array} . \tag{13}
$$

It is clear from this construction that P and Q always have the same shape; furthermore, since we always add elements on the periphery of Q, in increasing order, Q is a tableau.

Conversely, given two equal-shape tableaux P and Q, we can find the corresponding two-line array (11) as follows. Let the elements of Q be

$$ q_1 < q_2 < \cdots < q_n. $$

For $i = n, \ldots, 2, 1$ (in this order), let p_i be the element x that is removed when Algorithm D is applied to P, using the values s and t such that $Q_{st} = q_i$.

For example, this construction will start with (13) and will successively undo the calculation (12) until P is empty, and $\left(\begin{smallmatrix} 1 & 3 & 5 & 6 & 8 \\ 7 & 2 & 9 & 5 & 3 \end{smallmatrix}\right)$ is obtained.

Since Algorithms I and D are inverses of each other, the two constructions we have described are inverses of each other, and the one-to-one correspondence has been established. ∎

The correspondence defined in the poof of Theorem A has many startling properties, and we will now proceed to derive some of them. The reader is urged to work out the example in exercise 1, in order to become familiar with the construction, before proceeding further.

Once an element has been bumped from row 1 to row 2, it doesn't affect row 1 any longer; furthermore rows 2, 3, ... are built up from the sequence of bumped elements in exactly the same way as rows 1, 2, ... are built up from the original permutation. These facts suggest that we can look at the construction of Theorem A in another way, concentrating only on the first rows of P and Q. For example, the permutation $\left(\begin{smallmatrix} 1 & 3 & 5 & 6 & 8 \\ 7 & 2 & 9 & 5 & 3 \end{smallmatrix}\right)$ causes the following action in row 1, according to (12):

$$
\begin{array}{rl}
1: & \text{Insert } 7, \text{ set } Q_{11} \leftarrow 1. \\
3: & \text{Insert } 2, \text{ bump } 7. \\
5: & \text{Insert } 9, \text{ set } Q_{12} \leftarrow 5. \\
6: & \text{Insert } 5, \text{ bump } 9. \\
8: & \text{Insert } 3, \text{ bump } 5.
\end{array} \tag{14}
$$

Thus the first row of P is 2 3, and the first row of Q is 1 5. Furthermore, the remaining rows of P and Q are the tableaux corresponding to the "bumped" two-line array

$$
\begin{pmatrix} 3 & 6 & 8 \\ 7 & 9 & 5 \end{pmatrix}. \tag{15}
$$

In order to study the behavior of the construction on row 1, we can consider the elements that go into a given column of this row. Let us say that (q_i, p_i) is in *class* t with respect to the two-line array

$$\begin{pmatrix} q_1 & q_2 & \cdots & q_n \\ p_1 & p_2 & \cdots & p_n \end{pmatrix}, \qquad \begin{matrix} q_1 < q_2 < \cdots < q_n, \\ p_1, p_2, \ldots, p_n \text{ distinct,} \end{matrix} \tag{16}$$

if $p_i = P_{1t}$ after Algorithm I has been applied successively to $p_1, p_2, \ldots, p_i$, starting with an empty tableau P. (Remember that Algorithm I always inserts the given element into row 1.)

It is easy to see that (q_i, p_i) is in class 1 if and only if p_i has $i - 1$ inversions, that is, if and only if $p_i = \min\{p_1, p_2, \ldots, p_i\}$ is a "left-to-right minimum." If we cross out the columns of class 1 in (16), we obtain another two-line array

$$\begin{pmatrix} q_1' & q_2' & \cdots & q_m' \\ p_1' & p_2' & \cdots & p_m' \end{pmatrix} \tag{17}$$

such that (q, p) is in class t with respect to (17) if and only if it is in class $t+1$ with respect to (16). The operation of going from (16) to (17) represents removing the leftmost position of row 1. This gives us a systematic way to determine the classes. For example in $\begin{pmatrix} 1 & 3 & 5 & 6 & 8 \\ 7 & 2 & 9 & 5 & 3 \end{pmatrix}$ the elements that are left-to-right minima are 7 and 2, so class 1 is $\{(1, 7), (3, 2)\}$; in the remaining array $\begin{pmatrix} 5 & 6 & 8 \\ 9 & 5 & 3 \end{pmatrix}$ all elements are minima, so class 2 is $\{(5, 9), (6, 5), (8, 3)\}$. In the "bumped" array (15), class 1 is $\{(3, 7), (8, 5)\}$ and class 2 is $\{(6, 9)\}$.

For any fixed value of t, the elements of class t can be labeled

$$(q_{i_1}, p_{i_1}), \ldots, (q_{i_k}, p_{i_k})$$

in such a way that

$$\begin{matrix} q_{i_1} < q_{i_2} < \cdots < q_{i_k}, \\ p_{i_1} > p_{i_2} > \cdots > p_{i_k}, \end{matrix} \tag{18}$$

since the tableau position P_{1t} takes on the decreasing sequence of values $p_{i_1}, \ldots,$ p_{i_k} as the insertion algorithm proceeds. At the end of the construction we have

$$P_{1t} = p_{i_k}, \qquad Q_{1t} = q_{i_1}; \tag{19}$$

and the "bumped" two-line array that defines rows 2, 3, ... of P and Q contains the columns

$$\begin{pmatrix} q_{i_2} & q_{i_3} & \cdots & q_{i_k} \\ p_{i_1} & p_{i_2} & \cdots & p_{i_{k-1}} \end{pmatrix} \tag{20}$$

plus other columns formed in a similar way from the other classes.

These observations lead to a simple method for calculating P and Q by hand (see exercise 3), and they also provide us with the means to prove a rather unexpected result:

Theorem B. *If the permutation*

$$\begin{pmatrix} 1 & 2 & \cdots & n \\ a_1 & a_2 & \cdots & a_n \end{pmatrix}$$

corresponds to tableaux (P, Q) *in the construction of Theorem A, then the inverse permutation corresponds to* (Q, P).

This fact is quite startling, since P and Q are formed by such completely different methods in Theorem A, and since the inverse of a permutation is obtained by juggling the columns of the two-line array rather capriciously.

Proof. Suppose that we have a two-line array (16); interchanging the lines and sorting the columns so that the new top line is in increasing order gives the "inverse" array

$$\begin{pmatrix} q_1 & q_2 & \cdots & q_n \\ p_1 & p_2 & \cdots & p_n \end{pmatrix}^- = \begin{pmatrix} p_1 & p_2 & \cdots & p_n \\ q_1 & q_2 & \cdots & q_n \end{pmatrix}$$

$$= \begin{pmatrix} p_1' & p_2' & \cdots & p_n' \\ q_1' & q_2' & \cdots & q_n' \end{pmatrix}, \quad \begin{array}{l} p_1' < p_2' < \cdots < p_n'; \\ q_1', q_2', \ldots, q_n' \text{ distinct.} \end{array} \quad (21)$$

We will show that this operation corresponds to interchanging P and Q in the construction of Theorem A.

Exercise 2 reformulates our remarks about class determination so that the class of (q_i, p_i) doesn't depend on the fact that $q_1, q_2, \ldots, q_n$ are in ascending order. Since the resulting condition is symmetrical in the q's and the p's, the operation (21) does not destroy the class structure; if (q, p) is in class t with respect to (16), then (p, q) is in class t with respect to (21). If we therefore arrange the elements of the latter class t as

$$p_{i_k} < \cdots < p_{i_2} < p_{i_1}, \qquad (22)$$
$$q_{i_k} > \cdots > q_{i_2} > q_{i_1},$$

by analogy with (18), we have

$$P_{1t} = q_{i_1}, \qquad Q_{1t} = p_{i_k} \qquad (23)$$

as in (19), and the columns

$$\begin{pmatrix} p_{i_{k-1}} & \cdots & p_{i_2} & p_{i_1} \\ q_{i_k} & \cdots & q_{i_3} & q_{i_2} \end{pmatrix} \qquad (24)$$

go into the "bumped" array as in (20). Hence the first rows of P and Q are interchanged. Furthermore the "bumped" two-line array for (21) is the inverse of the "bumped" two-line array for (16), so the proof is completed by induction on the number of rows in the tableaux. ∎

Corollary. *The number of tableaux that can be formed from $\{1, 2, \ldots, n\}$ is the number of involutions on $\{1, 2, \ldots, n\}$.*

Proof. If π is an involution corresponding to (P, Q), then $\pi = \pi^-$ corresponds to (Q, P); hence $P = Q$. Conversely, if π is any permutation corresponding to (P, P), then π^- also corresponds to (P, P); hence $\pi = \pi^-$. So there is a one-to-one correspondence between involutions π and tableaux P. ∎

It is clear that the upper-left corner element of a tableau is always the smallest. This suggests a possible way to sort a set of numbers: First we can put the numbers into a tableau, by using Algorithm I repeatedly; this brings the smallest element to the corner. Then we delete the smallest element, rearranging the remaining elements so that they form another tableau; then we delete the new smallest element; and so on.

Let us therefore consider what happens when we delete the corner element from the tableau

$$
\begin{array}{|c|c|c|c|c|c|}
\hline
1 & 3 & 5 & 7 & 11 & 15 \\
\hline
2 & 6 & 8 & 14 \\
\cline{1-4}
4 & 9 & 13 \\
\cline{1-3}
10 & 12 \\
\cline{1-2}
16 \\
\cline{1-1}
\end{array}
\qquad (25)
$$

If the 1 is removed, the 2 must come to take its place. Then we can move the 4 up to where the 2 was, but we can't move the 10 to the position of the 4; the 9 can be moved instead, then the 12 in place of the 9. In general, we are led to the following procedure.

Algorithm S (*Delete corner element*). Given a tableau P, this algorithm deletes the upper left corner element of P and moves other elements so that the tableau properties are preserved. The notational conventions of Algorithms I and D are used.

S1. [Initialize.] Set $r \leftarrow 1$, $s \leftarrow 1$.

S2. [Done?] If $P_{rs} = \infty$, the process is complete.

S3. [Compare.] If $P_{(r+1)s} \lesssim P_{r(s+1)}$, go to step S5. (We examine the elements just below and to the right of the vacant cell, and we will move the smaller of the two.)

S4. [Shift left.] Set $P_{rs} \leftarrow P_{r(s+1)}$, $s \leftarrow s + 1$, and return to S3.

S5. [Shift up.] Set $P_{rs} \leftarrow P_{(r+1)s}$, $r \leftarrow r + 1$, and return to S2. ∎

It is easy to prove that P is still a tableau after Algorithm S has deleted its corner element (see exercise 10). So if we repeat Algorithm S until P is empty, we can read out its elements in increasing order. Unfortunately this doesn't turn out to be as efficient a sorting algorithm as other methods we will see; its minimum running time is proportional to $n^{1.5}$, but similar algorithms that use trees instead of tableau structures have an execution time on the order of $n \log n$.

In spite of the fact that Algorithm S doesn't lead to a superbly efficient sorting algorithm, it has some very interesting properties.

Theorem C (M. P. Schützenberger). *If P is the tableau formed by the construction of Theorem A from the permutation $a_1 a_2 \ldots a_n$, and if*

$$ a_i = \min\{a_1, a_2, \ldots, a_n\}, $$

then Algorithm S changes P to the tableau corresponding to $a_1 \ldots a_{i-1} a_{i+1} \ldots a_n$.

Proof. See exercise 13. ∎

After we apply Algorithm S to a tableau, let us put the deleted element into the newly vacated place P_{rs}, but in *italic type* to indicate that it isn't really part of the tableau. For example, after applying this procedure to the tableau (25) we would have

2	3	5	7	11	15
4	6	8	14		
9	12	13			
10	*1*				
16					

and two more applications yield

4	5	7	11	15	*2*
6	8	13	14		
9	12	*3*			
10	*1*				
16					

Continuing until all elements are removed gives

16	*14*	*13*	*12*	*10*	*2*
15	*9*	*6*	*4*		
11	*5*	*3*			
8	*1*				
7					

(26)

which has the same shape as the original tableau (25). This configuration may be called a *dual tableau*, since it is like a tableau except that the "dual order" has been used (reversing the roles of < and >). Let us denote the dual tableau formed from P in this way by the symbol P^S.

From P^S we can determine P uniquely; in fact, we can obtain the original tableau P from P^S, by applying exactly the same algorithm — but reversing the order and the roles of italic and regular type, since P^S is a dual tableau. For example, two steps of the algorithm applied to (26) give

14	*13*	*12*	*10*	*2*	15
11	*9*	*6*	*4*		
8	*5*	*3*			
7	*1*				
16					

and eventually (25) will be reproduced again! This remarkable fact is one of the consequences of our next theorem.

Theorem D (C. Schensted, M. P. Schützenberger). *Let*

$$\begin{pmatrix} q_1 & q_2 & \cdots & q_n \\ p_1 & p_2 & \cdots & p_n \end{pmatrix} \qquad (27)$$

be the two-line array corresponding to the tableaux (P, Q).

a) *Using dual (reverse) order on the q's, but not on the p's, the two-line array*

$$\begin{pmatrix} q_n & \cdots & q_2 & q_1 \\ p_n & \cdots & p_2 & p_1 \end{pmatrix} \qquad (28)$$

   corresponds to $\bigl(P^T, (Q^S)^T\bigr)$.

As usual, "T" denotes the operation of transposing rows and columns; P^T is a tableau, while $(Q^S)^T$ is a dual tableau, since the order of the q's is reversed.

b) *Using dual order on the p's, but not on the q's, the two-line array* (27) *corresponds to* $\bigl((P^S)^T, Q^T\bigr)$.

c) *Using dual order on both the p's and the q's, the two-line array* (28) *corresponds to* (P^S, Q^S).

Proof. No simple proof of this theorem is known. The fact that case (a) corresponds to (P^T, X) for some dual tableau X is proved in exercise 5; hence by Theorem B, case (b) corresponds to (Y, Q^T) for some dual tableau Y, and Y must have the shape of P^T.

Let $p_i = \min\{p_1, \ldots, p_n\}$; since p_i is the "largest" element in the dual order, it appears on the periphery of Y, and it doesn't bump any elements in the construction of Theorem A. Thus, if we successively insert $p_1, \ldots, p_{i-1}, p_{i+1}, \ldots, p_n$ using the dual order, we get $Y - \{p_i\}$, that is, Y with p_i removed. By Theorem C if we successively insert $p_1, \ldots, p_{i-1}, p_{i+1}, \ldots, p_n$ using the normal order, we get the tableau $d(P)$ obtained by applying Algorithm S to P. By induction on n, $Y - \{p_i\} = \bigl(d(P)^S\bigr)^T$. But since

$$(P^S)^T - \{p_i\} = \bigl(d(P)^S\bigr)^T, \qquad (29)$$

by definition of the operation S, and since Y has the same shape as $(P^S)^T$, we must have $Y = (P^S)^T$.

This proves part (b), and part (a) follows by an application of Theorem B. Applying parts (a) and (b) successively then shows that case (c) corresponds to $\bigl(((P^T)^S)^T, ((Q^S)^T)^T\bigr)$; and this is (P^S, Q^S) since $(P^S)^T = (P^T)^S$ by the row-column symmetry of operation S. ∎

In particular, this theorem establishes two surprising facts about the tableau insertion algorithm: If successive insertion of distinct elements $p_1, \ldots, p_n$ into an empty tableau yields tableau P, insertion in the opposite order $p_n, \ldots, p_1$ yields the *transposed* tableau P^T. And if we not only insert the p's in this order $p_n, \ldots, p_1$ but also interchange the roles of $<$ and $>$, as well as 0 and ∞, in the insertion process, we obtain the dual tableau P^S. The reader is urged to try out these processes on some simple examples. The unusual nature of these coincidences might lead us to suspect that some sort of witchcraft is operating behind the scenes! No simple explanation for these phenomena is yet known; there seems to be no obvious way to prove even that case (c) corresponds to tableaux having the same *shape* as P and Q, although the characterization of classes in exercise 2 does provide a significant clue.

The correspondence of Theorem A was given by G. de B. Robinson [*American J. Math.* **60** (1938), 745–760, §5], in a somewhat vague and different form, as part of his solution to a rather difficult problem in group theory. Robinson stated Theorem B without proof. Many years later, C. Schensted independently rediscovered the correspondence, which he described in terms of "bumping" as we have done in Algorithm I; Schensted also proved the "P" part of Theorem D(a) [see *Canadian J. Math.* **13** (1961), 179–191]. M. P. Schützenberger [*Math. Scand.* **12** (1963), 117–128] proved Theorem C and the "Q" part of Theorem D(a), from which (b) and (c) follow. It is possible to extend the correspondence to permutations of *multisets;* the case that $p_1, \ldots, p_n$ need not be distinct was considered by Schensted, and the "ultimate" generalization to the case that both the p's and the q's may contain repeated elements was investigated by Knuth [*Pacific J. Math.* **34** (1970), 709–727].

Let us now turn to a related question: *How many tableaux formed from* $\{1, 2, \ldots, n\}$ *have a given shape* $(n_1, n_2, \ldots, n_m)$, *where* $n_1 + n_2 + \cdots + n_m = n$? If we denote this number by $f(n_1, n_2, \ldots, n_m)$, and if we allow the parameters n_j to be arbitrary integers, the function f must satisfy the relations

$$f(n_1, n_2, \ldots, n_m) = 0 \quad \text{unless} \quad n_1 \geq n_2 \geq \cdots \geq n_m \geq 0; \tag{30}$$

$$f(n_1, n_2, \ldots, n_m, 0) = f(n_1, n_2, \ldots, n_m); \tag{31}$$

$$f(n_1, n_2, \ldots, n_m) = f(n_1 - 1, n_2, \ldots, n_m) + f(n_1, n_2 - 1, \ldots, n_m)$$
$$+ \cdots + f(n_1, n_2, \ldots, n_m - 1),$$
$$\text{if} \quad n_1 \geq n_2 \geq \cdots \geq n_m \geq 1. \tag{32}$$

Recurrence (32) comes from the fact that a tableau with its largest element removed is always another tableau; for example, the number of tableaux of shape $(6, 4, 4, 1)$ is $f(5, 4, 4, 1) + f(6, 3, 4, 1) + f(6, 4, 3, 1) + f(6, 4, 4, 0) = f(5, 4, 4, 1) + f(6, 4, 3, 1) + f(6, 4, 4)$, since every tableau of shape $(6, 4, 4, 1)$ on $\{1, 2, \ldots, 15\}$ is formed by inserting the element 15 into the appropriate place in a tableau of shape $(5, 4, 4, 1)$, $(6, 4, 3, 1)$, or $(6, 4, 4)$. Schematically,

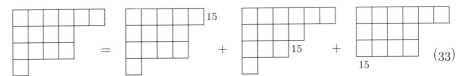

$$(33)$$

The function $f(n_1, n_2, \ldots, n_m)$ that satisfies these relations has a fairly simple form,

$$f(n_1, n_2, \ldots, n_m) = \frac{\Delta(n_1 + m - 1, n_2 + m - 2, \ldots, n_m) \, n!}{(n_1 + m - 1)! \, (n_2 + m - 2)! \, \ldots n_m!}, \tag{34}$$

provided that the relatively mild conditions

$$n_1 + m - 1 \geq n_2 + m - 2 \geq \cdots \geq n_m$$

are satisfied; here Δ denotes the "square root of the discriminant" function

$$\Delta(x_1, x_2, \ldots, x_m) = \det \begin{pmatrix} x_1^{m-1} & x_2^{m-1} & \cdots & x_m^{m-1} \\ \vdots & \vdots & & \vdots \\ x_1^2 & x_2^2 & & x_m^2 \\ x_1 & x_2 & & x_m \\ 1 & 1 & \cdots & 1 \end{pmatrix} = \prod_{1 \leq i < j \leq m} (x_i - x_j). \quad (35)$$

Formula (34) was derived by G. Frobenius [*Sitzungsberichte preuß. Akad. der Wissenschaften* (1900), 516–534, §3], in connection with an equivalent problem in group theory, using a rather deep group-theoretical argument; a combinatorial proof was given independently by MacMahon [*Philosophical Trans.* **A209** (1909), 153–175]. The formula can be established by induction, since relations (30) and (31) are readily proved and (32) follows by setting $y = -1$ in the identity of exercise 17.

Theorem A gives a remarkable identity in connection with this formula for the number of tableaux. If we sum over all shapes, we have

$$n! = \sum_{\substack{k_1 \geq k_2 \geq \cdots \geq k_n \geq 0 \\ k_1 + k_2 + \cdots + k_n = n}} f(k_1, k_2 \ldots, k_n)^2$$

$$= n!^2 \sum_{\substack{k_1 \geq k_2 \geq \cdots \geq k_n \geq 0 \\ k_1 + k_2 + \cdots + k_n = n}} \frac{\Delta(k_1 + n - 1, k_2 + n - 2, \ldots, k_n)^2}{(k_1 + n - 1)!^2 \, (k_2 + n - 2)!^2 \ldots k_n!^2}$$

$$= n!^2 \sum_{\substack{q_1 > q_2 > \cdots > q_n \geq 0 \\ q_1 + q_2 + \cdots + q_n = (n+1)n/2}} \frac{\Delta(q_1, q_2, \ldots, q_n)^2}{q_1!^2 \, q_2!^2 \ldots q_n!^2};$$

hence

$$\sum_{\substack{q_1 + q_2 + \cdots + q_n = (n+1)n/2 \\ q_1, q_2, \ldots, q_n \geq 0}} \frac{\Delta(q_1, q_2, \ldots, q_n)^2}{q_1!^2 \, q_2!^2 \ldots q_n!^2} = 1. \quad (36)$$

The inequalities $q_1 > q_2 > \cdots > q_n$ have been removed in the latter sum, since the summand is a symmetric function of the q's that vanishes when $q_i = q_j$. A similar identity appears in exercise 24.

The formula for the number of tableaux can also be expressed in much more interesting way, based on the idea of "hooks." The *hook* corresponding to a cell in a tableau is defined to be the cell itself plus the cells lying below and to its right. For example, the shaded area in Fig. 5 is the hook corresponding to cell $(2, 3)$ in row 2, column 3; it contains six cells. Each cell of Fig. 5 has been filled in with the length of its hook.

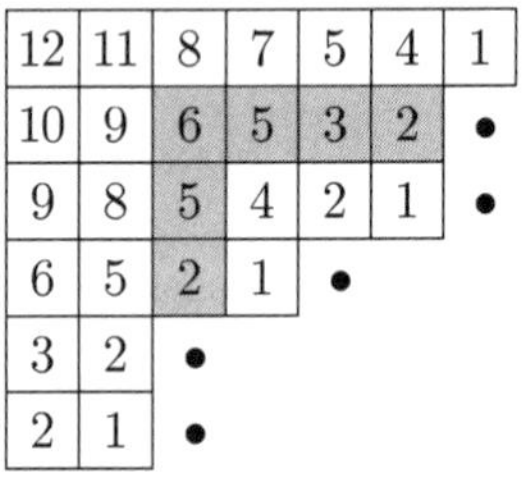

12	11	8	7	5	4	1
10	9	6	5	3	2	•
9	8	5	4	2	1	•
6	5	2	1	•		
3	2	•				
2	1	•				

Fig. 5. Hooks and hook lengths.

If the shape of the tableau is $(n_1, n_2, \ldots, n_m)$, the longest hook has length $n_1 + m - 1$. Further examination of the hook lengths shows that row 1 contains all the lengths $n_1 + m - 1$, $n_1 + m - 2$, ..., 1 *except* for $(n_1 + m - 1) - (n_m)$, $(n_1 + m - 1) - (n_{m-1} + 1)$, ..., $(n_1 + m - 1) - (n_2 + m - 1)$. In Fig. 5, for example, the hook lengths in row 1 are 12, 11, 10, ..., 1 except for 10, 9, 6, 3, 2; the exceptions correspond to five nonexistent hooks, from nonexistent cells $(6, 3)$, $(5, 3)$, $(4, 5)$, $(3, 7)$, $(2, 7)$ leading up to cell $(1, 7)$. Similarly, row j contains all lengths $n_j + m - j$, ..., 1, except for $(n_j + m - j) - (n_m)$, ..., $(n_j + m - j) - (n_{j+1} + m - j - 1)$. It follows that the product of all the hook lengths is equal to

$$\frac{(n_1 + m - 1)! \, (n_2 + m - 2)! \ldots n_m!}{\Delta(n_1 + m - 1, n_2 + m - 2, \ldots, n_m)}.$$

This is just what happens in Eq. (34), so we have derived the following celebrated result due to J. S. Frame, G. de B. Robinson, and R. M. Thrall [*Canadian J. Math.* **6** (1954), 316–318]:

Theorem H. *The number of tableaux on* $\{1, 2, \ldots, n\}$ *having a specified shape is* $n!$ *divided by the product of the hook lengths.* ∎

Since this is such a simple rule, it deserves a simple proof; a heuristic argument runs as follows: Each element of the tableau is the smallest in its hook. If we fill the tableau shape at random, the probability that cell (i, j) will contain the minimum element of the corresponding hook is the reciprocal of the hook length; multiplying these probabilities over all i and j gives Theorem H. But unfortunately this argument is fallacious, since the probabilities are far from independent! No direct proof of Theorem H, based on combinatorial properties of hooks used correctly, was known until 1992 (see exercise 39), although researchers did discover several instructive indirect proofs (exercises 35, 36, and 38).

Theorem H has an interesting connection with the enumeration of trees, which we considered in Chapter 2. We observed that binary trees with n nodes correspond to permutations that can be obtained with a stack, and that such permutations correspond to sequences $a_1 a_2 \ldots a_{2n}$ of n S's and n X's, where the number of S's is never less than the number of X's as we read from left to right. (See exercises 2.2.1–3 and 2.3.1–6.) The latter sequences correspond in a natural way to tableaux of shape (n, n); we place in row 1 the indices i such that $a_i = $ S, and in row 2 we put those indices with $a_i = $ X. For example, the sequence

$$\text{S S S X X S S X X S X X}$$

corresponds to the tableau

1	2	3	6	7	10
4	5	8	9	11	12

$$\tag{37}$$

The column constraint is satisfied in this tableau if and only if the number of X's never exceeds the number of S's from left to right. By Theorem H, the number of tableaux of shape (n, n) is

$$\frac{(2n)!}{(n+1)!\,n!};$$

so this is the number of binary trees, in agreement with Eq. 2.3.4.4–(14). Furthermore, this argument solves the more general "ballot problem" considered in the answer to exercise 2.2.1–4, if we use tableaux of shape (n, m) for $n \geq m$. So Theorem H includes some rather complex enumeration problems as simple special cases.

Any tableau A of shape (n, n) on the elements $\{1, 2, \ldots, 2n\}$ corresponds to two tableaux (P, Q) of the same shape, in the following way suggested by MacMahon [*Combinatory Analysis* **1** (1915), 130–131]: Let P consist of the elements $\{1, \ldots, n\}$ as they appear in A; then Q is formed by taking the remaining elements, rotating the configuration by $180°$, and replacing $n+1$, $n+2$, $\ldots$, $2n$ by n, $n-1$, $\ldots$, 1, respectively. For example, (37) splits into

1	2	3	6
4	5		

and

		7	10
8	9	11	12

;

rotation and renaming of the latter yields

$$P = \begin{array}{|c|c|c|c|} \hline 1 & 2 & 3 & 6 \\ \hline 4 & 5 \\ \cline{1-2} \end{array}, \quad Q = \begin{array}{|c|c|c|c|} \hline 1 & 2 & 4 & 5 \\ \hline 3 & 6 \\ \cline{1-2} \end{array}. \tag{38}$$

Conversely, any pair of equal-shape tableaux of at most two rows, each containing n cells, corresponds in this way to a tableau of shape (n, n). Hence by exercise 7 *the number of permutations* $a_1\, a_2 \ldots a_n$ *of* $\{1, 2, \ldots, n\}$ *containing no decreasing subsequence* $a_i > a_j > a_k$ *for* $i < j < k$ *is the number of binary trees with* n *nodes.* An interesting one-to-one correspondence between such permutations and binary trees, more direct than the roundabout method via Algorithm I that we have used here, has been found by D. Rotem [*Inf. Proc. Letters* **4** (1975), 58–61]; similarly there is a rather direct correspondence between binary trees and permutations having no instances of $a_j > a_k > a_i$ for $i < j < k$ (see exercise 2.2.1–5).

The number of ways to fill a tableau of shape (6,4,4,1) is obviously the number of ways to put the labels $\{1, 2, \ldots, 15\}$ onto the vertices of the directed graph

$$\tag{39}$$

in such a way that the label of vertex u is less than the label of vertex v whenever $u \to v$. In other words, it is the number of ways to sort the partial ordering (39) topologically, in the sense of Section 2.2.3.

In general, we can ask the same question for any directed graph that contains no oriented cycles. It would be nice if there were some simple formula generalizing Theorem H to the case of an arbitrary directed graph; but not all graphs have such pleasant properties as the graphs corresponding to tableaux. Some other classes of directed graphs for which the labeling problem has a simple solution are discussed in the exercises at the close of this section. Other exercises show that some directed graphs have *no* simple formula corresponding to Theorem H. For example, the number of ways to do the labeling is not always a divisor of $n!$.

To complete our investigations, let us count the total number of tableaux that can be formed from n distinct elements; we will denote this number by t_n. By the corollary to Theorem B, t_n is the number of involutions of $\{1, 2, \ldots, n\}$. A permutation is its own inverse if and only if its cycle form consists solely of one-cycles (fixed points) and two-cycles (transpositions). Since t_{n-1} of the t_n involutions have (n) as a one-cycle, and since t_{n-2} of them have $(j\ n)$ as a two-cycle, for fixed $j < n$, we obtain the formula

$$t_n = t_{n-1} + (n-1)t_{n-2}, \tag{40}$$

which Rothe devised in 1800 to tabulate t_n for small n. The values for $n \geq 0$ are 1, 1, 2, 4, 10, 26, 76, 232, 764, 2620, 9496, ...

Counting another way, let us suppose that there are k two-cycles and $(n-2k)$ one-cycles. There are $\binom{n}{2k}$ ways to choose the fixed points, and the multinomial coefficient $(2k)!/(2!)^k$ is the number of ways to arrange the other elements into k distinguishable transpositions; dividing by $k!$ to make the transpositions indistinguishable we therefore obtain

$$t_n = \sum_{k=0}^{\lfloor n/2 \rfloor} t_n(k), \qquad t_n(k) = \frac{n!}{(n-2k)!\, 2^k k!}. \tag{41}$$

Unfortunately, this sum has no simple closed form (unless we choose to regard the Hermite polynomial $i^n 2^{-n/2} H_n(-i/\sqrt{2})$ as simple), so we resort to two indirect approaches in order to understand t_n better:

a) We can find the generating function

$$\sum_n t_n z^n/n! = e^{z+z^2/2}; \tag{42}$$

see exercise 25.

b) We can determine the asymptotic behavior of t_n. This is an instructive problem, because it involves some general techniques that will be useful to us in other connections, so we will conclude this section with an analysis of the asymptotic behavior of t_n.

The first step in analyzing the asymptotic behavior of (41) is to locate the main contribution to the sum. Since

$$\frac{t_n(k+1)}{t_n(k)} = \frac{(n-2k)(n-2k-1)}{2(k+1)}, \tag{43}$$

we can see that the terms gradually increase from $k = 0$ until $t_n(k+1) \approx t_n(k)$ when k is approximately $\frac{1}{2}(n - \sqrt{n}\,)$; then they decrease to zero when k exceeds $\frac{1}{2}n$. The main contribution clearly comes from the vicinity of $k = \frac{1}{2}(n - \sqrt{n}\,)$. It is usually preferable to have the main contribution at the value 0, so we write

$$k = \tfrac{1}{2}(n - \sqrt{n}\,) + x, \tag{44}$$

and we will investigate the size of $t_n(k)$ as a function of x.

One useful way to get rid of the factorials in $t_n(k)$ is to use Stirling's approximation, Eq. 1.2.11.2–(18). For this purpose it is convenient (as we shall see in a moment) to restrict x to the range

$$-n^{\epsilon+1/4} \le x \le n^{\epsilon+1/4}, \tag{45}$$

where $\epsilon = 0.001$, say, so that an error term can be included. A somewhat laborious calculation, which the author did by hand in the 60s but which is now easily done with the help of computer algebra, yields the formula

$$t_n(k) = \exp\bigl(\tfrac{1}{2}\ln n - \tfrac{1}{2}n + \sqrt{n} - \tfrac{1}{4}\ln n - 2x^2/\sqrt{n} - \tfrac{1}{4} - \tfrac{1}{2}\ln \pi$$
$$- \tfrac{4}{3}x^3/n + 2x/\sqrt{n} + \tfrac{1}{3}/\sqrt{n} - \tfrac{4}{3}x^4/n\sqrt{n} + O(n^{5\epsilon-3/4})\bigr). \tag{46}$$

The restriction on x in (45) can be justified by the fact that we may set $x = \pm n^{\epsilon+1/4}$ to get an upper bound for all of the discarded terms, namely

$$e^{-2n^{2\epsilon}}\exp\bigl(\tfrac{1}{2}n\ln n - \tfrac{1}{2}n + \sqrt{n} - \tfrac{1}{4}\ln n - \tfrac{1}{4} - \tfrac{1}{2}\ln \pi + O(n^{3\epsilon-1/4})\bigr), \tag{47}$$

and if we multiply this by n we get an upper bound for the sum of the excluded terms. The upper bound is of lesser order than the terms we will compute for x in the restricted range (45), because of the factor $\exp(-2n^{2\epsilon})$, which is much smaller than any polynomial in n.

We can evidently remove the factor

$$\exp\bigl(\tfrac{1}{2}n\ln n - \tfrac{1}{2}n + \sqrt{n} - \tfrac{1}{4}\ln n - \tfrac{1}{4} - \tfrac{1}{2}\ln \pi + \tfrac{1}{3}/\sqrt{n}\,\bigr) \tag{48}$$

from the sum, and this leaves us with the task of summing

$$\exp\bigl(-2x^2/\sqrt{n} - \tfrac{4}{3}x^3/n + 2x/\sqrt{n} - \tfrac{4}{3}x^4/n\sqrt{n} + O(n^{5\epsilon-3/4})\bigr)$$
$$= \exp\left(\frac{-2x^2}{\sqrt{n}}\right)\left(1 - \frac{4}{3}\frac{x^3}{n} + \frac{x^6}{n^2}\right)\left(1 + 2\frac{x}{\sqrt{n}} + 2\frac{x^2}{n}\right)$$
$$\times \left(1 - \frac{4}{3}\frac{x^4}{n\sqrt{n}}\right)\bigl(1 + O(n^{9\epsilon-3/4})\bigr) \tag{49}$$

over the range $x = \alpha,\ \alpha+1,\ \ldots,\ \beta-2,\ \beta-1$, where $-\alpha$ and β are approximately equal to $n^{\epsilon+1/4}$ (and not necessarily integers). Euler's summation formula, Eq. 1.2.11.2–(10), can be written

$$\sum_{\alpha \le x < \beta} f(x) = \int_\alpha^\beta f(x)\, dx - \frac{1}{2} f(x) \bigg|_\alpha^\beta$$

$$+ \frac{1}{2} B_2 \frac{f'(x)}{1!} \bigg|_\alpha^\beta + \cdots + \frac{1}{m+1} B_{m+1} \frac{f^{(m)}(x)}{m!} \bigg|_\alpha^\beta + R_{m+1}, \quad (50)$$

by translation of the summation interval. Here $|R_m| \le (4/(2\pi)^m) \int_\alpha^\beta |f^{(m)}(x)|\, dx$. If we let $f(x) = x^t \exp(-2x^2/\sqrt{n}\,)$, where t is a fixed nonnegative integer, Euler's summation formula will give an asymptotic series for $\sum f(x)$ as $n \to \infty$, since

$$f^{(m)}(x) = n^{(t-m)/4} g^{(m)}(n^{-1/4}x), \qquad g(y) = y^t e^{-2y^2}, \qquad (51)$$

and $g(y)$ is a well-behaved function independent of n. The derivative $g^{(m)}(y)$ is e^{-2y^2} times a polynomial in y, hence $R_m = O(n^{(t+1-m)/4}) \int_{-\infty}^{+\infty} |g^{(m)}(y)|\, dy = O(n^{(t+1-m)/4})$. Furthermore if we replace α and β by $-\infty$ and $+\infty$ in the right-hand side of (50), we make an error of at most $O(\exp(-2n^\epsilon))$ in each term. Thus

$$\sum_{\alpha \le x < \beta} f(x) = \int_{-\infty}^\infty f(x)\, dx + O(n^{-m}), \qquad \text{for all } m \ge 0; \qquad (52)$$

only the integral is really significant, given this particular choice of $f(x)$! The integral is not difficult to evaluate (see exercise 26), so we can multiply out and sum formula (49), giving $\sqrt{\pi/2}(n^{1/4} - \frac{1}{24}n^{-1/4} + O(n^{-1/2}))$. Thus

$$t_n = \frac{1}{\sqrt{2}} n^{n/2} e^{-n/2+\sqrt{n}-1/4} \left(1 + \frac{7}{24}n^{-1/2} + O(n^{-3/4})\right). \qquad (53)$$

Actually the O terms here should have an extra 9ϵ in the exponent, but our manipulations make it clear that this 9ϵ would disappear if we had carried further accuracy in the intermediate calculations. In principle, the method we have used could be extended to obtain $O(n^{-k})$ for any k, instead of $O(n^{-3/4})$. This asymptotic series for t_n was first determined (using a different method) by Moser and Wyman, *Canadian J. Math.* **7** (1955), 159–168.

The method we have used to derive (53) is an extremely useful technique for asymptotic analysis that was introduced by P. S. Laplace [*Mémoires Acad. Sci. Paris* (1782), 1–88]; it is discussed under the name "trading tails" in *CMath*, §9.4. For further examples and extensions of tail-trading, see the conclusion of Section 5.2.2.

EXERCISES

1. [16] What tableaux (P, Q) correspond to the two-line array

$$\begin{pmatrix} 1 & 2 & 3 & 4 & 5 & 6 & 7 & 8 & 9 \\ 6 & 4 & 9 & 5 & 7 & 1 & 2 & 8 & 3 \end{pmatrix},$$

in the construction of Theorem A? What two-line array corresponds to the tableaux

$$P = \begin{array}{|c|c|c|}\hline 1 & 4 & 7 \\\hline 2 & 8 \\\cline{1-2} 5 & 9 \\\cline{1-2}\end{array} \quad , \quad Q = \begin{array}{|c|c|c|}\hline 1 & 3 & 7 \\\hline 4 & 5 \\\cline{1-2} 8 & 9 \\\cline{1-2}\end{array} \quad ?$$

2. [*M21*] Prove that (q,p) belongs to class t with respect to (16) if and only if t is the largest number of indices $i_1, \ldots, i_t$ such that

$$p_{i_1} < p_{i_2} < \cdots < p_{i_t} = p, \qquad q_{i_1} < q_{i_2} < \cdots < q_{i_t} = q.$$

▶ **3.** [*M24*] Show that the correspondence defined in the proof of Theorem A can also be carried out by constructing a table such as this:

Line 0	1	3	5	6	8
Line 1	7	2	9	5	3
Line 2	∞	7	∞	9	5
Line 3		∞		∞	7
Line 4				∞	

Here lines 0 and 1 constitute the given two-line array. For $k \geq 1$, line $k + 1$ is formed from line k by the following procedure:

a) Set $p \leftarrow \infty$.
b) Let column j be the leftmost column in which line k contains an integer $< p$, but line $k + 1$ is blank. If no such columns exist, and if $p = \infty$, line $k + 1$ is complete; if no such columns exist and $p < \infty$, return to (a).
c) Insert p into column j in line $k + 1$, then set p equal to the entry in column j of line k and return to (b).

Once the table has been constructed in this way, row k of P consists of those integers in line k that are not in line $(k + 1)$; row k of Q consists of those integers in line 0 that appear in a column containing ∞ in line $k + 1$.

▶ **4.** [*M30*] Let $a_1 \ldots a_{j-1} a_j \ldots a_n$ be a permutation of distinct elements, and assume that $1 < j \leq n$. The permutation $a_1 \ldots a_{j-2} a_j a_{j-1} a_{j+1} \ldots a_n$, obtained by interchanging a_{j-1} with a_j, is called "admissible" if either

i) $j \geq 3$ and a_{j-2} lies between a_{j-1} and a_j; or
ii) $j < n$ and a_{j+1} lies between a_{j-1} and a_j.

For example, exactly three admissible interchanges can be performed on the permutation $1\,5\,4\,6\,8\,3\,7$; we can interchange the 1 and the 5 since $1 < 4 < 5$; we can interchange the 8 and the 3 since $3 < 6 < 8$ (or since $3 < 7 < 8$); but we cannot interchange the 5 and the 4, or the 3 and the 7.

a) Prove that an admissible interchange does not change the tableau P formed from the permutation by successive insertion of the elements $a_1, a_2, \ldots, a_n$ into an initially empty tableau.
b) Conversely, prove that any two permutations that have the same P tableau can be transformed into each other by a sequence of one or more admissible interchanges. [*Hint:* Given that the shape of P is $(n_1, n_2, \ldots, n_m)$, show that any permutation that corresponds to P can be transformed into the "canonical permutation" $P_{m1} \ldots P_{mn_m} \cdots P_{21} \ldots P_{2n_2} P_{11} \ldots P_{1n_1}$ by a sequence of admissible interchanges.]

▶ **5.** [*M22*] Let P be the tableau corresponding to the permutation $a_1 a_2 \ldots a_n$; use exercise 4 to prove that P^T is the tableau corresponding to $a_n \ldots a_2 a_1$.

6. [*M26*] (M. P. Schützenberger.) Let π be an involution with k fixed points. Prove that the tableau corresponding to π, in the proof of the corollary to Theorem B, has exactly k columns of odd length.

7. [*M20*] (C. Schensted.) Let P be the tableau corresponding to the permutation $a_1 a_2 \ldots a_n$. Prove that the number of *columns* in P is the longest length c of an increasing subsequence $a_{i_1} < a_{i_2} < \cdots < a_{i_c}$, where $i_1 < i_2 < \cdots < i_c$; the number of *rows* in P is the longest length r of a decreasing subsequence $a_{j_1} > a_{j_2} > \cdots > a_{j_r}$ where $j_1 < j_2 < \cdots < j_r$.

8. [*M18*] (P. Erdős, G. Szekeres.) Prove that any permutation containing more than n^2 elements has a monotonic subsequence of length greater than n; but there are permutations of n^2 elements with no monotonic subsequences of length greater than n. [*Hint:* See the previous exercise.]

9. [*M24*] Continuing exercise 8, find a "simple" formula for the exact number of permutations of $\{1, 2, \ldots, n^2\}$ that have no monotonic subsequences of length greater than n.

10. [*M20*] Prove that P is a tableau when Algorithm S terminates, if it was a tableau initially.

11. [*20*] Given only the values of r and s after Algorithm S terminates, is it possible to restore P to its original condition?

12. [*M24*] How many times is step S3 performed, if Algorithm S is used repeatedly to delete all elements of a tableau P whose shape is $(n_1, n_2, \ldots, n_m)$? What is the minimum of this quantity, taken over all shapes with $n_1 + n_2 + \cdots + n_m = n$?

13. [*M28*] Prove Theorem C.

14. [*M43*] Find a more direct proof of Theorem D, part (c).

15. [*M20*] How many permutations of the multiset $\{l \cdot a, \, m \cdot b, \, n \cdot c\}$ have the property that, as we read the permutation from left to right, the number of c's never exceeds the number of b's, and the number of b's never exceeds the number of a's? (For example, $a\,a\,b\,c\,a\,b\,b\,c\,a\,c\,a$ is such a permutation.)

16. [*M08*] In how many ways can the partial ordering represented by (39) be sorted topologically?

17. [*HM25*] Let

$$g(x_1, x_2, \ldots, x_n; \, y) = x_1 \, \Delta(x_1 + y, x_2, \ldots, x_n) + x_2 \, \Delta(x_1, x_2 + y, \ldots, x_n)$$
$$+ \cdots + x_n \, \Delta(x_1, x_2, \ldots, x_n + y).$$

Prove that

$$g(x_1, x_2, \ldots, x_n; \, y) = \left(x_1 + x_2 + \cdots + x_n + \binom{n}{2} y \right) \Delta(x_1, x_2, \ldots, x_n).$$

[*Hint:* The polynomial g is homogeneous (all terms have the same total degree); and it is antisymmetric in the x's (interchanging x_i and x_j changes the sign of g).]

18. [*HM30*] Generalizing exercise 17, evaluate the sum

$$x_1^m \, \Delta(x_1 + y, x_2, \ldots, x_n) + x_2^m \, \Delta(x_1, x_2 + y, \ldots, x_n) + \cdots + x_n^m \, \Delta(x_1, x_2, \ldots, x_n + y),$$

when $m \geq 0$.

19. [*M40*] Find a formula for the number of ways to fill an array that is like a tableau but with two boxes removed at the left of row 1; for example,

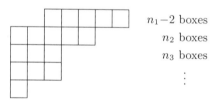

$n_1 - 2$ boxes
n_2 boxes
n_3 boxes
$\vdots$

is such a shape. (The rows and columns are to be in increasing order, as in ordinary tableaux.)

In other words, how many tableaux of shape $(n_1, n_2, \ldots, n_m)$ on the elements $\{1, 2, \ldots, n_1 + \cdots + n_m\}$ have both of the elements 1 and 2 in the first row?

▶ **20.** [*M24*] Prove that the number of ways to label the nodes of a given tree with the elements $\{1, 2, \ldots, n\}$, such that the label of each node is less than that of its descendants, is $n!$ divided by the product of the subtree sizes (the number of nodes in each subtree). For example, the number of ways to label the nodes of

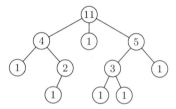

is $11! / 11 \cdot 4 \cdot 1 \cdot 5 \cdot 1 \cdot 2 \cdot 3 \cdot 1 \cdot 1 \cdot 1 \cdot 1 = 10 \cdot 9 \cdot 8 \cdot 7 \cdot 6$. (Compare with Theorem H.)

21. [*HM31*] (R. M. Thrall.) Let $n_1 > n_2 > \cdots > n_m$ specify the shape of a "shifted tableau" where row $i+1$ starts one position to the right of row i; for example, a shifted tableau of shape $(7, 5, 4, 1)$ has the form of the diagram

12	11	8	7	5	4	1
	9	6	5	3	2	
		5	4	2	1	
		1				

Prove that the number of ways to put the integers $1, 2, \ldots, n = n_1 + n_2 + \cdots + n_m$ into shifted tableaux of shape $(n_1, n_2, \ldots, n_m)$, so that rows and columns are in increasing order, is $n!$ divided by the product of the "generalized hook lengths"; a generalized hook of length 11, corresponding to the cell in row 1 column 2, has been shaded in the diagram above. (Hooks in the "inverted staircase" portion of the array, at the left, have a U-shape, tilted $90°$, instead of an L-shape.) Thus there are

$$17!/12 \cdot 11 \cdot 8 \cdot 7 \cdot 5 \cdot 4 \cdot 1 \cdot 9 \cdot 6 \cdot 5 \cdot 3 \cdot 2 \cdot 5 \cdot 4 \cdot 2 \cdot 1 \cdot 1$$

ways to fill the shape with rows and columns in increasing order.

22. [*M39*] In how many ways can an array of shape $(n_1, n_2, \ldots, n_m)$ be filled with elements from the set $\{1, 2, \ldots, N\}$ *with repetitions allowed*, so that the rows are nondecreasing and the columns are strictly increasing? For example, the simple m-rowed shape $(1, 1, \ldots, 1)$ can be filled in $\binom{N}{m}$ ways; the 1-rowed shape (m) can be filled in $\binom{m+N-1}{m}$ ways; the small square shape $(2, 2)$ in $\frac{1}{3}\binom{N+1}{2}\binom{N}{2}$ ways.

▶ **23.** [*HM30*] (D. André.) In how many ways, A_n, can the numbers $\{1, 2, \ldots, n\}$ be placed into the array of n cells

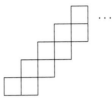

in such a way that the rows and columns are in increasing order? Find the generating function $g(z) = \sum A_n z^n / n!$.

24. [*M28*] Prove that

$$\sum_{\substack{q_1 + \cdots + q_n = t \\ 0 \le q_1, \ldots, q_n \le m}} \binom{m}{q_1} \cdots \binom{m}{q_n} \Delta(q_1, \ldots, q_n)^2$$

$$= n! \binom{nm - (n^2 - n)}{t - \frac{1}{2}(n^2 - n)} \binom{m}{n-1} \binom{m}{n-2} \cdots \binom{m}{0} \Delta(n-1, \ldots, 0)^2.$$

[*Hints:* Prove that $\Delta(k_1 + n - 1, \ldots, k_n) = \Delta(m - k_n + n - 1, \ldots, m - k_1)$; decompose an $n \times (m - n + 1)$ tableau in a fashion analogous to (38); and manipulate the sum as in the derivation of (36).]

25. [*M20*] Why is (42) the generating function for involutions?

26. [*HM21*] Evaluate $\int_{-\infty}^{\infty} x^t \exp(-2x^2/\sqrt{n}) \, dx$ when t is a nonnegative integer.

27. [*M24*] Let Q be a Young tableau on $\{1, 2, \ldots, n\}$; let the element i be in row r_i and column c_i. We say that i is "above" j when $r_i < r_j$.

a) Prove that, for $1 \le i < n$, i is above $i + 1$ if and only if $c_i \ge c_{i+1}$.

b) Given that Q is such that (P, Q) corresponds to the permutation

$$\begin{pmatrix} 1 & 2 & \cdots & n \\ a_1 & a_2 & \cdots & a_n \end{pmatrix},$$

prove that i is above $i + 1$ if and only if $a_i > a_{i+1}$. (Therefore we can determine the number of runs in the permutation, knowing only Q. This result is due to M. P. Schützenberger.)

c) Prove that, for $1 \le i < n$, i is above $i + 1$ in Q if and only if $i + 1$ is above i in Q^S.

28. [*M43*] Prove that the average length of the longest increasing subsequence of a random permutation of $\{1, 2, \ldots, n\}$ is asymptotically $2\sqrt{n}$. (This is the average length of row 1 in the correspondence of Theorem A.)

29. [*HM25*] Prove that a random permutation of n elements has an increasing subsequence of length $\ge l$ with probability $\le \binom{n}{l}/l!$. This probability is $O(1/\sqrt{n})$ when $l = e\sqrt{n} + O(1)$, and $O(\exp(-c\sqrt{n}))$ when $l = 3\sqrt{n}$, $c = 6\ln 3 - 6$.

30. [*M41*] (M. P. Schützenberger.) Show that the operation of going from P to P^S is a special case of an operation applicable in connection with *any* finite partially ordered set, not merely a tableau: Label the elements of a partially ordered set with the integers

$\{1, 2, \ldots, n\}$ in such a way that the partial order is consistent with the labeling. Find a dual labeling analogous to (26), by successively deleting the labels 1, 2, ... while moving the other labels in a fashion analogous to Algorithm S and placing $1, 2, \ldots$ in the vacated places. Show that this operation, when repeated on the dual labeling in reverse numerical order, yields the original labeling; and explore other properties of the operation.

31. [*HM30*] Let x_n be the number of ways to place n mutually nonattacking rooks on an $n \times n$ chessboard, where each arrangement is unchanged by reflection about both diagonals. Thus, $x_4 = 6$. (Involutions are required to be symmetrical about only one diagonal. Exercise 5.1.3–19 considers a related problem.) Find the asymptotic behavior of x_n.

32. [*HM21*] Prove that t_n is the expected value of X^n, when X is a normal deviate with mean 1 and variance 1.

33. [*M25*] (O. H. Mitchell, 1881.) True or false: $\Delta(a_1, a_2, \ldots, a_m)/\Delta(1, 2, \ldots, m)$ is an integer when $a_1, a_2, \ldots, a_m$ are integers.

34. [*25*] (T. Nakayama, 1940.) Prove that if a tableau shape contains a hook of length ab, it contains a hook of length a.

▶ **35.** [*30*] (A. P. Hillman and R. M. Grassl, 1976.) An arrangement of nonnegative integers p_{ij} in a tableau shape is called a *plane partition of m* if $\sum p_{ij} = m$ and

$$p_{i1} \geq \cdots \geq p_{in_i}, \qquad p_{1j} \geq \cdots \geq p_{n'_j j}, \qquad \text{for } 1 \leq i \leq n'_1, 1 \leq j \leq n_1,$$

when there are n_i cells in row i and n'_j cells in column j. It is called a *reverse plane partition* if instead

$$p_{i1} \leq \cdots \leq p_{in_i}, \qquad p_{1j} \leq \cdots \leq p_{n'_j j}, \qquad \text{for } 1 \leq i \leq n'_1, 1 \leq j \leq n_1.$$

Consider the following algorithm, which operates on reverse plane partitions of a given shape and constructs another array of numbers q_{ij} having the same shape:

G1. [Initialize.] Set $q_{ij} \leftarrow 0$ for $1 \leq j \leq n_i$ and $1 \leq i \leq n'_1$. Then set $j \leftarrow 1$.

G2. [Find nonzero cell.] If $p_{n'_j j} > 0$, set $i \leftarrow n'_j$, $k \leftarrow j$, and go on to step G3. Otherwise if $j < n_1$, increase j by 1 and repeat this step. Otherwise stop (the p array is now zero).

G3. [Decrease p.] Decrease p_{ik} by 1.

G4. [Move up or right.] If $i > 1$ and $p_{(i-1)k} > p_{ik}$, decrease i by 1 and return to G3. Otherwise if $k < n_i$, increase k by 1 and return to G3.

G5. [Increase q.] Increase q_{ij} by 1 and return to G2. ∎

Prove that this construction defines a one-to-one correspondence between reverse plane partitions of m and solutions of the equation

$$m = \sum h_{ij} q_{ij},$$

where the numbers h_{ij} are the hook lengths of the shape, by designing an algorithm that recomputes the p's from the q's.

36. [*HM27*] (R. P. Stanley, 1971.) (a) Prove that the number of reverse plane partitions of m in a given shape is $[z^m] 1/\prod(1 - z^{h_{ij}})$, where the numbers h_{ij} are the hook lengths of the shape. (b) Derive Theorem H from this result. [*Hint:* What is the asymptotic number of partitions as $m \to \infty$?]

37. [*M20*] (P. A. MacMahon, 1912.) What is the generating function for all plane partitions? (The coefficient of z^m should be the total number of plane partitions of m when the tableau shape is unbounded.)

▶ **38.** [*M30*] (Greene, Nijenhuis, and Wilf, 1979.) We can construct a directed acyclic graph on the cells T of any given tableau shape by letting arcs run from each cell to the other cells in its hook; the outdegree of cell (i,j) will then be $d_{ij} = h_{ij} - 1$, where h_{ij} is the hook length. Suppose we generate a random path in this digraph by choosing a random starting cell (i,j) and choosing further arcs at random, until coming to a corner cell from which there is no exit. Each random choice is made uniformly.

    a) Let (a,b) be a corner cell of T, and let $I = \{i_0, \ldots, i_k\}$ and $J = \{j_0, \ldots, j_l\}$ be sets of rows and columns with $i_0 < \cdots < i_k = a$ and $j_0 < \cdots < j_l = b$. The digraph contains $\binom{k+l}{k}$ paths whose row and columns sets are respectively I and J; let $P(I, J)$ be the probability that the random path is one of these. Prove that $P(I, J) = 1/(n\, d_{i_0 b} \ldots d_{i_{k-1} b}\, d_{a j_0} \ldots d_{a j_{l-1}})$, where $n = |T|$.

    b) Let $f(T) = n!/\prod h_{ij}$. Prove that the random path ends at corner (a,b) with probability $f(T \setminus \{(a,b)\})/f(T)$.

    c) Show that the result of (b) proves Theorem H and also gives us a way to generate a random tableau of shape T, with all $f(T)$ tableaux equally likely.

39. [*M38*] (I. M. Pak and A. V. Stoyanovskii, 1992.) Let P be an array of shape $(n_1, \ldots, n_m)$ that has been filled with any permutation of the integers $\{1, \ldots, n\}$, where $n = n_1 + \cdots + n_m$. The following procedure, which is analogous to the "siftup" algorithm in Section 5.2.3, can be used to convert P to a tableau. It also defines an array Q of the same shape, which can be used to provide a combinatorial proof of Theorem H.

    P1. [Loop on (i,j).] Perform steps P2 and P3 for all cells (i,j) of the array, in reverse lexicographic order (that is, from bottom to top, and from right to left in each row); then stop.

    P2. [Fix P at (i,j).] Set $K \leftarrow P_{ij}$ and perform Algorithm S' (see below).

    P3. [Adjust Q.] Set $Q_{ik} \leftarrow Q_{i(k+1)} + 1$ for $j \le k < s$, and set $Q_{is} \leftarrow i - r$. ∎

Here Algorithm S' is the same as Schützenberger's Algorithm S, except that steps S1 and S2 are generalized slightly:

    S1'. [Initialize.] Set $r \leftarrow i$, $s \leftarrow j$.

    S2'. [Done?] If $K \lesssim P_{(r+1)s}$ and $K \lesssim P_{r(s+1)}$, set $P_{rs} \leftarrow K$ and terminate.

(Algorithm S is essentially the special case $i = 1$, $j = 1$, $K = \infty$.)

    For example, Algorithm P straightens out one particular array of shape $(3, 3, 2)$ in the following way, if we view the contents of arrays P and Q at the beginning of step P2, with P_{ij} in boldface type:

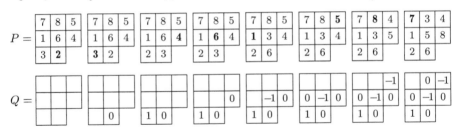

The final result is

$$P = \begin{array}{|c|c|c|} \hline 1 & 3 & 4 \\ \hline 2 & 5 & 8 \\ \hline 6 & 7 \\ \cline{1-2} \end{array}, \qquad Q = \begin{array}{|c|c|c|} \hline 1 & -2 & -1 \\ \hline 0 & -1 & 0 \\ \hline 1 & 0 \\ \cline{1-2} \end{array}.$$

a) If P is simply a $1 \times n$ array, Algorithm P sorts it into $\boxed{1}\ \cdots\ \boxed{n}$. Explain what the Q array will contain in that case.

b) Answer the same question if P is $n \times 1$ instead of $1 \times n$.

c) Prove that, in general, we will have

$$-b_{ij} \le Q_{ij} \le r_{ij},$$

where b_{ij} is the number of cells below (i, j) and r_{ij} is the number of cells to the right. Thus, the number of possible values for Q_{ij} is exactly h_{ij}, the size of the (i, j)th hook.

d) Theorem H will be proved constructively if we can show that Algorithm P defines a one-to-one correspondence between the $n!$ ways to fill the original shape and the pairs of output arrays (P, Q), where P is a tableau and the elements of Q satisfy the condition of part (c). Therefore we want to find an inverse of Algorithm P. For what initial permutations does Algorithm P produce the 2×2 array $Q = \left(\begin{smallmatrix} 0 & -1 \\ 0 & 0 \end{smallmatrix}\right)$?

e) What initial permutation does Algorithm P convert into the arrays

$$P = \begin{array}{|c|c|c|c|c|c|} \hline 1 & 3 & 5 & 7 & 11 & 15 \\ \hline 2 & 6 & 8 & 14 \\ \cline{1-4} 4 & 9 & 13 \\ \cline{1-3} 10 & 12 \\ \cline{1-2} 16 \\ \cline{1-1} \end{array}, \qquad Q = \begin{array}{|c|c|c|c|c|c|} \hline -2 & -3 & -1 & -1 & 1 & 0 \\ \hline 3 & -2 & -1 & 0 \\ \cline{1-4} 0 & -1 & 0 \\ \cline{1-3} -1 & 0 \\ \cline{1-2} 0 \\ \cline{1-1} \end{array} \qquad ?$$

f) Design an algorithm that inverts Algorithm P, given any pair of arrays (P, Q) such that P is a tableau and Q satisfies the condition of part (c). [*Hint:* Construct an oriented tree whose vertices are the cells (i, j), with arcs

$$\begin{aligned} (i, j) &\to (i, j - 1) \quad \text{if } P_{i(j-1)} > P_{(i-1)j}; \\ (i, j) &\to (i - 1, j) \quad \text{if } P_{i(j-1)} < P_{(i-1)j}. \end{aligned}$$

In the example of part (e) we have the tree

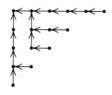

The paths of this tree hold the key to inverting Algorithm P.]

40. [*HM43*] Suppose a random Young tableau has been constructed by successively placing the numbers $1, 2, \ldots, n$ in such a way that each possibility is equally likely when a new number is placed. For example, the tableau (1) would be obtained with probability $\frac{1}{1} \cdot \frac{1}{2} \cdot \frac{1}{2} \cdot \frac{1}{3} \cdot \frac{1}{3} \cdot \frac{1}{3} \cdot \frac{1}{4} \cdot \frac{1}{3} \cdot \frac{1}{3} \cdot \frac{1}{4} \cdot \frac{1}{4} \cdot \frac{1}{5} \cdot \frac{1}{4}$ using this procedure.

Prove that, with high probability, the resulting shape $(n_1, n_2, \ldots, n_m)$ will have $m \approx \sqrt{6n}$ and $\sqrt{k} + \sqrt{n_{k+1}} \approx \sqrt{m}$ for $0 \le k \le m$.

41. [25] (*Disorder in a library.*) Casual users of a library often put books back on the shelves in the wrong place. One way to measure the amount of disorder present in a library is to consider the minimum number of times we would have to take a book out of one place and insert it in another, before all books are restored to the correct order.

Thus let $\pi = a_1 a_2 \ldots a_n$ be a permutation of $\{1, 2, \ldots, n\}$. A "deletion-insertion operation" changes π to

$$a_1 \ldots a_{i-1} \, a_{i+1} \ldots a_j \, a_i \, a_{j+1} \ldots a_n \qquad \text{or} \qquad a_1 \ldots a_j \, a_i \, a_{j+1} \ldots a_{i-1} \, a_{i+1} \ldots a_n,$$

for some i and j. Let $\mathrm{dis}(\pi)$ be the minimum number of deletion-insertion operations that will sort π into order. Can $\mathrm{dis}(\pi)$ be expressed in terms of simpler characteristics of π?

▶ **42.** [30] (*Disorder in a genome.*) The DNA of *Lobelia fervens* has genes occurring in the sequence $g_7^R g_1 g_2 g_4 g_5 g_3 g_6^R$, where g_7^R stands for the left-right reflection of g_7; the same genes occur in tobacco plants, but in the order $g_1 g_2 g_3 g_4 g_5 g_6 g_7$. Show that five "flip" operations on substrings are needed to get from $g_1 g_2 g_3 g_4 g_5 g_6 g_7$ to $g_7^R g_1 g_2 g_4 g_5 g_3 g_6^R$. (A flip takes $\alpha\beta\gamma$ to $\alpha\beta^R\gamma$, when α, β, and γ are strings.)

43. [35] Continuing the previous exercise, show that at most $n + 1$ flips are needed to sort any rearrangement of $g_1 g_2 \ldots g_n$. Construct examples that require $n + 1$ flips, for all $n > 3$.

44. [M37] Show that the average number of flips required to sort a random arrangement of n genes is greater than $n - H_n$, if all $2^n \, n!$ genome rearrangements are equally likely.

5.2. INTERNAL SORTING

LET'S BEGIN our discussion of good "sortsmanship" by conducting a little experiment. How would you solve the following programming problem?

"Memory locations R+1, R+2, R+3, R+4, and R+5 contain five numbers. Write a computer program that rearranges these numbers, if necessary, so that they are in ascending order."

(If you already are familiar with some sorting methods, please do your best to forget about them momentarily; imagine that you are attacking this problem for the first time, without any prior knowledge of how to proceed.)

Before reading any further, you are requested to construct a solution to this problem.

. . . .

The time you spent working on the challenge problem will pay dividends as you continue to read this chapter. Chances are your solution is one of the following types:

A. *An insertion sort.* The items are considered one at a time, and each new item is inserted into the appropriate position relative to the previously-sorted items. (This is the way many bridge players sort their hands, picking up one card at a time.)

B. *An exchange sort.* If two items are found to be out of order, they are interchanged. This process is repeated until no more exchanges are necessary.

C. *A selection sort.* First the smallest (or perhaps the largest) item is located, and it is somehow separated from the rest; then the next smallest (or next largest) is selected, and so on.

D. *An enumeration sort.* Each item is compared with each of the others; an item's final position is determined by the number of keys that it exceeds.

E. *A special-purpose sort,* which works nicely for sorting five elements as stated in the problem, but does not readily generalize to larger numbers of items.

F. *A lazy attitude,* with which you ignored the suggestion above and decided not to solve the problem at all. Sorry, by now you have read too far and you have lost your chance.

G. *A new, super sorting technique* that is a definite improvement over known methods. (Please communicate this to the author at once.)

If the problem had been posed for, say, 1000 items, not merely 5, you might also have discovered some of the more subtle techniques that will be mentioned later. At any rate, when attacking a new problem it is often wise to find some fairly obvious procedure that works, and then try to improve upon it. Cases A, B, and C above lead to important classes of sorting techniques that are refinements of the simple ideas stated.

Many different sorting algorithms have been invented, and we will be discussing about 25 of them in this book. This rather alarming number of methods is actually only a fraction of the algorithms that have been devised so far; many techniques that are now obsolete will be omitted from our discussion, or mentioned only briefly. Why are there so many sorting methods? For computer programming, this is a special case of the question, "Why are there so many x methods?", where x ranges over the set of problems; and the answer is that each method has its own advantages and disadvantages, so that it outperforms the others on some configurations of data and hardware. Unfortunately, there is no known "best" way to sort; there are *many* best methods, depending on what is to be sorted on what machine for what purpose. In the words of Rudyard Kipling, "There are nine and sixty ways of constructing tribal lays, and every single one of them is right."

It is a good idea to learn the characteristics of each sorting method, so that an intelligent choice can be made for particular applications. Fortunately, it is not a formidable task to learn these algorithms, since they are interrelated in interesting ways.

At the beginning of this chapter we defined the basic terminology and notation to be used in our study of sorting: The records

$$R_1, R_2, \ldots, R_N \tag{1}$$

are supposed to be sorted into nondecreasing order of their keys $K_1, K_2, \ldots, K_N$, essentially by discovering a permutation $p(1)\, p(2) \ldots p(N)$ such that

$$K_{p(1)} \leq K_{p(2)} \leq \cdots \leq K_{p(N)}. \tag{2}$$

In the present section we are concerned with *internal sorting*, when the number of records to be sorted is small enough that the entire process can be performed in a computer's high-speed memory.

In some cases we will want the records to be physically rearranged in memory so that their keys are in order, while in other cases it may be sufficient merely to have an auxiliary table of some sort that specifies the permutation. If the records and/or the keys each take up quite a few words of computer memory, it is often better to make up a new table of link addresses that point to the records, and to manipulate these link addresses instead of moving the bulky records around. This method is called *address table sorting* (see Fig. 6). If the key is short but the satellite information of the records is long, the key may be placed with the link addresses for greater speed; this is called *keysorting*. Other sorting schemes utilize an auxiliary link field that is included in each record; these links are manipulated in such a way that, in the final result, the records are linked together to form a straight linear list, with each link pointing to the following record. This is called *list sorting* (see Fig. 7).

After sorting with an address table or list method, the records can be rearranged into increasing order as desired. Exercises 10 and 12 discuss interesting ways to do this, requiring only enough additional memory space to hold one record; alternatively, we can simply move the records into a new area capable of holding all records. The latter method is usually about twice as fast as the former, but it demands nearly twice as much storage space. Many applications can get by without moving the records at all, since the link fields are often adequate for all of the subsequent processing.

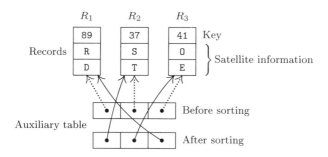

Fig. 6. Address table sorting.

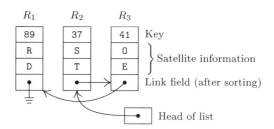

Fig. 7. List sorting.

All of the sorting methods that we shall examine in depth will be illustrated in four ways, by means of

a) an English-language description of the algorithm,

b) a flow diagram,

c) a MIX program, and

d) an example of the sorting method applied to a certain set of 16 numbers.

For convenience, the MIX programs will usually assume that the key is numeric and that it fits in a single word; sometimes we will even restrict the key to part of a word. The order relation < will be ordinary arithmetic order; and the record will consist of the key alone, with no satellite information. These assumptions make the programs shorter and easier to understand, and a reader should find it fairly easy to adapt any of the programs to the general case by using address table sorting or list sorting. An analysis of the running time of each sorting algorithm will be given with the MIX programs.

Sorting by counting. As a simple example of the way in which we shall study internal sorting methods, let us consider the "counting" idea mentioned near the beginning of this section. This simple method is based on the idea that the jth key in the final sorted sequence is greater than exactly $j-1$ of the other keys. Putting this another way, if we know that a certain key exceeds exactly 27 others, and if no two keys are equal, the corresponding record should go into position 28 after sorting. So the idea is to compare every pair of keys, counting how many are less than each particular one.

The obvious way to do the comparisons is to

$$\big((\text{compare } K_j \text{ with } K_i) \text{ for } 1 \le j \le N\big) \text{ for } 1 \le i \le N;$$

but it is easy to see that more than half of these comparisons are redundant, since it is unnecessary to compare a key with itself, and it is unnecessary to compare K_a with K_b and later to compare K_b with K_a. We need merely to

$$\big((\text{compare } K_j \text{ with } K_i) \text{ for } 1 \le j < i\big) \text{ for } 1 < i \le N.$$

Hence we are led to the following algorithm.

Algorithm C (*Comparison counting*). This algorithm sorts $R_1, \ldots, R_N$ on the keys $K_1, \ldots, K_N$ by maintaining an auxiliary table COUNT[1], ..., COUNT[N] to count the number of keys less than a given key. After the conclusion of the algorithm, COUNT[j] + 1 will specify the final position of record R_j.

C1. [Clear COUNTs.] Set COUNT[1] through COUNT[N] to zero.

C2. [Loop on i.] Perform step C3, for $i = N, N-1, \ldots, 2$; then terminate the algorithm.

C3. [Loop on j.] Perform step C4, for $j = i-1, i-2, \ldots, 1$.

C4. [Compare $K_i : K_j$.] If $K_i < K_j$, increase COUNT[j] by 1; otherwise increase COUNT[i] by 1. ∎

Note that this algorithm involves no movement of records. It is similar to an address table sort, since the COUNT table specifies the final arrangement of records; but it is somewhat different because COUNT[j] tells us where to move R_j, instead of indicating which record should be moved into the place of R_j. (Thus the COUNT table specifies the *inverse* of the permutation $p(1) \ldots p(N)$; see Section 5.1.1.)

Table 1 illustrates the typical behavior of comparison counting, by applying it to 16 numbers that were chosen at random by the author on March 19, 1963. The same 16 numbers will be used to illustrate almost all of other methods that we shall discuss later.

In our discussion preceding this algorithm we blithely assumed that no two keys were equal. This was a potentially dangerous assumption, for if equal keys corresponded to equal COUNTs the final rearrangement of records would be quite complicated. Fortunately, however, Algorithm C gives the correct result no matter how many equal keys are present; see exercise 2.

Program C (*Comparison counting*). The following MIX implementation of Algorithm C assumes that R_j is stored in location INPUT + j, and COUNT[j] in location COUNT + j, for $1 \le j \le N$; rI1 $\equiv i$; rI2 $\equiv j$; rA $\equiv K_i \equiv R_i$; rX $\equiv$ COUNT[i].

```
01  START  ENT1 N          1    C1. Clear COUNTs.
02         STZ  COUNT,1     N    COUNT[i] ← 0.
03         DEC1 1           N
04         J1P  *-2         N    N ≥ i > 0.
```

Table 2

SORTING BY COUNTING (ALGORITHM C)

KEYS:	503	087	512	061	908	170	897	275	653	426	154	509	612	677	765	703
COUNT (init.):	0	0	0	0	0	0	0	0	0	0	0	0	0	0	0	0
COUNT ($i = N$):	0	0	0	0	1	0	1	0	0	0	0	0	0	0	1	12
COUNT ($i = N-1$):	0	0	0	0	2	0	2	0	0	0	0	0	0	0	13	12
COUNT ($i = N-2$):	0	0	0	0	3	0	3	0	0	0	0	0	0	11	13	12
COUNT ($i = N-3$):	0	0	0	0	4	0	4	0	1	0	0	0	9	11	13	12
COUNT ($i = N-4$):	0	0	1	0	5	0	5	0	2	0	0	7	9	11	13	12
COUNT ($i = N-5$):	1	0	2	0	6	1	6	1	3	1	2	7	9	11	13	12
. . . .																
COUNT ($i = 2$):	6	1	8	0	15	3	14	4	10	5	2	7	9	11	13	12

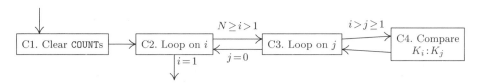

Fig. 8. Algorithm C: Comparison counting.

05		ENT1	N	1	C2. Loop on i.
06		JMP	1F	1	
07	2H	LDA	INPUT,1	$N-1$	
08		LDX	COUNT,1	$N-1$	
09	3H	CMPA	INPUT,2	A	C4. Compare $K_i : K_j$.
10		JGE	4F	A	Jump if $K_i \geq K_j$.
11		LD3	COUNT,2	B	COUNT[j]
12		INC3	1	B	+1
13		ST3	COUNT,2	B	$\to$ COUNT[j].
14		JMP	5F	B	
15	4H	INCX	1	$A - B$	COUNT[i] $\leftarrow$ COUNT[i] $+ 1$.
16	5H	DEC2	1	A	C3. Loop on j.
17		J2P	3B	A	
18		STX	COUNT,1	$N-1$	
19		DEC1	1	$N-1$	
20	1H	ENT2	-1,1	N	$N \geq i > j > 0$.
21		J2P	2B	N	▮

The running time of this program is $13N + 6A + 5B - 4$ units, where N is the number of records; A is the number of choices of two things from a set of N objects, namely $\binom{N}{2} = (N^2 - N)/2$; and B is the number of pairs of indices for which $j < i$ and $K_j > K_i$. Thus, B is the number of *inversions* of the permutation $K_1, \ldots, K_N$; this is the quantity that was analyzed extensively in Section 5.1.1, where we found in Eqs. 5.1.1–(12) and 5.1.1–(13) that, for unequal keys in random order, we have

$$B = \left(\min 0, \ \text{ave } (N^2-N)/4, \ \max (N^2-N)/2, \ \text{dev } \sqrt{N(N - 1)(N + 2.5)/6}\right).$$

Hence Program C requires between $3N^2 + 10N - 4$ and $5.5N^2 + 7.5N - 4$ units
of time, and the average running time lies halfway between these two extremes.
For example, the data in Table 1 has $N = 16$, $A = 120$, $B = 41$, so Program C
will sort it in $1129u$. See exercise 5 for a modification of Program C that has
slightly different timing characteristics.

The factor N^2 that dominates this running time shows that Algorithm C
is not an efficient way to sort when N is large; doubling the number of records
increases the running time fourfold. Since the method requires a comparison of
all distinct pairs of keys (K_i, K_j), there is no apparent way to get rid of the
dependence on N^2, although we will see later in this chapter that the worst-case
running time for sorting can be reduced to order $N \log N$ using other techniques.
Our main interest in Algorithm C is its simplicity, not its speed. Algorithm C
serves as an example of the style in which we will be describing more complex
(and more efficient) methods.

There is another way to sort by counting that *is* quite important from the
standpoint of efficiency; it is primarily applicable in the case that many equal
keys are present, and when all keys fall into the range $u \le K_j \le v$, where $(v - u)$
is small. These assumptions appear to be quite restrictive, but in fact we shall
see quite a few applications of the idea. For example, if we apply this method
to the leading digits of keys instead of applying it to entire keys, the file will be
partially sorted and it will be comparatively simple to complete the job.

In order to understand the principles involved, suppose that all keys lie
between 1 and 100. In one pass through the file we can count how many 1s, 2s,
..., 100s are present; and in a second pass we can move the records into the
appropriate place in an output area. The following algorithm spells things out
in complete detail:

Algorithm D (*Distribution counting*). Assuming that all keys are integers in
the range $u \le K_j \le v$ for $1 \le j \le N$, this algorithm sorts the records $R_1, \ldots, R_N$
by making use of an auxiliary table COUNT$[u], \ldots,$ COUNT$[v]$. At the conclusion
of the algorithm the records are moved to an output area $S_1, \ldots, S_N$ in the
desired order.

D1. [Clear COUNTs.] Set COUNT$[u]$ through COUNT$[v]$ all to zero.

D2. [Loop on j.] Perform step D3 for $1 \le j \le N$; then go to step D4.

D3. [Increase COUNT$[K_j]$.] Increase the value of COUNT$[K_j]$ by 1.

D4. [Accumulate.] (At this point COUNT$[i]$ is the number of keys that are equal
to i.) Set COUNT$[i] \leftarrow$ COUNT$[i] +$ COUNT$[i-1]$, for $i = u+1, u+2, \ldots, v$.

D5. [Loop on j.] (At this point COUNT$[i]$ is the number of keys that are less than
or equal to i; in particular, COUNT$[v] = N$.) Perform step D6 for $j = N$,
$N - 1, \ldots, 1$; then terminate the algorithm.

D6. [Output R_j.] Set $i \leftarrow$ COUNT$[K_j]$, $S_i \leftarrow R_j$, and COUNT$[K_j] \leftarrow i - 1$. ∎

An example of this algorithm is worked out in exercise 6; a MIX program appears
in exercise 9. When the range $v - u$ is small, this sorting procedure is very fast.

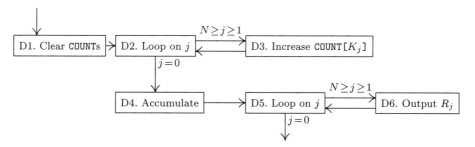

Fig. 9. Algorithm D: Distribution counting.

Sorting by comparison counting as in Algorithm C was first mentioned in print by E. H. Friend [*JACM* **3** (1956), 152], although he didn't claim it as his own invention. Distribution sorting as in Algorithm D was first developed by H. Seward in 1954 for use with radix sorting techniques that we will discuss later (see Section 5.2.5); it was also published under the name "Mathsort" by W. Feurzeig, *CACM* **3** (1960), 601.

EXERCISES

1. [*15*] Would Algorithm C still work if i varies from 2 up to N in step C2, instead of from N down to 2? What if j varies from 1 up to $i-1$ in step C3?

2. [*21*] Show that Algorithm C works properly when equal keys are present. If $K_j = K_i$ and $j < i$, does R_j come before or after R_i in the final ordering?

▸ **3.** [*21*] Would Algorithm C still work properly if the test in step C4 were changed from "$K_i < K_j$" to "$K_i \leq K_j$"?

4. [*16*] Write a MIX program that "finishes" the sorting begun by Program C; your program should transfer the keys to locations OUTPUT+1 through OUTPUT+N, in ascending order. How much time does your program require?

5. [*22*] Does the following set of changes improve Program C?

    New line 08a: INCX 0,2
   Change line 10: JGE   5F
   Change line 14: DECX 1
     Delete line 15.

6. [*18*] Simulate Algorithm D by hand, showing intermediate results when the 16 records 5T, 0C, 5U, 0O, 9., 1N, 8S, 2R, 6A, 4A, 1G, 5L, 6T, 6I, 7O, 7N are being sorted. Here the numeric digit is the key, and the alphabetic information is just carried along with the records.

7. [*13*] Is Algorithm D a stable sorting method?

8. [*15*] Would Algorithm D still work properly if j were to vary from 1 up to N in step D5, instead of from N down to 1?

9. [*23*] Write a MIX program for Algorithm D, analogous to Program C and exercise 4. What is the execution time of your program, as a function of N and $(v - u)$?

10. [*25*] Design an efficient algorithm that replaces the N quantities $(R_1, \ldots, R_N)$ by $(R_{p(1)}, \ldots, R_{p(N)})$, respectively, given the values of $R_1, \ldots, R_N$ and the permutation

$p(1)\ldots p(N)$ of $\{1,\ldots,N\}$. Try to avoid using excess memory space. (This problem arises if we wish to rearrange records in memory after an address table sort, without having enough room to store $2N$ records.)

11. [*M27*] Write a MIX program for the algorithm of exercise 10, and analyze its efficiency.

▶ **12.** [*25*] Design an efficient algorithm suitable for rearranging the records $R_1,\ldots,R_N$ into sorted order, after a list sort (Fig. 7) has been completed. Try to avoid using excess memory space.

▶ **13.** [*27*] Algorithm D requires space for $2N$ records $R_1,\ldots,R_N$ and $S_1,\ldots,S_N$. Show that it is possible to get by with only N records $R_1,\ldots,R_N$, if a new unshuffling procedure is substituted for steps D5 and D6. (Thus the problem is to design an algorithm that rearranges $R_1,\ldots,R_N$ in place, based on the values of COUNT[u], ..., COUNT[v] after step D4, without using additional memory space; this is essentially a generalization of the problem considered in exercise 10.)

5.2.1. Sorting by Insertion

One of the important families of sorting techniques is based on the "bridge player" method mentioned near the beginning of Section 5.2: Before examining record R_j, we assume that the preceding records $R_1,\ldots,R_{j-1}$ have already been sorted; then we insert R_j into its proper place among the previously sorted records. Several interesting variations on this basic theme are possible.

Straight insertion.   The simplest insertion sort is the most obvious one. Assume that $1 < j \le N$ and that records $R_1,\ldots,R_{j-1}$ have been rearranged so that

$$K_1 \le K_2 \le \cdots \le K_{j-1}.$$

(Remember that, throughout this chapter, K_j denotes the key portion of R_j.) We compare the new key K_j with K_{j-1}, K_{j-2}, ..., in turn, until discovering that R_j should be inserted between records R_i and R_{i+1}; then we move records R_{i+1}, ..., R_{j-1} up one space and put the new record into position $i + 1$. It is convenient to combine the comparison and moving operations, interleaving them as shown in the following algorithm; since R_j "settles to its proper level" this method of sorting has often been called the *sifting* or *sinking* technique.

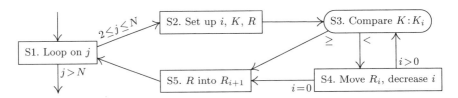

Fig. 10. Algorithm S: Straight insertion.

Algorithm S (*Straight insertion sort*).   Records $R_1,\ldots,R_N$ are rearranged in place; after sorting is complete, their keys will be in order, $K_1 \le \cdots \le K_N$.

S1. [Loop on j.] Perform steps S2 through S5 for $j = 2, 3, \ldots, N$; then terminate the algorithm.

S2. [Set up i, K, R.] Set $i \leftarrow j - 1$, $K \leftarrow K_j$, $R \leftarrow R_j$. (In the following steps we will attempt to insert R into the correct position, by comparing K with K_i for decreasing values of i.)

S3. [Compare $K : K_i$.] If $K \geq K_i$, go to step S5. (We have found the desired position for record R.)

S4. [Move R_i, decrease i.] Set $R_{i+1} \leftarrow R_i$, then $i \leftarrow i - 1$. If $i > 0$, go back to step S3. (If $i = 0$, K is the smallest key found so far, so record R belongs in position 1.)

S5. [R into R_{i+1}.] Set $R_{i+1} \leftarrow R$. ∎

Table 1 shows how our sixteen example numbers are sorted by Algorithm S. This method is extremely easy to implement on a computer; in fact the following MIX program is the shortest decent sorting routine in this book.

Table 1

EXAMPLE OF STRAIGHT INSERTION

```
 503 : 087
_∧
  087  503 : 512
           _∧
 087  503  512 : 061
_∧
  061  087  503  512 : 908
                      _∧
  061  087  503  512  908 : 170
           _∧
  061  087  170  503  512  908 : 897
                          _∧

  · · · · · · · · · · · · · · · · · · · · · · · · · ·

  061  087  154  170  275  426  503  509  512  612  653  677  765  897  908 : 703
                                                         _∧
  061  087  154  170  275  426  503  509  512  612  653  677  703  765  897  908
```

Program S (*Straight insertion sort*). The records to be sorted are in locations INPUT+1 through INPUT+N; they are sorted in place in the same area, on a full-word key. rI1 $\equiv j - N$; rI2 $\equiv i$; rA $\equiv R \equiv K$; assume that $N \geq 2$.

01	START	ENT1	2-N	1	S1. Loop on j. $j \leftarrow 2$.
02	2H	LDA	INPUT+N,1	$N - 1$	S2. Set up i, K, R.
03		ENT2	N-1,1	$N - 1$	$i \leftarrow j - 1$.
04	3H	CMPA	INPUT,2	$B + N - 1 - A$	S3. Compare $K : K_i$.
05		JGE	5F	$B + N - 1 - A$	To S5 if $K \geq K_i$.
06	4H	LDX	INPUT,2	B	S4. Move R_i, decrease i.
07		STX	INPUT+1,2	B	$R_{i+1} \leftarrow R_i$.
08		DEC2	1	B	$i \leftarrow i - 1$.
09		J2P	3B	B	To S3 if $i > 0$.
10	5H	STA	INPUT+1,2	$N - 1$	S5. R into R_{i+1}.
11		INC1	1	$N - 1$	
12		J1NP	2B	$N - 1$	$2 \leq j \leq N$. ∎

The running time of this program is $9B + 10N - 3A - 9$ units, where N is the number of records sorted, A is the number of times i decreases to zero in step S4, and B is the number of moves. Clearly A is the number of times $K_j < \min(K_1, \ldots, K_{j-1})$ for $1 < j \le N$; this is one less than the number of left-to-right minima, so A is equivalent to the quantity that was analyzed carefully in Section 1.2.10. Some reflection shows us that B is also a familiar quantity: The number of moves for fixed j is the number of inversions of K_j, so B is the total number of inversions of the permutation $K_1 K_2 \ldots K_N$. Hence by Eqs. 1.2.10–(16), 5.1.1–(12), and 5.1.1–(13), we have

$$A = \left(\min 0, \text{ ave } H_N - 1, \text{ max } N - 1, \text{ dev } \sqrt{H_N - H_N^{(2)}} \right);$$

$$B = \left(\min 0, \text{ ave } (N^2 - N)/4, \text{ max } (N^2 - N)/2, \text{ dev } \sqrt{N(N-1)(N+2.5)}/6 \right);$$

and the average running time of Program S, assuming that the input keys are distinct and randomly ordered, is $(2.25N^2 + 7.75N - 3H_N - 6)u$. Exercise 33 explains how to improve this slightly.

The example data in Table 1 involves 16 items; there are two changes to the left-to-right minimum, namely 087 and 061; and there are 41 inversions, as we have seen in the previous section. Hence $N = 16$, $A = 2$, $B = 41$, and the total sorting time is $514u$.

Binary insertion and two-way insertion. While the jth record is being processed during a straight insertion sort, we compare its key with about $j/2$ of the previously sorted keys, on the average; therefore the total number of comparisons performed comes to roughly $(1 + 2 + \cdots + N)/2 \approx N^2/4$, and this gets very large when N is only moderately large. In Section 6.2.1 we shall study "binary search" techniques, which show where to insert the jth item after only about $\lg j$ well-chosen comparisons have been made. For example, when inserting the 64th record we can start by comparing K_{64} with K_{32}; if it is less, we compare it with K_{16}, but if it is greater we compare it with K_{48}, etc., so that the proper place to insert R_{64} will be known after making only six comparisons. The total number of comparisons for inserting all N items comes to about $N \lg N$, a substantial improvement over $\frac{1}{4}N^2$; and Section 6.2.1 shows that the corresponding program need not be much more complicated than a program for straight insertion. This method is called *binary insertion*; it was mentioned by John Mauchly as early as 1946, in the first published discussion of computer sorting.

The unfortunate difficulty with binary insertion is that it solves only half of the problem; after we have found where record R_j is to be inserted, we still need to move about $\frac{1}{2}j$ of the previously sorted records in order to make room for R_j, so the total running time is still essentially proportional to N^2. Some early computers such as the IBM 705 had a built-in "tumble" instruction that did such move operations at high speed, and modern machines can do the moves even faster with special hardware attachments; but as N increases, the dependence on N^2 eventually takes over. For example, an analysis by H. Nagler [*CACM* **3**

(1960), 618–620] indicated that binary insertion could not be recommended for sorting more than about $N = 128$ records on the IBM 705, when each record was 80 characters long, and similar analyses apply to other machines.

Of course, a clever programmer can think of various ways to reduce the amount of moving that is necessary; the first such trick, proposed early in the 1950s, is illustrated in Table 2. Here the first item is placed in the center of an output area, and space is made for subsequent items by moving to the right or to the left, whichever is most convenient. This saves about half the running time of ordinary binary insertion, at the expense of a somewhat more complicated program. It is possible to use this method without using up more space than required for N records (see exercise 6); but we shall not dwell any longer on this "two-way" method of insertion, since considerably more interesting techniques have been developed.

Table 2

TWO-WAY INSERTION

			503				
		087	503				
		087	503	512			
	061	087	503	512			
	061	087	503	512	908		
	061	087	170	503	512	908	
	061	087	170	503	512	897	908
061	087	170	275	503	512	897	908

Shell's method. If we have a sorting algorithm that moves items only one position at a time, its average time will be, at best, proportional to N^2, since each record must travel an average of about $\frac{1}{3}N$ positions during the sorting process (see exercise 7). Therefore, if we want to make substantial improvements over straight insertion, we need some mechanism by which the records can take long leaps instead of short steps.

Such a method was proposed in 1959 by Donald L. Shell [*CACM* **2**, 7 (July 1959), 30–32], and it became known as *shellsort*. Table 3 illustrates the general idea behind the method: First we divide the 16 records into 8 groups of two each, namely $(R_1, R_9), (R_2, R_{10}), \ldots, (R_8, R_{16})$. Sorting each group of records separately takes us to the second line of Table 3; this is called the "first pass." Notice that 154 has changed places with 512; 908 and 897 have both jumped to the right. Now we divide the records into 4 groups of four each, namely $(R_1, R_5, R_9, R_{13}), \ldots, (R_4, R_8, R_{12}, R_{16})$, and again each group is sorted separately; this "second pass" takes us to line 3. A third pass sorts two groups of eight records, then a fourth pass completes the job by sorting all 16 records. Each of the intermediate sorting processes involves either a comparatively short file or a file that is comparatively well ordered, so straight insertion can be used

Table 3

SHELLSORT WITH INCREMENTS 8, 4, 2, 1

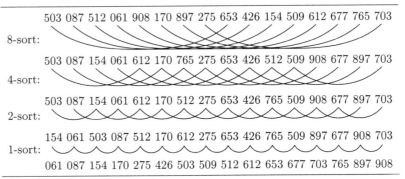

8-sort:

4-sort:

2-sort:

1-sort:

503 087 512 061 908 170 897 275 653 426 154 509 612 677 765 703

503 087 154 061 612 170 765 275 653 426 512 509 908 677 897 703

503 087 154 061 612 170 512 275 653 426 765 509 908 677 897 703

154 061 503 087 512 170 612 275 653 426 765 509 897 677 908 703

061 087 154 170 275 426 503 509 512 612 653 677 703 765 897 908

for each sorting operation. In this way the records tend to converge quickly to their final destinations.

Shellsort is also known as the "diminishing increment sort," since each pass is defined by an increment h such that w sort the records that are h units apart. The sequence of increments 8, 4, 2, 1 is not sacred; indeed, *any* sequence h_{t-1}, $h_{t-2}, \ldots, h_0$ can be used, so long as the last increment h_0 equals 1. For example, Table 4 shows the same data sorted with increments 7, 5, 3, 1. Some sequences are much better than others; we will discuss the choice of increments later.

Algorithm D (*Shellsort*). Records $R_1, \ldots, R_N$ are rearranged in place; after sorting is complete, their keys will be in order, $K_1 \le \cdots \le K_N$. An auxiliary sequence of increments $h_{t-1}, h_{t-2}, \ldots, h_0$ is used to control the sorting process, where $h_0 = 1$; proper choice of these increments can significantly decrease the sorting time. This algorithm reduces to Algorithm S when $t = 1$.

D1. [Loop on s.] Perform step D2 for $s = t - 1, t - 2, \ldots, 0$; then terminate the algorithm.

D2. [Loop on j.] Set $h \leftarrow h_s$, and perform steps D3 through D6 for $h < j \le N$. (We will use a straight insertion method to sort elements that are h positions apart, so that $K_i \le K_{i+h}$ for $1 \le i \le N - h$. Steps D3 through D6 are essentially the same as steps S2 through S5, respectively, in Algorithm S.)

D3. [Set up i, K, R.] Set $i \leftarrow j - h$, $K \leftarrow K_j$, $R \leftarrow R_j$.

D4. [Compare $K : K_i$.] If $K \ge K_i$, go to step D6.

D5. [Move R_i, decrease i.] Set $R_{i+h} \leftarrow R_i$, then $i \leftarrow i - h$. If $i > 0$, go back to step D4.

D6. [R into R_{i+h}.] Set $R_{i+h} \leftarrow R$. ∎

The corresponding MIX program is not much longer than our program for straight insertion. Lines 08–19 of the following code are a direct translation of Program S into the more general framework of Algorithm D.

Program D (*Shellsort*). We assume that the increments are stored in an auxiliary table, with h_s in location H + s; all increments are less than N. Register

Table 4

SHELLSORT WITH INCREMENTS 7, 5, 3, 1

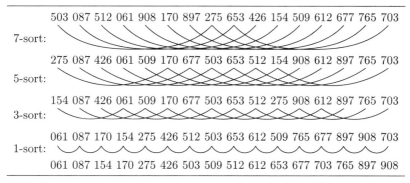

assignments: $rI1 \equiv j - N$; $rI2 \equiv i$; $rA \equiv R \equiv K$; $rI3 \equiv s$; $rI4 \equiv h$. Note that this program modifies itself, in order to obtain efficient execution of the inner loop.

01	START	ENT3 T-1	1	D1. Loop on s. $s \leftarrow t - 1$.
02	1H	LD4 H,3	T	D2. Loop on j. $h \leftarrow h_s$.
03		ENT1 INPUT,4	T	Modify the addresses of three
04		ST1 5F(0:2)	T	instructions in the main loop.
05		ST1 6F(0:2)	T	
06		ENN1 -N,4	T	$rI1 \leftarrow N - h$.
07		ST1 3F(0:2)	T	
08		ENT1 1-N,4	T	$j \leftarrow h + 1$.
09	2H	LDA INPUT+N,1	$NT - S$	D3. Set up i, K, R.
10	3H	ENT2 N-H,1	$NT - S$	$i \leftarrow j - h$. [Instruction modified]
11	4H	CMPA INPUT,2	$B+NT-S-A$	D4. Compare $K : K_i$.
12		JGE 6F	$B+NT-S-A$	To D6 if $K \geq K_i$.
13		LDX INPUT,2	B	D5. Move R_i, decrease i.
14	5H	STX INPUT+H,2	B	$R_{i+h} \leftarrow R_i$. [Instruction modified]
15		DEC2 0,4	B	$i \leftarrow i - h$.
16		J2P 4B	B	To D4 if $i > 0$.
17	6H	STA INPUT+H,2	$NT - S$	D6. R into R_{i+h}. [Instruction modified]
18	7H	INC1 1	$NT - S$	$j \leftarrow j + 1$.
19		J1NP 2B	$NT - S$	To D3 if $j \leq N$.
20		DEC3 1	T	
21		J3NN 1B	T	$t > s \geq 0$. ∎

*Analysis of shellsort.** In order to choose a good sequence of increments $h_{t-1}, \ldots, h_0$ for use in Algorithm D, we need to analyze the running time as a function of those increments. This leads to some fascinating mathematical problems, not yet completely resolved; nobody has been able to determine the best possible sequence of increments for large values of N. Yet a good many interesting facts are known about the behavior of shellsort, and we will summarize them here; details appear in the exercises below. [Readers who are not mathematically inclined should skim over the next few pages, continuing with the discussion of list insertion following (12).]

The frequency counts shown with Program D indicate that five factors determine the execution time: the size of the file, N; the number of passes (that is, the number of increments), $T = t$; the sum of the increments,

$$S = h_0 + \cdots + h_{t-1};$$

the number of comparisons, $B + NT - S - A$; and the number of moves, B. As in the analysis of Program S, A is essentially the number of left-to-right minima encountered in the intermediate sorting operations, and B is the number of inversions in the subfiles. The factor that governs the running time is B, so we shall devote most of our attention to it. For purposes of analysis we shall assume that the keys are distinct and initially in random order.

Let us call the operation of step D2 "h-sorting," so that shellsort consists of h_{t-1}-sorting, followed by h_{t-2} sorting, ..., followed by h_0-sorting. A file in which $K_i \leq K_{i+h}$ for $1 \leq i \leq N - h$ will be called "h-ordered."

Consider first the simplest generalization of straight insertion, when there are just two increments, $h_1 = 2$ and $h_0 = 1$. In this case the second pass begins with a 2-ordered sequence of keys, $K_1 K_2 \ldots K_N$. It is easy to see that the number of permutations $a_1 a_2 \ldots a_n$ of $\{1, 2, \ldots, n\}$ having $a_i \leq a_{i+2}$ for $1 \leq i \leq n - 2$ is

$$\binom{n}{\lfloor n/2 \rfloor},$$

since we obtain exactly one 2-ordered permutation for each choice of $\lfloor n/2 \rfloor$ elements to put in the even-numbered positions $a_2 a_4 \ldots$, while the remaining $\lceil n/2 \rceil$ elements occupy the odd-numbered positions. Each 2-ordered permutation is equally likely after a random file has been 2-sorted. What is the average number of inversions among all such permutations?

Let A_n be the total number of inversions among all 2-ordered permutations of $\{1, 2, \ldots, n\}$. Clearly $A_1 = 0$, $A_2 = 1$, $A_3 = 2$; and by considering the six cases

$$1\,3\,2\,4 \qquad 1\,2\,3\,4 \qquad 1\,2\,4\,3 \qquad 2\,1\,3\,4 \qquad 2\,1\,4\,3 \qquad 3\,1\,4\,2$$

we find that $A_4 = 1 + 0 + 1 + 1 + 2 + 3 = 8$. One way to investigate A_n in general is to consider the "lattice diagram" illustrated in Fig. 11 for $n = 15$. A 2-ordered permutation of $\{1, 2, \ldots, n\}$ can be represented as a path from the upper left corner point $(0,0)$ to the lower right corner point $(\lceil n/2 \rceil, \lfloor n/2 \rfloor)$, if we make the kth step of the path go downwards or to the right, respectively, according as k appears in an odd or an even position in the permutation. This rule defines a one-to-one correspondence between 2-ordered permutations and n-step paths from corner to corner of the lattice diagram; for example, the path shown by the heavy line in Fig. 11 corresponds to the permutation

$$2\ 1\ 3\ 4\ 6\ 5\ 7\ 10\ 8\ 11\ 9\ 12\ 14\ 13\ 15. \tag{1}$$

Furthermore, we can attach "weights" to the vertical lines of the path, as Fig. 11 shows; a line from (i, j) to $(i+1, j)$ gets weight $|i - j|$. A little study will convince the reader that the sum of these weights along each path is equal to the number of inversions of the corresponding permutation; this sum also equals the number

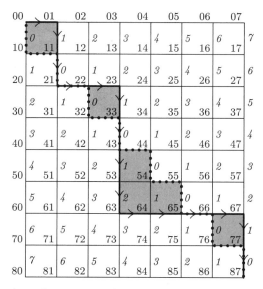

Fig. 11. Correspondence between 2-ordering and paths in a lattice. Italicized numbers are weights that yield the number of inversions in the 2-ordered permutation.

of shaded squares between the given path and the staircase path indicated by heavy dots in the figure. (See exercise 12.) Thus, for example, (1) has $1 + 0 + 1 + 0 + 1 + 2 + 1 + 0 = 6$ inversions.

When $a \leq a'$ and $b \leq b'$, the number of relevant paths from (a, b) to (a', b') is the number of ways to mix $a' - a$ vertical lines with $b' - b$ horizontal lines, namely

$$\binom{a' - a + b' - b}{a' - a};$$

hence the number of permutations whose corresponding path traverses the vertical line segment from (i, j) to $(i+1, j)$ is

$$\binom{i+j}{i}\binom{n-i-j-1}{\lfloor n/2 \rfloor - j}.$$

Multiplying by the associated weight and summing over all segments gives

$$A_{2n} = \sum_{\substack{0 \leq i \leq n \\ 0 \leq j \leq n}} |i - j| \binom{i+j}{i}\binom{2n-i-j-1}{n-j};$$

$$A_{2n+1} = \sum_{\substack{0 \leq i \leq n \\ 0 \leq j \leq n}} |i - j| \binom{i+j}{i}\binom{2n-i-j}{n-j}. \tag{2}$$

The absolute value signs in these sums make the calculations somewhat tricky, but exercise 14 shows that A_n has the surprisingly simple form $\lfloor n/2 \rfloor 2^{n-2}$. Hence the average number of inversions in a random 2-ordered permutation is

$$\lfloor n/2 \rfloor 2^{n-2} \Big/ \binom{n}{\lfloor n/2 \rfloor} ;$$

by Stirling's approximation this is asymptotically $\sqrt{\pi/128}\, n^{3/2} \approx 0.15 n^{3/2}$. The maximum number of inversions is easily seen to be

$$\binom{\lfloor n/2 \rfloor + 1}{2} \approx \frac{1}{8} n^2.$$

It is instructive to study the distribution of inversions more carefully, by examining the generating functions

$$\begin{aligned}
h_1(z) &= 1, \\
h_2(z) &= 1 + z, \\
h_3(z) &= 1 + 2z, \\
h_4(z) &= 1 + 3z + z^2 + z^3, \qquad \ldots,
\end{aligned} \tag{3}$$

as in exercise 15. In this way we find that the standard deviation is also proportional to $n^{3/2}$, so the distribution is not extremely stable about the mean.

Now let us consider the general two-pass case of Algorithm D, when the increments are h and 1:

Theorem H. *The average number of inversions in an h-ordered permutation of $\{1, 2, \ldots, n\}$ is*

$$f(n, h) = \frac{2^{2q-1} q!\, q!}{(2q+1)!} \left(\binom{h}{2} q(q+1) + \binom{r}{2}(q+1) - \frac{1}{2}\binom{h-r}{2} q \right), \tag{4}$$

where $q = \lfloor n/h \rfloor$ and $r = n \bmod h$.

This theorem is due to Douglas H. Hunt [Bachelor's thesis, Princeton University (April 1967)]. Note that when $h \geq n$ the formula correctly gives $f(n, h) = \frac{1}{2}\binom{n}{2}$.

Proof. An h-ordered permutation contains r sorted subsequences of length $q+1$, and $h-r$ of length q. Each inversion comes from a pair of distinct subsequences, and a given pair of distinct subsequences in a random h-ordered permutation defines a random 2-ordered permutation. The average number of inversions is therefore the sum of the average number of inversions between each pair of distinct subsequences, namely

$$\binom{r}{2} \frac{A_{2q+2}}{\binom{2q+2}{q+1}} + r(h-r) \frac{A_{2q+1}}{\binom{2q+1}{q}} + \binom{h-r}{2} \frac{A_{2q}}{\binom{2q}{q}} = f(n, h). \quad \blacksquare$$

Corollary. *If the sequence of increments $h_{t-1}, \ldots, h_1, h_0$ satisfies the condition*

$$h_{s+1} \bmod h_s = 0, \qquad \text{for} \qquad t - 1 > s \geq 0, \tag{5}$$

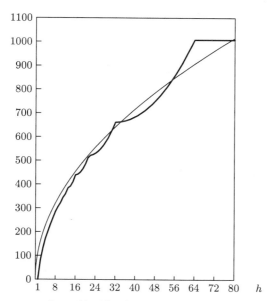

Fig. 12. The average number, $f(n, h)$, of inversions in an h-ordered file of n elements, shown for $n = 64$.

then the average number of move operations in Algorithm D is

$$\sum_{t>s\geq 0} \left(r_s f(q_s+1, h_{s+1}/h_s) + (h_s - r_s) f(q_s, h_{s+1}/h_s)\right), \qquad (6)$$

where $r_s = N \bmod h_s$, $q_s = \lfloor N/h_s \rfloor$, $h_t = Nh_{t-1}$, and f is defined in (4).

Proof. The process of h_s-sorting consists of a straight insertion sort on r_s (h_{s+1}/h_s)-ordered subfiles of length $q_s + 1$, and on $(h_s - r_s)$ such subfiles of length q_s. The divisibility condition implies that each of these subfiles is a random (h_{s+1}/h_s)-ordered permutation, in the sense that each (h_{s+1}/h_s)-ordered permutation is equally likely, since we are assuming that the original input was a random permutation of distinct elements. ∎

Condition (5) in this corollary is always satisfied for *two-pass* shellsorts, when the increments are h and 1. If $q = \lfloor N/h \rfloor$ and $r = N \bmod h$, the quantity B in Program D will have an average value of

$$r f(q+1, N) + (h - r) f(q, N) + f(N, h) = \frac{r}{2} \binom{q+1}{2} + \frac{h-r}{2} \binom{q}{2} + f(N, h).$$

To a first approximation, the function $f(n, h)$ equals $(\sqrt{\pi}/8) n^{3/2} h^{1/2}$; we can, for example, compare it to the smooth curve in Fig. 12 when $n = 64$. Hence the running time for a two-pass Program D is approximately proportional to

$$2N^2/h + \sqrt{\pi N^3 h}.$$

The best choice of h is therefore approximately $\sqrt[3]{16N/\pi} \approx 1.72 \sqrt[3]{N}$; and with this choice of h we get an average running time proportional to $N^{5/3}$.

Thus we can make a substantial improvement over straight insertion, from $O(N^2)$ to $O(N^{1.667})$, just by using shellsort with two increments. Clearly we can do even better when more increments are used. Exercise 18 discusses the optimum choice of $h_{t-1}, \ldots, h_0$ when t is fixed and when the h's are constrained by the divisibility condition; the running time decreases to $O(N^{1.5+\epsilon/2})$, where $\epsilon = 1/(2^t - 1)$, for large N. We cannot break the $N^{1.5}$ barrier by using the formulas above, since the last pass always contributes

$$f(N, h_1) \approx (\sqrt{\pi}/8)N^{3/2}h_1^{1/2}$$

inversions to the sum.

But our intuition tells us that we can do even better when the increments $h_t, \ldots, h_1$ do *not* satisfy the divisibility condition (5). For example, 8-sorting followed by 4-sorting followed by 2-sorting does not allow any interaction between keys in even and odd positions; therefore the final 1-sorting pass is inevitably faced with $\Theta(N^{3/2})$ inversions, on the average. By contrast, 7-sorting followed by 5-sorting followed by 3-sorting jumbles things up in such a way that the final 1-sorting pass cannot encounter more than $2N$ inversions! (See exercise 26.) Indeed, an astonishing phenomenon occurs:

Theorem K. *If a k-ordered file is h-sorted, it remains k-ordered.*

Thus a file that is first 7-sorted, then 5-sorted, becomes both 7-ordered and 5-ordered. And if we 3-sort it, the result is ordered by 7s, 5s, and 3s. Examples of this remarkable property can be seen in Table 4 on page 85.

Proof. Exercise 20 shows that Theorem K is a consequence of the following fact:

Lemma L. *Let m, n, r be nonnegative integers, and let $(x_1, \ldots, x_{m+r})$ and $(y_1, \ldots, y_{n+r})$ be any sequences of numbers such that*

$$y_1 \le x_{m+1}, \qquad y_2 \le x_{m+2}, \qquad \ldots, \qquad y_r \le x_{m+r}. \qquad (7)$$

If the x's and y's are sorted independently, so that $x_1 \le \cdots \le x_{m+r}$ and $y_1 \le \cdots \le y_{n+r}$, the relations (7) will still be valid.

Proof. All but m of the x's are known to dominate (that is, to be greater than or equal to) some y, where distinct x's dominate distinct y's. Let $1 \le j \le r$. Since x_{m+j} after sorting dominates $m + j$ of the x's, it dominates at least j of the y's; therefore it dominates the *smallest* j of the y's; hence $x_{m+j} \ge y_j$ after sorting. ∎ ∎

Theorem K suggests that it is desirable to sort with relatively prime increments, but it does not lead directly to exact estimates of the number of moves made in Algorithm D. Moreover, the number of permutations of $\{1, 2, \ldots, n\}$ that are both h-ordered and k-ordered is not always a divisor of $n!$, so we can see that Theorem K does not tell the whole story; some k- and h-ordered files are obtained more often than others after k- and h-sorting. Therefore the average-case analysis of Algorithm D for general increments $h_{t-1}, \ldots, h_0$ has baffled everyone so far when $t > 3$. There is not even an obvious way to find the *worst* case, when N and $(h_{t-1}, \ldots, h_0)$ are given. We can, however, derive several facts about the approximate maximum running time when the increments have certain forms:

Theorem P. *The running time of Algorithm D is $O(N^{3/2})$, when $h_s = 2^{s+1} - 1$ for $0 \le s < t = \lfloor \lg N \rfloor$.*

Proof. It suffices to bound B_s, the number of moves in pass s, in such a way that $B_{t-1} + \cdots + B_0 = O(N^{3/2})$. During the first $t/2$ passes, for $t > s \ge t/2$, we may use the obvious bound $B_s = O\bigl(h_s(N/h_s)^2\bigr)$; and for subsequent passes we may use the result of exercise 23, $B_s = O(Nh_{s+2}h_{s+1}/h_s)$. Consequently $B_{t-1} + \cdots + B_0 = O\bigl(N(2 + 2^2 + \cdots + 2^{t/2} + 2^{t/2} + \cdots + 2)\bigr) = O(N^{3/2})$. ∎

This theorem is due to A. A. Papernov and G. V. Stasevich, *Problemy Peredachi Informatsii* **1**, 3 (1965), 81–98. It gives an upper bound on the *worst case* running time of the algorithm, not merely a bound on the *average* running time. The result is not trivial since the maximum running time when the h's satisfy the divisibility constraint (5) is of order N^2; and exercise 24 shows that the exponent $3/2$ cannot be lowered.

An interesting improvement of Theorem P was discovered by Vaughan Pratt in 1969: *If the increments are chosen to be the set of all numbers of the form 2^p3^q that are less than N, the running time of Algorithm D is of order $N(\log N)^2$.* In this case we can also make several important simplifications to the algorithm; see exercises 30 and 31. However, even with these simplifications, Pratt's method requires a substantial overhead because it makes quite a few passes over the data. Therefore his increments don't actually sort faster than those of Theorem P in practice, unless N is astronomically large. The best sequences for real-world N appear to satisfy $h_s \approx \rho^s$, where the ratio $\rho \approx h_{s+1}/h_s$ is roughly independent of s but may depend on N.

We have observed that it is unwise to choose increments in such a way that each is a divisor of all its predecessors; but we should not conclude that the best increments are relatively prime to all of their predecessors. Indeed, every element of a file that is gh-sorted and gk-sorted with $h \perp k$ has at most $\frac{1}{2}(h-1)(k-1)$ inversions when we are g-sorting. (See exercise 21.) Pratt's sequence $\{2^p3^q\}$ wins as $N \to \infty$ by exploiting this fact, but it grows too slowly for practical use.

Janet Incerpi and Robert Sedgewick [*J. Comp. Syst. Sci.* **31** (1985), 210–224; see also *Lecture Notes in Comp. Sci.* **1136** (1996), 1–11] have found a way to have the best of both worlds, by showing how to construct a sequence of increments for which $h_s \approx \rho^s$ yet each increment is the gcd of two of its predecessors. Given any number $\rho > 1$, they start by defining a *base sequence* $a_1, a_2, \ldots$, where a_k is the least integer $\ge \rho^k$ such that $a_j \perp a_k$ for $1 \le j < k$. If $\rho = 2.5$, for example, the base sequence is

$$a_1, a_2, a_3, \ldots = 3, 7, 16, 41, 101, 247, 613, 1529, 3821, 9539, \ldots.$$

Now they define the increments by setting $h_0 = 1$ and

$$h_s = h_{s-r}a_r \qquad \text{for } \binom{r}{2} < s \le \binom{r+1}{2}. \tag{8}$$

Thus the sequence of increments starts

$$1; a_1; a_2, a_1a_2; a_1a_3, a_2a_3, a_1a_2a_3; \dots .$$

For example, when $\rho = 2.5$ we get

$$1, 3, 7, 21, 48, 112, 336, 861, 1968, 4592, 13776, 33936, 86961, 198768, \dots .$$

The crucial point is that we can turn recurrence (8) around:

$$h_s = h_{r+s}/a_r = h_{\binom{r}{2}}/a_{\binom{r}{2}-s} \qquad \text{for } \binom{r-1}{2} \le s \le \binom{r}{2}. \tag{9}$$

Therefore, by the argument in the previous paragraph, the number of inversions per element when we are h_0-sorting, h_1-sorting, $\dots$ is at most

$$b(a_2, a_1); b(a_3, a_2), b(a_3, a_1); b(a_4, a_3), b(a_4, a_2), b(a_4, a_1); \dots \tag{10}$$

where $b(h, k) = \frac{1}{2}(h-1)(k-1)$. If $\rho^{t-1} \le N < \rho^t$, the total number B of moves is at most N times the sum of the first t elements of this sequence. Therefore (see exercise 41) we can prove that the worst case running time is much better than order $N^{1.5}$:

Theorem I. *The running time for Algorithm D is $O(Ne^{c\sqrt{\ln n}})$ when the increments h_s are defined by (8). Here $c = \sqrt{8\ln\rho}$ and the constant implied by O depends on ρ.* ∎

This asymptotic upper bound is not especially important as $N \to \infty$, because Pratt's sequence does better. The main point of Theorem I is that a sequence of increments with the practical growth rate $h_s \approx \rho^s$ can have a running time that is guaranteed to be $O(N^{1+\epsilon})$ for arbitrarily small $\epsilon > 0$, when any value $\rho > 1$ is given.

Let's consider practical sizes of N more carefully by looking at the *total* running time of Program D, namely $(9B+10NT+13T-10S-3A+1)u$. Table 5 shows the average running time for various sequences of increments when $N = 8$. For this small value of N, bookkeeping operations are the most significant part of the cost, and the best results are obtained when $t = 1$; hence for $N = 8$ we are better off using simple straight insertion. (The average running time of Program S when $N = 8$ is only $191.85u$.) Curiously, the best two-pass algorithm occurs when $h_1 = 6$, since a large value of S is more important here than a small value of B. Similarly, the three increments 3 2 1 minimize the average number of moves, but they do not lead to the best three-pass sequence. It may be of interest to record here some "worst case" permutations that maximize the number of moves, since the general construction of such permutations is still unknown:

$$h_2 = 5, \quad h_1 = 3, \quad h_0 = 1: \qquad 8\,5\,2\,6\,3\,7\,4\,1 \qquad \text{(19 moves)}$$
$$h_2 = 3, \quad h_1 = 2, \quad h_0 = 1: \qquad 8\,3\,5\,7\,2\,4\,6\,1 \qquad \text{(17 moves)}$$

Table 5

ANALYSIS OF ALGORITHM D WHEN $N = 8$

Increments	A_{ave}	B_{ave}	S	T	MIX time
1	1.718	14.000	1	1	$204.85u$
2 1	2.667	9.657	3	2	$235.91u$
3 1	2.917	9.100	4	2	$220.15u$
4 1	3.083	10.000	5	2	$217.75u$
5 1	2.601	10.000	6	2	$209.20u$
6 1	2.135	10.667	7	2	$206.60u$
7 1	1.718	12.000	8	2	$209.85u$
4 2 1	3.500	8.324	7	3	$274.42u$
5 3 1	3.301	8.167	9	3	$253.60u$
3 2 1	3.320	7.829	6	3	$280.50u$

As N grows larger we have a slightly different picture. Table 6 shows the approximate number of moves for various sequences of increments when $N = 1000$. The first few entries satisfy the divisibility constraints (5), so that formula (6) and exercise 19 can be used; empirical tests were used to get approximate average values for the other cases. Ten thousand random files of 1000 elements were generated, and they each were sorted with each of the sequences of increments. The standard deviation of the number of left-to-right minima A was usually about 15; the standard deviation of the number of moves B was usually about 300.

Some patterns are evident in this data, but the behavior of Algorithm D still remains very obscure. Shell originally suggested using the increments $\lfloor N/2 \rfloor$, $\lfloor N/4 \rfloor$, $\lfloor N/8 \rfloor$, ..., but this is undesirable when the binary representation of N contains a long string of zeros. Lazarus and Frank [*CACM* **3** (1960), 20–22] suggested using essentially the same sequence, but adding 1 when necessary, to make all increments odd. Hibbard [*CACM* **6** (1963), 206–213] suggested using increments of the form $2^k - 1$; Papernov and Stasevich suggested the form $2^k + 1$. Other natural sequences investigated in Table 6 involve the numbers $(2^k - (-1)^k)/3$ and $(3^k - 1)/2$, as well as Fibonacci numbers and the Incerpi–Sedgewick sequences (8) for $\rho = 2.5$ and $\rho = 2$. Pratt-like sequences $\{5^p 11^q\}$ and $\{7^p 13^q\}$ are also shown, because they retain the asymptotic $O\big(N(\log N)^2\big)$ behavior but have lower overhead costs for small N. The final examples in Table 6 come from another sequence devised by Sedgewick, based on slightly different heuristics [*J. Algorithms* **7** (1986), 159–173]:

$$h_s = \begin{cases} 9 \cdot 2^s - 9 \cdot 2^{s/2} + 1, & \text{if } s \text{ is even;} \\ 8 \cdot 2^s - 6 \cdot 2^{(s+1)/2} + 1, & \text{if } s \text{ is odd.} \end{cases} \tag{11}$$

When these increments $(h_0, h_1, h_2, \ldots) = (1, 5, 19, 41, 109, 209, \ldots)$ are used, Sedgewick proved that the worst-case running time is $O(N^{4/3})$.

The minimum number of moves, about 6750, was observed for increments of the form $2^k + 1$, and also in the Incerpi–Sedgewick sequence for $\rho = 2$. But it is important to realize that the number of moves is not the only consideration,

Table 6

APPROXIMATE BEHAVIOR OF ALGORITHM D WHEN $N = 1000$

Increments													A_{ave}	B_{ave}	T
												1	6	249750	1
											17	1	65	41667	2
										60	6	1	158	26361	3
									140	20	4	1	262	21913	4
								256	64	16	4	1	362	20459	5
							576	192	48	16	4	1	419	20088	6
						729	243	81	27	9	3	1	378	18533	7
			512	256	128	64	32	16	8	4	2	1	493	16435	10
				500	250	125	62	31	15	7	3	1	516	7655	9
				501	251	125	63	31	15	7	3	1	558	7370	9
				511	255	127	63	31	15	7	3	1	559	7200	9
					255	127	63	31	15	7	3	1	436	7445	8
						127	63	31	15	7	3	1	299	8170	7
							63	31	15	7	3	1	190	9860	6
								31	15	7	3	1	114	13615	5
			513	257	129	65	33	17	9	5	3	1	561	6745	10
				257	129	65	33	17	9	5	3	1	440	6995	9
					129	65	33	17	9	5	3	1	304	7700	8
						65	33	17	9	5	3	1	197	9300	7
							33	17	9	5	3	1	122	12695	6
			683	341	171	85	43	21	11	5	3	1	511	7365	10
				341	171	85	43	21	11	5	3	1	490	7490	9
							255	63	15	7	3	1	373	8620	6
							257	65	17	5	3	1	375	8990	6
							341	85	21	5	3	1	410	9345	6
377	233	144	89	55	34	21	13	8	5	3	2	1	518	7400	13
	233	144	89	55	34	21	13	8	5	3	2	1	432	7610	12
						377	144	55	21	8	3	1	456	8795	7
						365	122	41	14	5	2	1	440	8085	7
							364	121	40	13	4	1	437	8900	6
								121	40	13	4	1	268	9790	5
						336	112	48	21	7	3	1	432	7840	7
				306	170	90	45	18	10	5	2	1	465	6755	9
							169	91	49	13	7	1	349	8698	6
					275	125	121	55	25	11	5	1	446	6788	8
					929	505	209	109	41	19	5	1	512	7725	8
						505	209	109	41	19	5	1	519	7790	7
							209	109	41	19	5	1	382	8165	6

even though it dominates the asymptotic running time. Since Program D takes $9B + 10NT + \cdots$ units of time, we see that saving one pass is about as desirable as saving $\frac{10}{9}N$ moves; when $N = 1000$ we are willing to add 1111 moves if we can save one pass. Therefore it seems unwise to start with h_{t-1} greater than, say, $\frac{1}{3}N$, since a large increment will not decrease the subsequent number of moves enough to justify the first pass.

Extensive empirical tests conducted by M. A. Weiss [*Comp. J.* **34** (1991), 88–91] suggest strongly that the average number of moves performed by Algorithm D with increments $2^k - 1, \ldots, 15, 7, 3, 1$ is approximately proportional to $N^{5/4}$. More precisely, Weiss found that $B_{\text{ave}} \approx 1.55N^{5/4} - 4.48N + O(N^{3/4})$ for $100 \le N \le 12000000$ when these increments are used; the empirical standard deviation was approximately $.065N^{5/4}$. He also discovered that Sedgewick's sequence (11) gives asymptotically better performance, $B_{\text{ave}} \approx 0.43N^{7/6} + 18.5N + O(N^{5/6})$. Surprisingly, the standard deviation for this sequence of increments appears to be quite small, approximately of order $N^{3/4}$.

Table 7 shows typical breakdowns of moves per pass obtained in three random experiments, using increments of the forms $2^k - 1$, $2^k + 1$, and (11). The same file of numbers was used in each case. The total number of moves, $\sum_s B_s$, comes to 346152, 329532, 248788 in the three cases, so sequence (11) is clearly superior in this example.

Table 7

MOVES PER PASS: EXPERIMENTS WITH $N = 20000$

h_s	B_s	h_s	B_s	h_s	B_s
4095	19458	4097	19459	3905	20714
2047	15201	2049	14852	2161	13428
1023	16363	1025	15966	929	18206
511	18867	513	18434	505	16444
255	23232	257	22746	209	21405
127	28034	129	27595	109	19605
63	33606	65	34528	41	26604
31	40350	33	45497	19	23441
15	66037	17	48717	5	38941
7	43915	9	38560	1	50000
3	24191	5	20271		
1	16898	3	9448		
		1	13459		

Although Algorithm D is gradually becoming better understood, more than three decades of research have failed to turn up any grounds for making strong assertions about what sequences of increments make it work best. If N is less than 1000, a simple rule such as

$$\text{Let } h_0 = 1, \; h_{s+1} = 3h_s + 1, \text{ and stop with } h_{t-1} \text{ when } 3h_t \ge N \qquad (12)$$

seems to be about as good as any other. For larger values of N, Sedgewick's sequence (11) can be recommended, again stopping with h_{t-1} when $3h_t \ge N$.

Exercise 43 explains how to remove the test "$i > 0$" from step D5. This change will make Program D run about 10% faster.

List insertion. Let us now leave shellsort and consider other types of improvements over straight insertion. One of the most important general ways to improve on a given algorithm is to examine its data structures carefully, since a reorganization of data structures to avoid unnecessary operations often leads to substantial savings. Further discussion of this general idea appears in Section 2.4, where a rather complex algorithm is studied; let us consider how it applies to a very simple algorithm like straight insertion. What is the most appropriate data structure for Algorithm S?

Straight insertion involves two basic operations:

i) scanning an ordered file to find the largest key less than or equal to a given key; and

ii) inserting a new record into a specified part of the ordered file.

The file is obviously a linear list, and Algorithm S handles this list by using sequential allocation (Section 2.2.2); therefore it is necessary to move roughly half of the records in order to accomplish each insertion operation. On the other hand, we know that linked allocation (Section 2.2.3) is ideally suited to insertion, since only a few links need to be changed; and the other operation, sequential scanning, is about as easy with linked allocation as with sequential allocation. Only one-way linkage is needed, since we always scan the list in the same direction. Therefore we conclude that the right data structure for straight insertion is a one-way, linked linear list. It also becomes convenient to revise Algorithm S so that the list is scanned in increasing order:

Algorithm L (*List insertion*). Records $R_1, \ldots, R_N$ are assumed to contain keys $K_1, \ldots, K_N$, together with link fields $L_1, \ldots, L_N$ capable of holding the numbers 0 through N; there is also an additional link field L_0, in an artificial record R_0 at the beginning of the file. This algorithm sets the link fields so that the records are linked together in ascending order. Thus, if $p(1) \ldots p(N)$ is the stable permutation that makes $K_{p(1)} \leq \cdots \leq K_{p(N)}$, this algorithm will yield

$$L_0 = p(1); \qquad L_{p(i)} = p(i+1), \quad \text{for} \quad 1 \leq i < N; \qquad L_{p(N)} = 0. \qquad (13)$$

L1. [Loop on j.] Set $L_0 \leftarrow N$, $L_N \leftarrow 0$. (Link L_0 acts as the "head" of the list, and 0 acts as a null link; hence the list is essentially circular.) Perform steps L2 through L5 for $j = N-1, N-2, \ldots, 1$; then terminate the algorithm.

L2. [Set up p, q, K.] Set $p \leftarrow L_0$, $q \leftarrow 0$, $K \leftarrow K_j$. (In the following steps we will insert R_j into its proper place in the linked list, by comparing K with the previous keys in ascending order. The variables p and q act as pointers to the current place in the list, with $p = L_q$ so that q is one step behind p.)

L3. [Compare $K : K_p$.] If $K \leq K_p$, go to step L5. (We have found the desired position for record R, between R_q and R_p in the list.)

L4. [Bump p, q.] Set $q \leftarrow p$, $p \leftarrow L_q$. If $p > 0$, go back to step L3. (If $p = 0$, K is the largest key found so far; hence record R belongs at the end of the list, between R_q and R_0.)

L5. [Insert into list.] Set $L_q \leftarrow j$, $L_j \leftarrow p$. ▮

This algorithm is important not only because it is a simple sorting method, but also because it occurs frequently as part of other list-processing algorithms.

Table 8 shows the first few steps that occur when our sixteen example numbers are sorted; exercise 32 gives the final link setting.

Table 8

EXAMPLE OF LIST INSERTION

j:	0	1	2	3	4	5	6	7	8	9	10	11	12	13	14	15	16
K_j:	–	503	087	512	061	908	170	897	275	653	426	154	509	612	677	765	703
L_j:	16	–	–	–	–	–	–	–	–	–	–	–	–	–	–	–	0
L_j:	16	–	–	–	–	–	–	–	–	–	–	–	–	–	–	0	15
L_j:	14	–	–	–	–	–	–	–	–	–	–	–	–	–	16	0	15

. . . .

Program L (*List insertion*). We assume that K_j is stored in INPUT$+j$ (0:3), and L_j is stored in INPUT$+j$ (4:5). rI1 $\equiv j$; rI2 $\equiv p$; rI3 $\equiv q$; rA(0:3) $\equiv K$.

```
01 KEY    EQU  0:3
02 LINK   EQU  4:5
03 START  ENT1 N                        1           L1. Loop on j. j ← N.
04        ST1  INPUT(LINK)              1           L0 ← N.
05        STZ  INPUT+N(LINK)            1           LN ← 0.
06        JMP  6F                       1           Go to decrease j.
07 2H     LD2  INPUT(LINK)             N − 1        L2. Set up p, q, K. p ← L0.
08        ENT3 0                       N − 1        q ← 0.
09        LDA  INPUT,1                 N − 1        K ← Kj.
10 3H     CMPA INPUT,2(KEY)      B + N − 1 − A      L3. Compare K : Kp.
11        JLE  5F               B + N − 1 − A       To L5 if K ≤ Kp.
12 4H     ENT3 0,2                      B           L4. Bump p, q. q ← p.
13        LD2  INPUT,3(LINK)           B           p ← Lq.
14        J2P  3B                       B           To L3 if p > 0.
15 5H     ST1  INPUT,3(LINK)          N − 1        L5. Insert into list. Lq ← j.
16        ST2  INPUT,1(LINK)          N − 1        Lj ← p.
17 6H     DEC1 1                        N
18        J1P  2B                       N           N > j ≥ 1.  ∎
```

The running time of this program is $7B + 14N - 3A - 6$ units, where N is the length of the file, $A + 1$ is the number of right-to-left maxima, and B is the number of inversions in the original permutation. (See the analysis of Program S. Note that Program L does not rearrange the records in memory; this can be done as in exercise 5.2–12, at a cost of about $20N$ additional units of time.) Program S requires $(9B + 10N - 3A - 9)u$, and since B is about $\frac{1}{4}N^2$, we can see that the extra memory space used for the link fields has saved about 22 percent of the execution time. Another 22 percent can be saved by careful programming (see exercise 33), but the running time remains proportional to N^2.

To summarize what we have done so far: We started with Algorithm S, a simple and natural sorting algorithm that does about $\frac{1}{4}N^2$ comparisons and $\frac{1}{4}N^2$ moves. We improved it in one direction by considering binary insertion, which does about $N \lg N$ comparisons and $\frac{1}{4}N^2$ moves. Changing the data

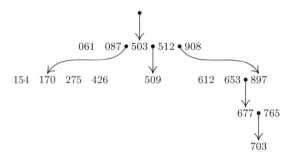

Fig. 13. Example of Wheeler's tree insertion scheme.

structure slightly with "two-way insertion" cuts the number of moves down to about $\frac{1}{8}N^2$. Shellsort cuts the number of comparisons and moves to about $N^{7/6}$, for N in a practical range; as $N \to \infty$ this number can be lowered to order $N(\log N)^2$. Another way to improve on Algorithm S, using a linked data structure, gave us the list insertion method, which does about $\frac{1}{4}N^2$ comparisons, 0 moves, and $2N$ changes of links.

Is it possible to marry the best features of these methods, reducing the number of comparisons to order $N \log N$ as in binary insertion, yet reducing the number of moves as in list insertion? The answer is yes, by going to a tree-structured arrangement. This possibility was first explored about 1957 by D. J. Wheeler, who suggested using two-way insertion until it becomes necessary to move some data; then instead of moving the data, a pointer to another area of memory is inserted, and the same technique is applied recursively to all items that are to be inserted into this new area of memory. Wheeler's original method [see A. S. Douglas, *Comp. J.* **2** (1959), 5] was a complicated combination of sequential and linked memory, with nodes of varying size; for our 16 example numbers the tree of Fig. 13 would be formed. A similar but simpler tree-insertion scheme, using binary trees, was devised by C. M. Berners-Lee about 1958 [see *Comp. J.* **3** (1960), 174, 184]. Since the binary tree method and its refinements are quite important for searching as well as sorting, they are discussed at length in Section 6.2.2.

Still another way to improve on straight insertion is to consider inserting several things at a time. For example, if we have a file of 1000 items, and if 998 of them have already been sorted, Algorithm S makes two more passes through the file (first inserting R_{999}, then R_{1000}). We can obviously save time if we compare K_{999} with K_{1000}, to see which is larger, then insert them *both* with one look at the file. A combined operation of this kind involves about $\frac{2}{3}N$ comparisons and moves (see exercise 3.4.2–5), instead of two passes each with about $\frac{1}{2}N$ comparisons and moves.

In other words, it is generally a good idea to "batch" operations that require long searches, so that multiple operations can be done together. If we carry this idea to its natural conclusion, we rediscover the method of sorting by merging, which is so important it is discussed below in Section 5.2.4.

Address calculation sorting. Surely by now we have exhausted all possible ways to improve on the simple method of straight insertion; but let's look again! Suppose you want to arrange several dozen books on your bookshelves, in order by authors' names, when the books are given to you in random order. You'll naturally try to estimate the final position of each book as you put it in place, thereby reducing the number of comparisons and moves that you'll have to make. And the whole process will be somewhat more efficient if you start with a little more shelf space than is absolutely necessary. This method was first suggested for computer sorting by Isaac and Singleton, *JACM* **3** (1956), 169–174, and it was developed further by Tarter and Kronmal, *Proc. ACM Nat'l Conf.* **21** (1966), 331–337.

Address calculation sorting usually requires additional storage space proportional to N, either to leave enough room so that excessive moving is not required, or to maintain auxiliary tables that account for irregularities in the distribution of keys. (See the "distribution counting" sort, Algorithm 5.2D, which is a form of address calculation.) We can probably make the best use of this additional memory space if we devote it to link fields, as in the list insertion method. In this way we can also avoid having separate areas for input and output; everything can be done in the same area of memory.

These considerations suggest that we generalize list insertion so that *several* lists are kept, not just one. Each list is used for certain ranges of keys. We make the important assumption that the keys are pretty evenly distributed, not "bunched up" irregularly: The set of all possible values of the keys is partitioned into M parts, and we assume a probability of $1/M$ that a given key falls into a given part. Then we provide additional storage for M list heads, and each list is maintained as in simple list insertion.

It is not necessary to give the algorithm in great detail here; the method simply begins with all list heads set to Λ. As each new item enters, we first decide which of the M parts its key falls into, then we insert it into the corresponding list as in Algorithm L.

To illustrate this approach, suppose that the 16 keys used in our examples are divided into the $M = 4$ ranges 0–249, 250–499, 500–749, 750–999. We obtain the following configurations as the keys $K_1, K_2, \ldots, K_{16}$ are successively inserted:

	After 4 items:	After 8 items:	After 12 items:	Final state:
List 1:	061, 087	061, 087, 170	061, 087, 154, 170	061, 087, 154, 170
List 2:		275	275, 426	275, 426
List 3:	503, 512	503, 512	503, 509, 512, 653	503, 509, 512, 612, 653, 677, 703
List 4:		897, 908	897, 908	765, 897, 908

(Program M below actually inserts the keys in reverse order, $K_{16}, \ldots, K_2, K_1$, but the final result is the same.) Because linked memory is used, the varying-length lists cause no storage allocation problem. All lists can be combined into a single list at the end, if desired (see exercise 35).

Program M (*Multiple list insertion*). In this program we make the same assumptions as in Program L, except that the keys must be *nonnegative*, thus

$$0 \le K_j < (\texttt{BYTESIZE})^3.$$

The program divides this range into M equal parts by multiplying each key by a suitable constant. The list heads are in locations HEAD+1 through HEAD+M.

```
01 KEY   EQU  1:3
02 LINK  EQU  4:5
03 START ENT2 M                          1
04       STZ  HEAD,2                      M        HEAD[p] ← Λ.
05       DEC2 1                           M
06       J2P  *-2                         M        M ≥ p ≥ 1.
07       ENT1 N                           1        j ← N.
08 2H    LDA  INPUT,1(KEY)                N
09       MUL  =M(1:3)=                    N        rA ← ⌊M · Kⱼ/BYTESIZE³⌋.
10       STA  *+1(1:2)                    N
11       ENT4 0                           N        rI4 ← rA.
12       ENT3 HEAD+1-INPUT,4              N        q ← LOC(HEAD[rA]).
13       LDA  INPUT,1                     N        K ← Kⱼ.
14       JMP  4F                          N        Jump to set p.
15 3H    CMPA INPUT,2(KEY)          B + N − A
16       JLE  5F                    B + N − A      Jump to insert, if K ≤ Kₚ.
17       ENT3 0,2                         B        q ← p.
18 4H    LD2  INPUT,3(LINK)           B + N        p ← LINK(q).
19       J2P  3B                      B + N        Jump if not end of list.
20 5H    ST1  INPUT,3(LINK)              N         LINK(q) ← LOC(Rⱼ).
21       ST2  INPUT,1(LINK)              N         LINK(LOC(Rⱼ)) ← p.
22 6H    DEC1 1                          N
23       J1P  2B                         N         N ≥ j ≥ 1.  ∎
```

This program is written for general M, but it would be better to fix M at some convenient value; for example, we might choose $M = $ BYTESIZE, so that the list heads could be cleared with a single MOVE instruction and the multiplication sequence of lines 08–11 could be replaced by the single instruction LD3 INPUT,1(1:1). The most notable contrast between Program L and Program M is the fact that Program M must consider the case of an empty list, when no comparisons are to be made.

How much time do we save by having M lists? The total running time of Program M is $7B + 31N - 3A + 4M + 2$ units, where M is the number of lists and N is the number of records sorted; A and B respectively count the right-to-left maxima and the inversions present among the keys belonging to each list. (In contrast to other time analyses of this section, the rightmost element of a nonempty permutation is included in the count A.) We have already studied A and B for $M = 1$, when their average values are respectively H_N and $\frac{1}{2}\binom{N}{2}$. By our assumption about the distribution of keys, the probability that a given list contains precisely n items at the conclusion of sorting is the "binomial" probability

$$\binom{N}{n}\left(\frac{1}{M}\right)^n\left(1 - \frac{1}{M}\right)^{N-n}. \tag{14}$$

Therefore the average values of A and B in the general case are

$$A_{\text{ave}} = M \sum_n \binom{N}{n} \left(\frac{1}{M}\right)^n \left(1 - \frac{1}{M}\right)^{N-n} H_n; \tag{15}$$

$$B_{\text{ave}} = M \sum_n \binom{N}{n} \left(\frac{1}{M}\right)^n \left(1 - \frac{1}{M}\right)^{N-n} \binom{n}{2} \Big/ 2. \tag{16}$$

Using the identity

$$\binom{N}{n}\binom{n}{2} = \binom{N}{2}\binom{N-2}{n-2},$$

which is a special case of Eq. 1.2.6–(20), we can easily evaluate the sum in (16):

$$B_{\text{ave}} = \frac{1}{2M}\binom{N}{2}. \tag{17}$$

And exercise 37 derives the standard deviation of B. But the sum in (15) is more difficult. By Theorem 1.2.7A, we have

$$\sum_n \binom{N}{n}(M-1)^{-n} H_n = \left(1 - \frac{1}{M}\right)^{-N}(H_N - \ln M) + \epsilon,$$

$$0 < \epsilon = \sum_{n>N} \frac{1}{n}\left(1 - \frac{1}{M}\right)^{n-N} < \frac{M-1}{N+1};$$

hence

$$A_{\text{ave}} = M(H_N - \ln M) + \delta, \qquad 0 < \delta < \frac{M^2}{N+1}\left(1 - \frac{1}{M}\right)^{N+1}. \tag{18}$$

(This formula is practically useless when $M \approx N$; exercise 40 gives a more detailed analysis of the asymptotic behavior of A_{ave} when $M = N/\alpha$.)

By combining (17) and (18) we can deduce the total running time of Program M, for fixed M as $N \to \infty$:

min $31N + M + 2$,

ave $1.75N^2/M + 31N - 3MH_N + 3M\ln M + 4M - 3\delta - 1.75N/M + 2$,

max $3.50N^2 + 24.5N + 4M + 2$. $\hspace{2cm}$ (19)

Notice that when M is not too large *we are speeding up the average time by a factor of* M; $M = 10$ will sort about ten times as fast as $M = 1$. However, the maximum time is much larger than the average time; this reiterates the assumption we have made about a fairly equal distribution of keys, since the worst case occurs when all records pile onto the same list.

If we set $M = N$, the average running time of Program M is approximately $34.36N$ units; when $M = \frac{1}{2}N$ it is slightly more, approximately $34.52N$; and when $M = \frac{1}{10}N$ it is approximately $48.04N$. The additional cost of the supplementary program in exercise 35, which links all M lists together in a single list, raises these times respectively to $44.99N$, $41.95N$, and $52.74N$. (Note that

$10N$ of these MIX time units are spent in the multiplication instruction alone!)
*We have achieved a sorting method of order N, provided only that the keys are
reasonably well spread out over their range.*

Improvements to multiple list insertion are discussed in Section 5.2.5.

EXERCISES

1. [*10*] Is Algorithm S a stable sorting algorithm?

2. [*11*] Would Algorithm S still sort numbers correctly if the relation "$K \geq K_i$" in
step S3 were replaced by "$K > K_i$"?

▶ **3.** [*30*] Is Program S the shortest possible sorting program that can be written for
MIX, or is there a shorter program that achieves the same effect?

▶ **4.** [*M20*] Find the minimum and maximum running times for Program S, as a
function of N.

▶ **5.** [*M27*] Find the generating function $g_N(z) = \sum_{k \geq 0} p_{Nk} z^k$ for the total running
time of Program S, where p_{Nk} is the probability that Program S takes exactly k units
of time, given a random permutation of $\{1, 2, \ldots, N\}$ as input. Also calculate the
standard deviation of the running time, given N.

6. [*23*] The two-way insertion method illustrated in Table 2 seems to imply that
there is an output area capable of holding up to $2N + 1$ records, in addition to the
input area containing N records. Show that two-way insertion can be done using only
enough space for $N + 1$ records, including both input and output.

7. [*M20*] If $a_1 a_2 \ldots a_n$ is a random permutation of $\{1, 2, \ldots, n\}$, what is the average
value of $|a_1 - 1| + |a_2 - 1| + \cdots + |a_n - n|$? (This is n times the average net distance
traveled by a record during a sorting process.)

8. [*10*] Is Algorithm D a stable sorting algorithm?

9. [*20*] What are the quantities A and B, and the total running time of Program D,
corresponding to Tables 3 and 4? Discuss the relative merits of shellsort versus straight
insertion in this case.

▶ **10.** [*22*] If $K_j \geq K_{j-h}$ when we begin step D3, Algorithm D specifies a lot of actions
that accomplish nothing. Show how to modify Program D so that this redundant
computation can be avoided, and discuss the merits of such a modification.

11. [*M10*] What path in a lattice like that of Fig. 11 corresponds to the permutation
1 2 5 3 7 4 8 6 9 11 10 12?

12. [*M20*] Prove that the area between a lattice path and the staircase path (as shown
in Fig. 11) equals the number of inversions in the corresponding 2-ordered permutation.

▶ **13.** [*M16*] Explain how to put weights on the *horizontal* line segments of a lattice,
instead of the vertical segments, so that the sum of the horizontal weights on a lattice
path is the number of inversions in the corresponding 2-ordered permutation.

14. [*M28*] (a) Show that, in the sums defined by Eq. (2), we have $A_{2n+1} = 2A_{2n}$.
(b) The general identity of exercise 1.2.6–26 simplifies to

$$\sum_k \binom{2k + s}{k} z^k = \frac{1}{\sqrt{1 - 4z}} \left(\frac{1 - \sqrt{1 - 4z}}{2z} \right)^s$$

if we set $r = s$, $t = -2$. By considering the sum $\sum_n A_{2n} z^n$, show that

$$A_{2n} = n \cdot 4^{n-1}.$$

▸ **15.** [*HM33*] Let $g_n(z)$, $\hat{g}_n(z)$, $h_n(z)$, and $\hat{h}_n(z)$ be $\sum z^{\text{total weight of path}}$ summed over all lattice paths of length $2n$ from $(0,0)$ to (n,n), where the weight is defined as in Fig. 11, subject to certain restrictions on the vertices on the paths: For $h_n(z)$, there is no restriction, but for $g_n(z)$ the path must avoid all vertices (i,j) with $i > j$; $\hat{h}_n(z)$ and $\hat{g}_n(z)$ are defined similarly, except that all vertices (i,i) are also excluded, for $0 < i < n$. Thus

$$g_0(z) = 1, \qquad g_1(z) = z, \qquad g_2(z) = z^3 + z^2; \qquad \hat{g}_1(z) = z, \qquad \hat{g}_2(z) = z^3;$$

$$h_0(z) = 1, \qquad h_1(z) = z + 1, \qquad h_2(z) = z^3 + z^2 + 3z + 1;$$

$$\hat{h}_1(z) = z + 1, \qquad \hat{h}_2(z) = z^3 + z.$$

Find recurrence relations defining these functions, and use these relations to prove that

$$h_n''(1) + h_n'(1) = \frac{7n^3 + 4n^2 + 4n}{30} \binom{2n}{n}.$$

(The exact formula for the variance of the number of inversions in a random 2-ordered permutation of $\{1, 2, \ldots, 2n\}$ is therefore easily found; it is asymptotically $(\frac{7}{30} - \frac{\pi}{16})n^3$.)

16. [*M24*] Find a formula for the maximum number of inversions in an h-ordered permutation of $\{1, 2, \ldots, n\}$. What is the maximum possible number of moves in Algorithm D when the increments satisfy the divisibility condition (5)?

17. [*M21*] Show that, when $N = 2^t$ and $h_s = 2^s$ for $t > s \geq 0$, there is a unique permutation of $\{1, 2, \ldots, n\}$ that maximizes the number of move operations performed by Algorithm D. Find a simple way to describe this permutation.

18. [*HM24*] For large N the sum (6) can be estimated as

$$\frac{1}{4}\frac{N^2}{h_{t-1}} + \frac{\sqrt{\pi}}{8}\left(\frac{N^{3/2}h_{t-1}^{1/2}}{h_{t-2}} + \cdots + \frac{N^{3/2}h_1^{1/2}}{h_0}\right).$$

What real values of $h_{t-1}, \ldots, h_0$ minimize this expression when N and t are fixed and $h_0 = 1$?

▸ **19.** [*M25*] What is the average value of the quantity A in the timing analysis of Program D, when the increments satisfy the divisibility condition (5)?

20. [*M22*] Show that Theorem K follows from Lemma L.

21. [*M25*] Let h and k be relatively prime positive integers, and say that an integer is *generable* if it equals $xh + yk$ for some nonnegative integers x and y. Show that n is generable if and only if $hk - h - k - n$ is not generable. (Since 0 is the smallest generable integer, the largest nongenerable integer must therefore be $hk - h - k$. It follows that $K_i \leq K_j$ whenever $j - i \geq (h-1)(k-1)$, in any file that is both h-ordered and k-ordered.)

22. [*M30*] Prove that all integers $\geq 2^s(2^s - 1)$ can be represented in the form

$$a_0(2^s - 1) + a_1(2^{s+1} - 1) + a_2(2^{s+2} - 1) + \cdots,$$

where the a_j's are nonnegative integers; but $2^s(2^s - 1) - 1$ cannot be so represented. Furthermore, exactly $2^{s-1}(2^s + s - 3)$ positive integers are unrepresentable in this form.

Find analogous formulas when the quantities $2^k - 1$ are replaced by $2^k + 1$ in the representations.

▶ **23.** [*M22*] Prove that if h_{s+2} and h_{s+1} are relatively prime, the number of moves that occur while Algorithm D is using the increment h_s is $O(Nh_{s+2}h_{s+1}/h_s)$. *Hint:* See exercise 21.

24. [*M42*] Prove that Theorem P is best possible, in the sense that the exponent $3/2$ cannot be lowered.

▶ **25.** [*M22*] How many permutations of $\{1, 2, \ldots, N\}$ are both 3-ordered and 2-ordered? What is the maximum number of inversions in such a permutation? What is the total number of inversions among all such permutations?

26. [*M35*] Can a file of N elements have more than N inversions if it is 3-, 5-, and 7-ordered? Estimate the maximum number of inversions when N is large.

27. [*M41*] (Bjorn Poonen.) (a) Prove that there is a constant c such that if m of the increments h_s in Algorithm D are less than $N/2$, the running time is $\Omega(N^{1+c/\sqrt{m}})$ in the worst case. (b) Consequently the worst-case running time is $\Omega(N(\log N/\log\log N)^2)$ for all sequences of increments.

28. [*15*] Which sequence of increments shown in Table 6 is best from the standpoint of Program D, considering the average total running time?

29. [*40*] For $N = 1000$ and various values of t, find empirical values of $h_{t-1}, \ldots, h_1, h_0$ for which the average number of moves, B_{ave}, is as small as you can make it.

30. [*M23*] (V. Pratt.) If the set of increments in shellsort is $\{2^p3^q \mid 2^p3^q < N\}$, show that the number of passes is approximately $\frac{1}{2}(\log_2 N)(\log_3 N)$, and the number of moves per pass is at most $N/2$. In fact, if $K_{j-h} > K_j$ on any pass, we will always have $K_{j-3h}, K_{j-2h} \leq K_j < K_{j-h} \leq K_{j+h}, K_{j+2h}$; so we may simply interchange K_{j-h} and K_j and increase j by $2h$, saving two of the comparisons of Algorithm D. *Hint:* See exercise 25.

▶ **31.** [*25*] Write a MIX program for Pratt's sorting algorithm (exercise 30). Express its running time in terms of quantities A, B, S, T, N analogous to those in Program D.

32. [*10*] What would be the final contents of $L_0 L_1 \ldots L_{16}$ if the list insertion sort in Table 8 were carried through to completion?

▶ **33.** [*25*] Find a way to improve on Program L so that its running time is dominated by $5B$ instead of $7B$, where B is the number of inversions. Discuss corresponding improvements to Program S.

34. [*M10*] Verify formula (14).

35. [*21*] Write a MIX program to follow Program M, so that all lists are combined into a single list. Your program should set the LINK fields exactly as they would have been set by Program L.

36. [*18*] Assume that the byte size of MIX is 100, and that the sixteen example keys in Table 8 are actually 503000, 087000, 512000, ..., 703000. Determine the running time of Programs L and M on this data, when $M = 4$.

37. [*M25*] Let $g_n(z)$ be the probability generating function for inversions in a random permutation of n objects, Eq. 5.1.1–(11). Let $g_{NM}(z)$ be the corresponding generating function for the quantity B in Program M. Show that

$$\sum_{N \geq 0} g_{NM}(z) \frac{M^N w^N}{N!} = \left(\sum_{n \geq 0} g_n(z) \frac{w^n}{n!} \right)^M,$$

and use this formula to derive the variance of B.

38. [*HM23*] (R. M. Karp.) Let $F(x)$ be a distribution function for a probability distribution, with $F(0) = 0$ and $F(1) = 1$. Given that the keys $K_1, K_2, \ldots, K_N$ are independently chosen at random from this distribution, and that $M = cN$, where c is constant and $N \to \infty$, prove that the running time of Program M is $O(N)$ when F is sufficiently smooth. (A key K is inserted into list j when $\lfloor MK \rfloor = j - 1$; this occurs with probability $F(j/M) - F((j-1)/M)$. Only the case $F(x) = x$, $0 \le x \le 1$, is treated in the text.)

39. [*HM16*] If a program runs in approximately $A/M + B$ units of time and uses $C + M$ locations in memory, what choice of M gives the minimum time × space?

▶ **40.** [*HM24*] Find the asymptotic value of the average number of right-to-left maxima that occur in multiple list insertion, Eq. (15), when $M = N/\alpha$ for fixed α as $N \to \infty$. Carry out the expansion to an absolute error of $O(N^{-1})$, expressing your answer in terms of the *exponential integral* function $E_1(z) = \int_z^\infty e^{-t} \, dt/t$.

41. [*HM26*] (a) Prove that the sum of the first $\binom{k}{2}$ elements of (10) is $O(\rho^{2k})$. (b) Now prove Theorem I.

42. [*HM43*] Analyze the average behavior of shellsort when there are $t = 3$ increments h, g, and 1, assuming that $h \perp g$. The first pass, h-sorting, obviously does a total of $\frac{1}{4}N^2/h + O(N)$ moves.

a) Prove that the second pass, g-sorting, does $\frac{\sqrt{\pi}}{8}(\sqrt{h} - 1/\sqrt{h})N/g + O(hN)$ moves.
b) Prove that the third pass, 1-sorting, does $\psi(h, g)N + O(g^3 h^2)$ moves, where

$$\psi(h, g) = \frac{1}{2} \sum_{d=1}^{g-1} \sum_j \binom{h-1}{j} \left(\frac{d}{g}\right)^j \left(1 - \frac{d}{g}\right)^{h-1-j} \left| j - \left\lfloor \frac{hd}{g} \right\rfloor \right|.$$

▶ **43.** [*25*] Exercise 33 uses a sentinel to speed up Algorithm S, by making the test "$i > 0$" unnecessary in step S4. This trick does not apply to Algorithm D. Nevertheless, show that there is an easy way to avoid testing "$i > 0$" in step D5, thereby speeding up the inner loop of shellsort.

44. [*M25*] If $\pi = a_1 \ldots a_n$ and $\pi' = a_1' \ldots a_n'$ are permutations of $\{1, \ldots, n\}$, say that $\pi \le \pi'$ if the ith-largest element of $\{a_1, \ldots, a_j\}$ is less than or equal to the ith-largest element of $\{a_1', \ldots, a_j'\}$, for $1 \le i \le j \le n$. (In other words, $\pi \le \pi'$ if straight insertion sorting of π is componentwise less than or equal to straight insertion sorting of π' after the first j elements have been inserted, for all j.)

a) If π is above π' in the sense of exercise 5.1.1–12, does it follow that $\pi \le \pi'$?
b) If $\pi \le \pi'$, does it follow that $\pi^R \ge \pi'^R$?
c) If $\pi \le \pi'$, does it follow that π is above π'?

5.2.2. Sorting by Exchanging

We come now to the second family of sorting algorithms mentioned near the beginning of Section 5.2: "exchange" or "transposition" methods that systematically interchange pairs of elements that are out of order until no more such pairs exist.

The process of straight insertion, Algorithm 5.2.1S, can be viewed as an exchange method: We take each new record R_j and essentially exchange it with its neighbors to the left until it has been inserted into the proper place. Thus the classification of sorting methods into various families such as "insertion,"

	Pass 1	Pass 2	Pass 3	Pass 4	Pass 5	Pass 6	Pass 7	Pass 8	Pass 9
703	908	908	908	908	908	908	908	908	908
765	703	897	897	897	897	897	897	897	897
677	765	703	765	765	765	765	765	765	765
612	677	765	703	703	703	703	703	703	703
509	612	677	677	677	677	677	677	677	677
154	509	612	653	653	653	653	653	653	653
426	154	509	612	612	612	612	612	612	612
653	426	154	509	512	512	512	512	512	512
275	653	426	154	509	509	509	509	509	509
897	275	653	426	154	503	503	503	503	503
170	897	275	512	426	154	426	426	426	426
908	170	512	275	503	426	154	275	275	275
061	512	170	503	275	275	275	154	170	170
512	061	503	170	170	170	170	170	154	154
087	503	061	087	087	087	087	087	087	087
503	087	087	061	061	061	061	061	061	061

Fig. 14. The bubble sort in action.

"exchange," "selection," etc., is not always clear-cut. In this section, we shall discuss four types of sorting methods for which exchanging is a dominant characteristic: *exchange selection* (the "bubble sort"); *merge exchange* (Batcher's parallel sort); *partition exchange* (Hoare's "quicksort"); and *radix exchange*.

The bubble sort. Perhaps the most obvious way to sort by exchanges is to compare K_1 with K_2, interchanging R_1 and R_2 if the keys are out of order; then do the same to records R_2 and R_3, R_3 and R_4, etc. During this sequence of operations, records with large keys tend to move to the right, and in fact the record with the largest key will move up to become R_N. Repetitions of the process will get the appropriate records into positions R_{N-1}, R_{N-2}, etc., so that all records will ultimately be sorted.

Figure 14 shows this sorting method in action on the sixteen keys 503 087 512 ... 703; it is convenient to represent the file of numbers vertically instead of horizontally, with R_N at the top and R_1 at the bottom. The method is called "bubble sorting" because large elements "bubble up" to their proper position, by contrast with the "sinking sort" (that is, straight insertion) in which elements sink down to an appropriate level. The bubble sort is also known by more prosaic names such as "exchange selection" or "propagation."

After each pass through the file, it is not hard to see that all records above and including the last one to be exchanged must be in their final position, so they need not be examined on subsequent passes. Horizontal lines in Fig. 14 show the progress of the sorting from this standpoint; notice, for example, that five more elements are known to be in final position as a result of Pass 4. On the final pass, no exchanges are performed at all. With these observations we are ready to formulate the algorithm.

Algorithm B (*Bubble sort*). Records $R_1, \ldots, R_N$ are rearranged in place; after sorting is complete their keys will be in order, $K_1 \leq \cdots \leq K_N$.

B1. [Initialize BOUND.] Set BOUND $\leftarrow N$. (BOUND is the highest index for which the record is not known to be in its final position; thus we are indicating that nothing is known at this point.)

B2. [Loop on j.] Set $t \leftarrow 0$. Perform step B3 for $j = 1, 2, \ldots,$ BOUND $- 1$, and then go to step B4. (If BOUND $= 1$, this means go directly to B4.)

B3. [Compare/exchange $R_j : R_{j+1}$.] If $K_j > K_{j+1}$, interchange $R_j \leftrightarrow R_{j+1}$ and set $t \leftarrow j$.

B4. [Any exchanges?] If $t = 0$, terminate the algorithm. Otherwise set BOUND $\leftarrow t$ and return to step B2. ∎

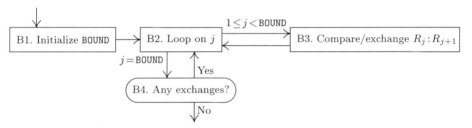

Fig. 15. Flow chart for bubble sorting.

Program B (*Bubble sort*). As in previous MIX programs of this chapter, we assume that the items to be sorted are in locations INPUT+1 through INPUT+N. rI1 ≡ t; rI2 ≡ j.

01	START	ENT1	N	1	*B1. Initialize* BOUND. $t \leftarrow N$.
02	1H	ST1	BOUND(1:2)	A	BOUND $\leftarrow t$.
03		ENT2	1	A	*B2. Loop on j.* $j \leftarrow 1$.
04		ENT1	0	A	$t \leftarrow 0$.
05		JMP	BOUND	A	Exit if $j \geq$ BOUND.
06	3H	LDA	INPUT,2	C	*B3. Compare/exchange $R_j : R_{j+1}$.*
07		CMPA	INPUT+1,2	C	
08		JLE	2F	C	No exchange if $K_j \leq K_{j+1}$.
09		LDX	INPUT+1,2	B	R_{j+1}
10		STX	INPUT,2	B	$\rightarrow R_j$.
11		STA	INPUT+1,2	B	(old R_j) $\rightarrow R_{j+1}$.
12		ENT1	0,2	B	$t \leftarrow j$.
13	2H	INC2	1	C	$j \leftarrow j + 1$.
14	BOUND	ENTX	-*,2	$A + C$	rX $\leftarrow j -$ BOUND. [Instruction modified]
15		JXN	3B	$A + C$	Do step B3 for $1 \leq j <$ BOUND.
16	4H	J1P	1B	A	*B4. Any exchanges?* To B2 if $t > 0$. ∎

Analysis of the bubble sort. It is quite instructive to analyze the running time of Algorithm B. Three quantities are involved in the timing: the number of passes, A; the number of exchanges, B; and the number of comparisons, C. If the input keys are distinct and in random order, we may assume that they form a random permutation of $\{1, 2, \ldots, n\}$. The idea of *inversion tables* (Section 5.1.1) leads to an easy way to describe the effect of each pass in a bubble sort.

Theorem I. *Let $a_1 a_2 \ldots a_n$ be a permutation of $\{1, 2, \ldots, n\}$, and let $b_1 b_2 \ldots b_n$ be the corresponding inversion table. If one pass of the bubble sort, Algorithm B, changes $a_1 a_2 \ldots a_n$ to the permutation $a'_1 a'_2 \ldots a'_n$, the corresponding inversion table $b'_1 b'_2 \ldots b'_n$ is obtained from $b_1 b_2 \ldots b_n$ by decreasing each nonzero entry by 1.*

Proof. If a_i is preceded by a larger element, the largest preceding element is exchanged with it, so b_{a_i} decreases by 1. But if a_i is not preceded by a larger element, it is never exchanged with a larger element, so b_{a_i} remains 0. ∎

Thus we can see what happens during a bubble sort by studying the sequence of inversion tables between passes. For example, the successive inversion tables corresponding to Fig. 14 are

$$
\begin{array}{l}
\qquad\qquad 3\ 1\ 8\ 3\ 4\ 5\ 0\ 4\ 0\ 3\ 2\ 2\ 3\ 2\ 1\ 0 \\
\text{Pass 1} \\
\qquad\qquad 2\ 0\ 7\ 2\ 3\ 4\ 0\ 3\ 0\ 2\ 1\ 1\ 2\ 1\ 0\ 0 \\
\text{Pass 2} \\
\qquad\qquad 1\ 0\ 6\ 1\ 2\ 3\ 0\ 2\ 0\ 1\ 0\ 0\ 1\ 0\ 0\ 0 \\
\text{Pass 3} \\
\qquad\qquad 0\ 0\ 5\ 0\ 1\ 2\ 0\ 1\ 0\ 0\ 0\ 0\ 0\ 0\ 0\ 0
\end{array}
\qquad (1)
$$

and so on. If $b_1 b_2 \ldots b_n$ is the inversion table of the input permutation, we must therefore have

$$A = 1 + \max(b_1, b_2, \ldots, b_n), \qquad (2)$$

$$B = b_1 + b_2 + \cdots + b_n, \qquad (3)$$

$$C = c_1 + c_2 + \cdots + c_A, \qquad (4)$$

where c_j is the value of $\mathtt{BOUND} - 1$ at the beginning of pass j. In terms of the inversion table,

$$c_j = \max\{b_i + i \mid b_i \geq j - 1\} - j \qquad (5)$$

(see exercise 5). In example (1) we therefore have $A = 9$, $B = 41$, $C = 15 + 14 + 13 + 12 + 7 + 5 + 4 + 3 + 2 = 75$. The total MIX sorting time for Fig. 14 is $960u$.

The distribution of B (the total number of inversions in a random permutation) is very well-known to us by now; so we are left with A and C to be analyzed.

The probability that $A \leq k$ is $1/n!$ times the number of inversion tables having no components $\geq k$, namely $k^{n-k}k!$, when $1 \leq k \leq n$. Hence the probability that exactly k passes are required is

$$A_k = \frac{1}{n!}\left(k^{n-k}k! - (k-1)^{n-k+1}(k-1)!\right). \qquad (6)$$

The mean value $\sum k A_k$ can now be calculated; summing by parts, it is

$$A_{\text{ave}} = n + 1 - \sum_{k=0}^{n} \frac{k^{n-k} k!}{n!} = n + 1 - P(n), \tag{7}$$

where $P(n)$ is the function whose asymptotic value was found to be $\sqrt{\pi n/2} - \frac{2}{3} + O(1/\sqrt{n})$ in Eq. 1.2.11.3–(24). Formula (7) was stated without proof by E. H. Friend in *JACM* **3** (1956), 150; a proof was given by Howard B. Demuth [Ph.D. Thesis (Stanford University, October 1956), 64–68]. For the standard deviation of A, see exercise 7.

The total number of comparisons, C, is somewhat harder to handle, and we will consider only C_{ave}. For fixed n, let $f_j(k)$ be the number of inversion tables $b_1 \ldots b_n$ such that for $1 \le i \le n$ we have either $b_i < j - 1$ or $b_i + i - j \le k$; then

$$f_j(k) = (j+k)!\,(j-1)^{n-j-k}, \qquad \text{for } 0 \le k \le n - j. \tag{8}$$

(See exercise 8.) The average value of c_j in (5) is $\left(\sum k\big(f_j(k) - f_j(k-1)\big)\right)/n!$; summing by parts and then summing on j leads to the formula

$$C_{\text{ave}} = \binom{n+1}{2} - \frac{1}{n!} \sum_{\substack{1 \le j \le n \\ 0 \le k \le n-j}} f_j(k) = \binom{n+1}{2} - \frac{1}{n!} \sum_{0 \le r < s \le n} s!\, r^{n-s}. \tag{9}$$

Here the asymptotic value is not easy to determine, and we shall return to it at the end of this section.

To summarize our analysis of the bubble sort, the formulas derived above and below may be written as follows:

$$A = \left(\text{min } 1,\ \text{ave } N - \sqrt{\pi N/2} + O(1),\ \text{max } N\right); \tag{10}$$

$$B = \left(\text{min } 0,\ \text{ave } \tfrac{1}{4}(N^2 - N),\ \text{max } \tfrac{1}{2}(N^2 - N)\right); \tag{11}$$

$$C = \Big(\text{min } N - 1,\ \text{ave } \tfrac{1}{2}\big(N^2 - N \ln N - (\gamma + \ln 2 - 1)N\big) + O\big(\sqrt{N}\big),$$
$$\text{max } \tfrac{1}{2}(N^2 - N)\Big). \tag{12}$$

In each case the minimum occurs when the input is already in order, and the maximum occurs when it is in reverse order; so the MIX running time is $8A + 7B + 8C + 1 = \left(\text{min } 8N + 1,\ \text{ave } 5.75N^2 + O(N \log N),\ \text{max } 7.5N^2 + 0.5N + 1\right)$.

Refinements of the bubble sort. It took a good deal of work to analyze the bubble sort; and although the techniques used in the calculations are instructive, the results are disappointing since they tell us that the bubble sort isn't really very good at all. Compared to straight insertion (Algorithm 5.2.1S), bubble sorting requires a more complicated program and takes more than twice as long!

Some of the bubble sort's deficiencies are easy to spot. For example, in Fig. 14, the first comparison in Pass 4 is redundant, as are the first two in Pass 5 and the first three in Passes 6 and 7. Notice also that elements can never move to the left more than one step per pass; so if the smallest item happens to be initially at the far right we are forced to make the maximum number of

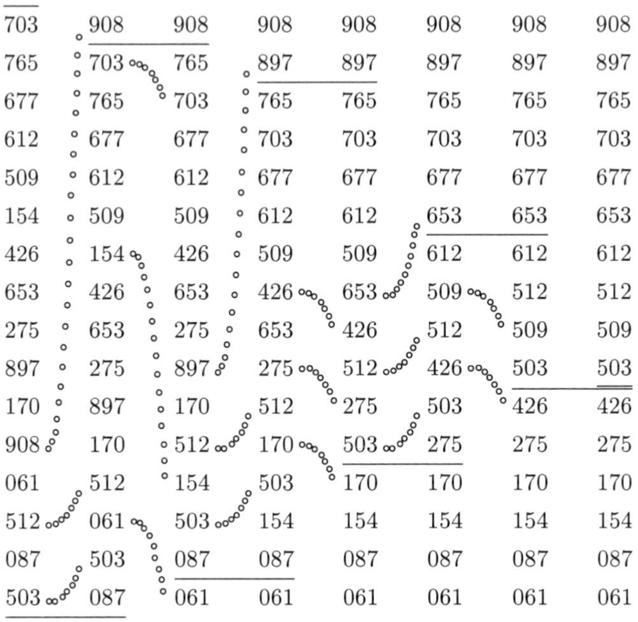

703	908	908	908	908	908	908	908
765	703	765	897	897	897	897	897
677	765	703	765	765	765	765	765
612	677	677	703	703	703	703	703
509	612	612	677	677	677	677	677
154	509	509	612	612	653	653	653
426	154	426	509	509	612	612	612
653	426	653	426	653	509	512	512
275	653	275	653	426	512	509	509
897	275	897	275	512	426	503	503
170	897	170	512	275	503	426	426
908	170	512	170	503	275	275	275
061	512	154	503	170	170	170	170
512	061	503	154	154	154	154	154
087	503	087	087	087	087	087	087
503	087	061	061	061	061	061	061

Fig. 16. The cocktail-shaker short [shic].

comparisons. This suggests the "cocktail-shaker sort," in which alternate passes go in opposite directions (see Fig. 16). The average number of comparisons is slightly reduced by this approach. K. E. Iverson [*A Programming Language* (Wiley, 1962), 218–219] made an interesting observation in this regard: If j is an index such that R_j and R_{j+1} are not exchanged with each other on two consecutive passes in opposite directions, then R_j and R_{j+1} must be in their final position, and they need not enter into any subsequent comparisons. For example, traversing 4 3 2 1 8 6 9 7 5 from left to right yields 3 2 1 4 6 8 7 5 9; no interchange occurred between R_4 and R_5. When we traverse the latter permutation from right to left, we find R_4 still less than (the new) R_5, so we may immediately conclude that R_4 and R_5 need not participate in any further comparisons.

But none of these refinements lead to an algorithm better than straight insertion; and we already know that straight insertion isn't suitable for large N. Another idea is to eliminate most of the exchanges; since most elements simply shift left one step during an exchange, we could achieve the same effect by viewing the array differently, shifting the origin of indexing! But the resulting algorithm is no better than straight *selection*, Algorithm 5.2.3S, which we shall study later.

In short, the bubble sort seems to have nothing to recommend it, except a catchy name and the fact that it leads to some interesting theoretical problems.

Batcher's parallel method. If we are going to have an exchange algorithm whose running time is faster than order N^2, we need to select some *nonadjacent* pairs of keys (K_i, K_j) for comparisons; otherwise we will need as many exchanges as the original permutation has inversions, and the average number of inversions is $\frac{1}{4}(N^2 - N)$. An ingenious way to program a sequence of comparisons, looking for potential exchanges, was discovered in 1964 by K. E. Batcher [see *Proc. AFIPS Spring Joint Computer Conference* **32** (1968), 307–314]. His method is not at all obvious; in fact, a fairly intricate proof is needed just to show that it is valid, since comparatively few comparisons are made. We shall discuss two proofs, one in this section and another in Section 5.3.4.

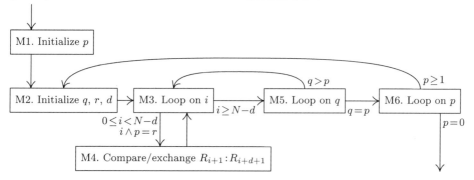

Fig. 17. Algorithm M.

Batcher's sorting scheme is similar to shellsort, but the comparisons are done in a novel way so that no propagation of exchanges is necessary. We can, for instance, compare Table 1 (on the next page) to Table 5.2.1–3; Batcher's method achieves the effect of 8-sorting, 4-sorting, 2-sorting, and 1-sorting, but the comparisons do not overlap. Since Batcher's algorithm essentially merges pairs of sorted subsequences, it may be called the "merge exchange sort."

Algorithm M (*Merge exchange*). Records $R_1, \ldots, R_N$ are rearranged in place; after sorting is complete their keys will be in order, $K_1 \leq \cdots \leq K_N$. We assume that $N \geq 2$.

M1. [Initialize p.] Set $p \leftarrow 2^{t-1}$, where $t = \lceil \lg N \rceil$ is the least integer such that $2^t \geq N$. (Steps M2 through M5 will be performed for $p = 2^{t-1}, 2^{t-2}, \ldots, 1$.)

M2. [Initialize q, r, d.] Set $q \leftarrow 2^{t-1}$, $r \leftarrow 0$, $d \leftarrow p$.

M3. [Loop on i.] For all i such that $0 \leq i < N - d$ and $i \wedge p = r$, do step M4. Then go to step M5. (Here $i \wedge p$ means the "bitwise and" of the binary representations of i and p; each bit of the result is zero except where both i and p have 1 bits in corresponding positions. Thus $13 \wedge 21 = (1101)_2 \wedge (10101)_2 = (00101)_2 = 5$. At this point, d is an odd multiple of p, and p is a power of 2, so that $i \wedge p \neq (i+d) \wedge p$; it follows that the actions of step M4 can be done for all relevant i in any order, even simultaneously.)

M4. [Compare/exchange $R_{i+1} : R_{i+d+1}$.] If $K_{i+1} > K_{i+d+1}$, interchange the records $R_{i+1} \leftrightarrow R_{i+d+1}$.

M5. [Loop on q.] If $q \neq p$, set $d \leftarrow q - p$, $q \leftarrow q/2$, $r \leftarrow p$, and return to M3.

M6. [Loop on p.] (At this point the permutation $K_1 K_2 \ldots K_N$ is p-ordered.) Set $p \leftarrow \lfloor p/2 \rfloor$. If $p > 0$, go back to M2. ∎

Table 1

MERGE-EXCHANGE SORTING (BATCHER'S METHOD)

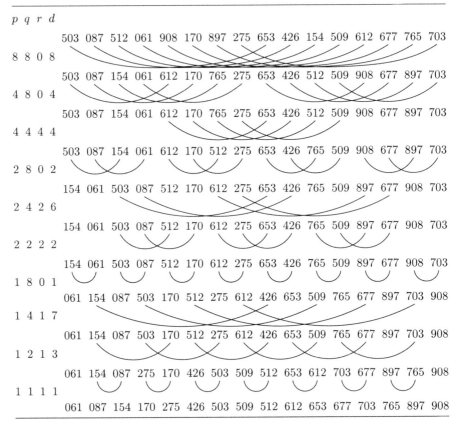

p	q	r	d
				503 087 512 061 908 170 897 275 653 426 154 509 612 677 765 703
8	8	0	8
				503 087 154 061 612 170 765 275 653 426 512 509 908 677 897 703
4	8	0	4
				503 087 154 061 612 170 765 275 653 426 512 509 908 677 897 703
4	4	4	4
				503 087 154 061 612 170 512 275 653 426 765 509 908 677 897 703
2	8	0	2
				154 061 503 087 512 170 612 275 653 426 765 509 897 677 908 703
2	4	2	6
				154 061 503 087 512 170 612 275 653 426 765 509 897 677 908 703
2	2	2	2
				154 061 503 087 512 170 612 275 653 426 765 509 897 677 908 703
1	8	0	1
				061 154 087 503 170 512 275 612 426 653 509 765 677 897 703 908
1	4	1	7
				061 154 087 503 170 512 275 612 426 653 509 765 677 897 703 908
1	2	1	3
				061 154 087 275 170 426 503 509 512 653 612 703 677 897 765 908
1	1	1	1
				061 087 154 170 275 426 503 509 512 612 653 677 703 765 897 908

Table 1 illustrates the method for $N = 16$. Notice that the algorithm sorts N elements essentially by sorting $R_1, R_3, R_5, \ldots$ and $R_2, R_4, R_6, \ldots$ independently; then we perform steps M2 through M5 for $p = 1$, in order to merge the two sorted sequences together.

In order to prove that the magic sequence of comparison/exchanges specified in Algorithm M actually will sort all possible input files $R_1 R_2 \ldots R_N$, we must show only that steps M2 through M5 will merge all 2-ordered files $R_1 R_2 \ldots R_N$ when $p = 1$. For this purpose we can use the lattice-path method of Section 5.2.1 (see Fig. 11 on page 87); each 2-ordered permutation of $\{1, 2, \ldots, N\}$ corresponds uniquely to a path from $(0,0)$ to $(\lceil N/2 \rceil, \lfloor N/2 \rfloor)$ in a lattice diagram. Figure 18(a) shows an example for $N = 16$, corresponding to the permutation 1 3 2 4 10 5 11 6 13 7 14 8 15 9 16 12. When we perform step M3 with $p = 1$, $q = 2^{t-1}$, $r = 0$, $d = 1$, the effect is to compare (and possibly exchange) $R_1 : R_2$, $R_3 : R_4$, etc. This operation corresponds to a simple transformation of the lattice path, "folding" it about the diagonal if necessary so that it never goes above the diagonal. (See Fig. 18(b) and the proof in exercise 10.) The next iterations of step M3 have $p = r = 1$, and $d = 2^{t-1} - 1, 2^{t-2} - 1, \ldots, 1$; their effect is to compare/exchange $R_2 : R_{2+d}$, $R_4 : R_{4+d}$, etc., and again there is a simple lattice interpretation: The path is "folded" about a line $\frac{1}{2}(d+1)$ units below the diagonal. See Fig. 18(c) and (d); eventually we get to the path in Fig. 18(e), which corresponds to a completely sorted permutation. This completes a "geometric proof" that Batcher's algorithm is valid; we might call it sorting by folding!

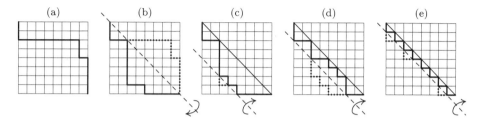

Fig. 18. A geometric interpretation of Batcher's method, $N = 16$.

A MIX program for Algorithm M appears in exercise 12. Unfortunately the amount of bookkeeping needed to control the sequence of comparisons is rather large, so the program is less efficient than other methods we have seen. But it has one important redeeming feature: All comparison/exchanges specified by a given iteration of step M3 can be done *simultaneously*, on computers or networks that allow parallel computations. With such parallel operations, sorting is completed in $\frac{1}{2}\lceil \lg N \rceil (\lceil \lg N \rceil + 1)$ steps, and this is about as fast as any general method known. For example, *1024 elements can be sorted in only 55 parallel steps by Batcher's method.* The nearest competitor is Pratt's method (see exercise 5.2.1–30), which uses either 40 or 73 steps, depending on how we count; if we are willing to allow overlapping comparisons as long as no overlapping exchanges are necessary, Pratt's method requires only 40 comparison/exchange cycles to sort 1024 elements. For further comments, see Section 5.3.4.

Quicksort. The sequence of comparisons in Batcher's method is predetermined; we compare the same pairs of keys each time, regardless of what we may have learned about the file from previous comparisons. The same is largely true of the bubble sort, although Algorithm B does make limited use of previous knowledge in order to reduce its work at the right end of the file. Let us now turn to a quite different strategy, which uses the result of each comparison to determine what keys are to be compared next. Such a strategy is inappropriate for parallel computations, but on computers that work serially it can be quite fruitful.

The basic idea of the following method is to take one record, say R_1, and to move it to the final position that it should occupy in the sorted file, say position s. While determining this final position, we will also rearrange the other records so that there will be none with greater keys to the left of position s, and none with smaller keys to the right. Thus the file will have been partitioned in such a way

that the original sorting problem is reduced to two simpler problems, namely
to sort $R_1 \ldots R_{s-1}$ and (independently) to sort $R_{s+1} \ldots R_N$. We can apply the
same technique to each of these subfiles, until the job is done.

There are several ways to achieve such a partitioning into left and right
subfiles; the following scheme due to R. Sedgewick seems to be best, for reasons
that will become clearer when we analyze the algorithm: Keep two pointers,
i and j, with $i = 2$ and $j = N$ initially. If R_i is eventually supposed to be
part of the left-hand subfile after partitioning (we can tell this by comparing
K_i with K_1), increase i by 1, and continue until encountering a record R_i that
belongs to the right-hand subfile. Similarly, decrease j by 1 until encountering
a record R_j belonging to the left-hand subfile. If $i < j$, exchange R_i with R_j;
then move on to process the next records in the same way, "burning the candle
at both ends" until $i \geq j$. The partitioning is finally completed by exchanging
R_j with R_1. For example, consider what happens to our file of sixteen numbers:

```
                      i                                                            j
                      ↓                                                            ↓
Initial file:     [503 087 512 061 908 170 897 275 653 426 154 509 612 677 765 703]
1st exchange:      503 087 512 061 908 170 897 275 653 426 154 509 612 677 765 703
2nd exchange:      503 087 154 061 908 170 897 275 653 426 512 509 612 677 765 703
3rd exchange:      503 087 154 061 426 170 897 275 653 908 512 509 612 677 765 703
Pointers cross:    503 087 154 061 426 170 275 897 653 908 512 509 612 677 765 703
Partitioned file:[275 087 154 061 426 170]503[897 653 908 512 509 612 677 765 703]
                                          ↑   ↑
                                          j   i
```

(In order to indicate the positions of i and j, keys K_i and K_j are shown here in
boldface type.)

Table 2 shows how our example file gets completely sorted by this approach,
in 11 stages. Brackets indicate subfiles that still need to be sorted; double
brackets identify the subfile of current interest. Inside a computer, the current
subfile can be represented by boundary values (l, r), and the other subfiles by
a stack of additional pairs (l_k, r_k). Whenever a file is subdivided, we put the
longer subfile on the stack and commence work on the shorter one, until we reach
trivially short files; this strategy guarantees that the stack will never contain
more than $\lg N$ entries (see exercise 20).

The sorting procedure just described may be called *partition-exchange sorting*; it is due to C. A. R. Hoare, whose interesting paper [*Comp. J.* **5** (1962),
10–15] contains one of the most comprehensive accounts of a sorting method that
has ever been published. Hoare dubbed his method "quicksort," and that name
is not inappropriate, since the inner loops of the computation are extremely fast
on most computers. All comparisons during a given stage are made against the
same key, so this key may be kept in a register. Only a single index needs to
be changed between comparisons. Furthermore, the amount of data movement

Table 2

QUICKSORTING

		(l,r)	Stack
[503 087 512 061 908 170 897 275 653 426 154 509 612 677 765 703]		(1,16)	—
[275 087 154 061 426 170] 503 [897 653 908 512 509 612 677 765 703]		(1,6)	(8,16)
[170 087 154 061] 275 426 503 [897 653 908 512 509 612 677 765 703]		(1,4)	(8,16)
[061 087 154] 170 275 426 503 [897 653 908 512 509 612 677 765 703]		(1,3)	(8,16)
061 [087 154] 170 275 426 503 [897 653 908 512 509 612 677 765 703]		(2,3)	(8,16)
061 087 154 170 275 426 503 [897 653 908 512 509 612 677 765 703]		(8,16)	—
061 087 154 170 275 426 503 [765 653 703 512 509 612 677] 897 908		(8,14)	—
061 087 154 170 275 426 503 [677 653 703 512 509 612] 765 897 908		(8,13)	—
061 087 154 170 275 426 503 [509 653 612 512] 677 703 765 897 908		(8,11)	—
061 087 154 170 275 426 503 509 [653 612 512] 677 703 765 897 908		(9,11)	—
061 087 154 170 275 426 503 509 [512 612] 653 677 703 765 897 908		(9,10)	—
061 087 154 170 275 426 503 509 512 612 653 677 703 765 897 908		—	—

is quite reasonable; the computation in Table 2, for example, makes only 17 exchanges.

The bookkeeping required to control i, j, and the stack is not difficult, but it makes the quicksort partitioning procedure most suitable for fairly large N. Therefore the following algorithm uses another strategy after the subfiles have become short.

Algorithm Q (*Quicksort*). Records $R_1, \ldots, R_N$ are rearranged in place; after sorting is complete their keys will be in order, $K_1 \leq \cdots \leq K_N$. An auxiliary stack with at most $\lfloor \lg N \rfloor$ entries is needed for temporary storage. This algorithm follows the quicksort partitioning procedure described in the text above, with slight modifications for extra efficiency:

a) We assume the presence of artificial keys $K_0 = -\infty$ and $K_{N+1} = +\infty$ such that

$$K_0 \leq K_i \leq K_{N+1} \qquad \text{for } 1 \leq i \leq N. \tag{13}$$

(Equality is allowed.)

b) Subfiles of M or fewer elements are left unsorted until the very end of the procedure; then a single pass of straight insertion is used to produce the final ordering. Here $M \geq 1$ is a parameter that should be chosen as described in the text below. (This idea, due to R. Sedgewick, saves some of the overhead that would be necessary if we applied straight insertion directly to each small subfile, unless locality of reference is significant.)

c) Records with equal keys are exchanged, although it is not strictly necessary to do so. (This idea, due to R. C. Singleton, keeps the inner loops fast and helps to split subfiles nearly in half when equal elements are present; see exercise 18.)

Q1. [Initialize.] If $N \leq M$, go to step Q9. Otherwise set the stack empty, and set $l \leftarrow 1$, $r \leftarrow N$.

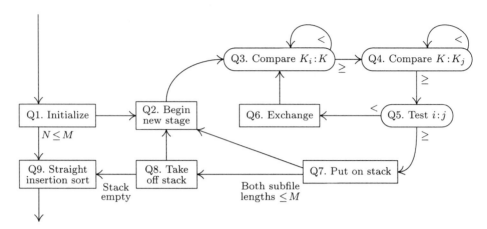

Fig. 19. Partition-exchange sorting (quicksort).

Q2. [Begin new stage.] (We now wish to sort the subfile $R_l \ldots R_r$; from the nature of the algorithm, we have $r \geq l + M$, and $K_{l-1} \leq K_i \leq K_{r+1}$ for $l \leq i \leq r$.) Set $i \leftarrow l$, $j \leftarrow r+1$; and set $K \leftarrow K_l$. (The text below discusses alternative choices for K that might be better.)

Q3. [Compare $K_i : K$.] (At this point the file has been rearranged so that

$$K_k \leq K \quad \text{for } l - 1 \leq k \leq i, \qquad K \leq K_k \quad \text{for } j \leq k \leq r + 1; \qquad (14)$$

and $l \leq i < j$.) Increase i by 1; then if $K_i < K$, repeat this step. (Since $K_j \geq K$, the iteration must terminate with $i \leq j$.)

Q4. [Compare $K : K_j$.] Decrease j by 1; then if $K < K_j$, repeat this step. (Since $K \geq K_{i-1}$, the iteration must terminate with $j \geq i - 1$.)

Q5. [Test $i : j$.] (At this point, (14) holds except for $k = i$ and $k = j$; also $K_i \geq K \geq K_j$, and $r \geq j \geq i - 1 \geq l$.) If $j \leq i$, interchange $R_l \leftrightarrow R_j$ and go to step Q7.

Q6. [Exchange.] Interchange $R_i \leftrightarrow R_j$ and go back to step Q3.

Q7. [Put on stack.] (Now the subfile $R_l \ldots R_j \ldots R_r$ has been partitioned so that $K_k \leq K_j$ for $l - 1 \leq k \leq j$ and $K_j \leq K_k$ for $j \leq k \leq r + 1$. If $r - j \geq j - l > M$, insert $(j+1, r)$ on top of the stack, set $r \leftarrow j - 1$, and go to Q2. If $j - l > r - j > M$, insert $(l, j-1)$ on top of the stack, set $l \leftarrow j+1$, and go to Q2. (Each entry (a, b) on the stack is a request to sort the subfile $R_a \ldots R_b$ at some future time.) Otherwise if $r - j > M \geq j - l$, set $l \leftarrow j+1$ and go to Q2; or if $j - l > M \geq r - j$, set $r \leftarrow j - 1$ and go to Q2.

Q8. [Take off stack.] If the stack is nonempty, remove its top entry (l', r'), set $l \leftarrow l'$, $r \leftarrow r'$, and return to step Q2.

Q9. [Straight insertion sort.] For $j = 2, 3, \ldots, N$, if $K_{j-1} > K_j$ do the following operations: Set $K \leftarrow K_j$, $R \leftarrow R_j$, $i \leftarrow j - 1$; then set $R_{i+1} \leftarrow R_i$ and $i \leftarrow i - 1$ one or more times until $K_i \leq K$; then set $R_{i+1} \leftarrow R$. (This is Algorithm 5.2.1S, modified as suggested in exercise 5.2.1–10 and answer 5.2.1–33. Step Q9 may be omitted if $M = 1$. *Caution:* The final straight insertion might conceal bugs in steps Q1–Q8; don't trust an implementation just because it gives the correct answers!) ∎

The corresponding MIX program is rather long, but not complicated; in fact, a large part of the coding is devoted to step Q7, which just fools around with the variables in a very straightforward way.

Program Q (*Quicksort*). Records to be sorted appear in locations INPUT+1 through INPUT+N; assume that locations INPUT and INPUT+N+1 contain, respectively, the smallest and largest values possible in MIX. The stack is kept in locations STACK+1, STACK+2, . . . ; see exercise 20 for the exact number of locations to set aside for the stack. rI2 ≡ l, rI3 ≡ r, rI4 ≡ i, rI5 ≡ j, rI6 ≡ size of stack, rA ≡ K ≡ R. We assume that $N > M$.

	A	EQU 2:3		First component of stack entry.
	B	EQU 4:5		Second component of stack entry.
01	START	ENT6 0	1	*Q1. Initialize.* Set stack empty.
02		ENT2 1	1	$l \leftarrow 1$.
03		ENT3 N	1	$r \leftarrow N$.
04	2H	ENT5 1,3	A	*Q2. Begin new stage.* $j \leftarrow r+1$.
05		LDA INPUT,2	A	$K \leftarrow K_l$.
06		ENT4 1,2	A	$i \leftarrow l+1$.
07		JMP 0F	A	To Q3 omitting "$i \leftarrow i+1$".
08	6H	LDX INPUT,4	B	*Q6. Exchange.*
09		ENT1 INPUT,4	B	
10		MOVE INPUT,5	B	
11		STX INPUT,5	B	$R_i \leftrightarrow R_j$.
12	3H	INC4 1	$C'-A$	*Q3. Compare $K_i:K$.* $i \leftarrow i+1$.
13	0H	CMPA INPUT,4	C'	
14		JG 3B	C'	Repeat if $K > K_i$.
15	4H	DEC5 1	$C-C'$	*Q4. Compare $K:K_j$.* $j \leftarrow j-1$.
16		CMPA INPUT,5	$C-C'$	
17		JL 4B	$C-C'$	Repeat if $K < K_j$.
18	5H	ENTX 0,5	$B+A$	*Q5. Test $i:j$.*
19		DECX 0,4	$B+A$	
20		JXP 6B	$B+A$	To Q6 if $j > i$.
21		LDX INPUT,5	A	
22		STX INPUT,2	A	$R_l \leftarrow R_j$.
23		STA INPUT,5	A	$R_j \leftarrow R$.
24	7H	ENT4 0,3	A	*Q7. Put on stack.*
25		DEC4 M,5	A	rI4 $\leftarrow r-j-M$.
26		ENT1 0,5	A	
27		DEC1 M,2	A	rI1 $\leftarrow j-l-M$.
28		ENTA 0,4	A	
29		DECA 0,1	A	
30		JANN 1F	A	Jump if $r-j \geq j-l$.
31		J1NP 8F	A'	To Q8 if $M \geq j-l > r-j$.
32		J4NP 3F	$S'+A''$	Jump if $j-l > M \geq r-j$.

33		INC6 1	S'	(Now $j-l > r-j > M$.)
34		ST2 STACK,6(A)	S'	
35		ENTA -1,5	S'	
36		STA STACK,6(B)	S'	$(l, j-1) \Rightarrow$ stack.
37	4H	ENT2 1,5	$S' + A'''$	$l \leftarrow j+1$.
38		JMP 2B	$S' + A'''$	To Q2.
39	1H	J4NP 8F	$A - A'$	To Q8 if $M \geq r - j \geq j - l$.
40		J1NP 4B	$S - S' + A'''$	Jump if $r - j > M \geq j - l$.
41		INC6 1	$S - S'$	(Now $r - j \geq j - l > M$.)
42		ST3 STACK,6(B)	$S - S'$	
43		ENTA 1,5	$S - S'$	
44		STA STACK,6(A)	$S - S'$	$(j+1, r) \Rightarrow$ stack.
45	3H	ENT3 -1,5	$S - S' + A''$	$r \leftarrow j - 1$.
46		JMP 2B	$S - S' + A''$	To Q2.
47	8H	LD2 STACK,6(A)	$S + 1$	*Q8. Take off stack.*
48		LD3 STACK,6(B)	$S + 1$	
49		DEC6 1	$S + 1$	$(l, r) \Leftarrow$ stack.
50		J6NN 2B	$S + 1$	To Q2 if stack wasn't empty.
51	9H	ENT5 2-N	1	*Q9. Straight insertion sort.* $j \leftarrow 2$.
52	2H	LDA INPUT+N,5	$N - 1$	$K \leftarrow K_j,\ R \leftarrow R_j$.
53		CMPA INPUT+N-1,5	$N - 1$	(In this loop, rI5 $\equiv j - N$)
54		JGE 6F	$N - 1$	Jump if $K \geq K_{j-1}$.
55	3H	ENT4 N-1,5	D	$i \leftarrow j - 1$.
56	4H	LDX INPUT,4	E	
57		STX INPUT+1,4	E	$R_{i+1} \leftarrow R_i$.
58		DEC4 1	E	$i \leftarrow i - 1$.
59		CMPA INPUT,4	E	
60		JL 4B	E	Repeat if $K < K_i$.
61	5H	STA INPUT+1,4	D	$R_{i+1} \leftarrow R$.
62	6H	INC5 1	$N - 1$	
63		J5NP 2B	$N - 1$	$2 \leq j \leq N$. ∎

Analysis of quicksort. The timing information shown with Program Q is not hard to derive using Kirchhoff's conservation law (Section 1.3.3) and the fact that everything put onto the stack is eventually removed again. Kirchhoff's law applied at Q2 also shows that

$$A = 1 + (S' + A''') + (S - S' + A'') + S = 2S + 1 + A'' + A''', \qquad (15)$$

hence the total running time comes to

$$24A + 11B + 4C + 3D + 8E + 7N + 9S \text{ units},$$

where

A = number of partitioning stages;
B = number of exchanges in step Q6;
C = number of comparisons made while partitioning;
D = number of times $K_{j-1} > K_j$ during straight insertion (step Q9);
E = number of inversions removed by straight insertion;
S = number of times an entry is put on the stack. $\qquad (16)$

By analyzing these six quantities, we will be able to make an intelligent choice of the parameter M that specifies the "threshold" between straight insertion and partitioning. The analysis is particularly instructive because the algorithm is rather complex; the unraveling of this complexity makes a particularly good illustration of important techniques. However, nonmathematical readers are advised to skip to Eq. (25).

As in most other analyses of this chapter, we shall assume that the keys to be sorted are distinct; exercise 18 indicates that equalities between keys do not seriously harm the efficiency of Algorithm Q, and in fact they seem to help it. Since the method depends only on the relative order of the keys, we may as well assume that they are simply $\{1, 2, \ldots, N\}$ in some order.

We can attack this problem by considering the behavior of the very first partitioning stage, which takes us to Q7 for the first time. Once this partitioning has been achieved, *both of the subfiles $R_1 \ldots R_{j-1}$ and $R_{j+1} \ldots R_N$ will be in random order if the original file was in random order*, since the relative order of elements in these subfiles has no effect on the partitioning algorithm. Therefore the contribution of subsequent partitionings can be determined by induction on N. (This is an important observation, since some alternative algorithms that violate this property have turned out to be significantly slower; see *Computing Surveys* **6** (1974), 287–289.)

Let s be the value of the first key, K_1, and assume that exactly t of the keys $K_1, \ldots, K_s$ are greater than s. (Remember that the keys being sorted are the integers $\{1, 2, \ldots, N\}$.) If $s = 1$, it is easy to see what happens during the first stage of partitioning: Step Q3 is performed once, step Q4 is performed N times, and then step Q5 takes us to Q7. So the contributions of the first stage in this case are $A = 1$, $B = 0$, $C = N + 1$. A similar but slightly more complicated argument when $s > 1$ (see exercise 21) shows that the contributions of the first stage to the total running time are, in general,

$$A = 1, \; B = t, \; C = N + 1, \qquad \text{for } 1 \leq s \leq N. \qquad (17)$$

To this we must add the contributions of the later stages, which sort subfiles of $s - 1$ and $N - s$ elements, respectively.

If we assume that the original file is in random order, it is now possible to write down formulas that define the generating functions for the probability distributions of $A, B, \ldots, S$ (see exercise 22). But for simplicity we shall consider here only the *average* values of these quantities, $A_N, B_N, \ldots, S_N$, as functions of N. Consider, for example, the average number of comparisons, C_N, that occur during the partitioning process. When $N \leq M$, $C_N = 0$. Otherwise, since any given value of s occurs with probability $1/N$, we have

$$C_N = \frac{1}{N} \sum_{s=1}^{N} (N + 1 + C_{s-1} + C_{N-s})$$

$$= N + 1 + \frac{2}{N} \sum_{0 \leq k < N} C_k, \qquad \text{for } N > M. \qquad (18)$$

Similar formulas hold for other quantities A_N, B_N, D_N, E_N, S_N (see exercise 23).

There is a simple way to solve recurrence relations of the form

$$x_n = f_n + \frac{2}{n} \sum_{0 \le k < n} x_k, \qquad \text{for } n \ge m. \tag{19}$$

The first step is to get rid of the summation sign: Since

$$(n+1)x_{n+1} = (n+1)f_{n+1} + 2 \sum_{0 \le k \le n} x_k,$$

$$nx_n = nf_n + 2 \sum_{0 \le k < n} x_k,$$

we may subtract, obtaining

$$(n+1)x_{n+1} - nx_n = g_n + 2x_n, \qquad \text{where } g_n = (n+1)f_{n+1} - nf_n.$$

Now the recurrence takes the much simpler form

$$(n+1)x_{n+1} = (n+2)x_n + g_n, \qquad \text{for } n \ge m. \tag{20}$$

Any recurrence relation that has the general form

$$a_n x_{n+1} = b_n x_n + g_n \tag{21}$$

can be reduced to a summation if we multiply both sides by the "summation factor" $a_0\, a_1 \ldots a_{n-1}/b_0\, b_1 \ldots b_n$; we obtain

$$y_{n+1} = y_n + c_n, \qquad \text{where} \quad y_n = \frac{a_0 \ldots a_{n-1}}{b_0 \ldots b_{n-1}} x_n, \quad c_n = \frac{a_0 \ldots a_{n-1}}{b_0\, b_1 \ldots b_n} g_n. \tag{22}$$

In our case (20), the summation factor is simply $n!/(n+2)! = 1/(n+1)(n+2)$, so we find that the simple relation

$$\frac{x_{n+1}}{n+2} = \frac{x_n}{n+1} + \frac{(n+1)f_{n+1} - nf_n}{(n+1)(n+2)}, \qquad \text{for } n \ge m, \tag{23}$$

is a consequence of (19).

For example, if we set $f_n = 1/n$, we get the unexpected result $x_n/(n+1) = x_m/(m+1)$ for all $n \ge m$. If we set $f_n = n+1$, we get

$$x_n/(n+1) = 2/(n+1) + 2/n + \cdots + 2/(m+2) + x_m/(m+1)$$
$$= 2\,(H_{n+1} - H_{m+1}) + x_m/(m+1),$$

for all $n \ge m$. Thus we obtain the solution to (18) by setting $m = M+1$ and $x_n = 0$ for $n \le M$; the required formula is

$$C_N = (N+1)\,(2H_{N+1} - 2H_{M+2} + 1)$$

$$\approx 2\,(N+1)\ln\left(\frac{N+1}{M+2}\right), \qquad \text{for } N > M. \tag{24}$$

Exercise 6.2.2–8 proves that, when $M = 1$, the standard deviation of C_N is asymptotically $\sqrt{(21 - 2\pi^2)/3}\,N$; this is reasonably small compared to (24).

The other quantities can be found in a similar way (see exercise 23); when $N > M$ we have

$$A_N = 2\,(N+1)/(M+2) - 1,$$

$$B_N = \frac{1}{6}\,(N+1)\left(2H_{N+1} - 2H_{M+2} + 1 - \frac{6}{M+2}\right) + \frac{1}{2},$$

$$D_N = (N+1)\big(1 - 2H_{M+1}/(M+2)\big),$$

$$E_N = \tfrac{1}{6}\,(N+1)M(M-1)/(M+2);$$

$$S_N = (N+1)/(2M+3) - 1, \qquad \text{for } N > 2M + 1. \qquad (25)$$

The discussion above shows that it is possible to carry out an exact analysis of the average running time of a fairly complex program, by using techniques that we have previously applied only to simpler cases.

Formulas (24) and (25) can be used to determine the best value of M on a particular computer. In MIX's case, Program Q requires $(35/3)(N+1)H_{N+1} + \frac{1}{6}(N+1)f(M) - 34.5$ units of time on the average, for $N > 2M+1$, where

$$f(M) = 8M - 70H_{M+2} + 71 - 36\,\frac{H_{M+1}}{M+2} + \frac{270}{M+2} + \frac{54}{2M+3}. \qquad (26)$$

We want to choose M so that $f(M)$ is a minimum, and a simple computer calculation shows that $M = 9$ is best. The average running time of Program Q is approximately $11.667(N+1)\ln N - 1.74N - 18.74$ units when $M = 9$, for large N.

So Program Q is quite fast, on the average, considering that it requires very little memory space. Its speed is primarily due to the fact that the inner loops, in steps Q3 and Q4, are extremely short—only three MIX instructions each (see lines 12–14 and 15–17). The number of exchanges, in step Q6, is only about $1/6$ of the number of comparisons in steps Q3 and Q4; hence we have saved a significant amount of time by not comparing i to j in the inner loops.

But what is the *worst* case of Algorithm Q? Are there some inputs that it does not handle efficiently? The answer to this question is quite embarrassing: If the original file is already in order, with $K_1 < K_2 < \cdots < K_N$, each "partitioning" operation is almost useless, since it reduces the size of the subfile by only one element! So this situation (which ought to be easiest of all to sort) makes quicksort anything but quick; the sorting time becomes proportional to N^2 instead of $N\lg N$. (See exercise 25.) Unlike the other sorting methods we have seen, Algorithm Q *likes* a disordered file.

Hoare suggested two ways to remedy the situation, in his original paper, by choosing a better value of the test key K that governs the partitioning. One of his recommendations was to choose a *random* integer q between l and r in the last part of step Q2; we can change the instruction "$K \leftarrow K_l$" to

$$K \leftarrow K_q, \qquad R \leftarrow R_q, \qquad R_q \leftarrow R_l, \qquad R_l \leftarrow R \qquad (27)$$

in that step. (The last assignment "$R_l \leftarrow R$" is necessary; otherwise step Q4 would stop with $j = l - 1$ when K is the smallest key of the subfile being partitioned.) According to Eqs. (25), such random integers need to be calculated only $2(N+1)/(M+2) - 1$ times on the average, so the additional running time is not substantial; and the random choice gives good protection against the occurrence of the worst case. Even a mildly random choice of q should be safe. Exercise 58 proves that, with truly random q, the probability of more than, say, $20N \ln N$ comparisons will surely be less than 10^{-8}.

Hoare's second suggestion was to look at a small sample of the file and to choose a median value of the sample. This approach was adopted by R. C. Singleton [*CACM* **12** (1969), 185–187], who suggested letting K_q be the median of the three values

$$K_l, \qquad K_{\lfloor (l+r)/2 \rfloor}, \qquad K_r. \tag{28}$$

Singleton's procedure cuts the number of comparisons down from $2N \ln N$ to about $\frac{12}{7} N \ln N$ (see exercise 29). It can be shown that B_N is asymptotically $C_N/5$ instead of $C_N/6$ in this case, so the median method slightly increases the amount of time spent in transferring the data; the total running time therefore decreases by roughly 8 percent. (See exercise 56 for a detailed analysis.) The worst case is still of order N^2, but such slow behavior will hardly ever occur.

W. D. Frazer and A. C. McKellar [*JACM* **17** (1970), 496–507] have suggested taking a much larger sample consisting of $2^k - 1$ records, where k is chosen so that $2^k \approx N/\ln N$. The sample can be sorted by the usual quicksort method, then inserted among the remaining records by taking k passes over the file (partitioning it into 2^k subfiles, bounded by the elements of the sample). Finally the subfiles are sorted. The average number of comparisons required by such a "samplesort" procedure is about the same as in Singleton's median method, when N is in a practical range, but it decreases to the asymptotic value $N \lg N$ as $N \to \infty$.

An absolute guarantee of $O(N \log N)$ sorting time in the worst case, together with fast running time on the average, can be obtained by combining quicksort with other schemes. For example, D. R. Musser [*Software Practice & Exper.* **27** (1997), 983–993] has suggested adding a "depth of partitioning" component to each entry on quicksort's stack. If any subfile is found to have been subdivided more than, say, $2 \lg N$ times, we can abandon Algorithm Q and switch to Algorithm 5.2.3H. The inner loop time remains unchanged, so the average total running time remains almost the same as before.

Robert Sedgewick has analyzed a number of optimized variants of quicksort in *Acta Informatica* **7** (1977), 327–356, and in *CACM* **21** (1978), 847–857, **22** (1979), 368. See also J. L. Bentley and M. D. McIlroy, *Software Practice & Exper.* **23** (1993), 1249–1265, for a version of quicksort that has been tuned up to fit the UNIX® software library, based on 15 further years of experience.

Radix exchange. We come now to a method that is quite different from any of the sorting schemes we have seen before; it makes use of the *binary representation* of the keys, so it is intended only for binary computers. Instead of comparing two keys with each other, this method inspects individual bits of the keys, to see if they are 0 or 1. In other respects it has the characteristics of exchange sorting, and, in fact, it is rather similar to quicksort. Since it depends on radix 2 representations, we call it "radix exchange sorting." The algorithm can be described roughly as follows:

i) Sort the sequence on its *most significant binary bit*, so that all keys that have a leading 0 come before all keys that have a leading 1. This sorting is done by finding the leftmost key K_i that has a leading 1, and the rightmost key K_j with a leading 0. Then R_i and R_j are exchanged and the process is repeated until $i > j$.

ii) Let F_0 be the elements with leading bit 0, and let F_1 be the others. Apply the radix exchange sorting method to F_0 (starting now at the *second* bit from the left instead of the most significant bit), until F_0 is completely sorted; then do the same for F_1.

For example, Table 3 shows how the radix exchange sort acts on our 16 random numbers, which have been converted to octal notation. Stage 1 in the table shows the initial input, and after exchanging on the first bit we get to stage 2. Stage 2 sorts the first group on bit 2, and stage 3 works on bit 3. (The reader should mentally convert the octal notation to 10-bit binary numbers. For example, *0232* stands for $(0\ 010\ 011\ 010)_2$.) When we reach stage 5, after sorting on bit 4, we find that each group remaining has but a single element, so this part of the file need not be further examined. The notation "$^4[0232\ 0252]$" means that the subfile *0232 0252* is waiting to be sorted on bit 4 from the left. In this particular case, no progress occurs when sorting on bit 4; we need to go to bit 5 before the items are separated.

The complete sorting process shown in Table 3 takes 22 stages, somewhat more than the comparable number for quicksort (Table 2). Similarly, the number of bit inspections, 82, is rather high; but we shall see that the number of bit inspections for large N is actually less than the number of comparisons made by quicksort, assuming a uniform distribution of keys. The total number of exchanges in Table 3 is 17, which is quite reasonable. Note that bit inspections never have to go past bit 7 here, although 10-bit numbers are being sorted.

As in quicksort, we can use a stack to keep track of the "boundary line information" for waiting subfiles. Instead of sorting the smallest subfile first, it is convenient simply to go from left to right, since the stack size in this case can never exceed the number of bits in the keys being sorted. In the following algorithm the stack entry (r, b) is used to indicate the right boundary r of a subfile waiting to be sorted on bit b; the left boundary need not be recorded in the stack — it is implicit because of the left-to-right nature of the procedure.

Algorithm R (*Radix exchange sort*). Records $R_1, \ldots, R_N$ are rearranged in place; after sorting is complete, their keys will be in order, $K_1 \leq \cdots \leq K_N$. Each key is assumed to be a nonnegative m-bit binary number, $(a_1\ a_2 \ldots a_m)_2$; the ith most significant bit, a_i, is called "bit i" of the key. An auxiliary stack with room for at most $m - 1$ entries is needed for temporary storage. This algorithm

Table 3
RADIX EXCHANGE SORTING

Stage																	l	r	b	Stack
1	^{1}[0767	0127	1000	0075	1614	0252	1601	1215	0423	0232	0652	0775	1144	1245	1375	1277]^{1}	1	16	1	—
2	^{2}[0767	0127	0775	0075	0652	0252	0232	0423]^{2}	^{2}[1215	1601	1614	1000	1144	1245	1375	1277]^{2}	1	8	2	(16,2)
3	^{3}[0232	0127	0252	0075]^{3}	^{3}[0652	0775	0767	0423]^{3}	^{2}[1215	1601	1614	1000	1144	1245	1375	1277]^{2}	1	4	3	(8,3)(16,2)
4	^{4}[0075	0127]^{4}	^{4}[0252	0232]^{4}	^{3}[0652	0775	0767	0423]^{3}	^{2}[1215	1601	1614	1000	1144	1245	1375	1277]^{2}	1	2	4	(4,4)(8,3)(16,2)
5	0075	0127	^{4}[0252	0232]^{4}	^{3}[0652	0775	0767	0423]^{3}	^{2}[1215	1601	1614	1000	1144	1245	1375	1277]^{2}	3	4	4	(8,3)(16,2)
6	0075	0127	^{5}[0252	0232]^{5}	^{3}[0652	0775	0767	0423]^{3}	^{2}[1215	1601	1614	1000	1144	1245	1375	1277]^{2}	3	4	5	(8,3)(16,2)
7	0075	0127	0232	0252	^{3}[0652	0775	0767	0423]^{3}	^{2}[1215	1601	1614	1000	1144	1245	1375	1277]^{2}	5	8	3	(16,2)
8	0075	0127	0232	0252	0423	^{4}[0775	0767	0652]^{4}	^{2}[1215	1601	1614	1000	1144	1245	1375	1277]^{2}	6	8	4	(16,2)
9	0075	0127	0232	0252	0423	0652	^{5}[0767	0775]^{5}	^{2}[1215	1601	1614	1000	1144	1245	1375	1277]^{2}	7	8	5	(16,2)
10	0075	0127	0232	0252	0423	0652	^{6}[0767	0775]^{6}	^{2}[1215	1601	1614	1000	1144	1245	1375	1277]^{2}	7	8	6	(16,2)
11	0075	0127	0232	0252	0423	0652	^{7}[0767	0775]^{7}	^{2}[1215	1601	1614	1000	1144	1245	1375	1277]^{2}	7	8	7	(16,2)
12	0075	0127	0232	0252	0423	0652	0767	0775	^{2}[1215	1601	1614	1000	1144	1245	1375	1277]^{2}	9	16	2	—
13	0075	0127	0232	0252	0423	0652	0767	0775	^{3}[1215	1277	1375	1000	1144	1245]^{3}	^{3}[1614	1601]^{3}	9	14	3	(16,3)
14	0075	0127	0232	0252	0423	0652	0767	0775	^{4}[1144	1000]^{4}	^{4}[1375	1277	1215	1245]^{4}	^{3}[1614	1601]^{3}	9	10	4	(14,4)(16,3)
15	0075	0127	0232	0252	0423	0652	0767	0775	1000	1144	^{4}[1375	1277	1215	1245]^{4}	^{3}[1614	1601]^{3}	11	14	4	(16,3)
16	0075	0127	0232	0252	0423	0652	0767	0775	1000	1144	^{5}[1245	1277	1215]^{5}	1375	^{3}[1614	1601]^{3}	11	13	5	(16,3)
17	0075	0127	0232	0252	0423	0652	0767	0775	1000	1144	1215	^{6}[1277	1245]^{6}	1375	^{3}[1614	1601]^{3}	12	13	6	(16,3)
18	0075	0127	0232	0252	0423	0652	0767	0775	1000	1144	1215	1245	1277	1375	^{3}[1614	1601]^{3}	15	16	3	—
19	0075	0127	0232	0252	0423	0652	0767	0775	1000	1144	1215	1245	1277	1375	^{4}[1614	1601]^{4}	15	16	4	—
20	0075	0127	0232	0252	0423	0652	0767	0775	1000	1144	1215	1245	1277	1375	^{5}[1614	1601]^{5}	15	16	5	—
21	0075	0127	0232	0252	0423	0652	0767	0775	1000	1144	1215	1245	1277	1375	^{6}[1614	1601]^{6}	15	16	6	—
22	0075	0127	0232	0252	0423	0652	0767	0775	1000	1144	1215	1245	1277	1375	^{7}[1614	1601]^{7}	15	16	7	—
23	0075	0127	0232	0252	0423	0652	0767	0775	1000	1144	1215	1245	1277	1375	1601	1614	17		—	—

The radix exchange method looks precisely once at every bit that is needed to determine the final order of the keys.

essentially follows the radix exchange partitioning procedure described in the text above; certain improvements in its efficiency are possible, as described in the text and exercises below.

R1. [Initialize.] Set the stack empty, and set $l \leftarrow 1$, $r \leftarrow N$, $b \leftarrow 1$.

R2. [Begin new stage.] (We now wish to sort the subfile $R_l \leq \cdots \leq R_r$ on bit b; from the nature of the algorithm, we have $l \leq r$.) If $l = r$, go to step R10 (since a one-word file is already sorted). Otherwise set $i \leftarrow l$, $j \leftarrow r$.

R3. [Inspect K_i for 1.] Examine bit b of K_i. If it is a 1, go to step R6.

R4. [Increase i.] Increase i by 1. If $i \leq j$, return to step R3; otherwise go to step R8.

R5. [Inspect K_{j+1} for 0.] Examine bit b of K_{j+1}. If it is a 0, go to step R7.

R6. [Decrease j.] Decrease j by 1. If $i \leq j$, go to step R5; otherwise go to step R8.

R7. [Exchange R_i, R_{j+1}.] Interchange records $R_i \leftrightarrow R_{j+1}$; then go to step R4.

R8. [Test special cases.] (At this point a partitioning stage has been completed; $i = j + 1$, bit b of keys $K_l, \ldots, K_j$ is 0, and bit b of keys $K_i, \ldots, K_r$ is 1.) Increase b by 1. If $b > m$, where m is the total number of bits in the keys, go to step R10. (In such a case, the subfile $R_l \ldots R_r$ has been sorted. This test need not be made if there is no chance of having equal keys present in the file.) Otherwise if $j < l$ or $j = r$, go back to step R2 (all bits examined were 1 or 0, respectively). Otherwise if $j = l$, increase l by 1 and go to step R2 (there was only one 0 bit).

R9. [Put on stack.] Insert the entry (r, b) on top of the stack; then set $r \leftarrow j$ and go to step R2.

R10. [Take off stack.] If the stack is empty, we are done sorting; otherwise set $l \leftarrow r + 1$, remove the top entry (r', b') of the stack, set $r \leftarrow r'$, $b \leftarrow b'$, and return to step R2. ▮

Program R (*Radix exchange sort*). The following MIX code uses essentially the same conventions as Program Q. We have rI1 $\equiv l - r$, rI2 $\equiv r$, rI3 $\equiv i$, rI4 $\equiv j$, rI5 $\equiv m - b$, rI6 $\equiv$ size of stack, except that it proves convenient for certain instructions (designated below) to leave rI3 $= i - j$ or rI4 $= j - i$. Because of the binary nature of radix exchange, this program uses the operations SRB (shift right AX binary), JAE (jump A even), and JAO (jump A odd), defined in Section 4.5.2. We assume that $N \geq 2$.

01	START	ENT6	0	1	R1. Initialize. Set stack empty.
02		ENT1	1-N	1	$l \leftarrow 1$.
03		ENT2	N	1	$r \leftarrow N$.
04		ENT5	M-1	1	$b \leftarrow 1$.
05		JMP	1F	1	To R2 (omit testing $l = r$).
06	9H	INC6	1	S	R9. Put on stack. $\qquad$ [rI4 $= l - j$]
07		ST2	STACK,6(A)	S	
08		ST5	STACK,6(B)	S	$(r, b) \Rightarrow$ stack.

09		ENN1	0,4	S	$rI1 \leftarrow l - j$.
10		ENT2	-1,3	S	$r \leftarrow j$.
11	1H	ENT3	0,1	A	R2. Begin new stage. [rI3 $= i - j$]
12		ENT4	0,2	A	$i \leftarrow l, j \leftarrow r$. [rI3 $= i - j$]
13	3H	INC3	0,4	C'	R3. Inspect K_i for 1.
14		LDA	INPUT,3	C'	
15		SRB	0,5	C'	units bit of rA $\leftarrow$ bit b of K_i.
16		JAE	4F	C'	To R4 if it is 0.
17	6H	DEC4	1,3	$C'' + X$	R6. Decrease j. $j \leftarrow j - 1$. [rI4 $= j - i$]
18		J4N	8F	$C'' + X$	To R8 if $j < i$. [rI4 $= j - i$]
19	5H	INC4	0,3	C''	R5. Inspect K_{j+1} for 0.
20		LDA	INPUT+1,4	C''	
21		SRB	0,5	C''	units bit of rA $\leftarrow$ bit b of K_{j+1}.
22		JAO	6B	C''	To R6 if it is 1.
23	7H	LDA	INPUT+1,4	B	R7. Exchange R_i, R_{j+1}.
24		LDX	INPUT,3	B	
25		STX	INPUT+1,4	B	
26		STA	INPUT,3	B	
27	4H	DEC3	-1,4	$C' - X$	R4. Increase i. $i \leftarrow i + 1$. [rI3 $= i - j$]
28		J3NP	3B	$C' - X$	To R3 if $i \leq j$. [rI3 $= i - j$]
29		INC3	0,4	$A - X$	$rI3 \leftarrow i$.
30	8H	J5Z	0F	A	R8. Test special cases. [rI4 unknown]
31		DEC5	1	$A - G$	To R10 if $b = m$, else $b \leftarrow b - 1$.
32		ENT4	-1,3	$A - G$	$rI4 \leftarrow j$.
33		DEC4	0,2	$A - G$	$rI4 \leftarrow j - r$.
34		J4Z	1B	$A - G$	To R2 if $j = r$.
35		DEC4	0,1	$A - G - R$	$rI4 \leftarrow j - l$.
36		J4N	1B	$A - G - R$	To R2 if $j < l$.
37		J4NZ	9B	$A-G-L-R$	To R9 if $j \neq l$.
38		INC1	1	K	$l \leftarrow l + 1$.
39	2H	J1NZ	1B	$K + S$	Jump if $l \neq r$.
40	0H	ENT1	1,2	$S + 1$	R10. Take off stack.
41		LD2	STACK,6(A)	$S + 1$	
42		DEC1	0,2	$S + 1$	
43		LD5	STACK,6(B)	$S + 1$	stack $\Rightarrow (r, b)$.
44		DEC6	1	$S + 1$	
45		J6NN	2B	$S + 1$	To R2 if stack was nonempty. ▌

The running time of this radix exchange program depends on

A = number of stages encountered with $l < r$;

B = number of exchanges;

$C = C' + C''$ = number of bit inspections;

G = number of times $b > m$ in step R8;

K = number of times $b \leq m$, $j = l$ in step R8;

L = number of times $b \leq m$, $j < l$ in step R8;

R = number of times $b \leq m$, $j = r$ in step R8;

S = number of times things are entered onto the stack;

X = number of times $j < i$ in step R6.

(29)

By Kirchhoff's law, $S = A - G - K - L - R$; so the total running time comes to $27A + 8B + 8C - 23G - 14K - 17L - 19R - X + 13$ units. The bit-inspection loops can be made somewhat faster, as shown in exercise 34, at the expense of a more complicated program. It is also possible to increase the speed of radix exchange by using straight insertion whenever $r - l$ is sufficiently small, as we did in Algorithm Q; but we shall not dwell on these refinements.

In order to analyze the running time of radix exchange, two kinds of input data suggest themselves. We can

i) assume that $N = 2^m$ and that the keys to be sorted are simply the integers $0, 1, 2, \ldots, 2^m - 1$ in random order; or

ii) assume that $m = \infty$ (unlimited precision) and that the keys to be sorted are independent uniformly distributed real numbers in $[0 .. 1)$.

The analysis of case (i) is relatively easy, so it has been left as an exercise for the reader (see exercise 35). Case (ii) is comparatively difficult, so it has *also* been left as an exercise (see exercise 38). The following table shows crude approximations to the results of these analyses:

Quantity	Case (i)	Case (ii)
A	N	αN
B	$\frac{1}{4} N \lg N$	$\frac{1}{4} N \lg N$
C	$N \lg N$	$N \lg N$
G	$\frac{1}{2} N$	0
K	0	$\frac{1}{2} N$
L	0	$\frac{1}{2}(\alpha - 1)N$
R	0	$\frac{1}{2}(\alpha - 1)N$
S	$\frac{1}{2} N$	$\frac{1}{2} N$
X	$\frac{1}{2} N$	$\frac{1}{4}(\alpha + 1)N \cdot$ (30)

Here $\alpha = 1/\ln 2 \approx 1.4427$. Notice that the average number of exchanges, bit inspections, and stack accesses is essentially the same for both kinds of data, even though case (ii) takes about 44 percent more stages. Our MIX program takes approximately $14.4 N \ln N$ units of time, on the average, to sort N items in case (ii), and this could be cut to about $11.5 N \ln N$ using the suggestion of exercise 34; the corresponding figure for Program Q is $11.7 N \ln N$, which can be decreased to about $10.6 N \ln N$ using Singleton's median-of-three suggestion.

Thus radix exchange sorting takes about as long as quicksort, on the average, when sorting uniformly distributed data; on some machines it is actually a little quicker than quicksort. Exercise 53 indicates to what extent the process slows down for a nonuniform distribution. It is important to note that our entire analysis is predicated on the assumption that keys are distinct; *radix exchange as defined above is not especially efficient when equal keys are present*, since it goes through several time-consuming stages trying to separate sets of identical keys before b becomes $> m$. One plausible way to remedy this defect is suggested in the answer to exercise 40.

Both radix exchange and quicksort are essentially based on the idea of partitioning. Records are exchanged until the file is split into two parts: a left-hand subfile, in which all keys are $\leq K$, for some K, and a right-hand subfile in which all keys are $\geq K$. Quicksort chooses K to be an actual key in the file, while radix exchange essentially chooses an artificial key K based on binary representations. From a historical standpoint, radix exchange was discovered by P. Hildebrandt, H. Isbitz, H. Rising, and J. Schwartz [*JACM* **6** (1959), 156–163], about a year earlier than quicksort. Other partitioning schemes are also possible; for example, John McCarthy has suggested setting $K \approx \frac{1}{2}(u + v)$, if all keys are known to lie between u and v. Yihsiao Wang has suggested that the mean of three key values such as (28) be used as the threshold for partitioning; he has proved that the number of comparisons required to sort uniformly distributed random data will then be asymptotic to $1.082 N \lg N$.

Still another partitioning strategy has been proposed by M. H. van Emden [*CACM* **13** (1970), 563–567]: Instead of choosing K in advance, we "learn" what a good K might be, by keeping track of $K' = \max(K_l, \ldots, K_i)$ and $K'' = \min(K_j, \ldots, K_r)$ as partitioning proceeds. We may increase i until encountering a key greater than K', then decrease j until encountering a key less than K'', then exchange and/or adjust K' and K''. Empirical tests on this "interval-exchange sort" method indicate that it is slightly slower than quicksort; its running time appears to be so difficult to analyze that an adequate theoretical explanation will never be found, especially since the subfiles after partitioning are no longer in random order.

A generalization of radix exchange to radices higher than 2 is discussed in Section 5.2.5.

*Asymptotic methods. The analysis of exchange sorting algorithms leads to some particularly instructive mathematical problems that enable us to learn more about how to find the asymptotic behavior of functions. For example, we came across the function

$$W_n = \frac{1}{n!} \sum_{0 \leq r < s \leq n} s! \, r^{n-s} \tag{31}$$

in (9), during our analysis of the bubble sort; what is its asymptotic value?

We can proceed as in our study of the number of involutions, Eq. 5.1.4–(41); the reader will find it helpful to review the discussion at the end of Section 5.1.4 before reading further.

Inspection of (31) shows that the contribution for $s = n$ is larger than that for $s = n - 1$, etc.; this suggests replacing s by $n - s$. In fact, we soon discover that it is most convenient to use the substitutions $t = n - s + 1$, $m = n + 1$, so that (31) becomes

$$\frac{1}{m} W_{m-1} = \frac{1}{m!} \sum_{1 \leq t < m} (m - t)! \sum_{0 \leq r < m - t} r^{t-1}. \tag{32}$$

The inner sum has a well-known asymptotic series obtained from Euler's summation formula, namely

$$\sum_{0 \le r < N} r^{t-1} = \frac{N^t}{t} - \frac{1}{2}(N^{t-1} - \delta_{t1}) + \frac{B_2}{2!}(t-1)(N^{t-2} - \delta_{t2}) + \cdots$$

$$= \frac{1}{t}\sum_{j=0}^{k}\binom{t}{j}B_j(N^{t-j} - \delta_{tj}) + O(N^{t-k}) \qquad (33)$$

(see exercise 1.2.11.2–4); hence our problem reduces to studying sums of the form

$$\frac{1}{m!}\sum_{1 \le t < m}(m-t)!\,(m-t)^t t^k, \qquad k \ge -1. \qquad (34)$$

As in Section 5.1.4 we can show that the value of this summand is negligible, $O\big(\exp(-n^\delta)\big)$, whenever t is greater than $m^{1/2+\epsilon}$; hence we may put $t = O(m^{1/2+\epsilon})$ and replace the factorials by Stirling's approximation:

$$\frac{(m-t)!\,(m-t)^t}{m!}$$

$$= \sqrt{1 - \frac{t}{m}}\,\exp\left(\frac{t}{12m^2} - \left(\frac{t^2}{2m} + \frac{t^3}{3m^2} + \frac{t^4}{4m^3} + \frac{t^5}{5m^4}\right) + O(m^{-2+6\epsilon})\right).$$

We are therefore interested in the asymptotic value of

$$r_k(m) = \sum_{1 \le t < m} e^{-t^2/2m} t^k, \qquad k \ge -1. \qquad (35)$$

The sum could also be extended to the full range $1 \le t < \infty$ without changing its asymptotic value, since the values for $t > m^{1/2+\epsilon}$ are negligible.
    Let $g_k(x) = x^k e^{-x^2}$ and $f_k(x) = g_k(x/\sqrt{2m})$. When $k \ge 0$, Euler's summation formula tells us that

$$\sum_{0 \le t < m} f_k(t) = \int_0^m f_k(x)\,dx + \sum_{j=1}^{p}\frac{B_j}{j!}\big(f_k^{(j-1)}(m) - f_k^{(j-1)}(0)\big) + R_p,$$

$$R_p = \frac{(-1)^{p+1}}{p!}\int_0^m B_p(\{x\})f_k^{(p)}(x)\,dx$$

$$= \left(\frac{1}{\sqrt{2m}}\right)^p O\left(\int_0^\infty |g_k^{(p)}(y)|\,dy\right) = O(m^{-p/2}); \qquad (36)$$

hence we can get an asymptotic series for $r_k(m)$ whenever $k \ge 0$ by using essentially the same ideas we have used before. But when $k = -1$ the method breaks down, since $f_{-1}(0)$ is undefined; we can't merely sum from 1 to m either, because the remainders don't give smaller and smaller powers of m when the lower limit is 1. (This is the crux of the matter, and the reader should pause to appreciate the problem before proceeding further.)

To resolve the dilemma we can define $g_{-1}(x) = (e^{-x^2} - 1)/x$ and $f_{-1} = g_{-1}(x/\sqrt{2m}\,)$; then $f_{-1}(0) = 0$, and $r_{-1}(m)$ can be obtained from $\sum_{0 \le t < m} f_{-1}(t)$ in a simple way. Equation (36) is now valid for $k = -1$, and the remaining integral is well known,

$$\frac{2}{\sqrt{2m}} \int_0^m f_{-1}(x)\,dx = 2 \int_0^m \frac{e^{-x^2/2m} - 1}{x}\,dx = \int_0^{m/2} \frac{e^{-y} - 1}{y}\,dy$$

$$= \int_0^1 \frac{e^{-y} - 1}{y}\,dy + \int_1^{m/2} \frac{e^{-y}}{y}\,dy - \ln \frac{m}{2}$$

$$= -\gamma - \ln m + \ln 2 + O(e^{-m/2}),$$

by exercise 43.

Now we have enough facts and formulas to grind out the answer,

$$W_n = \tfrac{1}{2}m \ln m + \tfrac{1}{2}(\gamma + \ln 2)m - \tfrac{2}{3}\sqrt{2\pi m} + \tfrac{49}{36} + O(n^{-1/2}), \quad m = n + 1, \quad (37)$$

as shown in exercise 44. This completes our analysis of the bubble sort.

For the analysis of radix exchange sorting, we need to know the asymptotic value of the finite sum

$$U_n = \sum_{k \ge 2} \binom{n}{k} (-1)^k \frac{1}{2^{k-1} - 1} \tag{38}$$

as $n \to \infty$. This question turns out to be harder than any of the other asymptotic problems we have met so far; the elementary methods of power series expansions, Euler's summation formula, etc., turn out to be inadequate. The following derivation has been suggested by N. G. de Bruijn.

To get rid of the cancellation effects of the large factors $\binom{n}{k}(-1)^k$ in (38), we start by rewriting the sum as an infinite series

$$U_n = \sum_{k \ge 2} \binom{n}{k} (-1)^k \sum_{j \ge 1} \left(\frac{1}{2^{k-1}} \right)^j = \sum_{j \ge 1} \left(2^j (1 - 2^{-j})^n - 2^j + n \right). \tag{39}$$

If we set $x = n/2^j$, the summand is

$$2^j (1 - 2^{-j})^n - 2^j + n = \frac{n}{x} \left(\left(1 - \frac{x}{n} \right)^n - 1 + x \right).$$

When $x \le n^\epsilon$, we have

$$\left(1 - \frac{x}{n} \right)^n = \exp\left(n \ln \left(1 - \frac{x}{n} \right) \right) = \exp\left(-x + x^2\, O(n^{-1}) \right), \tag{40}$$

and this suggests approximating (39) by

$$T_n = \sum_{j \ge 1} \left(2^j e^{-n/2^j} - 2^j + n \right). \tag{41}$$

To justify this approximation, we have $U_n - T_n = X_n + Y_n$, where

$$X_n = \sum_{\substack{j \geq 1 \\ 2^j < n^{1-\epsilon}}} \left(2^j(1-2^{-j})^n - 2^j e^{-n/2^j}\right) \qquad \text{[the terms for } x > n^\epsilon\text{]}$$

$$= \sum_{\substack{j \geq 1 \\ 2^j < n^{1-\epsilon}}} O(ne^{-n/2^j}) \qquad \text{[since } 0 < 1-2^{-j} < e^{-2^{-j}}\text{]}$$

$$= O(n \log n \, e^{-n^\epsilon}) \qquad \text{[since there are } O(\log n) \text{ terms];}$$

and

$$Y_n = \sum_{\substack{j \geq 1 \\ 2^j \geq n^{1-\epsilon}}} \left(2^j(1-2^{-j})^n - 2^j e^{-n/2^j}\right) \qquad \text{[the terms for } x \leq n^\epsilon\text{]}$$

$$= \sum_{\substack{j \geq 1 \\ 2^j \geq n^{1-\epsilon}}} \left(e^{-n/2^j} \frac{n}{2^j} O(1)\right) \qquad \text{[by (40)].}$$

Our discussion below will demonstrate that the latter sum is $O(1)$; consequently $U_n - T_n = O(1)$. (See exercise 47.)

So far we haven't applied any techniques that are really different from those we have used before. But the study of T_n requires a new idea, based on simple principles of complex variable theory: If x is any positive number, we have

$$e^{-x} = \frac{1}{2\pi i} \int_{1/2-i\infty}^{1/2+i\infty} \Gamma(z)x^{-z} \, dz = \frac{1}{2\pi} \int_{-\infty}^{\infty} \Gamma(\tfrac{1}{2} + it)x^{-(1/2+it)} \, dt. \qquad (42)$$

To prove this identity, consider the path of integration shown in Fig. 20(a), where N, N', and M are large. The value of the integral along this contour is the sum of the residues inside, namely

$$\sum_{0 \leq k < M} x^{-(-k)} \lim_{z \to -k}(z+k)\Gamma(z) = \sum_{0 \leq k < M} x^k \frac{(-1)^k}{k!}.$$

The integral on the top line is $O\left(\int_{-\infty}^{1/2} |\Gamma(t+iN)| \, x^{-t} \, dt\right)$, and we have the well-known bound

$$\Gamma(t + iN) = O\left(|t + iN|^{t-1/2} e^{-t-\pi N/2}\right) \qquad \text{as } N \to \infty.$$

[For properties of the gamma function see, for example, Erdélyi, Magnus, Oberhettinger, and Tricomi, *Higher Transcendental Functions* **1** (New York: McGraw–Hill, 1953), Chapter 1.] Therefore the top line integral is quite negligible, $O\left(e^{-\pi N/2} \int_{-\infty}^{1/2} (N/xe)^t \, dt\right)$. The bottom line integral has a similar innocuous behavior. For the integral along the left line we use the fact that

$$\Gamma(\tfrac{1}{2} + it - M) = \Gamma(\tfrac{1}{2} + it)/(-M + \tfrac{1}{2} + it) \ldots (-1 + \tfrac{1}{2} + it)$$
$$= \Gamma(\tfrac{1}{2} + it) O\left(1/(M-1)!\right);$$

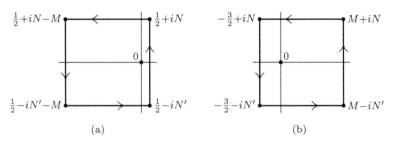

Fig. 20. Contours of integration for gamma-function identities.

hence the left-hand integral is $O\left(x^{M-1/2}/(M-1)!\right) \int_{-\infty}^{\infty} \left|\Gamma\left(\frac{1}{2}+it\right)\right| \, dt$. Therefore as M, N, $N' \to \infty$, only the right-hand integral survives, and this proves (42). In fact, (42) remains valid if we replace $\frac{1}{2}$ by any positive number.

The same argument can be used to derive many other useful relations involving the gamma function. We can replace x^{-z} by other functions of z; or we can replace the constant $\frac{1}{2}$ by other quantities. For example,

$$\frac{1}{2\pi i} \int_{-3/2-i\infty}^{-3/2+i\infty} \Gamma(z)x^{-z} \, dz = e^{-x} - 1 + x, \tag{43}$$

and this is the critical quantity in our formula (41) for T_n:

$$T_n = n \sum_{j\geq 1} \frac{1}{2\pi i} \int_{-3/2-i\infty}^{-3/2+i\infty} \Gamma(z)(n/2^j)^{-1-z} \, dz. \tag{44}$$

The sum may be placed inside the integrals, since its convergence is absolutely well-behaved; we have

$$\sum_{j\geq 1}(n/2^j)^w = n^w \sum_{j\geq 1}(1/2^w)^j = n^w/(2^w - 1), \qquad \text{when } \Re(w) > 0,$$

because $|2^w| = 2^{\Re(w)} > 1$. Therefore

$$T_n = \frac{n}{2\pi i} \int_{-3/2-i\infty}^{-3/2+i\infty} \frac{\Gamma(z)n^{-1-z}}{2^{-1-z} - 1} \, dz, \tag{45}$$

and it remains to evaluate the latter integral.

This time we integrate along a path that extends far to the *right*, as in Fig. 20(b). The top line integral is $O(n^{1/2}e^{-\pi N/2} \int_{-3/2}^{M} |M + iN|^t \, dt)$, if $2^{iN} \neq 1$, and the bottom line integral is equally negligible, when N and N' are much larger than M. The right-hand line integral is $O(n^{-1-M} \int_{-\infty}^{\infty} |\Gamma(M + it)| \, dt)$. Fixing M and letting N, $N' \to \infty$ shows that $-T_n/n$ is $O(n^{-1-M})$ plus the sum of the residues in the region $-3/2 < \Re(z) < M$. The factor $\Gamma(z)$ has simple poles at $z = -1$ and $z = 0$, while n^{-1-z} has no poles, and $1/(2^{-1-z} - 1)$ has simple poles when $z = -1 + 2\pi i k/\ln 2$.

The double pole at $z = -1$ is the hardest to handle. We can use the well-known relation

$$\Gamma(z+1) = \exp(-\gamma z + \zeta(2)z^2/2 - \zeta(3)z^3/3 + \zeta(4)z^4/4 - \cdots),$$

where $\zeta(s) = 1^{-s} + 2^{-s} + 3^{-s} + \cdots = H_\infty^{(s)}$, to deduce the following expansions when $w = z + 1$ is small:

$$\Gamma(z) = \frac{\Gamma(w+1)}{w(w-1)} = -w^{-1} + (\gamma - 1) + O(w),$$

$$n^{-1-z} = 1 - w \ln n + O(w^2),$$

$$1/(2^{-1-z} - 1) = -w^{-1}/\ln 2 - \tfrac{1}{2} + O(w).$$

The residue at $z = -1$ is the coefficient of w^{-1} in the product of these three formulas, namely $\tfrac{1}{2} - (\ln n + \gamma - 1)/\ln 2$. Adding the other residues gives the formula

$$\frac{T_n}{n} = \frac{\ln n + \gamma - 1}{\ln 2} - \frac{1}{2} + \delta(n) + \frac{2}{n} + O(n^{-M}), \qquad (46)$$

for arbitrarily large M, where $\delta(n)$ is a rather strange function,

$$\delta(n) = \frac{2}{\ln 2} \sum_{k \geq 1} \Re\big(\Gamma(-1 - 2\pi i k/\ln 2) \exp(2\pi i k \lg n)\big). \qquad (47)$$

Notice that $\delta(n) = \delta(2n)$. The average value of $\delta(n)$ is zero, since the average value of each term is zero. (We may assume that $(\lg n) \bmod 1$ is uniformly distributed, in view of the results about floating point numbers in Section 4.2.4.) Furthermore, since $|\Gamma(-1+it)| = |\pi/(t(1+t^2)\sinh \pi t)|^{1/2}$, it is not difficult to show that

$$\big|\delta(n)\big| < 0.000000173; \qquad (48)$$

thus we may safely ignore $\delta(n)$ for practical purposes. For theoretical purposes, however, we can't obtain a valid asymptotic expansion of U_n without it; that is why U_n is a comparatively difficult function to analyze.

From the definition of T_n in (41) we can see immediately that

$$\frac{T_{2n}}{2n} = \frac{T_n}{n} + 1 - \frac{1}{n} + \frac{e^{-n}}{n}. \qquad (49)$$

Therefore the error term $O(n^{-M})$ in (46) is essential; it cannot be replaced by zero. However, exercise 54 presents another approach to the analysis, which avoids such error terms by deriving a rather peculiar convergent series.

In summary, we have deduced the behavior of the difficult sum (38):

$$U_n = n \lg n + n \left(\frac{\gamma - 1}{\ln 2} - \frac{1}{2} + \delta(n) \right) + O(1). \qquad (50)$$

The gamma-function method we have used to obtain this result is a special case of the general technique of *Mellin transforms*, which are extremely useful in the study of radix-oriented recurrence relations. Other examples of this approach can be found in exercises 51–53 and in Section 6.3. An excellent introduction to Mellin transforms and their applications to algorithmic analysis has been presented by P. Flajolet, X. Gourdon, and P. Dumas in *Theoretical Computer Science* **144** (1995), 3–58.

EXERCISES

1. [*M20*] Let $a_1 \ldots a_n$ be a permutation of $\{1, \ldots, n\}$, and let i and j be indices such that $i < j$ and $a_i > a_j$. Let $a'_1 \ldots a'_n$ be the permutation obtained from $a_1 \ldots a_n$ by interchanging a_i and a_j. Can $a'_1 \ldots a'_n$ have more inversions than $a_1 \ldots a_n$?

▶ **2.** [*M25*] (a) What is the minimum number of exchanges that will sort the permutation 3 7 6 9 8 1 4 5 2? (b) In general, given any permutation $\pi = a_1 \ldots a_n$ of $\{1, \ldots, n\}$, let $\operatorname{xch}(\pi)$ be the minimum number of exchanges that will sort π into increasing order. Express $\operatorname{xch}(\pi)$ in terms of "simpler" characteristics of π. (See exercise 5.1.4–41 for another way to measure the disorder of a permutation.)

3. [*10*] Is the bubble sort Algorithm B a stable sorting algorithm?

4. [*M23*] If $t = 1$ in step B4, we could actually terminate Algorithm B immediately, because the subsequent step B2 will do nothing useful. What is the probability that $t = 1$ will occur in step B4 when sorting a random permutation?

5. [*M25*] Let $b_1 b_2 \ldots b_n$ be the inversion table for the permutation $a_1 a_2 \ldots a_n$. Show that the value of BOUND after r passes of the bubble sort is $\max \{b_i + i \mid b_i \geq r\} - r$, for $0 \leq r \leq \max(b_1, \ldots, b_n)$.

6. [*M22*] Let $a_1 \ldots a_n$ be a permutation of $\{1, \ldots, n\}$ and let $a'_1 \ldots a'_n$ be its inverse. Show that the number of passes to bubble-sort $a_1 \ldots a_n$ is $1 + \max(a'_1 - 1, a'_2 - 2, \ldots, a'_n - n)$.

7. [*M28*] Calculate the standard deviation of the number of passes for the bubble sort, and express it in terms of n and the function $P(n)$. [See Eqs. (6) and (7).]

8. [*M24*] Derive Eq. (8).

9. [*M48*] Analyze the number of passes and the number of comparisons in the cocktail-shaker sorting algorithm. *Note:* See exercise 5.4.8–9 for partial information.

10. [*M26*] Let $a_1 a_2 \ldots a_n$ be a 2-ordered permutation of $\{1, 2, \ldots, n\}$.
a) What are the coordinates of the endpoints of the a_ith step of the corresponding lattice path? (See Fig. 11 on page 87.)
b) Prove that the comparison/exchange of $a_1 : a_2$, $a_3 : a_4$, $\ldots$ corresponds to folding the path about the diagonal, as in Fig. 18(b).
c) Prove that the comparison/exchange of $a_2 : a_{2+d}$, $a_4 : a_{4+d}$, $\ldots$ corresponds to folding the path about a line m units below the diagonal, as in Figs. 18(c), (d), and (e), when $d = 2m - 1$.

▶ **11.** [*M25*] What permutation of $\{1, 2, \ldots, 16\}$ maximizes the number of exchanges done by Batcher's algorithm?

12. [*24*] Write a MIX program for Algorithm M, assuming that MIX is a binary computer with the operations AND, SRB. How much time does your program take to sort the sixteen records in Table 1?

13. [*10*] Is Batcher's method a stable sorting algorithm?

14. [*M21*] Let $c(N)$ be the number of key comparisons used to sort N elements by Batcher's method; this is the number of times step M4 is performed.

a) Show that $c(2^t) = 2c(2^{t-1}) + (t-1)2^{t-1} + 1$, for $t \geq 1$.

b) Find a simple expression for $c(2^t)$ as a function of t. *Hint:* Consider the sequence $x_t = c(2^t)/2^t$.

15. [*M38*] The object of this exercise is to analyze the function $c(N)$ of exercise 14, and to find a formula for $c(N)$ when $N = 2^{e_1} + 2^{e_2} + \cdots + 2^{e_r}$, $e_1 > e_2 > \cdots > e_r \geq 0$.

a) Let $a(N) = c(N+1) - c(N)$. Prove that $a(2n) = a(n) + \lfloor \lg(2n) \rfloor$, and $a(2n+1) = a(n) + 1$; hence

$$a(N) = \binom{e_1 + 1}{2} - r(e_1 - 1) + (e_1 + e_2 + \cdots + e_r).$$

b) Let $x(n) = a(n) - a(\lfloor n/2 \rfloor)$, so that $a(n) = x(n) + x(\lfloor n/2 \rfloor) + x(\lfloor n/4 \rfloor) + \cdots$. Let $y(n) = x(1) + x(2) + \cdots + x(n)$; and let $z(2n) = y(2n) - a(n)$, $z(2n+1) = y(2n+1)$. Prove that $c(N+1) = z(N) + 2z(\lfloor N/2 \rfloor) + 4z(\lfloor N/4 \rfloor) + \cdots$.

c) Prove that $y(N) = N + (\lfloor N/2 \rfloor + 1)(e_1 - 1) - 2^{e_1} + 2$.

d) Now put everything together and find a formula for $c(N)$ in terms of the exponents e_j, holding r fixed.

16. [*HM42*] Find the asymptotic value of the *average* number of exchanges occurring when Batcher's method is applied to a random permutation of N distinct elements, assuming that N is a power of two.

▶ **17.** [*20*] Where in Algorithm Q do we use the fact that K_0 and K_{N+1} have the values postulated in (13)?

▶ **18.** [*20*] Explain how the computation proceeds in Algorithm Q when all of the input keys are equal. What would happen if the "<" signs in steps Q3 and Q4 were changed to "≤" instead?

19. [*15*] Would Algorithm Q still work properly if a queue (first-in-first-out) were used instead of a stack (last-in-first-out)?

20. [*M20*] What is the largest possible number of elements that will ever be on the stack at once in Algorithm Q, as a function of M and N?

21. [*20*] Explain why the first partitioning phase of Algorithm Q takes the number of comparisons and exchanges specified in (17), when the keys are distinct.

22. [*M25*] Let p_{kN} be the probability that the quantity A in (16) will equal k, when Algorithm Q is applied to a random permutation of $\{1, 2, \ldots, N\}$, and let $A_N(z) = \sum_k p_{kN} z^k$ be the corresponding generating function. Prove that $A_N(z) = 1$ for $N \leq M$, and $A_N(z) = z(\sum_{1 \leq s \leq N} A_{s-1}(z) A_{N-s}(z))/N$ for $N > M$. Find similar recurrence relations defining the other probability distributions $B_N(z)$, $C_N(z)$, $D_N(z)$, $E_N(z)$, $S_N(z)$.

23. [*M23*] Let A_N, B_N, D_N, E_N, S_N be the average values of the corresponding quantities in (16), when sorting a random permutation of $\{1, 2, \ldots, N\}$. Find recurrence relations for these quantities, analogous to (18); and solve these recurrences to obtain (25).

24. [*M21*] Algorithm Q obviously does a few more comparisons than it needs to, since we can have $i = j$ in step Q3 and even $i > j$ in step Q4. How many comparisons C_N would be done on the average if we avoided all comparisons when $i \geq j$?

25. [*M20*] When the input keys are the numbers 1 2 ... N in order, what are the exact values of the quantities A, B, C, D, E, and S in the timing of Program Q? (Assume that $N > M$.)

▶ **26.** [*M24*] Construct an input file that makes Program Q go even more slowly than it does in exercise 25. (Try to find a really bad case.)

27. [*M28*] (R. Sedgewick.) Consider the *best* case of Algorithm Q: Find a permutation of $\{1, 2, \ldots, 23\}$ that takes the least time to be sorted when $N = 23$ and $M = 3$.

28. [*M26*] Find the recurrence relation analogous to (20) that is satisfied by the average number of comparisons in Singleton's modification of Algorithm Q (choosing s as the median of $\{K_1, K_{\lfloor (N+1)/2 \rfloor}, K_N\}$ instead of $s = K_1$).

29. [*HM40*] Continuing exercise 28, find the asymptotic value of the number of comparisons in Singleton's "median of three" method.

▶ **30.** [*25*] (P. Shackleton.) When *multiword keys* are being sorted, many sorting methods become progressively slower as the file gets closer to its final order, since equal and nearly-equal keys require an inspection of several words to determine the proper lexicographic order. (See exercise 5–5.) Files that arise in practice often involve such keys, so this phenomenon can have a significant impact on the sorting time.

Explain how Algorithm Q can be extended to avoid this difficulty; within a subfile in which the leading k words are known to have constant values for all keys, only the $(k + 1)$st words of the keys should be inspected.

▶ **31.** [*20*] (C. A. R. Hoare.) Suppose that, instead of sorting an entire file, we only want to determine the mth smallest of a given set of n elements. Show that quicksort can be adapted to this purpose, avoiding many of the computations required to do a complete sort.

32. [*M40*] Find a simple closed form expression for C_{nm}, the average number of key comparisons required to select the mth smallest of n elements by the "quickfind" method of exercise 31. (For simplicity, let $M = 1$; that is, don't assume the use of a special technique for short subfiles.) What is the asymptotic behavior of $C_{(2m-1)m}$, the average number of comparisons needed to find the median of $2m - 1$ elements by Hoare's method?

▶ **33.** [*15*] Design an algorithm that rearranges all the numbers in a given table so that all *negative* values precede all nonnegative ones. (The items need not be sorted completely, just separated between negative and nonnegative.) Your algorithm should use the minimum possible number of exchanges.

34. [*20*] How can the bit-inspection loops of radix exchange (in steps R3 through R6) be speeded up?

35. [*M23*] Analyze the values of the frequencies A, B, C, G, K, L, R, S, and X that arise in radix exchange sorting using "case (i) input."

36. [*M27*] Given a sequence of numbers $\langle a_n \rangle = a_0, a_1, a_2, \ldots$, define its *binomial transform* $\langle \hat{a}_n \rangle = \hat{a}_0, \hat{a}_1, \hat{a}_2, \ldots$ by the rule

$$\hat{a}_n = \sum_k \binom{n}{k} (-1)^k a_k.$$

a) Prove that $\langle \hat{\hat{a}}_n \rangle = \langle a_n \rangle$.
b) Find the binomial transforms of the sequences $\langle 1 \rangle$; $\langle n \rangle$; $\langle \binom{n}{m} \rangle$, for fixed m; $\langle a^n \rangle$, for fixed a; $\langle \binom{n}{m} a^n \rangle$, for fixed a and m.

c) Suppose that a sequence $\langle x_n \rangle$ satisfies the relation

$$x_n = a_n + 2^{1-n} \sum_{k \geq 2} \binom{n}{k} x_k, \qquad \text{for } n \geq 2; \qquad x_0 = x_1 = a_0 = a_1 = 0.$$

Prove that the solution to this recurrence is

$$x_n = \sum_{k \geq 2} \binom{n}{k} (-1)^k \frac{2^{k-1} \hat{a}_k}{2^{k-1} - 1} = a_n + \sum_{k \geq 2} \binom{n}{k} (-1)^k \frac{\hat{a}_k}{2^{k-1} - 1}.$$

37. [*M28*] Determine all sequences $\langle a_n \rangle$ such that $\langle \hat{a}_n \rangle = \langle a_n \rangle$, in the sense of exercise 36.

▸ **38.** [*M30*] Find A_N, B_N, C_N, G_N, K_N, L_N, R_N, and X_N, the average values of the quantities in (29), when radix exchange is applied to "case (ii) input." Express your answers in terms of N and the quantities

$$U_n = \sum_{k \geq 2} \binom{n}{k} \frac{(-1)^k}{2^{k-1} - 1} \qquad V_n = \sum_{k \geq 2} \binom{n}{k} \frac{(-1)^k k}{2^{k-1} - 1} = n(U_n - U_{n-1}).$$

[*Hint:* See exercise 36.]

39. [*20*] The results shown in (30) indicate that radix exchange sorting involves about $1.44N$ partitioning stages when it is applied to random input. Prove that quicksort will never require more than N stages; and explain why radix exchange often does.

40. [*21*] Explain how to modify Algorithm R so that it works with reasonable efficiency when sorting files containing numerous equal keys.

▸ **41.** [*30*] Devise a good way to exchange records $R_l \ldots R_r$ so that they are partitioned into three blocks, with (i) $K_k < K$ for $1 \leq k < i$; (ii) $K_k = K$ for $i \leq k \leq j$; (iii) $K_k > K$ for $j < k \leq r$. Schematically, the final arrangement should be

$< K$	$= K$	$> K$
l	i	j r

.

42. [*HM32*] For any real number $c > 0$, prove that the probability is less than e^{-c} that Algorithm Q will make more than $(c + 1)(N + 1)H_N$ comparisons when sorting random data. (This upper bound is especially interesting when c is, say, N^ϵ.)

43. [*HM21*] Prove that $\int_0^1 y^{-1}(e^{-y} - 1)\,dy + \int_1^\infty y^{-1} e^{-y}\,dy = -\gamma$. [*Hint:* Consider $\lim_{a \to 0+} y^{a-1}$.]

44. [*HM24*] Derive (37) as suggested in the text.

45. [*HM20*] Explain why (43) is true, when $x > 0$.

46. [*HM20*] What is the value of $(1/2\pi i) \int_{a-i\infty}^{a+i\infty} \Gamma(z) n^{s-z}\,dz/(2^{s-z} - 1)$, given that s is a positive integer and $0 < a < s$?

47. [*HM21*] Prove that $\sum_{j \geq 1}(n/2^j) e^{-n/2^j}$ is a bounded function of n.

48. [*HM24*] Find the asymptotic value of the quantity V_n defined in exercise 38, using a method analogous to the text's study of U_n, obtaining terms up to $O(1)$.

49. [*HM24*] Extend the asymptotic formula (47) for U_n to $O(n^{-1})$.

50. [*HM24*] Find the asymptotic value of the function

$$U_{mn} = \sum_{k \geq 2} \binom{n}{k} (-1)^k \frac{1}{m^{k-1} - 1},$$

when m is any fixed number greater than 1. (When m is an integer greater than 2, this quantity arises in the study of generalizations of radix exchange, as well as the trie memory search algorithms of Section 6.3.)

▶ **51.** [*HM28*] Show that the gamma-function approach to asymptotic problems can be used instead of Euler's summation formula to derive the asymptotic expansion of the quantity $r_k(m)$ in (35). (This gives us a uniform method for studying $r_k(m)$ for all k, without relying on tricks such as the text's introduction of $g_{-1}(x) = (e^{-x^2} - 1)/x$.)

52. [*HM35*] (N. G. de Bruijn.) What is the asymptotic behavior of the sum

$$S_n = \sum_{t \geq 1} \binom{2n}{n+t} d(t),$$

where $d(t)$ is the number of divisors of t? (Thus, $d(1) = 1$, $d(2) = d(3) = 2$, $d(4) = 3$, $d(5) = 2$, etc. This question arises in connection with the analysis of a tree traversal algorithm, exercise 2.3.1–11.) Find the value of $S_n / \binom{2n}{n}$ to terms of $O(n^{-1})$.

53. [*HM42*] Analyze the average number of bit inspections and exchanges done by radix exchange when the input data consists of infinite-precision binary numbers in $[0 . . 1)$, each of whose bits is independently equal to 1 with probability p. (Only the case $p = \frac{1}{2}$ is discussed in the text; the methods we have used can be generalized to arbitrary p.) Consider in particular the case $p = 1/\phi = .61803\ldots$.

54. [*HM24*] (S. O. Rice.) Show that U_n can be written

$$U_n = (-1)^n \frac{n!}{2\pi i} \oint_C \frac{dz}{z(z-1)\ldots(z-n)} \frac{1}{2^{z-1}-1},$$

where C is a skinny closed curve encircling the points $2, 3, \ldots, n$. Changing C to an arbitrarily large circle centered at the origin, derive the convergent series

$$U_n = \frac{(H_{n-1} - 1)n}{\ln 2} - \frac{n}{2} + 2 + \frac{2}{\ln 2} \sum_{m \geq 1} \Re\left(B(n+1, -1+ibm)\right),$$

where $b = 2\pi/\ln 2$, and $B(n+1, -1+ibm) = \Gamma(n+1)\Gamma(-1+ibm)/\Gamma(n+ibm) = n!/\prod_{k=0}^{n}(k-1+ibm)$.

▶ **55.** [*22*] Show how to modify Program Q so that the partitioning element is the median of the three keys (28).

56. [*M43*] Analyze the average behavior of the quantities that occur in the running time of Algorithm Q when the program has been modified to take the median of three elements as in exercise 55. (See exercise 29.)

5.2.3. Sorting by Selection

Another important family of sorting techniques is based on the idea of repeated selection. The simplest selection method is perhaps the following:

   i) Find the smallest key; transfer the corresponding record to the output area; then replace the key by the value ∞ (which is assumed to be higher than any actual key).

   ii) Repeat step (i). This time the second smallest key will be selected, since the smallest key has been replaced by ∞.

   iii) Continue repeating step (i) until N records have been selected.

A selection method requires all of the input items to be present before sorting may proceed, and it generates the final outputs one by one in sequence. This is essentially the opposite of insertion, where the inputs are received sequentially but we do not know any of the final outputs until sorting is completed.

Step (i) involves $N-1$ comparisons each time a new record is selected, and it also requires a separate output area in memory. But we can obviously do better: We can move the selected record into its proper final position, by exchanging it with the record currently occupying that position. Then we need not consider that position again in future selections, and we need not deal with infinite keys. This idea yields our first selection sorting algorithm.

Algorithm S (*Straight selection sort*). Records $R_1, \ldots, R_N$ are rearranged in place; after sorting is complete, their keys will be in order, $K_1 \leq \cdots \leq K_N$. Sorting is based on the method indicated above, except that it proves to be more convenient to select the *largest* element first, then the second largest, etc.

S1. [Loop on j.] Perform steps S2 and S3 for $j = N, N-1, \ldots, 2$.

S2. [Find $\max(K_1, \ldots, K_j)$.] Search through keys $K_j, K_{j-1}, \ldots, K_1$ to find a maximal one; let it be K_i, where i is as large as possible.

S3. [Exchange with R_j.] Interchange records $R_i \leftrightarrow R_j$. (Now records $R_j, \ldots, R_N$ are in their final position.) ∎

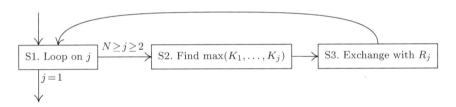

Fig. 21. Straight selection sorting.

Table 1 shows this algorithm in action on our sixteen example keys. Elements that are candidates for the maximum during the right-to-left search in step S2 are shown in boldface type.

Table 1

STRAIGHT SELECTION SORTING

503	087	512	061	**908**	170	**897**	275	653	426	154	509	612	677	**765**	**703**|
503	087	512	061	703	170	**897**	275	653	426	154	509	612	677	**765**|908	
503	087	512	061	703	170	**765**	275	653	426	154	509	612	**677**|897	908	
503	087	512	061	**703**	170	677	275	**653**	426	154	509	**612**|765	897	908	
503	087	512	061	612	170	**677**	275	**653**	426	154	**509**|703	765	897	908	
503	087	512	061	612	170	509	275	**653**	**426**	**154**|677	703	765	897	908	

. . .

061\|087 154 170 275 426 503 509 512 612 653 677 703 765 897 908

The corresponding MIX program is quite simple:

Program S (*Straight selection sort*). As in previous programs of this chapter, the records in locations INPUT+1 through INPUT+N are sorted in place, on a full-word key. rA ≡ current maximum, rI1 ≡ $j-1$, rI2 ≡ k (the current search position), rI3 ≡ i. Assume that $N \geq 2$.

01	START	ENT1	N-1	1	*S1. Loop on j.* $j \leftarrow N$.
02	2H	ENT2	0,1	$N-1$	*S2. Find* $\max(K_1,\ldots,K_j)$. $k \leftarrow j-1$.
03		ENT3	1,1	$N-1$	$i \leftarrow j$.
04		LDA	INPUT,3	$N-1$	rA $\leftarrow K_i$.
05	8H	CMPA	INPUT,2	A	
06		JGE	*+3	A	Jump if $K_i \geq K_k$.
07		ENT3	0,2	B	Otherwise set $i \leftarrow k$,
08		LDA	INPUT,3	B	rA $\leftarrow K_i$.
09		DEC2	1	A	$k \leftarrow k-1$.
10		J2P	8B	A	Repeat if $k > 0$.
11		LDX	INPUT+1,1	$N-1$	*S3. Exchange with R_j.*
12		STX	INPUT,3	$N-1$	$R_i \leftarrow R_j$.
13		STA	INPUT+1,1	$N-1$	$R_j \leftarrow$ rA.
14		DEC1	1	$N-1$	
15		J1P	2B	$N-1$	$N \geq j \geq 2$. ∎

The running time of this program depends on the number of items, N; the number of comparisons, A; and the number of changes to right-to-left maxima, B. It is easy to see that

$$A = \binom{N}{2} = \frac{1}{2}N(N-1),\tag{1}$$

regardless of the values of the input keys; hence only B is variable. In spite of the simplicity of straight selection, this quantity B is not easy to analyze precisely. Exercises 3 through 6 show that

$$B = \big(\min\, 0,\ \text{ave}\ (N+1)H_N - 2N,\ \max\,\lfloor N^2/4\rfloor\big);\tag{2}$$

in this case the maximum value turns out to be particularly interesting. The standard deviation of B is of order $N^{3/4}$; see exercise 7.

Thus the average running time of Program S is $2.5N^2 + 3(N+1)H_N + 3.5N - 11$ units, just slightly slower than straight insertion (Program 5.2.1S). It is interesting to compare Algorithm S to the bubble sort (Algorithm 5.2.2B), since bubble sorting may be regarded as a selection algorithm that sometimes selects more than one element at a time. For this reason bubble sorting usually does fewer comparisons than straight selection and it may seem to be preferable; but in fact Program 5.2.2B is more than twice as slow as Program S! Bubble sorting is handicapped by the fact that it does so many exchanges, while straight selection involves very little data movement.

Refinements of straight selection. Is there any way to improve on the selection method used in Algorithm S? For example, take the search for a maximum in step S2; is there a substantially faster way to find a maximum? The answer to the latter question is *no*!

Lemma M. *Every algorithm for finding the maximum of n elements, based on comparing pairs of elements, must make at least $n - 1$ comparisons.*

Proof. If we have made fewer than $n - 1$ comparisons, there will be at least two elements that have never been found to be less than any others. Therefore we do not know which of these two elements is larger, and we cannot have determined the maximum. ∎

Thus, any selection process that finds the largest element must perform at least $n - 1$ comparisons; and we might suspect that all sorting methods based on n repeated selections are doomed to require $\Omega(n^2)$ operations. But fortunately Lemma M applies only to the *first* selection step; subsequent selections can make use of previously gained information. For example, exercises 8 and 9 show that a comparatively simple change to Algorithm S will cut the average number of comparisons in half.

Consider the 16 numbers in Table 1; one way to save time on repeated selections is to regard them as four groups of four. We can start by determining the largest in each group, namely the respective keys

$$512, 908, 653, 765;$$

the largest of these four elements, 908, is then the largest of the entire file. To get the second largest we need only look at 512, 653, 765, and the other three elements of the group containing 908; the largest of $\{170, 897, 275\}$ is 897, and the largest of

$$512, 897, 653, 765$$

is 897. Similarly, to get the third largest element we determine the largest of $\{170, 175\}$ and then the largest of

$$512, 275, 653, 765.$$

Each selection after the first takes at most 5 additional comparisons. In general, if N is a perfect square, we can divide the file into $\sqrt{N}$ groups of $\sqrt{N}$ elements each; each selection after the first takes at most $\sqrt{N} - 2$ comparisons within the group of the previously selected item, plus $\sqrt{N} - 1$ comparisons among the "group leaders." This idea is called *quadratic selection*; its total execution time is $O(N\sqrt{N})$, which is substantially better than order N^2.

Quadratic selection was first published by E. H. Friend [*JACM* **3** (1956), 152–154], who pointed out that the same idea can be generalized to cubic, quartic, and higher degrees of selection. For example, cubic selection divides the file into $\sqrt[3]{N}$ large groups, each containing $\sqrt[3]{N}$ small groups, each containing $\sqrt[3]{N}$ records; the execution time is proportional to $N\sqrt[3]{N}$. If we carry this idea to its ultimate conclusion we arrive at what Friend called "nth degree selecting," based on a binary tree structure. This method has an execution time proportional to $N \log N$; we shall call it *tree selection*.

Tree selection. The principles of tree selection sorting are easy to understand in terms of matches in a typical "knockout tournament." Consider, for example, the results of the ping-pong contest shown in Fig. 22; at the bottom level, Kim beats Sandy and Chris beats Lou, then in the next round Chris beats Kim, etc.

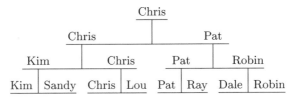

Fig. 22. A ping-pong tournament.

Figure 22 shows that Chris is the champion of the eight players, and $8-1 = 7$ matches/comparisons were required to determine this fact. Pat is not necessarily the second-best player; any of the people defeated by Chris, including the first-round loser Lou, might possibly be second best. We can determine the second-best player by having Lou play Kim, and the winner of that match plays Pat; only two additional matches are required to find the second-best player, because of the structure we have remembered from the earlier games.

In general, we can "output" the player at the root of the tree, and replay the tournament as if that player had been sick and unable to play a good game. Then the original second-best player will rise to the root; and to recalculate the winners in the upper levels of the tree, only one path must be changed. It follows that fewer than $\lceil \lg N \rceil$ further comparisons are needed to select the second-best player. The same procedure will find the third-best, etc.; hence the total time for such a selection sort will be roughly proportional to $N \log N$, as claimed above.

Figure 23 shows tree selection sorting in action, on our 16 example numbers. Notice that we need to know where the key at the root came from, in order to know where to insert the next "$-\infty$". Therefore each branch node of the tree should actually contain a pointer or index specifying the position of the relevant key, instead of the key itself. It follows that we need memory space for N input records, $N - 1$ pointers, and N output records or pointers to those records. (If the output goes to tape or disk, of course, we don't need to retain the output records in high-speed memory.)

The reader should pause at this point and work exercise 10, because a good understanding of the basic principles of tree selection will make it easier to appreciate the remarkable improvements we are about to discuss.

One way to modify tree selection, essentially introduced by K. E. Iverson [*A Programming Language* (Wiley, 1962), 223–227], does away with the need for pointers by "looking ahead" in the following way: When the winner of a match in the bottom level of the tree is moved up, the winning value can be replaced immediately by $-\infty$ at the bottom level; and whenever a winner moves up from one branch to another, we can replace the corresponding value by the one that should eventually move up into the vacated place (namely the larger of the two keys below). Repeating this operation as often as possible converts Fig. 23(a) into Fig. 24.

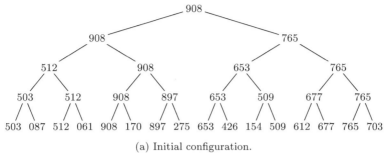

(a) Initial configuration.

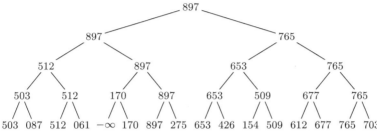

(b) Key 908 is replaced by $-\infty$, and the second highest element moves up to the root.

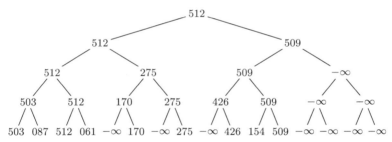

(c) Configuration after 908, 897, 765, 703, 677, 653, and 612 have been output.

Fig. 23. An example of tree selection sorting.

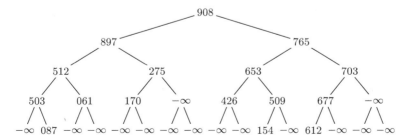

Fig. 24. The Peter Principle applied to sorting. Everyone rises to their level of incompetence in the hierarchy.

Once the tree has been set up in this way we can proceed to sort by a "top-down" method, instead of the "bottom up" method of Fig. 23: We output the root, then move up its largest descendant, then move up the latter's largest descendant, and so forth. The process begins to look less like a ping-pong tournament and more like a corporate system of promotions.

The reader should be able to see that this top-down method has the advantage that redundant comparisons of $-\infty$ with $-\infty$ can be avoided. (The bottom-up approach finds $-\infty$ omnipresent in the latter stages of sorting, but the top-down approach can stop modifying the tree during each stage as soon as a $-\infty$ has been stored.)

Figures 23 and 24 are *complete binary trees* with 16 terminal nodes (see Section 2.3.4.5), and it is convenient to represent such trees in consecutive locations as shown in Fig. 25. Note that the parent of node number k is node $\lfloor k/2 \rfloor$, and its children are nodes $2k$ and $2k+1$. This leads to another advantage of the top-down approach, since it is often considerably simpler to go top-down from node k to nodes $2k$ and $2k+1$ than bottom-up from node k to nodes $k \oplus 1$ and $\lfloor k/2 \rfloor$. (Here $k \oplus 1$ stands for $k+1$ or $k-1$, according as k is even or odd.)

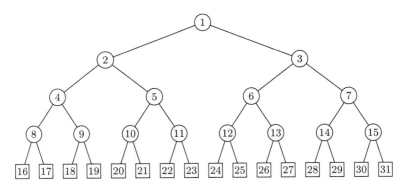

Fig. 25. Sequential storage allocation for a complete binary tree.

Our examples of tree selection so far have more or less assumed that N is a power of 2; but actually we can work with arbitrary N, since the complete binary tree with N terminal nodes is readily constructed for any N.

Now we come to the crucial question: Can't we do the top-down method without using $-\infty$ at all? Wouldn't it be nice if the important information of Fig. 24 were all in locations 1 through 16 of the complete binary tree, without the useless "holes" containing $-\infty$? Some reflection shows that it is indeed possible to achieve this goal, not only eliminating $-\infty$ but also avoiding the need for an auxiliary output area. This line of thinking leads us to an important sorting algorithm that was christened "heapsort" by its discoverer J. W. J. Williams [*CACM* **7** (1964), 347–348].

Heapsort. Let us say that a file of keys $K_1, K_2, \ldots, K_N$ is a *heap* if

$$K_{\lfloor j/2 \rfloor} \geq K_j \qquad \text{for } 1 \leq \lfloor j/2 \rfloor < j \leq N. \tag{3}$$

Thus, $K_1 \geq K_2$, $K_1 \geq K_3$, $K_2 \geq K_4$, etc.; this is exactly the condition that holds in Fig. 24, and it implies in particular that the largest key appears "on top of the heap,"

$$K_1 = \max{(K_1, K_2, \ldots, K_N)}. \tag{4}$$

If we can somehow transform an arbitrary input file into a heap, we can sort the elements by using a top-down selection procedure as described above.

An efficient approach to heap creation has been suggested by R. W. Floyd [*CACM* **7** (1964), 701]. Let us assume that we have been able to arrange the file so that

$$K_{\lfloor j/2 \rfloor} \geq K_j \qquad \text{for } l < \lfloor j/2 \rfloor < j \leq N, \tag{5}$$

where l is some number ≥ 1. (In the original file this condition holds vacuously for $l = \lfloor N/2 \rfloor$, since no subscript j satisfies the condition $\lfloor N/2 \rfloor < \lfloor j/2 \rfloor < j \leq N$.) It is not difficult to see how to transform the file so that the inequalities in (5) are extended to the case $l = \lfloor j/2 \rfloor$, working entirely in the subtree whose root is node l. Then we can decrease l by 1, until condition (3) is finally achieved. These ideas of Williams and Floyd lead to the following elegant algorithm, which merits careful study:

Algorithm H (*Heapsort*). Records $R_1, \ldots, R_N$ are rearranged in place; after sorting is complete, their keys will be in order, $K_1 \leq \cdots \leq K_N$. First we rearrange the file so that it forms a heap, then we repeatedly remove the top of the heap and transfer it to its proper final position. Assume that $N \geq 2$.

H1. [Initialize.] Set $l \leftarrow \lfloor N/2 \rfloor + 1$, $r \leftarrow N$.

H2. [Decrease l or r.] If $l > 1$, set $l \leftarrow l - 1$, $R \leftarrow R_l$, $K \leftarrow K_l$. (If $l > 1$, we are in the process of transforming the input file into a heap; on the other hand if $l = 1$, the keys $K_1 K_2 \ldots K_r$ presently constitute a heap.) Otherwise set $R \leftarrow R_r$, $K \leftarrow K_r$, $R_r \leftarrow R_1$, and $r \leftarrow r - 1$; if this makes $r = 1$, set $R_1 \leftarrow R$ and terminate the algorithm.

H3. [Prepare for siftup.] Set $j \leftarrow l$. (At this point we have

$$K_{\lfloor k/2 \rfloor} \geq K_k \qquad \text{for } l < \lfloor k/2 \rfloor < k \leq r; \tag{6}$$

and record R_k is in its final position for $r < k \leq N$. Steps H3–H8 are called the *siftup algorithm*; their effect is equivalent to setting $R_l \leftarrow R$ and then rearranging $R_l, \ldots, R_r$ so that condition (6) holds also for $l = \lfloor k/2 \rfloor$.)

H4. [Advance downward.] Set $i \leftarrow j$ and $j \leftarrow 2j$. (In the following steps we have $i = \lfloor j/2 \rfloor$.) If $j < r$, go right on to step H5; if $j = r$, go to step H6; and if $j > r$, go to H8.

H5. [Find larger child.] If $K_j < K_{j+1}$, then set $j \leftarrow j + 1$.

H6. [Larger than K?] If $K \geq K_j$, then go to step H8.

H7. [Move it up.] Set $R_i \leftarrow R_j$, and go back to step H4.

H8. [Store R.] Set $R_i \leftarrow R$. (This terminates the siftup algorithm initiated in step H3.) Return to step H2. ∎

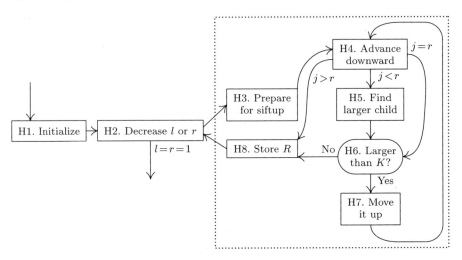

Fig. 26. Heapsort; dotted lines enclose the siftup algorithm.

Heapsort has sometimes been described as the $\not\!\!\!/$ algorithm, because of the motion of l and r. The upper triangle represents the heap-creation phase, when $r = N$ and l decreases to 1; and the lower triangle represents the selection phase, when $l = 1$ and r decreases to 1. Table 2 shows the process of heapsorting our sixteen example numbers. (Each line in that table shows the state of affairs at the beginning of step H2, and brackets indicate the position of l and r.)

Program H (*Heapsort*).   The records in locations INPUT+1 through INPUT+N are sorted by Algorithm H, with the following register assignments: rI1 $\equiv l - 1$, rI2 $\equiv r - 1$, rI3 $\equiv i$, rI4 $\equiv j$, rI5 $\equiv r - j$, rA $\equiv K \equiv R$, rX $\equiv R_j$.

01	START	ENT1	N/2	1	H1. Initialize. $l \leftarrow \lfloor N/2 \rfloor + 1$.
02		ENT2	N-1	1	$r \leftarrow N$.
03	1H	DEC1	1	$\lfloor N/2 \rfloor$	$l \leftarrow l - 1$.
04		LDA	INPUT+1,1	$\lfloor N/2 \rfloor$	$R \leftarrow R_l,\ K \leftarrow K_l$.
05	3H	ENT4	1,1	P	H3. Prepare for siftup. $j \leftarrow l$.
06		ENT5	0,2	P	
07		DEC5	0,1	P	rI5 $\leftarrow r - j$.
08		JMP	4F	P	To H4.
09	5H	LDX	INPUT,4	$B+A-D$	H5. Find larger child.
10		CMPX	INPUT+1,4	$B+A-D$	
11		JGE	6F	$B+A-D$	Jump if $K_j \geq K_{j+1}$.
12		INC4	1	C	Otherwise set $j \leftarrow j + 1$.
13		DEC5	1	C	
14	9H	LDX	INPUT,4	$C+D$	rX $\leftarrow R_j$.
15	6H	CMPA	INPUT,4	$B+A$	H6. Larger than K?
16		JGE	8F	$B+A$	To H8 if $K \geq K_j$.
17	7H	STX	INPUT,3	B	H7. Move it up. $R_i \leftarrow R_j$.
18	4H	ENT3	0,4	$B+P$	H4. Advance downward. $i \leftarrow j$.
19		DEC5	0,4	$B+P$	rI5 $\leftarrow$ rI5 $- j$.
20		INC4	0,4	$B+P$	$j \leftarrow j + j$.

Table 2

EXAMPLE OF HEAPSORT

K_1	K_2	K_3	K_4	K_5	K_6	K_7	K_8	K_9	K_{10}	K_{11}	K_{12}	K_{13}	K_{14}	K_{15}	K_{16}	l	r
503	087	512	061	908	170	897	275	[653	426	154	509	612	677	765	703]	9	16
503	087	512	061	908	170	897	[703	653	426	154	509	612	677	765	275]	8	16
503	087	512	061	908	170	[897	703	653	426	154	509	612	677	765	275]	7	16
503	087	512	061	908	[612	897	703	653	426	154	509	170	677	765	275]	6	16
503	087	512	061	[908	612	897	703	653	426	154	509	170	677	765	275]	5	16
503	087	512	[703	908	612	897	275	653	426	154	509	170	677	765	061]	4	16
503	087	[897	703	908	612	765	275	653	426	154	509	170	677	512	061]	3	16
503	[908	897	703	426	612	765	275	653	087	154	509	170	677	512	061]	2	16
[908	703	897	653	426	612	765	275	503	087	154	509	170	677	512	061]	1	16
[897	703	765	653	426	612	677	275	503	087	154	509	170	061	512]	908	1	15
[765	703	677	653	426	612	512	275	503	087	154	509	170	061]	897	908	1	14
[703	653	677	503	426	612	512	275	061	087	154	509	170]	765	897	908	1	13
[677	653	612	503	426	509	512	275	061	087	154	170]	703	765	897	908	1	12
[653	503	612	275	426	509	512	170	061	087	154]	677	703	765	897	908	1	11
[612	503	512	275	426	509	154	170	061	087]	653	677	703	765	897	908	1	10
[512	503	509	275	426	087	154	170	061]	612	653	677	703	765	897	908	1	9
[509	503	154	275	426	087	061	170]	512	612	653	677	703	765	897	908	1	8
[503	426	154	275	170	087	061]	509	512	612	653	677	703	765	897	908	1	7
[426	275	154	061	170	087]	503	509	512	612	653	677	703	765	897	908	1	6
[275	170	154	061	087]	426	503	509	512	612	653	677	703	765	897	908	1	5
[170	087	154	061]	275	426	503	509	512	612	653	677	703	765	897	908	1	4
[154	087	061]	170	275	426	503	509	512	612	653	677	703	765	897	908	1	3
[087	061]	154	170	275	426	503	509	512	612	653	677	703	765	897	908	1	2

21		J5P	5B	$B+P$	To H5 if $j < r$.	
22		J5Z	9B	$P-A+D$	To H6 if $j = r$.	
23	8H	STA	INPUT,3	P	<u>H8. Store R.</u> $R_i \leftarrow R$.	
24	2H	J1P	1B	P	<u>H2. Decrease l or r.</u>	
25		LDA	INPUT+1,2	$N-1$	If $l = 1$, set $R \leftarrow R_r$, $K \leftarrow K_r$.	
26		LDX	INPUT+1	$N-1$		
27		STX	INPUT+1,2	$N-1$	$R_r \leftarrow R_1$.	
28		DEC2	1	$N-1$	$r \leftarrow r-1$.	
29		J2P	3B	$N-1$	To H3 if $r > 1$.	
30		STA	INPUT+1	1	$R_1 \leftarrow R$. ∎	

Although this program is only about twice as long as Program S, it is much more efficient when N is large. Its running time depends on

$P = N + \lfloor N/2 \rfloor - 2$, the number of siftup passes;

A, the number of siftup passes in which the key K finally lands in an interior node of the heap;

B, the total number of keys promoted during siftups;

C, the number of times $j \leftarrow j + 1$ in step H5; and

D, the number of times $j = r$ in step H4.

These quantities are analyzed below; in practice they show comparatively little fluctuation about their average values,

$$A \approx 0.349N, \qquad\qquad B \approx N \lg N - 1.87N,$$
$$C \approx \tfrac{1}{2}N \lg N - 0.94N, \qquad D \approx \ln N. \tag{7}$$

For example, when $N = 1000$, four experiments on random input gave, respectively, $A = 371, 351, 341, 340$; $B = 8055, 8072, 8094, 8108$; $C = 4056, 4087, 4017, 4083$; and $D = 12, 14, 8, 13$. The total running time,

$$7A + 14B + 4C + 20N - 2D + 15\lfloor N/2 \rfloor - 28,$$

is therefore approximately $16N \lg N + 0.01N$ units on the average.

A glance at Table 2 makes it hard to believe that heapsort is very efficient; large keys migrate to the left before we stash them at the right! It is indeed a strange way to sort, when N is small; the sorting time for the 16 keys in Table 2 is $1068u$, while the simple method of straight insertion (Program 5.2.1S) takes only $514u$. Straight selection (Program S) takes $853u$.

For larger N, Program H is more efficient. It invites comparison with shellsort (Program 5.2.1D) and quicksort (Program 5.2.2Q), since all three programs sort by comparisons of keys and use little or no auxiliary storage. When $N = 1000$, the approximate average running times on MIX are

$$160000u \text{ for heapsort,}$$
$$130000u \text{ for shellsort,}$$
$$80000u \text{ for quicksort.}$$

(MIX is a typical computer, but particular machines will of course yield somewhat different relative values.) As N gets larger, heapsort will be superior to shellsort, but its asymptotic running time $16N \lg N \approx 23.08N \ln N$ will never beat quicksort's $11.67N \ln N$. A modification of heapsort discussed in exercise 18 will speed up the process by substantially reducing the number of comparisons, but even this improvement falls short of quicksort.

On the other hand, quicksort is efficient only on the average, and its worst case is of order N^2. Heapsort has the interesting property that its worst case isn't much worse than the average: We always have

$$A \le 1.5N, \qquad B \le N\lfloor \lg N \rfloor, \qquad C \le N\lfloor \lg N \rfloor, \tag{8}$$

so Program H will take no more than $18N\lfloor \lg N \rfloor + 38N$ units of time, regardless of the distribution of the input data. Heapsort is the first sorting method we have seen that is *guaranteed* to be of order $N \log N$. Merge sorting, discussed in Section 5.2.4 below, also has this property, but it requires more memory space.

Largest in, first out. We have seen in Chapter 2 that linear lists can often be classified in a meaningful way by the nature of the insertion and deletion operations that make them grow and shrink. A *stack* has last-in-first-out behavior, in the sense that every deletion removes the youngest item in the list — the item that was inserted most recently of all items currently present. A simple *queue* has first-in-first-out behavior, in the sense that every deletion removes the oldest remaining item. In more complex situations, such as the elevator simulation of Section 2.2.5, we want a smallest-in-first-out list, where every deletion removes the item having the smallest key. Such a list may be called a *priority queue*, since the key of each item reflects its relative ability to get out of the list quickly. Selection sorting is a special case of a priority queue in which we do N insertions followed by N deletions.

Priority queues arise in a wide variety of applications. For example, some numerical iterative schemes are based on repeated selection of an item having the largest (or smallest) value of some test criterion; parameters of the selected item are changed, and it is reinserted into the list with a new test value, based on the new values of its parameters. Operating systems often make use of priority queues for the scheduling of jobs. Exercises 15, 29, and 36 mention other typical applications of priority queues, and many other examples will appear in later chapters.

How shall we implement priority queues? One of the obvious methods is to maintain a sorted list, containing the items in order of their keys. Inserting a new item is then essentially the same problem we have treated in our study of insertion sorting, Section 5.2.1. Another even more obvious way to deal with priority queues is to keep the list of elements in arbitrary order, selecting the appropriate element each time a deletion is required by finding the largest (or smallest) key. The trouble with both of these obvious approaches is that they require $\Omega(N)$ steps either for insertion or deletion, when there are N entries in the list, so they are very time-consuming when N is large.

In his original paper on heapsorting, Williams pointed out that heaps are ideally suited to large priority queue applications, since we can insert or delete elements from a heap in $O(\log N)$ steps; furthermore, all elements of the heap are compactly located in consecutive memory locations. The selection phase of Algorithm H is a sequence of deletion steps of a *largest-in-first-out* process: To delete the largest element K_1 we remove it and sift K_N up into a new heap of $N - 1$ elements. (If we want a smallest-in-first-out algorithm, as in the elevator simulation, we can obviously change the definition of heap so that "$\geq$" becomes "$\leq$" in (3); for convenience, we shall consider only the largest-in-first-out case here.) In general, if we want to delete the largest item and then insert a new element x, we can do the siftup procedure with

$$l = 1, \qquad r = N, \qquad \text{and} \qquad K = x.$$

If we wish to insert an element x without a prior deletion, we can use the bottom-up procedure of exercise 16.

A linked representation for priority queues. An efficient way to represent priority queues as linked binary trees was discovered in 1971 by Clark A. Crane [Technical Report STAN-CS-72-259 (Computer Science Department, Stanford University, 1972)]. His method requires two link fields and a small count in every record, but it has the following advantages over a heap:

i) When the priority queue is being treated as a stack, the insertion and deletion operations take a fixed time independent of the queue size.

ii) The records never move, only the pointers change.

iii) Two disjoint priority queues, having a total of N elements, can easily be merged into a single priority queue, in only $O(\log N)$ steps.

Crane's original method, slightly modified, is illustrated in Fig. 27, which shows a special kind of binary tree structure. Each node contains a KEY field, a DIST field, and two link fields LEFT and RIGHT. The DIST field is always set to the length of a shortest path from that node to the null link Λ; in other words, it is the distance from that node to the nearest empty subtree. If we define DIST(Λ) = 0 and KEY(Λ) = $-\infty$, the KEY and DIST fields in the tree satisfy the following properties:

$$\text{KEY(P)} \geq \text{KEY(LEFT(P))}, \qquad \text{KEY(P)} \geq \text{KEY(RIGHT(P))}; \tag{9}$$

$$\text{DIST(P)} = 1 + \min(\text{DIST(LEFT(P))}, \text{DIST(RIGHT(P))}); \tag{10}$$

$$\text{DIST(LEFT(P))} \geq \text{DIST(RIGHT(P))}. \tag{11}$$

Relation (9) is analogous to the heap condition (3); it guarantees that the root of the tree has the largest key. Relation (10) is just the definition of the DIST fields as stated above. Relation (11) is the interesting innovation: It implies that a shortest path to Λ may always be obtained by moving to the right. We shall say that a binary tree with this property is a *leftist tree*, because it tends to lean so heavily to the left.

It is clear from these definitions that DIST(P) = n implies the existence of at least 2^n empty subtrees below P; otherwise there would be a shorter path from P to Λ. Thus, if there are N nodes in a leftist tree, the path leading downward from the root towards the right contains at most $\lfloor \lg(N+1) \rfloor$ nodes. It is possible to insert a new node into the priority queue by traversing this path (see exercise 33); hence only $O(\log N)$ steps are needed in the worst case. The best case occurs when the tree is linear (all RIGHT links are Λ), and the worst case occurs when the tree is perfectly balanced.

To remove the node at the root, we simply need to merge its two subtrees. The operation of merging two disjoint leftist trees, pointed to respectively by P and Q, is conceptually simple: If KEY(P) $\geq$ KEY(Q) we take P as the root and merge Q with P's right subtree; then DIST(P) is updated, and LEFT(P) is interchanged with RIGHT(P) if necessary. A detailed description of this process is not difficult to devise (see exercise 33).

Comparison of priority queue techniques. When the number of nodes, N, is small, it is best to use one of the straightforward linear list methods to maintain a priority queue; but when N is large, a $\log N$ method using heaps or leftist trees is obviously much faster. In Section 6.2.3 we shall discuss the representation of linear lists as *balanced trees*, and this leads to a third $\log N$ method suitable for priority queue implementation. It is therefore appropriate to compare these three techniques.

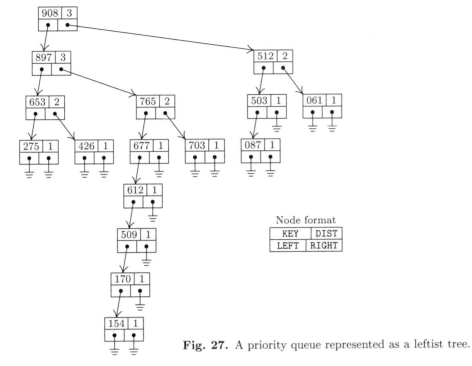

Node format

KEY	DIST
LEFT	RIGHT

Fig. 27. A priority queue represented as a leftist tree.

We have seen that leftist tree operations tend to be slightly faster than heap operations, although heaps consume less memory space because they have no link fields. Balanced trees take about the same space as leftist trees, perhaps slightly less; the operations are slower than heaps, and the programming is more complicated, but the balanced tree structure is considerably more flexible in several ways. When using a heap or a leftist tree we cannot predict very easily what will happen to two items with equal keys; it is impossible to guarantee that items with equal keys will be treated in a last-in-first-out or first-in-first-out manner, unless the key is extended to include an additional "serial number of insertion" field so that no equal keys are really present. With balanced trees, on the other hand, we can easily stipulate consistent conventions about equal keys, and we can also do things such as "insert x immediately before (or after) y." Balanced trees are symmetrical, so that we can delete either the largest or the smallest element at any time, while heaps and leftist trees must be oriented one way or the other. (See exercise 31, however, which shows how to construct *symmetrical* heaps). Balanced trees can be used for searching as well as for sorting; and we can rather quickly remove consecutive blocks of elements from a balanced tree. But $\Omega(N)$ steps are needed in general to merge two balanced trees, while leftist trees can be merged in only $O(\log N)$ steps.

In summary, heaps use minimum memory; leftist trees are great for merging disjoint priority queues; and the flexibility of balanced trees is available, if necessary, at reasonable cost.

Many new ways to represent priority queues have been discovered since the pioneering work of Williams and Crane discussed above. Programmers now have a large menu of options to ponder, besides simple lists, heaps, leftist or balanced trees:

- stratified trees, which provide symmetrical priority queue operations in only $O(\log \log M)$ steps when all keys lie in a given range $0 \le K < M$ [P. van Emde Boas, R. Kaas, and E. Zijlstra, *Math. Systems Theory* **10** (1977), 99–127];
- binomial queues [J. Vuillemin, *CACM* **12** (1978), 309–315; M. R. Brown, *SICOMP* **7** (1978), 298–319];
- pagodas [J. Françon, G. Viennot, and J. Vuillemin, *FOCS* **19** (1978), 1–7];
- pairing heaps [M. L. Fredman, R. Sedgewick, D. D. Sleator, and R. E. Tarjan, *Algorithmica* **1** (1986), 111–129; J. T. Stasko and J. S. Vitter, *CACM* **30** (1987), 234–249];
- skew heaps [D. D. Sleator and R. E. Tarjan, *SICOMP* **15** (1986), 52–59];
- Fibonacci heaps [M. L. Fredman and R. E. Tarjan, *JACM* **34** (1987), 596–615] and the more general AF-heaps [M. L. Fredman and D. E. Willard, *J. Computer and System Sci.* **48** (1994), 533–551];
- calendar queues [R. Brown, *CACM* **31** (1988), 1220–1227; G. A. Davison, *CACM* **32** (1989), 1241–1243];
- relaxed heaps [J. R. Driscoll, H. N. Gabow, R. Shrairman, and R. E. Tarjan, *CACM* **31** (1988), 1343–1354];
- fishspear [M. J. Fischer and M. S. Paterson, *JACM* **41** (1994), 3–30];
- hot queues [B. V. Cherkassky, A. V. Goldberg, and C. Silverstein, *SODA* **8** (1997), 83–92];

etc. Not all of these methods will survive the test of time; leftist trees are in fact already obsolete, except for applications with a strong tendency towards last-in-first-out behavior. Detailed implementations and expositions of binomial queues and Fibonacci heaps can be found in D. E. Knuth, The Stanford GraphBase (New York: ACM Press, 1994), 475–489.

*Analysis of heapsort. Algorithm H is rather complicated, so it probably will never submit to a complete mathematical analysis; but several of its properties can be deduced without great difficulty. Therefore we shall conclude this section by studying the anatomy of a heap in some detail.

Figure 28 shows the shape of a heap with 26 elements; each node has been labeled in binary notation corresponding to its subscript in the heap. Asterisks in this diagram denote the *special nodes*, those that lie on the path from 1 to N.

One of the most important attributes of a heap is the collection of its subtree sizes. For example, in Fig. 28 the sizes of the subtrees rooted at $1, 2, \ldots, 26$ are, respectively,

$$26^*, 15, 10^*, 7, 7, 6^*, 3, 3, 3, 3, 3, 3, 2^*, 1, 1, 1, 1, 1, 1, 1, 1, 1, 1, 1, 1, 1^*. \qquad (12)$$

Asterisks denote *special subtrees*, rooted at the special nodes; exercise 20 shows that if the binary representation of N is

$$N = (b_n b_{n-1} \ldots b_1 b_0)_2, \qquad n = \lfloor \lg N \rfloor, \qquad (13)$$

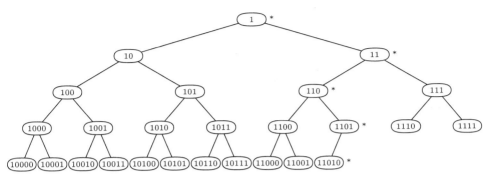

Fig. 28. A heap of $26 = (11010)_2$ elements looks like this.

then the special subtree sizes are always

$$(1b_{n-1}\ldots b_1 b_0)_2, \ (1b_{n-2}\ldots b_1 b_0)_2, \ldots, (1b_1 b_0)_2, \ (1b_0)_2, \ (1)_2. \qquad (14)$$

Nonspecial subtrees are always perfectly balanced, so their size is always of the form $2^k - 1$. Exercise 21 shows that the nonspecial sizes consist of exactly

$$\left\lfloor \frac{N-1}{2} \right\rfloor \ 1\text{s}, \ \left\lfloor \frac{N-2}{4} \right\rfloor \ 3\text{s}, \ \left\lfloor \frac{N-4}{8} \right\rfloor \ 7\text{s}, \ \ldots, \ \left\lfloor \frac{N-2^{n-1}}{2^n} \right\rfloor \ (2^n - 1)\text{s}. \quad (15)$$

For example, Fig. 28 contains twelve nonspecial subtrees of size 1, six of size 3, two of size 7, and one of size 15.

Let s_l be the size of the subtree whose root is l, and let M_N be the multiset $\{s_1, s_2, \ldots, s_N\}$ of all these sizes. We can calculate M_N easily for any given N by using (14) and (15). Exercise 5.1.4–20 tells us that the total number of ways to arrange the integers $\{1, 2, \ldots, N\}$ into a heap is

$$N!/s_1 s_2 \ldots s_N = N! \Big/ \prod \{s \mid s \in M_N\}. \qquad (16)$$

For example, the number of ways to place the 26 letters $\{A, B, C, \ldots, Z\}$ into Fig. 28 so that vertical lines preserve alphabetic order is

$$26!/(26 \cdot 10 \cdot 6 \cdot 2 \cdot 1 \cdot 1^{12} \cdot 3^6 \cdot 7^2 \cdot 15^1).$$

We are now in a position to analyze the heap-creation phase of Algorithm H, namely the computations that take place before the condition $l = 1$ occurs for the first time in step H2. Fortunately we can reduce the study of heap creation to the study of independent siftup operations, because of the following theorem.

Theorem H. *If Algorithm H is applied to a random permutation of $\{1, 2, \ldots, N\}$, each of the $N! / \prod \{s \mid s \in M_N\}$ possible heaps is an equally likely outcome of the heap-creation phase. Moreover, each of the $\lfloor N/2 \rfloor$ siftup operations performed during this phase is uniform, in the sense that each of the s_l possible values of i is equally likely when step H8 is reached.*

Proof. We can apply what numerical analysts might call a "backwards analysis"; given a possible result $K_1 \ldots K_N$ of the siftup operation rooted at l, we see that there are exactly s_l prior configurations $K_1' \ldots K_N'$ of the file that will sift up to that result. Each of these prior configurations has a different value of K_l'; hence, working backwards, there are exactly $s_l s_{l+1} \ldots s_N$ input permutations of $\{1, 2, \ldots, N\}$ that yield the configuration $K_1 \ldots K_N$ after the siftup at position l has been completed.

The case $l = 1$ is typical: Let $K_1 \ldots K_N$ be a heap, and let $K_1' \ldots K_N'$ be a file that is transformed by siftup into $K_1 \ldots K_N$ when $l = 1$, $K = K_1'$. If $K = K_i$, we must have $K_i' = K_{\lfloor i/2 \rfloor}$, $K_{\lfloor i/2 \rfloor}' = K_{\lfloor i/4 \rfloor}$, etc., while $K_j' = K_j$ for all j not on the path from 1 to i. Conversely, for each i this construction yields a file $K_1' \ldots K_N'$ such that (a) siftup transforms $K_1' \ldots K_N'$ into $K_1 \ldots K_N$, and (b) $K_{\lfloor j/2 \rfloor} \geq K_j$ for $2 \leq \lfloor j/2 \rfloor < j \leq N$. Therefore exactly N such files $K_1' \ldots K_N'$ are possible, and the siftup operation is uniform. (An example of the proof of this theorem appears in exercise 22.) ∎

Referring to the quantities A, B, C, D in the analysis of Program H, we can see that a uniform siftup operation on a subtree of size s contributes $\lfloor s/2 \rfloor / s$ to the average value of A; it contributes

$$\frac{1}{s}(0 + 1 + 1 + 2 + \cdots + \lfloor \lg s \rfloor) = \frac{1}{s} \sum_{k=1}^{s} \lfloor \lg k \rfloor = \frac{1}{s}\big((s+1)\lfloor \lg s \rfloor - 2^{\lfloor \lg s \rfloor + 1} + 2\big)$$

to the average value of B (see exercise 1.2.4–42); and it contributes either $2/s$ or 0 to the average value of D, according as s is even or odd. The corresponding contribution to C is somewhat more difficult to determine, so it has been left to the reader (see exercise 26). Summing over all siftups, we find that the average value of A during heap creation is

$$A_N' = \sum \{\lfloor s/2 \rfloor / s \mid s \in M_N\}, \tag{17}$$

and similar formulas hold for B, C, and D. It is therefore possible to compute these average values exactly without great difficulty, and the following table shows typical results:

N	A_N'	B_N'	C_N'	D_N'
99	19.18	68.35	42.95	0.00
100	19.93	69.39	42.71	1.84
999	196.16	734.66	464.53	0.00
1000	196.94	735.80	464.16	1.92
9999	1966.02	7428.18	4695.54	0.00
10000	1966.82	7429.39	4695.06	1.97
10001	1966.45	7430.07	4695.84	0.00
10002	1967.15	7430.97	4695.95	1.73

Asymptotically speaking, we may ignore the special subtree sizes in M_N, and we find for example that

$$A_N' = \frac{N}{2} \cdot \frac{0}{1} + \frac{N}{4} \cdot \frac{1}{3} + \frac{N}{8} \cdot \frac{3}{7} + \cdots + O(\log N) = \big(1 - \tfrac{1}{2}\alpha\big)N + O(\log N), \tag{18}$$

where

$$\alpha = \sum_{k \geq 1} \frac{1}{2^k - 1} = 1.60669\,51524\,15291\,76378\,33015\,23190\,92458\,04805 - . \quad (19)$$

(This value was first computed to high precision by J. W. Wrench, Jr., using the series transformation of exercise 27. Paul Erdős has proved that α is irrational [*J. Indian Math. Soc.* **12** (1948), 63–66], and Peter Borwein has demonstrated the irrationality of many similar constants [*Proc. Camb. Phil. Soc.* **112** (1992), 141–146].) For large N, we may use the approximate formulas

$$\begin{aligned}
A'_N &\approx 0.1967N + (-1)^N 0.3; \\
B'_N &\approx 0.74403N - 1.3 \ln N; \\
C'_N &\approx 0.47034N - 0.8 \ln N; \\
D'_N &\approx (1.8 \pm 0.2)[N \text{ even}].
\end{aligned} \quad (20)$$

The minimum and maximum values are also readily determined. Only $O(N)$ steps are needed to create the heap (see exercise 23).

This theory nicely explains the heap-creation phase of Algorithm H. But the selection phase is another story, which remains to be written! Let A''_N, B''_N, C''_N, and D''_N denote the average values of A, B, C, and D during the selection phase when N elements are being heapsorted. The behavior of Algorithm H on random input is subject to comparatively little fluctuation about the empirically determined average values

$$\begin{aligned}
A''_N &\approx 0.152N; \\
B''_N &\approx N \lg N - 2.61N; \\
C''_N &\approx \tfrac{1}{2}N \lg N - 1.41N; \\
D''_N &\approx \lg N \pm 2;
\end{aligned} \quad (21)$$

but no adequate theoretical explanation for the behavior of D''_N or for the conjectured constants 0.152, 2.61, or 1.41 has yet been found. The leading terms of B''_N and C''_N have, however, been established in an elegant manner by R. Schaffer and R. Sedgewick; see exercise 30. Schaffer has also proved that the minimum and maximum possible values of C''_N are respectively asymptotic to $\tfrac{1}{4}N \lg N$ and $\tfrac{3}{4}N \lg N$.

EXERCISES

1. [*10*] Is straight selection (Algorithm S) a stable sorting method?

2. [*15*] Why does it prove to be more convenient to select the largest key, then the second-largest, etc., in Algorithm S, instead of first finding the smallest, then the second-smallest, etc.?

3. [*M21*] (a) Prove that if the input to Algorithm S is a random permutation of $\{1, 2, \ldots, N\}$, then the first iteration of steps S2 and S3 yields a random permutation of $\{1, 2, \ldots, N-1\}$ followed by N. (In other words, the presence of each permutation of $\{1, 2, \ldots, N-1\}$ in $K_1 \ldots K_{N-1}$ is equally likely.) (b) Therefore if B_N denotes the

average value of the quantity B in Program S, given randomly ordered input, we have
$B_N = H_N - 1 + B_{N-1}$. [*Hint:* See Eq. 1.2.10–(16).]

▶ **4.** [*M25*] Step S3 of Algorithm S accomplishes nothing when $i = j$; is it a good idea to test whether or not $i = j$ before doing step S3? What is the average number of times the condition $i = j$ will occur in step S3 for random input?

5. [*20*] What is the value of the quantity B in the analysis of Program S, when the input is $N \ldots 3\,2\,1$?

6. [*M29*] (a) Let $a_1 a_2 \ldots a_N$ be a permutation of $\{1, 2, \ldots, N\}$ having C cycles, I inversions, and B changes to the right-to-left maxima when sorted by Program S. Prove that $2B \le I + N - C$. [*Hint:* See exercise 5.2.2–1.] (b) Show that $I + N - C \le \lfloor N^2/2 \rfloor$; hence B can never exceed $\lfloor N^2/4 \rfloor$.

7. [*M41*] Find the variance of the quantity B in Program S, as a function of N, assuming random input.

▶ **8.** [*24*] Show that if the search for $\max(K_1, \ldots, K_j)$ in step S2 is carried out by examining keys in left-to-right order $K_1, K_2, \ldots, K_j$, instead of going from right to left as in Program S, it is often possible to reduce the number of comparisons needed on the next iteration of step S2. Write a MIX program based on this observation.

9. [*M25*] What is the average number of comparisons performed by the algorithm of exercise 8, for random input?

10. [*12*] What will be the configuration of the tree in Fig. 23 after 14 of the original 16 items have been output?

11. [*10*] What will be the configuration of the tree in Fig. 24 after the element 908 has been output?

12. [*M20*] How many times will $-\infty$ be compared with $-\infty$ when the bottom-up method of Fig. 23 is used to sort a file of 2^n elements into order?

13. [*20*] (J. W. J. Williams.) Step H4 of Algorithm H distinguishes between the three cases $j < r$, $j = r$, and $j > r$. Show that if $K \ge K_{r+1}$ it would be possible to simplify step H4 so that only a two-way branch is made. How could the condition $K \ge K_{r+1}$ be ensured throughout the heapsort process, by modifying step H2?

14. [*10*] Show that simple queues are special cases of priority queues. (Explain how keys can be assigned to the elements so that a largest-in-first-out procedure is equivalent to first-in-first-out.) Is a stack also a special case of a priority queue?

▶ **15.** [*M22*] (B. A. Chartres.) Design a high-speed algorithm that builds a table of the prime numbers $\le N$, making use of a priority queue to avoid division operations. [*Hint:* Let the smallest key in the priority queue be the least odd nonprime number greater than the last odd number considered as a prime candidate. Try to minimize the number of elements in the queue.]

16. [*20*] Design an efficient algorithm that inserts a new key into a given heap of n elements, producing a heap of $n + 1$ elements.

17. [*20*] The algorithm of exercise 16 can be used for heap creation, instead of the "decrease l to 1" method used in Algorithm H. Do both methods create the same heap when they begin with the same input file?

▶ **18.** [*21*] (R. W. Floyd.) During the selection phase of heapsort, the key K tends to be quite small, so that nearly all of the comparisons in step H6 find $K < K_j$. Show how to modify the algorithm so that K is not compared with K_j in the main loop of the computation, thereby nearly cutting the average number of comparisons in half.

19. [*21*] Design an algorithm that *deletes* a given element of a heap of length N, producing a heap of length $N - 1$.

20. [*M20*] Prove that (14) gives the special subtree sizes in a heap.

21. [*M24*] Prove that (15) gives the nonspecial subtree sizes in a heap.

▸ **22.** [*20*] What permutations of $\{1, 2, 3, 4, 5\}$ are transformed into 5 3 4 1 2 by the heap-creation phase of Algorithm H?

23. [*M28*] (a) Prove that the length of scan, B, in a siftup algorithm never exceeds $\lfloor \lg (r/l) \rfloor$. (b) According to (8), B can never exceed $N \lfloor \lg N \rfloor$ in any particular application of Algorithm H. Find the maximum value of B as a function of N, taken over all possible input files. (You must prove that an input file exists such that B takes on this maximum value.)

24. [*M24*] Derive an exact formula for the standard deviation of B'_N (the total length of scan during the heap-creation phase of Algorithm H).

25. [*M20*] What is the average value of the contribution to C made during the siftup pass when $l = 1$ and $r = N$, if $N = 2^{n+1} - 1$?

26. [*M30*] Solve exercise 25, (a) for $N = 26$, (b) for general N.

27. [*M25*] (T. Clausen, 1828.) Prove that

$$\sum_{n \geq 1} \frac{x^n}{1 - x^n} = \sum_{n \geq 1} \frac{1 + x^n}{1 - x^n} x^{n^2}.$$

(Setting $x = \frac{1}{2}$ gives a very rapidly converging series for the evaluation of (19).)

28. [*35*] Explore the idea of *ternary heaps*, based on complete ternary trees instead of binary trees. Do ternary heaps sort faster than binary heaps?

29. [*26*] (W. S. Brown.) Design an algorithm for multiplication of polynomials or power series $(a_1 x^{i_1} + a_2 x^{i_2} + \cdots)(b_1 x^{j_1} + b_2 x^{j_2} + \cdots)$, in which the coefficients of the answer $c_1 x^{i_1 + j_1} + \cdots$ are generated in order as the input coefficients are being multiplied. [*Hint:* Use an appropriate priority queue.]

▸ **30.** [*HM35*] (R. Schaffer and R. Sedgewick.) Let h_{nm} be the number of heaps on the elements $\{1, 2, \ldots, n\}$ for which the selection phase of heapsort does exactly m promotions. Prove that $h_{nm} \leq 2^m \prod_{k=2}^{n} \lg k$, and use this relation to show that the average number of promotions performed by Algorithm H is $N \lg N + O(N \log \log N)$.

31. [*37*] (J. W. J. Williams.) Show that if two heaps are placed "back to back" in a suitable way, it is possible to maintain a structure in which either the smallest or the largest element can be deleted at any time in $O(\log n)$ steps. (Such a structure may be called a *priority deque*.)

32. [*M28*] Prove that the number of heapsort promotions, B, is always at least $\frac{1}{2} N \lg N + O(N)$, if the keys being sorted are distinct. *Hint:* Consider the movement of the largest $\lceil N/2 \rceil$ keys.

33. [*21*] Design an algorithm that merges two disjoint priority queues, represented as leftist trees, into one. (In particular, if one of the given queues contains a single element, your algorithm will insert it into the other queue.)

34. [*M41*] How many leftist trees with N nodes are possible, ignoring the KEY values? The sequence begins 1, 1, 2, 4, 8, 17, 38, 87, 203, 482, 1160, ...; show that the number is asymptotically $ab^N N^{-3/2}$ for suitable constants a and b, using techniques like those of exercise 2.3.4.4–4.

35. [*26*] If UP links are added to a leftist tree (see the discussion of triply linked trees in Section 6.2.3), it is possible to delete an arbitrary node P from within the priority queue as follows: Replace P by the merger of LEFT(P) and RIGHT(P); then adjust the DIST fields of P's ancestors, possibly swapping left and right subtrees, until either reaching the root or reaching a node whose DIST is unchanged.

Prove that this process never requires changing more than $O(\log N)$ of the DIST fields, if there are N nodes in the tree, even though the tree may contain very long upward paths.

36. [*18*] (*Least-recently-used page replacement.*) Many operating systems make use of the following type of algorithm: A collection of nodes is subjected to two operations, (i) "using" a node, and (ii) replacing the least-recently-used node by a new node. What data structure makes it easy to ascertain the least-recently-used node?

37. [*HM32*] Let $e_N(k)$ be the expected treewise distance of the kth-largest element from the root, in a random heap of N elements, and let $e(k) = \lim_{N\to\infty} e_N(k)$. Thus $e(1) = 0$, $e(2) = 1$, $e(3) = 1.5$, and $e(4) = 1.875$. Find the asymptotic value of $e(k)$ to within $O(k^{-1})$.

38. [*M21*] Find a simple recurrence relation for the multiset M_N of subtree sizes in a heap or in a complete binary tree with N internal nodes.

5.2.4. Sorting by Merging

Merging (or *collating*) means the combination of two or more ordered files into a single ordered file. For example, we can merge the two files 503 703 765 and 087 512 677 to obtain 087 503 512 677 703 765. A simple way to accomplish this is to compare the two smallest items, output the smallest, and then repeat the same process. Starting with

$$\left\{ \begin{array}{l} 503\ 703\ 765 \\ 087\ 512\ 677 \end{array} \right.$$

we obtain

$$087 \left\{ \begin{array}{l} 503\ 703\ 765 \\ 512\ 677 \end{array} \right.$$

then

$$087\ 503 \left\{ \begin{array}{l} 703\ 765 \\ 512\ 677 \end{array} \right.$$

and

$$087\ 503\ 512 \left\{ \begin{array}{l} 703\ 765 \\ 677 \end{array} \right.$$

and so on. Some care is necessary when one of the two files becomes exhausted; a detailed description of the process appears in the following algorithm:

Algorithm M (*Two-way merge*). This algorithm merges nonempty ordered files $x_1 \le x_2 \le \cdots \le x_m$ and $y_1 \le y_2 \le \cdots \le y_n$ into a single file $z_1 \le z_2 \le \cdots \le z_{m+n}$.

M1. [Initialize.] Set $i \leftarrow 1$, $j \leftarrow 1$, $k \leftarrow 1$.

M2. [Find smaller.] If $x_i \le y_j$, go to step M3, otherwise go to M5.

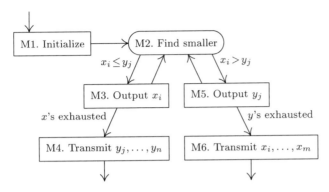

Fig. 29. Merging $x_1 \leq \cdots \leq x_m$ with $y_1 \leq \cdots \leq y_n$.

M3. [Output x_i.] Set $z_k \leftarrow x_i$, $k \leftarrow k+1$, $i \leftarrow i+1$. If $i \leq m$, return to M2.

M4. [Transmit $y_j, \ldots, y_n$.] Set $(z_k, \ldots, z_{m+n}) \leftarrow (y_j, \ldots, y_n)$ and terminate the algorithm.

M5. [Output y_j.] Set $z_k \leftarrow y_j$, $k \leftarrow k+1$, $j \leftarrow j+1$. If $j \leq n$, return to M2.

M6. [Transmit $x_i, \ldots, x_m$.] Set $(z_k, \ldots, z_{m+n}) \leftarrow (x_i, \ldots, x_m)$ and terminate the algorithm. ▮

We shall see in Section 5.3.2 that this straightforward procedure is essentially the best possible way to merge on a conventional computer, when $m \approx n$. (On the other hand, when m is much smaller than n, it is possible to devise more efficient merging algorithms, although they are rather complicated in general.) Algorithm M could be made slightly simpler without much loss of efficiency by placing sentinel elements $x_{m+1} = y_{n+1} = \infty$ at the end of the input files, stopping just before ∞ is output. For an analysis of Algorithm M, see exercise 2.

The total amount of work involved in Algorithm M is essentially proportional to $m + n$, so it is clear that merging is a simpler problem than sorting. Furthermore, we can reduce the problem of sorting to merging, because we can repeatedly merge longer and longer subfiles until everything is in sort. We may consider this to be an extension of the idea of insertion sorting: Inserting a new element into a sorted file is the special case $n = 1$ of merging. If we want to speed up the insertion process we can consider inserting several elements at a time, "batching" them, and this leads naturally to the general idea of merge sorting. From a historical point of view, merge sorting was one of the very first methods proposed for computer sorting; it was suggested by John von Neumann as early as 1945 (see Section 5.5).

We shall study merging in considerable detail in Section 5.4, with regard to external sorting algorithms; our main concern in the present section is the somewhat simpler question of merge sorting within a high-speed random-access memory.

Table 1 shows a merge sort that "burns the candle at both ends" in a manner similar to the scanning procedure we have used in quicksort and radix exchange: We examine the input from the left and from the right, working towards the middle. Ignoring the top line of the table for a moment, let us consider the transformation from line 2 to line 3. At the left we have the ascending run 503 703 765; at the right, reading leftwards, we have the run 087 512 677. Merging these two sequences leads to 087 503 512 677 703 765, which is placed at the left of line 3. Then the keys 061 612 908 in line 2 are merged with 170 509 897, and the result (061 170 509 612 897 908) is recorded at the *right* end of line 3. Finally, 154 275 426 653 is merged with 653 — discovering the overlap before it causes any harm — and the result is placed at the left, following the previous run. Line 2 of the table was formed in the same way from the original input in line 1.

Table 1
NATURAL TWO-WAY MERGE SORTING

```
503| 087 512| 061 908| 170 897| 275 |653| 426 154 |509 |612 |677 |765 703

503 703 765| 061 612 908| 154 275 426 |653||897 509 170 |677 512 087

087 503 512 677 703 765| 154 275 426 |653||908 897 612 509 170 061

061 087 170 503 509 512 612 677 703 765 897 |908| 653 426 275 154

061 087 154 170 275 426 503 509 512 612 653 677 703 765 897 |908|
```

Vertical lines in Table 1 represent the boundaries between runs. They are the so-called *stepdowns*, where a smaller element follows a larger one in the direction of reading. We generally encounter an ambiguous situation in the middle of the file, when we read the same key from both directions; this causes no problem if we are a little bit careful as in the following algorithm. The method is traditionally called a "natural" merge because it makes use of the runs that occur naturally in its input.

Algorithm N (*Natural two-way merge sort*). Records $R_1, \ldots, R_N$ are sorted using two areas of memory, each of which is capable of holding N records. For convenience, we shall say that the records of the second area are $R_{N+1}, \ldots, R_{2N}$, although it is not really necessary that R_{N+1} be adjacent to R_N. The initial contents of $R_{N+1}, \ldots, R_{2N}$ are immaterial. After sorting is complete, the keys will be in order, $K_1 \leq \cdots \leq K_N$.

N1. [Initialize.] Set $s \leftarrow 0$. (When $s = 0$, we will be transferring records from the $(R_1, \ldots, R_N)$ area to the $(R_{N+1}, \ldots, R_{2N})$ area; when $s = 1$, we will be going the other way.)

N2. [Prepare for pass.] If $s = 0$, set $i \leftarrow 1$, $j \leftarrow N$, $k \leftarrow N + 1$, $l \leftarrow 2N$; if $s = 1$, set $i \leftarrow N + 1$, $j \leftarrow 2N$, $k \leftarrow 1$, $l \leftarrow N$. (Variables i, j, k, l point to the current positions in the "source files" being read and the "destination files" being written.) Set $d \leftarrow 1$, $f \leftarrow 1$. (Variable d gives the current direction of output; f is set to zero if future passes are necessary.)

N3. [Compare $K_i : K_j$.] If $K_i > K_j$, go to step N8. If $i = j$, set $R_k \leftarrow R_i$ and go to N13.

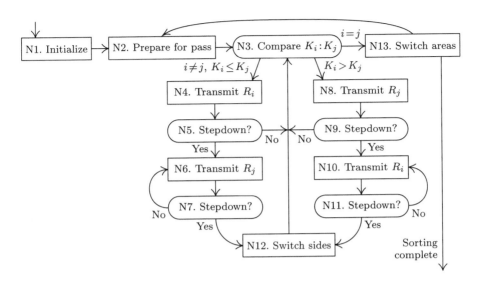

Fig. 30. Merge sorting.

N4. [Transmit R_i.] (Steps N4–N7 are analogous to steps M3–M4 of Algorithm M.) Set $R_k \leftarrow R_i$, $k \leftarrow k + d$.

N5. [Stepdown?] Increase i by 1. Then if $K_{i-1} \leq K_i$, go back to step N3.

N6. [Transmit R_j.] Set $R_k \leftarrow R_j$, $k \leftarrow k + d$.

N7. [Stepdown?] Decrease j by 1. Then if $K_{j+1} \leq K_j$, go back to step N6; otherwise go to step N12.

N8. [Transmit R_j.] (Steps N8–N11 are dual to steps N4–N7.) Set $R_k \leftarrow R_j$, $k \leftarrow k + d$.

N9. [Stepdown?] Decrease j by 1. Then if $K_{j+1} \leq K_j$, go back to step N3.

N10. [Transmit R_i.] Set $R_k \leftarrow R_i$, $k \leftarrow k + d$.

N11. [Stepdown?] Increase i by 1. Then if $K_{i-1} \leq K_i$, go back to step N10.

N12. [Switch sides.] Set $f \leftarrow 0$, $d \leftarrow -d$, and interchange $k \leftrightarrow l$. Return to step N3.

N13. [Switch areas.] If $f = 0$, set $s \leftarrow 1 - s$ and return to N2. Otherwise sorting is complete; if $s = 0$, set $(R_1, \ldots, R_N) \leftarrow (R_{N+1}, \ldots, R_{2N})$. (This last copying operation is unnecessary if it is acceptable to have the output in $(R_{N+1}, \ldots, R_{2N})$ about half of the time.) ∎

This algorithm contains one tricky feature that is explained in exercise 5.

It would not be difficult to program Algorithm N for MIX, but we can deduce the essential facts of its behavior without constructing the entire program. The number of ascending runs in the input will be about $\frac{1}{2}N$, under random conditions, since we have $K_i > K_{i+1}$ with probability $\frac{1}{2}$; detailed information about the number of runs, under slightly different hypotheses, has been derived in Section 5.1.3. Each pass cuts the number of runs in half (except in unusual cases such as the situation in exercise 6). So the number of passes will usually be about $\lg \frac{1}{2}N = \lg N - 1$. Each pass requires us to transmit each of the N records, and by exercise 2 most of the time is spent in steps N3, N4, N5, N8, N9. We can sketch the time in the inner loop as follows, if we assume that there is low probability of equal keys:

	Step	Operations	Time
	$N3$	CMPA, JG, JE	$3.5u$
Either $\{$	$N4$	STA, INC	$3u$
	$N5$	INC, LDA, CMPA, JGE	$6u$
Or $\{$	$N8$	STX, INC	$3u$
	$N9$	DEC, LDX, CMPX, JGE	$6u$

Thus about $12.5u$ is spent on each record in each pass, and the total running time will be asymptotically $12.5N \lg N$, for both the average case and the worst case. This is slower than quicksort's average time, and it may not be enough better than heapsort to justify taking twice as much memory space, since the asymptotic running time of Program 5.2.3H is never more than $18N \lg N$.

The boundary lines between runs are determined in Algorithm N entirely by stepdowns. This has the possible advantage that input files with a preponderance of increasing order can be handled very quickly, and so can input files with a preponderance of decreasing order; but it slows down the main loop of the calculation. Instead of testing stepdowns, we can determine the length of runs artificially, by saying that all runs in the input have length 1, all runs after the first pass (except possibly the last run) have length 2, ..., all runs after k passes (except possibly the last run) have length 2^k. This is called a *straight* two-merge, as opposed to the "natural" merge in Algorithm N.

Straight two-way merging is very similar to Algorithm N, and it has essentially the same flow chart; but things are sufficiently different that we had better write down the whole algorithm again:

Algorithm S (*Straight two-way merge sort*).   Records $R_1, \ldots, R_N$ are sorted using two memory areas as in Algorithm N.

S1. [Initialize.] Set $s \leftarrow 0$, $p \leftarrow 1$. (For the significance of variables s, i, j, k, l, and d, see Algorithm N. Here p represents the size of ascending runs to be merged on the current pass; further variables q and r will keep track of the number of unmerged items in a run.)

S2. [Prepare for pass.] If $s = 0$, set $i \leftarrow 1$, $j \leftarrow N$, $k \leftarrow N$, $l \leftarrow 2N+1$; if $s = 1$, set $i \leftarrow N+1$, $j \leftarrow 2N$, $k \leftarrow 0$, $l \leftarrow N+1$. Then set $d \leftarrow 1$, $q \leftarrow p$, $r \leftarrow p$.

S3. [Compare $K_i : K_j$.] If $K_i > K_j$, go to step S8.

S4. [Transmit R_i.] Set $k \leftarrow k + d$, $R_k \leftarrow R_i$.

S5. [End of run?] Set $i \leftarrow i + 1$, $q \leftarrow q - 1$. If $q > 0$, go back to step S3.

S6. [Transmit R_j.] Set $k \leftarrow k + d$. Then if $k = l$, go to step S13; otherwise set $R_k \leftarrow R_j$.

Table 2

STRAIGHT TWO-WAY MERGE SORTING

503	087	512	061	908	170	897	275	653	426	154	509	612	677	765	703
503	703	512	677	509	908	426	897	653	275	170	154	612	061	765	087
087	503	703	765	154	170	509	908	897	653	426	275	677	612	512	061
061	087	503	512	612	677	703	765	908	897	653	509	426	275	170	154
061	087	154	170	275	426	503	509	512	612	653	677	703	765	897	908

S7. [End of run?] Set $j \leftarrow j - 1$, $r \leftarrow r - 1$. If $r > 0$, go back to step S6; otherwise go to S12.

S8. [Transmit R_j.] Set $k \leftarrow k + d$, $R_k \leftarrow R_j$.

S9. [End of run?] Set $j \leftarrow j - 1$, $r \leftarrow r - 1$. If $r > 0$, go back to step S3.

S10. [Transmit R_i.] Set $k \leftarrow k + d$. Then if $k = l$, go to step S13; otherwise set $R_k \leftarrow R_i$.

S11. [End of run?] Set $i \leftarrow i + 1$, $q \leftarrow q - 1$. If $q > 0$, go back to step S10.

S12. [Switch sides.] Set $q \leftarrow p$, $r \leftarrow p$, $d \leftarrow -d$, and interchange $k \leftrightarrow l$. If $j - i < p$, return to step S10; otherwise return to S3.

S13. [Switch areas.] Set $p \leftarrow p + p$. If $p < N$, set $s \leftarrow 1 - s$ and return to S2. Otherwise sorting is complete; if $s = 0$, set

$$(R_1, \ldots, R_N) \leftarrow (R_{N+1}, \ldots, R_{2N}).$$

(The latter copying operation will be done if and only if $\lceil \lg N \rceil$ is odd, regardless of the distribution of the input. Therefore it is possible to predict the location of the sorted output in advance, and copying will usually be unnecessary.) ▌

An example of this algorithm appears in Table 2. It is somewhat amazing that the method works properly when N is not a power of 2; the runs being merged are not all of length 2^k, yet no provision has apparently been made for the exceptions! (See exercise 8.) The former tests for stepdowns have been replaced by decrementing q or r and testing the result for zero; this reduces the asymptotic MIX running time to $11N \lg N$ units, slightly faster than we were able to achieve with Algorithm N.

In practice it would be worthwhile to combine Algorithm S with straight insertion; we can sort groups of, say, 16 items using straight insertion, in place of the first four passes of Algorithm S, thereby avoiding the comparatively wasteful bookkeeping operations involved in short merges. As we saw with quicksort, such a combination of methods does not affect the asymptotic running time, but it gives us a reasonable improvement nevertheless.

Let us now study Algorithms N and S from the standpoint of data structures. Why did we need $2N$ record locations instead of N? The reason is comparatively simple: We were dealing with four lists of varying size (two source lists and two destination lists on each pass); and we were using the standard "growing together" idea discussed in Section 2.2.2, for each pair of sequentially allocated lists. But half of the memory space was always unused, and a little reflection shows that we could really make use of a *linked* allocation for the four lists. If we add one link field to each of the N records, we can do everything required by the merging algorithms using simple link manipulations, without moving the records at all! Adding N link fields is generally better than adding the space needed for N more records, and the reduced record movement may also save us time, unless our computer memory is especially good at sequential reading and writing. Therefore we ought to consider also a merging algorithm like the following one:

Algorithm L (*List merge sort*). Records $R_1, \ldots, R_N$ are assumed to contain keys $K_1, \ldots, K_N$, together with link fields $L_1, \ldots, L_N$ capable of holding the numbers $-(N+1)$ through $(N+1)$. There are two auxiliary link fields L_0 and L_{N+1} in artificial records R_0 and R_{N+1} at the beginning and end of the file. This algorithm is a "list sort" that sets the link fields so that the records are linked together in ascending order. After sorting is complete, L_0 will be the index of the record with the smallest key; and L_k, for $1 \le k \le N$, will be the index of the record that follows R_k, or $L_k = 0$ if R_k is the record with the largest key. (See Eq. 5.2.1–(13).)

During the course of this algorithm, R_0 and R_{N+1} serve as list heads for two linear lists whose sublists are being merged. A negative link denotes the end of a sublist known to be ordered; a zero link denotes the end of the entire list. We assume that $N \ge 2$.

The notation "$|L_s| \leftarrow p$" means "Set L_s to p or $-p$, retaining the previous sign of L_s." This operation is well-suited to MIX, but unfortunately not to most computers; it is possible to modify the algorithm in straightforward ways to obtain an equally efficient method for most other machines.

L1. [Prepare two lists.] Set $L_0 \leftarrow 1$, $L_{N+1} \leftarrow 2$, $L_i \leftarrow -(i+2)$ for $1 \le i \le N-2$, and $L_{N-1} \leftarrow L_N \leftarrow 0$. (We have created two lists containing $R_1, R_3, R_5, \ldots$ and $R_2, R_4, R_6, \ldots$, respectively; the negative links indicate that each ordered sublist consists of one element only. For another way to do this step, taking advantage of ordering that may be present in the initial data, see exercise 12.)

L2. [Begin new pass.] Set $s \leftarrow 0$, $t \leftarrow N+1$, $p \leftarrow L_s$, $q \leftarrow L_t$. If $q = 0$, the algorithm terminates. (During each pass, p and q traverse the lists being merged; s usually points to the most recently processed record of the current sublist, while t points to the end of the previously output sublist.)

L3. [Compare $K_p : K_q$.] If $K_p > K_q$, go to L6.

L4. [Advance p.] Set $|L_s| \leftarrow p$, $s \leftarrow p$, $p \leftarrow L_p$. If $p > 0$, return to L3.

L5. [Complete the sublist.] Set $L_s \leftarrow q$, $s \leftarrow t$. Then set $t \leftarrow q$ and $q \leftarrow L_q$, one or more times, until $q \le 0$. Finally go to L8.

L6. [Advance q.] (Steps L6 and L7 are dual to L4 and L5.) Set $|L_s| \leftarrow q$, $s \leftarrow q$, $q \leftarrow L_q$. If $q > 0$, return to L3.

Table 3

LIST MERGE SORTING

j	0	1	2	3	4	5	6	7	8	9	10	11	12	13	14	15	16	17
K_j	—	503	087	512	061	908	170	897	275	653	426	154	509	612	677	765	703	—
L_j	1	-3	-4	-5	-6	-7	-8	-9	-10	-11	-12	-13	-14	-15	-16	0	0	2
L_j	2	-6	1	-8	3	-10	5	-11	7	-13	9	12	-16	14	0	0	15	4
L_j	4	3	1	-11	2	-13	8	5	7	0	12	10	9	14	16	0	15	6
L_j	4	3	6	7	2	0	8	5	1	14	12	10	13	9	16	0	15	11
L_j	4	12	11	13	2	0	8	5	10	14	1	6	3	9	16	7	15	0

L7. [Complete the sublist.] Set $L_s \leftarrow p$, $s \leftarrow t$. Then set $t \leftarrow p$ and $p \leftarrow L_p$, one or more times, until $p \leq 0$.

L8. [End of pass?] (At this point, $p \leq 0$ and $q \leq 0$, since both pointers have moved to the end of their respective sublists.) Set $p \leftarrow -p$, $q \leftarrow -q$. If $q = 0$, set $|L_s| \leftarrow p$, $|L_t| \leftarrow 0$ and return to L2. Otherwise return to L3. ∎

An example of this algorithm in action appears in Table 3, where we can see the link settings each time step L2 is encountered. It is possible to rearrange the records $R_1, \ldots, R_N$ at the end of this algorithm so that their keys are in order, using the method of exercise 5.2–12. There is an interesting similarity between list merging and the addition of sparse polynomials (see Algorithm 2.2.4A).

Let us now construct a MIX program for Algorithm L, to see whether the list manipulation is advantageous from the standpoint of speed as well as space:

Program L (*List merge sort*). For convenience, we assume that records are one word long, with L_j in the (0:2) field and K_j in the (3:5) field of location INPUT + j; rI1 ≡ p, rI2 ≡ q, rI3 ≡ s, rI4 ≡ t, rA ≡ K_q; $N \geq 2$.

```
01  L       EQU   0:2                          Definition of field names
02  ABSL    EQU   1:2
03  KEY     EQU   3:5
04  START   ENT1  N-2            1             L1. Prepare two lists.
05          ENNA  2,1            N - 2
06          STA   INPUT,1(L)     N - 2         L_i ← -(i + 2).
07          DEC1  1              N - 2
08          J1P   *-3            N - 2         N - 2 ≥ i > 0.
09          ENTA  1              1
10          STA   INPUT(L)       1             L_0 ← 1.
11          ENTA  2              1
12          STA   INPUT+N+1(L)   1             L_{N+1} ← 2.
13          STZ   INPUT+N-1(L)   1             L_{N-1} ← 0.
14          STZ   INPUT+N(L)     1             L_N ← 0.
15          JMP   L2             1             To L2.
16  L3Q     LDA   INPUT,2        C'' + B'      L3. Compare K_p:K_q.
17  L3P     CMPA  INPUT,1(KEY)   C
18          JL    L6             C             To L6 if K_q < K_p.
19  L4      ST1   INPUT,3(ABSL)  C'            L4. Advance p. |L_s| ← p.
20          ENT3  0,1            C'            s ← p.
21          LD1   INPUT,1(L)     C'            p ← L_p.
22          J1P   L3P            C'            To L3 if p > 0.
```

23	L5	ST2	INPUT,3(L)	B'	*L5. Complete the sublist.* $L_s \leftarrow q$.
24		ENT3	0,4	B'	$s \leftarrow t$.
25		ENT4	0,2	D'	$t \leftarrow q$.
26		LD2	INPUT,2(L)	D'	$q \leftarrow L_q$.
27		J2P	*-2	D'	Repeat if $q > 0$.
28		JMP	L8	B'	To L8.
29	L6	ST2	INPUT,3(ABSL)	C''	*L6. Advance q.* $|L_s| \leftarrow q$.
30		ENT3	0,2	C''	$s \leftarrow q$.
31		LD2	INPUT,2(L)	C''	$q \leftarrow L_q$.
32		J2P	L3Q	C''	To L3 if $q > 0$.
33	L7	ST1	INPUT,3(L)	B''	*L7. Complete the sublist.* $L_s \leftarrow p$.
34		ENT3	0,4	B''	$s \leftarrow t$.
35		ENT4	0,1	D''	$t \leftarrow p$.
36		LD1	INPUT,1(L)	D''	$p \leftarrow L_p$.
37		J1P	*-2	D''	Repeat if $p > 0$.
38	L8	ENN1	0,1	B	*L8. End of pass?* $p \leftarrow -p$.
39		ENN2	0,2	B	$q \leftarrow -q$.
40		J2NZ	L3Q	B	To L3 if $q \neq 0$.
41		ST1	INPUT,3(ABSL)	A	$|L_s| \leftarrow p$.
42		STZ	INPUT,4(ABSL)	A	$|L_t| \leftarrow 0$.
43	L2	ENT3	0	$A+1$	*L2. Begin new pass.* $s \leftarrow 0$.
44		ENT4	N+1	$A+1$	$t \leftarrow N + 1$.
45		LD1	INPUT(L)	$A+1$	$p \leftarrow L_s$.
46		LD2	INPUT+N+1(L)	$A+1$	$q \leftarrow L_t$.
47		J2NZ	L3Q	$A+1$	To L3 if $q \neq 0$. ▮

The running time of this program can be deduced using techniques we have seen many times before (see exercises 13 and 14); it comes to approximately $(10N \lg N + 4.92N)u$ on the average, with a small standard deviation of order $\sqrt{N}$. Exercise 15 shows that the running time can be reduced to about $9N \lg N$ at the expense of a somewhat longer program.

Thus we have a clear victory for linked-memory techniques over sequential allocation, when internal merging is being done: Less memory space is required, and the program runs about 10 to 20 percent faster. Similar algorithms have been published by L. J. Woodrum [*IBM Systems J.* **8** (1969), 189–203] and A. D. Woodall [*Comp. J.* **13** (1970), 110–111.]

EXERCISES

1. [*21*] Generalize Algorithm M to a *k-way merge* of the input files $x_{i1} \leq \cdots \leq x_{im_i}$ for $i = 1, 2, \ldots, k$.

2. [*M24*] Assuming that each of the $\binom{m+n}{m}$ possible arrangement of m x's among n y's is equally likely, find the mean and standard deviation of the number of times step M2 is performed during Algorithm M. What are the maximum and minimum values of this quantity?

▶ **3.** [*20*] (*Updating.*) Given records $R_1, \ldots, R_M$ and $R'_1, \ldots, R'_N$ whose keys are distinct and in order, so that $K_1 < \cdots < K_M$ and $K'_1 < \cdots K'_N$, show how to modify Algorithm M to obtain a merged file in which records R_i of the first file have been *discarded* if their key appears also in the second file.

4. [*21*] The text observes that merge sorting may be regarded as a generalization of insertion sorting. Show that merge sorting is also strongly related to tree selection sorting as depicted in Fig. 23.

▶ **5.** [*21*] Prove that i can never be equal to j in steps N6 or N10. (Therefore it is unnecessary to test for a possible jump to N13 in those steps.)

6. [*22*] Find a permutation $K_1 K_2 \ldots K_{16}$ of $\{1, 2, \ldots, 16\}$ such that

$$K_2 > K_3, \quad K_4 > K_5, \quad K_6 > K_7, \quad K_8 > K_9, \quad K_{10} < K_{11}, \quad K_{12} < K_{13}, \quad K_{14} < K_{15},$$

yet Algorithm N will sort the file in only two passes. (Since there are eight or more runs, we would expect to have at least four runs after the first pass, two runs after the second pass, and sorting would ordinarily not be complete until after at least three passes. How can we get by with only two passes?)

7. [*16*] Give a formula for the exact number of passes required by Algorithm S, as a function of N.

8. [*22*] During Algorithm S, the variables q and r are supposed to represent the lengths of the unmerged elements in the runs currently being processed; q and r both start out equal to p, while the runs are not always this long. How can this possibly work?

9. [*24*] Write a MIX program for Algorithm S. Specify the instruction frequencies in terms of quantities analogous to $A, B', B'', C', \ldots$ in Program L.

10. [*25*] (D. A. Bell.) Show that sequentially allocated straight two-way merging can be done with at most $\frac{3}{2} N$ memory locations, instead of $2N$ as in Algorithm S.

11. [*21*] Is Algorithm L a stable sorting method?

▶ **12.** [*22*] Revise step L1 of Algorithm L so that the two-way merge is "natural," taking advantage of ascending runs that are initially present. (In particular, if the input is already sorted, step L2 should terminate the algorithm immediately after your step L1 has acted.)

▶ **13.** [*M34*] Give an analysis of the average running time of Program L, in the style of other analyses in this chapter: Interpret the quantities $A, B, B', \ldots$, and explain how to compute their exact average values. How long does Program L take to sort the 16 numbers in Table 3?

14. [*M24*] Let the binary representation of N be $2^{e_1} + 2^{e_2} + \cdots + 2^{e_t}$, where $e_1 > e_2 > \cdots > e_t \geq 0$, $t \geq 1$. Prove that the maximum number of key comparisons performed by Algorithm L is $1 - 2^{e_t} + \sum_{k=1}^{t} (e_k + k - 1) 2^{e_k}$.

15. [*20*] Hand simulation of Algorithm L reveals that it occasionally does redundant operations; the assignments $|L_s| \leftarrow p$, $|L_s| \leftarrow q$ in steps L4 and L6 are unnecessary about half of the time, since we have $L_s = p$ (or q) each time step L4 (or L6) returns to L3. How can Program L be improved so that this redundancy disappears?

16. [*28*] Design a list merging algorithm like Algorithm L but based on three-way merging.

17. [*20*] (J. McCarthy.) Let the binary representation of N be as in exercise 14, and assume that we are given N records arranged in t ordered subfiles of respective sizes $2^{e_1}, 2^{e_2}, \ldots, 2^{e_t}$. Show how to maintain this state of affairs when a new $(N+1)$st record is added and $N \leftarrow N+1$. (The resulting algorithm may be called an *online merge sort*.)

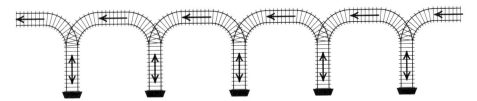

Fig. 31. A railway network with five "stacks."

18. *[40]* (M. A. Kronrod.) Given a file on N records containing only two runs,

$$K_1 \leq \cdots \leq K_M \qquad \text{and} \qquad K_{M+1} \leq \cdots \leq K_N,$$

is it possible to sort the file with $O(N)$ operations in a random-access memory, *using only a small fixed amount of additional memory space* regardless of the sizes of M and N? (All of the merging algorithms described in this section make use of extra memory space proportional to N.)

19. *[26]* Consider a railway switching network with n "stacks," as shown in Fig. 31 when $n = 5$; we considered one-stack networks in exercises 2.2.1–2 through 2.2.1–5. If N railroad cars enter at the right, we observed that only comparatively few of the $N!$ permutations of those cars could appear at the left, in the one-stack case.

In the n-stack network, assume that 2^n cars enter at the right. Prove that each of the $2^n!$ possible permutations of these cars *is* achievable at the left, by a suitable sequence of operations. (Each stack is actually much bigger than indicated in the illustration — big enough to accommodate all the cars, if necessary.)

20. *[47]* In the notation of exercise 2.2.1–4, at most a_N^n permutations of N elements can be produced with an n-stack railway network; hence the number of stacks needed to obtain all $N!$ permutations is at least $\log N! / \log a_N \approx \log_4 N$. Exercise 19 shows that at most $\lceil \lg N \rceil$ stacks are needed. What is the true rate of growth of the necessary number of stacks, as $N \to \infty$?

21. *[23]* (A. J. Smith.) Explain how to extend Algorithm L so that, in addition to sorting, it computes the number of *inversions* present in the input permutation.

22. *[28]* (J. K. R. Barnett.) Develop a way to speed up merge sorting on multiword keys. (Exercise 5.2.2–30 considers the analogous problem for quicksort.)

23. *[M30]* Exercises 13 and 14 analyze a "bottom-up" or iterative version of merge sort, where the cost $c(N)$ of sorting N items satisfies the recurrence

$$c(N) = c(2^k) + c(N - 2^k) + f(2^k, N - 2^k) \qquad \text{for } 2^k < N \leq 2^{k+1}$$

and $f(m, n)$ is the cost of merging m things with n. Study the "top-down" or divide-and-conquer recurrence

$$c(N) = c(\lceil N/2 \rceil) + c(\lfloor N/2 \rfloor) + f(\lceil N/2 \rceil, \lfloor N/2 \rfloor) \qquad \text{for } N > 1,$$

which arises when merge sort is programmed recursively.

5.2.5. Sorting by Distribution

We come now to an interesting class of sorting methods that are essentially the exact *opposite* of merging, when considered from a standpoint we shall discuss in Section 5.4.7. These methods were used to sort punched cards for many years, long before electronic computers existed. The same approach can be adapted to computer programming, and it is generally known as "bucket sorting," "radix sorting," or "digital sorting," because it is based on the digits of the keys.

Suppose we want to sort a 52-card deck of playing cards. We may define

$$A < 2 < 3 < 4 < 5 < 6 < 7 < 8 < 9 < 10 < J < Q < K,$$

as an ordering of the face values, and for the suits we may define

$$\clubsuit < \diamondsuit < \heartsuit < \spadesuit.$$

One card is to precede another if either (i) its suit is less than the other suit, or (ii) its suit equals the other suit but its face value is less. (This is a particular case of *lexicographic ordering* between ordered pairs of objects; see exercise 5–2.) Thus

$$A\clubsuit < 2\clubsuit < \cdots < K\clubsuit < A\diamondsuit < \cdots < Q\spadesuit < K\spadesuit.$$

We could sort the cards by any of the methods already discussed. Card players often use a technique somewhat analogous to the idea behind radix exchange: First they divide the cards into four piles, according to suit, then they fiddle with each individual pile until everything is in order.

But there is a faster way to do the trick! First deal the cards face up into 13 piles, one for each face value. Then collect these piles by putting the aces on the bottom, the 2s face up on top of them, then the 3s, etc., finally putting the kings (face up) on top. Turn the deck face down and deal again, this time into four piles for the four suits. (Again you turn the cards face up as you deal them.) By putting the resulting piles together, with clubs on the bottom, then diamonds, hearts, and spades, you'll get the deck in perfect order.

The same idea applies to the sorting of numbers and alphabetic data. Why does it work? Because (in our playing card example) if two cards go into different piles in the final deal, they have different suits, so the one with the lower suit is lowest. But if two cards have the same suit (and consequently go into the same pile), they are already in proper order because of the previous sorting. In other words, the face values will be in increasing order, on each of the four piles, as we deal the cards on the second pass. The same proof can be abstracted to show that any lexicographic ordering can be sorted in this way; for details, see the answer to exercise 5–2, at the beginning of this chapter.

The sorting method just described is not immediately obvious, and it isn't clear who first discovered the fact that it works so conveniently. A 19-page pamphlet entitled "The Inventory Simplified," published by the Tabulating Machines Company division of IBM in 1923, presented an interesting Digit Plan method for forming sums of products on their Electric Sorting Machine: Suppose, for example, that we want to multiply the number punched in columns 1–10 by the number punched in columns 23–25, and to sum all of these products for a large number of cards. We can sort first on column 25, then use the Tabulating Machine to find the quantities $a_1, a_2, \ldots, a_9$, where a_k is the total of columns 1–10 summed over all cards having k in column 25. Then we can sort on column 24, finding the analogous totals $b_1, b_2, \ldots, b_9$; also on column 23, obtaining $c_1, c_2, \ldots, c_9$. The desired sum of products is easily seen to be

$$a_1 + 2a_2 + \cdots + 9a_9 + 10b_1 + 20b_2 + \cdots + 90b_9 + 100c_1 + 200c_2 + \cdots + 900c_9.$$

This punched-card tabulating method leads naturally to the discovery of least-significant-digit-first radix sorting, so it probably became known to the machine operators. The first published reference to this principle for sorting appears in L. J. Comrie's early discussion of punched-card equipment [*Transactions of the Office Machinery Users' Assoc., Ltd.* (1929), 25–37, especially page 28].

In order to handle radix sorting inside a computer, we must decide what to do with the piles. Suppose that there are M piles; we could set aside M areas of memory, moving each record from an input area into its appropriate pile area. But this is unsatisfactory, since each area must be large enough to hold N items, and $(M+1)N$ record spaces would be required. Therefore most people rejected the idea of radix sorting within a computer, until H. H. Seward [Master's thesis, M.I.T. Digital Computer Laboratory Report R-232 (1954), 25–28] pointed out that we can achieve the same effect with only $2N$ record areas and M count fields. We simply count how many elements will lie in each of the M piles, by making a preliminary pass over the data; this tells us precisely how to allocate memory for the piles. We have already made use of the same idea in the "distribution counting sort," Algorithm 5.2D.

Thus radix sorting can be carried out as follows: Start with a distribution sort based on the *least significant digit* of the keys (in radix M notation), moving records from the input area to an auxiliary area. Then do another distribution sort, on the next least significant digit, moving the records back into the original input area; and so on, until the final pass (on the most significant digit) puts all records into the desired order.

If we have a decimal computer with 12-digit keys, and if N is rather large, we can choose $M = 1000$ (considering three decimal digits as one radix-1000 digit); then sorting will be complete in four passes, regardless of the size of N. Similarly, if we have a binary computer and a 40-bit key, we can set $M = 1024 = 2^{10}$ and complete the sorting in four passes. Actually each pass consists of three parts (counting, allocating, moving); E. H. Friend [*JACM* **3** (1956), 151] suggested combining two of those parts at the expense of M more memory locations, by accumulating the counts for pass $k+1$ while moving the records on pass k.

Table 1 shows how such a radix sort can be applied to our 16 example numbers, with $M = 10$. Radix sorting is generally not useful for such small N, so a small example like this is intended to illustrate the sufficiency rather than the efficiency of the method.

An alert, "modern" reader will note, however, that the whole idea of making digit counts for the storage allocation is tied to old-fashioned ideas about sequential data representation. We know that *linked* allocation is specifically designed to handle a set of tables of variable size, so it is natural to choose a linked data structure for radix sorting. Since we traverse each pile serially, all

Table 1

RADIX SORTING

Input area contents:	503 087 512 061 908 170 897 275 653 426 154 509 612 677 765 703
Counts for units digit distribution:	1 1 2 3 1 2 1 3 1 1
Storage allocations based on these counts:	1 2 4 7 8 10 11 14 15 16
Auxiliary area contents:	170 061 512 612 503 653 703 154 275 765 426 087 897 677 908 509
Counts for tens digit distribution:	4 2 1 0 0 2 2 3 1 1
Storage allocations based on these counts:	4 6 7 7 7 9 11 14 15 16
Input area contents:	503 703 908 509 512 612 426 653 154 061 765 170 275 677 087 897
Counts for hundreds digit distribution:	2 2 1 0 1 3 3 2 1 1
Storage allocations based on these counts:	2 4 5 5 6 9 12 14 15 16
Auxiliary area contents:	061 087 154 170 275 426 503 509 512 612 653 677 703 765 897 908

we need is a single link from each item to its successor. Furthermore, we never need to move the records; we merely adjust the links and proceed merrily down the lists. The amount of memory required is $(1 + \epsilon)N + 2\epsilon M$ records, where ϵ is the amount of space taken up by a link field. Formal details of this procedure are rather interesting since they furnish an excellent example of typical data structure manipulations, combining sequential and linked allocation:

Algorithm R (*Radix list sort*). Records $R_1, \ldots, R_N$ are each assumed to contain a LINK field. Their keys are assumed to be p-tuples

$$(a_1, a_2, \ldots, a_p), \qquad 0 \le a_i < M, \tag{1}$$

where the order is defined lexicographically so that

$$(a_1, a_2, \ldots, a_p) < (b_1, b_2, \ldots, b_p) \tag{2}$$

if and only if for some j, $1 \le j \le p$, we have

$$a_i = b_i \quad \text{for all } i < j, \qquad \text{but} \qquad a_j < b_j. \tag{3}$$

The keys may, in particular, be thought of as numbers written in radix M notation,

$$a_1 M^{p-1} + a_2 M^{p-2} \cdots + a_{p-1} M + a_p, \tag{4}$$

and in this case lexicographic order corresponds to the normal ordering of non-negative numbers. The keys may also be strings of alphabetic letters, etc.

Sorting is done by keeping M "piles" of records, in a manner that exactly parallels the action of a card sorting machine. The piles are really queues in the sense of Chapter 2, since we link them together so that they are traversed in a first-in-first-out manner. There are two pointer variables TOP[i] and BOTM[i] for each pile, $0 \le i < M$, and we assume as in Chapter 2 that

$$\text{LINK(LOC(BOTM}[i])) \equiv \text{BOTM}[i]. \tag{5}$$

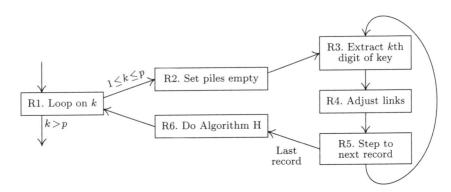

Fig. 32. Radix list sort.

R1. [Loop on k.] In the beginning, set P $\leftarrow$ LOC(R_N), a pointer to the last
record. Then perform steps R2 through R6 for $k = 1, 2, \ldots, p$. (Steps R2
through R6 constitute one "pass.") Then the algorithm terminates, with
P pointing to the record with the smallest key, LINK(P) to the record with
next smallest, then LINK(LINK(P)), etc.; the LINK in the final record will
be Λ.

R2. [Set piles empty.] Set TOP[i] $\leftarrow$ LOC(BOTM[i]) and BOTM[i] $\leftarrow$ Λ, for
$0 \le i < M$.

R3. [Extract kth digit of key.] Let KEY(P), the key in the record referenced by P,
be $(a_1, a_2, \ldots, a_p)$; set $i \leftarrow a_{p+1-k}$, the kth least significant digit of this key.

R4. [Adjust links.] Set LINK(TOP[i]) $\leftarrow$ P, then set TOP[i] $\leftarrow$ P.

R5. [Step to next record.] If $k = 1$ (the first pass) and if P = LOC(R_j), for some
$j \neq 1$, set P $\leftarrow$ LOC(R_{j-1}) and return to R3. If $k > 1$ (subsequent passes),
set P $\leftarrow$ LINK(P), and return to R3 if P $\neq \Lambda$.

R6. [Do Algorithm H.] (We are now done distributing all elements onto the
piles.) Perform Algorithm H below, which "hooks together" the individual
piles into one list, in preparation for the next pass. Then set P $\leftarrow$ BOTM[0],
a pointer to the first element of the hooked-up list. (See exercise 3.) ∎

Algorithm H (*Hooking-up of queues*). Given M queues, linked according to
the conventions of Algorithm R, this algorithm adjusts at most M links so that
a single queue is created, with BOTM[0] pointing to the first element, and with
pile 0 preceding pile 1 $\ldots$ preceding pile $M-1$.

H1. [Initialize.] Set $i \leftarrow 0$.

H2. [Point to top of pile.] Set P $\leftarrow$ TOP[i].

H3. [Next pile.] Increase i by 1. If $i = M$, set LINK(P) $\leftarrow \Lambda$ and terminate the
algorithm.

H4. [Is pile empty?] If BOTM[i] $= \Lambda$, go back to H3.

H5. [Tie piles together.] Set LINK(P) $\leftarrow$ BOTM[i]. Return to H2. ∎

Figure 33 shows the contents of the piles after each of the three passes, when our 16 example numbers are sorted with $M = 10$. Algorithm R is very easy to program for MIX, once a suitable way to treat the pass-by-pass variation of steps R3 and R5 has been found. The following program does this without sacrificing any speed in the inner loop, by overlaying two of the instructions. Note that TOP[i] and BOTM[i] can be packed into the same word.

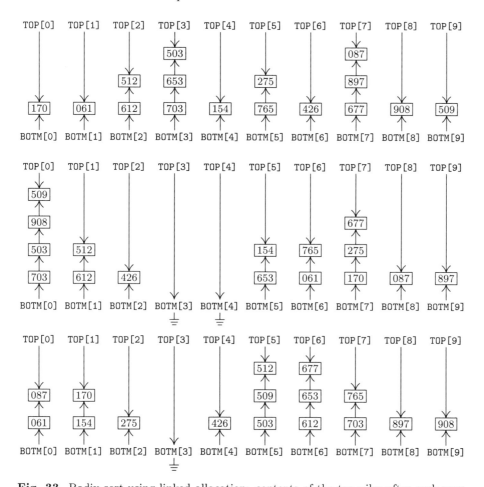

Fig. 33. Radix sort using linked allocation: contents of the ten piles after each pass.

Program R (*Radix list sort*). The given records in locations INPUT+1 through INPUT+N are assumed to have $p = 3$ components (a_1, a_2, a_3) stored respectively in the (1:1), (2:2), and (3:3) fields. (Thus M is assumed to be less than or equal to the byte size of MIX.) The (4:5) field of each record is its LINK. We let TOP[i] $\equiv$ PILES $+ i(1:2)$ and BOTM[i] $\equiv$ PILES $+ i(4:5)$, for $0 \le i < M$. It is convenient to make links relative to location INPUT, so that LOC(BOTM[i]) = PILES $+i-$ INPUT; to avoid negative links we therefore want the PILES table to be

in higher locations than the INPUT table. Index registers are assigned as follows:
rI1 ≡ P, rI2 ≡ i, rI3 ≡ $3 - k$, rI4 ≡ TOP[i]; during Algorithm H, rI2 ≡ $i - M$.

01	LINK	EQU	4:5	
02	TOP	EQU	1:2	
03	START	ENT1	N	1	R1. Loop on k. P = LOC(R_N).
04		ENT3	2	1	$k \leftarrow 1$.
05	2H	ENT2	M-1	3	R2. Set piles empty.
06		ENTA	PILES-INPUT,2	3M	LOC(BOTM[i])
07		STA	PILES,2(TOP)	3M	→ TOP[i]
08		STZ	PILES,2(LINK)	3M	BOTM[i] ← Λ.
09		DEC2	1	3M	
10		J2NN	*-4	3M	$M > i \geq 0$.
11		LDA	R3SW,3	3	
12		STA	3F	3	Modify instructions for pass k.
13		LDA	R5SW,3	3	
14		STA	5F	3	
15	3H	[LD2	INPUT,1(3:3)]		R3. Extract kth digit of key.
16	4H	LD4	PILES,2(TOP)	3N	R4. Adjust links.
17		ST1	INPUT,4(LINK)	3N	LINK(TOP[i]) ← P.
18		ST1	PILES,2(TOP)	3N	TOP[i] ← P.
19	5H	[DEC1	1]		R5. Step to next record.
20		J1NZ	3B	3N	To R3 if end of pass.
21	6H	ENN2	M	3	R6. Do Algorithm H.
22		JMP	7F	3	To H2 with $i \leftarrow 0$.
23	R3SW	LD2	INPUT,1(1:1)	N	Instruction for R3 when $k = 3$.
24		LD2	INPUT,1(2:2)	N	Instruction for R3 when $k = 2$.
25		LD2	INPUT,1(3:3)	N	Instruction for R3 when $k = 1$.
26	R5SW	LD1	INPUT,1(LINK)	N	Instruction for R5 when $k = 3$.
27		LD1	INPUT,1(LINK)	N	Instruction for R5 when $k = 2$.
28		DEC1	1	N	Instruction for R5 when $k = 1$.
29	9H	LDA	PILES+M,2(LINK)	3M-3	H4. Is pile empty?
30		JAZ	8F	3M-3	To H3 if BOTM[i] = Λ.
31		STA	INPUT,1(LINK)	3M-3-E	H5. Tie piles together.
32	7H	LD1	PILES+M,2(TOP)	3M - E	H2. Point to top of pile.
33	8H	INC2	1	3M	H3. Next pile. $i \leftarrow i + 1$.
34		J2NZ	9B	3M	To H4 if $i \neq M$.
35		STZ	INPUT,1(LINK)	3	LINK(P) ← Λ.
36		LD1	PILES(LINK)	3	P ← BOTM[0].
37		DEC3	1	3	
38		J3NN	2B	3	Loop for $1 \leq k \leq 3$. ∎

The running time of Program R is $32N + 48M + 38 - 4E$, where N is the
number of input records, M is the radix (the number of piles), and E is the
number of occurrences of empty piles. This compares very favorably with other
programs we have constructed based on similar assumptions (Programs 5.2.1M,
5.2.4L). A p-pass version of the program would take $(11p - 1)N + O(pM)$ units
of time; the critical factor in the timing is the inner loop, which involves five
references to memory and one branch. On a typical computer we will have
$M = b^r$ and $p = \lceil t/r \rceil$, where t is the number of radix-b digits in the keys;

increasing r will decrease p, so the formulas can be used to determine a best value of r.

The only variable in the timing is E, the number of empty piles observed in step H4. If we consider each of the M^N sequences of radix-M digits to be equally probable, we know from our study of the "poker test" in Section 3.3.2D that there are $M - r$ empty piles with probability

$$\frac{M(M - 1) \ldots (M - r + 1)}{M^N} \left\{ \begin{matrix} N \\ r \end{matrix} \right\} \tag{6}$$

on each pass, where $\left\{ \begin{smallmatrix} N \\ r \end{smallmatrix} \right\}$ is a Stirling number of the second kind. By exercise 6,

$$E = \left(\min \ \max(M - N, 0)p, \ \text{ave} \ M\left(1 - \frac{1}{M}\right)^N p, \ \max \ (M - 1)p \right). \tag{7}$$

An ever-increasing number of "pipeline" or "number-crunching" computers have appeared in recent years. These machines have multiple arithmetic units and look-ahead circuitry so that memory references and computation can be highly overlapped; but their efficiency deteriorates noticeably in the presence of conditional branch instructions unless the branch almost always goes the same way. The inner loop of a radix sort is well adapted to such machines, because it is a straight iterative calculation of typical number-crunching form. Therefore *radix sorting is usually more efficient than any other known method for internal sorting on such machines*, provided that N is not too small and the keys are not too long.

Of course, radix sorting is not very efficient when the keys are extremely long. For example, imagine sorting 60-digit decimal numbers with 20 passes of a radix sort, using $M = 10^3$; very few pairs of numbers will tend to have identical keys in their leading 9 digits, so the first 17 passes accomplish very little. In our analysis of radix exchange sorting, we found that it was unnecessary to inspect many bits of the key, when we looked at the keys from the left instead of the right. Let us therefore reconsider the idea of a radix sort that starts at the most significant digit (MSD) instead of the least significant digit (LSD).

We have already remarked that an MSD-first radix method suggests itself naturally; in fact, it is not hard to see why the post office uses such a method to sort mail. A large collection of letters can be sorted into separate bags for different geographical areas; each of these bags then contains a smaller number of letters that can be sorted independently of the other bags, into finer and finer geographical divisions. (Indeed, bags of letters can be transported nearer to their destinations before they are sorted further, or as they are being sorted further.) This principle of "divide and conquer" is quite appealing, and the only reason it doesn't work especially well for sorting punched cards is that it ultimately spends too much time fussing with very small piles. Algorithm R is relatively efficient, even though it considers LSD first, since we never have more than M piles, and the piles need to be hooked together only p times. On the other hand, it is not difficult to design an MSD-first radix method using linked memory, with negative links as in Algorithm 5.2.4L to denote the boundaries between piles. (See exercise 10.) The main difficulty is that empty piles tend to proliferate and to consume a great deal of time in an MSD-first method.

Perhaps the best compromise has been suggested by M. D. MacLaren [*JACM* **13** (1966), 404–411], who recommends an LSD-first sort as in Algorithm R, but *applied only to the most significant digits.* This does not completely sort the file, but it usually brings the file very nearly into order so that very few inversions remain; therefore straight insertion can be used to finish up. Our analysis of Program 5.2.1M applies also to this situation, so that if the keys are uniformly distributed we will have an average of $\frac{1}{4}N(N-1)M^{-p}$ inversions remaining in the file after sorting on the leading p digits. (See Eq. 5.2.1–(17) and exercise 5.2.1–38.) MacLaren has computed the average number of memory references per item sorted, and the optimum choice of M and p (assuming that M is a power of 2, that the keys are uniformly distributed, and that $N/M^p \le 0.1$ so that deviations from uniformity are tolerable) turns out to be given by the following table:

$N =$	100	1000	10000	100000	1000000	10^7	10^8	10^9
best $M =$	32	128	512	1024	8192	2^{15}	2^{17}	2^{19}
best $p =$	2	2	2	2	2	2	2	2
$\beta(N) =$	19.3	18.5	18.2	18.1	18.0	18.0	18.0	18.0

Here $\beta(N)$ denotes the average number of memory references per item sorted,

$$\beta(N) = 5p + 8 + \frac{2pM}{N} + \frac{N-1}{2M^p} - \frac{H_N}{N}; \qquad (8)$$

it is bounded as $N \to \infty$, if we take $p = 2$ and $M > \sqrt{N}$, so the average sorting time is actually $O(N)$ instead of order $N \log N$. This method is an improvement over multiple list insertion (Program 5.2.1M), which is essentially the case $p = 1$. Exercise 12 gives MacLaren's interesting procedure for final rearrangement of a partially list-sorted file.

It is also possible to avoid the link fields, using the methods of Algorithm 5.2D and exercise 5.2–13, so that only $O(\sqrt{N})$ memory locations are needed in addition to the space required for the records themselves. The average sorting time is proportional to N if the input records are uniformly distributed.

W. Dobosiewicz obtained good results by using an MSD-first distribution sort until reaching short subfiles, with the distribution process constrained so that the first $M/2$ piles were guaranteed to receive between 25% and 75% of the records [see *Inf. Proc. Letters* **7** (1978), 1–6; **8** (1979), 170–172]; this ensured that the average time to sort uniform keys would be $O(N)$ while the worst case would be $O(N \log N)$. His papers inspired several other researchers to devise new address calculation algorithms, of which the most instructive is perhaps the following 2-level scheme due to Markku Tamminen [*J. Algorithms* **6** (1985), 138–144]: Assume that all keys are fractions in the interval $[0 .. 1)$. First distribute the N records into $\lfloor N/8 \rfloor$ bins by mapping key K into bin $\lfloor KN/8 \rfloor$. Then suppose bin k has received N_k records; if $N_k \le 16$, sort it by straight insertion, otherwise sort if by a MacLaren-like distribution-plus-insertion sort into M^2 bins, where $M^2 \approx 10N_k$. Tamminen proved the following remarkable result:

Theorem T. *There is a constant T such that the sorting method just described performs at most TN operations on the average, whenever the keys are independent random numbers whose density function $f(x)$ is bounded and Riemann-integrable for $0 \le x \le 1$. (The constant T does not depend on f.)*

Proof. See exercise 18. Intuitively, the first distribution into $N/8$ piles finds intervals in which f is approximately constant; the second distribution will then make the expected bin size approximately constant. ∎

Several versions of radix sort that have been well tuned for sorting large arrays of alphabetic strings are described in an instructive article by P. M. McIlroy, K. Bostic, and M. D. McIlroy, *Computing Systems* **6** (1993), 5–27.

EXERCISES

▶ **1.** [*20*] The algorithm of exercise 5.2–13 shows how to do a distribution sort with only N record areas (and M count fields), instead of $2N$ record areas. Does this lead to an improvement over the radix sorting algorithm illustrated in Table 1?

2. [*13*] Is Algorithm R a stable sorting method?

3. [*15*] Explain why Algorithm H makes BOTM[0] point to the first record in the "hooked-up" queue, *even though pile 0 might be empty.*

▶ **4.** [*23*] Algorithm R keeps the M piles linked together as queues (first-in-first-out). Explore the idea of linking the piles as *stacks* instead. (The arrows in Fig. 33 would go downward instead of upward, and the BOTM table would be unnecessary.) Show that if the piles are "hooked together" in an appropriate order, it is possible to achieve a valid sorting method. Does this lead to a simpler or a faster algorithm?

5. [*20*] What changes are necessary to Program R so that it sorts eight-byte keys instead of three-byte keys? Assume that the most significant bytes of K_i are stored in location KEY$+i\,(1{:}5)$, while the three least significant bytes are in location INPUT$+i\,(1{:}3)$ as presently. What is the running time of the program, after these changes have been made?

6. [*M24*] Let $g_{MN}(z) = \sum p_{MNk}z^k$, where p_{MNk} is the probability that exactly k empty piles are present after a random radix-sort pass puts N elements into M piles.
a) Show that $g_{M(N+1)}(z) = g_{MN}(z) + ((1-z)/M)g'_{MN}(z)$.
b) Use this relation to find simple expressions for the mean and variance of this probability distribution, as a function of M and N.

7. [*20*] Discuss the similarities and differences between Algorithm R and radix exchange sorting (Algorithm 5.2.2R).

▶ **8.** [*20*] The radix-sorting algorithms discussed in the text assume that all keys being sorted are nonnegative. What changes should be made to the algorithms when the keys are numbers expressed in *two's complement* or *ones' complement* notation?

9. [*20*] Continuing exercise 8, what changes should be made to the algorithms when the keys are numbers expressed in *signed-magnitude* notation?

10. [*30*] Design an efficient most-significant-digit-first radix-sorting algorithm that uses linked memory. (As the size of the subfiles decreases, it is wise to decrease M, and to use a nonradix method on the really short subfiles.)

11. [*16*] The sixteen input numbers shown in Table 1 start with 41 inversions; after sorting is complete, of course, there are no inversions remaining. How many inversions would be present in the file if we omitted pass 1, doing a radix sort only on the tens and hundreds digits? How many inversions would be present if we omitted both pass 1 and pass 2?

12. [*24*] (M. D. MacLaren.) Suppose that Algorithm R has been applied only to the p leading digits of the actual keys; thus the file is nearly sorted when we read it in the order of the links, but keys that agree in their first p digits may be out of order. Design an algorithm that rearranges the records in place so that their keys are in order, $K_1 \le K_2 \le \cdots \le K_N$. [*Hint:* The special case that the file is perfectly sorted appears in the answer to exercise 5.2–12; it is possible to combine this with straight insertion without loss of efficiency, since few inversions remain in the file.]

13. [*40*] Implement the internal sorting method suggested in the text at the close of this section, producing a subroutine that sorts random data in $O(N)$ units of time with only $O(\sqrt{N})$ additional memory locations.

14. [*22*] The sequence of playing cards

can be sorted into increasing order A 2 ... J Q K from top to bottom in two passes, using just two piles for intermediate storage: Deal the cards face down into two piles containing respectively A 2 9 3 10 and 4 J 5 6 Q K 7 8 (from bottom to top); then put the second pile on the first, turn the deck face up, and deal into two piles A 2 3 4 5 6 7 8, 9 10 J Q K. Combine these piles, turn them face up, and you're done.

Prove that this sequence of cards cannot be sorted into *decreasing* order K Q J ... 2 A from top to bottom in two passes, even if you are allowed to use up to three piles for intermediate storage. (Dealing must always be from the top of the deck, turning the cards face down as they are dealt. Top to bottom is right to left in the illustration.)

15. [*M25*] Consider the problem of exercise 14 when all cards must be dealt face up instead of face down. Thus, one pass can be used to convert increasing order into decreasing order. How many passes are required?

▶ **16.** [*25*] Design an algorithm to sort strings $\alpha_1, \ldots, \alpha_n$ on an m-letter alphabet into lexicographic order. The total running time of your algorithm should be $O(m + n + N)$, where $N = |\alpha_1| + \cdots + |\alpha_n|$ is the total length of all the strings.

17. [*15*] In the two-level distribution sort proposed by Tamminen (see Theorem T), why is a MacLaren-like method used for the second level of distribution but not the first level?

18. [*HM26*] Prove Theorem T. *Hint:* Show first that MacLaren's distribution-plus-insertion algorithm does $O(BN)$ operations, on the average, when it is applied to independent random keys whose probability density function satisfies $f(x) \leq B$ for $0 \leq x \leq 1$.

> *For sorting the roots and words*
> *we had the use of 1100 lozenge boxes,*
> *and used trays for the forms.*
> — GEORGE V. WIGRAM (1843)

5.3. OPTIMUM SORTING

NOW THAT WE have analyzed a great many methods for internal sorting, it is time to turn to a broader question: *What is the best possible way to sort?* Can we place limits on the maximum sorting speeds that will ever be achievable, no matter how clever a programmer might be?

Of course there *is* no best possible way to sort; we must define precisely what is meant by "best," and there is no best possible way to define "best." We have discussed similar questions about the theoretical optimality of algorithms in Sections 4.3.3, 4.6.3, and 4.6.4, where high-precision multiplication and polynomial evaluation were considered. In each case it was necessary to formulate a rather simple definition of a "best possible" algorithm, in order to give sufficient structure to the problem to make it workable. And in each case we ran into interesting problems that are so difficult they still haven't been completely resolved. The same situation holds for sorting; some very interesting discoveries have been made, but many fascinating questions remain unanswered.

Studies of the inherent complexity of sorting have usually been directed towards minimizing the number of times we make comparisons between keys while sorting n items, or merging m items with n, or selecting the tth largest of an unordered set of n items. Sections 5.3.1, 5.3.2, and 5.3.3 discuss these questions in general, and Section 5.3.4 deals with similar issues under the interesting restriction that the pattern of comparisons must essentially be fixed in advance. Several other types of interesting theoretical questions related to optimum sorting appear in the exercises for Section 5.3.4, and in the discussion of external sorting (Sections 5.4.4, 5.4.8, and 5.4.9).

> As soon as an Analytical Engine exists,
> it will necessarily guide the future course of the science.
> Whenever any result is sought by its aid,
> the question will then arise —
> By what course of calculation can these
> results be arrived at by the machine
> in the shortest time?
> — CHARLES BABBAGE (1864)

5.3.1. Minimum-Comparison Sorting

The minimum number of key comparisons needed to sort n elements is obviously *zero*, because we have seen radix methods that do no comparisons at all. In fact, it is possible to write MIX programs that are able to sort, although they contain no conditional jump instructions at all! (See exercise 5–8 at the beginning of this chapter.) We have also seen several sorting methods that are based essentially on comparisons of keys, yet their running time in practice is dominated by other considerations such as data movement, housekeeping operations, etc.

Therefore it is clear that comparison counting is not the only way to measure the effectiveness of a sorting method. But it is fun to scrutinize the number of comparisons anyway, since a theoretical study of this subject gives us a good

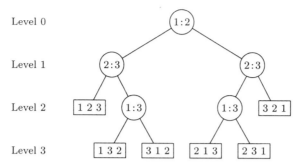

Fig. 34. A comparison tree for sorting three elements.

deal of useful insight into the nature of sorting processes, and it also helps us to sharpen our wits for the more mundane problems that confront us at other times.

In order to rule out radix-sorting methods, which do no comparisons at all, we shall restrict our discussion to sorting techniques that are based solely on an abstract linear ordering relation "$<$" between keys, as discussed at the beginning of this chapter. For simplicity, we shall also confine our discussion to the case of *distinct* keys, so that there are only two possible outcomes of any comparison of K_i versus K_j: either $K_i < K_j$ or $K_i > K_j$. (For an extension of the theory to the general case where equal keys are allowed, see exercises 3 through 12. For bounds on the worst-case running time that is needed to sort integers without the restriction to comparison-based methods, see Fredman and Willard, *J. Computer and Syst. Sci.* **47** (1993), 424–436; Ben-Amram and Galil, *J. Comp. Syst. Sci.* **54** (1997), 345–370; Thorup, *SODA* **9** (1998), 550–555.)

The problem of sorting by comparisons can also be expressed in other equivalent ways. Given a set of n distinct weights and a balance scale, we can ask for the least number of weighings necessary to completely rank the weights in order of magnitude, when the pans of the balance scale can each accommodate only one weight. Alternatively, given a set of n players in a tournament, we can ask for the smallest number of games that suffice to rank all contestants, assuming that the strengths of the players can be linearly ordered (with no ties).

All n-element sorting methods that satisfy the constraints above can be represented in terms of an extended binary tree structure such as that shown in Fig. 34. Each *internal node* (drawn as a circle) contains two indices "$i\,{:}\,j$" denoting a comparison of K_i versus K_j. The left subtree of this node represents the subsequent comparisons to be made if $K_i < K_j$, and the right subtree represents the actions to be taken when $K_i > K_j$. Each *external node* of the tree (drawn as a box) contains a permutation $a_1 a_2 \dots a_n$ of $\{1, 2, \dots, n\}$, denoting the fact that the ordering

$$K_{a_1} < K_{a_2} < \cdots < K_{a_n}$$

has been established. (If we look at the path from the root to this external node, each of the $n - 1$ relationships $K_{a_i} < K_{a_{i+1}}$ for $1 \le i < n$ will be the result of some comparison $a_i\,{:}\,a_{i+1}$ or $a_{i+1}\,{:}\,a_i$ on this path.)

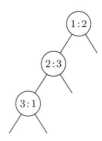

Fig. 35. Example of a redundant comparison.

Thus Fig. 34 represents a sorting method that first compares K_1 with K_2; if $K_1 > K_2$, it goes on (via the right subtree) to compare K_2 with K_3, and then if $K_2 < K_3$ it compares K_1 with K_3; finally if $K_1 > K_3$ it knows that $K_2 < K_3 < K_1$. An actual sorting algorithm will usually also move the keys around in the file, but we are interested here only in the comparisons, so we ignore all data movement. A comparison of K_i with K_j in this tree always means the *original* keys K_i and K_j, not the keys that might currently occupy the ith and jth positions of the file after the records have been shuffled around.

It is possible to make redundant comparisons; for example, in Fig. 35 there is no reason to compare 3:1, since $K_1 < K_2$ and $K_2 < K_3$ implies that $K_1 < K_3$. No permutation can possibly correspond to the left subtree of node 3:1 in Fig. 35; consequently that part of the algorithm will never be performed! Since we are interested in minimizing the number of comparisons, we may assume that no redundant comparisons are made. Hence we have an extended binary tree structure in which every external node corresponds to a permutation. All permutations of the input keys are possible, and every permutation defines a unique path from the root to an external node; it follows that *there are exactly $n!$ external nodes in a comparison tree that sorts n elements with no redundant comparisons.*

The best worst case.   The first problem that arises naturally is to find comparison trees that minimize the *maximum* number of comparisons made. (Later we shall consider the *average* number of comparisons.)

Let $S(n)$ be the minimum number of comparisons that will suffice to sort n elements. If all the internal nodes of a comparison tree are at levels $< k$, it is obvious that there can be at most 2^k external nodes in the tree. Hence, letting $k = S(n)$, we have

$$n! \le 2^{S(n)}.$$

Since $S(n)$ is an integer, we can rewrite this formula to obtain the lower bound

$$S(n) \ge \lceil \lg n! \rceil. \tag{1}$$

Stirling's approximation tells us that

$$\lceil \lg n! \rceil = n \lg n - n/\ln 2 + \tfrac{1}{2}\lg n + O(1), \tag{2}$$

hence roughly $n \lg n$ comparisons are needed.

Relation (1) is often called the *information-theoretic lower bound*, since cognoscenti of information theory would say that $\lg n!$ "bits of information" are being acquired during a sorting process; each comparison yields at most one bit of information. Trees such as Fig. 34 have also been called "questionnaires"; their mathematical properties were first explored systematically in Claude Picard's book *Théorie des Questionnaires* (Paris: Gauthier-Villars, 1965).

Of all the sorting methods we have seen, the three that require fewest comparisons are binary insertion (see Section 5.2.1), tree selection (see Section 5.2.3), and straight two-way merging (see Algorithm 5.2.4L). The maximum number of comparisons for binary insertion is readily seen to be

$$B(n) = \sum_{k=1}^{n} \lceil \lg k \rceil = n\lceil \lg n \rceil - 2^{\lceil \lg n \rceil} + 1, \tag{3}$$

by exercise 1.2.4–42, and the maximum number of comparisons in two-way merging is given in exercise 5.2.4–14. We will see in Section 5.3.3 that tree selection has the same bound on its comparisons as either binary insertion or two-way merging, depending on how the tree is set up. In all three cases we achieve an asymptotic value of $n \lg n$; combining these lower and upper bounds for $S(n)$ proves that

$$\lim_{n \to \infty} \frac{S(n)}{n \lg n} = 1. \tag{4}$$

Thus we have an approximate formula for $S(n)$, but it is desirable to obtain more precise information. The following table gives exact values of the lower and upper bounds discussed above, for small n:

$n =$	1	2	3	4	5	6	7	8	9	10	11	12	13	14	15	16	17
$\lceil \ln n! \rceil =$	0	1	3	5	7	10	13	16	19	22	26	29	33	37	41	45	49
$B(n) =$	0	1	3	5	8	11	14	17	21	25	29	33	37	41	45	49	54
$L(n) =$	0	1	3	5	9	11	14	17	25	27	30	33	38	41	45	49	65

Here $B(n)$ and $L(n)$ refer respectively to binary insertion and two-way list merging. It can be shown that $B(n) \le L(n)$ for all n (see exercise 2).

From the table above, we can see that $S(4) = 5$, but $S(5)$ might be either 7 or 8. This brings us back to a problem stated at the beginning of Section 5.2: What is the best way to sort five elements? Can five elements be sorted using only seven comparisons?

The answer is yes, but a seven-step procedure is not especially easy to discover. We begin as if we were sorting four elements by merging, first comparing $K_1:K_2$, then $K_3:K_4$, then the larger elements of these pairs. This produces a configuration that may be diagrammed as

$$\tag{5}$$

indicating that $a < b < d$ and $c < d$. (It is convenient to represent known ordering relations between elements by drawing directed graphs such as this, where x is known to be less than y if and only if there is a path from x to y in the graph.) At this point we insert the fifth element $K_5 = e$ into its proper place among $\{a, b, d\}$; only two comparisons are needed, since we may compare it first with b and then with a or d. This leaves one of four possibilities,

$$(6)$$

and in each case we can insert c among the remaining elements less than d in two more comparisons. This method for sorting five elements was first found by H. B. Demuth [Ph.D. thesis, Stanford University (1956), 41–43].

Merge insertion. A pleasant generalization of the method above has been discovered by Lester Ford, Jr. and Selmer Johnson. Since it involves some aspects of merging and some aspects of insertion, we shall call it *merge insertion*. For example, consider the problem of sorting 21 elements. We start by comparing the ten pairs $K_1:K_2, K_3:K_4, \ldots, K_{19}:K_{20}$; then we sort the ten larger elements of the pairs, using merge insertion. As a result we obtain the configuration

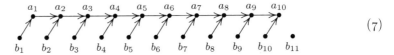

$$(7)$$

analogous to (5). The next step is to insert b_3 among $\{b_1, a_1, a_2\}$, then b_2 among the other elements less than a_2; we arrive at the configuration

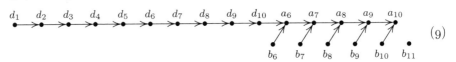

$$(8)$$

Let us call the upper-line elements the *main chain*. We can insert b_5 into its proper place in the main chain, using three comparisons (first comparing it to c_4, then c_2 or c_6, etc.); then b_4 can be moved into the main chain in three more steps, leading to

$$(9)$$

The next step is crucial; is it clear what to do? We insert b_{11} (*not* b_7) into the main chain, using only four comparisons. Then $b_{10}, b_9, b_8, b_7, b_6$ (in this order) can also be inserted into their proper places in the main chain, using at most four comparisons each.

A careful count of the comparisons involved here shows that the 21 elements have been sorted in at most $10 + S(10) + 2 + 2 + 3 + 3 + 4 + 4 + 4 + 4 + 4 + 4 = 66$

steps. Since

$$2^{65} < 21! < 2^{66},$$

we also know that no fewer than 66 would be possible in any event; hence

$$S(21) = 66. \tag{10}$$

(Binary insertion would have required 74 comparisons.)

    In general, merge insertion proceeds as follows for n elements:

i) Make pairwise comparisons of $\lfloor n/2 \rfloor$ disjoint pairs of elements. (If n is odd, leave one element out.)

ii) Sort the $\lfloor n/2 \rfloor$ larger numbers, found in step (i), by merge insertion.

iii) Name the elements $a_1, a_2, \ldots, a_{\lfloor n/2 \rfloor}, b_1, b_2, \ldots, b_{\lceil n/2 \rceil}$ as in (7), where $a_1 \leq a_2 \leq \cdots \leq a_{\lfloor n/2 \rfloor}$ and $b_i \leq a_i$ for $1 \leq i \leq \lfloor n/2 \rfloor$; call b_1 and the a's the "main chain." Insert the remaining b's into the main chain, using binary insertion, in the following order, leaving out all b_j for $j > \lceil n/2 \rceil$:

$$b_3, b_2; \; b_5, b_4; \; b_{11}, b_{10}, \ldots, b_6; \; \ldots; \; b_{t_k}, b_{t_k-1}, \ldots, b_{t_{k-1}+1}; \; \ldots \tag{11}$$

    We wish to define the sequence $(t_1, t_2, t_3, t_4, \ldots) = (1, 3, 5, 11, \ldots)$, which appears in (11), in such a way that each of $b_{t_k}, b_{t_k-1}, \ldots, b_{t_{k-1}+1}$ can be inserted into the main chain with at most k comparisons. Generalizing (7), (8), and (9), we obtain the diagram

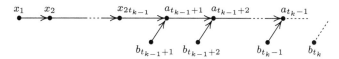

where the main chain up to and including a_{t_k-1} contains $2t_{k-1} + (t_k - t_{k-1} - 1)$ elements. This number must be less than 2^k; our best bet is to set it equal to $2^k - 1$, so that

$$t_{k-1} + t_k = 2^k. \tag{12}$$

Since $t_1 = 1$, we may set $t_0 = 1$ for convenience, and we find that

$$t_k = 2^k - t_{k-1} = 2^k - 2^{k-1} + t_{k-2} = \cdots = 2^k - 2^{k-1} + \cdots + (-1)^k 2^0$$
$$= \left(2^{k+1} + (-1)^k\right)/3 \tag{13}$$

by summing a geometric series. (Curiously, this same sequence arose in our study of an algorithm for calculating the greatest common divisor of two integers; see exercise 4.5.2–36.)

    Let $F(n)$ be the number of comparisons required to sort n elements by merge insertion. Clearly

$$F(n) = \lfloor n/2 \rfloor + F(\lfloor n/2 \rfloor) + G(\lceil n/2 \rceil), \tag{14}$$

where G represents the amount of work involved in step (iii). If $t_{k-1} \leq m \leq t_k$, we have

$$G(m) = \sum_{j=1}^{k-1} j(t_j - t_{j-1}) + k(m - t_{k-1}) = km - (t_0 + t_1 + \cdots + t_{k-1}), \tag{15}$$

summing by parts. Let us set

$$w_k = t_0 + t_1 + \cdots + t_{k-1} = \lfloor 2^{k+1}/3 \rfloor, \tag{16}$$

so that $(w_0, w_1, w_2, w_3, w_4, \ldots) = (0, 1, 2, 5, 10, 21, \ldots)$. Exercise 13 shows that

$$F(n) - F(n-1) = k \qquad \text{if and only if} \qquad w_k < n \le w_{k+1}, \tag{17}$$

and the latter condition is equivalent to

$$\frac{2^{k+1}}{3} < n \le \frac{2^{k+2}}{3},$$

or $k+1 < \lg 3n \le k+2$; hence

$$F(n) - F(n-1) = \lceil \lg \tfrac{3}{4} n \rceil. \tag{18}$$

(This formula is due to A. Hadian [Ph.D. thesis, Univ. of Minnesota (1969), 38–42].) It follows that $F(n)$ has a remarkably simple expression,

$$F(n) = \sum_{k=1}^{n} \lceil \lg \tfrac{3}{4} k \rceil, \tag{19}$$

quite similar to the corresponding formula (3) for binary insertion. A closed form for this sum appears in exercise 14.

Equation (19) makes it easy to construct a table of $F(n)$; we have

$n =$	1	2	3	4	5	6	7	8	9	10	11	12	13	14	15	16	17
$\lceil \lg n! \rceil =$	0	1	3	5	7	10	13	16	19	22	26	29	33	37	41	45	49
$F(n) =$	0	1	3	5	7	10	13	16	19	22	26	30	34	38	42	46	50

$n =$	18	19	20	21	22	23	24	25	26	27	28	29	30	31	32	33
$\lceil \lg n! \rceil =$	53	57	62	66	70	75	80	84	89	94	98	103	108	113	118	123
$F(n) =$	54	58	62	66	71	76	81	86	91	96	101	106	111	116	121	126

Notice that $F(n) = \lceil \lg n! \rceil$ for $1 \le n \le 11$ and for $20 \le n \le 21$, so we know that merge insertion is optimum for those n:

$$S(n) = \lceil \lg n! \rceil = F(n) \qquad \text{for } n = 1, \ldots, 11, 20, \text{ and } 21. \tag{20}$$

Hugo Steinhaus posed the problem of finding $S(n)$ in the second edition of his classic book *Mathematical Snapshots* (Oxford University Press, 1950), 38–39. He described the method of binary insertion, which is the best possible way to sort n objects if we start by sorting $n-1$ of them first before the nth is considered; and he conjectured that binary insertion would be optimum in general. Several years later [*Calcutta Math. Soc. Golden Jubilee Commemoration* **2** (1959), 323–327], he reported that two of his colleagues, S. Trybuła and P. Czen, had "recently" disproved his conjecture, and that they had determined $S(n)$ for $n \le 11$. Trybuła and Czen may have independently discovered the method of merge insertion, which was published soon afterwards by Ford and Johnson [*AMM* **66** (1959), 387–389].

After the discovery of merge insertion, the first unknown value of $S(n)$ was $S(12)$. Table 1 shows that $12!$ is quite close to 2^{29}, hence the existence of a

Table 1

VALUES OF FACTORIALS IN BINARY NOTATION

$$(1)_2 = 1!$$
$$(10)_2 = 2!$$
$$(110)_2 = 3!$$
$$(11000)_2 = 4!$$
$$(1111000)_2 = 5!$$
$$(1011010000)_2 = 6!$$
$$(1001110110000)_2 = 7!$$
$$(1001110110000000)_2 = 8!$$
$$(1011000100110000000)_2 = 9!$$
$$(110111010111100000000)_2 = 10!$$
$$(1001100001000101010000000)_2 = 11!$$
$$(1110010001100111110000000000)_2 = 12!$$
$$(10111001100101000110011000000000)_2 = 13!$$
$$(1010001001100001110110010100000000000)_2 = 14!$$
$$(10011000001110111011101110101100000000000)_2 = 15!$$
$$(100110000011101110111011101011000000000000000)_2 = 16!$$
$$(101000011011111101110111011001101100000000000000)_2 = 17!$$
$$(10110101111101110110011001010011100110000000000000000)_2 = 18!$$
$$(110110000001010111001001100000110100010010000000000000000)_2 = 19!$$
$$(10000111000011011001110111110010000010101101000000000000000000)_2 = 20!$$

29-step sorting procedure for 12 elements is somewhat unlikely. An exhaustive search (about 60 hours on a Maniac II computer) was therefore carried out by Mark Wells, who discovered that $S(12) = 30$ [*Proc. IFIP Congress 65* **2** (1965), 497–498; *Elements of Combinatorial Computing* (Pergamon, 1971), 213–215]. Thus the merge insertion procedure turns out to be optimum for $n = 12$ as well.

*A slightly deeper analysis. In order to study $S(n)$ more carefully, let us look more closely at partial ordering diagrams such as (5). After several comparisons have been made, we can represent the knowledge we have gained in terms of a directed graph. This directed graph contains no cycles, in view of the transitivity of the $<$ relation, so we can draw it in such a way that all arcs go from left to right; it is therefore convenient to leave arrows off the diagram. In this way (5) becomes

$$(21)$$

If G is such a directed graph, let $T(G)$ be the number of permutations consistent with G, that is, the number of ways to assign the integers $\{1, 2, \ldots, n\}$ to the vertices of G so that the number on vertex x is less than the number on vertex y whenever $x \to y$ in G. For example, one of the permutations consistent with (21) has $a = 1$, $b = 4$, $c = 2$, $d = 5$, $e = 3$. We have studied $T(G)$ for various G in Section 5.1.4, where we observed that $T(G)$ is the number of ways in which G can be sorted topologically.

If G is a graph on n elements that can be obtained after k comparisons, we define the *efficiency* of G to be

$$E(G) = \frac{n!}{2^k T(G)}. \tag{22}$$

(This idea is due to Frank Hwang and Shen Lin.) Strictly speaking, the efficiency is not a function of the graph G alone, it depends on the way we arrived at G during a sorting process, but it is convenient to be a little careless in our language. After making one more comparison, between elements i and j, we obtain two graphs G_1 and G_2, one for the case $K_i < K_j$ and one for the case $K_i > K_j$. Clearly

$$T(G) = T(G_1) + T(G_2).$$

If $T(G_1) \geq T(G_2)$, we have

$$T(G) \leq 2T(G_1),$$

$$E(G_1) = \frac{n!}{2^{k+1}T(G_1)} = \frac{E(G)T(G)}{2T(G_1)} \leq E(G). \tag{23}$$

Therefore each comparison leads to at least one graph of less or equal efficiency; we can't improve the efficiency by making further comparisons.

When G has no arcs at all, we have $k = 0$ and $T(G) = n!$, so the initial efficiency is 1. At the other extreme, when G is a graph representing the final result of sorting, G looks like a straight line and $T(G) = 1$. Thus, for example, if we want to find a sorting procedure that sorts five elements in at most seven steps, we must obtain the linear graph •—•—•—•—•, whose efficiency is $5!/(2^7 \times 1) = 120/128 = 15/16$. It follows that all of the graphs arising in the sorting procedure must have efficiency $\geq \frac{15}{16}$; if any less efficient graph were to appear, at least one of its descendants would also be less efficient, and we would ultimately reach a linear graph whose efficiency is $< \frac{15}{16}$. In general, this argument proves that all graphs corresponding to the tree nodes of a sorting procedure for n elements must have efficiency $\geq n!/2^l$, where l is the number of levels of the tree (not counting external nodes). This is another way to prove that $S(n) \geq \lceil \lg n! \rceil$, although the argument is not really much different from what we said before.

The graph (21) has efficiency 1, since $T(G) = 15$ and since G has been obtained in three comparisons. In order to see what vertices should be compared next, we can form the *comparison matrix*

$$C(G) = \begin{array}{c} \\ a \\ b \\ c \\ d \\ e \end{array} \begin{array}{c} \begin{array}{ccccc} a & b & c & d & e \end{array} \\ \left(\begin{array}{ccccc} 0 & 15 & 10 & 15 & 11 \\ 0 & 0 & 5 & 15 & 9 \\ 5 & 10 & 0 & 15 & 9 \\ 0 & 0 & 0 & 0 & 3 \\ 4 & 8 & 6 & 12 & 0 \end{array} \right) \end{array}, \tag{24}$$

where C_{ij} is $T(G_1)$ for the graph G_1 obtained by adding the arc $i \rightarrow j$ to G. For example, if we compare K_c with K_e, the 15 permutations consistent with G

split up into $C_{ec} = 6$ having $K_e < K_c$ and $C_{ce} = 9$ having $K_c < K_e$. The latter graph would have efficiency $15/(2 \times 9) = \frac{5}{6} < \frac{15}{16}$, so it could not lead to a seven-step sorting procedure. The next comparison *must* be $K_b : K_e$ in order to keep the efficiency $\geq \frac{15}{16}$.

The concept of efficiency is especially useful when we consider the connected components of graphs. Consider for example the graph

$$G = \quad \begin{array}{cc} a & b \\ \end{array} \quad \begin{array}{cc} d & e \\ \end{array} \quad ;$$

it has two components

$$G' = \quad \begin{array}{cc} a & b \\ \end{array} \quad \text{and} \quad G'' = \quad \begin{array}{cc} d & e \\ f & g \end{array}$$

with no arcs connecting G' to G'', so it has been formed by making some comparisons entirely within G' and others entirely within G''. In general, assume that $G = G' \oplus G''$ has no arcs between G' and G'', where G' and G'' have respectively n' and n'' vertices; it is easy to see that

$$T(G) = \binom{n' + n''}{n'} T(G') T(G''), \tag{25}$$

since each consistent permutation of G is obtained by choosing n' elements to assign to G' and then making consistent permutations within G' and G'' independently. If k' comparisons have been made within G' and k'' within G'', we have the basic result

$$E(G) = \frac{(n' + n'')!}{2^{k'+k''} T(G)} = \frac{n'!}{2^{k'} T(G')} \frac{n''!}{2^{k''} T(G')} = E(G') E(G''), \tag{26}$$

showing that the efficiency of a graph is related in a simple way to the efficiency of its components. Therefore we may restrict consideration to graphs having only one component.

Now suppose that G' and G'' are one-component graphs, and suppose that we want to hook them together by comparing a vertex x of G' with a vertex y of G''. We want to know how efficient this will be. For this purpose we need a function that can be denoted by

$$\binom{p \ < \ q}{m \quad n}, \tag{27}$$

defined to be the number of permutations consistent with the graph

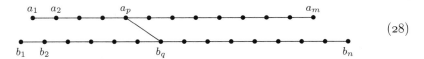

$$\tag{28}$$

Thus $\left({p\atop m}<{q\atop n}\right)$ is $\binom{m+n}{m}$ times the probability that the pth smallest of a set of m numbers is less than the qth smallest of an independently chosen set of n numbers. Exercise 17 shows that we can express $\left({p\atop m}<{q\atop n}\right)$ in two ways in terms of binomial coefficients,

$$\left({p\atop m}<{q\atop n}\right) = \sum_{0\le k<q}\binom{m-p+n-k}{m-p}\binom{p-1+k}{p-1}$$

$$= \sum_{p\le j\le m}\binom{n-q+m-j}{n-q}\binom{q-1+j}{q-1}. \tag{29}$$

(Incidentally, it is by no means obvious on algebraic grounds that these two sums of products of binomial coefficients should come out to be equal.) We also have the formulas

$$\left({p\atop m}<{q\atop n}\right) + \left({q\atop n}<{p\atop m}\right) = \binom{m+n}{m}; \tag{30}$$

$$\left({q\atop n}<{p\atop m}\right) = \left({m+1-p\atop m}<{n+1-q\atop n}\right); \tag{31}$$

$$\left({p\atop m}<{q\atop n}\right) = \left({p\atop m-1}<{q\atop n}\right) + \left({p\atop m}<{q\atop n-1}\right) + [p\le m][q=n]\binom{m+n-1}{m}. \tag{32}$$

For definiteness, let us now consider the two graphs

It is not hard to show by direct enumeration that $T(G') = 42$ and $T(G'') = 5$; so if G is the 11-vertex graph having G' and G'' as components, we have $T(G) = \binom{11}{4}\cdot 42\cdot 5 = 69300$ by Eq. (25). This is a formidable number of permutations to list, if we want to know how many of them have $x_i < y_j$ for each i and j. But the calculation can be done by hand, in less than an hour, as follows. We form the matrices $A(G')$ and $A(G'')$, where A_{ik} is the number of consistent permutations of G' (or G'') in which x_i (or y_i) is equal to k. Thus the number of permutations of G in which x_i is less than y_j is the (i,p) element of $A(G')$ times $\left({p\atop 7}<{q\atop 4}\right)$ times the (j,q) element of $A(G'')$, summed over $1\le p\le 7$ and $1\le q\le 4$. In other words, we want to form the matrix product $A(G')\cdot L\cdot A(G'')^T$, where $L_{pq} = \left({p\atop 7}<{q\atop 4}\right)$. This comes to

$$\begin{pmatrix} 21 & 16 & 5 & 0 & 0 & 0 & 0 \\ 0 & 5 & 10 & 12 & 10 & 5 & 0 \\ 21 & 16 & 5 & 0 & 0 & 0 & 0 \\ 0 & 0 & 12 & 18 & 12 & 0 & 0 \\ 0 & 0 & 0 & 0 & 5 & 16 & 21 \\ 0 & 5 & 10 & 12 & 10 & 5 & 0 \\ 0 & 0 & 0 & 0 & 5 & 16 & 21 \end{pmatrix} \begin{pmatrix} 210 & 294 & 322 & 329 \\ 126 & 238 & 301 & 325 \\ 70 & 175 & 265 & 315 \\ 35 & 115 & 215 & 295 \\ 15 & 65 & 155 & 260 \\ 5 & 29 & 92 & 204 \\ 1 & 8 & 36 & 120 \end{pmatrix} \begin{pmatrix} 2 & 3 & 0 & 0 \\ 2 & 2 & 0 & 1 \\ 1 & 0 & 2 & 2 \\ 0 & 0 & 3 & 2 \end{pmatrix} = \begin{pmatrix} 48169 & 42042 & 66858 & 64031 \\ 22825 & 16005 & 53295 & 46475 \\ 48169 & 42042 & 66858 & 64031 \\ 22110 & 14850 & 54450 & 47190 \\ 5269 & 2442 & 27258 & 21131 \\ 22825 & 16005 & 53295 & 46475 \\ 5269 & 2442 & 27258 & 21131 \end{pmatrix}.$$

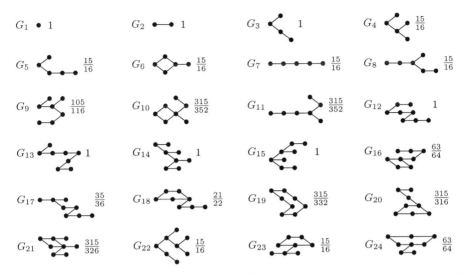

Fig. 36. Some graphs and their efficiencies, obtained at the beginning of a long proof that $S(12) > 29$.

Thus the "best" way to hook up G' and G'' is to compare x_1 with y_2; this gives 42042 cases with $x_1 < y_2$ and $69300 - 42042 = 27258$ cases with $x_1 > y_2$. (By symmetry, we could also compare x_3 with y_2, x_5 with y_3, or x_7 with y_3, leading to essentially the same results.) The efficiency of the resulting graph for $x_1 < y_2$ is

$$\frac{69300}{84084} E(G')E(G''),$$

which is none too good; hence it is probably a bad idea to hook G' up with G'' in any sorting method! The point of this example is that we are able to make such a decision without excessive calculation.

These ideas can be used to provide independent confirmation of Mark Wells's proof that $S(12) = 30$. Starting with a graph containing one vertex, we can repeatedly try to add a comparison to one of our graphs G or to $G' \oplus G''$ (a pair of graph components G' and G'') in such a way that the two resulting graphs have 12 or fewer vertices and efficiency $\geq 12!/2^{29} \approx 0.89221$. Whenever this is possible, we take the resulting graph of least efficiency and add it to our set, unless one of the two graphs is isomorphic to a graph we already have included. If both of the resulting graphs have the same efficiency, we arbitrarily choose one of them. A graph can be identified with its dual (obtained by reversing the order), so long as we consider adding comparisons to $G' \oplus \mathrm{dual}(G'')$ as well as to $G' \oplus G''$. A few of the smallest graphs obtained in this way are displayed in Fig. 36 together with their efficiencies.

Exactly 1649 graphs were generated, by computer, before this process terminated. Since the graph •—•—•—•—•—•—•—•—•—•—•—• was not obtained, we may conclude that $S(12) > 29$. It is plausible that a similar experiment could be performed to deduce that $S(22) > 70$ in a fairly reasonable amount of time, since

$22!/2^{70} \approx 0.952$ requires extremely high efficiency to sort in 70 steps. (Only 91 of the 1649 graphs found on 12 or fewer vertices had such high efficiency.)

The intermediate results suggest strongly that $S(13) = 33$, so that merge insertion would not be optimum when $n = 13$. It should certainly be possible to prove that $S(16) < F(16)$, since $F(16)$ takes no fewer comparisons than sorting ten elements with $S(10)$ comparisons and then inserting six others by binary insertion, one at a time. There must be a way to improve upon this! But at present, the smallest case where $F(n)$ is definitely known to be nonoptimum is $n = 47$: After sorting 5 and 42 elements with $F(5) + F(42) = 178$ comparisons, we can merge the results with 22 further comparisons, using a method due to J. Schulte Mönting, *Theoretical Comp. Sci.* **14** (1981), 19–37; this beats $F(47) = 201$. (Glenn K. Manacher [*JACM* **26** (1979), 441–456] had previously proved that infinitely many n exist with $S(n) < F(n)$, starting with $n = 189$.)

The average number of comparisons. So far we have been considering procedures that are best possible in the sense that their worst case isn't bad; in other words, we have looked for "minimax" procedures that minimize the *maximum* number of comparisons. Now let us look for a "minimean" procedure that minimizes the *average* number of comparisons, assuming that the input is random so that each permutation is equally likely.

Consider once again the tree representation of a sorting procedure, as shown in Fig. 34. The average number of comparisons in that tree is

$$\frac{2 + 3 + 3 + 3 + 3 + 2}{6} = 2\tfrac{2}{3},$$

averaging over all permutations. In general, the average number of comparisons in a sorting method is the *external path length* of the tree divided by $n!$. (Recall that the external path length is the sum of the distances from the root to each of the external nodes; see Section 2.3.4.5.) It is easy to see from the considerations of Section 2.3.4.5 that the minimum external path length occurs in a binary tree with N external nodes if there are $2^q - N$ external nodes at level $q - 1$ and $2N - 2^q$ at level q, where $q = \lceil \lg N \rceil$. (The root is at level zero.) The minimum external path length is therefore

$$(q-1)(2^q - N) + q(2N - 2^q) = (q+1)N - 2^q. \tag{34}$$

The minimum path length can also be characterized in another interesting way: *An extended binary tree has minimum external path length for a given number of external nodes if and only if there is a number l such that all external nodes appear on levels l and $l + 1$.* (See exercise 20.)

If we set $q = \lg N + \theta$, where $0 \le \theta < 1$, the formula for minimum external path length becomes

$$N(\lg N + 1 + \theta - 2^\theta). \tag{35}$$

The function $1 + \theta - 2^\theta$ is shown in Fig. 37; for $0 < \theta < 1$ it is positive but very small, never exceeding

$$1 - (1 + \ln \ln 2)/\ln 2 = 0.08607\ 13320\ 55934+. \tag{36}$$

Fig. 37. The function $1 + \theta - 2^\theta$.

Thus the minimum possible average number of comparisons, obtained by dividing (35) by N, is never less than $\lg N$ and never more than $\lg N + 0.0861$. (This result was first obtained by A. Gleason in 1956.)

Now if we set $N = n!$, we get a lower bound for the average number of comparisons in any sorting scheme. Asymptotically speaking, this lower bound is

$$\lg n! + O(1) = n \lg n - n/\ln 2 + O(\log n). \tag{37}$$

Let $\bar{F}(n)$ be the average number of comparisons performed by the merge insertion algorithm; we have

$n =$	1	2	3	4	5	6	7	8
lower bound (34) $=$	0	2	16	112	832	6896	62368	619904
$n!\,\bar{F}(n) =$	0	2	16	112	832	6912	62784	623232

Thus merge insertion is optimum in both senses for $n \leq 5$, but for $n = 6$ it averages $6912/720 = 9.6$ comparisons while our lower bound says that an average of $6896/720 = 9.577777\ldots$ comparisons might be possible. A moment's reflection shows why this is true: Some "fortunate" permutations of six elements are sorted by merge insertion after only eight comparisons, so the comparison tree has external nodes appearing on three levels instead of two. This forces the overall path length to be higher. Exercise 24 shows that it is possible to construct a six-element sorting procedure that requires nine or ten comparisons in each case; it follows that this method is superior to merge insertion, on the average, and no worse than merge insertion in its worst case.

When $n = 7$, Y. Césari [Thesis (Univ. of Paris, 1968), page 37] has shown that no sorting method can attain the lower bound 62368 on external path length. (It is possible to prove this fact without a computer, using the results of exercise 22.) On the other hand, he has constructed procedures that do achieve the lower bound (34) when $n = 9$ or 10. In general, the problem of minimizing the average number of comparisons turns out to be substantially more difficult than the problem of determining $S(n)$. It may even be true that, for some n, all methods that minimize the *average* number of comparisons require *more* than $S(n)$ comparisons in their worst case.

EXERCISES

1. [*20*] Draw the comparison trees for sorting four elements using the method of (a) binary insertion; (b) straight two-way merging. What are the external path lengths of these trees?

2. [*M24*] Prove that $B(n) \leq L(n)$, and find all n for which equality holds.

3. [*M22*] When equality between keys is allowed, there are 13 possible outcomes when sorting three elements:

$$K_1 = K_2 = K_3, \qquad K_1 = K_2 < K_3, \qquad K_1 = K_3 < K_2,$$
$$K_2 = K_3 < K_1, \qquad K_1 < K_2 = K_3, \qquad K_2 < K_1 = K_3,$$
$$K_3 < K_1 = K_2, \qquad K_1 < K_2 < K_3, \qquad K_1 < K_3 < K_2,$$
$$K_2 < K_1 < K_3, \qquad K_2 < K_3 < K_1, \qquad K_3 < K_1 < K_2, \qquad K_3 < K_2 < K_1.$$

Let P_n denote the number of possible outcomes when n elements are sorted with ties allowed, so that $(P_0, P_1, P_2, P_3, P_4, P_5, \dots) = (1, 1, 3, 13, 75, 541, \dots)$. Prove that the generating function $P(z) = \sum_{n \geq 0} P_n z^n / n!$ is equal to $1/(2 - e^z)$. *Hint:* Show that

$$P_n = \sum_{k > 0} \binom{n}{k} P_{n-k} \qquad \text{when } n > 0.$$

4. [*HM27*] (O. A. Gross.) Determine the asymptotic value of the numbers P_n of exercise 3, as $n \to \infty$. [*Possible hint:* Consider the partial fraction expansion of $\cot z$.]

5. [*16*] When keys can be equal, each comparison may have three results instead of two: $K_i < K_j$, $K_i = K_j$, $K_i > K_j$. Sorting algorithms for this general situation can be represented as extended *ternary* trees, in which each internal node $i:j$ has three subtrees; the left, middle, and right subtrees correspond respectively to the three possible outcomes of the comparison.

Draw an extended ternary tree that defines a sorting algorithm for $n = 3$, when equal keys are allowed. There should be 13 external nodes, corresponding to the 13 possible outcomes listed in exercise 3.

▶ **6.** [*M22*] Let $S'(n)$ be the minimum number of comparisons necessary to sort n elements and to determine all equalities between keys, when each comparison has three outcomes as in exercise 5. The information-theoretic argument of the text can readily be generalized to show that $S'(n) \geq \lceil \log_3 P_n \rceil$, where P_n is the function studied in exercises 3 and 4; but prove that, in fact, $S'(n) = S(n)$.

7. [*20*] Draw an extended ternary tree in the sense of exercise 5 for sorting four elements, when it is known that all keys are either 0 or 1. (Thus if $K_1 < K_2$ and $K_3 < K_4$, we know that $K_1 = K_3$ and $K_2 = K_4$!) Use the minimum average number of comparisons, assuming that the 2^4 possible inputs are equally likely. Be sure to determine all equalities that are present; for example, don't stop sorting when you know only that $K_1 \leq K_2 \leq K_3 \leq K_4$.

8. [*26*] Draw an extended ternary tree as in exercise 7 for sorting four elements, when it is known that all keys are either -1, 0, or $+1$. Use the minimum average number of comparisons, assuming that the 3^4 possible inputs are equally likely.

9. [*M20*] When sorting n elements as in exercise 7, knowing that all keys are 0 or 1, what is the minimum number of comparisons in the worst case?

▶ **10.** [*M25*] When sorting n elements as in exercise 7, knowing that all keys are 0 or 1, what is the minimum *average* number of comparisons as a function of n?

11. [*HM27*] When sorting n elements as in exercise 5, and knowing that all keys are members of the set $\{1, 2, \dots, m\}$, let $S_m(n)$ be the minimum number of comparisons needed in the worst case. [Thus by exercise 6, $S_n(n) = S(n)$.] Prove that, for fixed m, $S_m(n)$ is asymptotically $n \lg m + O(1)$ as $n \to \infty$.

▶ **12.** [*M25*] (W. G. Bouricius, circa 1954.) Suppose that equal keys may occur, but we merely want to sort the elements $\{K_1, K_2, \ldots, K_n\}$ so that a permutation $a_1 a_2 \ldots a_n$ is determined with $K_{a_1} \leq K_{a_2} \leq \cdots \leq K_{a_n}$; we do not need to know whether or not equality occurs between K_{a_i} and $K_{a_{i+1}}$.

Let us say that a comparison tree sorts a sequence of keys *strongly* if it will sort the sequence in the stated sense no matter which branch is taken below the nodes $i:j$ for which $K_i = K_j$. (The tree is binary, not ternary.)

  a) Prove that a comparison tree with no redundant comparisons sorts every sequence of keys strongly if and only if it sorts every sequence of distinct keys.

  b) Prove that a comparison tree sorts every sequence of keys strongly if and only if it sorts every sequence of zeros and ones strongly.

13. [*M28*] Prove (17).

14. [*M24*] Find a closed form for the sum (19).

15. [*M21*] Determine the asymptotic behavior of $B(n)$ and $F(n)$ up to $O(\log n)$. [*Hint:* Show that in both cases the coefficient of n involves the function shown in Fig. 37.]

16. [*HM26*] (F. Hwang and S. Lin.) Prove that $F(n) > \lceil \lg n! \rceil$ for $n \geq 22$.

17. [*M20*] Prove (29).

18. [*20*] If the procedure whose first steps are shown in Fig. 36 had produced the linear graph •━•━•━•━•━•━•━•━•━•━•━•━• with efficiency $12!/2^{29}$, would this have proved that $S(12) = 29$?

19. [*40*] Experiment with the following heuristic rule for deciding which pair of elements to compare next while designing a comparison tree: At each stage of sorting $\{K_1, \ldots, K_n\}$, let u_i be the number of keys known to be $\leq K_i$ as a result of the comparisons made so far, and let v_i be the number of keys known to be $\geq K_i$, for $1 \leq i \leq n$. Renumber the keys in terms of increasing u_i/v_i, so that $u_1/v_1 \leq u_2/v_2 \leq \cdots \leq u_n/v_n$. Now compare $K_i:K_{i+1}$ for some i that minimizes $|u_i v_{i+1} - u_{i+1} v_i|$. (Although this method is based on far less information than a full comparison matrix as in (24), it appears to give optimum results in many cases.)

▶ **20.** [*M26*] Prove that an extended binary tree has minimum external path length if and only if there is a number l such that all external nodes appear on levels l and $l+1$ (or perhaps all on a single level l).

21. [*M21*] The *height* of an extended binary tree is the maximum level number of its external nodes. If x is an internal node of an extended binary tree, let $t(x)$ be the number of external nodes below x, and let $l(x)$ denote the root of x's left subtree. If x is an external node, let $t(x) = 1$. Prove that an extended binary tree has minimum height among all binary trees with the same number of nodes if

$$\left| t(x) - 2t\big(l(x)\big) \right| \leq 2^{\lceil \lg t(x) \rceil} - t(x)$$

for all internal nodes x.

22. [*M24*] Continuing exercise 21, prove that a binary tree has minimum external path length among all binary trees with the same number of nodes if and only if

$$\left| t(x) - 2t\big(l(x)\big) \right| \leq 2^{\lceil \lg t(x) \rceil} - t(x) \qquad \text{and} \qquad \left| t(x) - 2t\big(l(x)\big) \right| \leq t(x) - 2^{\lfloor \lg t(x) \rfloor}$$

for all internal nodes x. [Thus, for example, if $t(x) = 67$, we must have $t(l(x)) = 32$, 33, 34, or 35. If we merely wanted to minimize the height of the tree we could have $3 \leq t(l(x)) \leq 64$, by the preceding exercise.]

23. [*10*] The text proves that the average number of comparisons made by any sorting method for n elements must be at least $\lceil \lg n! \rceil \approx n \lg n$. But multiple list insertion (Program 5.2.1M) takes only $O(n)$ units of time on the average. How can this be?

24. [*27*] (C. Picard.) Find a sorting tree for six elements such that all external nodes appear on levels 10 and 11.

25. [*11*] If there were a sorting procedure for seven elements that achieves the minimum average number of comparisons predicted by the use of Eq. (34), how many external nodes would there be on level 13?

26. [*M42*] Find a sorting procedure for seven elements that minimizes the average number of comparisons performed.

▶ **27.** [*20*] Suppose it is known that the configurations $K_1 < K_2 < K_3$, $K_1 < K_3 < K_2$, $K_2 < K_1 < K_3$, $K_2 < K_3 < K_1$, $K_3 < K_1 < K_2$, $K_3 < K_2 < K_1$ occur with respective probabilities .01, .25, .01, .24, .25, .24. Find a comparison tree that sorts these three elements with the smallest average number of comparisons.

28. [*40*] Write a MIX program that sorts five one-word keys in the minimum possible amount of time, and halts. (See the beginning of Section 5.2 for ground rules.)

29. [*M25*] (S. M. Chase.) Let $a_1 a_2 \ldots a_n$ be a permutation of $\{1, 2, \ldots, n\}$. Prove that any algorithm that decides whether this permutation is even or odd (that is, whether it has an even or odd number of inversions), based solely on comparisons between the a's, must make at least $n \lg n$ comparisons, even though the algorithm has only two possible outcomes.

30. [*M23*] (*Optimum exchange sorting.*) Every exchange sorting algorithm as defined in Section 5.2.2 can be represented as a *comparison-exchange tree*, namely a binary tree structure whose internal nodes have the form $i:j$ for $i < j$, interpreted as the following operation: "If $K_i \leq K_j$, continue by taking the left branch of the tree; if $K_i > K_j$, continue by interchanging records i and j and then taking the right branch of the tree." When an external node is encountered, it must be true that $K_1 \leq K_2 \leq \cdots \leq K_n$. Thus, a comparison-exchange tree differs from a comparison tree in that it specifies data movement as well as comparison operations.

Let $S_e(n)$ denote the minimum number of comparison-exchanges needed, in the worst case, to sort n elements by means of a comparison-exchange tree. Prove that $S_e(n) \leq S(n) + n - 1$.

31. [*M38*] Continuing exercise 30, prove that $S_e(5) = 8$.

32. [*M42*] Continuing exercise 31, investigate $S_e(n)$ for small values of $n > 5$.

33. [*M30*] (T. N. Hibbard.) A *real-valued search tree* of order x and resolution δ is an extended binary tree in which all nodes contain a nonnegative real value such that (i) the value in each external node is $\leq \delta$, (ii) the value in each internal node is at most the sum of the values in its two children, and (iii) the value in the root is x. The *weighted path length* of such a tree is defined to be the sum, over all external nodes, of the level of that node times the value it contains.

Prove that a real-valued search tree of order x and resolution 1 has minimum weighted path length, taken over all such trees of the same order and resolution, if and only if equality holds in (ii) and the following further conditions hold for all pairs of values x_0 and x_1 that are contained in sibling nodes: (iv) There is no integer $k \geq 0$ such that $x_0 < 2^k < x_1$ or $x_1 < 2^k < x_0$. (v) $\lceil x_0 \rceil - x_0 + \lceil x_1 \rceil - x_1 < 1$. (In particular if x is an integer, condition (v) implies that all values in the tree are integers, and condition (iv) is equivalent to the result of exercise 22.)

Also prove that the corresponding minimum weighted path length is $x\lceil \lg x\rceil + \lceil x\rceil - 2^{\lceil \lg x\rceil}$.

34. [*M50*] Determine the exact value of $S(n)$ for infinitely many n.

35. [*49*] Determine the exact value of $S(13)$.

36. [*M50*] (S. S. Kislitsyn, 1968.) Prove or disprove: Any directed acyclic graph G with $T(G) > 1$ has two vertices u and v such that the digraphs G_1 and G_2 obtained from G by adding the arcs $u \leftarrow v$ and $u \to v$ are acyclic and satisfy $1 \le T(G_1)/T(G_2) \le 2$. (Thus $T(G_1)/T(G)$ always lies between $\frac{1}{3}$ and $\frac{2}{3}$, for some u and v.)

*5.3.2. Minimum-Comparison Merging

Let us now consider a related question: What is the best way to merge an ordered set of m elements with an ordered set of n? Denoting the elements to be merged by

$$A_1 < A_2 < \cdots < A_m \qquad \text{and} \qquad B_1 < B_2 < \cdots < B_n, \qquad (1)$$

we shall assume as in Section 5.3.1 that the $m + n$ elements are distinct. The A's may appear among the B's in $\binom{m+n}{m}$ ways, so the arguments we have used for the sorting problem tell us immediately that at least

$$\left\lceil \lg\binom{m+n}{m} \right\rceil \qquad (2)$$

comparisons are required. If we set $m = \alpha n$ and let $n \to \infty$, while α is fixed, Stirling's approximation tells us that

$$\lg\binom{\alpha n+n}{\alpha n} = n\big((1+\alpha)\lg(1+\alpha) - \alpha\lg\alpha\big) - \tfrac{1}{2}\lg n + O(1). \qquad (3)$$

The normal merging procedure, Algorithm 5.2.4M, takes $m+n-1$ comparisons in its worst case.

Let $M(m, n)$ denote the function analogous to $S(n)$, namely the minimum number of comparisons that will always suffice to merge m things with n. By the observations we have just made,

$$\left\lceil \lg\binom{m+n}{m} \right\rceil \le M(m,n) \le m+n-1 \qquad \text{for all } m, n \ge 1. \qquad (4)$$

Formula (3) shows how far apart this lower bound and upper bound can be. When $\alpha = 1$ (that is, $m = n$), the lower bound is $2n - \tfrac{1}{2}\lg n + O(1)$, so both bounds have the right order of magnitude but the difference between them can be arbitrarily large. When $\alpha = 0.5$ (that is, $m = \tfrac{1}{2}n$), the lower bound is

$$\tfrac{3}{2}n(\lg 3 - \tfrac{2}{3}) + O(\log n),$$

which is about $\lg 3 - \tfrac{2}{3} \approx 0.918$ times the upper bound. And as α decreases, the bounds get farther and farther apart, since the standard merging algorithm is primarily designed for files with $m \approx n$.

When $m = n$, the merging problem has a fairly simple solution; it turns out that the *lower* bound of (4), not the upper bound, is at fault. The following theorem was discovered independently by R. L. Graham and R. M. Karp about 1968:

Theorem M. $M(m, m) = 2m - 1$, *for* $m \geq 1$.

Proof. Consider any algorithm that merges $A_1 < \cdots < A_m$ with $B_1 < \cdots < B_m$. When it compares $A_i : B_j$, take the branch $A_i < B_j$ if $i < j$, the branch $A_i > B_j$ if $i \geq j$. Merging must eventually terminate with the configuration

$$B_1 < A_1 < B_2 < A_2 < \cdots < B_m < A_m, \tag{5}$$

since this is consistent with all the branches taken. And each of the $2m - 1$ comparisons

$$B_1 : A_1, \quad A_1 : B_2, \quad B_2 : A_2, \quad \ldots, \quad B_m : A_m$$

must have been made explicitly, or else there would be at least two configurations consistent with the known facts. For example, if A_1 has not been compared to B_2, the configuration

$$B_1 < B_2 < A_1 < A_2 < \cdots < B_m < A_m$$

is indistinguishable from (5).   ∎

A simple modification of this proof yields the companion formula

$$M(m, m+1) = 2m, \qquad \text{for } m \geq 0. \tag{6}$$

Constructing lower bounds. Theorem M shows that the "information theoretic" lower bound (2) can be arbitrarily far from the true value; thus the technique used to prove Theorem M gives us another way to discover lower bounds. Such a proof technique is often viewed as the creation of an *adversary*, a pernicious being who tries to make algorithms run slowly. When an algorithm for merging decides to compare $A_i : B_j$, the adversary determines the fate of the comparison so as to force the algorithm down the more difficult path. If we can invent a suitable adversary, as in the proof of Theorem M, we can ensure that every valid merging algorithm will have to make quite a few comparisons.

We shall make use of *constrained adversaries*, whose power is limited with regard to the outcomes of certain comparisons. A merging method that is under the influence of a constrained adversary does not know about the constraints, so it must make the necessary comparisons even though their outcomes have been predetermined. For example, in our proof of Theorem M we constrained all outcomes by condition (5), yet the merging algorithm was unable to make use of that fact in order to avoid any of the comparisons.

The constraints we shall use in the following discussion apply to the left and right ends of the files. Left constraints are symbolized by

. (meaning no left constraint),

\ (meaning that all outcomes must be consistent with $A_1 < B_1$),

/ (meaning that all outcomes must be consistent with $A_1 > B_1$);

similarly, right constraints are symbolized by

. (meaning no right constraint),

\ (meaning that all outcomes must be consistent with $A_m < B_n$),

/ (meaning that all outcomes must be consistent with $A_m > B_n$).

There are nine kinds of adversaries, denoted by $\lambda M\rho$, where λ is a left constraint and ρ is a right constraint. For example, a $\backslash M\backslash$ adversary must say that $A_1 < B_j$ and $A_i < B_n$; a $.M.$ adversary is unconstrained. For small values of m and n, constrained adversaries of certain kinds are impossible; when $m = 1$ we obviously can't have a $\backslash M/$ adversary.

Let us now construct a rather complicated, but very formidable, adversary for merging. It does not always produce optimum results, but it gives lower bounds that cover a lot of interesting cases. Given m, n, and the left and right constraints λ and ρ, suppose the adversary is asked which is the greater of A_i or B_j. Six strategies can be used to reduce the problem to cases of smaller $m+n$:

Strategy A(k, l), *for* $i \leq k \leq m$ *and* $1 \leq l \leq j$. Say that $A_i < B_j$, and require that subsequent operations merge $\{A_1, \ldots, A_k\}$ with $\{B_1, \ldots, B_{l-1}\}$ and $\{A_{k+1}, \ldots, A_m\}$ with $\{B_l, \ldots, B_n\}$. Thus future comparisons $A_p:B_q$ will result in $A_p < B_q$ if $p \leq k$ and $q \geq l$; $A_p > B_q$ if $p > k$ and $q < l$; they will be handled by a $(k, l-1, \lambda, .)$ adversary if $p \leq k$ and $q < l$; they will be handled by an $(m-k, n+1-l, ., \rho)$ adversary if $p > k$ and $q \geq l$.

Strategy B(k, l), *for* $i \leq k \leq m$ *and* $1 \leq l < j$. Say that $A_i < B_j$, and require that subsequent operations merge $\{A_1, \ldots, A_k\}$ with $\{B_1, \ldots, B_l\}$ and $\{A_{k+1}, \ldots, A_m\}$ with $\{B_l, \ldots, B_n\}$, stipulating that $A_k < B_l < A_{k+1}$. (Note that B_l appears in both lists to be merged. The condition $A_k < B_l < A_{k+1}$ ensures that merging one group gives no information that could help to merge the other.) Thus future comparisons $A_p:B_q$ will result in $A_p < B_q$ if $p \leq k$ and $q \geq l$; $A_p > B_q$ if $p > k$ and $q \leq l$; they will be handled by a $(k, l, \lambda, \backslash)$ adversary if $p \leq k$ and $q \leq l$; by an $(m-k, n+1-l, /, \rho)$ adversary if $p > k$ and $q \geq l$.

Strategy C(k, l), *for* $i < k \leq m$ *and* $1 \leq l \leq j$. Say that $A_i < B_j$, and require that subsequent operations merge $\{A_1, \ldots, A_k\}$ with $\{B_1, \ldots, B_{l-1}\}$ and $\{A_k, \ldots, A_m\}$ with $\{B_l, \ldots, B_n\}$, stipulating that $B_{l-1} < A_k < B_l$. (Analogous to Strategy B, interchanging the roles of A and B.)

Strategy A'(k, l), *for* $1 \leq k \leq i$ *and* $j \leq l \leq n$. Say that $A_i > B_j$, and require the merging of $\{A_1, \ldots, A_{k-1}\}$ with $\{B_1, \ldots, B_l\}$ and $\{A_k, \ldots, A_m\}$ with $\{B_{l+1}, \ldots, B_n\}$. (Analogous to Strategy A.)

Strategy B'(k, l), *for* $1 \leq k \leq i$ *and* $j < l \leq n$. Say that $A_i > B_j$, and require the merging of $\{A_1, \ldots, A_{k-1}\}$ with $\{B_1, \ldots, B_l\}$ and $\{A_k, \ldots, A_m\}$ with $\{B_l, \ldots, B_n\}$, subject to $A_{k-1} < B_l < A_k$. (Analogous to Strategy B.)

Strategy C'(k, l), *for* $1 \leq k < i$ *and* $j \leq l \leq n$. Say that $A_i > B_j$, and require the merging of $\{A_1, \ldots, A_k\}$ with $\{B_1, \ldots, B_l\}$ and $\{A_k, \ldots, A_m\}$ with $\{B_{l+1}, \ldots, B_n\}$, subject to $B_l < A_k < B_{l+1}$. (Analogous to Strategy C.)

Because of the constraints, the strategies above cannot be used in certain cases summarized here:

Strategy	Must be omitted when
$A(k,1)$, $B(k,1)$, $C(k,1)$	$\lambda = /$
$A'(1,l)$, $B'(1,l)$, $C'(1,l)$	$\lambda = \backslash$
$A(m,l)$, $B(m,l)$, $C(m,l)$	$\rho = /$
$A'(k,n)$, $B'(k,n)$, $C'(k,n)$	$\rho = \backslash$

Let $\lambda M\rho(m,n)$ denote the maximum lower bound for merging that is obtainable by an adversary of the class described above. Each strategy, when applicable, gives us an inequality relating these nine functions, when the first comparison is $A_i : B_j$, namely,

$A(k,l)$: $\lambda M\rho(m,n) \geq 1 + \lambda M.(k,l-1) + .M\rho(m-k,n+1-l)$;

$B(k,l)$: $\lambda M\rho(m,n) \geq 1 + \lambda M\backslash(k,l) + /M\rho(m-k,n+1-l)$;

$C(k,l)$: $\lambda M\rho(m,n) \geq 1 + \lambda M/(k,l-1) + \backslash M\rho(m+1-k,n+1-l)$;

$A'(k,l)$: $\lambda M\rho(m,n) \geq 1 + \lambda M.(k-1,l) + .M\rho(m+1-k,n-l)$;

$B'(k,l)$: $\lambda M\rho(m,n) \geq 1 + \lambda M\backslash(k-1,l) + /M\rho(m+1-k,n+1-l)$;

$C'(k,l)$: $\lambda M\rho(m,n) \geq 1 + \lambda M/(k,l) + \backslash M\rho(m+1-k,n-l)$.

For fixed i and j, the adversary will adopt a strategy that maximizes the lower bound given by all possible right-hand sides, when k and l lie in the ranges permitted by i and j. Then we define $\lambda M\rho(m,n)$ to be the minimum of these lower bounds taken over $1 \leq i \leq m$ and $1 \leq j \leq n$. When m or n is zero, $\lambda M\rho(m,n)$ is zero.

For example, consider the case $m = 2$ and $n = 3$, and suppose that our adversary is unconstrained. If the first comparison is $A_1 : B_1$, the adversary may adopt strategy $A'(1,1)$, requiring $.M.(0,1) + .M.(2,2) = 3$ further comparisons. If the first comparison is $A_1 : B_3$, the adversary may adopt strategy $B(1,2)$, requiring $.M\backslash(1,2) + /M.(1,2) = 4$ further comparisons. No matter what comparison $A_i : B_j$ is made first, the adversary can guarantee that at least three further comparisons must be made. Hence $.M.(2,3) = 4$.

It isn't easy to do these calculations by hand, but a computer can grind out tables of $\lambda M\rho$ functions rather quickly. There are obvious symmetries, such as

$$/M.(m,n) = .M\backslash(m,n) = \backslash M.(n,m) = .M/(n,m), \qquad (7)$$

by means of which we can reduce the nine functions to just four,

$$.M.(m,n), \qquad /M.(m,n), \qquad /M\backslash(m,n), \qquad \text{and} \qquad /M/(m,n).$$

Table 1 shows the resulting values for all $m,n \leq 10$; our merging adversary has been defined in such a way that

$$.M.(m,n) \leq M(m,n) \qquad \text{for all} \qquad m,n \geq 0. \qquad (8)$$

Table 1

LOWER BOUNDS FOR MERGING, FROM THE "ADVERSARY"

$.M.(m,n)$ and $/M.(m,n)$

	1	2	3	4	5	6	7	8	9	10	n	1	2	3	4	5	6	7	8	9	10	
1	1	2	2	3	3	3	3	4	4	4		1	2	2	3	3	3	3	4	4	4	1
2	2	3	4	5	5	6	6	6	7	7		1	3	4	4	5	5	6	6	7	7	2
3	2	4	5	6	7	7	8	8	9	9		1	3	5	6	7	7	8	8	9	9	3
4	3	5	6	7	8	9	10	10	11	11		1	4	5	7	8	9	9	10	10	11	4
5	3	5	7	8	9	10	11	12	12	13		1	4	6	8	9	10	11	12	12	13	5
6	3	6	7	9	10	11	12	13	14	15		1	4	6	8	10	11	12	13	14	14	6
7	3	6	8	10	11	12	13	14	15	16		1	4	7	9	10	12	13	14	15	16	7
8	4	6	8	10	12	13	14	15	16	17		1	5	7	9	11	13	14	15	16	17	8
9	4	7	9	11	12	14	15	16	17	18		1	5	8	10	11	13	15	16	17	18	9
10	4	7	9	11	13	15	16	17	18	19		1	5	8	10	12	14	15	17	18	19	10

m ... $/M\backslash(m,n)$ and $/M/(m,n)$ ... m

	1	2	3	4	5	6	7	8	9	10	1	2	3	4	5	6	7	8	9	10	
1	$-\infty$	2	2	3	3	3	3	4	4	4	1	1	1	1	1	1	1	1	1	1	1
2	$-\infty$	2	4	4	5	5	6	6	7	7	1	3	3	4	4	4	4	5	5	5	2
3	$-\infty$	2	4	6	6	7	8	8	8	9	1	3	5	5	6	6	7	7	8	8	3
4	$-\infty$	2	5	6	8	8	9	10	10	11	1	4	5	7	7	8	9	9	9	10	4
5	$-\infty$	2	5	7	8	10	10	11	12	13	1	4	6	7	9	9	10	11	11	12	5
6	$-\infty$	2	5	7	9	10	12	13	14	14	1	4	6	8	9	11	11	12	13	14	6
7	$-\infty$	2	5	8	10	11	12	14	15	16	1	4	7	9	10	11	13	14	15	15	7
8	$-\infty$	2	6	8	10	12	13	15	16	17	1	5	7	9	11	12	14	15	16	17	8
9	$-\infty$	2	6	9	10	12	14	16	17	18	1	5	8	9	11	13	15	16	17	18	9
10	$-\infty$	2	6	9	11	13	15	16	18	19	1	5	8	10	12	14	15	17	18	19	10
	1	2	3	4	5	6	7	8	9	10	n	1	2	3	4	5	6	7	8	9	10

This relation includes Theorem M as a special case, because our adversary will use the simple strategy of that theorem when $|m - n| \le 1$.

Let us now consider some simple relations satisfied by the M function:

$$M(m,n) = M(n,m); \tag{9}$$
$$M(m,n) \le M(m,n+1); \tag{10}$$
$$M(k+m,n) \le M(k,n) + M(m,n); \tag{11}$$
$$M(m,n) \le \max\big(M(m,n-1) + 1, M(m-1,n) + 1\big), \quad \text{for } m \ge 1, n \ge 1; \tag{12}$$
$$M(m,n) \le \max\big(M(m,n-2) + 1, M(m-1,n) + 2\big), \quad \text{for } m \ge 1, n \ge 2. \tag{13}$$

Relation (12) comes from the usual merging procedure, if we first compare $A_1:B_1$. Relation (13) is derived similarly, by first comparing $A_1:B_2$; if $A_1 > B_2$, we need $M(m,n-2)$ more comparisons, but if $A_1 < B_2$, we can insert A_1 into its proper place and merge $\{A_2,\ldots,A_m\}$ with $\{B_1,\ldots,B_n\}$. Generalizing, we can see that if $m \ge 1$ and $n \ge k$ we have

$$M(m,n) \le \max\big(M(m,n-k) + 1, M(m-1,n) + 1 + \lceil \lg k \rceil\big), \tag{14}$$

by first comparing $A_1:B_k$ and using binary search if $A_1 < B_k$.

It turns out that $M(m,n) = .M.(m,n)$ for all $m, n \le 10$, so Table 1 actually gives the optimum values for merging. This can be proved by using (9)–(14) together with special constructions for $(m,n) = (2,8)$, $(3,6)$, and $(5,9)$ given in exercises 8, 9, and 10.

On the other hand, our adversary doesn't always give the best possible lower bounds; the simplest example is $m = 3$, $n = 11$, when $.M.(3, 11) = 9$ but $M(3, 11) = 10$. To see where the adversary has "failed" in this case, we must study the reasons for its decisions. Further scrutiny reveals that if $(i, j) \neq (2, 6)$, the adversary can find a strategy that demands 10 comparisons; but when $(i, j) = (2, 6)$, no strategy beats Strategy A(2, 4), leading to the lower bound $1 + .M.(2, 3) + .M.(1, 8) = 9$. It is necessary but not sufficient to finish by merging $\{A_1, A_2\}$ with $\{B_1, B_2, B_3\}$ and $\{A_3\}$ with $\{B_4, \ldots, B_{11}\}$, so the lower bound fails to be sharp in this case.

Similarly it can be shown that $.M.(2, 38) = 10$ while $M(2, 38) = 11$, so our adversary isn't even good enough to solve the case $m = 2$. But there is an infinite class of values for which it excels:

Theorem K. $M(m, m+2) = 2m + 1 \qquad$ for $m \geq 2$;

$\qquad\qquad\qquad M(m, m+3) = 2m + 2 \qquad$ for $m \geq 4$;

$\qquad\qquad\qquad M(m, m+4) = 2m + 3 \qquad$ for $m \geq 6$.

Proof. We can in fact prove the result with M replaced by $.M.$; for small m the results have been obtained by computer, so we may assume that m is sufficiently large. We may also assume that the first comparison is $A_i : B_j$ where $i \leq \lceil m/2 \rceil$. If $j \leq i$ we use strategy A$'(i, i)$, obtaining

$$.M.(m, m+d) \geq 1 + .M.(i-1, i) + .M.(m+1-i, m+d-i) = 2m + d - 1$$

by induction on d, for $d \leq 4$. If $j > i$ we use strategy A$(i, i+1)$, obtaining

$$.M.(m, m+d) \geq 1 + .M.(i, i) + .M.(m-i, m+d-i) = 2m + d - 1$$

by induction on m. ∎

The first two parts of Theorem K were obtained by F. Hwang and S. Lin in 1969. Paul Stockmeyer and Frances Yao showed several years later that the pattern evident in these three formulas holds in general, namely that the lower bounds derived by the adversarial strategies above suffice to establish the values $M(m, m+d) = 2m + d - 1$ for $m \geq 2d - 2$. [*SICOMP* **9** (1980), 85–90.]

Upper bounds. Now let us consider *upper* bounds for $M(m, n)$; good upper bounds correspond to efficient merging algorithms.

When $m = 1$ the merging problem is equivalent to an insertion problem, and there are $n + 1$ places in which A_1 might fall among $B_1, \ldots, B_n$. For this case it is easy to see that *any* extended binary tree with $n + 1$ external nodes is the tree for some merging method! (See exercise 2.) Hence we may choose an optimum binary tree, realizing the information-theoretic lower bound

$$1 + \lfloor \lg n \rfloor = M(1, n) = \lceil \lg(n + 1) \rceil. \tag{15}$$

Binary search (Section 6.2.1) is, of course, a simple way to attain this value.

The case $m = 2$ is extremely interesting, but considerably harder. It has been solved completely by R. L. Graham, F. K. Hwang, and S. Lin (see exercises

11, 12, and 13), who proved the general formula

$$M(2,n) = \left\lceil \lg \tfrac{7}{12}(n+1) \right\rceil + \left\lceil \lg \tfrac{14}{17}(n+1) \right\rceil. \tag{16}$$

We have seen that the usual merging procedure is optimum when $m = n$, while the rather different binary search procedure is optimum when $m = 1$. What we need is an in-between method that combines the normal merging algorithm with binary search in such a way that the best features of both are retained. Formula (14) suggests the following algorithm, due to F. K. Hwang and S. Lin [*SICOMP* **1** (1972), 31–39]:

Algorithm H (*Binary merging*).

H1. If m or n is zero, stop. Otherwise, if $m > n$, set $t \leftarrow \lfloor \lg(m/n) \rfloor$ and go to step H4. Otherwise set $t \leftarrow \lfloor \lg(n/m) \rfloor$.

H2. Compare $A_m : B_{n+1-2^t}$. If A_m is smaller, set $n \leftarrow n - 2^t$ and return to step H1.

H3. Using binary search (which requires exactly t more comparisons), insert A_m into its proper place among $\{B_{n+1-2^t}, \ldots, B_n\}$. If k is maximal such that $B_k < A_m$, set $m \leftarrow m - 1$ and $n \leftarrow k$. Return to H1.

H4. (Steps H4 and H5 are like H2 and H3, interchanging the roles of m and n, A and B.) If $B_n < A_{m+1-2^t}$, set $m \leftarrow m - 2^t$ and return to step H1.

H5. Insert B_n into its proper place among the A's. If k is maximal such that $A_k < B_n$, set $m \leftarrow k$ and $n \leftarrow n - 1$. Return to H1. ∎

As an example of this algorithm, Table 2 shows the process of merging the three keys $\{087, 503, 512\}$ with thirteen keys $\{061, 154, \ldots, 908\}$; eight comparisons are required in this example. The elements compared at each step are shown in boldface type.

Table 2

EXAMPLE OF BINARY MERGING

A	B	Output
087 503 **512**	061 154 170 275 426 509 612 653 677 **703** 765 897 908	
087 503 **512**	061 154 170 275 426 509 612 **653** 677	703 765 897 908
087 503 **512**	061 154 170 275 426 **509** 612	653 677 703 765 897 908
087 503 512	061 154 170 275 426 509 **612**	653 677 703 765 897 908
087 **503**	061 154 170 275 **426** 509	512 612 653 677 703 765 897 908
087 **503**	061 154 170 275 426 **509**	512 612 653 677 703 765 897 908
087	061 **154** 170 275 426	503 509 512 612 653 677 703 765 897 908
087	**061**	154 170 275 426 503 509 512 612 653 677 703 765 897 908
	061 087 154 170 275 426 503 509 512 612 653 677 703 765 897 908	

Let $H(m,n)$ be the maximum number of comparisons required by Hwang and Lin's algorithm. To calculate $H(m,n)$, we may assume that $k = n$ in step H3 and $k = m$ in step H5, since we shall prove that $H(m-1, n) \le H(m-1, n+1)$

for all $n \geq m - 1$ by induction on m. Thus when $m \leq n$ we have

$$H(m, n) = \max\bigl(M(m, n-2^t)+1,\ H(m-1, n)+t+1\bigr), \qquad (17)$$

for $2^t m \leq n < 2^{t+1} m$. Replace n by $2n + \epsilon$, with $\epsilon = 0$ or 1, to get

$$H(m, 2n+\epsilon) = \max\bigl(H(m, 2n+\epsilon-2^{t+1}) + 1,\ H(m-1, 2n+\epsilon)+t+2\bigr),$$

for $2^t m \leq n < 2^{t+1} m$; and it follows by induction on n that

$$H(m, 2n+\epsilon) = H(m, n) + m, \qquad \text{for } m \leq n \text{ and } \epsilon = 0 \text{ or } 1. \qquad (18)$$

It is also easy to see that $H(m, n) = m + n - 1$ when $m \leq n < 2m$; hence a repeated application of (18) yields the general formula

$$H(m, n) = m + \lfloor n/2^t \rfloor - 1 + tm, \quad \text{for} \quad m \leq n, \quad t = \lfloor \lg(n/m) \rfloor. \qquad (19)$$

This implies that $H(m, n) \leq H(m, n+1)$ for all $n \geq m$, verifying our inductive hypothesis about step H3.

Setting $m = \alpha n$ and $\theta = \lg(n/m) - t$ gives

$$H(\alpha n, n) = \alpha n(1 + 2^\theta - \theta - \lg \alpha) + O(1), \qquad (20)$$

as $n \to \infty$. We know by Eq. 5.3.1–(36) that $1.9139 < 1 + 2^\theta - \theta \leq 2$; hence (20) may be compared with the information-theoretic lower bound (3). Hwang and Lin have proved (see exercise 17) that

$$H(m, n) < \left\lceil \lg\binom{m+n}{m} \right\rceil + \min(m, n). \qquad (21)$$

The Hwang–Lin binary merging algorithm does not always give optimum results, but it has the great virtue that it can be programmed rather easily. It reduces to "uncentered binary search" when $m = 1$, and it reduces to the usual merging procedure when $m \approx n$, so it represents an excellent compromise between those two methods. Furthermore, it *is* optimum in many cases (see exercise 16). Improved algorithms have been found by F. K. Hwang and D. N. Deutsch, *JACM* **20** (1973), 148–159; G. K. Manacher, *JACM* **26** (1979), 434–440; and most notably by C. Christen, *FOCS* **19** (1978), 259–266. Christen's merging procedure, called *forward-testing-backward-insertion*, saves about $m/3$ comparisons over Algorithm H when $n/m \to \infty$. Moreover, Christen's procedure achieves the lower bound $.M.(m, n) = \lfloor (11m + n - 3)/4 \rfloor$ when $5m - 3 \leq n \leq 7m + 2[m \text{ even}]$; hence it is optimum in such cases (and, remarkably, so is our adversarial lower bound).

Formula (18) suggests that the M function itself might satisfy

$$M(m, n) \leq M(m, \lfloor n/2 \rfloor) + m. \qquad (22)$$

This is actually true (see exercise 19). Tables of $M(m, n)$ suggest several other plausible relations, such as

$$M(m+1, n) \geq 1 + M(m, n) \geq M(m, n+1), \qquad \text{for } m \leq n; \qquad (23)$$

$$M(m+1, n + 1) \geq 2 + M(m, n); \qquad (24)$$

but no proof of these inequalities is known.

EXERCISES

1. [*15*] Find an interesting relation between $M(m, n)$ and the function S defined in Section 5.3.1. [*Hint:* Consider $S(m + n)$.]

▶ **2.** [*22*] When $m = 1$, every merging algorithm without redundant comparisons defines an extended binary tree with $\binom{m+n}{m} = n + 1$ external nodes. Prove that, conversely, every extended binary tree with $n + 1$ external nodes corresponds to some merging algorithm with $m = 1$.

3. [*M24*] Prove that $.M.(1, n) = M(1, n)$ for all n.

4. [*M42*] Is $.M.(m, n) \geq \lceil \lg \binom{m+n}{m} \rceil$ for all m and n?

5. [*M30*] Prove that $.M.(m, n) \leq .M\backslash(m, n{+}1)$.

6. [*M26*] The stated proof of Theorem K requires that a lot of cases be verified by computer. How can the number of such cases be drastically reduced?

7. [*21*] Prove (11).

▶ **8.** [*24*] Prove that $M(2, 8) \leq 6$, by finding an algorithm that merges two elements with eight others using at most six comparisons.

9. [*27*] Prove that three elements can be merged with six in at most seven steps.

10. [*33*] Prove that five elements can be merged with nine in at most twelve steps. [*Hint:* Experience with the adversary suggests first comparing $A_1 : B_2$, then trying $A_5 : B_8$ if $A_1 < B_2$.]

11. [*M40*] (F. Hwang, S. Lin.) Let $g_{2k} = \lfloor 2^k \frac{17}{14} \rfloor$, $g_{2k+1} = \lfloor 2^k \frac{12}{7} \rfloor$, for $k \geq 0$, so that $(g_0, g_1, g_2, \dots) = (1, 1, 2, 3, 4, 6, 9, 13, 19, 27, 38, 54, 77, \dots)$. Prove that it takes more than t comparisons to merge two elements with g_t elements, in the worst case; but two elements can be merged with $g_t - 1$ in at most t steps. [*Hint:* Show that if $n = g_t$ or $n = g_t - 1$ and if we want to merge $\{A_1, A_2\}$ with $\{B_1, B_2, \dots, B_n\}$ in t comparisons, we can't do better than to compare $A_2 : B_{g_{t-1}}$ on the first step.]

12. [*M21*] Let $R_n(i, j)$ be the least number of comparisons required to sort the distinct objects $\{\alpha, \beta, X_1, \dots, X_n\}$, given the relations

$$\alpha < \beta, \qquad X_1 < X_2 < \cdots < X_n, \qquad \alpha < X_{i+1}, \qquad \beta > X_{n-j}.$$

(The condition $\alpha < X_{i+1}$ or $\beta > X_{n-j}$ becomes vacuous when $i \geq n$ or $j \geq n$. Therefore $R_n(n, n) = M(2, n)$.)

Clearly, $R_n(0, 0) = 0$. Prove that

$$R_n(i, j) = 1 + \min\Big(\min_{1 \leq k \leq i} \max\big(R_n(k{-}1, j),\ R_{n-k}(i{-}k, j)\big),$$
$$\min_{1 \leq k \leq j} \max\big(R_n(i, k{-}1),\ R_{n-k}(i, j{-}k)\big)\Big)$$

for $0 \leq i \leq n$, $0 \leq j \leq n$, $i + j > 0$.

13. [*M42*] (R. L. Graham.) Show that the solution to the recurrence in exercise 12 may be expressed as follows. Define the function $G(x)$, for $0 < x < \infty$, by the rules

$$G(x) = \begin{cases} 1, & \text{if } 0 < x \leq \frac{5}{7}; \\ \frac{1}{2} + \frac{1}{8}G(8x - 5), & \text{if } \frac{5}{7} < x \leq \frac{3}{4}; \\ \frac{1}{2}G(2x - 1), & \text{if } \frac{3}{4} < x \leq 1; \\ 0, & \text{if } 1 < x < \infty. \end{cases}$$

(See Fig. 38.) Since $R_n(i, j) = R_n(j, i)$ and since $R_n(0, j) = M(1, j)$, we may assume that $1 \le i \le j \le n$. Let $p = \lfloor \lg i \rfloor$, $q = \lfloor \lg j \rfloor$, $r = \lfloor \lg n \rfloor$, and let $t = n - 2^r + 1$. Then

$$R_n(i, j) = p + q + S_n(i, j) + T_n(i, j),$$

where S_n and T_n are functions that are either 0 or 1:

$$S_n(i, j) = 1 \quad \text{if and only if} \quad q < r \text{ or } (i - 2^p \ge u \text{ and } j - 2^r \ge u),$$
$$T_n(i, j) = 1 \quad \text{if and only if} \quad p < r \text{ or } (t > \tfrac{6}{7} 2^{r-2} \text{ and } i - 2^r \ge v),$$

where $u = 2^p G(t/2^p)$ and $v = 2^{r-2} G(t/2^{r-2})$.

(This may be the most formidable recurrence relation that will ever be solved!)

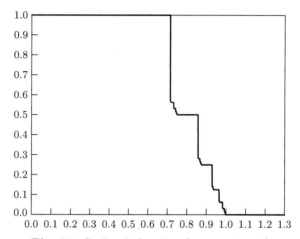

Fig. 38. Graham's function (see exercise 13).

14. [*41*] (F. K. Hwang.) Let $h_{3k} = \lfloor \frac{43}{28} 2^k \rfloor - 1$, $h_{3k+1} = h_{3k} + 3 \cdot 2^{k-3}$, $h_{3k+2} = \lfloor \frac{17}{7} 2^k - \frac{6}{7} \rfloor$ for $k \ge 3$, and let the initial values be defined so that

$$(h_0, h_1, h_2, \dots) = (1, 1, 2, 2, 3, 4, 5, 7, 9, 11, 14, 18, 23, 29, 38, 48, 60, 76, \dots).$$

Prove that $M(3, h_t) > t$ and $M(3, h_t - 1) \le t$ for all t, thereby establishing the exact values of $M(3, n)$ for all n.

15. [*12*] Step H1 of the binary merge algorithm may require the calculation of the expression $\lfloor \lg(n/m) \rfloor$, for $n \ge m$. Explain how to compute this easily without division or calculation of a logarithm.

16. [*18*] For which m and n is Hwang and Lin's binary merging algorithm optimum, for $1 \le m \le n \le 10$?

17. [*M25*] Prove (21). [*Hint:* The inequality isn't very tight.]

18. [*M40*] Study the *average* number of comparisons used by binary merge.

▶ **19.** [*23*] Prove that the M function satisfies (22).

20. [*20*] Show that if $M(m, n+1) \le M(m+1, n)$ for all $m \le n$, then $M(m, n+1) \le 1 + M(m, n)$ for all $m \le n$.

21. [*M47*] Prove or disprove (23) and (24).

22. [*M43*] Study the minimum *average* number of comparisons needed to merge m things with n.

23. [*M31*] (E. Reingold.) Let $\{A_1, \ldots, A_n\}$ and $\{B_1, \ldots, B_n\}$ be sets containing n elements each. Consider an algorithm that attempts to test *equality* of these two sets solely by making comparisons for equality between elements. Thus, the algorithm asks questions of the form "Is $A_i = B_j$?" for certain i and j, and it branches depending on the answer.

By defining a suitable adversary, prove that any such algorithm must make at least $\frac{1}{2}n(n+1)$ comparisons in its worst case.

24. [*22*] (E. L. Lawler.) What is the maximum number of comparisons needed by the following algorithm for merging m elements with $n \geq m$ elements? "Set $t \leftarrow \lfloor \lg(n/m) \rfloor$ and use Algorithm 5.2.4M to merge $A_1, A_2, \ldots, A_m$ with $B_{2^t}, B_{2 \cdot 2^t}, \ldots, B_{q \cdot 2^t}$, where $q = \lfloor n/2^t \rfloor$. Then insert each A_j into its proper place among the B_k."

▶ **25.** [*25*] Suppose (x_{ij}) is an $m \times n$ matrix with nondecreasing rows and columns: $x_{ij} \leq x_{(i+1)j}$ for $1 \leq i < m$ and $x_{ij} \leq x_{i(j+1)}$ for $1 \leq j < n$. Show that $M(m, n)$ is the minimum number of comparisons needed to determine whether a given number x is present in the matrix, if all comparisons are between x and some matrix element.

*5.3.3. Minimum-Comparison Selection

A similar class of interesting problems arises when we look for best possible procedures to select the tth largest of n elements.

The history of this question goes back to Rev. C. L. Dodgson's amusing (though serious) essay on lawn tennis tournaments, which appeared in *St. James's Gazette*, August 1, 1883, pages 5–6. Dodgson — who is of course better known as Lewis Carroll — was concerned about the unjust manner in which prizes were awarded in tennis tournaments. Consider, for example, Fig. 39, which shows a typical "knockout tournament" between 32 players labeled *01*, *02*, ..., *32*. In the finals, player *01* defeats player *05*, so it is clear that player *01* is the champion and deserves the first prize. The inequity arises because player *05* usually gets second prize, although someone else might well be the second best. You can win second prize even if you are worse than half of the players in the competition! In fact, as Dodgson observed, the second-best player wins second prize if and only if the champion and the next-best are originally in opposite halves of the tournament; this occurs with probability $2^{n-1}/(2^n - 1)$, when there are 2^n competitors, so the wrong player receives second prize almost half of the time. If the losers of the semifinal round (players *25* and *17* in Fig. 39) compete for third prize, it is highly unlikely that the third-best player receives third prize.

Dodgson therefore set out to design a tournament that determines the true second- and third-best players, assuming a transitive ranking. (In other words, if player A beats player B and B beats C, Dodgson assumed that A would beat C.) He devised a procedure in which losers are allowed to play further games until they are known to be definitely inferior to three other players. An example of Dodgson's scheme appears in Fig. 40, which is a supplementary tournament to be run in conjunction with Fig. 39. He tried to pair off players whose records in previous rounds were equivalent; he also tried to avoid matches in which both players had been defeated by the same person. In this particular example, *16* loses to *11* and *13* loses to *12* in Round 1; after *13* beats *16* in the second round, we can eliminate *16*, who is now known to be inferior to *11*, *12*, and *13*. In Round 3 Dodgson did not allow *19* to play with *21*, since they have both been defeated by *18* and we could not automatically eliminate the loser of *19* versus *21*.

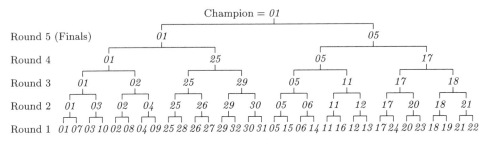

Fig. 39. A knockout tournament with 32 players.

It would be nice to report that Lewis Carroll's tournament turns out to be optimal, but unfortunately that is not the case. His diary entry for July 23, 1883, says that he composed the essay in about six hours, and he felt "we are now so late in the [tennis] season that it is better it should appear soon than be written well." His procedure makes more comparisons than necessary, and it is not formulated precisely enough to qualify as an algorithm. On the other hand, it has some rather interesting aspects from the standpoint of parallel computation. And it appears to be an excellent plan for a tennis tournament, because he built in some dramatic effects; for example, he specified that the two finalists should sit out round 5, playing an extended match during rounds 6 and 7. But tournament directors presumably thought the proposal was too logical, and so Carroll's system has apparently never been tried. Instead, a method of "seeding" is used to keep the supposedly best players in different parts of the tree.

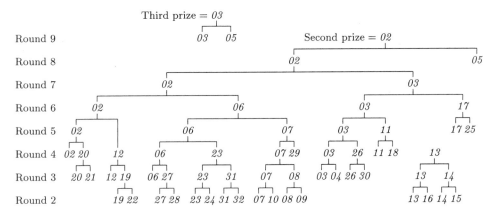

Fig. 40. Lewis Carroll's lawn tennis tournament (played in conjunction with Fig. 39).

In a mathematical seminar during 1929–1930, Hugo Steinhaus posed the problem of finding the *minimum* number of tennis matches required to determine the first and second best players in a tournament, when there are $n \geq 2$ players in all. J. Schreier [*Mathesis Polska* **7** (1932), 154–160] gave a procedure that requires at most $n - 2 + \lceil \lg n \rceil$ matches, using essentially the same method as the first two stages in what we have called tree selection sorting (see Section 5.2.3, Fig. 23), avoiding redundant comparisons that involve $-\infty$. Schreier also claimed that $n - 2 + \lceil \lg n \rceil$ is best possible, but his proof was incorrect, as was another attempted proof by J. Słupecki [*Colloquium Mathematicum* **2** (1951), 286–290]. Thirty-two years went by before a correct, although rather complicated, proof was finally published by S. S. Kislitsyn [*Sibirskiĭ Mat. Zhurnal* **5** (1964), 557–564].

Let $V_t(n)$ denote the minimum number of comparisons needed to determine the tth largest of n elements, for $1 \leq t \leq n$, and let $W_t(n)$ be the minimum number required to determine the largest, second largest, ..., and the tth largest, collectively. By symmetry, we have

$$V_t(n) = V_{n+1-t}(n), \tag{1}$$

and it is obvious that

$$V_1(n) = W_1(n), \tag{2}$$
$$V_t(n) \leq W_t(n), \tag{3}$$
$$W_n(n) = W_{n-1}(n) = S(n). \tag{4}$$

We have observed in Lemma 5.2.3M that

$$V_1(n) = n - 1. \tag{5}$$

In fact, there is an astonishingly simple proof of this fact, since everyone in a tournament except the champion must lose at least one game! By extending this idea and using an "adversary" as in Section 5.3.2, we can prove the Schreier–Kislitsyn theorem without much difficulty:

Theorem S. $V_2(n) = W_2(n) = n - 2 + \lceil \lg n \rceil$, for $n \geq 2$.

Proof. Assume that n players have participated in a tournament that has determined the second-best player by some given procedure, and let a_j be the number of players who have lost j or more matches. The total number of matches played is then $a_1 + a_2 + a_3 + \cdots$. We cannot determine the second-best player without also determining the champion (see exercise 2), so our previous argument shows that $a_1 = n - 1$. To complete the proof, we will show that there is always some sequence of outcomes of the matches that makes $a_2 \geq \lceil \lg n \rceil - 1$.

Suppose that at the end of the tournament the champion has played (and beaten) p players; one of these is the second best, and the others must have lost at least one other time, so $a_2 \geq p - 1$. Therefore we can complete the proof by constructing an adversary who decides the results of the games in such a way that the champion must play at least $\lceil \lg n \rceil$ other people.

Let the adversary declare A to be better than B if A is previously undefeated and B has lost at least once, or if both are undefeated and B has won fewer matches than A at that time. In other circumstances the adversary may make an arbitrary decision consistent with some partial ordering.

Consider the outcome of a complete tournament whose matches have been decided by such an adversary. Let us say that "A supersedes B" if and only if $A = B$ or A supersedes the player who first defeated B. (Only a player's first defeat is relevant in this relation; a loser's subsequent games are ignored. According to the mechanism of the adversary, any player who *first* defeats another must be previously unbeaten.) It follows that a player who won the first p matches supersedes at most 2^p players on the basis of those p contests. (This is clear for $p = 0$, and for $p > 0$ the pth match was against someone who was either previously beaten or who supersedes at most 2^{p-1} players.) Hence the champion, who supersedes everyone, must have played at least $\lceil \lg n \rceil$ matches. ∎

Theorem S completely resolves the problem of finding the second-best player, in the minimax sense. Exercise 6 shows, in fact, that it is possible to give a simple formula for the minimum number of comparisons needed to find the second largest element of a set when an *arbitrary* partial ordering of the elements is known beforehand.

What if $t > 2$? In the paper cited above, Kislitsyn went on to consider larger values of t, proving that

$$W_t(n) \leq n - t + \sum_{n+1-t<j\leq n} \lceil \lg j \rceil, \qquad \text{for } n \geq t. \tag{6}$$

For $t = 1$ and $t = 2$ we have seen that equality actually holds in this formula; for $t = 3$ it can be slightly improved (see exercise 21).

We shall prove Kislitsyn's theorem by showing that the first t stages of *tree selection* require at most $n - t + \sum_{n+1-t<j\leq n} \lceil \lg j \rceil$ comparisons, ignoring all of the comparisons that involve $-\infty$. It is interesting to note that, by Eq. 5.3.1–(3), the right-hand side of (6) equals $B(n)$ when $t = n$, and also when $t = n - 1$; hence tree selection and binary insertion yield the same upper bound for the sorting problem, although they are quite different methods.

Let α be an extended binary tree with n external nodes, and let π be a permutation of $\{1, 2, \ldots, n\}$. Place the elements of π into the external nodes, from left to right in symmetric order, and fill in the internal nodes according to the rules of a knockout tournament as in tree selection. When the resulting tree is subjected to repeated selection operations, it defines a sequence $c_{n-1} c_{n-2} \ldots c_1$, where c_j is the number of comparisons required to bring element j to the root of the tree when element $j + 1$ has been replaced by $-\infty$. For example, if α is the tree

$$\tag{7}$$

and if $\pi = 5\ 3\ 1\ 4\ 2$, we obtain the successive trees

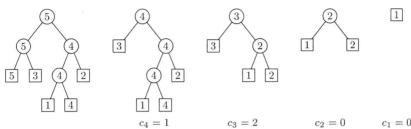

$$c_4 = 1 \qquad c_3 = 2 \qquad c_2 = 0 \qquad c_1 = 0$$

If π had been $3\ 1\ 5\ 4\ 2$, the sequence $c_4\ c_3\ c_2\ c_1$ would have been $2\ 1\ 1\ 0$ instead. It is not difficult to see that c_1 is always zero.

Let $\mu(\alpha, \pi)$ be the multiset $\{c_{n-1}, c_{n-2}, \ldots, c_1\}$ determined by α and π. If

$$\alpha = \begin{array}{c} \bigcirc \\ \diagup\ \diagdown \\ \alpha'\quad \alpha'' \end{array}$$

and if elements 1 and 2 do not both appear in α' or both in α'', it is easy to see that

$$\mu(\alpha, \pi) = \big(\mu(\alpha', \pi') + 1\big) \uplus \big(\mu(\alpha'', \pi'') + 1\big) \uplus \{0\} \qquad (8)$$

for appropriate permutations π' and π'', where $\mu+1$ denotes the multiset obtained by adding 1 to each element of μ. (See exercise 7.) On the other hand, if elements 1 and 2 both appear in α', we have

$$\mu(\alpha, \pi) = \big(\mu(\alpha', \pi') + \epsilon\big) \uplus \big(\mu(\alpha'', \pi'') + 1\big) \uplus \{0\},$$

where $\mu + \epsilon$ denotes a multiset obtained by adding 1 to some elements of μ and 0 to the others. A similar formula holds when 1 and 2 both appear in α''. Let us say that multiset μ_1 *dominates* μ_2 if both μ_1 and μ_2 contain the same number of elements, and if the kth largest element of μ_1 is greater than or equal to the kth largest element of μ_2 for all k; and let us define $\mu(\alpha)$ to be the dominant $\mu(\alpha, \pi)$, taken over all permutations π, in the sense that $\mu(\alpha)$ dominates $\mu(\alpha, \pi)$ for all π and $\mu(\alpha) = \mu(\alpha, \pi)$ for some π. The formulas above show that

$$\mu(\square) = \emptyset, \qquad \mu\!\left(\begin{array}{c}\bigcirc\\ \diagup\diagdown\\ \alpha'\ \alpha''\end{array}\right) = \big(\mu(\alpha') + 1\big) \uplus \big(\mu(\alpha'') + 1\big) \uplus \{0\}; \qquad (9)$$

hence $\mu(\alpha)$ *is the multiset of all distances from the root to the internal nodes of α.*

The reader who has followed this train of thought will now see that we are ready to prove Kislitsyn's theorem (6). Indeed, $W_t(n)$ is less than or equal to $n-1$ plus the $t-1$ largest elements of $\mu(\alpha)$, where α is any tree being used in tree selection sorting. We may take α to be the complete binary tree with n external nodes (see Section 2.3.4.5), when

$$\mu(\alpha) = \big\{\lfloor \lg 1 \rfloor, \lfloor \lg 2 \rfloor, \ldots, \lfloor \lg(n-1) \rfloor \big\}$$
$$= \big\{\lceil \lg 2 \rceil - 1, \lceil \lg 3 \rceil - 1, \ldots, \lceil \lg n \rceil - 1 \big\}. \qquad (10)$$

Formula (6) follows when we consider the $t-1$ largest elements of this multiset.

Kislitsyn's theorem gives a good upper bound for $W_t(n)$; he remarked that $V_3(5) = 6 < W_3(5) = 7$, but he was unable to find a better bound for $V_t(n)$ than for $W_t(n)$. A. Hadian and M. Sobel discovered a way to do this using *replacement selection* instead of tree selection; their formula [Univ. of Minnesota, Dept. of Statistics Report 121 (1969)],

$$V_t(n) \leq n - t + (t-1)\lceil \lg(n+2-t) \rceil, \qquad n \geq t, \qquad (11)$$

is similar to Kislitsyn's upper bound for $W_t(n)$ in (6), except that each term in the sum has been replaced by the smallest term.

Hadian and Sobel's theorem (11) can be proved by using the following construction: First set up a binary tree for a knockout tournament on $n - t + 2$ items. (This takes $n - t + 1$ comparisons.) The largest item is greater than $n - t + 1$ others, so it can't be tth largest. Replace it, where it appears at an external node of the tree, by one of the $t - 2$ elements held in reserve, and find the largest element of the resulting $n - t + 2$; this requires at most $\lceil \lg(n+2-t) \rceil$ comparisons, because we need to recompute only one path in the tree. Repeat this operation $t - 2$ times in all, for each element held in reserve. Finally, replace the currently largest element by $-\infty$, and determine the largest of the remaining $n + 1 - t$; this requires at most $\lceil \lg(n+2-t) \rceil - 1$ comparisons, and it brings the tth largest element of the original set to the root of the tree. Summing the comparisons yields (11).

In relation (11) we should of course replace t by $n+1-t$ on the right-hand side whenever $n+1-t$ gives a better value (as when $n = 6$ and $t = 3$). Curiously, the formula gives a smaller bound for $V_7(13)$ than it does for $V_6(13)$. The upper bound in (11) is exact for $n \leq 6$, but as n and t get larger it is possible to obtain much better estimates of $V_t(n)$.

For example, the following elegant method (due to David G. Doren) can be used to show that $V_4(8) \leq 12$. Let the elements be $X_1, \ldots, X_8$; first compare $X_1:X_2$ and $X_3:X_4$ and the two winners, and do the same to $X_5:X_6$ and $X_7:X_8$ and their winners. Relabel elements so that $X_1 < X_2 < X_4 > X_3$, $X_5 < X_6 < X_8 > X_7$, then compare $X_2:X_6$; by symmetry assume that $X_2 < X_6$, so that we have the configuration

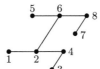

(Now X_1 and X_8 are out of contention and we must find the third largest of $\{X_2, \ldots, X_7\}$.) Compare $X_2:X_7$, and discard the smaller; in the worst case we have $X_2 < X_7$ and we must find the third largest of

```
5 •———• 6
           • 7
3 •———• 4
```

This can be done in $V_3(5) - 2 = 4$ more steps, since the procedure of (11) that achieves $V_3(5) = 6$ begins by comparing two disjoint pairs of elements.

Table 1

VALUES OF $V_t(n)$ FOR SMALL n

n	$V_1(n)$	$V_2(n)$	$V_3(n)$	$V_4(n)$	$V_5(n)$	$V_6(n)$	$V_7(n)$	$V_8(n)$	$V_9(n)$	$V_{10}(n)$
1	0									
2	1	1								
3	2	3	2							
4	3	4	4	3						
5	4	6	6	6	4					
6	5	7	8	8	7	5				
7	6	8	10	10*	10	8	6			
8	7	9	11	12	12	11	9	7		
9	8	11	12	14	14*	14	12	11	8	
10	9	12	14*	15	16**	16**	15	14*	12	9

* Exercises 10–12 give constructions that improve on Eq. (11) in these cases.

** See K. Noshita, *Trans. of the IECE of Japan* **E59**, 12 (December 1976), 17–18.

Other tricks of this kind can be used to produce the results shown in Table 1; no general method is evident as yet. The values listed for $V_4(9) = V_6(9)$ and $V_5(10) = V_6(10)$ were proved optimum in 1996 by W. Gasarch, W. Kelly, and W. Pugh [*SIGACT News* **27**, 2 (June 1996), 88–96], using a computer search.

A fairly good lower bound for the selection problem when t is small was obtained by David G. Kirkpatrick [*JACM* **28** (1981), 150–165]: If $2 \le t \le (n+1)/2$, we have

$$V_t(n) \ge n + t - 3 + \sum_{j=0}^{t-2} \left\lceil \lg \frac{n-t+2}{t+j} \right\rceil . \tag{12}$$

In his Ph.D. thesis [U. of Toronto, 1974], Kirkpatrick also proved that

$$V_3(n) \le n + 1 + \left\lceil \lg \frac{n-1}{4} \right\rceil + \left\lceil \lg \frac{n-1}{5} \right\rceil ; \tag{13}$$

this upper bound matches the lower bound (12) for $\lg \frac{5}{3} \approx 74\%$ of all integers n, and it exceeds (12) by at most 1. Kirkpatrick's analysis made it natural to conjecture that equality holds in (13) for all $n > 4$, but Jutta Eusterbrock found the surprising counterexample $V_3(22) = 28$ [*Discrete Applied Math.* **41** (1993), 131–137]. Improved lower bounds for larger values of t were found by S. W. Bent and J. W. John (see exercise 26):

$$V_t(n) \ge n + m - 2\lceil \sqrt{m} \rceil, \qquad m = 2 + \left\lceil \lg \left(\binom{n}{t} \middle/ (n+1-t) \right) \right\rceil . \tag{14}$$

This formula proves in particular that

$$V_{\alpha n}(n) \ge \left(1 + \alpha \lg \frac{1}{\alpha} + (1-\alpha) \lg \frac{1}{1-\alpha} \right) n + O(\sqrt{n}). \tag{15}$$

A linear method. When n is odd and $t = \lceil n/2 \rceil$, the tth largest (and tth smallest) element is called the median. According to (11), we can find the median of n elements in $\approx \frac{1}{2} n \lg n$ comparisons; but this is only about twice as fast as sorting, even though we are asking for much less information. For several years, concerted efforts were made by a number of people to find an improvement over (11) when t and n are large. Finally in 1971, Manuel Blum discovered a method that needed only $O(n \log \log n)$ steps. Blum's approach to the problem suggested a new class of techniques, which led to the following construction due to R. Rivest and R. Tarjan [*J. Comp. and Sys. Sci.* **7** (1973), 448–461]:

Theorem L. $V_t(n) \leq 15n - 163$ for $1 \leq t \leq n$, when $n > 32$.

Proof. The theorem is trivial when n is small, since $V_t(n) \leq S(n) \leq 10n \leq 15n - 163$ for $32 < n \leq 2^{10}$. By adding at most 13 dummy $-\infty$ elements, we may assume that $n = 7(2q + 1)$ for some integer $q \geq 73$. The following method may now be used to select the tth largest:

Step 1. Divide the elements into $2q + 1$ groups of seven elements each, and sort each of the groups. This takes at most $13(2q + 1)$ comparisons.

Step 2. Find the median of the $2q + 1$ median elements obtained in Step 1, and call it x. By induction on q, this takes at most $V_{q+1}(2q + 1) \leq 30q - 148$ comparisons.

Step 3. The $n - 1$ elements other than x have now been partitioned into three sets (see Fig. 41):

$4q + 3$ elements known to be greater than x (Region B);

$4q + 3$ elements known to be less than x (Region C);

$6q$ elements whose relation to x is unknown (Regions A and D).

By making $4q$ additional comparisons, we can tell exactly which of the elements in regions A and D are less than x. (We first test x against the middle element of each triple.)

Step 4. We have now found r elements greater than x and $n - 1 - r$ elements less than x, for some r. If $t = r + 1$, x is the answer; if $t < r + 1$, we need to find the tth largest of the r large elements; and if $t > r + 1$, we need to find the $(t-1-r)$th largest of the $n - 1 - r$ small elements. The point is that r and $n - 1 - r$ are both less than or equal to $10q + 3$ (the size of regions A and D, plus either B or C). By induction on q this step therefore requires at most $15(10q + 3) - 163$ comparisons.

The total number of comparisons comes to at most

$$13(2q + 1) + 30q - 148 + 4q + 15(10q + 3) - 163 = 15(14q - 6) - 163.$$

Since we started with at least $14q - 6$ elements, the proof is complete. ∎

Theorem L shows that selection can always be done in linear time, namely that $V_t(n) = O(n)$. Of course, the method used in this proof is rather crude, since it throws away good information in Step 4. Deeper study of the problem

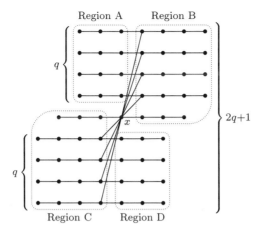

Fig. 41. The selection algorithm of Rivest and Tarjan ($q = 4$).

has led to much sharper bounds; for example, A. Schönhage, M. Paterson, and N. Pippenger [*J. Comp. Sys. Sci.* **13** (1976), 184–199] proved that the maximum number of comparisons required to find the median is at most $3n + O(n \log n)^{3/4}$. See exercise 23 for a lower bound and for references to more recent results.

The average number. Instead of minimizing the *maximum* number of comparisons, we can ask instead for an algorithm that minimizes the *average* number of comparisons, assuming random order. As usual, the minimean problem is considerably harder than the minimax problem; indeed, the minimean problem is still unsolved even in the case $t = 2$. Claude Picard mentioned the problem in his book *Théorie des Questionnaires* (1965), and an extensive exploration was undertaken by Milton Sobel [Univ. of Minnesota, Dept. of Statistics Reports 113 and 114 (November 1968); *Revue Française d'Automatique, Informatique et Recherche Opérationnelle* **6**, R-3 (December 1972), 23–68].

Sobel constructed the procedure of Fig. 42, which finds the second largest of six elements using only $6\frac{1}{2}$ comparisons on the average. In the worst case, 8 comparisons are required, and this is worse than $V_2(6) = 7$; in fact, an exhaustive computer search by D. Hoey has shown that the best procedure for this problem, if restricted to at most 7 comparisons, uses $6\frac{26}{45}$ comparisons on the average. Thus no procedure that finds the second largest of six elements can be optimum in both the minimax and the minimean senses simultaneously.

Let $\overline{V}_t(n)$ denote the minimum average number of comparisons needed to find the tth largest of n elements. Table 2 shows the exact values for small n, as computed by D. Hoey.

R. W. Floyd discovered in 1970 that the median of n elements can be found with only $\frac{3}{2}n + O(n^{2/3} \log n)$ comparisons, on the average. He and R. L. Rivest refined this method a few years later and constructed an elegant algorithm to prove that

$$\overline{V}_t(n) \leq n + \min(t, n-t) + O(\sqrt{n \log n}). \tag{16}$$

(See exercises 13 and 24.)

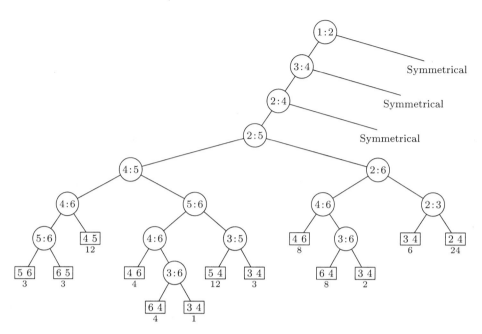

Fig. 42. A procedure that selects the second largest of $\{X_1, X_2, X_3, X_4, X_5, X_6\}$, using $6\frac{1}{2}$ comparisons on the average. Each "symmetrical" branch is identical to its sibling, with names permuted in some appropriate manner. External nodes contain "j k" when X_j is known to be the second largest and X_k the largest; the number of permutations leading to such a node appears immediately below it.

Using another approach, based on a generalization of one of Sobel's constructions for $t = 2$, David W. Matula [Washington Univ. Tech. Report AMCS-73-9 (1973)] showed that

$$\overline{V}_t(n) \le n + t \lceil \lg t \rceil (11 + \ln \ln n). \tag{17}$$

Thus, for fixed t the average amount of work can be reduced to $n + O(\log \log n)$ comparisons. An elegant lower bound on $\overline{V}_t(n)$ appears in exercise 25.

The sorting and selection problems are special cases of the much more general problem of finding a permutation of n given elements that is consistent with a given partial ordering. A. C. Yao [*SICOMP* **18** (1989), 679–689] has shown that, if the partial ordering is defined by an acyclic digraph G on n vertices with k connected components, the minimum number of comparisons necessary to solve such problems is always $\Theta\bigl(\lg\bigl(n!/T(G)\bigr) + n - k\bigr)$, in both the worst case and on the average, where $T(G)$ is the total number of permutations consistent with the partial ordering (the number of topological sortings of G).

EXERCISES

1. [*15*] In Lewis Carroll's tournament (Figs. 39 and 40), why was player *13* eliminated in spite of winning in Round 3?

Table 2

MINIMUM AVERAGE COMPARISONS FOR SELECTION

n	$\bar{V}_1(n)$	$\bar{V}_2(n)$	$\bar{V}_3(n)$	$\bar{V}_4(n)$	$\bar{V}_5(n)$	$\bar{V}_6(n)$	$\bar{V}_7(n)$
1	0						
2	1	1					
3	2	$2\frac{2}{3}$	2				
4	3	4	4	3			
5	4	$5\frac{4}{15}$	$5\frac{13}{15}$	$5\frac{4}{15}$	4		
6	5	$6\frac{1}{2}$	$7\frac{7}{18}$	$7\frac{7}{18}$	$6\frac{1}{2}$	5	
7	6	$7\frac{149}{210}$	$8\frac{509}{630}$	$9\frac{32}{105}$	$8\frac{509}{630}$	$7\frac{149}{210}$	6

▶ **2.** [*M25*] Prove that after we have found the tth largest of n elements by a sequence of comparisons, we also know which $t-1$ elements are greater than it, and which $n-t$ elements are less than it.

3. [*20*] Prove that $V_t(n) > V_t(n-1)$ and $W_t(n) > W_t(n-1)$, for $1 \le t < n$.

▶ **4.** [*M25*] (F. Fussenegger and H. N. Gabow.) Prove that $W_t(n) \ge n - t + \lceil \lg n\frac{t-1}{} \rceil$.

5. [*10*] Prove that $W_3(n) \le V_3(n) + 1$.

▶ **6.** [*M26*] (R. W. Floyd.) Given n distinct elements $\{X_1, \ldots, X_n\}$ and a set of relations $X_i < X_j$ for certain pairs (i, j), we wish to find the second largest element. If we know that $X_i < X_j$ and $X_i < X_k$ for $j \ne k$, X_i cannot possibly be the second largest, so it can be eliminated. The resulting relations now have a form such as

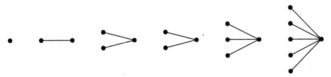

namely, m groups of elements that can be represented by a multiset $\{l_1, l_2, \ldots, l_m\}$; the jth group contains $l_j + 1$ elements, one of which is known to be greater than the others. For example, the configuration above can be described by the multiset $\{0, 1, 2, 2, 3, 5\}$; when no relations are known we have a multiset of n zeros.

Let $f(l_1, l_2, \ldots, l_m)$ be the minimum number of comparisons needed to find the second largest element of such a partially ordered set. Prove that

$$f(l_1, l_2, \ldots, l_m) = m - 2 + \lceil \lg(2^{l_1} + 2^{l_2} + \cdots + 2^{l_m}) \rceil.$$

[*Hint:* Show that the best strategy is always to compare the largest elements of the two smallest groups, until reducing m to unity; use induction on $l_1 + l_2 + \cdots + l_m + 2m$.]

7. [*M20*] Prove (8).

8. [*M21*] Kislitsyn's formula (6) is based on tree selection sorting using the complete binary tree with n external nodes. Would a tree selection method based on some *other* tree give a better bound, for any t and n?

▶ **9.** [*20*] Draw a comparison tree that finds the median of five elements in at most six steps, using the replacement-selection method of Hadian and Sobel [see (11)].

10. [*35*] Show that the median of seven elements can be found in at most 10 steps.

11. [*38*] (K. Noshita.) Show that the median of nine elements can be found in at most 14 steps, of which the first seven are identical to Doren's method.

12. [*21*] (Hadian and Sobel.) Prove that $V_3(n) \leq V_3(n-1) + 2$. [*Hint:* Start by discarding the smallest of $\{X_1, X_2, X_3, X_4\}$.]

▶ **13.** [*HM28*] (R. W. Floyd.) Show that if we start by finding the median element of $\{X_1, \ldots, X_{n^{2/3}}\}$, using a recursively defined method, we can go on to find the median of $\{X_1, \ldots, X_n\}$ with an average of $\frac{3}{2}n + O(n^{2/3} \log n)$ comparisons.

▶ **14.** [*20*] (M. Sobel.) Let $U_t(n)$ be the minimum number of comparisons needed to find the t largest of n elements, without necessarily knowing their relative order. Show that $U_2(5) \leq 5$.

15. [*22*] (I. Pohl.) Suppose that we are interested in minimizing space instead of time. What is the minimum number of data words needed in memory in order to compute the tth largest of n elements, if each element fills one word and if the elements are input one at a time into a single register?

▶ **16.** [*25*] (I. Pohl.) Show that we can find both the maximum and the minimum of a set of n elements, using at most $\lceil \frac{3}{2}n \rceil - 2$ comparisons; and the latter number cannot be lowered. [*Hint:* Any stage in such an algorithm can be represented as a quadruple (a, b, c, d), where a elements have never been compared, b have won but never lost, c have lost but never won, d have both won and lost. Construct an adversary.]

17. [*20*] (R. W. Floyd.) Show that it is possible to select, in order, both the k largest and the l smallest elements of a set of n elements, using at most $\lceil \frac{3}{2}n \rceil - k - l + \sum_{n+1-k<j\leq n} \lceil \lg j \rceil + \sum_{n+1-l<j\leq n} \lceil \lg j \rceil$ comparisons.

18. [*M20*] If groups of size 5, not 7, had been used in the proof of Theorem L, what theorem would have been obtained?

19. [*M42*] Extend Table 2 to $n = 8$.

20. [*M47*] What is the asymptotic value of $\overline{V}_2(n) - n$, as $n \to \infty$?

21. [*32*] (P. V. Ramanan and L. Hyafil.) Prove that $W_t(2^k + 2^{k+1-t}) \leq 2^k + 2^{k+1-t} + (t-1)(k-1)$, when $k \geq t \geq 2$; also show that equality holds for infinitely many k and t, because of exercise 4. [*Hint:* Maintain two knockout trees and merge their results cleverly.]

22. [*24*] (David G. Kirkpatrick.) Show that when $4 \cdot 2^k < n - 1 \leq 5 \cdot 2^k$, the upper bound (11) for $V_3(n)$ can be reduced by 1 as follows: (i) Form four knockout trees of size 2^k. (ii) Find the minimum of the four maxima, and discard all 2^k elements of its tree. (iii) Using the known information, build a single knockout tree of size $n - 1 - 2^k$. (iv) Continue as in the proof of (11).

23. [*M49*] What is the asymptotic value of $V_{\lceil n/2 \rceil}(n)$, as $n \to \infty$?

24. [*HM40*] Prove that $\overline{V}_t(n) \leq n + t + O(\sqrt{n \log n})$ for $t \leq \lceil n/2 \rceil$. *Hint:* Show that with this many comparisons we can in fact find both the $\lfloor t - \sqrt{t \ln n} \rfloor$th and $\lceil t + \sqrt{t \ln n} \rceil$th elements, after which the tth is easily located.

▶ **25.** [*M35*] (W. Cunto and J. I. Munro.) Prove that $\overline{V}_t(n) \geq n + t - 2$ when $t \leq \lceil n/2 \rceil$.

26. [*M32*] (A. Schönhage, 1974.) (a) In the notation of exercise 14, prove that $U_t(n) \geq \min(2 + U_t(n-1), 2 + U_{t-1}(n-1))$ for $n \geq 3$. [*Hint:* Construct an adversary by reducing from n to $n - 1$ as soon as the current partial ordering is not composed entirely of components having the form • or •——•.] (b) Similarly, prove that

$$U_t(n) \geq \min(2 + U_t(n-1), 3 + U_{t-1}(n-1), 3 + U_t(n-2))$$

for $n \geq 5$, by constructing an adversary that deals with components $\bullet$, $\longmapsto$, $\succ$, $\succcurlyeq$. (c) Therefore we have $U_t(n) \geq n + t + \min(\lfloor (n-t)/2 \rfloor, t) - 3$ for $1 \leq t \leq n/2$. [The inequalities in (a) and (b) apply also when V or W replaces U, thereby establishing the optimality of several entries in Table 1.]

▶ **27.** [*M34*] A *randomized adversary* is an adversary algorithm that is allowed to flip coins as it makes decisions.

a) Let A be a randomized adversary and let $\text{Pr}(l)$ be the probability that A reaches leaf l of a given comparison tree. Show that if $\text{Pr}(l) \leq p$ for all l, the height of the comparison tree is $\geq \lg(1/p)$.

b) Consider the following adversary for the problem of selecting the tth largest of n elements, given integer parameters q and r to be selected later:

  A1. Choose a random set T of t elements; all $\binom{n}{t}$ possibilities are equally likely. (We will ensure that the $t-1$ largest elements belong to T.) Let $S = \{1, \ldots, n\} \setminus T$ be the other elements, and set $S_0 \leftarrow S$, $T_0 \leftarrow T$; S_0 and T_0 will represent elements that might become the tth largest.

  A2. While $|T_0| > r$, decide all comparisons $x : y$ as follows: If $x \in S$ and $y \in T$, say that $x < y$. If $x \in S$ and $y \in S$, flip a coin to decide, and remove the smaller element from S_0 if it was in S_0. If $x \in T$ and $y \in T$, flip a coin to decide, and remove the larger element from T_0 if it was in T_0.

  A3. As soon as $|T_0| = r$, partition the elements into three classes P, Q, R as follows: If $|S_0| < q$, let $P = S$, $Q = T_0$, $R = T \setminus T_0$. Otherwise, for each $y \in T_0$, let $C(y)$ be the elements of S already compared with y, and choose y_0 so that $|C(y_0)|$ is minimum. Let $P = (S \setminus S_0) \cup C(y_0)$, $Q = (S_0 \setminus C(y_0)) \cup \{y_0\}$, $R = T \setminus \{y_0\}$. Decide all future comparisons $x : y$ by saying that elements of P are less than elements of Q, and elements of Q are less than elements of R; flip a coin when x and y are in the same class.

  Prove that if $1 \leq r \leq t$ and if $|C(y_0)| \leq q - r$ at the beginning of step A3, each leaf is reached with probability $\leq (n+1-t)/(2^{n-q}\binom{n}{t})$. *Hint:* Show that at least $n - q$ coin flips are made.

c) Continuing (b), show that we have

$$V_t(n) \geq \min\bigl(n - 1 + (r-1)(q+1-r), \, n - q + \lg(\binom{n}{t}/(n+1-t))\bigr),$$

  for all integers q and r.

d) Establish (14) by choosing q and r.

*5.3.4. Networks for Sorting

In this section we shall study a constrained type of sorting that is particularly interesting because of its applications and its rich underlying theory. The new constraint is to insist on an *oblivious* sequence of comparisons, in the sense that whenever we compare K_i versus K_j the subsequent comparisons for the case $K_i < K_j$ are exactly the same as for the case $K_i > K_j$, but with i and j interchanged.

Figure 43(a) shows a comparison tree in which this homogeneity condition is satisfied. Notice that every level has the same number of comparisons, so there are 2^m outcomes after m comparisons have been made. But $n!$ is not a power of 2; some of the comparisons must therefore be redundant, in the sense that

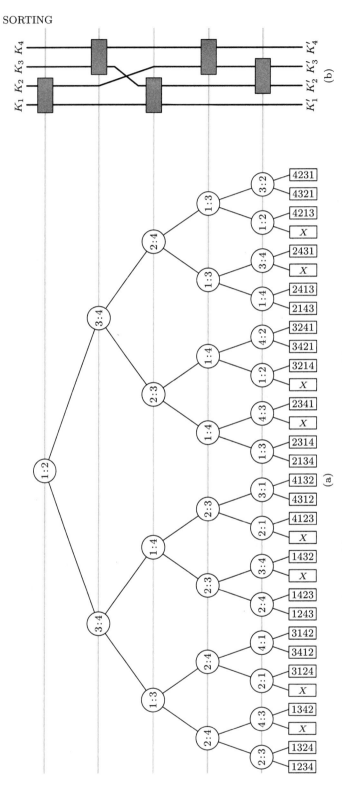

Fig. 43. (a) An oblivious comparison tree. (b) The corresponding network.

one of their subtrees can never arise in practice. In other words, some branches of the tree must make more comparisons than necessary, in order to ensure that all of the corresponding branches of the tree will sort properly.

Since each path from top to bottom of such a tree determines the entire tree, such a sorting scheme is most easily represented as a *network*; see Fig. 43(b). The boxes in such a network represent "comparator modules" that have two inputs (represented as lines coming into the module from above) and two outputs (represented as lines leading downward); the left-hand output is the smaller of the two inputs, and the right-hand output is the larger. At the bottom of the network, K_1' is the smallest of $\{K_1, K_2, K_3, K_4\}$, K_2' the second smallest, etc. It is not difficult to prove that any sorting network corresponds to an oblivious comparison tree in the sense above, and any oblivious tree corresponds to a network of comparator modules.

Incidentally, we may note that comparator modules are fairly easy to manufacture, from an engineering point of view. For example, assume that the lines contain binary numbers, where one bit enters each module per unit time, most significant bit first. Each comparator module has three states, and behaves as follows:

	Time t			Time $(t+1)$	
State	Inputs			State	Outputs
0	0	0		0	0 0
0	0	1		1	0 1
0	1	0		2	0 1
0	1	1		0	1 1
1	x	y		1	x y
2	x	y		2	y x

Initially all modules are in state 0 and are outputting 0 0. A module enters either state 1 or state 2 as soon as its inputs differ. Numbers that begin to be transmitted at the top of Fig. 43(b) at time t will begin to be output at the bottom, in sorted order, at time $t + 3$, if a suitable delay element is attached to the K_1' and K_4' lines.

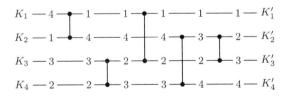

Fig. 44. Another way to represent the network of Fig. 43, as it sorts the sequence of four numbers $\langle 4, 1, 3, 2 \rangle$.

In order to develop the theory of sorting networks it is convenient to represent them in a slightly different way, illustrated in Fig. 44. Here numbers enter at the *left*, and comparator modules are represented by vertical connections between two lines; each comparator causes an interchange of its inputs, if necessary, so that the larger number sinks to the *lower* line after passing the comparator. At the right of the diagram all the numbers are in order from top to bottom.

Our previous studies of optimal sorting have concentrated on minimizing
the number of comparisons, with little or no regard for any underlying data
movement or for the complexity of the decision structure that may be necessary.
In this respect sorting networks have obvious advantages, since the data can be
maintained in n locations and the decision structure is "straight line" — there
is no need to remember the results of previous comparisons, since the plan is
immutably fixed in advance. Another important advantage of sorting networks
is that we can usually overlap several of the operations, performing them simultaneously (on a suitable machine). For example, the five steps in Figs. 43 and 44
can be collapsed into three when simultaneous nonoverlapping comparisons are
allowed, since the first two and the second two can be combined. We shall exploit
this property of sorting networks later in this section. Thus sorting networks can
be very useful, although it is not at all obvious that efficient n-element sorting
networks can be constructed for large n; we may find that many additional
comparisons are needed in order to keep the decision structure oblivious.

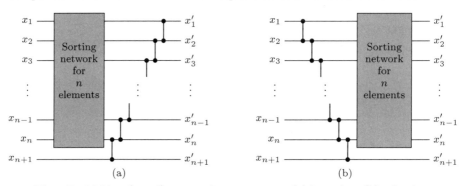

Fig. 45. Making $(n + 1)$-sorters from n-sorters: (a) insertion, (b) selection.

There are two simple ways to construct a sorting network for $n + 1$ elements
when an n-element network is given, using either the principle of *insertion* or
the principle of *selection*. Figure 45(a) shows how the $(n + 1)$st element can
be inserted into its proper place after the first n elements have been sorted;
and part (b) of the figure shows how the largest element can be selected before
we proceed to sort the remaining ones. Repeated application of Fig. 45(a) gives
the network analog of straight insertion sorting (Algorithm 5.2.1S), and repeated
application of Fig. 45(b) yields the network analog of the bubble sort (Algorithm
5.2.2B). Figure 46 shows the corresponding six-element networks.

(a)   (b)

Fig. 46. Network analogs of elementary internal sorting schemes, obtained by applying
the constructions of Fig. 45 repeatedly: (a) straight insertion, (b) bubble sort.

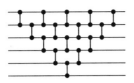

Fig. 47. With parallelism, straight insertion = bubble sort!

Notice that when we collapse either network together to allow simultaneous operations, both methods actually reduce to the same "triangular" $(2n - 3)$-stage procedure (Fig. 47).

It is easy to prove that the network of Figs. 43 and 44 will sort any set of four numbers into order, since the first four comparators route the smallest and the largest elements to the correct places, and the last comparator puts the remaining two elements in order. But it is not always so easy to tell whether or not a given network will sort all possible input sequences; for example, both

are valid 4-element sorting networks, but the proofs of their validity are not trivial. It would be sufficient to test each n-element network on all $n!$ permutations of n distinct numbers, but in fact we can get by with far fewer tests:

Theorem Z (Zero-one principle). *If a network with n input lines sorts all 2^n sequences of 0s and 1s into nondecreasing order, it will sort any arbitrary sequence of n numbers into nondecreasing order.*

Proof. (This is a special case of Bouricius's theorem, exercise 5.3.1–12.) If $f(x)$ is any monotonic function, with $f(x) \le f(y)$ whenever $x \le y$, and if a given network transforms $\langle x_1, \ldots, x_n \rangle$ into $\langle y_1, \ldots, y_n \rangle$, then it is easy to see that the network will transform $\langle f(x_1), \ldots, f(x_n) \rangle$ into $\langle f(y_1), \ldots, f(y_n) \rangle$. If $y_i > y_{i+1}$ for some i, consider the monotonic function f that takes all numbers $< y_i$ into 0 and all numbers $\ge y_i$ into 1; this defines a sequence $\langle f(x_1), \ldots, f(x_n) \rangle$ of 0s and 1s that is not sorted by the network. Hence if all 0–1 sequences are sorted, we have $y_i \le y_{i+1}$ for $1 \le i < n$. ∎

The zero-one principle is quite helpful in the construction of sorting networks. As a nontrivial example, we can derive a generalized version of Batcher's "merge exchange" sort (Algorithm 5.2.2M). The idea is to sort $m + n$ elements by sorting the first m and the last n independently, then applying an (m, n)-*merging network* to the result. An (m, n)-merging network can be constructed inductively as follows:

a) If $m = 0$ or $n = 0$, the network is empty. If $m = n = 1$, the network is a single comparator module.

b) If $mn > 1$, let the sequences to be merged be $\langle x_1, \ldots, x_m \rangle$ and $\langle y_1, \ldots, y_n \rangle$. Merge the "odd sequences" $\langle x_1, x_3, \ldots, x_{2\lceil m/2 \rceil - 1} \rangle$ and $\langle y_1, y_3, \ldots, y_{2\lceil n/2 \rceil - 1} \rangle$,

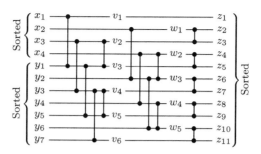

Fig. 48. The odd-even merge, when $m = 4$ and $n = 7$.

obtaining the sorted result $\langle v_1, v_2, \ldots, v_{\lceil m/2 \rceil + \lceil n/2 \rceil} \rangle$; and merge the "even sequences" $\langle x_2, x_4, \ldots, x_{2\lfloor m/2 \rfloor} \rangle$ and $\langle y_2, y_4, \ldots, y_{2\lfloor n/2 \rfloor} \rangle$, obtaining the sorted result $\langle w_1, w_2, \ldots, w_{\lfloor m/2 \rfloor + \lfloor n/2 \rfloor} \rangle$. Finally, apply the comparison-interchange operations

$$w_1 : v_2, \quad w_2 : v_3, \quad w_3 : v_4, \quad \ldots, \quad w_{\lfloor m/2 \rfloor + \lfloor n/2 \rfloor} : v^* \tag{1}$$

to the sequence

$$\langle v_1, w_1, v_2, w_2, v_3, w_3, \ldots, v_{\lfloor m/2 \rfloor + \lfloor n/2 \rfloor}, w_{\lfloor m/2 \rfloor + \lfloor n/2 \rfloor}, v^*, v^{**} \rangle; \tag{2}$$

the result will be sorted. (!) Here $v^* = v_{\lfloor m/2 \rfloor + \lfloor n/2 \rfloor + 1}$ does not exist if both m and n are even, and $v^{**} = v_{\lfloor m/2 \rfloor + \lfloor n/2 \rfloor + 2}$ does not exist unless both m and n are odd; the total number of comparator modules indicated in (1) is $\lfloor (m+n-1)/2 \rfloor$.

Batcher's (m, n)-merging network is called the *odd-even merge*. A $(4, 7)$-merge constructed according to these principles is illustrated in Fig. 48.

To prove that this rather strange merging procedure actually works, when $mn > 1$, we use the zero-one principle, testing it on all sequences of 0s and 1s. After the initial m-sort and n-sort, the sequence $\langle x_1, \ldots, x_m \rangle$ will consist of k 0s followed by $m - k$ 1s, and the sequence $\langle y_1, \ldots, y_m \rangle$ will be l 0s followed by $n - l$ 1s, for some k and l. Hence the sequence $\langle v_1, v_2, \ldots \rangle$ will consist of exactly $\lceil k/2 \rceil + \lceil l/2 \rceil$ 0s, followed by 1s; and $\langle w_1, w_2, \ldots \rangle$ will consist of $\lfloor k/2 \rfloor + \lfloor l/2 \rfloor$ 0s, followed by 1s. Now here's the point:

$$\big(\lceil k/2 \rceil + \lceil l/2 \rceil\big) - \big(\lfloor k/2 \rfloor + \lfloor l/2 \rfloor\big) = 0, 1, \text{ or } 2. \tag{3}$$

If this difference is 0 or 1, the sequence (2) is already in order, and if the difference is 2 one of the comparison-interchanges in (1) will fix everything up. This completes the proof. (Note that the zero-one principle reduces the merging problem from a consideration of $\binom{m+n}{m}$ cases to only $(m+1)(n+1)$, represented by the two parameters k and l.)

Let $C(m, n)$ be the number of comparator modules used in the odd-even merge for m and n, not counting the initial m-sort and n-sort; we have

$$C(m, n) = \begin{cases} mn, & \text{if } mn \leq 1; \\ C(\lceil m/2 \rceil, \lceil n/2 \rceil) + C(\lfloor m/2 \rfloor, \lfloor n/2 \rfloor) + \lfloor (m+n-1)/2 \rfloor, & \text{if } mn > 1. \end{cases} \tag{4}$$

This is not an especially simple function of m and n, in general, but by noting that $C(1, n) = n$ and that

$$C(m + 1, n + 1) - C(m, n)$$
$$= 1 + C(\lfloor m/2 \rfloor + 1, \lfloor n/2 \rfloor + 1) - C(\lfloor m/2 \rfloor, \lfloor n/2 \rfloor), \quad \text{if } mn \geq 1,$$

we can derive the relation

$$C(m + 1, n + 1) - C(m, n) = \lfloor \lg m \rfloor + 2 + \lfloor n/2^{\lfloor \lg m \rfloor + 1} \rfloor, \quad \text{if } n \geq m \geq 1. \quad (5)$$

Consequently

$$C(m, m + r) = B(m) + m + R_m(r), \quad \text{for } m \geq 0 \text{ and } r \geq 0, \quad (6)$$

where $B(m)$ is the "binary insertion" function $\sum_{k=1}^{m} \lceil \lg k \rceil$ of Eq. 5.3.1–(3), and where $R_m(r)$ denotes the sum of the first m terms of the series

$$\left\lfloor \frac{r+0}{1} \right\rfloor + \left\lfloor \frac{r+1}{2} \right\rfloor + \left\lfloor \frac{r+2}{4} \right\rfloor + \left\lfloor \frac{r+3}{4} \right\rfloor + \left\lfloor \frac{r+4}{8} \right\rfloor + \cdots + \left\lfloor \frac{r+j}{2^{\lfloor \lg j \rfloor + 1}} \right\rfloor + \cdots . \quad (7)$$

In particular, when $r = 0$ we have the important special case

$$C(m, m) = B(m) + m. \quad (8)$$

Furthermore if $t = \lceil \lg m \rceil$,

$$R_m(r + 2^t) = R_m(r) + 1 \cdot 2^{t-1} + 2 \cdot 2^{t-2} + \cdots + 2^{t-1} \cdot 2^0 + m$$
$$= R_m(r) + m + t \cdot 2^{t-1}.$$

Hence $C(m, n + 2^t) - C(m, n)$ has a simple form, and

$$C(m, n) = \left(\frac{t}{2} + \frac{m}{2^t} \right) n + O(1), \quad \text{for } m \text{ fixed}, n \to \infty, t = \lceil \lg m \rceil; \quad (9)$$

the $O(1)$ term is an eventually periodic function of n, with period length 2^t. As $n \to \infty$ we have $C(n, n) = n \lg n + O(n)$, by Eq. (8) and exercise 5.3.1–15.

Minimum-comparison networks. Let $\hat{S}(n)$ be the minimum number of comparators needed in a sorting network for n elements; clearly $\hat{S}(n) \geq S(n)$, where $S(n)$ is the minimum number of comparisons needed in an not-necessarily-oblivious sorting procedure (see Section 5.3.1). We have $\hat{S}(4) = 5 = S(4)$, so the new constraint causes no loss of efficiency when $n = 4$; but already when $n = 5$ it turns out that $\hat{S}(5) = 9$ while $S(5) = 7$. The problem of determining $\hat{S}(n)$ seems to be even harder than the problem of determining $S(n)$; even the asymptotic behavior of $\hat{S}(n)$ is still unknown.

It is interesting to trace the history of this problem, since each step was forged with some difficulty. Sorting networks were first explored by P. N. Armstrong, R. J. Nelson, and D. J. O'Connor, about 1954 [see *U.S. Patent 3029413*]; in the words of their patent attorney, "By the use of skill, it is possible to design economical n-line sorting switches using a reduced number of two-line sorting switches." After observing that $\hat{S}(n + 1) \leq \hat{S}(n) + n$, they gave special constructions for $4 \leq n \leq 8$, using 5, 9, 12, 18, and 19 comparators, respectively.

Then Nelson worked together with R. C. Bose to show that $\hat{S}(2^n) \leq 3^n - 2^n$ for all n; hence $\hat{S}(n) = O(n^{\lg 3}) = O(n^{1.585})$. Bose and Nelson published their interesting method in *JACM* **9** (1962), 282–296, where they conjectured that it was best possible; T. N. Hibbard [*JACM* **10** (1963), 142–150] found a similar but slightly simpler construction that used the same number of comparisons, thereby reinforcing the conjecture.

In 1964, R. W. Floyd and D. E. Knuth found a new way to approach the problem, leading to an asymptotic bound of the form $\hat{S}(n) = O(n^{1+c/\sqrt{\log n}})$. Working independently, K. E. Batcher discovered the general merging strategy outlined above. Using a number of comparators defined by the recursion

$$c(1) = 0, \quad c(n) = c(\lceil n/2 \rceil) + c(\lfloor n/2 \rfloor) + C(\lceil n/2 \rceil, \lfloor n/2 \rfloor) \quad \text{for } n \geq 2, \quad (10)$$

he proved (see exercise 5.2.2–14) that

$$c(2^t) = (t^2 - t + 4)2^{t-2} - 1;$$

consequently $\hat{S}(n) = O(n(\log n)^2)$. Neither Floyd and Knuth nor Batcher published their constructions until some time later [*Notices of the Amer. Math. Soc.* **14** (1967), 283; *Proc. AFIPS Spring Joint Computer Conf.* **32** (1968), 307–314].

Several people have found ways to reduce the number of comparators used by Batcher's merge-exchange construction; the following table shows the best upper bounds currently known for $\hat{S}(n)$:

$$
\begin{array}{rllllllllllllllll}
n = & 1 & 2 & 3 & 4 & 5 & 6 & 7 & 8 & 9 & 10 & 11 & 12 & 13 & 14 & 15 & 16 \\
c(n) = & 0 & 1 & 3 & 5 & 9 & 12 & 16 & 19 & 26 & 31 & 37 & 41 & 48 & 53 & 59 & 63 \\
\hat{S}(n) \leq & 0 & 1 & 3 & 5 & 9 & 12 & 16 & 19 & 25 & 29 & 35 & 39 & 45 & 51 & 56 & 60
\end{array}
\quad (11)
$$

Since $\hat{S}(n) < c(n)$ for $8 < n \leq 16$, merge exchange is nonoptimal for all $n > 8$. When $n \leq 8$, merge exchange uses the same number of comparators as the construction of Bose and Nelson. Floyd and Knuth proved in 1964–1966 that the values listed for $\hat{S}(n)$ are *exact* when $n \leq 8$ [see *A Survey of Combinatorial Theory* (North-Holland, 1973), 163–172]; the values of $\hat{S}(n)$ for $n > 8$ are still not known.

Constructions that lead to the values in (11) are shown in Fig. 49. The network for $n = 9$, based on an interesting three-way merge, was found by R. W. Floyd in 1964; its validity can be established by using the general principle described in exercise 27. The network for $n = 10$ was discovered by A. Waksman in 1969, by regarding the inputs as permutations of $\{1, 2, \ldots, 10\}$ and trying to reduce as much as possible the number of values that can appear on each line at a given stage, while maintaining some symmetry.

The network shown for $n = 13$ has quite a different pedigree: Hughes Juillé [*Lecture Notes in Comp. Sci.* **929** (1995), 246–260] used a computer program to construct it, by simulating an evolutionary process of genetic breeding. The network exhibits no obvious rhyme or reason, but it works — and it's shorter than any other construction devised so far by human ratiocination.

A 62-comparator sorting network for 16 elements was found by G. Shapiro in 1969, and this was rather surprising since Batcher's method (63 comparisons)

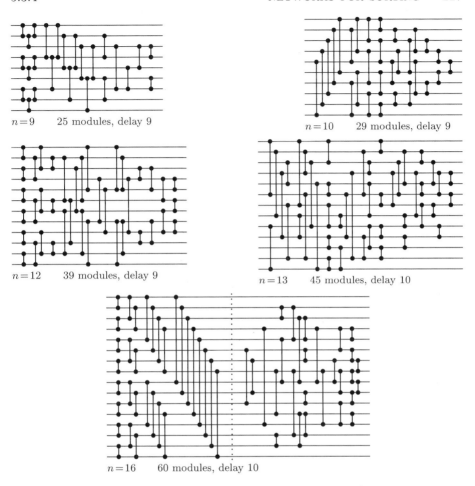

$n=9$ 25 modules, delay 9

$n=10$ 29 modules, delay 9

$n=12$ 39 modules, delay 9

$n=13$ 45 modules, delay 10

$n=16$ 60 modules, delay 10

Fig. 49. Efficient sorting networks.

would appear to be at its best when n is a power of 2. Soon after hearing of Shapiro's construction, M. W. Green tripled the amount of surprise by finding the 60-comparison sorter in Fig. 49. The first portion of Green's construction is fairly easy to understand; after the 32 comparison/interchanges to the left of the dotted line have been made, the lines can be labeled with the 16 subsets of $\{a, b, c, d\}$, in such a way that the line labeled s is known to contain a number less than or equal to the contents of the line labeled t whenever s is a subset of t. The state of the sort at this point is discussed further in exercise 32. Comparisons made on subsequent levels of Green's network become increasingly mysterious, however, and as yet nobody has seen how to generalize the construction in order to obtain correspondingly efficient networks for higher values of n.

Shapiro and Green also discovered the network shown for $n = 12$. When $n = 11$, 14, or 15, good networks can be found by removing the bottom line of the network for $n + 1$, together with all comparators touching that line.

The best sorting network currently known for 256 elements, due to D. Van Voorhis, shows that $\hat{S}(256) \leq 3651$, compared to 3839 by Batcher's method. [See R. L. Drysdale and F. H. Young, *SICOMP* **4** (1975), 264–270.] As $n \to \infty$, it turns out in fact that $\hat{S}(n) = O(n \log n)$; this astonishing upper bound was proved by Ajtai, Komlós, and Szemerédi in *Combinatorica* **3** (1983), 1–19. The networks they constructed are not of practical interest, since many comparators were introduced just to save a factor of $\log n$; Batcher's method is much better, unless n exceeds the total memory capacity of all computers on earth! But the theorem of Ajtai, Komlós, and Szemerédi does establish the true asymptotic growth rate of $\hat{S}(n)$, up to a constant factor.

Minimum-time networks. In physical realizations of sorting networks, and on parallel computers, it is possible to do nonoverlapping comparison-exchanges at the same time; therefore it is natural to try to minimize the delay time. A moment's reflection shows that the delay time of a sorting network is equal to the maximum number of comparators in contact with any "path" through the network, if we define a path to consist of any left-to-right route that possibly switches lines at the comparators. We can put a sequence number on each comparator indicating the earliest time it can be executed; this is one higher than the maximum of the sequence numbers of the comparators that occur earlier on its input lines. (See Fig. 50(a); part (b) of the figure shows the same network redrawn so that each comparison is done at the earliest possible moment.)

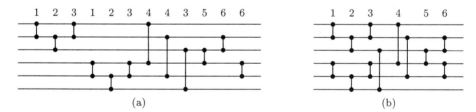

Fig. 50. Doing each comparison at the earliest possible time.

Batcher's odd-even merging network described above takes $T_B(m, n)$ units of time, where $T_B(m, 0) = T_B(0, n) = 0$, $T_B(1, 1) = 1$, and

$$T_B(m, n) = 1 + \max\bigl(T_B(\lfloor m/2 \rfloor, \lfloor n/2 \rfloor), T_B(\lceil m/2 \rceil, \lceil n/2 \rceil)\bigr) \quad \text{for } mn \geq 2.$$

We can use these relations to prove that $T_B(m, n+1) \geq T_B(m, n)$, by induction; hence $T_B(m, n) = 1 + T_B\bigl(\lceil m/2 \rceil, \lceil n/2 \rceil\bigr)$ for $mn \geq 2$, and it follows that

$$T_B(m, n) = 1 + \lceil \lg \max(m, n) \rceil, \qquad \text{for } mn \geq 1. \tag{12}$$

Exercise 5 shows that Batcher's sorting method therefore has a delay time of

$$\binom{1 + \lceil \lg n \rceil}{2}. \tag{13}$$

Let $\hat{T}(n)$ be the minimum achievable delay time in any sorting network for n elements. It is possible to improve some of the networks described above so

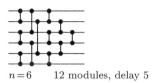

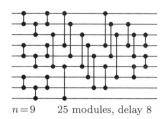

n=6   12 modules, delay 5

n=9   25 modules, delay 8

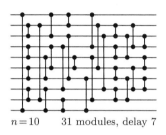

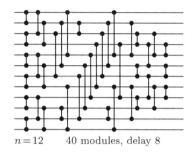

n=10   31 modules, delay 7

n=12   40 modules, delay 8

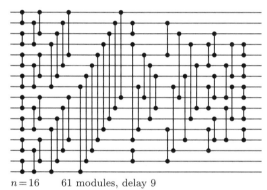

n=16   61 modules, delay 9

Fig. 51. Sorting networks that are the fastest known, when comparisons are performed in parallel.

that they have smaller delay time but use no more comparators, as shown for $n = 6$ and $n = 9$ in Fig. 51, and for $n = 10$ in exercise 7. Still smaller delay time can be achieved if we add one or two extra comparator modules, as shown in the remarkable networks for $n = 10$, 12, and 16 in Fig. 51. These constructions yield the following upper bounds on $\hat{T}(n)$ for small n:

$$
\begin{aligned}
n &= 1\ 2\ 3\ 4\ 5\ 6\ 7\ 8\ 9\ 10\ 11\ 12\ 13\ 14\ 15\ 16 \\
\hat{T}(n) &\leq 0\ 1\ 3\ 3\ 5\ 5\ 6\ 6\ 7\ \ 7\ \ 8\ \ 8\ \ 9\ \ 9\ \ 9\ \ 9
\end{aligned}
\tag{14}
$$

For $n \leq 10$ the values given here are known to be exact (see exercise 4). The networks in Fig. 51 merit careful study, because it is by no means obvious that they always sort; they were discovered in 1969–1971 by G. Shapiro ($n = 6$, 9, 12) and D. Van Voorhis ($n = 10$, 16).

Merging networks. Let $\hat{M}(m,n)$ denote the minimum number of comparator modules needed in a network that merges m elements $x_1 \leq \cdots \leq x_m$ with n elements $y_1 \leq \cdots \leq y_n$ to form the sorted sequence $z_1 \leq \cdots \leq z_{m+n}$. At present no merging networks have been discovered that are superior to the odd-even merge described above; hence the function $C(m,n)$ in (6) represents the best upper bound known for $\hat{M}(m,n)$.

R. W. Floyd has discovered an interesting way to find *lower* bounds for this merging problem.

Theorem F. $\hat{M}(2n,2n) \geq 2\hat{M}(n,n) + n$, for all $n \geq 1$.

Proof. Consider a network with $\hat{M}(2n,2n)$ comparator modules, capable of sorting all input sequences $\langle z_1, \ldots, z_{4n} \rangle$ such that $z_1 \leq z_3 \leq \cdots \leq z_{4n-1}$ and $z_2 \leq z_4 \leq \cdots \leq z_{4n}$. We may assume that each module replaces (z_i, z_j) by $\big(\min(z_i, z_j), \max(z_i, z_j)\big)$, for some $i < j$ (see exercise 16). The comparators can therefore be divided into three classes:

a) $i \leq 2n$ and $j \leq 2n$.

b) $i > 2n$ and $j > 2n$.

c) $i \leq 2n$ and $j > 2n$.

Class (a) must contain at least $\hat{M}(n,n)$ comparators, since $z_{2n+1}, z_{2n+2}, \ldots, z_{4n}$ may be already in their final position when the merge starts; similarly, there are at least $\hat{M}(n,n)$ comparators in class (b). Furthermore the input sequence $\langle 0, 1, 0, 1, \ldots, 0, 1 \rangle$ shows that class (c) contains at least n comparators, since n zeros must move from $\{z_{2n+1}, \ldots, z_{4n}\}$ to $\{z_1, \ldots, z_{2n}\}$. ∎

Repeated use of Theorem F proves that $\hat{M}(2^m, 2^m) \geq \frac{1}{2}(m+2)2^m$; hence $\hat{M}(n,n) \geq \frac{1}{2}n \lg n + O(n)$. We know from Theorem 5.3.2M that merging *without* the network restriction requires only $M(n,n) = 2n - 1$ comparisons; hence we have proved that merging with networks is intrinsically harder than merging in general.

The odd-even merge shows that

$$\hat{M}(m,n) \leq C(m,n) = \tfrac{1}{2}(m+n) \lg \min(m,n) + O(m+n).$$

P. B. Miltersen, M. Paterson, and J. Tarui [*JACM* **43** (1996), 147–165] have improved Theorem F by establishing the lower bound

$$\hat{M}(m,n) \geq \tfrac{1}{2}\big((m+n)\lg(m+1) - m/\ln 2\big) \qquad \text{for } 1 \leq m \leq n.$$

Consequently $\hat{M}(m,n) = \frac{1}{2}(m+n) \lg \min(m,n) + O(m+n)$.

The exact formula $\hat{M}(2,n) = C(2,n) = \lceil \frac{3}{2}n \rceil$ has been proved by A. C. Yao and F. F. Yao [*JACM* **23** (1976), 566–571]. The value of $\hat{M}(m,n)$ is also known to equal $C(m,n)$ for $m = n \leq 5$; see exercise 9.

Bitonic sorting. When simultaneous comparisons are allowed, we have seen in Eq. (12) that the odd-even merge uses $\lceil \lg(2n) \rceil$ units of delay time, when $1 \leq m \leq n$. Batcher has devised another type of network for merging, called a

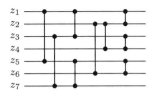

Fig. 52. Batcher's bitonic sorter of order 7.

bitonic sorter, which lowers the delay time to $\lceil \lg(m+n) \rceil$ although it requires more comparator modules. [See *U.S. Patent 3428946* (1969).]

Let us say that a sequence $\langle z_1, \ldots, z_p \rangle$ of p numbers is *bitonic* if $z_1 \geq \cdots \geq z_k \leq \cdots \leq z_p$ for some k, $1 \leq k \leq p$. (Compare this with the ordinary definition of "monotonic" sequences.) A bitonic sorter of order p is a comparator network that is capable of sorting any bitonic sequence of length p into nondecreasing order. The problem of merging $x_1 \leq \cdots \leq x_m$ with $y_1 \leq \cdots \leq y_n$ is a special case of the bitonic sorting problem, since merging can be done by applying a bitonic sorter of order $m+n$ to the sequence $\langle x_m, \ldots, x_1, y_1, \ldots, y_n \rangle$.

Notice that when a sequence $\langle z_1, \ldots, z_p \rangle$ is bitonic, so are all of its subsequences. Shortly after Batcher discovered the odd-even merging networks, he observed that we can construct a bitonic sorter of order p in an analogous way, by first sorting the bitonic subsequences $\langle z_1, z_3, z_5, \ldots \rangle$ and $\langle z_2, z_4, z_6, \ldots \rangle$ independently, then comparing and interchanging $z_1:z_2$, $z_3:z_4$, ... (See exercise 10 for a proof.) If $C'(p)$ is the corresponding number of comparator modules, we have

$$C'(p) = C'(\lceil p/2 \rceil) + C'(\lfloor p/2 \rfloor) + \lfloor p/2 \rfloor, \qquad \text{for } p \geq 2; \qquad (15)$$

and the delay time is clearly $\lceil \lg p \rceil$. Figure 52 shows the bitonic sorter of order 7 constructed in this way: It can be used as a (3,4)- as well as a (2,5)-merging network, with three units of delay; the odd-even merge for $m = 2$ and $n = 5$ saves one comparator but adds one more level of delay.

Batcher's bitonic sorter of order 2^t is particularly interesting; it consists of t levels of 2^{t-1} comparators each. If we number the input lines $z_0, z_1, \ldots, z_{2^t-1}$, element z_i is compared to z_j on level l if and only if i and j differ only in the lth most significant bit of their binary representations. This simple structure leads to parallel sorting networks that are as fast as merge exchange, Algorithm 5.2.2M, but considerably easier to implement. (See exercises 11 and 13.)

Bitonic merging is optimum, in the sense that no parallel merging method based on simultaneous disjoint comparisons can sort in fewer than $\lceil \lg(m+n) \rceil$ stages, whether it works obliviously or not. (See exercise 46.) Another way to achieve this optimum time, with fewer comparisons but a slightly more complicated control logic, is discussed in exercise 57.

When $1 \leq m \leq n$, the nth smallest output of an (m, n) merging network depends on $2m + [m < n]$ of the inputs (see exercise 29). If it can be computed by comparators with l levels of delay, it involves at most 2^l of the inputs; hence $2^l \geq 2m + [m < n]$, and $l \geq \lceil \lg(2m + [m < n]) \rceil$. Batcher has shown [Report GER-14122 (Akron, Ohio: Goodyear Aerospace Corporation, 1968)] that this

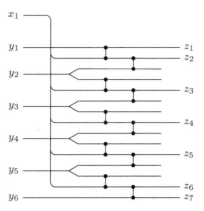

Fig. 53. Merging one item with six others, with multiple fanout, in order to achieve the minimum possible delay time.

minimum delay time is achievable if we allow "multiple fanout" in the network, namely the splitting of lines so that the same number is fed to many modules at once. For example, one of his networks, capable of merging one item with n others after only two levels of delay, is illustrated for $n = 6$ in Fig. 53. Of course, networks with multiple fanout do not conform to our conventions, and it is fairly easy to see that any $(1, n)$ merging network without multiple fanout must have a delay time of $\lg(n + 1)$ or more. (See exercise 45.)

Selection networks. We can also use networks to approach the problem of Section 5.3.3. Let $\hat{U}_t(n)$ denote the minimum number of comparators required in a network that moves the t largest of n distinct inputs into t specified output lines; the numbers are allowed to appear in any order on these output lines. Let $\hat{V}_t(n)$ denote the minimum number of comparators required to move the tth largest of n distinct inputs into a specified output line; and let $\hat{W}_t(n)$ denote the minimum number of comparators required to move the t largest of n distinct inputs into t specified output lines in nondecreasing order. It is not difficult to deduce (see exercise 17) that

$$\hat{U}_t(n) \leq \hat{V}_t(n) \leq \hat{W}_t(n). \tag{16}$$

Suppose first that we have $2t$ elements $\langle x_1, \ldots, x_{2t} \rangle$ and we wish to select the largest t. V. E. Alekseev [*Kibernetika* **5**, 5 (1969), 99–103] has observed that we can do the job by first sorting $\langle x_1, \ldots, x_t \rangle$ and $\langle x_{t+1}, \ldots, x_{2t} \rangle$, then comparing and interchanging

$$x_1 : x_{2t}, \qquad x_2 : x_{2t-1}, \qquad \ldots, \qquad x_t : x_{t+1}. \tag{17}$$

Since none of these pairs can contain more than one of the largest t elements (why?), Alekseev's procedure must select the largest t elements.

If we want to select the t largest of nt elements, we can apply Alekseev's procedure $n - 1$ times, eliminating t elements each time; hence

$$\hat{U}_t(nt) \leq (n - 1)\big(2\hat{S}(t) + t\big). \tag{18}$$

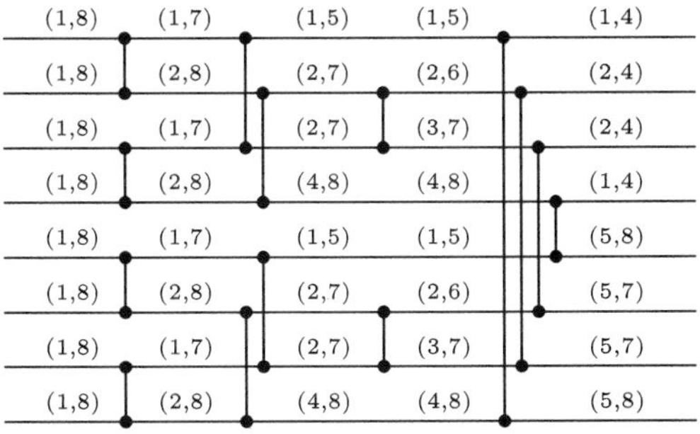

(1,8)	(1,7)	(1,5)	(1,5)	(1,4)
(1,8)	(2,8)	(2,7)	(2,6)	(2,4)
(1,8)	(1,7)	(2,7)	(3,7)	(2,4)
(1,8)	(2,8)	(4,8)	(4,8)	(1,4)
(1,8)	(1,7)	(1,5)	(1,5)	(5,8)
(1,8)	(2,8)	(2,7)	(2,6)	(5,7)
(1,8)	(1,7)	(2,7)	(3,7)	(5,7)
(1,8)	(2,8)	(4,8)	(4,8)	(5,8)

Fig. 54. Separating the largest four from the smallest four. (Numbers on these lines are used in the proof of Theorem A.)

Alekseev also derived an interesting *lower* bound for the selection problem:

Theorem A. $\hat{U}_t(n) \geq (n - t)\lceil \lg(t + 1)\rceil$.

Proof. It is most convenient to consider the equivalent problem of selecting the *smallest* t elements. We can attach numbers (l, u) to each line of a comparator network, as shown in Fig. 54, where l and u denote respectively the minimum and maximum values that can appear at that position when the input is a permutation of $\{1, 2, \ldots, n\}$. Let l_i and l_j be the lower bounds on lines i and j before a comparison of $x_i : x_j$, and let l'_i and l'_j be the corresponding lower bounds after the comparison. It is obvious that $l'_i = \min(l_i, l_j)$; exercise 24 proves the (nonobvious) relation

$$l'_j \leq l_i + l_j. \tag{19}$$

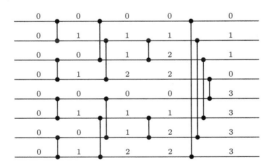

Fig. 55. Another interpretation for the network of Fig. 54.

Now let us reinterpret the network operations in another way (see Fig. 55): All input lines are assumed to contain zero, and each "comparator" now places the smaller of its inputs on the upper line and the larger *plus one* on the lower line. The resulting numbers $\langle m_1, m_2, \ldots, m_n \rangle$ have the property that

$$2^{m_i} \geq l_i \tag{20}$$

Table 1

COMPARISONS NEEDED IN SELECTION NETWORKS $(\hat{U}_t(n),\ \hat{V}_t(n),\ \hat{W}_t(n))$

	$t = 1$	$t = 2$	$t = 3$	$t = 4$	$t = 5$	$t = 6$
$n = 1$	$(0,0,0)$					
$n = 2$	$(1,1,1)$	$(0,1,1)$				
$n = 3$	$(2,2,2)$	$(2,3,3)$	$(0,2,3)$			
$n = 4$	$(3,3,3)$	$(4,5,5)$	$(3,5,5)$	$(0,3,5)$		
$n = 5$	$(4,4,4)$	$(6,7,7)$	$(6,7,8)$	$(4,7,9)$	$(0,4,9)$	
$n = 6$	$(5,5,5)$	$(8,9,9)$	$(8,10,10)$	$(8,10,12)$	$(5,9,12)$	$(0,5,12)$

throughout the network, since this holds initially and it is preserved by each comparator because of (19). Furthermore, the final value of

$$m_1 + m_2 + \cdots + m_n$$

is the total number of comparators in the network, since each comparator adds unity to this sum.

If the network selects the smallest t numbers, $n - t$ of the l_i are $\geq t + 1$; hence $n - t$ of the m_i must be $\geq \lceil \lg(t+1) \rceil$.   ∎

The lower bound in Theorem A turns out to be exact when $t = 1$ and when $t = 2$ (see exercise 19). Table 1 gives some values of $\hat{U}_t(n)$, $\hat{V}_t(n)$, and $\hat{W}_t(n)$ for small t and n. Andrew Yao [Ph.D. thesis, U. of Illinois (1975)] determined the asymptotic behavior of $\hat{U}_t(n)$ for fixed t, by showing that $\hat{U}_3(n) = 2n + \lg n + O(1)$ and $\hat{U}_t(n) = n \lceil \lg(t+1) \rceil + O\big((\log n)^{\lfloor \lg t \rfloor}\big)$ as $n \to \infty$; the minimum delay time is $\lg n + \lfloor \lg t \rfloor \lg \lg n + O(\log \log \log n)$. N. Pippenger [*SICOMP* **20** (1991), 878–887] has proved by nonconstructive methods that for any $\epsilon > 0$ there exist selection networks with $\hat{U}_{\lceil n/2 \rceil}(n) \leq (2 + \epsilon) n \lg n$, whenever n is sufficiently large (depending on ϵ).

EXERCISES — First Set

Several of the following exercises develop the theory of sorting networks in detail, and it is convenient to introduce some notation. We let $[i:j]$ stand for a comparison/interchange module. A network with n inputs and r comparator modules is written $[i_1 : j_1][i_2 : j_2] \ldots [i_r : j_r]$, where each of the i's and j's is $\leq n$; we shall call it an n-*network* for short. A network is called *standard* if $i_q < j_q$ for $1 \leq q \leq r$. Thus, for example, Fig. 44 on page 221 depicts a standard 4-network, denoted by the comparator sequence $[1:2][3:4][1:3][2:4][2:3]$.

The text's convention for drawing network diagrams represents only standard networks; all comparators $[i:j]$ are represented by a line from i to j, where $i < j$. When nonstandard networks must be drawn, we can use an *arrow* from i to j, indicating that the larger number goes to the point of the arrow. For example, Fig. 56 illustrates a nonstandard network for 16 elements, whose comparators are $[1:2][4:3][5:6][8:7]$ etc. Exercise 11 proves that Fig. 56 is a sorting network.

If $x = \langle x_1, \ldots, x_n \rangle$ is an n-vector and α is an n-network, we write $x\alpha$ for the vector of numbers $\langle (x\alpha)_1, \ldots, (x\alpha)_n \rangle$ produced by the network. For brevity, we also let $a \vee b = \max(a,b)$, $a \wedge b = \min(a,b)$, $\bar{a} = 1 - a$. Thus $(x[i:j])_i = x_i \wedge x_j$, $(x[i:j])_j = x_i \vee x_j$,

Stage 1   Stage 2   Stage 3   Stage 4

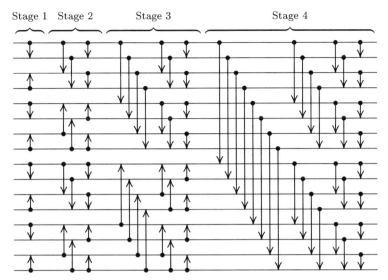

Fig. 56. A nonstandard sorting network based on bitonic sorting.

and $(x[i\!:\!j])_k = x_k$ when $i \neq k \neq j$. We say α is a *sorting network* if $(x\alpha)_i \leq (x\alpha)_{i+1}$ for all x and for $1 \leq i < n$.

The symbol $e^{(i)}$ stands for a vector that has 1 in position i, 0 elsewhere; thus $(e^{(i)})_j = \delta_{ij}$. The symbol D_n stands for the set of all 2^n n-place vectors of 0s and 1s, and P_n stands for the set of all $n!$ vectors that are permutations of $\{1, 2, \ldots, n\}$. We write $x \wedge y$ and $x \vee y$ for the vectors $\langle x_1 \wedge y_1, \ldots, x_n \wedge y_n \rangle$ and $\langle x_1 \vee y_1, \ldots, x_n \vee y_n \rangle$, and we write $x \leq y$ if $x_i \leq y_i$ for all i. Thus $x \leq y$ if and only if $x \vee y = y$ if and only if $x \wedge y = x$. If x and y are in D_n, we say that x *covers* y if $x = (y \vee e^{(i)}) \neq y$ for some i. Finally for all x in D_n we let $\nu(x)$ be the number of 1s in x, and $\zeta(x)$ the number of 0s; thus $\nu(x) + \zeta(x) = n$.

1. [*20*] Draw a network diagram for the odd-even merge when $m = 3$ and $n = 5$.

2. [*22*] Show that V. Pratt's sorting algorithm (exercise 5.2.1–30) leads to a sorting network for n elements that has approximately $(\log_2 n)(\log_3 n)$ levels of delay. Draw the corresponding network for $n = 12$.

3. [*M20*] (K. E. Batcher.) Find a simple relation between $C(m, m-1)$ and $C(m, m)$.

▶ **4.** [*M23*] Prove that $\hat{T}(6) = 5$.

5. [*M16*] Prove that (13) is the delay time associated with the sorting network outlined in (10).

6. [*28*] Let $T(n)$ be the minimum number of stages needed to sort n distinct numbers by making *simultaneous disjoint comparisons* (without necessarily obeying the network constraint); such comparisons can be represented as a node containing a set of pairs $\{i_1\!:\!j_1, i_2\!:\!j_2, \ldots, i_r\!:\!j_r\}$ where $i_1, j_1, i_2, j_2, \ldots, i_r, j_r$ are distinct, with 2^r branches below this node for the respective cases

$$\langle K_{i_1} < K_{j_1}, \ K_{i_2} < K_{j_2}, \ \ldots, \ K_{i_r} < K_{j_r} \rangle,$$
$$\langle K_{i_1} > K_{j_1}, \ K_{i_2} < K_{j_2}, \ \ldots, \ K_{i_r} < K_{j_r} \rangle, \qquad \text{etc.}$$

Prove that $T(5) = T(6) = 5$.

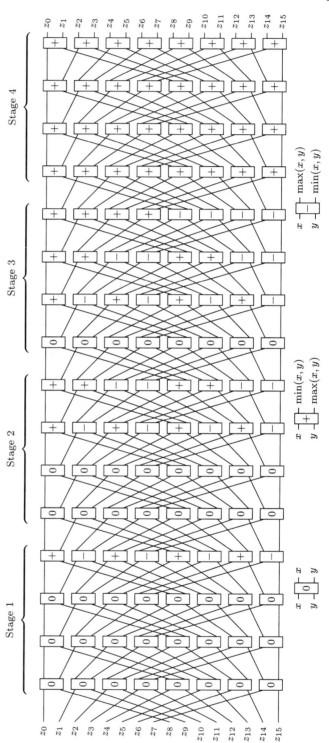

Fig. 57. Sorting 16 elements with perfect shuffles.

7. [*25*] Show that if the final three comparators of the network for $n = 10$ in Fig. 49 are replaced by the "weaker" sequence $[5\!:\!6][4\!:\!5][6\!:\!7]$, the network will still sort.

8. [*M20*] Prove that $\hat{M}(m_1+m_2, n_1+n_2) \geq \hat{M}(m_1, n_1) + \hat{M}(m_2, n_2) + \min(m_1, n_2)$, for $m_1, m_2, n_1, n_2 \geq 0$.

9. [*M25*] (R. W. Floyd.) Prove that $\hat{M}(3,3) = 6$, $\hat{M}(4,4) = 9$, $\hat{M}(5,5) = 13$.

10. [*M22*] Prove that Batcher's bitonic sorter, as defined in the remarks preceding (15), is valid. [*Hint:* It is only necessary to prove that all sequences consisting of k 1s followed by l 0s followed by $n - k - l$ 1s will be sorted.]

11. [*M23*] Prove that Batcher's bitonic sorter of order 2^t will not only sort sequences $\langle z_0, z_1, \ldots, z_{2^t-1} \rangle$ for which $z_0 \geq \cdots \geq z_k \leq \cdots \leq z_{2^t-1}$, it also will sort any sequence for which $z_0 \leq \cdots \leq z_k \geq \cdots \geq z_{2^t-1}$. [As a consequence, the network in Fig. 56 will sort 16 elements, since each stage consists of bitonic sorters or reverse-order bitonic sorters, applied to sequences that have been sorted in opposite directions.]

12. [*M20*] Prove or disprove: If x and y are bitonic sequences of the same length, so are $x \vee y$ and $x \wedge y$.

▶ **13.** [*24*] (H. S. Stone.) Show that a sorting network for 2^t elements can be constructed by following the pattern illustrated for $t = 4$ in Fig. 57. Each of the t^2 steps in this scheme consists of a "perfect shuffle" of the first 2^{t-1} elements with the last 2^{t-1}, followed by simultaneous operations performed on 2^{t-1} pairs of adjacent elements. Each of the latter operations is either "0" (no operation), "+" (a standard comparator module), or "−" (a reverse comparator module). The sorting proceeds in t stages of t steps each; during the last stage all operations are "+". During stage s, for $s < t$, we do $t-s$ steps in which all operations are "0", followed by s steps in which the operations within step q consist alternately of 2^{q-1} "+" followed by 2^{q-1} "−", for $q = 1, 2, \ldots, s$.

[Note that this sorting scheme could be performed by a fairly simple device whose circuitry performs one "shuffle-and-operate" step and feeds the output lines back into the input. The first three steps in Fig. 57 could of course be eliminated; they have been retained only to make the pattern clear. Stone notes that the same pattern "shuffle/operate" occurs in several other algorithms, such as the fast Fourier transform (see 4.6.4–(40)).]

▶ **14.** [*M27*] (V. E. Alekseev.) Let $\alpha = [i_1\!:\!j_1]\ldots[i_r\!:\!j_r]$ be an n-network; for $1 \leq s \leq r$ we define $\alpha^s = [i'_1\!:\!j'_1]\ldots[i'_{s-1}\!:\!j'_{s-1}][i_s\!:\!j_s]\ldots[i_r\!:\!j_r]$, where the i'_k and j'_k are obtained from i_k and j_k by changing i_s to j_s and changing j_s to i_s wherever they appear. For example, if $\alpha = [1\!:\!2][3\!:\!4][1\!:\!3][2\!:\!4][2\!:\!3]$, then $\alpha^4 = [1\!:\!4][3\!:\!2][1\!:\!3][2\!:\!4][2\!:\!3]$.

   a) Prove that $D_n\alpha = D_n(\alpha^s)$.

   b) Prove that $(\alpha^s)^t = (\alpha^t)^s$.

   c) A *conjugate* of α is any network of the form $(\ldots((\alpha^{s_1})^{s_2})\ldots)^{s_k}$. Prove that α has at most 2^{r-1} conjugates.

   d) Let $g_\alpha(x) = [x \in D_n\alpha]$, and let $f_\alpha(x) = (\bar{x}_{i_1} \vee x_{j_1}) \wedge \cdots \wedge (\bar{x}_{i_r} \vee x_{j_r})$. Prove that $g_\alpha(x) = \bigvee \{f_{\alpha'}(x) \mid \alpha' \text{ is a conjugate of } \alpha\}$.

   e) Let G_α be the directed graph with vertices $\{1, \ldots, n\}$ and with arcs $i_s \rightarrow j_s$ for $1 \leq s \leq r$. Prove that α is a sorting network if and only if $G_{\alpha'}$ has an oriented path from i to $i+1$ for $1 \leq i < n$ and for all α' conjugate to α. [This condition is somewhat remarkable, since G_α does not depend on the order of the comparators in α.]

15. [*20*] Find a nonstandard sorting network for four elements that has only five comparator modules.

16. [*M22*] Prove that the following algorithm transforms any sorting network $[i_1 : j_1]$ $\ldots [i_r : j_r]$ into a standard sorting network of the same length:

> **T1.** Let q be the smallest index such that $i_q > j_q$. If no such index exists, stop.
>
> **T2.** Change all occurrences of i_q to j_q, and all occurrences of j_q to i_q, in all comparators $[i_s : j_s]$ for $q \leq s \leq r$. Return to T1. ∎

Thus, $[4:1][3:2][1:3][2:4][1:2][3:4]$ is first transformed into $[1:4][3:2][4:3][2:1][4:2][3:1]$, then $[1:4][2:3][4:2][3:1][4:3][2:1]$, then $[1:4][2:3][2:4][3:1][2:3][4:1]$, etc., until the standard network $[1:4][2:3][2:4][1:3][1:2][3:4]$ is obtained.

17. [*M25*] Let D_{tn} be the set of all $\binom{n}{t}$ sequences $\langle x_1, \ldots, x_n \rangle$ of 0s and 1s having exactly t 1s. Show that $\hat{U}_t(n)$ is the minimum number of comparators needed in a network that sorts all the elements of D_{tn}; $\hat{V}_t(n)$ is the minimum number needed to sort $D_{tn} \cup D_{(t-1)n}$; and $\hat{W}_t(n)$ is the minimum number needed to sort $\bigcup_{0 \leq k \leq t} D_{kn}$.

▸ **18.** [*M20*] Prove that a network that finds the median of $2t - 1$ elements requires at least $(t-1)\lceil \lg(t+1) \rceil + \lceil \lg t \rceil$ comparator modules. [*Hint:* See the proof of Theorem A.]

19. [*M22*] Prove that $\hat{U}_2(n) = 2n - 4$ and $\hat{V}_2(n) = 2n - 3$, for all $n \geq 2$.

20. [*24*] Prove that $\hat{V}_3(5) = 7$.

21. [*21*] True or false: Inserting a new standard comparator into any standard sorting network yields another standard sorting network.

22. [*M17*] Let α be any n-network, and let x and y be n-vectors.
a) Prove that $x \leq y$ implies that $x\alpha \leq y\alpha$.
b) Prove that $x \cdot y \leq (x\alpha) \cdot (y\alpha)$, where $x \cdot y$ denotes the dot product $x_1 y_1 + \cdots + x_n y_n$.

23. [*M18*] Let α be an n-network. Prove that there is a permutation $p \in P_n$ such that $(p\alpha)_i = j$ if and only if there are vectors x and y in D_n such that x covers y, $(x\alpha)_i = 1$, $(y\alpha)_i = 0$ and $\zeta(y) = j$.

▸ **24.** [*M21*] (V. E. Alekseev.) Let α be an n-network, and for $1 \leq k \leq n$ let

$$l_k = \min\{(p\alpha)_k \mid p \in P_n\}, \qquad u_k = \max\{(p\alpha)_k \mid p \in P_n\}$$

denote the lower and upper bounds on the range of values that may appear in line k of the output. Let l'_k and u'_k be defined similarly for the network $\alpha' = \alpha[i:j]$. Prove that

$$l'_i = l_i \wedge l_j, \qquad l'_j \leq l_i + l_j, \qquad u'_i \geq u_i + u_j - (n+1), \qquad u'_j = u_i \vee u_j.$$

[*Hint:* Given vectors x and y in D_n with $(x\alpha)_i = (y\alpha)_j = 0$, $\zeta(x) = l_i$, and $\zeta(y) = l_j$, find a vector z in D_n with $(z\alpha')_j = 0$, $\zeta(z) \leq l_i + l_j$.]

25. [*M30*] Let l_k and u_k be as defined in exercise 24. Prove that all integers between l_k and u_k inclusive are in the set $\{(p\alpha)_k \mid p \text{ in } P_n\}$.

26. [*M24*] (R. W. Floyd.) Let α be an n-network. Prove that one can determine the set $D_n\alpha = \{x\alpha \mid x \text{ in } D_n\}$ from the set $P_n\alpha = \{p\alpha \mid p \text{ in } P_n\}$; conversely, $P_n\alpha$ can be determined from $D_n\alpha$.

▸ **27.** [*M20*] Let x and y be vectors, and let $x\alpha$ and $y\alpha$ be sorted. Prove that $(x\alpha)_i \leq (y\alpha)_j$ if and only if, for every choice of j elements from y, we can choose i elements from x such that every chosen x element is $\leq$ some chosen y element. Use this principle to prove that *if we sort the rows of any matrix, then sort the columns, the rows will remain in order*.

▶ **28.** [*M20*] The following diagram illustrates the fact that we can systematically write down formulas for the contents of all lines in a sorting network in terms of the inputs:

$$
\begin{array}{llll}
a & a \wedge b & (a \wedge b) \wedge (c \wedge d) & (a \wedge b) \wedge (c \wedge d) \\
b & a \vee b & (a \vee b) \wedge (c \vee d) & ((a \vee b) \wedge (c \vee d)) \wedge ((a \wedge b) \vee (c \wedge d)) \\
c & c \wedge d & (a \wedge b) \vee (c \wedge d) & ((a \vee b) \wedge (c \vee d)) \vee ((a \wedge b) \vee (c \wedge d)) \\
d & c \vee d & (a \vee b) \vee (c \vee d) & (a \vee b) \vee (c \vee d)
\end{array}
$$

Using the commutative laws $x \wedge y = y \wedge x$, $x \vee y = y \vee x$, the associative laws $x \wedge (y \wedge z) = (x \wedge y) \wedge z$, $x \vee (y \vee z) = (x \vee y) \vee z$, the distributive laws $x \wedge (y \vee z) = (x \wedge y) \vee (x \wedge z)$, $x \vee (y \wedge z) = (x \vee y) \wedge (x \vee z)$, the absorption laws $x \wedge (x \vee y) = x \vee (x \wedge y) = x$, and the idempotent laws $x \wedge x = x \vee x = x$, we can reduce the formulas at the right of this network to $(a \wedge b \wedge c \wedge d)$, $(a \wedge b \wedge c) \vee (a \wedge b \wedge d) \vee (a \wedge c \wedge d) \vee (b \wedge c \wedge d)$, $(a \wedge b) \vee (a \wedge c) \vee (a \wedge d) \vee (b \wedge c) \vee (b \wedge d) \vee (c \wedge d)$, and $a \vee b \vee c \vee d$, respectively.

Prove that, in general, the tth largest element of $\{x_1, \ldots, x_n\}$ is given by the "elementary symmetric function"

$$
\sigma_t(x_1, \ldots, x_n) = \bigvee \{x_{i_1} \wedge x_{i_2} \wedge \cdots \wedge x_{i_t} \mid 1 \le i_1 < i_2 < \cdots < i_t \le n\}.
$$

[There are $\binom{n}{t}$ terms being $\vee$'d together. Thus the problem of finding minimum-cost sorting networks is equivalent to the problem of computing the elementary symmetric functions with a minimum of "and/or" circuits, where at every stage we are required to replace two quantities ϕ and ψ by $\phi \wedge \psi$ and $\phi \vee \psi$.]

29. [*M20*] Given that $x_1 \le x_2 \le x_3$ and $y_1 \le y_2 \le y_3 \le y_4 \le y_5$, and that $z_1 \le z_2 \le \cdots \le z_8$ is the result of merging the x's with the y's, find formulas for each of the z's in terms of the x's and the y's, using the operators $\wedge$ and $\vee$.

30. [*HM24*] Prove that any formula involving $\wedge$ and $\vee$ and the independent variables $\{x_1, \ldots, x_n\}$ can be reduced using the identities in exercise 28 to a "canonical" form $\tau_1 \vee \tau_2 \vee \cdots \vee \tau_k$, where $k \ge 1$, each τ_i has the form $\bigwedge \{x_j \mid j \text{ in } S_i\}$ where S_i is a subset of $\{1, 2, \ldots, n\}$, and no set S_i is included in S_j for $i \ne j$. Prove also that two such canonical forms are equal for all $x_1, \ldots, x_n$ if and only if they are identical (up to order).

31. [*M24*] (R. Dedekind, 1897.) Let δ_n be the number of distinct canonical forms on $x_1, \ldots, x_n$ in the sense of exercise 30. Thus $\delta_1 = 1$, $\delta_2 = 4$, and $\delta_3 = 18$. What is δ_4?

32. [*M28*] (M. W. Green.) Let $G_1 = \{00, 01, 11\}$, and let G_{t+1} be the set of all strings $\theta \phi \psi \omega$ such that θ, ϕ, ψ, ω have length 2^{t-1} and $\theta\phi$, $\psi\omega$, $\theta\psi$, and $\phi\omega$ are in G_t. Let α be the network consisting of the first four levels of the 16-sorter shown in Fig. 49. Show that $D_{16}\alpha = G_4$, and prove that it has exactly $\delta_4 + 2$ elements. (See exercise 31.)

▶ **33.** [*M22*] Not all δ_n of the functions of $\langle x_1, \ldots, x_n \rangle$ in exercise 31 can appear in comparator networks. In fact, prove that the function $(x_1 \wedge x_2) \vee (x_2 \wedge x_3) \vee (x_3 \wedge x_4)$ cannot appear as an output of any comparator network on $\langle x_1, \ldots, x_n \rangle$.

34. [*23*] Is the following a sorting network?

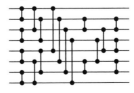

35. [*20*] Prove that any standard sorting network must contain each of the *adjacent* comparators $[i:i+1]$, for $1 \le i < n$, at least once.

▶ **36.** [*22*] The network of Fig. 47 involves only adjacent comparisons $[i:i+1]$; let us call such a network *primitive*.

a) Prove that a primitive sorting network for n elements must have at least $\binom{n}{2}$ comparators. [*Hint:* Consider the inversions of a permutation.]

b) (R. W. Floyd, 1964.) Let α be a primitive network for n elements, and let x be a vector such that $(x\alpha)_i > (x\alpha)_j$ for some $i < j$. Prove that $(y\alpha)_i > (y\alpha)_j$, where y is the vector $\langle n, n-1, \ldots, 1 \rangle$.

c) As a consequence of (b), a primitive network is a sorting network if and only if it sorts the single vector $\langle n, n-1, \ldots, 1 \rangle$.

37. [*M22*] The *odd-even transposition sort* for n numbers, $n \ge 3$, is a network n levels deep with $\frac{1}{2}n(n-1)$ comparators, arranged in a brick-like pattern as shown in Fig. 58. (When n is even, there are two possibilities.) Such a sort is especially easy to implement in hardware, since only two kinds of actions are performed alternatively. Prove that such a network is, in fact, a valid sorting network. [*Hint:* See exercise 36.]

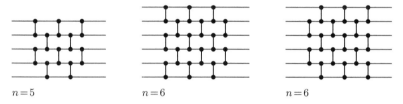

$n=5$ $n=6$ $n=6$

Fig. 58. The odd-even transposition sort.

▶ **38.** [*43*] Let $N = \binom{n}{2}$. Find a one-to-one correspondence between Young tableaux of shape $(n-1, n-2, \ldots, 1)$ and primitive sorting networks $[i_1:i_1+1]\ldots[i_N:i_N+1]$. [Consequently by Theorem 5.1.4H there are exactly

$$\frac{N!}{1^{n-1}\,3^{n-2}\,5^{n-3}\,\ldots\,(2n-3)^1}$$

such sorting networks.] *Hint:* Exercise 36(c) shows that primitive networks without redundant comparators correspond to paths from $1\,2\ldots n$ to $n\ldots 2\,1$ in polyhedra like Fig. 1 in Section 5.1.1.

39. [*25*] Suppose that a primitive comparator network on n lines is known to sort the single input $1\,0\,1\,0\,\ldots\,1\,0$ correctly. (See exercise 36; assume that n is even.) Show that its "middle third," consisting of all comparators that involve only lines $\lceil n/3 \rceil$ through $\lceil 2n/3 \rceil$ inclusive, will sort *all* inputs.

40. [*HM44*] Comparators $[i_1:i_1+1][i_2:i_2+1]\ldots[i_r:i_r+1]$ are chosen at random, with each value of $i_k \in \{1, 2, \ldots, n-1\}$ equally likely; the process stops when the network contains a bubble sort configuration like that of Fig. 47 as a subnetwork. Prove that $r \le 4n^2 + \sqrt{n}\,\lg n$, except with probability $O(n^{-1000})$.

41. [*M47*] Comparators $[i_1:j_1][i_2:j_2]\ldots[i_r:j_r]$ are chosen at random, with each *irredundant* choice $1 \le i_k < j_k \le n$ equally likely; the process stops when a sorting network has been obtained. Estimate the expected value of r; is it $O(n^{1+\epsilon})$ for all $\epsilon > 0$?

▶ **42.** [*25*] (D. Van Voorhis.) Prove that $\hat{S}(n) \ge \hat{S}(n-1) + \lceil \lg n \rceil$.

43. [*48*] Find an (m, n) merging network with fewer than $C(m, n)$ comparators, or prove that no such network exists.

44. [*50*] Find the exact value of $\hat{S}(n)$ for some $n > 8$.

45. [*M20*] Prove that any $(1, n)$-merging network without multiple fanout must have at least $\lceil \lg(n + 1) \rceil$ levels of delay.

▶ **46.** [*30*] (M. Aigner.) Show that the minimum number of stages needed to merge m elements with n, using any algorithm that does simultaneous disjoint comparisons as in exercise 6, is at least $\lceil \lg(m+n) \rceil$; hence the bitonic merging network has optimum delay.

47. [*47*] Is the function $T(n)$ of exercise 6 strictly less than $\hat{T}(n)$ for some n?

▶ **48.** [*26*] We can interpret sorting networks in another way, letting each line carry a multiset of m numbers instead of a single number; under this interpretation, the operation $[i:j]$ replaces x_i and x_j, respectively, by $x_i \wedge x_j$ and $x_i \vee x_j$, the least m and the greatest m of the $2m$ numbers $x_i \uplus x_j$. (For example, the diagram

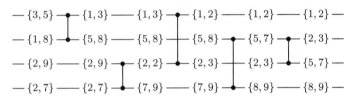

illustrates this interpretation when $m = 2$; each comparator merges its inputs and separates the lower half from the upper half.)

If a and b are multisets of m numbers each, we say that $a \ll b$ if and only if $a \wedge b = a$ (equivalently, $a \vee b = b$; the largest element of a is less than or equal to the smallest of b). Thus $a \wedge b \ll a \vee b$.

Let α be an n-network, and let $x = \langle x_1, \ldots, x_n \rangle$ be a vector in which each x_i is a multiset of m elements. Prove that if $(x\alpha)_i$ is not $\ll (x\alpha)_j$ in the interpretation above, there is a vector y in D_n such that $(y\alpha)_i = 1$ and $(y\alpha)_j = 0$. [Consequently, a sorting network for n elements becomes a sorting network for mn elements if we replace comparisons by m-way merges. Figure 59 shows an 8-element sorter constructed from a 4-element sorter by using this observation.]

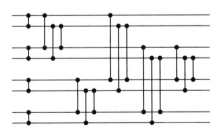

Fig. 59. An 8-sorter constructed from a 4-sorter, by using the merging interpretation.

49. [*M23*] Show that, in the notation of exercise 48, $(x \wedge y) \wedge z = x \wedge (y \wedge z)$ and $(x \vee y) \vee z = x \vee (y \vee z)$; however $(x \vee y) \wedge z$ is *not* always equal to $(x \wedge z) \vee (y \wedge z)$, and $(x \wedge y) \vee (x \wedge z) \vee (y \wedge z)$ does *not* always equal the middle m elements of $x \uplus y \uplus z$. Find a correct formula, in terms of x, y, z and the $\wedge$ and $\vee$ operations, for those middle elements.

50. [*HM46*] Explore the properties of the $\bigwedge$ and $\bigvee$ operations defined in exercise 48. Is it possible to characterize all of the identities in this algebra in some nice way, or to derive them all from a finite set of identities? In this regard, identities such as $x \bigwedge x \bigwedge x = x \bigwedge x$, or $x \bigwedge (x \bigvee (x \bigwedge (x \bigvee y))) = x \bigwedge (x \bigvee y)$, which hold only for $m \leq 2$, are of comparatively little interest; consider only the identities that are true for all m.

▶ **51.** [*M25*] (R. L. Graham.) The comparator $[i:j]$ is called *redundant* in the network $\alpha_1[i:j]\alpha_2$ if either $(x\alpha_1)_i \leq (x\alpha_1)_j$ for all vectors x, or $(x\alpha_1)_i \geq (x\alpha_1)_j$ for all vectors x. Prove that if α is a network with r irredundant comparators, there are at least r distinct ordered pairs (i, j) of distinct indices such that $(x\alpha)_i \leq (x\alpha)_j$ for all vectors x. (Consequently, a network with no redundant comparators contains at most $\binom{n}{2}$ modules.)

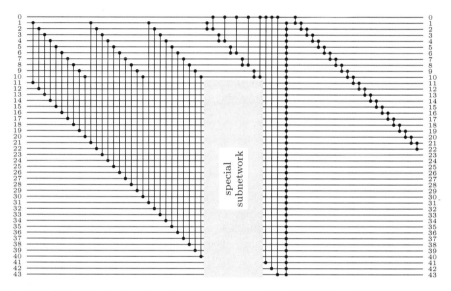

Fig. 61. A family of networks whose ability to sort is difficult to verify, illustrated for $m = 3$ and $n = 5$. (See exercise 52.)

▶ **52.** [*32*] (M. O. Rabin, 1980.) Prove that it is intrinsically difficult to decide in general whether a sequence of comparators defines a sorting network, by considering networks of the form sketched in Fig. 61. It is convenient to number the inputs x_0 to x_N, where $N = 2mn + m + 2n$; the positive integers m and n are parameters. The first comparators are $[j:j+2nk]$ for $1 \leq j \leq 2n$ and $1 \leq k \leq m$. Then we have $[2j-1:2j][0:2j]$ for $1 \leq j \leq n$, in parallel with a special subnetwork that uses only indices $> 2n$. Next we compare $[0:2mn+2n+j]$ for $1 \leq j \leq m$. And finally there is a complete sorting network for $\langle x_1, \ldots, x_N \rangle$, followed by $[0:1][1:2] \ldots [N-t-1:N-t]$, where $t = mn + n + 1$.

a) Describe all inputs $\langle x_0, x_1, \ldots, x_N \rangle$ that are *not* sorted by such a network, in terms of the behavior of the special subnetwork.

b) Given a set of clauses such as $(y_1 \vee y_2 \vee \bar{y}_3) \wedge (\bar{y}_2 \vee y_3 \vee \bar{y}_4) \wedge \ldots$, explain how to construct a special subnetwork such that Fig. 61 sorts all inputs if and only if the clauses are unsatisfiable. [Hence the task of deciding whether a comparator sequence forms a sorting network is co-NP-complete, in the sense of Section 7.9.]

53. [*30*] (*Periodic sorting networks.*) The following two 16-networks illustrate general recursive constructions of t-level networks for $n = 2^t$ in the case $t = 4$:

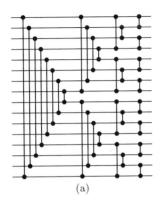 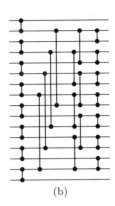

(a)   (b)

If we number the input lines from 0 to $2^t - 1$, the lth level in case (a) has comparators $[i:j]$ where $i \bmod 2^{t+1-l} < 2^{t-l}$ and $j = i \oplus (2^{t+1-l} - 1)$; there are $t2^{t-1}$ comparators altogether, as in the bitonic merge. In case (b) the first-level comparators are $[2j:2j+1]$ for $0 \le j < 2^{t-1}$, and the lth-level comparators for $2 \le l \le t$ are $[2j+1:2j+2^{t+1-l}]$ for $0 \le j < 2^{t-1} - 2^{t-l}$; there are $(t-1)2^{t-1} + 1$ comparators altogether, as in the odd-even merge.

If the input numbers are 2^k-ordered in the sense of Theorem 5.2.1H, for some $k \ge 1$, prove that both networks yield outputs that are 2^{k-1}-ordered. Therefore we can sort 2^t numbers by passing them through either network t times. [When t is large, these sorting networks use roughly twice as many comparisons as Algorithm 5.2.2M; but the total delay time is the same as in Fig. 57, and the implementation is simpler because the same network is used repeatedly.]

54. [*42*] Study the properties of sorting networks made from m-sorter modules instead of 2-sorters. (For example, G. Shapiro has constructed the network

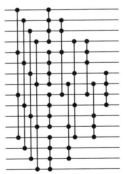

which sorts 16 elements using fourteen 4-sorters. Is this the best possible? Prove that m^2 elements can be sorted with at most 16 levels of m-sorters, when m is sufficiently large.)

55. [*23*] A *permutation network* is a sequence of modules $[i_1:j_1]\dots[i_r:j_r]$ where each module $[i:j]$ can be set by external controls to pass its inputs unchanged or to switch x_i and x_j (irrespective of the values of x_i and x_j), and such that each permutation of the inputs is achievable on the output lines by some setting of the modules. Every sorting network is clearly a permutation network, but the converse is not true: Find a permutation network for five elements that has only eight modules.

▶ **56.** [*25*] Suppose the bit vector $x \in D_n$ is not sorted. Show that there is a standard n-network α_x that fails to sort x, although it sorts all other elements of D_n.

57. [*M35*] The *even-odd merge* is similar to Batcher's odd-even merge, except that when $mn > 2$ it recursively merges the sequence $\langle x_{m \bmod 2 + 1}, \ldots, x_{m-3}, x_{m-1} \rangle$ with $\langle y_1, y_3, \ldots, y_{2\lceil n/2 \rceil - 1} \rangle$ and $\langle x_{(m+1) \bmod 2 + 1}, \ldots, x_{m-2}, x_m \rangle$ with $\langle y_2, y_4, \ldots, y_{2\lfloor n/2 \rfloor} \rangle$ before making a set of $\lceil m/2 \rceil + \lceil n/2 \rceil - 1$ comparison-interchanges analogous to (1). Show that the even-odd merge achieves the optimum delay time $\lceil \lg(m+n) \rceil$ of bitonic merging, without making more comparisons than the bitonic method. In fact, prove that the number of comparisons $A(m, n)$ made by even-odd merging satisfies $C(m, n) \leq A(m, n) < \frac{1}{2}(m + n) \lg \min(m, n) + m + \frac{3}{2}n$.

EXERCISES — Second Set

The following exercises deal with several different types of optimality questions related to sorting. The first few problems are based on an interesting "multihead" generalization of the bubble sort, investigated by P. N. Armstrong and R. J. Nelson as early as 1954. [See *U.S. Patents 3029413, 3034102*.] Let $1 = h_1 < h_2 < \cdots < h_m = n$ be an increasing sequence of integers; we shall call it a "head sequence" of length m and span n, and we shall use it to define a special kind of sorting method. The sorting of records $R_1 \ldots R_N$ proceeds in several passes, and each pass consists of $N + n - 1$ steps. On step j, for $j = 1 - n, 2 - n, \ldots, N - 1$, the records $R_{j+h[1]}, R_{j+h[2]}, \ldots, R_{j+h[m]}$ are examined and rearranged if necessary so that their keys are in order. (We say that $R_{j+h[1]}, \ldots, R_{j+h[m]}$ are "under the read-write heads." When $j + h[k]$ is < 1 or $> N$, record $R_{j+h[k]}$ is left out of consideration; in effect, the keys $K_0, K_{-1}, K_{-2}, \ldots$ are treated as $-\infty$ and $K_{N+1}, K_{N+2}, \ldots$ are treated as $+\infty$. Therefore step j is actually trivial when $j \leq -h[m - 1]$ or $j > N - h[2]$.)

For example, the following table shows one pass of a sort when $m = 3$, $N = 9$, and $h_1 = 1$, $h_2 = 2$, $h_3 = 4$:

	K_{-2}	K_{-1}	K_0	K_1	K_2	K_3	K_4	K_5	K_6	K_7	K_8	K_9	K_{10}	K_{11}	K_{12}
$j = -3$	—	—	3	1	4	5	9	2	6	8	7				
$j = -2$		—	—	3	1	4	5	9	2	6	8	7			
$j = -1$			—	3	1	4	5	9	2	6	8	7			
$j = 0$			—	1	3	4	5	9	2	6	8	7			
$j = 1$				1	3	4	5	9	2	6	8	7			
$j = 2$				1	3	2	4	9	5	6	8	7			
$j = 3$				1	3	2	4	6	5	9	8	7			
$j = 4$				1	3	2	4	5	6	9	8	7			
$j = 5$				1	3	2	4	5	6	7	8	9			
$j = 6$				1	3	2	4	5	6	7	8	9	—		
$j = 7$				1	3	2	4	5	6	7	8	9	—	—	
$j = 8$				1	3	2	4	5	6	7	8	9	—	—	—

When $m = 2$, $h_1 = 1$, and $h_2 = 2$, this multihead method reduces to the bubble sort (Algorithm 5.2.2B).

58. [*21*] (James Dugundji.) Prove that if $h[k+1] = h[k] + 1$ for some k, $1 \le k < m$, the multihead sorter defined above will eventually sort any input file in a finite number of passes. But if $h[k+1] \ge h[k] + 2$ for $1 \le k < m$, the input might *never* become sorted.

▶ **59.** [*30*] (Armstrong and Nelson.) Given that $h[k+1] \le h[k] + k$ for $1 \le k < m$, and $N \ge n - 1$, prove that the largest $n - 1$ elements always move to their final destination on the first pass. [*Hint:* Use the zero-one principle; when sorting 0s and 1s, with fewer than n 1s, prove that it is impossible to have all heads sensing a 1 unless all 0s lie to the left of the heads.]

Prove that sorting will be complete in at most $\lceil (N-1)/(n-1) \rceil$ passes when the heads satisfy the given conditions. Is there an input file that requires this many passes?

60. [*26*] If $n = N$, prove that the first pass can be guaranteed to place the smallest key into position R_1 if and only if $h[k+1] \le 2h[k]$ for $1 \le k < m$.

61. [*34*] (J. Hopcroft.) A "perfect sorter" for N elements is a multihead sorter with $N = n$ that always finishes in one pass. Exercise 59 proves that the sequence $\langle h_1, h_2, h_3, h_4, \ldots, h_m \rangle = \langle 1, 2, 4, 7, \ldots, 1 + \binom{m}{2} \rangle$ gives a perfect sorter for $N = \binom{m}{2} + 1$ elements, using $m = (\sqrt{8N-7}+1)/2$ heads. For example, the head sequence $\langle 1, 2, 4, 7, 11, 16, 22 \rangle$ is a perfect sorter for 22 elements.

Prove that, in fact, the head sequence $\langle 1, 2, 4, 7, 11, 16, 23 \rangle$ is a perfect sorter for 23 elements.

62. [*49*] Study the largest N for which m-head perfect sorters exist, given m. Is $N = O(m^2)$?

63. [*23*] (V. Pratt.) When each head h_k is in position 2^{k-1} for $1 \le k \le m$, how many passes are necessary to sort the sequence $z_1 z_2 \ldots z_{2^m-1}$ of 0s and 1s where $z_j = 0$ if and only if j is a power of 2?

64. [*24*] (*Uniform sorting.*) The tree of Fig. 34 in Section 5.3.1 makes the comparison 2:3 in both branches on level 1, and on level 2 it compares 1:3 in each branch unless that comparison would be redundant. In general, we can consider the class of all sorting algorithms whose comparisons are uniform in that way; assuming that the $M = \binom{N}{2}$ pairs $\{(a,b) \mid 1 \le a < b \le N\}$ have been arranged into a sequence

$$(a_1, b_1), (a_2, b_2), \ldots, (a_M, b_M),$$

we can successively make each of the comparisons $K_{a_1}:K_{b_1}$, $K_{a_2}:K_{b_2}$, ... whose outcome is not already known. Each of the $M!$ arrangements of the (a,b) pairs defines a uniform sorting algorithm. The concept of uniform sorting is due to H. L. Beus [*JACM* **17** (1970), 482–495], whose work has suggested the next few exercises.

It is convenient to define uniform sorting formally by means of graph theory. Let G be the directed graph on the vertices $\{1, 2, \ldots, N\}$ having no arcs. For $i = 1, 2, \ldots, M$ we add arcs to G as follows:

Case 1. G contains a path from a_i to b_i. Add the arc $a_i \to b_i$ to G.

Case 2. G contains a path from b_i to a_i. Add the arc $b_i \to a_i$ to G.

Case 3. G contains no path from a_i to b_i or b_i to a_i. Compare $K_{a_i}:K_{b_i}$; then add the arc $a_i \to b_i$ to G if $K_{a_i} \le K_{b_i}$, the arc $b_i \to a_i$ if $K_{a_i} > K_{b_i}$.

We are concerned primarily with the number of key comparisons made by a uniform sorting algorithm, not with the mechanism by which redundant comparisons are actually avoided. Thus the graph G need not be constructed explicitly; it is used here merely to help define the concept of uniform sorting.

We shall also consider *restricted uniform sorting*, in which only paths of length 2 are counted in cases 1, 2, and 3 above. (A restricted uniform sorting algorithm may make some redundant comparisons, but exercise 65 shows that the analysis is somewhat simpler in the restricted case.)

Prove that the restricted uniform algorithm is the same as the uniform algorithm when the sequence of pairs is taken in lexicographic order

$$(1, 2)(1, 3)(1, 4) \ldots (1, N)(2, 3)(2, 4) \ldots (2, N) \ldots (N-1, N).$$

Show in fact that both algorithms are equivalent to quicksort (Algorithm 5.2.2Q) when the keys are distinct and when quicksort's redundant comparisons are removed as in exercise 5.2.2–24. (Disregard the order in which the comparisons are actually made in quicksort; consider only which pairs of keys are compared.)

65. [*M38*] Given a pair sequence $(a_1, b_1) \ldots (a_M, b_M)$ as in exercise 64, let c_i be the number of pairs (j, k) such that $j < k < i$ and (a_i, b_i), (a_j, b_j), (a_k, b_k) forms a triangle.

a) Prove that the average number of comparisons made by the restricted uniform sorting algorithm is $\sum_{i=1}^{M} 2/(c_i + 2)$.

b) Use the results of (a) and exercise 64 to determine the average number of irredundant comparisons performed by quicksort.

c) The following pair sequence is inspired by (but not equivalent to) merge sorting:

$$(1, 2)(3, 4)(5, 6) \ldots (1, 3)(1, 4)(2, 3)(2, 4)(5, 7) \ldots (1, 5)(1, 6)(1, 7)(1, 8)(2, 5) \ldots$$

Does the uniform method based on this sequence do more or fewer comparisons than quicksort, on the average?

66. [*M29*] In the worst case, quicksort does $\binom{N}{2}$ comparisons. Do all restricted uniform sorting algorithms (in the sense of exercise 63) perform $\binom{N}{2}$ comparisons in their worst case?

67. [*M48*] (H. L. Beus.) Does quicksort have the minimum average number of comparisons, over all (restricted) uniform sorting algorithms?

68. [*25*] The Ph.D. thesis "Electronic Data Sorting" by Howard B. Demuth (Stanford University, October 1956) was perhaps the first publication to deal in any detail with questions of computational complexity. Demuth considered several abstract models for sorting devices, and established lower and upper bounds on the mean and maximum execution times achievable with each model. His simplest model, the "circular nonreversible memory" (Fig. 60), is the subject of this exercise.

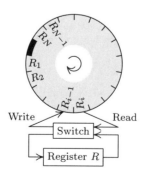

Fig. 60. A device for which the bubble-sort strategy is optimum.

Consider a machine that sorts $R_1 R_2 \ldots R_N$ in a number of passes, where each pass contains the following $N + 1$ steps:

Step 1. Set $R \leftarrow R_1$. (R is an internal machine register.)

Step i, for $1 \leq i \leq N$. Either (i) set $R_{i-1} \leftarrow R$, $R \leftarrow R_i$, or (ii) set $R_{i-1} \leftarrow R_i$, leaving R unchanged.

Step N+1. Set $R_N \leftarrow R$.

The problem is to find a way to choose between alternatives (i) and (ii) each time, in order to minimize the number of passes required to sort.

Prove that the "bubble sort" technique is optimum for this model. In other words, show that the strategy that selects alternative (i) whenever $R \leq R_i$ and alternative (ii) whenever $R > R_i$ will achieve the minimum number of passes.

They that weave networks shall be confounded.

— *Isaiah 19:9*

5.4. EXTERNAL SORTING

NOW IT IS TIME for us to study the interesting problems that arise when the number of records to be sorted is larger than our computer can hold in its high-speed internal memory. External sorting is quite different from internal sorting, even though the problem in both cases is to sort a given file into nondecreasing order, since efficient storage accessing on external files is rather severely limited. The data structures must be arranged so that comparatively slow peripheral memory devices (tapes, disks, drums, etc.) can quickly cope with the requirements of the sorting algorithm. Consequently most of the internal sorting techniques we have studied (insertion, exchange, selection) are virtually useless for external sorting, and it is necessary to reconsider the whole question.

Suppose, for example, that we are supposed to sort a file of five million records $R_1 R_2 \ldots R_{5000000}$, and that each record R_i is 20 words long (although the keys K_i are not necessarily this long). If only one million of these records will fit in the internal memory of our computer at one time, what shall we do?

One fairly obvious solution is to start by sorting each of the five subfiles $R_1 \ldots R_{1000000}$, $R_{1000001} \ldots R_{2000000}$, $\ldots$, $R_{4000001} \ldots R_{5000000}$ independently, then to merge the resulting subfiles together. Fortunately the process of merging uses only very simple data structures, namely linear lists that are traversed in a sequential manner as stacks or as queues; hence merging can be done without difficulty on the least expensive external memory devices.

The process just described — internal sorting followed by external merging — is very commonly used, and we shall devote most of our study of external sorting to variations on this theme.

The ascending sequences of records that are produced by the initial internal sorting phase are often called *strings* in the published literature about sorting; this terminology is fairly widespread, but it unfortunately conflicts with even more widespread usage in other branches of computer science, where "strings" are *arbitrary* sequences of symbols. Our study of permutations has already given us a perfectly good name for the sorted segments of a file, which are conventionally called ascending runs or simply *runs*. Therefore we shall consistently use the word "runs" to describe sorted portions of a file. In this way it is possible to distinguish between "strings of runs" and "runs of strings" without ambiguity. (Of course, "runs of a program" means something else again; we can't have everything.)

Let us consider first the process of external sorting when *magnetic tapes* are used for auxiliary storage. Perhaps the simplest and most appealing way to merge with tapes is the *balanced two-way merge* following the central idea that was used in Algorithms 5.2.4N, S, and L. We use four "working tapes" in this process. During the first phase, ascending runs produced by internal sorting are placed alternately on Tapes 1 and 2, until the input is exhausted. Then Tapes 1 and 2 are rewound to their beginnings, and we merge the runs from these tapes, obtaining new runs that are twice as long as the original ones; the new runs are written alternately on Tapes 3 and 4 as they are being formed. (If Tape 1 contains one more run than Tape 2, an extra "dummy" run of length 0 is assumed to be present on Tape 2.) Then all tapes are rewound, and the contents of Tapes 3 and 4 are merged into quadruple-length runs recorded alternately on Tapes 1 and 2. The process continues, doubling the length of runs each time, until only one run is left (namely the entire sorted file). If S runs were produced during the internal sorting phase, and if $2^{k-1} < S \leq 2^k$, this balanced two-way merge procedure makes exactly $k = \lceil \lg S \rceil$ merging passes over all the data.

For example, in the situation above where 5000000 records are to be sorted with an internal memory capacity of 1000000, we have $S = 5$. The initial distribution phase of the sorting process places five runs on tape as follows:

$$
\begin{array}{lll}
\text{Tape 1} & R_1 \ldots R_{1000000}; R_{2000001} \ldots R_{3000000}; R_{4000001} \ldots R_{5000000}. & \\
\text{Tape 2} & R_{1000001} \ldots R_{2000000}; R_{3000001} \ldots R_{4000000}. & \\
\text{Tape 3} & \text{(empty)} & (1) \\
\text{Tape 4} & \text{(empty)} &
\end{array}
$$

The first pass of merging then produces longer runs on Tapes 3 and 4, as it reads Tapes 1 and 2, as follows:

$$
\begin{array}{lll}
\text{Tape 3} & R_1 \ldots R_{2000000}; R_{4000001} \ldots R_{5000000}. & \\
\text{Tape 4} & R_{2000001} \ldots R_{4000000}. & (2)
\end{array}
$$

(A dummy run has implicitly been added at the end of Tape 2, so that the last run $R_{4000001} \ldots R_{5000000}$ on Tape 1 is merely copied onto Tape 3.) After all tapes are rewound, the next pass over the data produces

$$
\begin{array}{lll}
\text{Tape 1} & R_1 \ldots R_{4000000}. & \\
\text{Tape 2} & R_{4000001} \ldots R_{5000000}. & (3)
\end{array}
$$

(Again that run $R_{4000001} \ldots R_{5000000}$ was simply copied; but if we had started with 8000000 records, Tape 2 would have contained $R_{4000001} \ldots R_{8000000}$ at this point.) Finally, after another spell of rewinding, $R_1 \ldots R_{5000000}$ is produced on Tape 3, and the sorting is complete.

Balanced merging can easily be generalized to the case of T tapes, for any $T \geq 3$. Choose any number P with $1 \leq P < T$, and divide the T tapes into two "banks," with P tapes on the left bank and $T - P$ on the right. Distribute the initial runs as evenly as possible onto the P tapes in the left bank; then do a P-way merge from the left to the right, followed by a $(T - P)$-way merge from the right to the left, etc., until sorting is complete. The best choice of P usually turns out to be $\lceil T/2 \rceil$ (see exercises 3 and 4).

Balanced two-way merging is the special case $T = 4$, $P = 2$. Let us reconsider the example above using more tapes, taking $T = 6$ and $P = 3$. The initial distribution now gives us

$$
\begin{array}{lll}
\text{Tape 1} & R_1 \ldots R_{1000000}; R_{3000001} \ldots R_{4000000}. & \\
\text{Tape 2} & R_{1000001} \ldots R_{2000000}; R_{4000001} \ldots R_{5000000}. & (4) \\
\text{Tape 3} & R_{2000001} \ldots R_{3000000}. &
\end{array}
$$

And the first merging pass produces

$$\begin{aligned}
&\text{Tape 4} \qquad R_1 \dots R_{3000000}. \\
&\text{Tape 5} \qquad R_{3000001} \dots R_{5000000}. \qquad\qquad\qquad\qquad (5) \\
&\text{Tape 6} \qquad (\text{empty})
\end{aligned}$$

(A dummy run has been assumed on Tape 3.) The second merging pass completes the job, placing $R_1 \dots R_{5000000}$ on Tape 1. In this special case $T = 6$ is essentially the same as $T = 5$, since the sixth tape is used only when $S \geq 7$.

Three-way merging requires more computer processing than two-way merging; but this is generally negligible compared to the cost of reading, writing, and rewinding the tapes. We can get a fairly good estimate of the running time by considering only the amount of tape motion. The example in (4) and (5) required only two passes over the data, compared to three passes when $T = 4$, so the merging takes only about two-thirds as long when $T = 6$.

Balanced merging is quite simple, but if we look more closely, we find immediately that it isn't the *best* way to handle the particular cases treated above. Instead of going from (1) to (2) and rewinding all of the tapes, we should have stopped the first merging pass after Tapes 3 and 4 contained $R_1 \dots R_{2000000}$ and $R_{2000001} \dots R_{4000000}$, respectively, with Tape 1 poised ready to read the records $R_{4000001} \dots R_{5000000}$. Then Tapes 2, 3, 4 could be rewound and we could complete the sort by doing a three-way merge onto Tape 2. The total number of records read from tape during this procedure would be only $4000000 + 5000000 = 9000000$, compared to $5000000 + 5000000 + 5000000 = 15{,}000000$ in the balanced scheme. A smart computer would be able to figure this out!

Indeed, when we have five runs and four tapes we can do even better by distributing them as follows:

$$\begin{aligned}
&\text{Tape 1} \qquad R_1 \dots R_{1000000}; \; R_{3000001} \dots R_{4000000}. \\
&\text{Tape 2} \qquad R_{1000001} \dots R_{2000000}; \; R_{4000001} \dots R_{5000000}. \\
&\text{Tape 3} \qquad R_{2000001} \dots R_{3000000}. \\
&\text{Tape 4} \qquad (\text{empty})
\end{aligned}$$

Then a three-way merge to Tape 4, followed by a rewind of Tapes 3 and 4, followed by a three-way merge to Tape 3, would complete the sort with only $3000000 + 5000000 = 8000000$ records read.

And, of course, if we had six tapes we could put the initial runs on Tapes 1 through 5 and complete the sort in one pass by doing a five-way merge to Tape 6. These considerations indicate that simple balanced merging isn't the best, and it is interesting to look for improved merging patterns.

Subsequent portions of this chapter investigate external sorting more deeply. In Section 5.4.1, we will consider the internal sorting phase that produces the initial runs; of particular interest is the technique of "replacement selection," which takes advantage of the order present in most data to produce long initial runs that actually exceed the internal memory capacity by a significant amount. Section 5.4.1 also discusses a suitable data structure for multiway merging.

The most important merging patterns are discussed in Sections 5.4.2 through 5.4.5. It is convenient to have a rather naïve conception of tape sorting as we learn the characteristics of these patterns, before we come to grips with the harsh realities of real tape drives and real data to be sorted. For example, we may blithely assume (as we did above) that the original input records appear magically during the initial distribution phase; in fact, these input records might well occupy one of our tapes, and they may even fill several tape reels since tapes aren't of infinite length! It is best to ignore such mundane considerations until after an academic understanding of the classical merging patterns has been gained. Then Section 5.4.6 brings the discussion down to earth by discussing real-life constraints that strongly influence the choice of a pattern. Section 5.4.6 compares the basic merging patterns of Sections 5.4.2 through 5.4.5, using a variety of assumptions that arise in practice.

Some other approaches to external sorting, *not* based on merging, are discussed in Sections 5.4.7 and 5.4.8. Finally Section 5.4.9 completes our survey of external sorting by treating the important problem of sorting on bulk memories such as disks and drums.

When this book was first written, magnetic tapes were abundant and disk drives were expensive. But disks became enormously better during the 1980s, and by the late 1990s they had almost completely replaced magnetic tape units on most of the world's computer systems. Therefore the once-crucial topic of patterns for tape merging has become of limited relevance to current needs.

Yet many of the patterns are quite beautiful, and the associated algorithms reflect some of the best research done in computer science during its early years; the techniques are just too nice to be discarded abruptly onto the rubbish heap of history. Indeed, the ways in which these methods blend theory with practice are especially instructive. Therefore merging patterns are discussed carefully and completely below, in what may be their last grand appearance before they accept a final curtain call.

> *For all we know now,*
> *these techniques may well become crucial once again.*
> — PAVEL CURTIS (1997)

EXERCISES

1. [*15*] The text suggests internal sorting first, followed by external merging. Why don't we do away with the internal sorting phase, simply merging the records into longer and longer runs right from the start?

2. [*10*] What will the sequence of tape contents be, analogous to (1) through (3), when the example records $R_1 R_2 \ldots R_{5000000}$ are sorted using a 3-tape balanced method with $P = 2$? Compare this to the 4-tape merge; how many passes are made over all the data, after the initial distribution of runs?

3. [*20*] Show that the balanced $(P, T{-}P)$-way merge applied to S initial runs takes $2k$ passes, when $P^k(T - P)^{k-1} < S \le P^k(T - P)^k$; and it takes $2k + 1$ passes, when $P^k(T - P)^k < S \le P^{k+1}(T - P)^k$.

Give simple formulas for (a) the exact number of passes, as a function of S, when $T = 2P$; and (b) the approximate number of passes, as $S \to \infty$, for general P and T.

4. [*HM15*] What value of P, for $1 \le P < T$, makes $P(T - P)$ a maximum?

5.4.1. Multiway Merging and Replacement Selection

In Section 5.2.4, we studied internal sorting methods based on two-way merging, the process of combining two ordered sequences into a single ordered sequence. It is not difficult to extend this to the notion of P-way merging, where P runs of input are combined into a single run of output.

Let's assume that we have been given P ascending runs, that is, sequences of records whose keys are in nondecreasing order. The obvious way to merge them is to look at the first record of each run and to select the record whose key is smallest; this record is transferred to the output and removed from the input, and the process is repeated. At any given time we need to look at only P keys (one from each input run) and select the smallest. If two or more keys are smallest, an arbitrary one is selected.

When P isn't too large, it is convenient to make this selection by simply doing $P - 1$ comparisons to find the smallest of the current keys. But when P is, say, 8 or more, we can save work by using a *selection tree* as described in Section 5.2.3; then only about $\lg P$ comparisons are needed each time, once the tree has been set up.

Consider, for example, the case of four-way merging, with a two-level selection tree:

Step 1.
$$087 \begin{cases} 087 \begin{cases} 087\ 503\ \infty \\ 170\ 908\ \infty \end{cases} \\ 154 \begin{cases} 154\ 426\ 653\ \infty \\ 612\ \infty \end{cases} \end{cases}$$

Step 2.
$$087\ 154 \begin{cases} 170 \begin{cases} 503\ \infty \\ 170\ 908\ \infty \end{cases} \\ 154 \begin{cases} 154\ 426\ 653\ \infty \\ 612\ \infty \end{cases} \end{cases}$$

Step 3.
$$087\ 154\ 170 \begin{cases} 170 \begin{cases} 503\ \infty \\ 170\ 908\ \infty \end{cases} \\ 426 \begin{cases} 426\ 653\ \infty \\ 612\ \infty \end{cases} \end{cases}$$

$\vdots$

Step 9.
$$087\ 154\ 170\ 426\ 503\ 612\ 653\ 908\ \infty \begin{cases} \infty \begin{cases} \infty \\ \infty \end{cases} \\ \infty \begin{cases} \infty \\ \infty \end{cases} \end{cases}$$

An additional key "∞" has been placed at the end of each run in this example, so that the merging terminates gracefully. Since external merging generally deals with very long runs, the addition of records with ∞ keys does not add substantially to the length of the data or to the amount of work involved in merging, and such sentinel records frequently serve as a useful way to delimit the runs on a file.

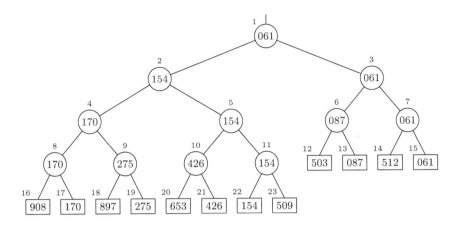

Fig. 62. A tournament to select the smallest key, using a complete binary tree whose nodes are numbered from 1 to 23.

Each step after the first in this process consists of replacing the smallest element by the succeeding element in its run, and changing the corresponding path in the selection tree. Thus the three positions of the tree that contain 087 in Step 1 are changed in Step 2; the three positions containing 154 in Step 2 are changed in Step 3; and so on. The process of replacing one key by another in the selection tree is called *replacement selection*.

We can look at this four-way merge in several ways. From one standpoint it is equivalent to three two-way merges performed concurrently as coroutines; each node in the selection tree represents one of the sequences involved in concurrent merging processes. The selection tree is also essentially operating as a priority queue, with a smallest-in-first-out discipline.

As in Section 5.2.3 we could implement the priority queue by using a heap instead of a selection tree. (The heap would, of course, be arranged so that the *smallest* element appears at the top, instead of the largest, reversing the order of Eq. 5.2.3–(3).) Since a heap does not have a fixed size, we could therefore avoid the use of ∞ keys; merging would be complete when the heap becomes empty. On the other hand, external sorting applications usually deal with comparatively long records and keys, so that the heap is filled with pointers to keys instead of the keys themselves; we shall see below that selection trees can be represented by pointers in such a convenient manner that they are probably superior to heaps in this situation.

A tree of losers. Figure 62 shows the complete binary tree with 12 external (rectangular) nodes and 11 internal (circular) nodes. The external nodes have been filled with keys, and the internal nodes have been filled with the "winners," if the tree is regarded as a tournament to select the smallest key. The smaller numbers above each node show the traditional way to allocate consecutive storage positions for complete binary trees.

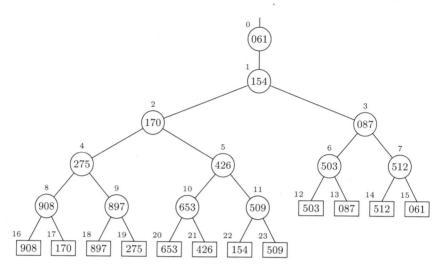

Fig. 63. The same tournament as Fig. 62, but showing the losers instead of the winners; the champion appears at the very top.

When the smallest key, 061, is to be replaced by another key in the selection tree of Fig. 62, we will have to look at the keys 512, 087, and 154, and no other existing keys, in order to determine the new state of the selection tree. Considering the tree as a tournament, these three keys are the losers in the matches played by 061. This suggests that the *loser* of a match should actually be stored in each internal node of the tree, instead of the winner; then the information required for updating the tree will be readily available.

Figure 63 shows the same tree as Fig. 62, but with the losers represented instead of the winners. An extra node number 0 has been appended at the top of the tree, to indicate the champion of the tournament. Each key except the champion is a loser exactly once (see Section 5.3.3), so each key appears just once in an external node and once in an internal node.

In practice, the external nodes at the bottom of Fig. 63 will represent fairly long records stored in computer memory, and the internal nodes will represent pointers to those records. Note that P-way merging calls for exactly P external nodes and P internal nodes, each in consecutive positions of memory, hence several efficient methods of storage allocation suggest themselves. It is not difficult to see how to use a loser-oriented tree for replacement selection; we shall discuss the details later.

Initial runs by replacement selection. The technique of replacement selection can be used also in the *first* phase of external sorting, if we essentially do a P-way merge of the input data with itself! In this case we take P to be quite large, so that the internal memory is essentially filled. When a record is output, it is replaced by the next record from the input. If the new record has a smaller key than the one just output, we cannot include it in the current run; but

Table 1

EXAMPLE OF FOUR-WAY REPLACEMENT SELECTION

Memory contents				Output
503	087	512	061	061
503	087	512	908	087
503	170	512	908	170
503	897	512	908	503
(275)	897	512	908	512
(275)	897	653	908	653
(275)	897	(426)	908	897
(275)	(154)	(426)	908	908
(275)	(154)	(426)	(509)	(end of run)
275	154	426	509	154
275	612	426	509	275
		etc.		

otherwise we can enter it into the selection tree in the usual way and it will form part of the run currently being produced. Thus the runs can contain more than P records each, even though we never have more than P in the selection tree at any time. Table 1 illustrates this process for $P = 4$; parenthesized numbers are waiting for inclusion in the following run.

This important method of forming initial runs was first described by Harold H. Seward [Master's Thesis, Digital Computer Laboratory Report R-232 (Mass. Inst. of Technology, 1954), 29–30], who gave reason to believe that the runs would contain more than $1.5P$ records when applied to random data. A. I. Dumey had also suggested the idea about 1950 in connection with a special sorting device planned by Engineering Research Associates, but he did not publish it. The name "replacement selecting" was coined by E. H. Friend [*JACM* **3** (1956), 154], who remarked that "the expected length of the sequences produced eludes formulation but experiment suggests that $2P$ is a reasonable expectation."

A clever way to show that $2P$ is indeed the expected run length was discovered by E. F. Moore, who compared the situation to a snowplow on a circular track [*U.S. Patent 2983904* (1961), columns 3–4]. Consider the situation shown in Fig. 64: Flakes of snow are falling uniformly on a circular road, and a lone snowplow is continually clearing the snow. Once the snow has been plowed off the road, it disappears from the system. Points on the road may be designated by real numbers x, $0 \le x < 1$; a flake of snow falling at position x represents an input record whose key is x, and the snowplow represents the output of replacement selection. The ground speed of the snowplow is inversely proportional to the height of snow it encounters, and the situation is perfectly balanced so that the total amount of snow on the road at all times is exactly P. A new run is formed in the output whenever the plow passes point 0.

After this system has been in operation for awhile, it is intuitively clear that it will approach a stable situation in which the snowplow runs at constant speed (because of the circular symmetry of the track). This means that the snow is at

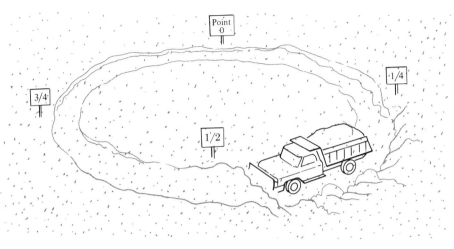

Fig. 64. The perpetual plow on its ceaseless cycle.

constant height when it meets the plow, and the height drops off linearly in front of the plow as shown in Fig. 65. It follows that the volume of snow removed in one revolution (namely the run length) is twice the amount present at any one time (namely P).

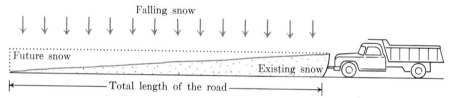

Fig. 65. Cross-section, showing the varying height of snow in front of the plow when the system is in its steady state.

In many commercial applications the input data is *not* completely random; it already has a certain amount of existing order. Therefore the runs produced by replacement selection will tend to contain even more than $2P$ records. We shall see that the time required for external merge sorting is largely governed by the number of runs produced by the initial distribution phase, so that replacement selection becomes especially desirable; other types of internal sorting would produce about twice as many initial runs because of the limitations on memory size.

Let us now consider the process of creating initial runs by replacement selection in detail. The following algorithm is due to John R. Walters, James Painter, and Martin Zalk, who used it in a merge-sort program for the Philco 2000 in 1958. It incorporates a rather nice way to initialize the selection tree and to distinguish records belonging to different runs, as well as to flush out the last run, with comparatively simple and uniform logic. (The proper handling of the last run produced by replacement selection turns out to be a bit tricky,

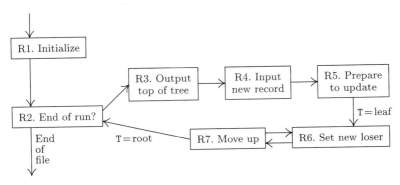

Fig. 66. Making initial runs by replacement selection.

and it has tended to be a stumbling block for programmers.) The principal idea is to consider each key as a pair (S, K), where K is the original key and S is the run number to which this record belongs. When such extended keys are lexicographically ordered, with S as major key and K as minor key, we obtain the output sequence produced by replacement selection.

The algorithm below uses a data structure containing P nodes to represent the selection tree; the jth node $X[j]$ is assumed to contain c words beginning in $\text{LOC}(X[j]) = L_0 + cj$, for $0 \leq j < P$, and it represents both internal node number j and external node number $P + j$ in Fig. 63. There are several named fields in each node:

KEY = the key stored in this external node;

RECORD = the record stored in this external node (including KEY as a subfield);

LOSER = pointer to the "loser" stored in this internal node;

RN = run number of the record pointed to by LOSER;

PE = pointer to internal node above this external node in the tree;

PI = pointer to internal node above this internal node in the tree.

For example, when $P = 12$, internal node number 5 and external node number 17 of Fig. 63 would both be represented in $X[5]$, by the fields KEY = 170, LOSER = $L_0 + 9c$ (the address of external node number 21), PE = $L_0 + 8c$, PI = $L_0 + 2c$.

The PE and PI fields have constant values, so they need not appear explicitly in memory; however, the initial phase of external sorting sometimes has trouble keeping up with the I/O devices, and it can be worthwhile to store these redundant values with the data instead of recomputing them each time.

Algorithm R (*Replacement selection*). This algorithm reads records sequentially from an input file and writes them sequentially onto an output file, producing RMAX runs whose length is P or more (except for the final run). There are $P \geq 2$ nodes, $X[0], \ldots, X[P-1]$, having fields as described above.

R1. [Initialize.] Set RMAX ← 0, RC ← 0, LASTKEY ← ∞, Q ← LOC($X[0]$), and RQ ← 0. (RC is the number of the current run and LASTKEY is the key of the last record output. The initial setting of LASTKEY should be larger than any possible key; see exercise 8.) For $0 \leq j < P$, set the initial contents of $X[j]$ as follows, when $J = \text{LOC}(X[j])$:

$$\text{LOSER}(J) \leftarrow J; \qquad \text{RN}(J) \leftarrow 0;$$
$$\text{PE}(J) \leftarrow \text{LOC}(X[\lfloor (P+j)/2 \rfloor]); \qquad \text{PI}(J) \leftarrow \text{LOC}(X[\lfloor j/2 \rfloor]).$$

(The settings of LOSER(J) and RN(J) are artificial ways to get the tree initialized by considering a fictitious run number 0 that is never output. This is tricky; see exercise 10.)

R2. [End of run?] If RQ = RC, go on to step R3. (Otherwise RQ = RC + 1 and we have just completed run number RC; any special actions required by a merging pattern for subsequent passes of the sort would be done at this point.) If RQ > RMAX, stop; otherwise set RC ← RQ.

R3. [Output top of tree.] (Now Q points to the "champion," and RQ is its run number.) If RQ ≠ 0, output RECORD(Q) and set LASTKEY ← KEY(Q).

R4. [Input new record.] If the input file is exhausted, set RQ ← RMAX + 1 and go on to step R5. Otherwise set RECORD(Q) to the next record from the input file. If KEY(Q) < LASTKEY (so that this new record does not belong to the current run), set RQ ← RQ + 1 and then if RQ > RMAX set RMAX ← RQ.

R5. [Prepare to update.] (Now Q points to a new record, whose run number is RQ.) Set T ← PE(Q). (T is a pointer variable that will move up the tree.)

R6. [Set new loser.] If RN(T) < RQ or if RN(T) = RQ and KEY(LOSER(T)) < KEY(Q), then interchange LOSER(T) ↔ Q, RN(T) ↔ RQ. (Variables Q and RQ keep track of the current winner and its run number.)

R7. [Move up.] If T = LOC($X[1]$) then go back to R2, otherwise set T ← PI(T) and return to R6. ∎

Algorithm R speaks of input and output of records one at a time, while in practice it is best to read and write relatively large blocks of records. Therefore some input and output buffers are actually present in memory, behind the scenes, effectively lowering the size of P. We shall illustrate this in Section 5.4.6.

*Delayed reconstitution of runs. A very interesting way to improve on replacement selection has been suggested by R. J. Dinsmore [*CACM* **8** (1965), 48] using a concept that we shall call *degrees of freedom*. As we have seen, each block of records on tape within a run is in nondecreasing order, so that its first element is the lowest and its last element is the highest. In the ordinary process of replacement selection, the lowest element of each block within a run is never less than the highest element of the preceding block in that run; this is "1 degree of freedom." Dinsmore suggests relaxing this condition to "m degrees of freedom," where the lowest element of each block may be less than the highest element of the preceding block so long as it is *not less than the highest elements in m different preceding blocks of the same run*. Records within individual blocks are ordered, as before, but adjacent blocks need not be in order.

For example, suppose that there are just two records per block; the following sequence of blocks is a run with three degrees of freedom:

$$| \ 08 \ 50 \ | \ 06 \ 90 \ | \ 17 \ 27 \ | \ 42 \ 67 \ | \ 51 \ 89 \ | \qquad (1)$$

A subsequent block that is to be part of the same run must begin with an element not less than the third largest element of $\{50, 90, 27, 67, 89\}$, namely 67. The sequence (1) would not be a run if there were only two degrees of freedom, since 17 is less than both 50 and 90.

A run with m degrees of freedom can be "reconstituted" while it is being read during the next phase of sorting, so that for all practical purposes it is a run in the ordinary sense. We start by reading the first m blocks into m buffers, and doing an m-way merge on them; when one buffer is exhausted, we replace it with the $(m + 1)$st block, and so on. In this way we can recover the run as a single sequence, for the first word of every newly read block must be greater than or equal to the last word of the just-exhausted block (lest it be less than the highest elements in m different blocks that precede it). This method of reconstituting the run is essentially like an m-way merge using a single tape unit for all the input blocks! The reconstitution procedure acts as a coroutine that is called upon to deliver one record of the run at a time. We could be reconstituting different runs from different tape units with different degrees of freedom, and merging the resulting runs, all at the same time, in essentially the same way as the four-way merge illustrated at the beginning of this section may be thought of as several two-way merges going on at once.

This ingenious idea is difficult to analyze precisely, but T. O. Espelid has shown how to extend the snowplow analogy to obtain an approximate formula for the behavior [*BIT* **16** (1976), 133–142]. According to his approximation, which agrees well with empirical tests, the run length will be about

$$2P + (m - 1.5) \left(\frac{2P + (m - 2)b}{2P + (2m - 3)b} \right) b,$$

when b is the block size and $m \geq 2$. Such an increase may not be enough to justify the added complication; on the other hand, it may be advantageous when there is room for a rather large number of buffers during the second phase of sorting.

*Natural selection. Another way to increase the run lengths produced by replacement selection has been explored by W. D. Frazer and C. K. Wong [*CACM* **15** (1972), 910–913]. Their idea is to proceed as in Algorithm R, except that a new record is not placed in the tree when its key is less than LASTKEY; it is output into an external *reservoir* instead, and another new record is read in. This process continues until the reservoir is filled with a certain number of records, P'; then the remainder of the current run is output from the tree, and the reservoir items are used as input for the next run.

The use of a reservoir tends to produce longer runs than replacement selection, because it reroutes the "dead" records that belong to the next run instead of letting them clutter up the tree; but it requires extra time for input and output

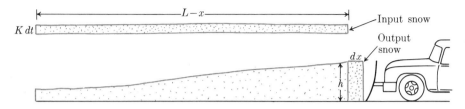

Fig. 67. Equal amounts of snow are input and output; the plow moves dx in time dt.

to and from the reservoir. When $P' > P$ it is possible that some records will be placed into the reservoir twice, but when $P' \leq P$ this will never happen.

Frazer and Wong made extensive empirical tests of their method, noticing that when P is reasonably large (say $P \geq 32$) and $P' = P$ the average run length for random data is approximately given by eP, where $e \approx 2.718$ is the base of natural logarithms. This phenomenon, and the fact that the method is an evolutionary improvement over simple replacement selection, naturally led them to call their method *natural selection*.

The "natural" law for run lengths can be proved by considering the snowplow of Fig. 64 again, and applying elementary calculus. Let L be the length of the track, and let $x(t)$ be the position of the snowplow at time t, for $0 \leq t \leq T$. The reservoir is assumed to be full at time T, when the snow stops temporarily while the plow returns to its starting position (clearing the P units of snow remaining in its path). The situation is the same as before except that the "balance condition" is different; instead of P units of snow on the road at all times, we have P units of snow in front of the plow, and the reservoir (behind the plow) gets up to $P' = P$ units. The snowplow advances by dx during a time interval dt if $h(x,t)\,dx$ records are output, where $h(x,t)$ is the height of the snow at time t and position $x = x(t)$, measured in suitable units; hence $h(x,t) = h(x,0) + Kt$ for all x, where K is the rate of snowfall. Since the number of records in memory stays constant, $h(x,t)\,dx$ is also the number of records that are input *ahead* of the plow, namely $K\,dt\,(L - x)$ (see Fig. 67). Thus

$$\frac{dx}{dt} = \frac{K(L - x)}{h(x,t)}. \tag{2}$$

Fortunately, it turns out that $h(x,t)$ is constant, equal to KT, whenever $x = x(t)$ and $0 \leq t \leq T$, since the snow falls steadily at position $x(t)$ for $T-t$ units of time after the plow passes that point, plus t units of time before it comes back. In other words, the plow sees all snow at the same height on its journey, assuming that a steady state has been reached where each journey is the same. Hence the total amount of snow cleared (the run length) is LKT; and the amount of snow in memory is the amount cleared after time T, namely $KT\big(L - x(T)\big)$. The solution to (2) such that $x(0) = 0$ is

$$x(t) = L\big(1 - e^{-t/T}\big); \tag{3}$$

hence $P = LKTe^{-1} = (\text{run length})/e$; and this is what we set out to prove.

Exercises 21 through 23 show that this analysis can be extended to the case of general P'; for example, when $P' = 2P$ the average run length turns out to be $e^\theta(e - \theta)P$, where $\theta = (e - \sqrt{e^2 - 4})/2$, a result that probably wouldn't have been guessed offhand! Table 2 shows the dependence of run length on reservoir size; the usefulness of natural selection in a given computer environment can be estimated by referring to this table. The table entries for reservoir size $< P$ use an improved technique that is discussed in exercise 27.

The ideas of delayed run reconstitution and natural selection can be combined, as discussed by T. C. Ting and Y. W. Wang in *Comp. J.* **20** (1977), 298–301.

Table 2
RUN LENGTHS BY NATURAL SELECTION

Reservoir size	Run length	$k + \theta$	Reservoir size	Run length	$k + \theta$
$0.10000P$	$2.15780P$	0.32071	$0.00000P$	$2.00000P$	0.00000
$0.50000P$	$2.54658P$	0.69952	$0.43428P$	$2.50000P$	0.65348
$1.00000P$	$2.71828P$	1.00000	$1.30432P$	$3.00000P$	1.15881
$2.00000P$	$3.53487P$	1.43867	$1.95014P$	$3.50000P$	1.42106
$3.00000P$	$4.16220P$	1.74773	$2.72294P$	$4.00000P$	1.66862
$4.00000P$	$4.69446P$	2.01212	$4.63853P$	$5.00000P$	2.16714
$5.00000P$	$5.16369P$	2.24938	$21.72222P$	$10.00000P$	4.66667
$10.00000P$	$7.00877P$	3.17122	$5.29143P$	$5.29143P$	2.31329

The quantity $k + \theta$ is defined in exercise 22, or (when $k = 0$) in exercise 27.

*Analysis of replacement selection.** Let us now return to the case of replacement selection without an auxiliary reservoir. The snowplow analogy gives us a fairly good indication of the average length of runs obtained by replacement selection in the steady-state limit, but it is possible to get much more precise information about Algorithm R by applying the facts about runs in permutations that we have studied in Section 5.1.3. For this purpose it is convenient to assume that the input file is an arbitrarily long sequence of independent random real numbers between 0 and 1.

Let

$$g_P(z_1, z_2, \ldots, z_k) = \sum_{l_1, l_2, \ldots, l_k \geq 0} a_P(l_1, l_2, \ldots, l_k) z_1^{l_1} z_2^{l_2} \ldots z_k^{l_k}$$

be the generating function for run lengths produced by P-way replacement selection on such a file, where $a_P(l_1, l_2, \ldots, l_k)$ is the probability that the first run has length l_1, the second has length l_2, ..., the kth has length l_k. The following "independence theorem" is basic, since it reduces the analysis to the case $P = 1$:

Theorem K. $g_P(z_1, z_2, \ldots, z_k) = g_1(z_1, z_2, \ldots, z_k)^P$.

Proof. Let the input keys be $X_1, X_2, X_3, \ldots$. Algorithm R partitions them into P subsequences, according to which external node position they occupy in the tree; the subsequence containing X_n is determined by the values of $X_1, \ldots, X_{n-1}$. Each of these subsequences is therefore an independent sequence of independent random numbers between 0 and 1. Furthermore, the output of replacement selection is precisely what would be obtained by doing a P-way merge on these subsequences; an element belongs to the jth run of a subsequence if and only if it belongs to the jth run produced by replacement selection (since LASTKEY and KEY(Q) belong to the same subsequence in step R4).

In other words, we might just as well assume that Algorithm R is being applied to P independent random input files, and that step R4 reads the next record from the file corresponding to external node Q; in this sense, the algorithm is equivalent to a P-way merge, with "stepdowns" marking the ends of the runs.

Thus the output has runs of lengths $(l_1, \ldots, l_k)$ if and only if the subsequences have runs of respective lengths $(l_{11}, \ldots, l_{1k}), \ldots, (l_{P1}, \ldots, l_{Pk})$, where the l_{ij} are some nonnegative integers satisfying $\sum_{1 \le i \le P} l_{ij} = l_j$ for $1 \le j \le k$. It follows that

$$a_P(l_1, \ldots, l_k) = \sum_{\substack{l_{11}+\cdots+l_{P1}=l_1 \\ \vdots \\ l_{1k}+\cdots+l_{Pk}=l_k}} a_1(l_{11}, \ldots, l_{1k}) \ldots a_1(l_{P1}, \ldots, l_{Pk}),$$

and this is equivalent to the desired result. ∎

We have discussed the average length L_k of the kth run, when $P = 1$, in Section 5.1.3, where the values are tabulated in Table 5.1.3–2. Theorem K implies that the average length of the kth run for general P is P times as long as the average when $P = 1$, namely $L_k P$; and the variance is also P times as large, so the standard deviation of the run length is proportional to $\sqrt{P}$. These results were first derived by B. J. Gassner about 1958.

Thus the first run produced by Algorithm R will be about $(e-1)P \approx 1.718P$ records long, for random data; the second run will be about $(e^2 - 2e)P \approx 1.952P$ records long; the third, about $1.996P$; and subsequent runs will be very close to $2P$ records long until we get to the last two runs (see exercise 14). The standard deviation of most of these run lengths is approximately $\sqrt{(4e - 10)P} \approx 0.934\sqrt{P}$ [CACM 6 (1963), 685–687]. Furthermore, exercise 5.1.3–10 shows that the *total* length of the first k runs will be fairly close to $\left(2k - \frac{1}{3}\right)P$, with a standard deviation of $\left(\left(\frac{2}{3}k + \frac{2}{9}\right)P\right)^{1/2}$. The generating functions $g_1(z, z, \ldots, z)$ and $g_1(1, \ldots, 1, z)$ are derived in exercises 5.1.3–9 and 11.

The analysis above has assumed that the input file is infinitely long, but the proof of Theorem K shows that the same probability $a_p(l_1, \ldots, l_k)$ would be obtained in any random input sequence containing at least $l_1 + \cdots + l_k + P$ elements. So the results above are applicable for, say, files of size $N > (2k+1)P$, in view of the small standard deviation.

We will be seeing some applications in which the merging pattern wants some of the runs to be ascending and some to be descending. Since the residue accumulated in memory at the end of an ascending run tends to contain numbers somewhat smaller on the average than random data, a change in the direction of ordering decreases the average length of the runs. Consider, for example, a snowplow that must make a U-turn every time it reaches an end of a straight road; it will go very speedily over the area just plowed. The run lengths when directions are reversed vary between $1.5P$ and $2P$ for random data (see exercise 24).

EXERCISES

1. [10] What is Step 4, in the example of four-way merging at the beginning of this section?

2. [12] What changes would be made to the tree of Fig. 63 if the key 061 were replaced by 612?

3. [16] (E. F. Moore.) What output is produced by four-way replacement selection when it is applied to successive words of the following sentence:

> fourscore and seven years ago our fathers brought forth
> on this continent a new nation conceived in liberty and
> dedicated to the proposition that all men are created equal.

(Use ordinary alphabetic order, treating each word as one key.)

4. [16] Apply four-way *natural* selection to the sentence in exercise 3, using a reservoir of capacity 4.

5. [00] True or false: Replacement selection using a tree works only when P is a power of 2 or the sum of two powers of 2.

6. [15] Algorithm R specifies that P must be ≥ 2; what comparatively small changes to the algorithm would make it valid for all $P \geq 1$?

7. [17] What does Algorithm R do when there is no input at all?

8. [20] Algorithm R makes use of an artificial key "∞" that must be larger than any possible key. Show that the algorithm might fail if an actual key were equal to ∞, and explain how to modify the algorithm in case the implementation of a true ∞ is inconvenient.

▶ **9.** [23] How would you modify Algorithm R so that it causes certain specified runs (depending on RC) to be output in ascending order, and others in descending order?

10. [26] The initial setting of the LOSER pointers in step R1 usually doesn't correspond to any actual tournament, since external node $P + j$ may not lie in the subtree below internal node j. Explain why Algorithm R works anyway. [*Hint:* Would the algorithm work if {LOSER(LOC($X[0]$)),...,LOSER(LOC($X[P-1]$))} were set to an *arbitrary* permutation of {LOC($X[0]$),...,LOC($X[P-1]$)} in step R1?]

11. [M25] True or false: The probability that KEY(Q) < LASTKEY in step R4 is approximately $\frac{1}{2}$, assuming random input.

12. [M46] Carry out a detailed analysis of the number of times each portion of Algorithm R is executed; for example, how often are interchanges made in step R6?

13. [13] Why is the second run produced by replacement selection usually longer than the first run?

▶ **14.** [HM25] Use the snowplow analogy to estimate the average length of the *last two runs* produced by replacement selection on a long sequence of input data.

15. [*20*] True or false: The final run produced by replacement selection never contains more than P records. Discuss your answer.

16. [*M26*] Find a "simple" necessary and sufficient condition that a file $R_1 R_2 \ldots R_N$ will be completely sorted in one pass by P-way replacement selection. What is the probability that this happens, as a function of P and N, when the input is a random permutation of $\{1, 2, \ldots, N\}$?

17. [*20*] What is output by Algorithm R when the input keys are in decreasing order, $K_1 \geq K_2 \geq \cdots \geq K_N$?

▶ **18.** [*22*] What happens if Algorithm R is applied *again* to an output file that was produced by Algorithm R?

19. [*HM22*] Use the snowplow analogy to prove that the first run produced by replacement selection is approximately $(e - 1)P$ records long.

20. [*HM24*] Approximately how long is the first run produced by natural selection, when $P = P'$?

▶ **21.** [*HM23*] Determine the approximate length of runs produced by natural selection when $P' < P$.

22. [*HM40*] The purpose of this exercise is to determine the average run length obtained in natural selection, when $P' > P$. Let $\kappa = k + \theta$ be a real number ≥ 1, where $k = \lfloor \kappa \rfloor$ and $\theta = \kappa \bmod 1$, and consider the function $F(\kappa) = F_k(\theta)$, where $F_k(\theta)$ is the polynomial defined by the generating function

$$\sum_{k \geq 0} F_k(\theta) z^k = e^{-\theta z}/(1 - ze^{1-z}).$$

Thus, $F_0(\theta) = 1$, $F_1(\theta) = e - \theta$, $F_2(\theta) = e^2 - e - e\theta + \frac{1}{2}\theta^2$, etc.

Suppose that a snowplow starts out at time 0 to simulate the process of natural selection, and suppose that after T units of time exactly P snowflakes have fallen behind it. At this point a second snowplow begins on the same journey, occupying the same position at time $t + T$ as the first snowplow did at time t. Finally, at time κT, exactly P' snowflakes have fallen behind the first snowplow; it instantaneously plows the rest of the road and disappears.

Using this model to represent the process of natural selection, show that a run length equal to $e^\theta F(\kappa)P$ is obtained when

$$P'/P = k + 1 + e^\theta \left(\kappa F(\kappa) - \sum_{j=0}^{k} F(\kappa - j) \right).$$

23. [*HM35*] The preceding exercise analyzes natural selection when the records from the reservoir are always read in the same order that they were written, first-in-first-out. Find the approximate run length that would be obtained if the reservoir contents from the preceding run were read in completely *random* order, as if the records in the reservoir had been thoroughly shuffled between runs.

24. [*HM39*] The purpose of this exercise is to analyze the effect caused by haphazardly changing the direction of runs in replacement selection.

a) Let $g_P(z_1, z_2, \ldots, z_k)$ be a generating function defined as in Theorem K, but with each of the k runs specified as to whether it is to be ascending or descending.

For example, we might say that all odd-numbered runs are ascending, all even-numbered runs are descending. Show that Theorem K is valid for each of the 2^k generating functions of this type.

b) As a consequence of (a), we may assume that $P = 1$. We may also assume that the input is a uniformly distributed sequence of independent random numbers between 0 and 1. Let

$$a(x, y) = \begin{cases} e^{1-x} - e^{y-x}, & \text{if } x \leq y; \\ e^{1-x}, & \text{if } x > y. \end{cases}$$

Given that $f(x) \, dx$ is the probability that a certain ascending run begins with x, prove that $\left(\int_0^1 a(x, y) f(x) \, dx \right) dy$ is the probability that the following run begins with y. [*Hint:* Consider, for each $n \geq 0$, the probability that $x \leq X_1 \leq \cdots \leq X_n > y$, when x and y are given.]

c) Consider runs that change direction with probability p; in other words, the direction of each run after the first is randomly chosen to be the same as that of the previous run, $q = (1 - p)$ of the time, but it is to be in the opposite direction p of the time. (Thus when $p = 0$, all runs have the same direction; when $p = 1$, the runs alternate in direction; and when $p = \frac{1}{2}$, the runs are independently random.) Let

$$f_1(x) = 1, \qquad f_{n+1}(y) = p \int_0^1 a(x, y) f_n(1 - x) \, dx + q \int_0^1 a(x, y) f_n(x) \, dx.$$

Show that the probability that the nth run begins with x is $f_n(x) \, dx$ when the $(n-1)$st run is ascending, $f_n(1-x) \, dx$ when the $(n-1)$st run is descending.

d) Find a solution f to the steady-state equations

$$f(y) = p \int_0^1 a(x, y) f(1 - x) \, dx + q \int_0^1 a(x, y) f(x) \, dx, \qquad \int_0^1 f(x) \, dx = 1.$$

[*Hint:* Show that $f''(x)$ is independent of x.]

e) Show that the sequence $f_n(x)$ in part (c) converges rather rapidly to the function $f(x)$ in part (d).

f) Show that the average length of an ascending run starting with x is e^{1-x}.

g) Finally, put all these results together to prove the following theorem: *If the directions of consecutive runs are independently reversed with probability p in replacement selection, the average run length approaches $(6/(3+p))P$.*

(The case $p = 1$ of this theorem was first derived by Knuth [*CACM* **6** (1963), 685–688]; the case $p = \frac{1}{2}$ was first proved by A. G. Konheim in 1970.)

25. [*HM40*] Consider the following procedure:

N1. Read a record into a one-word "reservoir." Then read another record, R, and let K be its key.

N2. Output the reservoir, set LASTKEY to its key, and set the reservoir empty.

N3. If K < LASTKEY then output R and set LASTKEY ← K and go to N5.

N4. If the reservoir is nonempty, return to N2; otherwise enter R into the reservoir.

N5. Read in a new record, R, and let K be its key. Go to N3. ∎

This is essentially equivalent to natural selection with $P = 1$ and with $P' = 1$ or 2 (depending on whether you choose to empty the reservoir at the moment it fills or at the moment it is about to overfill), except that it produces *descending* runs, and it never stops. The latter anomalies are convenient and harmless assumptions for the purposes of this problem.

Proceeding as in exercise 24, let $f_n(x, y)\, dy\, dx$ be the probability that x and y are the respective values of LASTKEY and K just after the nth time step N2 is performed. Prove that there is a function $g_n(x)$ of one variable such that $f_n(x, y) = g_n(x)$ when $x < y$, and $f_n(x, y) = g_n(x) - e^{-y}(g_n(x) - g_n(y))$ when $x > y$. This function $g_n(x)$ is defined by the relations $g_1(x) = 1$,

$$g_{n+1}(x) = \int_0^x e^u g_n(u)\, du + \int_0^x dv\, (v+1) \int_v^1 du\, ((e^v - 1)g_n(u) + g_n(v))$$
$$+ x \int_x^1 dv \int_v^1 du\, ((e^v - 1)g_n(u) + g_n(v)).$$

Show further that the expected length of the nth run is

$$\int_0^1 dx \int_0^x dy\, (g_n(x)(e^y - 1) + g_n(y))(2 - \tfrac{1}{2}y^2) + \int_0^1 dx\, (1 - x)g_n(x)e^x.$$

[*Note:* The steady-state solution to these equations appears to be very complicated; it has been obtained numerically by J. McKenna, who showed that the run lengths approach a limiting value ≈ 2.61307209. Theorem K does not apply to natural selection, so the case $P = 1$ does not carry over to other P.]

26. [*M33*] Considering the algorithm in exercise 25 as a definition of natural selection when $P' = 1$, find the expected length of the *first* run when $P' = r$, for any $r \geq 0$, as follows.

a) Show that the first run has length n with probability

$$(n+r) \begin{bmatrix} n+r \\ n \end{bmatrix} \Big/ (n+r+1)!.$$

b) Define "associated Stirling numbers" $[[\begin{smallmatrix} n \\ m \end{smallmatrix}]]$ by the rules

$$\begin{bmatrix}\begin{bmatrix} 0 \\ m \end{bmatrix}\end{bmatrix} = \delta_{m0}, \quad \begin{bmatrix}\begin{bmatrix} n \\ m \end{bmatrix}\end{bmatrix} = (n+m-1)\left(\begin{bmatrix}\begin{bmatrix} n-1 \\ m \end{bmatrix}\end{bmatrix} + \begin{bmatrix}\begin{bmatrix} n-1 \\ m-1 \end{bmatrix}\end{bmatrix} \right) \qquad \text{for } n > 0.$$

Prove that

$$\begin{bmatrix} n+r \\ n \end{bmatrix} = \sum_{k=0}^{r} \binom{n+r}{k+r} \begin{bmatrix}\begin{bmatrix} r \\ k \end{bmatrix}\end{bmatrix}.$$

c) Prove that the average length of the first run is therefore $c_r e - r - 1$, where

$$c_r = \sum_{k=0}^{r} \begin{bmatrix}\begin{bmatrix} r \\ k \end{bmatrix}\end{bmatrix} \frac{r+k+1}{(r+k)!}.$$

▶ **27.** [*HM30*] (W. Dobosiewicz.) When natural selection is used with $P' < P$, we need not stop forming a run when the reservoir becomes full; we can store records that do not belong to the current run in the main priority queue, as in replacement selection, until only P' records of the current run are left. Then we can flush them to the output and replace them with the reservoir contents.

How much better is this method than the simpler approach analyzed in exercise 21?

28. [*25*] The text considers only the case that all records to be sorted have a fixed size. How can replacement selection be done reasonably well on *variable-length* records?

29. [*22*] Consider the 2^k nodes of a complete binary tree that has been right-threaded, illustrated here when $k = 3$:

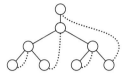

(Compare with 2.3.1–(10); the top node is the list head, and the dotted lines are thread links. In this exercise we are not concerned with sorting but rather with the structure of complete binary trees when a list-head-like node 0 has been added above node 1, as in the "tree of losers," Fig. 63.)

Show how to assign the 2^{n+k} internal nodes of a large tree of losers onto these 2^k host nodes so that (i) every host node holds exactly 2^n nodes of the large tree; (ii) adjacent nodes in the large tree either are assigned to the same host node or to host nodes that are adjacent (linked); and (iii) no two pairs of adjacent nodes in the large tree are separated by the same link in the host tree. [Multiple virtual processors in a large binary tree network can thereby be mapped to actual processors without undue congestion in the communication links.]

30. [*M29*] Prove that if $n \geq k \geq 1$, the construction in the preceding exercise is optimum, in the sense that *any* 2^k-node host graph satisfying (i), (ii), and (iii) must have at least $2^k + 2^{k-1} - 1$ edges (links) between nodes.

*5.4.2. The Polyphase Merge

Now that we have seen how initial runs can be built up, we shall consider various patterns that can be used to distribute them onto tapes and to merge them together until only a single run remains.

Let us begin by assuming that there are three tape units, T1, T2, and T3, available; the technique of "balanced merging," described near the beginning of Section 5.4, can be used with $P = 2$ and $T = 3$, when it takes the following form:

B1. Distribute initial runs alternately on tapes T1 and T2.

B2. Merge runs from T1 and T2 onto T3; then stop if T3 contains only one run.

B3. Copy the runs of T3 alternately onto T1 and T2, then return to B2. ▮

If the initial distribution pass produces S runs, the first merge pass will produce $\lceil S/2 \rceil$ runs on T3, the second will produce $\lceil S/4 \rceil$, etc. Thus if, say, $17 \leq S \leq 32$, we will have 1 distribution pass, 5 merge passes, and 4 copy passes; in general, if $S > 1$, the number of passes over all the data is $2\lceil \lg S \rceil$.

The copying passes in this procedure are undesirable, since they do not reduce the number of runs. Half of the copying can be avoided if we use a *two-phase* procedure:

A1. Distribute initial runs alternately on tapes T1 and T2.

A2. Merge runs from T1 and T2 onto T3; then stop if T3 contains only one run.

A3. Copy *half* of the runs from T3 onto T1.

A4. Merge runs from T1 and T3 onto T2; then stop if T2 contains only one run.

A5. Copy *half* of the runs from T2 onto T1. Return to A2. ▮

The number of passes over the data has been reduced to $\frac{3}{2}\lceil \lg S \rceil + \frac{1}{2}$, since steps A3 and A5 do only "half a pass"; about 25 percent of the time has therefore been saved.

The copying can actually be eliminated *entirely*, if we start with F_n runs on T1 and F_{n-1} runs on T2, where F_n and F_{n-1} are consecutive Fibonacci numbers. Consider, for example, the case $n = 7$, $S = F_n + F_{n-1} = 13 + 8 = 21$:

Phase	Contents of T1	Contents of T2	Contents of T3	Remarks
1	1,1,1,1,1,1,1,1,1,1,1,1,1	1,1,1,1,1,1,1,1		Initial distribution
2	1,1,1,1,1	—	2,2,2,2,2,2,2,2	Merge 8 runs to T3
3	—	3,3,3,3,3	2,2,2	Merge 5 runs to T2
4	5,5,5	3,3	—	Merge 3 runs to T1
5	5	—	8,8	Merge 2 runs to T3
6	—	13	8	Merge 1 run to T2
7	21	—	—	Merge 1 run to T1

Here, for example, "2,2,2,2,2,2,2,2" denotes eight runs of relative length 2, considering each initial run to be of relative length 1. Fibonacci numbers are omnipresent in this chart!

Only phases 1 and 7 are complete passes over the data; phase 2 processes only 16/21 of the initial runs, phase 3 only 15/21, etc., and so the total number of "passes" comes to $(21 + 16 + 15 + 15 + 16 + 13 + 21)/21 = 5\frac{4}{7}$ if we assume that the initial runs have approximately equal length. By comparison, the two-phase procedure above would have required 8 passes to sort these 21 initial runs. We shall see that in general this "Fibonacci" pattern requires approximately $1.04 \lg S + 0.99$ passes, making it competitive with a *four*-tape balanced merge although it requires only three tapes.

The same idea can be generalized to T tapes, for any $T \geq 3$, using $(T-1)$-way merging. We shall see, for example, that the four-tape case requires only about $.703 \lg S + 0.96$ passes over the data. The generalized pattern involves generalized Fibonacci numbers. Consider the following six-tape example:

Phase	T1	T2	T3	T4	T5	T6	Initial runs processed
1	1^{31}	1^{30}	1^{28}	1^{24}	1^{16}	—	$31 + 30 + 28 + 24 + 16 = 129$
2	1^{15}	1^{14}	1^{12}	1^{8}	—	5^{16}	$16 \times 5 = 80$
3	1^{7}	1^{6}	1^{4}	—	9^{8}	5^{8}	$8 \times 9 = 72$
4	1^{3}	1^{2}	—	17^{4}	9^{4}	5^{4}	$4 \times 17 = 68$
5	1^{1}	—	33^{2}	17^{2}	9^{2}	5^{2}	$2 \times 33 = 66$
6	—	65^{1}	33^{1}	17^{1}	9^{1}	5^{1}	$1 \times 65 = 65$
7	129^{1}	—	—	—	—	—	$1 \times 129 = 129$

Here 1^{31} stands for 31 runs of relative length 1, etc.; five-way merges have been used throughout. This general pattern was developed by R. L. Gilstad [*Proc. Eastern Joint Computer Conf.* **18** (1960), 143–148], who called it the *polyphase merge*. The three-tape case had been discovered earlier by B. K. Betz [unpublished memorandum, Minneapolis–Honeywell Regulator Co. (1956)].

In order to make polyphase merging work as in the examples above, we need to have a "perfect Fibonacci distribution" of runs on the tapes after each phase. By reading the table above from bottom to top, we can see that the first seven perfect Fibonacci distributions when $T = 6$ are $\{1,0,0,0,0\}$, $\{1,1,1,1,1\}$, $\{2,2,2,2,1\}$, $\{4,4,4,3,2\}$, $\{8,8,7,6,4\}$, $\{16,15,14,12,8\}$, and $\{31,30,28,24,16\}$. The big questions now facing us are

1. What is the rule underlying these perfect Fibonacci distributions?
2. What do we do if S does not correspond to a perfect Fibonacci distribution?
3. How should we design the initial distribution pass so that it produces the desired configuration on the tapes?
4. How many "passes" over the data will a T-tape polyphase merge require, as a function of S (the number of initial runs)?

We shall discuss these four questions in turn, first giving "easy answers" and then making a more intensive analysis.

The perfect Fibonacci distributions can be obtained by running the pattern backwards, cyclically rotating the tape contents. For example, when $T = 6$ we have the following distribution of runs:

Level	T1	T2	T3	T4	T5	Total	Final output will be on
0	1	0	0	0	0	1	T1
1	1	1	1	1	1	5	T6
2	2	2	2	2	1	9	T5
3	4	4	4	3	2	17	T4
4	8	8	7	6	4	33	T3
5	16	15	14	12	8	65	T2
6	31	30	28	24	16	129	T1
7	61	59	55	47	31	253	T6
8	120	116	108	92	61	497	T5
. . . . . .							. . .
n	a_n	b_n	c_n	d_n	e_n	t_n	$T(k)$
$n+1$	$a_n + b_n$	$a_n + c_n$	$a_n + d_n$	$a_n + e_n$	a_n	$t_n + 4a_n$	$T(k-1)$ (1)
. . . . . .							. . .

(Tape T6 will always be empty after the initial distribution.)

The rule for going from level n to level $n+1$ shows that the condition

$$a_n \geq b_n \geq c_n \geq d_n \geq e_n \tag{2}$$

will hold in every level. In fact, it is easy to see from (1) that

$$
\begin{aligned}
e_n &= a_{n-1}, \\
d_n &= a_{n-1} + e_{n-1} = a_{n-1} + a_{n-2}, \\
c_n &= a_{n-1} + d_{n-1} = a_{n-1} + a_{n-2} + a_{n-3}, \\
b_n &= a_{n-1} + c_{n-1} = a_{n-1} + a_{n-2} + a_{n-3} + a_{n-4}, \\
a_n &= a_{n-1} + b_{n-1} = a_{n-1} + a_{n-2} + a_{n-3} + a_{n-4} + a_{n-5},
\end{aligned}
\tag{3}
$$

where $a_0 = 1$ and where we let $a_n = 0$ for $n = -1, -2, -3, -4$.

The *pth-order Fibonacci numbers* $F_n^{(p)}$ are defined by the rules

$$F_n^{(p)} = F_{n-1}^{(p)} + F_{n-2}^{(p)} + \cdots + F_{n-p}^{(p)}, \quad \text{for } n \geq p;$$
$$F_n^{(p)} = 0, \quad \text{for } 0 \leq n \leq p - 2; \quad F_{p-1}^{(p)} = 1. \tag{4}$$

In other words, we start with $p - 1$ 0s, then 1, and then each number is the sum of the preceding p values. When $p = 2$, this is the usual Fibonacci sequence; for larger values of p the sequence was apparently first studied by V. Schlegel in *El Progreso Matemático* **4** (1894), 173–174. Schlegel derived the generating function

$$\sum_{n \geq 0} F_n^{(p)} z^n = \frac{z^{p-1}}{1 - z - z^2 - \cdots - z^p} = \frac{z^{p-1} - z^p}{1 - 2z + z^{p+1}}. \tag{5}$$

The last equation of (3) shows that the number of runs on T1 during a six-tape polyphase merge is a fifth-order Fibonacci number: $a_n = F_{n+4}^{(5)}$.

In general, if we set $P = T-1$, the polyphase merge distributions for T tapes will correspond to Pth order Fibonacci numbers in the same way. The kth tape gets

$$F_{n+P-2}^{(P)} + F_{n+P-3}^{(P)} + \cdots + F_{n+k-2}^{(P)}$$

initial runs in the perfect nth level distribution, for $1 \leq k \leq P$, and the total number of initial runs on all tapes is therefore

$$t_n = P F_{n+P-2}^{(P)} + (P - 1) F_{n+P-3}^{(P)} + \cdots + F_{n-1}^{(P)}. \tag{6}$$

This settles the issue of "perfect Fibonacci distributions." But what should we do if S is not exactly equal to t_n, for any n? And how do we get the runs onto the tapes in the first place?

When S isn't perfect (and so few values are), we can do just as we did in balanced P-way merging, adding artificial "dummy runs" so that we can pretend S is perfect after all. There are several ways to add the dummy runs, and we aren't ready yet to analyze the "best" way of doing this. We shall discuss first a method of distribution and dummy-run assignment that isn't strictly optimal, although it has the virtue of simplicity and appears to be better than all other equally simple methods.

Algorithm D (*Polyphase merge sorting with "horizontal" distribution*). This algorithm takes initial runs and disperses them to tapes, one run at a time, until the supply of initial runs is exhausted. Then it specifies how the tapes are to be merged, assuming that there are $T = P + 1 \geq 3$ available tape units, using P-way merging. Tape T may be used to hold the input, since it does not receive any initial runs. The following tables are maintained:

A[j], $1 \leq j \leq T$: The perfect Fibonacci distribution we are striving for.

D[j], $1 \leq j \leq T$: Number of dummy runs assumed to be present at the beginning of logical tape unit number j.

TAPE[j], $1 \leq j \leq T$: Number of the physical tape unit corresponding to logical tape unit number j.

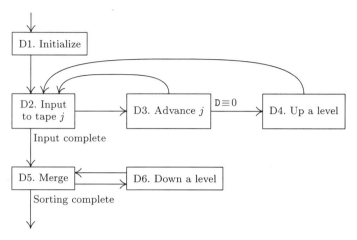

Fig. 68. Polyphase merge sorting.

(It is convenient to deal with "logical tape unit numbers" whose assignment to physical tape units varies as the algorithm proceeds.)

D1. [Initialize.] Set $A[j] \leftarrow D[j] - 1$ and $\mathtt{TAPE}[k] \leftarrow j$, for $1 \le j < T$. Set $A[T] \leftarrow D[T] \leftarrow 0$ and $\mathtt{TAPE}[T] \leftarrow T$. Then set $l \leftarrow 1$, $j \leftarrow 1$.

D2. [Input to tape j.] Write one run on tape number j, and decrease $D[j]$ by 1. Then if the input is exhausted, rewind all the tapes and go to step D5.

D3. [Advance j.] If $D[j] < D[j+1]$, increase j by 1 and return to D2. Otherwise if $D[j] = 0$, go on to D4. Otherwise set $j \leftarrow 1$ and return to D2.

D4. [Up a level.] Set $l \leftarrow l + 1$, $a \leftarrow A[1]$, and then for $j = 1, 2, \ldots, P$ (in this order) set $D[j] \leftarrow a + A[j+1] - A[j]$ and $A[j] \leftarrow a + A[j+1]$. (See (1) and note that $A[P+1]$ is always zero. At this point we will have $D[1] \ge D[2] \ge \cdots \ge D[T]$.) Now set $j \leftarrow 1$ and return to D2.

D5. [Merge.] If $l = 0$, sorting is complete and the output is on $\mathtt{TAPE}[1]$. Otherwise, merge runs from $\mathtt{TAPE}[1], \ldots, \mathtt{TAPE}[P]$ onto $\mathtt{TAPE}[T]$ until $\mathtt{TAPE}[P]$ is empty and $D[P] = 0$. The merging process should operate as follows, for each run merged: If $D[j] > 0$ for all j, $1 \le j \le P$, then increase $D[T]$ by 1 and decrease each $D[j]$ by 1 for $1 \le j \le P$; otherwise merge one run from each $\mathtt{TAPE}[j]$ such that $D[j] = 0$, and decrease $D[j]$ by 1 for each other j. (Thus the dummy runs are imagined to be at the *beginning* of the tape instead of at the ending.)

D6. [Down a level.] Set $l \leftarrow l - 1$. Rewind $\mathtt{TAPE}[P]$ and $\mathtt{TAPE}[T]$. (Actually the rewinding of $\mathtt{TAPE}[P]$ could have been initiated during step D5, just after its last block was input.) Then set $(\mathtt{TAPE}[1], \mathtt{TAPE}[2], \ldots, \mathtt{TAPE}[T]) \leftarrow (\mathtt{TAPE}[T], \mathtt{TAPE}[1], \ldots, \mathtt{TAPE}[T-1])$, $(D[1], D[2], \ldots, D[T]) \leftarrow (D[T], D[1], \ldots, D[T-1])$, and return to step D5. ∎

The distribution rule that is stated so succinctly in step D3 of this algorithm is intended to equalize the number of dummies on each tape as well as possible.

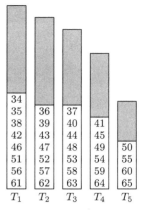

Fig. 69. The order in which runs 34 through 65 are distributed to tapes, when advancing from level 4 to level 5. (See the table of perfect distributions, Eq. (1).) Shaded areas represent the first 33 runs that were distributed when level 4 was reached. The bottom row corresponds to the beginning of each tape.

Figure 69 illustrates the order of distribution when we go from level 4 (33 runs) to level 5 (65 runs) in a six-tape sort; if there were only, say, 53 initial runs, all runs numbered 54 and higher would be treated as dummies. (The runs are actually being written at the end of the tape, but it is best to imagine them being written at the beginning, since the dummies are assumed to be at the beginning.)

We have now discussed the first three questions listed above, and it remains to consider the number of "passes" over the data. Comparing our six-tape example to the table (1), we see that the total number of initial runs processed when $S = t_6$ was $a_5 t_1 + a_4 t_2 + a_3 t_3 + a_2 t_4 + a_1 t_5 + a_0 t_6$, excluding the initial distribution pass. Exercise 4 derives the generating functions

$$a(z) = \sum_{n \geq 0} a_n z^n = \frac{1}{1 - z - z^2 - z^3 - z^4 - z^5},$$

$$t(z) = \sum_{n \geq 1} t_n z^n = \frac{5z + 4z^2 + 3z^3 + 2z^4 + z^5}{1 - z - z^2 - z^3 - z^4 - z^5}. \tag{7}$$

It follows that, in general, the number of initial runs processed when $S = t_n$ is exactly the coefficient of z^n in $a(z)t(z)$, plus t_n (for the initial distribution pass). This makes it possible to calculate the asymptotic behavior of polyphase merging, as shown in exercises 5 through 7, and we obtain the following results:

Table 1

APPROXIMATE BEHAVIOR OF POLYPHASE MERGE SORTING

Tapes	Phases	Passes	Pass/phase	Growth ratio
3	$2.078 \ln S + 0.672$	$1.504 \ln S + 0.992$	72%	1.6180340
4	$1.641 \ln S + 0.364$	$1.015 \ln S + 0.965$	62%	1.8392868
5	$1.524 \ln S + 0.078$	$0.863 \ln S + 0.921$	57%	1.9275620
6	$1.479 \ln S - 0.185$	$0.795 \ln S + 0.864$	54%	1.9659482
7	$1.460 \ln S - 0.424$	$0.762 \ln S + 0.797$	52%	1.9835828
8	$1.451 \ln S - 0.642$	$0.744 \ln S + 0.723$	51%	1.9919642
9	$1.447 \ln S - 0.838$	$0.734 \ln S + 0.646$	51%	1.9960312
10	$1.445 \ln S - 1.017$	$0.728 \ln S + 0.568$	50%	1.9980295
20	$1.443 \ln S - 2.170$	$0.721 \ln S - 0.030$	50%	1.9999981

In Table 1, the "growth ratio" is $\lim_{n\to\infty} t_{n+1}/t_n$, the approximate factor by which the number of runs increases at each level. "Passes" denotes the average number of times each record is processed, namely $1/S$ times the total number of initial runs processed during the distribution and merge phases. The stated number of passes and phases is correct in each case up to $O(S^{-\epsilon})$, for some $\epsilon > 0$, for perfect distributions as $S \to \infty$.

Figure 70 shows the average number of times each record is merged, as a function of S, when Algorithm D is used to handle the case of nonperfect numbers. Note that with three tapes there are "peaks" of relative inefficiency occurring just after the perfect distributions, but this phenomenon largely disappears when there are four or more tapes. The use of eight or more tapes gives comparatively little improvement over six or seven tapes.

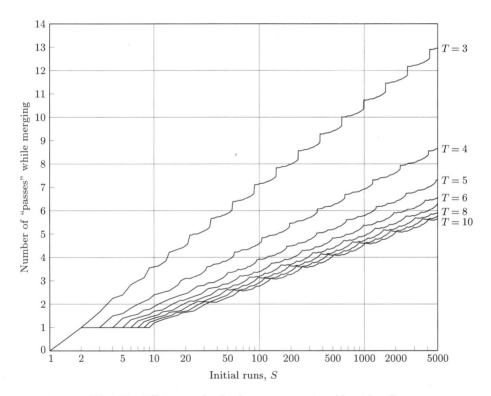

Fig. 70. Efficiency of polyphase merge using Algorithm D.

A closer look. In a balanced merge requiring k passes, every record is processed exactly k times during the course of the sort. But the polyphase procedure does not have this lack of bias; some records may get processed many more times than others, and we can gain speed if we arrange to put dummy runs into the oft-processed positions.

Let us therefore study the polyphase distribution more closely; instead of merely looking at the number of runs on each tape, as in (1), let us associate with each run its *merge number*, the number of times it will be processed during the complete polyphase sort. We get the following table in place of (1):

Level	T1	T2	T3	T4	T5
0	0	—	—	—	—
1	1	1	1	1	1
2	21	21	21	21	2
3	3221	3221	3221	322	32
4	43323221	43323221	4332322	433232	4332
5	5443433243323221	544343324332322	54434332433232	544343324332	54434332

$$
\begin{array}{cccccc}
\cdot & \cdot & \cdot & \cdot & \cdot & \cdot \\
n & A_n & B_n & C_n & D_n & E_n \\
n+1 & (A_n+1)B_n & (A_n+1)C_n & (A_n+1)D_n & (A_n+1)E_n & A_n+1 \quad (8)\\
\cdot & \cdot & \cdot & \cdot & \cdot & \cdot
\end{array}
$$

Here A_n is a string of a_n values representing the merge numbers for each run on T1, if we begin with the level n distribution; B_n is the corresponding string for T2; etc. The notation "$(A_n+1)B_n$" means "A_n with all values increased by 1, followed by B_n."

Figure 71(a) shows A_5, B_5, C_5, D_5, E_5 tipped on end, showing how the merge numbers for each run appear on tape; notice, for example, that the run at the beginning of each tape will be processed five times, while the run at the end of T1 will be processed only once. This discriminatory practice of the polyphase merge makes it much better to put a dummy run at the beginning of the tape than at the end. Figure 71(b) shows an optimum order in which to distribute runs for a five-level polyphase merge, placing each new run into a position with the smallest available merge number. Algorithm D is not quite as good (see Fig. 69), since it fills some "4" positions before all of the "3" positions are used up.

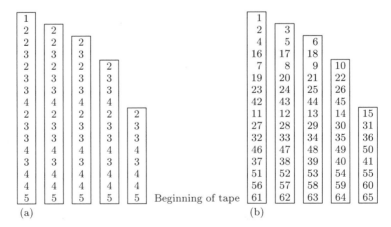

Fig. 71. Analysis of the fifth-level polyphase distribution for six tapes: (a) merge numbers, (b) optimum distribution order.

The recurrence relations (8) show that each of B_n, C_n, D_n, and E_n are initial substrings of A_n. In fact, we can use (8) to derive the formulas

$$
\begin{aligned}
E_n &= (A_{n-1}) + 1, \\
D_n &= (A_{n-1}A_{n-2}) + 1, \\
C_n &= (A_{n-1}A_{n-2}A_{n-3}) + 1, \\
B_n &= (A_{n-1}A_{n-2}A_{n-3}A_{n-4}) + 1, \\
A_n &= (A_{n-1}A_{n-2}A_{n-3}A_{n-4}A_{n-5}) + 1,
\end{aligned}
\tag{9}
$$

generalizing Eqs. (3), which treated only the lengths of these strings. Furthermore, the rule defining the A's implies that essentially the same structure is present at the beginning of every level; we have

$$
A_n = n - Q_n,
\tag{10}
$$

where Q_n is a string of a_n values defined by the law

$$
\begin{aligned}
Q_n &= Q_{n-1}(Q_{n-2}+1)(Q_{n-3}+2)(Q_{n-4}+3)(Q_{n-5}+4), \quad \text{for } n \geq 1; \\
Q_0 &= 0; \qquad\qquad Q_n = \epsilon \quad \text{(the empty string)} \quad \text{for } n < 0.
\end{aligned}
\tag{11}
$$

Since Q_n begins with Q_{n-1}, we can consider the *infinite* string Q_∞, whose first a_n elements are equal to Q_n; this string Q_∞ essentially characterizes all the merge numbers in polyphase distribution. In the six-tape case,

$$
Q_\infty = 0112122312232334122323342334344122323342334344523343445344545512232 \cdots.
\tag{12}
$$

Exercise 11 contains an interesting interpretation of this string.

Given that A_n is the string $m_1 m_2 \ldots m_{a_n}$, let

$$
A_n(x) = x^{m_1} + x^{m_2} + \cdots + x^{m_{a_n}}
$$

be the corresponding generating function that counts the number of times each merge number appears; and define $B_n(x)$, $C_n(x)$, $D_n(x)$, $E_n(x)$ similarly. For example, $A_4(x) = x^4 + x^3 + x^3 + x^2 + x^3 + x^2 + x^2 + x = x^4 + 3x^3 + 3x^2 + x$. Relations (9) tell us that

$$
\begin{aligned}
E_n(x) &= x\big(A_{n-1}(x)\big), \\
D_n(x) &= x\big(A_{n-1}(x) + A_{n-2}(x)\big), \\
C_n(x) &= x\big(A_{n-1}(x) + A_{n-2}(x) + A_{n-3}(x)\big), \\
B_n(x) &= x\big(A_{n-1}(x) + A_{n-2}(x) + A_{n-3}(x) + A_{n-4}(x)\big), \\
A_n(x) &= x\big(A_{n-1}(x) + A_{n-2}(x) + A_{n-3}(x) + A_{n-4}(x) + A_{n-5}(x)\big),
\end{aligned}
\tag{13}
$$

for $n \geq 1$, where $A_0(x) = 1$ and $A_n(x) = 0$ for $n = -1, -2, -3, -4$. Hence

$$
\sum_{n \geq 0} A_n(x) z^n = \frac{1}{1 - x(z + z^2 + z^3 + z^4 + z^5)} = \sum_{k \geq 0} x^k (z + z^2 + z^3 + z^4 + z^5)^k.
\tag{14}
$$

Considering the runs on all tapes, we let

$$T_n(x) = A_n(x) + B_n(x) + C_n(x) + D_n(x) + E_n(x), \qquad n \geq 1; \qquad (15)$$

from (13) we immediately have

$$T_n(x) = 5A_{n-1}(x) + 4A_{n-2}(x) + 3A_{n-3}(x) + 2A_{n-4}(x) + A_{n-5}(x),$$

hence

$$\sum_{n \geq 1} T_n(x) z^n = \frac{x(5z + 4z^2 + 3z^3 + 2z^4 + z^5)}{1 - x(z + z^2 + z^3 + z^4 + z^5)}. \qquad (16)$$

The form of (16) shows that it is easy to compute the coefficients of $T_n(x)$:

	z	z^2	z^3	z^4	z^5	z^6	z^7	z^8	z^9	z^{10}	z^{11}	z^{12}	z^{13}	z^{14}
x	5	4	3	2	1	0	0	0	0	0	0	0	0	0
x^2	0	5	9	12	14	15	10	6	3	1	0	0	0	0
x^3	0	0	5	14	26	40	55	60	57	48	35	20	10	4
x^4	0	0	0	5	19	45	85	140	195	238	260	255	220	170
x^5	0	0	0	0	5	24	69	154	294	484	703	918	1088	1168

(17)

The columns of this tableau give $T_n(x)$; for example, $T_4(x) = 2x + 12x^2 + 14x^3 + 5x^4$. After the first row, each entry in the tableau is the sum of the five entries just above and to the left in the previous row.

The number of runs in a "perfect" nth level distribution is $T_n(1)$, and the total amount of processing as these runs are merged is the derivative, $T'_n(1)$. Now

$$\sum_{n \geq 1} T'_n(x) z^n = \frac{5z + 4z^2 + 3z^3 + 2z^4 + z^5}{\left(1 - x(z + z^2 + z^3 + z^4 + z^5)\right)^2}; \qquad (18)$$

setting $x = 1$ in (16) and (18) gives a result in agreement with our earlier demonstration that the merge processing for a perfect nth level distribution is the coefficient of z^n in $a(z)t(z)$; see (7).

We can use the functions $T_n(x)$ to determine the work involved when dummy runs are added in an optimum way. Let $\Sigma_n(m)$ be the sum of the smallest m merge numbers in an nth level distribution. These values are readily calculated by looking at the columns of (17), and we find that $\Sigma_n(m)$ is given by

$m =$	1	2	3	4	5	6	7	8	9	10	11	12	13	14	15	16	17	18	19	20	21
$n = 1$	1	2	3	4	5	∞	∞	∞	∞	∞	∞	∞	∞	∞	∞	∞	∞	∞	∞	∞	∞
$n = 2$	1	2	3	4	6	8	10	12	14	∞	∞	∞	∞	∞	∞	∞	∞	∞	∞	∞	∞
$n = 3$	1	2	3	5	7	9	11	13	15	17	19	21	24	27	30	33	36	∞	∞	∞	∞
$n = 4$	1	2	4	6	8	10	12	14	16	18	20	22	24	26	29	32	35	38	41	44	47
$n = 5$	1	3	5	7	9	11	13	15	17	19	21	23	25	27	29	32	35	38	41	44	47
$n = 6$	2	4	6	8	10	12	14	16	18	20	22	24	26	28	30	33	36	39	42	45	48
$n = 7$	2	4	6	8	10	12	14	16	18	20	23	26	29	32	35	38	41	44	47	50	53

(19)

For example, if we wish to sort 17 runs using a level-3 distribution, the total amount of processing is $\Sigma_3(17) = 36$; but if we use a level-4 or level-5 distribution

Table 2

NUMBER OF RUNS FOR WHICH A GIVEN LEVEL IS OPTIMUM

Level	$T = 3$	$T = 4$	$T = 5$	$T = 6$	$T = 7$	$T = 8$	$T = 9$	$T = 10$	
1	2	2	2	2	2	2	2	2	M_1
2	3	4	5	6	7	8	9	10	M_2
3	4	6	8	10	12	14	16	18	M_3
4	6	10	14	14	17	20	23	26	M_4
5	9	18	23	29	20	24	28	32	M_5
6	14	32	35	43	53	27	32	37	M_6
7	22	55	76	61	73	88	35	41	M_7
8	35	96	109	154	98	115	136	44	M_8
9	56	173	244	216	283	148	171	199	M_9
10	90	280	359	269	386	168	213	243	M_{10}
11	145	535	456	779	481	640	240	295	M_{11}
12	234	820	1197	1034	555	792	1002	330	M_{12}
13	378	1635	1563	1249	1996	922	1228	1499	M_{13}
14	611	2401	4034	3910	2486	1017	1432	1818	M_{14}
15	988	4959	5379	4970	2901	4397	1598	2116	M_{15}
16	1598	7029	6456	5841	10578	5251	1713	2374	M_{16}
17	2574	14953	18561	19409	13097	5979	8683	2576	M_{17}
18	3955	20583	22876	23918	15336	6499	10069	2709	M_{18}
19	6528	44899	64189	27557	17029	30164	11259	15787	M_{19}

and position the dummy runs optimally, the total amount of processing during the merge phases is only $\Sigma_4(17) = \Sigma_5(17) = 35$. It is better to use level 4, even though 17 corresponds to a "perfect" level-3 distribution! Indeed, as S gets large it turns out that the optimum number of levels is many more than that used in Algorithm D.

Exercise 14 proves that there is a nondecreasing sequence of numbers M_n such that level n is optimum for $M_n \leq S < M_{n+1}$, but not for $S \geq M_{n+1}$. In the six-tape case the table of $\Sigma_n(m)$ we have just calculated shows that

$$M_0 = 0, \qquad M_1 = 2, \qquad M_2 = 6, \qquad M_3 = 10, \qquad M_4 = 14.$$

The discussion above treats only the case of six tapes, but it is clear that the same ideas apply to polyphase merging with T tapes for any $T \geq 3$; we simply replace 5 by $P = T - 1$ in all appropriate places. Table 2 shows the sequences M_n obtained for various values of T. Table 3 and Fig. 72 indicate the total number of initial runs that are processed after making an optimum distribution of dummy runs. (The formulas that appear at the bottom of Table 3 should be taken with a grain of salt, since they are least-squares fits over the range $1 \leq S \leq 5000$, or $1 \leq S \leq 10000$ for $T = 3$; this leads to somewhat erratic behavior because the given range of S values is not equally favorable for all T. As $S \to \infty$, the number of initial runs processed after an optimum polyphase distribution is asymptotically $S \log_P S$, but convergence to this asymptotic limit is extremely slow.)

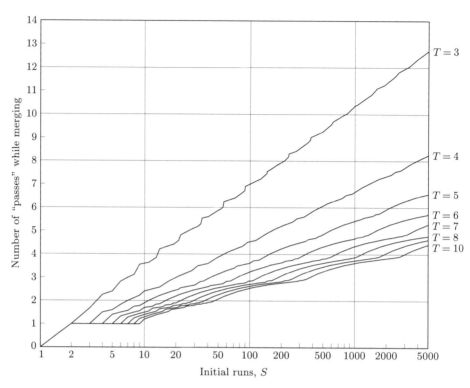

Fig. 72. Efficiency of polyphase merge with optimum initial distribution, using the same assumptions as Fig. 70.

Table 3

INITIAL RUNS PROCESSED DURING AN OPTIMUM POLYPHASE MERGE

S	$T = 3$	$T = 4$	$T = 5$	$T = 6$	$T = 7$	$T = 8$	$T = 9$	$T = 10$
10	36	24	19	17	15	14	13	12
20	90	60	49	44	38	36	34	33
50	294	194	158	135	128	121	113	104
100	702	454	362	325	285	271	263	254
500	4641	3041	2430	2163	1904	1816	1734	1632
1000	10371	6680	5430	4672	4347	3872	3739	3632
5000	63578	41286	32905	28620	26426	23880	23114	22073
$S\begin{cases} \\ \end{cases}$	(1.51	0.951	0.761	0.656	0.589	0.548	0.539	0.488) $\times S \ln S +$
	(−.11	+.14	+.16	+.19	+.21	+.20	+.02	+.18) $\times S$

Table 4 shows how the distribution method of Algorithm D compares with the results of optimum distribution in Table 3. It is clear that Algorithm D is not very close to the optimum when S and T become large; but it is not clear

Table 4

INITIAL RUNS PROCESSED DURING THE STANDARD POLYPHASE MERGE

S	$T = 3$	$T = 4$	$T = 5$	$T = 6$	$T = 7$	$T = 8$	$T = 9$	$T = 10$
10	36	24	19	17	15	14	13	12
20	90	62	49	44	41	37	34	33
50	294	194	167	143	134	131	120	114
100	714	459	393	339	319	312	292	277
500	4708	3114	2599	2416	2191	2100	2047	2025
1000	10730	6920	5774	5370	4913	4716	4597	4552
5000	64740	43210	36497	32781	31442	29533	28817	28080

how to do much better than Algorithm D without considerable complication in such cases, especially if we do not know S in advance. Fortunately, we rarely have to worry about large S (see Section 5.4.6), so Algorithm D is not too bad in practice; in fact, it's pretty good.

Polyphase sorting was first analyzed mathematically by W. C. Carter [*Proc. IFIP Congress* (1962), 62–66]. Many of the results stated above about optimal dummy run placement are due originally to B. Sackman and T. Singer ["A vector model for merge sort analysis," an unpublished paper presented at the ACM Sort Symposium (November 1962), 21 pages]. Sackman later suggested the horizontal method of distribution used in Algorithm D. Donald Shell [*CACM* **14** (1971), 713–719; **15** (1972), 28] developed the theory independently, noted relation (10), and made a detailed study of several different distribution algorithms. Further instructive developments and refinements have been made by Derek A. Zave [*SICOMP* **6** (1977), 1–39]; some of Zave's results are discussed in exercises 15 through 17. The generating function (16) was first investigated by W. Burge [*Proc. IFIP Congress* (1971), **1**, 454–459].

But what about rewind time? So far we have taken "initial runs processed" as the sole measure of efficiency for comparing tape merge strategies. But after each of phases 2 through 6, in the examples at the beginning of this section, it is necessary for the computer to wait for two tapes to rewind; both the previous output tape and the new current output tape must be repositioned at the beginning, before the next phase can proceed. This can cause a significant delay, since the previous output tape generally contains a significant percentage of the records being sorted (see the "Pass/phase" column in Table 1). It is a shame to have the computer twiddling its thumbs during all these rewind operations, since useful work could be done with the other tapes if we used a different merging pattern.

A simple modification of the polyphase procedure will overcome this problem, although it requires at least five tapes [see Y. Césari, Thesis, U. of Paris (1968), 25–27, where the idea is credited to J. Caron]. Each phase in Caron's scheme merges runs from $T - 3$ tapes onto another tape, while the remaining two tapes are rewinding.

For example, consider the case of six tapes and 49 initial runs. In the following tableau, R denotes rewinding during the phase, and T5 is assumed to contain the original input:

Phase	T1	T2	T3	T4	T5	T6	Write time	Rewind time
1	1^{11}	1^{17}	1^{13}	1^8	—	(R)	49	17
2	(R)	1^9	1^5	—	R	3^8	$8 \times 3 = 24$	$49 - 17 = 32$
3	1^6	1^4	—	R	3^5	R	$5 \times 3 = 15$	$\max(8, 24)$
4	1^2	—	R	5^4	R	3^4	$4 \times 5 = 20$	$\max(13, 15)$
5	—	R	7^2	R	3^3	3^2	$2 \times 7 = 14$	$\max(17, 20)$
6	R	11^2	R	5^2	3^1	—	$2 \times 11 = 22$	$\max(11, 14)$
7	15^1	R	7^1	5^1	—	R	$1 \times 15 = 15$	$\max(22, 24)$
8	R	11^1	7^0	—	R	23^1	$1 \times 23 = 23$	$\max(15, 15)$
9	15^1	11^1	—	R	33^0	R	$0 \times 33 = 0$	$\max(20, 23)$
10	(15^0)	—	R	49^1	(R)	(23^0)	$1 \times 49 = 49$	14

Here all the rewind time is essentially overlapped, except in phase 9 (a "dummy phase" that prepares for the final merge), and after the initial distribution phase (when all tapes are rewound). If t is the time to merge the number of records in one initial run, and if r is the time to rewind over one initial run, this process takes about $182t + 40r$ plus the time for initial distribution and final rewind. The corresponding figures for standard polyphase using Algorithm D are $140t + 104r$, which is slightly worse when $r = \frac{3}{4}t$, slightly better when $r = \frac{1}{2}t$.

Everything we have said about standard polyphase can be adapted to Caron's polyphase; for example, the sequence a_n now satisfies the recurrence

$$a_n = a_{n-2} + a_{n-3} + a_{n-4} \tag{20}$$

instead of (3). The reader will find it instructive to analyze this method in the same way we analyzed standard polyphase, since it will enhance an understanding of both methods. (See, for example, exercises 19 and 20.)

Table 5 gives statistics about Polyphase Caron that are analogous to the facts about Polyphase Ordinaire in Table 1. Notice that Caron's method actually becomes *superior* to polyphase on eight or more tapes, in the number of runs processed as well as in the rewind time, even though it does $(T-3)$-way merging instead of $(T-1)$-way merging!

Table 5
APPROXIMATE BEHAVIOR OF CARON'S POLYPHASE MERGE SORTING

Tapes	Phases	Passes	Pass/phase	Growth ratio
5	$3.556 \ln S + 0.158$	$1.463 \ln S + 1.016$	41%	1.3247180
6	$2.616 \ln S - 0.166$	$0.951 \ln S + 1.014$	36%	1.4655712
7	$2.337 \ln S - 0.472$	$0.781 \ln S + 1.001$	33%	1.5341577
8	$2.216 \ln S - 0.762$	$0.699 \ln S + 0.980$	32%	1.5701473
9	$2.156 \ln S - 1.034$	$0.654 \ln S + 0.954$	30%	1.5900054
10	$2.124 \ln S - 1.290$	$0.626 \ln S + 0.922$	29%	1.6013473
20	$2.078 \ln S - 3.093$	$0.575 \ln S + 0.524$	28%	1.6179086

This may seem paradoxical until we realize that *a high order of merge does not necessarily imply an efficient sort*. As an extreme example, consider placing one run on T1 and n runs on T2, T3, T4, T5; if we alternately do five-way merging to T6 and T1 until T2, T3, T4, T5 are empty, the processing time is $(2n^2 + 3n)$ initial run lengths, essentially proportional to S^2 instead of $S \log S$, although five-way merging was done throughout.

Tape splitting. Efficient overlapping of rewind time is a problem that arises in many applications, not just sorting, and there is a general approach that can often be used. Consider an iterative process that uses two tapes in the following way:

	T1	T2
Phase 1	Output 1	—
	Rewind	—
Phase 2	Input 1	Output 2
	Rewind	Rewind
Phase 3	Output 3	Input 2
	Rewind	Rewind
Phase 4	Input 3	Output 4
	Rewind	Rewind

and so on, where "Output k" means write the kth output file and "Input k" means read it. The rewind time can be avoided when three tapes are used, as suggested by C. Weisert [*CACM* **5** (1962), 102]:

	T1	T2	T3
Phase 1	Output 1.1	—	—
	Output 1.2	—	—
	Rewind	Output 1.3	—
Phase 2	Input 1.1	Output 2.1	—
	Input 1.2	Rewind	Output 2.2
	Rewind	Input 1.3	Output 2.3
Phase 3	Output 3.1	Input 2.1	Rewind
	Output 3.2	Rewind	Input 2.2
	Rewind	Output 3.3	Input 2.3
Phase 4	Input 3.1	Output 4.1	Rewind
	Input 3.2	Rewind	Output 4.2
	Rewind	Input 3.3	Output 4.3

and so on. Here "Output $k.j$" means write the jth third of the kth output file, and "Input $k.j$" means read it. Virtually all of the rewind time will be eliminated if rewinding is at least twice as fast as the read/write speed. Such a procedure, in which the output of each phase is divided between tapes, is called "tape splitting."

SORTING

R. L. McAllester [*CACM* **7** (1964), 158–159] has shown that tape splitting leads to an efficient way of overlapping the rewind time in a polyphase merge. His method can be used with four or more tapes, and it does $(T-2)$-way merging.

Assuming once again that we have six tapes, let us try to design a merge pattern that operates as follows, splitting the output on each level, where "I", "O", and "R", respectively, denote input, output, and rewinding:

Level	T1	T2	T3	T4	T5	T6	Number of runs output
7	I	I	I	I	R	O	u_7
	I	I	I	I	O	R	v_7
6	I	I	I	R	O	I	u_6
	I	I	I	O	R	I	v_6
5	I	I	R	O	I	I	u_5
	I	I	O	R	I	I	v_5
4	I	R	O	I	I	I	u_4
	I	O	R	I	I	I	v_4
3	R	O	I	I	I	I	u_3
	O	R	I	I	I	I	v_3
2	O	I	I	I	I	R	u_2
	R	I	I	I	I	O	v_2
1	I	I	I	I	R	O	u_1
	I	I	I	I	O	R	v_1
0	I	I	I	R	O	I	u_0
	I	I	I	O	R	I	v_0	(21)

In order to end with one run on T4 and all other tapes empty, we need to have

$$v_0 = 1,$$
$$u_0 + v_1 = 0,$$
$$u_1 + v_2 = u_0 + v_0,$$
$$u_2 + v_3 = u_1 + v_1 + u_0 + v_0,$$
$$u_3 + v_4 = u_2 + v_2 + u_1 + v_1 + u_0 + v_0,$$
$$u_4 + v_5 = u_3 + v_3 + u_2 + v_2 + u_1 + v_1 + u_0 + v_0,$$
$$u_5 + v_6 = u_4 + v_4 + u_3 + v_3 + u_2 + v_2 + u_1 + v_1 + u_0 + v_0,$$

etc.; in general, the requirement is that

$$u_n + v_{n+1} = u_{n-1} + v_{n-1} + u_{n-2} + v_{n-2} + u_{n-3} + v_{n-3} + u_{n-4} + v_{n-4} \quad (22)$$

for all $n \geq 0$, if we regard $u_j = v_j = 0$ for all $j < 0$.

There is no unique solution to these equations; indeed, if we let all the u's be zero, we get the usual polyphase merge with one tape wasted! But if we choose $u_n \approx v_{n+1}$, the rewind time will be satisfactorily overlapped.

McAllester suggested taking

$$u_n = v_{n-1} + v_{n-2} + v_{n-3} + v_{n-4},$$
$$v_{n+1} = u_{n-1} + u_{n-2} + u_{n-3} + u_{n-4},$$

so that the sequence

$$\langle x_0, x_1, x_2, x_3, x_4, x_5, \ldots \rangle = \langle v_0, u_0, v_1, u_1, v_2, u_2, \ldots \rangle$$

satisfies the uniform recurrence $x_n = x_{n-3} + x_{n-5} + x_{n-7} + x_{n-9}$. However, it turns out to be better to let

$$\begin{aligned} v_{n+1} &= u_{n-1} + v_{n-1} + u_{n-2} + v_{n-2}, \\ u_n &= u_{n-3} + v_{n-3} + u_{n-4} + v_{n-4}; \end{aligned} \tag{23}$$

this sequence not only leads to a slightly better merging time, it also has the great virtue that its merging time can be analyzed mathematically. McAllester's choice is extremely difficult to analyze because runs of different lengths may occur during a single phase; we shall see that this does not happen with (23).

We can deduce the number of runs on each tape on each level by working backwards in the pattern (21), and we obtain the following sorting scheme:

Level	T1	T2	T3	T4	T5	T6	Write time	Rewind time
	1^{23}	1^{21}	1^{17}	1^{10}	—	1^{11}	82	23
7	1^{19}	1^{17}	1^{13}	1^6	R	$1^{11}4^4$	$4 \times 4 = 16$	$82 - 23$
	1^{13}	1^{11}	1^7	—	4^6	R	$6 \times 4 = 24$	27
6	1^{10}	1^8	1^4	R	4^9	$1^8 4^4$	$3 \times 4 = 12$	10
	1^6	1^4	—	4^4	R	$1^4 4^4$	$4 \times 4 = 16$	36
5	1^5	1^3	R	$4^4 7^1$	4^8	$1^3 4^4$	$1 \times 7 = 7$	17
	1^2	—	7^3	R	4^5	4^4	$3 \times 7 = 21$	23
4	1^1	R	$7^3 13^1$	$4^3 7^1$	4^4	4^3	$1 \times 13 = 13$	21
	—	13^1	R	$4^2 7^1$	4^3	4^2	$1 \times 13 = 13$	34
3	R	$13^1 19^1$	$7^2 13^1$	$4^1 7^1$	4^2	4^1	$1 \times 19 = 19$	23
	19^1	R	$7^1 13^1$	7^1	4^1	—	$1 \times 19 = 19$	32
2	$19^1 31^0$	$13^1 19^1$	$7^1 13^1$	7^1	4^1	R	$0 \times 31 = 0$	27
	R	19^1	13^1	7^0	—	31^1	$1 \times 31 = 31$	19
1	$19^1 31^0$	19^1	13^1	7^0	R	$31^1 52^0$	$0 \times 52 = 0$	
	$19^1 31^0$	19^1	13^1	—	52^0	R	$0 \times 52 = 0$	$\}\ \max(36, 31, 23)$
0	$19^1 31^0$	19^1	13^1	R	$52^0 82^0$	$31^1 52^0$	$0 \times 82 = 0$	
	(31^0)	(19^0)	—	82^1	(R)	(52^0)	$1 \times 82 = 82$	0

Unoverlapped rewinding occurs in three places: when the input tape T5 is being rewound (82 units), during the first half of the level 2 phase (27 units), and during the final "dummy merge" phases in levels 1 and 0 (36 units). So we may estimate the time as $273t + 145r$; the corresponding amount for Algorithm D, $268t + 208r$, is almost always inferior.

Exercise 23 proves that the run lengths output during each phase are successively

$$4, 4, 7, 13, 19, 31, 52, 82, 133, \ldots, \tag{24}$$

a sequence $\langle t_1, t_2, t_3, \ldots \rangle$ satisfying the law

$$t_n = t_{n-2} + 2t_{n-3} + t_{n-4} \tag{25}$$

if we regard $t_n = 1$ for $n \le 0$. We can also analyze the optimum placement of dummy runs, by looking at strings of merge numbers as we did for standard polyphase in Eq. (8):

						Final
Level	T1	T2	T3	T4	T6	output on
1	1	1	1	1	—	T5
2	1	1	1	—	1	T4
3	21	21	2	2	1	T3
4	2221	222	222	22	2	T2
5	23222	23222	2322	23	222	T1
6	333323222	33332322	333323	3333	2322	T6
$\cdots$	$\cdots$	$\cdots$	$\cdots$	$\cdots$	$\cdots$	
n	A_n	B_n	C_n	D_n	E_n	T(k)
$n+1$	$(A_n''E_n+1)B_n$	$(A_n''E_n+1)C_n$	$(A_n''E_n+1)D_n$	$A_n''E_n+1$	A_n'	T$(k-1)$ (26)
$\cdots$	$\cdots$	$\cdots$	$\cdots$	$\cdots$	$\cdots$	

where $A_n = A_n'A_n''$, and A_n'' consists of the last u_n merge numbers of A_n. The rule
above for going from level n to level $n+1$ is valid for *any* scheme satisfying (22).
When we define the u's and v's by (23), the strings $A_n, \ldots, E_n$ can be expressed
in the following rather simple way analogous to (9):

$$A_n = (W_{n-1}W_{n-2}W_{n-3}W_{n-4}) + 1,$$
$$B_n = (W_{n-1}W_{n-2}W_{n-3}) + 1,$$
$$C_n = (W_{n-1}W_{n-2}) + 1,$$
$$D_n = (W_{n-1}) + 1,$$
$$E_n = (W_{n-2}W_{n-3}) + 1, \tag{27}$$

where

$$W_n = (W_{n-3}W_{n-4}W_{n-2}W_{n-3}) + 1 \qquad \text{for } n > 0,$$
$$W_0 = 0, \qquad \text{and} \qquad W_n = \epsilon \text{ for } n < 0. \tag{28}$$

From these relations it is easy to make a detailed analysis of the six-tape case.

In general, when there are $T \geq 5$ tapes, we let $P = T - 2$, and we define the
sequences $\langle u_n \rangle$, $\langle v_n \rangle$ by the rules

$$v_{n+1} = u_{n-1} + v_{n-1} + \cdots + u_{n-r} + v_{n-r},$$
$$u_n = u_{n-r-1} + v_{n-r-1} + \cdots + u_{n-P} + v_{n-P}, \qquad \text{for } n \geq 0, \tag{29}$$

where $r = \lfloor P/2 \rfloor$; $v_0 = 1$, and $u_n = v_n = 0$ for $n < 0$. So if $w_n = u_n + v_n$, we have

$$w_n = w_{n-2} + \cdots + w_{n-r} + 2w_{n-r-1} + w_{n-r-2} + \cdots + w_{n-P}, \qquad \text{for } n > 0; \tag{30}$$

$w_0 = 1$; and $w_n = 0$ for $n < 0$. The initial distribution on tapes for level
$n + 1$ places $w_n + w_{n-1} + \cdots + w_{n-P+k}$ runs on tape k, for $1 \leq k \leq P$, and
$w_{n-1} + \cdots + w_{n-r}$ on tape T; tape $T - 1$ is used for input. Then u_n runs are
merged to tape T while $T - 1$ is being rewound; v_n are merged to $T - 1$ while T
is rewinding; u_{n-1} to $T - 1$ while $T - 2$ is rewinding; etc.

Table 6 shows the approximate behavior of this procedure when S is not
too small. The "Pass/phase" column indicates approximately how much of the
entire file is being rewound during each half of a phase, and approximately how
much of the file is being written during each full phase. *The tape splitting method
is superior to standard polyphase on six or more tapes, and probably also on five,
at least for large S.*

Table 6

APPROXIMATE BEHAVIOR OF POLYPHASE MERGE WITH TAPE SPLITTING

Tapes	Phases	Passes	Pass/phase	Growth ratio
4	$2.885 \ln S + 0.000$	$1.443 \ln S + 1.000$	50%	1.4142136
5	$2.078 \ln S + 0.232$	$0.929 \ln S + 1.022$	45%	1.6180340
6	$2.078 \ln S - 0.170$	$0.752 \ln S + 1.024$	36%	1.6180340
7	$1.958 \ln S - 0.408$	$0.670 \ln S + 1.007$	34%	1.6663019
8	$2.008 \ln S - 0.762$	$0.624 \ln S + 0.994$	31%	1.6454116
9	$1.972 \ln S - 0.987$	$0.595 \ln S + 0.967$	30%	1.6604077
10	$2.013 \ln S - 1.300$	$0.580 \ln S + 0.941$	29%	1.6433803
20	$2.069 \ln S - 3.164$	$0.566 \ln S + 0.536$	27%	1.6214947

When $T = 4$ the procedure above would become essentially equivalent to balanced two-way merging, *without* overlapping the rewind time, since w_{2n+1} would be 0 for all n. So the entries in Table 6 for $T = 4$ have been obtained by making a slight modification, letting $v_2 = 0$, $u_1 = 1$, $v_1 = 0$, $u_0 = 0$, $v_0 = 1$, and $v_{n+1} = u_{n-1} + v_{n-1}$, $u_n = u_{n-2} + v_{n-2}$ for $n \geq 2$. This leads to a very interesting sorting scheme (see exercises 25 and 26).

EXERCISES

1. [*16*] Figure 69 shows the order in which runs 34 through 65 are distributed to five tapes with Algorithm D; in what order are runs 1 through 33 distributed?

▶ **2.** [*21*] True or false: After two merge phases in Algorithm D (that is, on the second time we reach step D6), all dummy runs have disappeared.

▶ **3.** [*22*] Prove that the condition $D[1] \geq D[2] \geq \cdots \geq D[T]$ is always satisfied at the conclusion of step D4. Explain why this condition is important, in the sense that the mechanism of steps D2 and D3 would not work properly otherwise.

4. [*M20*] Derive the generating functions (7).

5. [*HM26*] (E. P. Miles, Jr., 1960.) For all $p \geq 2$, prove that the polynomial $f_p(z) = z^p - z^{p-1} - \cdots - z - 1$ has p distinct roots, of which exactly one has magnitude greater than unity. [*Hint:* Consider the polynomial $z^{p+1} - 2z^p + 1$.]

6. [*HM24*] The purpose of this exercise is to consider how Tables 1, 5, and 6 were prepared. Assume that we have a merging pattern whose properties are characterized by polynomials $p(z)$ and $q(z)$ in the following way: (i) The number of initial runs present in a "perfect distribution" requiring n merging phases is $[z^n] p(z)/q(z)$. (ii) The number of initial runs processed during these n merging phases is $[z^n] p(z)/q(z)^2$. (iii) There is a "dominant root" α of $q(z^{-1})$ such that $q(\alpha^{-1}) = 0$, $q'(\alpha^{-1}) \neq 0$, $p(\alpha^{-1}) \neq 0$, and $q(\beta^{-1}) = 0$ implies that $\beta = \alpha$ or $|\beta| < |\alpha|$.

Prove that there is a number $\epsilon > 0$ such that, if S is the number of runs in a perfect distribution requiring n merging phases, and if ρS initial runs are processed during those phases, we have $n = a \ln S + b + O(S^{-\epsilon})$ and $\rho = c \ln S + d + O(S^{-\epsilon})$, where

$$a = (\ln \alpha)^{-1}, \qquad b = -a \ln \left(\frac{p(\alpha^{-1})}{-q'(\alpha^{-1})} \right) - 1, \qquad c = a \frac{\alpha}{-q'(\alpha^{-1})},$$

$$d = \frac{(b+1)\alpha - p'(\alpha^{-1})/p(\alpha^{-1}) + q''(\alpha^{-1})/q'(\alpha^{-1})}{-q'(\alpha^{-1})}.$$

7. [*HM22*] Let α_p be the dominant root of the polynomial $f_p(z)$ in exercise 5. What is the asymptotic behavior of α_p as $p \to \infty$?

8. [*M20*] (E. Netto, 1901.) Let $N_m^{(p)}$ be the number of ways to express m as an ordered sum of the integers $\{1, 2, \ldots, p\}$. For example, when $p = 3$ and $m = 5$, there are 13 ways, namely $1+1+1+1+1 = 1+1+1+2 = 1+1+2+1 = 1+1+3 = 1+2+1+1 = 1+2+2 = 1+3+1 = 2+1+1+1 = 2+1+2 = 2+2+1 = 2+3 = 3+1+1 = 3+2$. Show that $N_m^{(p)}$ is a generalized Fibonacci number.

9. [*M20*] Let $K_m^{(p)}$ be the number of sequences of m 0s and 1s such that there are no p consecutive 1s. For example, when $p = 3$ and $m = 5$ there are 24 such sequences: 00000, 00001, 00010, 00011, 00100, 00101, 00110, 01000, 01001, ..., 11011. Show that $K_m^{(p)}$ is a generalized Fibonacci number.

10. [*M27*] (*Generalized Fibonacci number system.*) Prove that every nonnegative integer n has a unique representation as a sum of distinct pth order Fibonacci numbers $F_j^{(p)}$, for $j \geq p$, subject to the condition that no p consecutive Fibonacci numbers are used.

11. [*M24*] Prove that the nth element of the string Q_∞ in (12) is equal to the number of distinct Fibonacci numbers in the fifth-order Fibonacci representation of $n - 1$. [See exercise 10.]

▶ **12.** [*M18*] Find a connection between powers of the matrix $\begin{pmatrix} 0 & 1 & 0 & 0 & 0 \\ 0 & 0 & 1 & 0 & 0 \\ 0 & 0 & 0 & 1 & 0 \\ 0 & 0 & 0 & 0 & 1 \\ 1 & 1 & 1 & 1 & 1 \end{pmatrix}$ and the perfect Fibonacci distributions in (1).

▶ **13.** [*22*] Prove the following rather odd property of perfect Fibonacci distributions: When the final output will be on tape number T, the number of runs on each other tape is *odd*; when the final output will be on some tape other than T, the number of runs will be *odd* on that tape, and it will be *even* on the others. [See (1).]

14. [*M35*] Let $T_n(x) = \sum_{k \geq 0} T_{nk} x^k$, where $T_n(x)$ is the polynomial defined in (16).
  a) Show that for each k there is a number $n(k)$ such that $T_{1k} \leq T_{2k} \leq \cdots \leq T_{n(k)k} > T_{(n(k)+1),k} \geq \cdots$.
  b) Given that $T_{n'k'} < T_{nk'}$ and $n' < n$, prove that $T_{n'k} \leq T_{nk}$ for all $k \geq k'$.
  c) Prove that there is a nondecreasing sequence $\langle M_n \rangle$ such that $\Sigma_n(S) = \min_{j \geq 1} \Sigma_j(S)$ when $M_n \leq S < M_{n+1}$, but $\Sigma_n(S) > \min_{j \geq 1} \Sigma_j(S)$ when $S \geq M_{n+1}$. [See (19).]

15. [*M43*] Prove or disprove: $\Sigma_{n-1}(m) < \Sigma_n(m)$ implies that $\Sigma_n(m) \leq \Sigma_{n+1}(m) \leq \Sigma_{n+2}(m) \leq \cdots$. [Such a result would greatly simplify the calculation of Table 2.]

16. [*HM43*] Determine the asymptotic behavior of the polyphase merge with optimum distribution of dummy runs.

17. [*32*] Prove or disprove: There is a way to disperse runs for an optimum polyphase distribution in such a way that the distribution for $S + 1$ initial runs is formed by adding one run (on an appropriate tape) to the distribution for S initial runs.

18. [*30*] Does the optimum polyphase distribution produce the best possible merging pattern, in the sense that the total number of initial runs processed is minimized, if we insist that the initial runs be placed on at most $T-1$ of the tapes? (Ignore rewind time.)

19. [*21*] Make a table analogous to (1), for Caron's polyphase sort on six tapes.

20. [*M24*] What generating functions for Caron's polyphase sort on six tapes correspond to (7) and to (16)? What relations, analogous to (9) and (27), define the strings of merge numbers?

21. [*11*] What should appear on level 7 in (26)?

22. [*M21*] Each term of the sequence (24) is approximately equal to the sum of the previous two. Does this phenomenon hold for the remaining numbers of the sequence? Formulate and prove a theorem about $t_n - t_{n-1} - t_{n-2}$.

▶ **23.** [*29*] What changes would be made to (25), (27), and (28), if (23) were changed to $v_{n+1} = u_{n-1} + v_{n-1} + u_{n-2}$, $u_n = v_{n-2} + u_{n-3} + v_{n-3} + u_{n-4} + v_{n-4}$?

24. [*HM41*] Compute the asymptotic behavior of the tape-splitting polyphase procedure, when v_{n+1} is defined to be the sum of the first q terms of $u_{n-1} + v_{n-1} + \cdots + u_{n-P} + v_{n-P}$, for various $P = T - 2$ and for $0 \le q \le 2P$. (The text treats only the case $q = 2\lfloor P/2 \rfloor$; see exercise 23.)

25. [*19*] Show how the tape-splitting polyphase merge on four tapes, mentioned at the end of this section, would sort 32 initial runs. (Give a phase-by-phase analysis like the 82-run six-tape example in the text.)

26. [*M21*] Analyze the behavior of the tape-splitting polyphase merge on four tapes, when $S = 2^n$ and when $S = 2^n + 2^{n-1}$. (See exercise 25.)

27. [*23*] Once the initial runs have been distributed to tapes in a perfect distribution, the polyphase strategy is simply to "merge until empty": We merge runs from all nonempty input tapes until one of them has been entirely read; then we use that tape as the next output tape, and let the previous output tape serve as an input.

Does this merge-until-empty strategy always sort, no matter how the initial runs are distributed, as long as we distribute them onto at least two tapes? (One tape will, of course, be left empty so that it can be the first output tape.)

28. [*M26*] The previous exercise defines a rather large family of merging patterns. Show that polyphase is the *best* of them, in the following sense: If there are six tapes, and if we consider the class of all initial distributions (a, b, c, d, e) such that the merge-until-empty strategy requires at most n phases to sort, then $a + b + c + d + e \le t_n$, where t_n is the corresponding value for polyphase sorting (1).

29. [*M47*] Exercise 28 shows that the polyphase distribution is optimal among all merge-until-empty patterns in the minimum-phase sense. But is it optimal also in the minimum-pass sense?

Let a be relatively prime to b, and assume that $a + b$ is the Fibonacci number F_n. Prove or disprove the following conjecture due to R. M. Karp: The number of initial runs processed during the merge-until-empty pattern starting with distribution (a, b) is greater than or equal to $((n - 5)F_{n+1} + (2n + 2)F_n)/5$. (The latter figure is achieved when $a = F_{n-1}$, $b = F_{n-2}$.)

30. [*42*] Prepare a table analogous to Table 2, for the tape-splitting polyphase merge.

31. [*M22*] (R. Kemp.) Let $K_d(n)$ be the number of n-node ordered trees in which every leaf is at distance d from the root. For example, $K_3(8) = 7$ because of the trees

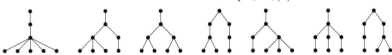

Show that $K_d(n)$ is a generalized Fibonacci number, and find a one-to-one correspondence between such trees and the ordered partitions considered in exercise 8.

*5.4.3. The Cascade Merge

Another basic pattern, called the "cascade merge," was actually discovered before polyphase [B. K. Betz and W. C. Carter, *ACM National Conf.* **14** (1959), Paper 14]. This approach is illustrated for six tapes and 190 initial runs in the following table, using the notation developed in Section 5.4.2:

	T1	T2	T3	T4	T5	T6	Initial runs processed
Pass 1	1^{55}	1^{50}	1^{41}	1^{29}	1^{15}	—	190
Pass 2	—	$*1^{5}$	2^{9}	3^{12}	4^{14}	5^{15}	190
Pass 3	15^{5}	14^{4}	12^{3}	9^{2}	$*5^{1}$	—	190
Pass 4	—	$*15^{1}$	29^{1}	41^{1}	50^{1}	55^{1}	190
Pass 5	190^{1}	—	—	—	—	—	190

A cascade merge, like polyphase, starts out with a "perfect distribution" of runs on tapes, although the rule for perfect distributions is somewhat different from those in Section 5.4.2. Each line in the table represents a complete pass over *all* the data. Pass 2, for example, is obtained by doing a five-way merge from $\{T1, T2, T3, T4, T5\}$ to T6, until T5 is empty (this puts 15 runs of relative length 5 on T6), then a four-way merge from $\{T1, T2, T3, T4\}$ to T5, then a three-way merge to T4, a two-way merge to T3, and finally a one-way merge (a copying operation) from T1 to T2. Pass 3 is obtained in the same way, first doing a five-way merge until one tape becomes empty, then a four-way merge, and so on. (Perhaps the present section of this book should be numbered 5.4.3.2.1 instead of 5.4.3!)

It is clear that the copying operations are unnecessary, and they could be omitted. Actually, however, in the six-tape case this copying takes only a small percentage of the total time. The items marked with an asterisk in the table above are those that were simply copied; only 25 of the 950 runs processed are of this type. Most of the time is devoted to five-way and four-way merging.

Table 1
APPROXIMATE BEHAVIOR OF CASCADE MERGE SORTING

Tapes	Passes (with copying)	Passes (without copying)	Growth ratio
3	$2.078 \ln S + 0.672$	$1.504 \ln S + 0.992$	1.6180340
4	$1.235 \ln S + 0.754$	$1.102 \ln S + 0.820$	2.2469796
5	$0.946 \ln S + 0.796$	$0.897 \ln S + 0.800$	2.8793852
6	$0.796 \ln S + 0.821$	$0.773 \ln S + 0.808$	3.5133371
7	$0.703 \ln S + 0.839$	$0.691 \ln S + 0.822$	4.1481149
8	$0.639 \ln S + 0.852$	$0.632 \ln S + 0.834$	4.7833861
9	$0.592 \ln S + 0.861$	$0.587 \ln S + 0.845$	5.4189757
10	$0.555 \ln S + 0.869$	$0.552 \ln S + 0.854$	6.0547828
20	$0.397 \ln S + 0.905$	$0.397 \ln S + 0.901$	12.4174426

At first it may seem that the cascade pattern is a rather poor choice, by comparison with polyphase, since standard polyphase uses $(T - 1)$-way merging throughout while the cascade uses $(T-1)$-way, $(T-2)$-way, $(T-3)$-way, etc. But in fact it is asymptotically *better* than polyphase, on six or more tapes! As we have observed in Section 5.4.2, a high order of merge is not a guarantee of efficiency. Table 1 shows the performance characteristics of cascade merge, by analogy with the similar tables in Section 5.4.2.

The "perfect distributions" for a cascade merge are easily derived by working backwards from the final state $(1, 0, \ldots, 0)$. With six tapes, they are

Level	T1	T2	T3	T4	T5
0	1	0	0	0	0
1	1	1	1	1	1
2	5	4	3	2	1
3	15	14	12	9	5
4	55	50	41	29	15
5	190	175	146	105	55
$\cdots$	$\cdots$	$\cdots$	$\cdots$	$\cdots$	$\cdots$
n	a_n	b_n	c_n	d_n	e_n
$n+1$	$a_n+b_n+c_n+d_n+e_n$	$a_n+b_n+c_n+d_n$	$a_n+b_n+c_n$	a_n+b_n	a_n

$$(1)$$

It is interesting to note that the relative magnitudes of these numbers appear also in the diagonals of a regular $(2T-1)$-sided polygon. For example, the five diagonals in the hendecagon of Fig. 73 have relative lengths very nearly equal to 190, 175, 146, 105, and 55! We shall prove this remarkable fact later in this section, and we shall also see that the relative amount of time spent in $(T-1)$-way merging, $(T-2)$-way merging, $\ldots$, 1-way merging is approximately proportional to the *squares* of the lengths of these diagonals.

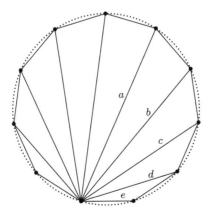

Fig. 73. Geometrical interpretation of cascade numbers.

Initial distribution of runs. When the actual number of initial runs isn't perfect, we can insert dummy runs as usual. A superficial analysis of this situation would indicate that the method of dummy run assignment is immaterial,

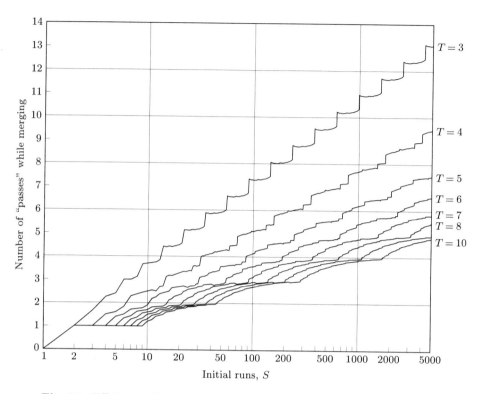

Fig. 74. Efficiency of cascade merge with the distribution of Algorithm D.

since cascade merging operates by complete passes; if we have 190 initial runs, each record is processed five times as in the example above, but if there are 191 we must apparently go up a level so that every record is processed six times. Fortunately this abrupt change is not actually necessary; David E. Ferguson has found a way to distribute initial runs so that many of the operations during the first merge pass reduce to copying the contents of a tape. When such copying relations are bypassed (by simply changing "logical" tape unit numbers relative to the "physical" numbers as in Algorithm 5.4.2D), we obtain a relatively smooth transition from level to level, as shown in Fig. 74.

Suppose that (a, b, c, d, e) is a perfect distribution, where $a \geq b \geq c \geq d \geq e$. By redefining the correspondence between logical and physical tape units, we can imagine that the distribution is actually (e, d, c, b, a), with a runs on T5, b on T4, etc. The next perfect distribution is $(a+b+c+d+e, a+b+c+d, a+b+c, a+b, a)$; and if the input is exhausted before we reach this next level, let us assume that the tapes contain, respectively, $(D_1, D_2, D_3, D_4, D_5)$ dummy runs, where

$$D_1 \leq a+b+c+d, \quad D_2 \leq a+b+c, \quad D_3 \leq a+b, \quad D_4 \leq a, \quad D_5 = 0;$$
$$D_1 \geq D_2 \geq D_3 \geq D_4 \geq D_5. \tag{2}$$

We are free to imagine that the dummy runs appear in any convenient place on the tapes. The first merge pass is supposed to produce a runs by five-way merging, then b by four-way merging, etc., and our goal is to arrange the dummies so as to replace merging by copying. It is convenient to do the first merge pass as follows:

1. If $D_4 = a$, subtract a from each of D_1, D_2, D_3, D_4 and pretend that T5 is the result of the merge. If $D_4 < a$, merge a runs from tapes T1 through T5, using the minimum possible number of dummies on tapes T1 through T5 so that the new values of D_1, D_2, D_3, D_4 will satisfy

$$D_1 \le b + c + d, \quad D_2 \le b + c, \quad D_3 \le b, \quad D_4 = 0;$$
$$D_1 \ge D_2 \ge D_3 \ge D_4. \tag{3}$$

Thus, if D_2 was originally $\le b + c$, we use no dummies from it at this step, while if $b + c < D_2 \le a + b + c$ we use exactly $D_2 - b - c$ of them.

2. (This step is similar to step 1, but "shifted.") If $D_3 = b$, subtract b from each of D_1, D_2, D_3 and pretend that T4 is the result of the merge. If $D_3 < b$, merge b runs from tapes T1 through T4, reducing the number of dummies if necessary in order to make

$$D_1 \le b + c, \quad D_2 \le b, \quad D_3 = 0; \quad D_1 \ge D_2 \ge D_3.$$

3. And so on.

Table 2
EXAMPLE OF CASCADE DISTRIBUTION STEPS

	Add to T1	Add to T2	Add to T3	Add to T4	Add to T5	"Amount saved"
Step (1,1)	9	0	0	0	0	15+14+12+5
Step (2,2)	3	12	0	0	0	15+14+9+5
Step (2,1)	9	0	0	0	0	15+14+5
Step (3,3)	2	2	14	0	0	15+12+5
Step (3,2)	3	12	0	0	0	15+9+5
Step (3,1)	9	0	0	0	0	15+5
Step (4,4)	1	1	1	15	0	14+5
Step (4,3)	2	2	14	0	0	12+5
Step (4,2)	3	12	0	0	0	9+5
Step (4,1)	9	0	0	0	0	5

Ferguson's method of distributing runs to tapes can be illustrated by considering the process of going from level 3 to level 4 in (1). Assume that "logical" tapes (T1, ..., T5) contain respectively $(5, 9, 12, 14, 15)$ runs and that we want eventually to bring this up to $(55, 50, 41, 29, 15)$. The procedure can be summarized as shown in Table 2. We first put nine runs on T1, then $(3, 12)$ on T1 and T2, etc. If the input becomes exhausted during, say, Step (3,2), then the "amount saved" is $15 + 9 + 5$, meaning that the five-way merge of 15 runs, the two-way merge of 9 runs, and the one-way merge of 5 runs are avoided by the dummy run assignment. In other words, $15 + 9 + 5$ of the runs present at level 3 are not processed during the first merge phase.

The following algorithm defines the process in detail.

Algorithm C (*Cascade merge sorting with special distribution*). This algorithm takes initial runs and disperses them to tapes, one run at a time, until the supply of initial runs is exhausted. Then it specifies how the tapes are to be merged, assuming that there are $T \geq 3$ available tape units, using at most $(T-1)$-way merging and avoiding unnecessary one-way merging. Tape T may be used to hold the input, since it does not receive any initial runs. The following tables are maintained:

A[j], $1 \leq j \leq T$: The perfect cascade distribution we have most recently reached.

AA[j], $1 \leq j \leq T$: The perfect cascade distribution we are striving for.

D[j], $1 \leq j \leq T$: Number of dummy runs assumed to be present on logical tape unit number j.

M[j], $1 \leq j < T$: Maximum number of dummy runs desired on logical tape unit number j.

TAPE[j], $1 \leq j \leq T$: Number of the physical tape unit corresponding to logical tape unit number j.

C1. [Initialize.] Set A[k] $\leftarrow$ AA[k] $\leftarrow$ D[k] $\leftarrow$ 0 for $2 \leq k \leq T$; and set A[1] $\leftarrow$ 0, AA[1] $\leftarrow$ 1, D[1] $\leftarrow$ 1. Set TAPE[k] $\leftarrow$ k for $1 \leq k \leq T$. Finally set $i \leftarrow T - 2$, $j \leftarrow 1$, $k \leftarrow 1$, $l \leftarrow 0$, $m \leftarrow 1$, and go to step C5. (This maneuvering is one way to get everything started, by jumping right into the inner loop with appropriate settings of the control variables.)

C2. [Begin new level.] (We have just reached a perfect distribution, and since there is more input we must get ready for the next level.) Increase l by 1. Set A[k] $\leftarrow$ AA[k], for $1 \leq k \leq T$; then set AA[$T - k$] $\leftarrow$ AA[$T - k + 1$]+A[k], for $k = 1, 2, \ldots, T-1$ in this order. Set (TAPE[1],..., TAPE[$T-1$]) $\leftarrow$ (TAPE[$T-1$],..., TAPE[1]), and set D[k] $\leftarrow$ AA[$k + 1$] for $1 \leq k < T$. Finally set $i \leftarrow 1$.

C3. [Begin ith sublevel.] Set $j \leftarrow i$. (The variables i and j represent "Step (i, j)" in the example shown in Table 2.)

C4. [Begin Step (i, j).] Set $k \leftarrow j$ and $m \leftarrow$ A[$T - j - 1$]. If $m = 0$ and $i = j$, set $i \leftarrow T - 2$ and return to C3; if $m = 0$ and $i \neq j$, return to C2. (Variable m represents the number of runs to be written onto TAPE[k]; $m = 0$ occurs only when $l = 1$.)

C5. [Input to TAPE[k].] Write one run on tape number TAPE[k], and decrease D[k] by 1. Then if the input is exhausted, rewind all the tapes and go to step C7.

C6. [Advance.] Decrease m by 1. If $m > 0$, return to C5. Otherwise decrease k by 1; if $k > 0$, set $m \leftarrow$ A[$T - j - 1$] $-$ A[$T - j$] and return to C5 if $m > 0$. Otherwise decrease j by 1; if $j > 0$, go to C4. Otherwise increase i by 1; if $i < T - 1$, return to C3. Otherwise go to C2.

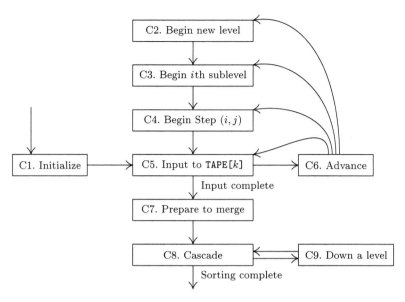

Fig. 75. The cascade merge, with special distribution.

C7. [Prepare to merge.] (At this point the initial distribution is complete, and the AA, D, and TAPE tables describe the present states of the tapes.) Set $M[k] \leftarrow AA[k+1]$ for $1 \leq k < T$, and set FIRST $\leftarrow 1$. (Variable FIRST is nonzero only during the first merge pass.)

C8. [Cascade.] If $l = 0$, stop; sorting is complete and the output is on TAPE[1]. Otherwise, for $p = T - 1, T - 2, \ldots, 1$, in this order, do a p-way merge from TAPE[1], ..., TAPE[p] to TAPE[$p + 1$] as follows:

If $p = 1$, simulate the one-way merge by simply rewinding TAPE[2], then interchanging TAPE[1] $\leftrightarrow$ TAPE[2].

Otherwise if FIRST $= 1$ and $D[p-1] = M[p-1]$, simulate the p-way merge by simply interchanging TAPE[p] $\leftrightarrow$ TAPE[$p+1$], rewinding TAPE[p], and subtracting $M[p-1]$ from each of $D[1],\ldots,D[p-1],M[1],\ldots,M[p-1]$.

Otherwise, subtract $M[p-1]$ from each of $M[1],\ldots,M[p-1]$. Then merge one run from each TAPE[j] such that $1 \leq j \leq p$ and $D[j] \leq M[j]$; subtract one from each $D[j]$ such that $1 \leq j \leq p$ and $D[j] > M[j]$; and put the output run on TAPE[$p+1$]. Continue doing this until TAPE[p] is empty. Then rewind TAPE[p] and TAPE[$p+1$].

C9. [Down a level.] Decrease l by 1, set FIRST $\leftarrow 0$, and set (TAPE[1],..., TAPE[T]) $\leftarrow$ (TAPE[T],...,TAPE[1]). (At this point all D's and M's are zero and will remain so.) Return to C8. ▌

Steps C1–C6 of this algorithm do the distribution, and steps C7–C9 do the merging; the two parts are fairly independent of each other, and it would be possible to store $M[k]$ and $AA[k+1]$ in the same memory locations.

Analysis of cascade merging. The cascade merge is somewhat harder to analyze than polyphase, but the analysis is especially interesting because so many remarkable formulas are present. Readers who enjoy discrete mathematics are urged to study the cascade distribution for themselves, *before reading further*, since the numbers have extraordinary properties that are a pleasure to discover. We shall discuss here one of the many ways to approach the analysis, emphasizing the way in which the results might be discovered.

For convenience, let us consider the six-tape case, looking for formulas that generalize to all T. Relations (1) lead to the first basic pattern:

$$
\begin{aligned}
a_n &= a_n && = \binom{0}{0}a_n, \\
b_n &= a_n - e_{n-1} \\
    &= a_n - a_{n-2} && = \binom{1}{0}a_n - \binom{2}{2}a_{n-2}, \\
c_n &= b_n - d_{n-1} \\
    &= b_n - a_{n-2} - b_{n-2} && = \binom{2}{0}a_n - \binom{3}{2}a_{n-2} + \binom{4}{4}a_{n-4}, &&(4)\\
d_n &= c_n - e_{n-1} \\
    &= c_n - a_{n-2} - b_{n-2} - c_{n-2} && = \binom{3}{0}a_n - \binom{4}{2}a_{n-2} + \binom{5}{4}a_{n-4} - \binom{6}{6}a_{n-6}, \\
e_n &= d_n - b_{n-1} \\
    &= d_n - a_{n-2} - b_{n-2} - c_{n-2} - d_{n-2} &&= \binom{4}{0}a_n - \binom{5}{2}a_{n-2} + \binom{6}{4}a_{n-4} - \binom{7}{6}a_{n-6} + \binom{8}{8}a_{n-8}.
\end{aligned}
$$

Let $A(z) = \sum_{n\geq 0} a_n z^n, \ldots, E(z) = \sum_{n\geq 0} e_n z^n$, and define the polynomials

$$
q_m(z) = \binom{m}{0} - \binom{m+1}{2}z^2 + \binom{m+2}{4}z^4 - \cdots
$$

$$
= \sum_k \binom{m+k}{2k}(-1)^k z^{2k} = \sum_{k=0}^{m} \binom{2m-k}{k}(-1)^{m-k}z^{2m-2k}. \qquad (5)
$$

The result of (4) can be summarized by saying that the generating functions $B(z) - q_1(z)A(z)$, $C(z) - q_2(z)A(z)$, $D(z) - q_3(z)A(z)$, and $E(z) - q_4(z)A(z)$ reduce to finite sums, corresponding to the values of $a_{-1}, a_{-2}, a_{-3}, \ldots$ that appear in (4) for small n but do not appear in $A(z)$. In order to supply appropriate boundary conditions, let us run the recurrence backwards to negative levels, through level -8:

n	a_n	b_n	c_n	d_n	e_n
0	1	0	0	0	0
-1	0	0	0	0	1
-2	1	-1	0	0	0
-3	0	0	0	-1	2
-4	2	-3	1	0	0
-5	0	0	1	-4	5
-6	5	-9	5	-1	0
-7	0	-1	6	-14	14
-8	14	-28	20	-7	1

(On seven tapes the table would be similar, with entries for odd n shifted right one column.) The sequence $a_0, a_{-2}, a_{-4}, \ldots = 1, 1, 2, 5, 14, \ldots$ is a dead giveaway for computer scientists, since it occurs in connection with so many recursive algorithms (see, for example, exercise 2.2.1–4 and Eq. 2.3.4.4–(14)); therefore we conjecture that in the T-tape case

$$a_{-2n} = \binom{2n}{n} \frac{1}{n+1}, \qquad \text{for } 0 \le n \le T - 2;$$

$$a_{-2n-1} = 0, \qquad \text{for } 0 \le n \le T - 3.$$
(6)

To verify that this choice is correct, it suffices to show that (6) and (4) yield the correct results for levels 0 and 1. On level 1 this is obvious, and on level 0 we have to verify that

$$\binom{m}{0} a_0 - \binom{m+1}{2} a_{-2} + \binom{m+2}{4} a_{-4} - \binom{m+3}{6} a_{-6} + \cdots$$

$$= \sum_{k \ge 0} \binom{m+k}{2k} \binom{2k}{k} \frac{(-1)^k}{k+1} = \delta_{m0} \quad (7)$$

for $0 \le m \le T - 2$. Fortunately this sum can be evaluated by standard techniques; it is, in fact, Example 2 in Section 1.2.6.

Now we can compute the coefficients of $B(z) - q_1(z)A(z)$, etc. For example, consider the coefficient of z^{2m} in $D(z) - q_3(z)A(z)$: It is

$$\sum_{k \ge 0} \binom{3+m+k}{2m+2k} (-1)^{m+k} a_{-2k} = \sum_{k \ge 0} \binom{3+m+k}{2m+2k} \binom{2k}{k} \frac{(-1)^{m+k}}{k+1}$$

$$= (-1)^m \left(\binom{2+m}{2m-1} - \binom{3+m}{2m} \right)$$

$$= (-1)^{m+1} \binom{2+m}{2m},$$

by the result of Example 3 in Section 1.2.6. Therefore we have deduced that

$$A(z) = q_0(z)A(z),$$
$$B(z) = q_1(z)A(z) - q_0(z), \qquad C(z) = q_2(z)A(z) - q_1(z),$$
$$D(z) = q_3(z)A(z) - q_2(z), \qquad E(z) = q_4(z)A(z) - q_3(z).$$
(8)

Furthermore we have $e_{n+1} = a_n$; hence $zA(z) = E(z)$, and

$$A(z) = q_3(z)/\big(q_4(z) - z\big).$$
(9)

The generating functions have now been derived in terms of the q polynomials, and so we want to understand the q's better. Exercise 1.2.9–15 is useful in this regard, since it gives us a closed form that may be written

$$q_m(z) = \frac{\big((\sqrt{4 - z^2} + iz)/2\big)^{2m+1} + \big((\sqrt{4 - z^2} - iz)/2\big)^{2m+1}}{\sqrt{4 - z^2}}.$$
(10)

Everything simplifies if we now set $z = 2 \sin \theta$:

$$q_m(2 \sin \theta) = \frac{(\cos \theta + i \sin \theta)^{2m+1} + (\cos \theta - i \sin \theta)^{2m+1}}{2 \cos \theta} = \frac{\cos(2m+1)\theta}{\cos \theta}. \quad (11)$$

(This coincidence leads us to suspect that the polynomial $q_m(z)$ is well known in mathematics; and indeed, a glance at appropriate tables will show that $q_m(z)$ is essentially a Chebyshev polynomial of the second kind, namely $(-1)^m U_{2m}(z/2)$ in conventional notation.)

We can now determine the roots of the denominator in (9): The equation $q_4(2 \sin \theta) = 2 \sin \theta$ reduces to

$$\cos 9\theta = 2 \sin \theta \cos \theta = \sin 2\theta.$$

We can obtain solutions to this relation whenever $\pm 9\theta = 2\theta + (2n - \frac{1}{2})\pi$; and all such θ yield roots of the denominator in (9) provided that $\cos \theta \neq 0$. (When $\cos \theta = 0$, $q_m(\pm 2) = (2m+1)$ is never equal to ± 2.) The following eight distinct roots for $q_4(z) - z = 0$ are therefore obtained:

$$2 \sin \tfrac{-5}{14}\pi, \; 2 \sin \tfrac{-1}{14}\pi, \; 2 \sin \tfrac{3}{14}\pi; \; 2 \sin \tfrac{-7}{22}\pi, \; 2 \sin \tfrac{-3}{22}\pi, \; 2 \sin \tfrac{1}{22}\pi, \; 2 \sin \tfrac{5}{22}\pi, \; 2 \sin \tfrac{9}{22}\pi.$$

Since $q_4(z)$ is a polynomial of degree 8, this accounts for all the roots. The first three of these values make $q_3(z) = 0$, so $q_3(z)$ and $q_4(z) - z$ have a polynomial of degree three as a common factor. The other five roots govern the asymptotic behavior of the coefficients of $A(z)$, if we expand (9) in partial fractions.

Considering the general T-tape case, let $\theta_k = (4k+1)\pi/(4T-2)$. The generating function $A(z)$ for the T-tape cascade distribution numbers takes the form

$$\frac{4}{2T-1} \sum_{-T/2 < k < \lfloor T/2 \rfloor} \frac{\cos^2 \theta_k}{1 - z/(2 \sin \theta_k)} \quad (12)$$

(see exercise 8); hence

$$a_n = \frac{4}{2T-1} \sum_{-T/2 < k < \lfloor T/2 \rfloor} \cos^2 \theta_k \left(\frac{1}{2 \sin \theta_k}\right)^n. \quad (13)$$

Eqs. (8) now lead to the similar formulas

$$b_n = \frac{4}{2T-1} \sum_{-T/2 < k < \lfloor T/2 \rfloor} \cos \theta_k \cos 3\theta_k \left(\frac{1}{2 \sin \theta_k}\right)^n,$$

$$c_n = \frac{4}{2T-1} \sum_{-T/2 < k < \lfloor T/2 \rfloor} \cos \theta_k \cos 5\theta_k \left(\frac{1}{2 \sin \theta_k}\right)^n, \quad (14)$$

$$d_n = \frac{4}{2T-1} \sum_{-T/2 < k < \lfloor T/2 \rfloor} \cos \theta_k \cos 7\theta_k \left(\frac{1}{2 \sin \theta_k}\right)^n,$$

and so on. Exercise 9 shows that these equations hold for all $n \geq 0$, not only for large n. In each sum the term for $k = 0$ dominates all the others, especially when n is reasonably large; therefore the "growth ratio" is

$$\frac{1}{2\sin\theta_0} = \frac{2}{\pi}T - \frac{1}{\pi} + \frac{\pi}{48T} + O(T^{-2}). \tag{15}$$

Cascade sorting was first analyzed by W. C. Carter [*Proc. IFIP Congress* (1962), 62–66], who obtained numerical results for small T, and by David E. Ferguson [see *CACM* **7** (1964), 297], who discovered the first two terms in the asymptotic behavior (15) of the growth ratio. During the summer of 1964, R. W. Floyd discovered the explicit form $1/(2\sin\theta_0)$ of the growth ratio, so that exact formulas could be used for all T. An intensive analysis of the cascade numbers was independently carried out by G. N. Raney [*Canadian J. Math.* **18** (1966), 332–349], who came across them in quite another way having nothing to do with sorting. Raney observed the "ratio of diagonals" principle of Fig. 73, and derived many other interesting properties of the numbers. Floyd and Raney used matrix manipulations in their proofs (see exercise 6).

Modifications of cascade sorting. If one more tape is added, it is possible to overlap nearly all of the rewind time during a cascade sort. For example, we can merge T1–T5 to T7, then T1–T4 to T6, then T1–T3 to T5 (which by now is rewound), then T1–T2 to T4, and the next pass can begin when the comparatively short data on T4 has been rewound. The efficiency of this process can be predicted from the analysis of cascading. (See Section 5.4.6 for further information.)

A "compromise merge" scheme, which includes both polyphase and cascade as special cases, was suggested by D. E. Knuth in *CACM* **6** (1963), 585–587. Each phase consists of $(T-1)$-way, $(T-2)$-way, $\ldots$, P-way merges, where P is any fixed number between 1 and $T-1$. When $P = T-1$, this is polyphase, and when $P = 1$ it is pure cascade; when $P = 2$ it is cascade without copy phases. Analyses of this scheme have been made by C. E. Radke [*IBM Systems J.* **5** (1966), 226–247] and by W. H. Burge [*Proc. IFIP Congress* (1971), **1**, 454–459]. Burge found the generating function $\sum T_n(x)z^n$ for each (P, T) compromise merge, generalizing Eq. 5.4.2–(16); he showed that the best value of P, from the standpoint of fewest initial runs processed as a function of S as $S \to \infty$ (using a straightforward distribution scheme and ignoring rewind time), is respectively $(2, 3, 3, 4, 4, 4, 3, 3, 4)$ for $T = (3, 4, 5, 6, 7, 8, 9, 10, 11)$. These values of P lean more towards cascade than polyphase as T increases; and it turns out that the compromise merge is never substantially better than cascade itself. On the other hand, with an optimum choice of levels and optimum distribution of dummy runs, as described in Section 5.4.2, pure polyphase seems to be best of all the compromise merges; unfortunately the optimum distribution is comparatively difficult to implement.

Th. L. Johnsen [*BIT* **6** (1966), 129–143] has studied a combination of balanced and polyphase merging; a rewind-overlap variation of balanced merging has been proposed by M. A. Goetz [*Digital Computer User's Handbook*, edited by M. Klerer and G. A. Korn (New York: McGraw–Hill, 1967), 1.311–1.312]; and many other hybrid schemes can be imagined.

EXERCISES

1. [*10*] Using Table 1, compare cascade merging with the tape-splitting version of polyphase described in Section 5.4.2. Which is better? (Ignore rewind time.)

▸ **2.** [*22*] Compare cascade sorting on three tapes, using Algorithm C, to polyphase sorting on three tapes, using Algorithm 5.4.2D. What similarities and differences can you find?

3. [*23*] Prepare a table that shows what happens when 100 initial runs are sorted on six tapes using Algorithm C.

4. [*M20*] (G. N. Raney.) An "nth level cascade distribution" is a multiset defined as follows (in the case of six tapes): $\{1, 0, 0, 0, 0\}$ is a 0th level cascade distribution; and if $\{a, b, c, d, e\}$ is an nth level cascade distribution, $\{a+b+c+d+e, a+b+c+d, a+b+c, a+b, a\}$ is an $(n + 1)$st level cascade distribution. (A multiset is unordered, hence up to 5! different $(n + 1)$st level distributions can be formed from a single nth level distribution.)

   a) Prove that *any* multiset $\{a, b, c, d, e\}$ of relatively prime integers is an nth level cascade distribution, for some n.

   b) Prove that the distribution defined for cascade sorting is *optimum*, in the sense that, if $\{a, b, c, d, e\}$ is any nth level distribution with $a \geq b \geq c \geq d \geq e$, we have $a \leq a_n$, $b \leq b_n$, $c \leq c_n$, $d \leq d_n$, $e \leq e_n$, where $(a_n, b_n, c_n, d_n, e_n)$ is the distribution defined in (1).

▸ **5.** [*20*] Prove that the cascade numbers defined in (1) satisfy the law

$$a_k a_{n-k} + b_k b_{n-k} + c_k c_{n-k} + d_k d_{n-k} + e_k e_{n-k} = a_n, \qquad \text{for } 0 \leq k \leq n.$$

[*Hint:* Interpret this relation by considering how many runs of various lengths are output during the kth pass of a complete cascade sort.]

6. [*M20*] Find a 5×5 matrix Q such that the first row of Q^n contains the six-tape cascade numbers $a_n\, b_n\, c_n\, d_n\, e_n$ for all $n \geq 0$.

7. [*M20*] Given that cascade merge is being applied to a perfect distribution of a_n initial runs, find a formula for the amount of processing saved when one-way merging is suppressed.

8. [*HM23*] Derive (12).

9. [*HM26*] Derive (14).

▸ **10.** [*M28*] Instead of using the pattern (4) to begin the study of the cascade numbers, start with the identities

$$e_n = a_{n-1} \qquad\qquad\qquad = \binom{1}{1} a_{n-1},$$
$$d_n = 2a_{n-1} - e_{n-2} \qquad\quad = \binom{2}{1} a_{n-1} - \binom{3}{3} a_{n-3},$$
$$c_n = 3a_{n-1} - d_{n-2} - 2e_{n-2} = \binom{3}{1} a_{n-1} - \binom{4}{3} a_{n-3} - \binom{5}{5} a_{n-5},$$

etc. Letting

$$r_m(z) = \binom{m}{1} z - \binom{m+1}{3} z^3 + \binom{m+2}{5} z^5 - \cdots,$$

express $A(z)$, $B(z)$, etc. in terms of these r polynomials.

11. [*M38*] Let

$$f_m(z) = \sum_{k=0}^{m} \binom{\lfloor (m+k)/2 \rfloor}{k} (-1)^{\lceil k/2 \rceil} z^k.$$

Prove that the generating function $A(z)$ for the T-tape cascade numbers is equal to $f_{T-3}(z)/f_{T-1}(z)$, where the numerator and denominator in this expression have no common factor.

12. [*M40*] Prove that Ferguson's distribution scheme is optimum, in the sense that no method of placing the dummy runs, satisfying (2), will cause fewer initial runs to be processed during the first pass, *provided* that the strategy of steps C7–C9 is used during this pass.

13. [*40*] The text suggests overlapping most of the rewind time, by adding an extra tape. Explore this idea. (For example, the text's scheme involves waiting for T4 to rewind; would it be better to omit T4 from the first merge phase of the next pass?)

*5.4.4. Reading Tape Backwards

Many magnetic tape units have the ability to read tape in the opposite direction from which it was written. The merging patterns we have encountered so far always write information onto tape in the "forward" direction, then rewind the tape, read it forwards, and rewind again. The tape files therefore behave as queues, operating in a first-in-first-out manner. Backwards reading allows us to eliminate both of these rewind operations: We write the tape forwards and read it backwards. In this case the files behave as stacks, since they are used in a last-in-first-out manner.

The balanced, polyphase, and cascade merge patterns can all be adapted to backward reading. The main difference is that *merging reverses the order of the runs* when we read backwards and write forwards. If two runs are in ascending order on tape, we can merge them while reading backwards, but this produces descending order. The descending runs produced in this way will subsequently become ascending on the next pass; so the merging algorithms must be capable of dealing with runs in either order. Programmer who are confronted with read-backwards for the first time often feel like they are standing on their heads!

As an example of backwards reading, consider the process of merging 8 initial runs, using a *balanced* merge on four tapes. The operations can be summarized as follows:

	T1	T2	T3	T4	
Pass 1	$A_1A_1A_1A_1$	$A_1A_1A_1A_1$	—	—	Initial distribution
Pass 2	—	—	D_2D_2	D_2D_2	Merge to T3 and T4
Pass 3	A_4	A_4	—	—	Merge to T1 and T2
Pass 4	—	—	D_8	—	Final merge to T3

Here A_r stands for a run of relative length r that appears on tape in ascending order, if the tape is read forwards as in our previous examples; D_r is the corresponding notation for a descending run of length r. During Pass 2 the ascending runs become descending: They appear to be descending in the input, since we are reading T1 and T2 backwards. Then the runs switch orientation again on Pass 3.

Notice that the process above finishes with the result on tape T3, in *descending* order. If this is bad (depending on whether the output is to be read backwards, or to be dismounted and put away for future use), we could copy it to another tape, reversing the direction. A faster way would be to rewind T1 and T2 after Pass 3, producing A_8 during Pass 4. Still faster would be to start with eight *descending* runs during Pass 1, since this would interchange all the A's and D's. However, the balanced merge on 16 initial runs would require the initial runs to be ascending; and we usually don't know in advance how many initial runs will be formed, so it is necessary to choose one consistent direction. Therefore the idea of rewinding after Pass 3 is probably best.

The *cascade* merge carries over in the same way. For example, consider sorting 14 initial runs on four tapes:

	T1	T2	T3	T4
Pass 1	$A_1A_1A_1A_1A_1A_1$	$A_1A_1A_1A_1A_1$	$A_1A_1A_1$	—
Pass 2	—	D_1	D_2D_2	$D_3D_3D_3$
Pass 3	A_6	A_5	A_3	—
Pass 4	—	—	—	D_{14}

Again, we could produce A_{14} instead of D_{14}, if we rewound T1, T2, T3 just before the final pass. This tableau illustrates a "pure" cascade merge, in the sense that all of the one-way merges have been performed explicitly. If we had suppressed the copying operations, as in Algorithm 5.4.3C, we would have been confronted with the situation

$$A_1 \qquad\qquad — \qquad\qquad D_2D_2 \qquad\qquad D_3D_3D_3$$

after Pass 2, and it would have been impossible to continue with a three-way merge since we cannot merge runs that are in opposite directions! The operation of copying T1 to T2 could be avoided if we rewound T1 and proceeded to read it forward during the next merge phase (while reading T3 and T4 backwards). But it would then be necessary to rewind T1 again after merging, so this trick trades one copy for two rewinds.

Thus the distribution method of Algorithm 5.4.3C does not work as efficiently for read-backwards as for read-forwards; the amount of time required jumps rather sharply every time the number of initial runs passes a "perfect" cascade distribution number. Another dispersion technique can be used to give a smoother transition between perfect cascade distributions (see exercise 17).

Read-backward polyphase. At first glance (and even at second and third glance), the polyphase merge scheme seems to be totally unfit for reading backwards. For example, suppose that we have 13 initial runs and three tapes:

	T1	T2	T3
Phase 1	$A_1A_1A_1A_1A_1$	$A_1A_1A_1A_1A_1A_1A_1A_1$	—
Phase 2	—	$A_1A_1A_1$	$D_2D_2D_2D_2D_2$

Now we're stuck; we could rewind either T2 or T3 and then read it forwards, while reading the other tape backwards, but this would jumble things up and we would have gained comparatively little by reading backwards.

An ingenious idea that saves the situation is to *alternate the direction of runs on each tape*. Then the merging can proceed in perfect synchronization:

	T1	T2	T3
Phase 1	$A_1 D_1 A_1 D_1 A_1$	$D_1 A_1 D_1 A_1 D_1 A_1 D_1 A_1$	—
Phase 2	—	$D_1 A_1 D_1$	$D_2 A_2 D_2 A_2 D_2$
Phase 3	$A_3 D_3 A_3$	—	$D_2 A_2$
Phase 4	A_3	$D_5 A_5$	—
Phase 5	—	D_5	D_8
Phase 6	A_{13}	—	—

This principle was mentioned briefly by R. L. Gilstad in his original article on polyphase merging, and he described it more fully in *CACM* **6** (1963), 220–223.

The *ADA*... technique works properly for polyphase merging on *any* number of tapes; for we can show that the A's and D's will be properly synchronized at each phase, provided only that the initial distribution pass produces alternating A's and D's on each tape and that each tape ends with A (or each tape ends with D): Since the last run written on the output file during one phase is in the opposite direction from the last runs used from the input files, the next phase always finds its runs in the proper orientation. Furthermore we have seen in exercise 5.4.2–13 that most of the perfect Fibonacci distributions call for an *odd* number of runs on one tape (the eventual output tape), and an *even* number of runs on each other tape. If T1 is designated as the final output tape, we can therefore guarantee that all tapes end with an A run, if we start T1 with an A and let the remaining tapes start with a D. A distribution method analogous to Algorithm 5.4.2D can be used, modified so that the distributions on each level have T1 as the final output tape. (We skip levels 1, $T+1$, $2T+1$, ..., since they are the levels in which the initially empty tape is the final output tape.) For example, in the six-tape case, we can use the following distribution numbers in place of 5.4.2–(1):

Level	T1	T2	T3	T4	T5	Total	Final output will be on
0	1	0	0	0	0	1	T1
2	1	2	2	2	2	9	T1
3	3	4	4	4	2	17	T1
4	7	8	8	6	4	33	T1 (1)
5	15	16	14	12	8	65	T1
6	31	30	28	24	16	129	T1
8	61	120	116	108	92	497	T1

Thus, T1 always gets an odd number of runs, while T2 through T5 get the even numbers, in decreasing order for flexibility in dummy run assignment. Such a distribution has the advantage that the final output tape is known in advance, regardless of the number of initial runs that happen to be present. It turns out (see exercise 3) that the output will always appear in *ascending* order on T1 when this scheme is used.

Another way to handle the distribution for read-backward polyphase has been suggested by D. T. Goodwin and J. L. Venn [*CACM* **7** (1964), 315]. We can distribute runs almost as in Algorithm 5.4.2D, beginning with a D run on each tape. When the input is exhausted, a dummy A run is imagined to be at the beginning of the unique "odd" tape, unless a distribution with all odd numbers has been reached. Other dummies are imagined at the end of the tapes, or grouped into pairs in the middle. The question of optimum placement of dummy runs is analyzed in exercise 5 below.

Optimum merge patterns. So far we have been discussing various patterns for merging on tape, without asking for "best possible" methods. It appears to be quite difficult to determine the optimal patterns, especially in the read-forward case where the interaction of rewind time with merge time is hard to handle. On the other hand, when merging is done by reading backwards and writing forwards, all rewinding is essentially eliminated, and it is possible to get a fairly good characterization of optimal ways to merge. Richard M. Karp has introduced some very interesting approaches to this problem, and we shall conclude this section by discussing the theory he has developed.

In the first place we need a more satisfactory way to describe merging patterns, instead of the rather mysterious tape-content tableaux that have been used above. Karp has suggested two ways to do this, the *vector representation* and the *tree representation* of a merge pattern. Both forms of representation are useful in practice, so we shall describe them in turn.

The vector representation of a merge pattern consists of a sequence of "merge vectors" $y^{(m)} \ldots y^{(1)} y^{(0)}$, each of which has T components. The ith-last merge step is represented by $y^{(i)}$ in the following way:

$$y_j^{(i)} = \begin{cases} +1, & \text{if tape number } j \text{ is an input to the merge;} \\ 0, & \text{if tape number } j \text{ is not used in the merge;} \\ -1, & \text{if tape number } j \text{ gets the output of the merge.} \end{cases} \quad (2)$$

Thus, exactly one component of $y^{(i)}$ is -1, and the other components are 0s and 1s. The final vector $y^{(0)}$ is special; it is a unit vector, having 1 in position j if the final sorted output appears on unit j, and 0 elsewhere. These definitions imply that the vector sum

$$v^{(i)} = y^{(i)} + y^{(i-1)} + \cdots + y^{(0)} \quad (3)$$

represents the distribution of runs on tape just before the ith-last merge step, with $v_j^{(i)}$ runs on tape j. In particular, $v^{(m)}$ tells how many runs the initial distribution pass places on each tape.

It may seem awkward to number these vectors backwards, with $y^{(m)}$ coming first and $y^{(0)}$ last, but this peculiar viewpoint turns out to be advantageous for developing the theory. One good way to search for an optimal method is to start with the sorted output and to imagine "unmerging" it to various tapes, then unmerging these, etc., considering the successive distributions $v^{(0)}, v^{(1)}, v^{(2)}, \ldots$ in the reverse order from which they actually occur during the sorting process.

In fact that is essentially the approach we have taken already in our analysis of polyphase and cascade merging.

The three merge patterns described in tabular form earlier in this section have the following vector representations:

Balanced $(T = 4, S = 8)$	Cascade $(T = 4, S = 14)$	Polyphase $(T = 3, S = 13)$
$v^{(7)} = (\ 4,\ \ 4,\ \ 0,\ \ 0)$	$v^{(10)} = (\ 6,\ \ 5,\ \ 3,\ \ 0)$	$v^{(12)} = (\ 5,\ \ 8,\ \ 0)$
$y^{(7)} = (+1, +1, -1,\ \ 0)$	$y^{(10)} = (+1, +1, +1, -1)$	$y^{(12)} = (+1, +1, -1)$
$y^{(6)} = (+1, +1,\ \ 0, -1)$	$y^{(9)} = (+1, +1, +1, -1)$	$y^{(11)} = (+1, +1, -1)$
$y^{(5)} = (+1, +1, -1,\ \ 0)$	$y^{(8)} = (+1, +1, +1, -1)$	$y^{(10)} = (+1, +1, -1)$
$y^{(4)} = (+1, +1,\ \ 0, -1)$	$y^{(7)} = (+1, +1, -1,\ \ 0)$	$y^{(9)} = (+1, +1, -1)$
$y^{(3)} = (-1,\ \ 0, +1, +1)$	$y^{(6)} = (+1, +1, -1,\ \ 0)$	$y^{(8)} = (+1, +1, -1)$
$y^{(2)} = (\ \ 0, -1, +1, +1)$	$y^{(5)} = (+1, -1,\ \ 0,\ \ 0)$	$y^{(7)} = (-1, +1, +1)$
$y^{(1)} = (+1, +1, -1,\ \ 0)$	$y^{(4)} = (-1, +1, +1, +1)$	$y^{(6)} = (-1, +1, +1)$
$y^{(0)} = (\ \ 0,\ \ 0,\ \ 1,\ \ 0)$	$y^{(3)} = (\ \ 0, -1, +1, +1)$	$y^{(5)} = (-1, +1, +1)$
	$y^{(2)} = (\ \ 0,\ \ 0, -1, +1)$	$y^{(4)} = (+1, -1, +1)$
	$y^{(1)} = (+1, +1, +1, -1)$	$y^{(3)} = (+1, -1, +1)$
	$y^{(0)} = (\ \ 0,\ \ 0,\ \ 0,\ \ 1)$	$y^{(2)} = (+1, +1, -1)$
		$y^{(1)} = (-1, +1, +1)$
		$y^{(0)} = (\ \ 1,\ \ 0,\ \ 0)$

Every merge pattern obviously has a vector representation. Conversely, it is easy to see that the sequence of vectors $y^{(m)} \ldots y^{(1)} y^{(0)}$ corresponds to an actual merge pattern if and only if the following three conditions are satisfied:

i) $y^{(0)}$ is a unit vector.

ii) $y^{(i)}$ has exactly one component equal to -1, all other components equal to 0 or $+1$, for $m \geq i \geq 1$.

iii) All components of $y^{(i)} + \cdots + y^{(1)} + y^{(0)}$ are nonnegative, for $m \geq i \geq 1$.

The tree representation of a merge pattern gives another picture of the same information. We construct a tree with one external leaf node for each initial run, and one internal node for each run that is merged, in such a way that the descendants of each internal node are the runs from which it was fabricated. Each internal node is labeled with the step number on which the corresponding run was formed, numbering steps backwards as in the vector representation; furthermore, the line just above each node is labeled with the name of the tape on which that run appears. For example, the three merge patterns above have the tree representations depicted in Fig. 76, if we call the tapes A, B, C, D instead of T1, T2, T3, T4.

This representation displays many of the relevant properties of the merge pattern in convenient form; for example, if the run on level 0 of the tree (the root) is to be ascending, then the runs on level 1 must be descending, those on level 2 must be ascending, etc.; an initial run is ascending if and only if the corresponding external node is on an even-numbered level. Furthermore the total number of initial runs processed during the merging (not including the initial distribution) is exactly equal to the *external path length* of the tree, since each initial run on level k is processed exactly k times.

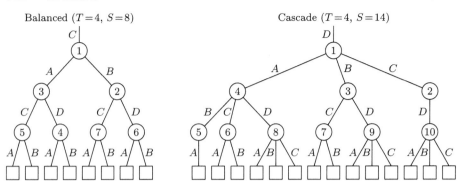

Balanced ($T=4$, $S=8$)   Cascade ($T=4$, $S=14$)

Polyphase ($T=3$, $S=13$)

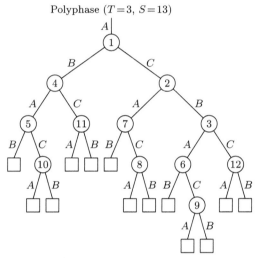

Fig. 76. Tree representations of three merge patterns.

Every merge pattern has a tree representation, but not every tree defines a merge pattern. A tree whose internal nodes have been labeled with the numbers 1 through m, and whose lines have been labeled with tape names, represents a valid read-backward merge pattern if and only if

a) no two lines adjacent to the same internal node have the same tape name;

b) if $i > j$, and if A is a tape name, the tree does not contain the configuration

c) if $i < j < k < l$, and if A is a tape name, the tree does not contain

both A and A or   both A and A .   (4)

Condition (a) is self-evident, since the input and output tapes in a merge must be distinct; similarly, (b) is obvious. The "no crossover" condition (c) mirrors the last-in-first-out restriction that characterizes read-backward operations on tape: The run formed at step k must be removed before any runs formed previously on that same tape; hence the configurations in (4) are impossible. It is not difficult to verify that any labeled tree satisfying conditions (a), (b), (c) does indeed correspond to a read-backward merge pattern.

If there are T tape units, condition (a) implies that the degree of each internal node is $T - 1$ or less. It is not always possible to attach suitable labels to all such trees; for example, when $T = 3$ there is no merge pattern whose tree has the shape

$$(5)$$

This shape would lead to an optimal merge pattern if we could attach step numbers and tape names in a suitable way, since it is the only way to achieve the minimum external path length in a tree having four external nodes. But there is essentially only one way to do the labeling according to conditions (a) and (b), because of the symmetries of the diagram, namely,

$$(6)$$

and this violates condition (c). A shape that *can* be labeled according to the conditions above, using at most T tape names, is called a *T-lifo* tree.

Another way to characterize all labeled trees that can arise from merge patterns is to consider how all such trees can be "grown." Start with some tape name, say A, and with the seedling

Step number i in the tree's growth consists of choosing distinct tape names $B, B_1, B_2, \ldots, B_k$, and changing the *most recently formed* external node corresponding to B

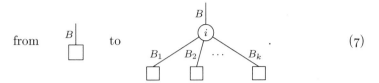

This "last formed, first grown on" rule explains how the tree representation can be constructed directly from the vector representation.

The determination of strictly optimum T-tape merge patterns—that is, of T-lifo trees whose path length is minimum for a given number of external nodes— seems to be quite difficult. For example, the following nonobvious pattern turns out to be an optimum way to merge seven initial runs on four tapes, reading backwards:

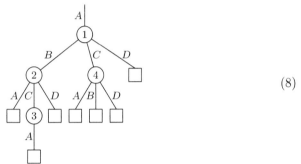

A one-way merge is actually necessary to achieve the optimum! (See exercise 8.) On the other hand, it is not so difficult to give constructions that are *asymptotically* optimal, for any fixed T.

Let $K_T(n)$ be the minimum external path length achievable in a T-lifo tree with n external nodes. From the theory developed in Section 2.3.4.5, it is not difficult to prove that

$$K_T(n) \geq nq - \lfloor((T-1)^q - n)/(T-2)\rfloor, \qquad q = \lceil \log_{T-1} n \rceil, \tag{9}$$

since this is the minimum external path length of *any* tree with n external nodes and all nodes of degree $< T$. At the present time comparatively few values of $K_T(n)$ are known exactly. Here are some upper bounds that are probably exact:

$n =$	1	2	3	4	5	6	7	8	9	10	11	12	13	14	15	
$K_3(n) \leq$	0	2	5	9	12	16	21	25	30	34	39	45	50	56	61	(10)
$K_4(n) \leq$	0	2	3	6	8	11	14	17	20	24	27	31	33	37	40	

Karp discovered that *any* tree whose internal nodes have degrees $< T$ is *almost* T-lifo, in the sense that it can be made T-lifo by changing some of the external nodes to one-way merges. In fact, the construction of a suitable labeling is fairly simple. Let A be a particular tape name, and proceed as follows:

Step 1. Attach tape names to the lines of the tree diagram, in any manner consistent with condition (a) above, provided that the special name A is used only in the leftmost line of a branch.

Step 2. Replace each external node of the form

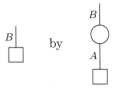

whenever $B \neq A$.

Step 3. Number the internal nodes of the tree in *preorder*. The result will be a labeling satisfying conditions (a), (b), and (c).

For example, if we start with the tree

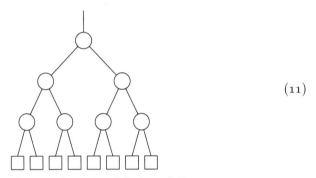

(11)

and three tapes, this procedure might assign labels as follows:

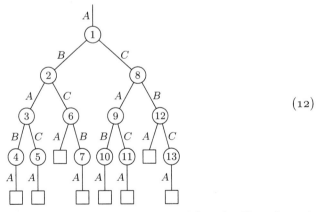

(12)

It is not difficult to verify that Karp's construction satisfies the "last formed, first grown on" discipline, because of the nature of preorder (see exercise 12).

The result of this construction is a merge pattern for which all of the initial runs appear on tape A. This suggests the following distribution and sorting scheme, which we may call the *preorder merge:*

P1. Distribute initial runs onto Tape A until the input is exhausted. Let S be the total number of initial runs.

P2. Carry out the construction above, using a minimum-path-length $(T-1)$-ary tree with S external nodes, obtaining a T-lifo tree whose external path length is within S of the lower bound in (9).

P3. Merge the runs according to this pattern. ▌

This scheme will produce its output on any desired tape. But *it has one serious flaw*—does the reader see what will go wrong? The problem is that the merge pattern requires some of the runs initially on tape A to be ascending, and some to be descending, depending on whether the corresponding external node appears on an odd or an even level. This problem can be resolved without knowing S in advance, by copying runs that should be descending onto an auxiliary tape or tapes, just before they are needed. Then the total amount of processing, in terms of initial run lengths, comes to

$$S \log_{T-1} S + O(S). \tag{13}$$

Thus the preorder merge is definitely better than polyphase or cascade, as $S \to \infty$; indeed, it is asymptotically *optimum*, since (9) shows that $S \log_{T-1} S + O(S)$ is the best we could ever hope to achieve on T tapes. On the other hand, for the comparatively small values of S that usually arise in practice, the preorder merge is rather inefficient; polyphase or cascade methods are simpler and faster, when S is reasonably small. Perhaps it will be possible to invent a simple distribution-and-merge scheme that is competitive with polyphase and cascade for small S, and that is asymptotically optimum for large S.

The second set of exercises below shows how Karp has formulated the question of *read-forward* merging in a similar way. The theory turns out to be rather more complicated in this case, although some very interesting results have been discovered.

EXERCISES — First Set

1. [*17*] It is often convenient, during read-forward merging, to mark the end of each run on tape by including an artificial sentinel record whose key is $+\infty$. How should this practice be modified, when reading backwards?

2. [*20*] Will the columns of an array like (1) always be nondecreasing, or is there a chance that we will have to "subtract" runs from some tape as we go from one level to the next?

▶ **3.** [*20*] Prove that when read-backward polyphase merging is used with the perfect distributions of (1), we will always obtain an A run on tape T1 when sorting is complete, if T1 originally starts with $ADA\ldots$ and T2 through T5 start with $DAD\ldots$.

4. [*M22*] Is it a good idea to do read-backward polyphase merging after distributing all runs in *ascending* order, imagining all the D positions to be initially filled with dummies?

▶ **5.** [*23*] What formulas for the strings of merge numbers replace (8), (9), (10), and (11) of Section 5.4.2, when read-backward polyphase merging is used? Show the merge numbers for the fifth level distribution on six tapes, by drawing a diagram like Fig. 71(a).

6. [*07*] What is the vector representation of the merge pattern whose tree representation is (8)?

7. [*16*] Draw the tree representation for the read-backward merge pattern defined by the following sequence of vectors:

$$v^{(33)} = (\ 20,\quad 9,\quad 5)$$
$$y^{(33)} = (+1,-1,+1)$$
$$y^{(32)} = (+1,+1,-1)$$
$$y^{(31)} = (+1,+1,-1)$$
$$y^{(30)} = (+1,+1,-1)$$
$$y^{(29)} = (+1,-1,+1)$$
$$y^{(28)} = (-1,+1,+1)$$
$$y^{(27)} = (+1,-1,+1)$$
$$y^{(26)} = (+1,-1,+1)$$
$$y^{(25)} = (+1,+1,-1)$$
$$y^{(24)} = (+1,-1,+1)$$
$$y^{(23)} = (+1,-1,+1)$$
$$y^{(22)} = (+1,-1,+1)$$
$$y^{(21)} = (-1,+1,+1)$$
$$y^{(20)} = (+1,+1,-1)$$
$$y^{(19)} = (-1,+1,+1)$$
$$y^{(18)} = (+1,+1,-1)$$
$$y^{(17)} = (+1,+1,-1)$$

$$y^{(16)} = (+1,+1,-1)$$
$$y^{(15)} = (+1,+1,-1)$$
$$y^{(14)} = (+1,-1,+1)$$
$$y^{(13)} = (+1,-1,+1)$$
$$y^{(12)} = (-1,+1,+1)$$
$$y^{(11)} = (+1,+1,-1)$$
$$y^{(10)} = (+1,+1,-1)$$
$$y^{(9)} = (+1,-1,+1)$$
$$y^{(8)} = (+1,+1,-1)$$
$$y^{(7)} = (+1,+1,-1)$$
$$y^{(6)} = (+1,+1,-1)$$
$$y^{(5)} = (-1,+1,+1)$$
$$y^{(4)} = (+1,-1,+1)$$
$$y^{(3)} = (-1,+1,+1)$$
$$y^{(2)} = (+1,-1,+1)$$
$$y^{(1)} = (-1,+1,+1)$$
$$y^{(0)} = (\ 1,\quad 0,\quad 0)$$

8. [*23*] Prove that (8) is an optimum way to merge, reading backwards, when $S = 7$ and $T = 4$, and that all methods that avoid one-way merging are inferior.

9. [*M22*] Prove the lower bound (9).

10. [*41*] Prepare a table of the exact values of $K_T(n)$, using a computer.

▶ **11.** [*20*] True or false: Any read-backward merge pattern that uses nothing but $(T-1)$-way merging must always have the runs alternating $ADAD\ldots$ on each tape; it will not work if two adjacent runs appear in the same order.

12. [*22*] Prove that Karp's preorder construction always yields a labeled tree satisfying conditions (a), (b), and (c).

13. [*16*] Make (12) more efficient, by removing as many of the one-way merges as possible so that preorder still gives a valid labeling of the internal nodes.

14. [*40*] Devise an algorithm that carries out the preorder merge without explicitly representing the tree in steps P2 and P3, using only $O(\log S)$ words of memory to control the merging pattern.

15. [*M39*] Karp's preorder construction in the text yields trees with one-way merges at several terminal nodes. Prove that when $T = 3$ it is possible to construct asymptotically optimal 3-lifo trees in which two-way merging is used throughout.

In other words, let $\hat{K}_T(n)$ be the minimum external path length over all T-lifo trees with n external nodes, such that every internal node has degree $T-1$. Prove that $\hat{K}_3(n) = n \lg n + O(n)$.

16. [*M46*] In the notation of exercise 15, is $\hat{K}_T(n) = n \log_{T-1} n + O(n)$ for all $T \geq 3$, when $n \equiv 1 \pmod{T-2}$?

▶ **17.** [*28*] (Richard D. Pratt.) To achieve ascending order in a read-backward cascade merge, we could insist on an *even* number of merging passes; this suggests a technique of initial distribution that is somewhat different from Algorithm 5.4.3C.

a) Change 5.4.3–(1) so that it shows only the perfect distributions that require an even number of merging passes.

b) Design an initial distribution scheme that interpolates between these perfect distributions. (Thus, if the number of initial runs falls between perfect distributions, it is desirable to merge some, but not all, of the runs twice, in order to reach a perfect distribution.)

▶ **18.** [*M38*] Suppose that T tape units are available, for some $T \geq 3$, and that T1 contains N records while the remaining tapes are empty. Is it possible to reverse the order of the records on T1 in fewer than $\Omega(N \log N)$ steps, *without* reading backwards? (The operation is, of course, trivial if backwards reading is allowed.) See exercise 5.2.5–14 for a class of such algorithms that *do* require order $N \log N$ steps.

EXERCISES — Second Set

The following exercises develop the theory of tape merging on read-forward tapes; in this case each tape acts as a queue instead of as a stack. A merge pattern can be represented as a sequence of vectors $y^{(m)} \ldots y^{(1)} y^{(0)}$ exactly as in the text, but when we convert the vector representation to a tree representation we change "last formed, first grown on" to "*first* formed, first grown on." Thus the invalid configurations (4) would be changed to

A tree that can be labeled so as to represent a read-forward merge on T tapes is called T-fifo, analogous to the term "T-lifo" in the read-backward case.

When tapes can be read backwards, they make very good stacks. But unfortunately they don't make very good general-purpose queues. If we randomly write and read, in a first-in-first-out manner, we waste a lot of time moving from one part of the tape to another. Even worse, we will soon run off the end of the tape! We run into the same problem as the queue overrunning memory in 2.2.2–(4) and (5), but the solution in 2.2.2–(6) and (7) doesn't apply to tapes since they aren't circular loops. Therefore we shall call a tree *strongly T-fifo* if it can be labeled so that the corresponding merge pattern makes each tape follow the special queue discipline "write, rewind, read all, rewind; write, rewind, read all, rewind; etc."

▶ **19.** [*22*] (R. M. Karp.) Find a binary tree that is not 3-fifo.

▶ **20.** [*22*] Formulate the condition "strongly T-fifo" in terms of a fairly simple rule about invalid configurations of tape labels, analogous to (4′).

21. [*18*] Draw the tree representation for the read-forwards merge pattern defined by the vectors in exercise 7. Is this tree strongly 3-fifo?

22. [*28*] (R. M. Karp.) Show that the tree representations for polyphase and cascade merging with perfect distributions are exactly the same for both the read-backward and the read-forward case, except for the numbers that label the internal nodes. Find a larger class of vector representations of merging patterns for which this is true.

23. [24] (R. M. Karp.) Let us say that a segment $y^{(q)} \ldots y^{(r)}$ of a merge pattern is a *stage* if no output tape is subsequently used as an input tape — that is, if there do not exist i, j, k with $q \geq i > k \geq r$, $y_j^{(i)} = -1$, and $y_j^{(k)} = +1$. The purpose of this exercise is to prove that *cascade merge minimizes the number of stages*, over all merge patterns having the same number of tapes and initial runs.

It is convenient to define some notation. Let us write $v \to w$ if v and w are T-vectors such that w reduces to v in the first stage of some merge pattern. (Thus there is a merge pattern $y^{(m)} \ldots y^{(0)}$ such that $y^{(m)} \ldots y^{(l+1)}$ is a stage, $w = y^{(m)} + \cdots + y^{(0)}$, and $v = y^{(l)} + \cdots + y^{(0)}$.) Let us write $v \preceq w$ if v and w are T-vectors such that the sum of the largest k elements of v is $\leq$ the sum of the largest k elements of w, for $1 \leq k \leq T$. Thus, for example, $(2, 1, 2, 2, 2, 1) \preceq (1, 2, 3, 0, 3, 1)$, since $2 \leq 3$, $2+2 \leq 3+3$, $\ldots$, $2 + 2 + 2 + 2 + 1 + 1 \leq 3 + 3 + 2 + 1 + 1 + 0$. Finally, if $v = (v_1, \ldots, v_T)$, let $C(v) = (s_T, s_{T-2}, s_{T-3}, \ldots, s_1, 0)$ where s_k is the sum of the largest k elements of v.
a) Prove that $v \to C(v)$.
b) Prove that $v \preceq w$ implies $C(v) \preceq C(w)$.
c) Assuming the result of exercise 24, prove that cascade merge minimizes the number of stages.

24. [M35] In the notation of exercise 23, prove that $v \to w$ implies $w \preceq C(v)$.

25. [M36] (R. M. Karp.) Let us say that a segment $y^{(q)} \ldots y^{(r)}$ of a merge pattern is a *phase* if no tape is used both for input and for output — that is, if there do not exist i, j, k with $q \geq i \geq r$, $q \geq k \geq r$, $y_j^{(i)} = +1$, and $y_j^{(k)} = -1$. The purpose of this exercise is to investigate merge patterns that minimize the number of phases. We shall write $v \Rightarrow w$ if w can be reduced to v in one phase (a similar notation was introduced in exercise 23); and we let

$$D_k(v) = (s_k + t_{k+1}, \; s_k + t_{k+2}, \; \ldots, \; s_k + t_T, \; 0, \; \ldots, \; 0),$$

where t_j denotes the jth largest element of v and $s_k = t_1 + \cdots + t_k$.
a) Prove that $v \Rightarrow D_k(v)$ for $1 \leq k < T$.
b) Prove that $v \preceq w$ implies $D_k(v) \preceq D_k(w)$, for $1 \leq k < T$.
c) Prove that $v \Rightarrow w$ implies $w \preceq D_k(v)$, for some k, $1 \leq k < T$.
d) Consequently, a merge pattern that sorts the maximum number of initial runs on T tapes in q phases can be represented by a sequence of integers $k_1 k_2 \ldots k_q$, such that the initial distribution is $D_{k_q}(\ldots (D_{k_2}(D_{k_1}(u))) \ldots)$, where $u = (1, 0, \ldots, 0)$. This minimum-phase strategy has a strongly T-fifo representation, and it also belongs to the class of patterns in exercise 22. When $T = 3$ it is the *polyphase* merge, and for $T = 4, 5, 6, 7$ it is a variation of the *balanced* merge.

26. [M46] (R. M. Karp.) Is the optimum sequence $k_1 k_2 \ldots k_q$ mentioned in exercise 25 equal to $1 \lceil T/2 \rceil \lfloor T/2 \rfloor \lceil T/2 \rceil \lfloor T/2 \rfloor \ldots$, for all $T \geq 4$ and all sufficiently large q?

*5.4.5. The Oscillating Sort

A somewhat different approach to merge sorting was introduced by Sheldon Sobel in *JACM* **9** (1962), 372–375. Instead of starting with a distribution pass where all the initial runs are dispersed to tapes, he proposed an algorithm that oscillates back and forth between distribution and merging, so that much of the sorting takes place before the input has been completely examined.

Suppose, for example, that there are five tapes available for merging. Sobel's method would sort 16 initial runs as follows:

	Operation	T1	T2	T3	T4	T5	Cost
Phase 1	Distribute	A_1	A_1	A_1	A_1	—	4
Phase 2	Merge	—	—	—	—	D_4	4
Phase 3	Distribute	—	A_1	A_1	A_1	$D_4 A_1$	4
Phase 4	Merge	D_4	—	—	—	D_4	4
Phase 5	Distribute	$D_4 A_1$	—	A_1	A_1	$D_4 A_1$	4
Phase 6	Merge	D_4	D_4	—	—	D_4	4
Phase 7	Distribute	$D_4 A_1$	$D_4 A_1$	—	A_1	$D_4 A_1$	4
Phase 8	Merge	D_4	D_4	D_4	—	D_4	4
Phase 9	Merge	—	—	—	A_{16}	—	16

Here, as in Section 5.4.4, we use A_r and D_r to stand respectively for ascending and descending runs of relative length r. The method begins by writing an initial run onto each of four tapes, and merges them (reading backwards) onto the fifth tape. Distribution resumes again, this time cyclically shifted one place to the right with respect to the tapes, and a second merge produces another run D_4. When four D_4's have been formed in this way, an additional merge creates A_{16}. We could go on to create three more A_{16}'s, merging them into a D_{64}, and so on until the input is exhausted. It isn't necessary to know the length of the input in advance.

When the number of initial runs, S, is 4^m, it is not difficult to see that this method processes each record exactly $m + 1$ times: once during the distribution, and m times during a merge. When S is between 4^{m-1} and 4^m, we could assume that dummy runs are present, bringing S up to 4^m; hence the total sorting time would essentially amount to $\lceil \log_4 S \rceil + 1$ passes over all the data. This is just what would be achieved by a balanced sort on *eight* tapes; in general, oscillating sort with T work tapes is equivalent to balanced merging with $2(T-1)$ tapes, since it makes

$$\lceil \log_{T-1} S \rceil + 1$$

passes over the data. When S is a power of $T - 1$, this is the best *any* T-tape method could possibly do, since it achieves the lower bound in Eq. 5.4.4–(9). On the other hand, when S is

$$(T - 1)^{m-1} + 1,$$

just one higher than a power of $T - 1$, the method wastes nearly a whole pass.

Exercise 2 shows how to eliminate part of this penalty for non-perfect-powers S, by using a special ending routine. A further refinement was discovered in 1966 by Dennis L. Bencher, who called his procedure the "criss-cross merge" [see H. Wedekind, *Datenorganisation* (Berlin: W. de Gruyter, 1970), 164–166; see also *U.S. Patent 3540000* (1970)]. The main idea is to delay merging until more knowledge of S has been gained. We shall discuss a slightly modified form of Bencher's original scheme.

This improved oscillating sort proceeds as follows:

	Operation	T1	T2	T3	T4	T5	Cost
Phase 1	Distribute	—	A_1	A_1	A_1	A_1	4
Phase 2	Distribute	—	A_1	$A_1 A_1$	$A_1 A_1$	$A_1 A_1$	3
Phase 3	Merge	D_4	—	A_1	A_1	A_1	4
Phase 4	Distribute	$D_4 A_1$	—	A_1	$A_1 A_1$	$A_1 A_1$	3
Phase 5	Merge	D_4	D_4	—	A_1	A_1	4
Phase 6	Distribute	$D_4 A_1$	$D_4 A_1$	—	A_1	$A_1 A_1$	3
Phase 7	Merge	D_4	D_4	D_4	—	A_1	4
Phase 8	Distribute	$D_4 A_1$	$D_4 A_1$	$D_4 A_1$	—	A_1	3
Phase 9	Merge	D_4	D_4	D_4	D_4	—	4

We do not merge the D_4's into an A_{16} at this point (unless the input happens to be exhausted); only after building up to

| Phase 15 | Merge | $D_4 D_4$ | $D_4 D_4$ | $D_4 D_4$ | D_4 | — | 4 |

will we get

| Phase 16 | Merge | D_4 | D_4 | D_4 | — | A_{16} | 16 |

The second A_{16} will occur after three more D_4's have been made,

| Phase 22 | Merge | $D_4 D_4$ | $D_4 D_4$ | D_4 | — | $A_{16} D_4$ | 4 |
| Phase 23 | Merge | D_4 | D_4 | — | A_{16} | A_{16} | 16 |

and so on (compare with Phases 1–5). The advantage of Bencher's scheme can be seen for example if there are only five initial runs: Oscillating sort as modified in exercise 2 would do a four-way merge (in Phase 2) followed by a two-way merge, for a total cost of $4 + 4 + 1 + 5 = 14$, while Bencher's scheme would do a two-way merge (in Phase 3) followed by a four-way merge, for a total cost of $4 + 1 + 2 + 5 = 12$. Both methods also involve a small additional cost, namely one unit of rewind before the final merge.

A precise description of Bencher's method appears in Algorithm B below. Unfortunately it seems to be a procedure that is harder to understand than to code; it is much easier to explain the technique to a computer than to a computer scientist! This is partly because it is an inherently recursive method that has been expressed in iterative form and then optimized somewhat; the reader may find it necessary to trace through the operation of this algorithm several times before discovering what is really going on.

Algorithm B (*Oscillating sort with "criss-cross" distribution*). This algorithm takes initial runs and disperses them to tapes, occasionally interrupting the distribution process in order to merge some of the tape contents. The algorithm uses P-way merging, assuming that $T = P + 1 \geq 3$ tape units are available — *not* counting the unit that may be necessary to hold the input data. The tape units must allow reading in both forward and backward directions, and they are designated by the numbers $0, 1, \ldots, P$. The following tables are maintained:

D[j], $0 \le j \le P$: Number of dummy runs assumed to be present at the end of tape j.

A[l, j], $0 \le l \le L$, Here L is a number such that at most P^{L+1} initial runs will $0 \le j \le P$ be input. When A[l, j] $= k \ge 0$, a run of nominal length P^k is present on tape j, corresponding to "level l" of the algorithm's operation. This run is ascending if k is even, descending if k is odd. When A[l, j] < 0, level l does not use tape j.

The statement "Write an initial run on tape j" is an abbreviation for the following operations:

Set A[l, j] $\leftarrow 0$. If the input is exhausted, increase D[j] by 1; otherwise write an initial run (in ascending order) onto tape j.

The statement "Merge to tape j" is an abbreviation for the following operations:

If D[i] > 0 for all $i \ne j$, decrease D[i] by 1 for all $i \ne j$ and increase D[j] by 1. Otherwise merge one run to tape j, from all tapes $i \ne j$ such that D[i] $= 0$, and decrease D[i] by 1 for all other $i \ne j$.

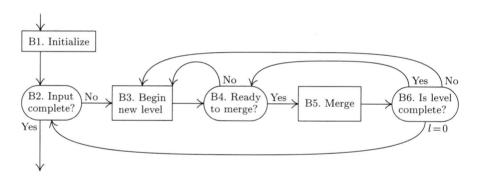

Fig. 77. Oscillating sort, with a "criss-cross" distribution.

B1. [Initialize.] Set D[j] $\leftarrow 0$ for $0 \le j \le P$. Set A[$0, 0$] $\leftarrow -1$, $l \leftarrow 0$, $q \leftarrow 0$. Then write an initial run on tape j, for $1 \le j \le P$.

B2. [Input complete?] (At this point tape q is empty and the other tapes contain at most one run each.) If there is more input, go on to step B3. But if the input is exhausted, rewind all tapes $j \ne q$ such that A[$0, j$] is even; then merge to tape q, reading forwards on tapes just rewound, and reading backwards on the other tapes. This completes the sort, with the output in ascending order on tape q.

B3. [Begin new level.] Set $l \leftarrow l + 1$, $r \leftarrow q$, $s \leftarrow 0$, and $q \leftarrow (q + 1) \bmod T$. Write an initial run on tape $(q + j) \bmod T$, for $1 \le j \le T - 2$. (Thus an initial run is written onto each tape except tapes q and r.) Set A[l, q] $\leftarrow -1$ and A[l, r] $\leftarrow -2$.

B4. [Ready to merge?] If A[$l-1, q$] $\ne s$, go back to step B3.

B5. [Merge.]   (At this point $A[l-1, q] = A[l, j] = s$ for all $j \neq q$, $j \neq r$.)
Merge to tape r, reading backwards. (See the definition of this operation
above.) Then set $s \leftarrow s + 1$, $l \leftarrow l - 1$, $A[l, r] \leftarrow s$, and $A[l, q] \leftarrow -1$. Set
$r \leftarrow (2q - r) \bmod T$. (In general, we have $r = (q - 1) \bmod T$ when s is even,
$r = (q + 1) \bmod T$ when s is odd.)

B6. [Is level complete?] If $l = 0$, go to B2. Otherwise if $A[l, j] = s$ for all $j \neq q$
and $j \neq r$, go to B4. Otherwise return to B3.   ▮

We can use a "recursion induction" style of proof to show that this algorithm is valid, just as we have done for Algorithm 2.3.1T. Suppose that
we begin at step B3 with $l = l_0$, $q = q_0$, $s_+ = A[l_0, (q_0+1) \bmod T]$, and
$s_- = A[l_0, (q_0-1) \bmod T]$; and assume furthermore that either $s_+ = 0$ or $s_- = 1$
or $s_+ = 2$ or $s_- = 3$ or $\cdots$. It is possible to verify by induction that the algorithm
will eventually get to step B5 without changing rows 0 through l_0 of A, and with
$l = l_0 + 1$, $q = q_0 \pm 1$, $r = q_0$, and $s = s_+$ or s_-, where we choose the $+$ sign if
$s_+ = 0$ or ($s_+ = 2$ and $s_- \neq 1$) or ($s_+ = 4$ and $s_- \neq 1, 3$) or $\cdots$, and we choose
the $-$ sign if ($s_- = 1$ and $s_+ \neq 0$) or ($s_- = 3$ and $s_+ \neq 0, 2$) or $\cdots$. The proof
sketched here is not very elegant, but the algorithm has been stated in a form
more suited to implementation than to verification.

Figure 78 shows the efficiency of Algorithm B, in terms of the average number of times each record is merged as a function of the number S of initial runs,
assuming that the initial runs are approximately equal in length. (Corresponding
graphs for polyphase and cascade sort have appeared in Figs. 70 and 74.) A slight
improvement, mentioned in exercise 3, has been used in preparing this chart.

A related method called the *gyrating sort* was developed by R. M. Karp,
based on the theory of preorder merging that we have discussed in Section 5.4.4;
see *Combinatorial Algorithms*, edited by Randall Rustin (Algorithmics Press,
1972), 21–29.

Reading forwards. The oscillating sort pattern appears to require a read-
backwards capability, since we need to store long runs somewhere as we merge
newly input short runs. However, M. A. Goetz [*Proc. AFIPS Spring Joint
Comp. Conf.* **25** (1964), 599–607] has discovered a way to perform an oscillating
sort using only forward reading and simple rewinding. His method is radically
different from the other schemes we have seen in this chapter, in two ways:

a) Data is sometimes written at the front of the tape, with the understanding
   that the existing data in the *middle* of the tape is not destroyed.

b) All initial runs have a fixed maximum length.

Condition (a) violates the first-in-first-out property we have assumed to be
characteristic of forward reading, but it can be implemented reliably if a sufficient
amount of blank tape is left between runs and if parity errors are ignored at
appropriate times. Condition (b) tends to be somewhat incompatible with an
efficient use of replacement selection.

Goetz's read-forward oscillating sort has the somewhat dubious distinction
of being one of the first algorithms to be patented as an algorithm instead of as a

physical device [*U.S. Patent 3380029* (1968)]; unless successfully contested, such a patent makes it illegal to use the algorithm in a program without permission of the patentee. Bencher's read-backward oscillating sort technique was patented by IBM several years later. [Alas, we have reached the end of the era when the joy of discovering a new algorithm was satisfaction enough! Fortunately the oscillating sort isn't especially good; let's hope that community-minded folks who invent the best algorithms continue to make their ideas freely available. Of course the specter of people keeping new techniques completely secret is far worse than the public appearance of algorithms that are proprietary for a limited time.]

The central idea in Goetz's method is to arrange things so that each tape begins with a run of relative length 1, followed by one of relative length P, then P^2, etc. For example, when $T = 5$ the sort begins as follows, using "." to indicate the current position of the read-write head on each tape:

	Operation	T1	T2	T3	T4	T5	"Cost"	Remarks
Phase 1	Distribute	$.A_1$	$.A_1$	$.A_1$	$.A_1$	$A_1.$	5	[T5 not rewound]
Phase 2	Merge	$\cancel{A}_1.$	$\cancel{A}_1.$	$\cancel{A}_1.$	$\cancel{A}_1.$	$A_1 A_4.$	4	[Now rewind all]
Phase 3	Distribute	$.A_1$	$.A_1$	$.A_1$	$A_1.$	$.A_1 A_4$	4	[T4 not rewound]
Phase 4	Merge	$\cancel{A}_1.$	$\cancel{A}_1.$	$\cancel{A}_1.$	$A_1 A_4.$	$\cancel{A}_1.A_4$	4	[Now rewind all]
Phase 5	Distribute	$.A_1$	$.A_1$	$.A_1$	$.A_1 A_4$	$.A_1 A_4$	4	[T3 not rewound]
Phase 6	Merge	$\cancel{A}_1.$	$\cancel{A}_1.$	$A_1 A_4.$	$\cancel{A}_1.A_4$	$\cancel{A}_1.A_4$	4	[Now rewind all]
Phase 7	Distribute	$.A_1$	$A_1.$	$.A_1 A_4$	$.A_1 A_4$	$.A_1 A_4$	4	[T2 not rewound]
Phase 8	Merge	$\cancel{A}_1.$	$A_1 A_4.$	$\cancel{A}_1.A_4$	$\cancel{A}_1.A_4$	$\cancel{A}_1.A_4$	4	[Now rewind all]
Phase 9	Distribute	$A_1.$	$.A_1 A_4$	$.A_1 A_4$	$.A_1 A_4$	$.A_1 A_4$	4	[T1 not rewound]
Phase 10	Merge	$A_1 A_4.$	$\cancel{A}_1.A_4$	$\cancel{A}_1.A_4$	$\cancel{A}_1.A_4$	$\cancel{A}_1.A_4$	4	[No rewinding]
Phase 11	Merge	$A_1 A_4 A_{16}.$	$\cancel{A}_1 \cancel{A}_4.$	$\cancel{A}_1 \cancel{A}_4.$	$\cancel{A}_1 \cancel{A}_4.$	$\cancel{A}_1 \cancel{A}_4.$	16	[Now rewind all]

And so on. During Phase 1, T1 was rewinding while T2 was receiving its input, then T2 was rewinding while T3 was receiving input, etc. Eventually, when the input is exhausted, dummy runs will start to appear, and we will sometimes need to imagine that they were written explicitly on the tape at full length. For example, if $S = 18$, the A_1's on T4 and T5 would be dummies during Phase 9; we would have to skip forwards on T4 and T5 while merging from T2 and T3 to T1 during Phase 10, because we have to get to the A_4's on T4 and T5 in preparation for Phase 11. On the other hand, the dummy A_1 on T1 need not appear explicitly. Thus the "endgame" is a bit tricky.

Another example of this method appears in the next section.

EXERCISES

1. [*22*] The text illustrates Sobel's original oscillating sort for $T = 5$ and $S = 16$. Give a precise specification of an algorithm that generalizes the procedure, sorting $S = P^L$ initial runs on $T = P + 1 \geq 3$ tapes. Strive for simplicity.

2. [*24*] If $S = 6$ in Sobel's original method, we could pretend that $S = 16$ and that 11 dummy runs were present. Then Phase 3 in the text's example would put dummy runs A_0 on T4 and T5; Phase 4 would merge the A_1's on T2 and T3 into a D_2 on T1; Phases 5–8 would do nothing; and Phase 9 would produce A_6 on T4. It would be better

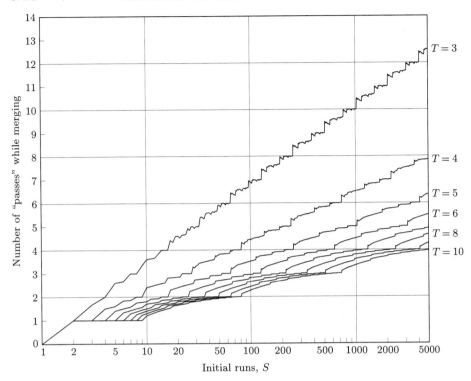

Fig. 78. Efficiency of oscillating sort, using the technique of Algorithm B and exercise 3.

to rewind T2 and T3 just after Phase 3, then to produce A_6 immediately on T4 by three-way merging.

Show how to modify the algorithm of exercise 1, so that an improved ending like this is obtained when S is not a perfect power of P.

▶ **3.** [*29*] Prepare a chart showing the behavior of Algorithm B when $T = 3$, assuming that there are nine initial runs. Show that the procedure is obviously inefficient in one place, and prescribe corrections to Algorithm B that will remedy the situation.

4. [*21*] Step B3 sets $A[l,q]$ and $A[l,r]$ to negative values. Show that one of these two operations is always superfluous, since the corresponding A table entry is never looked at.

5. [*M25*] Let S be the number of initial runs present in the input to Algorithm B. Which values of S require *no rewinding* in step B2?

*5.4.6. Practical Considerations for Tape Merging

Now comes the nitty-gritty: We have discussed the various families of merge patterns, so it is time to see how they actually apply to real configurations of computers and magnetic tapes, and to compare them in a meaningful way. Our study of internal sorting showed that we can't adequately judge the efficiency of a sorting method merely by counting the number of comparisons it performs; similarly we can't properly evaluate an external sorting method by simply knowing the number of passes it makes over the data.

In this section we shall discuss the characteristics of typical tape units, and the way they affect initial distribution and merging. In particular we shall study some schemes for buffer allocation, and the corresponding effects on running time. We also shall consider briefly the construction of *sort generator* programs.

How tape works. Different manufacturers have provided tape units with widely varying characteristics. For convenience, we shall define a hypothetical MIXT tape unit, which is reasonably typical of the equipment that was being manufactured at the time this book was first written. MIXT reads and writes 800 characters per inch of tape, at a rate of 75 inches per second. This means that one character is read or written every $\frac{1}{60}$ ms, or $16\frac{2}{3}$ microseconds, when the tape is active. Actual tape units that were available in 1970 had densities ranging from 200 to 1600 characters per inch, and tape speeds ranging from $37\frac{1}{2}$ to 150 inches per second, so their effective speed varied from 1/8 to 4 times as fast as MIXT.

Of course, we observed near the beginning of Section 5.4 that magnetic tapes in general are now pretty much obsolete. But many lessons were learned during the decades when tape sorting was of major importance, and those lessons are still valuable. Thus our main concern here is not to obtain particular answers; it is to learn how to combine theory and practice in a reasonable way. Methodology is much more important than phenomenology, because the principles of problem solving remain useful despite technological changes. Readers will benefit most from this material by transplanting themselves temporarily into the mindset of the 1970s. *Let us therefore pretend that we still live in that bygone era.*

One of the important considerations to keep in mind, as we adopt the perspective of the early days, is the fact that individual tapes have a strictly limited capacity. Each reel contains 2400 feet of tape or less; hence there is room for at most 23,000,000 or so characters per reel of MIXT tape, and it takes about $23000000/3600000 \approx 6.4$ minutes to read them all. If larger files must be sorted, it is generally best to sort one reelful at a time, and then to merge the individually sorted reels, in order to avoid excessive tape handling. This means that the number of initial runs, S, actually present in the merge patterns we have been studying is never extremely large. We will never find $S > 5000$, even with a very small internal memory that produces initial runs only 5000 characters long. Consequently the formulas that give asymptotic efficiency of the algorithms as $S \to \infty$ are primarily of academic interest.

Data appears on tape in *blocks* (Fig. 79), and each read/write instruction transmits a single block. Tape blocks are often called "records," but we shall avoid that terminology because it conflicts with the fact that we are sorting a file of "records" in another sense. Such a distinction was unnecessary on many of the early sorting programs written during the 1950s, since one record was written per block; but we shall see that it is usually advantageous to have quite a few records in every block on the tape.

An *interblock gap*, 480 character positions long, appears between adjacent blocks, in order to allow the tape to stop and to start between individual read or write commands. The effect of interblock gaps is to decrease the number of

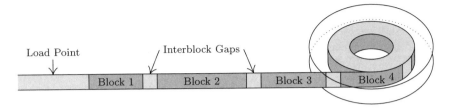

Fig. 79. Magnetic tape with variable-size blocks.

characters per reel of tape, depending on the number of characters per block (see Fig. 80); and the average number of characters transmitted per second decreases in the same way, since tape moves at a fairly constant speed.

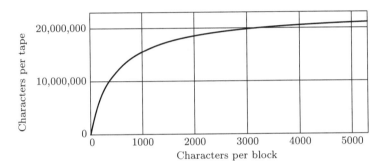

Fig. 80. The number of characters per reel of MIXT tape, as a function of the block size.

Many old-fashioned computers had fixed block sizes that were rather small; their design was reflected in the MIX computer as defined in Chapter 1, which always reads and writes 100-word blocks. But MIX's convention corresponds to about 500 characters per block, and 480 characters per gap, hence almost half the tape is wasted! Most machines of the 1970s therefore allowed the block size to be variable; we shall discuss the choice of appropriate block sizes below.

At the end of a read or write operation, the tape unit "coasts" at full speed over the first 66 characters (or so) of the gap. If the next operation for the same tape is initiated during this time, the tape motion continues without interruption. But if the next operation doesn't come soon enough, the tape will stop and it will also require some time to accelerate to full speed on the next operation. The combined stop/start time delay is 5 ms, 2 for the stop and 3 for the start (see Fig. 81). Thus if we just miss the chance to have continuous full-speed reading, the effect on running time is essentially the same as if there were 780 characters instead of 480 in the interblock gap.

Now let us consider the operation of *rewinding*. Unfortunately, the exact time needed to rewind over a given number n of characters is not easy to characterize. On some machines there is a high-speed rewind that applies only when n is greater than 5 million or so; for smaller values of n, rewinding goes at

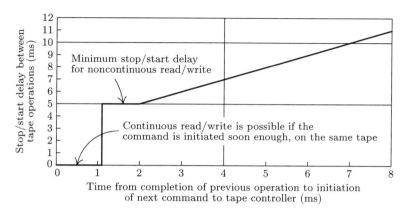

Fig. 81. How to compute the stop/start delay time. (This gets added to the time used for reading or writing the blocks and the gaps.)

normal read/write speed. On other machines a special motor is used to control all of the rewind operations; it gradually accelerates the tape reel to a certain number of revolutions per minute, then puts on the brakes when it is time to stop, and the actual tape speed varies with the fullness of the reel. For simplicity, we shall assume that MIXT requires $\max(30, n/150)$ ms to rewind over n character positions (including gaps), roughly two-fifths as long as it took to write them. This is a reasonably good approximation to the behavior of many actual tape units, where the ratio of read/write time to rewind time is generally between 2 and 3, but it does not adequately model the effect of combined low-speed and high-speed rewind that is present on many other machines. (See Fig. 82.)

Initial loading and/or rewinding will position a tape at "load point," and an extra 110 ms are necessary for any read or write operation initiated at load point. When the tape is not at load point, it may be read backwards; an extra 32 ms is added to the time of any backward operation following a forward operation or any forward operation following a backward one.

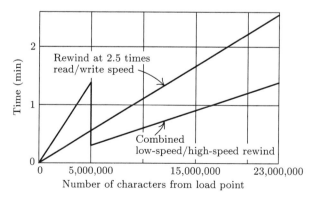

Fig. 82. Approximate running time for two commonly used rewind techniques.

Merging revisited. Let us now look again at the process of P-way merging, with an emphasis on input and output activities, assuming that $P+1$ tape units are being used for the input files and the output file. Our goal is to overlap the input/output operations as much as possible with each other and with the computations of the program, so that the overall merging time is minimized.

It is instructive to consider the following special case, in which serious restrictions are placed on the amount of simultaneity possible. Suppose that

a) at most one tape may be written on at any one time;

b) at most one tape may be read from at any one time;

c) reading, writing, and computing may take place simultaneously only when the read and write operations have been initiated simultaneously.

It turns out that a system of $2P$ input buffers and 2 output buffers is sufficient to keep the tape moving at essentially its maximum speed, even though these three restrictions are imposed, unless the computer is unusually slow. Note that condition (a) is not really a restriction, since there is only one output tape. Furthermore the amount of input is equal to the amount of output, so there is only one tape being read, on the average, at any given time; if condition (b) is not satisfied, there will necessarily be periods when no input at all is occurring. Thus we can minimize the merging time if we keep the output tape busy.

An important technique called *forecasting* leads to the desired effect. While we are doing a P-way merge, we generally have P *current input buffers*, which are being used as the source of data; some of them are more full than others, depending on how much of their data has already been scanned. If all of them become empty at about the same time, we will need to do a lot of reading before we can proceed further, unless we have foreseen this eventuality in advance. Fortunately it is always possible to tell which buffer will empty first, by simply looking at the *last* record in each buffer. The buffer whose last record has the smallest key will always be the first one empty, regardless of the values of any other keys; so we always know which file should be the source of our next input command. The following algorithm spells out this principle in detail.

Algorithm F (*Forecasting with floating buffers*). This algorithm controls the buffering during a P-way merge of long input files, for $P \geq 2$. Assume that the input tapes and files are numbered $1, 2, \ldots, P$. The algorithm uses $2P$ input buffers $I[1], \ldots, I[2P]$; two output buffers $O[0]$ and $O[1]$; and the following auxiliary tables:

$A[j], 1 \leq j \leq 2P$: 0 if $I[j]$ is available for input, 1 otherwise.

$B[i], 1 \leq i \leq P$: Index of the buffer holding the last block read so far from file i.

$C[i], 1 \leq i \leq P$: Index of the buffer currently being used for the input from file i.

$L[i], 1 \leq i \leq P$: The last key read so far from file i.

$S[j], 1 \leq j \leq 2P$: Index of the buffer to use when $I[j]$ becomes empty.

The algorithm described here does not terminate; an appropriate way to shut it off is discussed below.

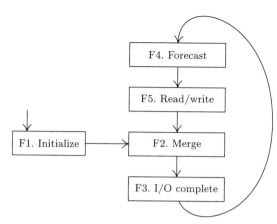

Fig. 83. Forecasting with floating buffers.

F1. [Initialize.] Read the first block from tape i into buffer $I[i]$, set $A[i] \leftarrow 1$, $A[P+i] \leftarrow 0$, $B[i] \leftarrow i$, $C[i] \leftarrow i$, and set $L[i]$ to the key of the final record in buffer $I[i]$, for $1 \leq i \leq P$. Then find m such that $L[m] = \min\{L[1],\ldots,L[P]\}$; and set $t \leftarrow 0$, $k \leftarrow P+1$. Begin to read from tape m into buffer $I[k]$.

F2. [Merge.] Merge records from buffers $I[C[1]],\ldots,I[C[P]]$ to $O[t]$, until $O[t]$ is full. If during this process an input buffer, say $I[C[i]]$, becomes empty and $O[t]$ is not yet full, set $A[C[i]] \leftarrow 0$, $C[i] \leftarrow S[C[i]]$, and continue to merge.

F3. [I/O complete.] Wait until the previous read (or read/write) operation is complete. Then set $A[k] \leftarrow 1$, $S[B[m]] \leftarrow k$, $B[m] \leftarrow k$, and set $L[m]$ to the key of the final record in $I[k]$.

F4. [Forecast.] Find m such that $L[m] = \min\{L[1],\ldots,L[P]\}$, and find k such that $A[k] = 0$.

F5. [Read/write.] Begin to read from tape m into buffer $I[k]$, and to write from buffer $O[t]$ onto the output tape. Then set $t \leftarrow 1-t$ and return to F2. ∎

The example in Fig. 84 shows how forecasting works when $P = 2$, assuming that each block on tape contains only two records. The input buffer contents are illustrated each time we get to the beginning of step F2. Algorithm F essentially forms P *queues of buffers*, with $C[i]$ pointing to the front and $B[i]$ to the rear of the ith queue, and with $S[j]$ pointing to the successor of buffer $I[j]$; these pointers are shown as arrows in Fig. 84. Line 1 illustrates the state of affairs after initialization: There is one buffer for each input file, and another block is being read from File 1 (since $03 < 05$). Line 2 shows the status of things after the first block has been merged: We are outputting a block containing $\boxed{01\ \ 02}$, and inputting the next block from File 2 (since $05 < 09$). Note that in line 3, three of the four input buffers are essentially committed to File 2, since we are reading from that file and we already have a full buffer and a partly full buffer in its

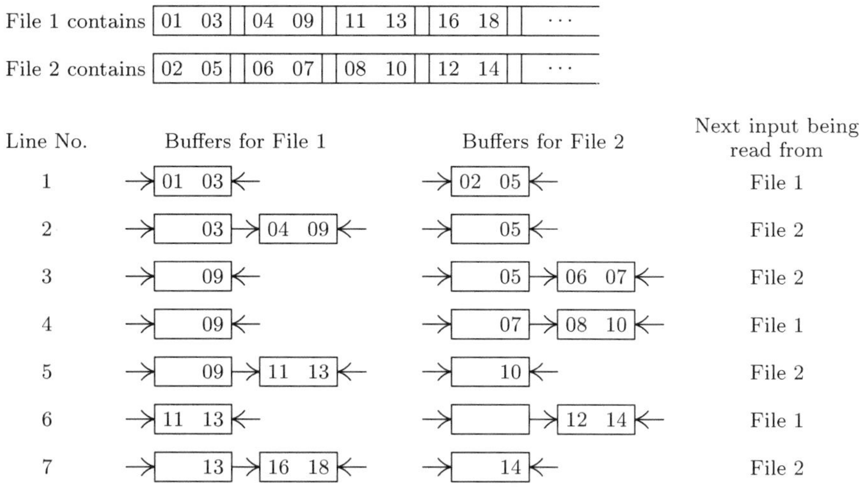

File 1 contains | 01 03 | | 04 09 | | 11 13 | | 16 18 | | · · ·

File 2 contains | 02 05 | | 06 07 | | 08 10 | | 12 14 | | · · ·

Line No.	Buffers for File 1	Buffers for File 2	Next input being read from
1	→ 01 03 ←	→ 02 05 ←	File 1
2	→ ⎵ 03 ⤏ 04 09 ←	→ ⎵ 05 ←	File 2
3	→ ⎵ 09 ←	→ ⎵ 05 ⤏ 06 07 ←	File 2
4	→ ⎵ 09 ←	→ ⎵ 07 ⤏ 08 10 ←	File 1
5	→ ⎵ 09 ⤏ 11 13 ←	→ ⎵ 10 ←	File 2
6	→ 11 13 ←	→ ⎵ ⤏ 12 14 ←	File 1
7	→ ⎵ 13 ⤏ 16 18 ←	→ ⎵ 14 ←	File 2

Fig. 84. Buffer queuing, according to Algorithm F.

queue. This floating-buffer arrangement is an important feature of Algorithm F, since we would be unable to proceed in line 4 if we had chosen File 1 instead of File 2 for the input on line 3.

In order to prove that Algorithm F is valid, we must show two things:

i) There is always an input buffer available (that is, we can always find a k in step F4).

ii) If an input buffer is exhausted while merging, its successor is already present in memory (that is, S[C[i]] is meaningful in step F2).

Suppose (i) is false, so that all buffers are unavailable at some point when we reach step F4. Each time we get to that step, the total amount of unprocessed data among all the buffers is exactly P bufferloads, just enough data to fill P buffers if it were redistributed, since we are inputting and outputting data at the same rate. Some of the buffers are only partially full; but at most one buffer for each file is partially full, so at most P buffers are in that condition. By hypothesis all $2P$ of the buffers are unavailable; therefore at least P of them must be completely full. This can happen only if P are full and P are empty, otherwise we would have too much data. But at most one buffer can be unavailable and empty at any one time; hence (i) cannot be false.

Suppose (ii) is false, so that we have no unprocessed records in memory, for some file, but the current output buffer is not yet full. By the principle of forecasting, we must have no more than one block of data for each of the other files, since we do not read in a block for a file unless that block will be needed before the buffers on any other file are exhausted. Therefore the total number of unprocessed records amounts to at most $P-1$ blocks; adding the unfilled output buffer leads to less than P bufferloads of data in memory, a contradiction.

This argument establishes the validity of Algorithm F; and it also indicates the possibility of pathological circumstances under which the algorithm just barely avoids disaster. An important subtlety that we have not mentioned, regarding the possibility of equal keys, is discussed in exercise 5. See also exercise 4, which considers the case $P = 1$.

One way to terminate Algorithm F gracefully is to set L$[m]$ to ∞ in step F3 if the block just read is the last of a run. (It is customary to indicate the end of a run in some special way.) After all of the data on all of the files has been read, we will eventually find all of the L's equal to ∞ in step F4; then it is usually possible to begin reading the first blocks of the next run on each file, beginning initialization of the next merge phase as the final $P + 1$ blocks are output.

Thus we can keep the output tape going at essentially full speed, without reading more than one tape at a time. An exception to this rule occurs in step F1, where it would be beneficial to read several tapes at once in order to get things going in the beginning; but step F1 can usually be arranged to overlap with the preceding part of the computation.

The idea of looking at the last record in each block, to predict which buffer will empty first, was discovered in 1953 by F. E. Holberton. The technique was first published by E. H. Friend [*JACM* **3** (1956), 144–145, 165]. His rather complicated algorithm used $3P$ input buffers, with three dedicated to each input file; Algorithm F improves the situation by making use of floating buffers, allowing any single file to claim as many as $P + 1$ input buffers at once, yet never needing more than $2P$ in all. A discussion of merging with fewer than $2P$ input buffers appears at the end of this section. Some interesting improvements to Algorithm F are discussed in Section 5.4.9.

Comparative behavior of merge patterns. Let us now use what we know about tapes and merging to compare the effectiveness of the various merge patterns that we have studied in Sections 5.4.2 through 5.4.5. It is very instructive to work out the details when each method is applied to the same task. Consider therefore the problem of sorting a file whose records each contain 100 characters, when there are 100,000 character positions of memory available for data storage — not counting the space needed for the program and its auxiliary variables, or the space occupied by links in a selection tree. (Remember that we are pretending to live in the days when memories were small.) The input appears in random order on tape, in blocks of 5000 characters each, and the output is to appear in the same format. There are five scratch tapes to work with, in addition to the unit containing the input tape.

The total number of records to be sorted is 100,000, but this information is not known in advance to the sorting algorithm.

The foldout illustration in Chart A summarizes the actions that transpire when ten different merging schemes are applied to this data. The best way to look at this important illustration is to imagine that you are actually watching the sort take place: Scan each line slowly from left to right, pretending that you can actually see six tapes reading, writing, rewinding, and/or reading backwards, as indicated on the diagram. During a P-way merge the input tapes will be moving only $1/P$ times as often as the output tape. When the original input tape has been completely read (and rewound "with lock"), Chart A assumes that a skilled computer operator dismounts it and replaces it with a scratch tape, in just 30 seconds. In examples 2, 3, and 4 this is "critical path time" when the computer is idly waiting for the operator to finish; but in the remaining examples, the dismount-reload operation is overlapped by other processing.

Example 1. Read-forward balanced merge. Let's review the specifications of the problem: The records are 100 characters long, there is enough internal memory to hold 1000 records at a time, and each block on the input tape contains 5000 characters (50 records). There are 100,000 records ($= 10,000,000$ characters $= 2000$ blocks) in all.

We are free to choose the block size for intermediate files. A six-tape balanced merge uses three-way merging, so the technique of Algorithm F calls for 8 buffers; we may therefore use blocks containing $1000/8 = 125$ records ($= 12500$ characters) each.

The initial distribution pass can make use of replacement selection (Algorithm 5.4.1R), and in order to keep the tapes running smoothly we may use two input buffers of 50 records each, plus two output buffers of 125 records each. This leaves room for 650 records in the replacement selection tree. Most of the initial runs will therefore be about 1300 records long (10 or 11 blocks); it turns out that 78 initial runs are produced in Chart A, the last one being rather short.

The first merge pass indicated shows nine runs merged to tape 4, instead of alternating between tapes 4, 5, and 6. This makes it possible to do useful work while the computer operator is loading a scratch tape onto unit 6; since the total number S of runs is known once the initial distribution has been completed, the algorithm knows that $\lceil S/9 \rceil$ runs should be merged to tape 4, then $\lceil (S-3)/9 \rceil$ to tape 5, then $\lceil (S-6)/9 \rceil$ to tape 6.

The entire sorting procedure for this example can be summarized in the following way, using the notation introduced in Section 5.4.2:

1^{26}	1^{26}	1^{26}	—	—	—
—	—	—	3^9	3^9	3^8
9^3	9^3	$9^2 6^1$	—	—	—
—	—	—	27^1	27^1	24^1
78^1	—	—	—	—	—

Example 2. Read-forward polyphase merge. The second example in Chart A carries out the polyphase merge, according to Algorithm 5.4.2D. In this case we do five-way merging, so the memory is split into 12 buffers of 83 records each. During the initial replacement selection we have two 50-record input buffers and two 83-record output buffers, leaving 734 records in the tree; so the initial runs this time are about 1468 records long (17 or 18 blocks). The situation illustrated shows that $S = 70$ initial runs were obtained, the last two

actually being only four blocks and one block long, respectively. The merge pattern can be summarized thus:

$0^{13}1^{18}$	$0^{13}1^{17}$	$0^{13}1^{15}$	$0^{12}1^{12}$	$0^{8}1^{8}$	—
1^{15}	1^{14}	1^{12}	1^{8}	—	$0^{8}1^{4}2^{1}5^{3}$
1^{7}	1^{6}	1^{4}	—	4^{8}	$1^{4}2^{1}5^{3}$
1^{3}	1^{2}	—	8^{4}	4^{4}	$2^{1}5^{3}$
1^{1}	—	$16^{1}19^{1}$	8^{2}	4^{2}	5^{2}
—	34^{1}	19^{1}	8^{1}	4^{1}	5^{1}
70^{1}	—	—	—	—	—

Curiously, polyphase actually took about 25 seconds *longer* than the far less sophisticated balanced merge! There are two main reasons for this:

1) Balanced merge was particularly lucky in this case, since $S = 78$ is just less than a perfect power of 3. If 82 initial runs had been produced, the balanced merge would have needed an extra pass.

2) Polyphase merge wasted 30 seconds while the input tape was being changed, and a total of more than 5 minutes went by while it was waiting for rewind operations to be completed. By contrast the balanced merge needed comparatively little rewind time. In the second phase of the polyphase merge, 13 seconds were saved because the 8 dummy runs on tape 6 could be assumed present even while that tape was rewinding; but no other rewind overlap occurred. Therefore polyphase lost out even though it required significantly less read/write time.

Example 3. Read-forward cascade merge. This case is analogous to the preceding, but using Algorithm 5.4.3C. The merging may be summarized thus:

1^{14}	1^{15}	1^{12}	1^{14}	1^{15}	—
1^{5}	1^{9}	—	1^{14}	1^{15}	$1^{3}2^{3}3^{6}$
$5^{1}6^{3}$	5^{3}	$5^{3}6^{2}$	—	1^{1}	2^{2}
—	12^{1}	6^{1}	18^{1}	18^{1}	16^{1}
70^{1}	—	—	—	—	—

(Remember to watch each of these examples in action, by scanning Chart A in the foldout illustration.)

Example 4. Tape-splitting polyphase merge. This procedure, described at the end of Section 5.4.2, allows most of the rewind time to be overlapped. It uses four-way merging, so we divide the memory into ten 100-record buffers; there are 700 records in the replacement selection tree, so it turns out that 72 initial runs are formed. The last run, again, is very short. A distribution scheme analogous to Algorithm 5.4.2D has been used, followed by a simple but somewhat ad hoc method of placing dummy runs:

1^{21}	1^{19}	1^{15}	1^8	—	0^21^9
0^21^{17}	0^21^{15}	0^21^{11}	0^21^4	—	$0^21^94^4$
1^{13}	1^{11}	1^7	—	0^24^4	$0^21^94^4$
1^{10}	1^8	1^4	—	$0^24^43^24^1$	1^84^4
1^6	1^4	—	4^4	$0^24^43^24^1$	1^44^4
1^5	1^3	—	4^43^1	$0^14^43^24^1$	1^34^4
1^2	—	3^17^2	4^43^1	$4^23^24^1$	4^4
1^1	—	$3^17^213^1$	4^33^1	$4^13^24^1$	4^3
—	13^1	$3^17^213^1$	4^23^1	3^24^1	4^2
—	13^114^1	7^213^1	4^13^1	3^14^1	4^1
18^1	13^114^1	7^113^1	3^1	4^1	—
18^1	14^1	13^1	—	—	27^1
—	—	—	72^1	—	—

This turns out to give the best running time of all the examples in Chart A that do not read backwards. Since S will never be very large, it would be possible to develop a more complicated algorithm that places dummy runs in an even better way; see Eq. 5.4.2–(26).

Example 5. Cascade merge with rewind overlap. This procedure runs almost as fast as the previous example, although the algorithm governing it is much simpler. We simply use the cascade sort method as in Algorithm 5.4.3C for the initial distribution, but with $T = 5$ instead of $T = 6$. Then each phase of each "cascade" staggers the tapes so that we ordinarily don't write on a tape until after it has had a chance to be rewound. The pattern, very briefly, is

1^{21}	1^{22}	1^{19}	1^{10}	—	—
1^4	1^7	—	—	$1^22^23^5$	4^{10}
7^2	—	8^3	7^28^2	—	4^1
—	26^1	—	8^1	22^1	16^1
72^1	—	—	—	—	—

Example 6. Read-backward balanced merge. This is like example 1 but with all the rewinding eliminated:

A_1^{26}	A_1^{26}	A_1^{26}	—	—	—
—	—	—	D_3^9	D_3^9	D_3^8
A_9^3	A_9^3	$A_9^2A_6^1$	—	—	—
—	—	—	D_{24}^1	D_{27}^1	D_{27}^1
A_{78}^1	—	—	—	—	—

Since there was comparatively little rewinding in example 1, this scheme is not a great deal better than the read-forward case. In fact, it turns out to be slightly slower than tape-splitting polyphase, in spite of the fortunate value $S = 78$.

Example 7. Read-backward polyphase merge. In this example only five of the six tapes are used, in order to eliminate the time for rewinding and changing the input tape. Thus, the merging is only four-way, and the buffer allocation is like that in examples 4 and 5. A distribution like Algorithm 5.4.2D is used, but with alternating directions of runs, and with tape 1 fixed as the final output tape. First an ascending run is written on tape 1; then descending runs on tapes 2, 3, 4; then ascending runs on 2, 3, 4; then descending on 1, 2, 3; etc. Each time we switch direction, replacement selection usually produces a shorter run, so it turns out that 77 initial runs are formed instead of the 72 in examples 4 and 5.

This procedure results in a distribution of $(22, 21, 19, 15)$ runs, and the next perfect distribution is $(29, 56, 52, 44)$. Exercise 5.4.4–5 shows how to generate strings of merge numbers that can be used to place dummy runs in optimum positions; such a procedure is feasible in practice because the finiteness of a tape reel ensures that S is never too large. Therefore the example in Chart A has been constructed using such a method for dummy run placement (see exercise 7). This turns out to be the fastest of all the examples illustrated.

Example 8. Read-backward cascade merge. As in example 7, only five tapes are used here. This procedure follows Algorithm 5.4.3C, using rewind and forward read to avoid one-way merging (since rewinding is more than twice as fast as reading on MIXT units). Distribution is therefore the same as in example 6. The pattern may be summarized briefly as follows, using $\downarrow$ to denote rewinding:

$$
\begin{array}{ccccc}
A_1^{21} & A_1^{22} & A_1^{19} & A_1^{10} & - \\[4pt]
A_1^4\!\downarrow & A_1^7\!\downarrow & - & D_1^2 D_2^2 D_3^5 & D_4^{10} \\[4pt]
A_8 A_7^2 & A_5^2 & A_9^4 & - & D_4^1\!\downarrow \\[4pt]
- & D_{17} & A_9\!\downarrow & D_{25} & D_{21} \\[4pt]
A_{72} & - & - & - & -
\end{array}
$$

Example 9. Read-backward oscillating sort. Oscillating sort with $T = 5$ (Algorithm 5.4.5B) can use buffer allocation as in examples 4, 5, 7, and 8, since it does four-way merging. However, replacement selection does not behave in the same way, since a run of length 700 (not 1400 or so) is output just before entering each merge phase, in order to clear the internal memory. Consequently 85 runs are produced in this example, instead of 72. Some of the key steps in the process are

$$
\begin{array}{ccccc}
- & A_1 & A_1 A_1 & A_1 A_1 & A_1 A_1 \\[4pt]
D_4 & - & A_1 & A_1 & A_1
\end{array}
$$

· ·

D_4D_4	D_4D_4	D_4D_4	D_4	—
D_4	D_4	D_4	—	A_{16}
$\cdots$				
D_4	$A_{16}D_4D_4$	$A_{16}D_4$	$A_{16}D_4A_1$	A_{16}
D_4	$A_{16}D_4D_4$	$A_{16}D_4D_1$	$A_{16}D_4$	A_{16}
—	$A_{16}D_4$	$A_{16}D_4$	A_{16}	$A_{16}A_{13}$
—	$A_{16}D_4$	A_{16}	$A_{16}A_4$	$A_{16}A_{13}$
—	A_{16}	$A_{16}A_4$	$A_{16}A_4$	$A_{16}A_{13}$
D_{37}	—	$A_{16}\downarrow$	$A_{16}\downarrow$	$A_{16}\downarrow$
—	A_{85}	—	—	—

Example 10. Read-forward oscillating sort. In the final example, replacement selection is not used because all initial runs must be the same length. Therefore full core loads of 1000 records are sorted internally whenever an initial run is required; this makes $S = 100$. Some key steps in the process are

A_1	A_1	A_1	A_1	A_1
—	—	—	—	A_1A_4
$\cdots$				
A_1	A_1	A_1	A_1	A_1A_4
—	—	—	A_1A_4	$\cancel{A_1}A_4$
—	—	—	A_1A_4	A_1A_4
$\cdots$				
A_1	A_1A_4	A_1A_4	A_1A_4	A_1A_4
A_1A_4	$\cancel{A_1}A_4$	$\cancel{A_1}A_4$	$\cancel{A_1}A_4$	$\cancel{A_1}A_4$
$A_1A_4A_{16}$	—	—	—	—
$\cdots$				
—	A_1A_4	A_1A_4	A_1A_4	$A_1A_4A_{16}A_{64}$
A_4	$\cancel{A_1}A_4$	$\cancel{A_1}A_4$	$\cancel{A_1}A_4$	$\cancel{A_1}A_4A_{16}A_{64}$
A_4A_{16}	—	—	—	$\cancel{A_1}\cancel{A_4}A_{16}A_{64}$
$\cancel{A_4}A_{16}$	A_4	—	—	$\cancel{A_1}\cancel{A_4}A_{16}A_{64}$
—	—	—	A_{36}	$\cancel{A_1}\cancel{A_4}\cancel{A_{16}}A_{64}$
A_{100}	—	—	—	—

This routine turns out to be slowest of all, partly because it does not use replacement selection, but mostly because of its rather awkward ending (a two-way merge).

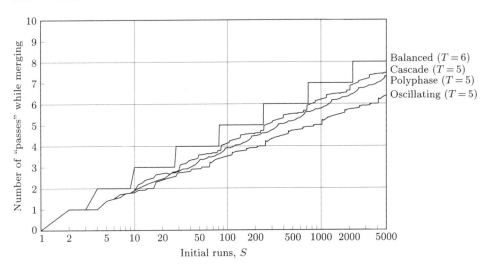

Fig. 85. A somewhat misleading way to compare merge patterns.

Estimating the running time. Let's see now how to figure out the approximate execution time of a sorting method using MIXT tapes. Could we have predicted the outcomes shown in Chart A without carrying out a detailed simulation?

One way that has traditionally been used to compare different merge patterns is to superimpose graphs such as we have seen in Figs. 70, 74, and 78. These graphs show the effective number of passes over the data, as a function of the number of initial runs, assuming that each initial run has approximately the same length. (See Fig. 85.) But this is *not* a very realistic comparison, because we have seen that different methods lead to different numbers of initial runs; furthermore there is a different overhead time caused by the relative frequency of interblock gaps, and the rewind time also has significant effects. All of these machine-dependent features make it impossible to prepare charts that provide a valid machine-independent comparison of the methods. On the other hand, Fig. 85 does show us that, except for balanced merge, the effective number of passes can be reasonably well approximated by smooth curves of the form $\alpha \ln S + \beta$. Therefore we can make a fairly good comparison of the methods in any particular situation, by studying formulas that approximate the running time. Our goal, of course, is to find formulas that are simple yet sufficiently realistic.

Let us now attempt to develop such formulas, in terms of the following parameters:

N = number of records to be sorted,

C = number of characters per record,

M = number of character positions available in the internal memory (assumed to be a multiple of C),

τ = number of seconds to read or write one character,

$\rho\tau$ = number of seconds to rewind over one character,

$\sigma\tau$ = number of seconds for stop/start time delay,

γ = number of characters per interblock gap,

δ = number of seconds for operator to dismount and replace input tape,

B_i = number of characters per block in the unsorted input,

B_o = number of characters per block in the sorted output.

For MIXT we have $\tau = 1/60000$, $\rho = 2/5$, $\sigma = 300$, $\gamma = 480$. The example application treated above has $N = 100000$, $C = 100$, $M = 100000$, $\delta = 30$, $B_i = B_o = 5000$. These parameters are usually the machine and data characteristics that affect sorting time most critically (although rewind time is often given by a more complicated expression than a simple ratio ρ). Given the parameters above and a merge pattern, we shall compute further quantities such as

P = maximum order of merge in the pattern,

P' = number of records in replacement selection tree,

S = number of initial runs,

$\pi = \alpha \ln S + \beta$ = approximate average number of times each character is read and written, not counting the initial distribution or the final merge,

$\pi' = \alpha' \ln S + \beta'$ = approximate average number of times rewinding over each character during intermediate merge phases,

B = number of characters per block in the intermediate merge phases,

$\omega_i, \omega, \omega_o$ = "overhead ratio," the effective time required to read or write a character (due to gaps and stop/start) divided by the hardware time τ.

The examples of Chart A have chosen block and buffer sizes according to the formula

$$B = \left\lfloor \frac{M}{C(2P+2)} \right\rfloor C, \qquad (1)$$

so that the blocks can be as large as possible consistent with the buffering scheme of Algorithm F. (In order to avoid trouble during the final pass, P should be small enough that (1) makes $B \geq B_o$.) The size of the tree during replacement selection is then

$$P' = (M - 2B_i - 2B)/C. \qquad (2)$$

For random data the number of initial runs S can be estimated as

$$S \approx \left\lceil \frac{N}{2P'} + \frac{7}{6} \right\rceil, \qquad (3)$$

using the results of Section 5.4.1. Assuming that $B_i < B$ and that the input tape can be run at full speed during the distribution (see below), it takes about $NC\omega_i\tau$ seconds to distribute the initial runs, where

$$\omega_i = (B_i + \gamma)/B_i. \tag{4}$$

While merging, the buffering scheme allows simultaneous reading, writing, and computing, but the frequent switching between input tapes means that we must add the stop/start time penalty; therefore we set

$$\omega = (B + \gamma + \sigma)/B, \tag{5}$$

and the merge time is approximately

$$(\pi + \rho\pi')NC\omega\tau. \tag{6}$$

This formula penalizes rewind slightly, since ω includes stop/start time, but other considerations, such as rewind interlock and the penalty for reading from load point, usually compensate for this. The final merge pass, assuming that $B_o \le B$, is constrained by the overhead ratio

$$\omega_o = (B_o + \gamma)/B_o. \tag{7}$$

We may estimate the running time of the final merge and rewind as

$$nC(1 + \rho)\omega_o\tau;$$

in practice it might take somewhat longer due to the presence of unequal block lengths (input and output are not synchronized as in Algorithm F), but the running time will be pretty much the same for all merge patterns.

Before going into more specific formulas for individual patterns, let us try to justify two of the assumptions made above.

a) *Can replacement selection keep up with the input tape?* In the examples of Chart A it probably can, since it takes about ten iterations of the inner loop of Algorithm 5.4.1R to select the next record, and we have $C\omega_i\tau > 1667$ microseconds in which to do this. With careful programming of the replacement selection loop, this can be done on most machines (even in the 1970s). Notice that the situation is somewhat less critical while merging: The computation time per record is almost always less than the tape time per record during a P-way merge, since P isn't very large.

b) *Should we really choose B to be the maximum possible buffer size, as in* (1)? A large buffer size cuts down the overhead ratio ω in (5); but it also increases the number of initial runs S, since P' is decreased. It is not immediately clear which factor is more important. Considering the merging time as a function of $x = CP'$, we can express it in the approximate form

$$\left(\theta_1 \ln\left(\frac{N}{x} + \frac{7}{6}\right) + \theta_2\right)\left(\frac{\theta_3 - x}{\theta_4 - x}\right) \tag{8}$$

for some appropriate constants $\theta_1, \theta_2, \theta_3, \theta_4$, with $\theta_3 > \theta_4$. Differentiating with respect to x shows that there is some N_0 such that for all $N \ge N_0$ it does not pay to increase x at the expense of buffer size. In the sorting application of Chart A, for example, N_0 turns out to be roughly 10000; when sorting more than 10000 records the large buffer size is superior.

Note, however, that with balanced merge the number of passes jumps sharply when S passes a power of P. If an approximation to N is known in advance, the buffer size should be chosen so that S will most likely be slightly less than a power of P. For example, the buffer size for the first line of Chart A was 12500; since $S = 78$, this was very satisfactory, but if S had turned out to be 82 it would have been much better to decrease the buffer size a little.

Formulas for the ten examples. Returning to Chart A, let us try to give formulas that approximate the running time in each of the ten methods. In most cases the basic formula

$$NC\omega_i\tau + (\pi + \rho\pi')NC\omega\tau + (1+\rho)NC\omega_o\tau \tag{9}$$

will be a sufficiently good approximation to the overall sorting time, once we have specified the number of intermediate merge passes $\pi = \alpha \ln S + \beta$ and the number of intermediate rewind passes $\pi' = \alpha' \ln S + \beta'$. Sometimes it is necessary to add a further correction to (9); details for each method can be worked out as follows:

Example 1. Read-forward balanced merge. The formulas

$$\pi = \lceil \ln S/\ln P \rceil - 1, \qquad \pi' = \lceil \ln S/\ln P \rceil / P$$

may be used for P-way merging on $2P$ tapes.

Example 2. Read-forward polyphase merge. We may take $\pi' \approx \pi$, since every phase is usually followed by a rewind of about the same length as the previous merge. From Table 5.4.2–1 we get the values $\alpha \approx 0.795$, $\beta \approx 0.864 - 2$, in the case of six tapes. (We subtract 2 because the table entry includes the initial and final passes as well as the intermediate ones.) The time for rewinding the input tape after the initial distribution, namely $\rho NC\omega_i\tau + \delta$, should be added to (9).

Example 3. Read-forward cascade merge. Table 5.4.3–1 gives the values $\alpha \approx 0.773$, $\beta \approx 0.808 - 2$. Rewind time is comparatively difficult to estimate; perhaps setting $\pi' \approx \pi$ is accurate enough. As in example 2, we need to add the initial rewind time to (9).

Example 4. Tape-splitting polyphase merge. Table 5.4.2–6 tells us that $\alpha \approx 0.752$, $\beta \approx 1.024 - 2$. The rewind time is almost overlapped except after the initialization ($\rho NC\omega_i\tau + \delta$) and two phases near the end ($2\rho NC\omega\tau$ times 36 percent). We may also subtract 0.18 from β since the first half phase is overlapped by the initial rewind.

Example 5. Cascade merge with rewind overlap. In this case we use Table 5.4.3–1 for $T = 5$, to get $\alpha \approx 0.897$, $\beta \approx 0.800 - 2$. Nearly all of the unoverlapped rewind occurs just after the initial distribution and just after each two-way merge. After a perfect initial distribution, the longest tape contains about $1/g$ of the data, where g is the "growth ratio." After each two-way merge the amount of rewind in the six-tape case is $d_k d_{n-k}$ (see exercise 5.4.3–5), hence the amount of rewind after two-way merges in the T-tape case can be shown to be approximately

$$\left(2/(2T-1)\right)\left(1 - \cos\left(4\pi/(2T-1)\right)\right)$$

of the file. In our case, $T = 5$, this is $\frac{2}{9}(1 - \cos 80°) \approx 0.184$ of the file, and the number of times it occurs is $0.946 \ln S + 0.796 - 2$.

Example 6. Read-backward balanced merge. This is like example 1, except that most of the rewinding is eliminated. The change in direction from forward to backward causes some delays, but they are not significant. There is a 50-50 chance that rewinding will be necessary before the final pass, so we may take $\pi' = 1/(2P)$.

Example 7. Read-backward polyphase merge. Since replacement selection in this case produces runs that change direction about every P times, we must replace (3) by another formula for S. A reasonably good approximation, suggested by exercise 5.4.1–24, is $S = \lceil N(3+1/P)/(6P')\rceil + 1$. All rewind time is eliminated, and Table 5.4.2–1 gives $\alpha \approx 0.863$, $\beta \approx 0.921 - 2$.

Example 8. Read-backward cascade merge. From Table 5.4.3–1 we have $\alpha \approx 0.897$, $\beta \approx 0.800 - 2$. The rewind time can be estimated as twice the difference between "passes with copying" minus "passes without copying" in that table, plus $1/(2P)$ in case the final merge must be preceded by rewinding to get ascending order.

Example 9. Read-backward oscillating sort. In this case replacement selection has to be started and stopped many times; bursts of $P - 1$ to $2P - 1$ runs are distributed at a time, averaging P in length; the average length of runs therefore turns out to be approximately $P'(2P - 4/3)/P$, and we may estimate $S = \lceil N/((2 - 4/(3P))P')\rceil + 1$. A little time is used to switch from merging to distribution and vice-versa; this is approximately the time to read in P' records from the input tape, namely $P'C\omega_i\tau$, and it occurs about S/P times. Rewind time and merging time may be estimated as in example 6.

Example 10. Read-forward oscillating sort. This method is not easy to analyze, because the final "cleanup" phases performed after the input is exhausted are not as efficient as the earlier phases. Ignoring this troublesome aspect, and simply calling it one extra pass, we can estimate the merging time by setting $\alpha = 1/\ln P$, $\beta = 0$, and $\pi' = \pi/P$. The distribution of runs is somewhat different in this case, since replacement selection is not used; we set $P' = M/C$ and $S = \lceil N/P'\rceil$. With care we will be able to overlap computing, reading, and writing during the distribution, with an additional factor of about $(M+2B)/M$ in the overhead. The "mode-switching" time mentioned in example 9 is not needed in the present case because it is overlapped by rewinding. So the estimated sorting time in this case is (9) plus $2BNC\omega_i\tau/M$.

Table 1

SUMMARY OF SORTING TIME ESTIMATES

Ex.	P	B	P'	S	ω	α	β	α'	β'	(9)	Additions to (9)	Est. total	Actual total
1	3	12500	650	79	1.062	0.910	−1.000	0.303	0.000	1064		1064	1076
2	5	8300	734	70	1.094	0.795	−1.136	0.795	−1.136	1010	$\rho NC\omega_i\tau + \delta$	1113	1103
3	5	8300	734	70	1.094	0.773	−1.192	0.773	−1.192	972	$\rho NC\omega_i\tau + \delta$	1075	1127
4	4	10000	700	73	1.078	0.752	−0.994	0.000	0.720	844	$\rho NC\omega_i\tau + \delta$	947	966
5	4	10000	700	73	1.078	0.897	−1.200	0.173	0.129	972		972	992
6	3	12500	650	79	1.062	0.910	−1.000	0.000	0.167	981		981	980
7	4	10000	700	79	1.078	0.863	−1.079	0.000	0.000	922		922	907
8	4	10000	700	73	1.078	0.897	−1.200	0.098	0.117	952		952	949
9	4	10000	700	87	1.078	0.721	−1.000	0.000	0.125	846	$P'SC\omega_i\tau/P$	874	928
10	4	10000	—	100	1.078	0.721	0.000	0.180	0.000	1095	$2BNC\omega_i\tau/M$	1131	1158

Table 1 shows that the estimates are not too bad in these examples, although in a few cases there is a discrepancy of 50 seconds or so. The formulas in examples 2 and 3 indicate that cascade merge should be preferable to polyphase on six tapes, yet in practice polyphase was better. The reason is that graphs like Fig. 85 (which shows the five-tape case) are more nearly straight lines for the polyphase algorithm; cascade is superior to polyphase on six tapes for $14 \le S \le 15$ and $43 \le S \le 55$, near the "perfect" cascade numbers 15 and 55, but the polyphase distribution of Algorithm 5.4.2D is equal or better for all other $S \le 100$. Cascade will win over polyphase as $S \to \infty$, but S doesn't actually approach ∞. The underestimate in example 9 is due to similar circumstances; polyphase was superior to oscillating even though the asymptotic theory tells us that oscillating will be better for large S.

Some miscellaneous remarks. It is now appropriate to make a few more or less random observations about tape merging.

• The formulas above show that the cost of tape sorting is essentially a function of N times C, not of N and C independently. Except for a few relatively minor considerations (such as the fact that B was taken to be a multiple of C), our formulas say that it takes about as long to sort one million records of 10 characters each as to sort 100,000 records of 100 characters each. Actually there may be a difference, not revealed in our formulas, because of the space used by link fields during replacement selection. In any event the size of the *key* makes hardly any difference, unless keys get so long and complicated that internal computation cannot keep up with the tapes.

With long records and short keys it is tempting to "detach" the keys, sort them first, and then somehow rearrange the records as a whole. But this idea doesn't really work; it merely postpones the agony, because the final rearrangement procedure takes about as long as a conventional merge sort would take.

• When writing a sort routine that is to be used repeatedly, it is wise to estimate the running time very carefully and to compare the theory with actual observed performance. Since the theory of sorting has been fairly well developed, this procedure has been known to turn up bugs in the input/output hardware or software on existing systems; the service was substantially slower than it should have been, yet nobody had noticed it until the sorting routine ran too slowly!

• Our analysis of replacement selection has been carried out for "random" files, but the files that actually arise in practice very often have a good deal of existing order. (In fact, sometimes people will sort a file that is already in order, just to be sure.) Therefore experience has shown that replacement selection is preferable to other kinds of internal sort, even more so than our formulas indicate. This advantage is slightly mitigated in the case of read-backward polyphase sorting, since a number of descending runs must be produced; indeed, R. L. Gilstad (who first published the polyphase merge) originally rejected the read-backward technique for that reason. But he noticed later that alternating directions will still pick up long ascending runs. Furthermore, read-backward polyphase is the only standard technique that likes descending input files as well as ascending ones.

• Another advantage of replacement selection is that it allows simultaneous reading, writing, and computing. If we merely did the internal sort in an obvious way — filling the memory, sorting it, then writing it out as it becomes filled with the next load — the distribution pass would take about twice as long.

The only other internal sort we have discussed that appears to be amenable to simultaneous reading, writing, and computing is heapsort. Suppose for convenience that the internal memory holds 1000 records, and that each block on tape holds 100. Example 10 of Chart A was prepared with the following strategy, letting $B_1 B_2 \ldots B_{10}$ stand for the contents of memory divided into ten 100-record blocks:

Step 0. Fill memory, and make the elements of $B_2 \ldots B_{10}$ satisfy the inequalities for a heap (with smallest element at the root).

Step 1. Make $B_1 \ldots B_{10}$ into a heap, then select out the least 100 records and move them to B_{10}.

Step 2. Write out B_{10}, while selecting the smallest 100 records of $B_1 \ldots B_9$ and moving them to B_9.

Step 3. Read into B_{10}, and write out B_9, while selecting the smallest 100 records of $B_1 \ldots B_8$ and moving them to B_8.

$$\vdots$$

Step 9. Read into B_4, and write out B_3, while selecting the smallest 100 records of $B_1 B_2$ and moving them to B_2 and while making the heap inequalities valid in $B_5 \ldots B_{10}$.

Step 10. Read into B_3, and write out B_2, while sorting B_1 and while making the heap inequalities valid in $B_4 \ldots B_{10}$.

Step 11. Read into B_2, and write out B_1, while making the heap inequalities valid in $B_3 \ldots B_{10}$.

Step 12. Read into B_1, while making the heap inequalities valid in $B_2 \ldots B_{10}$. Return to step 1. ∎

- We have been assuming that the number N of records to be sorted is not known in advance. Actually in most computer applications it would be possible to keep track of the number of records in all files at all times, and we could assume that our computer system is capable of telling us the value of N. How much help would this be? Unfortunately, not very much! We have seen that replacement selection is very advantageous, but it leads to an unpredictable number of initial runs. In a balanced merge we could use information about N to set the buffer size B in such a way that S will probably be just less than a power of P; and in a polyphase distribution with optimum placement of dummy runs we could use information about N to decide what level to shoot for (see Table 5.4.2–2).

- Tape drives tend to be the least reliable part of a computer. Therefore *the original input tape should never be destroyed until it is known that the entire sort has been satisfactorily completed.* The "operator dismount time" is annoying in some of the examples of Chart A, but it would be too risky to overwrite the input in view of the probability that something might go wrong during a long sort.

- When changing from forward write to backward read, we could save some time by never writing the last bufferload onto tape; it will just be read back in again anyway. But Chart A shows that this trick actually saves comparatively little time, except in the oscillating sort where directions are reversed frequently.

- Although a large computer system might have lots of tape units, we might be better off not using them all. The percentage difference between $\log_P S$ and $\log_{P+1} S$ is not very great when P is large, and a higher order of merge usually implies a smaller block size. (Consider also the poor computer operator who has to mount all those scratch tapes.) On the other hand, exercise 12 describes an interesting way to make use of additional tape units, grouping them so as to overlap input/output time without increasing the order of merge.

- On machines like MIX, which have fixed rather small block sizes, hardly any internal memory is needed while merging. Oscillating sort then becomes more attractive, because it becomes possible to maintain the replacement selection tree in memory while merging. In fact we can improve on oscillating sort in this case (as suggested by Colin J. Bell in 1962), merging a new initial run into the output every time we merge from the working tapes.

- We have observed that multireel files should be sorted one reel at a time, in order to avoid excessive tape handling. This is sometimes called a "reel time" application. Actually a balanced merge on six tapes can sort *three* reelfuls, up until the time of the final merge, if it has been programmed carefully.

To merge a fairly large number of individually sorted reels, a minimum-path-length merging tree will be fastest (see Section 5.4.4). This construction was first made by E. H. Friend [*JACM* **3** (1956), 166–167]; then W. H. Burge [*Information and Control* **1** (1958), 181–197] pointed out that an optimum way to merge runs of given (possibly unequal) lengths is obtained by constructing a tree with minimum *weighted* path length, using the run lengths as weights (see Sections 2.3.4.5 and 5.4.9), if we ignore tape handling time.

• Our discussions have blithely assumed that we have direct control over the input/output instructions for tape units, and that no complicated operating system keeps us from using tape as efficiently as the tape designers intended. These idealistic assumptions give us insights into the tape merging problem, and may give some insights into the proper design of operating system interfaces, but we should realize that multiprogramming and multiprocessing can make the situation considerably more complicated.

• The issues we have studied in this section were first discussed in print by E. H. Friend [*JACM* **3** (1956), 134–168], W. Zoberbier [*Elektronische Daten-verarbeitung* **5** (1960), 28–44], and M. A. Goetz [*Digital Computer User's Handbook* (New York: McGraw–Hill, 1967), 1.292–1.320].

Summary. We can sum up what we have learned about the relative efficiencies of different approaches to tape sorting in the following way:

Theorem A. *It is difficult to decide which merge pattern is best in a given situation.* ▌

The examples we have seen in Chart A show how 100,000 randomly ordered 100-character records (or 1 million 10-character records) might be sorted using six tapes under realistic assumptions. This much data fills about half of a tape, and it can be sorted in about 15 to 19 minutes on the MIXT tapes. However, there is considerable variation in available tape equipment, and running times for such a job could vary between about four minutes and about two hours on different machines of the 1970s. In our examples, about 3 minutes of the total time were used for initial distribution of runs and internal sorting; about $4\frac{1}{2}$ minutes were used for the final merge and rewinding the output tape; and about $7\frac{1}{2}$ to $11\frac{1}{2}$ minutes were spent in intermediate stages of merging.

Given six tapes that cannot read backwards, the best sorting method under our assumptions was the "tape-splitting polyphase merge" (example 4); and for tapes that do allow backward reading, the best method turned out to be read-backward polyphase with a complicated placement of dummy runs (example 7). Oscillating sort (example 9) was a close second. In both cases the cascade merge provided a simpler alternative that was only slightly slower (examples 5 and 8). In the read-forward case, a straightforward balanced merge (example 1) was surprisingly effective, partly by luck in this particular example but partly also because it spends comparatively little time rewinding.

The situation would change somewhat if we had a different number of available tapes.

Sort generators. Given the wide variability of data and equipment characteristics, it is almost impossible to write a single external sorting program that is satisfactory in a variety of different applications. And it is also rather difficult to prepare a program that really handles tapes efficiently. Therefore the preparation of sorting software is a particularly challenging job. A *sort generator* is a program that produces machine code specially tailored to particular sorting applications, based on parameters that describe the data format and the hardware configuration. Such a program is often tied to high-level languages such as COBOL or PL/I.

One of the features normally provided by a sort generator is the ability to insert the user's "own coding," a sequence of special instructions to be incorporated into the first and last passes of the sorting routine. First-pass own coding is usually used to edit the input records, often shrinking them or slightly expanding them into a form that is easier to sort. For example, suppose that the input records are to be sorted on a nine-character key that represents a date in month-day-year format:

> JUL041776 OCT311517 NOV051605 JUL141789 NOV071917

On the first pass the three-letter month code can be looked up in a table, and the month codes can be replaced by numbers with the most significant fields at the left:

> 17760704 15171031 16051105 17890714 19171107

This decreases the record length and makes subsequent comparisons much simpler. (An even more compact code could also be substituted.) Last-pass own coding can be used to restore the original format, and/or to make other desired changes to the file, and/or to compute some function of the output records. The merging algorithms we have studied are organized in such a way that it is easy to distinguish the last pass from other merges. Notice that when own coding is present there must be at least two passes over the file even if it is initially in order. Own coding that changes the record size can make it difficult for the oscillating sort to overlap some of its input/output operations.

Sort generators also take care of system details like tape label conventions, and they often provide for "hash totals" or other checks to make sure that none of the data has been lost or altered. Sometimes there are provisions for stopping the sort at convenient places and resuming later. The fanciest generators allow records to have dynamically varying lengths [see D. J. Waks, *CACM* **6** (1963), 267–272].

*Merging with fewer buffers. We have seen that $2P + 2$ buffers are sufficient to keep tapes moving rapidly during a P-way merge. Let us conclude this section by making a mathematical analysis of the merging time when *fewer* than $2P + 2$ buffers are present.

Two output buffers are clearly desirable, since we can be writing from one while forming the next block of output in the other. Therefore we may ignore the output question entirely, and concentrate only on the input.

Suppose there are $P + Q$ input buffers, where $1 \le Q \le P$. We shall use the following approximate model of the situation, as suggested by L. J. Woodrum [*IBM Systems J.* **9** (1970), 118–144]: It takes one unit of time to read a block of tape. During this time there is a probability p_0 that no input buffers have been emptied, p_1 that one has been emptied, $p_{\ge 2}$ that two or more have been, etc. When completing a tape read we are in one of $Q + 1$ states:

State 0. Q buffers are empty; we begin to read a block into one of them from the appropriate file, using the forecasting technique explained earlier in this section. After one unit of time we go to state 1 with probability p_0, otherwise we remain in state 0.

State 1. $Q - 1$ buffers are empty; we begin to read into one of them, forecasting the appropriate file. After one unit of time we go to state 2 with probability p_0, to state 1 with probability p_1, and to state 0 with probability $p_{\geq 2}$.

$$\vdots$$

State $Q - 1$. One buffer is empty; we begin to read into it, forecasting the appropriate file. After one unit of time we go to state Q with probability p_0, to state $Q - 1$ with probability p_1, ..., to state 1 with probability p_{Q-1}, and to state 0 with probability $p_{\geq Q}$.

State Q. All buffers are filled. Tape reading stops for an average of μ units of time and then we go to state $Q - 1$.

We start in state 0. This model of the situation corresponds to a *Markov process* (see exercise 2.3.4.2–26), which can be analyzed via generating functions in the following interesting way: Let z be an arbitrary parameter, and assume that each time we have a chance to read from tape we make a decision to do so with probability z, but we decide to terminate the algorithm with probability $1 - z$. Now let $g_Q(z) = \sum_{n \geq 0} a_n^{(Q)} z^n (1 - z)$ be the average number of times that state Q occurs in such a process; it follows that $a_n^{(Q)}$ is the average number of times state Q occurs when exactly n blocks have been read. Then $n + a_n^{(Q)} \mu$ is the average total time for input plus computation. If we had perfect overlap, as in the $(2P + 2)$-buffer algorithm, the total time would be only n units, so $a_n^{(Q)} \mu$ represents the "reading hangup" time.

Let A_{ij} be the probability that we go from state i to state j in this process, for $0 \leq i, j \leq Q + 1$, where $Q + 1$ is a new "stopped" state. For example, the A-matrix takes the following forms for small Q:

$$Q = 1: \quad \begin{pmatrix} p_{\geq 1}z & p_0 z & 1 - z \\ 1 & 0 & 0 \\ 0 & 0 & 0 \end{pmatrix},$$

$$Q = 2: \quad \begin{pmatrix} p_{\geq 1}z & p_0 z & 0 & 1 - z \\ p_{\geq 2}z & p_1 z & p_0 z & 1 - z \\ 0 & 1 & 0 & 0 \\ 0 & 0 & 0 & 0 \end{pmatrix},$$

$$Q = 3: \quad \begin{pmatrix} p_{\geq 1}z & p_0 z & 0 & 0 & 1 - z \\ p_{\geq 2}z & p_1 z & p_0 z & 0 & 1 - z \\ p_{\geq 3}z & p_2 z & p_1 z & p_0 z & 1 - z \\ 0 & 0 & 1 & 0 & 0 \\ 0 & 0 & 0 & 0 & 0 \end{pmatrix}.$$

Exercise 2.3.4.2–26(b) tells us that $g_Q(z) = \text{cofactor}_{Q0}(I - A)/\det(I - A)$. Thus for example when $Q = 1$ we have

$$g_1(z) = \det \begin{pmatrix} 0 & -p_0 z & z-1 \\ 1 & 0 & 0 \\ 0 & 0 & 1 \end{pmatrix} \Big/ \det \begin{pmatrix} 1 - p_{\geq 1}z & -p_0 z & z-1 \\ -1 & 1 & 0 \\ 0 & 0 & 1 \end{pmatrix}$$

$$= \frac{p_0 z}{1 - p_1 z - p_0 z} = \frac{p_0 z}{1 - z} = \sum_{n \geq 0} n p_0 z^n (1 - z),$$

so $a_n^{(1)} = np_0$. This of course was obvious *a priori*, since the problem is very simple when $Q = 1$. A similar calculation when $Q = 2$ (see exercise 14) gives the less obvious formula

$$a_n^{(2)} = \frac{p_0^2 n}{1 - p_1} - \frac{p_0^2(1 - p_1^n)}{(1 - p_1)^2}. \tag{10}$$

In general we can show that $a_n^{(Q)}$ has the form $\alpha^{(Q)} n + O(1)$ as $n \to \infty$, where the constant $\alpha^{(Q)}$ is not terribly difficult to calculate. (See exercise 15.) It turns out that $\alpha^{(3)} = p_0^3 / ((1 - p_1)^2 - p_0 p_2)$.

The nature of merging makes it fairly reasonable to assume that $\mu = 1/P$ and that we have a binomial distribution

$$p_k = \binom{P}{k} \left(\frac{1}{P}\right)^k \left(\frac{P-1}{P}\right)^{P-k}.$$

For example, when $P = 5$ we have $p_0 = .32768$, $p_1 = .4096$, $p_2 = .2048$, $p_3 = .0512$, $p_4 = .0064$, and $p_5 = .00032$; hence $\alpha^{(1)} \approx 0.328$, $\alpha^{(2)} \approx 0.182$, and $\alpha^{(3)} \approx 0.125$. In other words, if we use $5 + 3$ input buffers instead of $5 + 5$, we can expect an additional "reading hangup" time of about $0.125/5 \approx 2.5$ percent.

Of course this model is only a very rough approximation; we know that when $Q = P$ there is no hangup time at all, but the model says that there is. The extra reading hangup time for smaller Q just about counterbalances the savings in overhead gained by having larger blocks, so the simple scheme with $Q = P$ seems to be vindicated.

EXERCISES

1. [13] Give a formula for the exact number of characters per tape, when every block on the tape contains n characters. Assume that the tape could hold exactly 23000000 characters if there were no interblock gaps.

2. [15] Explain why the first buffer for File 2, in line 6 of Fig. 84, is completely blank.

3. [20] Would Algorithm F work properly if there were only $2P - 1$ input buffers instead of $2P$? If so, prove it; if not, give an example where it fails.

4. [20] How can Algorithm F be changed so that it works also when $P = 1$?

▶ 5. [21] When equal keys are present on different files, it is necessary to be very careful in the forecasting process. Explain why, and show how to avoid difficulty by defining the merging and forecasting operations of Algorithm F more precisely.

6. [*22*] What changes should be made to Algorithm 5.4.3C in order to convert it into an algorithm for cascade merge *with rewind overlap*, on $T + 1$ tapes?

▶ **7.** [*26*] The initial distribution in example 7 of Chart A produces

$$(A_1 D_1)^{11} \qquad D_1 (A_1 D_1)^{10} \qquad D_1 (A_1 D_1)^9 \qquad D_1 (A_1 D_1)^7$$

on tapes 1–4, where $(A_1 D_1)^7$ means $A_1 D_1 A_1 D_1 A_1 D_1 A_1 D_1 A_1 D_1 A_1 D_1 A_1 D_1$. Show how to insert additional A_0's and D_0's in a "best possible" way (in the sense that the overall number of initial runs processed while merging is minimized), bringing the distribution up to

$$A(DA)^{14} \qquad (DA)^{28} \qquad (DA)^{26} \qquad (DA)^{22}.$$

Hint: To preserve parity it is necessary to insert many of the A_0's and D_0's as adjacent pairs. The merge numbers for each initial run may be computed as in exercise 5.4.4–5; some simplification occurs since adjacent runs always have adjacent merge numbers.

8. [*20*] Chart A shows that most of the schemes for initial distribution of runs (with the exception of the initial distribution for the cascade merge) tend to put consecutive runs onto different tapes. If consecutive runs went onto the same tape we could save the stop/start time; would it therefore be a good idea to modify the distribution algorithms so that they switch tapes less often?

▶ **9.** [*22*] Estimate how long the read-backward polyphase algorithm would have taken in Chart A, if we had used all $T = 6$ tapes for sorting, instead of $T = 5$ as in example 7. Was it wise to avoid using the input tape?

10. [*M23*] Use the analyses in Sections 5.4.2 and 5.4.3 to show that the length of each rewind during a standard six-tape polyphase or cascade merge is rarely more than about 54 percent of the file (except for the initial and final rewinds, which cover the entire file).

11. [*23*] By modifying the appropriate entries in Table 1, estimate how long the first nine examples of Chart A would have taken if we had a combined low speed/high speed rewind. Assume that $\rho = 1$ when the tape is less than about one-fourth full, and that the rewind time for fuller tapes is approximately five seconds plus the time that would be obtained for $\rho = \frac{1}{5}$. Change example 8 so that it uses cascade merge *with* copying, since rewinding and reading forward is slower than copying in this case. [*Hint:* Use the result of exercise 10.]

12. [*40*] Consider partitioning six tapes into three pairs of tapes, with each pair playing the role of a single tape in a polyphase merge with $T = 3$. One tape of each pair will contains blocks $1, 3, 5, \ldots$ and the other tape will contain blocks $2, 4, 6, \ldots$; in this way we can essentially have two input tapes and two output tapes active at all times while merging, effectively doubling the merging speed.

    a) Find an appropriate way to extend Algorithm F to this situation. How many buffers should there be?

    b) Estimate the total running time that would be obtained if this method were used to sort 100,000 100-character records, considering both the read-forward and read-backward cases.

13. [*20*] Can a five-tape oscillating sort, as defined in Algorithm 5.4.5B, be used to sort four reelfuls of input data, up until the time of the final merge?

14. [*M19*] Derive (10).

15. [HM29] Prove that $g_Q(z) = h_Q(z)/(1-z)$, where $h_Q(z)$ is a rational function of z having no singularities inside the unit circle; hence $a_n^{(Q)} = h_Q(1)n + O(1)$ as $n \to \infty$. In particular, show that

$$h_3(1) = \det \begin{pmatrix} 0 & -p_0 & 0 & 0 \\ 0 & 1-p_1 & -p_0 & 0 \\ 0 & -p_2 & 1-p_1 & -p_0 \\ 1 & 0 & 0 & 0 \end{pmatrix} \bigg/ \det \begin{pmatrix} 1 & -p_0 & 0 & 0 \\ 1 & 1-p_1 & -p_0 & 0 \\ 1 & -p_2 & 1-p_1 & -p_0 \\ 0 & 0 & -1 & 1 \end{pmatrix}.$$

16. [41] Carry out detailed studies of the problem of sorting 100,000 100-character records, drawing charts such as those in Chart A, assuming that 3, 4, or 5 tapes are available.

*5.4.7. External Radix Sorting

The previous sections have discussed the process of tape sorting by merging; but there is another way to sort with tapes, based on the radix sorting principle that was once used in mechanical card sorters (see Section 5.2.5). This method is sometimes called distribution sorting, column sorting, pocket sorting, digital sorting, separation sorting, etc.; it turns out to be essentially the *opposite* of merging!

Suppose, for example, that we have four tapes and that there are only eight possible keys: 0, 1, 2, 3, 4, 5, 6, 7. If the input data is on tape T1, we can begin by transferring all even keys to T3, all odd keys to T4:

	T1	T2	T3	T4
Given	$\{0,1,2,3,4,5,6,7\}$	—	—	—
Pass 1	—	—	$\{0,2,4,6\}$	$\{1,3,5,7\}$

Now we rewind, and read T3 and then T4, putting $\{0, 1, 4, 5\}$ on T1 and $\{2, 3, 6, 7\}$ on T2:

| Pass 2 | $\{0,4\}\{1,5\}$ | $\{2,6\}\{3,7\}$ | — | — |

(The notation "$\{0,4\}\{1,5\}$" stands for a file that contains some records whose keys are all 0 or 4 followed by records whose keys are all 1 or 5. Notice that T1 now contains those keys whose middle binary digit is 0.) After rewinding again and distributing 0, 1, 2, 3 to T3 and 4, 5, 6, 7 to T4, we have

| Pass 3 | | | $\{0\}\{1\}\{2\}\{3\}$ | $\{4\}\{5\}\{6\}\{7\}$ |

Now we can finish up by copying T4 to the end of T3. In general, if the keys range from 0 to $2^k - 1$, we could sort the file in an analogous way using k passes, followed by a final collection phase that copies about half of the data from one tape to another. With six tapes we could use radix 3 representations in a similar way, to sort keys from 0 to $3^k - 1$ in k passes.

Partial-pass methods can also be used. For example, suppose that there are ten possible keys $\{0, 1, \ldots, 9\}$, and consider the following procedure due to

R. L. Ashenhurst [*Theory of Switching*, Progress Report BL-7 (Harvard Univ. Comp. Laboratory: May 1954), I.1–I.76]:

Phase	T1	T2	T3	T4	passes
	$\{0, 1, \ldots, 9\}$	—	—	—	
1	—	$\{0, 2, 4, 7\}$	$\{1, 5, 6\}$	$\{3, 8, 9\}$	1.0
2	$\{0\}$	—	$\{1, 5, 6\}\{2, 7\}$	$\{3, 8, 9\}\{4\}$	0.4
3	$\{0\}\{1\}\{2\}$	$\{6\}\{7\}$	—	$\{3, 8, 9\}\{4\}\{5\}$	0.5
4	$\{0\}\{1\}\{2\}\{3\}$	$\{6\}\{7\}\{8\}$	$\{9\}$	$\{4\}\{5\}$	0.3
C	$\{0\}\{1\}\{2\}\{3\}\{4\}\ldots\{9\}$				0.6
					—
					2.8

Here C represents the collection phase. If each key value occurs about one-tenth of the time, the procedure above takes only 2.8 passes to sort ten keys, while the first example required 3.5 passes to sort only eight keys. Therefore we find that a clever distribution pattern can make a significant difference, for radix sorting as well as for merging.

The distribution patterns in the examples above can conveniently be represented as tree structures:

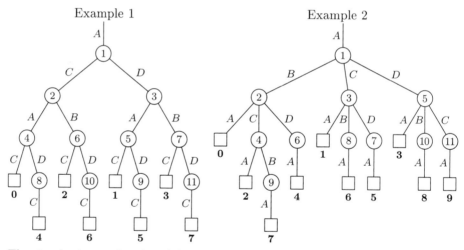

Example 1   Example 2

The circular internal nodes of these trees are numbered 1, 2, 3, ..., corresponding to steps 1, 2, 3, ... of the process. Tape names A, B, C, D (instead of T1, T2, T3, T4) have been placed next to the lines of the trees, in order to show where the records go. Square external nodes represent portions of a file that contain only one key, and that key is shown in boldface type just below the node. The lines just above square nodes all carry the name of the output tape (C in the first example, A in the second).

Thus, step 3 of example 1 consists of reading from tape D and writing 1s and 5s on tape A, 3s and 7s on tape B. It is not difficult to see that the number of passes performed is equal to the *external path length* of the tree divided by the number of external nodes, if we assume that each key occurs equally often.

Because of the sequential nature of tape, and the first-in-first-out discipline of forwards reading, we can't simply use *any* labeled tree as the basis of a distribution pattern. In the tree of example 1, data gets written on tape A during step 2 and step 3; it is necessary to use the data written during step 2 before we use the data written during step 3. In general if we write onto a tape during steps i and j, where $i < j$, we must use the data written during step i first; when the tree contains two branches of the form

$$
\begin{array}{cc}
\fbox{i} & \fbox{j} \\
A\Big| & A\Big| \\
\fbox{k} & \fbox{l}
\end{array}
\qquad i < j,
$$

we must have $k < l$. Furthermore we cannot write anything onto tape A *between* steps k and l, because we must rewind between reading and writing.

The reader who has worked the exercises of Section 5.4.4 will now immediately perceive that the allowable trees for read-forward radix sorting on T tapes are precisely the *strongly T-fifo trees*, which characterize read-forward *merge* sorting on T tapes! (See exercise 5.4.4–20.) The only difference is that all of the external nodes on the trees we are considering here have the same tape labels. We could remove this restriction by assuming a final collection phase that transfers all records to an output tape, or we could add that restriction to the rules for T-fifo trees by requiring that the initial distribution pass of a merge sort be explicitly represented in the corresponding merge tree.

In other words, *every merge pattern corresponds to a distribution pattern, and every distribution pattern corresponds to a merge pattern.* A moment's reflection shows why this is so: Consider running a merge sort backwards, "unmerging" the final output into subfiles, which are unmerged into others, etc.; finally we will have unmerged the file into S runs. Such a pattern is possible with tapes if and only if the corresponding radix sort distribution pattern, for S keys, is possible. This duality between merging and distribution is almost perfect; it breaks down only in one respect, namely that the input tape must be saved at different times.

The eight-key example treated at the beginning of this section is clearly dual to a balanced merge on four tapes. The ten-key example with partial passes corresponds to the following ten-run merge pattern (if we suppress the copy phases, steps 6–11 in the tree):

	T1	T2	T3	T4
Initial distribution	1^4	1^3	1^1	1^2
Tree step 5	1^3	1^2	—	$1^2 3^1$
Tree step 4	1^2	1^1	2^1	$1^2 3^1$
Tree step 3	1^1	—	$2^1 3^1$	$1^1 3^1$
Tree step 2	—	4^1	3^1	3^1
Tree step 1	10^1	—	—	—

If we compare this to the radix sort, we see that the methods have essentially the same structure but are reversed in time, with the tape contents also reversed from back to front: $1^2 3^1$ (two runs each of length 1 followed by one of length 3) corresponds to $\{3,8,9\}\{4\}\{5\}$ (two subfiles containing one key each, preceded by one subfile containing three).

Going the other way, we can in principle construct a radix sort dual to polyphase merge, another one dual to cascade merge, etc. For example, the 21-run polyphase merge on three tapes, illustrated at the beginning of Section 5.4.2, corresponds to the following interesting radix sort:

Phase	T1	T2	T3
	$\{0,1,\dots,20\}$	—	—
1	—	$\{0,2,4,5,7,9,10,12,13,15,17,18,20\}$	$\{1,3,6,8,11,14,16,19\}$
2	$\{0,5,10,13,18\}$	—	$\{1,3,6,8,11,14,16,19\}$ $\{2,4,7,9,12,15,17,20\}$
3	$\{0,5,10,13,18\}\{1,6,11,14,19\}$ $\{2,7,12,15,20\}$	$\{3,8,16\}\{4,9,17\}$	—
4	—	$\{3,8,16\}\{4,9,17\}\{5,10,18\}$ $\{6,11,19\}\{7,12,20\}$	$\{0,13\}\{1,14\}\{2,15\}$
5	$\{8\}\{9\}\{10\}\{11\}\{12\}$	—	$\{0,13\}\{1,14\}\{2,15\}$ $\{3,16\}\dots\{7,20\}$
6	$\{8\}\{9\}\{10\}\{11\}\{12\}\{13\}\dots\{20\}$	$\{0\}\{1\}\dots\{7\}$	—

The distribution rule used here to decide which keys go on which tapes at each step appears to be magic, but in fact it has a simple connection with the Fibonacci number system. (See exercise 2.)

Reading backwards. Duality between radix sorting and merging applies also to algorithms that read tapes backwards. We have defined "T-lifo trees" in Section 5.4.4, and it is easy to see that they correspond to radix sorts as well as to merge sorts.

A read-backward radix sort was actually considered by John Mauchly already in 1946, in one of the first papers ever to be published about sorting (see Section 5.5); Mauchly essentially gave the following construction:

Phase	T1	T2	T3	T4
	—	$\{0,1,2,\dots,9\}$	—	—
1	$\{4,5\}$	—	$\{2,3,6,7\}$	$\{0,1,8,9\}$
2	$\{4,5\}\{2,7\}$	$\{3,6\}$	—	$\{0,1,8,9\}$
3	$\{4,5\}\{2,7\}\{0,9\}$	$\{3,6\}\{1,8\}$	—	—
4	$\{4,5\}\{2,7\}$	$\{3,6\}\{1,8\}$	$\{9\}$	$\{0\}$
$\cdot\cdot\cdot\cdot\cdot\cdot$	$\cdot\cdot\cdot\cdot\cdot\cdot$	$\cdot\cdot\cdot\cdot\cdot\cdot$	$\cdot\cdot\cdot\cdot\cdot\cdot$	$\cdot\cdot\cdot\cdot\cdot\cdot$
8	—	—	$\{9\}\{8\}\{7\}\{6\}\{5\}$	$\{0\}\{1\}\{2\}\{3\}\{4\}$
C	—	—	—	$\{0\}\{1\}\{2\}\{3\}\{4\}\{5\}\dots\{9\}$

His scheme is not the most efficient one possible, but it is interesting because it shows that partial pass methods were considered for radix sorting already in 1946, although they did not appear in the literature for merging until about 1960.

An efficient construction of read-backward distribution patterns has been suggested by A. Bayes [*CACM* **11** (1968), 491–493]: Given $P + 1$ tapes and S keys, divide the keys into P subfiles each containing $\lfloor S/P \rfloor$ or $\lceil S/P \rceil$ keys, and apply this procedure recursively to each subfile. When $S < 2P$, one subfile should consist of the smallest key alone, and it should be written onto the output file. (R. M. Karp's general preorder construction, which appears at the end of Section 5.4.4, includes this method as a special case.)

Backward reading makes merging a little more complicated because it reverses the order of runs. There is a corresponding effect on radix sorting: The outcome is stable or "anti-stable" depending on what level is reached in the tree. After a read-backward radix sort in which some of the external nodes are at odd levels and some are at even levels, the relative order of different records with equal keys will be the *same* as the original order for some keys, but it will be the *opposite* of the original order for the other keys. (See exercise 6.)

Oscillating merge sorts have their counterparts too, under duality. In an *oscillating radix sort* we continue to separate out the keys until reaching subfiles that have only one key or are small enough to be internally sorted; such subfiles are sorted and written onto the output tape, then the separation process is resumed. For example, if we have three work tapes and one output tape, and if the keys are binary numbers, we may start by putting keys of the form $0x$ on tape T1, keys $1x$ on T2. If T1 receives more than one memory load, we scan it again and put $00x$ on T2 and $01x$ on T3. Now if the $00x$ subfile is short enough to be internally sorted, we do so and output the result, then continue by processing the $01x$ subfile. Such a method was called a "cascading pseudo-radix sort" by E. H. Friend [*JACM* **3** (1956), 157–159]; it was developed further by H. Nagler [*JACM* **6** (1959), 459–468], who gave it the colorful name "amphisbaenic sort," and by C. H. Gaudette [*IBM Tech. Disclosure Bull.* **12** (April 1970), 1849–1853].

Does radix sorting beat merging? One important consequence of the duality principle is that *radix sorting is usually inferior to merge sorting*. This happens because the technique of replacement selection gives merge sorting a definite advantage; there is no apparent way to arrange radix sorts so that we can make use of internal sorts encompassing more than one memory load at a time. Indeed, the oscillating radix sort will often produce subfiles that are somewhat smaller than one memory load, so the distribution pattern will correspond to a tree with many more external nodes than would be present if merging and replacement selection were used. Consequently the external path length of the tree — the sorting time — will be increased. (See exercise 5.3.1–33.)

On the other hand, external radix sorting does have its uses. Suppose, for example, that we have a file containing the names of all employees of a large corporation, in alphabetic order; the corporation has 10 divisions, and it is desired to sort the file by division, *retaining* the alphabetic order of the employees in each division. This is a perfect situation in which to apply a stable radix sort, if the file is long, since the number of records that belong to each of the 10 divisions is likely to be more than the number of records that would be obtained in initial runs produced by replacement selection. In general, if the range of key values is so small that the collection of records having a given key is expected to fill the internal memory more than twice, it is wise to use a radix sort technique.

We have seen in Section 5.2.5 that *internal* radix sorting is superior to merging, on certain high-speed computers, because the inner loop of the radix sort algorithm avoids complicated branching. If the external memory is especially fast, it may be impossible for such machines to merge data rapidly enough to keep up with the input/output equipment. Radix sorting may therefore turn out to be superior to merging in such a situation, especially if the keys are known to be uniformly distributed.

EXERCISES

1. [20] The general T-tape balanced merge with parameter P, $1 \leq P < T$, was defined near the beginning of Section 5.4. Show that this corresponds to a radix sort based on a mixed radix system.

2. [M28] The text illustrates the three-tape polyphase radix sort for 21 keys. Generalize to the case of F_n keys; explain what keys appear on what tapes at the end of each phase. [*Hint:* Consider the Fibonacci number system, exercise 1.2.8–34.]

3. [M35] Extend the results of exercise 2 to the polyphase radix sort on four or more tapes. (See exercise 5.4.2–10.)

4. [M23] Prove that Ashenhurst's distribution pattern is the best way to sort 10 keys on four tapes without reading backwards, in the sense that the associated tree has minimum external path length over all strongly 4-fifo trees. (Thus, it is essentially the best method if we ignore rewind time.)

5. [15] Draw the 4-lifo tree corresponding to Mauchly's read-backwards radix sort for 10 keys.

▶ **6.** [20] A certain file contains two-digit keys 00, 01, ..., 99. After performing Mauchly's radix sort on the least significant digits, we can repeat the same scheme on the most significant digits, interchanging the roles of tapes T2 and T4. In what order will the keys finally appear on T2?

7. [21] Does the duality principle apply also to multireel files?

*5.4.8. Two-Tape Sorting

Since we need three tapes to carry out a merge process without excessive tape motion, it is interesting to speculate about how we could preform a reasonable external sort using only two tapes.

One approach, suggested by H. B. Demuth in 1956, is sort of a combined replacement-selection and bubble sort. Assume that the input is on tape T1, and begin by reading $P + 1$ records into memory. Now output the record whose key is smallest, to tape T2, and replace it by the next input record. Continue outputting a record whose key is currently the smallest in memory, maintaining a selection tree or a priority queue of $P + 1$ elements. When the input is finally exhausted, the largest P keys of the file will be present in memory; output them in ascending order. Now rewind both tapes and repeat the process by reading from T2 and writing to T1; each such pass puts at least P more records into their proper place. A simple test can be built into the program that determines when the entire file is in sort. At most $\lceil (N - 1)/P \rceil$ passes will be necessary.

A few moments' reflection shows that each pass of this procedure is essentially equivalent to P consecutive passes of the bubble sort (Algorithm 5.2.2B). If an element has P or more inversions, it will be smaller than everything in the tree when it is input, so it will be output immediately — thereby losing P inversions. If an element has fewer than P inversions, it will go into the selection tree and will be output before all greater keys — thereby losing all its inversions. When $P = 1$, this is exactly what happens in the bubble sort, by Theorem 5.2.2I.

The total number of passes will therefore be $\lceil I/P \rceil$, where I is the maximum number of inversions of any element. By the theory developed in Section 5.2.2, the average value of I is $N - \sqrt{\pi N/2} + 2/3 + O(1/\sqrt{N})$.

If the file is not too much larger than the memory size, or if it is nearly in order to begin with, this order-P bubble sort will be fairly rapid; in fact, such a method might be advantageous even when extra tape units are available, because scratch tapes must be mounted by a human operator. But a two-tape bubble sort will run quite slowly on fairly long, randomly ordered files, since its average running time will be approximately proportional to N^2.

Let us consider how this method might be implemented for the 100,000-record example of Section 5.4.6. We need to choose P intelligently, in order to compensate for interblock gaps while doing simultaneous reading, writing, and computing. Since the example assumes that each record is 100 characters long and that 100,000 characters will fit into memory, we can make room for two input buffers and two output buffers of size B by setting

$$100(P + 1) + 4B = 100000. \tag{1}$$

Using the notation of Section 5.4.6, the running time for each pass will be about

$$NC\omega\tau(1 + \rho), \qquad \omega = (B + \gamma)/B. \tag{2}$$

Since the number of passes is inversely proportional to P, we want to choose B to be a multiple of 100 that minimizes the quantity ω/P. Elementary calculus shows that this occurs when B is approximately $\sqrt{24975\gamma + \gamma^2} - \gamma$, so we take $B = 3000$, $P = 879$. Setting $N = 100000$ in the formulas above shows that the number of passes $\lceil I/P \rceil$ will be about 114, and the total estimated running time will be approximately 8.57 hours (assuming for convenience that the initial input and the final output also have $B = 3000$). This represents approximately 0.44 reelfuls of data; a full reel would take about five times as long. Some improvements could be made if the algorithm were interrupted periodically, writing the records with largest keys onto an auxiliary tape that is dismounted, since such records are merely copied back and forth once they have been put into order.

Application of quicksort. Another internal sorting method that traverses the data in a nearly sequential manner is the partition exchange or quicksort procedure, Algorithm 5.2.2Q. Can we adapt it to two tapes? [N. B. Yoash, *CACM* **8** (1965), 649.]

It is not difficult to see how this can indeed be done, using backward reading. Assume that the two tapes are numbered 0 and 1, and imagine that the file is laid out as follows:

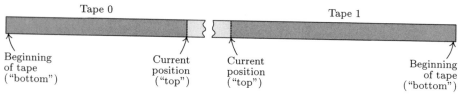

| Tape 0 | | Tape 1 |

Beginning of tape ("bottom") · Current position ("top") · Current position ("top") · Beginning of tape ("bottom")

Each tape serves as a stack; putting them together like this makes it possible to view the file as a linear list in which we can move the current position left or right by copying from one stack to the other. The following recursive subroutines define a suitable sorting procedure:

• SORT00 [Sort the top subfile on tape 0 and return it to tape 0].
If the subfile fits in the internal memory, sort it internally and return it to tape. Otherwise select one record R from the subfile, and let its key be K. Reading backwards on tape 0, copy all records whose key is $> K$, forming a new subfile on the top of tape 1. Now read forward on tape 0, copying all records whose key is $= K$ onto tape 1. Then read backwards again, copying all records whose key is $< K$ onto tape 1. Complete the sort by executing SORT10 on the $< K$ keys, then copying the $= K$ keys to tape 0, and finally executing SORT10 on the $> K$ keys.

• SORT01 [Sort the top subfile on tape 0 and write it on tape 1].
Same as SORT00, but the final "SORT10" is changed to "SORT11" followed by copying the $\le K$ keys to tape 1.

• SORT10 [Sort the top subfile on tape 1 and write it on Tape 0].
Same as SORT01, interchanging 0 with 1 and $<$ with $>$.

• SORT11 [Sort the top subfile on tape 1 and return it to tape 1].
Same as SORT00, interchanging 0 with 1 and $<$ with $>$.

The recursive nature of these subroutines can be handled without difficulty by storing appropriate control information on the tapes.

The running time for this algorithm can be estimated as follows, if we assume that the data are in random order, with negligible probability of equal keys. Let M be the number of records that fit into internal memory. Let X_N be the average number of records read while applying SORT00 or SORT11 to a subfile of N records, when $N > M$, and let Y_N be the corresponding quantity for SORT01 or SORT10. Then we have

$$X_N = \begin{cases} 0, & \text{if } N \le M; \\ 3N + 1 + \frac{1}{N}\sum_{0 \le k < N}(Y_k + Y_{N-1-k}), & \text{if } N > M; \end{cases}$$

$$Y_N = \begin{cases} 0, & \text{if } N \le M; \\ 3N + 2 + \frac{1}{N}\sum_{0 \le k < N}(Y_k + X_{N-1-k} + k), & \text{if } N > M. \end{cases} \tag{3}$$

The solution to these recurrences (see exercise 2) shows that the total amount of tape reading during the external partitioning phases will be $6\frac{2}{3}N \ln N + O(N)$, on the average, as $N \to \infty$. We also know from Eq. 5.2.2–(25) that the average number of internal sort phases will be $2(N+1)/(M+2) - 1$.

If we apply this analysis to the 100,000-record example of Section 5.4.6, using 25,000-character buffers and assuming that the sorting time is $2nC\omega\tau$ for a subfile of $n \le M = 1000$ records, we obtain an average sorting time of approximately 103 minutes (including the final rewind as in Chart A). Thus the quicksort method isn't bad, on the average; but of course its *worst* case turns out to be even more awful than the bubble sort discussed above. Randomization will make the worst case extremely unlikely.

Radix sorting. The radix exchange method (Algorithm 5.2.2R) can be adapted to two-tape sorting in a similar way, since it is so much like quicksort. The trick that makes both of these methods work is the idea of reading a file more than once, something we never did in our previous tape algorithms.

The same trick can be used to do a conventional least-significant-digit-first radix sort on two tapes. Given the input data on T1, we copy all records onto T2 whose key ends with 0 in binary notation; then after rewinding T1 we read it again, copying the records whose key ends with 1. Now both tapes are rewound and a similar pair of passes is made, interchanging the roles of T1 and T2, and using the *second* least significant binary digit. At this point T1 will contain all records whose keys are $(\dots 00)_2$, followed by those whose keys are $(\dots 01)_2$, then $(\dots 10)_2$, then $(\dots 11)_2$. If the keys are b bits long, we need only $2b$ passes over the file in order to complete the sort.

Such a radix sort could be applied only to the *leading* b bits of the keys, for some judiciously chosen number b; that would reduce the number of inversions by a factor of about 2^b, if the keys were uniformly distributed, so a few passes of the P-way bubble sort could then be used to complete the job. This approach reads tape in the forward direction only.

A novel but somewhat more complicated approach to two-tape distribution sorting has been suggested by A. I. Nikitin and L. I. Sholmov [*Kibernetika* **2**, 6 (1966), 79–84]. Counts are made of the number of keys having each possible configuration of leading bits, and artificial keys $\kappa_1, \kappa_2, \dots, \kappa_M$ based on these counts are constructed so that the number of actual keys lying between κ_i and κ_{i+1} is between predetermined limits P_1 and P_2, for each i. Thus, M lies between $\lceil N/P_2 \rceil$ and $\lceil N/P_1 \rceil$. If the leading bit counts do not give sufficient information to determine such $\kappa_1, \kappa_2, \dots, \kappa_M$, one or more further passes are made to count the frequency of less significant bit patterns, for certain configurations of most significant bits. After the table of artificial keys $\kappa_1, \kappa_2, \dots, \kappa_M$ has been constructed, $2\lceil \lg M \rceil$ further passes will suffice to complete the sort. (This method requires memory space proportional to N, so it can't be used for external sorting as $N \to \infty$. In practice we would not use the technique for multireel files, so M will be comparatively small and the table of artificial keys will fit comfortably in memory.)

Simulation of more tapes. F. C. Hennie and R. E. Stearns have devised a general technique for simulating k tapes on only two tapes, in such a way that the tape motion required is increased by a factor of only $O(\log L)$, where L is the maximum distance to be traveled on any one tape [*JACM* **13** (1966), 533–546].

	Zone 0	Zone 1		Zone 2				Zone 3					
Track 1	1	5	9	13	17	21	25	29	33	37	41	45	49
Track 2	2	6	10	14	18	22	26	30	34	38	42	46	50
Track 3	3	7	11	15	19	23	27	31	35	39	43	47	51
Track 4	4	8	12	16	20	24	28	32	36	40	44	48	52

Fig. 86. Layout of tape T1 in the Hennie–Stearns construction; nonblank zones are shaded.

Their construction can be simplified slightly in the case of sorting, as in the following method suggested by R. M. Karp.

We shall simulate an ordinary four-tape balanced merge, using two tapes T1 and T2. The first of these, T1, holds the simulated tape contents in a way that may be diagrammed as in Fig. 86; we imagine that the data is written in four "tracks," one for each simulated tape. (In actual fact the tape doesn't have such tracks; blocks 1, 5, 9, 13, ... are thought of as Track 1, blocks 2, 6, 10, 14, ... as Track 2, etc.) The other tape, T2, is used only for auxiliary storage, to help move things around on T1.

The blocks of each track are divided into *zones*, containing, respectively, 1, 2, 4, 8, ..., 2^k, ... blocks per zone. Zone k on each track is either filled with exactly 2^k blocks of data, or it is completely blank. In Fig. 86, for example, Track 1 has data in zones 1 and 3; Track 2 in zones 0, 1, 2; Track 3 in zones 0 and 2; Track 4 in zone 1; and the other zones are blank.

Suppose that we are merging data from Tracks 1 and 2 to Track 3. The internal computer memory contains two buffers used for input to a two-way merge, plus a third buffer for output. When the input buffer for Track 1 becomes empty, we can refill it as follows: Find the first nonempty zone on Track 1, say zone k, and copy its first block into the input buffer; then copy the other $2^k - 1$ blocks of data onto T2, and move them to zones 0, 1, ..., $k-1$ of Track 1. (Zones 0, 1, ..., $k-1$ are now full and zone k is blank.) An analogous procedure is used to refill the input buffer for Track 2, whenever it becomes empty. When the output buffer is ready to be written on Track 3, we reverse the process, scanning across T1 to find the first *blank* zone on Track 3, say zone k, while copying the data from zones 0, 1, ..., $k-1$ onto T2. The data on T2, augmented by the contents of the output buffer, is now used to fill zone k of Track 3.

This procedure requires the ability to write in the middle of tape T1, without destroying subsequent information on that tape. As in the case of read-forward oscillating sort (Section 5.4.5), it is possible to do this reliably if suitable precautions are taken.

The amount of tape motion required to bring $2^l - 1$ blocks of Track 1 into memory is $\sum_{0 \le k < l} 2^{l-1-k} \cdot c \cdot 2^k = cl2^{l-1}$, for some constant c, since we scan up to zone k only once in every 2^k steps. Thus each merge pass requires $O(N \log N)$ steps. Since there are $O(\log N)$ passes in a balanced merge, the total time to sort is guaranteed to be $O\big(N(\log N)^2\big)$ in the worst case; this is asymptotically much better than the worst case of quicksort.

But this method wouldn't work very well if we applied it to the 100,000-record example of Section 5.4.6, since the information specified for tape T1 would overflow the contents of one tape reel. Even if we ignore this fact, and if we use optimistic assumptions about read/write/compute overlap and interblock gap lengths, etc., we find that roughly 37 hours would be required to complete the sort! So this method is purely of academic interest; the constant in $O\big(N(\log N)^2\big)$ is much too high to be satisfactory when N is in a practical range.

One-tape sorting. Could we live with only one tape? It is not difficult to see that the order-P bubble sort described above could be converted into a one-tape sort, but the result would be ghastly.

H. B. Demuth [Ph.D. thesis (Stanford University, 1956), 85] observed that a computer with bounded internal memory cannot reduce the number of inversions of a permutation by more than a bounded amount as it moves a bounded distance on tape; hence every one-tape sorting algorithm must take at least N^2d units of time on the average, for some positive constant d that depends on the computer configuration.

R. M. Karp has pursued this topic in a very interesting way, discovering an essentially *optimum* way to sort with one tape. It is convenient to discuss Karp's algorithm by reformulating the problem as follows: *What is the fastest way to transport people between floors using a single elevator?* [See *Combinatorial Algorithms*, edited by Randall Rustin (Algorithmics Press, 1972), 17–21.]

Consider a building with n floors, having room for exactly b people on each floor. The building contains no doors, windows, or stairs, but it does have an elevator that can stop on each floor. There are bn people in the building, and exactly b of them want to be on each particular floor. The elevator holds at most m people, and it takes one unit of time to go from floor i to floor $i+1$. We wish to find the quickest way to get all the people onto the proper floors, if the elevator is required to start and finish on floor 1.

The connection between this elevator problem and one-tape sorting is not hard to see: The people are the records and the building is the tape. The floors are individual blocks on the tape, and the elevator is the internal computer memory. A computer program has more flexibility than an elevator operator (it can, for example, duplicate people, or temporarily chop them into two parts on different floors, etc.); but the solution below solves the problem in the fastest conceivable time without doing such operations.

The following two auxiliary tables are required by Karp's algorithm.

u_k, $1 \le k \le n$: Number of people on floors $\le k$ whose destination is $> k$; $\qquad$ (4)
d_k, $1 \le k \le n$: Number of people on floors $\ge k$ whose destination is $< k$.

When the elevator is empty, we always have $u_k = d_{k+1}$ for $1 \le k < n$, since there are b people on every floor; the number of misfits on floors $\{1, \ldots, k\}$ must equal the corresponding number on floors $\{k+1, \ldots, n\}$. By definition, $u_n = d_1 = 0$.

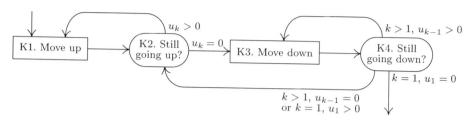

Fig. 87. Karp's elevator algorithm.

It is clear that the elevator must make at least $\lceil u_k/m \rceil$ trips from floor k to floor $k+1$, for $1 \leq k < n$, since only m passengers can ascend on each trip. Similarly it must make at least $\lceil d_k/m \rceil$ trips from floor k to floor $k-1$. Therefore the elevator must necessarily take at least

$$\sum_{k=1}^{n} \left(\lceil u_k/m \rceil + \lceil d_k/m \rceil \right) \tag{5}$$

units of time on any correct schedule. Karp discovered that this lower bound can actually be achieved, when $u_1, \ldots, u_{n-1}$ are nonzero.

Theorem K. *If $u_k > 0$ for $1 \leq k < n$, there is an elevator schedule that delivers everyone to the correct floor in the minimum time* (5).

Proof. Assume that there are m extra people in the building; they start in the elevator and their destination floor is artificially set to 0. The elevator can operate according to the following algorithm, starting with k (the current floor) equal to 1:

K1. [Move up.] From among the $b+m$ people currently in the elevator or on floor k, those m with the highest destinations get into the elevator, and the others remain on floor k.

   Let there be u people now in the elevator whose destination is $> k$, and d whose destination is $\leq k$. (It will turn out that $u = \min(m, u_k)$; if $u_k < m$ we may therefore be transporting some people away from their destination. This represents their sacrifice to the common good.) Decrease u_k by u, increase d_{k+1} by d, and then increase k by 1.

K2. [Still going up?] If $u_k > 0$, return to step K1.

K3. [Move down.] From among the $b+m$ people currently in the elevator or on floor k, those m with the lowest destinations get into the elevator, and the others remain on floor k.

   Let there be u people now in the elevator whose destination is $\geq k$, and d whose destination is $< k$. (It will always turn out that $u = 0$ and $d = m$, but the algorithm is described here in terms of general u and d in order to make the proof a little clearer.) Decrease d_k by d, increase u_{k-1} by u, and then decrease k by 1.

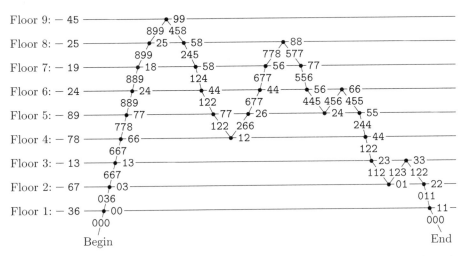

Fig. 88. An optimum way to rearrange people using a small, slow elevator. (People are each represented by the number of their destination floor.)

K4. [Still going down?] If $k > 1$ and $u_{k-1} > 0$, return to step K3. If $k = 1$ and $u_1 = 0$, terminate the algorithm (everyone has arrived safely and the m "extras" are back in the elevator). Otherwise return to step K2.

Figure 88 shows an example of this algorithm, with a nine-floor building and $b = 2$, $m = 3$. Note that one of the 6s is temporarily transported to floor 7, in spite of the fact that the elevator travels the minimum possible distance. The idea of testing u_{k-1} in step K4 is the crux of the algorithm, as we shall see.

To verify the validity of this algorithm, we note that steps K1 and K3 always keep the u and d tables (4) up to date, if we regard the people in the elevator as being on the "current" floor k. It is now possible to prove by induction that the following properties hold at the beginning of each step:

$$u_l = d_{l+1}, \qquad \text{for } k \le l < n; \tag{6}$$

$$u_l = d_{l+1} - m, \qquad \text{for } 1 \le l < k; \tag{7}$$

$$u_{l+1} = 0, \qquad \text{if } u_l = 0 \text{ and } k \le l < n. \tag{8}$$

Furthermore, at the beginning of step K1, the $\min(u_k, m)$ people with highest destinations, among all people on floors $\le k$ with destination $> k$, are in the elevator or on floor k. At the beginning of step K3, the $\min(d_k, m)$ people with lowest destinations, among all people on floors $\ge k$ with destination $< k$, are in the elevator or on floor k.

From these properties it follows that the parenthesized remarks in steps K1 and K3 are valid. Each execution of step K1 therefore decreases $\lceil u_k/m \rceil$ by 1 and leaves $\lceil d_{k+1}/m \rceil$ unchanged; each execution of K3 decreases $\lceil d_k/m \rceil$ by 1 and leaves $\lceil u_{k-1}/m \rceil$ unchanged. The algorithm must therefore terminate in a finite number of steps, and everybody must then be on the correct floor because of (6) and (8). ∎

When $u_k = 0$ and $u_{k+1} > 0$ we have a "disconnected" situation; the elevator must journey up to floor $k + 1$ in order to rearrange the people up there, even though nobody wants to move from floors $\leq k$ to floors $\geq k + 1$. Without loss of generality, we may assume that $u_{n-1} > 0$; then every valid elevator schedule must include at least

$$2 \sum_{1 \leq k < n} \max\bigl(1, \lceil u_k/m \rceil\bigr) \tag{9}$$

moves, since we require the elevator to return to floor 1. A schedule achieving this lower bound is readily constructed (exercise 4).

EXERCISES

1. [*20*] The order-P bubble sort discussed in the text uses only forward reading and rewinding. Can the algorithm be modified to take advantage of *backward* reading?

2. [*M26*] Find explicit closed-form solutions for the numbers X_N, Y_N defined in (3). [*Hint:* Study the solution to Eq. 5.2.2–(19).]

3. [*38*] Is there a two-tape sorting method, based only on comparisons of keys (not digital properties), whose tape motion is $O(N \log N)$ in the worst case, when sorting N records? [Quicksort achieves this on the average, but not in the worst case, and the Hennie–Stearns method (Fig. 86) achieves $O(N(\log N)^2)$.]

4. [*M23*] In the elevator problem, suppose there are indices p and q, with $q \geq p+2$, $u_p > 0$, $u_q > 0$, and $u_{p+1} = \cdots = u_{q-1} = 0$. Explain how to construct a schedule requiring at most (9) units of time.

▶ **5.** [*M23*] True or false: After step K1 of the algorithm in Theorem K, nobody on the elevator has a lower destination than any person on floors $< k$.

6. [*M30*] (R. M. Karp.) Generalize the elevator problem (Fig. 87) to the case that there are b_j passengers initially on floor j, and b'_j passengers whose destination is floor j, for $1 \leq j \leq n$. Show that a schedule exists that takes $2\sum_{k=1}^{n-1} \max(1, \lceil u_k/m \rceil, \lceil d_{k+1}/m \rceil)$ units of time, never allowing more than $\max(b_j, b'_j)$ passengers to be on floor j at any one time. [*Hint:* Introduce fictitious people, if necessary, to make $b_j = b'_j$ for all j.]

7. [*M40*] (R. M. Karp.) Generalize the problem of exercise 6, replacing the linear path of an elevator by a network of roads to be traveled by a bus, given that the network forms any *free tree*. The bus has finite capacity, and the goal is to transport passengers to their destinations in such a way that the bus travels a minimum distance.

8. [*M32*] Let $b = 1$ in the elevator problem treated in the text. How many permutations of the n people on the n floors will make $u_k \leq 1$ for $1 \leq k \leq n$ in (4)? [For example, 3 1 4 5 9 2 6 8 7 is such a permutation.]

▶ **9.** [*M25*] Find a significant connection between the "cocktail-shaker sort" described in Section 5.2.2, Fig. 16, and the numbers $u_1, u_2, \ldots, u_n$ of (4) in the case $b = 1$.

10. [*20*] How would you sort a multireel file with only two tapes?

*5.4.9. Disks and Drums

So far we have considered tapes as the vehicles for external sorting, but more flexible types of mass storage devices are generally available. Although such "bulk memory" or "direct-access storage" units come in many different forms, they may be roughly characterized by the following properties:

i) Any specified part of the stored information can be accessed quickly.

ii) Blocks of consecutive words can be transmitted rapidly between the internal and external memory.

Magnetic tape satisfies (ii) but not (i), because it takes a long time to get from one end of a tape to the other.

Every external memory unit has idiosyncrasies that ought to be studied carefully before major programs are written for it; but technology changes so rapidly, it is impossible to give a complete discussion here of all the available varieties of hardware. Therefore we shall consider only some typical memory devices that illustrate useful approaches to the sorting problem.

One of the most common types of external memories satisfying (i) and (ii) is a disk device (see Fig. 89). Data is kept on a number of rapidly rotating circular disks, covered with magnetic material; a comb-like access arm, containing one or more "read/write heads" for each disk surface, is used to store and retrieve the information. Each individual surface is divided into concentric rings called *tracks*, so that an entire track of data passes a read/write head every time the disk completes one revolution. The access arm can move in and out, shifting the read/write heads from track to track; but this motion takes time. A set of tracks that can be read or written without repositioning the access arm is called a *cylinder*. For example, Fig. 89 illustrates a disk unit that has just one read/write head per surface; the light gray circles show one of the cylinders, consisting of all tracks currently being scanned by the read/write heads.

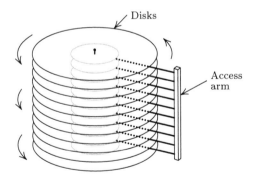

Fig. 89. A disk device.

To fix the ideas, let us consider hypothetical MIXTEC disk units, for which

$$1 \text{ track} = 5000 \text{ characters}$$
$$1 \text{ cylinder} = 20 \text{ tracks}$$
$$1 \text{ disk unit} = 200 \text{ cylinders}$$

Such a disk unit contains 20 million characters, slightly less than the amount of data that can be stored on a single MIXT magnetic tape. On some machines, tracks near the center have fewer characters than tracks near the rim; this tends to make the programming much more complicated, and MIXTEC fortunately avoids such problems. (See Section 5.4.6 for a discussion of MIXT tapes. As in that section, we are studying classical techniques by considering machine characteristics that were typical of the early 1970s; modern disks are much bigger and faster.)

The amount of time required to read or write on a disk device is essentially the sum of three quantities:

- seek time (the time to move the access arm to the proper cylinder);

- latency time (rotational delay until the read/write head reaches the right spot);

- transmission time (rotational delay while the data passes the read/write head).

On MIXTEC devices the seek time required to go from cylinder i to cylinder j is $25 + \frac{1}{2}|i - j|$ milliseconds. If i and j are randomly selected integers between 1 and 200, the average value of $|i - j|$ is $2\binom{201}{3}/200^2 \approx 66.7$, so the average seek time is about 60 ms. MIXTEC disks rotate once every 25 ms, so the latency time averages about 12.5 ms. The transmission time for n characters is $(n/5000) \times 25\,\text{ms} = 5n\,\mu\text{s}$. (This is about $3\frac{1}{3}$ times as fast as the transmission rate of the MIXT tapes that were used in the examples of Section 5.4.6.)

Thus the main differences between MIXTEC disks and MIXT tapes are these:

a) Tapes can only be accessed sequentially.

b) Individual disk operations tend to require significantly more overhead (seek time + latency time compared to stop/start time).

c) The disk transmission rate is faster.

By using clever merge patterns on tape, we were able to compensate somewhat for disadvantage (a). Our goal now is to think of some clever algorithms for disk sorting that will compensate for disadvantage (b).

Overcoming latency time. Let us consider first the problem of minimizing the delays caused by the fact that the disks aren't always positioned properly when we want to start an I/O command. We can't make the disk spin faster, but we can still apply some tricks that reduce or even eliminate all of the latency time. The addition of more access arms would obviously help, but that would be an expensive hardware modification. Here are some software ideas:

- If we read or write several tracks of a cylinder at a time, we avoid the latency time (*and* the seek time) on all tracks but the first. In general it is often possible to synchronize the computing time with the disk movement in such a way that a sequence of input/output instructions can be carried out without latency delays.

- Consider the problem of reading half a track of data (Fig. 90): If the read command begins when the heads are at axis A, there is no latency delay, and the total time for reading is just the transmission time, $\frac{1}{2} \times 25\,\text{ms}$. If the command begins with the heads at B, we need $\frac{1}{4}$ of a revolution for latency and $\frac{1}{2}$ for transmission, totalling $\frac{3}{4} \times 25\,\text{ms}$. The most interesting case occurs when the

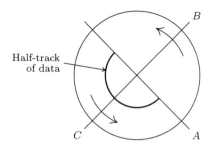

Fig. 90. Analysis of the latency time when reading half of a track.

heads are initially at C: With proper hardware and software we need *not* waste $\frac{3}{4}$ of a revolution for latency delay. Reading can begin immediately, into the second half of the input buffer; then after a $\frac{1}{2} \times 25$ ms pause, reading can resume into the first half of the buffer, so that the instruction is completed when axis C is reached again. In a similar manner, we can ensure that the total latency plus transmission time will never exceed the time for one revolution, regardless of the initial position of the disk. The average amount of latency delay is reduced by this scheme from half a revolution to $\frac{1}{2}(1 - x^2)$ of a revolution, if we are reading or writing a given fraction x of a track, for $0 < x \leq 1$. When an entire track is being read or written ($x = 1$), this technique eliminates *all* the latency time.

Drums: The no-seek case. Some external memory units, traditionally called drum memories, eliminate the seek time by having one read/write head for every track. If the technique of Fig. 90 is employed on such devices, both seek time and latency time reduce to zero, provided that we always read or write a track at a time; this is the ideal situation in which transmission time is the only limiting factor.

Let us consider again the example application of Section 5.4.6, sorting 100,000 records of 100 characters each, with a 100,000-character internal memory. The total amount of data to be sorted fills half of a MIXTEC disk. It is usually impossible to read and write simultaneously on a single disk unit; we shall assume that two disks are available, so that reading and writing can overlap each other. For the moment we shall assume, in fact, that the disks are actually drums, containing 4000 tracks of 5000 characters each, with no seek time required.

What sorting algorithm should be used? The method of merging is a fairly natural choice; other methods of internal sorting do not lend themselves so well to a disk implementation, except for the radix techniques of Section 5.2.5. The considerations of Section 5.4.7 show that radix sorting is usually inferior to merging for general-purpose applications, because the duality theorem of that section applies to disks as well as to tapes. Radix sorting does have a strong advantage, however, when the keys are uniformly distributed and many disks can be used in parallel, because an initial distribution by the most significant digits of the keys will divide the work up into independent subproblems that need no further communication. (See, for example, R. C. Agarwal, *SIGMOD Record* **25**, 2 (June 1996), 240–246.)

We will concentrate on merge sorting in the following discussion. To begin a merge sort for the stated problem we can use replacement selection, with two 5000-character input buffers and two 5000-character output buffers. In fact, it is possible to reduce this to *three* 5000-character buffers, if records in the current input buffer are replaced by records that come off the selection tree. That leaves 85,000 characters (850 records) for a selection tree, so one pass over our example data will form about 60 initial runs. (See Eq. 5.4.6–(3).) This pass takes only about 50 seconds, if we assume that the internal processing time is fast enough to keep up with the input/output rate, with one record moving to the output buffer every 500 microseconds. If the input to be sorted appeared on a MIXT tape, instead of a drum, this pass would be slower, governed by the tape speed.

With two drums and full-track reading/writing, it is not hard to see that the total transmission time for P-way merging is minimized if we let P be as large as possible. Unfortunately we can't simply do a 60-way merge on all of the initial runs, since there isn't room for 60 buffers in memory. (A buffer of fewer than 5000 characters would introduce unwanted latency time. Remember that we are still pretending to be living in the 1970s, when internal memory space was significantly limited.) If we do P-way merges, passing all the data from one drum to the other so that reading and writing are overlapped, the number of merge passes is $\lceil \log_P 60 \rceil$, so we may complete the job in two passes if $8 \leq P \leq 59$. The smallest such P reduces the amount of internal computing, so we choose $P = 8$; if 65 initial runs had been formed we would take $P = 9$. If 82 or more initial runs had been formed, we could take $P = 10$, but since there is room for only 18 input buffers and 2 output buffers there would be a possibility of hangup during the merge (see Algorithm 5.4.6F); it may be better in such a case to do two partial passes over a small portion of the data, reducing the number of initial runs to 81 or less.

Under our assumptions, both of the merging passes will take about 50 seconds, so the entire sort in this ideal situation will be completed in just 2.5 minutes (plus a few seconds for bookkeeping, initialization, etc.). This is six times faster than the best six-tape sort considered in Section 5.4.6; the reasons for this speedup are the improved external/internal transmission rate (3.5 times faster), the higher order of merge (we can't do an eight-way tape merge unless we have nine or more tapes), and the fact that the output was left on disk (no final rewind, etc., was necessary). If the initial input and sorted output were required to be on MIXT tapes, with the drums used for merging only, the corresponding sorting time would have been about 8.2 minutes.

If only one drum were available instead of two, the input-output time would take twice as long, since reading and writing must be done separately. (In fact, the input-output operations would take *three times* as long, since we would be overwriting the initial input data; in such a case it is prudent to follow each write by a "read-back check" operation, lest some of the input data be irretrievably lost, if the hardware does not provide automatic verification of written information.) But some of this excess time can be recovered because we can use partial pass methods that process some data records more often than others. The two-drum case requires all data to be processed an even number or an odd number of times, but the one-drum case can use more general merge patterns.

We observed in Section 5.4.4 that merge patterns can be represented by trees, and that the transmission time corresponding to a merge pattern is proportional to the external path length of its tree. Only certain trees (T-lifo or strongly T-fifo) could be used as efficient tape merging patterns, because some runs get buried in the middle of a tape as the merging proceeds. But *on disks or drums, all trees define usable merge patterns* if the degrees of their internal nodes are not too large for the available internal memory size.

Therefore we can minimize transmission time by choosing a tree with minimum external path length, such as a complete P-ary tree where P is as large as possible. By Eq. 5.4.4–(9), the external path length of such a tree is equal to

$$qS - \lfloor (P^q - S)/(P - 1) \rfloor, \qquad q = \lceil \log_P S \rceil, \tag{1}$$

if there are S external nodes (leaves).

It is particularly easy to design an algorithm that merges according to the complete P-ary tree pattern. See, for example, Fig. 91, which shows the case $P = 3$, $S = 6$. First we add dummy runs, if necessary, to make $S \equiv 1$ (modulo $P - 1$); then we combine runs according to a first-in-first-out discipline, at every stage merging the P oldest runs at the front of the queue into a single run that is placed at the rear.

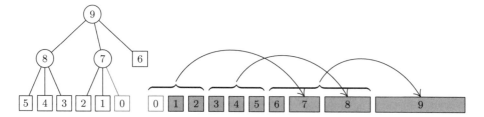

Fig. 91. Complete ternary tree with six leaves, and the corresponding merge pattern.

The complete P-ary tree gives an optimum pattern if all of the initial runs are the same length, but we can often do better if some runs are longer than others. An optimum pattern for this general situation can be constructed without difficulty by using Huffman's method (exercise 2.3.4.5–10), which may be stated in merging language as follows: "First add $(1 - S)$ mod $(P - 1)$ dummy runs of length 0. Then repeatedly merge together the P *shortest* existing runs until only one run is left." When all initial runs have the same length this method reduces to the FIFO discipline described above.

In our 100,000-record example we can do nine-way merging, since 18 input buffers and two output buffers will fit in memory and Algorithm 5.4.6F will overlap all compute time. The complete 9-ary tree with 60 leaves corresponds to a merging pattern with $1\frac{29}{30}$ passes, if all initial runs have the same length. The total sorting time with one drum, using read-back check after every write, therefore comes to about 7.4 minutes. A higher value of P may reduce this running time slightly; but the situation is complicated because "reading hangup" might occur when the buffers become too full or too empty.

The influence of seek time. Our discussion shows that it is relatively easy to construct optimum merging patterns for drums, because seek time and latency time can be essentially nonexistent. But when disks are used with small buffers we often spend more time seeking information than reading it, so the seek time has a considerable influence on the sorting strategy. Decreasing the order of merge, P, makes it possible to use larger buffers, so fewer seeks are required; this often compensates for the extra transmission time demanded by the smaller value of P.

Seek time depends on the distance traveled by the access arm, and we could try to arrange things so that this distance is minimized. For example, it may be wise to sort the records within cylinders first. However, large-scale merging requires a good deal of jumping around between cylinders (see exercise 2). Furthermore, the multiprogramming capability of modern operating systems means that users tend to lose control over the position of disk access arms. We are often justified, therefore, in assuming that each disk command involves a "random" seek.

Our goal is to discover a merge pattern that achieves the best balance between seek time and transmission time. For this purpose we need some way to estimate the goodness of any particular tree with respect to a particular hardware configuration. Consider, for example, the tree in Fig. 92; we want to estimate how long it will take to carry out the corresponding merge, so that we can compare this tree to other trees.

In the following discussion we shall make some simple assumptions about disk merging, in order to illustrate some of the general ideas. Let us suppose that (i) it takes $72.5 + 0.005n$ milliseconds to read or write n characters; (ii) 100,000 characters of internal memory are available for working storage; (iii) an average of 0.004 milliseconds of computation time are required to transmit each character from input to output; (iv) there is to be *no overlap* between reading, writing, or computing; and (v) the buffer size used on output need not be the same as the buffer size used to read the data on the following pass. An analysis of the sorting problem under these simple assumptions will give us some insights when we turn to more complicated situations.

If we do a P-way merge, we can divide the internal working storage into $P+1$ buffer areas, P for input and one for output, with $B = 100000/(P+1)$ characters per buffer. Suppose the files being merged contain a total of L characters; then we will do approximately L/B output operations and about the same number of input operations, so the total merging time under our assumptions will be approximately

$$2\left(72.5\frac{L}{B} + 0.005L\right) + 0.004L = (0.00145P + 0.01545)L \qquad (2)$$

milliseconds.

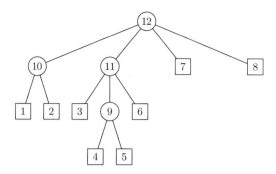

Fig. 92. A tree whose external path length is 16 and whose degree path length is 52.

In other words, a P-way merge of L characters takes about $(\alpha P + \beta)L$ units of time, for some constants α and β depending on the seek time, latency time, compute time, and memory size. This formula leads to an interesting way to construct good merge patterns for disks. Consider Fig. 92, for example, and assume that all initial runs (represented by square leaf nodes) have length L_0. Then the merges at nodes 9 and 10 each take $(2\alpha + \beta)(2L_0)$ units of time, the merge at node 11 takes $(3\alpha + \beta)(4L_0)$, and the final merge at node 12 takes $(4\alpha + \beta)(8L_0)$. The total merging time therefore comes to $(52\alpha + 16\beta)L_0$ units. The coefficient "16" here is well-known to us, it is simply the external path length of the tree. The coefficient "52" of α is, however, a new concept, which we may call the *degree path length* of the tree; it is the sum, taken over all leaf nodes, of the internal-node degrees on the path from the leaf to the root. For example, in Fig. 92 the degree path length is

$$(2+4) + (2+4) + (3+4) + (2+3+4) + (2+3+4) + (3+4) + (4) + (4)$$
$$= 52.$$

If $\mathcal{T}$ is any tree, let $D(\mathcal{T})$ and $E(\mathcal{T})$ denote its degree path length and its external path length, respectively. Our analysis may be summarized as follows:

Theorem H. *If the time required to do a P-way merge on L characters has the form $(\alpha P + \beta)L$, and if there are S equal-length runs to be merged, the best merge pattern corresponds to a tree $\mathcal{T}$ for which $\alpha D(\mathcal{T}) + \beta E(\mathcal{T})$ is a minimum, over all trees having S leaves.* ∎

(This theorem was implicitly contained in an unpublished paper that George U. Hubbard presented at the ACM National Conference in 1963.)

Let α and β be fixed constants; we shall say a tree is *optimal* if it has the minimum value of $\alpha D(\mathcal{T}) + \beta E(\mathcal{T})$ over all trees, $\mathcal{T}$, with the same number of leaves. It is not difficult to see that *all subtrees of an optimal tree are optimal*, and therefore we can construct optimal trees with n leaves by piecing together optimal trees with $< n$ leaves.

Theorem K. *Let the sequence of numbers $A_m(n)$ be defined for $1 \leq m \leq n$ by the rules*

$$A_1(1) = 0; \tag{3}$$

$$A_m(n) = \min_{1 \leq k \leq n/m} \left(A_1(k) + A_{m-1}(n-k)\right), \qquad \text{for } 2 \leq m \leq n; \tag{4}$$

$$A_1(n) = \min_{2 \leq m \leq n} \left(\alpha mn + \beta n + A_m(n)\right), \qquad \text{for } n \geq 2. \tag{5}$$

Then $A_1(n)$ is the minimum value of $\alpha D(\mathcal{T}) + \beta E(\mathcal{T})$, over all trees $\mathcal{T}$ with n leaves.

Proof. Equation (4) implies that $A_m(n)$ is the minimum value of $A_1(n_1) + \cdots + A_1(n_m)$ taken over all positive integers $n_1, \ldots, n_m$ such that $n_1 + \cdots + n_m = n$. The result now follows by induction on n. ∎

The recurrence relations (3), (4), (5) can also be used to construct the optimal trees themselves: Let $k_m(n)$ be a value for which the minimum occurs in the definition of $A_m(n)$. Then we can construct an optimal tree with n leaves by joining $m = k_1(n)$ subtrees at the root; the subtrees are optimal trees with $k_m(n)$, $k_{m-1}(n - k_m(n))$, $k_{m-2}(n - k_m(n) - k_{m-1}(n - k_m(n)))$, ... leaves, respectively.

For example, Table 1 illustrates this construction when $\alpha = \beta = 1$. A compact specification of the corresponding optimal trees appears at the right of the table; the entry "4:9:9" when $n = 22$ means, for example, that an optimal tree $\mathcal{T}_{22}$ with 22 leaves may be obtained by combining $\mathcal{T}_4$, $\mathcal{T}_9$, and $\mathcal{T}_9$ (see Fig. 93). Optimal trees are not unique; for instance, 5:8:9 would be just as good as 4:9:9.

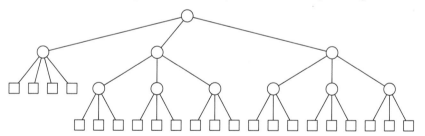

Fig. 93. An optimum way to merge 22 initial runs of equal length, when $\alpha = \beta$ in Theorem H. This pattern minimizes the seek time, under the assumptions leading to Eq. (2) in the text.

Our derivation of (2) shows that the relation $\alpha \leq \beta$ will hold whenever $P + 1$ equal buffer areas are used. The limiting case $\alpha = \beta$, shown in Table 1 and Fig. 93, occurs when the seek time itself is to be minimized without regard to transmission time.

Returning to our original application, we still haven't considered how to get the initial runs in the first place; without read/write/compute overlap, replacement selection loses some of its advantages. Perhaps we should fill the entire internal memory, sort it, and output the results; such input and output

Table 1

OPTIMAL TREE CHARACTERISTICS $A_m(n)$, $k_m(n)$ WHEN $\alpha = \beta = 1$

n	1	2	3	4	5	6	7	8	9	10	11	12	Tree	n
1	0,0												—	1
2	6,2	0,1											1:1	2
3	12,3	6,1	0,1										1:1:1	3
4	20,4	12,1	6,1	0,1									1:1:1:1	4
5	30,5	18,2	12,1	6,1	0,1								1:1:1:1:1	5
6	42,2	24,3	18,1	12,1	6,1	0,1							3:3	6
7	52,3	32,3	24,1	18,1	12,1	6,1	0,1						1:3:3	7
8	62,3	40,4	30,2	24,1	18,1	12,1	6,1	0,1					2:3:3	8
9	72,3	50,4	36,3	30,1	24,1	18,1	12,1	6,1	0,1				3:3:3	9
10	84,3	60,5	44,3	36,1	30,1	24,1	18,1	12,1	6,1	0,1			3:3:4	10
11	96,3	72,4	52,3	42,2	36,1	30,1	24,1	18,1	12,1	6,1	0,1		3:4:4	11
12	108,3	82,4	60,4	48,3	42,1	36,1	30,1	24,1	18,1	12,1	6,1	0,1	4:4:4	12
13	121,4	92,4	70,4	56,3	48,1	42,1	36,1	30,1	24,1	18,1	12,1	6,1	3:3:3:4	13
14	134,4	102,5	80,4	64,3	54,2	48,1	42,1	36,1	30,1	24,1	18,1	12,1	3:3:4:4	14
15	147,4	114,5	90,4	72,3	60,3	54,1	48,1	42,1	36,1	30,1	24,1	18,1	3:4:4:4	15
16	160,4	124,7	102,4	80,4	68,3	60,1	54,1	48,1	42,1	36,1	30,1	24,1	4:4:4:4	16
17	175,4	134,8	112,4	90,4	76,3	66,2	60,1	54,1	48,1	42,1	36,1	30,1	4:4:4:5	17
18	190,4	144,9	122,4	100,4	84,3	72,3	66,1	60,1	54,1	48,1	42,1	36,1	4:4:5:5	18
19	205,4	156,9	132,5	110,4	92,3	80,3	72,1	66,1	60,1	54,1	48,1	42,1	4:5:5:5	19
20	220,4	168,9	144,4	120,5	100,4	88,3	78,2	72,1	66,1	60,1	54,1	48,1	5:5:5:5	20
21	236,5	180,9	154,4	132,4	110,4	96,3	84,3	78,1	72,1	66,1	60,1	54,1	4:4:4:4:5	21
22	252,3	192,10	164,4	142,4	120,4	104,3	92,3	84,1	78,1	72,1	66,1	60,1	4:9:9	22
23	266,3	204,11	174,5	152,4	130,4	112,3	100,3	90,2	84,1	78,1	72,1	66,1	5:9:9	23
24	282,3	216,12	186,5	162,5	140,4	120,4	108,3	96,3	90,1	84,1	78,1	72,1	5:9:10	24
25	296,3	229,12	196,7	174,4	150,5	130,4	116,3	104,3	96,1	90,1	84,1	78,1	7:9:9	25

operations can each be done with one seek. Or perhaps we are better off using, say, 20 percent of the memory as a combination input/output buffer, and doing replacement selection. This requires five times as many seeks (an extra 60 seconds or so!), but it reduces the number of initial runs from 100 to 64; the reduction would be more dramatic if the input file were pretty much in order already.

If we decide not to use replacement selection, the optimum tree for $S = 100$, $\alpha = 0.00145$, $\beta = 0.01545$ [see (2)] turns out to be rather prosaic: It is simply a 10-way merge, completed in two passes over the data. Allowing 30 seconds for internal sorting (100 quicksorts, say), the initial distribution pass takes about 2.5 minutes, and the merge passes each take almost 5 minutes, for a total of 12.4 minutes. If we decide to use replacement selection, the optimal tree for $S = 64$ turns out to be equally uninteresting (two 8-way merge passes); the initial distribution pass takes about 3.5 minutes, the merge passes each take about 4.5 minutes, and the estimated total time comes to 12.6 minutes. Remember that both of these methods give up virtually all read/write/compute overlap in order to have larger buffers, reducing seek time. None of these estimated times includes the time that might be necessary for read-back check operations.

In practice the final merge pass tends to be quite different from the others; for example, the output is often expanded and/or written onto tape. In such cases the tree pattern should be chosen using a different optimality criterion at the root.

*A closer look at optimal trees. It is interesting to examine the extreme case $\beta = 0$ in Theorems H and K, even though practical situations usually lead to parameters with $0 \le \alpha \le \beta$. What tree with n leaves has the smallest possible degree path length? Curiously it turns out that three-way merging is best.

Theorem L. *The degree path length of a tree with n leaves is never less than*

$$f(n) = \begin{cases} 3qn + 2(n - 3^q), & \text{if } 2 \cdot 3^{q-1} \le n \le 3^q; \\ 3qn + 4(n - 3^q), & \text{if } 3^q \le n \le 2 \cdot 3^q. \end{cases} \tag{6}$$

Ternary trees $\mathcal{T}_n$ defined by the rules

$$\mathcal{T}_1 = \Box, \qquad \mathcal{T}_2 = \overset{\bigcirc}{\underset{\Box\ \Box}{\diagdown}}, \qquad \mathcal{T}_n = \overset{\bigcirc}{\mathcal{T}\left\lfloor\frac{n}{3}\right\rfloor \quad \mathcal{T}\left\lfloor\frac{n+1}{3}\right\rfloor \quad \mathcal{T}\left\lfloor\frac{n+2}{3}\right\rfloor} \tag{7}$$

have the minimum degree path length.

Proof. It is important to observe that $f(n)$ is a *convex function*, namely that

$$f(n + 1) - f(n) \ge f(n) - f(n - 1) \qquad \text{for all } n \ge 2. \tag{8}$$

The relevance of this property is due to the following lemma, which is dual to the result of exercise 2.3.4.5–17.

Lemma C. *A function $g(n)$ defined on the positive integers satisfies*

$$\min_{1 \le k < n} \big(g(k) + g(n - k)\big) = g(\lfloor n/2 \rfloor) + g(\lceil n/2 \rceil), \qquad n \ge 2, \tag{9}$$

if and only if it is convex.

Proof. If $g(n + 1) - g(n) < g(n) - g(n - 1)$ for some $n \ge 2$, we have $g(n + 1) + g(n - 1) < g(n) + g(n)$, contradicting (9). Conversely, if (8) holds for g, and if $1 \le k < n - k$, we have $g(k+1) + g(n - k - 1) \le g(k) + g(n - k)$ by convexity. ∎

The latter part of Lemma C's proof can be extended for any $m \ge 2$ to show that

$$\min_{\substack{n_1 + \cdots + n_m = n \\ n_1, \ldots, n_m \ge 1}} \big(g(n_1) + \cdots + g(n_m)\big)$$

$$= g(\lfloor n/m \rfloor) + g(\lfloor (n + 1)/m \rfloor) + \cdots + g(\lfloor (n + m - 1)/m \rfloor) \tag{10}$$

whenever g is convex. Let

$$f_m(n) = f(\lfloor n/m \rfloor) + f(\lfloor (n + 1)/m \rfloor) + \cdots + f(\lfloor (n + m - 1)/m \rfloor); \tag{11}$$

the proof of Theorem L is completed by proving that $f_3(n) + 3n = f(n)$ and $f_m(n) + mn \ge f(n)$ for all $m \ge 2$. (See exercise 11.) ∎

It would be very nice if optimal trees could always be characterized neatly as in Theorem L. But the results we have seen for $\alpha = \beta$ in Table 1 show that the function $A_1(n)$ is not always convex. In fact, Table 1 is sufficient to disprove most simple conjectures about optimal trees! We can, however, salvage part of Theorem L in the general case; M. Schlumberger and J. Vuillemin have shown that *large* orders of merge can always be avoided:

Theorem M. *Given α and β as in Theorem H, there exists an optimal tree in which the degree of every node is at most*

$$d(\alpha,\beta) = \left\lceil \min_{k \geq 1}\left(k + \left(1 + \frac{1}{k}\right)\left(1 + \frac{\beta}{\alpha}\right)\right)\right\rceil. \tag{12}$$

Proof. Let $n_1, \ldots, n_m$ be positive integers such that $n_1 + \cdots + n_m = n$, $A(n_1) + \cdots + A(n_m) = A_m(n)$, and $n_1 \leq \cdots \leq n_m$, and assume that $m \geq d(\alpha,\beta) + 1$. Let k be the value that minimizes (12); we shall show that

$$\alpha n(m - k) + \beta n + A_{m-k}(n) \leq \alpha nm + \beta n + A_m(n), \tag{13}$$

hence the minimum value in (4) is always achieved for some $m \leq d(\alpha,\beta)$.

By definition, since $m \geq k + 2$, we must have

$$
\begin{aligned}
A_{m-k}(n) &\leq A_1(n_1+\cdots+n_{k+1})+A_1(n_{k+2})+\cdots+A_1(n_m)\\
&\leq \alpha(n_1+\cdots+n_{k+1})(k+1)+\beta(n_1+\cdots+n_{k+1})+A_1(n_1)+\cdots+A_1(n_m)\\
&= \big(\alpha(k+1)+\beta\big)(n_1+\cdots+n_{k+1})+A_m(n)\\
&\leq \big(\alpha(k+1)+\beta\big)(k+1)n/m+A_m(n),
\end{aligned}
$$

and (13) now follows easily. (Careful inspection of this proof shows that (12) is best possible, in the sense that some optimal trees must have nodes of degree $d(\alpha,\beta)$; see exercise 13.) ∎

The construction in Theorem K needs $O(N^2)$ memory cells and $O(N^2 \log N)$ steps to evaluate $A_m(n)$ for $1 \leq m \leq n \leq N$; Theorem M shows that only $O(N)$ cells and $O(N^2)$ steps are needed. Schlumberger and Vuillemin have discovered several more very interesting properties of optimal trees [*Acta Informatica* **3** (1973), 25–36]. Furthermore the asymptotic value of $A_1(n)$ can be worked out as shown in exercise 9.

*Another way to allocate buffers. David E. Ferguson [*CACM* **14** (1971), 476–478] pointed out that seek time can be reduced if we don't make all buffers the same size. The same idea occurred at about the same time to several other people [S. J. Waters, *Comp. J.* **14** (1971), 109–112; Ewing S. Walker, *Software Age* **4** (August–September, 1970), 16–17].

Suppose we are doing a four-way merge on runs of equal length L_0, with M characters of memory. If we divide the memory into equal buffers of size $B = M/5$, we need about L_0/B seeks on each input file and $4L_0/B$ seeks for the output, totalling $8L_0/B = 40L_0/M$ seeks. But if we use four input buffers of size $M/6$ and one output buffer of size $M/3$, we need only about $4 \times (6L_0/M) + 4 \times (3L_0/M) = 36L_0/M$ seeks! The transmission time is the same in both cases, so we haven't lost anything by the change.

In general, suppose that we want to merge sorted files of lengths $L_1, \ldots, L_P$ into a sorted file of length

$$L_{P+1} = L_1 + \cdots + L_P,$$

and assume that a buffer of size B_k is being used for the kth file. Thus

$$B_1 + \cdots + B_P + B_{P+1} = M, \tag{14}$$

where M is the total size of available internal memory. The number of seeks will be approximately

$$\frac{L_1}{B_1} + \cdots + \frac{L_P}{B_P} + \frac{L_{P+1}}{B_{P+1}}. \tag{15}$$

Let's try to minimize this quantity, subject to condition (14), assuming for convenience that the B_k's don't have to be integers. If we increase B_j by δ and decrease B_k by the same amount, the number of seeks changes by

$$\frac{L_j}{B_j + \delta} - \frac{L_j}{B_j} + \frac{L_k}{B_k - \delta} - \frac{L_k}{B_k} = \left(\frac{L_k}{B_k(B_k - \delta)} - \frac{L_j}{B_j(B_j + \delta)} \right) \delta,$$

so the allocation can be improved if $L_j/B_j^2 \neq L_k/B_k^2$. Therefore we get the minimum number of seeks only if

$$\frac{L_1}{B_1^2} = \cdots = \frac{L_P}{B_P^2} = \frac{L_{P+1}}{B_{P+1}^2}. \tag{16}$$

Since a minimum does exist it must occur when

$$B_k = \sqrt{L_k}\, M / (\sqrt{L_1} + \cdots + \sqrt{L_{P+1}}), \qquad 1 \leq k \leq P+1; \tag{17}$$

these are the only values of $B_1, \ldots, B_{P+1}$ that satisfy both (14) and (16). Plugging (17) into (15) gives a fairly simple formula for the total number of seeks,

$$(\sqrt{L_1} + \cdots + \sqrt{L_{P+1}})^2/M, \tag{18}$$

which may be compared with the number $(P+1)(L_1 + \cdots + L_{P+1})/M$ obtained if all buffers are equal in length. By exercise 1.2.3–31, the improvement is

$$\sum_{1 \leq j < k \leq P+1} (\sqrt{L_j} - \sqrt{L_k})^2/M.$$

Unfortunately formula (18) does not lend itself to an easy determination of optimum merge patterns as in Theorem K (see exercise 14).

The use of chaining. M. A. Goetz [*CACM* **6** (1963), 245–248] has suggested an interesting way to avoid seek time on output, by linking individual tracks together. His idea requires a fairly fancy set of disk storage management routines, but it applies to many problems besides sorting, and it may therefore be a very worthwhile technique for general-purpose use.

The concept is simple: Instead of allocating tracks sequentially within cylinders of the disk, we link them together and maintain lists of available space, one for each cylinder. When it is time to output a track of information, we write it on the current cylinder (wherever the access arm happens to be), unless that cylinder is full. In this way the seek time usually disappears.

The catch is that we can't store a link-to-next-track within the track itself, since the necessary information isn't known at the right time. (We could store a link-to-previous-track and read the file backwards on the next pass, if that were suitable.) A table of link addresses for the tracks of each file can be maintained separately, because it requires comparatively little space. The available space lists can be represented compactly by using bit tables, with 1000 bits specifying the availability or unavailability of 1000 tracks.

Forecasting revisited. Algorithm 5.4.6F shows that we can forecast which input buffer of a P-way merge will empty first, by looking at the last keys in each buffer. Therefore we can be reading and computing at the same time. That algorithm uses floating input buffers, not dedicated to a particular file; so the buffers must all be the same size, and the buffer allocation technique above cannot be used. But the restriction to a uniform buffer size is no great loss, since computers now have much larger internal memories than they used to. Nowadays a natural buffer size, such as the capacity of a full disk track, often suggests itself.

Let us therefore imagine that the P runs to be merged each consist of a sequence of data *blocks*, where each block (except possibly the last) contains exactly B records. D. L. Whitlow and A. Sasson developed an interesting algorithm called SyncSort [*U.S. Patent 4210961* (1980)], which improves on Algorithm 5.4.6F by needing only three buffers of size B together with a memory pool holding PB records and PB pointers. By contrast, Algorithm 5.4.6F requires $2P$ input buffers and 2 output buffers, but no pointers.

The three SyncSort buffers are arranged in a circle. As merging proceeds, the computer is processing data in the current buffer, while input is being read into the next buffer and output is being written from the third. Many disk devices allow simultaneous reading and writing in the same cylinder; indeed, disk merging allows us to write new runs in place of the runs we are reading. Otherwise we could use two disks, one for reading and one for writing. If perfect synchronization between reading and writing is impossible (because of seek time, for example), we could also extend the circle to four or more buffers, as in Fig. 26 of Section 1.4.4.

SyncSort begins by reading the first block of each run and putting these PB records into the memory pool. Each record in the memory pool is linked to its successor in the run it belongs to, except that the final record in each block has no successor as yet. The smallest of the keys in those final records determines the run that will need to replenished first, so we begin to read the second block of that run. Merging begins as soon as that second block has been read; by looking at its final key we can accurately forecast the next relevant block, and we can continue in the same way to prefetch exactly the right blocks to input, just before they are needed.

The SyncSort merging algorithm exchanges each record in the current buffer with the next record of output, namely the record of the memory pool that has the smallest key. The selection tree and the successor links are also updated appropriately as we make each exchange. Once the end of the current buffer is reached, we are ready to rotate the buffer circle: The reading buffer becomes current, the writing buffer is used for reading, and we begin to write from the former current buffer.

Using several disks. Disk devices once were massive both in size and weight, but they became dramatically smaller, lighter, and less expensive during the late 1980s — although they began to hold more data than ever before. Therefore people began to design algorithms for once-unimaginable clusters of 5 or 10 or 50 disk devices or for even larger disk farms.

One easy way to gain speed with additional disks is to use the technique of *disk striping* for large files. Suppose we have D disk units, numbered 0, 1, ..., $D - 1$, and consider a file that consists of L blocks $a_0 a_1 \ldots a_{L-1}$. Striping this file on D disks means that we put block a_j on disk number $j \bmod D$; thus, disk 0 holds $a_0 a_D a_{2D} \ldots$, disk 1 holds $a_1 a_{D+1} a_{2D+1} \ldots$, etc. Then we can perform D reads or writes simultaneously on D-block groups $a_0 a_1 \ldots a_{D-1}$, $a_D a_{D+1} \ldots a_{2D-1}$, ..., which are called *superblocks*. The individual blocks of each superblock should be on corresponding cylinders on different disks so that the seek time will be the same on each unit. In essence, we are acting as if we had a single disk unit with blocks and buffers of size DB, but the input and output operations run D times faster.

An elegant improvement on superblock striping can be used when we're doing 2-way merging, or in general whenever we want to match records with equal keys in two files that are in order by keys. Suppose the blocks $a_0 a_1 a_2 \ldots$ of the first file are striped on D disks as above, but the blocks $b_0 b_1 b_2 \ldots$ of the other file are striped in the reverse direction, with block b_j on disk $(D - 1 - j) \bmod D$. For example, if $D = 5$ the blocks a_j appear respectively on disks 0, 1, 2, 3, 4, 0, 1, ..., while the blocks b_j for $j \geq 0$ appear on 4, 3, 2, 1, 0, 4, 3, ... Let α_j be the last key of block a_j and let β_j be the last key of block b_j. By examining the α's and β's we can forecast the sequence in which we will want to read the data blocks; this sequence might, for example, be

$$a_0 b_0 a_1 a_2 b_1 \quad a_3 a_4 b_2 a_5 a_6 \quad a_7 a_8 b_3 b_4 b_5 \quad b_6 b_7 b_8 b_9 b_{10} \quad \ldots \ .$$

These blocks appear respectively on disks

$$0 \ 4 \ 1 \ 2 \ 3 \quad 3 \ 4 \ 2 \ 0 \ 1 \quad 2 \ 3 \ 1 \ 0 \ 4 \quad 3 \ 2 \ 1 \ 0 \ 4 \quad \ldots$$

when $D = 5$, and if we read them five at a time we will be inputting successively from disks $\{0, 4, 1, 2, 3\}$, $\{3, 4, 2, 0, 1\}$, $\{2, 3, 1, 0, 4\}$, $\{3, 2, 1, 0, 4\}$, ...; there will never be a conflict in which we need to read two blocks from the same disk at the same time! In general, with D disks we can read D at a time without conflict, because the first group will have k blocks $a_0 \ldots a_{k-1}$ on disks 0 through $k-1$ and $D - k$ blocks $b_0 \ldots b_{D-k-1}$ on disks $D - 1$ through k, for some k; then we will be poised to continue in the same way but with disk numbers shifted cyclically by k.

This trick is well known to card magicians, who call it the *Gilbreath principle*; it was invented during the 1960s by Norman Gilbreath [see Martin Gardner, *Mathematical Magic Show* (New York: Knopf, 1977), Chapter 7; N. Gilbreath, *Genii* **52** (1989), 743–744]. We need to know the α's and β's, to decide what blocks should be read next, but that information takes up only a small fraction of the space needed by the a's and b's, and it can be kept in separate files. Therefore we need fewer buffers to keep the input going at full speed (see exercise 23).

Randomized striping. If we want to do P-way merging with D disks when P and D are large, we cannot keep reading the information simultaneously from D disks without conflict unless we have a large number of buffers, because there is no analog of the Gilbreath principle when $P > 2$. No matter how we allocate the blocks of a file to disks, there will be a chance that we might need to read many blocks into memory before we are ready to use them, because the blocks that we really need might all happen to reside on the same disk.

Suppose, for example, that we want to do 8-way merging on 5 disks, and suppose that the blocks $a_0 a_1 a_2 \ldots$, $b_0 b_1 b_2 \ldots$, $\ldots$, $h_0 h_1 h_2 \ldots$ of 8 runs have been striped with a_j on disk $j \bmod D$, b_j on disk $(j+1) \bmod D$, $\ldots$, h_j on disk $(j+7) \bmod D$. We might need to access these blocks in the order

$$a_0 b_0 c_0 d_0 e_0 \; f_0 g_0 h_0 d_1 e_1 \; d_2 e_2 d_3 a_1 f_1 \; b_1 g_1 a_2 f_2 e_3 \; d_4 c_1 h_1 b_2 g_2 \; a_3 f_3 e_4 d_5 d_6 \; \ldots; \quad (19)$$

then they appear on the respective disks

$$0 \; 1 \; 2 \; 3 \; 4 \; \; 0 \; 1 \; 2 \; 4 \; 0 \; \; 0 \; 1 \; 1 \; 1 \; 1 \; \; 2 \; 2 \; 2 \; 2 \; 2 \; \; 2 \; 3 \; 3 \; 3 \; 3 \; \; 3 \; 3 \; 3 \; 3 \; 4 \; \; \ldots, \quad (20)$$

so our best bet is to input them as follows:

Time 1	Time 2	Time 3	Time 4	Time 5
$a_0 b_0 c_0 d_0 e_0$	$f_0 g_0 h_0 c_1 d_1$	$e_1 e_2 b_1 h_1 d_6$	$d_2 d_3 g_1 b_2$?	? $a_1 a_2 g_2$?

Time 6	Time 7	Time 8	Time 9	
? $f_1 f_2 a_3$?	? ? $e_3 f_3$?	? ? $d_4 e_4$?	? ? ? d_5 ?	(21)

By the time we are able to look at block d_5, we need to have read d_6 as well as 15 blocks of future data denoted by "?", because of congestion on disk 3. And we will not yet be done with the seven buffers containing remnants of a_3, b_2, c_1, e_4, f_3, g_2, and b_1; so we will need buffer space for at least $(16 + 8 + 5)B$ input records in this particular example.

The simple superblock approach to disk striping would proceed instead to read blocks $a_0 a_1 a_2 a_3 a_4$ at time 1, $b_0 b_1 b_2 b_3 b_4$ at time 2, $\ldots$, $h_0 h_1 h_2 h_3 h_4$ at time 8, then $d_5 d_6 d_7 d_8 d_9$ at time 9 (since $d_5 d_6 d_7 d_8 d_9$ is the superblock needed next), and so on. Using the SyncSort strategy, it would require buffers for $(P + 3)DB$ records and PDB pointers in memory. The more versatile approach indicated above can be shown to need only about half as much buffer space; but the memory requirement is still approximately proportional to PDB when P and D are large (see exercise 24).

R. D. Barve, E. F. Grove, and J. S. Vitter [*Parallel Computing* **23** (1997), 601–631] showed that a slight modification of the independent-block approach leads to an algorithm that keeps the disk input/output running at nearly its full speed while needing only $O(P + D \log D)$ buffer blocks instead of $\Omega(PD)$. Their technique of *randomized striping* puts block j of run k on disk $(x_k + j) \bmod D$, where x_k is a random integer selected just before run k is first written. Instead of insisting that D blocks are constantly being input, one from each disk, they introduced a simple mechanism for holding back when there isn't enough space to keep reading ahead on certain disks, and they proved that their method is asymptotically optimal.

To do P-way merging on D disks with randomized striping, we can maintain $2D + P + Q - 1$ floating input buffers, each holding a block of B records. Input is typically being read into D of these buffers, called *active read buffers*, while P of the others contain the leading blocks from which records are currently being merged; these are called *active merge buffers*. The remaining $D + Q - 1$ "scratch buffers" are either empty or they hold prefetched data that will be needed later; Q is a nonnegative parameter that can be increased in order to lessen the chance that reading will be held back on any of the disks.

The blocks of all runs can be arranged into *chronological order* as in (19): First we list block 0 of each run, then we list the others by determining the order in which active merge buffers will become empty. As explained above, this order is determined by the final keys in each block, so we can readily forecast which blocks ought to be prefetched first.

Let's consider example (19) again, with $P = 8$, $D = 5$, and $Q = 4$. Now we will have only $2D + P + Q - 1 = 21$ input buffer blocks to work with instead of the 29 that were needed above for maximum-speed reading. We will use the offsets

$$x_1 = 3, \ x_2 = 1, \ x_3 = 4, \ x_4 = 1, \ x_5 = 0, \ x_6 = 4, \ x_7 = 2, \ x_8 = 1 \qquad (22)$$

(suggested by the decimal digits of π) for runs a, b, $\ldots$, h; thus the respective disks contain

Disk	Blocks									
0:		e_0			f_1	a_2	$d_4 c_1$			$\ldots$
1:	b_0	d_0	h_0	e_1		f_2		a_3	d_5	$\ldots$
2:		g_0	d_1	e_2	b_1		h_1	f_3	d_6 $\ldots$	(23)
3: a_0			d_2		g_1	e_3	b_2			$\ldots$
4:	c_0	f_0		$d_3 a_1$			g_2	e_4		$\ldots$

if we list their blocks in chronological order. The "random" offsets of (22), together with sequential striping within each run, will tend to minimize the congestion of any particular chronological sequence. The actual processing now goes like this:

	Active reading	Active merging	Scratch	Waiting for
Time 1	$e_0 b_0 g_0 a_0 c_0$	$- - - - - - - -$	$(- - - - - - - -)$	a_0
Time 2	$f_1 d_0 d_1 d_2 f_0$	$a_0 - - - - - - -$	$b_0 c_0 (e_0 g_0 - - - -)$	d_0
Time 3	$a_2 h_0 e_2 g_1 d_3$	$a_0 b_0 c_0 d_0 - - - -$	$e_0 f_0 g_0 (d_1 d_2 f_1 - -)$	h_0
Time 4	$a_2 e_1 b_1 g_1 a_1$	$a_0 b_0 c_0 d_0 e_0 f_0 g_0 h_0$	$d_1 (d_2 e_2 d_3 f_1 g_1 a_2 -)$	e_1 (24)
Time 5	$d_4 f_2 h_1 e_3 g_2$	$a_0 b_0 c_0 d_1 e_1 f_0 g_0 h_0$	$d_2 e_2 d_3 a_1 f_1 b_1 g_1 a_2()$	f_2
Time 6	$c_1 a_3 f_3 b_2 e_4$	$a_2 b_1 c_0 d_3 e_2 f_2 g_1 h_0$	$e_3 d_4 (h_1 g_2 - - - -)$	c_1
Time 7	$? \, d_5 d_6 \, ? \, ?$	$a_2 b_1 c_1 d_4 e_3 f_2 g_1 h_0$	$h_1 b_2 g_2 a_3 f_3 e_4 (- -)$	d_5

At each unit of time we are waiting for the chronologically first block that is not yet merged and not yet in a scratch buffer; this is one of the blocks that is currently being input to an active read buffer. We assume that the computer is much faster than the disks; thus, all blocks before the one we are waiting for will have already entered the merging process before input is complete. We also assume that sufficient output buffers are available so that merging will not be delayed by the lack of a place to place the output (see exercise 26). When a round of input is complete, the block we were waiting for is immediately classified as an active merge buffer, and the empty merge buffer it replaces will be used for the next active reading. The other $D-1$ active read buffers now trade places with the $D-1$ least important scratch buffers; scratch buffers are ranked by chronological order of their contents. On the next round we will wait for the first unmerged block that isn't present in the scratch buffers. Any scratch buffers preceding that block in chronological order will become part of the active merge before the next input cycle, but the others — shown in parentheses above — will be carried over and they will remain as scratch buffers on the next round. However, at most Q of the buffers in parentheses can be carried over, because we will need to convert $D-1$ scratch buffers to active read status immediately after the input is ready. Any additional scratch buffers are effectively blanked out, as if they hadn't been read. This blanking-out occurs at Time 4 in (24): We cannot carry all six of the blocks $d_2 e_2 d_3 f_1 g_1 a_2$ over to Time 5, because $Q = 4$, so we reread g_1 and a_2. Otherwise the reading operations in this example take place at full speed.

Exercise 29 proves that, given any chronological sequence of runs to be merged, the method of randomized striping will achieve the minimum number of disk reads within a factor of $r(D, Q+2)$, on the average, where the function r is tabulated in Table 2. For example, if $D = 4$ and $Q = 18$, the average time to do a P-way merge on L blocks of data with 4 disks and $P + 25$ input buffers will be at most the time to read $r(4, 20)L/D \approx 1.785L/4$ blocks on a single disk. This theoretical upper bound is quite conservative; in practice the performance is even better, very near the optimum time $L/4$.

Table 2

GUARANTEES ON THE PERFORMANCE OF RANDOMIZED STRIPING

	$r(d,d)$	$r(d,2d)$	$r(d,3d)$	$r(d,4d)$	$r(d,5d)$	$r(d,6d)$	$r(d,7d)$	$r(d,8d)$	$r(d,9d)$	$r(d,10d)$
$d=2$	1.500	1.500	1.499	1.467	1.444	1.422	1.393	1.370	1.353	1.339
$d=4$	2.460	2.190	1.986	1.888	1.785	1.724	1.683	1.633	1.597	1.570
$d=8$	3.328	2.698	2.365	2.183	2.056	1.969	1.889	1.836	1.787	1.743
$d=16$	4.087	3.103	2.662	2.434	2.277	2.156	2.067	1.997	1.933	1.890
$d=32$	4.503	3.392	2.917	2.654	2.458	2.319	2.218	2.130	2.062	2.005
$d=64$	5.175	3.718	3.165	2.847	2.613	2.465	2.346	2.249	2.174	2.107
$d=128$	5.431	3.972	3.356	2.992	2.759	2.603	2.459	2.358	2.273	2.201
$d=256$	5.909	4.222	3.536	3.155	2.910	2.714	2.567	2.464	2.363	2.289
$d=512$	6.278	4.455	3.747	3.316	3.024	2.820	2.675	2.556	2.450	2.375
$d=1024$	6.567	4.689	3.879	3.434	3.142	2.937	2.780	2.639	2.536	2.452

Will keysorting help? When records are long and keys are short, it is very tempting to create a new file consisting simply of the keys together with a serial number specifying their original file location. After sorting this key file, we can replace the keys by the successive numbers $1, 2, \ldots$; the new file can then be sorted by original file location and we will have a convenient specification of how to unshuffle the records for the final rearrangement. Schematically, the process has the following form:

i)	Original file	$(K_1, I_1)(K_2, I_2) \ldots (K_N, I_N)$	long
ii)	Key file	$(K_1, 1)(K_2, 2) \ldots (K_N, N)$	short
iii)	Sorted (ii)	$(K_{p_1}, p_1)(K_{p_2}, p_2) \ldots (K_{p_N}, p_N)$	short
iv)	Edited (iii)	$(1, p_1)(2, p_2) \ldots (N, p_N)$	short
v)	Sorted (iv)	$(q_1, 1)(q_2, 2) \ldots (q_N, N)$	short
vi)	Edited (i)	$(q_1, I_1)(q_2, I_2) \ldots (q_N, I_N)$	long

Here $p_j = k$ if and only if $q_k = j$. The two sorting processes in (iii) and (v) are comparatively fast (perhaps even internal sorts), since the records aren't very long. In stage (vi) we have reduced the problem to sorting a file whose keys are simply the numbers $\{1, 2, \ldots, N\}$; each record now specifies exactly where it is to be moved.

The external rearrangement problem that remains after stage (vi) seems trivial, at first glance; but in fact it is rather difficult, and no really good algorithms (significantly better than sorting) have yet been found. We could obviously do the rearrangement in N steps, moving one record at a time; for large enough N this is better than the $N \log N$ of a sorting method. But N is never that large; N is, however, sufficiently large that N seeks are unthinkable.

A radix sorting method can be used efficiently on the edited records of (vi), since their keys have a perfectly uniform distribution. On modern computers, the processing time for an eight-way distribution is much faster than the processing time for an eight-way merge; hence a distribution sort is probably the best procedure. (See Section 5.4.7, and see also exercise 19.)

On the other hand, it seems wasteful to do a full sort after the keys have already been sorted. One reason the external rearrangement problem is unexpectedly difficult has been discovered by R. W. Floyd, who found a nontrivial lower bound on the number of seeks required to rearrange records on a disk device [*Complexity of Computer Computations* (New York: Plenum, 1972), 105–109].

It is convenient to describe Floyd's result in terms of the elevator problem of Section 5.4.8; but this time we want to find an elevator schedule that minimizes the number of *stops*, instead of minimizing the distance traveled. Minimizing the number of stops is not precisely equivalent to finding the minimum-seek rearrangement algorithm, since a stop combines input to the elevator with output from the elevator; but the stop-minimization criterion is close enough to indicate the basic ideas.

We shall make use of the "discrete entropy" function

$$F(n) = \sum_{1 < k \leq n} \left(\lceil \lg k \rceil + 1 \right) = B(n) + n - 1 = n \lceil \lg n \rceil - 2^{\lceil \lg n \rceil} + n, \qquad (25)$$

where $B(n)$ is the binary insertion function, Eq. 5.3.1–(3). By Eq. 5.3.1–(34), $F(n)$ is the minimum external path length of a binary tree with n leaves, and

$$n \lg n \leq F(n) \leq n \lg n + 0.0861n. \qquad (26)$$

Since $F(n)$ is convex and satisfies $F(n) = n + F(\lfloor n/2 \rfloor) + F(\lceil n/2 \rceil)$, we know by Lemma C above that

$$F(n) \le F(k) + F(n-k) + n, \qquad \text{for } 0 \le k \le n. \tag{27}$$

This relation is also evident from the external path length characterization of F; it is the crucial fact we need in the following argument.

As in Section 5.4.8 we shall assume that each floor holds b people, the elevator holds m people, and there are n floors. Let s_{ij} be the number of people currently on floor i whose destination is floor j. The *togetherness rating* of any configuration of people in the building is defined to be the sum $\sum_{1 \le i,j \le n} F(s_{ij})$.

For example, assume that $b = m = n = 6$ and that the 36 people are initially scattered among the floors as follows:

$$\begin{matrix} \text{uuuuuu} \\ \text{123456} \quad \text{123456} \quad \text{123456} \quad \text{123456} \quad \text{123456} \quad \text{123456} \end{matrix} \tag{28}$$

The elevator is empty, sitting on floor 1; "u" denotes a vacant position. Each floor contains one person with each possible destination, so all s_{ij} are 1 and the togetherness rating is zero. If the elevator now transports six people to floor 2, we have the configuration

$$\begin{matrix} \text{123456} \\ \text{uuuuuu} \quad \text{123456} \quad \text{123456} \quad \text{123456} \quad \text{123456} \quad \text{123456} \end{matrix} \tag{29}$$

and the togetherness rating becomes $6F(0) + 24F(1) + 6F(2) = 12$. Suppose the elevator now carries 1, 1, 2, 3, 3, and 4 to floor 3:

$$\begin{matrix} \text{112334} \\ \text{uuuuuu} \quad \text{245566} \quad \text{123456} \quad \text{123456} \quad \text{123456} \quad \text{123456} \end{matrix} \tag{30}$$

The togetherness rating has jumped to $4F(2) + 2F(3) = 18$. When all people have finally been transported to their destinations, the togetherness rating will be $6F(6) = 96$.

Floyd observed that the togetherness rating can never increase by more than $b+m$ at each stop, since a set of s equal-destination people joining with a similar set of size s' improves the rating by $F(s+s') - F(s) - F(s') \le s+s'$. Therefore we have the following result.

Theorem F. *Let t be the togetherness rating of an initial configuration of bn people, in terms of the definitions above. The elevator must make at least*

$$\lceil (F(b)n - t)/(b+m) \rceil$$

stops in order to bring them all to their destinations. ∎

Translating this result into disk terminology, let there be bn records, with b per block, and suppose the internal memory can hold m records at a time. Every disk read brings one block into memory, every disk write stores one block, and s_{ij} is the number of records in block i that belong in block j. If $n \ge b$, there are initial configurations in which all the s_{ij} are ≤ 1; so $t = 0$ and at least $f(b)n/(b+m) \approx (bn \lg b)/m$ block-reading operations are necessary to rearrange the records. (The factor $\lg b$ makes this lower bound nontrivial when b is large.) Exercise 17 derives a substantially stronger lower bound for the common case that m is substantially larger than b.

EXERCISES

1. [*M22*] The text explains a method by which the average latency time required to read a fraction x of a track is reduced from $\frac{1}{2}$ to $\frac{1}{2}(1 - x^2)$ revolutions. This is the minimum possible value, when there is one access arm. What is the corresponding minimum average latency time if there are *two* access arms, $180°$ apart, assuming that only one arm can transmit data at any one time?

2. [*M30*] (A. G. Konheim.) The purpose of this problem is to investigate how far the access arm of a disk must move while merging files that are allocated "orthogonally" to the cylinders. Suppose there are P files, each containing L blocks of records, and assume that the first block of each file appears on cylinder 1, the second on cylinder 2, etc. The relative order of the last keys in each block governs the access arm motion during the merge, hence we may represent the situation in the following mathematically tractable way: Consider a set of PL ordered pairs

$$
\begin{array}{cccc}
(a_{11}, 1) & (a_{21}, 1) & \cdots & (a_{P1}, 1) \\
(a_{12}, 2) & (a_{22}, 2) & \cdots & (a_{P2}, 2) \\
\vdots & \vdots & & \vdots \\
(a_{1L}, L) & (a_{2L}, L) & \cdots & (a_{PL}, L)
\end{array}
$$

where the set $\{a_{ij} \mid 1 \le i \le P, \ 1 \le j \le L\}$ consists of the numbers $\{1, 2, \ldots, PL\}$ in some order, and where $a_{ij} < a_{i(j+1)}$ for $1 \le j < L$. (Rows represent cylinders, columns represent input files.) Sort the pairs on their first components and let the resulting sequence be $(1, j_1)(2, j_2) \ldots (PL, j_{PL})$. Show that, if each of the $(PL)!/L!^P$ choices of the a_{ij} is equally likely, the average value of

$$ |j_2 - j_1| + |j_3 - j_2| + \cdots + |j_{PL} - j_{PL-1}| $$

is

$$ (L - 1)\left(1 + (P - 1)2^{2L-2} \middle/ \binom{2L}{L}\right). $$

[*Hint:* See exercise 5.2.1–14.] Notice that as $L \to \infty$ this value is asymptotically equal to $\frac{1}{4}(P - 1)L\sqrt{\pi L} + O(PL)$.

3. [*M15*] Suppose the internal memory is limited so that 10-way merging is not feasible. How can recurrence relations (3), (4), (5) be modified so that $A_1(n)$ is the minimum value of $\alpha D(\mathcal{T}) + \beta E(\mathcal{T})$, over all n-leaved trees $\mathcal{T}$ having no internal nodes of degree greater than 9?

▶ **4.** [*M21*] Consider a modified form of the square root buffer allocation scheme, in which all P of the input buffers have equal length, but the output buffer size should be chosen so as to minimize seek time.

  a) Derive a formula corresponding to (2), for the running time of an L-character P-way merge.

  b) Show that the construction in Theorem K can be modified in order to obtain a merge pattern that is optimal according to your formula from part (a).

5. [*M20*] When two disks are being used, so that reading on one is overlapped with writing on the other, we cannot use merge patterns like that of Fig. 93 since some leaves are at even levels and some are at odd levels. Show how to modify the construction of Theorem K in order to produce trees that are optimal subject to the constraint that all leaves appear on even levels or all on odd levels.

▸ **6.** [*22*] Find a tree that is optimum in the sense of exercise 5, when $n = 23$ and $\alpha = \beta = 1$. (You may wish to use a computer.)

▸ **7.** [*M24*] When the initial runs are not all the same length, the best merge pattern (in the sense of Theorem H) minimizes $\alpha D(\mathcal{T}) + \beta E(\mathcal{T})$, where $D(\mathcal{T})$ and $E(\mathcal{T})$ now represent *weighted* path lengths: Weights $w_1, \ldots, w_n$ (corresponding to the lengths of the initial runs) are attached to each leaf of the tree, and the degree sums and path lengths are multiplied by the appropriate weights. For example, if $\mathcal{T}$ is the tree of Fig. 92, we would have $D(\mathcal{T}) = 6w_1 + 6w_2 + 7w_3 + 9w_4 + 9w_5 + 7w_3 + 4w_7 + 4w_8$, $E(\mathcal{T}) = 2w_1 + 2w_2 + 2w_3 + 3w_4 + 3w_5 + 2w_6 + w_7 + w_8$.

Prove that there is always an optimal pattern in which the *shortest k* runs are merged first, for some k.

8. [*49*] Is there an algorithm that finds optimal trees for given α, β and weights $w_1, \ldots, w_n$, in the sense of exercise 7, taking only $O(n^c)$ steps for some c?

9. [*HM39*] (L. Hyafil, F. Prusker, J. Vuillemin.) Prove that, for fixed α and β,

$$A_1(n) = \left(\min_{m \geq 2} \frac{\alpha m + \beta}{\log m} \right) n \log n + O(n)$$

as $n \to \infty$, where the $O(n)$ term is ≥ 0.

10. [*HM44*] (L. Hyafil, F. Prusker, J. Vuillemin.) Prove that when α and β are fixed, $A_1(n) = \alpha mn + \beta n + A_m(n)$ for all sufficiently large n, if m minimizes the coefficient in exercise 9.

11. [*M29*] In the notation of (6) and (11), prove that $f_m(n) + mn \geq f(n)$ for all $m \geq 2$ and $n \geq 2$, and determine all m and n for which equality holds.

12. [*25*] Prove that, for all $n > 0$, there is a tree with n leaves and minimum degree path length (6), with all leaves at the same level.

13. [*M24*] Show that for $2 \leq n \leq d(\alpha, \beta)$, where $d(\alpha, \beta)$ is defined in (12), the unique best merge pattern in the sense of Theorem H is an n-way merge.

14. [*40*] Using the square root method of buffer allocation, the seek time for the merge pattern in Fig. 92 would be proportional to $(\sqrt{2} + \sqrt{4} + \sqrt{1} + \sqrt{1} + \sqrt{8})^2 + (\sqrt{1} + \sqrt{1} + \sqrt{2})^2 + (\sqrt{1} + \sqrt{2} + \sqrt{1} + \sqrt{4})^2 + (\sqrt{1} + \sqrt{1} + \sqrt{2})^2$; this is the sum, over each internal node, of $(\sqrt{n_1} + \cdots + \sqrt{n_m} + \sqrt{n_1 + \cdots + n_m})^2$, where that node's respective subtrees have $(n_1, \ldots, n_m)$ leaves. Write a computer program that generates minimum-seek time trees having 1, 2, 3, ... leaves, based on this formula.

15. [*M22*] Show that Theorem F can be improved slightly if the elevator is initially empty and if $F(b)n \neq t$: At least $\lceil (F(b)n + m - t)/(b + m) \rceil$ stops are necessary in such a case.

16. [*23*] (R. W. Floyd.) Find an elevator schedule that transports all the people of (28) to their destinations in at most 12 stops. (Configuration (29) shows the situation after one stop, not two.)

▶ **17.** [*HM25*] (R. W. Floyd, 1980.) Show that the lower bound of Theorem F can be improved to

$$\frac{n(b \ln n - \ln b - 1)}{\ln n + b(1 + \ln(1 + m/b))},$$

in the sense that some initial configuration must require at least this many stops. [*Hint: Count the configurations that can be obtained after s stops.*]

18. [*HM26*] Let L be the lower bound of exercise 17. Show that the average number of elevator stops needed to take all people to their desired floors is at least $L - 1$, when the $(bn)!$ possible permutations of people into bn desks are equally likely.

▶ **19.** [*25*] (B. T. Bennett and A. C. McKellar.) Consider the following approach to keysorting, illustrated on an example file with 10 keys:

   i) Original file: $(50, I_0)(08, I_1)(51, I_2)(06, I_3)(90, I_4)(17, I_5)(89, I_6)(27, I_7)(65, I_8)(42, I_9)$

  ii) Key file: $(50, 0)(08, 1)(51, 2)(06, 3)(90, 4)(17, 5)(89, 6)(27, 7)(65, 8)(42, 9)$

 iii) Sorted (ii): $(06, 3)(08, 1)(17, 5)(27, 7)(42, 9)(50, 0)(51, 2)(65, 8)(89, 6)(90, 4)$

 iv) Bin assignments (see below): $(2, 1)(2, 3)(2, 5)(2, 7)(2, 8)(2, 9)(1, 0)(1, 2)(1, 4)(1, 6)$

  v) Sorted (iv): $(1, 0)(2, 1)(1, 2)(2, 3)(1, 4)(2, 5)(1, 6)(2, 7)(2, 8)(2, 9)$

 vi) (i) distributed into bins using (v):

     Bin 1: $(50, I_0)(51, I_2)(90, I_4)(89, I_6)$

     Bin 2: $(08, I_1)(06, I_3)(17, I_5)(27, I_7)(65, I_8)(42, I_9)$

 vii) The result of replacement selection, reading first bin 2, then bin 1:

     $(06, I_3)(08, I_1)(17, I_5)(27, I_7)(42, I_9)(50, I_0)(51, I_2)(65, I_8)(89, I_6)(90, I_4)$

The assignment of bin numbers in step (iv) is made by doing *replacement selection* on (iii), *from right to left*, in *decreasing* order of the second component. The bin number is the run number. The example above uses replacement selection with only two elements in the selection tree; the same size tree should be used for replacement selection in both (iv) and (vii). Notice that the bin contents are not necessarily in sorted order!

    Prove that this method will sort, namely that the replacement selection in (vii) will produce only one run. (This technique reduces the number of bins needed in a conventional keysort by distribution, especially if the input is largely in order already.)

▶ **20.** [*25*] Modern hardware/software systems provide programmers with a *virtual memory:* Programs are written as if there were a very large internal memory, able to contain all of the data. This memory is divided into *pages*, only a few of which are in the actual internal memory at any one time; the others are on disks or drums. Programmers need not concern themselves with such details, since the system takes care of everything; new pages are automatically brought into memory when needed.

    It would seem that the advent of virtual memory technology makes external sorting methods obsolete, since the job can simply be done using the techniques developed for internal sorting. Discuss this situation; in what ways might a hand-tailored external sorting method be better than the application of a general-purpose paging technique to an internal sorting method?

▶ **21.** [*M15*] How many blocks of an L-block file go on disk j when the file is striped on D disks?

22. [*22*] If you are merging two files with the Gilbreath principle and you want to store the keys α_j with the a blocks and the keys β_j with the b blocks, in which block should α_j be placed in order to have the information available when it is needed?

▸ **23.** [*20*] How much space is needed for input buffers to keep input going continuously when two-way merging is done by (a) superblock striping? (b) the Gilbreath principle?

24. [*M36*] Suppose P runs have been striped on D disks so that block j of run k appears on disk $(x_k + j) \bmod D$. A P-way merge will read those blocks in some chronological order such as (19). If groups of D blocks are to be input continuously, we will read at time t the chronologically tth block stored on each disk, as in (21). What is the minimum number of buffer records needed in memory to hold input data that has not yet been merged, regardless of the chronological order? Explain how to choose the offsets $x_1, x_2, \ldots, x_P$ so that the fewest buffers are needed in the worst case.

25. [*23*] Rework the text's example of randomized striping for the case $Q = 3$ instead of $Q = 4$. What buffer contents would occur in place of (24)?

26. [*26*] How many output buffers will guarantee that a P-way merge with randomized striping will never have to pause for lack of a place in internal memory to put newly merged output? Assume that the time to write a block equals the time to read a block.

27. [*HM27*] (*The cyclic occupancy problem.*) Suppose n empty urns have been arranged in a circle and assigned the numbers 0, 1, $\ldots$, $n - 1$. For $k = 1, 2, \ldots, p$, we throw m_k balls into urns $(X_k + j) \bmod n$ for $j = 0, 1, \ldots, m_k - 1$, where the integers X_k are chosen at random. Let $S_n(m_1, \ldots, m_p)$ be the number of balls in urn 0, and let $E_n(m_1, \ldots, m_p)$ be the expected number of balls in the fullest urn.
   a) Prove that $E_n(m_1, \ldots, m_p) \le \sum_{t=1}^{m} \min(1, n \Pr(S_n(m_1, \ldots, m_p) \ge t))$, where $m = m_1 + \cdots + m_p$.
   b) Use the tail inequality, Eq. 1.2.10–(25), to prove that

$$E_n(m_1, \ldots, m_p) \le \sum_{t=1}^{m} \min\left(1, \frac{n(1 + \alpha_t/n)^m}{(1 + \alpha_t)^t}\right)$$

   for any nonnegative real numbers $\alpha_1, \alpha_2, \ldots, \alpha_m$. What values of $\alpha_1, \ldots, \alpha_m$ give the best upper bound?

28. [*HM47*] Continuing exercise 27, is $E_n(m_1, \ldots, m_p) \ge E_n(m_1 + m_2, m_3, \ldots, m_p)$?

▸ **29.** [*M30*] The purpose of this exercise is to derive an upper bound on the average time needed to input any sequence of blocks in chronological order by the randomized striping procedure, when the blocks represent P runs and D disks. We say that the block being waited for at each time step as the algorithm proceeds (see (24)) is "marked"; thus the total input time is proportional to the number of marked blocks. Marking depends only on the chronological sequence of disk accesses (see (20)).
   a) Prove that if $Q + 1$ consecutive blocks in chronological order have N_j blocks on disk j, then at most $\max(N_0, N_1, \ldots, N_{D-1})$ of those blocks are marked.
   b) Strengthen the result of (a) by showing that it holds also for $Q + 2$ consecutive blocks.
   c) Now use the cyclic occupancy problem of exercise 27 to obtain an upper bound on the average running time in terms of a function $r(D, Q + 2)$ as in Table 2, given any chronological order.

30. [*HM30*] Prove that the function $r(d, m)$ of exercise 29 satisfies $r(d, sd \log d) = 1 + O(1/\sqrt{s})$ for fixed d as $s \to \infty$.

31. [*HM48*] Analyze randomized striping to determine its true average behavior, not merely an upper bound, as a function of P, Q, and D. (Even the case $Q = 0$, which needs an average of $\Theta(L/\sqrt{D})$ read cycles, is interesting.)

5.5. SUMMARY, HISTORY, AND BIBLIOGRAPHY

NOW THAT WE have nearly reached the end of this enormously long chapter, we
had better "sort out" the most important facts that we have studied.

An algorithm for sorting is a procedure that rearranges a file of records so
that the keys are in ascending order. This orderly arrangement is useful because
it brings equal-key records together, it allows efficient processing of several files
that are sorted on the same key, it leads to efficient retrieval algorithms, and it
makes computer output look less chaotic.

Internal sorting is used when all of the records fit in the computer's high
speed internal memory. We have studied more than two dozen algorithms for
internal sorting, in various degrees of detail; and perhaps we would be happier
if we didn't know so many different approaches to the problem! It was fun to
learn all the techniques, but now we must face the horrible prospect of actually
deciding which method ought to be used in a given situation.

It would be nice if only one or two of the sorting methods would dominate
all of the others, regardless of the application or the computer being used. But
in fact, each method has its own peculiar virtues. For example, the bubble sort
(Algorithm 5.2.2B) has no apparent redeeming features, since there is always
a better way to do what it does; but even this technique, suitably generalized,
turns out to be useful for two-tape sorting (see Section 5.4.8). Thus we find
that nearly all of the algorithms deserve to be remembered, since there are some
applications in which they turn out to be best.

The following brief survey gives the highlights of the most significant algorithms we have encountered for internal sorting. As usual, N stands for the
number of records in the given file.

1. *Distribution counting*, Algorithm 5.2D, is very useful when the keys have
a small range. It is stable (doesn't affect the order of records with equal keys),
but requires memory space for counters and for $2N$ records. A modification that
saves N of these record spaces at the cost of stability appears in exercise 5.2–13.

2. *Straight insertion*, Algorithm 5.2.1S, is the simplest method to program,
requires no extra space, and is quite efficient for small N (say $N \leq 25$). For
large N it is unbearably slow unless the input is nearly in order.

3. *Shellsort*, Algorithm 5.2.1D, is also quite easy to program, and uses
minimum memory space; and it is reasonably efficient for moderately large N
(say $N \leq 1000$).

4. *List insertion*, Algorithm 5.2.1L, uses the same basic idea as straight
insertion, so it is suitable only for small N. Like the other list sorting methods
described below, it saves the cost of moving long records by manipulating links;
this is particularly advantageous when the records have variable length or are
part of other data structures.

5. *Address calculation* techniques are efficient when the keys have a known
(usually uniform) distribution; the principal variants of this approach are *multiple list insertion* (Program 5.2.1M), and MacLaren's combined radix-insertion

method (discussed at the close of Section 5.2.5). The latter can be done with only $O(\sqrt{N})$ cells of additional memory. A two-pass method that learns a nonuniform distribution is discussed in Theorem 5.2.5T.

6. *Merge exchange*, Algorithm 5.2.2M (Batcher's method) and its cousin the *bitonic sort* (exercise 5.3.4–10) are useful when a large number of comparisons can be made simultaneously.

7. *Quicksort*, Algorithm 5.2.2Q (Hoare's method) is probably the most useful general-purpose technique for internal sorting, because it requires very little memory space and its average running time on most computers beats that of its competitors when it is well implemented. It can run *very* slowly in its worst case, however, so a careful choice of the partitioning elements should be made whenever nonrandom data are likely. Choosing the median of three elements, as suggested in exercise 5.2.2–55, makes the worst-case behavior extremely unlikely and also improves the average running time slightly.

8. *Straight selection*, Algorithm 5.2.3S, is a simple method especially suitable when special hardware is available to find the smallest element of a list rapidly.

9. *Heapsort*, Algorithm 5.2.3H, requires minimum memory and is guaranteed to run pretty fast; its average time and its maximum time are both roughly twice the average running time of quicksort.

10. *List merging*, Algorithm 5.2.4L, is a list sort that, like heapsort, is guaranteed to be rather fast even in its worst case; moreover, it is stable with respect to equal keys.

11. *Radix sorting*, using Algorithm 5.2.5R, is a list sort especially appropriate for keys that are either rather short or that have an unusual lexicographic collating sequence. The method of distribution counting (point 1 above) can also be used, as an alternative to linking; such a procedure requires $2N$ record spaces, plus a table of counters, but the simple form of its inner loop makes it especially good for ultra-fast, "number-crunching" computers that have look-ahead control. *Caution:* Radix sorting should not be used for small N!

12. *Merge insertion*, see Section 5.3.1, is especially suitable for very small values of N, in a "straight-line-coded" routine; for example, it would be the appropriate method in an application that requires the sorting of numerous five- or six-record groups.

13. Hybrid methods, combining one or more of the techniques above, are also possible. For example, merge insertion could be used for sorting short subfiles that arise in quicksort.

14. Finally, an unnamed method appearing in the answer to exercise 5.2.1–3 seems to require the shortest possible sorting program. But its average running time, proportional to N^3, makes it the slowest sorting routine in this book!

Table 1 summarizes the speed and space characteristics of many of these methods, when programmed for MIX. It is important to realize that the figures in this table are only rough indications of the relative sorting times; they apply to one computer only, and the assumptions made about input data are not

Table 1

A COMPARISON OF INTERNAL SORTING METHODS USING THE MIX COMPUTER

Method	Reference	Stable?	Length of MIX code	Space	Running Time				Notes
					Average	Maximum	$N = 16$	$N = 1000$	
Comparison counting	Ex. 5.2–5	Yes	22	$N(1+\epsilon)$	$4N^2 + 10N$	$5.5N^2$	1065	3992432	c
Distribution counting	Ex. 5.2–9	Yes	26	$2N + 1000\epsilon$	$22N + 10010$	$22N$	10362	32010	a
Straight insertion	Ex. 5.2.1–33	Yes	10	$N+1$	$1.5N^2 + 9.5N$	$3N^2$	412	1491928	
Shellsort	Prog. 5.2.1D	No	21	$N + \epsilon \lg N$	$3.9N^{7/6} + 10N\lg N + 166N$	$cN^{4/3}$	567	128758	d, h
List insertion	Ex. 5.2.1–33	Yes	19	$N(1+\epsilon)$	$1.25N^2 + 13.25N$	$2.5N^2$	433	1248615	b, c
Multiple list insertion	Prog. 5.2.1M	No	18	$N + \epsilon(N+100)$	$.0175N^2 + 18N$	$3.5N^2$	645	35246	b, c, f, i
Merge exchange	Ex. 5.2.2–12	No	35	N	$2.875N(\lg N)^2$	$4N(\lg N)^2$	939	284366	
Quicksort	Prog. 5.2.2Q	No	63	$N + 2\epsilon \lg N$	$11.67N \ln N - 1.74N$	$\geq 2N^2$	470	81486	
Median-of-3 quicksort	Ex. 5.2.2–55	No	100	$N + 2\epsilon \lg N$	$10.63N \ln N + 2.12N$	$\geq N^2$	487	74574	e
Radix exchange	Prog. 5.2.2R	No	45	$N + 68\epsilon$	$14.43N \ln N + 23.9N$	$272N$	1135	137614	g, i, j
Straight selection	Prog. 5.2.3S	No	15	N	$2.5N^2 + 3N \ln N$	$3.25N^2$	853	2525287	j
Heapsort	Prog. 5.2.3H	No	30	N	$23.08N \ln N + 0.01N$	$24.5N \ln N$	1068	159714	h, j
List merge	Prog. 5.2.4L	Yes	44	$N(1+\epsilon)$	$14.43N \ln N + 4.92N$	$14.4N \ln N$	761	104716	b, c, j
Radix list sort	Prog. 5.2.5R	Yes	36	$N + \epsilon(N+200)$	$32N + 4838$	$32N$	4250	36838	b, c

a: Three-digit keys only.

b: Six-digit (that is, three-byte) keys only.

c: Output not rearranged; final sequence is specified implicitly by links or counters.

d: Increments chosen as in 5.2.1–(11); a slightly better sequence appears in exercise 5.2.1–29.

e: $M = 9$, using **SRB**; for the version with DIV, add $1.60N$ to the average running time.

f: $M = 100$ (the byte size).

g: $M = 34$, since $2^{34} > 10^{10} > 2^{33}$.

h: The average time is based on an empirical estimate, since the theory is incomplete.

i: The average time is based on the assumption of uniformly distributed keys.

j: Further refinements, mentioned in the text and exercises accompanying this program, would reduce the running time.

completely consistent for all programs. Comparative tables such as this have been given by many authors, with no two people reaching the same conclusions. On the other hand, the timings do give at least an indication of the kind of speed to be expected from each algorithm, when sorting a rather small array of one-word records, since MIX is a fairly typical computer.

The "space" column in Table 1 gives some information about the amount of auxiliary memory used by each program, in units of record length. Here ϵ denotes the fraction of a record needed for one link field; thus, for example, $N(1 + \epsilon)$ means that the method requires space for N records plus N link fields.

The asymptotic average and maximum times appearing in Table 1 give only the leading terms that dominate for large N, assuming random input; c denotes an unspecified constant. These formulas can often be misleading, so actual total running times have also been listed, for sample runs of the program on two particular sequences of input data. The case $N = 16$ refers to the sixteen keys that appear in so many of the examples of Section 5.2; and the case $N = 1000$ refers to the sequence $K_1, K_2, \ldots, K_{1000}$ defined by

$$K_{1001} = 0; \qquad K_{n-1} = (3141592621 K_n + 2113148651) \bmod 10^{10}.$$

A MIX program of reasonably high quality has been used to represent each algorithm in the table, often incorporating improvements that have been suggested in the exercises. The byte size for these runs was 100.

External sorting techniques are different from internal sorting, because they must use comparatively primitive data structures, and because there is a great emphasis on minimizing their input/output time. Section 5.4.6 summarizes the interesting methods that have been developed for tape merging, and Section 5.4.9 discusses the use of disks and drums.

Of course, sorting isn't the whole story. While studying all of these sorting techniques, we have learned a good deal about how to handle data structures, how to deal with external memories, and how to analyze algorithms; and perhaps we have even learned a little about how to discover new algorithms.

Early developments. A search for the origin of today's sorting techniques takes us back to the nineteenth century, when the first machines for sorting were invented. The United States conducts a census of all its citizens at the beginning of each decade, and by 1880 the problem of processing the voluminous census data was becoming very acute; in fact, the total number of single (as opposed to married) people was never tabulated that year, although the necessary information had been gathered. Herman Hollerith, a 20-year-old employee of the Census Bureau, devised an ingenious electric tabulating machine to meet the need for better statistics-gathering, and about 100 of his machines were successfully used to tabulate the 1890 census rolls.

Figure 94 shows Hollerith's original battery-driven apparatus; of chief interest to us is the "sorting box" at the right, which has been opened to show half of the 26 inner compartments. The operator would insert a $6\frac{5}{8}'' \times 3\frac{1}{4}''$ punched card into the "press" and lower the handle; this caused spring-actuated pins in the upper plate to make contact with pools of mercury in the lower plate, wherever a hole was punched in the card. The corresponding completed circuits would cause associated dials on the panel to advance by one unit; and furthermore, one of the 26 lids of the sorting box would pop open. At this point the operator would reopen the press, put the card into the open compartment, and close the lid. One man reportedly ran 19071 cards through this machine in a single $6\frac{1}{2}$-hour working day, an average of about 49 cards per minute! (A typical operator would work at about one-third this speed.)

Fig. 94. Hollerith's original tabulating and sorting machine. (Photo courtesy of IBM archives.)

Population continued its inexorable growth, and the original tabulator-sorters were not fast enough to handle the 1900 census; so Hollerith devised another machine to stave off another data processing crisis. His new device (patented in 1901 and 1904) had an automatic card feed, and in fact it looked essentially like modern card sorters. The story of Hollerith's early machines has been told in interesting detail by Leon E. Truesdell, *The Development of Punch Card Tabulation* (Washington: U.S. Bureau of the Census, 1965); see also the contemporary accounts in *Columbia College School of Mines Quarterly* **10** (1889), 238–255; *J. Franklin Inst.* **129** (1890), 300–306; *The Electrical Engineer* **12** (November 11, 1891), 521–530; *J. Amer. Statistical Assn.* **2** (1891), 330–341, **4** (1895), 365; *J. Royal Statistical Soc.* **55** (1892), 326–327; *Allgemeines statistisches Archiv* **2** (1892), 78–126; *J. Soc. Statistique de Paris* **33** (1892), 87–96; *U.S. Patents 395781* (1889), *685608* (1901), *777209* (1904). Hollerith and another former Census Bureau employee, James Powers, went on to found rival companies that eventually became part of IBM and Remington Rand corporations, respectively.

Hollerith's sorting machine is, of course, the basis for radix sorting methods now used in digital computers. His patent mentions that two-column numerical items are to be sorted "separately for each column," but he didn't say whether the units or the tens columns should be considered first. Patent number 518240 by John K. Gore in 1894, which described another early machine for sorting cards, suggested starting with the tens column. The nonobvious trick of using the units column first was presumably discovered by some anonymous machine operator and passed on to others (see Section 5.2.5); it appears in the earliest extant IBM sorter manual (1936). The first known mention of this right-to-left technique is in a book by Robert Feindler, *Das Hollerith-Lochkarten-Verfahren* (Berlin: Reimar Hobbing, 1929), 126–130; it was also mentioned at about the same time in an article by L. J. Comrie, *Transactions of the Office Machinery Users' Association* (London: 1930), 25–37. Incidentally, Comrie was the first person to make the important observation that tabulating machines could fruitfully be employed in scientific calculations, even though they were originally designed for statistical and accounting applications. His article is especially interesting because it gives a detailed description of the tabulating equipment available in England in 1930. Sorting machines at that time processed 360 to 400 cards per minute, and could be rented for £9 per month.

The idea of merging goes back to another card-walloping machine, the *collator*, which was a much later invention (1938). With its two feeding stations, it could merge two sorted decks of cards into one, in only one pass; the technique for doing this was clearly explained in the first IBM collator manual (April 1939). [See James W. Bryce, *U.S. Patent 2189024* (1940).]

Then computers arrived on the scene, and sorting was intimately involved in this development; in fact, there is evidence that a sorting routine was the first program ever written for a stored program computer. The designers of EDVAC were especially interested in sorting, because it epitomized the potential nonnumerical applications of computers; they realized that a satisfactory order code should not only be capable of expressing programs for the solution of difference equations, it must also have enough flexibility to handle the combinatorial "decision-making" aspects of algorithms. John von Neumann therefore prepared programs for internal merge sorting in 1945, in order to test the adequacy of some instruction codes he was proposing for the EDVAC computer. The existence of efficient special-purpose sorting machines provided a natural standard by which the merits of his proposed computer organization could be evaluated. Details of this interesting development have been described in an article by D. E. Knuth, *Computing Surveys* **2** (1970), 247–260; see also von Neumann's *Collected Works* **5** (New York: Macmillan, 1963), 196–214, for the final polished form of his original sorting programs.

In Germany, K. Zuse independently constructed a program for straight insertion sorting in 1945, as one of the simplest examples of linear list operations in his

"Plankalkül" language. (This pioneering work remained unpublished for nearly 30 years; see *Berichte der Gesellschaft für Mathematik und Datenverarbeitung* **63** (Bonn: 1972), part 4, 84–85.)

The limited internal memory size planned for early computers made it natural to think of external sorting as well as internal sorting, and a "Progress Report on the EDVAC" prepared by J. P. Eckert and J. W. Mauchly of the Moore School of Electrical Engineering (30 September 1945) pointed out that a computer augmented with magnetic wire or tape devices could simulate the operations of card equipment, achieving a faster sorting speed. This progress report described balanced two-way radix sorting, and balanced two-way merging (called "collating"), using four magnetic wire or tape units, reading or writing "at least 5000 pulses per second."

John Mauchly lectured on "Sorting and Collating" at the special session on computing presented at the Moore School in 1946, and the notes of his lecture constitute the first published discussion of computer sorting [*Theory and Techniques for the Design of Electronic Digital Computers*, edited by G. W. Patterson, **3** (1946), 22.1–22.20]. Mauchly began his presentation with an interesting remark: "To ask that a single machine combine the abilities to compute and to sort might seem like asking that a single device be able to perform both as a can opener and a fountain pen." Then he observed that machines capable of carrying out sophisticated mathematical procedures must also have the ability to sort and classify data, and he showed that sorting may even be useful in connection with numerical calculations. He described straight insertion and binary insertion, observing that the former method uses about $N^2/4$ comparisons on the average, while the latter never needs more than about $N \lg N$. Yet binary insertion requires a rather complex data structure, and he went on to show that two-way merging achieves the same low number of comparisons using only sequential accessing of lists. The last half of his lecture notes were devoted to a discussion of partial-pass radix sorting methods that simulate digital card sorting on four tapes, using fewer than four passes per digit (see Section 5.4.7).

Shortly afterwards, Eckert and Mauchly started a company that produced some of the earliest electronic computers, the BINAC (for military applications) and the UNIVAC (for commercial applications). Again the U.S. Census Bureau played a part in this development, receiving the first UNIVAC. At this time it was not at all clear that computers would be economically profitable; computing machines could sort faster than card equipment, but they cost more. Therefore the UNIVAC programmers, led by Frances E. Holberton, put considerable effort into the design of high-speed external sorting routines, and their preliminary programs also influenced the hardware design. According to their estimates, 100 million 10-word records could be sorted on UNIVAC in 9000 hours, or 375 days.

UNIVAC I, officially dedicated in July 1951, had an internal memory of 1000 12-character (72-bit) words. It was designed to read and write 60-word blocks on tapes, at a rate of 500 words per second; reading could be either forward or backward, and simultaneous reading, writing, and computing was possible. In 1948, Mrs. Holberton devised an interesting way to do two-way merging with perfect overlap of reading, writing, and computing, using six input buffers: Let there be one "current buffer" and two "auxiliary buffers" for each input file; it is possible to merge in such a way that, whenever it is time to output one block, the two current input buffers contain a total of exactly one block's worth of unprocessed records. Therefore exactly one input buffer becomes empty while each output block is being formed, and we can arrange to have three of the four auxiliary buffers full at all times while we are reading into the other. This method is slightly faster than the forecasting method of Algorithm 5.4.6F, since it is not necessary to inspect the result of one input before initiating the next. [See "Collation Methods for the UNIVAC System," (Eckert-Mauchly Computer Corp., 1950), 2 volumes.]

The culmination of this work was a sort generator program, which was the first major software routine ever developed for automatic programming. The user would specify the record size, the positions of up to five keys in partial fields of each record, and the sentinel keys that mark file's end; then the sort generator would produce a copyrighted sorting program for one-reel files. The first pass of this program was an internal sort of 60-word blocks, using comparison counting (Algorithm 5.2C); then came a number of balanced two-way merge passes, reading backwards and avoiding tape interlock as described above. [See "Master Generating Routine for 2-way Sorting" (Eckert-Mauchly Division of Remington Rand, 1952); the first draft of this report was entitled "Master Prefabrication Routine for 2-way Collation." See also F. E. Holberton, *Symposium on Automatic Programming* (Office of Naval Research, 1954), 34–39.]

By 1952, many approaches to internal sorting were well known in the programming folklore, but comparatively little theory had been developed. Daniel Goldenberg ["Time analyses of various methods of sorting data," Digital Computer Laboratory memo M-1680 (Mass. Inst. of Tech., 17 October 1952)] coded five different methods for the Whirlwind computer, and made best-case and worst-case analyses of each program. When sorting one hundred 15-bit words on an 8-bit key, he found that the fastest method was to use a 256-word table, storing each record into a unique position corresponding to its key, then compressing the table. But this technique had an obvious disadvantage, since it would eliminate a record whenever a subsequent one had the same key. The other four methods he analyzed were ranked as follows: Straight two-way merging beat radix-2 sorting beat straight selection beat bubble sort.

Goldenberg's results were extended by Harold H. Seward in his 1954 Master's thesis ["Information sorting in the application of electronic digital computers to business operations," Digital Computer Lab. report R-232 (Mass. Inst. of Tech., 24 May 1954; 60 pages)]. Seward introduced the ideas of distribution counting and replacement selection; he showed that the first run in a random permutation has an average length of $e - 1$; and he analyzed external sorting as well as internal sorting, on various types of bulk memories as well as tapes.

An even more noteworthy thesis — a Ph.D. thesis in fact — was written by Howard B. Demuth in 1956 ["Electronic Data Sorting" (Stanford University, October 1956), 92 pages; *IEEE Trans.* **C-34** (1985), 296–310]. This work helped

to lay the foundations of computational complexity theory. It considered three
abstract models of the sorting problem, using cyclic, linear, and random-access
memories; and optimal or near-optimal methods were developed for each model.
(See exercise 5.3.4–68.) Although no practical consequences flowed immediately
from Demuth's thesis, it established important ideas about how to link theory
with practice.

Thus the history of sorting has been closely associated with many "firsts"
in computing: the first data-processing machines, the first stored programs, the
first software, the first buffering methods, the first work on algorithmic analysis
and computational complexity.

None of the computer-related documents mentioned so far actually appeared
in the "open literature"; in fact, most of the early history of computing appears
in comparatively inaccessible reports, because comparatively few people were
involved with computers at the time. Literature about sorting finally broke into
print in 1955–1956, in the form of three major survey articles.

The first paper was prepared by J. C. Hosken [*Proc. Eastern Joint Computer
Conference* **8** (1955), 39–55]. He began with an astute observation: "To lower
costs per unit of output, people usually increase the size of their operations. But
under these conditions, the unit cost of sorting, instead of falling, rises." Hosken
surveyed all the available special-purpose equipment then being marketed, as
well as the methods of sorting on computers. His bibliography of 54 items was
based mostly on manufacturers' brochures.

The comprehensive paper "Sorting on Electronic Computer Systems" by
E. H. Friend [*JACM* **3** (1956), 134–168] was a major milestone in the development of sorting. Although numerous techniques have been developed since
1956, this paper is still remarkably up-to-date in many respects. Friend gave
careful descriptions of quite a few internal and external sorting algorithms,
and he paid special attention to buffering techniques and the characteristics
of magnetic tape units. He introduced some new methods (for example, tree
selection, amphisbaenic sorting, and forecasting), and developed some of the
mathematical properties of the older methods.

The third survey of sorting to appear about this time was prepared by
D. W. Davies [*Proc. Inst. Elect. Engineers* **103B**, Supplement 1 (1956), 87–93].
In the following years several other notable surveys were published, by D. A. Bell
[*Comp. J.* **1** (1958), 71–77]; A. S. Douglas [*Comp. J.* **2** (1959), 1–9]; D. D. Mc-
Cracken, H. Weiss, and T. Lee [*Programming Business Computers* (New York:
Wiley, 1959), Chapter 15, pages 298–332]; I. Flores [*JACM* **8** (1961), 41–80];
K. E. Iverson [*A Programming Language* (New York: Wiley, 1962), Chapter 6,
176–245]; C. C. Gotlieb [*CACM* **6** (1963), 194–201]; T. N. Hibbard [*CACM* **6**
(1963), 206–213]; M. A. Goetz [*Digital Computer User's Handbook*, edited by
M. Klerer and G. A. Korn (New York: McGraw–Hill, 1967), Chapter 1.10, pages
1.292–1.320]. A symposium on sorting was sponsored by ACM in November
1962; most of the papers presented at that symposium were published in the
May 1963 issue of *CACM*, and they constitute a good representation of the state
of the art at that time. C. C. Gotlieb's survey of contemporary sort generators,

T. N. Hibbard's survey of minimal storage internal sorting, and G. U. Hubbard's early exploration of disk file sorting are particularly noteworthy articles in this collection.

New sorting methods were being discovered throughout this period: Address calculation (1956), merge insertion (1959), radix exchange (1959), cascade merge (1959), shellsort (1959), polyphase merge (1960), tree insertion (1960), oscillating sort (1962), Hoare's quicksort (1962), Williams's heapsort (1964), Batcher's merge exchange (1964). The history of each individual algorithm has been traced in the particular section of this chapter where that method is described. The late 1960s saw an intensive development of the corresponding theory.

A complete bibliography of all papers on sorting examined by the author as this chapter was first being written, compiled with the help of R. L. Rivest, appeared in *Computing Reviews* **13** (1972), 283–289.

Later developments. Dozens of sorting algorithms have been invented since 1970, although nearly all of them are variations on earlier themes. *Multikey quicksort*, which is discussed in the answer to exercise 5.2.2–30, is an excellent example of such more recent methods.

Another trend, primarily of theoretical interest so far, has been to study sorting schemes that are *adaptive*, in the sense that they are guaranteed to run faster when the input is already pretty much in order according to various criteria. See, for example, H. Mannila, *IEEE Transactions* **C-34** (1985), 318–325; V. Estivill-Castro and D. Wood, *Computing Surveys* **24** (1992), 441–476; C. Levcopoulos and O. Petersson, *Journal of Algorithms* **14** (1993), 395–413; A. Moffat, G. Eddy, and O. Petersson, *Software Practice & Experience* **26** (1996), 781–797.

Changes in computer hardware have prompted many interesting studies of the efficiency of sorting algorithms when the cost criteria change; see, for example, the discussion of virtual memory in exercise 5.4.9–20. The effect of hardware caches on internal sorting has been studied by A. LaMarca and R. E. Ladner, *SODA* **8** (1997), 370–379. One of their conclusions is that step Q9 of Algorithm 5.2.2Q is a bad idea on modern machines (although it worked well on traditional computers like MIX): Instead of finishing quicksort with a straight insertion sort, it is now better to sort the short subfiles earlier, while their keys are still in the cache.

What is the current state of the art for sorting large amounts of data? One popular benchmark since 1985 has been the task of sorting one million 100-character records that have uniformly random 10-character keys. The input and output are supposed to reside on disk, and the objective is to minimize the total elapsed time, including the time it takes to launch the program. R. C. Agarwal [*SIGMOD Record* **25**, 2 (June 1996), 240–246] used a desktop RISC computer, the IBM RS/6000 model 39H, to implement radix sorting with files that were striped on 8 disk units, and he finished this task in 5.1 seconds. Input/output was the main bottleneck; indeed, the processor needed only 0.6 seconds to control the actual sorting! Even faster times have been achieved when several processors are available: A network of 32 UltraSPARC I workstations, each with two internal disks, can sort a million records in 2.41 seconds using a hybrid method called NOW-Sort [A. C. Arpaci-Dusseau, R. H. Arpaci-Dusseau, D. E. Culler, J. M. Hellerstein, and D. A. Patterson, *SIGMOD Record* **26**, 2 (June 1997), 243–254].

Such advances mean that the million-record benchmark has become mostly a test of startup and shutdown time; larger data sets are needed to give more meaningful results. For example, the present world record for *terabyte sorting* — 10^{10} records of 100 characters each — is 2.5 hours, achieved in September 1997 on a Silicon Graphics Origin2000 system with 32 processors, 8 gigabytes of internal memory, and 559 disks of 4 gigabytes each. This record was set by a commercially available sorting routine called Nsort™, developed by C. Nyberg, C. Koester, and J. Gray using methods that have not yet been published.

Perhaps even the terabyte benchmark will be considered too small some day. The best current candidate for a benchmark that will live forever is *MinuteSort*: How many 100-character records can be sorted in 60 seconds? As this book went to press, the current record holder for this task was NOW-Sort; 95 workstations needed only 59.21 seconds to put 90.25 million records into order, on 30 March 1997. But present-day methods are not yet pushing up against any truly fundamental limitations on speed.

In summary, the problem of efficient sorting remains just as fascinating today as it ever was.

EXERCISES

1. [*05*] Summarize the contents of this chapter by stating a generalization of Theorem 5.4.6A.

2. [*20*] Based on the information in Table 1, what is the best list-sorting method for six-digit keys, for use on the MIX computer?

3. [*37*] (*Stable sorting in minimum storage.*) A sorting algorithm is said to require *minimum storage* if it uses only $O((\log N)^2)$ bits of memory space for its variables besides the space needed to store the N records. The algorithm must be general in the sense that it works for all N, not just for a particular value of N, assuming that a sufficient amount of random access memory has been made available whenever the algorithm is actually called upon to sort.

Many of the sorting methods we have studied violate this minimum-storage requirement; in particular, the use of N link fields is forbidden. Quicksort (Algorithm 5.2.2Q) satisfies the minimum-storage requirement, but its worst case running time is proportional to N^2. Heapsort (Algorithm 5.2.3H) is the only $O(N \log N)$ algorithm we have studied that uses minimum storage, although another such algorithm could be formulated using the idea of exercise 5.2.4–18.

The fastest general algorithm we have considered that sorts keys in a *stable* manner is the list merge sort (Algorithm 5.2.4L), but it does not use minimum storage. In fact, the only stable minimum-storage sorting algorithms we have seen are $\Omega(N^2)$ methods (straight insertion, bubble sorting, and a variant of straight selection).

Design a stable minimum-storage sorting algorithm that needs only $O(N(\log N)^2)$ units of time in its worst case. [*Hint:* It is possible to do stable minimum-storage merging in $O(N \log N)$ units of time.]

▶ **4.** [*28*] A sorting algorithm is called *parsimonious* if it makes decisions entirely by comparing keys, and if it never makes a comparison whose outcome could have been predicted from the results of previous comparisons. Which of the methods listed in Table 1 are parsimonious?

5. [*46*] It is much more difficult to sort nonrandom data with numerous equal keys than to sort uniformly random data. Devise a sorting benchmark that (i) is interesting now and will probably be interesting 100 years from now; (ii) does not involve uniformly random keys; and (iii) does not use data sets that change with time.

> *I shall have accomplished my purpose if I have sorted and put in logical order*
> *the gist of the great volume of material which has been generated about sorting*
> *over the past few years.*
> — J. C. HOSKEN (1955)

CHAPTER SIX

SEARCHING

Let's look at the record.
— AL SMITH (1928)

THIS CHAPTER might have been given the more pretentious title "Storage and Retrieval of Information"; on the other hand, it might simply have been called "Table Look-Up." We are concerned with the process of collecting information in a computer's memory, in such a way that the information can subsequently be recovered as quickly as possible. Sometimes we are confronted with more data than we can really use, and it may be wisest to forget and to destroy most of it; but at other times it is important to retain and organize the given facts in such a way that fast retrieval is possible.

Most of this chapter is devoted to the study of a very simple search problem: how to find the data that has been stored with a given identification. For example, in a numerical application we might want to find $f(x)$, given x and a table of the values of f; in a nonnumerical application, we might want to find the English translation of a given Russian word.

In general, we shall suppose that a set of N records has been stored, and the problem is to locate the appropriate one. As in the case of sorting, we assume that each record includes a special field called its *key*; this terminology is especially appropriate, because many people spend a great deal of time every day searching for their keys. We generally require the N keys to be distinct, so that each key uniquely identifies its record. The collection of all records is called a *table* or *file*, where the word "table" is usually used to indicate a small file, and "file" is usually used to indicate a large table. A large file or a group of files is frequently called a *database*.

Algorithms for searching are presented with a so-called *argument*, K, and the problem is to find which record has K as its key. After the search is complete, two possibilities can arise: Either the search was *successful*, having located the unique record containing K; or it was *unsuccessful*, having determined that K is nowhere to be found. After an unsuccessful search it is sometime desirable to enter a new record, containing K, into the table; a method that does this is called a *search-and-insertion* algorithm. Some hardware devices known as *associative memories* solve the search problem automatically, in a way that might resemble the functioning of a human brain; but we shall study techniques for searching on a conventional general-purpose digital computer.

Although the goal of searching is to find the information stored in the record associated with K, the algorithms in this chapter generally ignore everything but the keys themselves. In practice we can find the associated data once we have located K; for example, if K appears in location TABLE $+ i$, the associated data (or a pointer to it) might be in location TABLE $+ i + 1$, or in DATA $+ i$, etc. It is therefore convenient to gloss over the details of what should be done after K has been successfully found.

Searching is the most time-consuming part of many programs, and the substitution of a good search method for a bad one often leads to a substantial increase in speed. In fact we can often arrange the data or the data structure so that searching is eliminated entirely, by ensuring that we always know just where to find the information we need. Linked memory is a common way to achieve this; for example, a doubly linked list makes it unnecessary to search for the predecessor or successor of a given item. Another way to avoid searching occurs if we are allowed to choose the keys freely, since we might as well let them be the numbers $\{1, 2, \ldots, N\}$; then the record containing K can simply be placed in location TABLE $+ K$. Both of these techniques were used to eliminate searching from the topological sorting algorithm discussed in Section 2.2.3. However, searches would have been necessary if the objects in the topological sorting algorithm had been given symbolic names instead of numbers. Efficient algorithms for searching turn out to be quite important in practice.

Search methods can be classified in several ways. We might divide them into internal versus external searching, just as we divided the sorting algorithms of Chapter 5 into internal versus external sorting. Or we might divide search methods into static versus dynamic searching, where "static" means that the contents of the table are essentially unchanging (so that it is important to minimize the search time without regard for the time required to set up the table), and "dynamic" means that the table is subject to frequent insertions and perhaps also deletions. A third possible scheme is to classify search methods according to whether they are based on comparisons between keys or on digital properties of the keys, analogous to the distinction between sorting by comparison and sorting by distribution. Finally we might divide searching into those methods that use the actual keys and those that work with transformed keys.

The organization of this chapter is essentially a combination of the latter two modes of classification. Section 6.1 considers "brute force" sequential methods of search, then Section 6.2 discusses the improvements that can be made based on comparisons between keys, using alphabetic or numeric order to govern the decisions. Section 6.3 treats digital searching, and Section 6.4 discusses an important class of methods called hashing techniques, based on arithmetic transformations of the actual keys. Each of these sections treats both internal and external searching, in both the static and the dynamic case; and each section points out the relative advantages and disadvantages of the various algorithms.

Searching and sorting are often closely related to each other. For example, consider the following problem: *Given two sets of numbers, $A = \{a_1, a_2, \ldots, a_m\}$ and $B = \{b_1, b_2, \ldots, b_n\}$, determine whether or not $A \subseteq B$.* Three solutions suggest themselves:

1. Compare each a_i sequentially with the b_j's until finding a match.

2. Sort the a's and b's, then make one sequential pass through both files, checking the appropriate condition.

3. Enter the b_j's in a table, then search for each of the a_i.

Each of these solutions is attractive for a different range of values of m and n. Solution 1 will take roughly $c_1 mn$ units of time, for some constant c_1, and solution 2 will take about $c_2(m \lg m + n \lg n)$ units, for some (larger) constant c_2. With a suitable hashing method, solution 3 will take roughly $c_3 m + c_4 n$ units of time, for some (still larger) constants c_3 and c_4. It follows that solution 1 is good for very small m and n, but solution 2 soon becomes better as m and n grow larger. Eventually solution 3 becomes preferable, until n exceeds the internal memory size; then solution 2 is usually again superior until n gets much larger still. Thus we have a situation where sorting is sometimes a good substitute for searching, and searching is sometimes a good substitute for sorting.

More complicated search problems can often be reduced to the simpler case considered here. For example, suppose that the keys are words that might be slightly misspelled; we might want to find the correct record in spite of this error. If we make two copies of the file, one in which the keys are in normal lexicographic order and another in which they are ordered from right to left (as if the words were spelled backwards), a misspelled search argument will probably agree up to half or more of its length with an entry in one of these two files. The search methods of Sections 6.2 and 6.3 can therefore be adapted to find the key that was probably intended.

A related problem has received considerable attention in connection with airline reservation systems, and in other applications involving people's names when there is a good chance that the name will be misspelled due to poor handwriting or voice transmission. The goal is to transform the argument into some code that tends to bring together all variants of the same name. The following contemporary form of the "Soundex" method, a technique that was originally developed by Margaret K. Odell and Robert C. Russell [see *U.S. Patents 1261167* (1918), *1435663* (1922)], has often been used for encoding surnames:

1. Retain the first letter of the name, and drop all occurrences of a, e, h, i, o, u, w, y in other positions.

2. Assign the following numbers to the remaining letters after the first:

   b, f, p, v → 1   l → 4
   c, g, j, k, q, s, x, z → 2   m, n → 5
   d, t → 3   r → 6

3. If two or more letters with the same code were adjacent in the original name (before step 1), or adjacent except for intervening h's and w's, omit all but the first.

4. Convert to the form "letter, digit, digit, digit" by adding trailing zeros (if there are less than three digits), or by dropping rightmost digits (if there are more than three).

For example, the names Euler, Gauss, Hilbert, Knuth, Lloyd, Łukasiewicz, and Wachs have the respective codes E460, G200, H416, K530, L300, L222, W200. Of course this system will bring together names that are somewhat different, as well as names that are similar; the same seven codes would be obtained for Ellery, Ghosh, Heilbronn, Kant, Liddy, Lissajous, and Waugh. And on the other hand a few related names like Rogers and Rodgers, or Sinclair and St. Clair, or Tchebysheff and Chebyshev, remain separate. But by and large the Soundex code greatly increases the chance of finding a name in one of its disguises. [For further information, see C. P. Bourne and D. F. Ford, *JACM* **8** (1961), 538–552; Leon Davidson, *CACM* **5** (1962), 169–171; *Federal Population Censuses 1790–1890* (Washington, D.C.: National Archives, 1971), 90.]

When using a scheme like Soundex, we need not give up the assumption that all keys are distinct; we can make lists of all records with equivalent codes, treating each list as a unit.

Large databases tend to make the retrieval process more complex, since people often want to consider many different fields of each record as potential keys, with the ability to locate items when only part of the key information is specified. For example, given a large file about stage performers, a producer might wish to find all unemployed actresses between 25 and 30 with dancing talent and a French accent; given a large file of baseball statistics, a sportswriter may wish to determine the total number of runs scored by the Chicago White Sox in 1964, during the seventh inning of night games, against left-handed pitchers. Given a large file of data about anything, people like to ask arbitrarily complicated questions. Indeed, we might consider an entire library as a database, and a searcher may want to find everything that has been published about information retrieval. An introduction to the techniques for such *secondary key* (multi-attribute) retrieval problems appears below in Section 6.5.

Before entering into a detailed study of searching, it may be helpful to put things in historical perspective. During the pre-computer era, many books of logarithm tables, trigonometry tables, etc., were compiled, so that mathematical calculations could be replaced by searching. Eventually these tables were transferred to punched cards, and used for scientific problems in connection with collators, sorters, and duplicating punch machines. But when stored-program computers were introduced, it soon became apparent that it was now cheaper to recompute $\log x$ or $\cos x$ each time, instead of looking up the answer in a table.

Although the problem of sorting received considerable attention already in the earliest days of computers, comparatively little was done about algorithms for searching. With small internal memories, and with nothing but sequential media like tapes for storing large files, searching was either trivially easy or almost impossible.

But the development of larger and larger random-access memories during the 1950s eventually led to the recognition that searching was an interesting problem in its own right. After years of complaining about the limited amounts of space in the early machines, programmers were suddenly confronted with larger amounts of memory than they knew how to use efficiently.

The first surveys of the searching problem were published by A. I. Dumey, *Computers & Automation* **5**, 12 (December 1956), 6–9; W. W. Peterson, *IBM J. Research & Development* **1** (1957), 130–146; A. D. Booth, *Information and Control* **1** (1958), 159–164; A. S. Douglas, *Comp. J.* **2** (1959), 1–9. More extensive treatments were given later by Kenneth E. Iverson, *A Programming Language* (New York: Wiley, 1962), 133–158, and by Werner Buchholz, *IBM Systems J.* **2** (1963), 86–111.

During the early 1960s, a number of interesting new search procedures based on tree structures were introduced, as we shall see; and research about searching is still actively continuing at the present time.

6.1. SEQUENTIAL SEARCHING

"BEGIN AT THE BEGINNING, and go on till you find the right key; then stop." This sequential procedure is the obvious way to search, and it makes a useful starting point for our discussion of searching because many of the more intricate algorithms are based on it. We shall see that sequential searching involves some very interesting ideas, in spite of its simplicity.

The algorithm might be formulated more precisely as follows:

Algorithm S (*Sequential search*). Given a table of records $R_1, R_2, \ldots, R_N$, whose respective keys are $K_1, K_2, \ldots, K_N$, this algorithm searches for a given argument K. We assume that $N \geq 1$.

S1. [Initialize.] Set $i \leftarrow 1$.

S2. [Compare.] If $K = K_i$, the algorithm terminates successfully.

S3. [Advance.] Increase i by 1.

S4. [End of file?] If $i \leq N$, go back to S2. Otherwise the algorithm terminates unsuccessfully. ▮

Notice that this algorithm can terminate in two different ways, *successfully* (having located the desired key) or *unsuccessfully* (having established that the given argument is not present in the table). The same will be true of most other algorithms in this chapter.

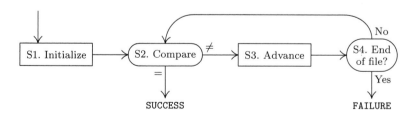

Fig. 1. Sequential or "house-to-house" search.

A MIX program can be written down immediately.

Program S (*Sequential search*). Assume that K_i appears in location KEY $+ i$, and that the remainder of record R_i appears in location INFO $+ i$. The following program uses rA $\equiv K$, rI1 $\equiv i - N$.

01	START	LDA K	1	*S1. Initialize.*
02		ENT1 1-N	1	$i \leftarrow 1$.
03	2H	CMPA KEY+N,1	C	*S2. Compare.*
04		JE SUCCESS	C	Exit if $K = K_i$.
05		INC1 1	$C - S$	*S3. Advance.*
06		J1NP 2B	$C - S$	*S4. End of file?*
07	FAILURE	EQU *	$1 - S$	Exit if not in table.

At location SUCCESS, the instruction "LDA INFO+N,1" will now bring the desired information into rA. ∎

The analysis of this program is straightforward; it shows that the running time of Algorithm S depends on two things,

$$C = \text{the number of key comparisons;}$$
$$S = 1 \text{ if successful, 0 if unsuccessful.} \tag{1}$$

Program S takes $5C - 2S + 3$ units of time. If the search successfully finds $K = K_i$, we have $C = i$, $S = 1$; hence the total time is $(5i + 1)u$. On the other hand if the search is unsuccessful, we have $C = N$, $S = 0$, for a total time of $(5N + 3)u$. If every input key occurs with equal probability, the average value of C in a successful search will be

$$\frac{1 + 2 + \cdots + N}{N} = \frac{N + 1}{2}; \tag{2}$$

the standard deviation is, of course, rather large, about $0.289N$ (see exercise 1).

The algorithm above is surely familiar to all programmers. But too few people know that it is *not* always the right way to do a sequential search! A straightforward change makes the algorithm faster, unless the list of records is quite short:

Algorithm Q (*Quick sequential search*). This algorithm is the same as Algorithm S, except that it assumes the presence of a dummy record R_{N+1} at the end of the file.

Q1. [Initialize.] Set $i \leftarrow 1$, and set $K_{N+1} \leftarrow K$.

Q2. [Compare.] If $K = K_i$, go to Q4.

Q3. [Advance.] Increase i by 1 and return to Q2.

Q4. [End of file?] If $i \leq N$, the algorithm terminates successfully; otherwise it terminates unsuccessfully $(i = N + 1)$. ∎

Program Q (*Quick sequential search*). rA $\equiv K$, rI1 $\equiv i - N$.

01	START	LDA K	1	*Q1. Initialize.*
02		STA KEY+N+1	1	$K_{N+1} \leftarrow K$.

03		ENT1 -N	1	$i \leftarrow 0$.
04		INC1 1	$C + 1 - S$	Q3. Advance.
05		CMPA KEY+N,1	$C + 1 - S$	Q2. Compare.
06		JNE *-2	$C + 1 - S$	To Q3 if $K_i \neq K$.
07		J1NP SUCCESS	1	Q4. End of file?
08	FAILURE	EQU *	$1 - S$	Exit if not in table. ∎

In terms of the quantities C and S in the analysis of Program S, the running time has decreased to $(4C - 4S + 10)u$; this is an improvement whenever $C \geq 6$ in a successful search, and whenever $N \geq 8$ in an unsuccessful search.

The transition from Algorithm S to Algorithm Q makes use of an important speed-up principle: When an inner loop of a program tests two or more conditions, we should try to reduce the testing to just one condition.

Another technique will make Program Q *still* faster.

Program Q' (*Quicker sequential search*). $rA \equiv K$, $rI1 \equiv i - N$.

01	START	LDA K	1	Q1. Initialize.
02		STA KEY+N+1	1	$K_{N+1} \leftarrow K$.
03		ENT1 -1-N	1	$i \leftarrow -1$.
04	3H	INC1 2	$\lfloor (C - S + 2)/2 \rfloor$	Q3. Advance. (twice)
05		CMPA KEY+N,1	$\lfloor (C - S + 2)/2 \rfloor$	Q2. Compare.
06		JE 4F	$\lfloor (C - S + 2)/2 \rfloor$	To Q4 if $K = K_i$.
07		CMPA KEY+N+1,1	$\lfloor (C - S + 1)/2 \rfloor$	Q2. Compare. (next)
08		JNE 3B	$\lfloor (C - S + 1)/2 \rfloor$	To Q3 if $K \neq K_{i+1}$.
09		INC1 1	$(C - S) \bmod 2$	Advance i.
10	4H	J1NP SUCCESS	1	Q4. End of file?
11	FAILURE	EQU *	$1 - S$	Exit if not in table. ∎

The inner loop has been duplicated; this avoids about half of the "$i \leftarrow i + 1$" instructions, so it reduces the running time to

$$3.5C - 3.5S + 10 + \frac{(C - S) \bmod 2}{2}$$

units. We have saved 30 percent of the running time of Program S, when large tables are being searched; many existing programs can be improved in this way. The same ideas apply to programming in high-level languages. [See, for example, D. E. Knuth, *Computing Surveys* **6** (1974), 266–269.]

A slight variation of the algorithm is appropriate if we know that the keys are in increasing order:

Algorithm T (*Sequential search in ordered table*). Given a table of records $R_1, R_2, \ldots, R_N$ whose keys are in increasing order $K_1 < K_2 < \cdots < K_N$, this algorithm searches for a given argument K. For convenience and speed, the algorithm assumes that there is a dummy record R_{N+1} whose key value is $K_{N+1} = \infty > K$.

T1. [Initialize.] Set $i \leftarrow 1$.

T2. [Compare.] If $K \leq K_i$, go to T4.

T3. [Advance.] Increase i by 1 and return to T2.

T4. [Equality?] If $K = K_i$, the algorithm terminates successfully. Otherwise it terminates unsuccessfully. ∎

If all input keys are equally likely, this algorithm takes essentially the same average time as Algorithm Q, for a successful search. But unsuccessful searches are performed about twice as fast, since the absence of a record can be established more quickly.

Each of the algorithms above uses subscripts to denote the table entries. It is convenient to describe the methods in terms of these subscripts, but the same search procedures can be used for tables that have a *linked* representation, since the data is being traversed sequentially. (See exercises 2, 3, and 4.)

Frequency of access. So far we have been assuming that every argument occurs as often as every other. This is not always a realistic assumption; in a general situation, key K_j will occur with probability p_j, where $p_1 + p_2 + \cdots + p_N = 1$. The time required to do a successful search is essentially proportional to the number of comparisons, C, which now has the average value

$$\bar{C}_N = p_1 + 2p_2 + \cdots + Np_N. \tag{3}$$

If we have the option of putting the records into the table in any desired order, this quantity $\bar{C}_N$ is smallest when

$$p_1 \geq p_2 \geq \cdots \geq p_N, \tag{4}$$

that is, when the most frequently used records appear near the beginning.

Let's look at several probability distributions, in order to see how much of a saving is possible when the records are arranged in the optimal manner specified in (4). If $p_1 = p_2 = \cdots = p_N = 1/N$, formula (3) reduces to $\bar{C}_N = (N+1)/2$; we have already derived this in Eq. (2). Suppose, on the other hand, that

$$p_1 = \frac{1}{2}, \quad p_2 = \frac{1}{4}, \quad \ldots, \quad p_{N-1} = \frac{1}{2^{N-1}}, \quad p_N = \frac{1}{2^{N-1}}. \tag{5}$$

Then $\bar{C}_N = 2 - 2^{1-N}$, by exercise 7; the average number of comparisons is *less than two*, for this distribution, if the records appear in the proper order within the table.

Another probability distribution that suggests itself is

$$p_1 = Nc, \quad p_2 = (N-1)c, \quad \ldots, \quad p_N = c, \quad \text{where } c = \frac{2}{N(N+1)}. \tag{6}$$

This wedge-shaped distribution is not as dramatic a departure from uniformity as (5). In this case we find

$$\bar{C}_N = c \sum_{k=1}^{N} k(N+1-k) = \frac{N+2}{3}; \tag{7}$$

the optimum arrangement saves about one-third of the search time that would have been obtained if the records had appeared in random order.

Of course the probability distributions in (5) and (6) are rather artificial, and they may never be a very good approximation to reality. A more typical sequence of probabilities, called "Zipf's law," has

$$p_1 = c/1, \quad p_2 = c/2, \quad \ldots, \quad p_N = c/N, \qquad \text{where } c = 1/H_N. \tag{8}$$

This distribution was popularized by G. K. Zipf, who observed that the nth most common word in natural language text seems to occur with a frequency approximately proportional to $1/n$. [*The Psycho-Biology of Language* (Boston, Mass.: Houghton Mifflin, 1935); *Human Behavior and the Principle of Least Effort* (Reading, Mass.: Addison–Wesley, 1949).] He observed the same phenomenon in census tables, when metropolitan areas are ranked in order of decreasing population. If Zipf's law governs the frequency of the keys in a table, we have immediately

$$\bar{C}_N = N/H_N; \tag{9}$$

searching such a file is about $\frac{1}{2}\ln N$ times faster than searching the same file with randomly ordered records. [See A. D. Booth, L. Brandwood, and J. P. Cleave, *Mechanical Resolution of Linguistic Problems* (New York: Academic Press, 1958), 79.]

Another approximation to realistic distributions is the "80-20" rule of thumb that has commonly been observed in commercial applications [see, for example, W. P. Heising, *IBM Systems J.* **2** (1963), 114–115]. This rule states that 80 percent of the transactions deal with the most active 20 percent of a file; and the same rule applies in fractal fashion to the top 20 percent, so that 64 percent of the transactions deal with the most active 4 percent, etc. In other words,

$$\frac{p_1 + p_2 + \cdots + p_{.20n}}{p_1 + p_2 + p_3 + \cdots + p_n} \approx .80 \qquad \text{for all } n. \tag{10}$$

One distribution that satisfies this rule exactly whenever n is a multiple of 5 is

$$p_1 = c, \quad p_2 = (2^\theta - 1)c, \quad p_3 = (3^\theta - 2^\theta)c, \quad \ldots, \quad p_N = \left(N^\theta - (N-1)^\theta\right)c, \tag{11}$$

where

$$c_1 = 1/N^\theta, \qquad \theta = \frac{\log .80}{\log .20} = 0.1386, \tag{12}$$

since $p_1 + p_2 + \cdots + p_n = cn^\theta$ for all n in this case. It is not especially easy to work with the probabilities in (11); we have, however, $n^\theta - (n - 1)^\theta = \theta n^{\theta-1}\left(1 + O(1/n)\right)$, so there is a simpler distribution that approximately fulfills the 80-20 rule, namely

$$p_1 = c/1^{1-\theta}, \quad p_2 = c/2^{1-\theta}, \quad \ldots, \quad p_N = c/N^{1-\theta}, \qquad \text{where } c = 1/H_N^{(1-\theta)}. \tag{13}$$

Here $\theta = \log .80/\log .20$ as before, and $H_N^{(s)}$ is the Nth harmonic number of order s, namely $1^{-s} + 2^{-s} + \cdots + N^{-s}$. Notice that this probability distribution is very similar to that of Zipf's law (8); as θ varies from 1 to 0, the probabilities vary from a uniform distribution to a Zipfian one. Applying (3) to (13) yields

$$\bar{C}_N = H_N^{(-\theta)} / H_N^{(1-\theta)} = \frac{\theta N}{\theta + 1} + O(N^{1-\theta}) \approx 0.122N \qquad (14)$$

as the mean number of comparisons for the 80-20 law (see exercise 8).

A study of word frequencies carried out by E. S. Schwartz [see the interesting graph on page 422 of *JACM* **10** (1963)] suggests that distribution (13) with a slightly *negative* value of θ gives a better fit to the data than Zipf's law (8). In this case the mean value

$$\bar{C}_N = H_N^{(-\theta)} / H_N^{(1-\theta)} = \frac{N^{1+\theta}}{(1+\theta)\zeta(1-\theta)} + O(N^{1+2\theta}) \qquad (15)$$

is substantially smaller than (9) as $N \to \infty$.

Distributions like (11) and (13) were first studied by Vilfredo Pareto in connection with disparities of personal income and wealth [*Cours d'Économie Politique* **2** (Lausanne: Rouge, 1897), 304–312]. If p_k is proportional to the wealth of the kth richest individual, the probability that a person's wealth exceeds or equals x times the wealth of the poorest individual is k/N when $x = p_k/p_N$. Thus, when $p_k = ck^{\theta-1}$ and $x = (k/N)^{\theta-1}$, the stated probability is $x^{-1/(1-\theta)}$; this is now called a *Pareto distribution* with parameter $1/(1-\theta)$.

Curiously, Pareto didn't understand his own distribution; he believed that a value of θ near 0 would correspond to a more egalitarian society than a value near 1! His error was corrected by Corrado Gini [*Atti della III Riunione della Società Italiana per il Progresso delle Scienze* (1910), reprinted in his *Memorie di Metodologia Statistica* **1** (Rome: 1955), 3–120], who was the first person to formulate and explain the significance of ratios like the 80-20 law (10). People still tend to misunderstand such distributions; they often speak about a "75-25 law" or a "90-10 law" as if an *a-b* law makes sense only when $a + b = 100$, while (12) shows that the sum $80 + 20$ is quite irrelevant.

Another discrete distribution analogous to (11) and (13) was introduced by G. Udny Yule when he studied the increase in biological species as a function of time, assuming various models of evolution [*Philos. Trans.* **B213** (1924), 21–87]. Yule's distribution applies when $\theta < 2$:

$$p_1 = c, \; p_2 = \frac{c}{2-\theta}, \; p_3 = \frac{2c}{(3-\theta)(2-\theta)}, \; \ldots, \; p_N = \frac{(N-1)! \, c}{(N-\theta)\ldots(2-\theta)} = \frac{c}{\binom{N-\theta}{N-1}};$$

$$c = \frac{\theta}{1-\theta} \frac{\binom{N-\theta}{N}}{1 - \binom{N-\theta}{N}}. \qquad (16)$$

The limiting value $c = 1/H_N$ or $c = 1/N$ is used when $\theta = 0$ or $\theta = 1$.

A "self-organizing" file. These calculations with probabilities are very nice, but in most cases we don't know what the probabilities are. We could keep a count in each record of how often it has been accessed, reallocating the records on the basis of those counts; the formulas derived above suggest that this procedure would often lead to a worthwhile savings. But we probably don't want to devote so much memory space to the count fields, since we can make better use of that memory by using one of the nonsequential search techniques that are explained later in this chapter.

A simple scheme, which has been in use for many years although its origin is unknown, can be used to keep the records in a pretty good order without auxiliary count fields: Whenever a record has been successfully located, it is moved to the front of the table.

The idea behind this "self-organizing" technique is that the oft-used items will tend to be located fairly near the beginning of the table, when we need them. If we assume that the N keys occur with respective probabilities $\{p_1, p_2, \ldots, p_N\}$, with each search being completely *independent* of previous searches, it can be shown that the average number of comparisons needed to find an item in such a self-organizing file tends to the limiting value

$$\widetilde{C}_N = 1 + 2 \sum_{1 \le i < j \le N} \frac{p_i p_j}{p_i + p_j} = \frac{1}{2} + \sum_{i,j} \frac{p_i p_j}{p_i + p_j}. \tag{17}$$

(See exercise 11.) For example, if $p_i = 1/N$ for $1 \le i \le N$, the self-organizing table is always in completely random order, and this formula reduces to the familiar expression $(N+1)/2$ derived above. In general, the average number of comparisons (17) is always less than twice the optimal value (3), since $\widetilde{C}_N \le 1 + 2\sum_{j=1}^{N}(j-1)p_j = 2\overline{C}_N - 1$. In fact, $\widetilde{C}_N$ is always less than $\pi/2$ times the optimal value $\overline{C}_N$ [Chung, Hajela, and Seymour, *J. Comp. Syst. Sci.* **36** (1988), 148–157]; this ratio is the best possible constant in general, since it is approached when p_j is proportional to $1/j^2$.

Let us see how well the self-organizing procedure works when the key probabilities obey Zipf's law (8). We have

$$\widetilde{C}_N = \frac{1}{2} + \sum_{1 \le i,j \le N} \frac{(c/i)(c/j)}{c/i + c/j} = \frac{1}{2} + c \sum_{1 \le i,j \le N} \frac{1}{i+j}$$

$$= \frac{1}{2} + c \sum_{i=1}^{N}(H_{N+i} - H_i) = \frac{1}{2} + c \sum_{i=1}^{2N} H_i - 2c \sum_{i=1}^{N} H_i$$

$$= \tfrac{1}{2} + c\big((2N+1)H_{2N} - 2N - 2(N+1)H_N + 2N\big)$$

$$= \tfrac{1}{2} + c\big(N \ln 4 - \ln N + O(1)\big) \approx 2N/\lg N, \tag{18}$$

by Eqs. 1.2.7–(8) and 1.2.7–(3). This is substantially better than $\frac{1}{2}N$, when N is reasonably large, and it is only about $\ln 4 \approx 1.386$ times as many comparisons as would be obtained in the optimum arrangement; see (9).

Computational experiments involving actual compiler symbol tables indicate that the self-organizing method works even better than our formulas predict, because successive searches are not independent (small groups of keys tend to occur in bunches).

This self-organizing scheme was first analyzed by John McCabe [*Operations Research* **13** (1965), 609–618], who established (17). McCabe also introduced another interesting scheme, under which each successfully located key that is not already at the beginning of the table is simply *interchanged with the preceding key*, instead of being moved all the way to the front. He conjectured that the limiting average search time for this method, assuming independent searches, never exceeds (17). Several years later, Ronald L. Rivest proved in fact that the transposition method uses strictly *fewer* comparisons than the move-to-front method, in the long run, except of course when $N \leq 2$ or when all the nonzero probabilities are equal [*CACM* **19** (1976), 63–67]. However, convergence to the asymptotic limit is much slower than for the move-to-front heuristic, so move-to-front is better unless the process is prolonged [J. R. Bitner, *SICOMP* **8** (1979), 82–110]. Moreover, J. L. Bentley, C. C. McGeoch, D. D. Sleator, and R. E. Tarjan have proved that the move-to-front method never makes more than four times the total number of memory accesses made by any algorithm on linear lists, given any sequence of accesses whatever to the data — even if the algorithm knows the future; the frequency-count and transposition methods do not have this property [*CACM* **28** (1985), 202–208, 404–411]. See *SODA* **8** (1997), 53–62, for a interesting empirical study of more than 40 heuristics for self-organizing lists, carried out by R. Bachrach and R. El-Yaniv.

Tape searching with unequal-length records. Now let's give the problem still another twist: Suppose the table we are searching is stored on tape, and the individual records have varying lengths. For example, in an old-fashioned operating system, the "system library tape" was such a file; standard system programs such as compilers, assemblers, loading routines, and report generators were the "records" on this tape, and most user jobs would start by searching down the tape until the appropriate routine had been input. This setup makes our previous analysis of Algorithm S inapplicable, since step S3 takes a variable amount of time each time we reach it. The number of comparisons is therefore not the only criterion of interest.

Let L_i be the length of record R_i, and let p_i be the probability that this record will be sought. The average running time of the search method will now be approximately proportional to

$$p_1 L_1 + p_2(L_1 + L_2) + \cdots + p_N(L_1 + L_2 + L_3 + \cdots + L_N). \qquad (19)$$

When $L_1 = L_2 = \cdots = L_N = 1$, this reduces to (3), the case already studied.

It seems logical to put the most frequently needed records at the beginning of the tape; but this is sometimes a bad idea! For example, assume that the tape contains just two programs, A and B, where A is needed twice as often as B but it is four times as long. Thus,

$$N = 2, \quad p_A = \tfrac{2}{3}, \quad L_A = 4, \quad p_B = \tfrac{1}{3}, \quad L_B = 1.$$

If we place A first on tape, according to the "logical" principle stated above, the average running time is $\tfrac{2}{3} \cdot 4 + \tfrac{1}{3} \cdot 5 = \tfrac{13}{3}$; but if we use an "illogical" idea, placing B first, the average running time is reduced to $\tfrac{1}{3} \cdot 1 + \tfrac{2}{3} \cdot 5 = \tfrac{11}{3}$.

The optimum arrangement of programs on a library tape may be determined as follows.

Theorem S. *Let L_i and p_i be as defined above. The arrangement of records in the table is optimal if and only if*

$$p_1/L_1 \geq p_2/L_2 \geq \cdots \geq p_N/L_N. \tag{20}$$

In other words, the minimum value of

$$p_{a_1} L_{a_1} + p_{a_2}(L_{a_1} + L_{a_2}) + \cdots + p_{a_N}(L_{a_1} + \cdots + L_{a_N}),$$

over all permutations $a_1 a_2 \ldots a_N$ of $\{1, 2, \ldots, N\}$, is equal to (19) if and only if (20) holds.

Proof. Suppose that R_i and R_{i+1} are interchanged on the tape; the cost (19) changes from

$$\cdots + p_i(L_1 + \cdots + L_{i-1} + L_i) + p_{i+1}(L_1 + \cdots + L_{i+1}) + \cdots$$

to

$$\cdots + p_{i+1}(L_1 + \cdots + L_{i-1} + L_{i+1}) + p_i(L_1 + \cdots + L_{i+1}) + \cdots,$$

a net change of $p_i L_{i+1} - p_{i+1} L_i$. Therefore if $p_i/L_i < p_{i+1}/L_{i+1}$, such an interchange will improve the average running time, and the given arrangement is not optimal. It follows that (20) holds in any optimal arrangement.

Conversely, assume that (20) holds; we need to prove that the arrangement is optimal. The argument just given shows that the arrangement is "locally optimal" in the sense that adjacent interchanges make no improvement; but there may conceivably be a long, complicated sequence of interchanges that leads to a better "global optimum." We shall consider two proofs, one that uses computer science and one that uses a mathematical trick.

First proof. Assume that (20) holds. We know that any permutation of the records can be sorted into the order $R_1 R_2 \ldots R_N$ by using a sequence of interchanges of adjacent records. Each of these interchanges replaces $\ldots R_j R_i \ldots$ by $\ldots R_i R_j \ldots$ for some $i < j$, so it decreases the search time by the nonnegative amount $p_i L_j - p_j L_i$. Therefore the order $R_1 R_2 \ldots R_N$ must have minimum search time.

Second proof. Replace each probability p_i by

$$p_i(\epsilon) = p_i + \epsilon^i - (\epsilon^1 + \epsilon^2 + \cdots + \epsilon^N)/N, \tag{21}$$

where ϵ is an extremely small positive number. When ϵ is sufficiently small, we will never have $x_1 p_1(\epsilon) + \cdots + x_N p_N(\epsilon) = y_1 p_1(\epsilon) + \cdots + y_N p_N(\epsilon)$ unless $x_1 = y_1$, $\ldots$, $x_N = y_N$; in particular, equality will not hold in (20). Consider now the $N!$ permutations of the records; at least one of them is optimum, and we know that it satisfies (20). But only one permutation satisfies (20) because there are no equalities. Therefore (20) uniquely characterizes the optimum arrangement of records in the table for the probabilities $p_i(\epsilon)$, whenever ϵ is sufficiently small. By continuity, the same arrangement must also be optimum when ϵ is set equal to zero. (This "tie-breaking" type of proof is often useful in connection with combinatorial optimization.) ∎

Theorem S is due to W. E. Smith, *Naval Research Logistics Quarterly* **3** (1956), 59–66. The exercises below contain further results about optimum file arrangements.

EXERCISES

1. [*M20*] When all the search keys are equally probable, what is the standard deviation of the number of comparisons made in a successful sequential search through a table of N records?

2. [*15*] Restate the steps of Algorithm S, using linked-memory notation instead of subscript notation. (If P points to a record in the table, assume that KEY(P) is the key, INFO(P) is the associated information, and LINK(P) is a pointer to the next record. Assume also that FIRST points to the first record, and that the last record points to Λ.)

3. [*16*] Write a MIX program for the algorithm of exercise 2. What is the running time of your program, in terms of the quantities C and S in (1)?

▶ **4.** [*17*] Does the idea of Algorithm Q carry over from subscript notation to linked-memory notation? (See exercise 2.)

5. [*20*] Program Q′ is, of course, noticeably faster than Program Q, when C is large. But are there any small values of C and S for which Program Q′ actually takes more time than Program Q?

▶ **6.** [*20*] Add three more instructions to Program Q′, reducing its running time to about $(3.33C + \text{constant})u$.

7. [*M20*] Evaluate the average number of comparisons, (3), using the "binary" probability distribution (5).

8. [*HM22*] Find an asymptotic series for $H_n^{(x)}$ as $n \to \infty$, when $x \neq 1$.

▶ **9.** [*HM28*] The text observes that the probability distributions given by (11), (13), and (16) are roughly equivalent when $0 < \theta < 1$, and that the mean number of comparisons using (13) is $\frac{\theta}{\theta+1} N + O(N^{1-\theta})$.

a) Is the mean number of comparisons equal to $\frac{\theta}{\theta+1} N + O(N^{1-\theta})$ also when the probabilities of (11) are used?

b) What about (16)?

c) How do (11) and (16) compare to (13) when $\theta < 0$?

10. [*M20*] The best arrangement of records in a sequential table is specified by (4); what is the *worst* arrangement? Show that the average number of comparisons in the worst arrangement has a simple relation to the average number of comparisons in the best arrangement.

11. [*M30*] The purpose of this exercise is to analyze the limiting behavior of a self-organizing file with the move-to-front heuristic. First we need to define some notation: Let $f_m(x_1, x_2, \ldots, x_m)$ be the infinite sum of all distinct ordered products $x_{i_1} x_{i_2} \ldots x_{i_k}$ such that $1 \leq i_1, \ldots, i_k \leq m$, where each of $x_1, x_2, \ldots, x_m$ appears in every term. For example,

$$f_2(x, y) = \sum_{j,k \geq 0} (x^{1+j} y (x+y)^k + y^{1+j} x (x+y)^k) = \frac{xy}{1-x-y} \left(\frac{1}{1-x} + \frac{1}{1-y} \right).$$

Given a set X of n variables $\{x_1, \ldots, x_n\}$, let

$$P_{nm} = \sum_{1 \le j_1 < \cdots < j_m \le n} f_m(x_{j_1}, \ldots, x_{j_m}); \qquad Q_{nm} = \sum_{1 \le j_1 < \cdots < j_m \le n} \frac{1}{1 - x_{j_1} - \cdots - x_{j_m}}.$$

For example, $P_{32} = f_2(x_1, x_2) + f_2(x_1, x_3) + f_2(x_2, x_3)$ and $Q_{32} = 1/(1 - x_1 - x_2) + 1/(1 - x_1 - x_3) + 1/(1 - x_2 - x_3)$. By convention we set $P_{n0} = Q_{n0} = 1$.

a) Assume that the text's self-organizing file has been servicing requests for item R_i with probability p_i. After the system has been running a long time, show that R_i will be the mth item from the front with limiting probability $p_i P_{(N-1)(m-1)}$, where the set of variables X is $\{p_1, \ldots, p_{i-1}, p_{i+1}, \ldots, p_N\}$.

b) By summing the result of (a) for $m = 1, 2, \ldots$, we obtain the identity

$$P_{nn} + P_{n(n-1)} + \cdots + P_{n0} = Q_{nn}.$$

Prove that, consequently,

$$P_{nm} + \binom{n-m+1}{1} P_{n(m-1)} + \cdots + \binom{n-m+m}{m} P_{n0} = Q_{nm};$$

$$Q_{nm} - \binom{n-m+1}{1} Q_{n(m-1)} + \cdots + (-1)^m \binom{n-m+m}{m} Q_{n0} = P_{nm}.$$

c) Compute the limiting average distance $d_i = \sum_{m \ge 1} m p_i P_{N-1,m-1}$ of R_i from the front of the list; then evaluate $\tilde{C}_N = \sum_{i=1}^{N} p_i d_i$.

12. [*M23*] Use (17) to evaluate the average number of comparisons needed to search the self-organizing file when the search keys have the binary probability distribution (5).

13. [*M27*] Use (17) to evaluate $\tilde{C}_N$ for the wedge-shaped probability distribution (6).

14. [*M21*] Given two sequences $\langle x_1, x_2, \ldots, x_n \rangle$ and $\langle y_1, y_2, \ldots, y_n \rangle$ of real numbers, what permutation $a_1 a_2 \ldots a_n$ of the subscripts will make $\sum_i x_i y_{a_i}$ a maximum? What permutation will make it a minimum?

▶ **15.** [*M22*] The text shows how to arrange programs optimally on a system library tape, when only one program is being sought. But another set of assumptions is more appropriate for a *subroutine* library tape, from which we may wish to load various subroutines called for in a user's program.

For this case let us suppose that subroutine j is desired with probability P_j, independently of whether or not other subroutines are desired. Then, for example, the probability that no subroutines at all are needed is $(1 - P_1)(1 - P_2) \ldots (1 - P_N)$; and the probability that the search will end just after loading the jth subroutine is $P_j(1 - P_{j+1}) \ldots (1 - P_N)$. If L_j is the length of subroutine j, the average search time will therefore be essentially proportional to

$$L_1 P_1 (1 - P_2) \ldots (1 - P_N) + (L_1 + L_2) P_2 (1 - P_3) \ldots (1 - P_N) + \cdots + (L_1 + \cdots + L_N) P_N.$$

What is the optimum arrangement of subroutines on the tape, under these assumptions?

16. [*M22*] (H. Riesel.) We often need to test whether or not n given conditions are all simultaneously true. (For example, we may want to test whether both $x > 0$ and $y < z^2$, and it is not immediately clear which condition should be tested first.) Suppose that the testing of condition j costs T_j units of time, and that the condition will be true with probability p_j, independent of the outcomes of all the other conditions. In what order should we make the tests?

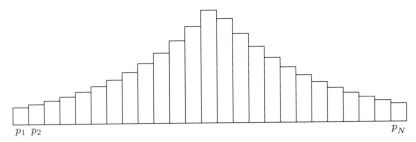

Fig. 2. An "organ-pipe arrangement" of probabilities minimizes the average seek time in a catenated search.

17. [*M23*] (W. E. Smith.) Suppose you have to do n jobs; the jth job takes T_j units of time, and it has a *deadline* D_j. In other words, the jth job is supposed to be finished after at most D_j units of time have elapsed. What schedule $a_1 a_2 \ldots a_n$ for processing the jobs will minimize the *maximum tardiness*, namely

$$\max(T_{a_1} - D_{a_1}, T_{a_1} + T_{a_2} - D_{a_2}, \ldots, T_{a_1} + T_{a_2} + \cdots + T_{a_n} - D_{a_n})\,?$$

18. [*M30*] (*Catenated search.*) Suppose that N records are located in a linear array $R_1 \ldots R_N$, with probability p_j that record R_j will be sought. A search process is called "catenated" if each search begins where the last one left off. If consecutive searches are independent, the average time required will be $\sum_{1 \le i,j \le N} p_i p_j d(i,j)$, where $d(i,j)$ represents the amount of time to do a search that starts at position i and ends at position j. This model can be applied, for example, to disk file seek time, if $d(i,j)$ is the time needed to travel from cylinder i to cylinder j.

The object of this exercise is to characterize the optimum placement of records for catenated searches, whenever $d(i,j)$ is an increasing function of $|i - j|$, that is, whenever we have $d(i,j) = d_{|i-j|}$ for $d_1 < d_2 < \cdots < d_{N-1}$. (The value of d_0 is irrelevant.) Prove that in this case the records are optimally placed, among all $N!$ permutations, if and only if either $p_1 \le p_N \le p_2 \le p_{N-1} \le \cdots \le p_{\lfloor N/2 \rfloor + 1}$ or $p_N \le p_1 \le p_{N-1} \le p_2 \le \cdots \le p_{\lceil N/2 \rceil}$. (Thus, an "organ pipe" arrangement of probabilities is best, as shown in Fig. 2.) *Hint:* Consider any arrangement where the respective probabilities are $q_1 q_2 \ldots q_k \, s \, r_k \ldots r_2 r_1 t_1 \ldots t_m$, for some $m \ge 0$ and $k > 0$; $N = 2k + m + 1$. Show that the rearrangement $q_1' q_2' \ldots q_k' \, s \, r_k' \ldots r_2' r_1' t_1 \ldots t_m$ is better, where $q_i' = \min(q_i, r_i)$ and $r_i' = \max(q_i, r_i)$, except when $q_i' = q_i$ and $r_i' = r_i$ for all i or when $q_i' = r_i$ and $r_i' = q_i$ and $t_j = 0$ for all i and j. The same holds true when s is not present and $N = 2k + m$.

19. [*M20*] Continuing exercise 18, what are the optimal arrangements for catenated searches when the function $d(i,j)$ has the property that $d(i,j) + d(j,i) = c$ for all $i \ne j$? [This situation occurs, for example, on tapes without read-backwards capability, when we do not know the appropriate direction to search; for $i < j$ we have, say, $d(i,j) = a + b(L_{i+1} + \cdots + L_j)$ and $d(j,i) = a + b(L_{j+1} + \cdots + L_N) + r + b(L_1 + \cdots + L_i)$, where r is the rewind time.]

20. [*M28*] Continuing exercise 18, what are the optimal arrangements for catenated searches when the function $d(i,j)$ is $\min(d_{|i-j|}, d_{n-|i-j|})$, for $d_1 < d_2 < \cdots$? [This situation occurs, for example, in a two-way linked circular list, or in a two-way shift-register storage device.]

21. [*M28*] Consider an n-dimensional cube whose vertices have coordinates $(d_1,\ldots,d_n)$ with $d_j = 0$ or 1; two vertices are called *adjacent* if they differ in exactly one coordinate. Suppose that a set of 2^n numbers $x_0 \le x_1 \le \cdots \le x_{2^n-1}$ is to be assigned to the 2^n vertices in such a way that $\sum_{i,j} |x_i - x_j|$ is minimized, where the sum is over all i and j such that x_i and x_j have been assigned to adjacent vertices. Prove that this minimum will be achieved if, for all j, x_j is assigned to the vertex whose coordinates are the binary representation of j.

▶ **22.** [*20*] Suppose you want to search a large file, not for equality but to find the 1000 records that are *closest* to a given key, in the sense that these 1000 records have the smallest values of $d(K_j, K)$ for some given distance function d. What data structure is most appropriate for such a sequential search?

> *Attempt the end, and never stand to doubt;*
> *Nothing's so hard, but search will find it out.*
> — ROBERT HERRICK, *Seeke and finde* (1648)

6.2. SEARCHING BY COMPARISON OF KEYS

IN THIS SECTION we shall discuss search methods that are based on a linear ordering of the keys, such as alphabetic order or numeric order. After comparing the given argument K to a key K_i in the table, the search continues in three different ways, depending on whether $K < K_i$, $K = K_i$, or $K > K_i$. The sequential search methods of Section 6.1 were essentially limited to a two-way decision ($K = K_i$ versus $K \neq K_i$), but if we free ourselves from the restriction of sequential access we are able to make effective use of an order relation.

6.2.1. Searching an Ordered Table

What would you do if someone handed you a large telephone directory and told you to find the name of the person whose number is 795-6841? There is no better way to tackle this problem than to use the sequential methods of Section 6.1. (Well, you might try to dial the number and talk to the person who answers; or you might know how to obtain a special directory that is sorted by number instead of by name.) The point is that it is much easier to find an entry by the party's name, instead of by number, although the telephone directory contains all the information necessary in both cases. When a large file must be searched, sequential scanning is almost out of the question, but an ordering relation simplifies the job enormously.

With so many sorting methods at our disposal (Chapter 5), we will have little difficulty rearranging a file into order so that it may be searched conveniently. Of course, if we need to search the table only once, a sequential search would be faster than to do a complete sort of the file; but if we need to make repeated searches in the same file, we are better off having it in order. Therefore in this section we shall concentrate on methods that are appropriate for searching a table whose keys satisfy

$$K_1 < K_2 < \cdots < K_N,$$

assuming that we can easily access the key in any given position. After comparing K to K_i in such a table, we have either

- $K < K_i$ $[R_i, R_{i+1}, \ldots, R_N$ are eliminated from consideration];

or   - $K = K_i$ [the search is done];

or   - $K > K_i$ $[R_1, R_2, \ldots, R_i$ are eliminated from consideration].

In each of these three cases, substantial progress has been made, unless i is near one of the ends of the table; this is why the ordering leads to an efficient algorithm.

Binary search. Perhaps the first such method that suggests itself is to start by comparing K to the middle key in the table; the result of this probe tells which half of the table should be searched next, and the same procedure can be used again, comparing K to the middle key of the selected half, etc. After at most about $\lg N$ comparisons, we will have found the key or we will have established

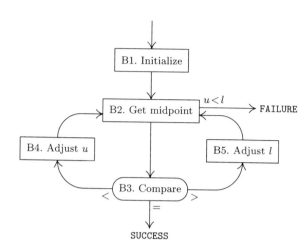

Fig. 3. Binary search.

that it is not present. This procedure is sometimes known as "logarithmic search" or "bisection," but it is most commonly called *binary search*.

Although the basic idea of binary search is comparatively straightforward, the details can be surprisingly tricky, and many good programmers have done it wrong the first few times they tried. One of the most popular correct forms of the algorithm makes use of two pointers, l and u, that indicate the current lower and upper limits for the search, as follows:

Algorithm B (*Binary search*). Given a table of records $R_1 R_2 \ldots R_N$ whose keys are in increasing order $K_1 < K_2 < \cdots < K_N$, this algorithm searches for a given argument K.

B1. [Initialize.] Set $l \leftarrow 1$, $u \leftarrow N$.

B2. [Get midpoint.] (At this point we know that if K is in the table, it satisfies $K_l \leq K \leq K_u$. A more precise statement of the situation appears in exercise 1 below.) If $u < l$, the algorithm terminates unsuccessfully. Otherwise, set $i \leftarrow \lfloor (l+u)/2 \rfloor$, the approximate midpoint of the relevant table area.

B3. [Compare.] If $K < K_i$, go to B4; if $K > K_i$, go to B5; and if $K = K_i$, the algorithm terminates successfully.

B4. [Adjust u.] Set $u \leftarrow i - 1$ and return to B2.

B5. [Adjust l.] Set $l \leftarrow i + 1$ and return to B2. ∎

Figure 4 illustrates two cases of this binary search algorithm: first to search for the argument 653, which is present in the table, and then to search for 400, which is absent. The brackets indicate l and u, and the underlined key represents K_i. In both examples the search terminates after making four comparisons.

a) Searching for 653:

[061 087 154 170 275 426 503 <u>509</u> 512 612 653 677 703 765 897 908]
061 087 154 170 275 426 503 509 [512 612 653 <u>677</u> 703 765 897 908]
061 087 154 170 275 426 503 509 [512 <u>612</u> 653] 677 703 765 897 908
061 087 154 170 275 426 503 509 512 612 [<u>653</u>] 677 703 765 897 908

b) Searching for 400:

[061 087 154 170 275 426 503 <u>509</u> 512 612 653 677 703 765 897 908]
[061 087 154 <u>170</u> 275 426 503] 509 512 612 653 677 703 765 897 908
061 087 154 170 [275 <u>426</u> 503] 509 512 612 653 677 703 765 897 908
061 087 154 170 [<u>275</u>] 426 503 509 512 612 653 677 703 765 897 908
061 087 154 170 275] [426 503 509 512 612 653 677 703 765 897 908

Fig. 4. Examples of binary search.

Program B (*Binary search*). As in the programs of Section 6.1, we assume here that K_i is a full-word key appearing in location KEY $+i$. The following code uses $rI1 \equiv l$, $rI2 \equiv u$, $rI3 \equiv i$.

01	START	ENT1	1	1	*B1. Initialize.* $l \leftarrow 1$.
02		ENT2	N	1	$u \leftarrow N$.
03		JMP	2F	1	To B2.
04	5H	JE	SUCCESS	$C1$	Jump if $K = K_i$.
05		ENT1	1,3	$C1 - S$	*B5. Adjust l.* $l \leftarrow i + 1$.
06	2H	ENTA	0,1	$C + 1 - S$	*B2. Get midpoint.*
07		INCA	0,2	$C + 1 - S$	$rA \leftarrow l + u$.
08		SRB	1	$C + 1 - S$	$rA \leftarrow \lfloor rA/2 \rfloor$. (rX changes too.)
09		STA	TEMP	$C + 1 - S$	
10		CMP1	TEMP	$C + 1 - S$	
11		JG	FAILURE	$C + 1 - S$	Jump if $u < l$.
12		LD3	TEMP	C	$i \leftarrow$ midpoint.
13	3H	LDA	K	C	*B3. Compare.*
14		CMPA	KEY,3	C	
15		JGE	5B	C	Jump if $K \geq K_i$.
16		ENT2	-1,3	$C2$	*B4. Adjust u.* $u \leftarrow i - 1$.
17		JMP	2B	$C2$	To B2. ∎

This procedure doesn't blend with MIX quite as smoothly as the other algorithms we have seen, because MIX does not allow much arithmetic in index registers. The running time is $(18C - 10S + 12)u$, where $C = C1 + C2$ is the number of comparisons made (the number of times step B3 is performed), and $S = $ [outcome is successful]. The operation on line 08 of this program is "shift right binary 1," which is legitimate only on binary versions of MIX; for general byte size, this instruction should be replaced by "MUL =1//2+1=", increasing the running time to $(26C - 18S + 20)u$.

A tree representation. In order to really understand what is happening in Algorithm B, our best bet is to think of the procedure as a binary decision tree, as shown in Fig. 5 for the case $N = 16$.

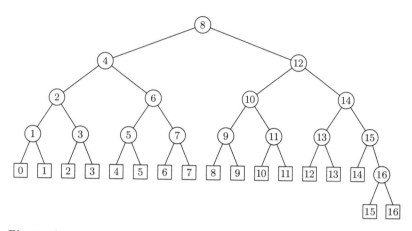

Fig. 5. A comparison tree that corresponds to binary search when $N = 16$.

When N is 16, the first comparison made by the algorithm is $K : K_8$; this is represented by the root node ⑧ in the figure. Then if $K < K_8$, the algorithm follows the left subtree, comparing K to K_4; similarly if $K > K_8$, the right subtree is used. An unsuccessful search will lead to one of the external square nodes numbered $\boxed{0}$ through $\boxed{N}$; for example, we reach node $\boxed{6}$ if and only if $K_6 < K < K_7$.

The binary tree corresponding to a binary search on N records can be constructed as follows: If $N = 0$, the tree is simply $\boxed{0}$. Otherwise the root node is

$$\left(\lceil N/2 \rceil\right),$$

the left subtree is the corresponding binary tree with $\lceil N/2 \rceil - 1$ nodes, and the right subtree is the corresponding binary tree with $\lfloor N/2 \rfloor$ nodes and with all node numbers increased by $\lceil N/2 \rceil$.

In an analogous fashion, *any* algorithm for searching an ordered table of length N by means of comparisons can be represented as an N-node binary tree in which the nodes are labeled with the numbers 1 to N (unless the algorithm makes redundant comparisons). Conversely, any binary tree corresponds to a valid method for searching an ordered table; we simply label the nodes

$$\boxed{0} \quad ① \quad \boxed{1} \quad ② \quad \boxed{2} \quad \dots \quad \boxed{N-1} \quad Ⓝ \quad \boxed{N} \qquad (1)$$

in symmetric order, from left to right.

If the search argument input to Algorithm B is K_{10}, the algorithm makes the comparisons $K > K_8$, $K < K_{12}$, $K = K_{10}$. This corresponds to the path from the root to ⑩ in Fig. 5. Similarly, the behavior of Algorithm B on other keys corresponds to the other paths leading from the root of the tree. The method of constructing the binary trees corresponding to Algorithm B therefore makes it easy to prove the following result by induction on N:

Theorem B. *If $2^{k-1} \le N < 2^k$, a successful search using Algorithm B requires* (min 1, max k) *comparisons. If $N = 2^k - 1$, an unsuccessful search requires*

k comparisons; and if $2^{k-1} \le N < 2^k - 1$, an unsuccessful search requires either $k - 1$ or k comparisons. ∎

Further analysis of binary search. (Nonmathematical readers should skip to Eq. (4).) The tree representation shows us also how to compute the *average* number of comparisons in a simple way. Let C_N be the average number of comparisons in a successful search, assuming that each of the N keys is an equally likely argument; and let C'_N be the average number of comparisons in an *unsuccessful* search, assuming that each of the $N + 1$ intervals between and outside the extreme values of the keys is equally likely. Then we have

$$C_N = 1 + \frac{\text{internal path length of tree}}{N}, \qquad C'_N = \frac{\text{external path length of tree}}{N + 1},$$

by the definition of internal and external path length. We saw in Eq. 2.3.4.5–(3) that the external path length is always $2N$ more than the internal path length. Hence there is a rather unexpected relationship between C_N and C'_N:

$$C_N = \left(1 + \frac{1}{N}\right)C'_N - 1. \tag{2}$$

This formula, which is due to T. N. Hibbard [*JACM* **9** (1962), 16–17], holds for all search methods that correspond to binary trees; in other words, it holds for all methods that are based on nonredundant comparisons. The variance of successful-search comparisons can also be expressed in terms of the corresponding variance for unsuccessful searches (see exercise 25).

From the formulas above we can see that the "best" way to search by comparisons is one whose tree has minimum external path length, over all binary trees with N internal nodes. Fortunately it can be proved that *Algorithm B is optimum* in this sense, for all N; for we have seen (exercise 5.3.1–20) that a binary tree has minimum path length if and only if its external nodes all occur on at most two adjacent levels. It follows that the external path length of the tree corresponding to Algorithm B is

$$(N + 1)\left(\lfloor \lg N \rfloor + 2\right) - 2^{\lfloor \lg N \rfloor + 1}. \tag{3}$$

(See Eq. 5.3.1–(34).) From this formula and (2) we can compute the exact average number of comparisons, assuming that all search arguments are equally probable.

$N = 1$	2	3	4	5	6	7	8	9	10	11	12	13	14	15	16
$C_N = 1$	$1\frac{1}{2}$	$1\frac{2}{3}$	2	$2\frac{1}{5}$	$2\frac{2}{6}$	$2\frac{3}{7}$	$2\frac{5}{8}$	$2\frac{7}{9}$	$2\frac{9}{10}$	3	$3\frac{1}{12}$	$3\frac{2}{13}$	$3\frac{3}{14}$	$3\frac{4}{15}$	$3\frac{6}{16}$
$C'_N = 1$	$1\frac{2}{3}$	2	$2\frac{2}{5}$	$2\frac{4}{6}$	$2\frac{6}{7}$	3	$3\frac{2}{9}$	$3\frac{4}{10}$	$3\frac{6}{11}$	$3\frac{8}{12}$	$3\frac{10}{13}$	$3\frac{12}{14}$	$3\frac{14}{15}$	4	$4\frac{2}{17}$

In general, if $k = \lfloor \lg N \rfloor$, we have

$$\begin{aligned} C_N &= k + 1 - (2^{k+1} - k - 2)/N &= \lg N - 1 + \epsilon + (k + 2)/N, \\ C'_N &= k + 2 - 2^{k+1}/(N + 1) &= \lg(N + 1) + \epsilon' \end{aligned} \tag{4}$$

where $0 \le \epsilon, \epsilon' < 0.0861$; see Eq. 5.3.1–(35).

To summarize: Algorithm B never makes more than $\lfloor \lg N \rfloor + 1$ comparisons, and it makes about $\lg N - 1$ comparisons in an average successful search. No search method based on comparisons can do better than this. The average running time of Program B is approximately

$$(18 \lg N - 16)u \qquad \text{for a successful search,}$$
$$(18 \lg N + 12)u \qquad \text{for an unsuccessful search,} \tag{5}$$

if we assume that all outcomes of the search are equally likely.

An important variation. Instead of using three pointers l, i and u in the search, it is tempting to use only two, namely the current position i and its rate of change, δ; after each unequal comparison, we could then set $i \leftarrow i \pm \delta$ and $\delta \leftarrow \delta/2$ (approximately). It is possible to do this, but only if extreme care is paid to the details, as in the following algorithm. Simpler approaches are doomed to failure!

Algorithm U (*Uniform binary search*). Given a table of records $R_1, R_2, \ldots, R_N$ whose keys are in increasing order $K_1 < K_2 < \cdots < K_N$, this algorithm searches for a given argument K. If N is even, the algorithm will sometimes refer to a dummy key K_0 that should be set to $-\infty$ (or any value less than K). We assume that $N \geq 1$.

U1. [Initialize.] Set $i \leftarrow \lceil N/2 \rceil$, $m \leftarrow \lfloor N/2 \rfloor$.

U2. [Compare.] If $K < K_i$, go to U3; if $K > K_i$, go to U4; and if $K = K_i$, the algorithm terminates successfully.

U3. [Decrease i.] (We have pinpointed the search to an interval that contains either m or $m-1$ records; i points just to the right of this interval.) If $m = 0$, the algorithm terminates unsuccessfully. Otherwise set $i \leftarrow i - \lceil m/2 \rceil$; then set $m \leftarrow \lfloor m/2 \rfloor$ and return to U2.

U4. [Increase i.] (We have pinpointed the search to an interval that contains either m or $m-1$ records; i points just to the left of this interval.) If $m = 0$, the algorithm terminates unsuccessfully. Otherwise set $i \leftarrow i + \lceil m/2 \rceil$; then set $m \leftarrow \lfloor m/2 \rfloor$ and return to U2. ∎

Figure 6 shows the corresponding binary tree for the search, when $N = 10$. In an unsuccessful search, the algorithm may make a redundant comparison just before termination; those nodes are shaded in the figure. We may call the search process *uniform* because the difference between the number of a node on level l and the number of its ancestor on level $l - 1$ has a constant value δ for all nodes on level l.

The theory underlying Algorithm U can be understood as follows: Suppose that we have an interval of length $n - 1$ to search; a comparison with the middle element (for n even) or with one of the two middle elements (for n odd) leaves us with two intervals of lengths $\lfloor n/2 \rfloor - 1$ and $\lceil n/2 \rceil - 1$. After repeating this process k times, we obtain 2^k intervals, of which the smallest has length $\lfloor n/2^k \rfloor - 1$ and the largest has length $\lceil n/2^k \rceil - 1$. Hence the lengths of two intervals at the same

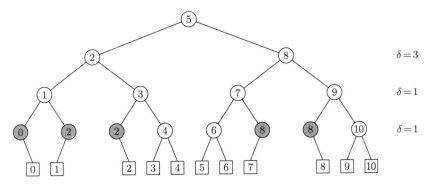

Fig. 6. The comparison tree for a "uniform" binary search, when $N = 10$.

level differ by at most unity; this makes it possible to choose an appropriate "middle" element, without keeping track of the exact lengths.

The principal advantage of Algorithm U is that we need not maintain the value of m at all; we need only refer to a short table of the various δ to use at each level of the tree. Thus the algorithm reduces to the following procedure, which is equally good on binary or decimal computers:

Algorithm C (*Uniform binary search*). This algorithm is just like Algorithm U, but it uses an auxiliary table in place of the calculations involving m. The table entries are

$$\text{DELTA}[j] = \left\lfloor \frac{N + 2^{j-1}}{2^j} \right\rfloor, \qquad \text{for } 1 \le j \le \lfloor \lg N \rfloor + 2. \tag{6}$$

C1. [Initialize.] Set $i \leftarrow \text{DELTA}[1]$, $j \leftarrow 2$.

C2. [Compare.] If $K < K_i$, go to C3; if $K > K_i$, go to C4; and if $K = K_i$, the algorithm terminates successfully.

C3. [Decrease i.] If $\text{DELTA}[j] = 0$, the algorithm terminates unsuccessfully. Otherwise, set $i \leftarrow i - \text{DELTA}[j]$, $j \leftarrow j + 1$, and go to C2.

C4. [Increase i.] If $\text{DELTA}[j] = 0$, the algorithm terminates unsuccessfully. Otherwise, set $i \leftarrow i + \text{DELTA}[j]$, $j \leftarrow j + 1$, and go to C2. ∎

Exercise 8 proves that this algorithm refers to the artificial key $K_0 = -\infty$ only when N is even.

Program C (*Uniform binary search*). This program does the same job as Program B, using Algorithm C with $\text{rA} \equiv K$, $\text{rI1} \equiv i$, $\text{rI2} \equiv j$, $\text{rI3} \equiv \text{DELTA}[j]$.

01	START	ENT1	N+1/2	1	*C1. Initialize.* $i \leftarrow \lfloor (N+1)/2 \rfloor$.
02		ENT2	2	1	$j \leftarrow 2$.
03		LDA	K	1	
04		JMP	2F	1	
05	3H	JE	SUCCESS	$C1$	Jump if $K = K_i$.
06		J3Z	FAILURE	$C1 - S$	Jump if $\text{DELTA}[j] = 0$.
07		DEC1	0,3	$C1 - S - A$	*C3. Decrease i.*

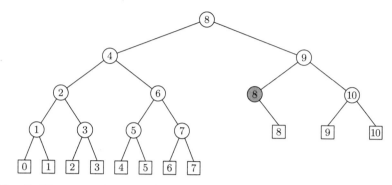

Fig. 7. The comparison tree for Shar's almost uniform search, when $N = 10$.

08	5H	INC2	1	$C - 1$	$j \leftarrow j + 1$.
09	2H	LD3	DELTA,2	C	*C2. Compare.*
10		CMPA	KEY,1	C	
11		JLE	3B	C	Jump if $K \leq K_i$.
12		INC1	0,3	$C2$	*C4. Increase i.*
13		J3NZ	5B	$C2$	Jump if DELTA[j] $\neq 0$.
14	FAILURE EQU		*	$1 - S$	Exit if not in table. ∎

In a successful search, this algorithm corresponds to a binary tree with the same internal path length as the tree of Algorithm B, so the average number of comparisons C_N is the same as before. In an unsuccessful search, Algorithm C always makes exactly $\lfloor \lg N \rfloor + 1$ comparisons. The total running time of Program C is not quite symmetrical between left and right branches, since C1 is weighted more heavily than C2, but exercise 11 shows that we have $K < K_i$ roughly as often as $K > K_i$; hence Program C takes approximately

$$(8.5 \lg N - 6)u \qquad \text{for a successful search,}$$
$$(8.5 \lfloor \lg N \rfloor + 12)u \qquad \text{for an unsuccessful search.} \tag{7}$$

This is more than twice as fast as Program B, without using any special properties of binary computers, even though the running times (5) for Program B assume that MIX has a "shift right binary" instruction.

Another modification of binary search, suggested in 1971 by L. E. Shar, will be still faster on some computers, because it is uniform after the first step, and it requires no table. The first step is to compare K with K_i, where $i = 2^k$, $k = \lfloor \lg N \rfloor$. If $K < K_i$, we use a uniform search with the δ's equal to 2^{k-1}, 2^{k-2}, ..., 1, 0. On the other hand, if $K > K_i$ we reset i to $i' = N + 1 - 2^l$, where $l = \lceil \lg(N - 2^k + 1) \rceil$, and pretend that the first comparison was actually $K > K_{i'}$, using a uniform search with the δ's equal to 2^{l-1}, 2^{l-2}, ..., 1, 0.

Shar's method is illustrated for $N = 10$ in Fig. 7. Like the previous algorithms, it never makes more than $\lfloor \lg N \rfloor + 1$ comparisons; hence it makes at most one more than the minimum possible average number of comparisons, in spite of the fact that it occasionally goes through several redundant steps in succession (see exercise 12).

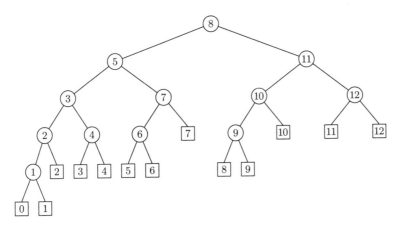

Fig. 8. The Fibonacci tree of order 6.

Still another modification of binary search, which increases the speed of *all* the methods above when N is extremely large, is discussed in exercise 23. See also exercise 24, for a method that is faster yet.

*Fibonaccian search. In the polyphase merge we have seen that the Fibonacci numbers can play a role analogous to the powers of 2. A similar phenomenon occurs in searching, where Fibonacci numbers provide us with an alternative to binary search. The resulting method is preferable on some computers, because it involves only addition and subtraction, not division by 2. The procedure we are about to discuss should be distinguished from an important numerical procedure called "Fibonacci search," which is used to locate the maximum of a unimodal function [see *Fibonacci Quarterly* **4** (1966), 265–269]; the similarity of names has led to some confusion.

The Fibonaccian search technique looks very mysterious at first glance, if we simply take the program and try to explain what is happening; it seems to work by magic. But the mystery disappears as soon as the corresponding search tree is displayed. Therefore we shall begin our study of the method by looking at *Fibonacci trees.*

Figure 8 shows the Fibonacci tree of order 6. It looks somewhat more like a real-life shrub than the other trees we have been considering, perhaps because many natural processes satisfy a Fibonacci law. In general, the Fibonacci tree of order k has $F_{k+1} - 1$ internal (circular) nodes and F_{k+1} external (square) nodes, and it is constructed as follows:

If $k = 0$ or $k = 1$, the tree is simply $\boxed{0}$.

If $k \geq 2$, the root is F_k; the left subtree is the Fibonacci tree of order $k - 1$; and the right subtree is the Fibonacci tree of order $k - 2$ with all numbers increased by F_k.

Except for the external nodes, the numbers on the two children of each internal node differ from their parent's number by the same amount, and this amount is a Fibonacci number. For example, $5 = 8 - F_4$ and $11 = 8 + F_4$ in Fig. 8. When the difference is F_j, the corresponding Fibonacci difference for the next branch on the left is F_{j-1}, while on the right it skips down to F_{j-2}. For example, $3 = 5 - F_3$ while $10 = 11 - F_2$.

If we combine these observations with an appropriate mechanism for recognizing the external nodes, we arrive at the following method:

Algorithm F (*Fibonaccian search*). Given a table of records $R_1 R_2 \ldots R_N$ whose keys are in increasing order $K_1 < K_2 < \cdots < K_N$, this algorithm searches for a given argument K.

For convenience in description, we assume that $N + 1$ is a perfect Fibonacci number, F_{k+1}. It is not difficult to make the method work for arbitrary N, if a suitable initialization is provided (see exercise 14).

F1. [Initialize.] Set $i \leftarrow F_k$, $p \leftarrow F_{k-1}$, $q \leftarrow F_{k-2}$. (Throughout the algorithm, p and q will be consecutive Fibonacci numbers.)

F2. [Compare.] If $K < K_i$, go to step F3; if $K > K_i$, go to F4; and if $K = K_i$, the algorithm terminates successfully.

F3. [Decrease i.] If $q = 0$, the algorithm terminates unsuccessfully. Otherwise set $i \leftarrow i - q$, and set $(p, q) \leftarrow (q, p-q)$; then return to F2.

F4. [Increase i.] If $p = 1$, the algorithm terminates unsuccessfully. Otherwise set $i \leftarrow i + q$, $p \leftarrow p - q$, then $q \leftarrow q - p$, and return to F2. ∎

The following MIX implementation gains speed by making two copies of the inner loop, one in which p is in rI2 and q in rI3, and one in which the registers are reversed; this simplifies step F3. In fact, the program actually keeps $p - 1$ and $q - 1$ in the registers, instead of p and q, in order to simplify the test "$p = 1$?" in step F4.

Program F (*Fibonaccian search*). We follow the previous conventions, with $\mathrm{rA} \equiv K$, $\mathrm{rI1} \equiv i$, (rI2 or rI3) $\equiv p - 1$, (rI3 or rI2) $\equiv q - 1$.

```
01 START LDA  K              1          F1. Initialize.
02       ENT1 Fk             1          i ← Fk.
03       ENT2 Fk−1−1         1          p ← Fk−1.
04       ENT3 Fk−2−1         1          q ← Fk−2.
05       JMP  F2A            1          To step F2.
06 F4A   INC1 1,3            C2−S−A     F4. Increase i. i ← i + q.
07       DEC2 1,3            C2−S−A     p ← p − q.
08       DEC3 1,2            C2−S−A     q ← q − p.
09 F2A   CMPA KEY,1          C          F2. Compare.
10       JL   F3A            C          To F3 if K < Ki.
11       JE   SUCCESS        C2         Exit if K = Ki.
12       J2NZ F4A            C2−S       To F4 if p ≠ 1.
13       JMP  FAILURE        A          Exit if not in table.
14 F3A   DEC1 1,3            C1         F3. Decrease i. i ← i − q.
15       DEC2 1,3            C1         p ← p − q.
16       J3NN F2B            C1         Swap registers if q > 0.
17       JMP  FAILURE        1−S−A      Exit if not in table.
```

```
18  F4B    INC1  1,2              (Lines 18–29 are parallel to 06–17.)
19         DEC3  1,2
20         DEC2  1,3
21  F2B    CMPA  KEY,1
22         JL    F3B
23         JE    SUCCESS
24         J3NZ  F4B
25         JMP   FAILURE
26  F3B    DEC1  1,2
27         DEC3  1,2
28         J2NN  F2A
29         JMP   FAILURE          ▮
```

The running time of this program is analyzed in exercise 18. Figure 8 shows, and the analysis proves, that a left branch is taken somewhat more often than a right branch. Let C, $C1$, and $(C2 - S)$ be the respective number of times steps F2, F3, and F4 are performed. Then we have

$$
\begin{aligned}
C &= (\text{ave} \quad \phi k/\sqrt{5} + O(1), \quad \max \ k - 1), \\
C1 &= (\text{ave} \quad k/\sqrt{5} + O(1), \quad \max \ k - 1), \\
C2 - S &= (\text{ave} \ \phi^{-1}k/\sqrt{5} + O(1), \quad \max \ \lfloor k/2 \rfloor).
\end{aligned} \tag{8}
$$

Thus the left branch is taken about $\phi \approx 1.618$ times as often as the right branch (a fact that we might have guessed, since each probe divides the remaining interval into two parts, with the left part about ϕ times as large as the right). The total average running time of Program F therefore comes to approximately

$$
\tfrac{1}{5}\big((18 + 4\phi)k + 31 - 26\phi\big)u \approx (7.050 \lg N + 1.08)u \tag{9}
$$

for a successful search, plus $(9 - 3\phi)u \approx 4.15u$ for an unsuccessful search. This is faster than Program C, although the worst case running time (roughly $8.6 \lg N$) is slightly slower.

Interpolation search. Let's forget computers for a moment, and consider how people actually carry out a search. Sometimes everyday life provides us with clues that lead to good algorithms.

Imagine yourself looking up a word in a dictionary. You probably *don't* begin by looking first at the middle page, then looking at the 1/4 or 3/4 point, etc., as in a binary search. It's even less likely that you use a Fibonaccian search!

If the word you want starts with the letter A, you probably begin near the front of the dictionary. In fact, many dictionaries have thumb indexes that show the starting page or the middle page for the words beginning with a fixed letter. This thumb-index technique can readily be adapted to computers, and it will speed up the search; such algorithms are explored in Section 6.3.

Yet even after the initial point of search has been found, your actions still are not much like the methods we have discussed. If you notice that the desired word is alphabetically much greater than the words on the page being examined, you will turn over a fairly large chunk of pages before making the next reference.

This is quite different from the algorithms above, which make no distinction between "much greater" and "slightly greater."

Such considerations suggest an algorithm that might be called *interpolation search:* When we know that K lies between K_l and K_u, we can choose the next probe to be about $(K - K_l)/(K_u - K_l)$ of the way between l and u, assuming that the keys are numeric and that they increase in a roughly constant manner throughout the interval.

Interpolation search is asymptotically superior to binary search. One step of binary search essentially reduces the amount of uncertainty from n to $\frac{1}{2}n$, while one step of interpolation search essentially reduces it to $\sqrt{n}$, when the keys in the table are randomly distributed. Hence interpolation search takes about $\lg \lg N$ steps, on the average, to reduce the uncertainty from N to 2. (See exercise 22.)

However, computer simulation experiments show that interpolation search does not decrease the number of comparisons enough to compensate for the extra computing time involved, unless the table is rather large. Typical files aren't sufficiently random, and the difference between $\lg \lg N$ and $\lg N$ is not substantial unless N exceeds, say, $2^{16} = 65{,}536$. Interpolation is most successful in the early stages of searching a large possibly external file; after the range has been narrowed down, binary search finishes things off more quickly. (Note that dictionary lookup by hand is essentially an external, not an internal, search. We shall discuss external searching later.)

History and bibliography. The earliest known example of a long list of items that was sorted into order to facilitate searching is the remarkable Babylonian reciprocal table of Inakibit-Anu, dating from about 200 B.C. This clay tablet contains more than 100 pairs of values, which appear to be the beginning of a list of approximately 500 multiple-precision sexagesimal numbers and their reciprocals, sorted into lexicographic order. For example, the list included the following sequence of entries:

01 13 09 34 29 08 08 53 20	49 12 27
01 13 14 31 52 30	49 09 07 12
01 13 43 40 48	48 49 41 15
01 13 48 40 30	48 46 22 59 25 25 55 33 20
01 14 04 26 40	48 36

The task of sorting 500 entries like this, given the technology available at that time, must have been phenomenal. [See D. E. Knuth, *Selected Papers on Computer Science* (Cambridge Univ. Press, 1996), Chapter 11, for further details.]

It is fairly natural to sort numerical values into order, but an order relation between letters or words does not suggest itself so readily. Yet a collating sequence for individual letters was present already in the most ancient alphabets. For example, many of the Biblical psalms have verses that follow a strict alphabetic sequence, the first verse starting with aleph, the second with beth, etc.; this was an aid to memory. Eventually the standard sequence of letters was used by Semitic and Greek peoples to denote numerals; for example, α, β, γ stood for 1, 2, 3, respectively.

The use of alphabetic order for entire words seems to be a much later invention; it is something we might think is obvious, yet it has to be taught to children, and at some point in history it was necessary to teach it to adults. Several lists from about 300 B.C. have been found on the Aegean Islands, giving the names of people in certain religious cults; these lists have been alphabetized, but only by the first letter, thus representing only the first pass of a left-to-right radix sort. Some Greek papyri from the years A.D. 134–135 contain fragments of ledgers that show the names of taxpayers alphabetized by the first two letters. Apollonius Sophista used alphabetic order on the first two letters, and often on subsequent letters, in his lengthy concordance of Homer's poetry (first century A.D.). A few examples of more perfect alphabetization are known, notably Galen's *Hippocratic Glosses* (c. 200), but they are very rare. Words were arranged by their first letter only in the *Etymologiarum* of St. Isidorus (c. 630, Book x); and the *Corpus Glossary* (c. 725) used only the first two letters of each word. The latter two works were perhaps the largest nonnumerical files of data to be compiled during the Middle Ages.

It is not until Giovanni di Genoa's *Catholicon* (1286) that we find a specific description of true alphabetical order. In his preface, Giovanni explained that

amo	precedes	*bibo*
abeo	precedes	*adeo*
amatus	precedes	*amor*
imprudens	precedes	*impudens*
iusticia	precedes	*iustus*
polisintheton	precedes	*polissenus*

(thereby giving examples of situations in which the ordering is determined by the 1st, 2nd, ..., 6th letters), "and so in like manner." He remarked that strenuous effort was required to devise these rules. "I beg of you, therefore, good reader, do not scorn this great labor of mine and this order as something worthless."

A detailed study of the development of alphabetic order, up to the time printing was invented, has been made by Lloyd W. Daly [*Collection Latomus* **90** (1967), 100 pages]. He found some interesting old manuscripts that were evidently used as worksheets while sorting words by their first letters (see pages 89–90 of his monograph).

The first dictionary of English, Robert Cawdrey's *Table Alphabeticall* (London, 1604), contains the following instructions:

> Nowe if the word, which thou art desirous to finde, beginne with (a) then looke in the beginning of this Table, but if with (v) looke towards the end. Againe, if thy word beginne with (ca) looke in the beginning of the letter (c) but if with (cu) then looke toward the end of that letter. And so of all the rest. &c.

Cawdrey seems to have been teaching *himself* how to alphabetize as he prepared his dictionary; numerous misplaced words appear on the first few pages, but the alphabetic order in the last part is not as bad.

Binary search was first mentioned by John Mauchly, in what was perhaps the first published discussion of nonnumerical programming methods [*Theory and Techniques for the Design of Electronic Digital Computers*, edited by G. W. Patterson, **1** (1946), 9.7–9.8; **3** (1946), 22.8–22.9]. The method became well known to programmers, but nobody seems to have worked out the details of what should be done when N does not have the special form $2^n - 1$. [See A. D. Booth, *Nature* **176** (1955), 565; A. I. Dumey, *Computers and Automation* **5** (December 1956), 7, where binary search is called "Twenty Questions"; Daniel D. McCracken, *Digital Computer Programming* (Wiley, 1957), 201–203; and M. Halpern, *CACM* **1**, 1 (February 1958), 1–3.]

D. H. Lehmer [*Proc. Symp. Appl. Math.* **10** (1960), 180–181] was apparently the first to publish a binary search algorithm that works for all N. The next step was taken by H. Bottenbruch [*JACM* **9** (1962), 214], who presented an interesting variation of Algorithm B that avoids a separate test for equality until the very end: Using

$$i \leftarrow \lceil (l + u)/2 \rceil$$

instead of $i \leftarrow \lfloor (l + u)/2 \rfloor$ in step B2, he set $l \leftarrow i$ whenever $K \geq K_i$; then $u - l$ decreases at every step. Eventually, when $l = u$, we have $K_l \leq K < K_{l+1}$, and we can test whether or not the search was successful by making one more comparison. (He assumed that $K \geq K_1$ initially.) This idea speeds up the inner loop slightly on many computers, and the same principle can be used with all of the algorithms we have discussed in this section; but a successful search will require about one more iteration, on the average, because of (2). Since the inner loop is performed only about $\lg N$ times, this tradeoff between an extra iteration and a faster loop does not save time unless n is extremely large. (See exercise 23.) On the other hand Bottenbruch's algorithm will find the rightmost occurrence of a given key when the table contains duplicates, and this property is occasionally important.

K. E. Iverson [*A Programming Language* (Wiley, 1962), 141] gave the procedure of Algorithm B, but without considering the possibility of an unsuccessful search. D. E. Knuth [*CACM* **6** (1963), 556–558] presented Algorithm B as an example used with an automated flowcharting system. The uniform binary search, Algorithm C, was suggested to the author by A. K. Chandra of Stanford University in 1971.

Fibonaccian searching was invented by David E. Ferguson [*CACM* **3** (1960), 648]. Binary trees similar to Fibonacci trees appeared in the pioneering work of the Norwegian mathematician Axel Thue as early as 1910 (see exercise 28). A Fibonacci tree without labels was also exhibited as a curiosity in the first edition of Hugo Steinhaus's popular book *Mathematical Snapshots* (New York: Stechert, 1938), page 28; he drew it upside down and made it look like a real tree, with right branches twice as long as left branches so that all the leaves would occur at the same level.

Interpolation searching was suggested by W. W. Peterson [*IBM J. Res. & Devel.* **1** (1957), 131–132]. A correct analysis of its average behavior was not discovered until many years later (see exercise 22).

EXERCISES

▶ **1.** [*21*] Prove that if $u < l$ in step B2 of the binary search, we have $u = l - 1$ and $K_u < K < K_l$. (Assume by convention that $K_0 = -\infty$ and $K_{N+1} = +\infty$, although these artificial keys are never really used by the algorithm so they need not be present in the actual table.)

▶ **2.** [*22*] Would Algorithm B still work properly when K is present in the table if we (a) changed step B5 to "$l \leftarrow i$" instead of "$l \leftarrow i+1$"? (b) changed step B4 to "$u \leftarrow i$" instead of "$u \leftarrow i - 1$"? (c) made both of these changes?

3. [*15*] What searching method corresponds to the tree ?

What is the average number of comparisons made in a successful search? in an unsuccessful search?

4. [*20*] If a search using Program 6.1S (sequential search) takes exactly 638 units of time, how long does it take with Program B (binary search)?

5. [*M24*] For what values of N is Program B actually *slower* than a sequential search (Program 6.1Q′) on the average, assuming that the search is successful?

6. [*28*] (K. E. Iverson.) Exercise 5 suggests that it would be best to have a hybrid method, changing from binary search to sequential search when the remaining interval has length less than some judiciously chosen value. Write an efficient MIX program for such a search and determine the best changeover value.

▶ **7.** [*M22*] Would Algorithm U still work properly if we changed step U1 so that
a) both i and m are set equal to $\lfloor N/2 \rfloor$?
b) both i and m are set equal to $\lceil N/2 \rceil$?
[*Hint:* Suppose the first step were "Set $i \leftarrow 0$, $m \leftarrow N$ (or $N + 1$), go to U4."]

8. [*M20*] Let $\delta_j =$ DELTA[j] be the jth increment in Algorithm C, as defined in (6).
a) What is the sum $\sum_{j=0}^{\lfloor \lg N \rfloor + 2} \delta_j$?
b) What are the minimum and maximum values of i that can occur in step C2?

9. [*20*] Is there any value of $N > 1$ for which Algorithm B and C are exactly equivalent, in the sense that they will both perform the same sequence of comparisons for all search arguments?

10. [*21*] Explain how to write a MIX program for Algorithm C containing approximately $7 \lg N$ instructions and having a running time of about $4.5 \lg N$ units.

11. [*M26*] Find exact formulas for the average values of $C1$, $C2$, and A in the frequency analysis of Program C, as a function of N and S.

12. [*20*] Draw the binary search tree corresponding to Shar's method when $N = 12$.

13. [*M24*] Tabulate the average number of comparisons made by Shar's method, for $1 \le N \le 16$, considering both successful and unsuccessful searches.

14. [*21*] Explain how to extend Algorithm F so that it will apply for all $N \ge 1$.

15. [*M19*] For what values of k does the Fibonacci tree of order k define an optimal search procedure, in the sense that the fewest comparisons are made on the average?

16. [*21*] Figure 9 shows the lineal chart of the rabbits in Fibonacci's original rabbit problem (see Section 1.2.8). Is there a simple relationship between this and the Fibonacci tree discussed in the text?

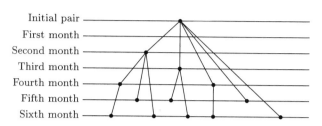

Fig. 9. Pairs of rabbits breeding by Fibonacci's rule.

17. [*M21*] From exercise 1.2.8–34 (or exercise 5.4.2–10) we know that every positive integer n has a unique representation as a sum of Fibonacci numbers

$$n = F_{a_1} + F_{a_2} + \cdots + F_{a_r},$$

where $r \geq 1$, $a_j \geq a_{j+1} + 2$ for $1 \leq j < r$, and $a_r \geq 2$. Prove that in the Fibonacci tree of order k, the path from the root to node (n) has length $k + 1 - r - a_r$.

18. [*M30*] Find exact formulas for the average values of $C1$, $C2$, and A in the frequency analysis of Program F, as a function of k, F_k, F_{k+1}, and S.

19. [*M42*] Carry out a detailed analysis of the average running time of the algorithm suggested in exercise 14.

20. [*M22*] The number of comparisons required in a binary search is approximately $\log_2 N$, and in the Fibonaccian search it is roughly $(\phi/\sqrt{5}) \log_\phi N$. The purpose of this exercise is to show that these formulas are special cases of a more general result.

Let p and q be positive numbers with $p + q = 1$. Consider a search algorithm that, given a table of N numbers in increasing order, starts by comparing the argument with the (pN)th key, and iterates this procedure on the smaller blocks. (The binary search has $p = q = 1/2$; the Fibonacci search has $p = 1/\phi$, $q = 1/\phi^2$.)

If $C(N)$ denotes the average number of comparisons required to search a table of size N, it approximately satisfies the relations

$$C(1) = 0; \qquad C(N) = 1 + pC(pN) + qC(qN) \quad \text{for } N > 1.$$

This happens because there is probability p (roughly) that the search reduces to a pN-element search, and probability q that it reduces to a qN-element search, after the first comparison. When N is large, we may ignore the small-order effect caused by the fact that pN and qN aren't exactly integers.

a) Show that $C(N) = \log_b N$ satisfies these relations exactly, for a certain choice of b. For binary and Fibonaccian search, this value of b agrees with the formulas derived earlier.

b) Consider the following argument: "With probability p, the size of the interval being scanned in this algorithm is divided by $1/p$; with probability q, the interval size is divided by $1/q$. Therefore the interval is divided by $p \cdot (1/p) + q \cdot (1/q) = 2$ on the average, so the algorithm is exactly as good as the binary search, regardless of p and q." Is there anything wrong with this reasoning?

21. [20] Draw the binary tree corresponding to interpolation search when $N = 10$.

22. [M41] (A. C. Yao and F. F. Yao.) Show that an appropriate formulation of interpolation search requires asymptotically $\lg\lg N$ comparisons, on the average, when applied to N independent uniform random keys that have been sorted. Furthermore *all* search algorithms on such tables must make asymptotically $\lg\lg N$ comparisons, on the average.

▶ **23.** [25] The binary search algorithm of H. Bottenbruch, mentioned at the close of this section, avoids testing for equality until the very end of the search. (During the algorithm we know that $K_l \le K < K_{u+1}$, and the case of equality is not examined until $l = u$.) Such a trick would make Program B run a little bit faster for large N, since the "JE" instruction could be removed from the inner loop. (However, the idea wouldn't really be practical since $\lg N$ is always rather small; we would need $N > 2^{66}$ in order to compensate for the extra work necessary on a successful search, because the running time $(18\lg N - 16)u$ of (5) is "decreased" to $(17.5\lg N + 17)u$!)

Show that *every* search algorithm corresponding to a binary tree can be adapted to a search algorithm that uses two-way branching ($<$ versus $\ge$) at the internal nodes of the tree, in place of the three-way branching ($<$, $=$, or $>$) used in the text's discussion. In particular, show how to modify Algorithm C in this way.

▶ **24.** [23] We have seen in Sections 2.3.4.5 and 5.2.3 that the complete binary tree is a convenient way to represent a minimum-path-length tree in consecutive locations. Devise an efficient search method based on this representation. [*Hint:* Is it possible to use multiplication by 2 instead of division by 2 in a binary search?]

▶ **25.** [M25] Suppose that a binary tree has a_k internal nodes and b_k external nodes on level k, for $k = 0, 1, \ldots$. (The root is at level zero.) Thus in Fig. 8 we have $(a_0, a_1, \ldots, a_5) = (1, 2, 4, 4, 1, 0)$ and $(b_0, b_1, \ldots, b_5) = (0, 0, 0, 4, 7, 2)$.

a) Show that a simple algebraic relationship holds between the generating functions $A(z) = \sum_k a_k z^k$ and $B(z) = \sum_k b_k z^k$.

b) The probability distribution for a successful search in a binary tree has the generating function $g(z) = zA(z)/N$, and for an unsuccessful search the generating function is $h(z) = B(z)/(N+1)$. (Thus in the text's notation we have $C_N = \text{mean}(g)$, $C'_N = \text{mean}(h)$, and Eq. (2) gives a relation between these quantities.) Find a relation between $\text{var}(g)$ and $\text{var}(h)$.

26. [22] Show that Fibonacci trees are related to polyphase merge sorting on three tapes.

27. [M30] (H. S. Stone and John Linn.) Consider a search process that uses k processors simultaneously and that is based solely on comparisons of keys. Thus at every step of the search, k indices $i_1, \ldots, i_k$ are specified, and we perform k simultaneous comparisons; if $K = K_{i_j}$ for some j, the search terminates successfully, otherwise the search proceeds to the next step based on the 2^k possible outcomes $K < K_{i_j}$ or $K > K_{i_j}$, for $1 \le j \le k$.

Prove that such a process must always take at least approximately $\log_{k+1} N$ steps on the average, as $N \to \infty$, assuming that each key of the table is equally likely as a search argument. (Hence the potential increase in speed over 1-processor binary search is only a factor of $\lg(k+1)$, not the factor of k we might expect. In this sense it is more efficient to assign each processor to a different, independent search problem, instead of making them cooperate on a single search.)

28. [*M23*] Define *Thue trees* T_n by means of algebraic expressions in a binary operator $*$ as follows: $T_0(x) = x * x$, $T_1(x) = x$, $T_{n+2}(x) = T_{n+1}(x) * T_n(x)$.
  a) The number of leaves of T_n is the number of occurrences of x when $T_n(x)$ is written
     out in full. Express this number in terms of Fibonacci numbers.
  b) Prove that if the binary operator $*$ satisfies the axiom

$$((x * x) * x) * ((x * x) * x) = x,$$

  then $T_m(T_n(x)) = T_{m+n-1}(x)$ for all $m \geq 0$ and $n \geq 1$.

▶ **29.** [*22*] (Paul Feldman, 1975.) Instead of assuming that $K_1 < K_2 < \cdots < K_N$,
assume only that $K_{p(1)} < K_{p(2)} < \cdots < K_{p(N)}$ where the permutation $p(1)p(2)\dots p(N)$
is an involution, and $p(j) = j$ for all even values of j. Show that we can locate any given
key K, or determine that K is not present, by making at most $2\lfloor \lg N \rfloor + 1$ comparisons.

30. [*27*] (*Involution coding.*) Using the idea of the previous exercise, find a way to
arrange N distinct keys in such a way that their relative order implicitly encodes an
arbitrarily given array of t-bit numbers x_1, x_2, $\dots$, x_m, when $m \leq N/4 + 1 - 2^t$.
With your arrangement it should be possible to determine the leading k bits of x_j by
making only k comparisons, for any given j, as well as to look up an arbitrary key with
$\leq 2\lfloor \lg N \rfloor + 1$ comparisons. (This result is used in theoretical studies of data structures
that are asymptotically efficient in both time and space.)

6.2.2. Binary Tree Searching

In the preceding section, we learned that an implicit binary tree structure makes
the behavior of binary search and Fibonaccian search easier to understand. For a
given value of N, the tree corresponding to binary search achieves the theoretical
minimum number of comparisons that are necessary to search a table by means
of key comparisons. But the methods of the preceding section are appropriate
mainly for fixed-size tables, since the sequential allocation of records makes
insertions and deletions rather expensive. If the table is changing dynamically,
we might spend more time maintaining it than we save in binary-searching it.

The use of an *explicit* binary tree structure makes it possible to insert and
delete records quickly, as well as to search the table efficiently. As a result, we
essentially have a method that is useful both for searching and for sorting. This
gain in flexibility is achieved by adding two link fields to each record of the table.

Techniques for searching a growing table are often called *symbol table algorithms*, because assemblers and compilers and other system routines generally
use such methods to keep track of user-defined symbols. For example, the key of
each record within a compiler might be a symbolic identifier denoting a variable
in some FORTRAN or C program, and the rest of the record might contain
information about the type of that variable and its storage allocation. Or the key
might be a symbol in a MIXAL program, with the rest of the record containing the
equivalent of that symbol. The tree search and insertion routines to be described
in this section are quite efficient for use as symbol table algorithms, especially in
applications where it is desirable to print out a list of the symbols in alphabetic
order. Other symbol table algorithms are described in Sections 6.3 and 6.4.

Figure 10 shows a binary search tree containing the names of eleven signs of
the zodiac. If we now search for the twelfth name, SAGITTARIUS, starting at the

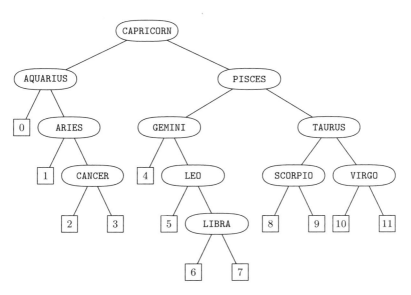

Fig. 10. A binary search tree.

root or apex of the tree, we find it is greater than CAPRICORN, so we move to the right; it is greater than PISCES, so we move right again; it is less than TAURUS, so we move left; and it is less than SCORPIO, so we arrive at external node $\boxed{8}$. The search was unsuccessful; we can now *insert* SAGITTARIUS at the place the search ended, by linking it into the tree in place of the external node $\boxed{8}$. In this way the table can grow without the necessity of moving any of the existing records. Figure 10 was formed by starting with an empty tree and successively inserting the keys CAPRICORN, AQUARIUS, PISCES, ARIES, TAURUS, GEMINI, CANCER, LEO, VIRGO, LIBRA, SCORPIO, in this order.

All of the keys in the left subtree of the root in Fig. 10 are alphabetically less than CAPRICORN, and all keys in the right subtree are alphabetically greater. A similar statement holds for the left and right subtrees of every node. It follows that the keys appear in strict alphabetic sequence from left to right,

AQUARIUS,   ARIES,   CANCER,   CAPRICORN,   GEMINI,   LEO,   ...,   VIRGO

if we traverse the tree in *symmetric order* (see Section 2.3.1), since symmetric order is based on traversing the left subtree of each node just before that node, then traversing the right subtree.

The following algorithm spells out the searching and insertion processes in detail.

Algorithm T (*Tree search and insertion*). Given a table of records that form a binary tree as described above, this algorithm searches for a given argument K. If K is not in the table, a new node containing K is inserted into the tree in the appropriate place.

The nodes of the tree are assumed to contain at least the following fields:

$$\text{KEY(P)} = \text{key stored in NODE(P);}$$
$$\text{LLINK(P)} = \text{pointer to left subtree of NODE(P);}$$
$$\text{RLINK(P)} = \text{pointer to right subtree of NODE(P).}$$

Null subtrees (the external nodes in Fig. 10) are represented by the null pointer Λ. The variable ROOT points to the root of the tree. For convenience, we assume that the tree is not empty (that is, ROOT $\neq \Lambda$), since the necessary operations are trivial when ROOT $= \Lambda$.

T1. [Initialize.] Set P $\leftarrow$ ROOT. (The pointer variable P will move down the tree.)

T2. [Compare.] If $K < \text{KEY(P)}$, go to T3; if $K > \text{KEY(P)}$, go to T4; and if $K = \text{KEY(P)}$, the search terminates successfully.

T3. [Move left.] If LLINK(P) $\neq \Lambda$, set P $\leftarrow$ LLINK(P) and go back to T2. Otherwise go to T5.

T4. [Move right.] If RLINK(P) $\neq \Lambda$, set P $\leftarrow$ RLINK(P) and go back to T2.

T5. [Insert into tree.] (The search is unsuccessful; we will now put K into the tree.) Set Q $\Leftarrow$ AVAIL, the address of a new node. Set KEY(Q) $\leftarrow K$, LLINK(Q) $\leftarrow$ RLINK(Q) $\leftarrow \Lambda$. (In practice, other fields of the new node should also be initialized.) If K was less than KEY(P), set LLINK(P) $\leftarrow$ Q, otherwise set RLINK(P) $\leftarrow$ Q. (At this point we could set P $\leftarrow$ Q and terminate the algorithm successfully.) ▍

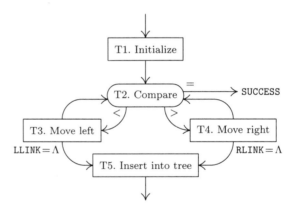

Fig. 11. Tree search and insertion.

This algorithm lends itself to a convenient machine language implementation. We may assume, for example, that the tree nodes have the form

$$\begin{array}{|c|c|c|c|} \hline + & 0 & \text{LLINK} & \text{RLINK} \\ \hline \multicolumn{4}{|c|}{\text{KEY}} \\ \hline \end{array} \tag{1}$$

followed perhaps by additional words of INFO. Using an AVAIL list for the free storage pool, as in Chapter 2, we can write the following MIX program:

Program T (*Tree search and insertion*). rA $\equiv K$, rI1 $\equiv$ P, rI2 $\equiv$ Q.

01		LLINK	EQU	2:3		
02		RLINK	EQU	4:5		
03	START	LDA	K	1	*T1. Initialize.*
04		LD1	ROOT	1	P $\leftarrow$ ROOT.
05		JMP	2F	1	
06	4H	LD2	0,1(RLINK)	$C2$	*T4. Move right.* Q $\leftarrow$ RLINK(P).
07		J2Z	5F	$C2$	To T5 if Q $= \Lambda$.
08	1H	ENT1	0,2	$C-1$	P $\leftarrow$ Q.
09	2H	CMPA	1,1	C	*T2. Compare.*
10		JG	4B	C	To T4 if $K >$ KEY(P).
11		JE	SUCCESS	$C1$	Exit if $K =$ KEY(P).
12		LD2	0,1(LLINK)	$C1-S$	*T3. Move left.* Q $\leftarrow$ LLINK(P).
13		J2NZ	1B	$C1-S$	To T2 if Q $\neq \Lambda$.
14	5H	LD2	AVAIL	$1-S$	*T5. Insert into tree.*
15		J2Z	OVERFLOW	$1-S$	
16		LDX	0,2(RLINK)	$1-S$	
17		STX	AVAIL	$1-S$	Q $\Leftarrow$ AVAIL.
18		STA	1,2	$1-S$	KEY(Q) $\leftarrow K$.
19		STZ	0,2	$1-S$	LLINK(Q) $\leftarrow$ RLINK(Q) $\leftarrow \Lambda$.
20		JL	1F	$1-S$	Was $K <$ KEY(P)?
21		ST2	0,1(RLINK)	A	RLINK(P) $\leftarrow$ Q.
22		JMP	*+2	A	
23	1H	ST2	0,1(LLINK)	$1-S-A$	LLINK(P) $\leftarrow$ Q.
24	DONE	EQU	*	$1-S$	Exit after insertion. ∎

The first 13 lines of this program do the search; the last 11 lines do the insertion. The running time for the searching phase is $(7C + C1 - 3S + 4)u$, where

$$C = \text{number of comparisons made};$$
$$C1 = \text{number of times } K \le \text{KEY(P)};$$
$$C2 = \text{number of times } K > \text{KEY(P)};$$
$$S = [\text{search is successful}].$$

On the average we have $C1 = \frac{1}{2}(C + S)$, since $C1 + C2 = C$ and $C1 - S$ has the same probability distribution as $C2$; so the running time is about $(7.5C - 2.5S + 4)u$. This compares favorably with the binary search algorithms that use an implicit tree (see Program 6.2.1C). By duplicating the code as in Program 6.2.1F we could effectively eliminate line 08 of Program T, reducing the running time to $(6.5C - 2.5S + 5)u$. If the search is unsuccessful, the insertion phase of the program costs an extra $14u$ or $15u$.

Algorithm T can conveniently be adapted to *variable-length keys* and variable-length records. For example, if we allocate the available space sequentially, in a last-in-first-out manner, we can easily create nodes of varying size; the first word of (1) could indicate the size. Since this is an efficient use of storage, symbol table algorithms based on trees are often especially attractive for use in compilers, assemblers, and loaders.

But what about the worst case? Programmers are often skeptical of Algorithm T when they first see it. If the keys of Fig. 10 had been entered into the tree in alphabetic order AQUARIUS, ..., VIRGO instead of the calendar order CAPRICORN, ..., SCORPIO, the algorithm would have built a degenerate tree that essentially specifies a *sequential* search. All LLINKs would be null. Similarly, if the keys come in the uncommon order

AQUARIUS, VIRGO, ARIES, TAURUS, CANCER, SCORPIO,

CAPRICORN, PISCES, GEMINI, LIBRA, LEO

we obtain a "zigzag" tree that is just as bad. (Try it!)

On the other hand, the particular tree in Fig. 10 requires only $3\frac{2}{11}$ comparisons, on the average, for a successful search; this is just a little higher than the minimum possible average number of comparisons, 3, achievable in the best possible binary tree.

When we have a fairly balanced tree, the search time is roughly proportional to $\log N$, but when we have a degenerate tree, the search time is roughly proportional to N. Exercise 2.3.4.5–5 proves that the average search time would be roughly proportional to $\sqrt{N}$ if we considered each N-node binary tree to be equally likely. What behavior can we really expect from Algorithm T?

Fortunately, it turns out that tree search will require only about $2 \ln N \approx 1.386 \lg N$ comparisons, if the keys are inserted into the tree in random order; well-balanced trees are common, and degenerate trees are very rare.

There is a surprisingly simple proof of this fact. Let us assume that each of the $N!$ possible orderings of the N keys is an equally likely sequence of insertions for building the tree. The number of comparisons needed to find a key is exactly one more than the number of comparisons that were needed when that key was entered into the tree. Therefore if C_N is the average number of comparisons involved in a successful search and C'_N is the average number in an unsuccessful search, we have

$$C_N = 1 + \frac{C'_0 + C'_1 + \cdots + C'_{N-1}}{N}. \tag{2}$$

But the relation between internal and external path length tells us that

$$C_N = \left(1 + \frac{1}{N}\right) C'_N - 1; \tag{3}$$

this is Eq. 6.2.1–(2). Putting (3) together with (2) yields

$$(N+1)C'_N = 2N + C'_0 + C'_1 + \cdots + C'_{N-1}. \tag{4}$$

This recurrence is easy to solve. Subtracting the equation

$$N C'_{N-1} = 2(N-1) + C'_0 + C'_1 + \cdots + C'_{N-2},$$

we obtain

$$(N+1)C'_N - N C'_{N-1} = 2 + C'_{N-1}, \qquad \text{hence} \qquad C'_N = C'_{N-1} + 2/(N+1).$$

Since $C'_0 = 0$, this means that

$$C'_N = 2H_{N+1} - 2. \tag{5}$$

Applying (3) and simplifying yields the desired result

$$C_N = 2\left(1 + \frac{1}{N}\right)H_N - 3. \tag{6}$$

Exercises 6, 7, and 8 below give more detailed information; it is possible to compute the exact probability distribution of C_N and C'_N, not merely the average values.

Tree insertion sorting. Algorithm T was developed for searching, but it can also be used as the basis of an internal *sorting* algorithm; in fact, we can view it as a natural generalization of list insertion, Algorithm 5.2.1L. When properly programmed, its average running time will be only a little slower than some of the best algorithms we discussed in Chapter 5. After the tree has been constructed for all keys, a symmetric tree traversal (Algorithm 2.3.1T) will visit the records in sorted order.

A few precautions are necessary, however. Something different needs to be done if $K = \text{KEY(P)}$ in step T2, since we are sorting instead of searching. One solution is to treat $K = \text{KEY(P)}$ exactly as if $K > \text{KEY(P)}$; this leads to a stable sorting method. (Equal keys will not necessarily be adjacent in the tree; they will only be adjacent in symmetric order.) But if many duplicate keys are present, this method will cause the tree to get badly unbalanced, and the sorting will slow down. Another idea is to keep a list, for each node, of all records having the same key; this requires another link field, but it will make the sorting faster when a lot of equal keys occur.

Thus if we are interested only in sorting, not in searching, Algorithm T isn't the best, but it isn't bad. And if we have an application that combines searching with sorting, the tree method can be warmly recommended.

It is interesting to note that there is a strong relation between the analysis of tree insertion sorting and the analysis of quicksort, although the methods are superficially dissimilar. If we successively insert N keys into an initially empty tree, we make the same average number of comparisons between keys as Algorithm 5.2.2Q does, with minor exceptions. For example, in tree insertion every key gets compared with K_1, and then every key less than K_1 gets compared with the first key less than K_1, etc.; in quicksort, every key gets compared to the first partitioning element K and then every key less than K gets compared to a particular element less than K, etc. The average number of comparisons needed in both cases is $NC_N - N$. (However, Algorithm 5.2.2Q actually makes a few more comparisons, in order to speed up the inner loops.)

Deletions. Sometimes we want to make the computer forget one of the table entries it knows. We can easily delete a node in which either LLINK or RLINK $= \Lambda$; but when both subtrees are nonempty, we have to do something special, since we can't point two ways at once.

For example, consider Fig. 10 again; how could we delete the root node, CAPRICORN? One solution is to delete the alphabetically *next* node, which always has a null LLINK, then reinsert it in place of the node we really wanted to delete. For example, in Fig. 10 we could delete GEMINI, then replace CAPRICORN by GEMINI. This operation preserves the essential left-to-right order of the table entries. The following algorithm gives a detailed description of such a deletion process.

Algorithm D (*Tree deletion*). Let Q be a variable that points to a node of a binary search tree represented as in Algorithm T. This algorithm deletes that node, leaving a binary search tree. (In practice, we will have either Q ≡ ROOT or Q ≡ LLINK(P) or RLINK(P) in some node of the tree. This algorithm resets the value of Q in memory, to reflect the deletion.)

D1. [Is RLINK null?] Set T ← Q. If RLINK(T) = Λ, set Q ← LLINK(T) and go to D4. (For example, if Q ≡ RLINK(P) for some P, we would set RLINK(P) ← LLINK(T).)

D2. [Find successor.] Set R ← RLINK(T). If LLINK(R) = Λ, set LLINK(R) ← LLINK(T), Q ← R, and go to D4.

D3. [Find null LLINK.] Set S ← LLINK(R). Then if LLINK(S) ≠ Λ, set R ← S and repeat this step until LLINK(S) = Λ. (At this point S will be equal to Q$, the symmetric successor of Q.) Finally, set LLINK(S) ← LLINK(T), LLINK(R) ← RLINK(S), RLINK(S) ← RLINK(T), Q ← S.

D4. [Free the node.] Set AVAIL ⇐ T, thus returning the deleted node to the free storage pool. ∎

The reader may wish to try this algorithm by deleting AQUARIUS, CANCER, and CAPRICORN from Fig. 10; each case is slightly different. An alert reader may have noticed that no special test has been made for the case RLINK(T) ≠ Λ, LLINK(T) = Λ; we will defer the discussion of this case until later, since the algorithm as it stands has some very interesting properties.

Since Algorithm D is quite unsymmetrical between left and right, it stands to reason that a sequence of deletions will make the tree get way out of balance, so that the efficiency estimates we have made will be invalid. But deletions don't actually make the trees degenerate at all!

Theorem H (T. N. Hibbard, 1962). *After a random element is deleted from a random tree by Algorithm D, the resulting tree is still random.*

[Nonmathematical readers, please skip to (10).] This statement of the theorem is admittedly quite vague. We can summarize the situation more precisely as follows: Let T be a tree of n elements, and let $P(T)$ be the probability that T occurs if its keys are inserted in random order by Algorithm T. Some trees are more probable than others. Let $Q(T)$ be the probability that T will occur if $n+1$ elements are inserted in random order by Algorithm T and then one of these elements is chosen at random and deleted by Algorithm D. In calculating $P(T)$, we assume that the $n!$ permutations of the keys are equally likely; in calculating

$Q(T)$, we assume that the $(n+1)!\,(n+1)$ permutations of keys and selections of the doomed key are equally likely. The theorem states that $P(T) = Q(T)$ for all T.

Proof. We are faced with the fact that permutations are equally probable, not trees, and therefore we shall prove the result by considering *permutations* as the random objects. We shall define a deletion from a permutation, and then we will prove that "a random element deleted from a random permutation leaves a random permutation."

Let $a_1\,a_2\ldots a_{n+1}$ be a permutation of $\{1, 2, \ldots, n+1\}$; we want to define the operation of deleting a_i, so as to obtain a permutation $b_1\,b_2\ldots b_n$ of $\{1, 2, \ldots, n\}$. This operation should correspond to Algorithms T and D, so that if we start with the tree constructed from the sequence of insertions $a_1, a_2, \ldots, a_{n+1}$ and delete a_i, renumbering the keys from 1 to n, we obtain the tree constructed from $b_1\,b_2\ldots b_n$.

It is not hard to define such a deletion operation. There are two cases:

Case 1: $a_i = n+1$, or $a_i + 1 = a_j$ for some $j < i$. (This is essentially the condition "$\mathtt{RLINK}(a_i) = \Lambda$.") Remove a_i from the sequence, and subtract unity from each element greater than a_i.

Case 2: $a_i + 1 = a_j$ for some $j > i$. Replace a_i by a_j, remove a_j from its original place, and subtract unity from each element greater than a_i.

For example, suppose we have the permutation 4 6 1 3 5 2. If we circle the element to be deleted, we have

$$\circled{4}\,6\ 1\ 3\ 5\ 2 = 4\ 5\ 1\ 3\ 2 \qquad 4\ 6\ 1\ \circled{3}\,5\ 2 = 3\ 5\ 1\ 4\ 2$$

$$4\ \circled{6}\,1\ 3\ 5\ 2 = 4\ 1\ 3\ 5\ 2 \qquad 4\ 6\ 1\ 3\ \circled{5}\,2 = 4\ 5\ 1\ 3\ 2$$

$$4\ 6\ \circled{1}\,3\ 5\ 2 = 3\ 5\ 1\ 2\ 4 \qquad 4\ 6\ 1\ 3\ 5\ \circled{2} = 3\ 5\ 1\ 2\ 4$$

Since there are $(n+1)!\,(n+1)$ possible deletion operations, the theorem will be established if we can show that every permutation of $\{1, 2, \ldots, n\}$ is the result of exactly $(n+1)^2$ deletions.

Let $b_1\,b_2\ldots b_n$ be a permutation of $\{1, 2, \ldots, n\}$. We shall define $(n+1)^2$ deletions, one for each pair i, j with $1 \le i, j \le n+1$, as follows:

If $i < j$, the deletion is

$$b'_1 \ldots b'_{i-1}\,\circled{b_i}\,b'_{i+1} \ldots b'_{j-1}\,(b_i{+}1)\,b'_j \ldots b'_n. \tag{7}$$

Here, as below, b'_k stands for either b_k or $b_k + 1$, depending on whether or not b_k is less than the circled element. This deletion corresponds to Case 2.

If $i > j$, the deletion is

$$b'_1 \ldots b'_{i-1}\,\circled{b_j}\,b'_i \ldots b'_n; \tag{8}$$

this deletion fits the definition of Case 1.

Finally, if $i = j$, we have another Case 1 deletion, namely

$$b'_1 \ldots b'_{i-1}\,\circled{n{+}1}\,b'_i \ldots b'_n. \tag{9}$$

As an example, let $n = 4$ and consider the 25 deletions that map into 3 1 4 2:

	$i = 1$	$i = 2$	$i = 3$	$i = 4$	$i = 5$
$j = 1$	⑤3 1 4 2	4③1 5 2	4 1③5 2	4 1 5③2	4 1 5 2③
$j = 2$	③4 1 5 2	3⑤1 4 2	4 2①5 3	4 2 5①3	4 2 5 3①
$j = 3$	③1 4 5 2	4①2 5 3	3 1⑤4 2	3 1 5④2	3 1 5 2④
$j = 4$	③1 5 4 2	4①5 2 3	3 1④5 2	3 1 4⑤2	4 1 5 3②
$j = 5$	③1 5 2 4	4①5 3 2	3 1④2 5	4 1 5②3	3 1 4 2⑤

The circled element is always in position i, and for fixed i we have constructed $n+1$ different deletions, one for each j; hence $(n+1)^2$ different deletions have been constructed for each permutation $b_1 b_2 \ldots b_n$. Since only $(n+1)^2 n!$ deletions are possible, we must have found all of them. ∎

The proof of Theorem H not only tells us about the result of deletions, it also helps us analyze the running time in an average deletion. Exercise 12 shows that we can expect to execute step D2 slightly less than half the time, on the average, when deleting a random element from a random table.

Let us now consider how often the loop in step D3 needs to be performed: Suppose that we are deleting a node on level l, and that the *external* node immediately following in symmetric order is on level k. For example, if we are deleting CAPRICORN from Fig. 10, we have $l = 0$ and $k = 3$ since node ④ is on level 3. If $k = l + 1$, we have RLINK(T) = Λ in step D1; and if $k > l + 1$, we will set S ← LLINK(R) exactly $k - l - 2$ times in step D3. The average value of l is (internal path length)$/N$; the average value of k is

(external path length − distance to leftmost external node)$/N$.

The distance to the leftmost external node is the number of left-to-right minima in the insertion sequence, so it has the average value H_N by the analysis of Section 1.2.10. Since external path length minus internal path length is $2N$, the average value of $k - l - 2$ is $-H_N/N$. Adding to this the average number of times that $k - l - 2$ is -1, we see that *the operation* S ← LLINK(R) *in step D3 is performed only*

$$\tfrac{1}{2} + \left(\tfrac{1}{2} - H_N\right)/N \qquad (10)$$

times, on the average, in a random deletion. This is reassuring, since the worst case can be pretty slow (see exercise 11).

Although Theorem H is rigorously true, in the precise form we have stated it, it *cannot* be applied, as we might expect, to a sequence of deletions followed by insertions. The shape of the tree is random after deletions, but the relative distribution of values in a given tree shape may change, and it turns out that the first random insertion after deletion actually *destroys* the randomness property on the shapes. This startling fact, first observed by Gary Knott in 1972, must be seen to be believed (see exercise 15). Even more startling is the empirical evidence gathered by J. L. Eppinger [*CACM* **26** (1983), 663–669, **27** (1984),

235], who found that the path length decreases slightly when a few random deletions and insertions are made, but then it *increases* until reaching a steady state after about n^2 deletion/insertion operations have been performed. This steady state is *worse* than the behavior of a random tree, when N is greater than about 150. Further study by Culberson and Munro [*Comp. J.* **32** (1989), 68–75; *Algorithmica* **5** (1990), 295–311] has led to a plausible conjecture that the average search time in the steady state is asymptotically $\sqrt{2N/9\pi}$. However, Eppinger also devised a simple modification that alternates between Algorithm D and a left-right reflection of the same algorithm; he found that this leads to an excellent steady state in which the path length is reduced to about 88% of its normal value for random trees. A theoretical explanation for this behavior is still lacking.

As mentioned above, Algorithm D does not test for the case LLINK(T) = Λ, although this is one of the easy cases for deletion. We could add a new step between D1 and D2, namely,

D1$\frac{1}{2}$. [Is LLINK null?] If LLINK(T) = Λ, set Q $\leftarrow$ RLINK(T) and go to D4.

Exercise 14 shows that Algorithm D with this extra step always leaves a tree that is at least as good as the original Algorithm D, in the path-length sense, and sometimes the result is even better. When this idea is combined with Eppinger's symmetric deletion strategy, the steady-state path length for repeated random deletion/insertion operations decreases to about 86% of its insertion-only value.

Frequency of access. So far we have assumed that each key was equally likely as a search argument. In a more general situation, let p_k be the probability that we will search for the kth element inserted, where $p_1 + \cdots + p_N = 1$. Then a straightforward modification of Eq. (2), if we retain the assumption of random order so that the shape of the tree stays random and Eq. (5) holds, shows that the average number of comparisons in a successful search will be

$$1 + \sum_{k=1}^{N} p_k(2H_k - 2) = 2\sum_{k=1}^{N} p_k H_k - 1. \tag{11}$$

For example, if the probabilities obey Zipf's law, Eq. 6.1–(8), the average number of comparisons reduces to

$$H_N - 1 + H_N^{(2)}/H_N \tag{12}$$

if we insert the keys in decreasing order of importance. (See exercise 18.) This is about half as many comparisons as predicted by the equal-frequency analysis, and it is fewer than we would make using binary search.

Fig. 12 shows the tree that results when the most common 31 words of English are entered in decreasing order of frequency. The relative frequency is shown with each word, using statistics from *Cryptanalysis* by H. F. Gaines (New York: Dover, 1956), 226. The average number of comparisons for a successful search in this tree is 4.042; the corresponding binary search, using Algorithm 6.2.1B or 6.2.1C, would require 4.393 comparisons.

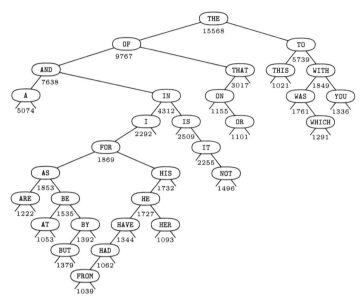

Fig. 12. The 31 most common English words, inserted in decreasing order of frequency.

Optimum binary search trees. These considerations make it natural to ask about the best possible tree for searching a table of keys with given frequencies. For example, the optimum tree for the 31 most common English words is shown in Fig. 13; it requires only 3.437 comparisons for an average successful search.

Let us now explore the problem of finding the optimum tree. When $N = 3$, for example, let us assume that the keys $K_1 < K_2 < K_3$ have respective probabilities p, q, r. There are five possible trees:

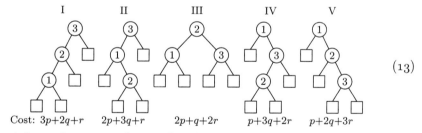

$$\text{Cost: } 3p+2q+r \quad 2p+3q+r \quad 2p+q+2r \quad p+3q+2r \quad p+2q+3r \tag{13}$$

Figure 14 shows the ranges of p, q, r for which each tree is optimum; the balanced tree is best about 45 percent of the time, if we choose p, q, r at random (see exercise 21).

Unfortunately, when N is large there are

$$\binom{2N}{N}\Big/(N+1) \approx 4^N\big/\big(\sqrt{\pi}\,N^{3/2}\big)$$

binary trees, so we can't just try them all and see which is best. Let us therefore study the properties of optimum binary search trees more closely, in order to discover a better way to find them.

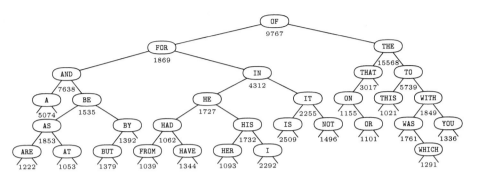

Fig. 13. An optimum search tree for the 31 most common English words.

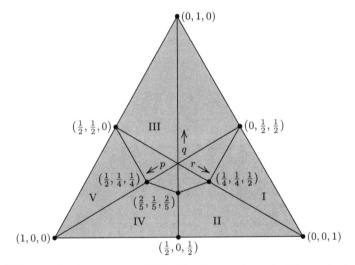

Fig. 14. If the relative frequencies of (K_1, K_2, K_3) are (p, q, r), this graph shows which of the five trees in (13) is best. The fact that $p + q + r = 1$ makes the graph two-dimensional although there are three coordinates.

So far we have considered only the probabilities for a successful search; in practice, the unsuccessful case must usually be considered as well. For example, the 31 words in Fig. 13 account for only about 36 percent of typical English text; the other 64 percent will certainly influence the structure of the optimum search tree.

Therefore let us set the problem up in the following way: We are given $2n+1$ probabilities $p_1, p_2, \ldots, p_n$ and $q_0, q_1, \ldots, q_n$, where

p_i = probability that K_i is the search argument;

q_i = probability that the search argument lies between K_i and K_{i+1}.

(By convention, q_0 is the probability that the search argument is less than K_1, and q_n is the probability that the search argument is greater than K_n.) Thus,

$p_1 + p_2 + \cdots + p_n + q_0 + q_1 + \cdots + q_n = 1$, and we want to find a binary tree that minimizes the expected number of comparisons in the search, namely

$$\sum_{j=1}^{n} p_j \left(\text{level}(\textcircled{j}) + 1\right) + \sum_{k=0}^{n} q_k \; \text{level}(\boxed{k}), \tag{14}$$

where $\textcircled{j}$ is the jth internal node in symmetric order and $\boxed{k}$ is the $(k+1)$st external node, and where the root has level zero. Thus the expected number of comparisons for the binary tree

$$(15)$$

is $2q_0 + 2p_1 + 3q_1 + 3p_2 + 3q_2 + p_3 + q_3$. Let us call this the *cost* of the tree; and let us say that a minimum-cost tree is *optimum*. In this definition there is no need to require that the p's and q's sum to unity; we can ask for a minimum-cost tree with any given sequence of "weights" $(p_1, \ldots, p_n; q_0, \ldots, q_n)$.

We have studied Huffman's procedure for constructing trees with minimum weighted path length, in Section 2.3.4.5; but that method requires all the p's to be zero, and the tree it produces will usually not have the external node weights $(q_0, \ldots, q_n)$ in the proper symmetric order from left to right. Therefore we need another approach.

What saves us is that *all subtrees of an optimum tree are optimum*. For example, if (15) is an optimum tree for the weights $(p_1, p_2, p_3; q_0, q_1, q_2, q_3)$, then the left subtree of the root must be optimum for $(p_1, p_2; q_0, q_1, q_2)$; any improvement to a subtree leads to an improvement in the whole tree.

This principle suggests a computation procedure that systematically finds larger and larger optimum subtrees. We have used much the same idea in Section 5.4.9 to construct optimum merge patterns; the general approach is known as "dynamic programming," and we shall consider it further in Section 7.7.

Let $c(i, j)$ be the cost of an optimum subtree with weights $(p_{i+1}, \ldots, p_j;\ q_i, \ldots, q_j)$; and let $w(i, j) = p_{i+1} + \cdots + p_j + q_i + \cdots + q_j$ be the sum of all those weights; thus $c(i, j)$ and $w(i, j)$ are defined for $0 \le i \le j \le n$. It follows that

$$c(i, i) = 0,$$
$$c(i, j) = w(i, j) + \min_{i < k \le j} \left(c(i, k-1) + c(k, j)\right), \qquad \text{for } i < j, \tag{16}$$

since the minimum possible cost of a tree with root $\textcircled{k}$ is $w(i, j) + c(i, k-1) + c(k, j)$. When $i < j$, let $R(i, j)$ be the set of all k for which the minimum is achieved in (16); this set specifies the possible roots of the optimum trees.

Equation (16) makes it possible to evaluate $c(i, j)$ for $j - i = 1, 2, \ldots, n$; there are about $\frac{1}{2}n^2$ such values, and the minimization operation is carried out for about $\frac{1}{6}n^3$ values of k. This means we can determine an optimum tree in $O(n^3)$ units of time, using $O(n^2)$ cells of memory.

A factor of n can actually be removed from the running time if we make use of a monotonicity property. Let $r(i,j)$ denote an element of $R(i,j)$; we need not compute the entire set $R(i,j)$, a single representative is sufficient. Once we have found $r(i,j-1)$ and $r(i+1,j)$, the result of exercise 27 proves that we may always assume that

$$r(i,j-1) \le r(i,j) \le r(i+1,j) \tag{17}$$

when the weights are nonnegative. This limits the search for the minimum, since only $r(i+1,j) - r(i,j-1) + 1$ values of k need to be examined in (16) instead of $j-i$. The total amount of work when $j-i = d$ is now bounded by the telescoping series

$$\sum_{\substack{d\le j\le n \\ i=j-d}} (r(i+1,j) - r(i,j-1) + 1) = r(n-d+1,n) - r(0,d-1) + n - d + 1 < 2n;$$

hence the total running time is reduced to $O(n^2)$.

The following algorithm describes this procedure in detail.

Algorithm K (*Find optimum binary search trees*). Given $2n+1$ nonnegative weights $(p_1,\ldots,p_n; q_0,\ldots,q_n)$, this algorithm constructs binary trees $t(i,j)$ that have minimum cost for the weights $(p_{i+1},\ldots,p_j; q_i,\ldots,q_j)$ in the sense defined above. Three arrays are computed, namely

$$\begin{array}{lll} c[i,j], & \text{for } 0 \le i \le j \le n, & \text{the cost of } t(i,j); \\ r[i,j], & \text{for } 0 \le i < j \le n, & \text{the root of } t(i,j); \\ w[i,j], & \text{for } 0 \le i \le j \le n, & \text{the total weight of } t(i,j). \end{array}$$

The results of the algorithm are specified by the r array: If $i = j$, $t(i,j)$ is null; otherwise its left subtree is $t(i, r[i,j]-1)$ and its right subtree is $t(r[i,j], j)$.

K1. [Initialize.] For $0 \le i \le n$, set $c[i,i] \leftarrow 0$ and $w[i,i] \leftarrow q_i$ and $w[i,j] \leftarrow w[i,j-1] + p_j + q_j$ for $j = i+1,\ldots,n$. Then for $1 \le j \le n$ set $c[j-1,j] \leftarrow w[j-1,j]$ and $r[j-1,j] \leftarrow j$. (This determines all the 1-node optimum trees.)

K2. [Loop on d.] Do step K3 for $d = 2,3,\ldots,n$, then terminate the algorithm.

K3. [Loop on j.] (We have already determined the optimum trees of fewer than d nodes. This step determines all the d-node optimum trees.) Do step K4 for $j = d, d+1, \ldots, n$.

K4. [Find $c[i,j]$, $r[i,j]$.] Set $i \leftarrow j - d$. Then set

$$c[i,j] \leftarrow w[i,j] + \min_{r[i,j-1]\le k\le r[i+1,j]}(c[i,k-1] + c[k,j]),$$

and set $r[i,j]$ to a value of k for which the minimum occurs. (Exercise 22 proves that $r[i,j-1] \le r[i+1,j]$.) ∎

As an example of Algorithm K, consider Fig. 15, which is based on a "keyword-in-context" (KWIC) indexing application. The titles of all articles in the first ten volumes of the *Journal of the ACM* were sorted to prepare a concordance in which there was one line for every word of every title. However, certain words like "THE" and "EQUATION" were felt to be sufficiently uninformative that they were left out of the index. These special words and their frequency of occurrence are shown in the internal nodes of Fig. 15. Notice that a title such as "On the solution of an equation for a certain new problem" would be so uninformative, it wouldn't appear in the index at all! The idea of KWIC indexing is due to H. P. Luhn, *Amer. Documentation* **11** (1960), 288–295. (See W. W. Youden, *JACM* **10** (1963), 583–646, where the full KWIC index appears.)

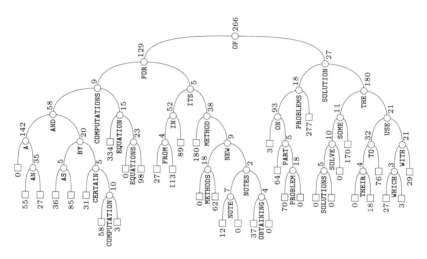

Fig. 15. An optimum binary search tree for a KWIC indexing application.

When preparing a KWIC index file for sorting, we might want to use a binary search tree in order to test whether or not each particular word is to be indexed. The other words fall between two of the unindexed words, with the frequencies shown in the external nodes of Fig. 15; thus, exactly 277 words that are alphabetically between "PROBLEMS" and "SOLUTION" appeared in the *JACM* titles during 1954–1963.

Figure 15 shows the optimum tree obtained by Algorithm K, with $n = 35$. The computed values of $r[0, j]$ for $j = 1, 2, \ldots, 35$ are $(1, 1, 2, 3, 3, 3, 3, 8, 8, 8, 8, 8, 8, 11, 11, \ldots, 11, 21, 21, 21, 21, 21, 21)$; the values of $r[i, 35]$ for $i = 0, 1, \ldots, 34$ are $(21, 21, \ldots, 21, 25, 25, 25, 25, 25, 25, 26, 26, 26, 30, 30, 30, 30, 30, 30, 33, 33, 33, 35, 35)$.

The "betweenness frequencies" q_j have a noticeable effect on the optimum tree structure; Fig. 16(a) shows the optimum tree that would have been obtained with the q_j set to zero. Similarly, the internal frequencies p_i are important; Fig. 16(b) shows the optimum tree when the p_i are set to zero. Considering the full set of frequencies, the tree of Fig. 15 requires only 4.15 comparisons, on the average, while the trees of Fig. 16 require, respectively, 4.69 and 4.55.

a)

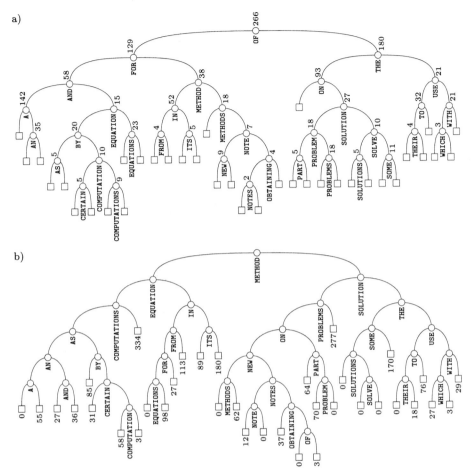

b)

Fig. 16. Optimum binary search trees based on half of the data of Fig. 15: (a) external frequencies suppressed; (b) internal frequencies suppressed.

Since Algorithm K requires time and space proportional to n^2, it becomes impractical when n is very large. Of course we may not really want to use binary search trees for large n, in view of the other search techniques to be discussed later in this chapter; but let's assume anyway that we want to find an optimum or nearly optimum tree when n is large.

We have seen that the idea of inserting the keys in order of decreasing frequency can tend to make a fairly good tree, on the average; but it can also be very bad (see exercise 20), and it is not usually very near the optimum, since it makes no use of the q_j weights. Another approach is to choose the root k so that the resulting maximum subtree weight, $\max(w(0, k-1), w(k, n))$, is as small as possible. This approach can also be fairly poor, because it may choose a node with very small p_k to be the root; however, Theorem M below shows that the resulting tree will not be extremely far from the optimum.

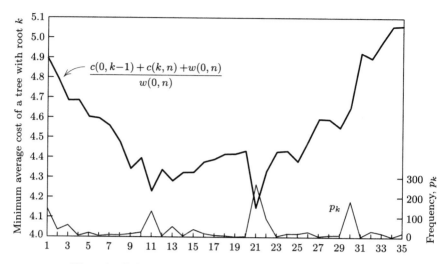

Fig. 17. Behavior of the cost as a function of the root, k.

A more satisfactory procedure can be obtained by combining these two methods, as suggested by W. A. Walker and C. C. Gotlieb [*Graph Theory and Computing* (Academic Press, 1972), 303–323]: Try to equalize the left-hand and right-hand weights, but be prepared to move the root a few steps to the left or right to find a node with relatively large p_k. Figure 17 shows why this method is reasonable: If we plot $c(0, k-1) + c(k, n)$ as a function of k, for the KWIC data of Fig. 15, we see that the result is quite sensitive to the magnitude of p_k.

A top-down method such as this can be used for large n to choose the root and then to work on the left and the right subtrees. When we get down to a sufficiently small subtree we can apply Algorithm K. The resulting method yields fairly good trees (reportedly within 2 or 3 percent of the optimum), and it requires only $O(n)$ units of space, $O(n \log n)$ units of time. In fact, M. Fredman has shown that $O(n)$ units of time suffice, if suitable data structures are used [*STOC* **7** (1975), 240–244]; see K. Mehlhorn, *Data Structures and Algorithms* **1** (Springer, 1984), Section 4.2.

Optimum trees and entropy. The minimum cost is closely related to a mathematical concept called *entropy*, which was introduced by Claude Shannon in his seminal work on information theory [*Bell System Tech. J.* **27** (1948), 379–423, 623–656]. If $p_1, p_2, \ldots, p_n$ are probabilities with $p_1 + p_2 + \cdots + p_n = 1$, we define the entropy $H(p_1, p_2, \ldots, p_n)$ by the formula

$$H(p_1, p_2, \ldots, p_n) = \sum_{k=1}^{n} p_k \lg \frac{1}{p_k}. \tag{18}$$

Intuitively, if n events are possible and the kth event occurs with probability p_k, we can imagine that we have received $\lg(1/p_k)$ bits of information when the kth event has occurred. (An event of probability $\frac{1}{32}$ gives 5 bits of information, etc.) Then $H(p_1, p_2, \ldots, p_n)$ is the expected number of bits of information in a random event. If $p_k = 0$, we define $p_k \lg(1/p_k) = 0$, because

$$\lim_{\epsilon \to 0+} \epsilon \lg \frac{1}{\epsilon} = \lim_{m \to \infty} \frac{1}{m} \lg m = 0.$$

This convention allows us to use (18) when some of the probabilities are zero.

The function $x \lg(1/x)$ is concave; that is, its second derivative, $-1/(x \ln 2)$, is negative. Therefore the maximum value of $H(p_1, p_2, \ldots, p_n)$ occurs when $p_1 = p_2 = \cdots = p_n = 1/n$, namely

$$H\left(\frac{1}{n}, \frac{1}{n}, \ldots, \frac{1}{n}\right) = \lg n. \tag{19}$$

In general, if we specify $p_1, \ldots, p_{n-k}$ but allow the other probabilities p_{n-k+1}, $\ldots, p_n$ to vary, we have

$$H(p_1, \ldots, p_{n-k}, p_{n-k+1}, \ldots, p_n) \le H\left(p_1, \ldots, p_{n-k}, \frac{q}{k}, \ldots, \frac{q}{k}\right)$$
$$= H(p_1, \ldots, p_{n-k}, q) + q \lg k, \tag{20}$$

$$H(p_1, \ldots, p_{n-k}, p_{n-k+1}, \ldots, p_n) \ge H(p_1, \ldots, p_{n-k}, q, 0, \ldots, 0)$$
$$= H(p_1, \ldots, p_{n-k}, q), \tag{21}$$

where $q = 1 - (p_1 + \cdots + p_{n-k})$.

Consider any not-necessarily-binary tree in which probabilities have been assigned to the leaves, say

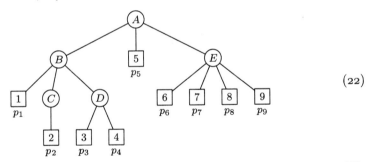

$$\tag{22}$$

Here p_k represents the probability that a search procedure will end at leaf $\boxed{k}$. Then the branching at each internal (nonleaf) node corresponds to a local probability distribution based on the sums of leaf probabilities below each branch. For example, at node $\textcircled{A}$ the first, second, and third branches are taken with the respective probabilities

$$(p_1 + p_2 + p_3 + p_4, \ p_5, \ p_6 + p_7 + p_8 + p_9),$$

and at node $\textcircled{B}$ the probabilities are

$$(p_1, p_2, p_3 + p_4)/(p_1 + p_2 + p_3 + p_4).$$

Let us say that each internal node has the entropy of its local probability distribution; thus

$$H(A) = (p_1+p_2+p_3+p_4) \lg \frac{1}{p_1+p_2+p_3+p_4}$$

$$+ p_5 \lg \frac{1}{p_5} + (p_6+p_7+p_8+p_9) \lg \frac{1}{p_6+p_7+p_8+p_9},$$

$$H(B) = \frac{p_1}{p_1+p_2+p_3+p_4} \lg \frac{p_1+p_2+p_3+p_4}{p_1} + \frac{p_2}{p_1+p_2+p_3+p_4} \lg \frac{p_1+p_2+p_3+p_4}{p_2}$$

$$+ \frac{p_3+p_4}{p_1+p_2+p_3+p_4} \lg \frac{p_1+p_2+p_3+p_4}{p_3+p_4},$$

$$H(C) = \frac{p_2}{p_2} \lg \frac{p_2}{p_2},$$

$$H(D) = \frac{p_3}{p_3+p_4} \lg \frac{p_3+p_4}{p_3} + \frac{p_4}{p_3+p_4} \lg \frac{p_3+p_4}{p_4},$$

$$H(E) = \frac{p_6}{p_6+p_7+p_8+p_9} \lg \frac{p_6+p_7+p_8+p_9}{p_6} + \frac{p_7}{p_6+p_7+p_8+p_9} \lg \frac{p_6+p_7+p_8+p_9}{p_7}$$

$$+ \frac{p_8}{p_6+p_7+p_8+p_9} \lg \frac{p_6+p_7+p_8+p_9}{p_8} + \frac{p_9}{p_6+p_7+p_8+p_9} \lg \frac{p_6+p_7+p_8+p_9}{p_9}.$$

Lemma E. *The sum of $p(\alpha)H(\alpha)$ over all internal nodes α of a tree, where $p(\alpha)$ is the probability of reaching node α and $H(\alpha)$ is the entropy of α, equals the entropy of the probability distribution on the leaves.*

Proof. It is easy to establish this identity by induction from bottom to top. For example, we have

$$H(A)+(p_1+p_2+p_3+p_4)H(B)+p_2 H(C)+(p_3+p_4)H(D)+(p_6+p_7+p_8+p_9)H(E)$$

$$= p_1 \lg \frac{1}{p_1} + p_2 \lg \frac{1}{p_2} + \cdots + p_9 \lg \frac{1}{p_9}$$

with respect to the formulas above; all terms involving $\lg(p_1 + p_2 + p_3 + p_4)$, $\lg(p_3 + p_4)$, and $\lg(p_6 + p_7 + p_8 + p_9)$ cancel out. ∎

As a consequence of Lemma E, we can use entropy to establish a convenient lower bound on the cost of any binary tree.

Theorem B. *Let $(p_1, \ldots, p_n; q_0, \ldots, q_n)$ be nonnegative weights as in Algorithm K, normalized so that $p_1+\cdots+p_n+q_0+\cdots+q_n = 1$, and let $P = p_1+\cdots+p_n$ be the probability of a successful search. Let*

$$H = H(p_1, \ldots, p_n, q_0, \ldots, q_n)$$

be the entropy of the corresponding probability distribution, and let C be the minimum cost, (14). Then if $H \geq 2P/e$ we have

$$C \geq H - P \lg \frac{eH}{2P}. \tag{23}$$

Proof. Take a binary tree of cost C and assign the probabilities q_k to its leaves. Also add a middle branch below each internal node, leading to a new leaf that has probability p_k. Then $C = \sum p(\alpha)$, summed over the internal nodes α of the resulting ternary tree, and $H = \sum p(\alpha)H(\alpha)$ by Lemma E.

The entropy $H(\alpha)$ corresponds to a three-way distribution, where one of the probabilities is $p_j/p(\alpha)$ if α is internal node ⓙ. Exercise 35 proves that

$$H(p,q,r) \le p\lg x + 1 + \lg\left(1 + \frac{1}{2x}\right) \tag{24}$$

for all $x > 0$, whenever $p + q + r = 1$. Therefore we have the inequality

$$H = \sum_{\alpha} p(\alpha)H(\alpha) \le \sum_{j=1}^{n} p_j \lg x + \left(1 + \lg\left(1 + \frac{1}{2x}\right)\right)C$$

for all positive x. Choosing $2x = H/P$ now leads to the desired result, since

$$
\begin{aligned}
C &\ge \frac{1}{1 + \lg(1 + P/H)}\left(H - P\lg\frac{H}{2P}\right) \\
&= \frac{1}{1 + \lg(1 + P/H)}(H + P\lg e) - \frac{P}{1 + \lg(1 + P/H)}\lg\frac{eH}{2P} \\
&\ge H - P\lg\frac{eH}{2P},
\end{aligned}
$$

because $\lg(1 + y) \le y\lg e$ for all $y > 0$. ▮

Eq. (23) does not necessarily hold when the entropy is extremely low. But the restriction to cases where $H \ge 2P/e$ is not severe, since the value of H is usually near $\lg n$; see exercise 37. Notice that the proof doesn't actually use the left-to-right order of the nodes; the lower bound (23) holds for any binary search tree that has internal node probabilities p_j and external node probabilities q_k in any order.

Entropy calculations also yield an upper bound that is not too far from (23), even when we do stick to the left-to-right order:

Theorem M. *Under the assumptions of Theorem B, we also have*

$$C < H + 2 - P. \tag{25}$$

Proof. Form the $n+1$ sums $s_0 = \frac{1}{2}q_0$, $s_1 = q_0 + p_1 + \frac{1}{2}q_1$, $s_2 = q_0 + p_1 + q_1 + p_2 + \frac{1}{2}q_2$, $\dots$, $s_n = q_0 + p_1 + \cdots + q_{n-1} + p_n + \frac{1}{2}q_n$; we may assume that $s_0 < s_1 < \cdots < s_n$ (see exercise 38). Express each s_k as a binary fraction, writing $s_n = (.111\ldots)_2$ if $s_n = 1$. Then let the string σ_k be the leading bits of s_k, retaining just enough bits to distinguish s_k from s_j for $j \ne k$. For example, we might have $n = 3$ and

$$
\begin{array}{ll}
s_0 = (.0000001)_2 & \sigma_0 = 00000 \\
s_1 = (.0000101)_2 & \sigma_1 = 00001 \\
s_2 = (.0001011)_2 & \sigma_2 = 0001 \\
s_3 = (.1100000)_2 & \sigma_3 = 1
\end{array}
$$

Construct a binary tree with $n+1$ leaves, in such a way that σ_k corresponds to the path from the root to $\boxed{k}$ for $0 \le k \le n$, where '0' denotes a left branch and '1' denotes a right branch. Also, if σ_{k-1} has the form $\alpha_k 0 \beta_k$ and σ_k has the form $\alpha_k 1 \gamma_k$ for some α_k, β_k, and γ_k, let the internal node $\textcircled{k}$ correspond to the path α_k. Thus we would have

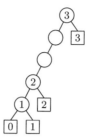

in the example above. There may be some internal nodes that are still nameless; replace each of them by their one and only child. The cost of the resulting tree is at most $\sum_{k=1}^{n} p_k(|\alpha_k|+1) + \sum_{k=0}^{n} q_k|\sigma_k|$.

We have

$$p_k \le \tfrac{1}{2}q_{k-1} + p_k + \tfrac{1}{2}q_k = s_k - s_{k-1} \le 2^{-|\alpha_k|}, \qquad (26)$$

because $s_k \le (.\alpha_k)_2 + 2^{-|\alpha_k|}$ and $s_{k-1} \ge (.\alpha_k)_2$. Furthermore, if $q_k \ge 2^{-t}$ we have $s_k \ge s_{k-1} + 2^{-t-1}$ and $s_{k+1} \ge s_k + 2^{-t-1}$, hence $|\sigma_k| \le t+1$. It follows that $q_k < 2^{-|\sigma_k|+2}$, and we have constructed a binary tree of cost

$$\le \sum_{k=1}^{n} p_k(1+|\alpha_k|) + \sum_{k=0}^{n} q_k|\sigma_k| \le \sum_{k=1}^{n} p_k\left(1 + \lg\frac{1}{p_k}\right) + \sum_{k=0}^{n} q_k\left(2 + \lg\frac{1}{q_k}\right)$$

$$= P + 2(1-P) + H = H + 2 - P. \quad \blacksquare$$

In the KWIC indexing application of Fig. 15, we have $P = 1304/3288 \approx 0.39659$, and $H(p_1, \ldots, p_{35}, q_0, \ldots, q_{35}) \approx 5.00635$. Therefore Theorem B tells us that $C \ge 3.3800$, and Theorem M tells us that $C < 6.6098$.

*The Garsia–Wachs algorithm. An amazing improvement on Algorithm K is possible in the special case that $p_1 = \cdots = p_n = 0$. This case, in which only the leaf probabilities $(q_0, q_1, \ldots, q_n)$ are relevant, is especially important because it arises in a several significant applications. Let us therefore assume in the remainder of this section that the probabilities p_j are zero. Notice that Theorems B and M reduce to the inequalities

$$H(q_0, q_1, \ldots, q_n) \le C(q_0, q_1, \ldots, q_n) < H(q_0, q_1, \ldots, q_n) + 2 \qquad (27)$$

in this case; and the cost function (14) simplifies to

$$C = \sum_{k=0}^{n} q_k l_k, \qquad l_k = \text{the level of } \boxed{k}. \qquad (28)$$

The key property that makes a simpler algorithm possible is the following observation:

Lemma W. *If $q_{k-1} > q_{k+1}$ then $l_k \leq l_{k+1}$ in every optimum tree. If $q_{k-1} = q_{k+1}$ then $l_k \leq l_{k+1}$ in some optimum tree.*

Proof. Suppose $q_{k-1} \geq q_{k+1}$ and consider a tree in which $l_k > l_{k+1}$. Then $\boxed{k}$ must be a right child, and its left sibling L is a subtree of cost $c \geq q_{k-1}$. Replace the parent of $\boxed{k}$ by L; replace $\boxed{k+1}$ by a node whose children are $\boxed{k}$ and $\boxed{k+1}$. This changes the overall cost by $-c - q_k(l_k - l_{k+1} - 1) + q_{k+1} \leq q_{k+1} - q_{k-1}$. So the given tree was not optimum if $q_{k-1} > q_{k+1}$, and it has been transformed into another optimum tree if $q_{k-1} = q_{k+1}$. In the latter case a sequence of such transformations will make $l_k \leq l_{k+1}$. ∎

A deeper analysis of the structure tells us considerably more.

Lemma X. *Suppose j and k are indices such that $j < k$ and we have*

  i) $q_{i-1} > q_{i+1}$ for $1 \leq i < k$;

  ii) $q_{k-1} \leq q_{k+1}$;

  iii) $q_i < q_{k-1} + q_k$ for $j \leq i < k - 1$; and

  iv) $q_{j-1} \geq q_{k-1} + q_k$.

Then there is an optimum tree in which $l_{k-1} = l_k$ and either

  a) $l_j = l_k - 1$, or

  b) $l_j = l_k$ and $\boxed{j}$ is a left child.

Proof. By reversing left and right in Lemma W, we see that (ii) implies the existence of an optimum tree in which $l_{k-1} \geq l_k$. But Lemma W and (i) also imply that $l_1 \leq l_2 \leq \cdots \leq l_k$. Therefore $l_{k-1} = l_k$.

Suppose $l_s < l_k - 1 \leq l_{s+1}$ for some s with $j \leq s < k$. Let t be the smallest index $< k$ such that $l_t = l_k$. Then $l_{s+1} = \cdots = l_{t-1} = l_k - 1$, and $\boxed{s+1}$ is a left child; hence $t - s$ is odd, and node $\boxed{i}$ is a left child for $i = s+1, s+3, \ldots, t$. Replace the parent of $\boxed{t}$ by $\boxed{t+1}$; replace $\boxed{i}$ by $\boxed{i+1}$ for $s < i < t$; and replace the external node $\boxed{s}$ by an internal node whose children are $\boxed{s}$ and $\boxed{s+1}$. This changes the cost by $\leq q_s - q_t - q_{t+1} \leq q_s - q_{k-1} - q_k$, so it is an improvement if $q_s < q_{k-1} + q_k$. Therefore, by (iii), $l_j \geq l_k - 1$.

We still have not used hypothesis (iv). If $l_j = l_k$ and $\boxed{j}$ is not a left child, $\boxed{j}$ must be the right sibling of $\boxed{j+1}$. Replace their parent by $\boxed{j+1}$; then replace leaf $\boxed{i}$ by $\boxed{i+1}$ for $j < i < k$; and replace the external node $\boxed{k}$ by an internal node whose children are $\boxed{k+1}$ and $\boxed{k}$. This changes the cost by $-q_{j-1} + q_{k-1} + q_k \leq 0$, so we obtain an optimum tree satisfying (b). ∎

Lemma Y. *Let j and k be as in Lemma X, and consider the modified probabilities $(q_0', \ldots, q_{n-1}') = (q_0, \ldots, q_{j-1}, q_{k-1} + q_k, q_j, \ldots, q_{k-2}, q_{k+1}, \ldots, q_n)$ obtained by removing q_{k-1} and q_k and inserting $q_{k-1} + q_k$ after q_{j-1}. Then*

$$C(q_0', \ldots, q_{n-1}') \leq (q_{k-1} + q_k) + C(q_0, \ldots, q_n). \tag{29}$$

Proof. It suffices to show that any optimum tree for $(q_0, \ldots, q_n)$ can be transformed into a tree of the same cost in which $\boxed{k-1}$ and $\boxed{k}$ are siblings and the leaves appear in permuted order

$$\boxed{0} \quad \boxed{j-1} \quad \boxed{k-1} \quad \boxed{k} \quad \boxed{j} \quad \cdots \quad \boxed{k-2} \quad \boxed{k+1} \quad \cdots \quad \boxed{n}. \tag{30}$$

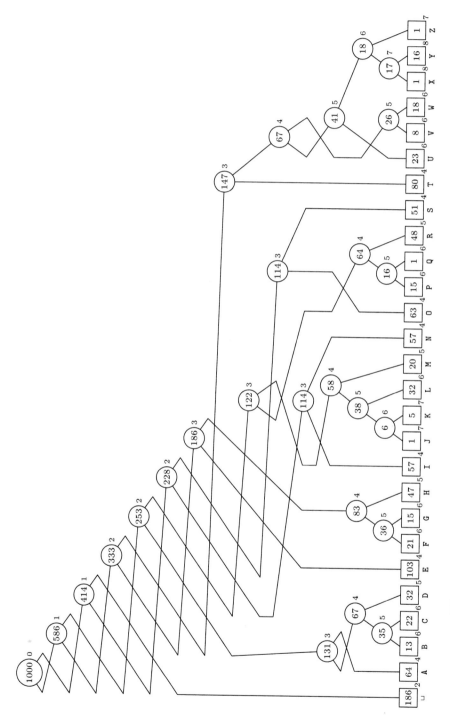

Fig. 18. The Garsia–Wachs algorithm applied to alphabetic frequency data: Phases 1 and 2.

We start with the tree constructed in Lemma X. If it is of type (b), we simply rename the leaves, sliding $\boxed{k-1}$ and $\boxed{k}$ to the left by $k-1-j$ places. If it is of type (a), suppose $l_{s-1} = l_k - 1$ and $l_s = l_k$; we proceed as follows: First slide $\boxed{k-1}$ and $\boxed{k}$ left by $k-1-s$ places; then replace their (new) parent by $\boxed{k-2}$; finally replace $\boxed{j}$ by a node whose children are $\boxed{k-1}$ and $\boxed{k}$, and replace node $\boxed{i}$ by $\boxed{i-1}$ for $j < i < k-1$. ∎

Lemma Z. *Under the hypotheses of Lemma Y, equality holds in* (29).

Proof. Every tree for $(q'_0, \ldots, q'_{n-1})$ corresponds to a tree with leaves (30) in which the two out-of-order leaf nodes $\boxed{k-1}$ and $\boxed{k}$ are siblings. Let internal node $\textcircled{x}$ be their parent. We want to show that any optimum tree of that type can be converted to a tree of the same cost in which the leaves appear in normal order $\boxed{0}$ $\cdots$ $\boxed{n}$.

There is nothing to prove if $j = k-1$. Otherwise we have $q'_{i-1} > q'_{i+1}$ for $j \le i < k-1$, because $q_{j-1} \ge q_{k-1} + q_k > q_j$. Therefore by Lemma W we have $l_x \le l_j \le \cdots \le l_{k-2}$, where l_x is the level of $\textcircled{x}$ and l_i is the level of $\boxed{i}$ for $j \le i < k-1$. If $l_x = l_{k-2}$, we simply slide node $\textcircled{x}$ to the right, replacing the sequence $\textcircled{x}$ $\boxed{j}$ $\cdots$ $\boxed{k-2}$ by $\boxed{j}$ $\cdots$ $\boxed{k-2}$ $\textcircled{x}$; this straightens out the leaves as desired.

Otherwise suppose $l_s = l_x$ and $l_{s+1} > l_x$. We first replace $\textcircled{x}$ $\boxed{j}$ $\cdots$ $\boxed{s}$ by $\boxed{j}$ $\cdots$ $\boxed{s}$ $\textcircled{x}$; this makes $l \le l_{s+1} \le \cdots \le l_{k-2}$, where $l = l_x + 1$ is the common level of nodes $\boxed{k-1}$ and $\boxed{k}$. Finally replace nodes

$$\boxed{k-1}\ \boxed{k}\ \boxed{s+1}\ \cdots\ \boxed{k-2}$$

by the cyclically shifted sequence

$$\boxed{s+1}\ \cdots\ \boxed{k-2}\ \boxed{k-1}\ \boxed{k}.$$

Exercise 40 proves that this decreases the cost, unless $l_{k-2} = l$. But the cost cannot decrease, because of Lemma Y. Therefore $l_{k-2} = l$, and the proof is complete. ∎

These lemmas show that the problem for $n+1$ weights $q_0, q_1, \ldots, q_n$ can be reduced to an n-weight problem: We first find the smallest index k with $q_{k-1} \le q_{k+1}$; then we find the largest $j < k$ with $q_{j-1} \ge q_{k-1} + q_k$; then we remove q_{k-1} and q_k from the list, and insert the sum $q_{k-1} + q_k$ just after q_{j-1}. In the special cases $j = 0$ or $k = n$, the proofs show that we should proceed as if infinite weights q_{-1} and q_{n+1} were present at the left and right. The proofs also show that any optimum tree T' that is obtained from the new weights $(q'_0, \ldots, q'_{n-1})$ can be rearranged into a tree T that has the original weights $(q_0, \ldots, q_n)$ in the correct left-to-right order; moreover, each weight will appear at the same level in both T and T'.

For example, Fig. 18 illustrates the construction when the weights q_k are the relative frequencies of the characters ␣, A, B, ..., Z in English text. The first few weights are

$$186, 64, 13, 22, 32, 103, \ldots$$

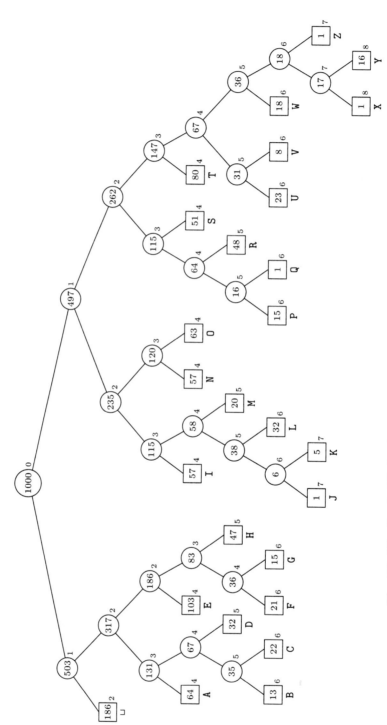

Fig. 19. The Garsia–Wachs algorithm applied to alphabetic frequency data: Phase 3.

and we have $186 > 13$, $64 > 22$, $13 \leq 32$; therefore we replace "$13, 22$" by 35. In the new sequence

$$186, \ 64, \ 35, \ 32, \ 103, \ \ldots$$

we replace "$35, 32$" by 67 and slide 67 to the left of 64, obtaining

$$186, \ 67, \ 64, \ 103, \ \ldots.$$

Then "$67, 64$" becomes 131, and we begin to examine the weights that follow 103. After the 27 original weights have been combined into the single weight 1000, the history of successive combinations specifies a binary tree whose weighted path length is the solution to the original problem.

But the leaves of the tree in Fig. 18 are not at all in the correct order, because they get tangled up when we slide $q_{k-1} + q_k$ to the left (see exercise 41). Still, the proof of Lemma Z guarantees that there is a tree whose leaves are in the correct order and on exactly the same levels as in the tangled tree. This untangled tree, Fig. 19, is therefore optimum; it is the binary tree output by the Garsia–Wachs algorithm.

Algorithm G (*Garsia–Wachs algorithm for optimum binary trees*). Given a sequence of nonnegative weights w_0, w_1, $\ldots$, w_n, this algorithm constructs a binary tree with n internal nodes for which $\sum_{k=0}^{n} w_k l_k$ is minimum, where l_k is the distance of external node $\boxed{k}$ from the root. It uses an array of $2n + 2$ nodes whose addresses are X_k for $0 \leq k \leq 2n + 1$; each node has four fields called WT, LLINK, RLINK, and LEVEL. The leaves of the constructed tree will be nodes $X_0 \ldots X_n$; the internal nodes will be $X_{n+1} \ldots X_{2n}$; the root will be X_{2n}; and X_{2n+1} is used as a temporary sentinel. The algorithm also maintains a working array of pointers P_0, P_1, $\ldots$, P_t, where $t \leq n + 1$.

G1. [Begin phase 1.] Set $\texttt{WT}(X_k) \leftarrow w_k$ and $\texttt{LLINK}(X_k) \leftarrow \texttt{RLINK}(X_k) \leftarrow \Lambda$ for $0 \leq k \leq n$. Also set $P_0 \leftarrow X_{2n+1}$, $\texttt{WT}(P_0) \leftarrow \infty$, $P_1 \leftarrow X_0$, $t \leftarrow 1$, $m \leftarrow n$. Then perform step G2 for $j = 1, 2, \ldots, n$, and go to G3.

G2. [Absorb w_j.] (At this point we have the basic condition

$$\texttt{WT}(P_{i-1}) > \texttt{WT}(P_{i+1}) \qquad \text{for } 1 \leq i < t; \tag{31}$$

in other words, the weights in the working array are "2-descending.") Perform Subroutine C below, zero or more times, until $\texttt{WT}(P_{t-1}) > w_j$. Then set $t \leftarrow t + 1$ and $P_t \leftarrow X_j$.

G3. [Finish phase 1.] Perform Subroutine C zero or more times, until $t = 1$.

G4. [Do phase 2.] (Now $P_1 = X_{2n}$ is the root of a binary tree, and $\texttt{WT}(P_1) = w_0 + \cdots + w_n$.) Set l_k to the distance of node X_k from node P_1, for $0 \leq k \leq n$. (See exercise 43. An example is shown in Fig. 18, where level numbers appear at the right of each node.)

G5. [Do phase 3.] By changing the links of $X_{n+1}, \ldots, X_{2n}$, construct a new binary tree having the same level numbers l_k, but with the leaf nodes in symmetric order $X_0, \ldots, X_n$. (See exercise 44; an example appears in Fig. 19.) ∎

Subroutine C (*Combination*). This subroutine is the heart of the Garsia–Wachs algorithm. It combines two weights, shifts them left as appropriate, and maintains the 2-descending condition (31).

C1. [Initialize.] Set $k \leftarrow t$.

C2. [Create a new node.] (At this point we have $k \geq 2$.) Set $m \leftarrow m + 1$, LLINK$(X_m) \leftarrow P_{k-1}$, RLINK$(X_m) \leftarrow P_k$, WT$(X_m) \leftarrow$ WT$(P_{k-1}) +$ WT(P_k).

C3. [Shift the following nodes left.] Set $t \leftarrow t - 1$, then $P_{j+1} \leftarrow P_j$ for $k \leq j \leq t$.

C4. [Shift the preceding nodes right.] Set $j \leftarrow k-2$; then while WT$(P_j) <$ WT(X_m) set $P_{j+1} \leftarrow P_j$ and $j \leftarrow j - 1$.

C5. [Insert the new node.] Set $P_{j+1} \leftarrow X_m$.

C6. [Done?] If $j > 0$ and WT$(P_{j-1}) \leq$ WT(X_m), set $k \leftarrow j$ and return to C2. ∎

As stated, Subroutine C might need $\Omega(n)$ steps to create and insert a new node, because it uses sequential memory instead of linked lists. Therefore the total running time of Algorithm G might be $\Omega(n^2)$. But more elaborate data structures can be used to guarantee that phase 1 will require at most $O(n \log n)$ steps (see exercise 45). Phases 2 and 3 need only $O(n)$ steps.

Kleitman and Saks [*SIAM J. Algeb. Discr. Methods* **2** (1981), 142–146] proved that the optimum weighted path length never exceeds the value of the optimum weighted path length that occurs when the q's have been rearranged in "sawtooth order":

$$q_0 \leq q_2 \leq q_4 \leq \cdots \leq q_{2\lfloor n/2 \rfloor} \leq q_{2\lceil n/2 \rceil - 1} \leq \cdots \leq q_3 \leq q_1. \qquad (32)$$

(This is the inverse of the organ-pipe order discussed in exercise 6.1–18.) In the latter case the Garsia–Wachs algorithm essentially reduces to Huffman's algorithm on the weights $q_0 + q_1$, $q_2 + q_3$, ..., because the weights in the working array will actually be nonincreasing (not merely "2-descending" as in (31)). Therefore we can improve the upper bound of Theorem M without knowing the order of the weights.

The optimum binary tree in Fig. 19 has an important application to coding theory as well as to searching: Using 0 to stand for a left branch in the tree and 1 to stand for a right branch, we obtain the following variable-length codewords:

␣	00	I	1000	R	11001	
A	0100	J	1001000	S	1101	
B	010100	K	1001001	T	1110	
C	010101	L	100101	U	111100	
D	01011	M	10011	V	111101	(33)
E	0110	N	1010	W	111110	
F	011100	O	1011	X	11111100	
G	011101	P	110000	Y	11111101	
H	01111	Q	110001	Z	1111111	

Thus a message like "RIGHT ON" would be encoded by the string

$$11001100001110101111111100010111010.$$

Decoding from left to right is easy, in spite of the variable length of the codewords, because the tree structure tells us when one codeword ends and another begins. This method of coding preserves the alphabetical order of messages, and it uses an average of about 4.2 bits per letter. Thus the code could be used to compress data files, without destroying lexicographic order of alphabetic information. (The figure of 4.2 bits per letter is minimum over all binary tree codes, although it could be reduced to 4.1 bits per letter if we disregarded the alphabetic ordering constraint. A further reduction, preserving alphabetic order, could be achieved if pairs of letters instead of single letters were encoded.)

History and bibliography. The tree search methods of this section were discovered independently by several people during the 1950s. In an unpublished memorandum dated August 1952, A. I. Dumey described a primitive form of tree insertion in the following way:

> Consider a drum with 2^n item storages in it, each having a binary address.
>
> Follow this program:
>
> 1. Read in the first item and store it in address 2^{n-1}, i.e., at the halfway storage place.
>
> 2. Read in the next item. Compare it with the first.
>
> 3. If it is larger, put it in address $2^{n-1} + 2^{n-2}$. It it is smaller, put it at 2^{n-2}. ...

Another early form of tree insertion was introduced by D. J. Wheeler, who actually allowed multiway branching similar to what we shall discuss in Section 6.2.4; and a binary tree insertion technique was devised by C. M. Berners-Lee [see *Comp. J.* **2** (1959), 5].

The first published descriptions of tree insertion were by P. F. Windley [*Comp. J.* **3** (1960), 84–88], A. D. Booth and A. J. T. Colin [*Information and Control* **3** (1960), 327–334], and Thomas N. Hibbard [*JACM* **9** (1962), 13–28]. Each of these authors seems to have developed the method independently of the others, and each paper derived the average number of comparisons (6) in a different way. The individual authors also went on to treat different aspects of the algorithm: Windley gave a detailed discussion of tree insertion sorting; Booth and Colin discussed the effect of preconditioning by making the first $2^n - 1$ elements form a perfectly balanced tree (see exercise 4); Hibbard introduced the idea of deletion and showed the connection between the analysis of tree insertion and the analysis of quicksort.

The idea of *optimum* binary search trees was first developed for the special case $p_1 = \cdots = p_n = 0$, in the context of alphabetic binary encodings like (33). A very interesting paper by E. N. Gilbert and E. F. Moore [*Bell System Tech. J.* **38** (1959), 933–968] discussed this problem and its relation to other coding problems. Gilbert and Moore proved Theorem M in the special case $P = 0$, and observed that an optimum tree could be constructed in $O(n^3)$ steps, using a method like Algorithm K but without making use of the monotonicity relation (17). K. E. Iverson [*A Programming Language* (Wiley, 1962), 142–144] independently considered the *other* case, when all the q's are zero. He suggested that an optimum tree would be obtained if the root is chosen so as to equalize the left and right subtree probabilities as much as possible; unfortunately we have seen that this idea doesn't work. D. E. Knuth [*Acta Informatica* **1** (1971), 14–25, 270] subsequently considered the case of general p and q weights and proved that the algorithm could be reduced to $O(n^2)$ steps; he also presented an example from a compiler application, where the keys in the tree are "reserved words" in an ALGOL-like language. T. C. Hu had been studying his own algorithm for the case $p_j = 0$ for several years; a rigorous proof of the validity of that algorithm was difficult to find because of the complexity of the problem, but he eventually obtained a proof jointly with A. C. Tucker [*SIAM J. Applied Math.* **21** (1971), 514–532]. Simplifications leading to Algorithm G were found several years later by A. M. Garsia and M. L. Wachs, *SICOMP* **6** (1977), 622–642, although their proof was still rather complicated. Lemmas W, X, Y, and Z above are due to J. H. Kingston, *J. Algorithms* **9** (1988), 129–136. See also the paper by Hu, Kleitman, and Tamaki, *SIAM J. Applied Math.* **37** (1979), 246–256, for an elementary proof of the Hu–Tucker algorithm and some generalizations to other cost functions.

Theorem B is due to Paul J. Bayer, report MIT/LCS/TM-69 (Mass. Inst. of Tech., 1975), who also proved a slightly weaker form of Theorem M. The stronger form above is due to K. Mehlhorn, *SICOMP* **6** (1977), 235–239.

EXERCISES

1. [*15*] Algorithm T has been stated only for nonempty trees. What changes should be made so that it works properly for the empty tree too?

2. [*20*] Modify Algorithm T so that it works with *right-threaded* trees. (See Section 2.3.1; symmetric traversal is easier in such trees.)

▶ **3.** [*20*] In Section 6.1 we found that a slight change to the sequential search Algorithm 6.1S made it faster (Algorithm 6.1Q). Can a similar trick be used to speed up Algorithm T?

4. [*M24*] (A. D. Booth and A. J. T. Colin.) Given N keys in random order, suppose that we use the first $2^n - 1$ to construct a perfectly balanced tree, placing 2^k keys on level k for $0 \le k < n$; then we use Algorithm T to insert the remaining keys. What is the average number of comparisons in a successful search? [*Hint:* Modify Eq. (2).]

▶ **5.** [*M25*] There are $11! = 39,916,800$ different orders in which the names CAPRICORN, AQUARIUS, etc. could have been inserted into a binary search tree.
   a) How many of these arrangements will produce Fig. 10?
   b) How many of these arrangements will produce a *degenerate* tree, in which LLINK or RLINK is Λ in each node?

6. [*M26*] Let P_{nk} be the number of permutations $a_1 a_2 \ldots a_n$ of $\{1, 2, \ldots, n\}$ such that, if Algorithm T is used to insert $a_1, a_2, \ldots, a_n$ successively into an initially empty tree, exactly k comparisons are made when a_n is inserted. (In this problem, we will ignore the comparisons made when $a_1, \ldots, a_{n-1}$ were inserted. In the notation of the text, we have $C'_{n-1} = (\sum_k k P_{nk})/n!$, since this is the average number of comparisons made in an unsuccessful search of a tree containing $n - 1$ elements.)

    a) Prove that $P_{(n+1)k} = 2P_{n(k-1)} + (n-1)P_{nk}$. [*Hint:* Consider whether or not a_{n+1} falls below a_n in the tree.]

    b) Find a simple formula for the generating function $G_n(z) = \sum_k P_{nk} z^k$, and use your formula to express P_{nk} in terms of Stirling numbers.

    c) What is the *variance* of this distribution?

  7. [*M25*] (S. R. Arora and W. T. Dent.) After n elements have been inserted into an initially empty tree, in random order, what is the average number of comparisons needed by Algorithm T to find the mth largest element, given the key of that element?

  8. [*M38*] Let $p(n, k)$ be the probability that k is the total internal path length of a tree built by Algorithm T from n randomly ordered keys. (The internal path length is the number of comparisons made by tree insertion sorting as the tree is being built.)

    a) Find a recurrence relation that defines the corresponding generating function.

    b) Compute the variance of this distribution. [Several of the exercises in Section 1.2.7 may be helpful here.]

  9. [*41*] We have proved that tree search and insertion requires only about $2 \ln N$ comparisons when the keys are inserted in random order; but in practice, the order may not be random. Make empirical studies to see how suitable tree insertion really is for symbol tables within a compiler and/or assembler. Do the identifiers used in typical large programs lead to fairly well-balanced binary search trees?

▶ **10.** [*22*] (R. W. Floyd.) Perhaps we are not interested in the sorting property of Algorithm T, but we expect that the input will come in nonrandom order. Devise a way to keep tree search efficient, by making the input "appear to be" in random order.

  11. [*20*] What is the maximum number of times the assignment S ← LLINK(R) might be performed in step D3, when deleting a node from a tree of size N? empirical data

  12. [*M22*] When making a random deletion from a random tree of N items, how often does step D1 go to D4, on the average? (See the proof of Theorem H.)

▶ **13.** [*M23*] If the root of a random tree is deleted by Algorithm D, is the resulting tree still random?

▶ **14.** [*22*] Prove that the path length of the tree produced by Algorithm D with step D1$\frac{1}{2}$ added is never more than the path length of the tree produced without that step. Find a case where step D1$\frac{1}{2}$ actually decreases the path length.

  15. [*23*] Let $a_1\, a_2\, a_3\, a_4$ be a permutation of $\{1, 2, 3, 4\}$, and let $j = 1$, 2, or 3. Take the one-element tree with key a_1 and insert a_2, a_3 using Algorithm T; then delete a_j using Algorithm D; then insert a_4 using Algorithm T. How many of the $4! \times 3$ possibilities produce trees of shape I, II, III, IV, V, respectively, in (13)?

▶ **16.** [*25*] Is the deletion operation *commutative*? That is, if Algorithm D is used to delete X and then Y, is the resulting tree the same as if Algorithm D is used to delete Y and then X?

  17. [*25*] Show that if the roles of left and right are completely reversed in Algorithm D, it is easy to extend the algorithm so that it deletes a given node from a *right-threaded* tree, preserving the necessary threads. (See exercise 2.)

  18. [*M21*] Show that Zipf's law yields (12).

19. [*M23*] What is the approximate average number of comparisons, (11), when the input probabilities satisfy the 80-20 law defined in Eq. 6.1–(11)?

20. [*M20*] Suppose we have inserted keys into a tree in order of decreasing frequency $p_1 \geq p_2 \geq \cdots \geq p_n$. Can this tree be substantially worse than the optimum search tree?

21. [*M20*] If p, q, r are probabilities chosen at random, subject to the condition that $p + q + r = 1$, what are the probabilities that trees I, II, III, IV, V of (13) are optimal, respectively? (Consider the relative areas of the regions in Fig. 14.)

22. [*M20*] Prove that $r[i, j-1]$ is never greater than $r[i+1, j]$ when step K4 of Algorithm K is performed.

▶ **23.** [*M23*] Find an optimum binary search tree for the case $N = 40$, with weights $p_1 = 9$, $p_2 = p_3 = \cdots = p_{40} = 1$, $q_0 = q_1 = \cdots = q_{40} = 0$. (Don't use a computer.)

24. [*M25*] Given that $p_n = q_n = 0$ and that the other weights are nonnegative, prove that an optimum tree for $(p_1, \ldots, p_n; q_0, \ldots, q_n)$ may be obtained by replacing

in any optimum tree for $(p_1, \ldots, p_{n-1}; q_0, \ldots, q_{n-1})$.

25. [*M20*] Let A and B be nonempty sets of real numbers, and define $A \leq B$ if the following property holds:

$$(a \in A, \ b \in B, \text{ and } b < a) \qquad \text{implies} \qquad (a \in B \text{ and } b \in A).$$

a) Prove that this relation is transitive on nonempty sets.

b) Prove or disprove: $A \leq B$ if and only if $A \leq A \cup B \leq B$.

26. [*M22*] Let $(p_1, \ldots, p_n; q_0, \ldots, q_n)$ be nonnegative weights, where $p_n + q_n = x$. Prove that as x varies from 0 to ∞, while $(p_1, \ldots, p_{n-1}; q_0, \ldots, q_{n-1})$ are held constant, the cost $c(0, n)$ of an optimum binary search tree is a concave, continuous, piecewise linear function of x with integer slopes. In other words, prove that there exist positive integers $l_0 > l_1 > \cdots > l_m$ and real constants $0 = x_0 < x_1 < \cdots < x_m < x_{m+1} = \infty$ and $y_0 < y_1 \cdots < y_m$ such that $c(0, n) = y_h + l_h x$ when $x_h \leq x \leq x_{h+1}$, for $0 \leq h \leq m$.

27. [*M33*] The object of this exercise is to prove that the sets of roots $R(i, j)$ of optimum binary search trees satisfy

$$R(i, j-1) \leq R(i, j) \leq R(i+1, j), \qquad \text{for } j - i \geq 2,$$

in terms of the relation defined in exercise 25, when the weights $(p_1, \ldots, p_n; q_0, \ldots, q_n)$ are nonnegative. The proof is by induction on $j-i$; our task is to prove that $R(0, n-1) \leq R(0, n)$, assuming that $n \geq 2$ and that the stated relation holds for $j - i < n$. [By left-right symmetry it follows that $R(0, n) \leq R(1, n)$.]

a) Prove that $R(0, n-1) \leq R(0, n)$ if $p_n = q_n = 0$. (See exercise 24.)

b) Let $p_n + q_n = x$. In the notation of exercise 26, let R_h be the set $R(0, n)$ of optimum roots when $x_h < x < x_{h+1}$, and let R'_h be the set of optimum roots when $x = x_h$. Prove that

$$R'_0 \leq R_0 \leq R'_1 \leq R_1 \leq \cdots \leq R'_m \leq R_m.$$

Hence by part (a) and exercise 25 we have $R(0, n-1) \leq R(0, n)$ for all x. [*Hint:* Consider the case $x = x_h$, and assume that both the trees

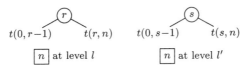

are optimum, with $s < r$ and $l \geq l'$. Use the induction hypothesis to prove that there is an optimum tree with root ⓡ such that $\boxed{n}$ is at level l', and an optimum tree with root ⓢ such that $\boxed{n}$ is at level l.]

28. [*24*] Use some macro language to define a "optimum binary search" macro, whose parameter is a nested specification of an optimum binary tree.

29. [*40*] What is the *worst* possible binary search tree for the 31 most common English words, using the frequency data of Fig. 12?

30. [*M34*] Prove that the costs of optimum binary search trees satisfy the "quadrangle inequality" $c(i, j) - c(i, j-1) \geq c(i+1, j) - c(i+1, j-1)$ when $j \geq i + 2$.

31. [*M35*] (K. C. Tan.) Prove that, among all possible sets of probabilities $(p_1, \ldots, p_n; q_0, \ldots, q_n)$ with $p_1 + \cdots + p_n + q_0 + \cdots + q_n = 1$, the most expensive minimum-cost tree occurs when $p_i = 0$ for all i, $q_j = 0$ for all even j, and $q_j = 1/\lceil n/2 \rceil$ for all odd j.

▶ **32.** [*M25*] Let $n + 1 = 2^m + k$, where $0 \leq k \leq 2^m$. There are exactly $\binom{2^m}{k}$ binary trees in which all external nodes appear on levels m and $m + 1$. Show that, among all these trees, we obtain one with the minimum cost for the weights $(p_1, \ldots, p_n; q_0, \ldots, q_n)$ if we apply Algorithm K to the weights $(p_1, \ldots, p_n; M+q_0, \ldots, M+q_n)$ for sufficiently large M.

33. [*M41*] In order to find the binary search tree that minimizes the running time of Program T, we should minimize the quantity $7C + C1$ instead of simply minimizing the number of comparisons C. Develop an algorithm that finds optimum binary search trees when different costs are associated with left and right branches in the tree. (Incidentally, when the right cost is twice the left cost, and the node frequencies are all equal, the Fibonacci trees turn out to be optimum; see L. E. Stanfel, *JACM* **17** (1970), 508–517. On machines that cannot make three-way comparisons at once, a program for Algorithm T will have to make two comparisons in step T2, one for equality and one for less-than; B. Sheil and V. R. Pratt have observed that these comparisons need not involve the same key, and it may well be best to have a binary tree whose internal nodes specify either an equality test *or* a less-than test but not both. This situation would be interesting to explore as an alternative to the stated problem.)

34. [*HM21*] Show that the asymptotic value of the multinomial coefficient

$$\binom{N}{p_1 N, \ p_2 N, \ \ldots, \ p_n N}$$

as $N \to \infty$ is related to the entropy $H(p_1, p_2, \ldots, p_n)$.

35. [*HM22*] Complete the proof of Theorem B by establishing the inequality (24).

▶ **36.** [*HM25*] (Claude Shannon.) Let X and Y be random variables with finite ranges $\{x_1, \ldots, x_m\}$ and $\{y_1, \ldots, y_n\}$, and let $p_i = \Pr(X = x_i)$, $q_j = \Pr(Y = y_j)$, $r_{ij} = \Pr(X = x_i$ and $Y = y_j)$. Let $H(X) = H(p_1, \ldots, p_m)$ and $H(Y) = H(q_1, \ldots, q_n)$ be the

respective entropies of the variables singly, and let $H(XY) = H(r_{11}, \ldots, r_{mn})$ be the
entropy of their joint distribution. Prove that

$$H(X) \leq H(XY) \leq H(X) + H(Y).$$

[*Hint:* If f is any concave function, we have $\mathrm{E}\, f(X) \leq f(\mathrm{E}\, X)$.]

37. [*HM26*] (P. J. Bayer, 1975.) Suppose $(P_1, \ldots, P_n)$ is a random probability distribution, namely a random point in the $(n-1)$-dimensional simplex defined by $P_k \geq 0$ for $1 \leq k \leq n$ and $P_1 + \cdots + P_n = 1$. (Equivalently, $(P_1, \ldots, P_n)$ is a set of random *spacings*, in the sense of exercise 3.3.2–26.) What is the expected value of the entropy $H(P_1, \ldots, P_n)$?

38. [*M20*] Explain why Theorem M holds in general, although we have only proved it in the case $s_0 < s_1 < s_2 < \cdots < s_n$.

▶ **39.** [*M25*] Let w_1, $\ldots$, w_n be nonnegative weights with $w_1 + \cdots + w_n = 1$. Prove that the weighted path length of the Huffman tree constructed in Section 2.3.4.5 is less than $H(w_1, \ldots, w_n) + 1$. *Hint:* See the proof of Theorem M.

40. [*M26*] Complete the proof of Lemma Z.

41. [*21*] Fig. 18 shows the construction of a tangled binary tree. List its leaves in left-to-right order.

42. [*23*] Explain why Subroutine C preserves the 2-descending condition (31).

43. [*20*] Explain how to implement phase 2 of the Garsia–Wachs algorithm efficiently.

▶ **44.** [*25*] Explain how to implement phase 3 of the Garsia–Wachs algorithm efficiently: Construct a binary tree, given the levels l_0, l_1, $\ldots$, l_n of its leaves in symmetric order.

▶ **45.** [*30*] Explain how to implement Subroutine C so that the total running time of the Garsia–Wachs algorithm is at most $O(n \log n)$.

46. [*M30*] (C. K. Wong and Shi-Kuo Chang.) Consider a scheme whereby a binary search tree is constructed by Algorithm T, except that whenever the number of nodes reaches a number of the form $2^n - 1$ the tree is reorganized into a perfectly balanced uniform tree, with 2^k nodes on level k for $0 \leq k < n$. Prove that the total number of comparisons made while constructing such a tree is $N \lg N + O(N)$ on the average. (It is not difficult to show that the amount of time needed for the reorganizations is $O(N)$.)

47. [*M40*] Generalize Theorems B and M from binary trees to t-ary trees. If possible, also allow the branching costs to be nonuniform as in exercise 33.

48. [*M47*] Carry out a rigorous analysis of the steady state of a binary search tree subjected to random insertions and deletions.

49. [*HM42*] Analyze the average height of a random binary search tree.

6.2.3. Balanced Trees

The tree insertion algorithm we have just learned will produce good search trees, when the input data is random, but there is still the annoying possibility that a degenerate tree will occur. Perhaps we could devise an algorithm that keeps the tree optimum at all times; but unfortunately that seems to be very difficult. Another idea is to keep track of the total path length, and to completely reorganize the tree whenever its path length exceeds $5N \lg N$, say. But such an approach might require about $\sqrt{N/2}$ reorganizations as the tree is being built.

A very pretty solution to the problem of maintaining a good search tree was discovered in 1962 by two Russian mathematicians, G. M. Adelson-Velsky and E. M. Landis [*Doklady Akademiiā Nauk SSSR* **146** (1962), 263–266; English translation in *Soviet Math.* **3**, 1259–1263]. Their method requires only two extra bits per node, and it never uses more than $O(\log N)$ operations to search the tree or to insert an item. In fact, we shall see that their approach also leads to a general technique that is good for representing arbitrary *linear lists* of length N, so that each of the following operations can be done in only $O(\log N)$ units of time:

i) Find an item having a given key.

ii) Find the kth item, given k.

iii) Insert an item at a specified place.

iv) Delete a specified item.

If we use sequential allocation for linear lists, operations (i) and (ii) are efficient but operations (iii) and (iv) take order N steps; on the other hand, if we use linked allocation, operations (iii) and (iv) are efficient but operations (i) and (ii) take order N steps. A tree representation of linear lists can do *all four* operations in $O(\log N)$ steps. And it is also possible to do other standard operations with comparable efficiency, so that, for example, we can concatenate a list of M elements with a list of N elements in $O\big(\log(M + N)\big)$ steps.

The method for achieving all this involves what we shall call *balanced trees*. (Many authors also call them *AVL trees*, where the AV stands for Adelson-Velsky and the L stands for Landis.) The preceding paragraph is an advertisement for balanced trees, which makes them sound like a universal panacea that makes all other forms of data representation obsolete; but of course we ought to have a balanced attitude about balanced trees! In applications that do not involve all four of the operations above, we may be able to get by with substantially less overhead and simpler programming. Furthermore, there is no advantage to balanced trees unless N is reasonably large; thus if we have an efficient method that takes $64 \lg N$ units of time and an inefficient method that takes $2N$ units of time, we should use the inefficient method unless N is greater than 256. On the other hand, N shouldn't be too large, either; balanced trees are appropriate chiefly for *internal* storage of data, and we shall study better methods for external direct-access files in Section 6.2.4. Since internal memories seem to be getting larger and larger as time goes by, balanced trees are becoming more and more important.

The *height* of a tree is defined to be its maximum level, the length of the longest path from the root to an external node. A binary tree is called *balanced* if the height of the left subtree of every node never differs by more than ±1 from the height of its right subtree. Figure 20 shows a balanced tree with 17 internal nodes and height 5; the *balance factor* within each node is shown as +, •, or − according as the right subtree height minus the left subtree height is +1, 0, or −1. The Fibonacci tree in Fig. 8 (Section 6.2.1) is another balanced binary tree of height 5, having only 12 internal nodes; most of the balance factors in that tree

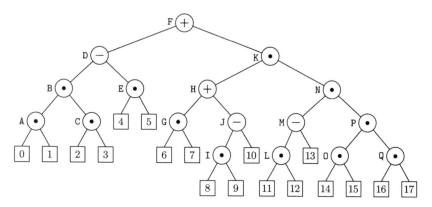

Fig. 20. A balanced binary tree.

are -1. The zodiac tree in Fig. 10 (Section 6.2.2) is *not* balanced, because the height restriction on subtrees fails at both the AQUARIUS and GEMINI nodes.

This definition of balance represents a compromise between *optimum* binary trees (with all external nodes required to be on two adjacent levels) and *arbitrary* binary trees (unrestricted). It is therefore natural to ask how far from optimum a balanced tree can be. The answer is that its search paths will never be more than 45 percent longer than the optimum:

Theorem A (Adelson-Velsky and Landis). *The height of a balanced tree with N internal nodes always lies between $\lg(N + 1)$ and $1.4404 \lg(N + 2) - 0.3277$.*

Proof. A binary tree of height h obviously cannot have more than 2^h external nodes; so $N + 1 \le 2^h$, that is, $h \ge \lceil \lg(N + 1) \rceil$ in any binary tree.

In order to find the maximum value of h, let us turn the problem around and ask for the minimum number of nodes possible in a balanced tree of height h. Let T_h be such a tree with fewest possible nodes; then one of the subtrees of the root, say the left subtree, has height $h - 1$, and the other subtree has height $h - 1$ or $h - 2$. Since we want T_h to have the minimum number of nodes, we may assume that the left subtree of the root is T_{h-1}, and that the right subtree is T_{h-2}. This argument shows that the *Fibonacci tree* of order $h + 1$ has the fewest possible nodes among all possible balanced trees of height h. (See the definition of Fibonacci trees in Section 6.2.1.) Thus

$$N \ge F_{h+2} - 1 > \phi^{h+2}/\sqrt{5} - 2,$$

and the stated result follows as in the corollary to Theorem 4.5.3F. ∎

The proof of this theorem shows that a search in a balanced tree will require more than 25 comparisons only if the tree contains at least $F_{28} - 1 = 317{,}810$ nodes.

Consider now what happens when a new node is inserted into a balanced tree using tree insertion (Algorithm 6.2.2T). In Fig. 20, the tree will still be balanced if the new node takes the place of $\boxed{4}$, $\boxed{5}$, $\boxed{6}$, $\boxed{7}$, $\boxed{10}$, or $\boxed{13}$, but some adjustment will be needed if the new node falls elsewhere. The problem arises when we have a node with a balance factor of $+1$ whose right subtree got higher after the insertion; or, dually, if the balance factor is -1 and the left subtree got higher. It is not difficult to see that trouble arises only in two cases:

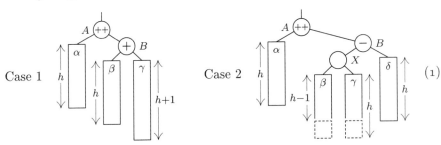

(Two other essentially identical cases occur if we reflect these diagrams, interchanging left and right.) In these diagrams the large rectangles α, β, γ, δ represent subtrees having the respective heights shown. Case 1 occurs when a new element has just increased the height of node B's right subtree from h to $h + 1$, and Case 2 occurs when the new element has increased the height of B's left subtree. In the second case, we have either $h = 0$ (so that X itself was the new node), or else node X has two subtrees of respective heights $(h-1, h)$ or $(h, h-1)$.

Simple transformations will restore balance in both of these cases, while preserving the symmetric order of the tree nodes:

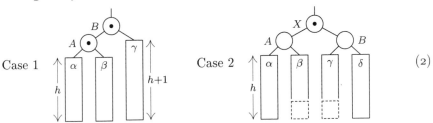

In Case 1 we simply "rotate" the tree to the left, attaching β to A instead of B. This transformation is like applying the associative law to an algebraic formula, replacing $\alpha(\beta\gamma)$ by $(\alpha\beta)\gamma$. In Case 2 we use a double rotation, first rotating (X, B) right, then (A, X) left. In both cases only a few links of the tree need to be changed. Furthermore, the new trees have height $h + 2$, which is exactly the height that was present before the insertion; hence the rest of the tree (if any) that was originally above node A always remains balanced.

For example, if we insert a new node into position $\boxed{17}$ of Fig. 20 we obtain the balanced tree shown in Fig. 21, after a single rotation (Case 1). Notice that several of the balance factors have changed.

The details of this insertion procedure can be worked out in several ways. At first glance an auxiliary stack seems to be necessary, in order to keep track of which nodes will be affected, but the following algorithm gains some speed by

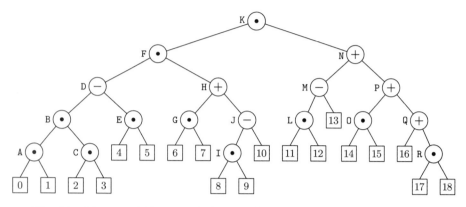

Fig. 21. The tree of Fig. 20, rebalanced after a new key R has been inserted.

exploiting the fact that the balance factor of node B in (1) was zero before the insertion.

Algorithm A (*Balanced tree search and insertion*). Given a table of records that form a balanced binary tree as described above, this algorithm searches for a given argument K. If K is not in the table, a new node containing K is inserted into the tree in the appropriate place and the tree is rebalanced if necessary.

The nodes of the tree are assumed to contain KEY, LLINK, and RLINK fields as in Algorithm 6.2.2T. We also have a new field

$$B(P) = \text{balance factor of NODE(P)},$$

the height of the right subtree minus the height of the left subtree; this field always contains either $+1$, 0, or -1. A special header node also appears at the top of the tree, in location HEAD; the value of RLINK(HEAD) is a pointer to the root of the tree, and LLINK(HEAD) is used to keep track of the overall height of the tree. (Knowledge of the height is not really necessary for this algorithm, but it is useful in the concatenation procedure discussed below.) We assume that the tree is *nonempty*, namely that RLINK(HEAD) $\neq \Lambda$.

For convenience in description, the algorithm uses the notation LINK(a,P) as a synonym for LLINK(P) if $a = -1$, and for RLINK(P) if $a = +1$.

A1. [Initialize.] Set T $\leftarrow$ HEAD, S $\leftarrow$ P $\leftarrow$ RLINK(HEAD). (The pointer variable P will move down the tree; S will point to the place where rebalancing may be necessary, and T always points to the parent of S.)

A2. [Compare.] If $K <$ KEY(P), go to A3; if $K >$ KEY(P), go to A4; and if $K =$ KEY(P), the search terminates successfully.

A3. [Move left.] Set Q $\leftarrow$ LLINK(P). If Q $= \Lambda$, set Q $\Leftarrow$ AVAIL and LLINK(P) $\leftarrow$ Q and go to step A5. Otherwise if B(Q) $\neq$ 0, set T $\leftarrow$ P and S $\leftarrow$ Q. Finally set P $\leftarrow$ Q and return to step A2.

A4. [Move right.] Set Q $\leftarrow$ RLINK(P). If Q $= \Lambda$, set Q $\Leftarrow$ AVAIL and RLINK(P) $\leftarrow$ Q and go to step A5. Otherwise if B(Q) $\neq$ 0, set T $\leftarrow$ P and S $\leftarrow$ Q. Finally set

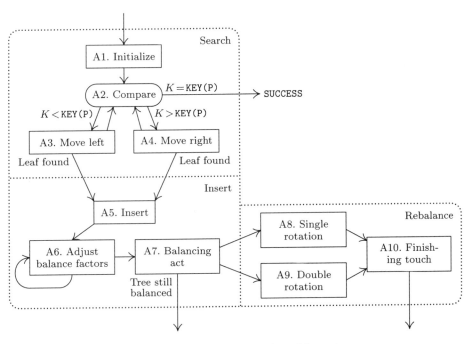

Fig. 22. Balanced tree search and insertion.

P ← Q and return to step A2. (The last part of this step may be combined with the last part of step A3.)

A5. [Insert.] (We have just linked a new node, NODE(Q), into the tree, and its fields need to be initialized.) Set KEY(Q) ← K, LLINK(Q) ← RLINK(Q) ← Λ, and B(Q) ← 0.

A6. [Adjust balance factors.] (Now the balance factors on nodes between S and Q need to be changed from zero to ±1.) If K < KEY(S) set a ← −1, otherwise set a ← +1. Then set R ← P ← LINK(a,S), and repeatedly do the following operations zero or more times until P = Q: If K < KEY(P) set B(P) ← −1 and P ← LLINK(P); if K > KEY(P), set B(P) ← +1 and P ← RLINK(P). (If K = KEY(P), then P = Q and we proceed to the next step.)

A7. [Balancing act.] Several cases now arise:
  i) If B(S) = 0 (the tree has grown higher), set B(S) ← a, LLINK(HEAD) ← LLINK(HEAD) + 1, and terminate the algorithm.
  ii) If B(S) = −a (the tree has gotten more balanced), set B(S) ← 0 and terminate the algorithm.
  iii) If B(S) = a (the tree has gotten out of balance), go to step A8 if B(R) = a, to A9 if B(R) = −a.
      (Case (iii) corresponds to the situations depicted in (1) when a = +1; S and R point, respectively, to nodes A and B, and LINK(−a,S) points to α, etc.)

A8. [Single rotation.] Set P ← R, LINK(a,S) ← LINK($-a$,R), LINK($-a$,R) ← S, B(S) ← B(R) ← 0. Go to A10.

A9. [Double rotation.] Set P ← LINK($-a$,R), LINK($-a$,R) ← LINK(a,P), LINK(a,P) ← R, LINK(a,S) ← LINK($-a$,P), LINK($-a$,P) ← S. Now set

$$(\text{B(S)}, \text{B(R)}) \leftarrow \begin{cases} (-a, 0), & \text{if } \text{B(P)} = a; \\ (0, 0), & \text{if } \text{B(P)} = 0; \\ (0, a), & \text{if } \text{B(P)} = -a; \end{cases} \tag{3}$$

and then set B(P) ← 0.

A10. [Finishing touch.] (We have completed the rebalancing transformation, taking (1) to (2), with P pointing to the new subtree root and T pointing to the parent of the old subtree root S.) If S = RLINK(T) then set RLINK(T) ← P, otherwise set LLINK(T) ← P. ∎

This algorithm is rather long, but it divides into three simple parts: Steps A1–A4 do the search, steps A5–A7 insert a new node, and steps A8–A10 rebalance the tree if necessary. Essentially the same method can be used if the tree is *threaded* (see exercise 6.2.2–2), since the balancing act never needs to make difficult changes to thread links.

We know that the algorithm takes about $C \log N$ units of time, for some C, but it is important to know the approximate value of C so that we can tell how large N should be in order to make balanced trees worth all the trouble. The following MIX implementation gives some insight into this question.

Program A (*Balanced tree search and insertion*). This program for Algorithm A uses tree nodes having the form

B	LLINK	RLINK
	KEY	

;   (4)

$rA \equiv K$, $rI1 \equiv P$, $rI2 \equiv Q$, $rI3 \equiv R$, $rI4 \equiv S$, $rI5 \equiv T$. The code for steps A7–A9 is duplicated so that the value of a appears implicitly (not explicitly) in the program.

```
01  B      EQU  0:1
02  LLINK  EQU  2:3
03  RLINK  EQU  4:5
04  START  LDA  K              1        A1. Initialize.
05         ENT5 HEAD           1        T ← HEAD.
06         LD2  0,5(RLINK)     1        Q ← RLINK(HEAD).
07         JMP  2F             1        To A2 with S ← P ← Q.
08  4H     LD2  0,1(RLINK)     C2       A4. Move right. Q ← RLINK(P).
09         J2Z  5F             C2       To A5 if Q = Λ.
10  1H     LDX  0,2(B)         C−1      rX ← B(Q).
11         JXZ  *+3            C−1      Jump if B(Q) = 0.
12         ENT5 0,1            D−1      T ← P.
```

13	2H	ENT4	0,2	D	S ← Q.
14		ENT1	0,2	C	P ← Q.
15		CMPA	1,1	C	*A2. Compare.*
16		JG	4B	C	To A4 if $K >$ KEY(P).
17		JE	SUCCESS	$C1$	Exit if $K =$ KEY(P).
18		LD2	0,1(LLINK)	$C1 - S$	*A3. Move left.* Q ← LLINK(P).
19		J2NZ	1B	$C1 - S$	Jump if Q ≠ Λ.
20	5H	LD2	AVAIL	$1 - S$	*A5. Insert.*
21		J2Z	OVERFLOW	$1 - S$	
22		LDX	0,2(RLINK)	$1 - S$	
23		STX	AVAIL	$1 - S$	Q ⇐ AVAIL.
24		STA	1,2	$1 - S$	KEY(Q) ← K.
25		STZ	0,2	$1 - S$	LLINK(Q) ← RLINK(Q) ← Λ.
26		JL	1F	$1 - S$	Was $K <$ KEY(P)?
27		ST2	0,1(RLINK)	A	RLINK(P) ← Q.
28		JMP	*+2	A	
29	1H	ST2	0,1(LLINK)	$1 - S - A$	LLINK(P) ← Q.
30	6H	CMPA	1,4	$1 - S$	*A6. Adjust balance factors.*
31		JL	*+3	$1 - S$	Jump if $K <$ KEY(S).
32		LD3	0,4(RLINK)	E	R ← RLINK(S).
33		JMP	*+2	E	
34		LD3	0,4(LLINK)	$1 - S - E$	R ← LLINK(S).
35		ENT1	0,3	$1 - S$	P ← R.
36		ENTX	-1	$1 - S$	rX ← −1.
37		JMP	1F	$1 - S$	To comparison loop.
38	4H	JE	7F	$F2 + 1 - S$	To A7 if $K =$ KEY(P).
39		STX	0,1(1:1)	$F2$	B(P) ← +1 (it was +0).
40		LD1	0,1(RLINK)	$F2$	P ← RLINK(P).
41	1H	CMPA	1,1	$F + 1 - S$	
42		JGE	4B	$F + 1 - S$	Jump if $K ≥$ KEY(P).
43		STX	0,1(B)	$F1$	B(P) ← −1.
44		LD1	0,1(LLINK)	$F1$	P ← LLINK(P).
45		JMP	1B	$F1$	To comparison loop.
46	7H	LD2	0,4(B)	$1 - S$	*A7. Balancing act.* rI2 ← B(S).
47		STZ	0,4(B)	$1 - S$	B(S) ← 0.
48		CMPA	1,4	$1 - S$	
49		JG	A7R	$1 - S$	To $a = +1$ routine if $K >$ KEY(S).
50	A7L	J2P	DONE	$U1$	Exit if rI2 = −a.
51		J2Z	7F	$G1 + J1$	Jump if B(S) was zero.
52		ENT1	0,3	$G1$	P ← R.
53		LD2	0,3(B)	$G1$	rI2 ← B(R).
54		J2N	A8L	$G1$	To A8 if rI2 = a.
55	A9L	LD1	0,3(RLINK)	$H1$	*A9. Double rotation.*
56		LDX	0,1(LLINK)	$H1$	LINK(a,P ← LINK(−a,R))
57		STX	0,3(RLINK)	$H1$	→ LINK(−a,R).
58		ST3	0,1(LLINK)	$H1$	LINK(a,P) ← R.
59		LD2	0,1(B)	$H1$	rI2 ← B(P).
60		LDX	T1,2	$H1$	−a, 0 or 0
61		STX	0,4(B)	$H1$	→ B(S).

62		LDX	T2,2	$H1$	0, 0, or a
63		STX	0,3(B)	$H1$	$\to$ B(R).
64	A8L	LDX	0,1(RLINK)	$G1$	*A8. Single rotation.*
65		STX	0,4(LLINK)	$G1$	LINK(a,S) $\leftarrow$ LINK($-a$,P).
66		ST4	0,1(RLINK)	$G1$	LINK($-a$,P) $\leftarrow$ S.
67		JMP	8F	$G1$	Join up with the other branch.
68	A7R	J2N	DONE	$U2$	Exit if rI2 $= -a$.
69		J2Z	6F	$G2 + J2$	Jump if B(S) was zero.
70		ENT1	0,3	$G2$	P $\leftarrow$ R.
71		LD2	0,3(B)	$G2$	rI2 $\leftarrow$ B(R).
72		J2P	A8R	$G2$	To A8 if rI2 $= a$.
73	A9R	LD1	0,3(LLINK)	$H2$	*A9. Double rotation.*
74		LDX	0,1(RLINK)	$H2$	LINK(a,P $\leftarrow$ LINK($-a$,R))
75		STX	0,3(LLINK)	$H2$	$\to$ LINK($-a$,R).
76		ST3	0,1(RLINK)	$H2$	LINK(a,P) $\leftarrow$ R.
77		LD2	0,1(B)	$H2$	rI2 $\leftarrow$ B(P).
78		LDX	T2,2	$H2$	$-a$, 0 or 0
79		STX	0,4(B)	$H2$	$\to$ B(S).
80		LDX	T1,2	$H2$	0, 0, or a
81		STX	0,3(B)	$H2$	$\to$ B(R).
82	A8R	LDX	0,1(LLINK)	$G2$	*A8. Single rotation.*
83		STX	0,4(RLINK)	$G2$	LINK(a,S) $\leftarrow$ LINK($-a$,P).
84		ST4	0,1(LLINK)	$G2$	LINK($-a$,P) $\leftarrow$ S.
85	8H	STZ	0,1(B)	G	B(P) $\leftarrow$ 0.
86	A10	CMP4	0,5(RLINK)	G	*A10. Finishing touch.*
87		JNE	*+3	G	Jump if RLINK(T) $\neq$ S.
88		ST1	0,5(RLINK)	$G3$	RLINK(T) $\leftarrow$ P.
89		JMP	DONE	$G3$	Exit.
90		ST1	0,5(LLINK)	$G4$	LLINK(T) $\leftarrow$ P.
91		JMP	DONE	$G4$	Exit.
92		CON	+1		
93	T1	CON	0		Table for (3).
94	T2	CON	0		
95		CON	-1		
96	6H	ENTX	+1	$J2$	rX $\leftarrow$ +1.
97	7H	STX	0,4(B)	J	B(S) $\leftarrow a$.
98		LDX	HEAD(LLINK)	J	LLINK(HEAD)
99		INCX	1	J	+ 1
100		STX	HEAD(LLINK)	J	$\to$ LLINK(HEAD).
101	DONE	EQU	*	$1 - S$	Insertion is complete. ∎

Analysis of balanced tree insertion. [Nonmathematical readers, please skip to (10).] In order to figure out the running time of Algorithm A, we would like to know the answers to the following questions:

- How many comparisons are made during the search?
- How far apart will nodes S and Q be? (In other words, how much adjustment is needed in step A6?)
- How often do we need to do a single or double rotation?

It is not difficult to derive upper bounds on the worst case running time, using Theorem A, but of course in practice we want to know the average behavior. No theoretical determination of the average behavior has been successfully completed as yet, since the algorithm appears to be quite complicated, but several interesting theoretical and empirical results have been obtained.

In the first place we can ask about the number B_{nh} of balanced binary trees with n internal nodes and height h. It is not difficult to compute the generating function $B_h(z) = \sum_{n \geq 0} B_{nh} z^n$ for small h, from the relations

$$B_0(z) = 1, \qquad B_1(z) = z, \qquad B_{h+1}(z) = zB_h(z)\big(B_h(z) + 2B_{h-1}(z)\big). \qquad (5)$$

(See exercise 6.) Thus

$$B_2(z) = 2z^2 + z^3,$$
$$B_3(z) = \qquad 4z^4 + 6z^5 + 4z^6 + z^7,$$
$$B_4(z) = \qquad\qquad\qquad 16z^7 + 32z^8 + 44z^9 + \cdots + 8z^{14} + z^{15},$$

and in general $B_h(z)$ has the form

$$2^{F_{h+1}-1} z^{F_{h+2}-1} + 2^{F_{h+1}-2} L_{h-1} z^{F_{h+2}} + \text{complicated terms} + 2^{h-1} z^{2^h-2} + z^{2^h-1} \tag{6}$$

for $h \geq 3$, where $L_k = F_{k+1} + F_{k-1}$. (This formula generalizes Theorem A.) The total number of balanced trees with height h is $B_h = B_h(1)$, which satisfies the recurrence

$$B_0 = B_1 = 1, \qquad B_{h+1} = B_h^2 + 2B_h B_{h-1}, \tag{7}$$

so that $B_2 = 3$, $B_3 = 3 \cdot 5$, $B_4 = 3^2 \cdot 5 \cdot 7$, $B_5 = 3^3 \cdot 5^2 \cdot 7 \cdot 23$; and, in general,

$$B_h = A_0^{F_h} A_1^{F_{h-1}} \cdots A_{h-1}^{F_1} A_h^{F_0}, \tag{8}$$

where $A_0 = 1$, $A_1 = 3$, $A_2 = 5$, $A_3 = 7$, $A_4 = 23$, $A_5 = 347$, $\ldots$, $A_h = A_{h-1} B_{h-2} + 2$. The sequences B_h and A_h grow very rapidly; in fact, they are *doubly exponential*: Exercise 7 shows that there is a real number $\theta \approx 1.43687$ such that

$$B_h = \lfloor \theta^{2^h} \rfloor - \lfloor \theta^{2^{h-1}} \rfloor + \lfloor \theta^{2^{h-2}} \rfloor - \cdots + (-1)^h \lfloor \theta^{2^0} \rfloor. \tag{9}$$

If we consider each of the B_h trees to be equally likely, exercise 8 shows that the average number of nodes in a tree of height h is

$$B_h'(1)/B_h(1) \approx (0.70118)2^h - 1. \tag{10}$$

This indicates that the height of a balanced tree with N nodes is usually much closer to $\log_2 N$ than to $\log_\phi N$.

Unfortunately, these results don't really have much to do with Algorithm A, since the mechanism of that algorithm makes some trees significantly more probable than others. For example, consider the case $N = 7$, where 17 balanced trees are possible. There are $7! = 5040$ possible orderings in which seven keys can be inserted, and the perfectly balanced "complete" tree

(11)

is obtained 2160 times. By contrast, the Fibonacci tree

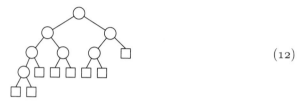

(12)

occurs only 144 times, and the similar tree

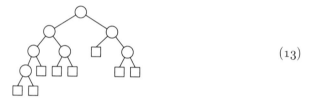

(13)

occurs 216 times. Replacing the left subtrees of (12) and (13) by arbitrary four-node balanced trees, and then reflecting left and right, yields 16 different trees; the eight generated from (12) each occur 144 times, and those generated from (13) each occur 216 times. It is surprising that (13) is more common than (12).

The fact that the perfectly balanced tree is obtained with such high probability — together with (10), which corresponds to the case of equal probabilities — makes it plausible that the average search time for a balanced tree should be about $\lg N + c$ comparisons for some small constant c. But R. W. Floyd has observed that the coefficient of $\lg N$ is unlikely to be exactly 1, because the root of the tree would then be near the median, and the roots of its two subtrees would be near the quartiles; then single and double rotation could not easily keep the root near the median. Empirical tests indicate that the true average number of comparisons needed to insert the Nth item is approximately $1.01 \lg N + 0.1$, except when N is small.

In order to study the behavior of the insertion and rebalancing phases of Algorithm A, we can classify the external nodes of balanced trees as shown in Fig. 23. The path leading up from an external node can be specified by a sequence of +'s and -'s (+ for a right link, - for a left link); we write down the link specifications until reaching the first node with a nonzero balance factor, or until reaching the root, if there is no such node. Then we write A or B according as the new tree will be balanced or unbalanced when an internal node is inserted in the given place. Thus the path up from ③ is ++-B, meaning "right link, right link, left link, unbalance." A specification ending in A requires

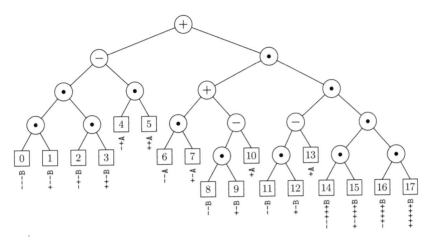

Fig. 23. Classification codes that specify the behavior of Algorithm A after insertion.

no rebalancing after insertion of a new node; a specification ending in ++B or --B requires a single rotation; and a specification ending in +-B or -+B requires a double rotation. When k links appear in the specification, step A6 has to adjust exactly $k-1$ balance factors. Thus the specifications give the essential facts that govern the running time of steps A6 to A10.

Empirical tests on random numbers for $100 \le N \le 2000$ gave the approximate probabilities shown in Table 1 for paths of various types; apparently these probabilities rapidly approach limiting values as $N \to \infty$. Table 2 gives the exact probabilities corresponding to Table 1 when $N = 10$, considering the 10! permutations of the input as equally probable. (The probabilities that show up as .143 in Table 1 are actually equal to 1/7, for all $N \ge 7$; see exercise 11. Single and double rotations are equally likely when $N \le 15$, but double rotations occur slightly less often when $N \ge 16$.)

Table 1

APPROXIMATE PROBABILITIES FOR INSERTING THE NTH ITEM

Path length k	No rebalancing	Single rotation	Double rotation
1	.143	.000	.000
2	.152	.143	.143
3	.092	.048	.048
4	.060	.024	.024
5	.036	.010	.010
> 5	.051	.009	.008
ave 2.78	total .534	.233	.232

From Table 1 we can see that k is ≤ 2 with probability about $.143 + .153 + .143 + .143 = .582$; thus, step A6 is quite simple almost 60 percent of the time. The average number of balance factors changed from 0 to ± 1 in that step is

Table 2
EXACT PROBABILITIES FOR INSERTING THE 10TH ITEM

Path length k	No rebalancing	Single rotation	Double rotation
1	1/7	0	0
2	6/35	1/7	1/7
3	4/21	2/35	2/35
4	0	1/21	1/21
ave 247/105	53/105	26/105	26/105

about 1.8. The average number of balanced factors changed from ± 1 to 0 in steps A7 through A10 is approximately $.534 + 2(.233 + .232) \approx 1.5$; thus, inserting one new node adds about $1.8 - 1.5 = 0.3$ unbalanced nodes, on the average. This agrees with the fact that about 68 percent of all nodes were found to be balanced in random trees built by Algorithm A.

An approximate model of the behavior of Algorithm A has been proposed by C. C. Foster [*Proc. ACM Nat. Conf.* **20** (1965), 192–205.] This model is not rigorously accurate, but it is close enough to the truth to give some insight. Let us assume that p is the probability that the balance factor of a given node in a large tree built by Algorithm A is 0; then the balance factor is $+1$ with probability $\frac{1}{2}(1 - p)$, and it is -1 with the same probability $\frac{1}{2}(1 - p)$. Let us assume further (without justification) that the balance factors of all nodes are independent. Then the probability that step A6 sets exactly $k-1$ balance factors nonzero is $p^{k-1}(1 - p)$, so the average value of k is $1/(1 - p)$. The probability that we need to rotate part of the tree is $q \approx \frac{1}{2}$. Inserting a new node should increase the number of balanced nodes by p, on the average; this number is actually increased by 1 in step A5, by $-p/(1 - p)$ in step A6, by q in step A7, and by $2q$ in step A8 or A9, so we should have

$$p = 1 - p/(1 - p) + 3q \approx 5/2 - p/(1 - p).$$

Solving for p yields fair agreement with Table 1:

$$p \approx \frac{9 - \sqrt{41}}{4} \approx 0.649; \qquad 1/(1 - p) \approx 2.851. \tag{14}$$

The running time of the search phase of Program A (lines 01–19) is

$$10C + C1 + 2D + 2 - 3S, \tag{15}$$

where C, $C1$, S are the same as in previous algorithms of this chapter and D is the number of unbalanced nodes encountered on the search path. Empirical tests show that we may take $D \approx \frac{1}{3}C$, $C1 \approx \frac{1}{2}(C + S)$, $C + S \approx 1.01 \lg N + 0.1$, so the average search time is approximately $11.3 \lg N + 3.3 - 13.7S$ units. (If searching is done much more often than insertion, we could of course use a separate, faster program for searching, since it would be unnecessary to look at the balance factors; the average running time for a successful search would then be only about $(6.6 \lg N - 3.4)u$, and the worst case running time would in fact be better than the average running time obtained with Program 6.2.2T.)

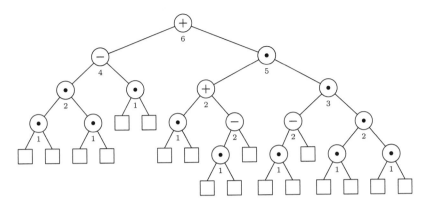

Fig. 24. RANK fields, used for searching by position.

The running time of the insertion phase of Program A (lines 20–45) is $8F + 26 + (0, 1, \text{ or } 2)$ units, when the search is unsuccessful. The data of Table 1 indicate that $F \approx 1.8$ on the average. The rebalancing phase (lines 46–101) takes either 16.5, 8, 27.5, or 45.5 (± 0.5) units, depending on whether we increase the total height, or simply exit without rebalancing, or do a single or double rotation. The first case almost never occurs, and the others occur with the approximate probabilities .534, .233, .232, so the average running time of the combined insertion-rebalancing portion of Program A is about $63u$.

These figures indicate that maintenance of a balanced tree in memory is reasonably fast, even though the program is rather lengthy. If the input data are random, the simple tree insertion algorithm of Section 5.2.2 is roughly $50u$ faster per insertion; but the balanced tree algorithm is guaranteed to be reliable even with nonrandom input data.

One way to compare Program A with Program 6.2.2T is to consider the worst case of the latter. If we study the amount of time necessary to insert N keys in increasing order into an initially empty tree, it turns out that Program A is slower for $N \leq 26$ and faster for $N \geq 27$.

Linear list representation. Now let us return to the claim made at the beginning of this section, that balanced trees can be used to represent linear lists in such a way that we can insert items rapidly (overcoming the difficulty of sequential allocation), yet we can also perform random accesses to list items (overcoming the difficulty of linked allocation).

The idea is to introduce a new field in each node, called the RANK field. The field indicates the relative position of that node in its subtree, namely one plus the number of nodes in its left subtree. Figure 24 shows the RANK values for the binary tree of Fig. 23. We can eliminate the KEY field entirely; or, if desired, we can have both KEY and RANK fields, so that it is possible to retrieve items either by their key value or by their relative position in the list.

Using such a RANK field, retrieval by position is a straightforward modifica-tion of the search algorithms we have been studying.

Algorithm B (*Tree search by position*). Given a linear list represented as a binary tree, this algorithm finds the kth element of the list (the kth node of the tree in symmetric order), given k. The binary tree is assumed to have LLINK and RLINK fields and a header as in Algorithm A, plus a RANK field as described above.

B1. [Initialize.] Set $M \leftarrow k$, $P \leftarrow$ RLINK(HEAD).

B2. [Compare.] If $P = \Lambda$, the algorithm terminates unsuccessfully. (This can happen only if k was greater than the number of nodes in the tree, or $k \leq 0$.) Otherwise if $M <$ RANK(P), go to B3; if $M >$ RANK(P), go to B4; and if $M =$ RANK(P), the algorithm terminates successfully (P points to the kth node).

B3. [Move left.] Set $P \leftarrow$ LLINK(P) and return to B2.

B4. [Move right.] Set $M \leftarrow M -$ RANK(P) and $P \leftarrow$ RLINK(P) and return to B2. ▮

The only new point of interest in this algorithm is the manipulation of M in step B4. We can modify the insertion procedure in a similar way, although the details are somewhat trickier:

Algorithm C (*Balanced tree insertion by position*). Given a linear list represented as a balanced binary tree, this algorithm inserts a new node just before the kth element of the list, given k and a pointer Q to the new node. If $k = N+1$, the new node is inserted just after the last element of the list.

The binary tree is assumed to be nonempty and to have LLINK, RLINK and B fields and a header, as in Algorithm A, plus a RANK field as described above. This algorithm is merely a transcription of Algorithm A; the difference is that it uses and updates the RANK fields instead of the KEY fields.

C1. [Initialize.] Set $T \leftarrow$ HEAD, $S \leftarrow P \leftarrow$ RLINK(HEAD), $U \leftarrow M \leftarrow k$.

C2. [Compare.] If $M \leq$ RANK(P), go to C3, otherwise go to C4.

C3. [Move left.] Set RANK(P) $\leftarrow$ RANK(P) $+ 1$ (we will be inserting a new node to the left of P). Set $R \leftarrow$ LLINK(P). If $R = \Lambda$, set LLINK(P) $\leftarrow$ Q and go to C5. Otherwise if B(R) $\neq 0$ set $T \leftarrow P$, $S \leftarrow R$, and $U \leftarrow M$. Finally set $P \leftarrow R$ and return to C2.

C4. [Move right.] Set $M \leftarrow M -$ RANK(P), and $R \leftarrow$ RLINK(P). If $R = \Lambda$, set RLINK(P) $\leftarrow$ Q and go to C5. Otherwise if B(R) $\neq 0$ set $T \leftarrow P$, $S \leftarrow R$, and $U \leftarrow M$. Finally set $P \leftarrow R$ and return to C2.

C5. [Insert.] Set RANK(Q) $\leftarrow 1$, LLINK(Q) $\leftarrow$ RLINK(Q) $\leftarrow \Lambda$, B(Q) $\leftarrow 0$.

C6. [Adjust balance factors.] Set $M \leftarrow U$. (This restores the former value of M when P was S; all RANK fields are now properly set.) If $M <$ RANK(S), set $R \leftarrow P \leftarrow$ LLINK(S) and $a \leftarrow -1$; otherwise set $R \leftarrow P \leftarrow$ RLINK(S), $a \leftarrow +1$, and $M \leftarrow M -$ RANK(S). Then repeatedly do the following operations until $P = Q$: If $M <$ RANK(P), set B(P) $\leftarrow -1$ and $P \leftarrow$ LLINK(P); if $M >$ RANK(P), set B(P) $\leftarrow +1$ and $M \leftarrow M -$ RANK(P) and $P \leftarrow$ RLINK(P). (If $M =$ RANK(P), then $P = Q$ and we proceed to the next step.)

C7. [Balancing act.] Several cases now arise.

i) If B(S) = 0, set B(S) ← a, LLINK(HEAD) ← LLINK(HEAD) + 1, and terminate the algorithm.

ii) If B(S) = $-a$, set B(S) ← 0 and terminate the algorithm.

iii) If B(S) = a, go to step C8 if B(R) = a, to C9 if B(R) = $-a$.

C8. [Single rotation.] Set P = R, LINK(a,S) ← LINK($-a$,R), LINK($-a$,R) ← S, B(S) ← B(R) ← 0. If $a = +1$, set RANK(R) ← RANK(R) + RANK(S); if $a = -1$, set RANK(S) ← RANK(S) − RANK(R). Go to C10.

C9. [Double rotation.] Do all the operations of step A9 (Algorithm A). Then if $a = +1$, set RANK(R) ← RANK(R) − RANK(P), RANK(P) ← RANK(P) + RANK(S); if $a = -1$, set RANK(P) ← RANK(P) + RANK(R), then RANK(S) ← RANK(S) − RANK(P).

C10. [Finishing touch.] If S = RLINK(T) then set RLINK(T) ← P, otherwise set LLINK(T) ← P. ∎

*Deletion, concatenation, etc. It is possible to do many other things to balanced trees and maintain the balance, but the algorithms are sufficiently lengthy that the details are beyond the scope of this book. We shall discuss the general ideas here, and an interested reader will be able to fill in the details without much difficulty.

The problem of deletion can be solved in $O(\log N)$ steps if we approach it correctly [C. C. Foster, "A Study of AVL Trees," Goodyear Aerospace Corp. report GER-12158 (April 1965)]. In the first place we can reduce deletion of an arbitrary node to the simple deletion of a node P for which LLINK(P) or RLINK(P) is Λ, as in Algorithm 6.2.2D. The algorithm should also be modified so that it constructs a list of pointers that specify the path to node P, namely

$$(P_0, a_0), \qquad (P_1, a_1), \qquad \ldots, \qquad (P_l, a_l), \qquad (16)$$

where $P_0 = $ HEAD, $a_0 = +1$; LINK(a_i, P_i) = P_{i+1}, for $0 \le i < l$; $P_l = $ P; and LINK(a_l, P_l) = Λ. This list can be placed on an auxiliary stack as we search down the tree. The process of deleting node P sets LINK(a_{l-1}, P_{l-1}) ← LINK($-a_l, P_l$), and we must adjust the balance factor at node P_{l-1}. Suppose that we need to adjust the balance factor at node P_k, because the a_k subtree of this node has just decreased in height; the following adjustment procedure should be used: If $k = 0$, set LLINK(HEAD) ← LLINK(HEAD) − 1 and terminate the algorithm, since the whole tree has decreased in height. Otherwise look at the balance factor B(P_k); there are three cases:

i) B(P_k) = a_k. Set B(P_k) ← 0, decrease k by 1, and repeat the adjustment procedure for this new value of k.

ii) B(P_k) = 0. Set B(P_k) to $-a_k$ and terminate the deletion algorithm.

iii) B(P_k) = $-a_k$. Rebalancing is required!

The situations that require rebalancing are almost the same as we met in the insertion algorithm; referring again to (1), A is node P_k, and B is the node LINK($-a_k, P_k$), on the *opposite* branch from where the deletion has occurred. The only new feature is that node B might be balanced; this leads to a new

Case 3, which is like Case 1 except that β has height $h + 1$. In Cases 1 and 2, rebalancing as in (2) means that we decrease the height, so we set LINK(a_{k-1}, P_{k-1}) to the root of (2), decrease k by 1, and restart the adjustment procedure for this new value of k. In Case 3 we do a single rotation, and this leaves the balance factors of both A and B nonzero without changing the overall height; after making LINK(a_{k-1}, P_{k-1}) point to node B, we therefore terminate the algorithm.

The important difference between deletion and insertion is that deletion might require up to $\log N$ rotations, while insertion never needs more than one. The reason for this becomes clear if we try to delete the rightmost node of a Fibonacci tree (see Fig. 8 in Section 6.2.1). But empirical tests show that only about 0.21 rotations per deletion are actually needed, on the average.

The use of balanced trees for linear list representation suggests also the need for a *concatenation* algorithm, where we want to insert an entire tree L_2 to the right of tree L_1, without destroying the balance. An elegant algorithm for concatenation was first devised by Clark A. Crane: Assume that height$(L_1) \geq$ height(L_2); the other case is similar. Delete the first node of L_2, calling it the *juncture node J*, and let L_2' be the new tree for $L_2 \setminus \{J\}$. Now go down the right links of L_1 until reaching a node P such that

$$\text{height}(P) - \text{height}(L_2') = 0 \text{ or } 1;$$

this is always possible, since the height changes by 1 or 2 each time we go down one level. Then replace $\widehat{P}$ by

and proceed to adjust L_1 as if the new node J had just been inserted by Algorithm A.

Crane also solved the more difficult inverse problem, to *split* a list into two parts whose concatenation would be the original list. Consider, for example, the problem of splitting the list in Fig. 20 to obtain two lists, one containing $\{\text{A}, \ldots, \text{I}\}$ and the other containing $\{\text{J}, \ldots, \text{Q}\}$; a major reassembly of the subtrees is required. In general, when we want to split a tree at some given node P, the path to P will be something like that in Fig. 25. We wish to construct a left tree that contains the nodes of $\alpha_1, P_1, \alpha_4, P_4, \alpha_6, P_6, \alpha_7, P_7, \alpha, P$ in symmetric order, and a right tree that contains $\beta, P_8, \beta_8, P_5, \beta_5, P_3, \beta_3, P_2, \beta_2$. This can be done by a sequence of concatenations: First insert P at the right of α, then concatenate β with β_8 using P_8 as juncture node, concatenate α_7 with αP using P_7 as juncture node, α_6 with $\alpha_7 P_7 \alpha P$ using P_6, $\beta P_8 \beta_8$ with β_5 using P_5, etc.; the nodes $P_8, P_7, \ldots, P_1$ on the path to P are used as juncture nodes. Crane proved that this splitting algorithm takes only $O(\log N)$ units of time, when the original tree contains N nodes; the essential reason is that concatenation using a given juncture node takes $O(k)$ steps, where k is the difference in heights between the

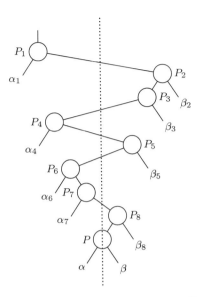

Fig. 25. The problem of splitting a list.

trees being concatenated, and the values of k that must be summed essentially form a telescoping series for both the left and right trees being constructed.

All of these algorithms can be used with either KEY or RANK fields or both (although in the case of concatenation the keys of L_2 must all be greater than the keys of L_1. For general purposes it is often preferable to use a *triply linked tree*, with UP links as well as LLINKs and RLINKs, together with a new one-bit field that specifies whether a node is the left or right child of its parent. The triply linked tree representation simplifies the algorithms slightly, and allows us to specify nodes in the tree without explicitly tracing the path to that node; we can write a subroutine to delete NODE(P), given P, or to delete the node that follows NODE(P) in symmetric order, or to find the list containing NODE(P), etc. In the deletion algorithm for triply linked trees it is unnecessary to construct the list (16), since the UP links provide the information we need. Of course, a triply linked tree requires us to change a few more links when insertions, deletions, and rotations are being performed. The use of a triply linked tree instead of a doubly linked tree is analogous to the use of two-way linking instead of one-way: We can start at any point and go either forward or backward. A complete description of list algorithms based on triply linked balanced trees appears in Clark A. Crane's Ph.D. thesis (Stanford University, 1972).

Alternatives to AVL trees. Many other ways have been proposed to organize trees so that logarithmic accessing time is guaranteed. For example, C. C. Foster [*CACM* **16** (1973), 513–517] considered the binary trees that arise when we allow the height difference of subtrees to be at most k. Such structures have been called HB(k) (meaning "height-balanced"), so that ordinary balanced trees represent the special case HB(1).

The interesting concept of *weight-balanced trees* has been studied by J. Nievergelt, E. Reingold, and C. K. Wong. Instead of considering the height of trees, they stipulate that the subtrees of all nodes must satisfy

$$\sqrt{2} - 1 < \frac{\text{left weight}}{\text{right weight}} < \sqrt{2} + 1, \qquad (17)$$

where the left and right weights count the number of *external* nodes in the left and right subtrees, respectively. It is possible to show that weight balance can be maintained under insertion, using only single and double rotations for rebalancing as in Algorithm A (see exercise 25). However, it may be necessary to do many rebalancings during a single insertion. It is possible to relax the conditions of (17), decreasing the amount of rebalancing at the expense of increased search time.

Weight-balanced trees may seem at first glance to require more memory than plain balanced trees, but in fact they sometimes require slightly less! If we already have a RANK field in each node, for the linear list representation, this is precisely the left weight, and it is possible to keep track of the corresponding right weights as we move down the tree. However, it appears that the bookkeeping required for maintaining weight balance takes more time than Algorithm A, and the elimination of two bits per node is probably not worth the trouble.

> *Why don't you pair 'em up in threes?*
> — attributed to YOGI BERRA (c. 1970)

Another interesting alternative to AVL trees, called "2-3 trees," was introduced by John Hopcroft in 1970 [see Aho, Hopcroft, and Ullman, *The Design and Analysis of Computer Algorithms* (Reading, Mass.: Addison–Wesley, 1974), Chapter 4]. The idea is to have either 2-way or 3-way branching at each node, and to stipulate that all external nodes appear on the same level. Every internal node contains either one or two keys, as shown in Fig. 26.

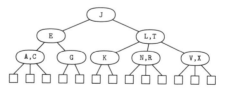

Fig. 26. A 2-3 tree.

Insertion into a 2-3 tree is somewhat easier to explain than insertion into an AVL tree: If we want to put a new key into a node that contains just one key, we simply insert it as the second key. On the other hand, if the node already contains two keys, we divide it into two one-key nodes, and insert the middle key into the parent node. This may cause the parent node to be divided in a similar way, if it already contains two keys. Figure 27 shows the process of inserting a new key into the 2-3 tree of Fig. 26.

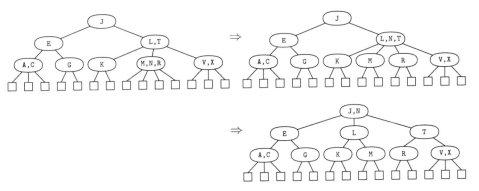

Fig. 27. Inserting the new key "M" into the 2-3 tree of Fig. 26.

Hopcroft observed that deletion, concatenation, and splitting can all be done with 2-3 trees, in a reasonably straightforward manner analogous to the corresponding operations with AVL trees.

R. Bayer [*Proc. ACM–SIGFIDET Workshop* (1971), 219–235] proposed an interesting binary tree representation for 2-3 trees. See Fig. 28, which shows the binary tree representation of Fig. 26; one bit in each node is used to distinguish "horizontal" RLINKs from "vertical" ones. Note that the keys of the tree appear from left to right in symmetric order, just as in any binary search tree. It turns out that the transformations we need to perform on such a binary tree, while inserting a new key as in Fig. 27, are precisely the single and double rotations used while inserting a new key into an AVL tree, although we need just one version of each rotation, not the left-right reflections needed by Algorithms A and C.

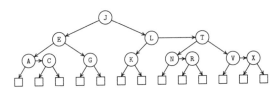

Fig. 28. The 2-3 tree of Fig. 26 represented as a binary search tree.

Elaboration of these ideas has led to many additional flavors of balanced trees, most notably the *red-black trees*, also called symmetric binary B-trees or half-balanced trees [R. Bayer, *Acta Informatica* **1** (1972), 290–306; L. Guibas and R. Sedgewick, *FOCS* **19** (1978), 8–21; H. J. Olivié, *RAIRO Informatique Théorique* **16** (1982), 51–71; R. E. Tarjan, *Inf. Proc. Letters* **16** (1983), 253–257; T. H. Cormen, C. E. Leiserson, and R. L. Rivest, *Introduction to Algorithms* (MIT Press, 1989), Chapter 14; R. Sedgewick, *Algorithms in C* (Addison–Wesley, 1997), §13.4]. There is also a strongly related family called hysterical B-trees or (a, b)-trees, notably $(2, 4)$-trees [D. Maier and S. C. Salveter, *Inf. Proc. Letters* **12** (1981), 199–202; S. Huddleston and K. Mehlhorn, *Acta Informatica* **17** (1982), 157–184].

When some keys are accessed much more frequently than others, we want the important ones to be relatively close to the root, as in the optimum binary search trees of Section 6.2.2. Dynamic trees that make it possible to maintain weighted balance within a constant factor of the optimum, called *biased trees*, have been developed by S. W. Bent, D. D. Sleator, and R. E. Tarjan, *SICOMP* **14** (1985), 545–568; J. Feigenbaum and R. E. Tarjan, *Bell System Tech. J.* **62** (1983), 3139–3158. The algorithms are, however, quite complicated.

A much simpler self-adjusting data structure called a *splay tree* was developed subsequently by D. D. Sleator and R. E. Tarjan [*JACM* **32** (1985), 652–686], based on ideas like the move-to-front and transposition heuristics discussed in Section 6.1; similar techniques had previously been explored by B. Allen and I. Munro [*JACM* **25** (1978), 526–535] and by J. Bitner [*SICOMP* **8** (1979), 82–110]. Splay trees, like the other kinds of balanced trees already mentioned, support the operations of concatenation and splitting as well as insertion and deletion, and in a particularly simple way. Moreover, the time needed to access data in a splay tree is known to be at most a small constant multiple of the access time of a statically optimum tree, when amortized over any series of operations. Indeed, Sleator and Tarjan conjectured that the total splay tree access time is at most a constant multiple of the optimum time to access data and to perform rotations dynamically by any binary tree algorithm whatsoever.

Randomization leads to methods that appear to be even simpler and faster than splay trees. Jean Vuillemin [*CACM* **23** (1980), 229–239] introduced *Cartesian trees*, in which every node has two keys (x, y). The x parts are ordered from left to right as in binary search trees; the y parts are ordered from top to bottom as in the priority queue trees of Section 5.2.3. C. R. Aragon and R. G. Seidel gave this data structure the more colorful name *treap*, because it neatly combines the notions of trees and heaps. Exactly one treap can be formed with n given key pairs $(x_1, y_1), \ldots, (x_n, y_n)$, if the x's and y's are distinct. One way to obtain it is to insert the x's by Algorithm 6.2.2T according to the order of the y's; but there is also a simple algorithm that inserts any new key pair directly into any treap. Aragon and Seidel observed [*FOCS* **30** (1989), 540–546] that if the x's are ordinary keys while the y's are chosen at random, we can be sure that the treap has the shape of a random binary search tree. In particular, a treap with random y values will always be reasonably well balanced, except with exponentially small probability (see exercise 5.2.2–42). Aragon and Seidel also showed that treaps can readily be biased so that, for example, a key x with relative frequency f will appear suitably near the root when it is associated with $y = U^{1/f}$, where U is a random number between 0 and 1. Treaps performed consistently better than splay trees in some experiments conducted by D. E. Knuth relating to the calculation of convex hulls [*Lecture Notes in Comp. Sci.* **606** (1992), 53–55].

A new Section 6.2.5 devoted to randomized data structures is planned for the next edition of the present book. It will discuss "skip lists" [W. Pugh, *CACM* **33** (1990), 668–676] and "randomized binary search trees" [S. Roura and C. Martínez, *Lecture Notes in Comp. Sci.* **1136** (1996), 91–106] as well as treaps.

EXERCISES

1. [*01*] In Case 2 of (1), why isn't it a good idea to restore the balance by simply interchanging the left subtrees of A and B?

2. [*16*] Explain why the tree has gotten one level higher if we reach step A7 with B(S) = 0.

▶ **3.** [*M25*] Prove that a balanced tree with N internal nodes never contains more than $(\phi - 1)N \approx 0.61803N$ nodes whose balance factor is nonzero.

4. [*M22*] Prove or disprove: Among all balanced trees with $F_{h+1} - 1$ internal nodes, the Fibonacci tree of order h has the greatest internal path length.

▶ **5.** [*M25*] Prove or disprove: If Algorithm A is used to insert the keys $K_2, \ldots, K_N$ successively in increasing order into a tree that initially contains only the single key K_1, where $K_1 < K_2 < \cdots < K_N$, then the tree produced is always *optimum* (that is, it has minimum internal path length over all N-node binary trees).

6. [*M21*] Prove that Eq. (5) defines the generating function for balanced trees of height h.

7. [*M27*] (N. J. A. Sloane and A. V. Aho.) Prove the remarkable formula (9) for the number of balanced trees of height h. [*Hint:* Let $C_n = B_n + B_{n-1}$, and use the fact that $\log(C_{n+1}/C_n^2)$ is exceedingly small for large n.]

8. [*M24*] (L. A. Khizder.) Show that there is a constant β such that $B'_h(1)/B_h(1) = 2^h \beta - 1 + O(2^h/B_{h-1})$ as $h \to \infty$.

9. [*HM44*] What is the asymptotic number of balanced binary trees with n internal nodes, $\sum_{h\geq 0} B_{nh}$? What is the asymptotic average height, $\sum_{h\geq 0} h B_{nh} / \sum_{h\geq 0} B_{nh}$?

▶ **10.** [*27*] (R. C. Richards.) Show that the shape of a balanced tree can be constructed uniquely from the list of its balance factors B(1)B(2)...B(N) in symmetric order.

11. [*M24*] (Mark R. Brown.) Prove that when $n \geq 6$ the average number of external nodes of each of the types +A, −A, ++B, +−B, −+B, −−B is exactly $(n+1)/14$, in a random balanced tree of n internal nodes constructed by Algorithm A.

▶ **12.** [*24*] What is the maximum possible running time of Program A when the eighth node is inserted into a balanced tree? What is the minimum possible running time for this insertion?

13. [*05*] Why is it better to use RANK fields as defined in the text, instead of simply to store the index of each node as its key (calling the first node "1", the second node "2", and so on)?

14. [*11*] Could Algorithms 6.2.2T and 6.2.2D be adapted to work with linear lists, using a RANK field, just as the balanced tree algorithms of this section have been so adapted?

15. [*18*] (C. A. Crane.) Suppose that an ordered linear list is being represented as a binary tree, with both KEY and RANK fields in each node. Design an algorithm that searches the tree for a given key, K, and determines the position of K in the list; that is, it finds the number m such that K is the mth smallest key.

▶ **16.** [*20*] Draw the balanced tree that is obtained after node E and the root node F are deleted from Fig. 20, using the deletion algorithm suggested in the text.

▶ **17.** [*21*] Draw the balanced trees that are obtained after the Fibonacci tree (12) is concatenated (a) to the right, (b) to the left, of the tree in Fig. 20, using the concatenation algorithm suggested in the text.

18. [*22*] Draw the balanced trees that are obtained after Fig. 20 is split into two parts {A, ..., I} and {J, ..., Q}, using the splitting algorithm suggested in the text.

▸ **19.** [*26*] Find a way to transform a given balanced tree so that the balance factor at the root is not −1. Your transformation should preserve the symmetric order of the nodes; and it should produce another balanced tree in $O(1)$ units of time, regardless of the size of the original tree.

20. [*40*] Explore the idea of using the restricted class of balanced trees whose nodes all have balance factors of 0 or +1. (Then the length of the B field can be reduced to one bit.) Is there a reasonably efficient insertion procedure for such trees?

▸ **21.** [*30*] (*Perfect balancing.*) Design an algorithm to construct N-node binary trees that are optimum in the sense of exercise 5. Your algorithm should use $O(N)$ steps and it should be "online," in the sense that it inputs the nodes one by one in increasing order and builds partial trees as it goes, without knowing the final value of N in advance. (It would be appropriate to use such an algorithm when restructuring a badly balanced tree, or when merging the keys of two trees into a single tree.)

22. [*M20*] What is the analog of Theorem A, for weight-balanced trees?

23. [*M20*] (E. Reingold.)   Demonstrate that there is no simple relation between height-balanced trees and weight-balanced trees:

a) Prove that there exist height-balanced trees that have an arbitrarily small ratio (left weight)/(right weight) in the sense of (17).

b) Prove that there exist weight-balanced trees that have an arbitrarily large difference between left and right subtree heights.

24. [*M22*] (E. Reingold.) Prove that if we strengthen condition (17) to

$$\frac{1}{2} < \frac{\text{left weight}}{\text{right weight}} < 2,$$

the only binary trees that satisfy this condition are perfectly balanced trees with $2^n - 1$ internal nodes. (In such trees, the left and right weights are exactly equal at all nodes.)

25. [*27*] (J. Nievergelt, E. Reingold, C. Wong.) Show that it is possible to design an insertion algorithm for weight-balanced trees so that condition (17) is preserved, making at most $O(\log N)$ rotations per insertion.

26. [*40*] Explore the properties of balanced t-ary trees, for $t > 2$.

▸ **27.** [*M23*] Estimate the maximum number of comparisons needed to search in a 2-3 tree with N internal nodes.

28. [*41*] Prepare efficient implementations of 2-3 tree algorithms.

29. [*M47*] Analyze the average behavior of 2-3 trees under random insertions.

30. [*26*] (E. McCreight.) Section 2.5 discusses several strategies for dynamic storage allocation, including best-fit (choosing an available area as small as possible from among all those that fulfill the request) and first-fit (choosing the available area with lowest address among all those that fulfill the request). Show that if the available space is linked together as a balanced tree in an appropriate way, it is possible to do (a) best-fit (b) first-fit allocation in only $O(\log n)$ units of time, where n is the number of available areas. (The algorithms given for those methods in Section 2.5 take order n steps.)

31. [*34*] (M. L. Fredman, 1975.)   Invent a representation of linear lists with the property that insertion of a new item between positions $m - 1$ and m, given m, takes $O(\log m)$ units of time.

32. [*M27*] Given two n-node binary trees, T and T', let us say that $T \preceq T'$ if T' can be obtained from T by a sequence of zero or more rotations to the right. Prove that $T \preceq T'$ if and only if $r_k \leq r'_k$ for $1 \leq k \leq n$, where r_k and r'_k denote the respective sizes of the right subtrees of the kth nodes of T and T' in symmetric order.

▶ **33.** [*25*] (A. L. Buchsbaum.) Explain how to encode the balance factors of an AVL tree implicitly, thus saving two bits per node, at the expense of additional work when the tree is accessed.

> Samuel considered the nation of Israel, tribe by tribe,
> and the tribe of Benjamin was picked by lot.
> Then he considered the tribe of Benjamin, family by family,
> and the family of Matri was picked by lot.
> Then he considered the family of Matri, man by man,
> and Saul son of Kish was picked by lot.
> But when they looked for Saul he could not be found.
> — 1 Samuel 10:20–21

6.2.4. Multiway Trees

The tree search methods we have been discussing were developed primarily for *internal searching*, when we want to look at a table that is contained entirely within a computer's high-speed internal memory. Let's now consider the problem of *external* searching, when we want to retrieve information from a very large file that appears on direct access storage units such as disks or drums. (An introduction to disks and drums appears in Section 5.4.9.)

Tree structures lend themselves nicely to external searching, if we choose an appropriate way to represent the tree. Consider the large binary search tree shown in Fig. 29, and imagine that it has been stored in a disk file. (The LLINKs and RLINKs of the tree are now disk addresses instead of internal memory addresses.) If we search this tree in a naïve manner, simply applying the algorithms we have learned for internal tree searching, we will have to make about $\lg N$ disk accesses before our search is complete. When N is a million, this means we will need 20 or so seeks. But suppose we divide the table into 7-node "pages," as shown by the dotted lines in Fig. 29; if we access one page at a time, we need only about one third as many seeks, so the search goes about three times as fast!

Grouping the nodes into pages in this way essentially changes the tree from a binary tree to an octonary tree, with 8-way branching at each page-node. If we let the pages be still larger, with 128-way branching after each disk access, we can find any desired key in a million-entry table after looking at only three pages. We can keep the root page in the internal memory at all times, so that only two references to the disk are required even though the internal memory never needs to hold more than 254 keys at any time.

Of course we don't want to make the pages arbitrarily large, since the internal memory size is limited and also since it takes a long time to read a large page. For example, suppose that it takes $72.5 + 0.05m$ milliseconds to read a page that allows m-way branching. The internal processing time per page will

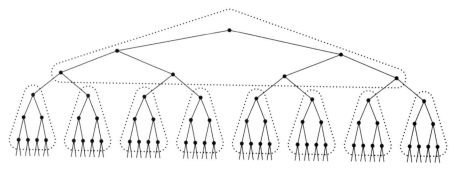

Fig. 29. A large binary search tree can be divided into "pages."

be about $a + b \lg m$, where a is small compared to 72.5 ms, so the total amount of time needed for searching a large table is approximately proportional to $\lg N$ times

$$(72.5 + 0.05m)/\lg m + b.$$

This quantity achieves a minimum when $m \approx 307$; actually the minimum is very "broad" — a nearly optimum value is achieved for all m between 200 and 500. In practice there will be a similar range of good values for m, based on the characteristics of particular external memory devices and on the length of the records in the table.

W. I. Landauer [*IEEE Trans.* **EC-12** (1963), 863–871] suggested building an m-ary tree by requiring level l to become nearly full before anything is allowed to appear on level $l + 1$. This scheme requires a rather complicated rotation method, since we may have to make major changes throughout the tree just to insert a single new item; Landauer was assuming that we need to search for items in the tree much more often than we need to insert or delete them.

When a file is stored on disk, and is subject to comparatively few insertions and deletions, a three-level tree is appropriate, where the first level of branching determines what cylinder is to be used, the second level of branching determines the appropriate track on that cylinder, and the third level contains the records themselves. This method is called *indexed-sequential* file organization [see *JACM* **16** (1969), 569–571].

R. Muntz and R. Uzgalis [*Proc. Princeton Conf. on Inf. Sciences and Systems* **4** (1970), 345–349] suggested modifying the tree search and insertion method, Algorithm 6.2.2T, so that all insertions go onto nodes belonging to the same page as their parent node, whenever possible; if that page is full, a new page is started, whenever possible. If the number of pages is unlimited, and if the data arrives in random order, it can be shown that the average number of page accesses is approximately $H_N/(H_m - 1)$, only slightly more than we would obtain in the best possible m-ary tree. (See exercise 8.)

B-trees. A new approach to external searching by means of multiway tree branching was discovered in 1970 by R. Bayer and E. McCreight [*Acta Informa-*

tica **1** (1972), 173–189], and independently at about the same time by M. Kauf-
man [unpublished]. Their idea, based on a versatile new kind of data structure
called a *B-tree*, makes it possible both to search and to update a large file with
guaranteed efficiency, in the worst case, using comparatively simple algorithms.

A *B-tree of order m* is a tree that satisfies the following properties:

i) Every node has at most m children.

ii) Every node, except for the root and the leaves, has at least $m/2$ children.

iii) The root has at least 2 children (unless it is a leaf).

iv) All leaves appear on the same level, and carry no information.

v) A nonleaf node with k children contains $k - 1$ keys.

(As usual, a "leaf" is a terminal node, one with no children. Since the leaves
carry no information, we may regard them as external nodes that aren't really
in the tree, so that Λ is a pointer to a leaf.)

Figure 30 shows a *B*-tree of order 7. Each node (except for the root and the
leaves) has between $\lceil 7/2 \rceil$ and 7 children, so it contains 3, 4, 5, or 6 keys. The
root node is allowed to contain from 1 to 6 keys; in this case it has 2. All of the
leaves are at level 3. Notice that (a) the keys appear in increasing order from
left to right, using a natural extension of the concept of symmetric order; and
(b) the number of leaves is exactly one greater than the number of keys.

B-trees of order 1 or 2 are obviously uninteresting, so we will consider only
the case $m \geq 3$. The 2-3 trees defined at the close of Section 6.2.3 are equivalent
to *B*-trees of order 3. (Bayer and McCreight considered only the case that m is
odd; some authors consider a *B*-tree of order m to be what we are calling a
B-tree of order $2m + 1$.)

A node that contains j keys and $j + 1$ pointers can be represented as

$$\mathsf{P}_0, K_1, \mathsf{P}_1, K_2, \mathsf{P}_2, \ldots, \mathsf{P}_{j-1}, K_j, \mathsf{P}_j \qquad (1)$$

where $K_1 < K_2 < \cdots < K_j$ and P_i points to the subtree for keys between
K_i and K_{i+1}. Therefore searching in a *B*-tree is quite straightforward: After
node (1) has been fetched into the internal memory, we search for the given
argument among the keys $K_1, K_2, \ldots, K_j$. (When j is large, we probably do a
binary search; but when j is smallish, a sequential search is best.) If the search
is successful, we have found the desired key; but if the search is unsuccessful
because the argument lies between K_i and K_{i+1}, we fetch the node indicated
by P_i and continue the process. The pointer P_0 is used if the argument is less
than K_1, and P_j is used if the argument is greater than K_j. If $\mathsf{P}_i = \Lambda$, the search
is unsuccessful.

The nice thing about *B*-trees is that insertion is also quite simple. Consider
Fig. 30, for example; every leaf corresponds to a place where a new insertion
might happen. If we want to insert the new key 337, we simply change the

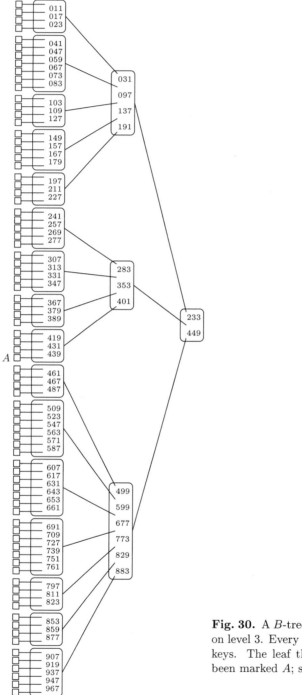

Fig. 30. A B-tree of order 7, with all leaves on level 3. Every node contains 3, 4, 5, or 6 keys. The leaf that precedes key 449 has been marked A; see (8).

appropriate node from

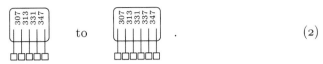

to   .   (2)

On the other hand, if we want to insert the new key 071, there is no room since the corresponding node on level 2 is already "full." This case can be handled by splitting the node into two parts, with three keys in each part, and passing the middle key up to level 1:

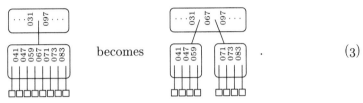

becomes   .   (3)

   In general, if we want to insert a new item into a B-tree of order m, when all the leaves are at level l, we insert the new key into the appropriate node on level $l - 1$. If that node now contains m keys, so that it has the form (1) with $j = m$, we split it into two nodes

$$\left(P_0, K_1, P_1, \ldots, K_{\lceil m/2 \rceil - 1}, P_{\lceil m/2 \rceil - 1} \right) \xleftarrow{\quad P\quad} \xrightarrow{\quad P'\quad} \left(P_{\lceil m/2 \rceil}, K_{\lceil m/2 \rceil + 1}, P_{\lceil m/2 \rceil + 1}, \ldots, K_m, P_m \right) \quad (4)$$

and insert the key $K_{\lceil m/2 \rceil}$ into the parent of the original node. (Thus the pointer P in the parent node is replaced by the sequence P, $K_{\lceil m/2 \rceil}$, P'.) This insertion may cause the parent node to contain m keys, and if so, it should be split in the same way. (Fig. 27 in the previous section illustrates the case $m = 3$.) If we need to split the root node, which has no parent, we simply create a new root node containing the single key $K_{\lceil m/2 \rceil}$; the tree gets one level taller in this case.

   This insertion procedure neatly preserves all of the B-tree properties; in order to appreciate the full beauty of the idea, the reader should work exercise 1. The tree essentially grows up from the top, instead of down from the bottom, since it gains in height only when the root splits.

   Deletion from B-trees is only slightly more complicated than insertion (see exercise 6).

Upper bounds on the running time. Let us now see how many nodes have to be accessed in the worst case, while searching in a B-tree of order m. Suppose that there are N keys, and that the $N + 1$ leaves appear on level l. Then the number of nodes on levels $1, 2, 3, \ldots$ is at least $2, 2\lceil m/2 \rceil, 2\lceil m/2 \rceil^2, \ldots$; hence

$$N + 1 \geq 2\lceil m/2 \rceil^{l-1}. \tag{5}$$

In other words,

$$l \leq 1 + \log_{\lceil m/2 \rceil}\left(\frac{N+1}{2}\right); \tag{6}$$

this means, for example, that if $N = 1{,}999{,}998$ and $m = 199$, then l is at most 3. Since we need to access at most l nodes during a search, this formula guarantees that the running time is quite small.

When a new key is being inserted, we may have to split as many as l nodes. However, the average number of nodes that need to be split is much less, since the total number of splittings that occur while the entire tree is being constructed is just the total number of internal nodes in the tree, minus l. If there are p internal nodes, there are at least $1 + (\lceil m/2 \rceil - 1)(p - 1)$ keys; hence

$$p \le 1 + \frac{N - 1}{\lceil m/2 \rceil - 1}. \tag{7}$$

It follows that the average number of times we need to split a node while building a tree of N keys is less than $1/(\lceil m/2 \rceil - 1)$ split per insertion.

Refinements and variations. There are several ways to improve upon the basic B-tree structure defined above, by breaking the rules a little.

In the first place, we note that all of the pointers in the level $l - 1$ nodes are Λ, and none of the pointers in the other levels are Λ. This often represents a significant amount of wasted space, so we can save both time and space by eliminating all the Λ's and using a different value of m for all of the "bottom" nodes. This use of two different m's does not foul up the insertion algorithm, since both halves of a node that is being split remain on the same level as the original node. We could in fact define a generalized B-tree of orders $m_1, m_2, m_3, \ldots$ by requiring all nonroot nodes on level $l - k$ to have between $m_k/2$ and m_k children; such a B-tree has different m's on each level, yet the insertion algorithm still works essentially as before.

To carry the idea in the preceding paragraph even further, we might use a completely different node format in each level of the tree, and we might also store information in the leaves. Sometimes the keys form only a small part of the records in a file, and in such cases it is a mistake to store the entire records in the branch nodes near the root of the tree; this would make m too small for efficient multiway branching.

We can therefore reconsider Fig. 30, imagining that all the records of the file are now stored in the leaves, and that only a few of the keys have been duplicated in the branch nodes. Under this interpretation, the leftmost leaf contains all records whose key is ≤ 011; the leaf marked A contains all records whose key satisfies

$$439 < K \le 449; \tag{8}$$

and so on. Under this interpretation the leaf nodes grow and split just as the branch nodes do, except that a record is never passed up from a leaf to the next level. Thus the leaves are always at least half filled to capacity. A new key enters the nonleaf part of the tree whenever a leaf splits. If each leaf is linked to its successor in symmetric order, we gain the ability to traverse the file both sequentially and randomly in an efficient and convenient manner. This variant has become known as a B^+-tree.

Some calculations by S. P. Ghosh and M. E. Senko [*JACM* **16** (1969), 569–579] suggest that it might be a good idea to make the leaves fairly large, say up to about 10 consecutive pages long. By linear interpolation in the known range of keys for each leaf, we can guess which of the 10 pages probably contains a given search argument. If our guess is wrong, we lose time, but experiments indicate that this loss might be less than the time we save by decreasing the size of the tree.

T. H. Martin [unpublished] has pointed out that the idea underlying B-trees can be used also for *variable-length* keys. We need not put bounds $[m/2 .. m]$ on the number of children of each node; instead we can say merely that each node should be at least about half full of data. The insertion and splitting mechanism still works fine, even though the exact number of keys per node depends on whether the keys are long or short. However, the keys shouldn't be allowed to get extremely long, or they can mess things up. (See exercise 5.)

Another important modification to the basic B-tree scheme is the idea of *overflow* introduced by Bayer and McCreight. The idea is to improve the insertion algorithm by resisting its temptation to split nodes so often; a local rotation is used instead. Suppose we have a node that is over-full because it contain m keys and $m+1$ pointers; instead of splitting it, we can look first at its sibling node on the right, which has say j keys and $j+1$ pointers. In the parent node there is a key $\overline{K}_f$ that separates the keys of the two siblings; schematically,

$$
\begin{array}{c}
\overbrace{\cdots\; \overline{K}_f \;\cdots} \\[2pt]
P\swarrow \qquad \searrow P' \\[2pt]
\boxed{K_1 \;\cdots\; K_m} \quad \boxed{K'_1 \;\cdots\; K'_j} \\[2pt]
P_0\; P_1 \;\; P_m \qquad P'_0\; P'_1 \;\; P'_j
\end{array}
\tag{9}
$$

If $j < m - 1$, a simple rearrangement makes splitting unnecessary: We leave $\lfloor (m + j)/2 \rfloor$ keys in the left node, we replace $\overline{K}_f$ by $K_{\lfloor (m+j)/2 \rfloor +1}$ in the parent node, and we put the $\lceil (m + j)/2 \rceil$ remaining keys (including $\overline{K}_f$) and the corresponding pointers into the right node. Thus the full node "flows over" into its sibling node. On the other hand, if the sibling node is already full ($j = m-1$), we can split *both* of the nodes, making three nodes each about two-thirds full, containing, respectively, $\lfloor (2m - 2)/3 \rfloor$, $\lfloor (2m - 1)/3 \rfloor$, and $\lfloor 2m/3 \rfloor$ keys:

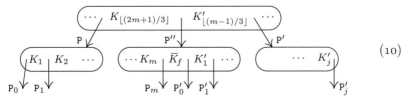

$$\tag{10}$$

If the original node has no right sibling, we can look at its left sibling in essentially the same way. (If the original node has both a right and a left sibling, we could even refrain from splitting off a new node unless *both* left and right siblings are full.) Finally if the original node to be split has no siblings at all, it must be the root; we can change the definition of B-tree, allowing the root to contain as many as $2\lfloor(2m-2)/3\rfloor$ keys, so that when the root splits it produces two nodes of $\lfloor(2m-2)/3\rfloor$ keys each.

The effect of all the technicalities in the preceding paragraph is to produce a superior breed of tree, say a B^*-tree of order m, which can be defined as follows:

i) Every node except the root has at most m children.

ii) Every node, except for the root and the leaves, has at least $(2m-1)/3$ children.

iii) The root has at least 2 and at most $2\lfloor(2m-2)/3\rfloor+1$ children.

iv) All leaves appear on the same level.

v) A nonleaf node with k children contains $k-1$ keys.

The important change is condition (ii), which asserts that we utilize at least two-thirds of the available space in every node. This change not only uses space more efficiently, it also makes the search process faster, since we may replace $\lceil m/2\rceil$ by $\lceil(2m-1)/3\rceil$ in (6) and (7). However, the insertion process gets slower, because nodes tend to need more attention as they fill up; see B. Zhang and M. Hsu, *Acta Informatica* **26** (1989), 421–438, for an approximate analysis of the tradeoffs involved.

At the other extreme, it is sometimes better to let nodes become less than half full in a tree that changes quite frequently, especially if insertions tend to outnumber deletions. This situation has been analyzed by T. Johnson and D. Shasha, *J. Comput. Syst. Sci.* **47** (1993), 45–76.

Perhaps the reader has been skeptical of B-trees because the degree of the root can be as low as 2. Why should we waste a whole disk access on merely a 2-way decision?! A simple buffering scheme, called *least-recently-used page replacement*, overcomes this objection; we can keep several bufferloads of information in the internal memory, so that input commands can be avoided when the corresponding page is already present. Under this scheme, the algorithms for searching or insertion issue "virtual read" commands that are translated into actual input instructions only when the necessary page is not in memory; a subsequent "release" command is issued when the buffer has been read and possibly modified by the algorithm. When an actual read is required, the buffer that has least recently been released is chosen; we write out that buffer, if its contents have changed since they were read in, then we read the desired page into the chosen buffer.

Since the number of levels in the tree is generally small compared to the number of buffers, this paging scheme will ensure that the root page is always present in memory; and if the root has only 2 or 3 children, the first-level pages will almost surely stay there too. Any pages that might need to be split during an insertion are automatically present in memory when they are needed, because they will be remembered from the immediately preceding search.

Experiments by E. McCreight have shown that this policy is quite successful. For example, he found that with 10 buffers and $m = 121$, the process of inserting

100,000 keys in ascending order required only 22 actual read commands, and only 857 actual write commands; thus most of the activity took place in the internal memory. Furthermore the tree contained only 835 nodes, just one higher than the minimum possible value $\lceil 100000/(m-1) \rceil = 834$; thus the storage utilization was nearly 100 percent. For this experiment he used the overflow technique, but with only 2-way node splitting as in (4), not 3-way splitting as in (10). (See exercise 3.)

In another experiment, again with 10 buffers and $m = 121$ and the overflow technique, he inserted 5000 keys into an initially empty tree, in *random* order; this produced a 2-level tree with 48 nodes (87 percent storage utilization), after making 2762 actual reads and 2739 actual writes. Then 1000 random searches required 786 actual reads. The same experiment *without* the overflow feature produced a 2-level tree with 62 nodes (67 percent storage utilization), after making 2743 actual reads and 2800 actual writes; 1000 subsequent random searches required 836 actual reads. This shows not only that the paging scheme is effective but also that it is wise to handle overflows locally before deciding to split a node.

Andrew Yao has proved that the average number of nodes after random insertions without the overflow feature will be

$$N/(m \ln 2) + O(N/m^2),$$

for large N and m, so the storage utilization will be approximately $\ln 2 = 69.3$ percent [*Acta Informatica* **9** (1978), 159–170]. See also the more detailed analyses by B. Eisenbarth, N. Ziviani, G. H. Gonnet, K. Mehlhorn, and D. Wood, *Information and Control* **55** (1982), 125–174; R. A. Baeza-Yates, *Acta Informatica* **26** (1989), 439–471.

B-trees became popular soon after they were invented. See, for example, the article by Douglas Comer in *Computing Surveys* **11** (1979), 121–138, 412, which discusses early developments and describes a widely used system called VSAM (Virtual Storage Access Method) developed by IBM Corporation. One of the innovations of VSAM was to replicate blocks on a disk track so that latency time was minimized.

Two of the most interesting developments of the basic *B*-tree strategy have unfortunately been given almost identical names: "*SB*-trees" and "SB-trees." The *SB*-tree of P. E. O'Neil [*Acta Inf.* **29** (1992), 241–265] is designed to minimize disk I/O time by allocating nearby records to the same track or cylinder, maintaining efficiency in applications where many consecutive records need to be accessed at the same time; in this case "*SB*" is in italic type and the *S* connotes "sequential." The SB-tree of P. Ferragina and R. Grossi [*STOC* **27** (1995), 693–702; *SODA* **7** (1996), 373–382] is an elegant combination of *B*-tree structure with the Patricia trees that we will consider in Section 6.3; in this case "SB" is in roman type and the S connotes "string." SB-trees have many applications to large-scale text processing, and they provide a basis for efficient sorting of variable-length strings on disk [see Arge, Ferragina, Grossi, and Vitter, *STOC* **29** (1997), 540–548].

EXERCISES

1. [*10*] What B-tree of order 7 is obtained after the key 613 is inserted into Fig. 30? (Do not use the overflow technique.)

2. [*15*] Work exercise 1, but use the overflow technique, with 3-way splitting as in (10).

▸ **3.** [*23*] Suppose we insert the keys 1, 2, 3, ... in ascending order into an initially empty B-tree of order 101. Which key causes the leaves to be on level 4 for the first time
a) when we use no overflow?
b) when we use overflow and only 2-way splitting as in (4)?
c) when we use a B*-tree of order 101, with overflow and 3-way splitting as in (10)?

4. [*21*] (Bayer and McCreight.) Explain how to handle insertions into a generalized B-tree so that all nodes except the root and leaves will be guaranteed to have at least $\frac{3}{4}m - \frac{1}{2}$ children.

▸ **5.** [*21*] Suppose that a node represents 1000 character positions of external memory. If each pointer occupies 5 characters, and if the keys are variable in length, between 5 and 50 characters long but always a multiple of 5 characters, what is the minimum number of character positions occupied in a node after it splits during an insertion? (Consider only a simple splitting procedure analogous to that described in the text for fixed-length-key B-trees, without overflowing; move up the key that makes the remaining two parts most nearly equal in size.)

6. [*23*] Design a deletion algorithm for B-trees.

7. [*28*] Design a concatenation algorithm for B-trees (see Section 6.2.3).

▸ **8.** [*HM37*] Consider the generalization of tree insertion suggested by Muntz and Uzgalis, where each page can hold M keys. After N random items have been inserted into such a tree, so that there are $N+1$ external nodes, let $b_{Nk}^{(j)}$ be the probability that an unsuccessful search requires k page accesses and that it ends at an external node whose parent node belongs to a page containing j keys. If $B_N^{(j)}(z) = \sum b_{Nk}^{(j)} z^k$ is the corresponding generating function, prove that we have $B_1^{(j)}(z) = \delta_{j1} z$ and

$$B_N^{(j)}(z) = \frac{N-j-1}{N+1} B_{N-1}^{(j)}(z) + \frac{j+1}{N+1} B_{N-1}^{(j-1)}(z), \qquad \text{for } 1 < j < M;$$

$$B_N^{(1)}(z) = \frac{N-2}{N+1} B_{N-1}^{(1)}(z) + \frac{2z}{N+1} B_{N-1}^{(M)}(z);$$

$$B_N^{(M)}(z) = \frac{N-1}{N+1} B_{N-1}^{(M)}(z) + \frac{M+1}{N+1} B_{N-1}^{(M-1)}(z).$$

Find the asymptotic behavior of $C_N' = \sum_{j=1}^{M} B_N^{(j)\prime}(1)$, the average number of page accesses per unsuccessful search. [*Hint:* Express the recurrence in terms of the matrix

$$W(z) = \begin{pmatrix} -3 & 0 & \cdots & 0 & 2z \\ 3 & -4 & \cdots & 0 & 0 \\ 0 & 4 & \cdots & 0 & 0 \\ \vdots & \vdots & & \vdots & \vdots \\ 0 & 0 & \cdots & -M-1 & 0 \\ 0 & 0 & \cdots & M+1 & -2 \end{pmatrix},$$

and relate C_N' to an Nth degree polynomial in $W(1)$.]

9. [*22*] Can the *B*-tree idea be used to retrieve items of a linear list by position instead of by key value? (See Algorithm 6.2.3B.)

▶ **10.** [*35*] Discuss how a large file, organized as a *B*-tree, can be used for concurrent accessing and updating by a large number of simultaneous users, in such a way that users of different pages rarely interfere with each other.

Little is known, even for otherwise equivalent algorithms,
about the optimization of storage allocation,
minimization of the number of required operations,
and so on. This area of investigation
must draw upon the most powerful resources
of both pure and applied mathematics
for further progress.
— ANTHONY G. OETTINGER (1961)

6.3. DIGITAL SEARCHING

INSTEAD OF BASING a search method on comparisons between keys, we can make use of their representation as a sequence of digits or alphabetic characters. Consider, for example, the thumb index on a large dictionary; from the first letter of a given word, we can immediately locate the pages that contain all words beginning with that letter.

If we pursue the thumb-index idea to one of its logical conclusions, we come up with a searching scheme based on repeated "subscripting" as illustrated in Table 1. Suppose that we want to test a given search argument to see whether it is one of the 31 most common words of English (see Figs. 12 and 13 in Section 6.2.2). The data is represented in Table 1 as a *trie structure*; this name was suggested by E. Fredkin [*CACM* **3** (1960), 490–500] because it is a part of information re*trie*val. A trie — pronounced "try" — is essentially an M-ary tree, whose nodes are M-place vectors with components corresponding to digits or characters. Each node on level l represents the set of all keys that begin with a certain sequence of l characters called its *prefix*; the node specifies an M-way branch, depending on the $(l + 1)$st character.

For example, the trie of Table 1 has 12 nodes; node (1) is the root, and we look up the first letter here. If the first letter is, say, N, the table tells us that our word must be NOT (or else it isn't in the table). On the other hand, if the first letter is W, node (1) tells us to go on to node (9), looking up the second letter in the same way; node (9) says that the second letter should be A, H, or I. The prefix of node (10) is HA. Blank entries in the table stand for null links.

The node vectors in Table 1 are arranged according to MIX character code. This means that a trie search will be quite fast, since we are merely fetching words of an array by using the characters of our keys as subscripts. Techniques for making quick multiway decisions by subscripting have been called "table look-at" as opposed to "table look-up" [see P. M. Sherman, *CACM* **4** (1961), 172–173, 175].

Algorithm T (*Trie search*). Given a table of records that form an M-ary trie, this algorithm searches for a given argument K. The nodes of the trie are vectors whose subscripts run from 0 to $M - 1$; each component of these vectors is either a key or a link (possibly null).

T1. [Initialize.] Set the link variable P so that it points to the root of the trie.

T2. [Branch.] Set k to the next character of the input argument, K, from left to right. (If the argument has been completely scanned, we set k to a "blank" or end-of-word symbol. The character should be represented as a number in the range $0 \le k < M$.) Let X be table entry number k in NODE(P). If X is a link, go to T3; but if X is a key, go to T4.

T3. [Advance.] If $X \ne \Lambda$, set P $\leftarrow X$ and return to step T2; otherwise the algorithm terminates unsuccessfully.

T4. [Compare.] If $X = K$, the algorithm terminates successfully; otherwise it terminates unsuccessfully. ∎

Table 1
A TRIE FOR THE 31 MOST COMMON ENGLISH WORDS

	(1)	(2)	(3)	(4)	(5)	(6)	(7)	(8)	(9)	(10)	(11)	(12)
␣		A				I					HE	
A	(2)				(10)				WAS			THAT
B	(3)											
C												
D										HAD		
E		BE			(11)							THE
F	(4)						OF					
G												
H	(5)							(12)	WHICH			
I	(6)			HIS					WITH			THIS
θ												
J												
K												
L												
M												
N	NOT	AND				IN	ON					
O	(7)			FOR				TO				
P												
Q												
R		ARE		FROM			OR				HER	
Φ												
Π												
S		AS				IS						
T	(8)	AT				IT						
U			BUT									
V										HAVE		
W	(9)											
X												
Y	YOU		BY									
Z												

Notice that if the search is unsuccessful, the *longest match* has been found. This property is occasionally useful in applications.

In order to compare the speed of this algorithm to the others in this chapter, we can write a short MIX program assuming that the characters are bytes and that the keys are at most five bytes long.

Program T (*Trie search*). This program assumes that all keys are represented in one MIX word, with blank spaces at the right whenever the key has less than five characters. Since we use MIX character code, each byte of the search argument is assumed to contain a number less than 30. Links are represented as negative numbers in the $0:2$ field of a node word. $\text{rI1} \equiv \text{P}$, $\text{rX} \equiv$ unscanned part of K.

```
01  START  LDX   K            1   T1. Initialize.
02         ENT1  ROOT         1   P ← pointer to root of trie.
03  2H     SLAX  1            C   T2. Branch.
04         STA   *+1(2:2)     C   Extract next character, k.
05         ENT2  0,1          C   Q ← P + k.
06         LD1N  0,2(0:2)     C   P = LINK(Q).
07         J1P   2B           C   T3. Advance. To T2 if P is a link ≠ Λ.
```

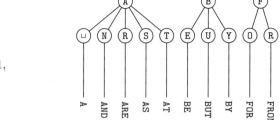

Fig. 31. The trie of Table 1,
converted into a "forest."

```
08              LDA  0,2       1   T4. Compare. rA ← KEY(Q).
09              CMPA K         1
10              JE   SUCCESS   1   Exit successfully if rA = K.
11  FAILURE EQU *                  Exit if not in the trie.  ▮
```

The running time of this program is $8C + 8$ units, where C is the number of characters examined. Since $C \leq 5$, the search will never take more than 48 units of time.

If we now compare the efficiency of this program (using the trie of Table 1) to Program 6.2.2T (using the *optimum* binary search tree of Fig. 13), we can make the following observations.

1. The trie takes much more memory space; we are using 360 words just to represent 31 keys, while the binary search tree uses only 62 words of memory. (However, exercise 4 shows that, with some fiddling around, we can actually fit the trie of Table 1 into only 49 words.)

2. A successful search takes about 26 units of time for both programs. But an unsuccessful search will go faster in the trie, slower in the binary search tree. For this data the search will be unsuccessful more often than it is successful, so the trie is preferable from the standpoint of speed.

3. If we consider the KWIC indexing application of Fig. 15 instead of the 31 commonest English words, the trie loses its advantage because of the nature of the data. For example, a trie requires 12 iterations to distinguish between COMPUTATION and COMPUTATIONS. In this case it would be better to build the trie so that words are scanned from right to left instead of from left to right.

The abstract concept of a trie to represent a family of strings was introduced by Axel Thue, in a paper about strings that do not contain adjacent repeated substrings [*Skrifter udgivne af Videnskabs-Selskabet i Christiania*, Mathematisk-Naturvidenskabelig Klasse (1912), No. 1; reprinted in Thue's *Selected Mathematical Papers* (Oslo: Universitetsforlaget, 1977), 413–477].

Trie memory for computer searching was first recommended by René de la Briandais [*Proc. Western Joint Computer Conf.* **15** (1959), 295–298]. He pointed out that we can save memory space at the expense of running time if we use a linked list for each node vector, since most of the entries in the vectors tend to be empty. In effect, this idea amounts to replacing the trie of Table 1 by the forest of trees shown in Fig. 31. Searching in such a forest proceeds by finding

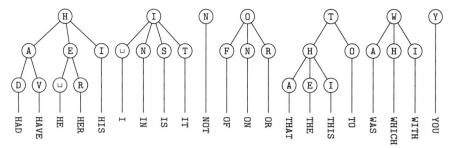

the root that matches the first character, then finding the child node of that root that matches the second character, etc.

In his article, de la Briandais did not actually stop the tree branching exactly as shown in Table 1 or Fig. 31; instead, he continued to represent each key, character by character, until reaching the end-of-word delimiter. Thus he would actually have used

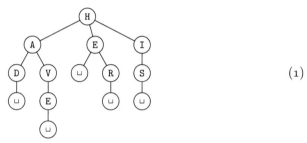

(1)

in place of the "H" tree in Fig. 31. This representation requires more storage, but it makes the processing of variable-length data especially easy. If we use two link fields per character, dynamic insertions and deletions can be handled in a simple manner.

If we use the normal way of representing trees as binary trees, (1) becomes the binary tree

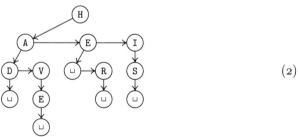

(2)

(In the representation of the full forest, Fig. 31, we would also have a pointer leading to the right from H to its neighboring root I.) The search in this binary tree proceeds by comparing a character of the argument to the character in the tree, and following RLINKs until finding a match; then the LLINK is taken and we treat the next character of the argument in the same way.

With such a binary tree, we are more or less doing a search by comparison, with equal-unequal branching instead of less-greater branching. The elementary theory of Section 6.2.1 tells that we must make at least $\lg N$ comparisons, on the average, to distinguish between N keys; the average number of tests made when searching a tree like that of Fig. 31 must be at least as many as we make when doing a binary search using the techniques of Section 6.2.

On the other hand, the trie in Table 1 is capable of making an M-way branch all at once; we shall see that the average search time for large N involves only about

$$\log_M N = \lg N / \lg M$$

iterations, if the input data is random. We shall also see that a "pure" trie scheme like that in Algorithm T requires a total of approximately $N/\ln M$ nodes to distinguish between N random inputs; hence the total amount of space is proportional to $MN/\ln M$.

From these considerations it is clear that the trie idea pays off only in the first few levels of the tree. We can get better performance by mixing two strategies, using a trie for the first few characters and then switching to some other technique. For example, E. H. Sussenguth, Jr. [*CACM* **6** (1963), 272–279] suggested using a character-by-character scheme until we reach part of the tree where only, say, six or fewer keys of the file are possible, and then we can sequentially run through the short list of remaining keys. We shall see that this mixed strategy decreases the number of trie nodes by roughly a factor of six, without substantially changing the running time.

T. N. Turba [*CACM* **25** (1982), 522–526] points out that it is sometimes most convenient to search for variable-length keys by having one search tree or trie for each different length.

The binary case. Let us now consider the special case $M = 2$, in which we scan the search argument one bit at a time. Two interesting methods have been developed that are especially appropriate for this case.

The first method, which we call *digital tree search*, is due to E. G. Coffman and J. Eve [*CACM* **13** (1970), 427–432, 436]. The idea is to store full keys in the nodes just as we did in the tree search algorithm of Section 6.2.2, but to use bits of the argument (instead of results of the comparisons) to govern whether to take the left or right branch at each step. Figure 32 shows the binary tree constructed by this method when we insert the 31 most common English words in order of decreasing frequency. In order to provide binary data for this illustration, the words have been expressed in MIX character code, and the codes have been converted into binary numbers with 5 bits per byte. Thus, the word WHICH is represented as the bit sequence 11010 01000 01001 00011 01000.

To search for this word WHICH in Fig. 32, we compare it first with the word THE at the root of the tree. Since there is no match and since the first bit of WHICH is 1, we move to the right and compare with OF. Since there is no match and since the second bit of WHICH is 1, we move to the right and compare with WITH; and so on. Alphabetic order of the keys in a digital search tree no longer corresponds to symmetric order of the nodes.

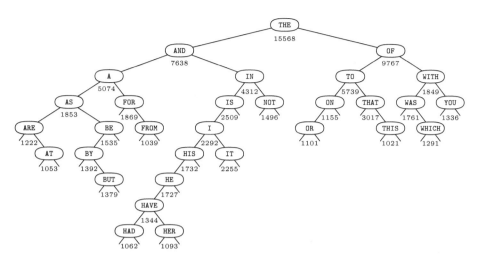

Fig. 32. A digital search tree for the 31 most common English words, inserted in decreasing order of frequency.

It is interesting to note the contrast between Fig. 32 and Fig. 12 in Section 6.2.2, since the latter tree was formed in the same way but using comparisons instead of key bits for the branching. If we consider the given frequencies, the digital search tree of Fig. 32 requires an average of 3.42 comparisons per successful search; this is somewhat better than the 4.04 comparisons needed by Fig. 12, although of course the computing time per comparison will probably be different.

Algorithm D (*Digital tree search and insertion*). Given a table of records that form a binary tree as described above, this algorithm searches for a given argument K. If K is not in the table, a new node containing K is inserted into the tree in the appropriate place.

This algorithm assumes that the tree is nonempty and that its nodes have KEY, LLINK, and RLINK fields just as in Algorithm 6.2.2T. In fact, the two algorithms are almost identical, as the reader may verify.

D1. [Initialize.] Set P ← ROOT, and $K' \leftarrow K$.

D2. [Compare.] If $K =$ KEY(P), the search terminates successfully. Otherwise set b to the leading bit of K', and shift K' left one place (thereby removing that bit and introducing a 0 at the right). If $b = 0$, go to D3, otherwise go to D4.

D3. [Move left.] If LLINK(P) $\neq \Lambda$, set P ← LLINK(P) and go back to D2. Otherwise go to D5.

D4. [Move right.] If RLINK(P) $\neq \Lambda$, set P ← RLINK(P) and go back to D2.

D5. [Insert into tree.] Set Q $\Leftarrow$ AVAIL, KEY(Q) ← K, LLINK(Q) ← RLINK(Q) ← Λ. If $b = 0$ set LLINK(P) ← Q, otherwise set RLINK(P) ← Q. ∎

Although the tree search of Algorithm 6.2.2T is inherently binary, it is not difficult to see that the present algorithm could be extended to an M-ary digital search for any $M \geq 2$ (see exercise 13).

Donald R. Morrison [*JACM* **15** (1968), 514–534] has discovered a very pretty way to form N-node search trees based on the binary representation of keys, *without* storing keys in the nodes. His method, called "Patricia" (Practical Algorithm To Retrieve Information Coded In Alphanumeric), is especially suitable for dealing with extremely long, variable-length keys such as titles or phrases stored within a large bulk file. A closely related algorithm was published at almost exactly the same time in Germany by G. Gwehenberger, *Elektronische Rechenanlagen* **10** (1968), 223–226.

Patricia's basic idea is to build a binary trie, but to avoid one-way branching by including in each node the number of bits to skip over before making the next test. There are several ways to exploit this idea; perhaps the simplest to explain is illustrated in Fig. 33. We have a TEXT array of bits, which is usually quite long; it may be stored as an external direct-access file, since each search accesses TEXT only once. Each key to be stored in our table is specified by a starting place in the text, and it can be imagined to go from this starting place all the way to the end of the text. (Patricia does not search for strict equality between key and argument; instead, it will determine whether or not there exists a key *beginning* with the argument.)

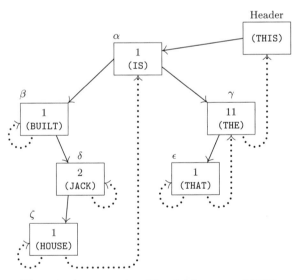

Fig. 33. An example of Patricia's tree and TEXT.

The situation depicted in Fig. 33 involves seven keys, one starting at each word, namely "THIS IS THE HOUSE THAT JACK BUILT?" and "IS THE HOUSE THAT

JACK BUILT?" and ... and "BUILT?". There is one important restriction, namely
that *no one key may be a prefix of another*; this restriction can be met if we end
the text with a unique end-of-text code (in this case "?") that appears nowhere
else. The same restriction was implicit in the trie scheme of Algorithm T, where
"␣" was the termination code.

The tree that Patricia uses for searching should be contained in random-
access memory, or it should be arranged on pages as suggested in Section 6.2.4.
It consists of a header and $N - 1$ nodes, where the nodes contain several fields:

KEY, a pointer to the text. This field must be at least $\lg C$ bits long, if the
   text contains C characters. In Fig. 33 the words shown within each node
   would really be represented by pointers to the text; for example, instead
   of "(JACK)" the node would contain the number 24 (which indicates the
   starting place of "JACK BUILT?" in the text string).

LLINK and RLINK, pointers within the tree. These fields must be at least
   $\lg N$ bits long.

LTAG and RTAG, one-bit fields that tell whether or not LLINK and RLINK,
   respectively, are pointers to children or to ancestors of the node. The
   dotted lines in Fig. 33 correspond to pointers whose TAG bit is 1.

SKIP, a number that tells how many bits to skip when searching, as explained
   below. This field should be large enough to hold the largest number k
   such that all keys with prefix σ agree in the next k bits following σ, for
   some string σ that is a prefix of at least two different keys; in practice,
   we may usually assume that k isn't too large, and an error indication
   can be given if the size of the SKIP field is exceeded. The SKIP fields
   are shown as numbers within each non-header node of Fig. 33.

The header contains only KEY, LLINK, and LTAG fields.

A search in Patricia's tree is carried out as follows: Suppose we are looking
up the word THE (bit pattern 10111 01000 00101). We start by looking at the
SKIP field of the root node α, which tells us to examine bit 1 of the argument.
That bit is 1, so we move to the right. The SKIP field in the next node, γ, tells
us to look at the $1 + 11 = 12$th bit of the argument. It is 0, so we move to the
left. The SKIP field of the next node, ϵ, tells us to look at the $(12 + 1)$st bit,
which is 1; now we find RTAG = 1, so we go back to node γ, which refers us to
the TEXT. The search path we have taken would occur for any argument whose
bit pattern is 1xxxx xxxxx x01..., and we must check to see if it matches the
unique key beginning with that pattern, namely THE.

Suppose, on the other hand, that we are looking for any or all keys starting
with TH. The search process begins as above, but it eventually tries to look at
the (nonexistent) 12th bit of the 10-bit argument. At this point we compare the
argument to the TEXT at the point specified in the current node (in this case
node γ). If it does not match, the argument is not the beginning of any key;
but if it does match, the argument is the beginning of every key represented by
dotted links in node γ and its descendants (namely THIS, THAT, THE).

The search process can be spelled out more precisely in the following way.

Algorithm P (*Patricia*). Given a TEXT array and a tree with KEY, LLINK, RLINK, LTAG, RTAG, and SKIP fields, as described above, this algorithm determines whether or not there is a key in the TEXT that begins with a specified argument K. (If r such keys exist, for $r \geq 1$, it is subsequently possible to locate them all in $O(r)$ steps; see exercise 14.) We assume that at least one key is present.

P1. [Initialize.] Set P ← HEAD and $j \leftarrow 0$. (Variable P is a pointer that will move down the tree, and j is a counter that will designate bit positions of the argument.) See $n \leftarrow$ number of bits in K.

P2. [Move left.] Set Q ← P and P ← LLINK(Q). If LTAG(Q) = 1, go to P6.

P3. [Skip bits.] (At this point we know that if the first j bits of K match any key whatsoever, they match the key that starts at KEY(P).) Set $j \leftarrow j+$SKIP(P). If $j > n$, go to P6.

P4. [Test bit.] (At this point we know that if the first $j-1$ bits of K match any key, they match the key starting at KEY(P).) If the jth bit of K is 0, go to P2, otherwise go to P5.

P5. [Move right.] Set Q ← P and P ← RLINK(Q). If RTAG(Q) = 0, go to P3.

P6. [Compare.] (At this point we know that if K matches any key, it matches the key starting at KEY(P).) Compare K to the key that starts at position KEY(P) in the TEXT array. If they are equal (up to n bits, the length of K), the algorithm terminates successfully; if unequal, it terminates unsuccessfully. ∎

Exercise 15 shows how Patricia's tree can be built in the first place. We can also add to the text and insert new keys, provided that the new text material always ends with a unique delimiter (for example, an end-of-text symbol followed by a serial number).

Patricia is a little tricky, and she requires careful scrutiny before all of her beauties are revealed.

Analyses of the algorithms. We shall conclude this section by making a mathematical study of tries, digital search trees, and Patricia. A summary of the main consequences of these analyses appears at the very end.

Let us consider first the case of binary tries, namely tries with $M = 2$. Figure 34 shows the binary trie that is formed when the sixteen keys from the sorting examples of Chapter 5 are treated as 10-bit binary numbers. (The keys are shown in octal notation, so that for example *1144* represents the 10-bit number $612 = (1001100100)_2$.) As in Algorithm T, we use the trie to store information about the leading bits of the keys until we get to the first point where the key is uniquely identified; then the key is recorded in full.

If Fig. 34 is compared to Table 5.2.2–3, an amazing relationship between trie memory and radix exchange sorting is revealed. (Then again, perhaps this relationship is obvious.) The 22 nodes of Fig. 34 correspond precisely to the 22

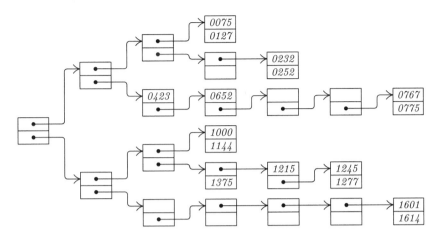

Fig. 34. Example of a random binary trie.

partitioning stages in Table 5.2.2–3, with the pth node in preorder corresponding to Stage p. The number of bit inspections in a partitioning stage is equal to the number of keys within the corresponding node and its subtries; consequently we may state the following result.

Theorem T. *If N distinct binary numbers are put into a binary trie as described above, then* (i) *the number of nodes of the trie is equal to the number of partitioning stages required if these numbers are sorted by radix exchange; and* (ii) *the average number of bit inspections required to retrieve a key by means of Algorithm T is $1/N$ times the number of bit inspections required by the radix exchange sort.* $\blacksquare$

Because of this theorem, we can make use of all the mathematical machinery that was developed for radix exchange in Section 5.2.2. For example, if we assume that our keys are infinite-precision random uniformly distributed real numbers between 0 and 1, the number of bit inspections needed for retrieval will be $\lg N + \gamma/\ln 2 + 1/2 + \delta(N) + O(N^{-1})$, and the number of trie nodes will be $N/\ln 2 + N\bar{\delta}(N) + O(1)$. Here $\delta(N)$ and $\bar{\delta}(N)$ are complicated functions that may be neglected since their absolute value is always less than 10^{-6} (see exercises 5.2.2–38 and 5.2.2–48).

Of course there is still more work to be done, since we need to generalize from binary tries to M-ary tries. We shall describe only the starting point of the investigations here, leaving the instructive details as exercises.

Let A_N be the average number of internal nodes in a random M-ary search trie that contains N keys. Then $A_0 = A_1 = 0$, and for $N \geq 2$ we have

$$A_N = 1 + \sum_{k_1 + \cdots + k_M = N} \left(\frac{N!}{k_1! \dots k_M!} M^{-N} \right) (A_{k_1} + \cdots + A_{k_M}), \qquad (3)$$

since $N!\,M^{-N}/k_1!\ldots k_M!$ is the probability that k_1 of the keys are in the first subtrie, $\ldots$, k_M in the Mth. This equation can be rewritten

$$A_N = 1 + M^{1-N} \sum_{k_1+\cdots+k_M=N} \left(\frac{N!}{k_1!\ldots k_M!}\right) A_{k_1}$$

$$= 1 + M^{1-N} \sum_{k} \binom{N}{k}(M-1)^{N-k} A_k, \qquad \text{for } N \geq 2, \qquad (4)$$

by using symmetry and then summing over $k_2, \ldots, k_M$. Similarly, if C_N denotes the average total number of digit inspections needed to look up all N keys in the trie, we find $C_0 = C_1 = 0$ and

$$C_N = N + M^{1-N} \sum_{k} \binom{N}{k}(M-1)^{N-k} C_k \qquad \text{for } N \geq 2. \qquad (5)$$

Exercise 17 shows how to deal with general recurrences of this type, and exercises 18–25 work out the corresponding theory of random tries. [The analysis of A_N was first approached from another point of view by L. R. Johnson and M. H. McAndrew, *IBM J. Res. and Devel.* **8** (1964), 189–193, in connection with an equivalent hardware-oriented sorting algorithm.]

If we now turn to a study of digital search trees, we find that the formulas are similar, yet different enough that it is not easy to see how to deduce the asymptotic behavior. For example, if $\bar{C}_N$ denotes the average total number of digit inspections made when looking up all N keys in an M-ary digital search tree, it is not difficult to deduce as above that $\bar{C}_0 = \bar{C}_1 = 0$, and

$$\bar{C}_{N+1} = N + M^{1-N} \sum_{k} \binom{N}{k}(M-1)^{N-k} \bar{C}_k \qquad \text{for } N \geq 0. \qquad (6)$$

This is almost identical to Eq. (5); but the appearance of $N+1$ instead of N on the left-hand side of this equation is enough to change the entire character of the recurrence, so the methods we have used to study (5) are wiped out.

Let's consider the binary case first. Figure 35 shows the digital search tree corresponding to the sixteen example keys of Fig. 34, when they have been inserted in the order used in the examples of Chapter 5. If we want to determine the average number of bit inspections made in a random successful search, this is just the internal path length of the tree divided by N, since we need l bit inspections to find a node on level l. Notice, however, that the average number of bit inspections made in a random *unsuccessful* search is *not* simply related to the external path length of the tree, since unsuccessful searches are more likely to occur at external nodes near the root; thus, the probability of reaching the left sub-branch of node *0075* in Fig. 35 is $\frac{1}{8}$ (assuming infinitely precise keys), and the left sub-branch of node *0232* will be encountered with probability only $\frac{1}{32}$. For this reason, digital search trees tend to stay better balanced than the binary search trees of Algorithm 6.2.2T, when the keys are uniformly distributed.

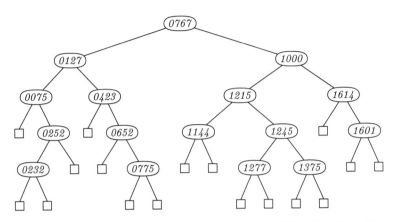

Fig. 35. A random digital search tree constructed by Algorithm D.

We can use a generating function to describe the pertinent characteristics of a digital search tree. If there are a_l internal nodes on level l, consider the generating function $a(z) = \sum_l a_l z^l$; for example, the generating function corresponding to Fig. 35 is $a(z) = 1 + 2z + 4z^2 + 5z^3 + 4z^4$. If there are b_l external nodes on level l, and if $b(z) = \sum_l b_l z^l$, we have

$$b(z) = 1 + (2z - 1)a(z) \tag{7}$$

by exercise 6.2.1–25. For example, $1 + (2z - 1)(1 + 2z + 4z^2 + 5z^3 + 4z^4) = 3z^3 + 6z^4 + 8z^5$. The average number of bit inspections made in a random successful search is $a'(1)/a(1)$, since $a'(1)$ is the internal path length of the tree and $a(1)$ is the number of internal nodes. The average number of bit inspections made in a random *unsuccessful* search is $\sum_l l b_l 2^{-l} = \frac{1}{2}b'(\frac{1}{2}) = a(\frac{1}{2})$, since we end up at a given external node on level l with probability 2^{-l}. The number of comparisons is the same as the number of bit inspections, plus one in a successful search. For example, in Fig. 35, a successful search will take $2\frac{9}{16}$ bit inspections and $3\frac{9}{16}$ comparisons, on the average; an unsuccessful search will take $3\frac{7}{8}$ of each.

Now let $g_N(z)$ be the "average" $a(z)$ for trees with N nodes; in other words, $g_N(z)$ is the sum $\sum p_T a_T(z)$ over all binary digital search trees T with N internal nodes, where $a_T(z)$ is the generating function for the internal nodes of T and p_T is the probability that T occurs when N random numbers are inserted using Algorithm D. Then the average number of bit inspections will be $g'_N(1)/N$ in a successful search, $g_N(\frac{1}{2})$ in an unsuccessful search.

We can compute $g_N(z)$ by mimicking the tree construction process, as follows. If $a(z)$ is the generating function for a tree of N nodes, we can form $N+1$ trees from it by making the next insertion into any one of the external node positions. The insertion goes into a given external node on level l with probability 2^{-l}; hence the sum of the generating functions for the $N+1$ new trees, multiplied by the probability of occurrence, is $a(z) + b(\frac{1}{2}z) = a(z) + 1 + (z-1)a(\frac{1}{2}z)$.

Averaging over all trees for N nodes, it follows that

$$g_{N+1}(z) = g_N(z) + 1 + (z-1)g_N\left(\tfrac{1}{2}z\right); \qquad g_0(z) = 0. \tag{8}$$

The corresponding generating function for external nodes,

$$h_N(z) = 1 + (2z-1)g_N(z),$$

is somewhat easier to work with, because (8) is equivalent to the formula

$$h_{N+1}(z) = h_N(z) + (2z-1)h_N\left(\tfrac{1}{2}z\right); \qquad h_0(z) = 1. \tag{9}$$

Applying this rule repeatedly, we find that

$$
\begin{aligned}
h_{N+1}(z) &= h_{N-1}(z) + 2(2z-1)h_{N-1}\left(\tfrac{1}{2}z\right) + (2z-1)(z-1)h_{N-1}\left(\tfrac{1}{4}z\right)\\
&= h_{N-2}(z) + 3(2z-1)h_{N-2}\left(\tfrac{1}{2}z\right) + 3(2z-1)(z-1)h_{N-2}\left(\tfrac{1}{4}z\right)\\
&\quad + (2z-1)(z-1)\left(\tfrac{1}{2}z-1\right)h_{N-2}\left(\tfrac{1}{8}z\right)
\end{aligned}
$$

and so on, so that eventually we have

$$h_N(z) = \sum_k \binom{N}{k} \prod_{j=0}^{k-1}(2^{1-j}z - 1); \tag{10}$$

$$g_N(z) = \sum_{k\geq 0} \binom{N}{k+1} \prod_{j=0}^{k-1}(2^{-j}z - 1). \tag{11}$$

For example, $g_4(z) = 4 + 6(z-1) + 4(z-1)\left(\tfrac{1}{2}z - 1\right) + (z-1)\left(\tfrac{1}{2}z - 1\right)\left(\tfrac{1}{4}z - 1\right)$. These formulas make it possible to express the quantities we are looking for as sums of products:

$$\bar{C}_N = g'_N(1) = \sum_{k\geq 0} \binom{N}{k+2} \prod_{j=1}^{k}(2^{-j} - 1); \tag{12}$$

$$g_N\left(\tfrac{1}{2}\right) = \sum_{k\geq 0} \binom{N}{k+1} \prod_{j=1}^{k}(2^{-j} - 1) = \bar{C}_{N+1} - \bar{C}_N. \tag{13}$$

It is not at all obvious that this formula for $\bar{C}_N$ satisfies (6)!

Unfortunately, these expressions are not suitable for calculation or for finding an asymptotic expansion, since $2^{-j} - 1$ is negative; we get large terms and a lot of cancellation. A more useful formula for $\bar{C}_N$ can be obtained by applying the partition identities of exercise 5.1.1–16. We have

$$
\begin{aligned}
\bar{C}_N &= \left(\prod_{j\geq 1}(1 - 2^{-j})\right) \sum_{k\geq 0} \binom{N}{k+2}(-1)^k \prod_{l\geq 0}(1 - 2^{-l-k-1})^{-1}\\
&= \left(\prod_{j\geq 1}(1 - 2^{-j})\right) \sum_{k\geq 0} \binom{N}{k+2}(-1)^k \sum_{m\geq 0}(2^{-k-1})^m \prod_{r=1}^{m}(1 - 2^{-r})^{-1}
\end{aligned}
$$

$$= \sum_{m \geq 0} 2^m \left(\sum_k \binom{N}{k} (-2^{-m})^k - 1 + 2^{-m} N \right) \prod_{j \geq 0} (1 - 2^{-j-m-1})$$

$$= \sum_{m \geq 0} 2^m \left((1-2^{-m})^N - 1 + 2^{-m} N \right) \sum_{n \geq 0} (-2^{-m-1})^n \frac{2^{-n(n-1)/2}}{\prod_{r=1}^n (1 - 2^{-r})}. \quad (14)$$

This may not seem at first glance to be an improvement over Eq. (12), but it has the great advantage that the sum on m converges rapidly for each fixed n. A precisely analogous situation occurred for the trie case in Eqs. 5.2.2–(38) and 5.2.2–(39); in fact, if we consider only the terms of (14) with $n = 0$, we have exactly $N - 1$ plus the number of bit inspections in a binary trie. We can now proceed to get the asymptotic value in essentially the same way as before; see exercise 27. [The derivation above is largely based on an approach suggested by A. J. Konheim and D. J. Newman, *Discrete Mathematics* **4** (1973), 57–63.]

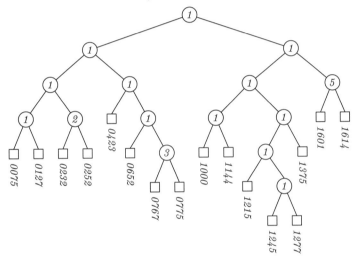

Fig. 36. Patricia constructs this tree instead of Fig. 34.

Finally let us take a mathematical look at Patricia. In her case the binary tree is like the corresponding binary trie on the same keys, but squashed together (because the SKIP fields eliminate 1-way branching), so that there are always exactly $N-1$ internal nodes and N external nodes. Figure 36 shows the Patrician tree corresponding to the sixteen keys in the trie of Fig. 34. The number shown in each branch node is the amount of SKIP; the keys are indicated with the external nodes, although the external node is not explicitly present (there is actually a tagged link to an internal node that references the TEXT, in place of each external node.) For the purposes of analysis, we may assume that external nodes exist as shown.

Since successful searches with Patricia end at external nodes, the average number of bit inspections made in a random successful search will be the external path length, divided by N. If we form the generating function $b(z)$ for external

nodes as above, this will be $b'(1)/b(1)$. An *unsuccessful* search with Patricia also
ends at an external node, but weighted with probability 2^{-l} for external nodes
on level l, so the average number of bit inspections is $\frac{1}{2}b'(\frac{1}{2})$. For example, in
Fig. 36 we have $b(z) = 3z^3+8z^4+3z^5+2z^6$; therefore there are $4\frac{1}{4}$ bit inspections
per successful search and $3\frac{25}{32}$ per unsuccessful search, on the average.

Let $h_n(z)$ be the "average" $b(z)$ for a Patrician tree constructed with n
external nodes, using uniformly distributed keys. The recurrence relation

$$h_n(z) = 2^{1-n}\sum_k \binom{n}{k} h_k(z)(z + \delta_{kn}(1 - z)), \quad h_0(z) = 0, \quad h_1(z) = 1 \quad (15)$$

appears to have no simple solution. But fortunately, there is a simple recurrence
for the average external path length $h_n'(1)$, since

$$h_n'(1) = 2^{1-n}\sum_k \binom{n}{k} h_k'(1) + 2^{1-n}\sum_k \binom{n}{k}k(1 - \delta_{kn})$$

$$= n - 2^{1-n}n + 2^{1-n}\sum_k \binom{n}{k} h_k'(1). \quad (16)$$

Since this has the form of (6), we can use the methods already developed to solve
for $h_n'(1)$, which turns out to be exactly n less than the corresponding number
of bit inspections in a random binary trie. Thus, the SKIP fields save us about
one bit inspection per successful search, on random data. (See exercise 31.) The
redundancy of typical real data will lead to greater savings.

When we try to find the average number of bit inspections for a random
unsuccessful search by Patricia, we obtain the recurrence

$$a_n = 1 + \frac{1}{2^n - 2}\sum_{k<n} \binom{n}{k} a_k, \quad \text{for } n \geq 2; \quad a_0 = a_1 = 0. \quad (17)$$

Here $a_n = \frac{1}{2}h_n'(\frac{1}{2})$. This does *not* have the form of any recurrence we have
studied, nor is it easily transformed into such a recurrence. The theory of Mellin
transforms, introduced in Section 5.2.2 and the references cited there, provides
a high-level way to deal with recurrences that have a digital character. It turns
out that the solution to (17) involves the Bernoulli numbers:

$$\frac{na_{n-1}}{2} - n + 2 = \sum_{k=2}^{n-1} \binom{n}{k}\frac{B_k}{2^{k-1} - 1}, \quad \text{for } n \geq 2. \quad (18)$$

This formula is probably the hardest asymptotic nut we have yet had to crack;
the solution in exercise 34 is an instructive review of many things we have done
before, with some slightly different twists.

Summary of the analyses. As a result of all the complicated mathematics in
this section, the following facts are perhaps the most noteworthy:

a) The number of nodes needed to store N random keys in an M-ary trie,
with the trie branching terminated for subfiles of $\leq s$ keys, is approximately
$N/(s \ln M)$. This approximation is valid for large N, small s, and small M.

Since a trie node involves M link fields, we will need only about $N/\ln M$ link fields if we choose $s = M$.

b) The number of digits or characters examined during a random search is approximately $\log_M N$ for all methods considered. When $M = 2$, the various analyses give us the following more accurate approximations to the number of bit inspections:

	Successful	Unsuccessful
Trie search	$\lg N + 1.33275$	$\lg N - 0.10995$
Digital tree search	$\lg N - 1.71665$	$\lg N - 0.27395$
Patricia	$\lg N + 0.33275$	$\lg N - 0.31875$

(These approximations can all be expressed in terms of fundamental mathematical constants; for example, 0.31875 stands for $(\ln \pi - \gamma)/\ln 2 - 1/2$.)

c) "Random" data here means that the M-ary digits are uniformly distributed, as if the keys were real numbers between 0 and 1 expressed in M-ary notation. Digital search methods are insensitive to the order in which keys are entered into the file (except for Algorithm D, which is only slightly sensitive to the order); but they are very sensitive to the distribution of digits. For example, if 0 bits are much more common than 1 bits, the trees will become much more skewed than they would be for random data as considered in the analyses cited above. Exercise 5.2.2–53 works out one example of what happens when the data is biased in this way.

EXERCISES

1. [*00*] If a tree has leaves, what does a trie have?

2. [*20*] Design an algorithm for the insertion of a new key into an M-ary trie, using the conventions of Algorithm T.

3. [*21*] Design an algorithm for the deletion of a key from an M-ary trie, using the conventions of Algorithm T.

▶ **4.** [*21*] Most of the 360 entries in Table 1 are blank (null links). But we can compress the table into only 49 entries, by overlapping nonblank entries with blank ones as follows:

Position	1	2	3	4	5	6	7	8	9	10	11	12	13	14	15	16	17	18	19	20	21	22	23	24	25
Entry	(10)		WAS	THAT	(11)	OF	BE	THE	HIS	WHICH	WITH	THIS		(12)	ON	I	HE	A	OR	(2)	(3)	TO	HAD		

Position	26	27	28	29	30	31	32	33	34	35	36	37	38	39	40	41	42	43	44	45	46	47	48	49
Entry	(4)	BUT	(5)	(6)	FOR	BY	IN	FROM	AND	NOT	(7)	HER	ARE	IS	IT	AS	AT	(8)		HAVE	(9)		YOU	

(Nodes (1), (2), $\ldots$, (12) of Table 1 begin, respectively, at positions 20, 19, 3, 14, 1, 17, 1, 7, 3, 20, 18, 4 within this compressed table.)

Show that if the compressed table is substituted for Table 1, Program T will still work, but not quite as fast.

▶ **5.** [*M26*] (Y. N. Patt.) The trees of Fig. 31 have their letters arranged in alphabetic order within each family. This order is not necessary, and if we rearrange the order of nodes within the families before constructing binary tree representations such as (2) we may get a faster search. What rearrangement of Fig. 31 is optimum from this standpoint? (Use the frequency assumptions of Fig. 32, and find the forest that minimizes the successful search time when it has been represented as a binary tree.)

6. [*15*] What digital search tree is obtained if the fifteen 4-bit binary keys 0001, 0010, 0011, ..., 1111 are inserted in increasing order by Algorithm D? (Start with 0001 at the root and then do fourteen insertions.)

▶ **7.** [*M26*] If the fifteen keys of exercise 6 are inserted in a different order, we might get a different tree. Of all the 15! possible permutations of these keys, which is the *worst*, in the sense that it produces a tree with the greatest internal path length?

8. [*20*] Consider the following changes to Algorithm D, which have the effect of eliminating variable K': Change "K'" to "K" in both places in step D2, and delete the operation "$K' \leftarrow K$" from step D1. Will the resulting algorithm still be valid for searching and insertion?

9. [*21*] Write a MIX program for Algorithm D, and compare it to Program 6.2.2T. You may use binary operations such as SLB (shift left AX binary), JAE (jump if A even), etc.; and you may also use the idea of exercise 8 if it helps.

10. [*23*] Given a file in which all the keys are n-bit binary numbers, and given a search argument $K = b_1 b_2 \ldots b_n$, suppose we want to find the maximum value of k such that there is a key in the file beginning with the bit pattern $b_1 b_2 \ldots b_k$. How can we do this efficiently if the file is represented as
a) a binary search tree (Algorithm 6.2.2T)?
b) a binary trie (Algorithm T)?
c) a binary digital search tree (Algorithm D)?

11. [*21*] Can Algorithm 6.2.2D be used without change to delete a node from a digital search tree?

12. [*25*] After a random element is deleted from a random digital search tree constructed by Algorithm D, is the resulting tree still random? (See exercise 11 and Theorem 6.2.2H.)

13. [*20*] (*M-ary digital searching.*) Explain how Algorithms T and D can be combined into a generalized algorithm that is essentially the same as Algorithm D when $M = 2$. What changes would be made to Table 1, if your algorithm is used for $M = 30$?

▶ **14.** [*25*] Design an efficient algorithm that can be performed just after Algorithm P has terminated successfully, to locate *all* places where K appears in the TEXT.

15. [*28*] Design an efficient algorithm that can be used to construct the tree used by Patricia, or to insert new TEXT references into an existing tree. Your insertion algorithm should refer to the TEXT array at most twice.

16. [*22*] Why is it desirable for Patricia to make the restriction that no key is a prefix of another?

17. [*M25*] Find a way to express the solution of the recurrence

$$x_0 = x_1 = 0, \qquad x_n = a_n + m^{1-n} \sum_k \binom{m}{k} (m-1)^{n-k} x_k, \qquad n \geq 2,$$

in terms of binomial transforms, by generalizing the technique of exercise 5.2.2–36.

18. [*M21*] Use the result of exercise 17 to express the solutions to (4) and (5) in terms of functions U_n and V_n analogous to those defined in exercise 5.2.2–38.

19. [*HM23*] Find the asymptotic value of the function

$$K(n, s, m) = \sum_{k \geq 2} \binom{n}{k}\binom{k}{s} \frac{(-1)^k}{m^{k-1} - 1}$$

to $O(1)$ as $n \to \infty$, for fixed $s \geq 0$ and $m > 1$. [The case $s = 0$ has already been solved in exercise 5.2.2–50, and the case $s = 1$, $m = 2$ has been solved in exercise 5.2.2–48.]

▶ **20.** [*M30*] Consider M-ary trie memory in which we use a sequential search whenever reaching a subfile of s or fewer keys. (Algorithm T is the special case $s = 1$.) Apply the results of the preceding exercises to analyze

     a) the average number of trie nodes;

     b) the average number of digit or character inspections in a successful search; and

     c) the average number of comparisons made in a successful search.

State your answers as asymptotic formulas as $N \to \infty$, for fixed M and s; the answer for (a) should be correct to within $O(1)$, and the answers for (b) and (c) should be correct to within $O(N^{-1})$. [When $M = 2$, this analysis applies also to the modified radix exchange sort, in which subfiles of size $\leq s$ are sorted by insertion.]

21. [*M25*] How many of the nodes, in a random M-ary trie containing N keys, have a null pointer in table entry 0? (For example, 9 of the 12 nodes in Table 1 have a null pointer in the "␣" position. "Random" in this exercise means as usual that the digits of the keys are uniformly distributed between 0 and $M - 1$.)

22. [*M25*] How many trie nodes are on level l of a random M-ary trie containing N keys, for $l = 0, 1, 2, \ldots$?

23. [*M26*] How many digit inspections are made on the average during an *unsuccessful* search in an M-ary trie containing N random keys?

24. [*M30*] Consider an M-ary trie that has been represented as a forest (see Fig. 31). Find exact and asymptotic expressions for

     a) the average number of nodes in the forest;

     b) the average number of times "P ← RLINK(P)" is performed during a random successful search.

▶ **25.** [*M24*] The mathematical derivations of asymptotic values in this section have been quite difficult, involving complex variable theory, because it is desirable to get more than just the leading term of the asymptotic behavior (and the second term is intrinsically complicated). The purpose of this exercise is to show that elementary methods are good enough to deduce some of the results in weaker form.

     a) Prove by induction that the solution to (4) satisfies $A_N \leq M(N - 1)/(M - 1)$.

     b) Let $D_N = C_N - N H_{N-1}/\ln M$, where C_N is defined by (5). Prove that $D_N = O(N)$; hence $C_N = N \log_M N + O(N)$. [*Hint:* Use (a) and Theorem 1.2.7A.]

26. [*23*] Determine the value of the infinite product

$$\left(1 - \tfrac{1}{2}\right)\left(1 - \tfrac{1}{4}\right)\left(1 - \tfrac{1}{8}\right)\left(1 - \tfrac{1}{16}\right)\cdots$$

correct to five decimal places, by hand calculation. [*Hint:* See exercise 5.1.1–16.]

27. [*HM31*] What is the asymptotic value of $\bar{C}_N$, as given by (14), to within $O(1)$?

28. [*HM26*] Find the asymptotic average number of digit inspections when searching in a random M-ary digital search tree, for general $M \geq 2$. Consider both successful and unsuccessful search, and give your answer to within $O(N^{-1})$.

29. [*HM40*] What is the asymptotic average number of nodes, in an M-ary digital search tree, for which all M links are null? (We might save memory space by eliminating such nodes; see exercise 13.)

30. [*M24*] Show that the Patrician generating function $h_n(z)$ defined in (15) can be expressed in the rather horrible form

$$n \sum_{m \geq 1} z^m \left(\sum_{\substack{a_1 + \cdots + a_m = n-1 \\ a_1, \ldots, a_m \geq 1}} \binom{n-1}{a_1, \ldots, a_m} \frac{1}{(2^{a_1} - 1)(2^{a_1 + a_2} - 1) \ldots (2^{a_1 + \cdots + a_m} - 1)} \right).$$

[Thus, if there is a simple formula for $h_n(z)$, we will be able to simplify this rather ungainly expression.]

31. [*M21*] Solve the recurrence (16).

32. [*M21*] What is the average value of the sum of all SKIP fields in a random Patrician tree with $N - 1$ internal nodes?

33. [*M30*] Prove that (18) is a solution to the recurrence (17). [*Hint:* Consider the generating function $A(z) = \sum_{n \geq 0} a_n z^n / n!$.]

34. [*HM40*] The purpose of this exercise is to find the asymptotic behavior of (18).

a) Prove that, if $n \geq 2$,

$$\frac{1}{n} \sum_{2 \leq k < n} \binom{n}{k} \frac{B_k}{2^{k-1} - 1} = \sum_{j \geq 1} \left(\frac{1^{n-1} + 2^{n-1} + \cdots + (2^j - 1)^{n-1}}{2^{j(n-1)}} - \frac{2^j}{n} + \frac{1}{2} \right).$$

b) Show that the summand in (a) is approximately $1/(e^x - 1) - 1/x + 1/2$, where $x = n/2^j$; the resulting sum equals the original sum plus $O(n^{-1})$.

c) Show that

$$\frac{1}{e^x - 1} - \frac{1}{x} + \frac{1}{2} = \frac{1}{2\pi i} \int_{-\frac{1}{2} - i\infty}^{-\frac{1}{2} + i\infty} \zeta(z) \Gamma(z) x^{-z} dz, \qquad \text{for real } x > 0.$$

d) Therefore the sum equals

$$\frac{1}{2\pi i} \int_{-\frac{1}{2} - i\infty}^{-\frac{1}{2} + i\infty} \frac{\zeta(z) \Gamma(z) n^{-z}}{2^{-z} - 1} dz + O(n^{-1});$$

evaluate this integral.

▶ **35.** [*M20*] What is the probability that Patricia's tree on five keys will be

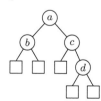

with the SKIP fields a, b, c, d as shown? (Assume that the keys have independent random bits, and give your answer as a function of a, b, c, and d.)

36. [*M25*] There are five binary trees with three internal nodes. If we consider how frequently each particular one of these occurs as the search tree in various algorithms, for random data, we find the following different probabilities:

Tree search (Algorithm 6.2.2T)	$\frac{1}{6}$	$\frac{1}{6}$	$\frac{1}{3}$	$\frac{1}{6}$	$\frac{1}{6}$
Digital tree search (Algorithm D)	$\frac{1}{8}$	$\frac{1}{8}$	$\frac{1}{2}$	$\frac{1}{8}$	$\frac{1}{8}$
Patricia (Algorithm P)	$\frac{1}{7}$	$\frac{1}{7}$	$\frac{3}{7}$	$\frac{1}{7}$	$\frac{1}{7}$

(Notice that the digital search tree tends to be balanced more often than the others.) In exercise 6.2.2–5 we found that the probability of a tree in the tree search algorithm was $\prod(1/s(x))$, where the product is over all internal nodes x, and $s(x)$ is the number of internal nodes in the subtree rooted at x. Find similar formulas for the probability of a tree in the case of (a) Algorithm D; (b) Algorithm P.

▶ **37.** [*M22*] Consider a binary tree with b_l external nodes on level l. The text observes that the running time for unsuccessful searching in digital search trees is not directly related to the external path length $\sum lb_l$, but instead it is essentially proportional to the *modified external path length* $\sum lb_l 2^{-l}$. Prove or disprove: The smallest modified external path length, over all trees with N external nodes, occurs when all of the external nodes appear on at most two adjacent levels. (See exercise 5.3.1–20.)

38. [*M40*] Develop an algorithm to find the n-node tree having the minimum value of $\alpha \cdot$ (internal path length) $+ \beta \cdot$ (modified external path length), given α and β, in the sense of exercise 37.

39. [*M43*] Develop an algorithm to find optimum digital search trees, analogous to the optimum binary search trees considered in Section 6.2.2.

▶ **40.** [*25*] Let $a_0 a_1 a_2 \ldots$ be a periodic binary sequence with $a_{N+k} = a_k$ for all $k \geq 0$. Show that there is a way to represent any fixed sequence of this type in $O(N)$ memory locations, so that the following operation can be done in only $O(N)$ steps: Given any binary pattern $b_0 b_1 \ldots b_{n-1}$, determine how often the pattern occurs in the period (thus, find how many values of p exist with $0 \leq p < N$ and $b_k = a_{p+k}$ for $0 \leq k < n$). The length n of the pattern is variable as well as the pattern itself. Assume that each memory location is big enough to hold arbitrary integers between 0 and N. [*Hint:* See exercise 14.]

41. [*HM28*] This is an application to group theory. Let G be the free group on the letters $\{a_1, \ldots, a_n\}$, namely the set of all strings $\alpha = b_1 \ldots b_r$, where each b_i is one of the a_j or a_j^- and no adjacent pair $a_j a_j^-$ or $a_j^- a_j$ occurs. The inverse of α is $b_r^- \ldots b_1^-$, and we multiply two such strings by concatenating them and cancelling adjacent inverse pairs. Let H be the subgroup of G generated by the strings $\{\beta_1, \ldots, \beta_p\}$, namely the set of all elements of G that can written as products of the β's and their inverses. According to a well-known theorem of Jakob Nielsen (see Marshall Hall, *The Theory of Groups* (New

York: Macmillan, 1959), Chapter 7), we can always find generators $\theta_1, \ldots, \theta_m$ of H, with $m \le p$, having the property that the middle character of θ_i (or at least one of the two central characters of θ_i if it has even length) is never cancelled in the expressions $\theta_i\theta_j^e$ or $\theta_j^e\theta_i$, $e = \pm 1$, unless $j = i$ and $e = -1$. This property implies that there is a simple algorithm for testing whether an arbitrary element of G is in H: Record the $2m$ keys $\theta_1, \ldots, \theta_m, \theta_1^-, \ldots, \theta_m^-$ in a character-oriented search tree, using the $2n$ letters $a_1, \ldots, a_n, a_1^-, \ldots, a_n^-$. Let $\alpha = b_1 \ldots b_r$ be a given element of G; if $r = 0$, α is obviously in H. Otherwise look up α, finding the longest prefix $b_1 \ldots b_k$ that matches a key. If there is more than one key beginning with $b_1 \ldots b_k$, α is not in H; otherwise let the unique such key be $b_1 \ldots b_k c_1 \ldots c_l = \theta_i^e$, and replace α by $\theta_i^{-e}\alpha = c_l^- \ldots c_1^- b_{k+1} \ldots b_r$. If this new value of α is longer than the old (that is, if $l > k$), α is not in H; otherwise repeat the process on the new value of α. The Nielsen property implies that this algorithm will always terminate. If α is eventually reduced to the null string, we can reconstruct the representation of the original α as a product of θ's.

For example, let $\{\theta_1, \theta_2, \theta_3\} = \{bbb, b^-a^-b^-, ba^-b\}$ and $\alpha = bbabaab$. The forest

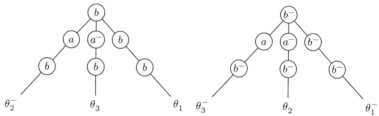

can be used with the algorithm above to deduce that $\alpha = \theta_1\theta_3^-\theta_1\theta_3^-\theta_2^-$. Implement this algorithm, given the θ's as input to your program.

42. [*23*] (*Front and rear compression.*) When a set of binary keys is being used as an index, to partition a larger file, we need not store the full keys. For example, if the sixteen keys of Fig. 34 are used, they can be truncated at the right, as soon as enough digits have been given to identify them uniquely: 0000, 0001, 00100, 00101, 010, ..., 1110001. These truncated keys can be used to partition a file into seventeen parts, where for example the fifth part consists of all keys beginning with 0011 or 010, and the last part contains all keys beginning with 111001, 11101, or 1111. The truncated keys can be represented more compactly if we suppress all leading digits common to the previous key: 0000, ◊◊◊1, ◊◊100, ◊◊◊◊1, ◊10, ..., ◊◊◊◊◊◊1. The bit following a ◊ is always 1, so it may be suppressed. A large file will have many ◊'s, and we need store only the number of ◊'s and the values of the following bits.

Show that the total number of bits in the compressed file, excluding ◊'s and the following 1 bits, is always equal to the number of nodes in the binary trie for the keys.

(Consequently the average total number of such bits in the entire index is about $N/\ln 2$, only 1.44 bits per key. This compression technique was shown to the author by A. Heller and R. L. Johnsen. Still further compression is possible, since we need only represent the trie structure; see Theorem 2.3.1A.)

43. [*HM42*] Analyze the height of a random M-ary trie that has N keys and cutoff parameter s as in exercise 20. (When $s = 1$, this is the length of the longest common prefix of N long random words in an M-ary alphabet.)

▶ **44.** [*30*] (J. L. Bentley and R. Sedgewick.) Explore a ternary representation of tries, in which left and right links correspond to the horizontal branches of (2) while middle links correspond to the downward branches.

6.4. HASHING

SO FAR WE HAVE CONSIDERED search methods based on comparing the given
argument K to the keys in the table, or using its digits to govern a branching
process. A third possibility is to avoid all this rummaging around by doing some
arithmetical calculation on K, computing a function $f(K)$ that is the location
of K and the associated data in the table.

For example, let's consider again the set of 31 English words that we have
subjected to various search strategies in Sections 6.2.2 and 6.3. Table 1 shows
a short MIX program that transforms each of the 31 keys into a unique number
$f(K)$ between -10 and 30. If we compare this method to the MIX programs
for the other methods we have considered (for example, binary search, optimal
tree search, trie memory, digital tree search), we find that it is superior from
the standpoint of both space and speed, except that binary search uses slightly
less space. In fact, the average time for a successful search, using the program
of Table 1 with the frequency data of Fig. 12, is only about $17.8u$, and only 41
table locations are needed to store the 31 keys.

Unfortunately, such functions $f(K)$ aren't very easy to discover. There are
$41^{31} \approx 10^{50}$ possible functions from a 31-element set into a 41-element set, and
only $41 \cdot 40 \cdot \ldots \cdot 11 = 41!/10! \approx 10^{43}$ of them will give distinct values for each
argument; thus only about one of every 10 million functions will be suitable.

Functions that avoid duplicate values are surprisingly rare, even with a fairly
large table. For example, the famous "birthday paradox" asserts that if 23 or
more people are present in a room, chances are good that two of them will have
the same month and day of birth! In other words, if we select a random function
that maps 23 keys into a table of size 365, the probability that no two keys map
into the same location is only 0.4927 (less than one-half). Skeptics who doubt
this result should try to find the birthday mates at the next large parties they
attend. [The birthday paradox was discussed informally by mathematicians in
the 1930s, but its origin is obscure; see I. J. Good, *Probability and the Weighing
of Evidence* (Griffin, 1950), 38. See also R. von Mises, *İstanbul Üniversitesi
Fen Fakültesi Mecmuasi* **4** (1939), 145–163, and W. Feller, *An Introduction to
Probability Theory* (New York: Wiley, 1950), Section 2.3.]

On the other hand, the approach used in Table 1 is fairly flexible [see
M. Greniewski and W. Turski, *CACM* **6** (1963), 322–323], and for a medium-
sized table a suitable function can be found after about a day's work. In
fact it is rather amusing to solve a puzzle like this. Suitable techniques have
been discussed by many people, including for example R. Sprugnoli, *CACM* **20**
(1977), 841–850, **22** (1979), 104, 553; R. J. Cichelli, *CACM* **23** (1980), 17–19;
T. J. Sager, *CACM* **28** (1985), 523–532, **29** (1986), 557; B. S. Majewski, N. C.
Wormald, G. Havas, and Z. J. Czech, *Comp. J.* **39** (1996), 547–554; Czech,
Havas, and Majewski, *Theoretical Comp. Sci.* **182** (1997), 1–143. See also the
article by J. Körner and K. Marton, *Europ. J. Combinatorics* **9** (1988), 523–530,
for theoretical limitations on perfect hash functions.

Of course this method has a serious flaw, since the contents of the table
must be known in advance; adding one more key will probably ruin everything,

Table 1
TRANSFORMING A SET OF KEYS INTO UNIQUE ADDRESSES

Instruction	A	AND	ARE	AS	AT	BE	BUT	BY	FOR	FROM	HAD	HAVE	HE	HER
LD1N K(1:1)	−1	−1	−1	−1	−1	−2	−2	−2	−6	−6	−8	−8	−8	−8
LD2 K(2:2)	−1	−1	−1	−1	−1	−2	−2	−2	−6	−6	−8	−8	−8	−8
INC1 -8,2	−9	6	10	13	14	−5	14	18	2	5	−15	−15	−11	−11
J1P *+2	−9	6	10	13	14	−5	14	18	2	5	−15	−15	−11	−11
INC1 16,2	7	.	.	.	.	16	.	.	.	.	2	2	10	10
LD2 K(3,3)	7	6	10	13	14	16	14	18	2	5	2	2	10	10
J2Z 9F	7	6	10	13	14	16	14	18	2	5	2	2	10	10
INC1 -28,2	.	−18	−13	.	.	.	9	.	−7	−7	−22	−1	.	−1
J1P 9F	.	−18	−13	.	.	.	9	.	−7	−7	−22	−1	.	−1
INC1 11,2	.	−3	3	.	.	.	.	.	23	20	−7	35	.	.
LDA K(4:4)	.	−3	3	.	.	.	.	.	23	20	−7	35	.	.
JAZ 9F	.	−3	3	.	.	.	.	.	23	20	−7	35	.	.
DEC1 -5,2	.	.	.	.	.	.	.	.	.	9	.	15	.	.
J1N 9F	.	.	.	.	.	.	.	.	.	9	.	15	.	.
INC1 10	.	.	.	.	.	.	.	.	.	19	.	25	.	.
9H LDA K	7	−3	3	13	14	16	9	18	23	19	−7	25	10	1
CMPA TABLE,1	7	−3	3	13	14	16	9	18	23	19	−7	25	10	1
JNE FAILURE	7	−3	3	13	14	16	9	18	23	19	−7	25	10	1

making it necessary to start over almost from scratch. We can obtain a much more versatile method if we give up the idea of uniqueness, permitting different keys to yield the same value $f(K)$, and using a special method to resolve any ambiguity after $f(K)$ has been computed.

These considerations lead to a popular class of search methods commonly known as *hashing* or *scatter storage* techniques. The verb "to hash" means to chop something up or to make a mess out of it; the idea in hashing is to scramble some aspects of the key and to use this partial information as the basis for searching. We compute a *hash address* $h(K)$ and begin searching there.

The birthday paradox tells us that there will probably be distinct keys $K_i \neq K_j$ that hash to the same value $h(K_i) = h(K_j)$. Such an occurrence is called a *collision*, and several interesting approaches have been devised to handle the collision problem. In order to use a hash table, programmers must make two almost independent decisions: They must choose a hash function $h(K)$, and they must select a method for collision resolution. We shall now consider these two aspects of the problem in turn.

Hash functions. To make things more explicit, let us assume throughout this section that our hash function h takes on at most M different values, with

$$0 \leq h(K) < M, \tag{1}$$

for all keys K. The keys in actual files that arise in practice usually have a great deal of redundancy; we must be careful to find a hash function that breaks up clusters of almost identical keys, in order to reduce the number of collisions.

HIS	I	IN	IS	IT	NOT	OF	ON	OR	THAT	THE	THIS	TO	WAS	WHICH	WITH	YOU
								Contents of rI1 after executing the instruction, given a particular key K								
−8	−9	−9	−9	−9	−15	−16	−16	−16	−23	−23	−23	−23	−26	−26	−26	−28
−8	−9	−9	−9	−9	−15	−16	−16	−16	−23	−23	−23	−23	−26	−26	−26	−28
−7	−17	−2	5	6	−7	−18	−9	−5	−23	−23	−23	−15	−33	−26	−25	−20
−7	−17	−2	5	6	−7	−18	−9	−5	−23	−23	−23	−15	−33	−26	−25	−20
18	−1	29	.	.	25	4	22	30	1	1	1	17	−16	−2	0	12
18	−1	29	5	6	25	4	22	30	1	1	1	17	−16	−2	0	12
18	−1	29	5	6	25	4	22	30	1	1	1	17	−16	−2	0	12
12	.	.	.	.	20	.	.	.	−26	−22	−18	.	−22	−21	−5	8
12	.	.	.	.	20	.	.	.	−26	−22	−18	.	−22	−21	−5	8
.	.	.	.	.	.	.	.	.	−14	−6	2	.	11	−1	29	.
.	.	.	.	.	.	.	.	.	−14	−6	2	.	11	−1	29	.
.	.	.	.	.	.	.	.	.	−14	−6	2	.	11	−1	29	.
.	.	.	.	.	.	.	.	.	−10	.	−2	.	.	−5	11	.
.	.	.	.	.	.	.	.	.	−10	.	−2	.	.	−5	11	.
.	.	.	.	.	.	.	.	.	.	.	.	.	.	.	21	.
12	−1	29	5	6	20	4	22	30	−10	−6	−2	17	11	−5	21	8
12	−1	29	5	6	20	4	22	30	−10	−6	−2	17	11	−5	21	8
12	−1	29	5	6	20	4	22	30	−10	−6	−2	17	11	−5	21	8

It is theoretically impossible to define a hash function that creates truly random data from the nonrandom data in actual files. But in practice it is not difficult to produce a pretty good imitation of random data, by using simple arithmetic as we have discussed in Chapter 3. And in fact we can often do even better, by exploiting the nonrandom properties of actual data to construct a hash function that leads to fewer collisions than truly random keys would produce.

Consider, for example, the case of 10-digit keys on a decimal computer. One hash function that suggests itself is to let $M = 1000$, say, and to let $h(K)$ be three digits chosen from somewhere near the middle of the 20-digit product $K \times K$. This would seem to yield a fairly good good spread of values between 000 and 999, with low probability of collisions. Experiments with actual data show, in fact, that this "middle square" method isn't bad, provided that the keys do not have a lot of leading or trailing zeros; but it turns out that there are safer and saner ways to proceed, just as we found in Chapter 3 that the middle square method is not an especially good random number generator.

Extensive tests on typical files have shown that two major types of hash functions work quite well. One is based on division, and the other is based on multiplication.

The division method is particularly easy; we simply use the remainder modulo M:

$$h(K) = K \bmod M. \tag{2}$$

In this case, some values of M are obviously much better than others. For example, if M is an even number, $h(K)$ will be even when K is even and odd when K is odd, and this will lead to a substantial bias in many files. It would be even worse to let M be a power of the radix of the computer, since $K \bmod M$ would then be simply the least significant digits of K (independent of the other digits). Similarly we can argue that M probably shouldn't be a multiple of 3; for if the keys are alphabetic, two keys that differ only by permutation of letters would then differ in numeric value by a multiple of 3. (This occurs because $2^{2n} \bmod 3 = 1$ and $10^n \bmod 3 = 1$.) In general, we want to avoid values of M that divide $r^k \pm a$, where k and a are small numbers and r is the radix of the alphabetic character set (usually $r = 64, 256$, or 100), since a remainder modulo such a value of M tends to be largely a simple superposition of the key digits. Such considerations suggest that we *choose M to be a prime number* such that $r^k \not\equiv \pm a$ (modulo M) for small k and a. This choice has been found to be quite satisfactory in most cases.

For example, on the MIX computer we could choose $M = 1009$, computing $h(K)$ by the sequence

$$
\begin{array}{lll}
\texttt{LDX} & \texttt{K} & \text{rX} \leftarrow K. \\
\texttt{ENTA} & \texttt{0} & \text{rA} \leftarrow 0. \\
\texttt{DIV} & \texttt{=1009=} & \text{rX} \leftarrow K \bmod 1009.
\end{array}
\tag{3}
$$

The multiplicative hashing scheme is equally easy to do, but it is slightly harder to describe because we must imagine ourselves working with fractions instead of with integers. Let w be the word size of the computer, so that w is usually 10^{10} or 2^{30} for MIX; we can regard an integer A as the fraction A/w if we imagine the radix point to be at the left of the word. The method is to choose some integer constant A relatively prime to w, and to let

$$
h(K) = \left\lfloor M \left(\left(\frac{A}{w} K \right) \bmod 1 \right) \right\rfloor.
\tag{4}
$$

In this case we usually let M be a power of 2 on a binary computer, so that $h(K)$ consists of the leading bits of the least significant half of the product AK.

In MIX code, if we let $M = 2^m$ and assume a binary radix, the multiplicative hash function is

$$
\begin{array}{lll}
\texttt{LDA} & \texttt{K} & \text{rA} \leftarrow K. \\
\texttt{MUL} & \texttt{A} & \text{rAX} \leftarrow AK. \\
\texttt{ENTA} & \texttt{0} & \text{rAX} \leftarrow AK \bmod w. \\
\texttt{SLB} & \texttt{m} & \text{Shift rAX } m \text{ bits to the left.}
\end{array}
\tag{5}
$$

Now $h(K)$ appears in register A. Since MIX has rather slow multiplication and shift instructions, this sequence takes exactly as long to compute as (3); but on many machines multiplication is significantly faster than division.

In a sense this method can be regarded as a generalization of (3), since we could for example take A to be an approximation to $w/1009$; multiplying by the reciprocal of a constant is often faster than dividing by that constant. The technique of (5) is almost a "middle square" method, but there is one important difference: We shall see that multiplication by a suitable constant has demonstrably good properties.

One of the nice features of the multiplicative scheme is that no information is lost when we blank out the A register in (5); we could determine K again, given only the contents of rAX after (5) has finished. The reason is that A is relatively prime to w, so Euclid's algorithm can be used to find a constant A' with $AA' \bmod w = 1$; this implies that $K = \bigl(A'(AK \bmod w)\bigr) \bmod w$. In other words, if $f(K)$ denotes the contents of register X just before the SLB instruction in (5), then

$$K_1 \neq K_2 \qquad \text{implies} \qquad f(K_1) \neq f(K_2). \tag{6}$$

Of course $f(K)$ takes on values in the range 0 to $w - 1$, so it isn't any good as a hash function, but it can be very useful as a *scrambling function*, namely a function satisfying (6) that tends to randomize the keys. Such a function can be very useful in connection with the tree search algorithms of Section 6.2.2, if the order of keys is unimportant, since it removes the danger of degeneracy when keys enter the tree in increasing order. (See exercise 6.2.2–10.) A scrambling function is also useful in connection with the digital tree search algorithm of Section 6.3, if the bits of the actual keys are biased.

Another feature of the multiplicative hash method is that it makes good use of the nonrandomness found in many files. Actual sets of keys often have a preponderance of arithmetic progressions, where $\{K, K+d, K+2d, \ldots, K+td\}$ all appear in the file; for example, consider alphabetic names like {PART1, PART2, PART3} or {TYPEA, TYPEB, TYPEC}. The multiplicative hash method converts an arithmetic progression into an approximate arithmetic progression $h(K)$, $h(K+d)$, $h(K+2d)$, ... of distinct hash values, reducing the number of collisions from what we would expect in a random situation. The division method has this same property.

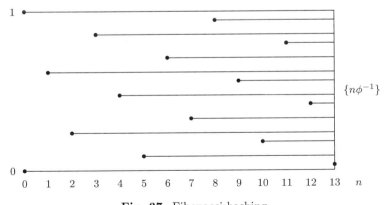

Fig. 37. Fibonacci hashing.

Figure 37 illustrates this aspect of multiplicative hashing in a particularly interesting case. Suppose that A/w is approximately the golden ratio $\phi^{-1} = (\sqrt{5}-1)/2 \approx 0.6180339887$; then the successive values $h(K)$, $h(K+1)$, $h(K+2)$, ... have essentially the same behavior as the successive hash values $h(0)$, $h(1)$,

$h(2)$, ..., so the following experiment suggests itself: Starting with the line segment $[0\,..\,1]$, we successively mark off the points $\{\phi^{-1}\}$, $\{2\phi^{-1}\}$, $\{3\phi^{-1}\}$, ..., where $\{x\}$ denotes the fractional part of x (namely $x - \lfloor x \rfloor$, or x mod 1). As shown in Fig. 37, these points stay very well separated from each other; in fact, each newly added point falls into one of the largest remaining intervals, and divides it in the golden ratio! [This phenomenon was first conjectured by J. Oderfeld and proved by S. Świerczkowski, *Fundamenta Math.* **46** (1958), 187–189. Fibonacci numbers play an important role in the proof.]

    The remarkable scattering property of the golden ratio is actually just a special case of a very general result, originally conjectured by Hugo Steinhaus and first proved by Vera Turán Sós [*Acta Math. Acad. Sci. Hung.* **8** (1957), 461–471; *Ann. Univ. Sci. Budapest. Eötvös Sect. Math.* **1** (1958), 127–134]:

Theorem S. *Let θ be any irrational number. When the points $\{\theta\}$, $\{2\theta\}$, ..., $\{n\theta\}$ are placed in the line segment $[0\,..\,1]$, the $n + 1$ line segments formed have at most three different lengths. Moreover, the next point $\{(n+1)\theta\}$ will fall in one of the largest existing segments.* ∎

Thus, the points $\{\theta\}, \{2\theta\}, \ldots, \{n\theta\}$ are spread out very evenly between 0 and 1. If θ is rational, the same theorem holds if we give a suitable interpretation to the segments of length 0 that appear when n is greater than or equal to the denominator of θ. A proof of Theorem S, together with a detailed analysis of the underlying structure of the situation, appears in exercise 8; it turns out that the segments of a given length are created and destroyed in a first-in-first-out manner. Of course, some θ's are better than others, since for example a value that is near 0 or 1 will start out with many small segments and one large segment. Exercise 9 shows that the two numbers ϕ^{-1} and $\phi^{-2} = 1 - \phi^{-1}$ lead to the "most uniformly distributed" sequences, among all numbers θ between 0 and 1.

    The theory above suggests *Fibonacci hashing*, where we choose the constant A to be the nearest integer to $\phi^{-1}w$ that is relatively prime to w. For example if MIX were a decimal computer we would take

$$A = \boxed{\;+\;|\;61\;|\;80\;|\;33\;|\;98\;|\;87\;}\;. \tag{7}$$

This multiplier will spread out alphabetic keys like LIST1, LIST2, LIST3 very nicely. But notice what happens when we have an arithmetic series in the fourth character position, as in the keys SUM1␣, SUM2␣, SUM3␣: The effect is as if Theorem S were being used with $\theta = \{100A/w\} = .80339887$ instead of $\theta = .6180339887 = A/w$. The resulting behavior is still all right, in spite of the fact that this value of θ is not quite as good as ϕ^{-1}. On the other hand, if the progression occurs in the second character position, as in A1␣␣␣, A2␣␣␣, A3␣␣␣, the effective θ is .9887, and this is probably too close to 1.

    Therefore we might do better with a multiplier like

$$A = \boxed{\;+\;|\;61\;|\;61\;|\;61\;|\;61\;|\;61\;}$$

in place of (7); such a multiplier will separate out consecutive sequences of keys that differ in *any* character position. Unfortunately this choice suffers from another problem analogous to the difficulty of dividing by $r^k \pm 1$: Keys such as XY and YX will tend to hash to the same location! One way out of this difficulty is to look more closely at the structure underlying Theorem S. For short progressions of keys, only the first few partial quotients of the continued fraction representation of θ are relevant, and small partial quotients correspond to good distribution properties. Therefore we find that the best values of θ lie in the ranges

$$\tfrac{1}{4} < \theta < \tfrac{3}{10}, \qquad \tfrac{1}{3} < \theta < \tfrac{3}{7}, \qquad \tfrac{4}{7} < \theta < \tfrac{2}{3}, \qquad \tfrac{7}{10} < \theta < \tfrac{3}{4}.$$

A value of A can be found so that each of its bytes lies in a good range and is not too close to the values of the other bytes or their complements, for example

$$A = \boxed{+\ \vert\ 61\ \vert\ 25\ \vert\ 42\ \vert\ 33\ \vert\ 71}\ . \tag{8}$$

Such a multiplier can be recommended. (These ideas about multiplicative hashing are due largely to R. W. Floyd.)

A good hash function should satisfy two requirements:

a) Its computation should be very fast.

b) It should minimize collisions.

Property (a) is machine-dependent, and property (b) is data-dependent. If the keys were truly random, we could simply extract a few bits from them and use those bits for the hash function; but in practice we nearly always need to have a hash function that depends on all bits of the key in order to satisfy (b).

So far we have considered how to hash one-word keys. Multiword or variable-length keys can be handled by multiple-precision extensions of the methods above, but it is generally adequate to speed things up by combining the individual words together into a single word, then doing a single multiplication or division as above. The combination can be done by addition mod w, or by exclusive-or on a binary computer; both of these operations have the advantage that they are invertible, namely that they depend on all bits of both arguments, and exclusive-or is sometimes preferable because it avoids arithmetic overflow. However, both of these operations are commutative, hence (X, Y) and (Y, X) will hash to the same address; G. D. Knott has suggested avoiding this problem by doing a cyclic shift just before adding or exclusive-oring.

An even better way to hash l-character or l-word keys $K = x_1 x_2 \ldots x_l$ is to compute

$$h(K) = \bigl(h_1(x_1) + h_2(x_2) + \cdots + h_l(x_l) \bigr) \bmod M, \tag{9}$$

where each h_j is an independent hash function. This idea, introduced by J. L. Carter and M. N. Wegman in 1977, is especially efficient when each x_j is a single character, because we can then use a precomputed array for each h_j. Such arrays make multiplication unnecessary; and if M is a power of 2, we can avoid the division in (9) by substituting exclusive-or for addition. Therefore (9) certainly satisfies property (a). Moreover, Carter and Wegman proved that if the h_j are chosen at random, property (b) will hold *regardless of the input data*. (See exercise 72.)

Many more methods for hashing have been suggested, but none of them have proved to be superior to the simple methods described above. For a survey of several approaches together with detailed statistics on their performance with actual files, see the article by V. Y. Lum, P. S. T. Yuen, and M. Dodd, *CACM* **14** (1971), 228–239.

Of all the other hash methods that have been tried, perhaps the most interesting is a technique based on algebraic coding theory; the idea is analogous to the division method above, but we divide by a polynomial modulo 2 instead of dividing by an integer. (As observed in Section 4.6, this operation is analogous to division, just as addition is analogous to exclusive-or.) For this method, M should be a power of 2, say $M = 2^m$, and we make use of an mth degree polynomial $P(x) = x^m + p_{m-1}x^{m-1} + \cdots + p_0$. An n-digit binary key $K = (k_{n-1}\ldots k_1 k_0)_2$ can be regarded as the polynomial $K(x) = k_{n-1}x^{n-1} + \cdots + k_1 x + k_0$, and we compute the remainder

$$K(x) \bmod P(x) = h_{m-1}x^{m-1} + \cdots + h_1 x + h_0$$

using polynomial arithmetic modulo 2; then $h(K) = (h_{m-1}\ldots h_1 h_0)_2$. If $P(x)$ is chosen properly, this hash function can be guaranteed to avoid collisions between nearly equal keys. For example if $n = 15$, $m = 10$, and

$$P(x) = x^{10} + x^8 + x^5 + x^4 + x^2 + x + 1, \tag{10}$$

it can be shown that $h(K_1)$ will be unequal to $h(K_2)$ whenever K_1 and K_2 are distinct keys that differ in fewer than seven bit positions. (See exercise 7 for further information about this scheme; it is, of course, more suitable for hardware or microprogramming implementation than for software.)

It is often convenient to use the constant hash function $h(K) = 0$ when debugging a program, since all keys will be stored together; an efficient $h(K)$ can be substituted later.

Collision resolution by "chaining." We have observed that some hash addresses will probably be burdened with more than their share of keys. Perhaps the most obvious way to solve this problem is to maintain M linked lists, one for each possible hash code. A LINK field should be included in each record, and there will also be M list heads, numbered say from 1 through M. After hashing the key, we simply do a sequential search in list number $h(K) + 1$. (See exercise 6.1–2. The situation is very similar to multiple-list-insertion sorting, Program 5.2.1M.)

Figure 38 illustrates this simple chaining scheme when $M = 9$, for the sequence of seven keys

$$K = \text{EN, TO, TRE, FIRE, FEM, SEKS, SYV} \tag{11}$$

(the numbers 1 through 7 in Norwegian), having the respective hash codes

$$h(K) + 1 = 3,\ 1,\ 4,\ 1,\ 5,\ 9,\ 2. \tag{12}$$

The first list has two elements, and three of the lists are empty.

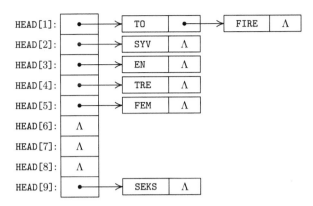

Fig. 38. Separate chaining.

Chaining is quite fast, because the lists are short. If 365 people are gathered together in one room, there will probably be many pairs having the same birthday, but the average number of people with any given birthday will be only 1! In general, if there are N keys and M lists, the average list size is N/M; thus hashing decreases the average amount of work needed for sequential searching by roughly a factor of M. (A precise formula is worked out in exercise 34.)

This method is a straightforward combination of techniques we have discussed before, so we do not need to formulate a detailed algorithm for chained hash tables. It is often a good idea to keep the individual lists in order by key, so that insertions and unsuccessful searches go faster. Thus if we choose to make the lists ascending, the TO and FIRE nodes of Fig. 38 would be interchanged, and all the Λ links would be replaced by pointers to a dummy record whose key is ∞. (See Algorithm 6.1T.) Alternatively we could make use of the "self-organizing" concept discussed in Section 6.1; instead of keeping the lists in order by key, they may be kept in order according to the time of most recent occurrence.

For the sake of speed we would like to make M rather large. But when M is large, many of the lists will be empty and much of the space for the M list heads will be wasted. This suggests another approach, when the records are small: We can overlap the record storage with the list heads, making room for a total of M records and M links instead of for N records and $M + N$ links. Sometimes it is possible to make one pass over all the data to find out which list heads will be used, then to make another pass inserting all the "overflow" records into the empty slots. But this is often impractical or impossible, and we'd rather have a technique that processes each record only once when it first enters the system. The following algorithm, due to F. A. Williams [*CACM* **2**, 6 (June 1959), 21–24], is a convenient way to solve the problem.

Algorithm C (*Chained hash table search and insertion*). This algorithm looks for a given key K in an M-node table. If K is not in the table and the table is not full, K is inserted.

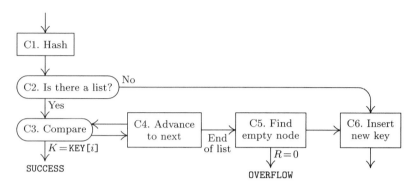

Fig. 39. Chained hash table search and insertion.

The nodes of the table are denoted by TABLE[i], for $0 \leq i \leq M$, and they are of two distinguishable types, *empty* and *occupied.* An occupied node contains a key field KEY[i], a link field LINK[i], and possibly other fields.

The algorithm makes use of a hash function $h(K)$. An auxiliary variable R is also used, to help find empty spaces; when the table is empty, we have $R = M + 1$, and as insertions are made it will always be true that TABLE[j] is occupied for all j in the range $R \leq j \leq M$. By convention, TABLE[0] will always be empty.

C1. [Hash.] Set $i \leftarrow h(K) + 1$. (Now $1 \leq i \leq M$.)

C2. [Is there a list?] If TABLE[i] is empty, go to C6. (Otherwise TABLE[i] is occupied; we will look at the list of occupied nodes that starts here.)

C3. [Compare.] If $K = $ KEY[i], the algorithm terminates successfully.

C4. [Advance to next.] If LINK[i] $\neq 0$, set $i \leftarrow$ LINK[i] and go back to step C3.

C5. [Find empty node.] (The search was unsuccessful, and we want to find an empty position in the table.) Decrease R one or more times until finding a value such that TABLE[R] is empty. If $R = 0$, the algorithm terminates with overflow (there are no empty nodes left); otherwise set LINK[i] $\leftarrow R$, $i \leftarrow R$.

C6. [Insert new key.] Mark TABLE[i] as an occupied node, with KEY[i] $\leftarrow K$ and LINK[i] $\leftarrow 0$. ∎

This algorithm allows several lists to coalesce, so that records need not be moved after they have been inserted into the table. For example, see Fig. 40, where SEKS appears in the list containing TO and FIRE since the latter had already been inserted into position 9.

In order to see how Algorithm C compares with others in this chapter, we can write the following MIX program. The analysis worked out below indicates that the lists of occupied cells tend to be short, and the program has been designed with this fact in mind.

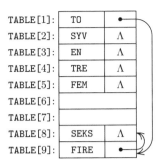

Fig. 40. Coalesced chaining.

Program C (*Chained hash table search and insertion*). For convenience, the keys are assumed to be only three bytes long, and nodes are represented as follows:

$$\text{empty node} \qquad \boxed{-\;|\;1\;|\;0\;|\;0\;|\;0\;|\;0}\;;$$

$$\text{occupied node} \qquad \boxed{+\;|\;\text{LINK}\;\;|\;\;\text{KEY}}\;.$$

(13)

The table size M is assumed to be prime; TABLE[i] is stored in location TABLE+i. rI1 $\equiv i$, rA $\equiv K$.

```
01 KEY    EQU  3:5
02 LINK   EQU  0:2
03 START  LDX  K              1        C1. Hash.
04        ENTA 0              1
05        DIV  =M=            1
06        STX  *+1(0:2)       1
07        ENT1 *              1        i ← h(K)
08        INC1 1              1              + 1.
09        LDA  K              1
10        LD2  TABLE,1(LINK)  1        C2. Is there a list?
11        J2N  6F             1        To C6 if TABLE[i] empty.
12        CMPA TABLE,1(KEY)   A        C3. Compare.
13        JE   SUCCESS        A        Exit if K = KEY[i].
14        J2Z  5F             A − S1   To C5 if LINK[i] = 0.
15 4H     ENT1 0,2            C − 1    C4. Advance to next.
16        CMPA TABLE,1(KEY)   C − 1    C3. Compare.
17        JE   SUCCESS        C − 1    Exit if K = KEY[i].
18        LD2  TABLE,1(LINK)  C − 1 − S2
19        J2NZ 4B             C − 1 − S2  Advance if LINK[i] ≠ 0.
20 5H     LD2  R              A − S    C5. Find empty node.
21        DEC2 1              T        R ← R − 1.
22        LDX  TABLE,2        T
23        JXNN *-2            T        Repeat until TABLE[R] empty.
24        J2Z  OVERFLOW       A − S    Exit if no empty nodes left.
25        ST2  TABLE,1(LINK)  A − S    LINK[i] ← R.
26        ENT1 0,2            A − S    i ← R.
```

27		ST2	R	$A - S$	Update R in memory.
28	6H	STZ	TABLE,1(LINK)	$1 - S$	C6. Insert new key. LINK[i] $\leftarrow$ 0.
29		STA	TABLE,1(KEY)	$1 - S$	KEY[i] $\leftarrow K$. ∎

The running time of this program depends on

C = number of table entries probed while searching;

A = [initial probe found an occupied node];

S = [search was successful];

T = number of table entries probed while looking for an empty space.

Here $S = S1 + S2$, where $S1 = 1$ if successful on the first try. The total running time for the searching phase of Program C is $(7C + 4A + 17 - 3S + 2S1)u$, and the insertion of a new key when $S = 0$ takes an additional $(8A + 4T + 4)u$.

Suppose there are N keys in the table at the start of this program, and let

$$\alpha = N/M = \text{load factor of the table.} \tag{14}$$

Then the average value of A in an unsuccessful search is obviously α, if the hash function is random; and exercise 39 proves that the average value of C in an unsuccessful search is

$$C'_N = 1 + \frac{1}{4}\left(\left(1 + \frac{2}{M}\right)^N - 1 - \frac{2N}{M}\right) \approx 1 + \frac{e^{2\alpha} - 1 - 2\alpha}{4}. \tag{15}$$

Thus when the table is half full, the average number of probes made in an unsuccessful search is about $\frac{1}{4}(e + 2) \approx 1.18$; and even when the table gets completely full, the average number of probes made just before inserting the final item will be only about $\frac{1}{4}(e^2 + 1) \approx 2.10$. The standard deviation is also small, as shown in exercise 40. These statistics prove that *the lists stay short even though the algorithm occasionally allows them to coalesce*, when the hash function is random. Of course C can be as high as N, if the hash function is bad or if we are extremely unlucky.

In a successful search, we always have $A = 1$. The average number of probes during a successful search may be computed by summing the quantity $C + A$ over the first N unsuccessful searches and dividing by N, if we assume that each key is equally likely. Thus we obtain

$$C_N = \frac{1}{N}\sum_{0 \le k < N}\left(C'_k + \frac{k}{M}\right) = 1 + \frac{1}{8}\frac{M}{N}\left(\left(1 + \frac{2}{M}\right)^N - 1 - \frac{2N}{M}\right) + \frac{1}{4}\frac{N-1}{M}$$

$$\approx 1 + \frac{e^{2\alpha} - 1 - 2\alpha}{8\alpha} + \frac{\alpha}{4} \tag{16}$$

as the average number of probes in a random successful search. Even a full table will require only about 1.80 probes, on the average, to find an item! Similarly (see exercise 42), the average value of $S1$ turns out to be

$$S1_N = 1 - \tfrac{1}{2}((N - 1)/M) \approx 1 - \tfrac{1}{2}\alpha. \tag{17}$$

At first glance it may appear that step C5 is inefficient, since it has to search sequentially for an empty position. But actually the total number of table probes made in step C5 as a table is being built will never exceed the number of items in the table; so we make an average of at most one of these probes per insertion. Exercise 41 proves that T is approximately αe^{α} in a random unsuccessful search.

It would be possible to modify Algorithm C so that no two lists coalesce, but then it would become necessary to move records around. For example, consider the situation in Fig. 40 just before we wanted to insert SEKS into position 9; in order to keep the lists separate, it would be necessary to move FIRE, and for this purpose it would be necessary to discover which node points to FIRE. We could solve this problem without providing two-way linkage by hashing FIRE and searching down its list, as suggested by D. E. Ferguson, since the lists are short. Exercise 34 shows that the average number of probes, when lists aren't coalesced, is reduced to

$$C'_N = 1 + \frac{N(N-1)}{2M^2} \approx 1 + \frac{\alpha^2}{2} \quad \text{(unsuccessful search)}; \qquad (18)$$

$$C_N = 1 + \frac{N-1}{2} \approx 1 + \frac{\alpha}{2} \quad \text{(successful search)}; \qquad (19)$$

This is not enough of an improvement over (15) and (16) to warrant changing the algorithm.

On the other hand, Butler Lampson has observed that most of the space actually needed for links can actually be saved in the chaining method, if we avoid coalescing the lists. This leads to an interesting algorithm that is discussed in exercise 13. Lampson's method introduces a tag bit in each entry, and causes the average number of probes needed in an unsuccessful search to decrease slightly, from (18) to

$$\left(1 - \frac{1}{M}\right)^N + \frac{N}{M} \approx e^{-\alpha} + \alpha. \qquad (18')$$

Separate chaining as in Fig. 38 can be used when $N > M$, so overflow is not a serious problem in that case. When the lists coalesce as in Fig. 40 and Algorithm C, we can link extra items into an auxiliary storage pool; L. Guibas has proved that the average number of probes to insert the $(M + L + 1)$st item is then $\left(L/2M + \frac{1}{4}\right)\left((1 + 2/M)^M - 1\right) + \frac{1}{2}$. However, it is usually preferable to use an alternative scheme that puts the first colliding elements into an auxiliary storage area, allowing lists to coalesce only when this auxiliary area has filled up; see exercise 43.

Collision resolution by "open addressing." Another way to resolve the problem of collisions is to do away with links entirely, simply looking at various entries of the table one by one until either finding the key K or finding an empty position. The idea is to formulate some rule by which every key K determines a "probe sequence," namely a sequence of table positions that are to be inspected whenever K is inserted or looked up. If we encounter an open position while searching for K, using the probe sequence determined by K, we can conclude that K is not in the table, since the same sequence of probes will be made every time K is processed. This general class of methods was named *open addressing* by W. W. Peterson [*IBM J. Research & Development* **1** (1957), 130–146].

The simplest open addressing scheme, known as *linear probing*, uses the cyclic probe sequence

$$h(K),\ h(K) - 1,\ \ldots,\ 0,\ M - 1,\ M - 2,\ \ldots,\ h(K) + 1 \qquad (20)$$

as in the following algorithm.

Algorithm L (*Linear probing and insertion*). This algorithm searches an M-node table, looking for a given key K. If K is not in the table and the table is not full, K is inserted.

The nodes of the table are denoted by TABLE[i], for $0 \leq i < M$, and they are of two distinguishable types, *empty* and *occupied*. An occupied node contains a key, called KEY[i], and possibly other fields. An auxiliary variable N is used to keep track of how many nodes are occupied; this variable is considered to be part of the table, and it is increased by 1 whenever a new key is inserted.

This algorithm makes use of a hash function $h(K)$, and it uses the linear probing sequence (20) to address the table. Modifications of that sequence are discussed below.

L1. [Hash.] Set $i \leftarrow h(K)$. (Now $0 \leq i < M$.)

L2. [Compare.] If TABLE[i] is empty, go to step L4. Otherwise if KEY[i] = K, the algorithm terminates successfully.

L3. [Advance to next.] Set $i \leftarrow i - 1$; if now $i < 0$, set $i \leftarrow i + M$. Go back to step L2.

L4. [Insert.] (The search was unsuccessful.) If $N = M - 1$, the algorithm terminates with overflow. (This algorithm considers the table to be full when $N = M - 1$, not when $N = M$; see exercise 15.) Otherwise set $N \leftarrow N + 1$, mark TABLE[i] occupied, and set KEY[i] $\leftarrow K$. ∎

Figure 41 shows what happens when the seven example keys (11) are inserted by Algorithm L, using the respective hash codes 2, 7, 1, 8, 2, 8, 1: The last three keys, FEM, SEKS, and SYV, have been displaced from their initial locations $h(K)$.

0	FEM
1	TRE
2	EN
3	
4	
5	SYV
6	SEKS
7	TO
8	FIRE

Fig. 41. Linear open addressing.

Program L (*Linear probing and insertion*). This program deals with full-word keys; but a key of 0 is not allowed, since 0 is used to signal an empty position in the table. (Alternatively, we could require the keys to be non-negative, letting empty positions contain -1.) The table size M is assumed to be prime, and TABLE[i] is stored in location TABLE $+ i$ for $0 \le i < M$. For speed in the inner loop, location TABLE -1 is assumed to contain 0. Location VACANCIES is assumed to contain the value $M - 1 - N$; and rA $\equiv K$, rI1 $\equiv i$.

In order to speed up the inner loop of this program, the test "$i < 0$" has been removed from the loop so that only the essential parts of steps L2 and L3 remain. The total running time for the searching phase comes to $(7C + 9E + 21 - 4S)u$, and the insertion after an unsuccessful search adds an extra $8u$.

01	START	LDX	K	1	*L1. Hash.*
02		ENTA	0	1	
03		DIV	=M=	1	
04		STX	*+1(0:2)	1	
05		ENT1	*	1	$i \leftarrow h(K)$.
06		LDA	K	1	
07		JMP	2F	1	
08	8H	INC1	M+1	E	*L3. Advance to next.*
09	3H	DEC1	1	$C+E-1$	$i \leftarrow i - 1$.
10	2H	CMPA	TABLE,1	$C+E$	*L2. Compare.*
11		JE	SUCCESS	$C+E$	Exit if $K =$ KEY[i].
12		LDX	TABLE,1	$C+E-S$	
13		JXNZ	3B	$C+E-S$	To L3 if TABLE[i] nonempty.
14		J1N	8B	$E+1-S$	To L3 with $i \leftarrow M$ if $i = -1$.
15	4H	LDX	VACANCIES	$1-S$	*L4. Insert.*
16		JXZ	OVERFLOW	$1-S$	Exit with overflow if $N = M - 1$.
17		DECX	1	$1-S$	
18		STX	VACANCIES	$1-S$	Increase N by 1.
19		STA	TABLE,1	$1-S$	TABLE[i] $\leftarrow K$. ∎

As in Program C, the variable C denotes the number of probes, and S tells whether or not the search was successful. We may ignore the variable E, which is 1 only if a spurious probe of TABLE$[-1]$ has been made, since its average value is $(C-1)/M$.

Experience with linear probing shows that the algorithm works fine until the table begins to get full; but eventually the process slows down, with long drawn-out searches becoming increasingly frequent. The reason for this behavior can be understood by considering the following hypothetical hash table in which $M = 19$ and $N = 9$:

0	1	2	3	4	5	6	7	8	9	10	11	12	13	14	15	16	17	18

(21)

Shaded squares represent occupied positions. The next key K to be inserted into the table will go into one of the ten empty spaces, but these are not equally likely; in fact, K will be inserted into position 11 if $11 \le h(K) \le 15$, while it will fall into position 8 only if $h(K) = 8$. Therefore position 11 is five times as likely as position 8; long lists tend to grow even longer.

This phenomenon isn't enough by itself to account for the relatively poor behavior of linear probing, since a similar thing occurs in Algorithm C. (A list of length 4 is four times as likely to grow in Algorithm C as a list of length 1.) The real problem occurs when a cell like 4 or 16 becomes occupied in (21); then two separate lists are combined, while the lists in Algorithm C never grow by more than one step at a time. Consequently the performance of linear probing degrades rapidly when N approaches M.

We shall prove later in this section that the average number of probes needed by Algorithm L is approximately

$$C'_N \approx \frac{1}{2}\left(1 + \left(\frac{1}{1-\alpha}\right)^2\right) \quad \text{(unsuccessful search)};\qquad (22)$$

$$C_N \approx \frac{1}{2}\left(1 + \frac{1}{1-\alpha}\right) \qquad \text{(successful search)},\qquad (23)$$

where $\alpha = N/M$ is the load factor of the table. Therefore Program L is almost as fast as Program C, when the table is less than 75 percent full, in spite of the fact that Program C deals with unrealistically short keys. On the other hand, when α approaches 1 the best thing we can say about Program L is that it works, slowly but surely. In fact, when $N = M - 1$, there is only one vacant space in the table, so the average number of probes in an unsuccessful search is $(M + 1)/2$; we shall also prove that the average number of probes in a successful search is approximately $\sqrt{\pi M/8}$ when the table is full.

The pileup phenomenon that makes linear probing costly on a nearly full table is aggravated by the use of division hashing, if consecutive key values $\{K, K+1, K+2, \ldots\}$ are likely to occur, since these keys will have consecutive hash codes. Multiplicative hashing will break up these clusters satisfactorily.

Another way to protect against the consecutive hash code problem is to set $i \leftarrow i - c$ in step L3, instead of $i \leftarrow i - 1$. Any positive value of c will do, so long as it is *relatively prime* to M, since the probe sequence will still examine every position of the table in this case. Such a change would make Program L a bit slower, because of the test for $i < 0$. Decreasing by c instead of by 1 won't alter the pileup phenomenon, since groups of c-apart records will still be formed; equations (22) and (23) will still apply. But the appearance of consecutive keys $\{K, K+1, K+2, \ldots\}$ will now actually be a help instead of a hindrance.

Although a fixed value of c does not reduce the pileup phenomenon, we can improve the situation nicely by letting c depend on K. This idea leads to an important modification of Algorithm L, first introduced by Guy de Balbine [Ph.D. thesis, Calif. Inst. of Technology (1968), 149–150]:

Algorithm D (*Open addressing with double hashing*). This algorithm is almost identical to Algorithm L, but it probes the table in a slightly different fashion by making use of two hash functions $h_1(K)$ and $h_2(K)$. As usual $h_1(K)$ produces a value between 0 and $M - 1$, inclusive; but $h_2(K)$ must produce a value between

1 and $M - 1$ that is *relatively prime* to M. (For example, if M is prime, $h_2(K)$ can be any value between 1 and $M - 1$ inclusive; or if $M = 2^m$, $h_2(K)$ can be any *odd* value between 1 and $2^m - 1$.)

D1. [First hash.] Set $i \leftarrow h_1(K)$.

D2. [First probe.] If TABLE$[i]$ is empty, go to D6. Otherwise if KEY$[i] = K$, the algorithm terminates successfully.

D3. [Second hash.] Set $c \leftarrow h_2(K)$.

D4. [Advance to next.] Set $i \leftarrow i - c$; if now $i < 0$, set $i \leftarrow i + M$.

D5. [Compare.] If TABLE$[i]$ is empty, go to D6. Otherwise if KEY$[i] = K$, the algorithm terminates successfully. Otherwise go back to D4.

D6. [Insert.] If $N = M - 1$, the algorithm terminates with overflow. Otherwise set $N \leftarrow N + 1$, mark TABLE$[i]$ occupied, and set KEY$[i] \leftarrow K$.   ∎

Several possibilities have been suggested for computing $h_2(K)$. If M is prime and $h_1(K) = K \bmod M$, we might let $h_2(K) = 1 + (K \bmod (M - 1))$; but since $M - 1$ is even, it would be better to let $h_2(K) = 1 + (K \bmod (M - 2))$. This suggests choosing M so that M and $M - 2$ are "twin primes" like 1021 and 1019. Alternatively, we could set $h_2(K) = 1 + (\lfloor K/M \rfloor \bmod (M - 2))$, since the quotient $\lfloor K/M \rfloor$ might be available in a register as a by-product of the computation of $h_1(K)$.

If $M = 2^m$ and we are using multiplicative hashing, $h_2(K)$ can be computed simply by shifting left m more bits and "oring in" a 1, so that the coding sequence in (5) would be followed by

ENTA	0	Clear rA.
SLB	m	Shift rAX m bits left. (24)
OR	=1=	rA $\leftarrow$ rA $\vee$ 1.

This is faster than the division method.

In each of the techniques suggested above, $h_1(K)$ and $h_2(K)$ are essentially independent, in the sense that different keys will yield the same values for both h_1 and h_2 with probability approximately proportional to $1/M^2$ instead of to $1/M$. Empirical tests show that the behavior of Algorithm D with independent hash functions is essentially indistinguishable from the number of probes that would be required if the keys were inserted at random into the table; there is practically no "piling up" or "clustering" as in Algorithm L.

It is also possible to let $h_2(K)$ depend on $h_1(K)$, as suggested by Gary Knott in 1968; for example, if M is prime we could let

$$h_2(K) = \begin{cases} 1, & \text{if } h_1(K) = 0; \\ M - h_1(K), & \text{if } h_1(K) > 0. \end{cases} \qquad (25)$$

This would be faster than doing another division, but we shall see that it does cause a certain amount of *secondary clustering*, requiring slightly more probes because of the increased chance that two or more keys will follow the same path. The formulas derived below can be used to determine whether the gain in hashing time outweighs the loss of probing time.

Algorithms L and D are very similar, yet there are enough differences that it is instructive to compare the running time of the corresponding MIX programs.

Program D (*Open addressing with double hashing*). Since this program is substantially like Program L, it is presented without comments. $rI2 \equiv c - 1$.

01	START	LDX	K	1	15	3H	DEC1 1,2	$C-1$
02		ENTA	0	1	16		J1NN *+2	$C-1$
03		DIV	=M=	1	17		INC1 M	B
04		STX	*+1(0:2)	1	18		CMPA TABLE,1	$C-1$
05		ENT1	*	1	19		JE SUCCESS	$C-1$
06		LDX	TABLE,1	1	20		LDX TABLE,1	$C-1-S2$
07		CMPX	K	1	21		JXNZ 3B	$C-1-S2$
08		JE	SUCCESS	1	22	4H	LDX VACANCIES	$1-S$
09		JXZ	4F	$1-S1$	23		JXZ OVERFLOW	$1-S$
10		SRAX	5	$A-S1$	24		DECX 1	$1-S$
11		DIV	=M-2=	$A-S1$	25		STX VACANCIES	$1-S$
12		STX	*+1(0:2)	$A-S1$	26		LDA K	$1-S$
13		ENT2	*	$A-S1$	27		STA TABLE,1	$1-S$
14		LDA	K	$A-S1$				

The frequency counts A, C, $S1$, $S2$ in this program have a similar interpretation to those in Program C above. The other variable B will be about $(C-1)/2$ on the average. (If we restricted the range of $h_2(K)$ to, say, $1 \leq h_2(K) \leq M/2$, B would be only about $(C-1)/4$; this increase of speed will probably *not* be offset by a noticeable increase in the number of probes.) When there are $N = \alpha M$ keys in the table, the average value of A is, of course, α in an unsuccessful search, and $A = 1$ in a successful search. As in Algorithm C, the average value of $S1$ in a successful search is $1 - \frac{1}{2}((N-1)/M) \approx 1 - \frac{1}{2}\alpha$. The average number of probes is difficult to determine exactly, but empirical tests show good agreement with formulas derived below for "uniform probing," namely

$$C'_N = \frac{M+1}{M+1-N} \approx (1-\alpha)^{-1} \qquad \text{(unsuccessful search),} \quad (26)$$

$$C_N = \frac{M+1}{N}(H_{M+1} - H_{M+1-N}) \approx -\alpha^{-1}\ln(1-\alpha) \quad \text{(successful search),} \quad (27)$$

when $h_1(K)$ and $h_2(K)$ are independent. When $h_2(K)$ depends on $h_1(K)$ as in (25), the secondary clustering causes (26) and (27) to be increased to

$$C'_N = \frac{M+1}{M+1-n} - \frac{N}{M+1} + H_{M+1} - H_{M+1-N} + O(M^{-1})$$
$$\approx (1-\alpha)^{-1} - \alpha - \ln(1-\alpha); \quad (28)$$

$$C_N = 1 + H_{M+1} - H_{M+1-N} - \frac{N}{2(M+1)} - (H_{M+1} - H_{M+1-N})/N + O(N^{-1})$$
$$\approx 1 - \ln(1-\alpha) - \tfrac{1}{2}\alpha. \quad (29)$$

(See exercise 44.) Note that as the table gets full, these values of C_N approach $H_{M+1} - 1$ and $H_{M+1} - \frac{1}{2}$, respectively, when $N = M$; this is much better than we observed in Algorithm L, but not as good as in the chaining methods.

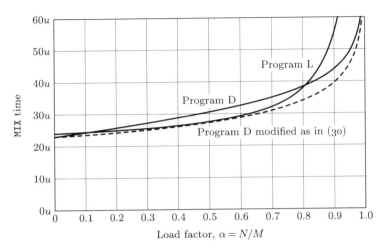

Fig. 42. The running time for successful searching by three open addressing schemes.

Since each probe takes slightly less time in Algorithm L, double hashing is advantageous only when the table gets full. Figure 42 compares the average running time of Program L, Program D, and a modified Program D that involves secondary clustering, replacing the rather slow calculation of $h_2(K)$ in lines 10–13 by the following three instructions:

$$\begin{array}{lll}
\text{ENN2 } \texttt{1-M,1} & c \leftarrow M - i. & \\
\text{J1NZ } \texttt{*+2} & & (30) \\
\text{ENT2 } \texttt{0} & \text{If } i = 0,\ c \leftarrow 1. &
\end{array}$$

Program D takes a total of $8C + 19A + B + 26 - 13S - 17S1$ units of time; modification (30) saves about $15(A - S1) \approx 7.5\alpha$ of these in a successful search. In this case, secondary clustering is preferable to independent double hashing.

On a binary computer, we could speed up the computation of $h_2(K)$ in another way, if M is prime greater than, say, 512, replacing lines 10–13 by

$$\begin{array}{lll}
\text{AND } \texttt{=511=} & \text{rA} \leftarrow \text{rA mod } 512. & \\
\text{STA } \texttt{*+1(0:2)} & & (31) \\
\text{ENT2 } \texttt{*} & c \leftarrow \text{rA} + 1. &
\end{array}$$

This idea (suggested by Bell and Kaman, *CACM* **13** (1970), 675–677, who discovered Algorithm D independently) avoids secondary clustering without the expense of another division.

Many other probe sequences have been proposed as improvements on Algorithm L, but none seem to be superior to Algorithm D except possibly the method described in exercise 20.

By using the relative order of keys we can reduce the average running time for unsuccessful searches by Algorithms L or D to the average running time for successful search; see exercise 66. This technique can be important in applications for which unsuccessful searches are common; for example, TEX uses such an algorithm when looking for exceptions to its hyphenation rules.

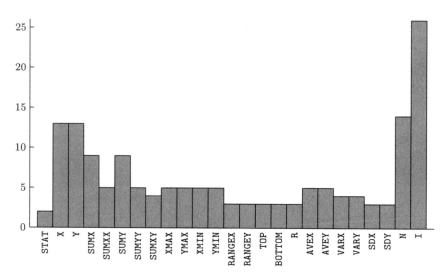

Fig. 43. The number of times a compiler typically searches for variable names. The names are listed from left to right in order of their first appearance.

Brent's Variation. Richard P. Brent has discovered a way to modify Algorithm D so that the average successful search time remains bounded as the table gets full. His method [*CACM* **16** (1973), 105–109] is based on the fact that successful searches are much more common than insertions, in many applications; therefore he proposes doing more work when inserting an item, moving records in order to reduce the expected retrieval time.

For example, Fig. 43 shows the number of times each identifier was actually found to appear, in a typical PL/I procedure. This data indicates that a PL/I compiler that uses a hash table to keep track of variable names will be looking up many of the names five or more times but inserting them only once. Similarly, Bell and Kaman found that a COBOL compiler used its symbol table algorithm 10988 times while compiling a program, but made only 735 insertions into the table; this is an average of about 14 successful searches per unsuccessful search. Sometimes a table is actually created only once (for example, a table of symbolic opcodes in an assembler), and it is used thereafter purely for retrieval.

Brent's idea is to change the insertion process in Algorithm D as follows. Suppose an unsuccessful search has probed locations $p_0, p_1, \ldots, p_{t-1}, p_t$, where $p_j = \big(h_1(K) - jh_2(K)\big) \bmod M$ and TABLE$[p_t]$ is empty. If $t \le 1$, we insert K in position p_t as usual; but if $t \ge 2$, we compute $c_0 = h_2(K_0)$, where $K_0 = \text{KEY}[p_0]$, and see if TABLE$[(p_0 - c_0) \bmod M]$ is empty. If it is, we set it to TABLE$[p_0]$ and then insert K in position p_0. This increases the retrieval time for K_0 by one step, but it decreases the retrieval time for K by $t \ge 2$ steps, so it results in a net improvement. Similarly, if TABLE$[(p_0 - c_0) \bmod M]$ is occupied and $t \ge 3$, we try TABLE$[(p_0 - 2c_0) \bmod M]$; if that is full too, we compute $c_1 = h_2(\text{KEY}[p_1])$ and try TABLE$[(p_0 - c_1) \bmod M]$; etc. In general, let $c_j = h_2(\text{KEY}[p_j])$ and

$p_{j,k} = (p_j - kc_j) \bmod M$; if we have found TABLE$[p_{j,k}]$ occupied for all indices j and k such that $j+k < r$, and if $t \geq r+1$, we look at TABLE$[p_{0,r}]$, TABLE$[p_{1,r-1}]$, $\ldots$, TABLE$[p_{r-1,1}]$. If the first empty space occurs at position $p_{j,r-j}$ we set TABLE$[p_{j,r-j}] \leftarrow$ TABLE$[p_j]$ and insert K in position p_j.

Brent's analysis indicates that the average number of probes per successful search is reduced to the levels shown in Fig. 44, on page 545, with a maximum value of about 2.49.

The number $t+1$ of probes in an unsuccessful search is not reduced by Brent's variation; it remains at the level indicated by Eq. (26), approaching $\frac{1}{2}(M+1)$ as the table gets full. The average number of times h_2 needs to be computed per insertion is $\alpha^2 + \alpha^5 + \frac{1}{3}\alpha^6 + \cdots$, according to Brent's analysis, eventually approaching $\Theta(\sqrt{M})$; and the number of additional table positions probed while deciding how to make the insertion is about $\alpha^2 + \alpha^4 + \frac{4}{3}\alpha^5 + \alpha^6 + \cdots$.

E. G. Mallach [*Comp. J.* **20** (1977), 137–140] has experimented with refinements of Brent's variation, and further results have been obtained by Gaston H. Gonnet and J. Ian Munro [*SICOMP* **8** (1979), 463–478].

Deletions. Many computer programmers have great faith in algorithms, and they are surprised to find that *the obvious way to delete records from a hash table doesn't work.* For example, if we try to delete the key EN from Fig. 41, we can't simply mark that table position empty, because another key FEM would suddenly be forgotten! (Recall that EN and FEM both hashed to the same location. When looking up FEM, we would find an empty place, indicating an unsuccessful search.) A similar problem occurs with Algorithm C, due to the coalescing of lists; imagine the deletion of both TO and FIRE from Fig. 40.

In general, we can handle deletions by putting a special code value in the corresponding cell, so that there are three kinds of table entries: empty, occupied, and deleted. When searching for a key, we should skip over deleted cells, as if they were occupied. If the search is unsuccessful, the key can be inserted in place of the first deleted or empty position that was encountered.

But this idea is workable only when deletions are very rare, because the entries of the table never become empty again once they have been occupied. After a long sequence of repeated insertions and deletions, all of the empty spaces will eventually disappear, and every unsuccessful search will take M probes! Furthermore the time per probe will be increased, since we will have to test whether i has returned to its starting value in step D4; and the number of probes in a successful search will drift upward from C_N to C'_N.

When linear probing is being used (Algorithm L), we can make deletions in a way that avoids such a sorry state of affairs, if we are willing to do some extra work for the deletion.

Algorithm R (*Deletion with linear probing*). Assuming that an open hash table has been constructed by Algorithm L, this algorithm deletes the record from a given position TABLE$[i]$.

R1. [Empty a cell.] Mark TABLE$[i]$ empty, and set $j \leftarrow i$.

R2. [Decrease i.] Set $i \leftarrow i - 1$, and if this makes i negative set $i \leftarrow i + M$.

R3. [Inspect TABLE[i].] If TABLE[i] is empty, the algorithm terminates. Otherwise set $r \leftarrow h(\text{KEY}[i])$, the original hash address of the key now stored at position i. If $i \leq r < j$ or if $r < j < i$ or $j < i \leq r$ (in other words, if r lies cyclically between i and j), go back to R2.

R4. [Move a record.] Set TABLE[j] $\leftarrow$ TABLE[i], and return to step R2.   ▮

Exercise 22 shows that this algorithm causes no degradation in performance; in other words, the average number of probes predicted in Eqs. (22) and (23) will remain the same. (A weaker result for tree insertion was proved in Theorem 6.2.2H.) But the validity of Algorithm R depends heavily on the fact that linear probing is involved, and no analogous deletion procedure for use with Algorithm D is possible. The average running time of Algorithm R is analyzed in exercise 64.

Of course when chaining is used with separate lists for each possible hash value, deletion causes no problems since it is simply a deletion from a linked linear list. Deletion with Algorithm C is discussed in exercise 23.

Algorithm R may move some of the table entries, and this is undesirable if they are being pointed to from elsewhere. Another approach to deletions is possible by adapting some of the ideas used in garbage collection (see Section 2.3.5): We might keep a reference count with each key telling how many other keys collide with it; then it is possible to convert unoccupied cells to empty status when their reference drops to zero. Alternatively we might go through the entire table whenever too many deleted entries have accumulated, changing all the unoccupied positions to empty and then looking up all remaining keys, in order to see which unoccupied positions still require "deleted" status. These procedures, which avoid relocation and work with any hash technique, were originally suggested by T. Gunji and E. Goto [*J. Information Proc.* **3** (1980), 1–12].

*Analysis of the algorithms. It is especially important to know the average behavior of a hashing method, because we are committed to trusting in the laws of probability whenever we hash. The worst case of these algorithms is almost unthinkably bad, so we need to be reassured that the average behavior is very good.

Before we get into the analysis of linear probing, etc., let us consider an approximate model of the situation, called *uniform probing*. In this model, which was suggested by W. W. Peterson [*IBM J. Research & Development* **1** (1957), 135–136], we assume that each key is placed in a completely random location of the table, so that each of the $\binom{M}{N}$ possible configurations of N occupied cells and $M - N$ empty cells is equally likely. This model ignores any effect of primary or secondary clustering; the occupancy of each cell in the table is essentially independent of all the others. Then the probability that exactly r probes are needed to insert the $(N+1)$st item is the number of configurations in which $r - 1$ given cells are occupied and another is empty, divided by $\binom{M}{N}$, namely

$$P_r = \binom{M - r}{N - r + 1} \Big/ \binom{M}{N};$$

therefore the average number of probes for uniform probing is

$$C'_N = \sum_{r=1}^{M} r P_r = M + 1 - \sum_{r=1}^{M}(M+1-r)P_r$$

$$= M + 1 - \sum_{r=1}^{M}(M+1-r)\binom{M-r}{M-N-1} \Big/ \binom{M}{N}$$

$$= M + 1 - \sum_{r=1}^{M}(M-N)\binom{M+1-r}{M-N} \Big/ \binom{M}{N}$$

$$= M + 1 - (M-N)\binom{M+1}{M-N+1} \Big/ \binom{M}{N}$$

$$= M + 1 - (M-N)\frac{M+1}{M-N+1} = \frac{M+1}{M-N+1}, \quad \text{for } 1 \le N < M. \quad (32)$$

(We have already solved essentially the same problem in connection with random sampling, in exercise 3.4.2–5.) Setting $\alpha = N/M$, this exact formula for C'_N is approximately equal to

$$\frac{1}{1-\alpha} = 1 + \alpha + \alpha^2 + \alpha^3 + \cdots, \quad (33)$$

a series that has a rough intuitive interpretation: With probability α we need more than one probe, with probability α^2 we need more than two, etc. The corresponding average number of probes for a successful search is

$$C_N = \frac{1}{N}\sum_{k=0}^{N-1} C'_k = \frac{M+1}{N}\left(\frac{1}{M+1} + \frac{1}{M} + \cdots + \frac{1}{M-N+2}\right)$$

$$= \frac{M+1}{N}\left(H_{M+1} - H_{M-N+1}\right) \approx \frac{1}{\alpha}\ln\frac{1}{1-\alpha}. \quad (34)$$

As remarked above, extensive tests show that Algorithm D with two independent hash functions behaves essentially like uniform probing, for all practical purposes. In fact, double hashing is asymptotically equivalent to uniform probing, in the limit as $M \to \infty$ (see exercise 70).

This completes our analysis of uniform probing. In order to study linear probing and other types of collision resolution, we need to set up the theory in a different, more realistic way. The probabilistic model we shall use for this purpose assumes that each of the M^N possible "hash sequences"

$$a_1 a_2 \ldots a_N, \quad 0 \le a_j < M, \quad (35)$$

is equally likely, where a_j denotes the initial hash address of the jth key inserted into the table. The average number of probes in a successful search, given any particular searching algorithm, will be denoted by C_N as above; this is assumed to be the average number of probes needed to find the kth key, averaged over $1 \le k \le N$ with each key equally likely, and averaged over all hash sequences (35) with each sequence equally likely. Similarly, the average number of probes needed when the Nth key is inserted, considering all sequences (35) to be equally likely, will be denoted by C'_{N-1}; this is the average number of probes in an unsuccessful search starting with $N-1$ elements in the table. When open addressing is used,

$$C_N = \frac{1}{N} \sum_{k=0}^{N-1} C'_k, \qquad (36)$$

so that we can deduce one quantity from the other as we have done in (34).

Strictly speaking, there are two defects even in this more accurate model. In the first place, the different hash sequences aren't all equally probable, because the keys themselves are distinct. This makes the probability that $a_1 = a_2$ slightly less than $1/M$; but the difference is usually negligible since the set of all possible keys is typically very large compared to M. (See exercise 24.) Furthermore a good hash function will exploit the nonrandomness of typical data, making it even less likely that $a_1 = a_2$; as a result, our estimates for the number of probes will be pessimistic. Another inaccuracy in the model is indicated in Fig. 43: Keys that occur earlier are (with some exceptions) more likely to be looked up than keys that occur later. Therefore our estimate of C_N tends to be doubly pessimistic, and the algorithms should perform slightly better in practice than our analysis predicts.

With these precautions, we are ready to make an "exact" analysis of linear probing.* Let $f(M, N)$ be the number of hash sequences (35) such that position 0 of the table will be empty after the keys have been inserted by Algorithm L. The circular symmetry of linear probing implies that position 0 is empty just as often as any other position, so it is empty with probability $1 - N/M$; in other words

$$f(M, N) = \left(1 - \frac{N}{M}\right) M^N. \qquad (37)$$

By convention we also set $f(0,0) = 1$. Now let $g(M, N, k)$ be the number of hash sequences (35) such that the algorithm leaves position 0 empty, positions 1 through k occupied, and position $k + 1$ empty. We have

$$g(M, N, k) = \binom{N}{k} f(k+1, k) f(M-k-1, N-k), \qquad (38)$$

because all such hash sequences are composed of two subsequences, one (containing k elements $a_i \leq k$) that leaves position 0 empty and positions 1 through k occupied and one (containing $N - k$ elements $a_j \geq k + 1$) that leaves position $k + 1$ empty; there are $f(k+1, k)$ subsequences of the former type and $f(M-k-1, N-k)$ of the latter type, and there are $\binom{N}{k}$ ways to intersperse two such subsequences. Finally let P_k be the probability that exactly $k + 1$ probes will be needed when the $(N + 1)$st key is inserted; it follows (see exercise 25)

---

* The author cannot resist inserting a biographical note at this point: I first formulated the following derivation in 1962, shortly after beginning work on *The Art of Computer Programming*. Since this was the first nontrivial algorithm I had ever analyzed satisfactorily, it had a strong influence on the structure of these books. Ever since that day, the analysis of algorithms has in fact been one of the major themes of my life.

that

$$P_k = M^{-N}\big(g(M,N,k) + g(M,N,k+1) + \cdots + g(M,N,N)\big). \qquad (39)$$

Now $C'_N = \sum_{k=0}^{N}(k+1)P_k$; putting this equation together with (36)–(39) and simplifying yields the following result.

Theorem K. *The average number of probes needed by Algorithm L, assuming that all M^N hash sequences (35) are equally likely, is*

$$C_N = \tfrac{1}{2}\big(1 + Q_0(M, N{-}1)\big) \quad \text{(successful search)}, \qquad (40)$$

$$C'_N = \tfrac{1}{2}\big(1 + Q_1(M, N)\big) \qquad \text{(unsuccessful search)}, \qquad (41)$$

where

$$Q_r(M, N) = \binom{r}{0} + \binom{r+1}{1}\frac{N}{M} + \binom{r+2}{2}\frac{N(N-1)}{M^2} + \cdots$$

$$= \sum_{k \ge 0}\binom{r+k}{k}\frac{N}{M}\frac{N-1}{M}\cdots\frac{N-k+1}{M}. \qquad (42)$$

Proof. Details of the calculation are worked out in exercise 27. (For the variance, see exercises 28, 67, and 68.) ∎

The rather strange-looking function $Q_r(M, N)$ that appears in this theorem is really not hard to deal with. We have

$$N^k - \binom{k}{2}N^{k-1} \le N(N-1)\ldots(N-k+1) \le N^k;$$

hence if $N/M = \alpha$,

$$\sum_{k \ge 0}\binom{r+k}{k}\left(N^k - \binom{k}{2}N^{k-1}\right)\Big/M^k \le Q_r(M, N) \le \sum_{k \ge 0}\binom{r+k}{k}N^k/M^k,$$

$$\sum_{k \ge 0}\binom{r+k}{k}\alpha^k - \frac{\alpha}{M}\sum_{k \ge 0}\binom{r+k}{k}\binom{k}{2}\alpha^{k-2} \le Q_r(M, \alpha M) \le \sum_{k \ge 0}\binom{r+k}{k}\alpha^k;$$

that is,

$$\frac{1}{(1-\alpha)^{r+1}} - \frac{1}{M}\binom{r+2}{2}\frac{\alpha}{(1-\alpha)^{r+3}} \le Q_r(M, \alpha M) \le \frac{1}{(1-\alpha)^{r+1}}. \qquad (43)$$

This relation gives us a good estimate of $Q_r(M, N)$ when M is large and α is not too close to 1. (The lower bound is a better approximation than the upper bound.) When α approaches 1, these formulas become useless, but fortunately $Q_0(M, M{-}1)$ is the function $Q(M)$ whose asymptotic behavior was studied in great detail in Section 1.2.11.3; and $Q_1(M, M{-}1)$ is simply equal to M (see exercise 50). In terms of the standard notation for hypergeometric functions, Eq. 1.2.6–39, we have $Q_r(M, N) = F(r+1, -N; ; -1/M) = F\left(\begin{smallmatrix} r+1, -N, 1 \\ 1 \end{smallmatrix}\,\middle|\, -\frac{1}{M}\right)$.

Another approach to the analysis of linear probing was taken in the early days by G. Schay, Jr. and W. G. Spruth [*CACM* **5** (1962), 459–462]. Although their method yielded only an approximation to the exact formulas in Theorem K, it sheds further light on the algorithm, so we shall sketch it briefly here. First let us consider a surprising property of linear probing that was first noticed by W. W. Peterson in 1957:

Theorem P. *The average number of probes in a successful search by Algorithm L is independent of the order in which the keys were inserted; it depends only on the number of keys that hash to each address.*

In other words, any rearrangement of a hash sequence $a_1 a_2 \ldots a_N$ yields a hash sequence with the same average displacement of keys from their hash addresses. (We are assuming, as stated earlier, that all keys in the table have equal importance. If some keys are more frequently accessed than others, the proof can be extended to show that an optimal arrangement occurs if we insert them in decreasing order of frequency, using the method of Theorem 6.1S.)

Proof. It suffices to show that the total number of probes needed to insert keys for the hash sequence $a_1 a_2 \ldots a_N$ is the same as the total number needed for $a_1 \ldots a_{i-1} a_{i+1} a_i a_{i+2} \ldots a_N$, $1 \le i < N$. There is clearly no difference unless the $(i + 1)$st key in the second sequence falls into the position occupied by the ith in the first sequence. But then the ith and $(i + 1)$st merely exchange places, so the number of probes for the $(i+1)$st is decreased by the same amount that the number for the ith is increased. ∎

Theorem P tells us that the average search length for a hash sequence $a_1 a_2 \ldots a_N$ can be determined from the numbers $b_0 b_1 \ldots b_{M-1}$, where b_j is the number of a's that equal j. From this sequence we can determine the "carry sequence" $c_0 c_1 \ldots c_{M-1}$, where c_j is the number of keys for which both locations j and $j - 1$ are probed as the key is inserted. This sequence is determined by the rule

$$c_j = \begin{cases} 0, & \text{if } b_j = c_{(j+1) \bmod M} = 0; \\ b_j + c_{(j+1) \bmod M} - 1, & \text{otherwise.} \end{cases} \tag{44}$$

For example, let $M = 10$, $N = 8$, and $b_0 \ldots b_9 = 0\ 3\ 2\ 0\ 1\ 0\ 0\ 0\ 0\ 2$; then $c_0 \ldots c_9 = 2\ 3\ 1\ 0\ 0\ 0\ 0\ 1\ 2\ 3$, since one key needs to be "carried over" from position 2 to position 1, three from position 1 to position 0, two of these from position 0 to position 9, etc. We have $b_0 + b_1 + \cdots + b_{M-1} = N$, and the average number of probes needed for retrieval of the N keys is

$$1 + (c_0 + c_1 + \cdots + c_{M-1})/N. \tag{45}$$

Rule (44) seems to be a circular definition of the c's in terms of themselves, but actually there is a unique solution to the stated equations whenever $N < M$ (see exercise 32).

Schay and Spruth used this idea to determine the probability q_k that $c_j = k$, in terms of the probability p_k that $b_j = k$. (These probabilities are independent of j.) Thus

$$q_0 = p_0q_0 + p_1q_0 + p_0q_1,$$
$$q_1 = p_2q_0 + p_1q_1 + p_0q_2, \tag{46}$$
$$q_2 = p_3q_0 + p_2q_1 + p_1q_2 + p_0q_3,$$

etc., since, for example, the probability that $c_j = 2$ is the probability that $b_j + c_{(j+1) \bmod M} = 3$. Let $B(z) = \sum p_k z^k$ and $C(z) = \sum q_k z^k$ be the generating functions for these probability distributions; the equations (46) are equivalent to

$$B(z)C(z) = p_0q_0 + (q_0 - p_0q_0)z + q_1 z^2 + \cdots = p_0q_0(1 - z) + zC(z).$$

Since $B(1) = 1$, we may write $B(z) = 1 + (z - 1)D(z)$, and it follows that

$$C(z) = \frac{p_0q_0}{1 - D(z)} = \frac{1 - D(1)}{1 - D(z)}, \tag{47}$$

since $C(1) = 1$. The average number of probes needed for retrieval, according to (45), will therefore be

$$1 + \frac{M}{N}C'(1) = 1 + \frac{M}{N}\frac{D'(1)}{1 - D(1)} = 1 + \frac{M}{2N}\frac{B''(1)}{1 - B'(1)}. \tag{48}$$

Since we are assuming that each hash sequence $a_1 \ldots a_N$ is equally likely, we have

$$p_k = \Pr(\text{exactly } k \text{ of the } a_i \text{ are equal to } j, \text{ for fixed } j)$$

$$= \binom{N}{k}\left(\frac{1}{M}\right)^k\left(1 - \frac{1}{M}\right)^{N-k}; \tag{49}$$

hence

$$B(z) = \left(1 + \frac{z-1}{M}\right)^N, \qquad B'(1) = \frac{N}{M}, \qquad B''(1) = \frac{N(N-1)}{M^2}, \tag{50}$$

and the average number of probes according to (48) will be

$$C_N = \frac{1}{2}\left(1 + \frac{M-1}{M-N}\right). \tag{51}$$

Can the reader spot the incorrect reasoning that has caused this answer to be different from the correct result in Theorem K? (See exercise 33.)

*Optimality considerations.** We have seen several examples of probe sequences for open addressing, and it is natural to ask for one that can be proved *best possible* in some meaningful sense. This problem has been set up in the following interesting way by J. D. Ullman [*JACM* **19** (1972), 569–575]: Instead of computing a hash address $h(K)$, we map each key K into an entire permutation of $\{0, 1, \ldots, M-1\}$, which represents the probe sequence to use for K. Each of the $M!$ permutations is assigned a probability, and the generalized hash function is supposed to select each permutation with that probability. The question is, "What assignment of probabilities to permutations gives the best performance, in the sense that the corresponding average number of probes C_N or C'_N is minimized?"

For example, if we assign the probability $1/M!$ to each permutation, it is easy to see that we have exactly the behavior of *uniform probing* that we have analyzed above in (32) and (34). However, Ullman found an example with $M = 4$ and $N = 2$ for which C'_N is smaller than the value $\frac{5}{3}$ obtained with uniform probing. His construction assigns zero probability to all but the following six permutations:

Permutation	Probability	Permutation	Probability	
0 1 2 3	$(1+2\epsilon)/6$	1 0 3 2	$(1+2\epsilon)/6$	
2 0 1 3	$(1-\epsilon)/6$	2 1 0 3	$(1-\epsilon)/6$	(52)
3 0 1 2	$(1-\epsilon)/6$	3 1 0 2	$(1-\epsilon)/6$	

Roughly speaking, the first probe tends to be either 2 or 3, but the second probe is always 0 or 1. The average number of probes needed to insert the third item, C'_3, turns out to be $\frac{5}{3} - \frac{1}{9}\epsilon + O(\epsilon^2)$, so we can improve on uniform probing by taking ϵ to be a small positive value.

However, the corresponding value of C'_1 for these probabilities is $\frac{23}{18} + O(\epsilon)$, which is larger than $\frac{5}{4}$ (the uniform probing value). Ullman proved that any assignment of probabilities such that $C'_N < (M+1)/(M+1-N)$ for some N always implies that $C'_n > (M+1)/(M+1-n)$ for some $n < N$; you can't win all the time over uniform probing.

Actually the number of probes C_N for a *successful* search is a better measure than C'_N. The permutations in (52) do not lead to an improved value of C_N for any N, and indeed Ullman conjectured that no assignment of probabilities will be able to make C_N less than the uniform value $((M+1)/N)(H_{M+1} - H_{M+1-N})$. Andrew Yao proved an asymptotic form of this conjecture by showing that the limiting cost when $N = \alpha M$ and $M \to \infty$ is always $\geq \frac{1}{\alpha} \ln \frac{1}{1-\alpha}$ [*JACM* **32** (1985), 687–693].

The strong form of Ullman's conjecture appears to be very difficult to prove, especially because there are many ways to assign probabilities to achieve the effect of uniform probing; we do not need to assign $1/M!$ to each permutation. For example, the following assignment for $M = 4$ is equivalent to uniform probing:

Permutation	Probability	Permutation	Probability	
0 1 2 3	1/6	0 2 1 3	1/12	
1 2 3 0	1/6	1 3 2 0	1/12	(53)
2 3 0 1	1/6	2 0 3 1	1/12	
3 0 1 2	1/6	3 1 0 2	1/12	

with zero probability assigned to the other 16 permutations.

The following theorem characterizes *all* assignments that produce the behavior of uniform probing.

Theorem U. *An assignment of probabilities to permutations will make each of the $\binom{M}{N}$ configurations of empty and occupied cells equally likely after N*

insertions, for $0 < N < M$, if and only if the sum of probabilities assigned to all permutations whose first N elements are the members of a given N-element set is $1/\binom{M}{N}$, for all N and for all N-element sets.

For example, the sum of probabilities assigned to each of the $3!(M-3)!$ permutations beginning with the numbers $\{0, 1, 2\}$ in some order must be $1/\binom{M}{3} = 3!(M-3)!/M!$. Observe that the condition of this theorem holds in (53), because $1/6 + 1/12 = 1/4$.

Proof. Let $A \subseteq \{0, 1, \ldots, M-1\}$, and let $\Pi(A)$ be the set of all permutations whose first $|A|$ elements are members of A; also let $S(A)$ be the sum of the probabilities assigned to those permutations. Let $P_k(A)$ be the probability that the first $|A|$ insertions of the open addressing procedure occupy the locations specified by A, and that the last insertion required exactly k probes. Finally, let $P(A) = P_1(A) + P_2(A) + \cdots$. The proof is by induction on $N \geq 1$, assuming that

$$P(A) = S(A) = 1 \Big/ \binom{M}{N}$$

for all sets A with $|A| = n < N$. Let B be any N-element set. Then

$$P_k(B) = \sum_{\substack{A \subseteq B \\ |A|=k}} \sum_{\pi \in \Pi(A)} \Pr(\pi) P(B \setminus \{\pi_k\}),$$

where $\Pr(\pi)$ is the probability assigned to permutation π and π_k is its kth element. By induction

$$P_k(B) = \sum_{\substack{A \subseteq B \\ |A|=k}} \frac{1}{\binom{M}{N-1}} \sum_{\pi \in \Pi(A)} \Pr(\pi),$$

which equals

$$\binom{N}{k} \Big/ \binom{M}{N-1}\binom{M}{k}, \qquad \text{if } k < N;$$

hence

$$P(B) = \frac{1}{\binom{M}{N-1}} \left(S(B) + \sum_{k=1}^{N-1} \frac{\binom{N}{k}}{\binom{M}{k}} \right),$$

and this can be equal to $1/\binom{M}{N}$ if and only if $S(B)$ has the correct value.   ∎

External searching. Hashing techniques lend themselves well to external searching on direct-access storage devices like disks or drums. For such applications, as in Section 6.2.4, we want to minimize the number of accesses to the file, and this has two major effects on the choice of algorithms:

1) It is reasonable to spend more time computing the hash function, since the penalty for bad hashing is much greater than the cost of the extra time needed to do a careful job.

2) The records are usually grouped into pages or *buckets*, so that several records are fetched from the external memory each time.

The file is divided into M buckets containing b records each. Collisions now cause no problem unless more than b keys have the same hash address. The following three approaches to collision resolution seem to be best:

A) *Chaining with separate lists.* If more than b records fall into the same bucket, a link to an overflow record can be inserted at the end of the first bucket. These overflow records are kept in a special overflow area. There is usually no advantage in having buckets in the overflow area, since comparatively few overflows occur; thus, the extra records are usually linked together so that the $(b + k)$th record of a list requires $1 + k$ accesses. It is usually a good idea to leave some room for overflows on each cylinder of a disk file, so that most accesses are to the same cylinder.

Although this method of handling overflows seems inefficient, the number of overflows is statistically small enough that the average search time is very good. See Tables 2 and 3, which show the average number of accesses required as a function of the load factor

$$\alpha = N/Mb, \tag{54}$$

for fixed α as M, $N \to \infty$. Curiously when $\alpha = 1$ the asymptotic number of accesses for an unsuccessful search increases with increasing b.

Table 2
AVERAGE ACCESSES IN AN UNSUCCESSFUL SEARCH BY SEPARATE CHAINING

Bucket size, b	Load factor, α									
	10%	20%	30%	40%	50%	60%	70%	80%	90%	95%
1	1.0048	1.0187	1.0408	1.0703	1.1065	1.1488	1.197	1.249	1.307	1.34
2	1.0012	1.0088	1.0269	1.0581	1.1036	1.1638	1.238	1.327	1.428	1.48
3	1.0003	1.0038	1.0162	1.0433	1.0898	1.1588	1.252	1.369	1.509	1.59
4	1.0001	1.0016	1.0095	1.0314	1.0751	1.1476	1.253	1.394	1.571	1.67
5	1.0000	1.0007	1.0056	1.0225	1.0619	1.1346	1.249	1.410	1.620	1.74
10	1.0000	1.0000	1.0004	1.0041	1.0222	1.0773	1.201	1.426	1.773	2.00
20	1.0000	1.0000	1.0000	1.0001	1.0028	1.0234	1.113	1.367	1.898	2.29
50	1.0000	1.0000	1.0000	1.0000	1.0000	1.0007	1.018	1.182	1.920	2.70

Table 3
AVERAGE ACCESSES IN A SUCCESSFUL SEARCH BY SEPARATE CHAINING

Bucket size, b	Load factor, α									
	10%	20%	30%	40%	50%	60%	70%	80%	90%	95%
1	1.0500	1.1000	1.1500	1.2000	1.2500	1.3000	1.350	1.400	1.450	1.48
2	1.0063	1.0242	1.0520	1.0883	1.1321	1.1823	1.238	1.299	1.364	1.40
3	1.0010	1.0071	1.0215	1.0458	1.0806	1.1259	1.181	1.246	1.319	1.36
4	1.0002	1.0023	1.0097	1.0257	1.0527	1.0922	1.145	1.211	1.290	1.33
5	1.0000	1.0008	1.0046	1.0151	1.0358	1.0699	1.119	1.186	1.268	1.32
10	1.0000	1.0000	1.0002	1.0015	1.0070	1.0226	1.056	1.115	1.206	1.27
20	1.0000	1.0000	1.0000	1.0000	1.0005	1.0038	1.018	1.059	1.150	1.22
50	1.0000	1.0000	1.0000	1.0000	1.0000	1.0000	1.001	1.015	1.083	1.16

B) *Chaining with coalescing lists.* Instead of providing a separate overflow area, we can adapt Algorithm C to external files. A doubly linked list of available space can be maintained for each cylinder, linking together each bucket that is not yet full. Under this scheme, every bucket contains a count of how many record positions are empty, and the bucket is removed from the doubly linked list only when its count becomes zero. A "roving pointer" can be used to distribute overflows (see exercise 2.5–6), so that different chains tend to use different overflow buckets. This method has not yet been analyzed, but it might prove to be quite useful.

C) *Open addressing.* We can also do without links, using an "open" method. Linear probing is probably better than random probing when we consider external searching, because the increment c can often be chosen so that it minimizes latency delays between consecutive accesses. The approximate theoretical model of linear probing that was worked out above can be generalized to account for the influence of buckets, and it shows that linear probing is indeed satisfactory unless the table has gotten very full. For example, see Table 4; when the load factor is 90 percent and the bucket size is 50, the average number of accesses in a successful search is only 1.04. This is actually *better* than the 1.08 accesses required by the chaining method (A) with the same bucket size!

Table 4

AVERAGE ACCESSES IN A SUCCESSFUL SEARCH BY LINEAR PROBING

Bucket size, b	Load factor, α									
	10%	20%	30%	40%	50%	60%	70%	80%	90%	95%
1	1.0556	1.1250	1.2143	1.3333	1.5000	1.7500	2.167	3.000	5.500	10.50
2	1.0062	1.0242	1.0553	1.1033	1.1767	1.2930	1.494	1.903	3.147	5.64
3	1.0009	1.0066	1.0201	1.0450	1.0872	1.1584	1.286	1.554	2.378	4.04
4	1.0001	1.0021	1.0085	1.0227	1.0497	1.0984	1.190	1.386	2.000	3.24
5	1.0000	1.0007	1.0039	1.0124	1.0307	1.0661	1.136	1.289	1.777	2.77
10	1.0000	1.0000	1.0001	1.0011	1.0047	1.0154	1.042	1.110	1.345	1.84
20	1.0000	1.0000	1.0000	1.0000	1.0003	1.0020	1.010	1.036	1.144	1.39
50	1.0000	1.0000	1.0000	1.0000	1.0000	1.0000	1.001	1.005	1.040	1.13

The analysis of methods (A) and (C) involves some very interesting mathematics; we shall merely summarize the results here, since the details are worked out in exercises 49 and 55. The formulas involve two functions strongly related to the Q-functions of Theorem K, namely

$$R(\alpha, n) = \frac{n}{n+1} + \frac{n^2\alpha}{(n+1)(n+2)} + \frac{n^3\alpha^2}{(n+1)(n+2)(n+3)} + \cdots, \qquad (55)$$

and

$$t_n(\alpha) = e^{-n\alpha}\left(\frac{(\alpha n)^n}{(n+1)!} + 2\frac{(\alpha n)^{n+1}}{(n+2)!} + 3\frac{(\alpha n)^{n+2}}{(n+3)!} + \cdots\right)$$

$$= \frac{e^{-n\alpha}n^n\alpha^n}{n!}\left(1 - (1-\alpha)R(\alpha, n)\right). \qquad (56)$$

In terms of these functions, the average number of accesses made by the chaining method (A) in an unsuccessful search is

$$C'_N = 1 + \alpha b t_b(\alpha) + O\left(\frac{1}{M}\right) \tag{57}$$

as M, $N \to \infty$, and the corresponding number in a successful search is

$$C_N = 1 + \frac{e^{-b\alpha} b^b \alpha^b}{2b!}\left(2 + (\alpha-1)b + \left(\alpha^2 + (\alpha-1)^2(b-1)\right)R(\alpha,b)\right) + O\left(\frac{1}{M}\right). \tag{58}$$

The limiting values of these formulas are the quantities shown in Tables 2 and 3.

Since chaining method (A) requires a separate overflow area, we need to estimate how many overflows will occur. The average number of overflows will be $M(C'_N - 1) = N t_b(\alpha)$, since $C'_N - 1$ is the average number of overflows in any given list. Therefore Table 2 can be used to deduce the amount of overflow space required. For fixed α, the standard deviation of the total number of overflows will be roughly proportional to $\sqrt{M}$ as $M \to \infty$.

Asymptotic values for C'_N and C_N appear in exercise 53, but the approximations aren't very good when b is small or α is large; fortunately the series for $R(\alpha, n)$ converges rather rapidly even when α is large, so the formulas can be evaluated to any desired precision without much difficulty. The maximum values occur for $\alpha = 1$, when

$$\max C'_N = 1 + \frac{e^{-b} b^{b+1}}{b!} = \sqrt{\frac{b}{2\pi}} + 1 + O(b^{-1/2}), \tag{59}$$

$$\max C_N = 1 + \frac{e^{-b} b^b}{2b!}\left(R(b) + 1\right) = \frac{5}{4} + \sqrt{\frac{2}{9\pi b}} + O(b^{-1}), \tag{60}$$

as $b \to \infty$, by Stirling's approximation and the analysis of the function $R(n) = R(1, n) - 1$ in Section 1.2.11.3.

The average number of accesses in a successful external search with *linear probing* has the remarkably simple expression

$$C_N \approx 1 + t_b(\alpha) + t_{2b}(\alpha) + t_{3b}(\alpha) + \cdots, \tag{61}$$

which can be understood as follows: The average total number of accesses to look up all N keys is $N C_N$, and this is $N + T_1 + T_2 + \cdots$, where T_k is the average number of keys that require more than k accesses. Theorem P says that we can enter the keys in any order without affecting C_N, and it follows that T_k is the average number of overflow records that would occur in the chaining method if we had M/k buckets of size kb, namely $N t_{kb}(\alpha)$ by what we said above. Further justification of Eq. (61) appears in exercise 55.

An excellent early discussion of practical considerations involved in the design of external hash tables was given by Charles A. Olson, *Proc. ACM Nat. Conf.* **24** (1969), 539–549. He included several worked examples and pointed out that the number of overflow records will increase substantially if the file is subject to frequent insertion/deletion activity without relocating records. He also presented an analysis of this situation that was obtained jointly with J. A. de Peyster.

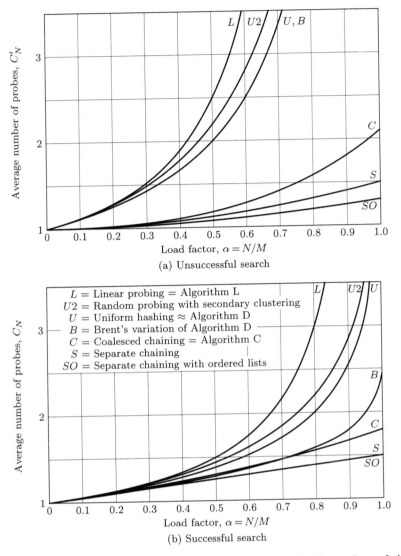

Fig. 44. Comparison of collision resolution methods: limiting values of the average number of probes as $M \to \infty$.

Comparison of the methods. We have now studied a large number of techniques for searching; how can we select the right one for a given application? It is difficult to summarize in a few words all the relevant details of the trade-offs involved in the choice of a search method, but the following things seem to be of primary importance with respect to the speed of searching and the requisite storage space.

Figure 44 summarizes the analyses of this section, showing that the various methods for collision resolution lead to different numbers of probes. But probe counting does not tell the whole story, since the time per probe varies in different methods, and the latter variation has a noticeable effect on the running time (as we have seen in Fig. 42). Linear probing accesses the table more frequently than the other methods shown in Fig. 44, but it has the advantage of simplicity. Furthermore, even linear probing isn't terribly bad: When the table is 90 percent full, Algorithm L requires fewer than 5.5 probes, on the average, to locate a random item in the table. (However, a 90-percent-full table does require about 50.5 probes for every *new* item inserted by Algorithm L.)

Figure 44 shows that the chaining methods are quite economical with respect to the number of probes, but the extra memory space needed for link fields sometimes makes open addressing more attractive for small records. For example, if we have to choose between a chained hash table of capacity 500 and an open hash table of capacity 1000, the latter is clearly preferable, since it allows efficient searching when 500 records are present and it is capable of absorbing twice as much data. On the other hand, sometimes the record size and format will allow space for link fields at virtually no extra cost. (See exercise 65.)

How do hash methods compare with the other search strategies we have studied in this chapter? From the standpoint of speed we can argue that they are better, when the number of records is large, because the average search time for a hash method stays bounded as $N \to \infty$ if we stipulate that the table never gets too full. For example, Program L will take only about 55 units of time for a successful search when the table is 90 percent full; this beats the fastest MIX binary search routine we have seen (exercise 6.2.1–24) when N is greater than 600 or so, at the cost of only 11 percent in storage space. Moreover the binary search is suitable only for fixed tables, while a hash table allows efficient insertions.

We can also compare Program L to the tree-oriented search methods that allow dynamic insertions. Program L with a 90-percent-full table is faster than Program 6.2.2T when N is greater than about 90, and faster than Program 6.3D (exercise 6.3–9) when N is greater than about 75.

Only one search method in this chapter is efficient for successful searching with virtually no storage overhead, namely Brent's variation of Algorithm D. His method allows us to put N records into a table of size $M = N + 1$, and to find any record in about 2.5 probes on the average. No extra space for link fields or tag bits is needed; however, an unsuccessful search will be very slow, requiring about $N/2$ probes.

Thus hashing has several advantages. On the other hand, there are three important respects in which hash table searching is inferior to other methods:

a) After an unsuccessful search in a hash table, we know only that the desired key is not present. Search methods based on comparisons always yield more information; they allow us to find the largest key $\le K$ and/or the smallest key $\ge K$. This is important in many applications; for example, it allows us to interpolate function values from a stored table. We can also use comparison-based algorithms to locate all keys that lie *between* two given values K and K'. Furthermore the tree search algorithms of Section 6.2 make it easy to traverse the contents of a table in ascending order, without sorting it separately.

b) The storage allocation for hash tables is often somewhat difficult; we have to dedicate a certain area of the memory for use as the hash table, and it may not be obvious how much space should be allotted. If we provide too much memory, we may be wasting storage at the expense of other lists or other computer users; but if we don't provide enough room, the table will overflow. By contrast, the tree search and insertion algorithms deal with trees that grow no larger than necessary. In a virtual memory environment we can keep memory accesses localized if we use tree search or digital tree search, instead of creating a large hash table that requires the operating system to access a new page nearly every time we hash a key.

c) Finally, we need a great deal of faith in probability theory when we use hashing methods, since they are efficient only on the average, while their worst case is terrible! As in the case of random number generators, we can never be completely sure that a hash function will perform properly when it is applied to a new set of data. Therefore hash tables are inappropriate for certain real-time applications such as air traffic control, where people's lives are at stake; the balanced tree algorithms of Sections 6.2.3 and 6.2.4 are much safer, since they provide guaranteed upper bounds on the search time.

History. The idea of hashing appears to have been originated by H. P. Luhn, who wrote an internal IBM memorandum in January 1953 that suggested the use of chaining; in fact, his suggestion was one of the first applications of linked linear lists. He pointed out the desirability of using buckets that contain more than one element, for external searching. Shortly afterwards, A. D. Lin carried Luhn's analysis further, and suggested a technique for handling overflows that used "degenerative addresses"; for example, the overflows from primary bucket 2748 were put in secondary bucket 274; overflows from that bucket went to tertiary bucket 27, and so on, assuming the presence of 10000 primary buckets, 1000 secondary buckets, 100 tertiary buckets, etc. The hash functions originally suggested by Luhn were digital in nature; for example, he combined adjacent pairs of key digits by adding them mod 10, so that 31415926 would be compressed to 4548.

At about the same time the idea of hashing occurred independently to another group of IBMers: Gene M. Amdahl, Elaine M. Boehme, N. Rochester, and Arthur L. Samuel, who were building an assembly program for the IBM 701. In order to handle the collision problem, Amdahl originated the idea of open addressing with linear probing.

Hash coding was first described in the open literature by Arnold I. Dumey, *Computers and Automation* **5**, 12 (December 1956), 6–9. He was the first to mention the idea of dividing by a prime number and using the remainder as the hash address. Dumey's interesting article mentions chaining but not open addressing. A. P. Ershov of Russia independently discovered linear open addressing in 1957 [*Doklady Akad. Nauk SSSR* **118** (1958), 427–430]; he published empirical results about the number of probes, conjecturing correctly that the average number of probes per successful search is < 2 when $N/M < 2/3$.

A classic article by W. W. Peterson, *IBM J. Research & Development* **1** (1957), 130–146, was the first major paper dealing with the problem of searching in large files. Peterson defined open addressing in general, analyzed the performance of uniform probing, and gave numerous empirical statistics about the behavior of linear open addressing with various bucket sizes, noting the degradation in performance that occurred when items were deleted. Another comprehensive survey of the subject was published six years later by Werner Buchholz [*IBM Systems J.* **2** (1963), 86–111], who gave an especially good discussion of hash functions. Correct analyses of Algorithm L were first published by A. G. Konheim and B. Weiss, *SIAM J. Appl. Math.* **14** (1966), 1266–1274; V. Podderjugin, *Wissenschaftliche Zeitschrift der Technischen Universität Dresden* **17** (1968), 1087–1089.

Up to this time linear probing was the only type of open addressing scheme that had appeared in the literature, but another scheme based on repeated random probing by independent hash functions had independently been developed by several people (see exercise 48). During the next few years hashing became very widely used, but hardly anything more was published about it. Then Robert Morris wrote a very influential survey of the subject [*CACM* **11** (1968), 38–44], in which he introduced the idea of random probing with secondary clustering. Morris's paper touched off a flurry of activity that culminated in Algorithm D and its refinements.

It is interesting to note that the word "hashing" apparently never appeared in print, with its present meaning, until the late 1960s, although it had already become common jargon in several parts of the world by that time. The first published appearance of the word seems to have been in H. Hellerman's book *Digital Computer System Principles* (New York: McGraw–Hill, 1967), 152; the only previous occurrence among approximately 60 relevant documents studied by the author as this section was being written was in an unpublished memorandum written by W. W. Peterson in 1961. Somehow the verb "to hash" magically became standard terminology for key transformation during the mid-1960s, yet nobody was rash enough to use such an undignified word in print until 1967!

Later developments. Many advances in the theory and practice of hashing have been made since the author first prepared this chapter in 1972, although the basic ideas discussed above still remain useful for ordinary applications. For example, the book *Design and Analysis of Coalesced Hashing* by J. S. Vitter and W.-C. Chen (New York: Oxford Univ. Press, 1987) discusses and analyzes several instructive variants of Algorithm C.

From a practical standpoint, the most important hash technique invented in the late 1970s is probably the method that Witold Lipski called *linear hashing* [*Proc. 6th International Conf. on Very Large Databases* (1980), 212–223]. Linear hashing — which incidentally has nothing to do with the classical technique of linear probing — allows the number of hash addresses to grow and/or contract gracefully as items are inserted and/or deleted. An excellent discussion of linear hashing, including comparisons with other methods for internal searching, has been given by Per-Åke Larson in *CACM* **31** (1988), 446–457; see also W. G. Griswold and G. M. Townsend, *Software Practice & Exp.* **23** (1993), 351–367, for improvements when many large and/or small tables are present simultaneously. Linear hashing can also be used for huge databases that are distributed between many different sites on a network [see Litwin, Neimat, and Schneider, *ACM Trans. Database Syst.* **21** (1996), 480–525]. An alternative scheme called *extendible hashing*, which has the property that at most two references to external pages are needed to retrieve any record, was proposed at about the same time by R. Fagin, J. Nievergelt, N. Pippenger, and H. R. Strong [*ACM Trans. Database Syst.* **4** (1979), 315–344]. Both linear hashing and extendible hashing are preferable to the B-trees of Section 6.2.4, when the order of keys is unimportant.

In the theoretical realm, more complicated methods have been devised by which it is possible to guarantee $O(1)$ maximum time per access, with $O(1)$ average amortized time per insertion and deletion, regardless of the keys being examined; moreover, the total storage used at any time is bounded by a constant times the number of items currently present, plus another additive constant. This result, which builds on ideas of Fredman, Komlós, and Szemerédi [*JACM* **31** (1984), 538–544], is due to Dietzfelbinger, Karlin, Mehlhorn, Meyer auf der Heide, Rohnert, and Tarjan [*SICOMP* **23** (1994), 738–761].

EXERCISES

1. [*20*] When the instruction 9H in Table 1 is reached, how small and how large can the contents of rI1 possibly be, assuming that bytes 1, 2, 3 of K each contain alphabetic character codes less than 30?

2. [*20*] Find a reasonably common English word not in Table 1 that could be added to that table without changing the program.

3. [*23*] Explain why no program beginning with the five instructions

```
LD1   K(1:1)   or   LD1N   K(1:1)
LD2   K(2:2)   or   LD2N   K(2:2)
INC1  a,2
LD2   K(3:3)
J2Z   9F
```

could be used in place of the more complicated program in Table 1, for any constant a, since unique addresses would not be produced for the given keys.

4. [*M30*] How many people should be invited to a party in order to make it likely that there are *three* with the same birthday?

5. [*15*] Mr. B. C. Dull was writing a FORTRAN compiler using a decimal MIX computer, and he needed a symbol table to keep track of the names of variables in the FORTRAN program being compiled. These names were restricted to be at most ten characters in length. He decided to use a hash table with $M = 100$, and to use the fast hash function $h(K) = $ leftmost byte of K. Was this a good idea?

6. [*15*] Would it be wise to change the first two instructions of (3) to LDA K; ENTX 0?

7. [*HM30*] (*Polynomial hashing.*) The purpose of this exercise is to consider the construction of polynomials $P(x)$ such as (10), which convert n-bit keys into m-bit addresses, in such a way that distinct keys differing in t or fewer bits will hash to different addresses. Given n and $t \leq n$, and given an integer k such that n divides $2^k - 1$, we shall construct polynomial whose degree m is a function of n, t, and k. (Usually n is increased, if necessary, so that k can be chosen to be reasonably small.)

Let S be the smallest set of integers such that $\{1, 2, \ldots, t\} \subseteq S$ and $(2j) \bmod n \in S$ for all $j \in S$. For example, when $n = 15$, $k = 4$, and $t = 6$, we have $S = \{1, 2, 3, 4, 5, 6, 8, 10, 12, 9\}$. We now define the polynomial $P(x) = \prod_{j \in S}(x - \alpha^j)$, where α is an element of order n in the finite field $\mathrm{GF}(2^k)$, and where the coefficients of $P(x)$ are computed in this field. The degree m of $P(x)$ is the number of elements of S. Since α^{2j} is a root of $P(x)$ whenever α^j is a root, it follows that the coefficients p_j of $P(x)$ satisfy $p_i^2 = p_i$, so they are 0 or 1.

Prove that if $R(x) = r_{n-1}x^{n-1} + \cdots + r_1 x + r_0$ is any nonzero polynomial modulo 2, with at most t nonzero coefficients, then $R(x)$ is not a multiple of $P(x)$ modulo 2. [It follows that the corresponding hash function behaves as advertised.]

8. [*M34*] (*The three-distance theorem.*) Let θ be an irrational number between 0 and 1, whose regular continued fraction representation in the notation of Section 4.5.3 is $\theta = //a_1, a_2, a_3, \ldots //$. Let $q_0 = 0$, $p_0 = 1$, $q_1 = 1$, $p_1 = 0$, and $q_{k+1} = a_k q_k + q_{k-1}$, $p_{k+1} = a_k p_k + p_{k-1}$ for $k \geq 1$. Let $\{x\}$ denote $x \bmod 1 = x - \lfloor x \rfloor$, and let $\{x\}^+$ denote $x - \lceil x \rceil + 1$. As the points $\{\theta\}, \{2\theta\}, \{3\theta\}, \ldots$ are successively inserted into the interval $[0 \mathinner{.\,.} 1]$, let the line segments be numbered as they appear in such a way that the first segment of a given length is number 0, the next is number 1, etc. Prove that the following statements are all true: Interval number s of length $\{t\theta\}$, where $t = rq_k + q_{k-1}$ and $0 \leq r < a_k$ and k is even and $0 \leq s < q_k$, has left endpoint $\{s\theta\}$ and right endpoint $\{(s+t)\theta\}^+$. Interval number s of length $1 - \{t\theta\}$, where $t = rq_k + q_{k-1}$ and $0 \leq r < a_k$ and k is odd and $0 \leq s < q_k$, has left endpoint $\{(s+t)\theta\}$ and right endpoint $\{s\theta\}^+$. Every positive integer n can be uniquely represented as $n = rq_k + q_{k-1} + s$ for some $k \geq 1$, $1 \leq r \leq a_k$, and $0 \leq s < q_k$. In terms of this representation, just before the point $\{n\theta\}$ is inserted the n intervals present are

the first s intervals (numbered $0, \ldots, s-1$) of length $\{(-1)^k(rq_k + q_{k-1})\theta\}$;

the first $n - q_k$ intervals (numbered $0, \ldots, n - q_k - 1$) of length $\{(-1)^k q_k \theta\}$;

the last $q_k - s$ intervals (numbered $s, \ldots, q_k - 1$) of length $\{(-1)^k((r-1)q_k + q_{k-1})\theta\}$.

The operation of inserting $\{n\theta\}$ removes interval number s of the third type and converts it into interval number s of the first type, number $n - q_k$ of the second type.

9. [*M30*] When we successively insert the points $\{\theta\}, \{2\theta\}, \ldots$ into the interval $[0 \mathinner{.\,.} 1]$, Theorem S asserts that each new point always breaks up one of the largest remaining intervals. If the interval $[a \mathinner{.\,.} c]$ is thereby broken into two parts $[a \mathinner{.\,.} b]$, $[b \mathinner{.\,.} c]$, we may call it a *bad break* if one of these parts is more than twice as long as the other, namely if $b - a > 2(c - b)$ or $c - b > 2(b - a)$.

Prove that bad breaks will occur for some $\{n\theta\}$ unless $\theta \bmod 1 = \phi^{-1}$ or ϕ^{-2}; and the latter values of θ *never* produce bad breaks.

10. [*M38*] (R. L. Graham.) If $\theta, \alpha_1, \ldots, \alpha_d$ are real numbers with $\alpha_1 = 0$, and if $n_1, \ldots, n_d$ are positive integers, and if the points $\{n\theta + \alpha_j\}$ are inserted into the interval $[0 \mathinner{.\,.} 1]$ for $0 \leq n < n_j$ and $1 \leq j \leq d$, prove that the resulting $n_1 + \cdots + n_d$ (possibly empty) intervals have at most $3d$ different lengths.

11. [*16*] Successful searches are often more frequent than unsuccessful ones. Would it therefore be a good idea to interchange lines 12–13 of Program C with lines 10–11?

▶ **12.** [*21*] Show that Program C can be rewritten so that there is only one conditional jump instruction in the inner loop. Compare the running time of the modified program with the original.

▶ **13.** [*24*] (*Abbreviated keys.*) Let $h(K)$ be a hash function, and let $q(K)$ be a function of K such that K can be determined once $h(K)$ and $q(K)$ are given. For example, in division hashing we may let $h(K) = K \bmod M$ and $q(K) = \lfloor K/M \rfloor$; in multiplicative hashing we may let $h(K)$ be the leading bits of $(AK/w) \bmod 1$, and $q(K)$ can be the other bits.

Show that when chaining is used without overlapping lists, we need only store $q(K)$ instead of K in each record. (This almost saves the space needed for the link fields.) Modify Algorithm C so that it allows such abbreviated keys by avoiding overlapping lists, yet uses no auxiliary storage locations for overflow records.

14. [*24*] (E. W. Elcock.) Show that it is possible to let a large hash table *share memory* with any number of other linked lists. Let every word of the list area have a 2-bit TAG field and two link fields called LINK and AUX, with the following interpretation:

TAG(P) = 0 indicates a word in the list of available space; LINK(P) points to the next entry in this list, and AUX(P) is unused.

TAG(P) = 1 indicates a word in use where P is not the hash address of any key in the hash table; the other fields of the word in location P may have any desired format.

TAG(P) = 2 indicates that P is the hash address of at least one key; AUX(P) points to a linked list specifying all such keys, and LINK(P) points to another word in the list memory. Whenever a word with TAG(P) = 2 is accessed during the processing of any list, we set P ← LINK(P) repeatedly until reaching a word with TAG(P) ≤ 1. (For efficiency we might also then change prior links so that it will not be necessary to skip over the same entries again and again.)

Define suitable algorithms for inserting and retrieving keys in such a hash table.

15. [*16*] Why is it a good idea for Algorithm L and Algorithm D to signal overflow when $N = M - 1$ instead of when $N = M$?

16. [*10*] Program L says that K should not be zero. But doesn't it actually work even when K is zero?

17. [*15*] Why not simply define $h_2(K) = h_1(K)$ in (25), when $h_1(K) \neq 0$?

▶ **18.** [*21*] Is (31) better or worse than (30), as a substitute for lines 10–13 of Program D? Give your answer on the basis of the average values of A, $S1$, and C.

19. [*40*] Empirically test the effect of restricting the range of $h_2(K)$ in Algorithm D, so that (a) $1 \leq h_2(K) \leq r$ for $r = 1, 2, 3, \ldots, 10$; (b) $1 \leq h_2(K) \leq \rho M$ for $\rho = \frac{1}{10}, \frac{2}{10}, \ldots, \frac{9}{10}$.

20. [*M25*] (R. Krutar.) Change Algorithm D as follows, avoiding the hash function $h_2(K)$: In step D3, set $c \leftarrow 0$; and at the beginning of step D4, set $c \leftarrow c + 1$. Prove that if $M = 2^m$, the corresponding probe sequence $h_1(K)$, $(h_1(K) - 1) \bmod M$, $\ldots$, $(h_1(K) - \binom{M}{2}) \bmod M$ will be a permutation of $\{0, 1, \ldots, M-1\}$. When this "quadratic probing" method is programmed for MIX, how does it compare with the three programs considered in Fig. 42, assuming that the algorithm behaves like random probing with secondary clustering?

▶ **21.** [*20*] Suppose that we wish to delete a record from a table constructed by Algorithm D, marking it "deleted" as suggested in the text. Should we also decrease the variable N that is used to govern Algorithm D?

22. [*27*] Prove that Algorithm R leaves the table exactly as it would have been if KEY[i] had never been inserted in the first place.

▶ **23.** [*33*] Design an algorithm analogous to Algorithm R, for deleting entries from a chained hash table that has been constructed by Algorithm C.

24. [*M20*] Suppose that the set of all possible keys that can occur has MP elements, where exactly P keys hash to any given address. (In practical cases, P is very large; for example, if the keys are arbitrary 10-digit numbers and if $M = 10^3$, we have $P = 10^7$.) Assume that $M \geq 7$ and $N = 7$. If seven distinct keys are selected at random from the set of all possible keys, what is the exact probability that the hash sequence 1 2 6 2 1 6 1 will be obtained (namely that $h(K_1) = 1$, $h(K_2) = 2$, ..., $h(K_7) = 1$), as a function of M and P?

25. [*M19*] Explain why Eq. (39) is true.

26. [*M20*] How many hash sequences $a_1 a_2 \ldots a_9$ yield the pattern of occupied cells (21), using linear probing?

27. [*M27*] Complete the proof of Theorem K. [*Hint:* Let

$$s(n, x, y) = \sum_k \binom{n}{k}(x + k)^{k+1}(y - k)^{n-k-1}(y - n);$$

use Abel's binomial theorem, Eq. 1.2.6–(16), to prove that $s(n, x, y) = x(x + y)^n + ns(n-1, x+1, y-1)$.]

28. [*M30*] In the old days when computers were much slower than they are now, it was possible to watch the lights flashing and see how fast Algorithm L was running. When the table began to fill up, some entries would be processed very quickly, while others took a great deal of time.

  This experience suggests that the standard deviation of the number of probes in an unsuccessful search is rather high, when linear probing is used. Find a formula that expresses the variance in terms of the Q_r functions defined in Theorem K, and estimate the variance when $N = \alpha M$ as $M \to \infty$.

29. [*M21*] (*The parking problem.*) A certain one-way street has m parking spaces in a row, numbered 1 through m. A man and his dozing wife drive by, and suddenly she wakes up and orders him to park immediately. He dutifully parks at the first available space; but if there are no places left that he can get to without backing up (that is, if his wife awoke when the car approached space k, but spaces k, $k + 1$, ..., m are all full), he expresses his regrets and drives on.

  Suppose, in fact, that this happens for n different cars, where the jth wife wakes up just in time to park at space a_j. In how many of the sequences $a_1 \ldots a_n$ will all of the cars get safely parked, assuming that the street is initially empty and that nobody leaves after parking? For example, when $m = n = 9$ and $a_1 \ldots a_9 = 3\ 1\ 4\ 1\ 5\ 9\ 2\ 6\ 5$, the cars get parked as follows:

[*Hint:* Use the analysis of linear probing.]

30. [*M38*] When $n = m$ in the parking problem of exercise 29, show that all cars get parked if and only if there exists a permutation $p_1 p_2 \ldots p_n$ of $\{1, 2, \ldots, n\}$ such that $a_j \leq p_j$ for all j.

31. [*M40*] When $n = m$ in the parking problem of exercise 29, the number of solutions turns out to be $(n+1)^{n-1}$; and from exercise 2.3.4.4–22 we know that this is the same as the number of free trees on $n + 1$ labeled vertices! Find an interesting connection between parking sequences and trees.

32. [*M27*] Prove that the system of equations (44) has a unique solution $(c_0, c_1, \ldots, c_{M-1})$, whenever $b_0, b_1, \ldots, b_{M-1}$ are nonnegative integers whose sum is less than M. Design an algorithm to find that solution.

▸ **33.** [*M23*] Explain why (51) is only an approximation to the true average number of probes made by Algorithm L. What was there about the derivation of (51) that wasn't rigorously exact?

▸ **34.** [*M23*] The purpose of this exercise is to investigate the average number of probes in a chained hash table when the lists are kept separate as in Fig. 38.

   a) What is P_{Nk}, the probability that a given list has length k, when the M^N hash sequences (35) are equally likely?
   b) Find the generating function $P_n(z) = \sum_{k \geq 0} P_{Nk} z^k$.
   c) Express the average number of probes for a successful search in terms of this generating function.
   d) Deduce the average number of probes in an *unsuccessful* search, considering variants of the data structure in which the following conventions are used: (i) hashing is always to a list head (see Fig. 38); (ii) hashing is to a table position (see Fig. 40), but all keys except the first of a list go into a separate overflow area; (iii) hashing is to a table position and all entries appear in the hash table.

35. [*M24*] Continuing exercise 34, what is the average number of probes in an unsuccessful search when the individual lists are kept in order by their key values? Consider data structures (i), (ii), and (iii).

36. [*M23*] Continuing exercise 34(d), find the *variance* of the number of probes when the search is unsuccessful, using data structures (i) and (ii).

▸ **37.** [*M29*] Eq. (19) gives the average number of probes in separate chaining when the search is successful; what is the *variance* of that number of probes?

38. [*M32*] (*Tree hashing.*) A clever programmer might try to use binary search trees instead of linear lists in the chaining method, thereby combining Algorithm 6.2.2T with hashing. Analyze the average number of probes that would be required by this compound algorithm, for both successful and unsuccessful searches. [*Hint:* See Eq. 5.2.1–(15).]

39. [*M28*] Let $c_N(k)$ be the total number of lists of length k formed when Algorithm C is applied to all M^N hash sequences (35). Find a recurrence relation on the numbers $c_N(k)$ that makes it possible to determine a simple formula for the sum

$$S_N = \sum_k \binom{k}{2} c_N(k).$$

How is S_N related to the number of probes in an unsuccessful search by Algorithm C?

40. [*M33*] Eq. (15) gives the average number of probes used by Algorithm C in an unsuccessful search; what is the *variance* of that number of probes?

41. [*M40*] Analyze T_N, the average number of times the index R is decreased by 1 when the $(N+1)$st item is being inserted by Algorithm C.

▶ **42.** [*M20*] Derive (17), the probability that Algorithm C succeeds immediately.

43. [*HM44*] Analyze a modification of Algorithm C that uses a table of size $M' \geq M$. Only the first M locations are used for hashing, so the first $M'-M$ empty nodes found in step C5 will be in the extra locations of the table. For fixed M', what choice of M in the range $1 \leq M \leq M'$ leads to the best performance?

44. [*M43*] (*Random probing with secondary clustering.*) The object of this exercise is to determine the expected number of probes in the open addressing scheme with probe sequence

$$h(K), \quad (h(K)+p_1) \bmod M, \quad (h(K)+p_2) \bmod M, \quad \ldots, \quad (h(K)+p_{M-1}) \bmod M,$$

where $p_1\,p_2\ldots p_{M-1}$ is a randomly chosen permutation of $\{1,2,\ldots,M-1\}$ that depends on $h(K)$. In other words, all keys with the same value of $h(K)$ follow the same probe sequence, and the $(M-1)!^M$ possible choices of M probe sequences with this property are equally likely.

This situation can be modeled accurately by the following experimental procedure performed on an initially empty linear array of size m. Do the following operation n times: "With probability p, occupy the leftmost empty position. Otherwise (that is, with probability $q = 1-p$), select any table position except the one at the extreme left, with each of these $m-1$ positions equally likely. If the selected position is empty, occupy it; otherwise select *any* empty position (including the leftmost) and occupy it, considering each of the empty positions equally likely."

For example, when $m = 5$ and $n = 3$, the array configuration after such an experiment will be (occupied, occupied, empty, occupied, empty) with probability

$$\tfrac{7}{192}qqq + \tfrac{1}{6}pqq + \tfrac{1}{6}qpq + \tfrac{11}{64}qqp + \tfrac{1}{3}ppq + \tfrac{1}{4}pqp + \tfrac{1}{4}qpp.$$

(This procedure corresponds to random probing with secondary clustering, when $p = 1/m$, since we can renumber the table entries so that a particular probe sequence is 0, 1, 2, ... and all the others are random.)

Find a formula for the average number of occupied positions at the left of the array (namely 2 in the example above). Also find the asymptotic value of this quantity when $p = 1/m$, $n = \alpha(m+1)$, and $m \to \infty$.

45. [*M43*] Solve the analog of exercise 44 with *tertiary clustering*, when the probe sequence begins $h_1(K)$, $((h_1(K) + h_2(K)) \bmod M$, and the succeeding probes are randomly chosen depending only on $h_1(K)$ and $h_2(K)$. (Thus the $(M-2)!^{M(M-1)}$ possible choices of $M(M-1)$ probe sequences with this property are considered to be equally likely.) Is this procedure asymptotically equivalent to uniform probing?

46. [*M42*] Determine C'_N and C_N for the open addressing method that uses the probe sequence

$$h(K),\ 0,\ 1,\ \ldots,\ h(K)-1,\ h(K)+1,\ \ldots,\ M-1.$$

47. [*M25*] Find the average number of probes needed by open addressing when the probe sequence is

$$h(K),\ h(K)-1,\ h(K)+1,\ h(K)-2,\ h(K)+2,\ \ldots.$$

This probe sequence was once suggested because all the distances between consecutive probes are distinct when M is even. [*Hint:* Find the trick and this problem is easy.]

▶ **48.** [*M21*] Analyze the open addressing method that probes locations $h_1(K)$, $h_2(K)$, $h_3(K), \ldots$, given an infinite sequence of mutually independent random hash functions $\langle h_n(K) \rangle$. In this setup it is possible to probe the same location twice, for example if $h_1(K) = h_2(K)$, but such coincidences are rather unlikely until the table gets full.

49. [*HM24*] Generalizing exercise 34 to the case of b records per bucket, determine the average number of probes (external memory accesses) C_N and C'_N, for chaining with separate lists, assuming that a list containing k elements requires $\max(1, k - b + 1)$ probes in an unsuccessful search. Instead of using the exact probability P_{Nk} as in exercise 34, use the *Poisson approximation*

$$\binom{N}{k}\left(\frac{1}{M}\right)^k\left(1 - \frac{1}{M}\right)^{N-k} = \frac{N}{M}\frac{N-1}{M}\cdots\frac{N-k+1}{M}\left(1 - \frac{1}{M}\right)^N\left(1 - \frac{1}{M}\right)^{-k}\frac{1}{k!}$$

$$= \frac{e^{-\rho}\rho^k}{k!}(1 + O(k^2/M)),$$

which is valid for $N = \rho M$ and $k \le \sqrt{M}$ as $M \to \infty$; derive formulas (57) and (58).

50. [*M20*] Show that $Q_1(M, N) = M - (M - N - 1)Q_0(M, N)$, in the notation of (42). [*Hint:* Prove first that $Q_1(M, N) = (N + 1)Q_0(M, N) - NQ_0(M, N-1)$.]

51. [*HM17*] Express the function $R(\alpha, n)$ defined in (55) in terms of the function Q_0 defined in (42).

52. [*HM20*] Prove that $Q_0(M, N) = \int_0^\infty e^{-t}(1 + t/M)^N\, dt$.

53. [*HM20*] Prove that the function $R(\alpha, n)$ can be expressed in terms of the incomplete gamma function, and use the result of exercise 1.2.11.3–9 to find the asymptotic value of $R(\alpha, n)$ to $O(n^{-2})$ as $n \to \infty$, for fixed $\alpha < 1$.

54. [*HM28*] Show that when $b = 1$, Eq. (61) is equivalent to Eq. (23). *Hint:* We have

$$t_n(\alpha) = \frac{(-1)^{n-1}}{n!\,\alpha} \sum_{m > n} \frac{(-n\alpha)^m}{m(m-1)(m-n-1)!}.$$

55. [*HM43*] Generalize the Schay–Spruth model, discussed after Theorem P, to the case of M buckets of size b. Prove that $C(z)$ is equal to $Q(z)/(B(z) - z^b)$, where $Q(z)$ is a polynomial of degree b and $Q(1) = 0$. Show that the average number of probes is

$$1 + \frac{M}{N}C'(1) = 1 + \frac{1}{b}\left(\frac{1}{1 - q_1} + \cdots + \frac{1}{1 - q_{b-1}} - \frac{1}{2}\frac{B''(1) - b(b-1)}{B'(1) - b}\right),$$

where $q_1, \ldots, q_{b-1}$ are the roots of $Q(z)/(z - 1)$. Replacing the binomial probability distribution $B(z)$ by the Poisson approximation $P(z) = e^{b\alpha(z-1)}$, where $\alpha = N/Mb$, and using Lagrange's inversion formula (see Eq. 2.3.4.4–(9) and exercise 4.7–8), reduce your answer to Eq. (61).

56. [*HM43*] Generalize Theorem K, obtaining an exact analysis of linear probing with buckets of size b. What is the asymptotic number of probes in a successful search when the table is full ($N = Mb$)?

57. [*M47*] Does the uniform assignment of probabilities to probe sequences give the minimum value of C_N, over all open addressing methods?

58. [*M21*] (S. C. Johnson.) Find ten permutations on $\{0, 1, 2, 3, 4\}$ that are equivalent to uniform probing in the sense of Theorem U.

59. [*M25*] Prove that if an assignment of probabilities to permutations is equivalent to uniform probing, in the sense of Theorem U, the number of permutations with nonzero probabilities exceeds M^a for any fixed exponent a, when M is sufficiently large.

60. [*M47*] Let us say that an open addressing scheme involves *single hashing* if it uses exactly M probe sequences, one beginning with each possible value of $h(K)$, each of which occurs with probability $1/M$.

   Are the best single-hashing schemes (in the sense of minimum C_N) asymptotically better than the random ones described by (29)? In particular, is $C_{\alpha M} \geq 1 + \frac{1}{2}\alpha + \frac{1}{2}\alpha^2 + O(\alpha^3)$ as $M \to \infty$?

61. [*M46*] Is the method analyzed in exercise 46 the worst possible single-hashing scheme, in the sense of exercise 60?

62. [*M49*] A single hashing scheme is called *cyclic* if the increments $p_1\,p_2\ldots p_{M-1}$ in the notation of exercise 44 are fixed for all K. (Examples of such methods are linear probing and the sequences considered in exercises 20 and 47.) An *optimum* single hashing scheme is one for which C_M is minimum, over all $(M-1)!^M$ single hashing schemes for a given M. When $M \leq 5$ the best single hashing schemes are cyclic. Is this true for all M?

63. [*M25*] If repeated random insertions and deletions are made in a hash table, how many independent insertions are needed on the average before all M locations have become occupied at one time or another? (This is the mean time to failure of the deletion method that simply marks cells "deleted.")

64. [*M41*] Analyze the expected behavior of Algorithm R (deletion with linear probing). How many times will step R4 be performed, on the average?

▶ **65.** [*20*] (*Variable-length keys.*) Many applications of hash tables deal with keys that can be any number of characters long. In such cases we can't simply store the key in the table as in the programs of this section. What would be a good way to deal with variable-length keys in a hash table on the MIX computer?

▶ **66.** [*25*] (Ole Amble, 1973.) Is it possible to insert keys into an open hash table making use also of their numerical or alphabetic order, so that a search with Algorithm L or Algorithm D is known to be unsuccessful whenever a key *smaller* than the search argument is encountered?

67. [*M41*] If Algorithm L inserts N keys with respective hash addresses $a_1\,a_2\ldots a_N$, let d_j be the displacement of the jth key from its home address a_j; then $C_N = 1 + (d_1 + d_2 + \cdots + d_N)/N$. Theorem P tells us that permutation of the a's has no effect on the sum $d_1 + d_2 + \cdots + d_N$. However, such permutation might drastically change the sum $d_1^2 + d_2^2 + \cdots + d_N^2$. For example, the hash sequence $1\ 2\ \ldots\ N{-}1\ N{-}1$ makes $d_1\,d_2\ldots d_{N-1}\,d_N = 0\ 0\ \ldots\ 0\ N{-}1$ and $\sum d_j^2 = (N-1)^2$, while its reflection $N{-}1\ N{-}1\ \ldots\ 2\ 1$ leads to much more civilized displacements $0\ 1\ \ldots\ 1\ 1$ for which $\sum d_j^2 = N - 1$.

   a) Which rearrangement of $a_1\,a_2\ldots a_N$ minimizes $\sum d_j^2$?
   b) Explain how to modify Algorithm L so that it maintains a least-variance set of displacements after every insertion.
   c) Determine the average value of $\sum d_j^2$ with and without this modification.

68. [*M41*] What is the variance of the average number of probes in a successful search by Algorithm L? In particular, what is the average of $(d_1 + d_2 + \cdots + d_N)^2$ in the notation of exercise 67?

69. [*M25*] (Andrew Yao.) Prove that all cyclic single hashing schemes in the sense of exercise 62 satisfy the inequality $C'_{\alpha M} \geq \frac{1}{2}(1 + 1/(1 - \alpha))$. [*Hint:* Show that an unsuccessful search takes exactly k probes with probability $p_k \leq (M - N)/M$.]

70. [*HM43*] Prove that the expected number of probes that are needed to insert the $(\alpha M + 1)$st item with double hashing is at most the expected number needed to insert the $(\alpha M + \sqrt{O(\log M)/M})$th item with uniform probing.

71. [*40*] Experiment with the behavior of Algorithm C when it has been adapted to external searching as described in the text.

▶ **72.** [*M28*] (*Universal hashing.*) Imagine a gigantic matrix H that has one column for every possible key K. The entries of H are numbers between 0 and $M-1$; the rows of H represent hash functions. We say that H defines a *universal family of hash functions* if any two columns agree in at most R/M rows, where R is the total number of rows.

a) Prove that if H is universal in this sense, and if we select a hash function h by choosing a row of H at random, than the expected size of the list containing any given key K in the method of separate chaining (Fig. 38) will be $\leq 1 + N/M$, after we have inserted any set of N distinct keys $K_1, K_2, \ldots, K_N$.

b) Suppose each h_j in (9) is a randomly chosen mapping from the set of all characters to the set $\{0, 1, \ldots, M - 1\}$. Show that this corresponds to a universal family of hash functions.

c) Would the result of (b) still be true if $h_j(0) = 0$ for all j, but $h_j(x)$ is random for $x \neq 0$?

73. [*M26*] (Carter and Wegman.) Show that part (b) of the previous exercise holds even when the h_j are not completely random functions, but they have either of the following special forms: (i) Let x_j be the binary number $(b_{j(n-1)} \ldots b_{j1} b_{j0})_2$. Then $h_j(x_j) = (a_{j(n-1)} b_{j(n-1)} + \cdots + a_{j1} b_{j1} + a_{j0} b_{j0}) \bmod M$, where each a_{jk} is chosen randomly modulo M. (ii) Let M be prime and assume that $0 \leq x_j < M$. Then $h_j(x_j) = (a_j x_j + b_j) \bmod M$, where a_j and b_j are chosen randomly modulo M.

74. [*M29*] Let H define a universal family of hash functions. Prove or disprove: Given any N distinct columns, and any row chosen at random, the expected number of zeros in those columns is $O(1) + O(N/M)$. [Thus, every list in the method of separate chaining will have this expected size.]

75. [*M26*] Prove or disprove the following statements about the hash function h of (9), when the h_j are independent random functions:

a) The probability that $h(K) = m$ is $1/M$, for all $0 \leq m < M$.

b) If $K \neq K'$, the probability that $h(K) = m$ and $h(K') = m'$ is $1/M^2$, for all $0 \leq m, m' < M$.

c) If K, K', and K'' are distinct, the probability that $h(K) = m$, $h(K') = m'$, and $h(K'') = m''$ is $1/M^3$, for all $0 \leq m, m', m'' < M$.

d) If K, K', K'', and K''' are distinct, the probability that $h(K) = m$, $h(K') = m'$, $h(K'') = m''$, and $h(K''') = m'''$ is $1/M^4$, for all $0 \leq m, m', m'', m''' < M$.

▶ **76.** [*M21*] Suggest a way to modify (9) for keys with variable length, preserving the properties of universal hashing.

77. [*M22*] Let H define a universal family of hash functions from 32-bit keys to 16-bit keys. (Thus H has 2^{32} columns, and $M = 2^{16}$, in the notation of exercise 72.) A 256-bit key can be regarded as the concatenation of eight 32-bit parts $x_1 x_2 x_3 x_4 x_5 x_6 x_7 x_8$; we can map it into a 16-bit address with the hash function

$$h_4\big(h_3\big(h_2(h_1(x_1)h_1(x_2))h_2(h_1(x_3)h_1(x_4))\big)h_3\big(h_2(h_1(x_5)h_1(x_6))h_2(h_1(x_7)h_1(x_8))\big)\big),$$

where h_1, h_2, h_3, and h_4 are randomly and independently chosen rows of H. (Here, for example, $h_1(x_1)h_1(x_2)$ stands for the 32-bit number obtained by concatenating $h_1(x_1)$ with $h_1(x_2)$.) Prove that the probability is less than 2^{-14} that two distinct keys hash to the same address. [This scheme requires substantially fewer random choices than (9).]

She made a hash of the proper names, to be sure.
— GRANT ALLEN (*The Tents of Shem*, 1889)

HASH, x.   There is no definition
for this word —
nobody knows what hash is.
— AMBROSE BIERCE (*The Devil's Dictionary*, 1906)

6.5. RETRIEVAL ON SECONDARY KEYS

WE HAVE NOW COMPLETED our study of searching for *primary keys*, namely for keys that uniquely specify a record in a file. But it is sometimes necessary to conduct a search based on the values of other fields in the records besides the primary key; these other fields are often called *secondary keys* or *attributes* of the record. For example, in an enrollment file that contains information about the students at a university, it may be desirable to search for all sophomores from Ohio who are not majoring in mathematics or statistics; or to search for all unmarried French-speaking graduate student women; etc.

In general, we assume that each record contains several attributes, and we want to search for all records that have certain values of certain attributes. The specification of the desired records is called a *query*. Queries are usually restricted to at most the following three types:

a) A *simple query* that gives a specific value of a specific attribute; for example, "MAJOR = MATHEMATICS", or "RESIDENCE.STATE = OHIO".

b) A *range query* that gives a specific range of values for a specific attribute; for example, "COST < $18.00", or "21 < AGE ≤ 23".

c) A *Boolean query* that consists of the previous types combined with the operations AND, OR, NOT; for example,

   "(CLASS = SOPHOMORE) AND (RESIDENCE.STATE = OHIO)
      AND NOT ((MAJOR = MATHEMATICS) OR (MAJOR = STATISTICS))".

The problem of discovering efficient search techniques for these three types of queries is already quite difficult, and therefore queries of more complicated types are usually not considered. For example, a railroad company might have a file giving the current status of all its freight cars; a query such as "find all empty refrigerator cars within 500 miles of Seattle" would not be explicitly allowed, unless "distance from Seattle" were an attribute stored within each record instead of a complicated function to be deduced from other attributes. And the use of logical quantifiers, in addition to AND, OR, and NOT, would introduce further complications, limited only by the imagination of the query-poser; given a file of baseball statistics, for example, we might ask for the longest consecutive hitting streak in night games. These examples are complicated, but they can still be handled by taking one pass through a suitably arranged file. Other queries are even more difficult — for example, to find all pairs of records that have the same values on five or more attributes (without specifying which attributes must match). Such queries may be regarded as general programming tasks that are beyond the scope of this discussion, although they can often be broken down into subproblems of the kind considered here.

Before we begin to study the various techniques for secondary key retrieval, it is important to put the subject in a proper economic context. Although a vast number of applications fit into the general framework of the three types of queries outlined above, not many of these applications are really suited to the sophisticated techniques we shall be studying, and some of them are better done by hand than by machine! People climb Mt. Everest "because it is there" and because tools have been developed that make the climb possible; similarly, when faced with a mountain of data, people are tempted to use a computer to find the answer to the most difficult queries they can dream up, in an online real-time environment, without properly balancing the cost. The desired calculations are possible, but they're not right for everyone's application.

For example, consider the following simple approach to secondary key retrieval: After *batching* a number of queries, we can do a sequential search through the entire file, retrieving all the relevant records. ("Batching" means that we accumulate a number of queries before doing anything about them.) This method is quite satisfactory if the file isn't too large and if the queries don't have to be handled immediately. It can be used even with tape files, and it only ties up the computer at odd intervals, so it will tend to be very economical in terms of equipment costs. Moreover, it will even handle computational queries of the "distance to Seattle" type discussed above.

Another simple way to facilitate secondary key retrieval is to let *people* do part of the work, by providing them with suitable printed indexes to the information. This method is often the most reasonable and economical way to proceed (provided, of course, that the old paper is recycled whenever a new index is printed), especially because people tend to notice interesting patterns when they have convenient access to masses of data.

The applications that are not satisfactorily handled by the simple schemes given above involve very large files for which quick responses to queries are important. Such a situation would occur, for example, if the file were continuously being queried by a number of simultaneous users, or if the queries were being generated by machine instead of by people. Our goal in this section will be to see how well we can do secondary key retrieval with conventional computers, under various assumptions about the file structure. Fortunately, the methods we will discuss are becoming more and more feasible in practice, as the cost of computation continues to decrease dramatically.

A lot of good ideas have been developed for dealing with the problem, but (as the reader will have guessed from all these precautionary remarks) the algorithms are by no means as good as those available for primary key retrieval. Because of the wide variety of files and applications, we will not be able to give a complete discussion of all the possibilities that have been considered, or to analyze the behavior of each algorithm in typical environments. The remainder of this section presents the basic approaches that have been proposed, and it is left to the reader's imagination to decide what combination of techniques is most appropriate in each particular case.

Inverted files. The first important class of techniques for secondary key retrieval is based on the idea of an *inverted file*. This does not mean that the file is turned upside down; it means that the roles of records and attributes are reversed. Instead of listing the attributes of a given record, we list the records having a given attribute.

We encounter inverted files (under other names) quite often in our daily lives. For example, the inverted file corresponding to a Russian-English dictionary is an English-Russian dictionary. The inverted file corresponding to this book is the index that appears at the close of the book. Accountants traditionally use "double-entry bookkeeping," where all transactions are entered both in a cash account and in a customer account, so that the current cash position and the current customer liability are both readily accessible.

In general, an inverted file usually doesn't stand by itself; it is to be used together with the original uninverted file. It provides duplicate, redundant information in order to speed up secondary key retrieval. The components of an inverted file are called *inverted lists*, namely the lists of all records having a given value of some attribute.

Like all lists, the inverted lists can be represented in many ways within a computer, and different modes of representation are appropriate at different times. Some secondary key fields have only two values (for example, "SEX"), and the corresponding inverted lists are quite long; but other fields typically have a great many values with few duplications (for example, "PHONENUMBER").

Imagine that we want to store the information in a telephone directory so that all entries can be retrieved on the basis of either name, phone number, or residence address. One solution is simply to make three separate files, oriented to retrieval on each type of key. Another idea is to combine the files, for example by making three hash tables that serve as the list heads for the chaining method. In the latter scheme, each record of the file would be an element of three lists, and it would therefore contain three link fields; this is the so-called *multilist* method illustrated in Fig. 13 of Section 2.2.6 and discussed further below. A third possibility is to combine the three files into one super file, by analogy with library card catalogues in which author cards, title cards, and subject cards are all alphabetized together.

A consideration of the format used in the index to this book leads to further ideas on inverted list representation. For secondary key fields in which there are typically five or so entries per attribute value, we can simply make a short sequential list of the record locations (analogous to page locations in a book index), following the key value. If related records tend to be clustered consecutively, a range specification code (for examples, pages 559–582) is useful. If the records in the file tend to be reallocated frequently, it may be better to use primary keys instead of record locations in the inverted files, so that no updating needs to be done when the locations change; for example, references to Bible passages are always given by chapter and verse, and the index to some books is based on paragraph numbers instead of page numbers.

None of these ideas is especially appropriate for the case of a two-valued attribute like "SEX". In such a case only one inverted list is needed, of course, since the non-males will be female and conversely. If each value relates to about half the items of the file, the inverted list will be horribly long, but we can solve the problem rather nicely on a binary computer by using a bit string representation, with each bit specifying the value of a particular record. Thus the bit string 01001011101... might mean that the first record in the file refers to a male, the second female, the next two male, etc.

Such methods suffice to handle simple queries about specific attribute values. A slight extension makes it possible to treat range queries, except that a comparison-based search scheme (Section 6.2) must be used instead of hashing.

For Boolean queries like "(MAJOR = MATHEMATICS) AND (RESIDENCE.STATE = OHIO)", we need to intersect two inverted lists. This can be done in several ways; for example, if both lists are ordered, one pass through each will pick out all common entries. Alternatively, we could select the *shortest* list and look up each of its records, checking the other attributes; but this method works only for AND's, not for OR's, and it is unattractive on external files because it requires many accesses to records that will not satisfy the query.

The same considerations show that a multilist organization as described above is inefficient for Boolean queries on an external file, since it implies many unnecessary accesses. For example, imagine what would happen if the index to this book were organized in a multilist manner: Each entry of the index would refer only to the last page on which its particular subject was mentioned; then on every page there would be a further reference, for each subject on that page, to the previous occurrence of that subject. In order to find all pages relevant to "[Analysis of algorithms] and [(External sorting) or (External searching)]", we would need to turn many pages. On the other hand, the same query can be resolved by looking at only two pages of the real index as it actually appears, doing simple operations on the inverted lists in order to find the small subset of pages that satisfy the query.

When an inverted list is represented as a bit string, Boolean combinations of simple queries are, of course, easily performed, because computers can manipulate bit strings at relatively high speed. For mixed queries in which some attributes are represented as sequential lists of record numbers while other attributes are represented as bit strings, it is not difficult to convert the sequential lists into bit strings, then to perform the Boolean operations on these bit strings.

A quantitative example of a hypothetical application may be helpful at this point. Assume that we have 1,000,000 records of 40 characters each, and that our file is stored on MIXTEC disks, as described in Section 5.4.9. The file itself therefore fills two disk units, and the inverted lists will probably fill several more. Each track contains 5000 characters = 30,000 bits, so an inverted list for a particular attribute will take up at most 34 tracks. (This maximum number of tracks occurs when the bitstring representation is the shortest possible one.) Suppose that we have a rather involved query that refers to a Boolean combination of 10 inverted lists; in the worst case we will have to read 340 tracks of information from the inverted file, for a total read time of 340×25 ms = 8.5 sec. The average latency delay will be about one half of the read time, but by careful programming we may be able to eliminate the latency. By storing the first track of each bitstring list in one cylinder, and the second track of each list in the next, etc., most of the seek time will be eliminated, so we can estimate the maximum seek time as about 34×26 ms ≈ 0.9 sec (or twice this if two independent disk units are involved). Finally, if q records satisfy the query, we will need about $q \times \big(60\,\text{ms (seek)} + 12.5\,\text{ms (latency)} + 0.2\,\text{ms (read)}\big)$ extra time to fetch each one for subsequent processing. Thus an optimistic estimate of the total expected time to process this rather complicated query is roughly $(10 + .073q)$ seconds. This may be contrasted with about 210 seconds to read through the entire file at top speed under the same assumptions without using any inverted lists.

This example shows that space optimization is closely related to time optimization in a disk memory; the time to process the inverted lists is roughly the time needed to seek and to read them.

The discussion above has more or less assumed that the file is not growing or shrinking as we query it; what should we do if frequent updates are necessary? In many applications it is sufficient to batch a number of requests for updates, and to take care of them in dull moments when no queries need to be answered. Alternatively, if updating the file has high priority, the method of B-trees (Section 6.2.4) is attractive. The entire collection of inverted lists could be made into one huge B-tree, with special conventions for the leaves so that the branch nodes contain key values while the leaves contain both keys and lists of pointers of records. File updates can also be handled by other methods that we shall discuss below.

Geometric data. A great many applications deal with points, lines, and shapes in spaces of two or more dimensions. One of the first approaches to distance-oriented queries was the "post-office tree" proposed in 1972 by Bruce McNutt. Suppose, for example, that we wish to handle queries like "What is the nearest city to point x?", given the value of x. Each node of McNutt's tree corresponds to a city y and a "test radius" r; the left subtree of this node corresponds to all cities z entered subsequently into this part of the tree such that the distance from y to z is $\leq r + \delta$, and the right subtree similarly is for distances $\geq r - \delta$. Here δ is a given tolerance; cities between $r - \delta$ and $r + \delta$ away from y must be entered in *both* subtrees. Searching in such a tree makes it possible to locate all cities within distance δ of a given point. (See Fig. 45.)

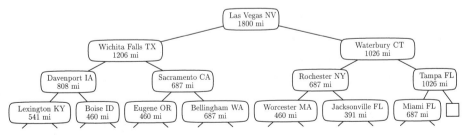

Fig. 45. The top levels of an example "post-office tree." To search for all cities near a given point x, start at the root: If x is within 1800 miles of Las Vegas, go left, otherwise go to the right; then repeat the process until encountering a terminal node. The method of tree construction ensures that all cities within 20 miles of x will be encountered during this search.

Several experiments based on this idea were conducted by McNutt and Edward Pring, using the 231 most populous cities in the continental United States in random order as an example database. They let the test radii shrink in a regular manner, replacing r by $0.67r$ when going to the left, and by $0.57r$ when going to the right, except that r was left unchanged when taking the second of two consecutive right branches. The result was that 610 nodes were required in the tree for $\delta = 20$ miles, and 1600 nodes were required for $\delta = 35$ miles. The top levels of their smaller tree are shown in Fig. 45. (In the remaining levels of this tree, Orlando FL appeared below both Jacksonville and Miami. Some cities occurred quite often; for example, 17 of the nodes were for Brockton MA!)

The rapid file growth as δ increases indicates that post-office trees probably have limited utility. We can do better by working directly with the *coordinates* of each point, regarding the coordinates as attributes or secondary keys; then we can make Boolean queries based on ranges of the keys. For example, suppose that the records of the file refer to North American cities, and that the query asks for all cities with

$$(21.49° \leq \text{LATITUDE} \leq 37.41°) \quad \text{AND} \quad (70.34° \leq \text{LONGITUDE} \leq 75.72°).$$

Reference to a map will show that many cities satisfy this LATITUDE range, and many satisfy the LONGITUDE range, but hardly any cities lie in both ranges. One approach to such *orthogonal range queries* is to partition the set of all possible LATITUDE and LONGITUDE values rather coarsely, with only a few classes per attribute (for example, by truncating to the next lower multiple of 5°), then to have one inverted list for each combined (LATITUDE, LONGITUDE) class. This is like having maps with one page for each local region. Using 5° intervals, the query above would refer to eight pages, namely $(20°, 70°)$, $(25°, 70°)$, $\ldots$, $(35°, 75°)$. The range query needs to be processed for each of these pages, either by going to a finer partition within the page or by direct reference to the records themselves, depending on the number of records corresponding to that page. In a sense this is a tree structure with two-dimensional branching at each internal node.

A substantial elaboration of this approach, called a *grid file*, was developed by J. Nievergelt, H. Hinterberger, and K. C. Sevcik [*ACM Trans. Database Systems* **9** (1984), 38–71]. If each point x has k coordinates $(x_1, \ldots, x_k)$, they divide the ith coordinate values into ranges

$$-\infty = g_{i0} < g_{i1} < \cdots < g_{ir_i} = +\infty \tag{1}$$

and locate x by determining indices $(j_1, \ldots, j_k)$ such that

$$0 \leq j_i < r_i, \qquad g_{ij_i} \leq x_i < g_{i(j_i+1)} \qquad \text{for } 1 \leq i \leq k. \tag{2}$$

All points that have a given value of $(j_1, \ldots, j_k)$ are called *cells*. Records for points in the same cell are stored in the same bucket in an external memory. Buckets are also allowed to contain points from several adjacent cells, provided that each bucket corresponds to a k-dimensional rectangular region or "super-cell." Various strategies for updating the grid boundary values g_{ij} and for splitting or combining buckets are possible; see, for example, K. Hinrichs, *BIT* **25**

(1985), 569–592. The characteristics of grid files with random data have been analyzed by M. Regnier, *BIT* **25** (1985), 335–357; P. Flajolet and C. Puech, *JACM* **33** (1986), 371–407, §4.2.

A simpler way to deal with orthogonal range queries was introduced by J. L. Bentley and R. A. Finkel, using structures called *quadtrees* [*Acta Informatica* **4** (1974), 1–9]. In the two-dimensional case of their construction, every node of such a tree represents a rectangle and also contains one of the points in that rectangle; there are four subtrees, corresponding to the four quadrants of the original rectangle relative to the coordinates of the given point. Similarly, in three dimensions there is eight-way branching, and the trees are sometimes called *octrees*. A k-dimensional quadtree has 2^k-way branching.

The mathematical analysis of random quadtrees is quite difficult, but in 1988 the asymptotic form of the expected insertion time for the N-th node in a random k-dimensional quadtree was determined to be

$$\frac{2}{k} \ln N + O(1), \tag{3}$$

by two groups of researchers working independently: See L. Devroye and L. La-forest, *SICOMP* **19** (1990), 821–832; P. Flajolet, G. Gonnet, C. Puech, and J. M. Robson, *Algorithmica* **10** (1993), 473–500. Notice that when $k = 1$, this result agrees with the well-known formula for insertion into a binary search tree, Eq. 6.2.2–(5). Further work by P. Flajolet, G. Labelle, L. Laforest, and B. Salvy showed in fact that the average internal path length can be expressed in the surprisingly elegant form

$$\sum_{l \geq 2} \binom{N}{l} (-1)^l \prod_{j=3}^{l} \left(1 - \frac{2^k}{j^k}\right), \tag{4}$$

and further analysis of random quadtrees was therefore possible with the help of hypergeometric functions [see *Random Structures and Algorithms* **7** (1995), 117–144].

Bentley went on to simplify the quadtree representation even further by introducing "k-d trees," which have only two-way branching at each node [*CACM* **18** (1975), 509–517; *IEEE Transactions* **SE-5** (1979), 333–340]. A 1-d tree is just an ordinary binary search tree, as in Section 6.2.2; a 2-d tree is similar, but the nodes on even levels compare x-coordinates and the nodes on odd levels compare y-coordinates when branching. In general, a k-d tree has nodes with k coordinates, and the branching on each level is based on only one of the coordinates; for example, we might branch on coordinate number $(k \bmod l) + 1$ on level l. A tie-breaking rule based on a record's serial number or location in memory can be used to ensure that no two records agree in any coordinate position. Randomly grown k-d trees turn out to have exactly the same average path length and shape distribution as ordinary binary search trees, because the assumptions underlying their growth are the same as in the one-dimensional case (see exercise 6.2.2–6).

If the file is not changing dynamically, we can balance any N-node k-d tree so that its height is $\approx \lg N$, by choosing a median value for branching at each node. Then we can be sure that several fundamental types of queries will be handled efficiently. For example, Bentley proved that we can identify all records that have t specified coordinates in $O(N^{1-t/k})$ steps. We can also find all records that lie in a given rectangular region in at most $O(tN^{1-1/k} + q)$ steps, if t of the coordinates are restricted to subranges and there are q such records altogether [D. T. Lee and C. K. Wong, *Acta Informatica* **23** (1977), 23–29]. In fact, if the given region is nearly cubical and q is small, and if the coordinate chosen for branching at each node has the greatest spread of attribute values, Friedman, Bentley, and Finkel [*ACM Trans. Math. Software* **3** (1977), 209–226] showed that the average time for such a region query will be only $O(\log N + q)$. The same formula applies when searching such k-d trees for the nearest neighbor of a given point in k-dimensional space.

When k-d trees are random instead of perfectly balanced, the average running time for partial matches of t specified coordinates increases slightly to $\Theta(N^{1-t/k+f(t/k)})$; here the function f is defined implicitly by the equation

$$\bigl(f(x) + 3 - x\bigr)^x \bigl(f(x) + 2 - x\bigr)^{1-x} = 2, \tag{5}$$

and it is quite small: We have

$$0 \le f(x) < 0.06329\,33881\,23738\,85718\,14011\,27797\,33590\,58170-, \tag{6}$$

and the maximum occurs when x is near 0.585. [See P. Flajolet and C. Puech, *JACM* **33** (1986), 371–407, §3.]

Because of the aesthetic appeal and great significance of geometric algorithms, there has been an enormous growth in techniques for solving higher-dimensional search problems and related questions of many kinds. Indeed, a new subfield of mathematics and computer science called Computational Geometry has developed rapidly since the 1970s. The *Handbook of Discrete and Computational Geometry*, edited by J. E. Goodman and J. O'Rourke (Boca Raton, Florida: CRC Press, 1997), is an excellent reference to the state of the art in that field as of 1997.

A comprehensive survey of data structures and algorithms for the important special cases of two- and three-dimensional objects has been prepared by Hanan Samet in a pair of complementary books, *The Design and Analysis of Spatial Data Structures* and *Applications of Spatial Data Structures* (Addison–Wesley, 1990). Samet points out that the original quadtrees of Bentley and Finkel are now more properly called "point quadtrees"; the name "quadtree" itself has become a generic term for any hierarchical decomposition of geometric data.

Compound attributes. It is possible to combine two or more attributes into one super-attribute. For example, a "(CLASS, MAJOR) attribute" could be created by combining the CLASS and MAJOR fields of a university enrollment file. In this way queries can often be satisfied by taking the union of disjoint, short lists instead of the intersection of longer lists.

The idea of attribute combination was developed further by V. Y. Lum [*CACM* **13** (1970), 660–665], who suggested ordering the inverted lists of combined attributes lexicographically from left to right, and making multiple copies, with the individual attributes permuted in a clever way. For example, suppose that we have three attributes A, B, and C; we can form three compound attributes

$$(A, B, C), \qquad (B, C, A), \qquad (C, A, B) \tag{7}$$

and construct ordered inverted lists for each of these. (Thus in the first list, the records occur in order of their A values, with all records of the same A value in order by B and then by C.) This organization makes it possible to satisfy queries based on any combination of the three attributes; for example, all records having specified values for A and C will appear consecutively in the third list.

Similarly, from four attributes A, B, C, D, we can form the six combined attributes

$$(A, B, C, D), \ (B, C, D, A), \ (B, D, A, C), \ (C, A, D, B), \ (C, D, A, B), \ (D, A, B, C), \tag{8}$$

which suffice to answer all combinations of simple queries relating to the simultaneous values of one, two, three, or four of the attributes. There is a general procedure for constructing $\binom{n}{k}$ combined attributes from n attributes, where $k \leq \frac{1}{2}n$, such that all records having specified combinations of at most k or at least $n - k$ of the attribute values will appear consecutively in one of the combined attribute lists (see exercise 1). Alternatively, we can get by with fewer combinations when some attributes have a limited number of values. For example, if D is simply a two-valued attribute, the three combinations

$$(D, A, B, C), \qquad (D, B, C, A), \qquad (D, C, A, B) \tag{9}$$

obtained by placing D in front of (7) will be almost as good as (8) with only half the redundancy, since queries that do not depend on D can be treated by looking in just two places in one of the lists.

Binary attributes. It is instructive to consider the special case in which all attributes are two-valued. In a sense this is the *opposite* of combining attributes, since we can represent any value as a binary number and regard the individual bits of that number as separate attributes. Table 1 shows a typical file involving "yes-no" attributes; in this case the records stand for selected cookie recipes, and the attributes specify which ingredients are used. For example, Almond Lace Wafers are made from butter, flour, milk, nuts, and granulated sugar. If we think of Table 1 as a matrix of zeros and ones, the transpose of the matrix is the inverted file, in bitstring form.

The right-hand column of Table 1 is used to indicate special items that occur only rarely. These can be coded in a more efficient way than to devote an entire column to each one; and the "Cornstarch" column could be treated similarly. Dually, we could find a more efficient way to encode the "Flour" column, since flour occurs in everything except Meringues. For the present, however, let us sidestep these considerations and simply ignore the "Special ingredients" column.

Table 1

A FILE WITH BINARY ATTRIBUTES

	Allspice	Anise seed	Baking powder	Baking soda	Butter	Cardamom	Chocolate	Cinnamon	Cloves	Coconut	Coffee	Cornstarch	Dates	Egg whites	Egg yolk	Flour	Ginger	Lemon juice	Lemon peel	Milk	Molasses	Nutmeg	Nuts	Oatmeal	Raisins	Salt	Sugar, brown	Sugar, granulated	Sugar, powdered	Vanilla extract	Special ingredients
Almond Lace Wafers	0	0	0	0	1	0	0	0	0	0	0	0	0	0	0	1	0	0	0	1	0	0	1	0	0	0	0	1	0	0	—
Applesauce-Spice Squares	0	0	0	1	1	0	0	1	1	0	0	0	0	0	1	1	0	0	0	0	0	1	1	1	1	1	1	0	0	0	Applesauce
Banana-Oatmeal Cookies	0	0	1	1	1	0	0	1	0	0	0	0	0	0	1	1	0	0	0	0	1	1	1	1	0	1	1	1	0	1	Bananas
Chocolate Chip Cookies	0	0	0	1	1	0	1	0	0	0	0	0	0	0	1	1	0	0	0	0	0	0	1	0	0	1	1	1	0	1	—
Coconut Macaroons	0	0	0	0	0	0	0	0	0	1	0	0	0	1	0	0	0	0	0	0	0	0	0	0	0	0	0	1	0	1	—
Cream-Cheese Cookies	0	0	1	0	1	0	0	0	0	0	0	0	0	0	1	1	0	0	0	0	0	0	0	0	0	0	0	1	0	1	Cream cheese
Delicious Prune Bars	0	0	0	1	1	0	0	1	1	0	0	0	0	0	1	1	0	0	0	0	0	1	1	0	0	1	1	1	0	1	Oranges, prunes
Double-Chocolate Drops	0	0	0	0	1	0	1	0	0	0	0	0	0	0	1	1	0	0	0	1	0	0	1	0	0	1	0	1	0	1	—
Dream Bars	0	0	1	0	1	0	0	0	0	1	0	0	0	0	1	1	0	0	0	0	0	0	1	0	0	1	1	0	0	1	—
Filled Turnovers	0	0	1	0	1	0	0	0	0	0	0	0	0	0	1	1	0	1	1	0	0	0	0	0	0	1	0	1	0	1	—
Finska Kakor	0	0	0	0	1	0	0	0	0	0	0	0	0	1	0	1	0	0	0	0	0	0	1	0	0	0	0	1	0	1	Almond extract
Glazed Gingersnaps	0	0	0	1	1	0	0	1	1	0	0	0	0	0	0	1	1	0	0	0	1	0	0	0	0	1	1	0	0	0	Vinegar
Hermits	1	0	1	0	1	0	0	1	1	0	0	0	0	0	1	1	0	0	0	1	0	1	1	0	1	1	1	1	0	0	Apricots
Jewel Cookies	0	0	0	0	1	0	0	0	0	0	0	0	0	1	1	1	0	0	0	0	0	0	1	0	0	0	0	1	0	1	Currant jelly
Jumbles	0	0	1	0	1	0	0	0	0	0	0	0	0	0	0	1	0	0	0	1	0	0	1	0	0	1	0	1	0	1	—
Kris Kringles	0	0	0	1	1	0	0	0	0	0	0	0	0	0	1	1	0	0	0	0	0	0	1	0	0	0	1	0	0	0	Vinegar
Lebkuchen Rounds	1	0	0	0	0	0	0	1	1	0	0	0	0	0	1	1	0	1	1	0	0	1	1	0	0	0	0	1	0	0	Apricots
Meringues	0	0	0	0	0	0	0	0	0	0	0	0	0	1	0	0	0	0	0	0	0	0	1	0	0	0	0	1	0	0	Currant jelly
Moravian Spice Cookies	1	0	0	1	1	0	0	1	1	0	0	0	0	0	0	1	1	0	0	0	1	0	0	0	0	1	1	0	0	0	—
Oatmeal-Date Bars	0	0	1	0	0	0	0	0	0	0	0	0	1	0	0	1	0	0	0	0	0	0	1	1	0	1	1	0	0	1	Salad oil
Old-Fashioned Sugar Cookies	0	0	1	0	1	0	0	0	0	0	0	0	0	0	1	1	0	0	0	1	0	1	0	0	0	1	0	1	0	1	—
Peanut-Butter Pinwheels	0	0	0	0	1	0	1	0	0	0	0	0	0	0	1	1	0	0	0	1	0	0	0	0	0	1	1	1	0	1	Honey
Petticoat Tails	0	0	0	0	1	0	0	0	0	0	0	0	0	0	1	1	0	0	0	1	0	0	0	0	0	0	0	1	0	1	Candied cherries
Pfeffernuesse	1	1	0	0	0	1	0	1	1	0	0	0	0	0	0	1	0	0	1	0	0	1	1	0	0	0	0	0	1	0	Citron, mace, pepper
Scotch Oatmeal Shortbread	0	0	0	0	1	0	0	0	0	0	0	0	0	0	0	1	0	0	0	0	0	0	0	1	0	1	1	0	0	0	—
Shortbread Stars	0	0	0	0	1	0	0	0	0	0	0	1	0	0	1	1	0	0	0	0	0	0	0	0	0	1	0	1	0	1	—
Springerle	0	1	0	0	0	0	0	0	0	0	0	0	0	0	0	1	0	0	1	0	0	0	0	0	0	0	0	1	0	0	Sour cream
Spritz Cookies	0	0	0	0	1	0	0	0	0	0	0	0	0	0	1	1	0	0	0	0	0	0	0	0	0	1	0	1	0	1	Peanut butter
Swedish Kringler	0	0	1	0	1	0	0	0	0	0	0	0	0	1	0	1	0	0	0	1	0	0	1	0	0	0	0	0	1	0	—
Swiss-Cinnamon Crisps	0	0	0	0	1	0	1	1	0	0	0	0	0	1	0	1	0	0	0	0	0	0	1	0	0	0	0	1	0	0	—
Toffee Bars	0	0	0	0	1	0	1	0	0	0	0	0	0	0	1	1	0	0	0	0	0	0	1	0	0	1	1	0	0	1	—
Vanilla-Nut Icebox Cookies	0	0	1	0	1	0	0	0	0	0	0	0	0	0	0	1	0	0	0	1	0	1	1	0	0	1	0	1	0	1	—

Reference: *McCall's Cook Book* (New York: Random House, 1963), Chapter 9.

Let us define a *basic query* in a binary attribute file as a request for all records having 0's in certain columns, 1's in other columns, and arbitrary values in the remaining columns. Using "*" to stand for an arbitrary value, we can represent any basic query as a sequence of 0's, 1's, and *'s. For example, consider a man who is in the mood for some coconut cookies, but he is allergic to chocolate, hates anise, and has run out of vanilla extract; he can formulate the query

$$* \ 0 \ * \ * \ * \ * \ 0 \ * \ * \ 1 \ * \ * \ * \ * \ * \ * \ * \ * \ * \ * \ * \ * \ * \ * \ * \ 0. \qquad (10)$$

Table 1 now says that Delicious Prune Bars are just the thing.

Before we consider the general problem of organizing a file for basic queries, it is important to look at the special case where no 0's are specified, only 1's and *'s. This may be called an *inclusive query*, because it asks for all records that include a certain set of attributes, if we assume that 1's denote attributes that are present and 0's denote attributes that are absent. For example, the recipes in Table 1 that call for both baking powder and baking soda are Glazed Gingersnaps and Old-Fashioned Sugar Cookies.

In some applications it is sufficient to provide for the special case of inclusive queries. This occurs, for example, in the case of many manual card-filing systems, such as "edge-notched cards" or "feature cards." An edge-notched card system corresponding to Table 1 would have one card for every recipe, with holes cut out for each ingredient (see Fig. 46). In order to process an inclusive query, the file of cards is arranged into a neat deck and needles are put in each column position corresponding to an attribute that is to be included. After raising the needles, all cards having the appropriate attributes will drop out.

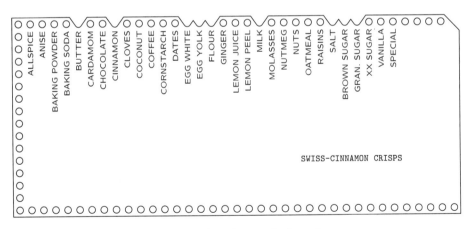

Fig. 46. An edge-notched card.

A feature-card system works on the inverse file in a similar way. In this case there is one card for every attribute, and holes are punched in designated positions on the surface of the card for every record possessing that attribute. An ordinary 80-column card can therefore be used to tell which of $12 \times 80 = 960$

records have a given attribute. To process an inclusive query, the feature cards for the specified attributes are selected and put together; then light will shine through all positions corresponding to the desired records. This operation is analogous to the treatment of Boolean queries by intersecting inverted bit strings as explained above.

Table 2

AN EXAMPLE OF SUPERIMPOSED CODING

Codes for individual flavorings

Almond extract	0100000001	Dates	1000000100
Allspice	0000100001	Ginger	0000110000
Anise seed	0000011000	Honey	0000000011
Applesauce	0010010000	Lemon juice	1000100000
Apricots	1000010000	Lemon peel	0011000000
Bananas	0000100010	Mace	0000010100
Candied cherries	0000101000	Molasses	1001000000
Cardamom	1000000001	Nutmeg	0000010010
Chocolate	0010001000	Nuts	0000100100
Cinnamon	1000000010	Oranges	0100000100
Citron	0100000010	Peanut butter	0000000101
Cloves	0001100000	Pepper	0010000100
Coconut	0001010000	Prunes	0010000010
Coffee	0001000100	Raisins	0101000000
Currant jelly	0010000001	Vanilla extract	0000001001

Superimposed codes

Almond Lace Wafers	0000100100	Lebkuchen Rounds	1011110111
Applesauce-Spice Squares	1111111111	Meringues	1000101100
Banana-Oatmeal Cookies	1000111111	Moravian Spice Cookies	1001110011
Chocolate Chip Cookies	0010101101	Oatmeal-Date Bars	1000100100
Coconut Macaroons	0001111101	Old-Fashioned Sugar Cookies	0000011011
Cream-Cheese Cookies	0010001001	Peanut-Butter Pinwheels	0010001101
Delicious Prune Bars	0111110110	Petticoat Tails	0000001001
Double-Chocolate Drops	0010101100	Pfeffernuesse	1111111111
Dream Bars	0001111101	Scotch Oatmeal Shortbread	0000001001
Filled Turnovers	1011101101	Shortbread Stars	0000000000
Finska Kakor	0100100101	Springerle	0011011000
Glazed Gingersnaps	1001110010	Spritz Cookies	0000001001
Hermits	1101010110	Swedish Kringler	0000000000
Jewel Cookies	0010101101	Swiss-Cinnamon Crisps	1000000010
Jumbles	1000001011	Toffee Bars	0010101101
Kris Kringles	1011100101	Vanilla-Nut Icebox Cookies	0000101101

Superimposed coding. The reason these manual card systems are of special interest to us is that ingenious schemes have been devised to save space on edge-notched cards; the same principles can be applied in the representation of computer files. Superimposed coding is a technique similar to hashing, and it was actually invented several years before hashing itself was discovered. The idea is to map attributes into random k-bit codes in an n-bit field, and to superimpose the codes for each attribute that is present in a record. An inclusive query for some set of attributes can be converted into an inclusive query for the corresponding superimposed bit codes. A few extra records may satisfy this query, but the number of such "false drops" can be statistically controlled. [See Calvin N. Mooers, *Amer. Chem. Soc. Meeting* **112** (September 1947), 14E–15E; *American Documentation* **2** (1951), 20–32.]

As an example of superimposed coding, let's consider Table 1 again, but only the flavorings instead of the basic ingredients like baking powder, shortening, eggs, and flour. Table 2 shows what happens if we assign random 2-bit codes in a 10-bit field to each of the flavoring attributes and superimpose the coding. For example, the entry for Chocolate Chip Cookies is obtained by superimposing the codes for chocolate, nuts, and vanilla:

$$0010001000 \lor 0000100100 \lor 0000001001 = 0010101101.$$

The superimposition of these codes also yields some spurious attributes, in this case allspice, candied cherries, currant jelly, peanut butter, and pepper; these will cause false drops to occur on certain queries (and they also suggest the creation of a new recipe called False Drop Cookies!).

Superimposed coding actually doesn't work very well in Table 2, because that table is a small example with lots of attributes present. In fact, Applesauce-Spice Squares will drop out for *every* query, since it was obtained by superimposing seven codes that cover all ten positions; and Pfeffernuesse is even worse, obtained by superimposing twelve codes. On the other hand Table 2 works surprisingly well in some respects; for example, if we try the query "Vanilla extract", only the record for Pfeffernuesse comes out as a false drop.

A more appropriate example of superimposed coding occurs if we have, say, a 32-bit field and a set of $\binom{32}{3} = 4960$ different attributes, where each record is allowed to possess up to six attributes and each attribute is encoded by specifying 3 of the 32 bits. In this situation, if we assume that each record has six randomly selected attributes, the probability of a false drop in an inclusive query

on one attribute is	.07948358	
on two attributes is	.00708659	
on three attributes is	.00067094;	(11)
on four attributes is	.00006786;	
on five attributes is	.00000728;	
on six attributes is	.00000082.	

Thus if there are M records that do not actually satisfy a two-attribute query, about $.007M$ will have a superimposed code that spuriously matches all code bits of the two specified attributes. (These probabilities are computed in exercise 4.) The total number of bits needed in the inverted file is only 32 times the number of records, which is less than half the number of bits needed to specify the attributes themselves in the original file.

If carefully selected nonrandom codes are used, it is possible to avoid false drops entirely in superimposed coding, as shown by W. H. Kautz and R. C. Singleton, *IEEE Trans.* **IT-10** (1964), 363–377; one of their constructions appears in exercise 16.

Malcolm C. Harrison [*CACM* **14** (1971), 777–779] has observed that superimposed coding can be used to speed up *text searching*. Assume that we want to locate all occurrences of a particular string of characters in a long body of text, without building an extensive table as in Algorithm 6.3P; and assume, for example, that the text is divided into individual lines $c_1 c_2 \ldots c_{50}$ of 50 characters each. Harrison suggests encoding each of the 49 pairs $c_1 c_2$, $c_2 c_3$, $\ldots$, $c_{49} c_{50}$ by hashing each of them into a number between 0 and 127, say; then the "signature" of the line $c_1 c_2 \ldots c_{50}$ is the string of 128 bits $b_0 b_1 \ldots b_{127}$, where $b_i = 1$ if and only if $h(c_j c_{j+1}) = i$ for some j.

If now we want to search for all occurrences of the word NEEDLE in a large text file called HAYSTACK, we simply look for all lines whose signature contains 1-bits in positions $h(\text{NE})$, $h(\text{EE})$, $h(\text{ED})$, $h(\text{DL})$, and $h(\text{LE})$. Assuming that the hash function is random, the probability that a random line contains all these bits in its signature is only 0.00341 (see exercise 4); hence the intersection of five inverted-list bit strings will rapidly identify all the lines containing NEEDLE, together with a few false drops.

The assumption of randomness is not really justified in this application, since typical text has so much redundancy; the distribution of adjacent letter pairs in English words is highly biased. For example, it will probably be very helpful to discard all pairs $c_j c_{j+1}$ containing a blank character, since blanks are usually much more common than any other symbol.

Another interesting application of superimposed coding to search problems has been suggested by Burton H. Bloom [*CACM* **13** (1970), 422–426]; his method actually applies to *primary* key retrieval, although it is most appropriate for us to discuss it in this section. Imagine a search application with a large database in which no calculation needs to be done if the search was unsuccessful. For example, we might want to check somebody's credit rating or passport number, and if no record for that person appears in the file we don't have to investigate further. Similarly in an application to computerized typesetting, we might have a simple algorithm that hyphenates most words correctly, but it fails on some 50,000 exceptional words; if we don't find the word in the exception file we are free to use the simple algorithm.

In such situations it is possible to maintain a bit table in internal memory so that most keys not in the file can be recognized as absent without making *any* references to the external memory. Here's how: Let the internal bit table be $b_0 b_1 \ldots b_{M-1}$, where M is rather large. For each key K_j in the file, compute k independent hash functions $h_1(K_j), \ldots, h_k(K_j)$, and set the corresponding k b's equal to 1. (These k values need not be distinct.) Thus $b_i = 1$ if and only if $h_l(K_j) = i$ for some j and l. Now to determine if a search argument K is in the external file, first test whether or not $b_{h_l(K)} = 1$ for $1 \le l \le k$; if not, there is no need to access the external memory, but if so, a conventional search will probably find K if k and M have been chosen properly. The chance of a false drop when there are N records in the file is approximately $(1 - e^{-kN/M})^k$. In a sense, Bloom's method treats the entire file as one record, with the primary keys as the attributes that are present, and with superimposed coding in a huge M-bit field.

Still another variation of superimposed coding has been developed by Richard A. Gustafson [Ph.D. thesis (Univ. South Carolina, 1969)]. Suppose that we have N records and that each record possesses six attributes chosen from a set of 10,000 possibilities. The records may, for example, stand for technical articles and the attributes may be keywords describing the article. Let h be a hash function that maps each attribute into a number between 0 and 15. If a record has attributes $a_1, a_2, \ldots, a_6$, Gustafson suggests mapping the record into the 16-bit number $b_0 b_1 \ldots b_{15}$, where $b_i = 1$ if and only if $h(a_j) = i$ for some j; and furthermore if this method results in only k of the b's equal to 1, for $k < 6$, another $6 - k$ 1s are supplied by some random method (not necessarily depending on the record itself). There are $\binom{16}{6} = 8008$ sixteen-bit codes in which exactly six 1 bits are present, and with luck about $N/8008$ records will be mapped into each value. We can keep 8008 lists of records, directly calculating the address corresponding to $b_0 b_1 \ldots b_{15}$ using a suitable formula. In fact, if the 1s occur in positions $0 \le p_1 < p_2 < \cdots < p_6$, the function

$$\binom{p_1}{1} + \binom{p_2}{2} + \cdots + \binom{p_6}{6}$$

will convert each string $b_0 b_1 \ldots b_{15}$ into a unique number between 0 and 8007, as we have seen in exercises 1.2.6–56 and 2.2.6–7.

Now if we want to find all records having three particular attributes A_1, A_2, A_3, we compute $h(A_1)$, $h(A_2)$, $h(A_3)$; assuming that these three values are distinct, we need only look at the records stored in the $\binom{13}{3} = 286$ lists whose bit code $b_0 b_1 \ldots b_{15}$ contains 1s in those three positions. In other words, only $286/8008 \approx 3.5$ percent of the records need to be examined in the search.

See the article by C. S. Roberts, *Proc. IEEE/ 67* (1979), 1624–1642, for an excellent exposition of superimposed coding, together with an application to a large database of telephone-directory listings. An application to spelling-check software is discussed by J. K. Mullin and D. J. Margoliash, *Software Practice & Exper.* **20** (1990), 625–630.

Combinatorial hashing. The idea underlying Gustafson's method just described is to find some way to map the records into memory locations so that comparatively few locations are relevant to a particular query. But his method applies only to inclusive queries when the individual records possess few attributes. Another type of mapping, designed to handle arbitrary basic queries like (10) consisting of 0's, 1's, and *'s, was discovered by Ronald L. Rivest in 1971. [See *SICOMP* **5** (1976), 19–50.]

Suppose first that we wish to construct a crossword-puzzle dictionary for all six-letter words of English; a typical query asks for all words of the form N**D*E, say, and gets the reply {NEEDLE, NIDDLE, NODDLE, NOODLE, NUDDLE}. We can solve this problem nicely by keeping 2^{12} lists, putting the word NEEDLE into list number

$$h(\text{N}) \, h(\text{E}) \, h(\text{E}) \, h(\text{D}) \, h(\text{L}) \, h(\text{E}).$$

Here h is a hash function taking each letter into a 2-bit value, and we get a 12-bit list address by putting the six bit-pairs together. Then the query N**D*E can be answered by looking through just 64 of the 4096 lists.

Similarly let's suppose that we have 1,000,000 records each containing 10 secondary keys, where each secondary key has a fairly large number of possible values. We can map the records whose secondary keys are $(K_1, K_2, \ldots, K_{10})$ into the 20-bit number

$$h(K_1) \, h(K_2) \, \ldots \, h(K_{10}), \tag{12}$$

where h is a hash function taking each secondary key into a 2-bit value, and (12) stands for the juxtaposition of these ten pairs of bits. This scheme maps 1,000,000 records into $2^{20} = 1{,}048{,}576$ possible values, and we can consider the total mapping as a hash function with $M = 2^{20}$; chaining can be used to resolve collisions. If we want to retrieve all records having specified values of any five secondary keys, we need to look at only 2^{10} lists, corresponding to the five unspecified bit pairs in (12); thus only about $1000 = \sqrt{N}$ records need to be examined on the average. (A similar approach was suggested by M. Arisawa, *J. Inf. Proc. Soc. Japan* **12** (1971), 163–167, and by B. Dwyer (unpublished). Dwyer suggested using a more flexible mapping than (12), namely

$$\bigl(h_1(K_1) + h_2(K_2) + \cdots + h_{10}(K_{10})\bigr) \bmod M,$$

where M is any convenient number, and the h_i are arbitrary hash functions possibly of the form $w_i K_i$ for "random" w_i.)

Rivest has developed this idea further so that in many cases we have the following situation. Assume that there are $N \approx 2^n$ records, each having m secondary keys. Each record is mapped into an n-bit hash address, in such a way that a query that leaves the values of k keys unspecified corresponds to approximately $N^{k/m}$ hash addresses. All the other methods we have discussed in this section (except Gustafson's) require order N steps for retrieval, although the constant of proportionality is small; for large enough N, Rivest's method will be faster, and it requires no inverted files.

But we have to define an appropriate mapping before we can apply this technique. Here is an example with small parameters, when $m = 4$ and $n = 3$ and when all secondary keys are binary-valued; we can map 4-bit records into eight addresses as follows:

$$
\begin{array}{ll}
* \; 0 \; 0 \; 1 \; \to \; 0 \qquad\qquad & * \; 1 \; 1 \; 0 \; \to \; 4 \\
0 \; * \; 0 \; 0 \; \to \; 1 & 1 \; * \; 1 \; 1 \; \to \; 5 \\
1 \; 0 \; * \; 0 \; \to \; 2 & 0 \; 1 \; * \; 1 \; \to \; 6 \\
1 \; 1 \; 0 \; * \; \to \; 3 & 0 \; 0 \; 1 \; * \; \to \; 7
\end{array} \tag{13}
$$

An examination of this table reveals that all records corresponding to the query 0 * * * are mapped into locations 1, 2, 5, 7, and 8; and similarly *any* basic query with three *'s corresponds to exactly five locations. The basic queries with two $*$'s correspond to three locations each; and the basic queries with one $*$ correspond to either one or two locations, $(8 \times 1 + 24 \times 2)/32 = 1.75$ on the average. Thus we have

Number of unspecified bits in the query	Number of locations to search	
4	$8 = 8^{4/4}$	
3	$5 \approx 8^{3/4}$	(14)
2	$3 \approx 8^{2/4}$	
1	$1.75 \approx 8^{1/4}$	
0	$1 = 8^{0/4}$	

Of course this is such a small example, we could handle it more easily by brute force. But it leads to nontrivial applications, since we can use it also when $m = 4r$ and $n = 3r$, mapping $4r$-bit records into $2^{3r} \approx N$ locations by dividing the secondary keys into r groups of 4 bits each and applying (13) in each group. The resulting mapping has the desired property: *A query that leaves k of the m bits unspecified will correspond to approximately $N^{k/m}$ locations.* (See exercise 6.)

In 1997, A. E. Brouwer found an attractive way to compress 8 bits to 5, with a mapping analogous to (13). Every 8-bit byte belongs to exactly one of the following 32 classes:

$$
\begin{array}{llll}
0*000*0* & 01*0**11 & 00*11**1 & *11**101 \\
1*000*0* & 11*0**11 & 10*11**1 & *11**010 \\
0*010*0* & 01*1**11 & 00*0*01* & *10*0*10 \\
1*010*0* & 11*1**11 & 10*0*01* & *10*1*01 \\
0*10*1*0 & 0*1*000* & *01*01*1 & *0*1001* \\
1*10*1*0 & 1*1*000* & *10*10*0 & *0*0100* \\
0*11*1*0 & 0*0*11*0 & *00*011* & *0*011*1 \\
1*11*1*0 & 1*0*11*0 & *11*100* & *0*110*0
\end{array} \qquad (15)
$$

The $*$'s in this design are arranged in such a way that there are 3 in each row and 12 in each column. Exercise 18 explains how to obtain similar schemes that will compress records having, say, $m = 4^r$ bits into addresses having $n = 3^r$ bits. In practice, buckets of size b would be used, and we would take $N \approx 2^n b$; the case $b = 1$ has been used in the discussion above for simplicity in exposition.

Rivest has also suggested another simple way to handle basic queries. Suppose we have, say, $N \approx 2^{10}$ records of 30 bits each, where we wish to answer arbitrary 30-bit basic queries like (10). Then we can simply divide the 30 bits into three 10-bit fields, and keep three separate hash tables of size $M = 2^{10}$. Each record is stored three places, in lists corresponding to its bit configurations in the three fields. Under suitable conditions, each list will contain about one element. Given a basic query with k unspecified bits, at least one of the fields will have $\lfloor k/3 \rfloor$ or fewer bits unspecified; hence we need to look in at most $2^{\lfloor k/3 \rfloor} \approx N^{k/30}$ of the lists to find all answers to the query. Or we could use any other technique for handling basic queries in the selected field.

Generalized tries. Rivest went on to suggest yet another approach, based on a data structure like the tries in Section 6.3. We can let each internal node of a generalized binary trie specify which bit of the record it represents. For example, in the data of Table 1 we could let the root of the trie represent Vanilla extract; then the left subtrie would correspond to those 16 cookie recipes that omit Vanilla extract, while the right subtrie would be for the 15 that use it. This 16–15 split nicely bisects the file; and we can handle each subfile in a similar way. When a subfile becomes suitably small, we represent it by a terminal node.

To process a basic query, we start at the root of the trie. When searching a generalized trie whose root specifies an attribute where the query has 0 or 1, we search the left or right subtrie, respectively; and if the query has $*$ in that bit position, we search both subtries.

Suppose the attributes are not binary, but they are represented in binary notation. We can build a trie by looking first at the first bit of attribute 1, then the first bit of attribute 2, ..., the first bit of attribute m, then the second bit of attribute 1, etc. Such a structure is called an "m-d trie," by analogy with m-d trees (which branch by comparisons instead of by bit inspections). P. Flajolet and C. Puech have shown that the average time to answer a partial match query in a random m-d trie of N nodes is $\Theta(N^{k/m})$ when k/m of the attributes are unspecified [*JACM* **33** (1986), 371–407, §4.1]; the variance has been calculated by W. Schachinger, *Random Structures and Algorithms* **7** (1995), 81–95.

Similar algorithms can be developed for m-dimensional versions of the digital search trees and Patricia trees of Section 6.3. These structures, which tend to be slightly better balanced than m-d tries, have been analyzed by P. Kirschenhofer and H. Prodinger, *Random Structures and Algorithms* **5** (1994), 123–134.

*Balanced filing schemes. Another combinatorial approach to information retrieval, based on *balanced incomplete block designs*, has been the subject of considerable investigation. Although the subject is quite interesting from a mathematical point of view, it has unfortunately not yet proved to be more useful than the other methods described above. A brief introduction to the theory will be presented here in order to indicate the flavor of the results, in hopes that readers might think of good ways to put the ideas to practical use.

A *Steiner triple system* is an arrangement of v objects into unordered triples in such a way that every pair of objects occurs in exactly one triple. For example, when $v = 7$ there is essentially only one Steiner triple system, namely

Triple	Pairs included	
$\{1, 2, 4\}$	$\{1, 2\}, \{1, 4\}, \{2, 4\}$	
$\{2, 3, 5\}$	$\{2, 3\}, \{2, 5\}, \{3, 5\}$	
$\{3, 4, 6\}$	$\{3, 4\}, \{3, 6\}, \{4, 6\}$	
$\{4, 5, 0\}$	$\{0, 4\}, \{0, 5\}, \{4, 5\}$	(16)
$\{5, 6, 1\}$	$\{1, 5\}, \{1, 6\}, \{5, 6\}$	
$\{6, 0, 2\}$	$\{0, 2\}, \{0, 6\}, \{2, 6\}$	
$\{0, 1, 3\}$	$\{0, 1\}, \{0, 3\}, \{1, 3\}$	

Since there are $\frac{1}{2}v(v-1)$ pairs of objects and three pairs per triple, there must be $\frac{1}{6}v(v-1)$ triples in all; and since each object must be paired with $v-1$ others, each object must appear in exactly $\frac{1}{2}(v-1)$ triples, These conditions imply that a Steiner triple system can't exist unless $\frac{1}{6}v(v-1)$ and $\frac{1}{2}(v-1)$ are integers, and this is equivalent to saying that v is odd and not congruent to 2 modulo 3; thus

$$v \bmod 6 = 1 \text{ or } 3. \tag{17}$$

Conversely, T. P. Kirkman proved in 1847 that Steiner triple systems do exist for all $v \geq 1$ such that (17) holds. His interesting construction is given in exercise 10.

Steiner triple systems can be used to reduce the redundancy of combined inverted file indexes. For example, consider again the cookie recipe file of Table 1, and convert the rightmost column into a 31st attribute that is 1 if any special ingredients are necessary, 0 otherwise. Assume that we want to answer all inclusive queries on pairs of attributes, such as "What recipes use both coconut and raisins?" We could make up an inverted list for each of the $\binom{31}{2} = 465$ possible queries. But it would turn out that this takes a lot of space since Pfeffernuesse (for example) would appear in $\binom{17}{2} = 136$ of the lists, and a record with all 31 attributes would appear in every list! A Steiner triple system can be used to make a slight improvement in this situation. There is a Steiner triple system on 31 objects, with 155 triples and each pair of objects occurring in exactly one of the triples. We can associate four lists with each triple $\{a, b, c\}$, one list for all records having attributes a, b, $\bar{c}$ (that is, a and b but not c); another for a, $\bar{b}$, c; another for $\bar{a}$, b, c; and another for records having all three attributes a, b, c. This guarantees that no record will be included in more than 155 of the inverted lists, and it saves space whenever a record has three attributes that correspond to a triple of the system.

Triple systems are special cases of block designs that have blocks of three or more objects. For example, there is a way to arrange 31 objects into sextuples so that every pair of objects appears in exactly one sextuple:

$$\{0, 4, 16, 21, 22, 24\}, \ \{1, 5, 17, 22, 23, 25\}, \ \ldots, \ \{30, 3, 15, 20, 21, 23\} \tag{18}$$

(This design is formed from the first block by addition mod 31. To verify that it has the stated property, note that the 30 values $(a_i - a_j) \bmod 31$, for $i \neq j$, are distinct, where $(a_1, a_2, \ldots, a_6) = (0, 4, 16, 21, 22, 24)$. To find the sextuple containing a pair (x, y), choose i and j such that $a_i - a_j \equiv x - y$ (modulo 31); now if $k = (x - a_i) \bmod 31$, we have $(a_i + k) \bmod 31 = x$ and $(a_j + k) \bmod 31 = y$.)

We can use the design above to store the inverted lists in such a way that no record can appear more than 31 times. Each sextuple $\{a, b, c, d, e, f\}$ is associated with 57 lists, for the various possibilities of records having two or more of the attributes a, b, c, d, e, f, namely $(a, b, \bar{c}, \bar{d}, \bar{e}, \bar{f})$, $(a, \bar{b}, c, \bar{d}, \bar{e}, \bar{f})$, $\ldots$, (a, b, c, d, e, f); and the answer to each inclusive 2-attribute query is the disjoint union of 16 appropriate lists in the appropriate sextuple. For this design, Pfeffernuesse would be stored in 29 of the 31 blocks, since that record has two of the six attributes in all but blocks $\{19, 23, 4, 9, 10, 12\}$ and $\{13, 17, 29, 3, 4, 6\}$ if we number the columns from 0 to 30.

The theory of block designs and related patterns is developed in detail in Marshall Hall, Jr.'s book *Combinatorial Theory* (Waltham, Mass.: Blaisdell, 1967). Although such combinatorial configurations are very beautiful, their main application to information retrieval so far has been to decrease the redundancy incurred when compound inverted lists are being used; and David K. Chow [*Information and Control* **15** (1969), 377–396] has observed that this type of decrease can be obtained even without using combinatorial designs.

A short history and bibliography. The first published article dealing with a technique for secondary key retrieval was by L. R. Johnson in *CACM* **4** (1961), 218–222. The multilist system was developed independently by Noah S. Prywes, H. J. Gray, W. I. Landauer, D. Lefkowitz, and S. Litwin at about the same time; see *IEEE Trans. on Communication and Electronics* **82** (1963), 488–492. Another rather early publication that influenced later work was by D. R. Davis and A. D. Lin, *CACM* **8** (1965), 243–246.

Since then a large literature on the subject grew up rapidly, but much of it dealt with the user interface and with programming language considerations, which are not within the scope of this book. In addition to the papers already cited, the following published articles were found to be most helpful to the author as this section was first being written in 1972: Jack Minker and Jerome Sable, *Ann. Rev. of Information Science and Technology* **2** (1967), 123–160; Robert E. Bleier, *Proc. ACM Nat. Conf.* **22** (1967), 41–49; Jerome A. Feldman and Paul D. Rovner, *CACM* **12** (1969), 439–449; Burton H. Bloom, *Proc. ACM Nat. Conf.* **24** (1969), 83–95; H. S. Heaps and L. H. Thiel, *Information Storage and Retrieval* **6** (1970), 137–153; Vincent Y. Lum and Huei Ling, *Proc. ACM Nat. Conf.* **26** (1971), 349–356. A good survey of manual card-filing systems appears in *Methods of Information Handling* by C. P. Bourne (New York: Wiley, 1963), Chapter 5. Balanced filing schemes were originally developed by C. T. Abraham, S. P. Ghosh, and D. K. Ray-Chaudhuri in 1965; see the article by R. C. Bose and Gary G. Koch, *SIAM J. Appl. Math.* **17** (1969), 1203–1214.

Most of the classical algorithms for multi-attribute data that are known to be of practical importance have been discussed above; but a few more topics are planned for the next edition of this book, including the following:

- E. M. McCreight introduced *priority search trees* [*SICOMP* **14** (1985), 257–276], which are specially designed to represent intersections of dynamically changing families of intervals, and to handle range queries of the form "Find all records with $x_0 \leq x \leq x_1$ and $y \leq y_1$." (Notice that the lower bound on y must be $-\infty$, but x can be bounded on both sides.)

- M. L. Fredman has proved several fundamental lower bounds, which show that a sequence of N intermixed insertions, deletions, and k-dimensional range queries must take $\Omega(N(\log N)^k)$ operations in the worst case, regardless of the data structure being used. See *JACM* **28** (1981), 696–705; *SICOMP* **10** (1981), 1–10; *J. Algorithms* **1** (1981), 77–87.

Basic algorithms for pattern matching and approximate pattern matching in text strings will be discussed in Chapter 9.

It is interesting to note that the human brain is much better at secondary key retrieval than computers are; in fact, people find it rather easy to recognize faces or melodies from only fragmentary information, while computers have barely been able to do this at all. Therefore it is not unlikely that a completely new approach to machine design will someday be discovered that solves the problem of secondary key retrieval once and for all, making this entire section obsolete.

EXERCISES

▶ **1.** [*M27*] Let $0 \le k \le n/2$. Prove that the following construction produces $\binom{n}{k}$ permutations of $\{1, 2, \ldots, n\}$ such that every t-element subset of $\{1, 2, \ldots, n\}$ appears as the first t elements of at least one of the permutations, for $t \le k$ or $t \ge n - k$: Consider a path in the plane from $(0,0)$ to (n, r) where $r \ge n - 2k$, in which the ith step is from $(i-1, j)$ to $(i, j+1)$ or to $(i, j-1)$; the latter possibility is allowed only if $j \ge 1$, so that the path never goes below the x axis. There are exactly $\binom{n}{k}$ such paths. For each path of this kind, a permutation is constructed as follows, using three lists that are initially empty: For $i = 1, 2, \ldots, n$, if the ith step of the path goes up, put the number i into list B; if the step goes down, put i into list A and move the currently largest element of list B into list C. The resulting permutation is equal to the final contents of list A, then list B, then list C, each list in increasing order.

For example, when $n = 4$ and $k = 2$, the six paths and permutations defined by this procedure are

|1 2 3 4| 2|3 4|1   2 4||1 3   3|1 4|2   3 4||1 2   4|1 2|3

(Vertical lines show the division between lists A, B, and C. These six permutations correspond to the compound attributes in (8).)

Hint: Represent each t-element subset S by a path that goes from $(0,0)$ to $(n, n-2t)$, whose ith step runs from $(i-1, j)$ to $(i, j+1)$ if $i \notin S$ and to $(i, j-1)$ if $i \in S$. Convert every such path into an appropriate path having the special form stated above.

2. [*M25*] (Sakti P. Ghosh.) Find the minimum possible length l of a list $r_1 r_2 \ldots r_l$ of references to records, such that the set of all responses to any of the inclusive queries $**1$, $*1*$, $1**$, $*11$, $1*1$, $11*$, 111 on three binary-valued secondary keys will appear in consecutive locations $r_i \ldots r_j$.

3. [*19*] In Table 2, what inclusive queries will cause (a) Old-Fashioned Sugar Cookies, (b) Oatmeal-Date Bars, to be obtained among the false drops?

4. [*M30*] Find exact formulas for the probabilities in (11), assuming that each record has r distinct attributes chosen randomly from among the $\binom{n}{k}$ k-bit codes in an n-bit field and that the query involves q distinct but otherwise random attributes. (Don't be alarmed if the formulas do not simplify.)

5. [*40*] Experiment with various ways to avoid the redundancy of text when using Harrison's technique for substring searching.

▶ **6.** [*M20*] The total number of m-bit basic queries with t bits specified is $s = \binom{m}{t} 2^t$. If a combinatorial hashing function like that in (13) converts these queries into l_1, l_2,

$\ldots$, l_s locations, respectively, $L(t) = (l_1 + l_2 + \cdots + l_s)/s$ is the average number of locations per query. [For example, in (13) we have $L(3) = 1.75$.]

Consider now a composite hash function on an $(m_1 + m_2)$-bit field, formed by mapping the first m_1 bits with one hash function and the remaining m_2 with another, where $L_1(t)$ and $L_2(t)$ are the corresponding average numbers of locations per query. Find a formula that expresses $L(t)$, for the composite function, in terms of L_1 and L_2.

7. [*M24*] (R. L. Rivest.) Find the functions $L(t)$, as defined in the previous exercise, for the following combinatorial hash functions:

(a) $m = 3$, $n = 2$

$$0\ 0\ * \to 0$$
$$1\ *\ 0 \to 1$$
$$*\ 1\ 1 \to 2$$
$$1\ 0\ 1 \to 3$$
$$0\ 1\ 0 \to 3$$

(b) $m = 4$, $n = 2$

$$0\ 0\ *\ * \to 0$$
$$*\ 1\ *\ 0 \to 1$$
$$*\ 1\ 1\ 1 \to 2$$
$$1\ 0\ 1\ * \to 2$$
$$*\ 1\ 0\ 1 \to 3$$
$$1\ 0\ 0\ * \to 3$$

8. [*M32*] (R. L. Rivest.) Consider the set $Q_{t,m}$ of all $2^t \binom{m}{t}$ basic m-bit queries like (10) in which there are exactly t specified bits. Given a set S of m-bit records, let $f_t(S)$ denote the number of queries in $Q_{t,m}$ whose answer contains a member of S; and let $f_t(s, m)$ be the minimum $f_t(S)$ over all such sets S having s elements, for $0 \le s \le 2^m$. By convention, $f_t(0,0) = 0$ and $f_t(1,0) = \delta_{t0}$.

a) Prove that, for all $t \ge 1$ and $m \ge 1$, and for $0 \le s \le 2^m$,

$$f_t(s, m) = f_t(\lceil s/2 \rceil, m - 1) + f_{t-1}(\lceil s/2 \rceil, m - 1) + f_{t-1}(\lfloor s/2 \rfloor, m - 1).$$

b) Consider any combinatorial hash function h from the 2^m possible records to 2^n lists, with each list corresponding to 2^{m-n} records. If each of the queries $Q_{t,m}$ is equally likely, the average number of lists that need to be examined per query is $1/2^t \binom{m}{t}$ times

$$\sum_{Q \in Q_{t,m}} (\text{lists examined for } Q) = \sum_{\text{lists } S} (\text{queries of } Q_{t,m} \text{ relevant to } S) \ge 2^n f_t(2^{m-n}, m).$$

Show that h is optimal, in the sense that this lower bound is achieved, when each of the lists is a "subcube"; in other words, show that equality holds in the case when each list corresponds to a set of records that satisfies some basic query with exactly n specified bits.

9. [*M20*] Prove that when $v = 3^n$, the set of all triples of the form

$$\{(a_1 \ldots a_{k-1}\, 0\, b_1 \ldots b_{n-k})_3,\ (a_1 \ldots a_{k-1}\, 1\, c_1 \ldots c_{n-k})_3,\ (a_1 \ldots a_{k-1}\, 2\, d_1 \ldots d_{n-k})_3\},$$

$1 \le k \le n$, forms a Steiner triple system, where the a's, b's, c's, and d's range over all combinations of 0s, 1s, and 2s such that $b_j + c_j + d_j \equiv 0$ (modulo 3) for $1 \le j \le n - k$.

10. [*M32*] (Thomas P. Kirkman, *Cambridge and Dublin Math. Journal* **2** (1847), 191–204.) Let us say that a *Kirkman triple system* of order v is an arrangement of $v + 1$ objects $\{x_0, x_1, \ldots, x_v\}$ into triples such that every pair $\{x_i, x_j\}$ for $i \ne j$ occurs in exactly one triple, except that the v pairs $\{x_i, x_{(i+1) \bmod v}\}$ do not ever occur in the same triple, for $0 \le i < v$. For example,

$$\{x_0, x_2, x_4\}, \quad \{x_1, x_3, x_4\}$$

is a Kirkman triple system of order 4.

a) Prove that a Kirkman triple system can exist only when $v \bmod 6 = 0$ or 4.

b) Given a Steiner triple system S on v objects $\{x_1, \ldots, x_v\}$, prove that the following construction yields another Steiner system S' on $2v + 1$ objects and a Kirkman triple system K' of order $2v - 2$: The triples of S' are those of S plus

   i) $\{x_i, y_j, y_k\}$ where $j + k \equiv i$ (modulo v) and $j < k$, $1 \le i, j, k \le v$;

   ii) $\{x_i, y_j, z\}$ where $2j \equiv i$ (modulo v), $1 \le i, j \le v$.

The triples of K' are those of S' minus all those containing y_1 and/or y_v.

c) Given a Kirkman triple system K on $\{x_0, x_1, \ldots, x_v\}$, where $v = 2u$, prove that the following construction yields a Steiner triple system S' on $2v + 1$ objects and a Kirkman triple system K' of order $2v - 2$: The triples of S' are those of K plus

   i) $\{x_i, x_{(i+1) \bmod v}, y_{i+1}\}$, $0 \le i < v$;

   ii) $\{x_i, y_j, y_k\}$, $j + k \equiv 2i + 1$ (modulo $v-1$), $1 \le j < k - 1 \le v - 2$, $1 \le i \le v - 2$;

   iii) $\{x_i, y_j, y_v\}$, $2j \equiv 2i + 1$ (modulo $v-1$), $1 \le j \le v - 1$, $1 \le i \le v - 2$;

   iv) $\{x_0, y_{2j}, y_{2j+1}\}$, $\{x_{v-1}, y_{2j-1}, y_{2j}\}$, $\{x_v, y_j, y_{v-j}\}$, for $1 \le j < u$;

   v) $\{x_v, y_u, y_v\}$.

The triples of K' are those of S' minus all those containing y_1 and/or y_{v-1}.

d) Use the preceding results to prove that Kirkman triple systems of order v exist for all $v \ge 0$ of the form $6k$ or $6k + 4$, and Steiner triple systems on v objects exist for all $v \ge 1$ of the form $6k + 1$ or $6k + 3$.

11. [*M25*] The text describes the use of Steiner triple systems in connection with inclusive queries; in order to extend this to all basic queries it is natural to define the following concept. A *complemented triple system* of order v is an arrangement of $2v$ objects $\{x_1, \ldots, x_v, \bar{x}_1, \ldots, \bar{x}_v\}$ into triples such that every pair of objects occurs together in exactly one triple, except that complementary pairs $\{x_i, \bar{x}_i\}$ never occur together. For example,

$$\{x_1, x_2, x_3\}, \quad \{x_1, \bar{x}_2, \bar{x}_3\}, \quad \{\bar{x}_1, x_2, \bar{x}_3\}, \quad \{\bar{x}_1, \bar{x}_2, x_3\}$$

is a complemented triple system of order three.

Prove that complemented triple systems of order v exist for all $v \ge 0$ not of the form $3k + 2$.

12. [*M23*] Continuing exercise 11, construct a complemented *quadruple* system of order 7.

13. [*M25*] Construct quadruple systems with $v = 4^n$ elements, analogous to the triple system of exercise 9.

14. [*28*] Discuss the problem of deleting nodes from quadtrees, k-d trees, and post-office trees like Fig. 45.

15. [*HM30*] (P. Elias.) Given a large collection of m-bit records, suppose we want to find a record closest to a given search argument, in the sense that it agrees in the most bits. Devise an algorithm for solving this problem efficiently, assuming that an m-bit t-error-correcting code of 2^n elements is given, and that each record has been hashed onto one of 2^n lists corresponding to the nearest codeword.

▶ **16.** [*25*] (W. H. Kautz and R. C. Singleton.) Show that a Steiner triple system of order v can be used to construct $v(v - 1)/6$ codewords of v bits each such that no codeword is contained in the superposition of any two others.

▶ **17.** [*M30*] Consider the following way to reduce $(2n+1)$-bit keys $a_{-n} \ldots a_0 \ldots a_n$ to $(n+1)$-bit bucket addresses $b_0 \ldots b_n$:

$$b_0 \leftarrow a_0;$$
$$\text{if } b_{k-1} = 0 \text{ then } b_k \leftarrow a_{-k} \text{ else } b_k \leftarrow a_k, \text{ for } 1 \le k \le n.$$

a) Describe the keys that appear in bucket $b_0 \ldots b_n$.

b) What is the largest number of buckets that need to be examined, in a basic query that has t bits specified?

▶ **18.** [*M35*] (*Associative block designs.*) A set of m-tuples like (13), with exactly $m-n$ *'s in each of 2^n rows, is called an ABD(m,n) if every column contains the same number of *'s and if every pair of rows has a "mismatch" (0 versus 1) in some column. Every m-bit binary number will then match exactly one row. For example, (13) is an ABD$(4,3)$.

a) Prove that an ABD(m,n) is impossible unless m is a divisor of $2^{n-1}n$ and $n^2 \ge 2m(1-2^{-n})$.

b) A row of an ABD is said to have *odd parity* if it contains an odd number of 1s. Show that, for every choice of $m-n$ columns in an ABD(m,n), the number of odd-parity rows with *'s in these columns equals the number of even-parity rows. In particular, each pattern of asterisks must occur in an even number of rows.

c) Find an ABD$(4,3)$ that cannot be obtained from (13) by permuting and/or complementing columns.

d) Construct an ABD$(16,9)$.

e) Construct an ABD$(16,10)$. Start with the ABD$(16,9)$ of part (d), instead of the ABD$(8,5)$ of (15).

19. [*M22*] Analyze the ABD$(8,5)$ of (15), as (13) has been analyzed in (14): How many of the 32 locations must be searched for an average query with k bits unspecified? How many must be searched in the worst case?

20. [*M47*] Find all ABD(m,n) when $n = 5$ or $n = 6$.

A new Section 6.6 devoted to "persistent data structures" is planned for the next edition of the present book. Persistent structures are able to represent changing information in such a way that the past history can be reconstructed efficiently. In other words, we might do many insertions and deletions, but we can still conduct searches as if the updates after a given time had not been made. Relevant early references to this topic include the following papers:

- J. K. Mullin, *Comp. J.* **24** (1981), 367–373;
- M. H. Overmars, *Lecture Notes in Comp. Sci.* **156** (1983), Chapter 9;
- E. W. Myers, *ACM Symp. Principles of Prog. Lang.* **11** (1984), 66–75;
- B. Chazelle, *Information and Control* **63** (1985), 77–99;
- D. Dobkin and J. I. Munro, *J. Algorithms* **6** (1985), 455–465;
- R. Cole, *J. Algorithms* **7** (1986), 202–220;
- D. Field, *Information Processing Letters* **24** (1987), 95–96;
- C. W. Fraser and E. W. Myers, *ACM Trans. Prog. Lang. and Systems* **9** (1987), 277–295;
- J. R. Driscoll, N. Sarnak, D. D. Sleator, and R. E. Tarjan, *J. Comp. Syst. Sci.* **38** (1989), 86–124;
- R. B. Dannenberg, *Software Practice & Experience* **20** (1990), 109–132;
- J. R. Driscoll, D. D. K. Sleator, and R. E. Tarjan, *JACM* **41** (1994), 943–959.

> *Instruction tables [programs] will have to be made up*
> *by mathematicians with computing experience*
> *and perhaps a certain puzzle solving ability.*
> *There will probably be a great deal of work of this kind to be done,*
> *for every known process has got to be*
> *translated into instruction table form at some stage. ...*
> *This process of constructing instruction tables should be very fascinating.*
> *There need be no real danger of it ever becoming a drudge,*
> *for any processes that are quite mechanical*
> *may be turned over to the machine itself.*
>
> — ALAN M. TURING (1945)

ANSWERS TO EXERCISES

"I have answered three questions, and that is enough,"
Said his father, "don't give yourself airs!
"Do you think I can listen all day to such stuff?
Be off, or I'll kick you down stairs!"
— LEWIS CARROLL, *Alice's Adventures Under Ground* (1862)

NOTES ON THE EXERCISES

1. An average problem for a mathematically inclined reader.

3. See W. J. LeVeque, *Topics in Number Theory* **2** (Reading, Mass.: Addison–Wesley, 1956), Chapter 3; P. Ribenboim, *13 Lectures on Fermat's Last Theorem* (New York: Springer-Verlag, 1979); A. Wiles, *Annals of Mathematics* **141** (1995), 443–551.

SECTION 5

1. Let $p(1)\ldots p(n)$ and $q(1)\ldots q(n)$ be different permutations satisfying the conditions, and let i be minimal with $p(i) \neq q(i)$. Then $p(i) = q(j)$ for some $j > i$, and $q(i) = p(k)$ for some $k > i$. Since $K_{p(i)} \leq K_{p(k)} = K_{q(i)} \leq K_{q(j)} = K_{p(i)}$ we have $K_{p(i)} = K_{q(i)}$; hence by stability $p(i) < p(k) = q(i) < q(j) = p(i)$, a contradiction.

2. Yes, if the sorting operations were all stable. (If they were not stable we cannot say.) Alice and Chris certainly have the same result; and so does Bill, since the stability shows that equal major keys in his result are accompanied by minor keys in nondecreasing order.

Formally, assume that Bill obtains $R_{p(n)}\ldots R_{p(N)} = R'_1 \ldots R'_N$ after sorting the minor keys, then $R'_{q(1)} \ldots R'_{q(N)} = R_{p(q(1))} \ldots R_{p(q(N))}$ after sorting the major keys; we want to show that

$$\big(K_{p(q(i))}, k_{p(q(i))}\big) \leq \big(K_{p(q(i+1))}, k_{p(q(i+1))}\big)$$

for $1 \leq i < N$. If $K_{p(q(i))} \neq K_{p(q(i+1))}$, we have $K_{p(q(i))} < K_{p(q(i+1))}$; and if $K_{p(q(i))} = K_{p(q(i+1))}$, then $K'_{q(i)} = K'_{q(i+1)}$, hence $q(i) < q(i+1)$, hence $k'_{q(i)} \leq k'_{q(i+1)}$; that is, $k_{p(q(i))} \leq k_{p(q(i+1))}$.

3. We can always bring all records with equal keys together, preserving their relative order, treating these groups of records as a unit in further operations; hence we may assume that all keys are distinct. Let $a < b < c < a$; then we can arrange things so that the first three keys are abc, bca, or cab. Now if $N - 1$ distinct keys can be sorted in three ways, so can N; for if $K_1 < \cdots < K_{N-1} > K_N$ we always have either $K_{i-1} < K_N < K_i$ for some i, or $K_N < K_1$.

4. First compare words without case distinction, then use case to break ties. More precisely, replace each word α by the pair (α', α) where α' is obtained from α by mapping A $\to$ a, ..., Z $\to$ z; then sort the pairs lexicographically. This procedure gives, for example, tex < Tex < TeX < TEX < text.

Dictionaries must also deal with accented letters, prefixes, suffixes, and abbreviations; for example,

a < A < Å < a- < a. < -a < A- < A. < aa < a.a.
$$< \bar{\text{a}}\text{a} < \bar{\text{a}}\bar{\text{a}} < \text{AA} < \text{A.A.} < \text{AAA} < \cdots < \text{zz} < \text{Zz.} < \text{ZZ} < \text{zzz} < \text{ZZZ}.$$

In this more general situation we obtain α' by mapping $\bar{\text{a}} \to$ a, Å $\to$ a, etc., and dropping the hyphens and periods.

5. Let $\rho(0) = 0$ and $\rho((1\alpha)_2) = 1\rho(|\alpha|)\alpha$; here $(1\alpha)_2$ is the ordinary binary representation of a positive integer, and $|\alpha|$ is the length of the string α. We have $\rho(1) = 10$, $\rho(2) = 1100$, $\rho(3) = 1101$, $\rho(4) = 1110000$, ..., $\rho(1009) = 111101001111110001$, ..., $\rho(65536) = 1^50^{24}$, ..., $\rho(2^{65536}) = 1^60^{65560}$, etc. The length of $\rho(n)$ is

$$|\rho(n)| = \lambda(n) + \lambda(\lambda(n)) + \lambda(\lambda(\lambda(n))) + \cdots + \lg^* n + 1,$$

where $\lambda(0) = 0$, $\lambda(n) = \lfloor \lg n \rfloor$ for $n \geq 1$, and $\lg^* n$ is the least integer $m \geq 0$ such that $\lambda^{[m]}(n) = 0$. [This construction is due to V. I. Levenshtein, *Problemy Kibernetiki* **20** (1968), 173–179; see also D. E. Knuth in *The Mathematical Gardner*, edited by D. A. Klarner (Belmont, California: Wadsworth International, 1981), 310–325.]

6. Overflow is possible, and it can lead to a false equality indication. He should have written, "LDA A; CMPA B" and tested the comparison indicator. (The inability to make full-word comparisons by subtraction is a problem on essentially all computers; it is the chief reason for including CMPA, ..., CMPX in MIX's repertoire.)

7.

```
   COMPARE STJ  9F              DEC1 1
   1H      LDX  A,1             J1P  1B
           CMPX B,1          9H JMP  *
           JNE  9F
```

8. *Solution 1*, based on the identity $\min(a, b) = \frac{1}{2}(a + b - |a - b|)$:

```
SOL1 LDA  A                    SRAX 1
     SRAX 5                    ADD  AB1
     DIV  =2=                  ENTX 1
     STA  A1    a = 2a₁ + a₂   SLAX 5
     STX  A2    |a₂| ≤ 1       MUL  AB2
     LDA  B                    STX  AB3    (a₂ − b₂) sign(a − b)
     SRAX 5                    LDA  A2
     DIV  =2=                  ADD  B2
     STA  B1    b = 2b₁ + b₂   SUB  AB3
     STX  B2    |b₂| ≤ 1       SRAX 5
     LDA  A1                   DIV  =2=
     SUB  B1    no overflow    ADD  A1
                possible
     STA  AB1   a₁ − b₁        ADD  B1    no overflow possible
     LDA  A2                   SUB  AB1(1:5)
     SUB  B2                   STA  C
     STA  AB2   a₂ − b₂
```

Solution 2, based on the fact that indexing can cause interchanges in a tricky way:

```
SOL2 LDA  A
     STA  C
     STA  TA
     LDA  B
     STA  TB
```

Now duplicate the following code k times, where $2^k > 10^{10}$:

```
     LDA  TA
     SRAX 5
     DIV  =2=
     STX  TEMP
     LD1  TEMP
     STA  TA
     LDA  TB
     SRAX 5
     DIV  =2=
     STX  TEMP
     LD2  TEMP
     STA  TB
     INC1 0,2
     INC1 0,2
     INC1 0,2
     LD3  TMIN,1
     LDA  0,3
     STA  C
```

(This scans the binary representations of a and b from right to left, preserving their signs.) The program concludes with a table:

```
     HLT
     CON  C    -1  -1
     CON  B     0  -1
     CON  B    +1  -1
     CON  A    -1   0
TMIN CON  C     0   0
     CON  B     1   0
     CON  A    -1   1
     CON  A     0   1
     CON  C     1   1   ▮
```

9. $\sum_j \binom{r+j-1}{j}(-1)^j \binom{N}{r+j} x^{r+j}$, by the method of inclusion and exclusion (exercise 1.3.3–26). This can also be written $r\binom{N}{r}\int_0^x t^{r-1}(1-t)^{N-r}\,dt$, a beta distribution.

10. Sort the tape contents, then count. (Some sorting methods make it convenient to drop records whose keys appear more than once as the sorting progresses.)

11. Assign each person an identification number, which must appear on all forms concerning that individual. Sort the information forms and the tax forms separately, with this identification number as the key. Denote the sorted tax forms by $R_1, \ldots, R_N$, with keys $K_1 < \cdots < K_N$. (There should be no two tax forms with equal keys.) Add a new $(N+1)$st record whose key is ∞, and set $i \leftarrow 1$. Then, for each record in the information file, check if it has been reported, as follows: Let K denote the key on the information form being processed.

a) If $K > K_i$, increase i by 1 and repeat this step.
b) If $K < K_i$, or if $K = K_i$ and the information is not reflected on tax form R_i, signal an error.

Try to do all this processing without wasting the taxpayers' money.

12. One way is to attach the key (j, i) to the entry $a_{i,j}$ and to sort using lexicographic order, then omit the keys. (A similar idea can be used to obtain *any* desired reordering of information, when a simple formula for the reordering can be given.)

In the special case considered in this problem, the method of "balanced two-way merge sorting" treats the keys in such a simple manner that it is unnecessary to write any keys explicitly on the tapes. Given an $n \times n$ matrix, we may proceed as follows: First put odd-numbered rows on tape 1, even-numbered rows on tape 2, etc., obtaining

Tape 1: $a_{11}\,a_{12}\ldots a_{1n}\,a_{31}\,a_{32}\ldots a_{3n}\,a_{51}\,a_{52}\ldots a_{5n}\ldots$
Tape 2: $a_{21}\,a_{22}\ldots a_{2n}\,a_{41}\,a_{42}\ldots a_{4n}\,a_{61}\,a_{62}\ldots a_{6n}\ldots$

Then rewind these tapes, and process them synchronously, to obtain

Tape 3: $a_{11}\,a_{21}\,a_{12}\,a_{22}\ldots a_{1n}\,a_{2n}\,a_{51}\,a_{61}\,a_{52}\,a_{62}\ldots a_{5n}\,a_{6n}\ldots$
Tape 4: $a_{31}\,a_{41}\,a_{32}\,a_{42}\ldots a_{3n}\,a_{4n}\,a_{71}\,a_{81}\,a_{72}\,a_{82}\ldots a_{7n}\,a_{8n}\ldots$

Rewind these tapes, and process them synchronously, to obtain

Tape 1: $a_{11}\,a_{21}\,a_{31}\,a_{41}\,a_{12}\ldots a_{42}\ldots a_{4n}\,a_{9,1}\ldots$
Tape 2: $a_{51}\,a_{61}\,a_{71}\,a_{81}\,a_{52}\ldots a_{82}\ldots a_{8n}\,a_{13,1}\ldots$

And so on, until the desired transpose is obtained after $\lceil \lg n \rceil$ passes.

13. One way is to attach random distinct key values, sort on those keys, then discard the keys. (See exercise 12; a similar method for obtaining a random *sample* was discussed in Section 3.4.2.) Another technique, involving about the same amount of work but apparently not straining the accuracy of the random number generator as much, is to attach a random integer in the range $0 \le K_i \le N - i$ to R_i, then rearrange using the technique of exercise 5.1.1–5.

14. With a character-conversion table, you can design a lexicographic comparison routine that simulates the order used on the other machine. Alternatively, you could create artificial keys, different from the actual characters but giving the desired ordering. The latter method has the advantage that it needs to be done only once; but it takes more space and requires conversion of the entire key. The former method can often determine the result of a comparison by converting only one or two letters of the keys; during later stages of sorting, the comparison will be between nearly equal keys, however, and the former method may find it advantageous to check for equality of letters before converting them.

15. For this problem, just run through the file once keeping 50 or so individual counts. But if "city" were substituted for "state," and if the total number of cities were quite large, it would be a good idea to sort on the city name.

16. As in exercise 15, it depends on the size of the problem. If the total number of cross-reference entries fits into high-speed memory, the best approach is probably to use a symbol table algorithm (Chapter 6) with each identifier associated with the head of a linked list of references. For larger problems, create a file of records, one record for each cross-reference citation to be put in the index, and sort it.

17. Carry along with each card a "shadow key" that, sorted lexicographically in the usual simple way, will define the desired ordering. This key is to be supplied by library personnel and attached to the catalog data when it first enters the system, although it is not visible to normal users. A possible key uses the following two-letter codes to separate words from each other:

⊔0	end of key;
⊔1	end of cross-reference;
⊔2	end of surname;
⊔3	hyphen of multiple surname;
⊔4	end of author name;
⊔5	end of place name;
⊔6	end of subject heading;
⊔7	end of book title;
⊔8	space between words.

The given example would come out as follows (showing only the first 25 characters):

```
ACCADEMIA⊔8NAZIONALE⊔8DEI        I⊔8HA⊔8EHAD⊔7⊔0
ACHTZEHNHUNDERT⊔8ZWOLF⊔8E        IA⊔8A⊔8LOVE⊔8STORY⊔7⊔0
BIBLIOTHEQUE⊔8D⊔8HISTOIRE        INTERNATIONAL⊔8BUSINESS⊔8
BIBLIOTHEQUE⊔8DES⊔8CURIOS        KHUWARIZMI⊔2MUHAMMAD⊔8IBN
BROWN⊔2J⊔8CROSBY⊔4⊔0             LABOR⊔7A⊔8MAGAZINE⊔8FOR⊔8
BROWN⊔2JOHN⊔4⊔0                  LABOR⊔8RESEARCH⊔8ASSOCIAT
BROWN⊔2JOHN⊔4MATHEMATICIA        LABOUR⊔1⊔0
BROWN⊔2JOHN⊔4OF⊔8BOSTON⊔0        MACCALLS⊔8COOKBOOK⊔7⊔0
BROWN⊔2JOHN⊔41715⊔0              MACCARTHY⊔2JOHN⊔41927⊔0
BROWN⊔2JOHN⊔41715⊔6⊔0            MACHINE⊔8INDEPENDENT⊔8COM
BROWN⊔2JOHN⊔41761⊔0              MACMAHON⊔2PERCY⊔8ALEXANDE
BROWN⊔2JOHN⊔41810⊔0              MISTRESS⊔8DALLOWAY⊔7⊔0
BROWN⊔3WILLIAMS⊔2REGINALD        MISTRESS⊔8OF⊔8MISTRESSES⊔
BROWN⊔8AMERICA⊔7⊔0               ROYAL⊔8SOCIETY⊔8OF⊔8LONDO
BROWN⊔8AND⊔8DALLISONS⊔8NE        SAINT⊔8PETERSBURGER⊔8ZEIT
BROWNJOHN⊔2ALAN⊔4⊔0              SAINT⊔8SAENS⊔2CAMILLE⊔418
DEN⊔2VLADIMIR⊔8EDUARDOVIC        SAINTE⊔8MARIE⊔2GASTON⊔8P⊔
DEN⊔7⊔0                          SEMINUMERICAL⊔8ALGORITHMS
DEN⊔8LIEBEN⊔8SUSSEN⊔8MADE        UNCLE⊔8TOMS⊔8CABIN⊔7⊔0
DIX⊔2MORGAN⊔41827⊔0              UNITED⊔8STATES⊔8BUREAU⊔8O
DIX⊔8HUIT⊔8CENT⊔8DOUZE⊔8O        VANDERMONDE⊔2ALEXANDER⊔8T
DIX⊔8NEUVIEME⊔8SIECLE⊔8FR        VANVALKENBURG⊔2MAC⊔8ELWYN
EIGHTEEN⊔8FORTY⊔8SEVEN⊔8I        VONNEUMANN⊔2JOHN⊔41903⊔0
EIGHTEEN⊔8TWELVE⊔8OVERTUR        WHOLE⊔8ART⊔8OF⊔8LEGERDEMA
I⊔8AM⊔8A⊔8MATHEMATICIAN⊔7        WHOS⊔8AFRAID⊔8OF⊔8VIRGINI
I⊔8B⊔8M⊔8JOURNAL⊔8OF⊔8RES        WIJNGAARDEN⊔2ADRIAAN⊔8VAN
```

This auxiliary key should be followed by the card data, so that unequal cards having the same auxiliary key (e.g., Sir John = John) are distinguished properly. Notice that "Saint-Saëns" is a hyphenated name but not a compound name. The birth year of al-Khuwārizmī should be given as, say, ⊔40779 with a leading zero. (This scheme will work until the year 9999, after which the world will face a huge software crisis.)

Careful study of this example reveals how to deal with many other unusual types of order that are needed in human-computer interaction.

18. For example, we can make two files containing values of $(u^6 + v^6 + w^6) \bmod m$ and $(z^6 - x^6 - y^6) \bmod m$ for $u \le v \le w$, $x \le y \le z$, where m is the word size of our computer. Sort these and look for duplicates, then subject the duplicates to further tests. (Some congruences modulo small primes might also be used to place further restrictions on u, v, w, x, y, z.)

19. In general, to find all pairs of numbers (x_i, x_j) with $x_i + x_j = c$, where c is given: Sort the file so that $x_1 < x_2 < \cdots < x_N$. Set $i \leftarrow 1$, $j \leftarrow N$, and then repeat the following operation until $j \le i$:

> If $x_i + x_j = c$, output $\{x_i, x_j\}$, set $i \leftarrow i + 1$, $j \leftarrow j - 1$;
> If $x_i + x_j < c$, set $i \leftarrow i + 1$;
> If $x_i + x_j > c$, set $j \leftarrow j - 1$.

Finally if $j = i$ and $2x_i = c$, output (x_i, x_i). This process is like those of exercises 18 and 19: We are essentially making two sorted files, one containing $x_1, \ldots, x_N$ and the other containing $c - x_N, \ldots, c - x_1$, and checking for duplicates. But the second file doesn't need to be explicitly formed in this case. Another approach when c is odd is to sort on a key such as (x odd $\Rightarrow x$, x even $\Rightarrow c - x$).

A similar algorithm can be used to find $\max\{x_i + x_j \mid x_i + x_j \le c\}$; or to find, say, $\min\{x_i + y_j \mid x_i + y_j > t\}$ given t and two sorted files $x_1 \le \cdots \le x_m$, $y_1 \le \cdots \le y_n$.

20. Some of the alternatives are: (a) For each of the 499,500 pairs i, j, with $1 \le i < j \le 1000$, set $y_1 \leftarrow x_i \oplus x_j$, $y_2 \leftarrow y_1 \wedge (y_1 - 1)$, $y_3 \leftarrow y_2 \wedge (y_2 - 1)$; then print (x_i, x_j) if and only if $y_3 = 0$. Here $\oplus$ denotes "exclusive or" and $\wedge$ denotes "bitwise and". (b) Create a file with 31,000 entries, forming 31 entries from each original word x_i by including x_i and the 30 words that differ from x_i in one position. Sort this file and look for duplicates. (c) Do a test analogous to (a) on

  i) all pairs of words that agree in their first 10 bits;

  ii) all pairs of words that agree in their middle 10 bits, but not the first 10;

  iii) all pairs of words that agree in their last 10 bits, but neither the first nor middle 10.

This involves three sorts of the data, using a specified 10-bit key each time. The expected number of pairs in each of the three cases is at most $499500/2^{10}$, which is less than 500, if the original words are randomly distributed.

21. First prepare a file containing all five-letter English words. (Be sure to consider adding suffixes such as -ED, -ER, ERS, -S to shorter words.) Now take each five-letter word α and sort its letters into ascending order, obtaining the sorted five-letter sequence α'. Finally sort all pairs (α', α) to bring all anagrams together.

Experiments by Kim D. Gibson in 1967 showed that the second longest set of commonly known five-letter anagrams is LEAST, SLATE, STALE, STEAL, TAELS, TALES, TEALS. But if he had been able to use larger dictionaries, he would have been able to catapult this set into first place, by adding the words ALETS (steel shoulderplates), ASTEL (a splinter), ATLES (intends), LAETS (people who rank between slaves and freemen), LASET (an ermine), LATES (a Nile perch), LEATS (watercourses), SALET (a mediæval helmet), SETAL (pertaining to setae), SLEAT (to incite), STELA (a column), and TESLA (a unit of magnetic flux density). Together with the old spellings SATEL, TASEL, and TASLE for "settle" and "teasel," we obtain 22 mutually permutable words, none of which needs to be spelled with an uppercase letter. And with a bit more daring we might add the Old English *tæsl*, German *altes*, and Madame de Staël! The set {LAPSE, LEAPS, PALES, PEALS, PLEAS, SALEP, SEPAL} can also be extended to at least 14 words when we turn to unabridged dictionaries. [See H. E. Dudeney, *300 Best Word Puzzles*, edited by

Martin Gardner (New York: Chas. Scribner's Sons, 1968), Puzzles 190 and 194; Ross Eckler, *Making the Alphabet Dance* (N.Y.: St. Martin's Griffin, 1997), Fig. 46c.]

The first and last sets of three or more five-letter English anagrams are {ALBAS, BALAS, BALSA, BASAL} and {STRUT, STURT, TRUST}, if proper names are not allowed. However, the proper names Alban, Balan, Laban, and Nabal lead to an earlier set {ALBAN, BALAN, BANAL, LABAN, NABAL, NABLA} if that restriction is dropped. The most striking example of longer anagram words in common English is perhaps the amazingly mathematical set {ALERTING, ALTERING, INTEGRAL, RELATING, TRIANGLE}.

A faster way to proceed is to compute $f(\alpha) = (h(a_1) + h(a_2) + \cdots + h(a_5)) \bmod m$, where $a_1, \ldots, a_5$ are numerical codes for the individual letters in α, and $(h(1), h(2), \ldots)$ are 26 randomly selected constants; here m is the computer word size. Sorting the file $(f(\alpha), \alpha)$ will bring anagrams together; afterwards when $f(\alpha) = f(\beta)$ we must make sure that we have a true anagram with $\alpha' = \beta'$. The value $f(\alpha)$ can be calculated more rapidly than α', and this method avoids the determination of α' for most of the words α in the file.

Note: A similar technique can be used when we want to bring together all sets of records that have equal multiword keys $(a_1, \ldots, a_n)$. Suppose that we don't care about the order of the file, except that records with equal keys are to be brought together; it is sometimes faster to sort on the one-word key $(a_1 x^{n-1} + a_2 x^{n-2} + \cdots + a_n) \bmod m$, where x is any fixed value, instead of sorting on the original multiword key.

22. Find isomorphic invariants of the graphs (functions that take equal values on isomorphic directed graphs) and sort on these invariants, to separate "obviously nonisomorphic" graphs from each other. Examples of isomorphic invariants: (a) Represent vertex v_i by (a_i, b_i), where a_i is its in-degree and b_i is its out-degree; then sort the pairs (a_i, b_i) into lexicographic order. The resulting file is an isomorphic invariant. (b) Represent an arc from v_i to v_j by (a_i, b_i, a_j, b_j), and sort these quadruples into lexicographic order. (c) Separate the directed graph into connected components (see Algorithm 2.3.3E), determine invariants of each component, and sort the components into order of their invariants in some way. See also the discussion in exercise 21.

After sorting the directed graphs on their invariants, it will still be necessary to make secondary tests to see whether directed graphs with identical invariants are in fact isomorphic. The invariants are helpful for these tests too. In the case of free trees it is possible to find "characteristic" or "canonical" invariants that completely characterize the tree, so that secondary testing is unnecessary [see J. Hopcroft and R. E. Tarjan, in *Complexity of Computer Computations* (New York: Plenum, 1972), 140–142.]

23. One way is to form a file containing all three-person cliques, then transform it into a file containing all four-person cliques, etc.; if there are no large cliques, this method will be quite satisfactory. (On the other hand, if there is a clique of size n, there are at least $\binom{n}{k}$ cliques of size k; so this method can blow up even when n is only 25 or so.)

Given a file that lists all $(k-1)$-person cliques, in the form $(a_1, \ldots, a_{k-1})$ where $a_1 < \cdots < a_{k-1}$, we can find the k-person cliques by (i) creating a new file containing the entries $(b, c, a_1, \ldots, a_{k-2})$ for each pair of $(k-1)$-person cliques of the respective forms $(a_1, \ldots, a_{k-2}, b)$, $(a_1, \ldots, a_{k-2}, c)$ with $b < c$; (ii) sorting this file on its first two components; (iii) for each entry $(b, c, a_1, \ldots, a_{k-2})$ in this new file that matches a pair (b, c) of acquaintances in the originally given file, output the k-person clique $(a_1, \ldots, a_{k-2}, b, c)$.

24. (Solution by Norman Hardy, c. 1967.) Make another copy of the input file; sort one copy on the first components and the other on the second. Passing over these files in sequence now allows us to create a new file containing all pairs (x_i, x_{i+2}) for $1 \leq i \leq N-2$, and to identify (x_{N-1}, x_N). The pairs $(N-1, x_{N-1})$ and (N, x_N) should be written on still another file.

The process continues inductively. Assume that file F contains all pairs (x_i, x_{i+t}) for $1 \leq i \leq N - t$, in random order, and that file G contains all pairs (i, x_i) for $N - t < i \leq N$ in order of the second components. Let H be a copy of file F, and sort H by first components, F by second. Now go through F, G, and H, creating two new files F' and G', as follows. If the current records of files F, G, H are, respectively (x, x'), (y, y'), (z, z'), then:

  i) If $x' = z$, output (x, z') to F' and advance files F and H.

 ii) If $x' = y'$, output $(y-t, x)$ to G' and advance files F and G.

iii) If $x' > y'$, advance file G.

iv) If $x' > z$, advance file H.

When file F is exhausted, sort G' by second components and merge G with it; then replace t by $2t$, F by F', G by G'.

Thus t takes the values $2, 4, 8, \ldots$; and for fixed t we do $O(\log N)$ passes over the data to sort it. Hence the total number of passes is $O((\log N)^2)$. Eventually $t \geq N$, so F is empty; then we simply sort G on its *first* components.

25. (An idea due to D. Shanks.) Prepare two files, one containing $a^{mn} \bmod p$ and the other containing $ba^{-n} \bmod p$ for $0 \leq n < m$. Sort these files and find a common entry.

Note: This reduces the worst-case running time from $\Theta(p)$ to $\Theta(\sqrt{p} \log p)$. Significant further improvements are often possible; for example, we can easily determine if n is even or odd, in $\log p$ steps, by testing whether $b^{(p-1)/2} \bmod p = 1$ or $(p-1)$. In general if f is any divisor of $p - 1$ and d is any divisor of $\gcd(f, n)$, we can similarly determine $(n/d) \bmod f$ by looking up the value of $b^{(p-1)/f}$ in a table of length f/d. If $p - 1$ has the prime factors $q_1 \leq q_2 \leq \cdots \leq q_t$ and if q_t is small, we can therefore compute n rapidly by finding the digits from right to left in its mixed-radix representation, for radices $q_1, \ldots, q_t$. (This idea is due to R. L. Silver, 1964; see also S. C. Pohlig and M. Hellman, *IEEE Transactions* **IT-24** (1978), 106–110.)

John M. Pollard discovered an elegant way to compute discrete logs with about $O(\sqrt{p})$ operations mod p, requiring very little memory, based on the theory of random mappings. See *Math. Comp.* **32** (1978), 918–924, where he also suggests another method based on numbers $n_j = r^j \bmod p$ that have only small prime factors.

Asymptotically faster methods are discussed in exercise 4.5.4–46.

SECTION 5.1.1

1. 205223000; 27354186.

2. $b_1 = (m - 1) \bmod n$; $b_{j+1} = (b_j + m - 1) \bmod (n - j)$.

3. $\bar{a}_j = a_{n+1-j}$ (the "reflected" permutation). This idea was used by O. Terquem [*Journ. de Math.* **3** (1838), 559–560] to prove that the average number of inversions in a random permutation is $\frac{1}{2}\binom{n}{2}$.

4. C1. Set $x_0 \leftarrow 0$. (It is possible to let x_j share memory with b_j in what follows, for $1 \leq j \leq n$.)

    C2. For $k = n, n-1, \ldots, 1$ (in this order) do the following: Set $j \leftarrow 0$; then set $j \leftarrow x_j$ exactly b_k times; then set $x_k \leftarrow x_j$ and $x_j \leftarrow k$.

    C3. Set $j \leftarrow 0$.

C4. For $k = 1, 2, \ldots, n$ (in this order), do the following: Set $a_k \leftarrow x_j$; then set $j \leftarrow x_j$. ∎

To save memory space, see exercise 5.2–12.

5. Let α be a string $[m_1, n_1] \ldots [m_k, n_k]$ of ordered pairs of nonnegative integers; we write $|\alpha| = k$, the length of α. Let ϵ denote the empty (length 0) string. Consider the binary operation $\circ$ defined recursively on pairs of such strings as follows:

$$\epsilon \circ \alpha = \alpha \circ \epsilon = \alpha;$$

$$([m, n]\alpha) \circ ([m', n']\beta) = \begin{cases} [m, n]\,(\alpha \circ ([m'-m, n']\beta)), & \text{if } m \leq m', \\ [m', n']\,(([m-m'-1, n]\alpha) \circ \beta), & \text{if } m > m'. \end{cases}$$

It follows that the computation time required to evaluate $\alpha \circ \beta$ is proportional to $|\alpha \circ \beta| = |\alpha| + |\beta|$. Furthermore, we can prove that $\circ$ is associative and that $[b_1, 1] \circ [b_2, 2] \circ \cdots \circ [b_n, n] = [0, a_1][0, a_2] \ldots [0, a_n]$. The expression on the left can be evaluated in $\lceil \lg n \rceil$ passes, each pass combining pairs of strings, for a total of $O(n \log n)$ steps.

Example: Starting from (2), we want to evaluate $[2, 1] \circ [3, 2] \circ [6, 3] \circ [4, 4] \circ [0, 5] \circ [2, 6] \circ [2, 7] \circ [1, 8] \circ [0, 9]$. The first pass reduces this to $[2, 1][1, 2] \circ [4, 4][1, 3] \circ [0, 5][2, 6] \circ [1, 8][0, 7] \circ [0, 9]$. The second pass reduces it to $[2, 1][1, 2][1, 4][1, 3] \circ [0, 5][1, 8][0, 6][0, 7] \circ [0, 9]$. The third pass yields $[0, 5][1, 1][0, 8][0, 2][0, 6][0, 4][0, 7][0, 3] \circ [0, 9]$. The fourth pass yields (1).

Motivation: A string such as $[4,4][1,3]$ stands for "␣␣␣␣4␣3␣$^\infty$", where "␣" denotes a blank; the operation $\alpha \circ \beta$ inserts the blanks and nonblanks of β into the blanks of α. Note that, together with exercise 2, we obtain an algorithm for the Josephus problem that is $O(n \log n)$ instead of $O(mn)$, partially answering a question raised in exercise 1.3.2–22.

Another $O(n \log n)$ solution to this problem, using a random-access memory, follows from the use of balanced trees in a straightforward manner.

6. Start with $b_1 = b_2 = \cdots = b_n = 0$. For $k = \lfloor \lg n \rfloor, \lfloor \lg n \rfloor - 1, \ldots, 0$ do the following: Set $x_s \leftarrow 0$ for $0 \leq s \leq n/2^{k+1}$; then for $j = 1, 2, \ldots, n$ do the following: Set $r \leftarrow \lfloor a_j/2^k \rfloor \bmod 2$, $s \leftarrow \lfloor a_j/2^{k+1} \rfloor$ (these are essentially bit extractions); if $r = 0$, set $b_{a_j} \leftarrow b_{a_j} + x_s$, and if $r = 1$ set $x_s \leftarrow x_s + 1$.

Another solution appears in exercise 5.2.4–21.

7. $B_j < j$ and $C_j \leq n - j$, since a_j has $j - 1$ elements to its left and $n - j$ elements to its right. To reconstruct $a_1 a_2 \ldots a_n$ from $B_1 B_2 \ldots B_n$, start with the element 1; then for $k = 2, \ldots, n$ add one to each element $\geq k - B_k$ and append $k - B_k$ at the right. (See Method 2 in Section 1.2.5). A similar procedure works for the C's. Alternatively, we could use the result of the following exercise. [The c inversion table was discussed by Rodriguez, *J. de Math.* **4** (1839), 236–240; the C inversion table appears in Netto's *Lehrbuch der Combinatorik* (1901), §5.]

8. $b' = C$, $c' = B$, $B' = c$, $C' = b$, since each inversion (a_i, a_j) of $a_1 \ldots a_n$ corresponds to the inversion (j, i) of $a'_1 \ldots a'_n$. Some further relations: (a) $c_j = j - 1$ if and only if $(b_i > b_j$ for all $i < j)$; (b) $b_j = n - j$ if and only if $(c_i > c_j$ for all $i > j)$; (c) $b_j = 0$ if and only if $(c_i - i < c_j - j$ for all $i > j)$; (d) $c_j = 0$ if and only if $(b_i + i < b_j + j$ for all $i < j)$; (e) $b_i \leq b_{i+1}$ if and only if $a'_i < a'_{i+1}$, if and only if $c_i \geq c_{i+1}$; (f) $a_j = j + C_j - B_j$; $a'_j = j + b_j - c_j$.

9. $b = C = b'$ is equivalent to $a = a'$.

10. $\sqrt{10}$. (One way to coordinatize the truncated octahedron lets the respective vectors $(1, 0, 0)$, $(0, 1, 0)$, $\frac{1}{2}(1, 1, \sqrt{2})$, $\frac{1}{2}(1, -1, \sqrt{2})$, $\frac{1}{2}(-1, 1, \sqrt{2})$, $\frac{1}{2}(-1, -1, \sqrt{2})$ stand for adjacent interchanges of the respective pairs 21, 43, 41, 31, 42, 32. The sum of these vectors gives $(1, 1, 2\sqrt{2})$ as the difference between vertices 4321 and 1234.)

A more symmetric solution is to represent vertex π in *four* dimensions by

$$\sum\{\mathbf{e}_u - \mathbf{e}_v \mid (u, v) \text{ is an inversion of } \pi\},$$

where $\mathbf{e}_1 = (1, 0, 0, 0)$, $\mathbf{e}_2 = (0, 1, 0, 0)$, $\mathbf{e}_3 = (0, 0, 1, 0)$, $\mathbf{e}_4 = (0, 0, 0, 1)$. Thus, $1234 \leftrightarrow (0, 0, 0, 0)$; $1243 \leftrightarrow (0, 0, -1, 1)$; $\ldots$; $4321 \leftrightarrow (-3, -1, 1, 3)$. All points lie on the three-dimensional subspace $\{(w, x, y, z) \mid w + x + y + z = 0\}$; the distance between adjacent vertices is $\sqrt{2}$. Equivalently $\left(\text{see answer 8(f)}\right)$ we may represent $\pi = a_1 a_2 a_3 a_4$ by the vector (a_1', a_2', a_3', a_4'), where $a_1' a_2' a_3' a_4'$ is the inverse permutation. (This 4-D representation of the truncated octahedron with permutations as coordinates was discussed together with its n-dimensional generalization by C. Howard Hinton in *The Fourth Dimension* (London, 1904), Chapter 10. Further properties were found many years later by Guilbaud and Rosenstiehl, who called Fig. 1 the "permutahedron"; see exercise 12.)

Replicas of the truncated octahedron will fill three-dimensional space in what has been called the simplest possible way [see H. Steinhaus, *Mathematical Snapshots* (Oxford, 1960), 200–203; C. S. Smith, *Scientific American* **190**, 1 (January 1954), 58–64]. Book V of Pappus's *Collection* (c. A.D. 300) mentions the truncated octahedron as one of 13 special solid figures studied by Archimedes. Illustrations of the Archimedean solids — the nonprism polyhedra that have symmetries taking any vertex into any other, and whose faces are regular polygons but not all identical — can be found, for example, in books by W. W. Rouse Ball, *Mathematical Recreations and Essays*, revised by H. S. M. Coxeter (Macmillan, 1939), Chapter 5; H. Martyn Cundy and A. P. Rollett, *Mathematical Models* (Oxford, 1952), 94–109.

11. (a) Obvious. (b) Construct a directed graph with vertices $\{1, 2, \ldots, n\}$ and arcs $x \to y$ if either $x > y$ and $(x, y) \in E$ or $x < y$ and $(y, x) \in \bar{E}$. If there are no oriented cycles, this directed graph can be topologically sorted, and the resulting linear order is the desired permutation. If there is an oriented cycle, the shortest has length 3, since there are none of length 1 or 2 and since a longer cycle $a_1 \to a_2 \to a_3 \to a_4 \to \cdots \to a_1$ can be shortened (either $a_1 \to a_3$ or $a_3 \to a_1$). But an oriented cycle of length 3 contains two arcs of either E or $\bar{E}$, and proves that E or $\bar{E}$ is not transitive after all.

12. [G. T. Guilbaud and P. Rosenstiehl, *Math. et Sciences Humaines* **4** (1963), 9–33.] Suppose that $(a, b) \in \bar{E}$, $(b, c) \in \bar{E}$, $(a, c) \notin \bar{E}$. Then for some $k \geq 1$ we have $a = x_0 > x_1 > \cdots > x_k = c$, where $(x_i, x_{i+1}) \in E(\pi_1) \cup E(\pi_2)$ for $0 \leq i < k$. Consider a counterexample of this type where k is minimal. Since $(a, b) \notin E(\pi_1)$ and $(b, c) \notin E(\pi_1)$, we have $(a, c) \notin E(\pi_1)$, and similarly $(a, c) \notin E(\pi_2)$; hence $k > 1$. But if $x_1 > b$, then $(x_1, b) \in \bar{E}$ contradicts the minimality of k, while $(x_1, b) \in E$ implies that $(a, b) \in E$. Similarly if $x_1 < b$ we find that both $(b, x_1) \in \bar{E}$ and $(b, x_1) \in E$ are impossible.

13. For any fixed choice of $b_1, \ldots, b_{m-1}, b_{m+1}, \ldots, b_n$ in the inversion table, the total $\sum_i b_i$ will assume each residue modulo m exactly once as b_m runs through its possible values 0, 1, $\ldots$, $m - 1$.

14. The hinted construction takes pairs of distinct-part partitions into each other, except in the two cases $j = k = p_k$ and $j = k = p_k - 1$. In the exceptional cases, n is $(2j - 1) + \cdots + j = (3j^2 - j)/2$ and $(2j) + \cdots + (j + 1) = (3j^2 + j)/2$, respectively, and there is a unique unpaired partition with j parts. [Euler's original proof, in *Novi Comment. Acad. Sci. Pet.* **5** (1754), 75–83, was also very interesting. He showed by simple manipulations that the infinite product equals s_1, if we define s_n as the power series $1 - z^{2n-1} - z^{3n-1}s_{n+1}$, for $n \geq 1$. Finite versions of Euler's infinite sum are discussed by Knuth and Paterson in *Fibonacci Quarterly* **16** (1978), 198–212.]

15. Transpose the dot diagram, to go from the p's to the P's. The generating function for the P's is easily obtained, since we first choose any number of 1s (generating function $1/(1-z)$), then independently choose any number of 2s (generating function $1/(1-z^2)$), ..., finally any number of n's.

16. The coefficient of $z^n q^m$ in the first identity is the number of partitions of m into at most n parts. In the second identity it is the number of partitions of m into n distinct nonnegative parts, namely sums of the form $m = p_1 + p_2 + \cdots + p_n$, where $p_1 > p_2 > \cdots > p_n \geq 0$. This is the same as $m - \binom{n}{2} = q_1 + q_2 + \cdots + q_n$, where $q_1 \geq q_2 \geq \cdots \geq q_n \geq 0$, under the correspondence $q_i = p_i - n + i$. [*Commentarii Academiæ Scientiarum Petropolitanæ* **13** (1741), 64–93.]

Notes: The second identity is the limit as $n \to \infty$ of the q-nomial theorem, exercise 1.2.6–58. The first identity, similarly, is the limit as $r \to \infty$ of the dual form of that theorem, proved in the answer to that exercise.

Let $n!_q = \prod_{k=1}^{n}(1 + q + \cdots + q^{k-1})$, and let $\exp_q(z) = \sum_{n=0}^{\infty} z^n/n!_q$. The first identity tells us that $\exp_q(z)$ is equal to $1/\prod_{k=0}^{\infty}(1 - q^k z(1 - q))$ when $|q| < 1$; the second tells us that it equals $\prod_{k=0}^{\infty}(1 + q^{-k}z(1 - q^{-1}))$ when $|q| > 1$. The resulting formal power series identity $\exp_q(z)\exp_{q^{-1}}(-z) = 1$ is equivalent to the formula

$$\sum_{k=0}^{n} \frac{(-1)^k q^{k(k-1)/2}}{(1-q)\ldots(1-q^k)(1-q)\ldots(1-q^{n-k})} = \delta_{n0}, \qquad \text{integer } n \geq 0,$$

which is a consequence of the q-nomial theorem with $x = -1$.

17.

0 0 0 0	0 1 0 0	0 0 1 0	0 0 0 1
1 1 0 1	1 2 0 1	1 0 2 1	1 0 1 2
1 0 1 0	0 1 1 0	0 1 2 0	0 1 0 2
1 0 1 1	0 1 1 1	0 1 2 1	0 1 1 2
1 0 0 1	0 1 0 1	0 0 1 1	0 0 1 2
2 0 1 2	0 2 1 2	0 1 2 2	0 1 2 3

18. Let $q = 1 - p$. The sum $\sum \Pr(\alpha)$ over all instances α of inversions may be evaluated by summing on k, where $0 \leq k < n$ is the exact number of leftmost bit positions in which there is equality between i and j as well as between X_i and X_j, in an inversion $X_i \oplus i > X_j \oplus j$ for $i < j$. In this way we obtain the formula $\sum_{0 \leq k < n} 2^k (p^2 + q^2)^k (p^2 2^{n-k-1} 2^{n-k-1} + 2pq 2^{n-k-1}(2^{n-k-1} - 1))$; summing and simplifying yields $2^{n-1}(p(2-p)(2^n - (p^2 + q^2)^n)/(2 - p^2 - q^2) + (p^2 + q^2)^n - 1)$.

19. The number of inversions is $\sum_{0 < i < j < n}(\lfloor mj/n \rfloor - \lfloor mi/n \rfloor - \lfloor m(j - i)/n \rfloor) = \sum_{0 < i < j < n}[mj \bmod n < mi \bmod n] = \sum_{0 < r < n} \lfloor mr/n \rfloor (r - (n - r) - (n - r - 1))$, which can be transformed to $\frac{1}{4}(n - 1)(n - 2) - \frac{1}{4}n\sigma(m, n, 0)$. [*Crelle* **198** (1957), 162–166.]

20. See E. M. Wright, *J. London Math. Soc.* **40** (1965), 55–57; and J. Zolnowski, *Discrete Math.* **9** (1974), 293–298.

Jacobi's identity can be proved rapidly as follows. Since

$$\prod_{k=1}^{n}(1 - u^k v^{k-1}) = (-1)^n u^{\binom{n+1}{2}} v^{\binom{n}{2}} \prod_{k=1}^{n}(1 - u^{-k} v^{1-k}),$$

the q-nomial theorem of exercise 1.2.6–58 with $q = uv$ tells us that

$$\prod_{k=1}^{n}(1 - u^k v^{k-1})(1 - u^{k-1}v^k) = (-1)^n u^{\binom{n+1}{2}} v^{\binom{n}{2}} \prod_{k=-n+1}^{n}(1 - u^{k-1}v^k)$$

$$= (-1)^n u^{\binom{n+1}{2}} v^{\binom{n}{2}} \sum_{j} \binom{2n}{j}_{uv} (uv)^{\binom{k}{2}}(-u^{-n}v^{1-n})^k$$

$$= \sum_{j} \binom{2n}{n+j}_{uv} (-1)^j u^{\binom{j}{2}} v^{\binom{j+1}{2}}.$$

Multiply both sides by $\prod_{k=1}^{n}(1 - u^k v^k) = \prod_{k=1}^{n}(1 - q^k)$ and note that, for fixed j, we have $\binom{2n}{n+j}_q \prod_{k=1}^{n}(1 - q^k) = 1 + O(q^{n+1-|j|})$. Jacobi's identity follows as $n \to \infty$.

21. Interpret C_j as the number of elements on the stack after the jth output. (See exercise 2.3.3–19 for characterizations of the b and B tables of stack permutations.)

22. (a) Arrange the numbers $\{1, 2, \ldots, n\}$ in a circle as on the face of a clock, and point at 1. Then for $j = n, n - 1, \ldots, 1$ (in this order), move the pointer counterclockwise $h_j + 1$ steps, remove the number pointed to from the circle, and call it a_j.

(b) Each i is counted as often as the sequence $a_i a_{i+1} \ldots a_n$ wraps around; this is the number of times that $a_j > a_{j+1}$ for $j \geq i$. Therefore each j with $a_j > a_{j+1}$ corresponds to the indices $1, \ldots, j$ being counted once. [Guo-Niu Han, *Advances in Math.* **105** (1994), 28–29; an equivalent result had been obtained by Rawlings, in the context of the next exercise.]

23. Suppose, for example, that $n = 5$ and $a_1 a_2 a_3 a_4 a_5 = 3\,1\,4\,2\,5$. The number of missed shots before each death must then be $2 + 5k_1$, $2 + 4k_2$, $1 + 3k_3$, $1 + 2k_2$, k_5, for some nonnegative integers k_j. Note that the dual permutation $1\,4\,2\,5\,3$ has h-table $0\,1\,1\,2\,2$ in the notation of the previous exercise. In general, the probability of obtaining $a_1 a_2 \ldots a_n$ will be

$$\sum_{k_1,\ldots,k_n \geq 0} (q_1^{h_n + nk_1} p_1)(q_2^{h_{n-1} + (n-1)k_2} p_2) \ldots (q_n^{h_1 + k_1} p_n)$$

$$= \frac{1 - q_1}{1 - q_1^n}\frac{1 - q_2}{1 - q_2^{n-1}} \cdots \frac{1 - q_n}{1 - q_n^1} q_1^{h_n} q_2^{h_{n-1}} \cdots q_n^{h_1},$$

where $p_j = 1 - q_j$ is the probability of fatality after $j - 1$ deaths, and $h_1 h_2 \ldots h_n$ corresponds to the dual of $a_1 a_2 \ldots a_n$. In particular, when $p_1 = \cdots = p_n = p = 1 - q$, the probability is $q^{h_1 + \cdots + h_n}/G_n(q)$. The least likely order is therefore $n \ldots 2\,1$. [J. Treadway and D. Rawlings, *Math. Mag.* **67** (1994), 345–354; Rawlings generalized the process to multiset permutations in *Int. J. Math. & Math. Sci.* **15** (1992), 291–312.]

24. Let $a_0 = 0$, and say that a *generalized descent* occurs at $j < n$ if $a_j > t(a_{j+1})$. Inserting n between a_{j-1} and a_j causes a new generalized descent if and only if $a_{j-1} \leq t(a_j) < n$. Suppose this occurs when j has the values $j_1 > j_2 > \cdots > j_k > 0$; let the other values of j be $j_n > j_{n-1} > \cdots > j_{k+1}$. Then $j_n = n$, and it can be shown that the generalized index increases by $n - k$ when n is inserted just before a_{j_k}. [The special case in which $t(j) = j + d$ for some $d \geq 0$ is due to D. Rawlings, *J. Combinatorial Theory* **A31** (1981), 175–183; he generalized this special case to multiset permutations in *Linear and Multilinear Algebra* **10** (1981), 253–260.]

This exercise defines $n!$ different statistics on permutations, each of which has the generating function $G_n(z)$ that appears in (7) and (8). We can define many more such statistics by generalizing Russian roulette as follows: After $j - 1$ deaths, the person who begins the next round of shooting is $f_j(a_1, \ldots, a_{j-1})$, where f_j is an arbitrary function taking values in $\{1, \ldots, n\} \backslash \{a_1, \ldots, a_{j-1}\}$. [See Guo-Niu Han, *Calcul Denertien* (Thesis, Univ. Strasbourg, 1992), Part 1.3, §7.]

25. (a) If $a_1 < a_n$, $h(\alpha)$ has exactly as many inversions as α, because the elements of α_j now invert x_j instead of a_n. But if $a_1 > a_n$, $h(\alpha)$ has $n-1$ fewer inversions, because x_j loses its inversion of a_n and of each element in α_j. Therefore if we set $x_n = a_n$ and recursively let $x_1 \ldots x_{n-1} = f(h(\alpha))$, the permutation $f(\alpha) = x_1 \ldots x_n$ has the desired properties. We have $f(1\,9\,8\,2\,6\,3\,7\,4\,5) = 9\,1\,2\,6\,3\,8\,7\,4\,5$, and $f^{[-1]}(1\,9\,8\,2\,6\,3\,7\,4\,5) = 1\,9\,2\,6\,8\,7\,3\,4\,5$.

(b) The key point is that $\operatorname{inv}(\alpha) = \operatorname{inv}(\alpha^-)$ and $\operatorname{ind}(\alpha^-) = \operatorname{ind}(f(\alpha)^-)$, when α^- is the inverse of α. Therefore if $\alpha_1 = \alpha^-$, $\alpha_2 = f(\alpha_1)$, $\alpha_3 = \alpha_2^-$, $\alpha_4 = f^{[-1]}(\alpha_3)$, and $\alpha_5 = \alpha_4^-$, we have

$$\operatorname{inv}(\alpha_5) = \operatorname{inv}(\alpha_4) = \operatorname{ind}(\alpha_3) = \operatorname{ind}(\alpha_2^-) = \operatorname{ind}(\alpha_1^-) = \operatorname{ind}(\alpha);$$
$$\operatorname{ind}(\alpha_5) = \operatorname{ind}(\alpha_4^-) = \operatorname{ind}(\alpha_3^-) = \operatorname{ind}(\alpha_2) = \operatorname{inv}(\alpha_1) = \operatorname{inv}(\alpha).$$

[*Math. Nachrichten* **83** (1978), 143–159.]

26. (Solution by Doron Zeilberger.) The average of $\operatorname{inv}(\alpha) \operatorname{ind}(\alpha)$ is

$$\frac{1}{n!} \sum_\alpha \sum_{1 \le j < k \le n} \sum_{1 \le l < n} [a_j > a_k] \, l \, [a_l > a_{l+1}],$$

which is a polynomial in n of degree ≤ 4. Evaluating this sum for $1 \le n \le 5$ gives the respective values 0, $\frac{1}{2}$, $\frac{6}{2}$, $\frac{21}{2}$, $\frac{55}{2}$; so the polynomial must be $\frac{1}{8}n(n-1) + \frac{1}{16}n^2(n-1)^2$. Subtracting $\operatorname{mean}(g_n)^2$ and dividing by $\operatorname{var}(g_n)$ gives the answer $9/(2n+5)$ for $n \ge 2$, by (12) and (13).

27. We have $\operatorname{inv}(a_1 a_2 \ldots a_n) = \operatorname{inv}(q_n \ldots q_2 q_1)$, when $q_n \ldots q_2 q_1$ is regarded as a permutation of a multiset (see Section 5.1.2). It follows that

$$\sum_n \frac{H_n(w, z)}{(1-z) \ldots (1-z^n)} = \sum_{a_1 \ldots a_n} w^{\operatorname{inv}(a_1 \ldots a_n)} z^{\operatorname{ind}(a_1 \ldots a_n)} \sum_{p_1 \ge \cdots \ge p_n \ge 0} z^{p_1 + \cdots + p_n}$$

$$= \sum_{q_1, q_2, \ldots, q_n \ge 0} w^{\operatorname{inv}(q_n \ldots q_2 q_1)} z^{q_1 + q_2 + \cdots + q_n}$$

$$= \sum_{k_0 + k_1 + k_2 + \cdots = n} \binom{n}{k_0, k_1, k_2, \ldots}_w z^{k_1 + 2k_2 + \cdots}$$

$$= n!_w \, [u^n] \sum_{k_0, k_1, k_2, \ldots} \prod_{j=0}^\infty \frac{(z^j u)^{k_j}}{k_j!_w}$$

$$= n!_w \, [u^n] \prod_{j=0}^\infty \exp_w(z^j u)$$

$$= n!_w \, [u^n] \prod_{j=0}^\infty \prod_{k=0}^\infty \frac{1}{1 - z^j w^k u(1-w)},$$

using the notation of answer 16 and the result of exercise 5.1.2–16. Thus we have the elegant identity

$$\prod_{j,k \ge 0} \frac{1}{1 - w^j z^k u} = \sum_{n \ge 0} \frac{H_n(w, z) \, u^n}{(1-w)(1-w^2) \ldots (1-w^n)(1-z)(1-z^2) \ldots (1-z^n)},$$

which was established for the generating function $H_n(w, z) = \sum_\alpha w^{\mathrm{ind}(\alpha^-)} z^{\mathrm{ind}(\alpha)}$ by D. P. Roselle in *Proc. Amer. Math. Soc.* **45** (1974), 144–150. Exercise 25 shows that the same bivariate generating function counts indexes and inversions. The proof given here is due to Garsia and Gessel [*Advances in Math.* **31** (1979), 288–305], who went on to obtain considerably more general results.

Setting $m = \infty$ in exercise 4.7–27 leads to the recurrence

$$H_n(w, z) = \sum_{k=1}^{n} \binom{n}{k}_w z^{n-k} \left(\prod_{j=1}^{k-1} (1 - z^{n-j}) \right) H_{n-k}(w, z).$$

28. Interchanging two adjacent elements changes the total displacement by 0 or ± 2; hence $\mathrm{td}(a_1 a_2 \ldots a_n) \leq 2 \mathrm{inv}(a_1 a_2 \ldots a_n)$.

We can also prove that $\mathrm{td}(a_1 a_2 \ldots a_n) \geq \mathrm{inv}(a_1 a_2 \ldots a_n)$. Suppose j is the smallest element out of place, and let $a_k = j$. Let l be maximum with $l < k$ and $a_l \geq k$. Interchanging a_l with a_k reduces the inversions by $2(k-l) - 1$, and reduces the total displacement by $2(k-l)$. Therefore if m repetitions of this algorithm are needed to sort a given permutation $a_1 a_2 \ldots a_n$, we have $\mathrm{td}(a_1 a_2 \ldots a_n) = \mathrm{inv}(a_1 a_2 \ldots a_n) + m$.

Note: The average total displacement of a random permutation is $(n^2 - 1)/3$; see exercise 5.2.1–7. The generating function for total displacement does not appear to have a simple form.

29. We can obtain π as a product of $\mathrm{inv}(\pi)$ transpositions τ_j, where τ_j interchanges j and $j + 1$. For example, the path $1234 \to 1324 \to 1342 \to 3142$ in Fig. 1 corresponds to τ_2, then τ_3, then τ_1; hence $3142 = \tau_1 \tau_3 \tau_2$. Therefore $\pi\pi'$ is obtainable from π' by making $\mathrm{inv}(\pi)$ transpositions, each of which changes the number of inversions by ± 1. It follows that $\mathrm{inv}(\pi\pi') \leq \mathrm{inv}(\pi) + \mathrm{inv}(\pi')$. If equality holds, each transposition adds a new inversion, hence $E(\pi\pi') \supseteq E(\pi')$.

Conversely, if $E(\pi\pi') \supseteq E(\pi')$, we want to show that some sequence of $|E(\pi\pi')| - |E(\pi')|= \mathrm{inv}(\pi\pi') - \mathrm{inv}(\pi')$ transpositions will transform π' to $\pi\pi'$. Such transpositions define π, so this will prove that $\mathrm{inv}(\pi) \leq \mathrm{inv}(\pi\pi') - \mathrm{inv}(\pi')$; hence equality must hold. Suppose, for example, that $\pi' = 314592687$ and that $E(\pi\pi') \supseteq E(\pi')$. If $E(\pi\pi')$ does not contain $(4, 1)$ or $(5, 4)$ or $(9, 5)$ or $(6, 2)$ or $(8, 6)$, then $\pi\pi'$ must be equal to π'. Otherwise $E(\pi\pi')$ contains one of them, say $(9, 5)$; then $E(\pi\pi')$ contains $E(\tau_4 \pi') = E(314952687)$. In this way we can prove the result by induction on $|E(\pi\pi')| - |E(\pi')|$.

SECTION 5.1.2

1. False, because of a reasonably important technicality. If you said "true," you probably didn't know the definition of $M_1 \cup M_2$ given in Section 4.6.3, which has the property that $M_1 \cup M_2$ is a set whenever M_1 and M_2 are sets. Actually, $\alpha \top \beta$ is a permutation of $M_1 \uplus M_2$.

2. *b c a d d a d a d b.*

3. Certainly not, since we may have $\alpha = \beta$. (The unique factorization theorem shows that there aren't too many possibilities, however.)

4. $(d) \top (b\, c\, d) \top (b\, b\, c\, a\, d) \top (b\, a\, b\, c\, d) \top (d)$.

5. The number of occurrences of the pair $\ldots xx \ldots$ is equal to the number of $\frac{x}{x}$ columns, minus 0 or 1. When x is the smallest element, the numbers of occurrences are equal if and only if x is not first in the permutation.

6. Counting the associated number of two-line arrays is easy: $\binom{m}{k}\binom{n}{k}$.

7. Using part (a) of Theorem B, a derivation like that of (20) gives

$$\binom{A-1}{A-k-m-1}\binom{B}{m}\binom{C}{k}\binom{B+k}{B-l}\binom{C-k}{l};$$

$$\binom{A-1}{A-k-m}\binom{B}{m}\binom{C}{k}\binom{B+k-1}{B-l-1}\binom{C-k}{l};$$

$$\binom{A-1}{A-k-m}\binom{B}{m}\binom{C}{k}\binom{B+k-1}{B-l}\binom{C-k}{l}.$$

8. The complete factorization into primes is $(d)_\top (b\ c\ d)_\top (b)_\top (a\ d\ b\ c)_\top (a\ b)_\top (b\ c\ d)_\top (d)$, which is unique since no adjacent pairs commute. So there are eight solutions, with $\alpha = \epsilon,\ (d),\ (d)_\top (b\ c\ d),\ \ldots$.

10. False, but true in interesting cases. Given any linear ordering of the primes, there is at least one factorization of the stated form, since whenever the condition is violated we can make an interchange that reduces the number of "inversions" in the factorization. So the condition fails only because some permutations have more than one such factorization.

Let $\rho \sim \sigma$ mean that ρ commutes with σ. The following condition is necessary and sufficient for the uniqueness of the factorization as stated:

$$\rho \sim \sigma \sim \tau \quad \text{and} \quad \rho \prec \sigma \prec \tau \quad \text{implies} \quad \rho \sim \tau.$$

Proof. If $\rho \sim \sigma \sim \tau$ and $\rho \prec \sigma \prec \tau$ and $\rho \not\sim \tau$, we would have two factorizations $\sigma_\top \tau_\top \rho = \tau_\top \rho_\top \sigma$; hence the condition is necessary. Conversely, to show that it is sufficient for uniqueness, let $\rho_1 \top \cdots \top \rho_n = \sigma_1 \top \cdots \top \sigma_n$ be two distinct factorizations satisfying the condition. We may assume that $\sigma_1 \prec \rho_1$, and hence $\sigma_1 = \rho_k$ for some $k > 1$; furthermore $\sigma_1 \sim \rho_j$ for $1 \le j < k$. Since $\rho_{k-1} \sim \sigma_1 = \rho_k$, we have $\rho_{k-1} \prec \sigma_1$; hence $k > 2$. Let j be such that $\sigma_1 \prec \rho_j$ and $\rho_i \prec \sigma_1$ for $j < i < k$. Then $\rho_{j+1} \sim \sigma_1 \sim \rho_j$ and $\rho_{j+1} \prec \sigma_1 \prec \rho_j$ implies that $\rho_{j+1} \sim \rho_j$; hence $\rho_j \prec \rho_{j+1}$, a contradiction.

Therefore if we are given an ordering relation on a set S of primes, satisfying the condition above, and if we know that all prime factors of a permutation π belongs to S, we can conclude that π has a unique factorization of the stated type. Such a condition holds, for example, when S is the set of cycles in (29).

But the set of *all* primes cannot be so ordered. For if we have, say, $(a\ b) \prec (d\ e)$, then we are forced to define

$$(a\ b) \prec (d\ e) \succ (b\ c) \prec (e\ a) \succ (c\ d) \prec (a\ b) \succ (d\ e),$$

a contradiction. (See also the following exercise.)

11. We wish to show that, if $p(1) \ldots p(t)$ is a permutation of $\{1, \ldots, t\}$, the permutation $x_{p(1)} \ldots x_{p(t)}$ is topologically sorted if and only if $\sigma_{p(1)} \top \cdots \top \sigma_{p(t)} = \sigma_1 \top \cdots \top \sigma_t$; and that if $x_{p(1)} \ldots x_{p(t)}$ and $x_{q(1)} \ldots x_{q(t)}$ are distinct topological sortings, we have $\sigma_{p(j)} \ne \sigma_{q(j)}$ for some j. The first property follows by observing that $x_{p(1)}$ can be first in a topological sort if and only if $\sigma_{p(1)}$ commutes with (yet is distinct from) $\sigma_{p(1)-1}, \ldots, \sigma_1$; and this condition implies that $\sigma_{p(2)} \top \cdots \top \sigma_{p(t)} = \sigma_1 \top \cdots \top \sigma_{p(1)-1} \top \sigma_{p(1)+1} \top \cdots \top \sigma_t$, so induction can be used. The second property follows because if j is minimal with $p(j) \ne q(j)$, we have, say, $p(j) < q(j)$ and $x_{p(j)} \not\prec x_{q(j)}$ by definition of topological sorting; hence $\sigma_{p(j)}$ has no letters in common with $\sigma_{q(j)}$.

To get an arbitrary partial ordering, let the cycle σ_k consist of all ordered pairs (i, j) such that $x_i \prec x_j$ and either $i = k$ or $j = k$; these ordered pairs are to appear in some arbitrary order as individual elements of the cycle. Thus the cycles for the partial ordering $x_1 \prec x_2$, $x_3 \prec x_4$, $x_1 \prec x_4$ would be $\sigma_1 = ((1,2)(1,4))$, $\sigma_2 = ((1,2))$, $\sigma_3 = ((3,4))$, $\sigma_4 = ((1,4)(3,4))$.

12. No other cycles can be formed, since, for example, the original permutation contains no $\begin{smallmatrix}a\\c\end{smallmatrix}$ columns. If $(a\ b\ c\ d)$ occurs s times, then $(a\ b)$ must occur $A - r - s$ times, since there are $A - r$ columns $\begin{smallmatrix}a\\b\end{smallmatrix}$, and only two kinds of cycles contribute to such columns.

13. In the two-line notation, first place $A - t$ columns of the form $\begin{smallmatrix}d\\a\end{smallmatrix}$, then put the other t a's in the second line, then place the b's, and finally the remaining letters.

14. Since the elements below any given letter in the two-line notation for π^- are in nondecreasing order, we do not always have $(\pi^-)^- = \pi$; but it is true that $((\pi^-)^-)^- = \pi^-$. In fact, the identity

$$(\alpha \top \beta)^- = ((\alpha^- \top \beta^-)^-)^-$$

holds for all α and β. (See exercise 5–2.)

Given a multiset whose distinct letters are $x_1 < \cdots < x_m$, we can characterize its self-inverse permutations by observing that they each have a unique prime factorization of the form $\beta_1 \top \cdots \top \beta_m$, where β_j has zero or more prime factors $(x_j) \top \cdots \top (x_j) \top (x_j x_{k_1}) \top \cdots \top (x_j x_{k_t})$, $j < k_1 \leq \cdots \leq k_t$. For example, $(a) \top (a\ b) \top (a\ b) \top (b\ c) \top (c)$ is a self-inverse permutation. The number of self-inverse permutations of $\{m \cdot a, n \cdot b\}$ is therefore $\min(m, n) + 1$; and the corresponding number for $(l \cdot a, m \cdot b, n \cdot c)$ is the number of solutions of the inequalities $x + y \leq l$, $x + z \leq m$, $y + z \leq n$ in nonnegative integers x, y, z. The number of self-inverse permutations of a *set* is considered in Section 5.1.4.

The number of permutations of $(n_1 \cdot x_1, \ldots, n_m \cdot x_m)$ having n_{ij} occurrences of $\begin{smallmatrix}x_i\\x_j\end{smallmatrix}$ in their two-line notation is $\prod_i n_i! / \prod_{i,j} n_{ij}!$, the same as the number having n_{ij} occurrences of $\begin{smallmatrix}x_j\\x_i\end{smallmatrix}$ in the two-line notation. Hence there ought to be a better way to define the inverse of a multiset permutation. For example, if the prime factorization of π is $\sigma_1 \top \sigma_2 \top \cdots \top \sigma_t$ as in Theorem C, we can define $\pi^- = \sigma_t^- \top \cdots \top \sigma_2^- \top \sigma_1^-$, where $(x_1 \ldots x_n)^- = (x_n \ldots x_1)$.

Dominique Foata and Guo-Niu Han have observed that it would be even more desirable to define inverses in such a way that π and π^- have the same number of inversions, because the generating function for inversions given the numbers n_{ij} is $\prod_i n_i! z / \prod_{i,j} n_{ij}! z$; see exercise 16. However, there does not seem to be any natural way to define an involution having that property.

15. See Theorem 2.3.4.2D. Removing one arc of the directed graph must leave an oriented tree.

16. If $x_1 < x_2 < \cdots$, the inversion table entries for the x_j's must have the form $b_{j1} \leq \cdots \leq b_{jn_j}$ where b_{jn_j} (the number of inversions of the rightmost x_j) is at most $n_{j+1} + n_{j+2} + \cdots$. So the generating function for the jth part of the inversion table is the generating function for partitions into at most n_j parts, no part exceeding $n_{j+1} + n_{j+2} + \cdots$. The generating function for partitions into at most m parts, no part exceeding n, is the z-nomial coefficient $\binom{m+n}{m}_z$; this is readily proved by induction, and it can also be proved by means of an ingenious construction due to F. Franklin [*Amer. J. Math.* **5** (1882), 268–269; see also Pólya and Alexanderson, *Elemente der Mathematik* **26** (1971), 102–109]. Multiplying the generating functions for $j = 1, 2$,

... gives the desired formula for inversions of multiset permutations, which MacMahon published in *Proc. London Math. Soc.* (2) **15** (1916), 314–321.

17. Let $h_n(z) = (n!_z)/n!$; then the desired probability generating function is

$$g(z) = h_n(z)/h_{n_1}(z)h_{n_2}(z)\cdots.$$

The mean of $h_n(z)$ is $\frac{1}{2}\binom{n}{2}$, by Eq. 5.1.1–(12), so the mean of g is

$$\frac{1}{2}\left(\binom{n}{2} - \binom{n_1}{2} - \binom{n_2}{2} - \cdots\right) = \frac{1}{4}(n^2 - n_1^2 - n_2^2 - \cdots) = \frac{1}{2}\sum_{i<j} n_i n_j.$$

The variance is, similarly,

$$\frac{1}{72}\left(n(n-1)(2n+5) - n_1(n_1-1)(2n_1+5) - \cdots\right)$$
$$= \frac{1}{36}(n^3 - n_1^3 - n_2^3 - \cdots) + \frac{1}{24}(n^2 - n_1^2 - n_2^2 - \cdots).$$

18. Yes; the construction of exercise 5.1.1–25 can be extended in a straightforward way. Alternatively we can generalize the proof following 5.1.1–(14), by constructing a one-to-one correspondence between m-tuples $(q_1, \ldots, q_m)$ where q_j is a multiset containing n_j nonnegative integers, on the one hand, and ordered pairs of n-tuples $((a_1, \ldots, a_n), (p_1, \ldots, p_n))$ on the other hand, where $a_1 \ldots a_n$ is a permutation of $\{n_1 \cdot 1, \ldots, n_m \cdot m\}$, and $p_1 \geq \cdots \geq p_n \geq 0$. This correspondence is defined as before, giving all elements of q_j the subscript j; it satisfies the condition

$$\Sigma(q_1) + \cdots + \Sigma(q_m) = \text{ind}(a_1 \ldots a_n) + (p_1 + \cdots + p_n)$$

where $\Sigma(q_j)$ denotes the sum of the elements of q_j. [For a further generalization of the technique used in this proof and in the derivation of Eq. 5.1.3–(8), see D. E. Knuth, *Math. Comp.* **24** (1970), 955–961. See also the comprehensive treatment by Richard P. Stanley in *Memoirs Amer. Math. Soc.* **119** (1972).]

19. (a) Let $S = \{\sigma \mid \sigma \text{ is prime}, \sigma \text{ is a left factor of } \pi\}$. If S has k elements, the left factors λ of π such that $\mu(\lambda) \neq 0$ are precisely the 2^k intercalations of the subsets of S (see the proof of Theorem C); hence $\sum \mu(\lambda) = \prod_{\sigma \in S}(1 + \mu(\sigma)) = 0$, since $\mu(\sigma) = -1$ and S is nonempty.   (b) Clearly $\epsilon(i_1 \ldots i_n) = \mu(\pi) = 0$ if $i_j = i_k$ for some $j \neq k$. Otherwise $\epsilon(i_1 \ldots i_n) = (-1)^r$ where $i_1 \ldots i_n$ has r inversions; this is $(-1)^s$, where $i_1 \ldots i_n$ has s even cycles; and this is $(-1)^{n+t}$ where $i_1 \ldots i_n$ has t cycles.

20. (a) Obvious, by definition of intercalation.   (b) By definition,

$$\det(b_{ij}) = \sum_{1 \leq i_1, \ldots, i_m \leq m} \epsilon(i_1 \ldots i_m)\, b_{1i_1} \ldots b_{mi_m}.$$

Setting $b_{ij} = \delta_{ij} - a_{ij}x_j$ and applying exercise 19(b), we obtain

$$\sum_{n \geq 0} \sum_{1 \leq i_1, \ldots, i_n \leq m} x_{i_1} \ldots x_{i_n} \mu(x_{i_1} \ldots x_{i_n}) \nu(x_{i_1} \ldots x_{i_n}),$$

since $\mu(\pi)$ is usually zero.

(c) Use exercise 19(a) to show that $D_\top G = 1$ when we regard the products of x's as permutations of noncommutative variables, using the natural algebraic convention $(\alpha + \beta)_\top \pi = \alpha_\top \pi + \beta_\top \pi$.

A succinct rendition of this combinatorial proof and similar proofs of other important theorems has been given by D. Zeilberger, *Discrete Math.* **56** (1985), 61–72.

21. $\prod_{k=1}^{m}\binom{n_k+\cdots+n_k-d}{n_k}$, if we let $n_k=0$ for $k\le 0$, since there are $\binom{n_m+\cdots+n_m-d}{n_m}$ ways to insert the m's into such a permutation of $\{n_1\cdot 1,\ldots,n_{m-1}\cdot(m-1)\}$.

22. (a) The left-right reversal of $l(\pi)$ is in $P_0(0^k 1^{n_1}\ldots t^{n_t})$, for some k; but instead of reversing $l(\pi)$, we will give it a two-line form by placing 0 last instead of first in the top line. The number k of 0s in $l(\pi)$ and $r(\pi)$ is the number of columns $\frac{j}{k}$ in the two-line form of π for which $j \le t < k$; this is also the number of columns with $k \le t < j$. We can easily reconstruct π from the two-line forms of $l(\pi)$ and $r(\pi)$, because each column $\frac{j}{k}$ with $j,k \le t$ occurs in $l(\pi)$, each column with $t < j,k$ occurs in $r(\pi)$, and the remaining columns are obtained by merging $\frac{j}{0}$ or $\frac{0}{k}$ of $l(\pi)$ with $\frac{0}{k}$ or $\frac{j}{0}$ of $r(\pi)$ from left to right.

(b) Let π be a permutation of the stated form, and let σ be any permutation of $P_0(0^{n_0} 1^{n_1}\ldots m^{n_m})$. Construct λ as follows: Delete the first n_0 entries of σ; then replace the 0s by x's, subscripted with the first n_0 entries of π; replace the other elements by y's, subscripted with the remaining nonzero entries of π. Also construct ρ as follows: Delete the 0s of σ, and replace the n_j occurrences of j with x_j or y_j according as the columns $\frac{j}{k}$ of π have $k=0$ or $k\ne 0$, from left to right. For example, if $\pi = \frac{0000011111222233333}{23131302310102032010}$ and $\sigma = \frac{0000011111222233333}{32313201103201300201}$, we have $\lambda = x_2 y_2 y_3 x_3 y_1 y_1 x_1 y_2 y_3 x_3 x_1 y_2 x_3 y_1$ and $\rho = y_3 y_2 y_3 x_1 x_3 x_2 y_1 y_1 y_3 y_2 y_1 x_3 x_2 x_1$. Conversely, we can reconstruct π and σ from λ and ρ.

(c) We have $w(\pi) = w(l(\pi))\, w(r(\pi))$ in the construction of (a), because column $\frac{j}{k}$ of π either becomes $\frac{j}{k}$ of weight w_j/w_k in $l(\pi)$ or $r(\pi)$, or it is factored into columns $\frac{j}{0}$ and $\frac{0}{k}$ having weights z_j/z_0 and z_0/z_k. If $l(\pi)$ has p_j columns $\frac{j}{0}$ and q_j columns $\frac{0}{j}$, its weight is $\prod_{j=1}^{t}(z_j^{q_j} w_j^{n_j-q_j}/z_j^{p_j} w_j^{n_j-p_j}) = \prod_{j=1}^{t}(w_j/z_j)^{p_j-q_j}$. Now $\prod_{j=1}^{t}(w_j/z_j)^{-q_j}$ is the complex conjugate of $\prod_{j=1}^{t}(w_j/z_j)^{q_j}$; so the sum of weights over all elements of $P_0(0^k 1^{n_1}\ldots t^{n_t})$ simplifies to

$$\frac{k!\,(n_1+\cdots+n_t-k)!}{n_1!\ldots n_t!}\;\left|\;\sum_{p_1+\cdots+p_t=k}\binom{n_1}{p_1}\cdots\binom{n_t}{p_t}\left(\frac{w_1}{z_1}\right)^{p_1}\cdots\left(\frac{w_t}{z_t}\right)^{p_t}\right|^2.$$

Similar remarks apply to $r(\pi)$. The stated sum is positive because the term for $k=0$ is nonzero.

23. We can assume that the original strand was sorted. Let $t = 2$, $m = 4$, $w_1 = w_3 = z_1 = z_2 = +1$, $w_2 = w_4 = z_3 = z_4 = -1$ in part (c) of the previous exercise. Then $w(\pi) = (-1)^d$, where d is the number of columns $\frac{j}{k}$ with $j \ne k$. [See Gillis and Zeilberger, *European J. Comb.* **4** (1983), 221–223. This result was first proved in a completely different way by Askey, Ismail, and Koornwinder, *J. Comb. Theory* **A25** (1978), 277–287, who found intriguing connections between multiset permutations and integrals of products of the Laguerre polynomials $L_n^\alpha(x) = \sum_{k=0}^{n}\binom{n+\alpha}{n-k}(-x)^k/k!$.] The analogous result for a five-letter alphabet is false, because the 5! permutations of $\{1,2,3,4,5\}$ include $1 + 10 + 45$ with an even number of differences, $0 + 20 + 44$ with an odd number.

24. (a) Transposing $\begin{smallmatrix}w & x\\ y & z\end{smallmatrix}$ twice restores $\begin{smallmatrix}w & x\\ y & z\end{smallmatrix}$. Given $\mathrm{sort}\left(\begin{smallmatrix}x_1 & \cdots & x_n\\ y_1 & \cdots & y_n\end{smallmatrix}\right) = \left(\begin{smallmatrix}x_1'' & \cdots & x_n''\\ y_1'' & \cdots & y_n''\end{smallmatrix}\right)$, unsort it by finding the leftmost x in the top row and transposing it to the left. This brings out the proper y. (The value of $\mathrm{sort}\left(\begin{smallmatrix}x_2' & \cdots & x_n'\\ y_2' & \cdots & y_n'\end{smallmatrix}\right)$ is also uniquely determined.)

(b) We are essentially expressing the two-line notation of π in the form

$$\pi = \mathrm{sort}\left(\begin{array}{ccccccc}y_1 & \cdots\; x_{1n_1} & y_2 & \cdots\; x_{2n_2} & \cdots & y_t & \cdots\; x_{tn_t}\\ x_{11} & \cdots\quad y_1 & x_{21} & \cdots\quad y_2 & \cdots & x_{t1} & \cdots\quad y_t\end{array}\right),$$

and part (a) provides us with precisely the tools we need. [When R preserves certain statistics of the two-line notation, this construction provides combinatorial proofs of interesting theorems. See Guo-Niu Han, *Advances in Math.* **105** (1994), 26–41.]

SECTION 5.1.3

1. We must only show that this value makes (11) valid for $x = k$, when $k \geq 1$. Using (7), the formula becomes

$$k^n = \sum_{r=0}^{k} \left\langle {n \atop r-1} \right\rangle \binom{k+n-r}{n} = \sum_{0 \leq j \leq r \leq k} (-1)^j (r-j)^n \binom{n+1}{j} \binom{n+k-r}{n}$$

$$= \sum_{s=0}^{k} s^n \sum_{j=0}^{k-s} (-1)^j \binom{n+1}{j} \binom{n+k-s-j}{n}.$$

For $s < k$, the sum on j can be extended to the range $0 \leq j \leq n+1$, and it is zero (the $(n+1)$st difference of an nth-degree polynomial in j).

2. (a) The number of sequences $a_1 a_2 \ldots a_n$ containing each of the elements $(1, 2, \ldots, q)$ at least once is $\left\{ {n \atop q} \right\} q!$, by exercise 1.2.6–64; the number of such sequences satisfying the analog of (10), for $m = q$, is $\binom{n-k}{n-q}$, since we must choose $n-q$ of the possible $=$ signs. (b) Add the results of (a) for $m = n - q$ and $n - q - 1$.

3. By (20),

$$\sum_n \frac{x^n}{n!} \sum_k \left\langle {n \atop k} \right\rangle (-1)^k = \frac{2}{e^{-2x}+1} = \frac{1}{x}\left(\frac{(-4x)}{e^{-4x}-1} - \frac{(-2x)}{e^{-2x}-1} \right)$$

$$= \frac{1}{x} \sum_{n \geq 0} \frac{B_n x^n}{n!} ((-4)^n - (-2)^n);$$

hence the result is $(-1)^{n+1} B_{n+1} 2^{n+1} (2^{n+1} - 1)/(n+1)$. Alternatively, the identity $2/(e^{-2x}+1) = 1 + \tanh x$ lets us express the answer as $(-1)^{(n-1)/2} T_n$ when n is odd, where T_n denotes the tangent number defined by the formula

$$\tan z = T_1 z + T_3 z^3/3! + T_5 z^5/5! + \cdots.$$

When $n > 0$ is even, the sum obviously vanishes, by (7).

Incidentally, (18) now yields the curious Stirling number identity

$$\sum_k \left\{ {n \atop k} \right\} \frac{k!}{(-2)^k} = \frac{2B_{n+1}(1 - 2^{n+1})}{n+1}.$$

4. $(-1)^{n+m} \left\langle {n \atop m} \right\rangle$. (Consider the coefficient of z^{m+1} in (18).)

5. $\left\langle {p \atop k} \right\rangle \equiv (k+1)^p - k^p \equiv (k+1) - k \equiv 1$ (modulo p) for $0 \leq k < p$, by formula (13), exercise 1.2.6–10, and Theorem 1.2.4F.

6. Summing first on k is not allowed, because the terms are nonzero for arbitrarily large j and k, and the sum of the absolute values is infinite.

For a simpler example of the fallacy, let $a_{jk} = (k-j)[|j-k| = 1]$. Then

$$\sum_{j \geq 0} \left(\sum_{k \geq 0} a_{jk} \right) = \sum_{j \geq 0} (\delta_{j0}) = +1, \quad \text{while} \quad \sum_{k \geq 0} \left(\sum_{j \geq 0} a_{jk} \right) = \sum_{k \geq 0} (-\delta_{k0}) = -1.$$

7. Yes. [F. N. David and D. E. Barton, *Combinatorial Chance* (1962), 150–154; see also the answer to exercise 25.]

8. [*Combinatory Analysis* **1** (1915), 190.] By inclusion and exclusion. For example, $1/(l_1 + l_2)!\, l_3!\, (l_4 + l_5 + l_6)!$ is the probability that $x_1 < \cdots < x_{l_1+l_2}$, $x_{l_1+l_2+1} < \cdots < x_{l_1+l_2+l_3}$, and $x_{l_1+l_2+l_3+1} < \cdots < x_{l_1+l_2+l_3+l_4+l_5+l_6}$.

A simple $O(n^2)$ algorithm to count the number of permutations of $\{1,\ldots,n\}$ having respective run lengths $(l_1,\ldots,l_k)$ has been given by N. G. de Bruijn, *Nieuw Archief voor Wiskunde* (3) **18** (1970), 61–65.

9. $p_{km} = q_{km} - q_{k(m+1)}$ in (23). Since $\sum_{k,m} q_{km} z^m x^k = \frac{x}{1-x} g(x,z)$ and $g(x,0) = 1$, we have

$$h(z,x) = \sum h_k(z) x^k = \frac{x}{1-x} g(x,z)(1 - z^{-1}) + \frac{x}{1-x} z^{-1} = \frac{(1 - z^{-1})x}{e^{(x-1)z} - x} + \frac{z^{-1}x}{1-x}.$$

Thus $h_1(z) = e^z - (e^z - 1)/z$; $h_2(z) = (e^{2z} - ze^z) + e^z - (e^{2z} - 1)/z$.

10. Let $M_n = L_1 + \cdots + L_n$ be the mean; then $\sum M_n x^n = h'(1,x)$, where the derivative is taken with respect to z, and this is $x/(e^{x-1} - x) - x/(1 - x) = M(x)$, say. By the residue theorem

$$\frac{1}{2\pi i} \oint M(z) z^{-n-1}\, dz = M_n - 2(n + \tfrac{1}{3}) + 1 + \frac{z_1^{-n}}{z_1 - 1} + \frac{\bar{z}_1^{-n}}{\bar{z}_1 - 1},$$

if we integrate around a circle of radius r where $|z_1| < r < |z_2|$. (Note the double pole at $z = 1$.) Furthermore, the absolute value of this integral is less than $\oint |M(z)|\, r^{-n-1}\, dz = O(r^{-n})$. Integrating over larger and larger circles gives the convergent series $M_n = 2n - \tfrac{1}{3} + \sum_{k \geq 1} 2\Re(1/z_k^n (1 - z_k))$.

To find the variance, we have $h''(1,x) = -2h'(1,x) - 2x(x-1)e^{x-1}/(e^{x-1} - x)^2$. An argument similar to that used for the mean, this time with a triple pole, shows that the coefficients of $h''(1,x)$ are asymptotically $4n^2 + \tfrac{4}{3}n - 2M_n$ plus smaller terms; this leads to the asymptotic formula $\tfrac{2}{3}n + \tfrac{2}{9}$ (plus exponentially smaller terms) for the variance.

11. $P_{kn} = \sum_{t_1 \geq 1,\ldots,t_k \geq 1} D(t_1, \ldots, t_{k-1}, n, 1)$, where $D(l_1, l_2, \ldots, l_k)$ is MacMahon's determinant of exercise 8. Evaluating this determinant by its first row, we find $P_{kn} = c_0 P_{(k-1)n} + c_1 P_{(k-2)n} + \cdots + c_{k-2} P_{1n} - E_k(n)$, where c_j and E_k are defined as follows:

$$c_j = (-1)^j \sum_{t_1,\ldots,t_{j+1} \geq 1} \frac{1}{(t_1 + \cdots + t_{j+1})!} = (-1)^j \sum_{m \geq 0} \binom{m}{j} \frac{1}{(m+1)!}$$

$$= (-1)^j \sum_{r,m \geq 0} \binom{-1}{j-r} \binom{m+1}{r} \frac{1}{(m+1)!} = -1 + e\left(\frac{1}{0!} - \frac{1}{1!} + \cdots + (-1)^j \frac{1}{j!}\right);$$

$$E_1(n) = 1/(n+1)! - 1/n!; \qquad E_2(n) = 1/(n+1)!;$$

$$E_k(n) = (-1)^k \sum_{m \geq 0} \binom{m}{k-3} \frac{1}{(n+2+m)!}, \qquad k \geq 3.$$

Let $P_{0n} = 0$, $C(z) = \sum c_j z^j = (e^{1-z} - 1)/(1 - z)$, and let

$$E(z,x) = \sum_{n,k} E_{k+1}(n) z^n x^k = 1 - e^z + \frac{(e^{1-x} - 1)x^2}{(1-x)^2} - \frac{x^2(e^{1-x} - e^z)}{(1-x)(1-x-z)} + \frac{e^z - 1 - z}{z(1-x)}.$$

The recurrence relation we have derived is equivalent to the formula $C(x)H(z,x) = H(z,x)/x + E(z,x)$; hence $H(z,x) = E(z,x)x(1-x)/(xe^{1-x} - 1)$. Expanding this power series gives $H_1(z) = h_1(z)$ (see exercise 9); $H_2(z) = eh_1(z) + 1 - e^z$.

[*Note:* The generating functions for the first three runs were derived by Knuth, *CACM* **6** (1963), 685–688. Barton and Mallows, *Ann. Math. Statistics* **36** (1965), 249, stated the formula $1 - H_{n+1}(z) = (1 - H_n(z))/(1 - z) - L_n h_1(z)$ for $n \geq 1$, together with (25). Another way to attack this problem is illustrated in exercise 23. Because adjacent runs are not independent, there is no simple relation between the problem solved here and the simpler (probably more useful) result of exercise 9.]

12. [*Combinatory Analysis* **1** (1915), 209–211.] The number of ways to put the multiset into t distinguishable boxes is

$$N_t = \binom{t + n_1 - 1}{n_1} \binom{t + n_2 - 1}{n_2} \cdots \binom{t + n_m - 1}{n_m},$$

since there are $\binom{t+n_1-1}{n_1}$ ways to place the 1s, etc. If we require that no box be empty, the method of inclusion and exclusion tells us that the number of ways is

$$M_t = N_t - \binom{t}{1} N_{t-1} + \binom{t}{2} N_{t-2} - \cdots.$$

Let P_k be the number of permutations having k runs; if we put $k - 1$ vertical lines between the runs, and $t - k$ additional vertical lines in any of the $n - k$ remaining places, we get one of the M_t ways to divide the multiset into t nonempty distinguishable parts. Hence

$$M_t = P_t + \binom{n - t + 1}{1} P_{t-1} + \binom{n - t + 2}{2} P_{t-2} + \cdots.$$

Equating the two values of M_t allows us to determine P_1, P_2, ... successively in terms of N_1, N_2, ... (A more direct proof would be desirable.)

13. $1 + \frac{1}{2} 13 \times 3 = 20.5$.

14. By Foata's correspondence the given permutation corresponds to

$$(3\,1)_\top (1)_\top \cdots _\top (4) = \begin{pmatrix} 1\ 1\ 1\ 1\ 2\ 2\ 2\ 2\ 3\ 3\ 3\ 3\ 4\ 4\ 4\ 4 \\ 3\ 1\ 1\ 2\ 3\ 4\ 3\ 2\ 1\ 1\ 3\ 4\ 2\ 2\ 4\ 4 \end{pmatrix};$$

by (33) this corresponds to

$$\begin{pmatrix} 1\ 1\ 1\ 1\ 2\ 2\ 2\ 2\ 3\ 3\ 3\ 3\ 4\ 4\ 4\ 4 \\ 2\ 4\ 4\ 3\ 3\ 3\ 1\ 1\ 4\ 4\ 2\ 1\ 2\ 1\ 2\ 3 \end{pmatrix},$$

which corresponds to $2\,3\,4\,2\,3\,4\,1\,4\,2\,1\,4\,3\,2\,1\,3\,1$ with 9 runs.

15. The number of alternating runs is 1 plus the number of j such that $1 < j < n$ and either $a_{j-1} < a_j > a_{j+1}$ or $a_{j-1} > a_j < a_{j+1}$. For fixed j, the probability is $\frac{2}{3}$; hence the average, for $n \geq 2$, is $1 + \frac{2}{3}(n - 2)$.

16. Each permutation of $\{1, 2, \ldots, n-1\}$, having k alternating runs, yields k permutations with k such runs, 2 with $k+1$, and $n - k - 2$ with $k+2$, when the new element n is inserted in all possible places. Hence

$$\left|{n \atop k}\right| = k \left|{n-1 \atop k}\right| + 2\left|{n-1 \atop k-1}\right| + (n - k) \left|{n-1 \atop k-2}\right|.$$

It is convenient to let $\left|{1 \atop k}\right| = \delta_{k0}$, $G_1(z) = 1$. Then

$$G_n(z) = \frac{z}{n}\left((1 - z^2)G'_{n-1}(z) + (2 + (n - 2)z)G_{n-1}(z)\right).$$

Differentiation leads to the recurrence

$$x_n = \frac{1}{n}\left((n - 2)x_{n-1} + 2n - 2\right)$$

for $x_n = G'_n(1)$, and this has the solution $x_n = \frac{2}{3}n - \frac{1}{3}$ for $n \geq 2$. Another differentiation leads to the recurrence

$$y_n = \frac{1}{n}\left((n-4)y_{n-1} + \tfrac{8}{3}n^2 - \tfrac{26}{3}n + 6\right)$$

for $y_n = G''_n(1)$. Set $y_n = \alpha n^2 + \beta n + \gamma$ and solve for α, β, γ to get $y_n = \frac{4}{9}n^2 - \frac{14}{15}n + \frac{11}{90}$ for $n \geq 4$. Hence $\operatorname{var}(g_n) = \frac{1}{90}(16n - 29)$, $n \geq 4$.

These formulas for the mean and variance are due to J. Bienaymé, who stated them without proof [*Bull. Soc. Math. de France* **2** (1874), 153–154; *Comptes Rendus Acad. Sci. Paris* **81** (1875), 417–423, see also Bertrand's remarks on p. 458]. The recurrence relation for $\langle\langle {n \atop k} \rangle\rangle$ is due to D. André [*Comptes Rendus Acad. Sci. Paris* **97** (1883), 1356–1358; *Annales Scientifiques de l'École Normale Supérieure* (3) **1** (Paris: 1884), 121–134]. André noted that $g_n(-1) = 0$ for $n \geq 4$; thus, the number of permutations with an even number of alternating runs is $n!/2$. He also proved the formula for the mean, and determined the number of permutations that have the maximum number of alternating runs (see exercise 5.1.4–23). It can be shown that

$$G_n(z) = \left(\frac{1+z}{2}\right)^{n-1}(1+w)^{n+1}g_n\left(\frac{1-w}{1+w}\right), \qquad w = \sqrt{\frac{1-z}{1+z}}, \qquad n \geq 2,$$

where $g_n(z)$ is the generating function (18) for ascending runs. [See David and Barton, *Combinatorial Chance* (London: Griffin, 1962), 157–162.]

17. $\binom{n+1}{2k-1}$; $\binom{n}{2k-2}$ end with 0, $\binom{n}{2k-1}$ end with 1.

18. (a) Let the given sequence be an inversion table as in Section 5.1.1. If it has k descents, the inverse of the corresponding permutation has k descents (see answer 5.1.1–8(e)); hence the answer is $\langle {n \atop k} \rangle$. (b) This quantity satisfies $f(n,k) = kf(n-1,k) + (n-k+1)f(n-1,k-1)$, so it must be $\langle {n \atop k-1} \rangle$. [See D. Dumont, *Duke Math. J.* **41** (1974), 313–315.]

19. (a) $\langle {n \atop k} \rangle$, by the correspondence of Theorem 5.1.2B. (b) There are $(n-k)!$ ways to put $n-k$ further nonattacking rooks on the entire board; hence the answer is $1/(n-k)!$ times $\sum_{j \geq 0} a_{nj}\binom{j}{k}$, where $a_{nj} = \langle {n \atop j} \rangle$ by part (a). This comes to $\{{n \atop n-k}\}$, by exercise 2. [Chapter 5 of Riordan's *Introduction to Combinatorial Analysis* (Wiley, 1958) discusses rook placement in general.]

A direct proof of this result, due to E. A. Bender, associates each partition of $\{1,2,\ldots,n\}$ into k nonempty disjoint subsets with an arrangement of $n-k$ rooks: Let the partition be

$$\{1,2,\ldots,n\} = \{a_{11}, a_{12}, \ldots, a_{1n_1}\} \cup \cdots \cup \{a_{k1}, \ldots, a_{kn_k}\},$$

where $a_{ij} < a_{i(j+1)}$ for $1 \leq j < n_i$, $1 \leq i \leq k$. The corresponding arrangement puts rooks in column a_{ij} of row $a_{i(j+1)}$, for $1 \leq j < n_i$, $1 \leq i \leq k$. For example, the configuration illustrated in Fig. 4 corresponds to the partition $\{1,3,8\} \cup \{2\} \cup \{4,6\} \cup \{5\} \cup \{7\}$.

20. The number of readings is the number of runs in the inverse permutation. The first run corresponds to the first reading, etc.

21. It has $n+1-k$ runs and requires $n+1-j$ readings.

22. [*J. Combinatorial Theory* **1** (1966), 350–374.] If $rs < n$, some reading will pick up $t > r$ elements, $a_{i_1} = j+1$, $\ldots$, $a_{i_t} = j+t$, where $i_1 < \cdots < i_t$. We cannot have $a_m > a_{m+1}$ for all m in the range $i_k \leq m < i_{k+1}$, so the permutation contains at least $t-1$ places with $a_m < a_{m+1}$; it therefore has at most $n-t+1$ runs.

On the other hand, consider the permutation $\alpha_r \ldots \alpha_2 \alpha_1$, where block α_j contains the numbers $\equiv j$ (modulo r), in decreasing order; for example, when $n = 9$ and $r = 4$, this permutation is 8 4 7 3 6 2 9 5 1. If $n \geq 2r - 1$, this permutation has $r - 1$ ascents, so it has $n + 1 - r$ runs. Moreover, it requires exactly $n + 1 - \lceil n/r \rceil$ readings, if $r > 1$. We can rearrange the elements of $\{kr + 1, \ldots, kr + r\}$ arbitrarily without changing the number of runs; in this way we can reduce the number of readings to any desired value $\geq \lceil n/r \rceil$.

Now suppose $rs \geq n$ and $r + s \leq n + 1$ and $r, s \geq 1$. By exercises 20 and 21 we can assume that $r \leq s$, since the reflection of the inverse of a permutation with $n + 1 - r$ runs and s readings has $n + 1 - s$ runs and r readings. Then the construction in the preceding paragraph handles all cases except those where $s > n + 1 - \lceil n/r \rceil$ and $r \geq 2$. To complete the proof we may use a permutation of the form

$$2k{+}1 \; 2k{-}1 \; \ldots \; 1 \; n{+}2{-}r \; n{+}1{-}r \; \ldots \; 2k{+}2 \; 2k \; \ldots \; 2 \; n{+}3{-}r \; \ldots \; n{-}1 \; n,$$

which has $n + 1 - r$ runs and $n + 1 - r - k$ readings, for $0 \leq k \leq \frac{1}{2}(n - r)$.

23. [*SIAM Review* **3** (1967), 121–122.] Assume that the infinite permutation consists of independent samples from the uniform distribution. Let $f_k(x)\, dx$ be the probability that the kth long run begins with x; and let $g(u, x)\, dx$ be the probability that a long run begins with x, when the preceding long run begins with u. Then $f_1(x) = 1$, $f_{k+1}(x) = \int_0^1 f_k(u) g(u, x)\, du$. We have $g(u, x) = \sum_{m \geq 1} g_m(u, x)$, where

$$g_m(u, x) = \Pr(u < X_1 < \cdots < X_m > x \text{ or } u > X_1 > \cdots > X_m < x)$$
$$= \Pr(u < X_1 < \cdots < X_m) + \Pr(u > X_1 > \cdots > X_m)$$
$$- \Pr(u < X_1 < \cdots < X_m < x) - \Pr(u > X_1 > \cdots > X_m > x)$$
$$= (u^m + (1 - u)^m + |u - x|^m)/m! \,;$$

hence $g(u, x) = e^u + e^{1-u} - 1 - e^{|u-x|}$, and we find $f_2(x) = 2e - 1 - e^x - e^{1-x}$. One can show that $f_k(x)$ approaches the limiting value $(2\cos(x - \frac{1}{2}) - \sin\frac{1}{2} - \cos\frac{1}{2})/(3\sin\frac{1}{2} - \cos\frac{1}{2})$. The average length of a run starting with x is $e^x + e^{1-x} - 1$; hence the length $\mathcal{L}_k$ of the kth long run is $\int_0^1 f_k(x)(e^x + e^{1-x} - 1)\, dx$; $\mathcal{L}_1 = 2e - 3 \approx 2.43656$; $\mathcal{L}_2 = 3e^2 - 8e + 2 \approx 2.42091$. See Section 5.4.1 for similar results.

24. Arguing as before, the result is

$$1 + \sum_{0 \leq k < n} 2^k (p^2 + q^2)^k (p^2 + 2pq(2^{n-k-1} - 1 + q^2((2pq)^{n-k-1} - 1)/(2pq - 1)));$$

carrying out the sum and simplifying yields

$$2^n(p^2 + q^2)^n (p(p - q)/(p^2 + q^2 - pq) - \tfrac{1}{2}) + (2pq)^n pq^3/(p^2 + q^2)(p^2 + q^2 - pq)$$
$$+ q^2/(p^2 + q^2) + 2^{n-1}.$$

25. Let $V_j = (U_1 + \cdots + U_j) \bmod 1$; then $V_1, \ldots, V_n$ are independent uniform random numbers in $[0 \ldots 1)$, forming a permutation that has k descents if and only if $\lfloor U_1 + \cdots + U_n \rfloor = k$. Hence the answer is $\left\langle {n \atop k} \right\rangle / n!$, a property first noticed by S. Tanny [*Duke Math. J.* **40** (1973), 717–722].

26. For example, $\vartheta^5 (1 - z)^{-1} = (z + 26z^2 + 66z^3 + 26z^4 + z^5)/(1 - z)^6$.

27. The following rule defines a one-to-one correspondence that takes a permutation $a_1 a_2 \ldots a_n$ with k descents into an n-node increasing forest with $k + 1$ leaves: The first root is a_1, and its descendants are the forest corresponding to $a_2 \ldots a_k$, where k is minimal such that $a_{k+1} < a_1$ or $k = n$. [R. P. Stanley, *Enumerative Combinatorics* **1** (Wadsworth, 1986), Proposition 1.3.16.]

SECTION 5.1.4

1.

1	2	3	8
4	5	7	
6	9		

1	3	5	8
2	4	9	
6	7		

;

$$\begin{pmatrix} 1 & 3 & 4 & 5 & 7 & 8 & 9 \\ 5 & 9 & 2 & 4 & 8 & 1 & 7 \end{pmatrix}.$$

2. When p_i is inserted into column t, let the element in column $t-1$ be p_j. Then (q_j, p_j) is in class $t-1$, $q_j < q_i$, and $p_j < p_i$; so, by induction, indices $i_1, \ldots, i_t$ exist with the property. Conversely, if $q_j < q_i$ and $p_j < p_i$ and if (q_j, p_j) is in class $t-1$, then column $t-1$ contains an element $< p_i$ when p_i is inserted, so (q_i, p_i) is in class $\geq t$.

3. The columns are the bumping sequences (9) when p_i is inserted. Lines 1 and 2 reflect the operations on row 1, see (14). If we remove columns in which line 2 has ∞ entries, lines 0 and 2 constitute the bumped array, as in (15). The stated method for going from line k to line $k+1$ is just the class-determination algorithm of the text.

4. (a) Use a case analysis, by induction on the size of the tableau, considering first the effect on row 1 and then the effect on the sequence of elements bumped from row 1. (b) Admissible interchanges can simulate the operations of Algorithm I, with the tableau represented as a canonical permutation before and after the algorithm. For example, we can transform

$$17\ 11\ 4\ 13\ 14\ 2\ 6\ 10\ 15\ 1\ 3\ 5\ 9\ 12\ 16\ 8$$

into

$$17\ 11\ 13\ 4\ 10\ 14\ 2\ 6\ 9\ 15\ 1\ 3\ 5\ 8\ 12\ 16$$

by a sequence of admissible interchanges (see (4) and (5)).

5. Admissible interchanges are symmetrical between left and right, and the canonical permutation for P obviously goes into P^T when the insertion order is reversed.

6. Let there be t classes in all; exactly k of them have an odd number of elements, since the elements of a class have the form

$$(p_{i_k}, p_{i_1}), \qquad (p_{i_{k-1}}, p_{i_2}), \qquad \ldots, \qquad (p_{i_1}, p_{i_k}).$$

(See (18) and (22).) The bumped two-line array has exactly $t-k$ fixed points, because of the way it is constructed; hence by induction the tableau minus its first row has $t-k$ columns of odd length. So the t elements in the first row lead to k odd-length columns in the whole tableau.

7. The number of columns, namely the length of row 1, is the number of classes (exercise 2). The number of rows is the number of columns of P^T, so exercise 5 (or Theorem D) completes the proof.

8. With more than n^2 elements, the corresponding P tableau must either have more than n rows or more than n columns. But there are $n \times n$ tableaux. [This result was originally proved in *Compositio Math.* **2** (1935), 463–470.]

9. Such permutations are in 1–1 correspondence with pairs of tableaux of shape $(n, n, \ldots, n)$; so by (34) the answer is

$$\left(\frac{n^2!\,\Delta(2n-1, 2n-2, \ldots, n)}{(2n-1)!\,(2n-2)!\ldots n!} \right)^2 = \left(\frac{n^2!}{(2n-1)(2n-2)^2 \ldots n^n(n-1)^{n-1}\ldots 1^1} \right)^2.$$

The existence of such a simple formula for this problem is truly amazing. We can also count the number of permutations of $\{1, 2, \ldots, mn\}$ with no increasing subsequences longer than m, no decreasing subsequences longer than n.

10. We prove inductively that, at step S3, $P_{(r-1)s}$ and $P_{r(s-1)}$ are both less than $P_{(r+1)s}$ and $P_{r(s+1)}$.

11. We also need to know, of course, the element that was originally P_{11}. Then it is possible to restore things using an algorithm remarkably similar to Algorithm S.

12. $\binom{n_1+1}{2} + \binom{n_2+2}{2} + \cdots + \binom{n_m+m}{2} - \binom{m+1}{3}$, the total distance traveled.
The minimum is the sum of the first n terms of the sequence $1, 2, 2, 3, 3, 3, 4, 4, 4, 4 \ldots$ of exercise 1.2.4–41; this sum is approximately $\sqrt{8/9}\, n^{3/2}$. (Nearly all tableaux on n elements come reasonably close to this lower bound, according to exercise 29, so the average number of times is $\Theta(n^{3/2})$.)

13. Assume that the elements permuted are $\{1, 2, \ldots, n\}$, so that $a_i = 1$; and assume that $a_j = 2$. *Case 1*, $j < i$. Then 1 bumps 2, so row 1 of the tableau corresponding to $a_1 \ldots a_{i-1}\, a_{i+1} \ldots a_n$ is row 1 of P^S; and the bumped permutation is the former bumped permutation except for its smallest element, 2, so we may use induction on n. *Case 2*, $j > i$. Apply Case 1 to P^T, in view of exercise 5 and the fact that $(P^T)^S = (P^S)^T$.

15. As in (37), the example permutation corresponds to the tableau

1	2	5	9	11
3	6	7		
4	8	10		

;

hence the number is $f(l, m, n) = (l + m + n)!\, (l - m + 1)(l - n + 2)(m - n + 1)/(l + 2)!\, (m + 1)!\, (n)!$, provided, of course, that $l \geq m \geq n$.

16. By Theorem H, 80080.

17. Since g is antisymmetric in the x's, it is zero when $x_i = x_j$, so it is divisible by $x_i - x_j$ for all $i < j$. Hence $g(x_1, \ldots, x_n; y) = h(x_1, \ldots, x_n; y)\Delta(x_1, \ldots, x_n)$. Here h must be homogeneous in $x_1, \ldots, x_n, y$, of total degree 1, and symmetric in $x_1, \ldots, x_n$; so $h(x_1, \ldots, x_n; y) = a(x_1 + \cdots + x_n) + by$ for some a, b depending only on n. We can evaluate a by setting $y = 0$; we can evaluate b by taking the partial derivative with respect to y and then setting $y = 0$. We have

$$\frac{\partial}{\partial y}\Delta(x_1, \ldots, x_i + y, \ldots, x_n)|_{y=0} = \frac{\partial}{\partial x_i}\Delta(x_1, \ldots, x_n) = \Delta(x_1, \ldots, x_n)\sum_{j \neq i}\frac{1}{x_i - x_j}.$$

Finally,

$$\sum_i \sum_{j \neq i}(x_i/(x_i - x_j)) = \sum_i \sum_{j < i}(x_i/(x_i - x_j) + x_j/(x_j - x_i)) = \binom{n}{2}.$$

18. It must be $\Delta(x_1, \ldots, x_n) \cdot (b_0 + b_1 y + \cdots + b_m y^m)$, where each b_k is a homogeneous symmetric polynomial of degree $m - k$ in the x's. We have

$$\frac{\partial^k}{k!\, \partial y^k}\Delta(x_1, \ldots, x_i + y, \ldots, x_n)|_{y=0} = \Delta(x_1, \ldots, x_n)\sum\left(1 \Big/ \prod_{l=1}^{k}(x_i - x_{j_l})\right)$$

summed over all $\binom{n-1}{k}$ choices of distinct indices $j_1, \ldots, j_k \neq i$. Now, in the expression $b_k = \sum x_i^m / \prod_{l=1}^{k}(x_i - x_{j_l})$, we may combine those groups of $k+1$ terms having a given set of indices $\{i, j_1, \ldots, j_k\}$; for example, when $k = 2$, we group sets of three terms of the form $a^m/(a - b)(a - c) + b^m/(b - a)(b - c) + c^m/(c - a)(c - b)$. The sum of every such group is $[z^{m-k}]\,1/(1 - x_i z)(1 - x_{j_1} z)\ldots(1 - x_{j_k} z)$, by exercise 1.2.3–33. We find therefore that

$$b_k = \sum_j \binom{n - j}{k + 1 - j} \sum s(p_1, \ldots, p_j),$$

where $s(p_1, \ldots, p_j)$ is the monomial symmetric function consisting of all distinct terms having the form $x_{i_1}^{p_1} \ldots x_{i_j}^{p_j}$, for distinct indices $i_1, \ldots, i_j \in \{1, \ldots, n\}$; and the inner sum is over all partitions of $m - k$ into exactly j parts, namely $p_1 \geq \cdots \geq p_j \geq 1$, $p_1 + \cdots + p_j = m - k$. (This result was obtained jointly with E. A. Bender in 1969.)
　　When $m = 2$ the answer is $\left(s(2) + (n - 1)s(1)y + \binom{n}{3}y^2\right)\Delta(x_1, \ldots, x_n)$; for $m = 3$ we get $\left(s(3) + ((n - 1)s(2) + s(1, 1))y + \binom{n-1}{2}s(1)y^2 + \binom{n}{4}y^3\right)\Delta(x_1, \ldots, x_n)$; etc.
　　Another expression gives b_k as the coefficient of z^m in

$$\left(\binom{n}{k + 1}z^k - \binom{n - 1}{k + 1}a_1 z^{k+1} + \binom{n - 2}{k + 1}a_2 z^{k+2} - \cdots\right)\Big/(1 - a_1 z + a_2 z^2 - \cdots),$$

where $a_l = \sum_{1 \leq i_1 < \cdots < i_l \leq n} x_{i_1} \ldots x_{i_l}$ is an elementary symmetric function. Multiplying by y^k and summing on k gives the answer as the coefficient of z^m in

$$\frac{1}{yz}\left(\frac{(1 + z(y - x_1))\ldots(1 + z(y - x_n))}{(1 - zx_1)\ldots(1 - zx_n)} - 1\right)\Delta(x_1, \ldots, x_n).$$

19. Let the shape of the transposed tableau be $(n_1', n_2', \ldots, n_r')$; the answer is

$$\frac{1}{2}f(n_1, n_2, \ldots, n_m)\left(\frac{(\sum n_i^2 - \sum n_j'^2)}{n(n - 1)} + 1\right),$$

where $n = \sum n_i = \sum n_j'$. (This formula can be expressed in a less symmetrical form using the relation $\sum i n_i = \frac{1}{2}(n + \sum n_j'^2)$.)
　　Note: W. Feit [*Proc. Amer. Math. Soc.* **4** (1953), 740–744] showed that the number of ways to place the integers $\{1, 2, \ldots, n\}$ into an array that is the "difference" of two tableau shapes $(n_1, \ldots, n_m) \setminus (l_1, \ldots, l_m)$, where $0 \leq l_j \leq n_j$ and $n = \sum(n_j - l_j)$, is $n! \det(1/((n_j - j) - (l_i - i))!)$.

20. The fallacious argument in the discussion following Theorem H is actually valid for this case (the corresponding probabilities *are* independent).
　　Note: If we consider all $n!$ ways to label the nodes, the labelings considered here are those having no "inversions." Inversions in permutations are the same as inversions in tree labelings, in the special case when the tree is simply a path. See A. Björner and M. L. Wachs, *J. Combinatorial Theory* **A52** (1989), 165–187.

21. [*Michigan Math. J.* **1** (1952), 81–88.] Let $g(n_1, \ldots, n_m) = (n_1 + \cdots + n_m)!\,\Delta(n_1, \ldots, n_m)/n_1! \ldots n_m!\,\sigma(n_1, \ldots, n_m)$, where $\sigma(x_1, \ldots, x_m) = \prod_{1 \leq i < j \leq m}(x_i + x_j)$. To prove that $g(n_1, \ldots, n_m)$ is the number of ways to fill the shifted tableau, we must prove that $g(n_1, \ldots, n_m) = g(n_1 - 1, \ldots, n_m) + \cdots + g(n_1, \ldots, n_m - 1)$. The identity corresponding to exercise 17 is $x_1 \Delta(x_1 + y, \ldots, x_n)/\sigma(x_1 + y, \ldots, x_n) + \cdots + x_n \Delta(x_1, \ldots, x_n + y)/\sigma(x_1, \ldots, x_n + y) = (x_1 + \cdots + x_n)\Delta(x_1, \ldots, x_n)/\sigma(x_1, \ldots, x_n)$, independent of y; for if we calculate the derivative as in exercise 17, we find that $2x_i x_j/(x_j^2 - x_i^2) + 2x_j x_i/(x_i^2 - x_j^2) = 0$.

22. Assume that $m = N$, by adding 0s to the shape if necessary; if $m > N$ and $n_m > 0$, the number of ways is clearly zero. When $m = N$ the answer is

$$\det \begin{pmatrix} \binom{n_1 + m - 1}{m - 1} & \binom{n_2 + m - 2}{m - 1} & \cdots & \binom{n_m}{m - 1} \\ \vdots & \vdots & & \vdots \\ \binom{n_1 + m - 1}{0} & \binom{n_2 + m - 2}{0} & \cdots & \binom{n_m}{0} \end{pmatrix}.$$

Proof. We may assume that $n_m = 0$, for if $n_m > 0$, the first n_m columns of the array must be filled with i in row i, and we may consider the remaining shape $(n_1 - n_m, \ldots, n_m - n_m)$. By induction on m, the number of ways is

$$\sum_{\substack{n_2 \le k_1 \le n_1 \\ \vdots \\ n_m \le k_{m-1} \le n_{m-1}}} \det \begin{pmatrix} \binom{k_1 + m - 2}{m - 2} & \binom{k_2 + m - 3}{m - 2} & \cdots & \binom{k_{m-1}}{m - 2} \\ \vdots & \vdots & & \vdots \\ \binom{k_1 + m - 2}{0} & \binom{k_2 + m - 3}{0} & \cdots & \binom{k_{m-1}}{0} \end{pmatrix},$$

where $n_j - k_j$ represents the number of m's in row j. The sum on each k_j may be carried out independently, giving

$$\det \begin{pmatrix} \binom{n_1+m-1}{m-1} - \binom{n_2+m-2}{m-1} & \binom{n_2+m-2}{m-1} - \binom{n_3+m-3}{m-1} & \cdots & \binom{n_{m-1}+1}{m-1} - \binom{n_m}{m-1} \\ \vdots & \vdots & & \vdots \\ \binom{n_1+m-1}{1} - \binom{n_2+m-2}{1} & \binom{n_2+m-2}{1} - \binom{n_3+m-3}{1} & \cdots & \binom{n_{m-1}+1}{1} - \binom{n_m}{1} \end{pmatrix},$$

which is the desired answer since $n_m = 0$. The answer can be converted into a Vandermonde determinant by row operations, giving $\Delta(n_1+m-1, n_2+m-2, \ldots, n_m)/ (m-1)! \, (m-2)! \ldots 0!$. [The answer to this exercise, in connection with an equivalent problem in group theory, appears in D. E. Littlewood's *Theory of Group Characters* (Oxford, 1940), 189.]

23. [*Journal de Math.* (3) **7** (1881), 167–184.] (This is a special case of exercise 5.1.3–8, with all runs of length 2 except that the final run might have length 1.) When $n \ge 2$, element n must appear in one of the rightmost positions of a row; once it has been placed in the rightmost box on row k, we have $\binom{n-1}{2k-1} A_{2k-1} A_{n-2k}$ ways to complete the job. Let

$$h(z) = \sum_{n \ge 1} A_{2n-1} z^{2n-1}/(2n-1)! = \tfrac{1}{2}(g(z) - g(-z));$$

then

$$h(z)g(z) = \sum_{k,n \ge 1} \binom{n}{2k-1} A_{2k-1} A_{n-2k+1} z^n/n! = \left(\sum_{n \ge 1} A_{n+1} z^n/n! \right) - 1 = g'(z) - 1.$$

Replace z by $-z$ and add, obtaining $h(z)^2 = h'(z) - 1$; hence $h(z) = \tan z$. Setting $k(z) = g(z) - h(z)$, we have $h(z)\,k(z) = k'(z)$; hence $k(z) = \sec z$ and $g(z) = \sec z + \tan z = \tan(\tfrac{1}{2}z + \tfrac{1}{4}\pi)$. The coefficients A_{2n} are therefore the Euler numbers $|E_{2n}|$; the coefficients A_{2n-1} are the tangent numbers $T_{2n-1} = (-1)^{n-1} 4^n (4^n - 1) B_{2n}/(2n)$. Tables of these numbers appear in *Math. Comp.* **21** (1967), 663–688; the sequence begins $(A_0, A_1, A_2, \ldots) = (1, 1, 1, 2, 5, 16, 61, 272, 1385, 7936, \ldots)$. The easiest way to compute tangent numbers and Euler numbers is probably to form the triangular array

$$
\begin{array}{ccccccc}
& & & 1 & & & \\
& & 0 & & 1 & & \\
& 1 & & 1 & & 0 & \\
0 & & 1 & & 2 & & 2 \\
5 & & 5 & & 4 & & 2 & & 0 \\
\end{array}
$$

$$
\begin{array}{ccccccc}
1 & & & & & & \\
0 & 1 & & & & & \\
1 & 1 & 0 & & & & \\
0 & 1 & 2 & 2 & & & \\
5 & 5 & 4 & 2 & 0 & & \\
0 & 5 & 10 & 14 & 16 & 16 & \\
61 & 61 & 56 & 46 & 32 & 16 & 0 \\
\end{array}
$$

in which partial sums are alternately formed from left to right and right to left [A. J. Kempner, *Tôhoku Math. J.* **37** (1933), 348–349].

25. In general, if u_{nk} is the number of permutations on $\{1, 2, \ldots, n\}$ having no cycles of length $> k$, $\sum u_{nk} z^n/n! = \exp(z + z^2/2 + \cdots + z^k/k)$; this is proved by multiplying $\exp(z) \times \cdots \times \exp(z^k/k)$, obtaining

$$
\sum_n z^n \left(\sum_{j_1 + 2j_2 + \cdots + kj_k = n} 1/1^{j_1} j_1! \, 2^{j_2} j_2! \, \cdots \right);
$$

see also exercise 1.3.3–21. Similarly, $\exp(\sum_{s \in S} z^s/s)$ is the corresponding generating function for permutations whose cycle lengths are all members of a given set S.

26. The integral from 0 to ∞ is $n^{(t+1)/4} \Gamma((t+1)/2)/2^{(t+3)/2}$, by the gamma function integral (exercise 1.2.5–20, $t = 2x^2/\sqrt{n}$). So, from $-\infty$ to ∞, we get 0 when t is odd, otherwise $n^{(t+1)/4} \sqrt{\pi} \, t!/2^{(3t+1)/2} (t/2)!$.

27. (a) If $r_i < r_{i+1}$ and $c_i < c_{i+1}$, the condition $i < Q_{r_i c_{i+1}} < i + 1$ is impossible. If $r_i \geq r_{i+1}$ and $c_i \geq c_{i+1}$, we certainly cannot have $i + 1 \leq Q_{r_i c_{i+1}} \leq i$. (b) Prove, by induction on the number of rows in the tableau for $a_1 \ldots a_i$, that $a_i < a_{i+1}$ implies $c_i < c_{i+1}$, and $a_i > a_{i+1}$ implies $c_i \geq c_{i+1}$. (Consider row 1 and the "bumped" sequences.) (c) This follows from Theorem D(c).

28. This result is due to A. M. Vershik and S. V. Kerov, *Dokl. Akad. Nauk SSSR* **233** (1977), 1024–1028; see also B. F. Logan and L. A. Shepp, *Advances in Math.* **26** (1977), 206–222. [M. Talagrand, *Annals of Probability* **24** (1996), 1–34, Theorem 6.5, has shown that the standard deviation is $O(n^{1/4})$. Numerical computations by A. M. Odlyzko and E. Rains in 1994 suggest that it actually is $\Theta(n^{1/6})$.]

29. $\binom{n}{l}/l!$ is the average number of increasing subsequences of length l. (By exercises 8 and 29, the probability is $O(1/\sqrt{n})$ that the largest increasing sequence has length $\geq e\sqrt{n}$ or $\leq \sqrt{n}/e$. [J. D. Dixon, *Discrete Math.* **12** (1975), 139–142.]

30. [*Discrete Math.* **2** (1972), 73–94; a simplified proof has been given by Marc van Leeuwen, *Electronic J. Combinatorics* **3**, 2 (1996), paper #R15.]

31. $x_n = a_{\lfloor n/2 \rfloor}$ where $a_0 = 1$, $a_1 = 2$, $a_n = 2a_{n-1} + (2n - 2)a_{n-2}$; $\sum a_n z^n/n! = \exp(2z + z^2) = (\sum t_n z^n/n!)^2$; $x_n \approx \exp(\frac{1}{4} n \ln n - \frac{1}{4} n + \sqrt{n} - \frac{1}{2} - \frac{1}{2} \ln 2)$ for n even. [See E. Lucas, *Théorie des Nombres* (1891), 217–223.]

32. Let $m_n = \int_{-\infty}^{\infty} t^n e^{-(t-1)^2/2} dt/\sqrt{2\pi}$. Then $m_0 = m_1 = 1$, and $m_{n+1} - m_n = nm_{n-1}$ if we integrate by parts. So $m_n = t_n$ by (40).

33. True; it is $\det_{i,j=1}^{m} \binom{a_i}{j-1}$. [Mitchell, in *Amer. J. Math.* **4** (1881), 341–344, showed that it is the number of terms in the expansion of a certain symmetric function, now called a Schur function. Indeed, if $0 < a_1 < \cdots < a_m$, it is the number of terms in $S_{n_1 n_2 \ldots n_m}(x_1, x_2, \ldots, x_m)$ where $n_1 = a_m - m$, $n_2 = a_{m-1} - (m-1)$, $\ldots$, $n_m = a_1 - 1$.

This Schur function is the sum over all generalized tableaux of shape $(n_1, \ldots, n_m)$ with elements in $\{1, \ldots, m\}$ of the products of x_j for all j in the tableau, where a generalized tableau is like an ordinary tableau except that equal elements are allowed in the rows. In this definition we allow the parameters n_k to be zero. For example, $S_{210}(x_1, x_2, x_3) = x_1^2 x_2 + x_1^2 x_3 + x_1 x_2^2 + x_1 x_2 x_3 + x_1 x_2 x_3 + x_1 x_3^2 + x_2^2 x_3 + x_2 x_3^2$, because of the generalized tableaux $\frac{11}{2}, \frac{11}{3}, \frac{12}{2}, \frac{12}{3}, \frac{13}{2}, \frac{13}{3}, \frac{22}{3}, \frac{23}{3}$. The number of such tableaux is $\Delta(1, 3, 5)/\Delta(1, 2, 3) = 8$. By extending Algorithms I and D to generalized tableaux [*Pacific J. Math.* **34** (1970), 709–727], we can obtain combinatorial proofs of the remarkable identities

$$\sum_\lambda S_\lambda(x_1, \ldots, x_m) S_\lambda(y_1, \ldots, y_n) = \prod_{i=1}^m \prod_{j=1}^n \frac{1}{1 - x_i y_j},$$

$$\sum_\lambda S_\lambda(x_1, \ldots, x_m) S_{\lambda^T}(y_1, \ldots, y_n) = \prod_{i=1}^m \prod_{j=1}^n (1 + x_i y_j);$$

here the sum is over all possible shapes λ, and λ^T denotes the transposed shape. These identities were first discovered by D. E. Littlewood, *Proc. London Math. Soc.* (2) **40** (1936), 40–70, Theorem V.]

Notes: It follows, for example, that any product of consecutive binomial coefficients $\binom{a}{k}\binom{a+1}{k}\ldots\binom{a+l}{k}$ is divisible by $\binom{k}{k}\binom{k+1}{k}\ldots\binom{k+l}{k}$, since the ratio is $\Delta(a + l, \ldots, a + 1, a, k - 1, \ldots, 1, 0)/\Delta(l, \ldots, 1, 0)$. The value of $\Delta(l, \ldots, 1, 0) = (l - 1)! \ldots 1! \, 0!$ is sometimes called a "superfactorial."

34. The length of a hook is also the length of any zigzag path from the hook's bottom left cell (x, y) to its top right cell (x', y'). We prove a stronger result: If there is a hook of length $a + b$, then there is either a hook of length a or a hook of length b. Consider the cells $(x, y) = (x_1, y_1), (x_2, y_2), \ldots, (x_{a+b}, y_{a+b}) = (x', y')$ that hug the bottom of the shape. If $x_{a+1} = x_a$, the cell (x_a, y_1) has a hook of length a; otherwise (x_{a+1}, y_{a+b}) has a hook of length b. [*Reference: Japanese J. Math.* **17** (1940), 165–184, 411–423. Nakayama was the first to consider hooks in the study of permutation groups, and he came close to discovering Theorem H.]

35. The execution of steps G3–G5 decreases exactly h_{ij} elements of the p array by 1 when q_{ij} is increased, because the algorithm follows a zigzag path from $p_{n'_j j}$ to $p_{i n_i}$. The next execution of those steps either starts with a larger value of j or stays above or equal to the preceding zigzag. Therefore the q array is filled from left to right and bottom to top; to reverse the process we proceed from right to left and top to bottom:

H1. [Initialize.] Set $p_{ij} \leftarrow 0$ for $1 \le j \le n_i$ and $1 \le i \le n'_1$. Then set $i \leftarrow 1$ and $j \leftarrow n_1$.

H2. [Find nonzero cell.] If $q_{ij} > 0$, go on to step H3. Otherwise if $i < n'_j$, increase i by 1 and repeat this step. Otherwise if $j > 1$, decrease j by 1, set $i \leftarrow 1$, and repeat this step. Otherwise stop (the q array is now zero).

H3. [Decrease q, prepare for zigzag.] Decrease q_{ij} by 1 and set $l \leftarrow i$, $k \leftarrow n_i$.

H4. [Move down or left.] If $l < n'_k$ and $p_{lk} > p_{(l+1)k}$, increase l by 1 and return to H4. Otherwise if $k > j$, decrease k by 1 and return to H4. Otherwise return to H2. ∎

The first zigzag path for a given column j ends by incrementing $p_{n'_j j}$, because $p_{1j} \le \cdots \le p_{n'_j j}$ implies that $p_{n'_j j} > 0$. Each subsequent path for column j stays below or equal to the previous one, so it also ends at $p_{n'_j j}$. The inequalities encountered on the way show that this algorithm inverts the other. [*J. Combinatorial Theory* **A21** (1976), 216–221.]

36. (a) The stated coefficient of z^m is the number of solutions to $m = \sum h_{ij} q_{ij}$, so we can apply the result of the previous exercise. (b) If $a_1, \ldots, a_k$ are any positive integers, we can prove by induction on k that

$$[z^m] 1/(1 - z)(1 - z^{a_1}) \ldots (1 - z^{a_k}) = \binom{m}{k}/a_1 \ldots a_k + O(m^{k-1}).$$

The number of partitions of m with at most n parts is therefore $\binom{m}{n-1}/n! + O(m^{n-2})$ for fixed n, by exercise 5.1.1–15. This is also the asymptotic number of partitions $m = p_1 + \cdots + p_n$ with *distinct* parts $p_1 > \cdots > p_n > 0$ (see exercise 5.1.1–16). So the number of reverse plane partitions is asymptotically $N\binom{m}{n-1}/n! + O(m^{n-2})$ when there are N tableaux of a given n-cell shape. By part (a) this is also $\binom{m}{n-1}/\prod h_{ij} + O(m^{n-2})$. [*Studies in Applied Math.* **50** (1971), 167–188, 259–279.]

37. Plane partitions in a rectangle are equivalent to reverse plane partitions, so the hook lengths tell us the generating function $1/\prod_{i=1}^{r} \prod_{j=1}^{c}(1 - z^{i+j-1})$ in an $r \times c$ rectangle. Letting $r, c \to \infty$ yields the elegant answer $1/(1 - z)(1 - z^2)^2(1 - z^3)^3 \ldots$. [MacMahon's original derivation in *Philosophical Transactions* **211** (1912), 75–110, 345–373, was extremely complicated. The first reasonably simple proof was found by Leonard Carlitz, *Acta Arithmetica* **13** (1967), 29–47.]

38. (a) The probability is $1/n$ when $k = l = 1$; otherwise it is

$$\frac{nP(I \setminus \{i_0\}, J) + nP(I, J \setminus \{j_0\})}{n \, d_{i_0 j_0}} = \frac{(d_{i_0 b} + d_{a j_0})/(n \, d_{i_0 b} \ldots d_{i_k - 1 b} \, d_{a j_0} \ldots d_{a j_{l-1}})}{d_{i_0 b} + d_{a j_0}},$$

by induction on $k + l$.

(b) Summing over all I and J gives

$$n^{-1}(1 + d_{1b}^{-1}) \ldots (1 + d_{(a-1)b}^{-1})(1 + d_{a1}^{-1}) \ldots (1 + d_{a(b-1)}^{-1}),$$

which is easily seen to equal $f(T \setminus \{(a, b)\})/f(T)$.

(c) The sum over all corners yields 1, because every path ends at a corner. Therefore $\sum f(T \setminus \{(a, b)\}) = f(T)$, and this proves Theorem H by induction on n. Furthermore, if we put n into the corner cell at the end of the random path and repeat the process on the remaining $n - 1$ cells, we get each tableau with probability $1/f(T)$. [*Advances in Math.* **31** (1979), 104–109.]

39. (a) $Q_{11} \ldots Q_{1n}$ will be $b_1 \ldots b_n$, the inversion table of the original permutations $P_{11} \ldots P_{1n}$. (See Section 5.1.1.)

(b) $Q_{11} \ldots Q_{n1}$ is the negated inversion table $(-C_1) \ldots (-C_n)$ of exercise 5.1.1–7.

(c) This condition is clearly preserved by step P3.

(d) $\left(\begin{smallmatrix} 1 & 4 \\ 2 & 3 \end{smallmatrix} \right) \to \left(\left(\begin{smallmatrix} 1 & 3 \\ 2 & 4 \end{smallmatrix} \right), \left(\begin{smallmatrix} 0 & -1 \\ 0 & 0 \end{smallmatrix} \right) \right)$; $\left(\begin{smallmatrix} 4 & 3 \\ 1 & 2 \end{smallmatrix} \right) \to \left(\left(\begin{smallmatrix} 1 & 2 \\ 3 & 4 \end{smallmatrix} \right), \left(\begin{smallmatrix} 0 & -1 \\ 0 & 0 \end{smallmatrix} \right) \right)$. This example shows that we cannot run step P3 backwards without looking at the array P.

(e)

12	10	8	14	15	11
9	13	7	1		
6	4	5			
16	3				
2					

.

(f) The following algorithm is correct, but not obviously so.

Q1. [Loop on (i,j).] Perform steps Q2 and Q3 for all cells (i,j) of the array in lexicographic order (that is, from top to bottom, and from left to right in each row); then stop.

Q2. [Adjust Q.] Find the "first candidate" (r,s) by the rule below. Then set $Q_{i(k+1)} \leftarrow Q_{ik} - 1$ for $j \le k < s$.

Q3. [Unfix P at (i,j).] Set $K \leftarrow P_{rs}$. Then do the following operations until $(r,s) = (i,j)$: If $P_{(r-1)s} > P_{r(s-1)}$, set $P_{rs} \leftarrow P_{(r-1)s}$ and $r \leftarrow r-1$; otherwise set $P_{rs} \leftarrow P_{r(s-1)}$ and $s \leftarrow s - 1$. Finally set $P_{ij} \leftarrow K$. ∎

In step Q2, cell (r,s) is a *candidate* when $s \ge j$ and $Q_{is} \le 0$ and $r = i - Q_{is}$. Let T be the oriented tree of the hint. One of the basic invariants of Algorithm Q is that there will be a path from (r,s) to (i,j) in T whenever (r,s) is a candidate in step Q2. The reverse of that path can be encoded by a sequence of letters D, Q, and R, meaning that we start at (i,j), then go down (D) or to the right (R) or quit (Q). The *first candidate* is the one whose code is lexicographically first in alphabetic order; intuitively, it is the candidate with the "leftmost and bottommost" path.

For example, the candidates when $(i,j) = (1,1)$ in the example of part (e) are $(3,1)$, $(4,2)$, $(2,3)$, $(2,4)$, and $(1,6)$. Their respective codes are DDQ, DDDRQ, RDRQ, RDRRQ, and RRRRRQ; so the first is $(4,2)$.

Algorithm P is a slightly simplified version of a construction stated without proof in *Funkts. Analiz i Ego Priloz.* **26**, 3 (1992), 80–82. The proof of correctness is nontrivial; a proof was given by J.-C. Novelli, I. Pak, and A. V. Stoyanovskii in *Disc. Math. and Theoretical Comp. Sci.* **1** (1997), 53–67.

40. An equivalent process was analyzed by H. Rost, *Zeitschrift für Wahrscheinlich-keitstheorie und verwandte Gebiete* **58** (1981), 41–53.

41. (Solution by R. W. Floyd.) A deletion-insertion operation essentially moves only a_i. In a sequence of such operations, unmoved elements retain their relative order. Therefore if π can be sorted with k deletion-insertions, it has an increasing subsequence of length $n - k$; and conversely. Hence $\mathrm{dis}(\pi) = n -$ (length of longest increasing subsequence of π) $= n +$ (length of row 1 in Theorem A).

M. L. Fredman has proved that the minimum number of comparisons needed to compute this length is $n \lg n - n \lg \lg n + O(n)$ [*Discrete Math.* **11** (1975), 29–35].

42. Construct a multigraph that has vertices $\{0_R, 1_L, 1_R, \ldots, n_L, n_R, (n+1)_L\}$ and edges k_R — $(k+1)_L$ for $0 \le k \le n$; also include the edges 0_R — 7_R, 7_L — 1_L, 1_R — 2_L, 2_R — 4_L, 4_R — 5_L, 5_R — 3_L, 3_R — 6_R, 6_L — 8_L, which define the "bonds" of *Lobelia fervens*. Exactly two edges touch each vertex, so the connected components are cycles: $(0_R 1_L 7_L 6_R 3_R 4_L 2_R 3_L 5_R 6_L 8_L 7_R)(1_R 2_L)(4_R 5_L)$. Any flip operation changes the number of cycles by -1, 0, or $+1$. Therefore we need at least five flips to reach the eight cycles $(0_R 1_L)(1_R 2_L) \ldots (7_R 8_L)$. [J. Kececioglu and D. Sankoff, *Lecture Notes in Comp. Sci.* **807** (1994), 307–325.]

The first flip must break the bond 6_L — 8_L, because we get no new cycle when we break two bonds that have the same left-to-right orientation in the linear arrangement. This leaves five possibilities after one flip, namely $g_7^R g_6 g_3^R g_5^R g_4^R g_2^R g_1^R$, $g_7^R g_1 g_2 g_4 g_5 g_3 g_6$, $g_7^R g_1 g_2 g_6 g_3^R g_5^R g_4^R$, $g_7^R g_1 g_2 g_4 g_5 g_6 g_3^R$, and $g_6 g_3^R g_5^R g_4^R g_2^R g_1^R g_7$; four more flips suffice to sort all but the second of these.

Incidentally, there are $2^7 \cdot 7! = 645120$ different possible arrangements of $g_1 \ldots g_7$, and 179904 of them are at distance ≤ 5 from tobacco order.

[An efficient algorithm to find the best way to sort any signed permutation by reversals was developed by S. Hannenhalli and P. Pevzner, *STOC* **27** (1995), 178–189, and improved to run in $O(n^2)$ time by Kaplan, Shamir, and Tarjan, *SODA* **8** (1997), 344–351.]

43. Denote an arrangement like $g_7^R g_1 g_2 g_4 g_5 g_3 g_6^R$ by the signed permutation $\overline{7}12453\overline{6}$. If there is a negated element, say $\overline{k}$ is present but not $\overline{k-1}$, one flip will create the 2-cycle $((k-1)_R k_L)$. Similarly, if $\overline{k}$ is present but not $\overline{k+1}$, a single flip creates $(k_R (k+1)_L)$. And if all flips of that special kind remove all negated elements, a single flip creates two 2-cycles. If no negated elements are present and the permutation isn't sorted, some flip will preserve the number of cycles. Hence we can sort in $\le n$ flips if the given permutation has a negated element, $\le n+1$ otherwise.

When n is even, the permutation $n(n-1)\dots 1$ requires $n+1$ flips, because it has one cycle after the first flip. When $n > 3$ is odd, the permutation $213n(n-1)\dots 4$ requires $n+1$ by a similar argument.

44. Let c_k be the number of cycles of length $2k$ in the multigraph of the previous answers. An upper bound on the average value of c_k can be found as follows: The total number of potential $2k$-cycles is $2^k(n+1)^{\underline{k}}/(2k)$, because we can choose a sequence of k distinct edges from $\{0_R - 1_L, \dots, n_R - (n+1)_L\}$ in $(n+1)^{\underline{k}}$ ways and orient them in 2^k ways; this counts each cycle $2k$ times, including impossible cases like $(1_R 2_L 2_R 3_L)$ or $(1_R 2_L 3_L 2_R 3_R 4_L)$ or $(1_R 2_L 6_R 7_L 4_L 3_R 2_R 3_L 6_L 5_R)$. When $k \le n$, every possible $2k$-cycle occurs in exactly $2^{n-k}(n-k)!$ signed permutations. For example, consider the case $k = 5$, $n = 9$, and the cycle $(0_R 1_L 9_L 8_R 7_R 8_L 1_R 2_L 5_L 4_R)$. This cycle occurs in the multigraph if and only if the signed permutation begins with $\overline{4}$ and contains the substrings $\overline{9}18\overline{7}$ and $\overline{2}5$ or their reverses; we obtain all solutions by finding all signed permutations of $\{1, 2, 3, 6\}$ and replacing 1 by $\overline{9}18\overline{7}$, 2 by $\overline{2}5$. Therefore $\mathrm{E}\,c_k \le 1/(2k)\,2^k(n+1)^{\underline{k}}2^{n-k}(n-k)!/2^n n! = \frac{1}{2}(1/k + 1/(n+1-k))$. It follows that $\mathrm{E}\,c = \sum_{k=1}^{n}\mathrm{E}\,c_k + \mathrm{E}\,c_{n+1} < H_n + 1$. Since $n+1-c$ is a lower bound on the number of flips, we need $\ge n+1 - \mathrm{E}\,c > n - H_n$ of them.

[This proof uses ideas of V. Bafna and P. Pevzner, *SICOMP* **25** (1996), 272–289, who studied the more difficult problem of sorting *unsigned* permutations by reversals. In that problem, an interesting permutation that can be written as the product of non-disjoint cycles $(1\,2\,3)(3\,4\,5)(5\,6\,7)\dots$, ending with either $(n-1\,n)$ or $(n-2\,n-1\,n)$ depending on whether n is even or odd, turns out to be the hardest to sort.]

SECTION 5.2

1. Yes; i and j may run through the set of values $1 \le j < i \le N$ in any order, possibly in parallel and/or as records are being read in.

2. The sorting is *stable* in the sense defined at the beginning of this chapter, because the algorithm is essentially sorting by lexicographic order on the *distinct* key-pairs $(K_1, 1), (K_2, 2), \dots, (K_N, N)$. (If we think of each key as extended on the right by its location in the file, no equal keys are present, and the sorting is stable.)

3. It would sort, but not in a stable manner; if $K_j = K_i$ and $j < i$, R_j will come *after* R_i in the final ordering. This change would also make Program C run more slowly.

4.

ENT1	N	1	STA	OUTPUT+1,2	N	
LD2	COUNT,1	N	DEC1	1	N	
LDA	INPUT,1	N	J1P	*-4	N	∎

5. The running time is decreased by $A + 1 - N - B$ units, and this is almost always an improvement.

6. $u = 0$, $v = 9$.

After D1,	COUNT =	0	0	0	0	0	0	0	0	0	0
After D2,	COUNT =	2	2	1	0	1	3	3	2	1	1
After D4,	COUNT =	2	4	5	5	6	9	12	14	15	16
During D5,	COUNT =	2	3	5	5	5	8	9	12	15	16

$j = 8$

OUTPUT = -- -- -- 1G -- 4A -- -- 5L 6A 6T 6I 7O 7N -- --

After D5, OUTPUT = 0C 0O 1N 1G 2R 4A 5T 5U 5L 6A 6T 6I 7O 7N 8S 9.

7. Yes; note that COUNT$[K_j]$ is decreased in step D6, and j decreases.

8. It would sort, but not in a stable manner (see exercise 7).

9. Let $M = v - u$; assume that $|u|$ and $|v|$ fit in two bytes. LOC$(R_j) \equiv$ INPUT$+ j$; LOC(COUNT$[j]$) $\equiv$ COUNT$+ j$; LOC$(S_j) \equiv$ OUTPUT$+ j$; rI1 $\equiv i$; rI2 $\equiv j$; rI3 $\equiv i - v$ or rI3 $\equiv K_j$.

M	EQU	V-U		
KEY	EQU	0:2		(Satellite information is in bytes 3:5)
1H	ENN3	M	1	*D1. Clear COUNTs.*
	STZ	COUNT+V,3	$M+1$	COUNT$[v-k] \leftarrow 0$.
	INC3	1	$M+1$	
	J3NP	*-2	$M+1$	$u \leq i \leq v$.
2H	ENT2	N	1	*D2. Loop on j.*
3H	LD3	INPUT,2(KEY)	N	*D3. Increase COUNT$[K_j]$.*
	LDA	COUNT,3	N	
	INCA	1	N	
	STA	COUNT,3	N	
	DEC2	1	N	
	J2P	3B	N	$N \geq j > 0$.
	ENN3	M-1	1	*D4. Accumulate.*
	LDA	COUNT+U	1	rA $\leftarrow$ COUNT$[i-1]$.
4H	ADD	COUNT+V,3	M	COUNT$[i-1] +$ COUNT$[i]$
	STA	COUNT+V,3	M	$\rightarrow$ COUNT$[i]$.
	INC3	1	M	
	J3NP	4B	M	$u \leq i \leq v$.
5H	ENT2	N	1	*D5. Loop on j.*
6H	LD3	INPUT,2(KEY)	N	*D6. Output R_j.*
	LD1	COUNT,3	N	$i \leftarrow$ COUNT$[K_j]$.
	LDA	INPUT,2	N	rA $\leftarrow R_j$.
	STA	OUTPUT,1	N	$S_i \leftarrow$ rA.
	DEC1	1	N	
	ST1	COUNT,3	N	COUNT$[K_j] \leftarrow i - 1$.
	DEC2	1	N	
	J2P	6B	N	$N \geq j > 0$. ∎

The running time is $(10M + 22N + 10)u$.

10. In order to avoid using N extra "tag" bits [see Section 1.3.3 and *Cybernetics* **1** (1965), 95], yet keep the running time essentially proportional to N, we may use the following algorithm based on the cycle structure of the permutation:

P1. [Loop on i.] Do step P2 for $1 \leq i \leq N$; then terminate the algorithm.

P2. [Is $p(i) = i$?] Do steps P3 through P5, if $p(i) \neq i$.

P3. [Begin cycle.] Set $t \leftarrow R_i$, $j \leftarrow i$.

P4. [Fix R_j.] Set $k \leftarrow p(j)$, $R_j \leftarrow R_k$, $p(j) \leftarrow j$, $j \leftarrow k$. If $p(j) \neq i$, repeat this step.

P5. [End cycle.] Set $R_j \leftarrow t$, $p(j) \leftarrow j$. ∎

This algorithm changes $p(i)$, since the sorting application lets us assume that $p(i)$ is stored in memory. On the other hand, there are applications such as matrix transposition where $p(i)$ is a function of i that is to be computed (not tabulated) in order to save memory space. In such a case we can use the following method, performing steps B1 through B3 for $1 \leq i \leq N$.

B1. Set $k \leftarrow p(i)$.

B2. If $k > i$, set $k \leftarrow p(k)$ and repeat this step.

B3. If $k < i$, do nothing; but if $k = i$ (this means that i is smallest in its cycle), we permute the cycle containing i as follows: Set $t \leftarrow R_i$; then while $p(k) \neq i$ repeatedly set $R_k \leftarrow R_{p(k)}$ and $k \leftarrow p(k)$; finally set $R_k \leftarrow t$. ∎

This algorithm is similar to the procedure of J. Boothroyd [*Comp. J.* **10** (1967), 310], but it requires less data movement; some refinements have been suggested by I. D. G. MacLeod [*Australian Comp. J.* **2** (1970), 16–19]. For random permutations the analysis in exercise 1.3.3–14 shows that step B2 is performed $(N+1)H_N - N$ steps on the average. See also the references in the answer to exercise 1.3.3–12. Similar algorithms can be designed to replace $(R_{p(1)}, \ldots, R_{p(N)})$ by $(R_1, \ldots, R_N)$, for example if the rearrangement in exercise 4 were to be done with OUTPUT = INPUT.

11. Let $rI1 \equiv i$; $rI2 \equiv j$; $rI3 \equiv k$; $rX \equiv t$.

1H	ENT1 N	1	*P1. Loop on i.*
2H	CMP1 P,1	N	*P2. Is $p(i) = i$?*
	JE 8F	N	Jump if $p(i) = i$.
3H	LDX INPUT,1	$A - B$	*P3. Begin cycle.* $t \leftarrow R_i$.
	ENT2 0,1	$A - B$	$j \leftarrow i$.
4H	LD3 P,2	$N - A$	*P4. Fix R_j.* $k \leftarrow p(j)$.
	LDA INPUT,3	$N - A$	
	STA INPUT,2	$N - A$	$R_j \leftarrow R_k$.
	ST2 P,2	$N - A$	$p(j) \leftarrow j$.
	ENT2 0,3	$N - A$	$j \leftarrow k$.
	CMP1 P,2	$N - A$	
	JNE 4B	$N - A$	Repeat if $p(j) \neq i$.
5H	STX INPUT,2	$A - B$	*P5. End cycle.* $R_j \leftarrow t$.
	ST2 P,2	$A - B$	$p(j) \leftarrow j$.
8H	DEC1 1	N	
	J1P 2B	N	$N \geq i \geq 1$. ∎

The running time is $(17N - 5A - 7B + 1)u$, where A is the number of cycles in the permutation $p(1) \ldots p(N)$ and B is the number of fixed points (1-cycles). We have

$$A = \left(\min 1, \text{ ave } H_N, \max N, \text{ dev } \sqrt{H_N - H_N^{(2)}}\right) \text{ and } B = \left(\min 0, \text{ ave } 1, \max N, \text{ dev } 1\right),$$

for $N \geq 2$, by Eqs. 1.3.3–(21) and 1.3.3–(28).

12. The obvious way is to run through the list, replacing the link of the kth element by the number k, and then to rearrange the elements in a second pass. The following more direct method, due to M. D. MacLaren, is shorter and faster if the records are not too long. (Assume for convenience that $0 \le \text{LINK(P)} \le N$, for $1 \le \text{P} \le N$, where $\Lambda \equiv 0$.)

M1. [Initialize.] Set P ← HEAD, $k \leftarrow 1$.

M2. [Done?] If P = Λ (or equivalently if $k = N + 1$), the algorithm terminates.

M3. [Ensure P ≥ k.] If P < k, set P ← LINK(P) and repeat this step.

M4. [Exchange.] Interchange R_k and R[P]. (Assume that LINK(k) and LINK(P) are also interchanged in this process.) Then set Q ← LINK(k), LINK(k) ← P, P ← Q, $k \leftarrow k + 1$, and return to step M2. ∎

A proof that MacLaren's method is valid can be based on an inductive verification of the following property that holds at the beginning of step M2: The entries that are $\ge k$ in the sequence P, LINK(P), LINK(LINK(P)), ..., Λ are $a_1, a_2, \ldots, a_{N+1-k}$, where $R_1 \le \cdots \le R_{k-1} \le R_{a_1} \le \cdots \le R_{a_{N+1-k}}$ is the desired final order of the records. Furthermore LINK(j) $\ge j$ for $1 \le j < k$, so that LINK(j) = Λ implies $j \ge k$.

It is quite interesting to analyze MacLaren's algorithm; one of its remarkable properties is that it can be run backwards, reconstructing the original set of links from the final values of LINK(1) ... LINK(N). Each of the $N!$ possible output configurations with $j \le \text{LINK}(j) \le N$ corresponds to exactly one of the $N!$ possible input configurations. If A is the number of times P ← LINK(P) in step M3, then $N - A$ is the number of j such that LINK(j) = j at the conclusion of the algorithm; this occurs if and only if j was largest in its cycle; hence $N - A$ is the number of cycles in the permutation, and $A = (\min 0, \text{ave } N - H_N, \max N-1)$.

References: M. D. MacLaren, *JACM* **13** (1966), 404–411; D. Gries and J. F. Prins, *Science of Computer Programming* **8** (1987), 139–145.

13. **D5'.** Set $r \leftarrow N$.

D6'. If $r = 0$, stop. Otherwise, if COUNT[K_r] < r set $r \leftarrow r - 1$ and repeat this step; if COUNT[K_r] = r, decrease both COUNT[K_r] and r by 1 and repeat this step. Otherwise set $R \leftarrow R_r$, $j \leftarrow$ COUNT[K_r], COUNT[K_r] ← $j - 1$.

D7'. Set $S \leftarrow R_j$, $k \leftarrow$ COUNT[K_j], COUNT[K_j] ← $k - 1$, $R_j \leftarrow R$, $R \leftarrow S$, $j \leftarrow k$. Then if $j \ne r$ repeat this step; if $j = r$ set $R_j \leftarrow R$, $r \leftarrow r - 1$, and go back to D6'. ∎

To prove that this procedure is valid, observe that at the beginning of step D6' all records R_j such that $j > r$ that are not in their final resting place must move to the left; when $r = 0$ there can't be any such records since *somebody* must move right. The algorithm is elegant but not stable for equal keys. It is intimately related to Foata's construction in Theorem 5.1.2B.

SECTION 5.2.1

1. Yes; equal elements are never moved across each other.

2. Yes. But the running time would be slower when equal elements are present, and the sorting would be just the opposite of stable.

3. The following eight-liner is conjectured to be the shortest MIX sorting routine, although it is not recommended for speed. We assume that the numbers appear in locations $1, \ldots, N$ (that is, INPUT EQU 0); otherwise another line of code is necessary.

```
2H       LDA   0,1    B
         CMPA  1,1    B
         JLE   1F     B
         MOVE  1,1    A
         STA   0,1    A
START    ENT1  N      A + 1
1H       DEC1  1      B + 1
         J1P   2B     B + 1    ▌
```

Note: To estimate the running time of this program, note that A is the number of inversions. The quantity B is a reasonably simple function of the inversion table, and (assuming distinct inputs in random order) it has the generating function

$$z^{N-1}(1 + z)(1 + z^2 + z^{2+1})$$
$$\times (1 + z^3 + z^{3+2} + z^{3+2+1}) \ldots (1 + z^{N-1} + z^{2N-3} + \cdots + z^{N(N-1)/2})/N!.$$

The mean value of B is $N - 1 + \sum_{k=1}^{N}(k-1)(2k-1)/6 = (N-1)(4N^2 + N + 36)/36$; hence the average running time of this program is roughly $\frac{7}{9}N^3 u$.

4. Consider the inversion table $B_1 \ldots B_N$ of the given input permutation, in the sense of exercise 5.1.1–7. Then A is one less than the number of B_j's that are equal to $j - 1$, and B is the sum of the B_j's. Hence both $B - A$ and B are maximized when the input permutation is $N \ldots 2\ 1$; they both are minimized when the input is $1\ 2 \ldots N$. The minimum achievable time therefore occurs for $A = 0$ and $B = 0$, namely $(10N - 9)u$; the maximum occurs for $A = N - 1$ and $B = \binom{N}{2}$, namely $(4.5N^2 + 2.5N - 6)u$.

5. The generating function is z^{10N-9} times the generating function for $9B - 3A$. By considering the inversion table as in the previous exercise, remembering that individual entries of the inversion table are independent of each other, the desired generating function is $z^{10N-9} \prod_{1<j\leq N}((1 + z^9 + \cdots + z^{9j-18} + z^{9j-12})/j)$. The variance comes to $2.25N^3 + 3.375N^2 - 32.625N + 36H_N - 9H_N^{(2)}$.

6. Treat the input area as a circular list, with position N adjacent to position 1. Take new elements to be inserted from either the left or the right of the current segment of unsorted elements, according as the previously inserted element fell to the right or left of the center of the sorted elements, respectively. Afterwards it will usually be necessary to "rotate" the area, moving each record k places around the circle for some fixed k; this can be done efficiently as in exercise 1.3.3–34.

7. The average value of $|a_j - j|$ is

$$\frac{1}{n}(|1 - j| + |2 - j| + \cdots + |n - j|) = \frac{1}{n}\left(\binom{j}{2} + \binom{n-j+1}{2}\right);$$

summing on j gives $\frac{1}{n}\left(\binom{n+1}{3} + \binom{n+1}{3}\right) = \frac{1}{3}(n^2 - 1)$.

8. No; for example, consider the keys 2 1 1 1 1 1 1 1 1 1 1.

9. For Table 3, $A = 3 + 0 + 2 + 1 = 6$, $B = 3 + 1 + 4 + 21 = 29$; in Table 4, $A = 4 + 2 + 2 + 0 = 8$, $B = 4 + 3 + 8 + 10 = 25$; hence the running time of Program D comes to $786u$ and $734u$, respectively. Although the number of moves has been cut from 41 to 25, the running time is not competitive with Program S since the bookkeeping time for four passes is wasted when $N = 16$. When sorting 16 items we will be better off using only two passes; a two-pass Program D begins to beat Program S at about $N = 13$, although they are fairly equal for awhile (and for such small N the length of the program is perhaps significant).

10. Insert "INC1 INPUT; ST1 3F(0:2)" between lines 07 and 08, and change lines 10–17 to:

```
3H CMPA INPUT+N-H,1     NT - S
   JGE  8F               NT - S
4H ENT2 N-H,1            NT - S - C
5H LDX  INPUT,2             B
6H STX  INPUT+H,2           B
   DEC2 0,4                 B
   J2NP 7F                  B
   CMPA INPUT,2           B - A
   JL   5B                B - A
7H STA  INPUT+H,2        NT - S - C
```

For a net increase of four instructions, this saves $3(C - T)$ units of time, where C is the number of times $K_j \geq K_{j-h}$. In Tables 3 and 4 the time savings is approximately 87 and 88, respectively; empirically the value of $C/(NT - S)$ seems to be about 0.4 when $h_{s+1}/h_s \approx 2$ and about 0.3 when $h_{s+1}/h_s \approx 3$, so the improvement is worth while. (On the other hand, the analogous change to Program S is not desirable, since the savings in that case is only proportional to $\log N$ unless the input is known to be pretty well ordered.)

11.

12. Changing ⌐ to ⌐ always changes the number of inversions by ± 1, depending on whether the change is above or below the diagonal.

13. Put the weight $|i - j|$ on the segment from $(i, j-1)$ to (i, j).

14. (a) Interchange i and j in the sum for A_{2n} and add the two sums. (b) Taking half of this result, we see that

$$A_{2n} = \sum_{0 \leq i \leq j} (j - i) \binom{i+j}{i} \binom{2n - i - j}{n - j} = \sum_{i, k \geq 0} k \binom{2i + k}{i} \binom{2n - 2i - k}{n - i - k};$$

hence $\sum A_{2n} z^n = \sum_{k \geq 0} k z^k \alpha^{2k}/(1 - 4z) = z/(1 - 4z)^2$, where $\alpha = (1 - \sqrt{1 - 4z})/2z$.

The proof above was suggested to the author by Leonard Carlitz. Another proof can be based on interplay between horizontal and vertical weights (see exercise 13), and still another by the identity in the answer to exercise 5.2.2–16 with $f(k) = k$; but no simple combinatorial derivation of the formula $A_n = \lfloor n/2 \rfloor 2^{n-2}$ is apparent.

15. For $n > 0$,

$$\hat{g}_n(z) = z^n g_{n-1}; \qquad\qquad \hat{h}_n(z) = \hat{g}_n(z) + z^{-n} \hat{g}_n(z);$$

$$g_n(z) = \sum_{k=1}^{n} \hat{g}_k(z) g_{n-k}(z); \quad h_n(z) = \sum_{k=1}^{n} \hat{h}_k(z) h_{n-k}(z).$$

Letting $G(w, z) = \sum_n g_n(z) w^n$, we find that $wzG(w, z)G(wz, z) = G(w, z) - 1$. From this representation we can deduce that, if $t = \sqrt{1 - 4w} = 1 - 2w - 2w^2 - 4w^3 - \cdots$, we have $G(w, 1) = (1 - t)/(2w)$; $G_{\prime}(w, 1) = 1/(wt) - (1 - t)/(2w^2)$; $G'(w, 1) = 1/(2t^2) - 1/(2t)$; $G_{\prime\prime}(w, 1) = 2/(wt^3) - 2/(w^2t) + (1 - t)/w^3$; $G'_{\prime}(w, 1) = 2/t^4 - 1/t^3$; and

$G''(w, 1) = 1/t^3 - (1 - 2w)/t^4 + 10w^2/t^5$. Here lower primes denote differentiation with respect to the first parameter, and upper primes denote differentiation with respect to the second parameter. Similarly, from the formula

$$w(zG(wz, z) + G(w, z))H(w, z) = H(w, z) - 1$$

we deduce that

$$H'(w, 1) = w/t^4, \qquad H''(w, 1) = -w/t^3 - w/t^4 + 2w/t^5 + (2w^2 + 20w^3)/t^7.$$

The formula manipulation summarized here was originally done by hand, but today it can readily be done by computer. In principle all moments of the distribution are obtainable in this way.

The generating function $g_n(z)$ also represents $\sum z^{\text{internal path length}}$ over all trees with $n + 1$ nodes; see exercise 2.3.4.5–5. It is interesting to note that $G(w, z)$ is equal to $F(-wz, z)/F(-w, z)$, where $F(z, q) = \sum_{n \geq 0} z^n q^{n^2}/\prod_{k=1}^{n}(1 - q^k)$; the coefficient of $q^m z^n$ in $F(z, q)$ is the number of partitions $m = p_1 + \cdots + p_n$ such that $p_j \geq p_{j+1} + 2$ for $1 \leq j < n$ and $p_n > 0$ (see exercise 5.1.1–16).

16. For $h = 2$ the maximum clearly occurs for the path that goes through the upper right corner of the lattice diagram, namely

$$\binom{\lfloor n/2 \rfloor + 1}{2}.$$

For general h the corresponding number is

$$\hat{f}(n, h) = \binom{h}{2}\binom{q + 1}{2} + \binom{r}{2}(q + 1),$$

where q and r are defined in Theorem H; the permutation with

$$a_{i+jh} = 1 + q(h - i) + (r - i)[i \leq r] \qquad \text{for } 1 \leq i \leq h \text{ and } j \geq 0$$

maximizes the number of inversions between each of the $\binom{h}{2}$ pairs of sorted subsequences. The maximum number of moves is obtained if we replace f by $\hat{f}$ in (6).

17. The only two-ordered permutation of $\{1, 2, \ldots, 2n\}$ that has as many as $\binom{n+1}{2}$ inversions is $n+1\ 1\ n+2\ 2\ \ldots\ 2n\ n$. Using this idea recursively, we obtain the permutation defined by adding unity to each element of the sequence $(2^t - 1)^R \ldots 1^R 0^R$, where R denotes the operation of writing an integer as a t-bit binary number, then reversing the left-to-right order of the bits.(!)

18. Take out a common factor and let $h_t = 4N/\pi$; we want to minimize the sum $\sum_{s=1}^{t} h_s^{1/2}/h_{s-1}$, when $h_0 = 1$. Differentiation yields $h_s^3 = 4h_{s-1}^2 h_{s+1}$, and we find $(2^t - 1) \lg h_1 = 2^{t+1} - 2(t+1) + \lg h_t$. The minimum value of the stated estimate comes to $(1 - 2^{-t})\pi^{(2^{t-1}-1)/(2^t-1)}N^{1+2^{t-1}/(2^t-1)}/2^{1+(t-1)/(2^t-1)}$, which rapidly approaches the limiting value $N\sqrt{\pi N}/2$ as $t \to \infty$.

Typical examples of "optimum" h's when $N = 1000$ (see also Table 6) are:

$$h_2 \approx 57.64, \qquad h_1 \approx 6.13, \qquad h_0 = 1;$$

$$h_3 \approx 135.30, \qquad h_2 \approx 22.05, \qquad h_1 \approx 4.45, \qquad h_0 = 1;$$

$$h_4 \approx 284.46, \qquad h_3 \approx 67.23, \qquad h_2 \approx 16.34, \qquad h_1 \approx 4.03, \qquad h_0 = 1;$$

$$h_9 \approx 9164.74, \quad h_8 \approx 12294.05, \quad h_7 \approx 7119.55, \quad h_6 \approx 2708.95, \quad h_5 \approx 835.50,$$
$$h_4 \approx 232.00, \quad h_3 \approx 61.13, \quad h_2 \approx 15.69, \quad h_1 \approx 3.97, \quad h_0 = 1.$$

19. Let $g(n, h) = H_r - 1 + \sum_{r < j \leq h} q/(qj + r)$, where q and r are defined in Theorem H; then replace f by g in (6).

20. (This is much harder to write down than to understand.) Assume that a k-ordered file $R_1, \ldots, R_N$ has been h-sorted, and let $1 \leq i \leq N - k$; we want to show that $K_i \leq K_{i+k}$. Find u, v such that $i \equiv u$ and $i + k \equiv v$ (modulo h), $1 \leq u, v \leq h$; and apply Lemma L with $x_j = K_{v+(j-1)h}$, $y_j = K_{u+(j-1)h}$. Then the first r elements K_u, K_{u+h}, $\ldots$, $K_{u+(r-1)h}$ of the y's are respectively $\leq$ the last r elements K_{u+k}, K_{u+k+h}, $\ldots$, $K_{u+k+(r-1)h}$ of the x's, where r is the greatest integer such that $u + k + (r - 1)h \leq N$.

21. If $xh + yk = x'h + y'k$, we have $(x - x')h = (y' - y)k$, so $x' = x + tk$ and $y' = y - th$ for some integer t. Let $h'h + k'k = 1$; then $n = (nh')h + (nk')k$, so every integer n has a unique representation of the form $n = xh + yk$ where $0 \leq x < k$, and n is generable if and only if $y \geq 0$. Let, similarly, $hk - h - k - n = x'h + y'k$; then $(x + x')h + (y + y')k = hk - h - k$. Hence $x + x' \equiv k - 1$ (modulo k) and we must have $x + x' = k - 1$. Hence $y + y' = -1$, and $y \geq 0$ if and only if $y' < 0$.

The symmetry of this result shows that exactly $\frac{1}{2}(h-1)(k-1)$ positive integers are unrepresentable in the stated form, a result originally due to Sylvester [*Mathematical Questions, with their Solutions, from the 'Educational Times'* **41** (1884), 21].

22. To avoid cumbersome notation, consider $s = 4$, which is representative of the general case. Let n_k be the smallest number that is congruent to k (modulo 15) and representable in the form $15a_0 + 31a_1 + \cdots$; then we find easily that

$$
\begin{array}{rccccccccccccccc}
k = & 0 & 1 & 2 & 3 & 4 & 5 & 6 & 7 & 8 & 9 & 10 & 11 & 12 & 13 & 14 \\
n_k = & 0 & 31 & 62 & 63 & 94 & 125 & 126 & 127 & 158 & 189 & 190 & 221 & 252 & 253 & 254.
\end{array}
$$

Hence $239 = 2^4(2^4 - 1) - 1$ is the largest unrepresentable number, and the total number of unrepresentables is

$$
\begin{aligned}
x_4 &= (n_1 - 1 + n_2 - 2 + \cdots + n_{14} - 14)/15 \\
&= (2 + 4 + 4 + 6 + 8 + 8) + 8 + (10 + 12 + 12 + 14 + 16 + 16) + 16 \\
&= 2x_3 + 8 \cdot 9;
\end{aligned}
$$

in general, $x_s = 2x_{s-1} + 2^{s-1}(2^{s-1} + 1)$.

For the other problem the answers are $2^{2s} + 2^s + 2$ and $2^{s-1}(2^s + s - 1) + 2$, respectively.

23. Each of the N numbers has at most $\lceil (h_{s+2} - 1)(h_{s+1} - 1)/h_s \rceil$ inversions in its subfile.

24. (Solution obtained jointly with V. Pratt.) Construct the "h-recidivous permutation" of $\{1, 2, \ldots, N\}$ as follows. Start with $a_1 \ldots a_N$ blank; then for $j = 2, 3, 4, \ldots$ do Step j: Fill in all blank positions a_i from left to right, using the smallest number that has not yet appeared in the permutation, whenever $(2^h - 1)j - i$ is a positive integer representable as in exercise 22. Continue until all positions are filled. Thus the 2-recidivous permutation for $N = 20$ is

$$6 \; 2 \; 1 \; 9 \; 4 \; 3 \; 12 \; 7 \; 5 \; 15 \; 10 \; 8 \; 17 \; 13 \; 11 \; 19 \; 16 \; 14 \; 20 \; 18.$$

The h-recidivous permutation is $(2^k - 1)$-ordered for all $k \geq h$. When $2^h < j \leq N/(2^h - 1)$, exactly $2^h - 1$ positions are filled during step j; the $(k+1)$st of them adds at least $2^{h-1} - 2k$ to the number of moves required to $(2^{h-1} - 1)$-sort the permutation. Hence the number of moves to sort the h-recidivous permutation with increments $h_s = 2^s - 1$ when $N = 2^{h+1}(2^h - 1)$ is $> 2^{3h-4} > \frac{1}{64}N^{3/2}$. Pratt generalized this construction to a large family of similar sequences, including (12), in his Ph.D. thesis (Stanford University, 1972). Heuristics that find permutations needing even more moves are discussed by H. Erkiö, *BIT* **20** (1980), 130–136. See also Weiss and Sedgewick, *J. Algorithms* **11** (1990), 242–251, for improvements on Pratt's construction.

25. F_{N+1} [this result is due to H. B. Mann, *Econometrica* **13** (1945), 256]; for the permutation must begin with either 1 or 2 1. There are at most $\lfloor N/2 \rfloor$ inversions; and the total number of inversions is

$$\frac{N-1}{5} F_N + \frac{2N}{5} F_{N-1}.$$

(See exercise 1.2.8–12.) Note that the F_{N+1} permutations can conveniently be represented by "Morse code" sequences of dots and dashes, where a dash corresponds to an inversion; see exercise 4.5.3–32. Hence we have found the total number of dashes among all Morse code sequences of length N.

Our derivation shows that a random 3- and 2-ordered permutation has roughly $\frac{1}{5}(\phi^{-1} + 2\phi^{-2})N = \phi^{-1}N/\sqrt{5} \approx .276N$ inversions. But if a random permutation is 3-sorted, then 2-sorted, exercise 42 shows that it has $\approx N/4$ inversions; if it is 2-sorted, then 3-sorted, it has $\approx N/3$.

26. Yes; a shortest example is 4 1 3 7 2 6 8 5, which has nine inversions. In general, the construction $a_{3k+s} = 3k + 4s$ for $-1 \le s \le 1$ yields files that are 3-, 5-, and 7-ordered, having approximately $\frac{4}{3}N$ inversions. When $N \bmod 3 = 2$ this construction is best possible.

27. (a) See *J. Algorithms* **15** (1993), 101–124. A simpler proof, which shows that c can be any constant $< \frac{1}{2}$, was found independently by C. G. Plaxton and T. Suel, *J. Algorithms* **23** (1997), 221–240. (b) This is obvious if $m > \frac{1}{4}c^2(\ln N/\ln\ln N)^2$. Otherwise $N^{1+c/\sqrt{m}} \ge N(\ln N)^2$. R. E. Cypher [*SICOMP* **22** (1993), 62–71] has proved the slightly stronger bound $\Omega(N(\log N)^2/\log\log N)$ when the increments satisfy $h_{s+1} > h_s$ for all s and when a sorting network is constructed as in exercise 5.3.4–2. No nontrivial lower bounds are yet known for the asymptotic *average* running time.

28. 209 109 41 19 5 1, from (11). But better sequences are possible; see exercise 29.

29. Experiments by C. Tribolet in 1971 resulted in the choices 373 137 53 19 7 3 1 ($B_{ave} \approx 7210$) and 317 101 31 11 3 1 ($B_{ave} \approx 8170$). [The first of these yields a sorting time of $\approx 127720u$, compared to $\approx 128593u$ when the same data are sorted using increments (11).] In general Tribolet suggests letting h_s be the nearest prime number to $N^{s/t}$. Experiments by Shelby Siegel in 1972 indicate that the best number of increments in such a method, for $N \le 10000$, is $t \approx \frac{4}{3}\ln(N/5.75)$.

Another good sequence, found by Robert L. Tomlinson, Jr., is 199 79 31 11 5 1 ($B_{ave} \approx 7950$). Its average running time, $\approx 127260u$, is the best known so far.

The best three-increment sequence, according to extensive tests by Carole M. McNamee, appears to be 45 7 1 ($B_{ave} \approx 18240$). For four increments, 91 23 7 1 was the winner in her tests ($B_{ave} \approx 11865$), but a rather broad range of increments gave roughly the same performance.

30. The number of integer points in the triangular region

$$\{x \ln 2 + y \ln 3 < \ln N, \ x \ge 0, \ y \ge 0\} \qquad \text{is} \qquad \tfrac{1}{2}(\log_2 N)(\log_3 N) + O(\log N).$$

While we are h-sorting, the file is already $2h$-ordered and $3h$-ordered, by Theorem K; hence exercise 25 applies.

31.

01	START	ENT3	T	1
02	1H	LD4	H,3	T
03		ENN2	-INPUT-N,4	T
04		ST2	6F(0:2)	T
05		ST2	7F(0:2)	T
06		ST2	4F(0:2)	T
07		ENT2	0,4	T
08		JMP	9F	T
09	2H	LDA	INPUT+N,1	$NT - S - B + A$
10	4H	CMPA	INPUT+N-H,1	$NT - S - B + A$
11		JGE	8F	$NT - S - B + A$
12	6H	LDX	INPUT+N-H,1	B
13		STX	INPUT+N,1	B
14	7H	STA	INPUT+N-H,1	B
15		INC1	0,4	B
16	8H	INC1	0,4	$NT - B + A$
17		J1NP	2B	$NT - B + A$
18		DEC2	1	S
19	9H	ENT1	-N,2	$T + S$
20		J2P	8B	$T + S$
21		DEC3	1	T
22		J3P	1B	T ∎

Here A is related to right-to-left maxima in the same way that A in Program D is the related to left-to-right minima; both quantities have the same statistical behavior. The simplifications in the inner loop have cut the running time to $7NT + 7A - 2S + 1 + 15T$ units, curiously independent of B!

When $N = 8$ the increments are 6, 4, 3, 2, 1, and we have $A_{\text{ave}} = 3.892$, $B_{\text{ave}} = 6.762$; the average total running time is $276.24u$. (Compare with Table 5.) Both A and B are maximized in the permutation 7 3 8 4 5 1 6 2. When $N = 1000$ there are 40 increments, $972, 864, 768, 729, \ldots, 8, 6, 4, 3, 2, 1$; empirical tests like those in Table 6 give $A \approx 875$, $B \approx 4250$, and a total time of about $268000u$ (more than twice as long as Program D with the increments of exercise 28).

Instead of storing the increments in an auxiliary table, it is convenient to generate them as follows on a binary machine:

P1. Set $m \leftarrow 2^{\lceil \lg N \rceil - 1}$, the largest power of 2 less than N.

P2. Set $h \leftarrow m$.

P3. Use h as the increment for one sorting pass.

P4. If h is even, set $h \leftarrow h + h/2$; then if $h < N$, return to P3.

P5. Set $m \leftarrow \lfloor m/2 \rfloor$ and if $m \geq 1$ return to P2. ∎

Although the increments are not being generated in descending order, the order specified here is sufficient to make the sorting algorithm valid.

32. 4 12 11 13 2 0 8 5 10 14 1 6 3 9 16 7 15.

33. Two types of improvements can be made. First, by assuming that the artificial key K_0 is ∞, we can omit testing whether or not $p > 0$. (This idea has been used, for example, in Algorithm 2.2.4A.) Secondly, a standard optimization technique: We can make two copies of the inner loop with the register assignments for p and q interchanged; this avoids the assignment $q \leftarrow p$. (This idea has been used in exercise 1.1–3.)

Thus we assume that location INPUT contains the largest possible value in its $(0:3)$ field, and we replace lines 07 and following of Program L by:

07	8H	LD3	INPUT,2(LINK)	B'	$p \leftarrow L_q$. (Here $p \equiv$ rI3, $q \equiv$ rI2.)
08		CMPA	INPUT,3(KEY)	B'	
09		JG	4F	B'	To L4 with $q \leftrightarrow p$ if $K > K_p$.
10	7H	ST1	INPUT,2(LINK)	N'	$L_q \leftarrow j$.
11		ST3	INPUT,1(LINK)	N'	$L_j \leftarrow p$.
12		JMP	6F	N'	Go to decrease j.
13	4H	LD2	INPUT,3(LINK)	B''	$p \leftarrow L_q$. (Here $p \equiv$ rI2, $q \equiv$ rI3.)
14		CMPA	INPUT,2(KEY)	B''	
15		JG	8B	B''	To L4 with $q \leftrightarrow p$ if $K > K_p$.
16	5H	ST1	INPUT,3(LINK)	N''	$L_q \leftarrow j$.
17		ST2	INPUT,1(LINK)	N''	$L_j \leftarrow p$.
18	6H	DEC1	1	N	$j \leftarrow j - 1$.
19		ENT3	0	N	$q \leftarrow 0$.
20		LDA	INPUT,1	N	$K \leftarrow K_j$.
21		J1P	4B	N	$N > j \geq 1$. ∎

Here $B' + B'' = B + N - 1$, $N' + N'' = N - 1$, so the total running time is $5B + 14N + N' - 3$ units. Since N' is the number of elements with an odd number of lesser elements to their right, it has the statistics

$$\left(\text{min } 0, \text{ ave } \tfrac{1}{2}N + \tfrac{1}{4}H_{\lfloor N/2 \rfloor} - \tfrac{1}{2}H_N, \text{ max } N - 1\right).$$

The ∞ trick also speeds up Program S; the following code suggested by J. H. Halperin uses this idea and the MOVE instruction to reduce the running time to $(6B + 11N - 10)u$, assuming that location INPUT+N+1 already contains the largest possible one-word value:

01	START	ENT2	N-1	1
02	2H	LDA	INPUT,2	$N - 1$
03		ENT1	INPUT,2	$N - 1$
04		JMP	3F	$N - 1$
05	4H	MOVE	1,1(1)	B
06	3H	CMPA	1,1	$B + N - 1$
07		JG	4B	$B + N - 1$
08	5H	STA	0,1	$N - 1$
09		DEC2	1	$N - 1$
10		J2P	2B	$N - 1$

Doubling up the inner loop would save an additional $B/2$ or so units of time.

34. There are $\binom{N}{n}$ sequences of N choices in which the given list is chosen n times; every such sequence has probability $(1/M)^n (1 - 1/M)^{N-n}$ of occurring, since the given list is chosen with probability $1/M$.

35.

24		ENT1	0	1	29		ENT1	0,3	N
25		ENT2	1-M	1	30		LD3	INPUT,1(LINK)	N
26	7H	LD3	HEAD+M,2	M	31		J3P	*-2	N
27		J3Z	8F	M	32	8H	INC2	1	M
28		ST3	INPUT,1(LINK)	$M - E$	33		J2NP	7B	M

Note: If Program M were modified to keep track of the current end of each list, by inserting "ST1 END,4" between lines 19 and 20, we could save time by hooking the lists together as in Algorithm 5.2.5H.

36. Program L: $A = 3$, $B = 41$, $N = 16$, time $= 496u$. Program M: $A = 2 + 1 + 1 + 3 = 7$, $B = 2+0+3+3 = 8$, $N = 16$, time $= 549u$. (We should also add the time needed by exercise 35, $94u$, in order to make a strictly fair comparison. The multiplications are slow!) Notice also that the improved Program L in exercise 33 takes only $358u$.)

37. The stated identity is equivalent to

$$g_{NM}(z) = M^{-N} \sum_{n_1 + \cdots + n_M = N} \left(\frac{N!}{n_1! \ldots n_M!} \right) g_{n_1}(z) \ldots g_{n_M}(z),$$

which is proved as in exercise 34. It may be of interest to tabulate some of these generating functions, to indicate the trend for increasing M:

$$g_{41}(z) = (216 + 648z + 1080z^2 + 1296z^3 + 1080z^4 + 648z^5 + 216z^6)/5184,$$
$$g_{42}(z) = (945 + 1917z + 1485z^2 + 594z^3 + 135z^4 + 81z^5 + 27z^6)/5184,$$
$$g_{43}(z) = (1704 + 2264z + 840z^2 + 304z^3 + 40z^4 + 24z^5 + 8z^6)/5184.$$

If $G_M(w, z)$ is the stated double generating function, differentiation by z gives

$$G'_M(w, z) = M \left(\sum_{n \geq 0} g_n(z) \frac{w^n}{n!} \right)^{M-1} \sum_{n \geq 0} g'_n(z) \frac{w^n}{n!},$$

hence

$$\sum_{N \geq 0} g'_{MN}(1) \frac{M^N w^N}{N!} = M e^{(M-1)w} \left(\frac{w^2}{4} e^w \right) = \frac{M}{4} w^2 e^{Mw};$$

similarly, the formula $g''_n(1) = \frac{3}{2} \binom{n}{4} + \frac{5}{3} \binom{n}{3}$ yields

$$\sum_{N \geq 0} g''_{MN}(1) \frac{M^N w^N}{N!} = M(M-1) e^{(M-2)w} \left(\frac{w^2}{4} e^w \right)^2 + M e^{(M-1)w} \left(\frac{3}{2} w^4 + \frac{5}{3} w^3 \right) e^w.$$

Equating coefficients of w^N gives $g'_{NM}(1) = \frac{1}{2} \binom{N}{2} M^{-1}$, $g''_{NM}(1) = \left(\frac{3}{2} \binom{N}{4} + \frac{5}{3} \binom{N}{3} \right) M^{-2}$, and the variance is $\left(\frac{1}{6} \binom{N}{3} + \frac{2M-1}{4} \binom{N}{2} \right) M^{-2}$.

38. $\sum_{j,n} \binom{N}{n} p_j^n (1 - p_j)^{N-n} \binom{n}{2} = \binom{N}{2} \sum_j p_j^2$; setting $p_j = F(j/M) - F((j-1)/M)$, and $F'(x) = f(x)$, this converges to $\binom{N}{2}/M$ times $\int_0^1 f(x)^2 \, dx$ when F is reasonably well behaved. [However, $\int_0^1 f(x)^2 \, dx$ might be quite large. See Theorem 5.2.5T for a refinement that applies to *all* bounded integrable densities.]

39. To minimize $AC/M + BM$ we need $M = \sqrt{AC/B}$, so M is one of the integers just above or below this quantity. (In the case of Program M we would choose M proportional to N.)

40. The asymptotic series for

$$\sum_{n > N} n^{-1}(1 - \alpha/N)^{n-N} = -N^{-1} + \sum_{k \geq 0} (N + k)^{-1}(1 - \alpha/N)^k$$

can be obtained by restricting k to $O(N^{1+\epsilon})$, expanding $(1 - \alpha/N)^k$ as $e^{-\alpha k/N}$ times $(1 - k\alpha^2/2N^2 + \cdots)$, and using Euler's summation formula; it begins with the terms $e^\alpha E_1(\alpha)(1 + \alpha^2/2N) - (1 + \alpha)/2N + O(N^{-2})$. Hence the asymptotic value of $(\mathbf{15})$ is

$N\big(\ln\alpha+\gamma+E_1(\alpha)\big)/\alpha+\big(1-e^{-\alpha}(1+\alpha)\big)/2\alpha+O(N^{-1})$. [The coefficient of N is ≈ 0.7966, 0.6596, 0.2880, respectively, for $\alpha=1,2,10$.] Note that we have $\ln\alpha+\gamma+E_1(\alpha)=\int_0^\alpha(1-e^{-t})t^{-1}\,dt$, by exercise 5.2.2–43.

41. We have $a_k=O(\rho^k)$, because the prime number theorem implies that the number of primes between ρ^k and ρ^{k+1} is $\rho^{k+1}/(k+1)-\rho^k/k+O(\rho^k/k^2)$; this is positive for all sufficiently large k. Therefore the sum of the first $\binom{k}{2}$ elements of (10) is $\sum_{1\le i<j\le k}b(a_i,a_j)=\sum_{1\le i<j\le k}O(\rho^{i+j})$; and we have

$$\sum_{1\le i<j\le k}\rho^{i+j}=\frac{\rho^3(\rho^k-1)(\rho^{k-1}-1)}{(\rho^2-1)(\rho-1)}.$$

(b) If $\binom{k-1}{2}<\log_\rho N\le\binom{k}{2}$ we have $(k-1)^2<2\log_\rho N$, hence $\rho^{2k}=O(\exp c\sqrt{\ln N}\,)$.

Notice that as $\rho\to1$, the base sequence $a_1,a_2,\dots$ becomes equal to the sequence of prime numbers, and the bound in Theorem I reduces to $O\big(N(\log N)^4(\log\log N)^{-3}\big)$.

42. (a) [A. C. Yao, *J. Algorithms* **1** (1980), 14–50.] We can show that each of the $\binom{h}{2}$ pairs of lists contributes $\frac{\sqrt{\pi}}{4}g^{-2}h^{-3/2}N^{3/2}+O(N/gh)$ inversions to each subfile $(K_a,K_{a+g},K_{a+2g},\dots)$, $1\le a\le g$. For example, suppose $h=12$, $g=5$, $a=1$, and consider inversions where the lists $K_3<K_{15}<K_{27}<\cdots$ and $K_7<K_{19}<K_{31}<\cdots$ intersect the subfile $(K_1,K_6,K_{11},\dots)$. After the first pass, $(K_3,K_7,K_{15},K_{19},K_{27},K_{31},\dots)$ is a random 2-ordered permutation. The elements K_j of concern to us have $j\equiv1$ (modulo 5) and $j\equiv3$ or 7 (modulo 12); hence $j\equiv51$ or 31 (modulo 60), and we want to compute the average value of $g(51,31)$ where

$$g(x,y)=\sum_{j<k}\big([K_{x+ghj}>K_{y+ghk}]+[K_{y+ghj}>K_{x+ghk}]\big)+r(x,y),$$

$$r(x,y)=\sum_j[K_{\min(x,y)+ghj}>K_{\max(x,y)+ghj}]<N/gh.$$

If $|p|\le g$ and $|q|\le g$ we have

$$[K_{j+ph-gh}>K_{k+qh+gh}]\le[K_j>K_k]\le[K_{j+ph+gh}>K_{k+qh-gh}];$$

hence

$$[K_{x+ghj}>K_{y+ghk}]+[K_{y+ghj}>K_{x+ghk}]$$
$$\le[K_{x+ph+gh(j+1)}>K_{y+qh+gh(k-1)}]+[K_{y+qh+gh(j+1)}>K_{x+ph+gh(k-1)}]$$

and it follows that $g(x,y)\le g(x+ph,y+qh)+8N/gh$. Similarly we find $g(x,y)\ge g(x+ph,y+qh)-8N/gh$. But the sum of $g(x,y)$ over all g^2 pairs (x,y) such that $x\bmod h=b$ and $y\bmod h=c$, for any given $b\ne c$, is the total number of inversions in a random 2-ordered permutation of $2N/h$ elements. Therefore by exercise 14, the average value of $g(x,y)$ is $g^{-2}\sqrt{\pi/128}\,(2N/h)^{3/2}+O(N/gh)$.

(b) See S. Janson and D. E. Knuth, *Random Structures and Algs.* **10** (1997), 125–142. When h and g are large we have $\psi(h,g)=\sqrt{\pi h/128}\,g+O(g^{-1/2}h^{1/2})+O(gh^{-1/2})$.

43. If $K<K_l$ after step D3, set $(K_l,\dots,K_{j-h},K_j)\leftarrow(K,K_l,\dots,K_{j-h})$; otherwise do steps D4 and D5 until $K\ge K_i$. Here $l=1$ when $j=h+1$, and $l\leftarrow l+1-h\,[l=h]$ when j increases by 1. [See H. W. Thimbleby, *Software Practice & Exper.* **19** (1989), 303–307.]

Another idea for speeding up the program [see W. Dobosiewicz, *Inf. Proc. Letters* **11** (1980), 5–6] is to sort only partially when $h > 1$, not attempting to propagate K_j further left than position $j - h$; but that approach seems to require more increments.

44. (a) Yes. This is clear whenever π' is one step above π, and exercise 5.1.1–29 shows that there is a path of adjacent transpositions from π to any permutation above it.

(b) Yes. Similarly, if π is above π', π^R is below π'^R.

(c) No; $2\,1\,3$ is neither above nor below $3\,1\,2$, but $2\,1\,3 \le 3\,1\,2$.

[The partial ordering $\pi \le \pi'$ was first discussed by C. Ehresmann, *Annals of Math.* (2) **35** (1934), 396–443, §20, in the context of algebraic topology. Many mathematicians now call it the "Bruhat order" of permutations, while aboveness is called the "weak Bruhat order" — although aboveness is actually a stronger condition, because it holds less often. Only the weak order defines a lattice.]

SECTION 5.2.2

1. No; it has $2m+1$ *fewer* inversions, where $m \ge 0$ is the number of elements a_k such that $i < k < j$ and $a_i > a_k > a_j$. (Hence *all* exchange-sorting methods will eventually converge to a sorted permutation.)

2. (a) 6. (b) [A. Cayley, *Philos. Mag.* **34** (1849), 527–529.] Consider the cycle representation of π. Any exchange of elements in the *same* cycle increases the number of cycles by 1; any exchange of elements in *different* cycles decreases the number by 1. (This is essentially the content of exercise 2.2.4–3.) A completely sorted permutation is characterized by having n cycles. Hence $\mathrm{xch}(\pi)$ is n minus the number of cycles in π. (Algorithm 5.2.3S does exactly $\mathrm{xch}(\pi)$ exchanges; see exercise 5.2.3–4.)

3. Yes; equal elements are never moved across each other.

4. It is the probability that $b_1 > \max(b_2, \dots, b_n)$ in the inversion table, namely

$$\left(\sum_{1 \le k < n} k!\, k^{n-k-1} \right) \Big/ n! = \sqrt{\pi/2n} + O(n^{-1}) = \text{negligible}.$$

5. We may assume that $r > 0$. Let $b'_i = (b_i - r + 1)[b_i \ge r]$ be the inversion table after $r - 1$ passes. If $b'_i > 0$, element i is preceded by b'_i larger elements, the largest of which will bubble up at least to position $b'_i + i$, because there are i elements $\le i$. Furthermore if element j is the rightmost to be exchanged, we have $b'_j > 0$ and $\mathtt{BOUND} = b'_j + j - 1$ after the rth pass.

6. *Solution 1:* An element displaced farthest to the right of its final position moves one step left on each pass except the last. *Solution 2* (higher level): By exercise 5.1.1–8, answer (f), $a'_i - i = b_i - c_i$, for $1 \le i \le n$, where $c_1 c_2 \dots c_n$ is the dual inversion table. If $b_j = \max(b_1, \dots, b_n)$ then $c_j = 0$.

7. $(2(n+1)(1 + P(n) - P(n+1)) - P(n) - P(n)^2)^{1/2} = \sqrt{(2 - \pi/2)n} + O(1)$.

8. For $i < k + 2$ there are $j + k - i + 1$ choices for b_i; for $k + 2 \le i < n - j + 2$ there are $j - 1$ choices; and for $i \ge n - j + 2$ there are $n - i + 1$.

10. (a) If $i = 2k-1$, from $(k-1, a_i - k)$ to $(k, a_i - k)$. If $i = 2k$, from $(a_i - k, k-1)$ to $(a_i - k, k)$. (b) Step a_{2k-1} is above the diagonal $\iff k \le a_{2k-1} - k \iff a_{2k-1} \ge 2k \iff a_{2k-1} > a_{2k} \iff a_{2k} \le 2k - 1 \iff a_{2k} - k \le k - 1 \iff$ step a_{2k} is above the diagonal. Exchanging them interchanges horizontal and vertical steps. (c) Step a_{2k+d} is at least m below the diagonal $\iff k + m - 1 \ge a_{2k+d} - (k + m) + m \iff a_{2k+d} < 2k + m \iff a_{2k} \ge 2k + m \iff a_{2k} - k \ge k + m \iff$ step a_{2k} is at least m

below the diagonal. (If $a_{2k+d} < 2k+m$ and $a_{2k} < 2k+m$, there are at least $(k+m)+k$ elements less than $2k+m$; that's impossible. If $a_{2k+d} \geq 2k+m$ and $a_{2k} \geq 2k+m$, one of the $\geq$ must be $>$; but we can't fit all of the elements $\leq 2k+m$ into fewer than $(k+m)+k$ positions. Hence $a_{2k+2m-1} < a_{2k}$ if and only if $a_{2k+2m-1} < 2k+m$ if and only if $2k+m \leq a_{2k}$. A rather unexpected result!)

11. 16 10 13 5 14 6 9 2 15 8 11 3 12 4 7 1 (61 exchanges), by considering the lattice diagram. The situation becomes more complicated when N is larger; in general, the set $\{K_2, K_4, \dots\}$ should be $\{1, 2, \dots, M-1, M, M+2, M+4, \dots, 2\lfloor N/2 \rfloor - M\}$, permuted so as to maximize the exchanges for $\lfloor N/2 \rfloor$ elements. Here $M = \lceil 2^k/3 \rceil$, where k maximizes $k\lfloor N/2 \rfloor - \frac{1}{9}((3k-2)2^{k-1} + (-1)^k)$. The maximum total number of exchanges is $1 - 2 \lg \lg N / \lg N + O(1/\log N)$ times the number of comparisons [R. Sedgewick, *SICOMP* **7** (1978), 239–272].

12. The following program by W. Panny avoids the AND instruction by noting that step M4 is performed for $i = r + 2kp + s$, $k \geq 0$, and $0 \leq s < p$. Here TT $\equiv 2^{t-1}$, $p \equiv$ rI1, $r \equiv$ rI2, $i \equiv$ rI3, $i+d-N \equiv$ rI4, and $p-1-s \equiv$ rI5; we assume that $N \geq 2$.

```
01  START  ENT1  TT              1      M1. Initialize p. p ← 2^(t-1).
02  2H     ENT2  TT              T      M2. Initialize q, r, d.
03         ST2   Q(1:2)          T      q ← 2^(t-1).
04         ENT2  0               T      r ← 0.
05         ENT4  0,1             T      rI4 ← d.
05  3H     ENT3  0,2             A      M3. Loop on i. i ← r.
07         INC4  -N,3            A      rI4 ← i + d - N.
08  8H     ENT5  -1,1            D+E    s ← 0.
09  4H     LDA   INPUT+1,3       C      M4. Compare/exchange R_{i+1}:R_{i+d+1}.
10         CMPA  INPUT+N+1,4     C
11         JLE   *+4             C      Jump if K_{i+1} ≤ K_{i+d+1}.
12         LDX   INPUT+N+1,4     B
13         STX   INPUT+1,3       B      R_{i+1} ↔ R_{i+d+1}.
14         STA   INPUT+N+1,4     B
15         J5Z   7F              C      Jump if s = p - 1.
16         DEC5  1               C-D    s ← s + 1.
17         INC3  1               C-D    i ← i + 1.
18         INC4  1               C-D
19         J4N   4B              C-D    Repeat loop if i + d < N.
20         JMP   5F              E      Otherwise go to M5.
21  7H     INC3  1,1             D      i ← i + p + 1.
22         INC4  1,1             D
23         J4N   4B              D      Repeat loop if i + d < N.
24  5H     ENT2  0,1             A      M5. Loop on q. r ← p.
25  Q      ENT4  *               A      rI4 ← q.
26         ENTA  0,4             A
27         SRB   1               A
28         STA   Q(1:2)          A      q ← q/2.
29         DEC4  0,1             A      rI4 ← d.
30         J4P   3B              A      To M3 if d ≠ 0.
31  6H     ENTA  0,1             T      M6. Loop on p.
32         SRB   1               T
33         STA   *+1(1:2)        T
```

| 34 | ENT1 * | T | $p \leftarrow \lfloor p/2 \rfloor$. |
| 35 | J1NZ 2B | T | To M2 if $p \neq 0$. |

The running time depends on six quantities, only one of which depends on the input data (the remaining five are functions of N alone): $T = t$, the number of "major cycles"; $A = t(t+1)/2$, the number of passes or "minor cycles"; B = the (variable) number of exchanges; C = the number of comparisons; D = the number of blocks of consecutive comparisons; and E = the number of incomplete blocks. When $N = 2^t$, it is not difficult to prove that $D = (t-2)N + t + 2$ and $E = 0$. For Table 1, we have $T = 4$, $A = 10$, $B = 3+0+1+4+0+0+8+0+4+5 = 25$, $C = 63$, $D = 38$, $E = 0$, so the total running time is $11A + 6B + 10C + 2E + 12T + 1 = 939u$.

In general when $N = 2^{e_1} + \cdots + 2^{e_r}$, Panny has shown that $D = e_1(N+1) - 2(2^{e_1}-1)$, $E = \binom{e_1-e_r}{2} + (e_1 + e_2 + \cdots + e_{r-1}) - (e_1-1)(r-1)$.

13. No, nor are Algorithms Q or R.

14. (a) When $p = 1$ we do $(2^{t-1} - 0) + (2^{t-1} - 1) + (2^{t-1} - 2) + (2^{t-1} - 4) + \cdots + (2^{t-1} - 2^{t-2}) = (t-1)2^{t-1} + 1$ comparisons for the final merge. (b) $x_t = x_{t-1} + \frac{1}{2}(t-1) + 2^{-t} = \cdots = x_0 + \sum_{0 \leq k < t}(\frac{1}{2}k + 2^{-k-1}) = \frac{1}{2}\binom{t}{2} + 1 - 2^{-t}$. Hence $c(2^t) = 2^{t-2}(t^2 - t + 4) - 1$.

15. (a) Consider the number of comparisons such that $i + d = N$; then use induction on r. (b) If $b(n) = c(n+1)$, we have $b(2n) = a(1) + \cdots + a(2n) = a(0) + a(1) + a(1) + \cdots + a(n-1) + a(n) + x(1) + x(2) + \cdots + x(2n) = 2b(n) + y(2n) - a(n)$; similarly $b(2n+1) = 2b(n) + y(2n+1)$. (c) See exercise 1.2.4–42. (d) A rather laborious calculation of $\big(z(N) + 2z(\lfloor N/2 \rfloor) + \cdots \big) - a(N)$, using formulas such as

$$\sum_{k=0}^{n} 2^k(n-k) = 2^{n+1} - n - 2, \qquad \sum_{k=0}^{n} 2^k \binom{n-k}{2} = 2^{n+1} - \binom{n+2}{2} - 1,$$

leads to the result

$$c(N) = N\left(\frac{1}{2}\binom{e_1}{2} + 2e_1 - 1\right) - 2^{e_1}(e_1 - 1) - 1$$
$$+ \sum_{j=1}^{r} 2^{e_j}\left(e_1 + \cdots + e_{j-1} - j(e_1 - 1) + \frac{1}{2}\binom{e_1 - e_j}{2}\right).$$

16. Consider the $\binom{2n}{n}$ lattice paths from $(0,0)$ to (n,n) as in Figs. 11 and 18, and attach weight $f(i-j)$ if $i \geq j$, $f(j-i-1) + 1$ if $i < j$, to the line from (i,j) to $(i+1,j)$; here $f(k)$ is the number of bit variations $b_r \neq b_{r+1}$ in the binary expansion $k = (\ldots b_2 b_1 b_0)_2$. The total number of exchanges on the final merge when $N = 2n$ is then $\sum_{0 \leq j \leq i < n}(2f(j)+1)\binom{2i-j}{i-j}\binom{2n-2i+j-1}{n-i-1}$. R. Sedgewick showed that this sum simplifies, for general f, to $\frac{n}{2}\binom{2n}{n} + 2\sum_{k \geq 1}\binom{2n}{n-k}\sum_{0 \leq j < k} f(j)$; then he used the gamma function method to obtain the asymptotic formula

$$\binom{2n}{n}\left(\frac{1}{4}n \lg n + \left(\lg \frac{\Gamma(1/4)^2}{2\pi} + \frac{1}{4} + \frac{\gamma + 2}{4 \ln 2} + \delta(n)\right)n + O(\sqrt{n}\log n)\right),$$

where $\delta(n)$ is a periodic function of $\lg n$ with magnitude bounded by .0005. Hence about $1/4$ of the comparisons lead to exchanges, on the average, as $n \to \infty$. [*SICOMP* **7** (1978), 239–272; see also Flajolet and Odlyzko, *SIAM J. Discrete Math.* **3** (1990), 238–239.]

17. K_{N+1} is inspected when we are sorting a subfile with $r = N$ and K_l the largest key. K_0 is inspected during step Q9 if left-to-right minima sink to position R_1.

18. Steps Q3 and Q4 make only a single change to i and j before exiting to Q5; the partitioning process for $R_l \ldots R_r$ ends with $j = \lceil (l+r)/2 \rceil$ in step Q7, bisecting the subfile as perfectly as possible. Quantitatively speaking, we replace (17) by $A = 1$, $B = \lfloor (N-1)/2 \rfloor$, $C = N + (N \bmod 2)$; this puts us essentially in the *best* case of the algorithm (see exercise 27), except that $B \approx \frac{1}{2}C$. If the "<" signs in steps Q3 and Q4 are changed to "≤," the algorithm won't sort any more; even if we assume "<" signs in (13), it will interchange R_0 with R_1, then the third partitioning phase will move the original R_0 to position R_2, etc. — a real catastrophe.

19. Yes, the other subfiles may be processed in any order. But the queue will contain $\Omega(N/\sqrt{\log N})$ items when each partitioning step divides the file equally, while a stack is guaranteed to stay much smaller than this (see the next exercise).

20. $\max(0, \lfloor \lg(N+2)/(M+2) \rfloor)$. (The worst case occurs when $N = 2^k(M+2)-1$ and all subfiles are perfectly bisected when they are partitioned.)

21. Exactly t records move to the area $R_{s+1} \ldots R_N$ in step Q6, hence $B = t$. The partitioning phase ends with $j = s$, hence $C - C' = N+1-s$ is the number of times j decreases. We must also have $i = s+1$ in step Q7 when the keys are distinct, since $i = j$ implies $K_j = K$; thus $C' = s$.

22. The stated relations for $A_N(z)$ follow because $A_{s-1}(z)A_{N-s}(z)$ is the generating function for the value of A after independently sorting randomly and independently ordered files of sizes $s-1$ and $N-s$. Similarly, we obtain the relations

$$B_N(z) = \sum_{s=1}^{N} \sum_{t=0}^{s} b_{stN}\, z^t\, B_{s-1}(z)\,B_{N-s}(z),$$

$$C_N(z) = \frac{1}{N} \sum_{s=1}^{N} z^{N+1} C_{s-1}(z)\,C_{N-s}(z),$$

$$D_N(z) = \frac{1}{N} \sum_{s=1}^{N} D_{s-1}(z)\,D_{N-s}(z),$$

$$E_N(z) = \frac{1}{N} \sum_{s=1}^{N} E_{s-1}(z)\,E_{N-s}(z),$$

$$S_N(z) = \frac{1}{N} \sum_{s=1}^{N} z^{[M+1<s<N-M]} S_{s-1}(z)\,S_{N-s}(z),$$

for $N > M$. Here b_{stN} is the probability that s and t have given values in a file of length N, namely

$$\binom{s-1}{t}\binom{N-s}{t} \Big/ N\binom{N-1}{s-1},$$

which is $(1/N!)$ times the $(s-1)!$ ways to permute $\{1, \ldots, s-1\}$ times the $(N-s)!$ ways to permute $\{s+1, \ldots, N\}$ times the $\binom{s-1}{t}\binom{N-s}{t}$ patterns with t displaced elements on each side. For $0 \le N \le M$, we have $B_N(z) = C_N(z) = S_N(z) = 1$; $D_N(z) = \prod_{k=1}^{N}((1+(k-1)z)/k)$; and $E_N(z) = \prod_{k=1}^{N}((1+z+\cdots+z^{k-1})/k)$.

[It is interesting to consider the behavior of these generating functions when N is large; a sequence analogous to $C_N(z)$, but with z^{N+1} replaced by z^{N-1}, is known to converge to a non-normal probability distribution that has not yet been fully analyzed.

See the articles by P. Hennequin, M. Regnier, and U. Rösler in *RAIRO Theoretical Informatics and Applications* **23** (1989), 317–333; **23** (1989), 335–343; **25** (1991), 85–100.]

23. When $N > M$, $A_N = 1 + (2/N)\sum_{0 \le k < N} A_k$; $B_N = \sum_{0 \le t < s \le N} b_{stN}(t + B_{s-1} + B_{N-s}) = (1/N)\sum_{s=1}^{N}((s-1)(N-s)/(N-1) + B_{s-1} + B_{N-s}) = (N-2)/6 + (2/N)\sum_{0 \le k < N} B_k$ [see exercise 22]; $D_N = (2/N)\sum_{0 \le k < N} D_k$; E_N is similar. When $N > 2M + 1$, $S_N = (2/N)\sum_{0 \le k < N} S_k + (N - 2M - 2)/N$. Each of these recurrences has the form (20) for some function f_n.

24. The recurrence $C_N = N - 1 + (2/N)\sum_{0 \le k < N} C_k$, for $N > M$, has the solution $(N+1)(2H_{N+1} - 2H_{M+2} + 1 - 4/(M+2) + 2/(N+1))$, for $N > M$. (So we could save about $4N/M$ comparisons. But each comparison takes longer if it must be followed by a test of i versus j, so we lose, unless the cost of a key comparison exceeds $\frac{1}{2}M \ln N$ times the cost of a register comparison. Many texts on sorting fail to realize that such an "improvement" makes quicksort significantly less quick!)

25. (Use (17) repeatedly with $s = 1$.) $A = N - M$, $B = 0$, $C = \binom{N+2}{2} - \binom{M+2}{2}$, $D = E = S = 0$.

26. Actually you can't do worse than to sort

$$1\ 2\ 3\ \ldots\ N{-}M\ N\ N{-}1\ \ldots\ N{-}M{+}1;$$

the subtler answer $N\ M{-}1\ M{-}2\ \ldots\ 1\ M\ M{+}1\ \ldots\ N{-}1$ is an equally bad case. This is only a little worse than exercise 25, because it makes $D = M - 1$, $E = \binom{M}{2}$.

27. 12 2 3 1 8 6 7 5 9 10 11 4 16 14 15 13 20 18 19 17 21 22 23, which requires $546u$. It can be shown that the best case for $N = 3(M+1)2^k - 1$ occurs when the subfiles are bisected by each partitioning until reaching size $3M + 2$; then a trisection is performed to avoid stack-pushing overhead. We have $A = 3 \cdot 2^k - 1$, $C = (k + \frac{5}{3})(N + 1)$, $S = 2^k - 1$, $B = D = E = 0$. (The behavior of the best case for general M and N makes an interesting but complex pattern.)

28. The recurrence

$$C_n = n + 1 + \frac{2}{\binom{n}{3}} \sum_{k=1}^{n} (k-1)(n-k)C_{k-1}$$

can be transformed into

$$\binom{n}{3}C_n - 2\binom{n-1}{3}C_{n-1} + \binom{n-2}{3}C_{n-2} = 2(n-1)(n-2) + 2(n-2)C_{n-2}.$$

29. In general, consider the recurrence

$$C_n = n + 1 + \frac{2}{\binom{n}{2t+1}} \sum_{k=1}^{n} \binom{k-1}{t}\binom{n-k}{t} C_{k-1},$$

which arises when the median of $2t + 1$ elements governs the partitioning. Letting $C(z) = \sum_n C_n z^n$, the recurrence can be transformed to $(1-z)^{t+1}C^{(2t+1)}(z)/(2t+2)! = 1/(1-z)^{t+2} + C^{(t)}(z)/(t+1)!$. Let $f(x) = C^{(t)}(1-x)$; then $p_t(\vartheta)f(x) = (2t+2)!/x^{t+2}$, where ϑ denotes the operator $x(d/dx)$, and $p_t(x) = (t-x)^{\underline{t+1}} - (2t+2)^{\underline{t+1}}$. The general solution to $(\vartheta - \alpha)g(x) = x^\beta$ is $g(x) = x^\beta/(\beta - \alpha) + Cx^\alpha$, for $\alpha \neq \beta$; $g(x) = x^\beta(\ln x + C)$ for $\alpha = \beta$. We have $p_t(-t-2) = 0$; so the general solution to our differential equation is

$$C^{(t)}(z) = (2t+2)!\ln(1-z)/p_t'(-t-2)(1-z)^{t+2} + \sum_{j=0}^{t} c_j(1-z)^{\alpha_j}$$

where $\alpha_0, \ldots, \alpha_t$ are the roots of $p_t(x) = 0$, and the constants c_i depend on the initial values $C_t, \ldots, C_{2t}$. The handy identity

$$\frac{1}{(1-z)^{m+1}}\ln\left(\frac{1}{1-z}\right) = \sum_{n\geq 0}(H_{n+m} - H_m)\binom{n+m}{m}z^n, \qquad m \geq 0,$$

now leads to the surprisingly simple *closed form solution*

$$C_n = \frac{H_{n+1} - H_{t+1}}{H_{2t+2} - H_{t+1}}(n+1) + \frac{1}{n!}\sum_{j=0}^{t} c_j(-\alpha_j)^{\overline{n-t}},$$

from which the asymptotic formula is easily deduced. (The leading term $n\ln n/ (H_{2t+2} - H_{t+1})$ was discovered by M. H. van Emden [*CACM* **13** (1970), 563–567] using an information-theoretic approach. In fact, suppose we wish to analyze any partitioning process such that the left subfile contains at most xN elements with asymptotic probability $\int_0^x f(x)\,dx$, as $N \to \infty$, for $0 \leq x \leq 1$; van Emden proved that the average number of comparisons required to sort the file completely is asymptotic to $\alpha^{-1}n\ln n$, where $\alpha = -1/\int_0^1 (f(x) + f(1-x))x\ln x\,dx$. This formula applies to radix exchange as well as to quicksort and various other methods. See also H. Hurwitz, *CACM* **14** (1971), 99–102.)

30. *Solution 1* (of historic interest): Each subfile may be identified by four quantities (l, r, k, X), where l and r are the boundaries (as presently), k indicates the number of words of the keys that are known to be equal throughout the subfile, and X is a lower bound for the $(k+1)$st words of the key. Assuming nonnegative keys, we have $(l, r, k, X) = (1, N, 0, 0)$ initially. When partitioning a file, we let K be the $(k+1)$st word of the test key K_q. If $K > X$, partitioning takes place with all keys $\geq K$ at the right and all keys $< K$ at the left (looking only at the $(k+1)$st word of the key each time); the partitioned subfiles get the respective identifications $(l, j-1, k, X)$ and (j, r, k, K). But if $K = X$, partitioning takes place with all keys $> K$ at the right and all keys $\leq K$ [actually $= K$] at the left; the partitioned subfiles get the respective identifications $(l, j, k+1, 0)$ and $(j+1, r, k, K)$. In both cases we are unsure that R_j is in its final position since we haven't looked at the $(k+2)$nd words. Obvious further changes are made to handle boundary conditions properly. By adding a fifth "upper bound" component, the method could be made symmetrical between left and right.

   Solution 2, by Bentley and Sedgewick [*SODA* **8** (1997), 360–369]: In a subfile identified by (l, r, k), let K be word $k+1$ of K_q as in solution 1, but use the algorithm of exercise 41 to tripartition the subfile into $(l, i-1, k)$, $(i, j, k+1)$, $(j+1, r, k)$ for the cases $<K$, $=K$, $>K$. This approach, which the authors call *multikey quicksort*, is significantly better than solution 1, and it is competitive with the fastest known methods for sorting strings of characters.

31. Go through a normal partitioning process, with R_1 finally falling into position R_s. If $s = m$, stop; if $s < m$, use the same technique to find the $(m-s)$th smallest element of the right-hand subfile; and if $s > m$, find the mth smallest element of the left-hand subfile. [*CACM* **4** (1961), 321–322; **14** (1971), 39–45.]

R. G. Dromey [*Software Practice & Experience* **16** (1986), 981–986] has observed that fewer comparisons and exchanges are needed if we stop each partitioning stage as soon as i or j has reached position m.

32. The recurrence is $C_{11} = 0$ and $C_{nm} = n + 1 + (A_{nm} + B_{nm})/n$ for $n > 1$, where

$$ A_{nm} = \sum_{1 \le s < m} C_{(n-s)(m-s)} \quad \text{and} \quad B_{nm} = \sum_{m < s \le n} C_{(s-1)m}, $$

for $1 \le m \le n$. Since $A_{(n+1)(m+1)} = A_{nm} + C_{nm}$ and $B_{(n+1)m} = B_{nm} + C_{nm}$, we can first find a formula for the quantity $D_n = (n+1)C_{(n+1)(m+1)} - nC_{nm}$, then sum this to obtain the answer $2((n+1)H_n - (n+2-m)H_{n+1-m} - (m+1)H_m + n + \frac{5}{3}) - \frac{1}{3}\delta_{mn} - \frac{1}{3}\delta_{m1} - \frac{2}{3}\delta_{mn}\delta_{m1}$. When $n = 2m-1$, it becomes $4m(H_{2m-1} - H_m) + 4m - 4H_m + \frac{4}{3}(1 - \delta_{m1}) = (4 + 4\ln 2)m - 4\ln m - 4\gamma - \frac{5}{3} + O(m^{-1}) \approx 3.39n$. [See D. E. Knuth, *Proc. IFIP Congress* (1971), 19–27.]

Another solution follows from the theory of Section 6.2.2: Suppose the keys are $\{1, 2, \ldots, n\}$, and let X_{jk} be the number of common ancestors of nodes j and k in the binary search tree corresponding to quicksort. Then the number of comparisons made by the algorithm of exercise 31 can be shown to be $\sum_{j=1}^{n} X_{jm} + X_{mm} - 2[\text{node } m \text{ is a leaf}]$. The probability that node i is a common ancestor of nodes j and k in a random binary search tree is $1/(\max(i, j, k) - \min(i, j, k) + 1)$. We obtain the average number of comparisons from the facts that $\mathrm{E}\,X_{jk} = H_j + H_{n+1-k} + 1 - 2H_{k-j+1}$ for $1 \le j \le k$, and $\Pr(\text{node } m \text{ is a leaf}) = \Pr(m \text{ isn't followed by } m \pm 1 \text{ in a random permutation}) = \frac{1}{3} + \frac{1}{6}\delta_{m1} + \frac{1}{6}\delta_{mn} + \frac{1}{3}\delta_{m1}\delta_{mn}$. [See R. Raman, *SIGACT News* **25**, 2 (June 1994), 86–89.]

For an analysis of a similar selection algorithm that uses median-of-three partitioning, see Kirschenhofer, Prodinger, and Martínez, *Random Structures and Algorithms* **10** (1997), 143–156. Asymptotically faster methods are discussed in exercise 5.3.3–24.

33. Proceed as in the first stage of radix exchange, using the sign instead of bit 1.

34. We can avoid testing whether or not $i \le j$, as soon as we have found at least one 0 bit and at least one 1 bit in each stage — that is, after making the first exchange in each stage. This saves approximately $2C$ units of time in Program R.

35. $A = N - 1$, $B = (\min 0, \text{ave } \frac{1}{4}N \lg N, \max \frac{1}{2}N \lg N)$, $C = N \lg N$, $G = \frac{1}{2}N$, $K = L = R = 0$, $S = \frac{1}{2}N - 1$, $X = (\min 0, \text{ave } \frac{1}{2}(N-1), \max N - 1)$. In general, the quantities A, C, G, K, L, R, and S depend only on the set of keys in the file, not on their initial order; only B and X are influenced by the initial order of the keys.

36. (a) $\sum \binom{n}{k}\binom{k}{j}(-1)^{k+j}a_j = \sum \binom{n}{j}\binom{n-j}{k-j}(-1)^{k-j}a_j = \sum \binom{n}{j}\delta_{nj}a_j = a_n$. (b) $\langle \delta_{n0} \rangle$; $\langle -\delta_{n1} \rangle$; $\langle (-1)^m \delta_{nm} \rangle$; $\langle (1-a)^n \rangle$; $\langle \binom{n}{m}(-a)^m(1-a)^{n-m} \rangle$. (c) Writing the relations to be proved as $x_n = y_n = a_n + z_n$, we have $y_n = a_n + z_n$ by part (a); also $2^{1-n}\sum_{k \ge 2}\binom{n}{k}y_k = z_n$, so y_n satisfies the same recurrence as x_n. [See exercises 53 and 6.3–17 for some generalizations of this result. It does not appear to be easy to prove *directly* that $\hat{x}_n = \hat{a}_n 2^{n-1}/(2^{n-1} - 1)$.]

37. $\langle \sum_m c_m \binom{n}{2m} 2^{-n} \rangle$ for an arbitrary sequence of constants $c_0, c_1, c_2, \ldots$. [This answer, although correct, does not reveal immediately that $\langle 1/(n+1) \rangle$ and $\langle n - \delta_{n1} \rangle$ are such sequences! Sequences having the form $\langle a_n + \hat{a}_n \rangle$ are always self-dual. Notice that, in terms of the generating function $A(z) = \sum a_n z^n/n!$, we have $\hat{A}(z) = e^z A(-z)$; hence $A = \hat{A}$ is equivalent to saying that $A(z)e^{-z/2}$ is an even function.]

38. A partitioning stage that yields a left subfile of size s and a right subfile of size $N - s$ makes the following contributions to the total running time:

$$A = 1, \quad B = t, \quad C = N, \quad K = \delta_{s1}, \quad L = \delta_{s0}, \quad R = \delta_{sN}, \quad X = h,$$

where t is the number of keys $K_1, \ldots, K_s$ with bit b equal to 1, and h is bit b of K_{s+1}; if $s = N$, then $h = 0$. (See (17).) This leads to recurrence equations such as

$$B_N = 2^{-N} \sum_{0 \le t \le s \le N} \binom{s}{t} \binom{N-s}{t} (t + B_s + B_{N-s})$$

$$= \frac{1}{4}(N - 1) + 2^{1-N} \sum_{s \ge 2} \binom{N}{s} B_s, \quad \text{for } N \ge 2; \qquad B_0 = B_1 = 0.$$

(See exercise 23.) Solving these recurrences by the method of exercise 36 yields the formulas $A_N = V_N - U_N + 1$, $B_N = \frac{1}{4}(U_N + N - 1)$, $C_N = V_N + N$, $K_N = N/2$, $L_N = R_N = \frac{1}{2}(V_N - U_N - N) + 1$, $X_N = \frac{1}{2}(A_N - L_N)$. Clearly $G_N = 0$.

39. Each stage of quicksort puts at least one element into its final position, but this need not happen during radix exchange (see Table 3).

40. If we switch to straight insertion whenever $r - l < M$ in step R2, the problem doesn't arise unless more than M equal elements occur. If the latter is a likely prospect, we can test whether or not $K_l = \cdots = K_r$ whenever $j < l$ or $j = r$ in step R8.

41. Lutz M. Wegner [*IEEE Trans.* **C-34** (1985), 362–367] has discussed several approaches, of which the following (as simplified by Bentley and McIlroy in *Software Practice & Exp.* **23** (1993), 1256–1258) appears to be best in practice. The basic idea is to work with the five-part array

$= K$	$< K$	?	$> K$	$= K$
l	a	b	c	d	r

until the middle part is empty, then swap the two ends into the middle.

D1. [Initialize.] Set $a \leftarrow b \leftarrow l$, $c \leftarrow d \leftarrow r$.

D2. [Increase b until $K_b > K$.] If $b \le c$ and $K_b < K$, increase b by 1 and repeat this step. If $b \le c$ and $K_b = K$, exchange $R_a \leftrightarrow R_b$, increase a and b by 1, and repeat this step.

D3. [Decrease c until $K_c < K$.] If $b \le c$ and $K_c > K$, decrease c by 1 and repeat this step. If $b \le c$ and $K_c = K$, exchange $R_c \leftrightarrow R_d$, decrease c and d by 1, and repeat this step.

D4. [Exchange.] If $b < c$, exchange $R_b \leftrightarrow R_c$, increase b by 1, decrease c by 1, and return to D2.

D5. [Cleanup.] Exchange $R_{l+k} \leftrightarrow R_{c-k}$ for $0 \le k < \min(a-l, b-a)$; also exchange $R_{b+k} \leftrightarrow R_{r-k}$ for $0 \le k < \min(d - c, r - d)$. Finally set $i \leftarrow l + b - a$, $j \leftarrow r - d + c$. ∎

Straightforward modifications to step D1 will handle degenerate cases efficiently and ensure that $a < b$ and $c < d$ before we get to D2. Then the tests "$b \le c$" in D2 and D3 will be unnecessary; see exercise 24. Furthermore, this change will keep those steps from needlessly exchanging records with themselves.

One of the main applications of sorting is to bring records with equal keys together. Therefore this tripartitioning scheme is often preferable to the bipartitioning of Algorithm Q. The exchanges in step D5 are efficient because all records with keys equal to K are now in their final resting place.

This exercise is due to W. H. J. Feijen, who called it the "Dutch national flag problem": Given a set of red, white, and blue tokens arranged randomly in a column, decide how to swap pairs of tokens so that the red ones will all be at the top and the blue ones all at the bottom, while looking at each token only once and using only a few auxiliary variables to control the process. [See E. W. Dijkstra, *A Discipline of Programming* (Prentice–Hall, 1976), Chapter 11.]

42. This is a special case of a general theorem due to R. M. Karp; see *JACM* **41** (1994), 1136–1150, §2.8. Significantly sharper asymptotic bounds for tails of the quicksort distribution have been obtained by McDiarmid and Hayward, *J. Algorithms* **21** (1996), 476–507.

43. As $a \to 0+$, we have $\int_0^1 y^{a-1}(e^{-y} - 1)\,dy + \int_1^\infty y^{a-1}e^{-y}\,dy = \Gamma(a) - 1/a = (\Gamma(a+1) - \Gamma(1))/a \to \Gamma'(1) = -\gamma$, by exercise 1.2.7–24.

44. For $k \geq 0$, we have $r_k(m) \sim \frac{1}{2}(2m)^{(k+1)/2}\Gamma((k+1)/2) - \delta_{k0} - \sum_{j\geq0}(-1)^j B_{k+2j+1}/((k+2j+1)j!\,(2m)^j)$. When $k = -1$, the contributions from $f_k^{(j-1)}(m)$ in (36) cancel with similar terms in the expansion of H_{m-1}, and we have $r_{-1}(m) = H_{m-1} + (1/\sqrt{2m})\sum_{t\geq0} f_{-1}(t) \sim \frac{1}{2}(\ln(2m) + \gamma) - \sum_{j\geq1}(-1)^j B_{2j}/(2j)j!\,(2m)^j$. Therefore the contribution to W_{m-1} from the term N^t/t of (33) is obtained from the sum $m\sum_{t\geq1} t^{-1}\exp(-t^2/2m)(1 - t^3/3m^2 + t^6/18m^4)(1 - t^4/4m^3)(1 - t/2m - t^2/8m^2) + O(m^{-1/2}) = \frac{1}{2}m\ln m + \frac{1}{2}(\ln 2 + \gamma)m - \frac{5}{12}\sqrt{2\pi m} + \frac{4}{9} + O(m^{-1/2})$. The term $-\frac{1}{2}N^{t-1}$ contributes $-\frac{1}{2}\sum_{t\geq1}\exp(-t^2/2m)(1 - t^3/3m^2)(1 - t/2m)(1 + t/m) + O(m^{-1/2}) = -\frac{1}{4}\sqrt{2\pi m} + \frac{1}{3}$. The term $\frac{1}{2}\delta_{t1}$ yields $\frac{1}{2}$. And finally the term $\frac{1}{2}(t-1)B_2 N^{t-2}$ contributes $\frac{1}{12}m^{-1}\sum_{t\geq1} t\exp(-t^2/2m) + O(m^{-1/2}) = \frac{1}{12} + O(m^{-1/2})$.

45. The argument used to derive (42) is also valid for (43), except that we leave out the residues at $z = -1$ and $z = 0$.

46. Proceeding as we did with (45), we obtain $(s - 1)!/\ln 2 + \delta_s(n)$, where

$$\delta_s(n) = \frac{2}{\ln 2}\sum_{k\geq1}\Re(\Gamma(s - 2\pi ik/\ln 2)\exp(2\pi ik\lg n)).$$

[Note that $|\Gamma(s + it)|^2 = (\prod_{0\leq k<s}(k^2 + t^2))\pi/(t\sinh \pi t)$, for integer $s \geq 0$, so we can bound $\delta_s(n)$.]

47. In fact, $\sum_{j\geq1} e^{-n/2^j}(n/2^j)^s$ equals the integral in exercise 46, for all $s > 0$.

48. Making use of the intermediate identity

$$1 - e^{-x} = \frac{-1}{2\pi i}\int_{-1/2-i\infty}^{-1/2+i\infty}\Gamma(z)x^{-z}\,dz,$$

we proceed as in the text, with $1 - e^{-x}$ playing the role of $e^{-x} - 1 + x$; $V_{n+1}/(n+1) = (-1/2\pi i)\int_{-1/2-i\infty}^{-1/2+i\infty}\Gamma(z)n^{-z}\,dz/(2^{-z} - 1) + O(n^{-1})$, and the integral equals $\lg n + \gamma/\ln 2 - \frac{1}{2} - \delta_0(n)$ in the notation of exercise 46. [Thus the quantity A_N in exercise 38 is $N(1/\ln 2 - \delta_0(N - 1) - \delta_{-1}(N)) + O(1)$.]

49. The right-hand side of Eq. (40) can be improved to $e^{-x}(n/x + \frac{1}{2}x + x^3 O(n^{-1}))$. The effect is to subtract $\frac{1}{2}$ times the sum in exercise 47, replacing $O(1)$ in (47) by $2 - \frac{1}{2}(1/\ln 2 + \delta_1(n)) + O(n^{-1})$. (The "2" comes from the "$2/n$" in (45).)

50. $U_{mn} = n \log_m n + n((\gamma - 1)/\ln m - \frac{1}{2} + \delta_{-1}(n)) + m/(m-1) - 1/(2 \ln m) - \frac{1}{2}\delta_1(n) + O(n^{-1})$, where $\delta_s(n)$ is defined as in exercise 46 but with $\ln 2$ and $\lg$ replaced by $\ln m$ and $\log_m$. [*Note:* For $m = 2$, 3, 4, 5, 10, 100, 1000, and 10^6 we have $\delta_{-1}(n) < .0000001725$, .00041227, .000296, .00085, .00627, .068, .153, .341, respectively.]

51. Let $N = 2m$. We may extend the sum (35) over all $t \geq 1$, when it equals

$$\sum_{t \geq 1} \frac{1}{2\pi i} \int_{a-i\infty}^{a+i\infty} \Gamma(z)(t^2/N)^{-z} t^k \, dz = \frac{1}{2\pi i} \int_{a-i\infty}^{a+i\infty} \Gamma(z) N^z \zeta(2z - k) \, dz,$$

provided that $a > (k+1)/2$. So we need to know properties of the zeta function. When $\Re(w) \geq -q$, we have $\zeta(w) = O(|w|^{q+1})$ as $|w| \to \infty$; hence we can shift the line of integration to the left as far as we please if we only take the residues into account. The factor $\Gamma(z)$ has poles at 0, -1, -2, $\ldots$, and $\zeta(2z - k)$ has a pole only at $z = (k+1)/2$. The residue at $z = -j$ is $N^{-j}(-1)^j \zeta(-2j - k)/j!$, and $\zeta(-n) = (-1)^n B_{n+1}/(n+1)$. The residue at $z = (k+1)/2$ is $\frac{1}{2}\Gamma((k+1)/2)N^{(k+1)/2}$. But when $k = -1$ there is a double pole at $z = 0$; and $\zeta(z) = 1/(z-1) + \gamma + O(|z-1|)$, so the residue at 0 in this case is $\gamma + \frac{1}{2}\ln N - \frac{1}{2}\gamma$. We therefore obtain the asymptotic series mentioned in the answer to exercise 44.

52. Set $x = t/n$; then

$$\binom{2n}{n+t} \Big/ \binom{2n}{n} = \exp(-2n(x^2/1 \cdot 2 + x^4/3 \cdot 4 + \cdots) + (x^2/2 + x^4/4 + \cdots)$$
$$- (1/6n)(x^2 - x^4 + \cdots) + \cdots);$$

the desired sum can now be expressed in terms of $\sum_{t \geq 1} t^k d(t) e^{-t^2/n}$, for various k. Proceeding as in exercise 51, since $\zeta(z)^2 = \sum_{t \geq 1} d(t) t^{-z}$, we wish to evaluate the residues of $\Gamma(z) n^z \zeta(2z - k)^2$ when $k \geq 0$. At $z = -j$ the residue is

$$n^{-j}(-1)^j (B_{2j+k+1}/(2j + k + 1))^2/j!,$$

and at $z = (k+1)/2$ it is $n^{(k+1)/2}\Gamma((k+1)/2)(\gamma + \frac{1}{4}\ln n + \frac{1}{4}\psi((k+1)/2))$, where $\psi(z) = \Gamma'(z)/\Gamma(z) = H_{z-1} - \gamma$; thus, for example, when $k = 0$, $\sum_{t \geq 1} e^{-t^2/n} d(t) = \frac{1}{4}\sqrt{\pi n} \ln n + (\frac{3}{4}\gamma - \frac{1}{2}\ln 2)\sqrt{\pi n} + \frac{1}{4} + O(n^{-M})$ for all M. For $S_n/\binom{2n}{n}$, add $(\frac{1}{32}\ln n + \frac{3}{32}\gamma + \frac{1}{24} - \frac{1}{16}\ln 2)\sqrt{\pi/n} + O(n^{-1})$ to this quantity. (See exercises 1.2.7–23 and 1.2.9–19.)

53. Let $q = 1 - p$. Generalizing exercise 36(c), if

$$x_n = a_n + \sum_{k \geq 2}\binom{n}{k}(p^k q^{n-k} + q^k p^{n-k})x_n,$$

then

$$x_n = a_n + \sum_{k \geq 2}\binom{n}{k}(-1)^k \hat{a}_k(p^k + q^k)/(1 - p^k - q^k).$$

We can therefore find B_N and C_N as before; the factor $\frac{1}{4}$ in B_N should be replaced by pq. The asymptotic examination of U_N proceeds essentially as in the text, with

$$T_n = \sum_{r \geq 1, s \geq 0}\binom{r}{s}(e^{-np^s q^{r-s}} - 1 + np^s q^{r-s})$$

$$= \frac{1}{2\pi i}\int_{-3/2-i\infty}^{-3/2+i\infty} \Gamma(z) n^{-z}(p^{-z} + q^{-z}) \, dz/(1 - p^{-z} - q^{-z})$$

$$= (n/h_p)(\ln n + \gamma - 1 + h_p^{(2)}/2h_p - h_p + \delta(n)) + O(1),$$

where $h_p = -(p \ln p + q \ln q)$, $h_p^{(2)} = p(\ln p)^2 + q(\ln q)^2$, and $\delta(n) = \sum \Gamma(z) n^{-1-z}/h_p$ summed over all complex $z \neq 1$ such that $p^{-z} + q^{-z} = 1$. The latter set of points seems to be difficult to analyze in general; but when $p = \phi^{-1}$, $q = \phi^{-2}$, the solutions are $z = (-1)^{k+1} + k\pi i/\ln\phi$. The dominant term, $(n \ln n)/h_p$, could also have been obtained from van Emden's general formula quoted in the answer to exercise 29. For $p = \phi^{-1}$ we have $1/h_p \approx 1.503718$, compared to $1/h_{1/2} \approx 1.442695$.

54. Let C be a circle of radius $(M + \frac{1}{2})b$, so that the integral vanishes on C as $M \to \infty$. (The asymptotic form of U_n can now be derived in a new way, expanding $\Gamma(n+1)/\Gamma(n+ibm)$. The method of this exercise applies to *all* sums of the form

$$\sum_k \binom{n}{k} (-1)^{n-k} f(k) = \frac{-1}{2\pi i} \oint B(n+1, -z) f(z)\, dz,$$

when f is reasonably well behaved. The latter formula can be found in N. E. Nörlund's *Vorlesungen Über Differenzenrechnung* (Berlin: Springer, 1924), §103.)

55. Replace lines 04–06 of Program Q by

```
2H ENTA 0,2              STA  INPUT,3  c≤b<a      JGE  5F
   INCA 0,3              STX  INPUT,2             CMPX INPUT,4  a<b,c
   SRB  1             5H LDA  INPUT,4  rA←b       JGE  5B
   STA  *+1(0:2)         JMP  6F                  LDA  INPUT,3  a<c<b
   ENT4 *             4H LDA  INPUT,3  b<c≤a      LDX  INPUT,4
   LDA  INPUT,2  rA←a     LDX  INPUT,2            STX  INPUT,3
   LDX  INPUT,3  rX←c     STX  INPUT,3            JMP  6F
   CMPA INPUT,3          JMP  5F                5H LDX  INPUT,4  b≤a<c
   JL   1F            3H STX  INPUT,2  c≤a≤b       STX  INPUT,2
   CMPA INPUT,4  rA:b     LDX  INPUT,4          6H LDX  INPUT+1,2
   JLE  3F              STX  INPUT,3             STX  INPUT,4
   CMPX INPUT,4  rX:b     JMP  6F                ENT4 2,2
   JG   4F            1H CMPA INPUT,4             ENT5 0,3
```

followed by 'STA INPUT+1,2' (see the remark after (27)); and change the instruction in line 22 to 'STX INPUT+1,2'. The first three of these instructions should be replaced by 'ENTX 0,2; INCX 0,3; ENTA 0; DIV =2=' if binary shifting is not available.

  This program essentially exchanges R_{i+1} with $R_{\lfloor(l+r)/2\rfloor}$ and sorts the three records R_l, R_{l+1}, R_r, then applies normal partitioning to $R_{l+1} \ldots R_{r-1}$. It is tempting to save a few lines of code by simply putting the median element in rA, moving R_l to the median's former place, and using Program Q as it stands. But such an approach has bad consequences, since it requires order N^2 steps to sort the file N $N-1$ $\ldots$ 1. (This amazing result, first noticed by D. B. Coldrick, has to be seen to be believed — try it!) The technique recommended above, due to R. Sedgewick, appears to be free of such simple worst-case anomalies, and runs faster too.

  With this median-of-three partitioning scheme, the algorithm does not look at K_0 and K_{N+1}; hence sentinel values aren't needed to keep the inner loop fast.

56. We can solve the recurrence $\binom{n}{3} x_n = b_n + 2\sum_{k=1}^{n}(k-1)(n-k)x_{k-1}$, for $n > m$, by letting $y_n = n x_n$, $u_n = n y_{n+1} - (n+2)y_n$, $v_n = n u_{n+1} - (n-5)u_n$; it follows that $v_n = 6(b_{n+2} - 2b_{n+1} + b_n)$, for $n > m$. *Example:* Let $x_n = \delta_{n1}$ for $n \leq m$, and let $b_n \equiv 0$. Then $v_n = 0$ for all $n > m$, hence $n^5 u_{n+1} = m^5 u_{m+1}$. Since $y_{m+1} = 12/m$ and $y_{m+2} = 12/(m+1)$, we ultimately find $x_n = \frac{48}{7}(n+1)/m(m+1)(m+2) + \frac{36}{7}(m-1)^4/n^6$, for $n > m$. In general, let $f_n = (12/(n-1)(n-2))\sum_{k=1}^{n}(k-1)(n-k)x_{k-1}$; the solution for $n > m$ when b_n is identically zero is

$$x_n = (n+1)\frac{(m+1)f_{m+2} - (m-4)f_{m+1}}{7(m+1)(m+2)} - \frac{((m+1)f_{m+2} - (m+3)f_{m+1})m^{\underline{5}}}{7n^{\underline{6}}}.$$

When $b_n = \binom{n}{3}/n^{\underline{p}}$ and $x_n = 0$ for $n \le m$, the solution is

$$\frac{x_n}{n+1} = \frac{(p-3)(p-2)}{(p-6)(p+1)(n+1)^{\underline{p+1}}} + \frac{12}{7}\frac{1}{(p+1)(m+2)^{\underline{p+1}}} - \frac{12}{7}\frac{(m+1-p)^{\underline{6-p}}}{(p-6)(n+1)^{\underline{7}}},$$

for $n > m$; except that when $p = -1$ we have $x_n/(n+1) = \frac{12}{7}(H_{n+1} - H_{m+2}) + \frac{37}{49} + \frac{12}{49}(m+2)^{\underline{7}}/(n+1)^{\underline{7}}$, and when $p = 6$, $x_n/(n+1) = -\frac{12}{7}(H_{n-6} - H_{m-5})/(n+1)^{\underline{7}} + \frac{12}{49}/(m+2)^{\underline{7}} + \frac{37}{49}/(n+1)^{\underline{7}}$.

Arguing as in exercises 21–23, we find that the first partitioning phase now contributes 1 to A, t to B, and $N-1$ to C, where t is defined as before but *after* the rearrangement made in exercise 55. Under the new assumptions we find $b_{stN} = 6\binom{s-2}{t}\binom{N-s-1}{t}/N\binom{N-1}{s-1}$; hence the recurrence stated above arises in the following ways:

	Value for $N \le M$	$b_N/\binom{N}{3}$ for $N > M$	Solution for $N > M$
A_N	0	1	$(N+1)(\frac{12}{7}/(M+2))-1+O(N^{-6})$
B_N	0	$(N-4)/5$	$(C_N - 3A_N)/5$
C_N	0	$N-1$	$(N+1)(\frac{12}{7}(H_{N+1}-H_{M+2})+\frac{37}{49}-\frac{24}{7}/(M+2))+2+O(N^{-6})$
D_N	$N-H_N$	0	$(N+1)(1-\frac{12}{7}H_{M+1}/(M+2)-\frac{4}{7}/(M+2))+O(N^{-6})$
E_N	$N(N-1)/4$	0	$(N+1)(\frac{6}{35}M-\frac{17}{35}+\frac{6}{7}/(M+2))+O(N^{-6})$

Similarly $S_N = \frac{3}{7}(N+1)(5M+3)/(2M+3)(2M+1) - 1 + O(N^{-6})$. The total average running time of the program in exercise 55 is $53\frac{1}{2}A_N + 11B_N + 4C_N + 3D_N + 8E_N + 9S_N + 7N$; the choice $M = 9$ is very slightly better than $M = 10$, producing an average time of approximately $10\frac{22}{35}N \ln N + 2.116N$ [*Acta Inf.* **7** (1977), 336–341]. With DIV instead of SRB, add $11A_N$ to the average running time and take $M = 10$.

SECTION 5.2.3

1. No; consider the case $K_1 > K_2 = \cdots = K_N$. But the method using ∞ (described just before Algorithm S) is stable.

2. Traversing a linear list stored sequentially in memory is often slightly faster if we scan the list from higher indices to lower, since it is usually easier for a computer to test if an index is zero than to test if it exceeds N. (For the same reason, the search in step S2 runs from j down to 1; but see exercise 8!)

3. (a) The permutation $a_1 \ldots a_{N-1} N$ occurs for inputs

$$N a_2 \ldots a_{N-1} a_1, \quad a_1 N a_3 \ldots a_{N-1} a_2, \quad \ldots, \quad a_1 a_2 \ldots a_{N-2} N a_{N-1}, \quad a_1 \ldots a_{N-1} N.$$

(b) The average number of times the maximum is changed during the first iteration of step S2 is $H_N - 1$, as shown in Section 1.2.10. [Hence B_N can be found from Eq. 1.2.7–(8).]

4. If the input is a permutation of $\{1, 2, \ldots, N\}$, the number of times $i = j$ in step S3 is exactly one less than the number of cycles in the permutation. (Indeed, it is not hard to show that steps S2 and S3 simply remove element j from its cycle; hence S3 is inactive only when j was the smallest element in its cycle.) By Eq. 1.3.3–(21) we could save $H_N - 1$ of the $N - 1$ executions of step S3, on the average.

Thus it is inefficient to insert an extra test "$i = j$?" before step S3. Instead of testing i versus j, however, we could lengthen the program for S2 slightly, duplicating part of the code, so that S3 never is encountered if the initial guess K_j is not changed during the search for the maximum; this would make Program S a wee bit faster.

5. $(N - 1) + (N - 3) + \cdots = \lfloor N^2/4 \rfloor$.

6. (a) If $i \neq j$ in step S3, that step decreases the number of inversions by $2m - 1$, where m is one more than the number of keys in $K_{i+1} \ldots K_{j-1}$ that lie between K_i and K_j; clearly m is not less than the contribution to B on the previous step S2. Now apply the observation of exercise 4, connecting cycles to the condition $i = j$. (b) Every permutation can be obtained from $N \ldots 2\ 1$ by successive interchanges of adjacent elements that are out of order. (Apply, in reverse sequence, the interchanges that sort the permutation into decreasing order.) Every such operation decreases I by one and changes C by ± 1. Hence no permutation has a value of $I - C$ exceeding the corresponding value for $N \ldots 2\ 1$. [By exercise 5 the inequality $B \leq \lfloor N^2/4 \rfloor$ is best possible.]

7. A. C. Yao, "On straight selection sort," Computer Science Technical Report 185 (Princeton University, 1988), showed that the variance is $\alpha N^{1.5} + O(N^{1.495} \log N)$, where $\alpha = \frac{4}{3}\sqrt{\pi} \ln \frac{4}{e} \approx 0.9129$; he also conjectured that the actual error term is significantly smaller.

8. We can start the next iteration of step S2 at position K_i, provided that we have remembered $\max(K_1, \ldots, K_{i-1})$. One way to keep all of this auxiliary information is to use a link table $L_1 \ldots L_N$ such that K_{L_k} is the previous boldface element whenever K_k is boldface; $L_1 = 0$. [We could also get by with less auxiliary storage, at the expense of some redundant comparisons.]

The following MIX program uses address modification so that the inner loop is fast. $r_{I1} \equiv j$, $r_{I2} \equiv k - j$, $r_{I3} \equiv i$, $rA \equiv K_i$.

01	START	ENT1	N	1	$j \leftarrow N$.	
02		STZ	LINK+1	1		
03		JMP	9F	1		
04	1H	ST1	6F(0:2)	$N - D$	Modify addresses in loop.	
05		ENT4	INPUT,1	$N - D$		
06		ST4	7F(0:2)	$N - D$		
07		ENT4	LINK,1	$N - D$		
08		ST4	8F(0:2)	$N - D$		
09	7H	CMPA	INPUT+J,2	A		[Address modified]
10		JGE	*+4	A	Jump if $K_i \geq K_k$.	
11	8H	ST3	LINK+J,2	$N + 1 - C$	Otherwise $L_k \leftarrow i$,	[Address modified]
12	6H	ENT3	J,2	$N + 1 - C$	$i \leftarrow k$.	[Address modified]
13		LDA	INPUT,3	$N + 1 - C$		
14		INC2	1	A	$k \leftarrow k + 1$.	
15		J2NP	7B	A	Jump if $k \leq j$.	
16	4H	LDX	INPUT,1	N		
17		STX	INPUT,3	N	$R_i \leftarrow R_j$.	
18		STA	INPUT,1	N	$R_j \leftarrow$ former R_i.	
19		DEC1	1	N	$j \leftarrow j - 1$.	
20		ENT2	0,3	N	$r_{I2} \leftarrow i$.	

21		LD3 LINK,3	N	$i \leftarrow L_i$.
22		J3NZ 5F	N	If $i > 0$, k will start at i.
23	9H	ENT3 1	C	Otherwise $i \leftarrow 1$.
24		ENT2 2	C	k will start at 2.
25	5H	DEC2 0,1	$N+1$	
26		LDA INPUT,3	$N+1$	rA $\leftarrow K_i$.
27		J2NP 1B	$N+1$	Jump if $k \leq j$.
28		J1P 4B	$D+1$	Jump if $j > 0$. ∎

9. $N - 1 + \sum_{N \geq k \geq 2}((k-1)/2 - 1/k) = \frac{1}{2}\binom{N}{2} + N - H_N$. [The average values of C and D are, respectively, $H_N + 1$ and $H_N - \frac{1}{2}$; hence the average running time of the program is $(1.25N^2 + 31.75N - 15H_N + 14.5)u$.] Program H is much better.

10.

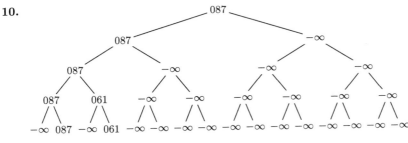

11.

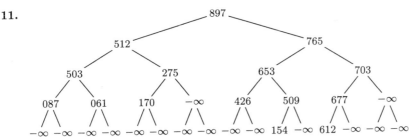

12. $2^n - 1$, once for each $-\infty$ in a branch node.

13. If $K \geq K_{r+1}$, then step H4 may go to step H5 if $j = r$. (Step H5 is inactive unless $K_r < K_{r+1}$, when step H6 will go to H8 anyway.) To ensure that $K \geq K_{r+1}$ throughout the algorithm, we may start with $K_{N+1} \leq \min(K_1, \ldots, K_N)$; instead of setting $R_r \leftarrow R_1$ in step H2, set $R_{r+1} \leftarrow R_{N+1}$ and $R_{N+1} \leftarrow R_1$; also set $R_2 \leftarrow R_{N+1}$ after $r = 1$. (This trick does not speed up the algorithm nor does it make Program H any shorter.)

14. When inserting an element, give it a key that is less (or greater) than all previously assigned keys, to get the effect of a simple queue (or stack, respectively).

15. For efficiency, the following solution is a little bit tricky, avoiding all multiples of 3 [*CACM* **10** (1967), 570].

    Step 1. Set $p[1] \leftarrow 2$, $p[2] \leftarrow 3$, $k \leftarrow 2$, $n \leftarrow 5$, $d \leftarrow 2$, $r \leftarrow 1$, $t \leftarrow 25$, and place $(25, 10, 30)$ in the priority queue. (In this algorithm, $p[i] = i$th prime; $k =$ number of primes found so far; $n =$ prime candidate; $d =$ distance to next candidate; $r =$ number of elements in the queue; $t = p[r+2]^2$, the next n for which we should increase r. The queue entries have the form $(u, v, 6p)$, where p is the smallest prime divisor of u, $v = 2p$ or $4p$, and $u + v$ is not a multiple of 3.)

Step 2. Let (q, q', q'') be the queue element having the smallest first component. Replace it in the queue by $(q + q', q'' - q', q'')$. (This denotes the next multiple of $q''/6$ that must be excluded.) If $n > q$, repeat this step until $n \leq q$.

Step 3. If $n > N$, terminate the algorithm. Otherwise, if $n < q$, set $k \leftarrow k + 1$, $p[k] \leftarrow n$, $n \leftarrow n + d$, $d \leftarrow 6 - d$, and repeat this step.

Step 4. (Now $n = q$ is not prime.) If $n = t$, set $r \leftarrow r + 1$, $u \leftarrow p[r + 2]$, $t \leftarrow u^2$, and insert $(t, 2u, 6u)$ or $(t, 4u, 6u)$ into the queue according as $u \bmod 3 = 2$ or $u \bmod 3 = 1$.

Step 5. Set $n \leftarrow n + d$, $d \leftarrow 6 - d$, and return to (b).

Thus the computation begins as follows:

Queue contents	Primes found
(25, 10, 30)	5, 7, 11, 13, 17, 19, 23
(35, 20, 30)(49, 28, 42)	29, 31
(49, 28, 42)(55, 10, 30)	37, 41, 43, 47
(55, 10, 30)(77, 14, 42)(121, 22, 66)	53

If the queue is maintained as a heap, we can find all primes $\leq N$ in $O(N \log N)$ steps; the length of the heap is at most the number of primes $\leq \sqrt{N}$. The sieve of Eratosthenes, as implemented in exercise 4.5.4–8, is a $O(N \log \log N)$ method requiring considerably more random access storage. More efficient implementations are discussed in Section 7.1.

16. Step 1. Set $K \leftarrow$ key to be inserted; $j \leftarrow n + 1$.
   Step 2. Set $i \leftarrow \lfloor j/2 \rfloor$.
   Step 3. If $i = 0$ or $K_i \geq K$, set $K_j \leftarrow K$ and terminate the algorithm.
   Step 4. Set $K_j \leftarrow K_i$, $j \leftarrow i$, and return to step 2.

[T. Porter and I. Simon showed in *IEEE Trans.* **SE-1** (1975), 292–298, that if A_{n+1} denotes the average number of times step 4 is executed, given a random heap of uniformly random numbers, we have $A_n = \lfloor \lg n \rfloor + (1 - n^{-1})A_{n'}$ for $n > 1$, where $n = (1b_{l-1}b_{l-2}\ldots b_0)_2$ implies $n' = (1b_{l-2}\ldots b_0)_2$. If $l = \lfloor \lg n \rfloor$, this value is always $\geq A_{2^{l+1}-1} = (2^{l+1} - 2)/(2^{l+1} - 1)$, and always $\leq A_{2^l} < \alpha$, where α is the constant in (19).]

17. The file 1 2 3 goes into the heap 3 2 1 with Algorithm H, but into 3 1 2 with exercise 16. (*Note:* The latter method of heap creation has a worst case of order $N \log N$; but empirical tests have shown that the average number of iterations of step 2 during the creation of a heap is less than about $2.28N$, for random input. R. Hayward and C. McDiarmid [*J. Algorithms* **12** (1991), 126–153] have proved rigorously that the constant of proportionality lies between 2.2778 and 2.2994.)

18. Delete step H6, and replace H8 by:

   H8′. [Move back up.] Set $j \leftarrow i$, $i \leftarrow \lfloor j/2 \rfloor$.

   H9′. [Does K fit?] If $K \leq K_i$ or $j = l$, set $R_j \leftarrow R$ and return to H2. Otherwise set $R_j \leftarrow R_i$ and return to H8′. ▌

The method is essentially the same as in exercise 16, but with a different starting place in the heap. The net change to the file is the same as in Algorithm H. Empirical tests on this method show that the number of times $R_j \leftarrow R_i$ occurs per siftup during the selection phase is $(0, 1, 2)$ with respective probabilities $(.837, .135, .016)$. This method makes Program H somewhat longer but improves its asymptotic speed to

$13N \lg N + O(N)$. A **MIX** instruction to halve the value of an index register would be desirable.

C. J. H. McDiarmid and B. A. Reed [*J. Algorithms* **10** (1989), 352–365] have proved that this modification also saves an average of $(3\beta - 8)N \approx 0.232N$ comparisons during the heap-creation phase, where β is defined in the answer to exercise 27. For further analysis of Floyd's improvement, see I. Wegener, *Theoretical Comp. Sci.* **118** (1993), 81–98.

J. Wu and H. Zhu [*J. Comp. Sci. and Tech.* **9** (1994), 261–266] have observed that binary search can also be used, so that each siftup of the selection phase involves at most $\lg N + \lg \lg N$ comparisons and $\lg N$ moves.

19. Proceed as in the revised siftup algorithm of exercise 18, with $K = K_N$, $l = 1$, and $r = N - 1$, starting with a given value of j in step H3.

20. For $0 \le k \le n$, the number of positive integers $\le N$ whose binary representation has the form $(b_n \ldots b_k a_1 \ldots a_q)_2$ for some $q \ge 0$ is clearly $(b_{k-1} \ldots b_0)_2 + 1 + \sum_{0 \le q < k} 2^q = (1 b_{k-1} \ldots b_0)_2$.

21. Let $j = (c_r \ldots c_0)_2$ be in the range $\lfloor N/2^{k+1} \rfloor = (b_n \ldots b_{k+1})_2 < j < (b_n \ldots b_k)_2 = \lfloor N/2^k \rfloor$. Then s_j is the number of positive integers $\le N$ whose binary representation has the form $(c_r \ldots c_0 a_1 \ldots a_q)_2$ for some $q \ge 0$, namely $\sum_{0 \le q < k} 2^q = 2^{k+1} - 1$. Hence the number of nonspecial subtrees of size $2^{k+1} - 1$ is

$$\lfloor N/2^k \rfloor - \lfloor N/2^{k+1} \rfloor - 1 = \lfloor (N - 2^k)/2^{k+1} \rfloor.$$

[To prove the latter identity, use the replicative law in exercise 1.2.4–38 with $n = 2$ and $x = N/2^{k+1}$.]

22. The five possibilities before $l = 1$ are $5\,3\,4\,1\,2$, $3\,5\,4\,1\,2$, $4\,3\,5\,1\,2$, $1\,5\,4\,3\,2$, and $2\,5\,4\,1\,3$. Each of these possibilities $a_1 a_2 a_3 a_4 a_5$ leads to three possible permutations $a_1 a_2 a_3 a_4 a_5$, $a_1 a_4 a_3 a_2 a_5$, $a_1 a_5 a_3 a_4 a_2$ before $l = 2$.

23. (a) After B iterations, $j \ge 2^B l$; hence $2^B l \le r$. (b) We have $\sum_{l=1}^{n} \lfloor \log_2 (N/l) \rfloor = (\lfloor N/2 \rfloor - \lfloor N/4 \rfloor) + 2(\lfloor N/4 \rfloor - \lfloor N/8 \rfloor) + 3(\lfloor N/8 \rfloor - \lfloor N/16 \rfloor) + \cdots = \lfloor N/2 \rfloor + \lfloor N/4 \rfloor + \lfloor N/8 \rfloor + \cdots = N - \nu(N)$, where $\nu(N)$ is the number of ones in the binary representation of N. Also by exercise 1.2.4–42 we have $\sum_{r=1}^{N-1} \lfloor \lg r \rfloor = N \lfloor \lg N \rfloor - 2^{\lfloor \lg N \rfloor + 1} + 2$. We know by Theorem H that this upper bound on B is best possible during the heap-creation phase. Furthermore it is interesting to note that there is a unique heap containing the keys $\{1, 2, \ldots, N\}$ such that K is identically equal to 1 throughout the selection phase of Algorithm H. (For example, when $N = 7$ that heap is $7\,5\,6\,2\,4\,3\,1$; it is not difficult to pass from N to $N + 1$.) This heap gives the maximum value of B (as well as the maximum value $\lfloor N/2 \rfloor$ of D) for the selection phase of heapsort, so the best possible upper bound on B for the entire sort is $N - \nu(N) + N \lfloor \lg N \rfloor - 2^{\lfloor \lg N \rfloor + 1} + 2$.

24. $\sum_{k=1}^{N} \lfloor \lg k \rfloor^2 = (N + 1 - 2^n)n^2 + \sum_{0 \le k < n} k^2 2^k = (N + 1)n^2 - (2n - 3)2^{n+1} - 6$, where $n = \lfloor \lg N \rfloor$ (see exercise 4.5.2–22); hence the variance of the last siftup is $\beta_N = ((N + 1)n^2 - (2n - 3)2^{n+1} - 6)/N - ((N + 1)n + 2 - 2^{n+1})^2/N^2 = O(1)$. The standard deviation of B'_N is $(\sum \{\beta_s \mid s \in M_N\})^{1/2} = O(\sqrt{N})$.

25. The siftup is "uniform," and each comparison $K_j : K_{j+1}$ has probability $\frac{1}{2}$ of coming out $<$. The average contribution to C in this case is just one-half the sum of the average contributions to A and B, namely $((2n - 3)2^{n-1} + \frac{1}{2})/(2^{n+1} - 1)$.

26. (a) $(\frac{10}{25} + \frac{1}{2} + 1\frac{3}{9} + \frac{1}{2} + 1\frac{1}{2} + 1\frac{2}{5} + 2\frac{1}{2} + \frac{1}{2} + 1\frac{1}{2} + 1\frac{1}{2} + 2\frac{1}{2} + 1\frac{1}{2} + 2 + 2 + 3 + 0 + 1 + 1 + 2 + 1 + 2 + 2 + 3 + 1 + 2 + 2)/26 = 1189/780 \approx 1.524$.

(b) $(\sum_{k=1}^{N} \nu(k) - N + \frac{1}{2} \lfloor N/2 \rfloor - \frac{1}{2} n + \sum_{k=1}^{n-1} \min(\alpha_{k-1}, \alpha_k - \alpha_{k-1} - 1)/(\alpha_k - 1))/N$, where $\nu(k)$ is the number of one bits in the binary representation of k, and $\alpha_k = (1b_k \ldots b_0)_2$. If $N = 2^{e_1} + 2^{e_2} + \cdots + 2^{e_t}$, with $e_1 > e_2 > \cdots > e_t \geq 0$, it can be shown that $\sum_{k=0}^{N} \nu(k) = \frac{1}{2}((e_1 + 2)2^{e_1} + (e_2 + 4)2^{e_2} + \cdots + (e_t + 2t)2^{e_t}) + t - N$. [The asymptotic properties of such sums can be analyzed perspicuously with the help of Mellin transforms; see Flajolet, Grabner, Kirschenhofer, Prodinger, and Tichy, *Theoretical Comp. Sci.* **123** (1994), 291–314.]

27. J. W. Wrench, Jr. has observed that the general Lambert series $\sum_{n \geq 1} a_n x^n / (1 - x^n)$ can be expanded as $\sum_{N \geq 1} (\sum_{d \backslash N} a_d) x^N = \sum_{m \geq 1} (a_m + \sum_{k \geq 1} (a_m + a_{m+k}) x^{km}) x^{m^2}$.

[The cases $a_n = 1$ and $a_n = n$ were introduced by J. H. Lambert in his *Anlage zur Architectonic* **2** (Riga: 1771), §875; Clausen stated his formula for the case $a_n = 1$ in *Crelle* **3** (1828), 95, and H. F. Scherk presented a proof in *Crelle* **9** (1832), 162–163. When $a_n = n$ and $x = \frac{1}{2}$ we obtain the relation

$$\beta = \sum_{n \geq 1} \frac{n}{2^n - 1} = \sum_{m \geq 1} \left(m \left(\frac{2^m + 1}{2^m - 1} \right) + \frac{2^m}{(2^m - 1)^2} \right) 2^{-m^2}$$

$$= 2.74403\ 38887\ 59488\ 36048\ 02148\ 91492\ 27216\ 43114+;$$

this constant arises in (20), where we have $B'_N \sim (\beta - 2)N$ and $C'_N \sim (\frac{1}{2}\beta - \frac{1}{4}\alpha - \frac{1}{2})N$.]

Incidentally, if we set $q = x$ and $z = xy$ in the first identity of exercise 5.1.1–16, then evaluate $\frac{\partial}{\partial y}$ at $y = 1$, we get the interesting identity

$$\sum_{n \geq 1} \frac{x^n}{1 - x^n} = \sum_{k \geq 1} k x^k (1 - x^{k+1})(1 - x^{k+2}) \ldots$$

28. The children of node k are nodes $3k - 1$, $3k$, and $3k + 1$; the parent is $\lfloor (k+1)/3 \rfloor$. A MIX program analogous to Program H takes asymptotically $21\frac{2}{3}N \log N \approx 13.7 N \lg N$ units of time. Using the idea of exercise 18 lowers this to $18\frac{2}{3}N \log_3 N \approx 11.8 N \lg N$, although the division by 3 will add a large $\Theta(N)$ term.

For further information about t-ary heaps, see S. Okoma, *Lecture Notes in Comp. Sci.* **88** (1980), 439–451.

30. Suppose $n = 2^t - 1 + r$, where $t = \lfloor \lg n \rfloor$ and $1 \leq r \leq 2^t$. Then $h_{2m} = [m = 0]$ and

$$h_{(n+1)m} \leq \sum_{j=0}^{t-2} (2^j - 1) h_{n(m-j)} + 2^{t-1} h_{n(m-t+1)} + r h_{n(m-t)} \qquad \text{for } n \geq 2,$$

by considering the number of elements on level j that could be the final resting place of K_{n+1} after it has been sifted up in place of K_1. Therefore, if $g_{nm} = h_{nm}/2^m$, we have

$$g_{(n+1)m} \leq \sum_{j=0}^{t-1} \frac{2^j - 1}{2^j} g_{n(m-j)} + g_{n(m-t+1)} + \frac{r}{2^t} g_{n(m-t)} \leq (\lg(n+1)) \max_{m \geq 0} g_{nm},$$

and it follows by induction that $g_{nm} \leq L_n = \prod_{k=2}^{n} \lg k$.

The average total number of promotions during the selection phase is $B''_N = h_N^{-1} \sum_{m \geq 0} m h_{Nm}$, where $h_N = \sum_{m \geq 0} h_{Nm}$ is the total number of possible heaps (Theorem H). We know that $B''_N \leq N \lceil \lg N \rceil$. On the other hand, we have $B''_N \geq m - h_N^{-1} \sum_{k=1}^{m} (m-k) h_{Nk} \geq m - h_N^{-1} L_N \sum_{k=1}^{m} (m-k) 2^k > m - 2^{m+1} h_N^{-1} L_N$, for all m. Choosing $m = \lg(h_N/L_N) + O(1)$ now gives $B''_N \geq \lg(h_N/L_N) + O(1)$.

The number of comparisons needed to create a heap is at most $2N$, by exercise 23(b); hence $h_N \geq N!/2^{2N}$. Clearly $L_N \leq (\lg N)^N$, so we have $\lg(h_N/L_N) \geq N \lg N - N \lg \lg N + O(N)$. [*J. Algorithms* **15** (1993), 76–100.]

31. (Solution by J. Edighoffer, 1981.) Let A be an array of $2n$ elements such that $A[2\lfloor i/2 \rfloor] \leq A[2i]$ and $A[2\lfloor i/2 \rfloor - 1] \geq A[2i - 1]$ for $1 < i \leq n$; furthermore we require that $A[2i - 1] \geq A[2i]$ for $1 \leq i \leq n$. (The latter condition holds for all i if and only if it holds for $n/2 < i \leq n$, because of the heap structure.) This "twin heap" contains $2n$ elements; to handle an odd number of elements, we simply keep one element off to the side. Appropriate modifications of the other algorithms in this section can be used to maintain twin heaps, and it is interesting to work out the details. This idea was independently discovered and developed further by J. van Leeuwen and D. Wood [*Comp. J.* **36** (1993), 209–216], who called the structure an "interval heap."

32. In any heap of N distinct elements, the largest $m = \lceil N/2 \rceil$ elements form a subtree. At least $\lfloor m/2 \rfloor$ of them must be nonleaves of that subtree, since a binary tree with k leaves has at least $k - 1$ nonleaves. Therefore at least $\lfloor m/2 \rfloor$ of the largest m elements appear in the first $\lfloor N/2 \rfloor$ positions of the heap. Those elements must be promoted to the root position before reaching their final destinations; so their movement contributes at least $\sum_{k=1}^{\lfloor m/2 \rfloor} \lfloor \lg k \rfloor = \frac{1}{2} m \lg m + O(m)$ to B, by exercise 1.2.4–42. Thus $B_{\min}(N) \geq \frac{1}{4} N \lg N + O(N) + B_{\min}(\lfloor N/2 \rfloor)$, and the result follows by induction on N. [I. Wegener, *Theoretical Comp. Sci.* **118** (1993), 81–98, Theorem 5.1. Schaffer and Sedgewick, and independently Bollobás, Fenner, and Frieze, have constructed permutations that require no more than $\frac{1}{2} N \lg N + O(N \log \log N)$ promotions; see *J. Algorithms* **15** (1993), 76–100; **20** (1996), 205–217. Such permutations are quite rare, by the result of exercise 30.]

33. Let P and Q point to the given priority queues. The following algorithm uses the convention $\text{DIST}(\Lambda) = 0$, as in the text, although Λ isn't really a node.

M1. [Initialize.] Set R ← Λ.

M2. [List merge.] If Q = Λ, set D ← DIST(P) and go to M3. If P = Λ, set P ← Q, D ← DIST(P), and go to M3. Otherwise if KEY(P) ≥ KEY(Q), set T ← RIGHT(P), RIGHT(P) ← R, R ← P, P ← T and repeat step M2. If KEY(P) < KEY(Q), set T ← RIGHT(Q), RIGHT(Q) ← R, R ← Q, Q ← T and repeat step M2. (This step essentially merges the two "right lists" of the given trees, temporarily inserting upward pointers into the RIGHT fields.)

M3. [Done?] If R = Λ, terminate the algorithm; P points to the answer.

M4. [Fix DISTs.] Set Q ← RIGHT(R). If DIST(LEFT(R)) < D, then set D ← DIST(LEFT(R)) + 1, RIGHT(R) ← LEFT(R), LEFT(R) ← P; otherwise set D ← D + 1, RIGHT(R) ← P. Finally set DIST(R) ← D, P ← R, R ← Q, and return to M3. ▮

34. Starting with the recurrence

$$L_1(z) = z, \qquad L_{m+1}(z) = L_m(z)\left(L(z) - \sum_{k=1}^{m-1} L_k(z)\right),$$

for parts of the overall generating function $L(z) = \sum_{n \geq 0} l_n z^n = \sum_{m \geq 1} L_m(z)$, where $L_m(z) = z^{2^{m-1}} + \cdots$ generates leftist trees with shortest path length m from root to Λ, Rainer Kemp has proved that $L(z) = z + \frac{1}{2} L(z)^2 + \frac{1}{2} \sum_{m \geq 1} L_m(z)^2$, and that $a \approx 0.25036$ and $b \approx 2.7494879$ [*Inf. Proc. Letters* **25** (1987), 227–232; *Random Graphs '87* (1990), 103–130]. Luis Trabb Pardo noticed in 1978 that the generating function $G(z) = zL(z)$ satisfies the elegant relation $G(z) = z + G(zG(z))$.

35. Let the DIST field of the deleted node be d_0, and let the DIST field of the merged subtrees be d_1. If $d_0 = d_1$, we need not go up at all. If $d_0 > d_1$, then $d_1 = d_0 - 1$; and if we go up n levels, the new DIST fields of the ancestors of P must be, respectively, $d_1 + 1$, $d_1 + 2$, $\ldots$, $d_1 + n$. If $d_0 < d_1$, the upward path must go only leftwards.

36. Instead of a general priority queue, it is simplest to use a doubly linked list; move nodes to one end of the list whenever they are used, and delete nodes from the other end. [See the discussion of self-organizing files in Section 6.1.]

37. In an infinite heap, the kth-largest element is equally likely to appear in the left or the right subheap of its larger ancestors. Thus we can use the theory of digital search trees, obtaining $e(k) = \overline{C}_k - \overline{C}_{k-1}$ in the notation of Eq. 6.3–(13). By exercise 6.3–28 we have $e(k) = \lg k + \gamma/(\ln 2) + \frac{1}{2} - \alpha + \delta_0(k) + O(k^{-1}) \approx \lg k - .274$, where α is defined in (19) and $\delta_0(k)$ is a periodic function of $\lg k$. [P. V. Poblete, *BIT* **33** (1993), 411–412.]

38. $M_0 = \emptyset$; $M_1 = \{1\}$; $M_N = \{N\} \uplus M_{2^k - 1} \uplus M_{N - 2^k}$ for $N > 1$, where $k = \lfloor \lg(2N/3) \rfloor$.

SECTION 5.2.4

1. Start with $i_1 = \cdots = i_k = 1$, $j = 1$. Repeatedly find $\min(x_{1i_1}, \ldots, x_{ki_k}) = x_{ri_r}$, and set $z_j = x_{ri_r}$, $j \leftarrow j + 1$, $i_r \leftarrow i_r + 1$. (In this case the use of $x_{i(m_i + 1)} = \infty$ is a decided convenience.)

When k is moderately large, it is desirable to keep the keys $x_{1i_1}, \ldots, x_{ki_k}$ in a tree structure suited to repeated selection, as discussed in Section 5.2.3, so that only $\lfloor \lg k \rfloor$ comparisons are needed to find the new minimum each time after the first. Indeed, this is a typical application of the principle of "smallest in, first out" in a priority queue. The keys can be maintained as a heap, and ∞ can be avoided entirely. See the further discussion in Section 5.4.1.

2. Let C be the number of comparisons; we have $C = m + n - S$, where S is the number of elements transmitted in step M4 or M6. The probability that $S \geq s$ is easily seen to be

$$q_s = \left(\binom{m+n-s}{m} + \binom{m+n-s}{n} \right) \Big/ \binom{m+n}{m}$$

for $1 \leq s \leq m+n$; $q_s = 0$ for $s > m+n$. Hence the mean of S is $\mu_{mn} = q_1 + q_2 + \cdots = m/(n+1) + n/(m+1)$ [see exercises 3.4.2–5, 6], and the variance is $\sigma_{mn}^2 = (q_1 + 3q_2 + 5q_3 + \cdots) - \mu_{mn}^2 = m(2m+n)/(n+1)(n+2) + (m+2n)n/(m+1)(m+2) - \mu_{mn}^2$. Thus

$$C = (\min\ \min(m, n),\ \text{ave}\ m + n - \mu_{mn},\ \max\ m + n - 1,\ \text{dev}\ \sigma_{mn}).$$

When $m = n$ the average was first computed by H. Nagler, *CACM* **3** (1960), 618–620; it is asymptotically $2n - 2 + O(n^{-1})$, with a standard deviation of $\sqrt{2} + O(n^{-1})$. Thus C hovers close to its maximum value.

3. **M2'.** If $K_i < K'_j$, go to M3'; if $K_i = K'_j$, go to M7'; if $K_i > K'_j$, go to M5'.

M7'. Set $K''_k \leftarrow K'_j$, $k \leftarrow k+1$, $i \leftarrow i+1$, $j \leftarrow j+1$. If $i > M$, go to M4'; otherwise if $j > N$, go to M6'; otherwise return to M2'. ∎

(Appropriate modifications are made to other steps of Algorithm M. Again many special cases disappear if we insert artificial keys $K_{M+1} = K'_{N+1} = \infty$ at the end of the files.)

4. The sequence of elements that appears at a fixed internal node of the selection tree, as time passes, is obtained by merging the sequences of elements that appear at the children of that node. (The discussion in Section 5.2.3 is based on selecting the *largest* element, but it could equally well have reversed the order.) So the operations involved in tree selection are essentially the same as those involved in merging, but they are performed in a different sequence and using different data structures.

Another relation between merging and tree selection is indicated in exercise 1. Note that an N-way merge of one-element files is a selection sort; compare also four-way merging of (A, B, C, D) to two-way merging of (A, B), (C, D), then (AB, CD).

5. In step N6 we always have $K_i < K_{i-1} \leq K_j$; in N10, $K_j < K_{j+1} < K_i$.

6. 2 6 4 10 8 14 12 16 15 11 13 7 9 3 5 1. After one pass, two of the expected stepdowns disappear: 1 2 5 6 7 8 13 14 16 15 12 11 10 9 4 3. This possibility was first noted by D. A. Bell, *Comp. J.* **1** (1958), 74. Quirks like this make it almost hopeless to carry out a precise analysis of Algorithm N.

7. $\lceil \lg N \rceil$, if $N > 1$. (Consider how many times p must be doubled until it is $\geq N$.)

8. If N is not a multiple of $2p$, there is one short run on the pass, and it is always near the middle; letting its length be t, we have $0 \leq t < p$. Step S12 handles the cases where the short run is to be "merged" with an empty run, or where $t = 0$; otherwise we have essentially $x_1 \leq x_2 \leq \cdots \leq x_p \mid y_t \geq \cdots \geq y_1$. If $x_p \leq y_t$, the left-hand run is exhausted first, and step S6 will take us to S13 after x_p has been transmitted. On the other hand, if $x_p > y_t$, the right-hand side will be artificially exhausted, but $K_j = x_p$ will never be $< K_i$ in step S3! Thus S6 will eventually take us to S13 in all cases.

10. For example, Algorithm M can merge elements $x_{j+1} \ldots x_{j+m}$ with $x_{j+m+1} \ldots x_{j+m+n}$ into positions $x_1 \ldots x_{m+n}$ of an array without conflict, if $j \geq n$. With care we can exploit this idea so that $N + 2^{\lfloor \lg N \rfloor - 1}$ locations are required for an entire sort. But the program seems to be rather complicated compared to Algorithm S. [*Comp. J.* **1** (1958), 75; see also L. S. Lozinskii, *Kibernetika* **1, 3** (1965), 58–62.]

11. Yes. This can be seen, for example, by considering the relation to tree selection mentioned in exercise 4. But Algorithms N and S are obviously not stable.

12. Set $L_0 \leftarrow 1$, $t \leftarrow N + 1$; then for $p = 1, 2, \ldots, N - 1$, do the following:

$$\text{If } K_p \leq K_{p+1} \text{ set } L_p \leftarrow p + 1; \text{ otherwise set } L_t \leftarrow -(p+1), \ t \leftarrow p.$$

Finally, set $L_t \leftarrow 0$, $L_N \leftarrow 0$, $L_{N+1} \leftarrow |L_{N+1}|$.

(Stability is preserved. The number of passes is $\lceil \lg r \rceil$, where r is the number of ascending runs in the input; the exact distribution of r is analyzed in Section 5.1.3. We may conclude that natural merging is preferable to straight merging when linked allocation is being used, although it was inferior for sequential allocation.)

13. The running time for $N \geq 3$ is $(11A + 6B + 3B' + 9C + 2C'' + 4D + 5N + 9)u$, where A is the number of passes; $B = B' + B''$ is the number of subfile-merge operations performed, where B' is the number of such merges in which the p subfile was exhausted first; $C = C' + C''$ is the number of comparisons performed, where C' is the number of such comparisons with $K_p \leq K_q$; $D = D' + D''$ is the number of elements remaining in subfiles when the other subfile has been exhausted, where D' is the number of such elements belonging to the q subfile. In Table 3 we have $A = 4$, $B' = 6$, $B'' = 9$, $C' = 22$, $C'' = 22$, $D' = 10$, $D'' = 10$, total time $= 761u$. (The comparable Program 5.2.1L takes only $433u$, when improved as in exercise 5.2.1–33, so we can see that merging isn't especially efficient when N is small.)

Algorithm L does a sequence of merges on subfiles whose sizes (m, n) can be determined as follows: Let $N - 1 = (b_k \ldots b_1 b_0)_2$ in binary notation. There are

$(b_k \ldots b_{j+1})_2$ "ordinary" merges with $(m, n) = (2^j, 2^j)$, for $0 \le j < k$; and there are
"special" merges with $(m, n) = (2^j, 1 + (b_{j-1} \ldots b_0)_2)$ whenever $b_j = 1$, for $0 \le j \le k$.
For example, when $N = 14$ there are six ordinary $(1, 1)$ merges, three ordinary $(2, 2)$
merges, one ordinary $(4, 4)$ merge, and the special merges deal with subfiles of sizes
$(1, 1)$, $(4, 2)$, $(8, 6)$. The multiset M_N of merge sizes (m, n) can also be described by
the recurrence relations

$$M_1 = \emptyset; \qquad M_{2^k+r} = \{(2^k, r)\} \uplus M_{2^k} \uplus M_r \quad \text{for } 0 < r \le 2^k.$$

It follows that, regardless of the input distribution, we have $A = \lceil \lg N \rceil$, $B = N-1$,
$C' + D'' = \sum_{j=0}^{k} b_j 2^j (1 + \frac{1}{2}j)$, $C'' + D' = \sum_{j=0}^{k} b_j (1 + 2^j (\frac{1}{2}j + b_{j+1} + \cdots + b_k))$; hence
only B', C', D' need to be analyzed further.

If the input to Algorithm L is random, each of the merging operations satisfies
the conditions of exercise 2, and is independent of the behavior of the other merges;
so the distribution of B', C', D' is the convolution of their individual distributions
for each subfile merge. The average values for such a merge are $B' = n/(m + n)$,
$C' = mn/(n + 1)$, $D' = n/(m + 1)$. Sum these over all relevant (m, n) to get the exact
average values.

When $N = 2^k$ we have, of course, the simplest situation; $B'_{\text{ave}} = \frac{1}{2}B$, $C'_{\text{ave}} = \frac{1}{2}C_{\text{ave}}$,
$C + D = kN$, and $D_{\text{ave}} = \sum_{j=1}^{k} (2^{k-j} 2^j / (2^{j-1} + 1)) = \alpha' N + O(1)$, where

$$\alpha' = \sum_{n \ge 0} \frac{1}{2^n + 1} = \alpha + \frac{1}{2} - 2 \sum_{n \ge 1} \frac{1}{4^n - 1}$$

$$= 1.26449\ 97803\ 48444\ 20919\ 13197\ 47255\ 49848\ 25577-$$

can be evaluated to high precision as in exercise 5.2.3–27. This special case was first
analyzed by A. Gleason [unpublished, 1956] and H. Nagler [*CACM* **3** (1960), 618–620].

14. Set $D = B$ in exercise 13 to maximize C. [A detailed analysis of Algorithm L has
been carried out by W. Panny and H. Prodinger, *Algorithmica* **14** (1995), 340–354.]

15. Make extra copies of steps L3, L4, L6 for the cases that L_s is known to equal p or q.
[A *further* improvement can also be made, removing the assignment $s \leftarrow p$ (or $s \leftarrow q$)
from the inner loop, by simply renaming the registers! For example, change lines 20
and 21 to 'LD3 INPUT,1(L)' and continue with p in rI3, s in rI1 and L_s known to equal p.
With twelve copies of the inner loop, corresponding to the different permutations of
(p, q, r) with respect to (rI1, rI2, rI3), and the different knowledge about L_s, we can
cut the average running time to $8N \lg N + O(N)$.]

16. (The result will be slightly faster than Algorithm L; see exercise 5.2.3–28.)

17. Consider the new record as a subfile of length 1. Repeatedly merge the smallest
two subfiles if they have the same length. (The resulting sorting algorithm is essentially
the same as Algorithm L, but the subfiles are merged at different relative times.)

18. Yes, but it seems to be a complicated job. The first solution to be found used
the following ingenious construction [*Doklady Akad. Nauk SSSR* **186** (1969), 1256–
1258]: Let n be $\approx \sqrt{N}$. Divide the file into $m + 2$ "zones" $Z_1 \ldots Z_m Z_{m+1} Z_{m+2}$, where
Z_{m+2} contains $N \bmod n$ records while each other zone contains exactly n records.
Interchange the records of Z_{m+1} with the zone containing R_M; the file now takes the
form $Z_1 \ldots Z_m A$, where each of the $Z_1 \ldots Z_m$ contains exactly n records in order and
where A is an auxiliary area containing s records, for some s in the range $n \le s < 2n$.

Find the zone with smallest leading element, and exchange that entire zone with Z_1;
if more than one zone has the smallest leading element, choose one that has the smallest

trailing element. (This takes $O(m + n)$ operations.) Then find the zone with the next smallest leading and trailing elements, and exchange it with Z_2, etc. Finally in $O(m(m + n)) = O(N)$ operations we will have rearranged the m zones so that their leading elements are in order. Furthermore, because of our original assumptions about the file, each of the keys in $Z_1 \ldots Z_m$ will now have fewer than n inversions.

We can merge Z_1 with Z_2, using the following trick: Interchange Z_1 with the first n elements A' of A; then merge Z_2 with A' in the usual way but exchanging elements with the elements of $Z_1 Z_2$ as they are output. For example, if $n = 3$ and $x_1 < y_1 < x_2 < y_2 < x_3 < y_3$, we have

	Zone 1			Zone 2			Auxiliary		
Initial contents:	x_1	x_2	x_3	y_1	y_2	y_3	a_1	a_2	a_3
Exchange Z_1:	a_1	a_2	a_3	y_1	y_2	y_3	x_1	x_2	x_3
Exchange x_1:	x_1	a_2	a_3	y_1	y_2	y_3	a_1	x_2	x_3
Exchange y_1:	x_1	y_1	a_3	a_2	y_2	y_3	a_1	x_2	x_3
Exchange x_2:	x_1	y_1	x_2	a_2	y_2	y_3	a_1	a_3	x_3
Exchange y_2:	x_1	y_1	x_2	y_2	a_2	y_3	a_1	a_3	x_3
Exchange x_3:	x_1	y_1	x_2	y_2	x_3	y_3	a_1	a_3	a_2

(The merge is always complete when the nth element of the auxiliary area has been exchanged; this method generally permutes the auxiliary records.)

The trick above is used to merge Z_1 with Z_2, then Z_2 with Z_3, $\ldots$, Z_{m-1} with Z_m, requiring a total of $O(mn) = O(N)$ operations. Since no element has more than n inversions, the $Z_1 \ldots Z_m$ portion of the file has been completely sorted.

For the final "cleanup," we sort $R_{N+1-2s} \ldots R_N$ by insertion, in $O(s^2) = O(N)$ steps; this brings the s largest elements into area A. Then we merge $R_1 \ldots R_{N-2s}$ with $R_{N+1-2s} \ldots R_{N-s}$, using the trick above with auxiliary storage area A (but interchanging the roles of right and left, less and greater, throughout). Finally, we sort $R_{N+1-s} \ldots R_N$ by insertion.

Subsequent refinements are discussed by J. Katajainen, T. Pasanen, and J. Teuhola in *Nordic J. Computing* **3** (1996), 27–40. See answer 5.5–3 for the problem of *stable merging in place*.

19. We may number the input cars so that the final permutation has them in order, 1 2 ... 2^n; so this is essentially a sorting problem. First move the first 2^{n-1} cars through $n - 1$ stacks, putting them in decreasing order, and transfer them to the nth stack so that the smallest is on top. Then move the other 2^{n-1} cars through $n - 1$ stacks, putting them into increasing order and leaving them positioned just before the nth stack. Finally, merge the two sequences together in the obvious way.

20. For further information, see R. E. Tarjan, *JACM* **19** (1972), 341–346.

22. See *Information Processing Letters* **2** (1973), 127–128.

23. The merges can be represented by a binary tree that has all external nodes on levels $\lfloor \lg N \rfloor$ and $\lceil \lg N \rceil$. Therefore the maximum number of comparisons is the minimum external path length of a binary tree with N external nodes, Eq. 5.3.1–(34), minus $N - 1$, since $f(m, n) = m + n - 1$ gives the maximum and there are $N - 1$ merges. (See also Eq. 5.4.9–(1).)

General techniques for studying the asymptotic properties of such recurrences with the help of Mellin transforms have been presented by P. Flajolet and M. Golin in *Acta Informatica* **31** (1994), 673–696; in particular, they show that the average number of comparisons is $N \lg N - \theta N + \delta(\lg N)N + O(1)$ and the variance is $\approx .345N$, where δ is a continuous function of period 1 and average value 0, and

$$\theta = \frac{1}{\ln 2} - \frac{1}{2} + \frac{1}{\ln 2}\sum_{m=1}^{\infty}\frac{2}{(m+1)(m+2)}\ln\frac{2m+1}{2m}$$

$$= 1.24815\ 20420\ 99653\ 84890\ 29565\ 64329\ 53240\ 16127+.$$

The total number of comparisons is well approximated by a normal distribution as $N \to \infty$; see the complementary analyses by H.-K. Hwang and M. Cramer in *Random Structures and Algorithms* **8** (1996), 319–336; **11** (1997), 81–96.

SECTION 5.2.5

1. No, because radix sorting doesn't work at all unless the distribution sorting is stable, after the first pass. (But the suggested distribution sort *could* be used in a most-significant-digit-first radix sorting method, generalizing radix exchange, as suggested in the last paragraph of the text.)

2. It is "anti-stable," just the opposite; elements with equal keys appear in reverse order, since the first pass goes through the records from R_N to R_1. (This proves to be convenient because of lines 28 and 20 of Program R, equating Λ with 0; but of course it is not necessary to make the first pass go backwards.)

3. If pile 0 is not empty, BOTM[0] already points to the first element; if it is empty, we set P ← LOC(BOTM[0]) and later make LINK(P) point to the bottom of the first nonempty pile.

4. When there are an even number of passes remaining, take pile 0 first (top to bottom), followed by pile 1, ..., pile $(M-1)$; the result will be in order with respect to the digits examined so far. When there are an odd number of passes remaining, take pile $(M-1)$ first, then pile $(M-2)$, ..., pile 0; the result will be in *reverse* order with respect to the digits examined so far. (This rule was apparently first published by E. H. Friend [*JACM* **3** (1956), 156, 165–166].)

5. Change line 04 to 'ENT3 7', and change the R3SW and R5SW tables to:

```
R3SW    LD2    KEY,1(1:1)
        LD2    KEY,1(2:2)
        LD2    KEY,1(3:3)
        LD2    KEY,1(4:4)
        LD2    KEY,1(5:5)
        LD2    INPUT,1(1:1)
        LD2    INPUT,1(2:2)
        LD2    INPUT,1(3:3)
R5SW    LD1    INPUT,1(LINK)
         ⋮     (repeat the previous line six more times)
        DEC1   1
```

The new running time is found by changing "3" to "8" everywhere; it amounts to $(11p-1)N + 16pM + 12p - 4E + 2$, for $p = 8$.

6. (a) Consider placing an $(N+1)$st element. The recurrence

$$p_{M(N+1)k} = \frac{k+1}{M}p_{MN(k+1)} + \frac{M-k}{M}p_{MNk}$$

is equivalent to the stated formula. (b) The nth derivative satisfies $g_{M(N+1)}^{(n)}(z) = (1 - n/M)g_{MN}^{(n)}(z) + ((1 - z)/M)g_{MN}^{(n+1)}(z)$, by induction on n. Setting $z = 1$, we find $g_{MN}^{(n)}(1) = (1 - n/M)^N M^{\underline{n}}$, since $g_{M0}(z) = z^M$. Hence mean$(g_{MN}) = (1 - 1/M)^N M$, var$(g_{MN}) = (1 - 2/M)^N M(M - 1) + (1 - 1/M)^N M - (1 - 1/M)^{2N} M^2$. (Notice that the generating function for E in Program R is $g_{MN}(z)^p$.)

7. Let R = radix sort, RX = radix exchange. Some of the important similarities and differences: RX goes from most significant digit to least significant, while R goes the other way. Both methods sort by digit inspections, without making comparisons of keys. RX always has $M = 2$ (but see exercise 1). The running time for R is almost unvarying, while RX is sensitive to the distribution of the digits. In both cases the running time is $O(N \log K)$, where K is the range of keys, but the constant of proportionality is higher for RX; on the other hand, when the keys are uniformly distributed in their leading digits, RX has an average running time of $O(N \log N)$ regardless of the size of K. R requires link fields while RX runs in minimal space. The inner loop of R is more suited to pipeline computers.

8. On the final pass, the piles should be hooked together in another order; for example, if $M = 256$, pile $(10000000)_2$ comes first, then pile $(10000001)_2$, ..., pile $(11111111)_2$, pile $(00000000)_2$, pile $(00000001)_2$, ..., pile $(01111111)_2$. This change in hooking order can be done easily by modifying Algorithm H, or (in Table 1) by changing the storage allocation strategy, on the last pass.

9. We could first separate the negative keys from the positive keys, as in exercise 5.2.2–33; or we could change the keys to complement notation on the first pass. Alternatively, after the last pass we could separate the positive keys from the negative ones, reversing the order of the latter, although the method of exercise 5.2.2–33 no longer applies.

11. Without the first pass the method would still sort perfectly, because (by coincidence) 503 already precedes 509. Without the first two passes, the number of inversions would be $1 + 1 + 0 + 0 + 0 + 1 + 1 + 1 + 0 + 0 = 5$.

12. After exchanging R_k with $R[P]$ in step M4 (exercise 5.2–12), we can compare K_k to K_{k-1}. If K_k is less, we compare it to $K_{k-2}, K_{k-3}, \ldots$, until finding $K_k \geq K_j$. Then set $(R_{j+1}, \ldots, R_{k-1}, R_k) \leftarrow (R_k, R_{j+1}, \ldots, R_{k-1})$, *without* changing the LINK fields. It is convenient to place an artificial key K_0, which is $\leq$ all other keys, at the left of the file.

14. If the original permutation of the cards requires k readings, in the sense of exercise 5.1.3–20, and if we use m piles per pass, we must make at least $\lceil \log_m k \rceil$ passes. (Consider going back from a sorted deck to the original one; the number of readings increases by at most a factor of m on each pass.) The given permutation requires 4 increasing readings, 10 decreasing readings; hence decreasing order requires 4 passes with two piles or 3 passes with three piles.

Conversely, this optimum number of passes can be achieved: Number the cards from 0 to $k - 1$ according to which reading it belongs to, and use a radix sort (least significant digit first in radix m). [See *Martin Gardner's Sixth Book of Mathematical Games* (San Francisco: W. H. Freeman, 1971), 111–112.]

15. Let there be k readings and m piles. The order is reversed on each pass; if there are k readings in one order, the number of readings in the opposite order is $n + 1 - k$. The minimum number of passes is either the smallest even number greater than or equal to $\log_m k$ or the smallest odd number greater than or equal to $\log_m (n + 1 - k)$. (Going backwards, there are at most m decreasing readings after one pass, m^2 increasing readings after two passes, etc.) The example can be sorted into increasing order in $\min(2, 5) = 2$ passes, into decreasing order in $\min(3, 4) = 3$ passes, using only two piles.

16. Assume that each string is followed by a special null character that is less than any letter of the alphabet. Perform a left-to-right radix sort by starting with all strings linked together in a single block of data. Then for $k = 1, 2, \ldots$, refine every block that contains more than one distinct string by splitting it into subblocks based on the kth letter of each string, meanwhile keeping the blocks sorted by their already-examined prefixes. When a block has only one item, or when its kth characters are all null (so that its keys are identical), we can arrange to avoid examining it again. [R. Paige and R. E. Tarjan, *SICOMP* **16** (1987), 973–989, §2.] This process is essentially that of constructing a trie as in Section 6.3. A simpler but slightly less efficient algorithm based on right-to-left radix sort was given for this problem by Aho, Hopcroft, and Ullman, *The Design and Analysis of Computer Algorithms* (Addison–Wesley, 1974), 79–84. The methods of McIlroy, Bostic, and McIlroy, cited in the text, are faster yet in practice.

17. MacLaren's method speeds up the second level, but it cannot be used at the top level because it does not compute the numbers N_k.

18. First we prove the hint: Let $p_k = \int_{k/CN}^{(k+1)/CN} f(x)\,dx$ be the probability that a key falls into bin k when there are CN bins. The time needed to distribute the records is $O(N)$, and the average number of inversions remaining after distribution is
$\frac{1}{2}\sum_{k=0}^{CN-1}\binom{N}{j}p_k^j(1-p_k)^{N-j}\binom{j}{2} = \frac{1}{2}\sum_{k=0}^{CN-1}\binom{N}{2}p_k^2 \le \frac{N-1}{4}p_k B/C$, because $p_k \le B/CN$.

Now consider two levels of distribution, with cN top-level bins, and let $b_k = \sup\{f(x) \mid k/cN \le x < (k+1)/cN\}$. Then the average total running time is $O(N)$ plus $\sum_{k=0}^{cN-1} T_k$, where T_k is the average time needed by MacLaren's method to sort N_k keys having the density function $f_k(x) = f((k+x)/cN)/cNp_k$. By the hint, we have $T_k = \mathrm{E}\,O(b_k N_k/cNp_k)$, because $f_k(x)$ is bounded by b_k/cNp_k. But $\mathrm{E}\,N_k = Np_k$, so $T_k = O(b_k/c)$. And as $N \to \infty$ we have $\sum_{k=0}^{cN-1} b_k \to N\int_0^1 f(x)\,dx = N$, by the definition of Riemann integrability.

SECTION 5.3.1

1. (a) 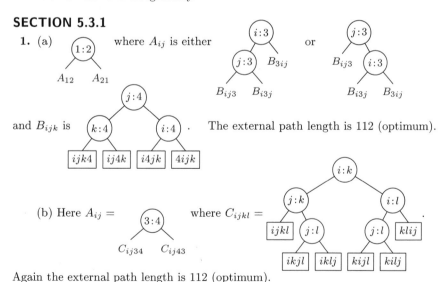 where A_{ij} is either   or

and B_{ijk} is   .   The external path length is 112 (optimum).

(b) Here $A_{ij} =$ where $C_{ijkl} =$.

Again the external path length is 112 (optimum).

2. In the notation of exercise 5.2.4–14,

$$L(n) - B(n) = \sum_{k=1}^{t} \left((e_k + k - 1)2^{e_k} - (e_1 + 1)2^{e_k} \right) + 2^{e_1+1} - 2^{e_t}$$

$$= 2^{e_1} - 2^{e_t} - \sum_{k=2}^{t} (e_1 - e_k + 2 - k)2^{e_k}$$

$$\geq 2^{e_1} - (2^{e_1-1} + \cdots + 2^{e_1-t+1} + 2^{e_t}) \geq 0,$$

with equality if and only if $n = 2^k - 2^j$ for some $k > j \geq 0$. [When merging is done "top-down" as in exercise 5.2.4–23, the maximum number of comparisons is $B(n)$.]

3. When $n > 0$, the number of outcomes such that the smallest key appears exactly k times is $\binom{n}{k}P_{n-k}$. Thus $2P_n = \sum_k \binom{n}{k}P_{n-k}$, for $n > 0$, and we have $2P(z) = e^z P(z) + 1$ by Eq. 1.2.9–(10).)

Another proof comes from the fact that $P_n = \sum_{k \geq 0} \left\{ {n \atop k} \right\} k!$, since $\left\{ {n \atop k} \right\}$ is the number of ways to partition n elements into k nonempty parts and these parts can be permuted in $k!$ ways. Thus $\sum_{n \geq 0} P_n z^n/n! = \sum_{k \geq 0} (e^z - 1)^k = 1/(2 - e^z)$ by Eq. 1.2.9–(23).

Still *another* proof, perhaps the most interesting, arises if we arrange the elements in sequence in a stable manner, so that K_i precedes K_j if and only if $K_i < K_j$ or ($K_i = K_j$ and $i < j$). Among all P_n outcomes, a given arrangement $K_{a_1} \ldots K_{a_n}$ now occurs exactly 2^k times if the permutation $a_1 \ldots a_n$ contains k ascents; hence P_n can be expressed in terms of the Eulerian numbers, $P_n = \sum_k \left\langle {n \atop k} \right\rangle 2^k$. Eq. 5.1.3–(20) with $z = 2$ now establishes the desired result.

This generating function was obtained by A. Cayley [*Phil. Mag.* **18** (1859), 374–378] in connection with the enumeration of an imprecisely defined class of trees. See also P. A. MacMahon, *Proc. London Math. Soc.* **22** (1891), 341–344; J. Touchard, *Ann. Soc. Sci. Bruxelles* **53** (1933), 21–31; and O. A. Gross, *AMM* **69** (1962), 4–8, who gave the interesting formula $P_n = \sum_{k \geq 1} k^n/2^{1+k}$, $n \geq 1$.

4. The representation

$$2P(z) = \frac{1}{2}\left(1 - i \cot \frac{i(z - \ln 2)}{2}\right) = \frac{1}{2} - \frac{1}{z - \ln 2} - \sum_{k \geq 1}\left(\frac{1}{z - \ln 2 - 2\pi i k} + \frac{1}{z - \ln 2 + 2\pi i k}\right)$$

yields the convergent series $P_n/n! = \frac{1}{2}(\ln 2)^{-n-1} + \sum_{k \geq 1} \Re((\ln 2 + 2\pi i k)^{-n-1})$.

5.

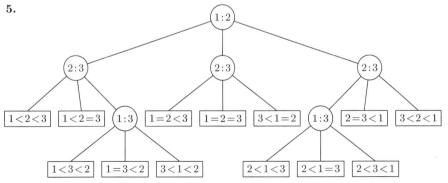

6. $S'(n) \geq S(n)$, since the keys might all be distinct; thus we must show that $S'(n) \leq S(n)$. Given a sorting algorithm that takes $S(n)$ steps on distinct keys, we can construct a sorting algorithm for the general case by defining the $=$ branch to be identical to the

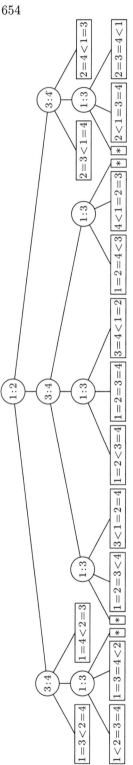

Fig. A–1. Solution to exercise 7. ("*" denotes an impossible case.)

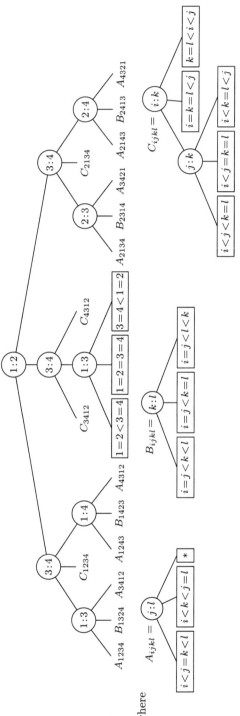

Fig. A–2. Solution to exercise 8.

< branch, removing redundancies. When an external node appears, we know all of the equality relations, since we have $K_{a_1} \leq K_{a_2} \leq \cdots \leq K_{a_n}$ and an explicit comparison $K_{a_i} : K_{a_{i+1}}$ has been made for $1 \leq i < n$.

M. Paterson observes that if the multiplicities of keys are $(n_1, \ldots, n_m)$, the number of comparisons can be reduced to $n \lg n - \sum n_j \lg n_j + O(n)$; see *SICOMP* **5** (1976), 2. This lower bound can almost be reached without substantial auxiliary memory by adapting heapsort to equal keys as suggested by Munro and Raman in *Lecture Notes in Comp. Sci.* **519** (1991), 473–480.

7. See Fig. A–1. The average number of comparisons is $(2 + 3 + 3 + 2 + 3 + 3 + 3 + 6 + 3 + 3 + 3 + 2 + 3 + 3 + 2)/16 = 2\frac{3}{4}$.

8. See Fig. A–2. The average number of comparisons is $3\frac{56}{81}$.

9. We need at least $n - 1$ comparisons to discover that all keys are equal, if they are. Conversely, $n - 1$ comparisons always suffice, since we can always deduce the final ordering after comparing K_1 with all of the other keys.

10. Let $f(n)$ be the desired function, and let $g(n)$ be the minimum average number of comparisons needed to sort $n+k$ elements when $k > 0$ and exactly k of the elements have known values (0 or 1). Then $f(0) = f(1) = g(0) = 0$, $g(1) = 1$; $f(n) = 1 + \frac{1}{2}f(n-1) + \frac{1}{2}g(n-2)$, $g(n) = 1 + \min(g(n-1), \frac{1}{2}g(n-1) + \frac{1}{2}g(n-2)) = 1 + \frac{1}{2}g(n-1) + \frac{1}{2}g(n-2)$, for $n \geq 2$. (Thus the best strategy is to compare two unknown elements whenever possible.) It follows that $f(n) - g(n) = \frac{1}{2}(f(n-1) - g(n-1))$ for $n \geq 2$, and $g(n) = \frac{2}{3}(n + \frac{1}{3}(1 - (-\frac{1}{2})^n))$ for $n \geq 0$. Hence the answer is

$$\frac{2}{3}n + \frac{2}{9} - \frac{2}{9}(-\frac{1}{2})^n - (\frac{1}{2})^{n-1}, \quad \text{for } n \geq 1.$$

(This exact formula may be compared with the information-theoretic lower bound, $\log_3(2^n - 1) \approx 0.6309n$.)

11. Binary insertion proves that $S_m(n) \leq B(m) + (n - m)\lceil \lg(m + 1) \rceil$, for $n \geq m$. On the other hand $S_m(n) \geq \lceil \lg \sum_{k=1}^{m} \{ {n \atop k} \} k! \rceil$, and this is asymptotically $n \lg m + O(((m-1)/m)^n)$; see Eq. 1.2.6–(53).

12. (a) If there are no redundant comparisons, we can arbitrarily assign an order to keys that are actually equal, when they are first compared, since no order can be deduced from previously made comparisons. (b) Assume that the tree strongly sorts every sequence of zeros and ones; we shall prove that it strongly sorts every permutation of $\{1, 2, \ldots, n\}$. Suppose it doesn't; then there is a permutation for which it claims that $K_{a_1} \leq K_{a_2} \leq \cdots \leq K_{a_n}$, whereas in fact $K_{a_i} > K_{a_{i+1}}$ for some i. Replace all elements $< K_{a_i}$ by 0 and all elements $\geq K_{a_i}$ by 1; by assumption the method will now sort when we take the path that leads to $K_{a_1} \leq K_{a_2} \leq \cdots \leq K_{a_n}$, a contradiction.

13. If n is even, $F(n) - F(n-1) = 1 + F(\lfloor n/2 \rfloor) - F(\lfloor n/2 \rfloor - 1)$ so we must prove that $w_{k-1} < \lfloor n/2 \rfloor \leq w_k$; this is obvious since $w_{k-1} = \lfloor w_k/2 \rfloor$. If n is odd, $F(n) - F(n-1) = G(\lceil n/2 \rceil) - G(\lfloor n/2 \rfloor)$, so we must prove that $t_{k-1} < \lceil n/2 \rceil \leq t_k$; this is obvious since $t_{k-1} = \lceil w_k/2 \rceil$.

14. By exercise 1.2.4–42, the sum is $n\lceil \lg \frac{3}{4}n \rceil - (w_1 + \cdots + w_j)$ where $w_j < n \leq w_{j+1}$. The latter sum is $w_{j+1} - \lfloor j/2 \rfloor - 1$. We can therefore express $F(n)$ in the form $n\lceil \lg \frac{3}{4}n \rceil - \lfloor 2^{\lfloor \lg(6n) \rfloor}/3 \rfloor + \lfloor \frac{1}{2}\lg(6n) \rfloor$ (and in many other ways).

15. If $\lceil \lg \frac{3}{4}n \rceil = \lg(\frac{3}{4}n) + \theta$, $F(n) = n \lg n - (3 - \lg 3)n + n(\theta + 1 - 2^\theta) + O(\log n)$. If $\lceil \lg n \rceil = \lg n + \theta$, $B(n) = n \lg n - n + n(\theta + 1 - 2^\theta) + O(\log n)$. [Note that $\lg n! = n \lg n - n/(\ln 2) + O(\log n)$; $1/(\ln 2) \approx 1.443$; $3 - \lg 3 \approx 1.415$.]

17. The number of cases with $b_k < a_p < b_{k+1}$ is

$$\binom{m-p+n-k}{m-p}\binom{p-1+k}{p-1},$$

and the number of cases with $a_j < b_q < a_{j+1}$ is

$$\binom{n-q+m-j}{n-q}\binom{q-1+j}{q-1}.$$

18. No, since we are considering only the less efficient branch of the tree below each comparison. One of the more efficient branches might turn out to be harder to handle.

20. Let L be the maximum level on which an external node appears, and let l be the minimum such level. If $L \geq l + 2$, we can remove two nodes from level L and place them below a node at level l; this decreases the external path length by $l + 2L - (L - 1 + 2(l + 1)) = L - l - 1 \geq 1$. Conversely, if $L \leq l + 1$, let there be k external nodes on level l and $N - k$ on level $l + 1$, where $0 < k \leq N$. By exercise 2.3.4.5–3, $k2^{-l} + (N - k)2^{-l-1} = 1$; hence $N + k = 2^{l+1}$. The inequalities $2^l \leq N < 2^{l+1}$ now show that $l = \lfloor \lg N \rfloor$; this defines k and yields the external path length (34).

21. Let $r(x)$ be the root of x's right subtree. All subtrees have minimum height if and only if $\lceil \lg t(l(x)) \rceil \leq \lceil \lg t(x) \rceil - 1$ and $\lceil \lg t(r(x)) \rceil \leq \lceil \lg t(x) \rceil - 1$ for all x. The first condition is equivalent to $2t(l(x)) - t(x) \leq 2^{\lceil \lg t(x) \rceil} - t(x)$, and the second condition is equivalent to $t(x) - 2t(l(x)) \leq 2^{\lceil \lg t(x) \rceil} - t(x)$.

22. By exercise 20, the four conditions $\lfloor \lg t(l(x)) \rfloor$, $\lfloor \lg t(r(x)) \rfloor \geq \lfloor \lg t(x) \rfloor - 1$ and $\lceil \lg t(l(x)) \rceil$, $\lceil \lg t(r(x)) \rceil \leq \lceil \lg t(x) \rceil - 1$ are necessary and sufficient. Arguing as in exercise 21, we can prove them equivalent to the stated conditions. [Martin Sandelius, *AMM* **68** (1961), 133–134.] See exercise 33 for a generalization.

23. Multiple list insertion assumes that the keys are uniformly distributed in a known range, so it isn't a "pure comparison" method satisfying the restrictions considered in this section.

24. First proceed as if sorting five elements, until after five comparisons we reach one of the configurations in (6). In the first three cases, complete sorting the five elements in two more comparisons, then insert the sixth element f. In the other case, first compare $f:b$, insert f into the main chain, then insert c. [Picard, *Théorie des Questionnaires*, page 116.]

25. Since $N = 7! = 5040$ and $q = 13$, there would be $8192 - 5040 = 3152$ external nodes on level 12 and $5040 - 3152 = 1888$ on level 13.

26. Ľ. Kollár [*Lecture Notes in Comp. Sci.* **233** (1986), 449–457] has presented an excellent way to verify that the optimum method has an external path length of 62416.

27.

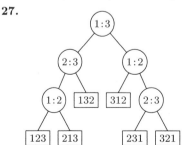

is the *only* way to recognize the two most frequent permutations with two comparisons, even though the first comparison produces a .27/.73 split!

28. Lun Kwan has constructed an 873-line program whose average running time is $38.925u$. Its maximum running time is $43u$; the latter appears to be optimal since it is the time for 7 compares, 7 tests, 6 loads, 5 stores.

29. We must make at least $S(n)$ comparisons, because it is impossible to know whether a permutation is even or odd unless we have made enough comparisons to determine it uniquely. For we can assume that enough comparisons have been made to narrow things down to two possibilities that depend on whether or not a_i is less than a_j, for some i and j; one of the two possibilities is even, the other is odd. [On the other hand there *is* an $O(n)$ algorithm for this problem, which simply counts the number of cycles and uses no comparisons at all; see exercise 5.2.2–2.]

30. Start with an optimal comparison tree of height $S(n)$; repeatedly interchange $i \leftrightarrow j$ in the right subtree of a node labeled $i:j$, from top to bottom. Interpreting the result as a comparison-exchange tree, every terminal node defines a unique permutation that can be sorted by at most $n-1$ more comparison-exchanges (by exercise 5.2.2–2).

[The idea of a comparison-exchange tree is due to T. N. Hibbard.]

31. At least 8 are required, since every tree of height 7 will produce the configuration

(or its dual) in some branch after 4 steps, with $a \neq 1$. This configuration cannot be sorted in 3 more comparison/exchange operations. On the other hand the following tree achieves the desired bound (and perhaps also the minimum *average* number of comparison/exchanges):

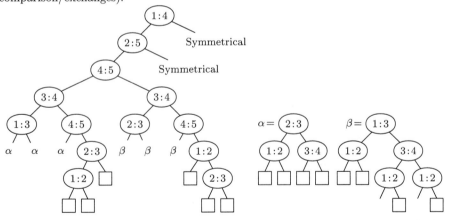

33. Simple operations applied to any tree of order x and resolution 1 can be applied to yield another whose weighted path length is no greater, where all external nodes lie on levels k and $k-1$ for some k, and at most one external node is noninteger, Furthermore, the noninteger external node lies on level k, if such a node is present. The weighted path length of any such tree has the stated value, so this must be minimal. Conversely, if (iv) and (v) hold in any real-valued search tree it is possible to show by induction that the weighted path length has the stated value, since there is a simple formula for the weighted path length of a tree in terms of the weighted path lengths of the two subtrees of the root.

35. The unsuccessful experiments by Knuth and Kaehler in *Information Processing Letters* **1** (1972), 173–176 may provide a clue.

36. [*Mat. Zametki* **4** (1968), 511–518.] See S. Felsner and W. T. Trotter, *Combinatorics, Paul Erdős is Eighty* **1** (1993), 145–157, for a summary of progress on this problem, and for a proof that we can always achieve

$$1 \leq T(G_1)/T(G_2) \leq \rho,$$

where the constant ρ is slightly less than 8/3.

SECTION 5.3.2

1. $S(m+n) \leq S(n) + S(n) + M(m,n)$.

2. The internal node that is kth in symmetric order corresponds to the comparison $A_1 : B_k$.

3. Strategy B$(1,l)$ is no better than strategy A$(1,l+1)$, and strategy B$'(1,l)$ no better than A$'(1,l-1)$; hence we must solve the recurrence

$$.M.(1,n) = \min_{1 \leq j \leq n} \max\big(\max_{1 \leq l \leq j}(1+.M.(1,l-1)),\ \max_{j \leq l \leq n}(1+.M.(1,n-l))\big), \quad n \geq 1;$$
$$.M.(1,0) = 0.$$

It is not difficult to verify that $\lceil \lg(n+1) \rceil$ satisfies this recurrence.

4. No. [C. Christen, *FOCS* **19** (1978), 259–266.]

6. Strategy A$'(i,i+1)$ can be used when $j = i+1$, except when $i \leq 2$. And we can use strategy A$(i,i+2)$ when $j \geq i+2$.

7. To insert $k+m$ elements among n others, independently insert k elements and m elements. (When k and m are large, an improved procedure is possible; see exercise 19.)

8, 9. In the following diagrams, $i:j$ denotes the comparison $A_i : B_j$, M_{ij} denotes merging i elements with j in $M(i,j)$ steps, and A denotes sorting the pattern ⸚ or ⸚ in three steps.

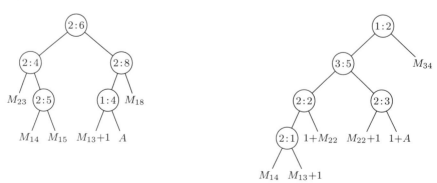

10.

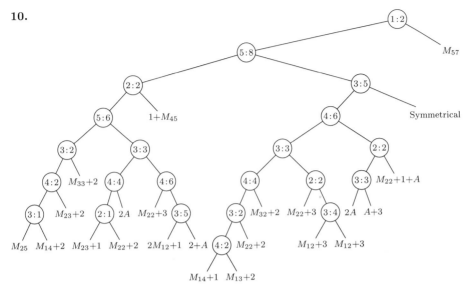

11. Let $n = g_t$ as in the hint. We may assume that $t \geq 6$. Without loss of generality let $A_2 : B_j$ be the first comparison. If $j > g_{t-1}$, the outcome $A_2 < B_j$ will require $\geq t$ more steps. If $j \leq g_{t-1}$, the outcome $A_2 < B_j$ would be no problem, so only the case $A_2 > B_j$ needs study, and we get the most information when $j = g_{t-1}$. If $t = 2k + 1$, we might have to merge A_2 with the $g_t - g_{t-1} = 2^{k-1}$ elements $> B_{g_{t-1}}$, and merge A_1 with the g_{t-1} others, but this requires $k + (k + 1) = t$ further steps. On the other hand if $n = g_t - 1$, we could merge A_2 with $2^{k-1} - 1$ elements, then A_1 with n elements, in $(k - 1) + (k + 1)$ further steps, hence $M(2, g_t - 1) \leq t$.

    The case $t = 2k$ is considerably more difficult; note that $g_t - g_{t-1} \geq 2^{k-2}$. After $A_2 > B_{g_{t-1}}$, suppose we compare $A_1 : B_j$. If $j > 2^{k-1}$ the outcome $A_1 < B_j$ requires $k + (k - 1)$ further comparisons (too many). If $j \leq 2^{k-1}$, we can argue as before that $j = 2^{k-1}$ gives most information. After $A_1 > B_{2^{k-1}}$, the next comparisons with A_1 might as well be with $B_{2^{k-1}+2^{k-2}}$, then $B_{2^{k-1}+2^{k-2}+2^{k-3}}$; since $2^{k-1} + 2^{k-2} + 2^{k-3} > g_{t-1}$, the remaining problem is to merge $\{A_1, A_2\}$ with $n - (2^{k-1} + 2^{k-2} + 2^{k-3})$ elements. Of course we needn't make any comparisons with A_1 right away; we could instead compare $A_2 : B_{n+1-j}$. If $j \leq 2^{k-3}$, we consider the case $A_2 < B_{n+1-j}$, while if $j > 2^{k-3}$ we consider $A_2 > B_{n+1-j}$. The latter case requires at least $(k - 2) + (k + 1)$ more steps. Continuing, we find that the *only* potentially fruitful line is $A_2 > B_{g_{t-1}}$, $A_2 < B_{n+1-2^{k-3}}$, $A_1 > B_{2^{k-1}}$, $A_1 > B_{2^{k-1}+2^{k-2}}$, $A_1 > B_{2^{k-1}+2^{k-2}+2^{k-3}}$, but then we have exactly g_{t-5} elements left! Conversely, if $n = g_t - 1$, this line works. [*Acta Informatica* **1** (1971), 145–158.]

12. The first comparison must be either $\alpha : X_k$ for $1 \leq k \leq i$, or (symmetrically) $\beta : X_{n-k}$ for $1 \leq k \leq j$. In the former case the response $\alpha < X_k$ leaves us with $R_n(k-1, j)$ more comparisons to make; the response $\alpha > X_k$ leaves us with the problem of sorting $\alpha < \beta$, $Y_1 < \cdots < Y_{n-k}$, $\alpha < Y_{i-k+1}$, $\beta > Y_{n-k-j}$, where $Y_r = X_{r-k}$.

13. [*Computers in Number Theory* (New York: Academic Press, 1971), 263–269.]

14. [*SICOMP* **9** (1980), 298–320. The complete solution for $M(4, n)$ was obtained shortly afterwards by J. Schulte Mönting, who also gave a conjectured solution for $M(5, n)$, in *Theor. Comp. Sci.* **14** (1981), 19–37.]

15. Double m until it exceeds n. This involves $\lfloor \lg(n/m) \rfloor + 1$ doublings.

16. All except $(m,n) = (2,8)$, $(3,6)$, $(3,8)$, $(3,10)$, $(4,8)$, $(4,10)$, $(5,9)$, $(5,10)$, when it's one over.

17. Assume that $m \le n$ and let $t = \lg(n/m) - \theta$. Then $\lg \binom{m+n}{m} > \lg n^m - \lg m! \ge m \lg n - (m \lg m - m + 1) = m(t + \theta) + m - 1 = H(m,n) + \theta m - \lfloor 2^\theta m \rfloor \ge H(m,n) + \theta m - 2^\theta m \ge H(m,n) - m$. (The inequality $m! \le m^m 2^{1-m}$ is a consequence of the fact that $k(m-k) \le (m/2)^2$ for $1 \le k < m$.)

19. First merge $\{A_1, \ldots, A_m\}$ with $\{B_2, B_4, \ldots, B_{2\lfloor n/2 \rfloor}\}$. Then we must insert the odd elements B_{2i-1} among a_i of the A's for $1 \le i \le \lceil n/2 \rceil$, where $a_1 + a_2 + \cdots + a_{\lceil n/2 \rceil} \le m$. The latter operation requires at most a_i operations for each i, so at most m more comparisons will finish the job.

20. Apply (12).

22. R. Michael Tanner [*SICOMP* **7** (1978), 18–38] has shown that a "fractile insertion" algorithm makes at most $1.06 \lg \binom{m+n}{m}$ comparisons on the average. Ľ. Kollár [*Computers and Artificial Int.* **5** (1986), 335–344] has studied the average behavior of Algorithm H.

23. The adversary keeps an $n \times n$ matrix X whose entries x_{ij} are initially all 1. When the algorithm asks if $A_i = B_j$, the adversary sets x_{ij} to 0. The answer is "No," unless the permanent of X has just become zero. In the latter case, the adversary answers "Yes" (as it must, lest the algorithm terminate immediately!), and deletes row i and column j from X; the resulting $(n-1) \times (n-1)$ matrix will have a nonzero permanent. The adversary continues in this way until only a 0×0 matrix is left.

   If the permanent is about to become zero, we can rearrange rows and columns so that $i = j = 1$ and the matrix has all 1s on the diagonal, yet its permanent vanishes when $x_{11} \leftarrow 1$; then we must have $x_{1k}x_{k1} = 0$ for all $k > 1$. It follows that at least n zeros are deleted when the adversary first answers "Yes," and $n-1$ the second time, etc. The algorithm will terminate only after receiving n "Yes" answers to nonredundant questions, and after asking at least $n + (n-1) + \cdots + 1$ questions [*JACM* **19** (1972), 649–659]. A similar argument shows that $n + (n-1) + \cdots + (n-m+1)$ questions are needed to determine that $A \subseteq B$ when $|A| = m \le n = |B|$.

24. The coarse preliminary merge needs at most $m + q - 1$ comparisons, and the subsequent insertions need at most t each. These upper bounds cannot be decreased. So the maximum is the same as for Algorithm H (see (19)).

25. The general problem is as hard as the special case where each x_{ij} is 0 or 1 and $x = \frac{1}{2}$. Then each comparison is equivalent to looking at the bit x_{ij}, and we want to determine the entire matrix by inspecting the fewest bits. Any merging problem (1) corresponds to such a 0–1 matrix if we set $x_{ij} = [A_i > B_{n+1-j}]$. (N. Linial and M. Saks, in *J. Algorithms* **6** (1985), 86–103, attribute this observation to J. Shearer. A similar result connects searching and sorting with respect to any partial order.)

SECTION 5.3.3

1. Player *11* lost to *05*; so *13* was known to be worse than *05*, *11*, and *12*.

2. Let x be the tth largest, and let S be the set of all elements y such that the comparisons made are insufficient to prove either that $x < y$ or $y < x$. There are permutations, consistent with all the comparisons made, in which all elements of S are less than x; for we can stipulate that all elements of S are less than x and embed the resulting partial ordering in a linear ordering. Similarly there are consistent permutations in which all elements of S are greater than x. Hence we don't know the rank of x unless S is empty.

3. An adversary may regard the loser of the first comparison as the worst player of all.

4. Suppose the largest $t-1$ elements are $\{a_1,\ldots,a_{t-1}\}$. Any path in the comparison tree to determine the largest t elements, consistent with this assumption, must include at least $n-t$ comparisons to determine the largest of the remaining $n-t+1$ elements. Such paths have at least $n-t$ binary choice points, so there are at least 2^{n-t} of them. Thus, each of the $n^{\underline{t-1}}$ choices for the largest $t-1$ elements must appear in at least 2^{n-t} leaves of the tree.

5. In fact, $W_t(n) \le V_t(n) + S(t-1)$, by exercise 2.

6. Let $g(l_1, l_2, \ldots, l_m) = m - 2 + \lceil \lg(2^{l_1} + 2^{l_2} + \cdots + 2^{l_m}) \rceil$, and assume that $f = g$ whenever $l_1 + l_2 + \cdots + l_m + 2m < N$. We shall prove that $f = g$ when $l_1 + l_2 + \cdots + l_m + 2m = N$. We may assume that $l_1 \ge l_2 \ge \cdots \ge l_m$. There are only a few possible ways to make the first comparison:

Strategy A(j, k), for $j < k$. Compare the largest element of group j with the largest of group k. This gives the relation

$$f(l_1, \ldots, l_m) \le 1 + g(l_1, \ldots, l_{j-1}, l_j+1, l_{j+1}, \ldots, l_{k-1}, l_{k+1}, \ldots, l_m)$$
$$= g(l_1, \ldots, l_{j-1}, l_j, l_{j+1}, \ldots, l_{k-1}, l_j, l_{k+1}, \ldots, l_m) \ge g(l_1, \ldots, l_m).$$

Strategy B(j, k), for $l_k > 0$. Compare the largest element of group j with one of the small elements of group k. This gives the relation

$$f(l_1, \ldots, l_m) \le 1 + \max(\alpha, \beta) = 1 + \beta,$$

where

$$\alpha = g(l_1, \ldots, l_{j-1}, l_{j+1}, \ldots, l_m) \le g(l_1, \ldots, l_m) - 1,$$
$$\beta = g(l_1, \ldots, l_{k-1}, l_k-1, l_{k+1}, \ldots, l_m) \ge g(l_1, \ldots, l_m) - 1.$$

Strategy C(j, k), for $j \le k$, $l_j > 0$, $l_k > 0$. Compare a small element from group j with a small element from group k. The corresponding relation is

$$f(l_1, \ldots, l_m) \le 1 + g(l_1, \ldots, l_{k-1}, l_k - 1, l_{k+1}, \ldots, l_m) \ge g(l_1, \ldots, l_m).$$

The value of $f(l_1, \ldots, l_m)$ is found by taking the minimum right-hand side over all these strategies; hence $f(l_1, \ldots, l_m) \ge g(l_1, \ldots, l_m)$. When $m > 1$, Strategy A$(m-1, m)$ shows that $f(l_1, \ldots, l_m) \le g(l_1, \ldots, l_m)$, since $g(l_1, \ldots, l_{m-1}, l_m) = g(l_1, \ldots, l_{m-1}, l_{m-1})$ when $l_1 \ge \cdots \ge l_m$. (*Proof:* $\lceil \lg(M + 2^a) \rceil = \lceil \lg(M + 2^b) \rceil$ for $0 \le a \le b$, when M is a positive multiple of 2^b.) When $m = 1$, use Strategy C$(1, 1)$.

[S. S. Kislitsyn's paper determined the optimum strategy A$(m-1, m)$ and evaluated $f(l, l, \ldots, l)$ in closed form; the general formula for f and this simplified proof were discovered by Floyd in 1970.]

7. For $j > 1$, if $j + 1$ is in α', c_j is 1 plus the number of comparisons needed to select the next largest element of α'. Similar reasoning applies if $j + 1$ is in α''; and c_1 is always 0, since the tree always looks the same at the end.

8. In other words, is there an extended binary tree with n external nodes such that the sum of the distances to the $t-1$ farthest internal nodes from the root is less than the corresponding sum for the complete binary tree? The answer is no, since it is not hard to show that the kth largest element of $\mu(\alpha)$ is at least $\lfloor \lg(n-k) \rfloor$ for all α.

9. (All paths use six comparisons, yet the procedure is not optimum for $\overline{V}_3(5)$.)

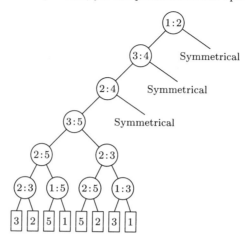

10. (Found manually by trial and error, using exercise 6 to help find fruitful lines.)

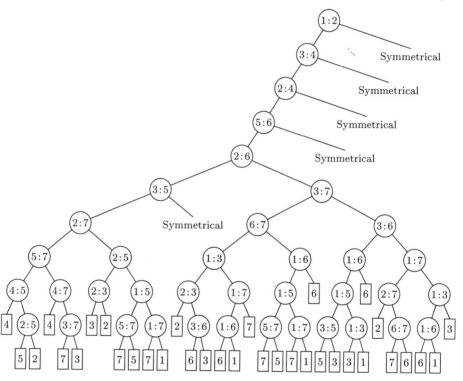

11. See *Information Processing Letters* **3** (1974), 8–12.

12. After discarding the smallest of $\{X_1, X_2, X_3, X_4\}$, we have the configuration •—•
plus $n - 3$ isolated elements; the third largest of them can be found in $V_3(n - 1) - 1$
further steps.

13. After finding the median of the first $f(n)$ elements, say X_j, compare it to each of the others; this splits the elements into approximately $n/2-k$ less than X_j and $n/2+k$ greater than X_j, for some k. It remains to find the $|k|$th largest or smallest element of the bigger set, which requires $n/2+O(|k|\log n)$ further comparisons. The average value of $|k|$ (consider points uniformly distributed in $[0..1]$) is $O(1/\sqrt{n})+O(n/\sqrt{f(n)})$. Let $T(n)$ be the average number of comparisons when $f(n)=n^{2/3}$; then $T(n)-n=T(n^{2/3})-n^{2/3}+n/2+O(n^{2/3})$, and the result follows.

It is interesting to note that when $n=5$, this method requires only $5\frac{13}{15}$ comparisons on the average, slightly better than the tree of exercise 9.

14. In general, the t largest can be found in $U_t(n)\le V_t(n-1)+1$ comparisons, by finding the tth largest of $\{X_1,\ldots,X_{n-1}\}$ and comparing it with X_n, because of exercise 2. (Kirkpatrick actually proved that (12) is a lower bound for $U_t(n+1)-1$. For larger t, an improved bound for $U_t(n)$ was found by J. W. John, *SICOMP* **17** (1988), 640–647.)

15. $\min(t,n+1-t)$. Assuming that $t\le n+1-t$, if we don't save each of the first t words when they are first read in, we may have forgotten the tth largest, depending on the subsequent values still unknown to us. Conversely, t locations are sufficient, since we can compare a newly input item with the previous tth largest, storing the register if and only if it is greater.

16. The algorithm starts with $(a,b,c,d)=(n,0,0,0)$ and ends with $(0,1,1,n-2)$. If the adversary avoids "surprising" outcomes, the only transitions possible after each comparison are from (a,b,c,d) to itself or to

$$
\begin{aligned}
(a-2,\,b+1,\,c+1,\,d), &\quad \text{if } a\ge 2;\\
(a-1,\,b,\,c+1,\,d) \text{ or } (a-1,\,b+1,\,c,\,d), &\quad \text{if } a\ge 1;\\
(a,\,b-1,\,c,\,d+1), &\quad \text{if } b\ge 2;\\
(a,\,b,\,c-1,\,d+1), &\quad \text{if } c\ge 2.
\end{aligned}
$$

It follows that $\lceil\frac{3}{2}a\rceil+b+c-2$ comparisons are needed to get from (a,b,c,d) to $(0,1,1,a+b+c+d-2)$. [*Reference: CACM* **15** (1972), 462–464. In *FOCS* **16** (1975), 71–74, Pohl proved that the algorithm also minimizes the *average* number of comparisons.]

17. Use (6) first for the largest, then for the smallest, noting that $\lfloor n/2\rfloor$ of the comparisons are common to both.

18. $V_t(n)\le 18n-151$, for all sufficiently large n.

21. Step 0. Build two knockout trees of sizes 2^k and 2^{k-t+1}.

Step j, for $1\le j\le t$. (At this point we have output the largest $j-1$ elements. The remaining elements, together with a set of dummy placeholders that each equal $-\infty$, now appear in two knockout trees A and B, where A has 2^k leaves and B has 2^{k-t+j}.) Let a be the champion of A, and assume that a has beaten $a_0, a_1, \ldots, a_{k-1}$, where a_l is a champion of 2^l elements. Similarly, let b and $b_0, b_1, \ldots, b_{k-t+j-1}$ be the champion and subchampions of B. If $j=t$, output $\max(a,b)$ and stop. Otherwise, "grow" another level at the bottom of B by introducing 2^{k-t+j} dummies who each have lost their first game to the players of B. (Our strategy will be to merge B into A, if possible, by exchanging it with the subtree A' of A that contains $a_0, a_1, \ldots, a_{k-t+j}$; notice that A', like the newly enlarged B, is a knockout tree with $2^{k-t+j+1}$ leaves.) Compare b to $a_{k-t+j+1}$, then compare the winner to $a_{k-t+j+2}$, etc., until $c=\max(b,a_{k-t+j-1},\ldots,a_{k-1})$ has been found. Case 1, $b<c$: Output a and interchange

B with A'. Case 2, $b = c$ and $b < a$: Output a and interchange B with A'. Case 3, $b = c$ and $b > a$: Output b. After handling these three cases we are left with (possibly new) knockout trees A and B in which the champion of B has just been output. Remove that element from B and replace it by $-\infty$, making any necessary comparisons to restore the knockout tournament structure (as in tree selection). This completes Step j.

Step 0 makes $2^k - 1 + 2^{k+1-t} - 1$ comparisons, and Step t makes 1. Steps 1, 2, $\ldots$, $t - 1$ each make at most $k - 1$ comparisons, except in Case 2 when there might be k. But whenever Case 2 occurs, we'll save one comparison the next time we're in Case 1 or Case 2, because a_0 will then be $-\infty$. Thus steps 1 through $t - 1$ make at most $(t - 1)(k - 1) + 1$ comparisons altogether.

By exercise 3 we have $W_t(n) \le n + (t - 1)(k - 1)$ for all $n \le 2^k + 2^{k+1-t}$, when $k \ge t \ge 2$. If $n \ge 2^k + t - 2$, exercise 4 says that $W_t(n) \ge n - t + \lceil \lg(2^k + t - 2)\frac{t-1}{} \rceil$, which is $n - t + (t-1)k + 1$ if $t \ge 3$. Thus the method is optimum for $2^k + t - 2 \le n \le 2^k + 2^{k+1-t}$ when $k \ge t \ge 3$. (Also for several smaller values of n, if t is large.)

A similar method, which uses a reserved element instead of $-\infty$ when rebuilding B at the end of steps 1, $\ldots$, $t-2$ (see the proof of (11)), proves that $V_t(n) \le n + (t-1)(k-1)$ when $n \le 2^k + 2^{k+1-t} + t - 2$ and $k \ge t \ge 3$. [See *J. Algorithms* **5** (1984), 557–578.]

22. In general when $2^r \cdot 2^k < n + 2 - t \le (2^r + 1) \cdot 2^k$ and $t < 2^r \le 2t$, this procedure starting with $t + 1$ knockout trees of size 2^k will yield $\lfloor (t - 1)/2 \rfloor$ fewer comparisons than (11), since at least this many of the comparisons that were used to find the minimum in (ii) can be "reused" in (iii).

23. According to (15), the quantity $V_{\lceil n/2 \rceil}(n)/n$ is bounded below by 2 as $n \to \infty$; but D. Dor [Ph.D. thesis, Tel Aviv University, 1995] has shown that the actual lower limit is strictly greater than 2. Dor and U. Zwick have also established the upper limit 2.942 [*SODA* **6** (1995), 28–37]; and they have proved an asymptotic upper bound

$$V_{an}(n) \le \left(1 + \alpha \lg \frac{1}{\alpha} + O\left(\alpha \log \log \frac{1}{\alpha}\right)\right) n$$

which is not extremely far from (15) when α is small [*Combinatorica* **16** (1996), 41–58].

24. Since $W_t(n) = n + O(t \log n)$ by Eq. (6), the statement in the hint is surely true when $t \le \sqrt{n}/\ln n$. Suppose that statement holds for n, and let u and v have ranks $t_- = \lfloor t - \sqrt{t \ln n} \rfloor$ and $t_+ = \lceil t + \sqrt{t \ln n} \rceil$ in the first n of $2n$ randomly ordered elements. (The smallest element has rank 1.) Compare the other n elements to v, and compare those less than v also to u. The probability p_s that an element x of rank t in the first n has rank s overall is $\binom{s-1}{t-1}\binom{2n-s}{n-t}/\binom{2n}{n}$. The average value of s is $\sum s p_s = \frac{2n+1}{n+1}t$; this is the average number of elements $< x$, hence the average number of comparisons to u is $\binom{n}{n+1}t_+ = t + O(n \log n)^{1/2}$. Let u and v have ranks s_- and s_+ among all $2n$ elements, and let $T_- = \lfloor 2t - \sqrt{2t \ln 2n} \rfloor$, $T_+ = \lceil 2t + \sqrt{2t \ln 2n} \rceil$. If $s_- \le T_-$ and $s_+ \ge T_+$, we can find the elements of ranks T_- and T_+ by selecting from the $s_+ - s_- + 1$ elements between u and v. We will prove that it's very unlikely to have $s_- > T_-$ or $s_- < T_- - 2\sqrt{n \ln n}$ or $s_+ < T_+$ or $s_+ > T_+ + 2\sqrt{n \ln n}$; therefore $O(n \log n)^{1/2}$ further comparisons will almost always suffice. The hint will follow by induction on n if we can show that "very unlikely" means "with probability $O(n^{-1-\epsilon})$ for all sufficiently large n."

Notice that $p_{s+1}/p_s = s(n - s + t)/(s + 1 - t)(2n - s)$ decreases as s increases from t to $n + t$, and it is ≤ 1 if and only if $s \ge 2n(t - 1)/(n - 1)$; it is $\le 1 - \frac{1}{2}cn^{-1/2} + O(n^{-1})$ when $s = \bar{s}(c) = 2t + ct(n - t)/n^{3/2}$. Therefore the probability that $s \ge \bar{s}(c)$ is $\le 2c^{-1}n^{1/2}p_{\bar{s}(c)}(1 + O(n^{-1/2}))$. Similarly, $p_{s-1}/p_s < 1 - \frac{1}{2}cn^{-1/2} - O(n^{-1})$

when $s = \underline{s}(c) = 2t - 1 - c(t - 1)(n + 1 - t)/n^{3/2}$, so $s \le \underline{s}(c)$ with probability $\le 2c^{-1}n^{1/2}p_{\underline{s}(c)}(1 + O(n^{-1/2}))$. In the cases we need, the relevant values of c are $\ge .55n^{3/2}(\ln n)^{1/2}t^{-1/2}(n - t)^{-1}$ for all large n, and Stirling's approximation implies that $p_{\bar{s}(c)}$ and $p_{\underline{s}(c)}$ are both

$$O\big(n^{1/2}s^{-1/2}(2n - s)^{-1/2}\big)\exp\big(-2sc^2(n - t)^2/n^3 - 2(2n - s)c^2t^2/n^3\big)$$
$$\le O\big(t^{-1/2}\exp(-4t(n - t)c^2/n^2)\big) \le O(t^{-1/2}n^{-1.2}).$$

Thus the probability $O(n^{-1.2}(\log n)^{1/2})$ is indeed very unlikely. [A similar construction appeared in *CACM* **18** (1975), 165–172, but the analysis was incorrect.]

25. Given a selection algorithm and a permutation π of $\{1,\ldots,n\}$, let's charge each comparison $\pi_i\!:\!\pi_j$ to π_i if $|\pi_i - t| > |\pi_j - t|$; if $|\pi_i - t| = |\pi_j - t|$, we charge $\frac{1}{2}$ to each. A charge to π_i is called *useful* if $\pi_i < \pi_j \le t$ or $\pi_i > \pi_j \ge t$; otherwise it's *useless*. Let x_k be the total charge to k. Then the total number of comparisons is $x_1 + \cdots + x_n$. Clearly $x_t = 0$; but $x_k \ge 1$ for all $k \ne t$, because every element other than t has a useful charge. We will prove that $\mathrm{E}\,x_{t+k} + \mathrm{E}\,x_{t-k} \ge 3$ for $0 < k < t$.

Let $A_k(\pi) = $ [the first charge to $t + k$ was useless]. Then $A_k(\pi) = 1 - A_{-k}(\pi')$, where π' is like π but with the elements $(t - k, \ldots, t + k - 1, t + k)$ replaced respectively by $(t-k+1, \ldots, t+k, t-k)$. Therefore $\mathrm{E}\,A_k + \mathrm{E}\,A_{-k} = 1$.

Let $B_k(\pi) = $ [the first charge to both $t + k$ and $t - k$ was $\frac{1}{2}$, and $t + k$ received its second charge before $t - k$ did]. Also let $C_k(\pi) = [x_{t+k} \ge 2 + A_k]$. Then $B_k(\pi) \le C_k(\pi')$, where π' is like π but with the elements $(t - k, t - k + 1, \ldots, t + k - 1)$ replaced by $(t + k - 1, t - k, \ldots, t + k - 2)$. Similarly, $B_{-k}(\pi) \le C_{-k}(\pi'')$, where π'' is obtained from π by changing $(t-k+1, \ldots, t+k-1, t+k)$ to $(t-k+2, \ldots, t+k, t-k+1)$. It follows that $\mathrm{E}\,B_k \le \mathrm{E}\,C_k$ and $\mathrm{E}\,B_{-k} \le \mathrm{E}\,C_{-k}$.

The proof is completed by observing that $x_{t-k} + x_{t+k} \ge 2 + A_k + A_{-k} - B_k - B_{-k} + C_k + C_{-k}$. [See *JACM* **36** (1989), 270–279, for further results.]

The upper bound in (17) also has a matching lower bound: Andrew and Frances Yao proved that $\overline{V}_t(n) \ge n + \frac{1}{2}t\,(\ln\ln n - \ln t - 9)$ for $t > 1$ and $n \ge (8t)^{18t}$, in *SICOMP* **11** (1982), 428–447.

26. (a) Let the vertices of the two types of components be designated a; $b < c$. The adversary acts as follows on nonredundant comparisons: Case 1, $a\!:\!a'$, make an arbitrary decision. Case 2, $x\!:\!b$, say that $x > b$; all future comparisons $y\!:\!b$ with this particular b will result in $y > b$, otherwise the comparisons are decided by an adversary for $U_t(n-1)$, yielding $\ge 2 + U_t(n - 1)$ comparisons in all. This reduction will be abbreviated "let $b = \min; 2 + U_t(n - 1)$." Case 3, $x\!:\!c$, let $c = \max; 2 + U_{t-1}(n - 1)$.

(b) Let the new types of vertices be designated $d_1, d_2 < e$; $f < g < h > i$. Case 1, $a\!:\!a'$ or $c\!:\!c'$, arbitrary decision. Case 2, $a\!:\!c$, say that $a < c$. Case 3, $x\!:\!b$, let $b = \min$; $2 + U_t(n - 1)$. Case 4, $x\!:\!d$, let $d = \min$; $2 + U_t(n - 1)$. Case 5, $x\!:\!e$, let $e = \max$; $3 + U_{t-1}(n-1)$. Case 6, $x\!:\!f$, let $f = \min$; $2 + U_t(n-1)$. Case 7, $x\!:\!g$, let f and $g = \min$; $3 + U_t(n - 2)$. Case 8, $x\!:\!h$, let $h = \max$; $3 + U_{t-1}(n - 1)$. Case 9, $x\!:\!i$, let $i = \min$; $2 + U_t(n - 1)$.

(c) For $t = 1$ we have $U_t(n) = n - 1$, so the inequality holds. For $1 < t \le n/2 - 1$, use induction and (b). For $t = (n - 1)/2$, use induction and (a). For $t = n/2$, $U_t(n - 1) = U_{t-1}(n - 1)$; use induction and (a).

27. (a) The height h satisfies $2^h \ge \sum_l 1 \ge \sum_l \Pr(l)/p = 1/p$.

(b) If $r \le t$, we reach A3 after at least $n - |S_0| - |T_0| = n - |S_0| - r$ flips. The tth largest element will be either the smallest or largest element of Q, and the elements of

Q have not yet been compared to each other, so we will need at least $|Q|-1$ more flips. If $|S_0| < q$ we have $|Q| = r$, and if not we have $|Q| \geq |S_0| - |C(y_0)| + 1 \geq |S_0| - (q-r) + 1$; so in both cases at least $n-q$ flips will be made. There are $n+1-t$ sets T containing the $t-1$ largest elements determined by a given leaf, and for every such T the probability of reaching that leaf is either zero or $2^{-f}/\binom{n}{t}$, where $f \geq n - q$ is the number of flips corresponding to T. [This adversary is implicit in the paper of Bent and John, *STOC* **17** (1985), 213–216.]

(c) If $t < r$, change t to $n + 1 - t$; this will make $t \geq r$ when r maximizes the right-hand side, since r will be $O(\sqrt{n})$. If it is possible to reach A3 with $|C(y)| > q - r$ for all $y \in T_0$, the algorithm will make $n - 1$ comparisons to relate the tth largest element to all the others, in addition to at least $(r - 1)(q - r + 1)$ comparisons that it made between S and $T \setminus \{y_0\}$.

(d) Choose $r = \lceil \sqrt{m} \rceil$ and $q = 2r - 2$. (It is slightly better to let $q = r + \lfloor \sqrt{m} + \frac{1}{2} \rfloor - 2$; this choice maximizes the lower bound derived in (c).)

SECTION 5.3.4

1. (When $m = 2k - 1$ is odd it is best to have v_k followed by v_{k+1}, w_{k+1}, v_{k+2}, $\ldots$ instead of by w_{k+1}, v_{k+1}, w_{k+2}, $\ldots$ in the diagram. This change is valid because the swapped lines are being compared to each other.)

(3,5) odd-even merge

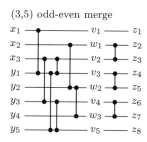

Pratt eight-sort

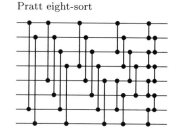

2. The increment h needs $2 - \lceil 2h \geq n \rceil$ levels; see the diagram above for $n = 8$.

3. $C(m, m-1) = C(m, m) - 1$, for $m \geq 1$.

4. If $\hat{T}(6) = 4$, there would be three comparators acting at each time, since $\hat{S}(6) = 12$. But then removing the bottom line and its four comparators would give $\hat{S}(5) \leq 8$, a contradiction. [The same argument yields $\hat{T}(7) = \hat{T}(8) = 6$. Ian Parberry has shown by exhaustive computer search that $\hat{T}(9) = \hat{T}(10) = 7$; see *Math. Systems Theory* **24** (1991), 101–116.]

5. Let $f(n) = f(\lceil n/2 \rceil) + 1 + \lceil \lg \lceil n/2 \rceil \rceil$, if $n \geq 2$. Then $f(n) = (1 + \lceil \lg n \rceil) \lceil \lg n \rceil / 2$ by induction on n.

6. We may assume that each stage makes $\lfloor n/2 \rfloor$ comparisons (extra comparisons can't hurt). Since $\hat{T}(6) = 5$, it suffices to show that $T(5) = 5$. After two stages when $n = 5$, we cannot avoid the partial orderings $\nearrow\!\!\!\searrow$ or $\leq$, which cannot be sorted in two more stages.

7. Assume that the input keys are $\{1, 2, \ldots, 10\}$. The key fact is that after the first 16 comparators, lines 2, 3, 4, and 6 cannot contain 8 or 9, nor can they contain both 6 and 7.

8. Straightforward generalization of Theorem F.

9. $\hat{M}(3,3) \geq \hat{S}(6) - 2\hat{S}(3)$; $\hat{M}(4,4) \geq \hat{S}(8) - 2\hat{S}(4)$; $\hat{M}(5,5) \geq 2\hat{M}(2,3) + 3$ by exercise 8; and $\hat{M}(2,3) \geq \hat{S}(5) - \hat{S}(2) - \hat{S}(3)$. Similarly $\hat{M}(3,4) = 8$. But what are $\hat{M}(3,5)$ and $\hat{M}(4,5)$?

10. The hint follows by the method of proof in Theorem Z. Then show that the number of 0s in the even subsequence minus the number of 0s in the odd subsequence is ± 1 or 0.

11. (Solution by M. W. Green.) The network is symmetric in the sense that, whenever z_i is compared to z_j, there is a corresponding comparison of $z_{2^t-1-j} : z_{2^t-1-i}$. Any symmetric network capable of sorting a sequence $\langle z_0, \ldots, z_{2^t-1} \rangle$ will also sort the sequence $\langle -z_{2^t-1}, \ldots, -z_0 \rangle$.

Batcher has observed that the network will actually sort any cyclic shift $\langle z_j, z_{j+1}, \ldots, z_{2^t-1}, z_0, \ldots, z_{j-1} \rangle$ of a bitonic sequence. This is a consequence of the 0–1 principle.

[These results do *not* hold for bitonic sorters when the order is not a power of 2. For example, Fig. 52 does not sort $\langle 0,0,0,0,0,1,0 \rangle$. Batcher's original definition of bitonic sequences was more complicated and less useful than the definition we have adopted.]

12. $x \vee y$ is (consider 0–1 sequences), but not $x \wedge y$ (consider $\langle 3,1,4,5 \rangle \wedge \langle 6,7,8,2 \rangle$).

13. A perfect shuffle has the effect of replacing z_i by z_j, where the binary representation of j is that of i rotated cyclically to the right one place (see exercise 3.4.2–13). Consider shuffling the comparators instead of the lines; then the first column of comparators acts on the pairs $z[i]$ and $z[i \oplus 2^{r-1}]$, the next column on $z[i]$ and $z[i \oplus 2^{r-2}]$, ..., the tth column on $z[i]$ and $z[i \oplus 1]$, the $(t+1)$st column on $z[i]$ and $z[i \oplus 2^{r-1}]$ again, etc. Here $\oplus$ denotes exclusive-or on the binary representation. This shows that Fig. 57 is equivalent to Fig. 56; after s stages we have groups of 2^s elements that are alternatively sorted and reverse-sorted.

C. G. Plaxton and T. Suel [*Math. Systems Theory* **27** (1994), 491–508] have shown that any such network requires at least $\Omega((\log n)^2/\log\log n)$ levels of delay.

14. (a) Let $y_{i_s} = x_{j_s}$, $y_{j_s} = x_{i_s}$, $y_k = x_k$ for $i_s \neq k \neq j_s$; then $y\alpha^s = x\alpha$. (b) This is obvious unless the set $\{i_s, j_s, i_t, j_t\}$ has only three distinct elements; suppose that $i_s = i_t$. Then if $s < t$ the first $s-1$ comparators have (i_s, j_s, j_t) replaced, respectively, by (j_s, j_t, i_s) in both $(\alpha^s)^t$ and $(\alpha^t)^s$. (c) $(\alpha^s)^s = \alpha$, and $\alpha^1 = \alpha$, so we can assume that $s_1 > s_2 > \cdots > s_k > 1$. (d) Let $\beta = \alpha[i:j]$; then $g_\beta(x_1, \ldots, x_n) = (\bar{x}_i \vee x_j) \wedge \left(g_\alpha(x_1, \ldots, x_i, \ldots, x_j, \ldots, x_n) \vee g_\alpha(x_1, \ldots, x_j, \ldots, x_i, \ldots, x_n) \right)$. Iterating this identity yields the result. (e) $f_\alpha(x) = 1$ if and only if no path in G_α goes from i to j where $x_i > x_j$. If α is a sorting network, the conjugates of α are also; and $f_\alpha(x) = 0$ for all x with $x_i > x_{i+1}$. Take $x = e^{(i)}$; this shows that G has an arc from i to k_1 for some $k_1 \neq i$. If $k_1 \neq i+1$, $x = e^{(i)} \vee e^{(k_1)}$ shows that G has an arc from i or k_1 to k_2 for some $k_2 \notin \{i, k_1\}$. If $k_2 \neq i+1$, continue in the same way until finding a path in G from i to $i+1$. Conversely if α is not a sorting network, let x be a vector with $x_i > x_{i+1}$ and $g_\alpha(x) = 1$. Some conjugate α' has $f_{\alpha'}(x) = 1$, so $G_{\alpha'}$ can have no path from i to $i+1$. [In general, $(x\alpha)_i \leq (x\alpha)_j$ for all x if and only if $G_{\alpha'}$ has an oriented path from i to j for all α' conjugate to α.]

15. $[1\!:\!4][3\!:\!2][1\!:\!3][2\!:\!4][2\!:\!3]$.

16. The process clearly terminates. Each execution of step T2 has the effect of interchanging the i_qth and j_qth outputs, so the result of the algorithm is to permute the output lines in some way. Since the resulting (standard) network makes no change to the input $\langle 1, 2, \ldots, n \rangle$, the output lines must have been returned to their original position.

17. Make the network standard by the algorithm of exercise 16; then by considering the input sequence $\langle 1, 2, \ldots, n \rangle$, we see that standard selection networks must take the t largest elements into the t highest-numbered lines; and a $\hat{V}_t(n)$ network must take the tth largest into line $n + 1 - t$. Apply the zero-one principle.

18. The proof in Theorem A shows that $\hat{V}_t(n) \geq (n - t)\lceil \lg(t + 1) \rceil + \lceil \lg t \rceil$.

19. The network $[1{:}n][2{:}n] \ldots [1{:}3][2{:}3]$ selects the smallest two elements with $2n - 4$ comparators; add $[1{:}2]$ for $\hat{V}_2(n)$. The lower bounds come from the proof of Theorem A (see the previous answer).

20. First note that $\hat{V}_3(n) \geq \hat{V}_3(n-1)+2$ when $n \geq 4$; by symmetry the first comparator may be assumed to be $[1{:}n]$; after this must come a network to select the third largest of $\langle x_2, x_3, \ldots, x_n \rangle$, and another comparator touching line 1. On the other hand, $\hat{V}_3(5) \leq 7$, since four comparators find the min and max of $\{x_1, x_2, x_3, x_4\}$ and it remains to sort three elements.

21. False; consider, for example, the two networks $[1{:}2][3{:}4][2{:}3][1{:}4][1{:}2][3{:}4]$ and $[1{:}2][3{:}4][2{:}3][3{:}4][1{:}4][1{:}2][3{:}4]$. (However, N. G. de Bruijn proved in *Discrete Math.* **9** (1974), 337, that new comparators do not mess up sorting networks that are *primitive* in the sense of exercise 36.)

22. (a) By induction on the length of α, since $x_i \leq y_i$ and $x_j \leq y_j$ implies that $x_i \wedge x_j \leq y_i \wedge y_j$ and $x_i \vee x_j \leq y_i \vee y_j$. (b) By induction on the length of α, since $(x_i \wedge x_j)(y_i \wedge y_j)+(x_i \vee x_j)(y_i \vee y_j) \geq x_i y_i + x_j y_j$. [Consequently $\nu(x \wedge y) \leq \nu(x\alpha \wedge y\alpha)$, an observation due to W. Shockley.]

23. Let $x_k = 1$ if and only if $p_k \geq j$, $y_k = 1$ if and only if $p_k > j$; then $(x\alpha)_k = 1$ if and only if $(p\alpha)_k \geq j$, etc.

24. The formula for l_i' is obvious and for l_j' take $z = x \wedge y$ as in the hint and observe that $(z\alpha)_i = (z\alpha)_j = 0$ by exercise 21. Adding additional 1s to z shows the existence of a permutation p with $(pa')_j \leq \zeta(z)$, by exercise 23. The relations for u_i' and u_j' follow by reversing the order.

25. (Solution by H. Shapiro.) Let p and q be permutations with $(p\alpha)_k = l_k$ and $(q\alpha)_k = u_k$. It is possible to transform p into q by a sequence of steps, each of which interchanges a pair $(i, i+1)$ of adjacent integers; such an interchange in the input affects the kth output by at most ± 1.

26. There is a one-to-one correspondence that takes the element $\langle p_1, \ldots, p_n \rangle$ of $P_n\alpha$ into the "covering sequence" $x^{(0)}$ covers $x^{(1)}$ covers $\ldots$ covers $x^{(n)}$, where the $x^{(i)}$ are in $D_n\alpha$; in this correspondence, $x^{(i-1)} = x^{(i)} \vee e^{(j)}$ if and only if $p_j = i$. For example, $\langle 3, 1, 4, 2 \rangle$ corresponds to the sequence $\langle 1, 1, 1, 1 \rangle$ covers $\langle 1, 0, 1, 1 \rangle$ covers $\langle 1, 0, 1, 0 \rangle$ covers $\langle 0, 0, 1, 0 \rangle$ covers $\langle 0, 0, 0, 0 \rangle$. [Andrew Yao observes that consequently it suffices to test a sorting network on $\binom{n}{\lfloor n/2 \rfloor} - 1$ suitably chosen permutations. For example, any 4-network that sorts $\langle 4, 1, 2, 3 \rangle$, $\langle 3, 1, 4, 2 \rangle$, $\langle 3, 4, 1, 2 \rangle$, $\langle 2, 4, 1, 3 \rangle$, and $\langle 2, 3, 4, 1 \rangle$ sorts everything. See exercise 6.5–1; see also exercise 56.]

27. The principle holds because $(x\alpha)_i$ is the ith smallest element of x. If x and y denote different columns of a matrix whose rows are sorted, so that $x_i \leq y_i$ for all i, and if $x\alpha$ and $y\alpha$ denote the result of sorting the columns, the stated principle shows that $(x\alpha)_i \leq (y\alpha)_i$ for all i, since we can choose i elements of x in the same rows as any i given elements of y. [We have used this principle to prove the invariance property of shellsort, Theorem 5.2.1K. Further exploitation of the idea appears in an interesting paper by David Gale and R. M. Karp, *J. Computer and System Sciences* **6** (1972), 103–115. The fact that column sorting does not mess up sorted rows was apparently first observed in connection with the manipulation of tableaux; see Hermann Boerner, *Darstellung von Gruppen* (Springer, 1955), Chapter V, §5.]

28. If $\{x_{i_1}, \ldots, x_{i_t}\}$ are the t largest elements, then $x_{i_1} \wedge \ldots \wedge x_{i_t}$ is the tth largest. If $\{x_{i_1}, \ldots, x_{i_t}\}$ are *not* the t largest, then $x_{i_1} \wedge \ldots \wedge x_{i_t}$ is *less than* the tth largest.

29. $\langle x_1 \wedge y_1, (x_2 \wedge y_1) \vee (x_1 \wedge y_2), (x_3 \wedge y_1) \vee (x_2 \wedge y_2) \vee (x_1 \wedge y_3), y_1 \vee (x_3 \wedge y_2) \vee (x_2 \wedge y_3) \vee (x_1 \wedge y_4), y_2 \vee (x_3 \wedge y_3) \vee (x_2 \wedge y_4) \vee (x_1 \wedge y_5), y_3 \vee (x_3 \wedge y_4) \vee (x_2 \wedge y_5) \vee x_1, y_4 \vee (x_3 \wedge y_5) \vee x_2, y_5 \vee x_3 \rangle$.

30. Applying the distributive and associative laws reduces any formula to $\vee$'s of $\wedge$'s; then the commutative, idempotent, and absorption laws lead to canonical form. The S_i are precisely those sets S such that the formula is 1 when $x_j = [j \in S]$ while the formula is 0 when $x_j = [j \in S']$ for any proper subset S' of S.

31. $\delta_4 = 166$. R. Church [*Duke Math. J.* **6** (1940), 732–734] found $\delta_5 = 7579$, M. Ward [*Bull. Amer. Math. Soc.* **52** (1946), 423] found $\delta_6 = 7828352$, and the next values are $\delta_7 = 2414682040996$, $\delta_8 = 56130437228687557907786$ [R. Church, *Notices Amer. Math. Soc.* **12** (1965), 724; J. Berman and P. Köhler, *Mitteilungen Math. Seminar Gießen* **121** (1976), 103–124; D. Wiedemann, *Order* **8** (1991), 5–6]. No simple formula for δ_n is apparent; D. Kleitman [*Proc. Amer. Math. Soc.* **21** (1969), 677–682] proved that $(\lg \delta_n)/\binom{n}{\lfloor n/2 \rfloor} \to 1$ as $n \to \infty$, using an extremely complicated argument.

32. G_{t+1} is also the set of all strings $\theta\psi$ where θ and ψ are in G_t and $\theta \leq \psi$ as vectors of 0s and 1s. It follows that G_t is the set of all strings $z_0 \ldots z_{2^t-1}$ of 0s and 1s having the property that $z_i \leq z_j$ whenever the binary representation of i is "$\leq$" the binary representation of j in the 0–1 vector sense. Each element $z_0 \ldots z_{2^t-1}$ of G_T, except $00 \ldots 0$ and $11 \ldots 1$, represents a $\wedge$–$\vee$ function $f(x_1, \ldots, x_t)$ from D_{2^t} into $\{0,1\}$, under the correspondence $f(x_1, \ldots, x_t) = z[(x_1 \ldots x_t)_2]$.

33. If such a network existed we would have $(x_1 \wedge x_2) \vee (x_2 \wedge x_3) \vee (x_3 \wedge x_4) = f(x_1 \wedge x_2, x_1 \vee x_2, x_3, x_4)$ or $f(x_1 \wedge x_3, x_2, x_1 \vee x_3, x_4)$ or $\ldots$ or $f(x_1, x_2, x_3 \wedge x_4, x_3 \vee x_4)$ for some function f. The choices $\langle x_1, x_2, x_3, x_4 \rangle = \langle x, \bar{x}, 1, 0 \rangle$, $\langle x, 0, \bar{x}, 1 \rangle$, $\langle x, 1, 0, \bar{x} \rangle$, $\langle 1, x, \bar{x}, 0 \rangle$, $\langle 1, x, 0, \bar{x} \rangle$, $\langle 0, 1, x, \bar{x} \rangle$ show that no such f exists.

34. Yes; after proving this, you are ready to tackle the network for $n = 16$ in Fig. 49 (unless you simply checked all 2^n bit vectors by brute force using Theorem Z).

35. Otherwise the permutation in which only i and $i+1$ are misplaced would never be sorted. Let D_k be the number of comparators $[i:i+k]$ in a standard sorting network. Then $D_1 + 2D_2 + D_3 \geq 2(n-2)$ since there must be two comparators from $\{i, i+1\}$ to $\{i+2, i+3\}$, for $1 \leq i \leq n-3$, as well as $[1:2]$ and $[n-1:n]$. Similarly $D_1 + 2D_2 + \cdots + kD_k + (k-1)D_{k-1} + \cdots + D_{2k-1} \geq k(n-k)$, a formula suggested by J. M. Pollard. We can also prove that $2D_1 + D_2 \geq 3n-4$: If we strike out the first comparators of the form $[j:j+1]$ for all j there must be at least one more comparator lying within $\{i, i+1, i+2\}$, for $1 \leq i \leq n-2$. Similarly $kD_1 + (k-1)D_2 + \cdots + D_k \geq S(k+1)(n-k) + k(k-1)$.

36. (a) Each adjacent comparator reduces the number of inversions by 0 or 1, and $\langle n, n-1, \ldots, 1 \rangle$ has $\binom{n}{2}$ inversions. (b) Let $\alpha = \beta[p:p+1]$, and argue by induction on the length of α. If $p = i$, then $j > p + 1$, and $(x\beta)_p > (x\beta)_j$, $(x\beta)_{p+1} > (x\beta)_j$; hence $(y\beta)_p > (y\beta)_j$ and $(y\beta)_{p+1} > (y\beta)_j$. If $p = i - 1$, then either $(x\beta)_p$ or $(x\beta)_{p+1}$ is $> (x\beta)_j$; hence either $(y\beta)_p$ or $(y\beta)_{p+1}$ is $> (y\beta)_j$. If $p = j-1$ or j, the arguments are similar. For other p the argument is trivial.

Notes: If α is a primitive sorting network, so is α^R (the comparators in reverse order). For generalizations and another proof of (c), see N. G. de Bruijn, *Discrete Mathematics* **9** (1974), 333–339; *Indagationes Math.* **45** (1983), 125–132. In the latter paper, de Bruijn proved that a primitive network sorts all permutations of the multiset $\{n_1 \cdot 1, \ldots, n_m \cdot m\}$ if and only if it sorts the single permutation $m^{c_m} \ldots 1^{c_1}$. The relation $x \preceq y$, defined for permutations x and y to mean that there exists a standard network α such that $x = y\alpha$, is called *Bruhat order*; the analogous relation restricted to primitive α is *weak Bruhat order* (see the answer to exercise 5.2.1–44).

37. It suffices to show that if each comparator is replaced by an *interchange* operation we obtain a "reflection network" that transforms $\langle x_1, \ldots, x_n \rangle$ into $\langle x_n, \ldots, x_1 \rangle$. But in this interpretation it is not difficult to trace the route of x_k. Note that the permutation $\pi = (1\ 2)(3\ 4) \ldots (2n{-}1\ 2n)(2\ 3)(4\ 5) \ldots (2n{-}2\ 2n{-}1) = (1\ 3\ 5\ \ldots\ 2n{-}1\ 2n\ 2n{-}2\ \ldots\ 2)$ satisfies $\pi^n = (1\ 2n)(2\ 2n{-}1) \ldots (n{-}1\ n)$. The odd-even transposition sort was mentioned briefly by H. Seward in 1954; it has been discussed by A. Grasselli [*IRE Trans.* **EC-11** (1962), 483] and by Kautz, Levitt, and Waksman [*IEEE Trans.* **C-17** (1968), 443–451]. The reflective property of this network was introduced much earlier by H. E. Dudeney in one of his "frog puzzles" [*Amusements in Mathematics* (1917), 193].

38. Insert the elements $i_1, \ldots, i_N$ into an initially empty tableau using Algorithm 5.1.4I but with one crucial change: Set $P_{ij} \leftarrow x_i$ in step I3 only if $x_i \neq P_{i(j-1)}$. It can be proved that x_i will equal $P_{i(j-1)}$ in that step only if $x_i + 1 = P_{ij}$, when the inputs $i_1 \ldots i_N$ define a primitive sorting network. (The parenthesized assertions of the algorithm need to be modified.) After i_j has been inserted into P, set $Q_{st} \leftarrow j$ as in Theorem 5.1.4A. After N steps, the tableau P will always contain $(r, r+1, \ldots, n-1)$ in row r, while Q will be a tableau from which the sequence $i_1 \ldots i_N$ can be reconstructed by working backwards.

For example, when $n = 6$ the sequence $i_1 \ldots i_N = 4\,1\,3\,2\,4\,3\,5\,4\,3\,1\,2\,3\,5\,1\,4$ corresponds to

$$P = \begin{array}{|c|c|c|c|c|}
\hline 1 & 2 & 3 & 4 & 5 \\\hline
2 & 3 & 4 & 5 \\\cline{1-4}
3 & 4 & 5 \\\cline{1-3}
4 & 5 \\\cline{1-2}
5 \\\cline{1-1}
\end{array}
\qquad , \qquad
Q = \begin{array}{|c|c|c|c|c|}
\hline 1 & 4 & 5 & 8 & 13 \\\hline
2 & 6 & 7 & 15 \\\cline{1-4}
3 & 9 & 12 \\\cline{1-3}
10 & 11 \\\cline{1-2}
14 \\\cline{1-1}
\end{array}\ .$$

The transpose of Q corresponds to the complementary network $[n{-}i_1 : n{-}i_1{+}1] \ldots [n{-}i_N : n{-}i_N{+}1]$.

References: A. Lascoux and M. P. Schützenberger, *Comptes Rendus Acad. Sci. Paris* (I) **295** (1982), 629–633; R. P. Stanley, *Eur. J. Combinatorics* **5** (1984), 359–372; P. H. Edelman and C. Greene, *Advances in Math.* **63** (1987), 42–99. The diagrams of primitive sorting networks also correspond to arrangements of pseudolines and to other abstractions of two-dimensional convexity; see D. E. Knuth, *Lecture Notes in Comp. Sci.* **606** (1992), for further information.

39. When $n = 8$, for example, such a network must include the comparators shown here; all other comparators are ineffective on 10101010. Then lines $\lceil n/3 \rceil \ldots \lceil 2n/3 \rceil = 3 \ldots 6$ sort 4 elements, as in exercise 37. (This exercise is based on an idea of David B. Wilson.)

Notes: There is a one-to-one correspondence between minimal-length primitive networks that sort a given bit string and Young tableaux whose shape is bounded by the zigzag path defined by that bit string. Thus, exercise 38 yields a one-to-one correspondence between primitive networks of $\binom{n/2+1}{2}$ comparators that sort $(10)^{n/2}$ and primitive networks of $\binom{n/2+1}{2}$ comparators that sort $n/2 + 1$ arbitrary numbers. If a primitive network sorts the bit string $1^{n/2}0^{n/2}$, we can make a stronger statement: All of its "halves," consisting of the subnetworks on lines k through $k+n/2$ inclusive, are sorting networks, for $1 \le k \le n/2$. (See also de Bruijn's theorem, cited in the answer to exercise 36.)

40. This follows by applying the tail inequalities to the interesting construction in Proposition 7 of a paper by H. Rost, *Zeitschrift für Wahrscheinlichkeitstheorie und verwandte Gebiete* **58** (1981), 41–53, setting $b = \frac{1}{2}$, $a = \frac{1}{4}$, and $t = 4n$.

Curiously, R. P. Stanley and S. V. Fomin have proved that if the comparators $[i_k : i_k + 1]$ are chosen nonuniformly in such a way that $i_k = j$ occurs with probability $j / \binom{n}{2}$, then the expected time to reach a primitive sorting network (not necessarily the bubble sort) is exactly $\binom{n}{2} H_{\binom{n}{2}}$.

42. There must exist a path of length $\lceil \lg n \rceil$ or more, from some input to the largest output (consider m_n in Theorem A); when that input is set to ∞, the comparators on this path have a predetermined behavior, and the remaining network must be an $(n-1)$-sorter. [*IEEE Trans. on Computers* **C-21** (1972), 612–613.]

45. After l levels the input x_1 can be in at most 2^t different places. After merging is complete, x_1 can be in $n + 1$ different places.

46. [*J. Algorithms* **3** (1982), 79–88; the following alternative proof is due to V. S. Grinberg.] We may assume that $1 \le m \le n$ and that every stage makes m comparisons. Let $l = \lceil (n-m)/2 \rceil$ and suppose we are merging $x_1 \le \cdots \le x_m$ with $y_1 \le \cdots \le y_n$. An adversary can force $\lceil \lg(m+n) \rceil$ stages as follows: In the first stage some x_j is compared to an element y_k where we have either $k \le l$ or $k \ge l + m$. The adversary decides that $x_{j-1} < y_1$ and $x_{j+1} > y_n$; also that $x_j > y_k$ if $k \le l$, $x_j < y_k$ if $k \ge l+m$. The remaining task is essentially to merge x_j with either $y_{k+1} \le \cdots \le y_n$ or $y_1 \le \cdots \le y_{k-1}$; so at least $\min(n-k+1, k) \ge \min(n-l+1, l+m) = \lceil (m+n)/2 \rceil$ outcomes remain. At least $\lceil \lg \lceil (m+n)/2 \rceil \rceil = \lceil \lg(m+n) \rceil - 1$ subsequent stages are therefore necessary.

48. Let u be the smallest element of $(x\alpha)_j$, and let $y^{(0)}$ be any vector in D_n such that $(y^{(0)})_k = 0$ implies $(x\alpha)_k$ contains an element $\le u$, $(y^{(0)})_k = 1$ implies $(x\alpha)_k$ contains an element $> u$. If $\alpha = \beta[p:q]$, it is possible to find a vector $y^{(1)}$ satisfying the same conditions but with α replaced by β, and such that $y^{(1)}[p:q] = y^{(0)}$. Starting with $(y^{(0)})_i = 1$, $(y^{(0)})_j = 0$, we eventually have a vector $y = y^{(r)}$ satisfying the desired condition.

G. Baudet and D. Stevenson have observed that exercises 37 and 48 combine to yield a simple sorting method with $(n \ln n)/k + O(n)$ comparison cycles on k processors: First sort k subfiles of size $\le \lceil n/k \rceil$, then merge them in k passes using the "odd-even transposition merge" of order k. [*IEEE Trans.* **C-27** (1978), 84–87.]

49. Both $(x \lor y) \lor z$ and $x \lor (y \lor z)$ represent the largest m elements of the multiset $x \uplus y \uplus z$; $(x \land y) \land z$ and $x \land (y \land z)$ represent the smallest m. If $x = y = z = \{0,1\}$, $(x \land z) \lor (y \land z) = (x \land y) \lor (x \land z) \lor (y \land z) = \{0,0\}$, but the middle elements of $\{0,0,0,1,1,1\}$ are $\{0,1\}$. Sorting networks for three elements and the result of exercise 48 imply that the middle elements of $x \uplus y \uplus z$ may be expressed either as $((x \lor y) \land z) \lor (x \land y)$ or $((x \land y) \lor z) \land (x \lor y)$ or any other formula obtained by permuting x, y, z in these expressions. (There seems to be no symmetrical formula for the middle elements.)

50. Equivalently by Theorem Z, we must find all identities satisfied by the operations

$$x \lor\!\!\!\lor y = \min(x{+}y, 1), \qquad x \land\!\!\!\land y = \max(0, x{+}y{-}1)$$

on rational values x, y in $[0\mathbin{.\,.}1]$. [This is the operation of pouring as much liquid as possible from a glass that is x full into another that is y full, as observed by J. M. Pollard.] All such identities can be obtained from a system of four axioms and a rule of inference for multivalued logic due to Łukasiewicz; see Rose and Rosser, *Trans. Amer. Math. Soc.* **87** (1958), 1–53.

51. Let $\alpha' = \alpha[i{:}j]$, and let k be an index $\neq i, j$. If $(x\alpha)_i \leq (x\alpha)_k$ for all x, then $(x\alpha')_i \leq (x\alpha')_k$; if $(x\alpha)_k \leq (x\alpha)_i$ and $(x\alpha)_k \leq (x\alpha)_j$ for all x, the same holds when α is replaced by α'; if $(x\alpha)_k \leq (x\alpha)_i$ for all x, then $(x\alpha')_k \leq (x\alpha')_j$. In this way we see that α' has at least as many known relations as α, plus one more if $[i{:}j]$ isn't redundant. [*Bell System Tech. J.* **49** (1970), 1627–1644.]

52. (a) Consider sorting 0s and 1s; let $w = x_0 + x_1 + \cdots + x_N$. The network fails if and only if $w \leq t$ and $x_0 = 1$ before the complete N-sort. If $x_0 = 1$ at this point, it must have been 1 initially, and for $1 \leq j \leq n$ we must have initially had either $x_{2j-1+2nk} = 1$ for $0 \leq k \leq m$ or $x_{2j+2nk} = 1$ for $0 \leq k \leq m$; therefore $w \geq 1+(m+1)n = t$. So failure implies that $w = t$ and $x_j = x_{j+2nk}$ for $1 \leq k \leq m$ and $x_{2j} = \bar{x}_{2j-1}$ for $1 \leq j \leq n$. Furthermore the special subnetwork must transform such inputs so that $x_{2m+2n+j} = 1$ for $1 \leq j \leq m$.

(b) For example, the special subnetwork for $(y_1 \lor y_2 \lor \bar{y}_3) \land (\bar{y}_2 \lor y_3 \lor \bar{y}_4) \land \dots$ could be

$$[1 + 2n{:}2mn + 2n + 1][3 + 2n{:}2mn + 2n + 1][6 + 2n{:}2mn + 2n + 1]$$
$$[4 + 4n{:}2mn + 2n + 2][5 + 4n{:}2mn + 2n + 2][8 + 4n{:}2mn + 2n + 2]\dots,$$

using $x_{2j-1+2kn}$ and x_{2j+2kn} to represent y_j and $\bar{y}_j$ in the kth clause, and $x_{2m+2n+k}$ to represent that clause itself.

53. Paint the lines red or blue according to the following rule:

if $i \bmod 4$ is	then line i in case (a) is	and in case (b) it is
0	red	red;
1	blue	red;
2	blue	blue;
3	red	blue.

Now observe that the first $t-1$ levels of the network consists of two separate networks, one for the 2^{t-1} red lines and another for the 2^{t-1} blue lines. The comparators on the tth level complete a merging network, as in the bitonic or odd-even merge. This establishes the desired result for $k = 1$.

The red-blue decomposition also establishes the case $k = 2$. For if the input is 4-ordered, the red lines contain 2^{t-1} numbers that are 2-ordered, and so do the blue lines, so we are left with

$$x_0 y_0 y_1 x_1 x_2 y_2 y_3 x_3 \dots \text{ (case (a))} \qquad \text{or} \qquad x_0 x_1 y_0 y_1 x_2 x_3 y_2 y_3 \dots \text{ (case (b))}$$

after $t-1$ levels; the final result

$$(x_0 \land y_0)(x_0 \lor y_0)(y_1 \land x_1)(y_1 \lor x_1) \dots \qquad \text{or} \qquad x_0 (x_1 \land y_0)(x_1 \lor y_0)(y_1 \land x_2)(y_1 \lor x_2) \dots$$

is clearly 2-ordered.

Now for $k \geq 2$, we can assume that $k \leq t$. The first $t - k + 2$ levels decompose into 2^{k-2} separate networks of size 2^{t-k+2}, which each are 2-ordered by the case $k = 2$; hence the lines are 2^{k-1}-ordered after $t - k + 2$ levels. The subsequent levels clearly preserve 2^{k-1}-ordering, because they have a "vertical" periodicity of order 2^{k-2}. (We can imagine $-\infty$ on lines $-1, -2, \ldots$ and $+\infty$ on lines $2^t, 2^t + 1, \ldots$.)

References: Network (a) was introduced by M. Dowd, Y. Perl, L. Rudolph, and M. Saks, *JACM* **36** (1989), 738–757; network (b) by E. R. Canfield and S. G. Williamson, *Linear and Multilinear Algebra* **29** (1991), 43–51. It is interesting to note that in case (a) we have $D_n \alpha = G_t$, where G_t is defined in exercise 32 [Dowd et al., Theorem 17]; thus the image of D_n is not enough by itself to characterize the behavior of a periodic network.

54. The following construction by Ajtai, Komlós, and Szemerédi [*FOCS* **33** (1992), 686–692] shows how to sort m^3 elements with four levels of m^2-sorters: We may suppose that the elements being sorted are 0s and 1s; let the lines be numbered $(a, b, c) = am^2 + bm + c$ for $0 \leq a, b, c < m$. The first level sorts the lines $\{(a, b, (b + k) \bmod m) \mid 0 \leq a, b < m\}$ for $0 \leq k < m$; let a_k be the number of 1s in the kth group of m^2 lines. The second level sorts $\{(a, b, k) \mid 0 \leq a, b < m\}$ for $0 \leq k < m$; the number of 1s in the kth group is then

$$b_k = \sum_{j=0}^{m^2 - 1} \left\lfloor \frac{a_{(k-j) \bmod m} + j}{m^2} \right\rfloor,$$

and it follows that $b_0 \leq b_1 + 1, b_1 \leq b_2 + 1, \ldots, b_{m-1} \leq b_0 + 1$. In the third level we sort $\{(k, a, b) \mid 0 \leq a, b < m\}$ for $0 \leq k < m$; the number of 1s in the kth group is

$$c_k = \sum_{i=0}^{m-1} \sum_{j=0}^{m-1} \left\lfloor \frac{b_i + km + j}{m^2} \right\rfloor.$$

If $0 < c_{k+1} < m^2$ we have $c_k \leq \binom{m-1}{2}$ and $c_j = 0$ for $j < k$. Similarly, if $0 < c_k < m^2$ we have $c_{k+1} \geq m^2 - \binom{m-1}{2}$ and $c_j = 0$ for $j > k + 1$. Consequently a fourth level that sorts lines $m^2 k - \binom{m-1}{2} . . m^2 k + \binom{m-1}{2} - 1$ for $0 < k < m$ will complete the sorting.

It follows that four levels of m-sorters will sort $f(m) = \lfloor \sqrt{m} \rfloor^3$ elements, and 16 levels will sort $f(f(m))$ elements. This proves the stated result, since $f(f(m)) > m^2$ when $m > 24$. (The construction is not "tight," so we can probably do the job with substantially fewer than 16 levels.)

55. ———————————— [If $P(n)$ denotes the minimum number of switches needed in a permutation network, it is clear that $P(n) \geq \lceil \lg n! \rceil$. By slightly extending a construction due to L. J. Goldstein and S. W. Leibholz, *IEEE Trans.* **EC-16** (1967), 637–641, one can show that $P(n) \leq P(\lfloor n/2 \rfloor) + P(\lceil n/2 \rceil) + n - 1$, hence $P(n) \leq B(n)$ for all n, where $B(n)$ is the binary insertion function of Eq. 5.3.1–(3). M. W. Green has proved (unpublished) that $P(5) = 8$.]

56. In fact we can construct α_x inductively so that $x\alpha_x = 0^{k-1}101^{n-k-1}$, when x has k zeros. The base case, α_{10}, is empty. Otherwise at least one of the following four cases applies, where y is not sorted: (1) $x = y0$, $\alpha_x = \alpha_y[n-1:n][n-2:n-1] \ldots [1:2]$. (2) $x = y1$, $\alpha_x = \alpha_y[1:n][2:n] \ldots [n-1:n]$. (3) $x = 0y$, $\alpha_x = \alpha_y^+[1:n][1:n-1] \ldots [1:2]$. (4) $x = 1y$, $\alpha_x = \alpha_y^+[1:2][2:3] \ldots [n-1:n]$. The network α^+ is obtained from α by changing each comparator $[i:j]$ to $[i+1:j+1]$. [See M. J. Chung and B. Ravikumar,

Discrete Math. **81** (1990), 1–9.] This construction uses $\binom{n}{2} - 1$ comparators; can it be done with substantially fewer?

57. [See H. Zhu and R. Sedgewick, *STOC* **14** (1982), 296–302.] The stated delay time is easily verified by induction. But the problem of analyzing the recurrence

$$A(m, n) = A(\lfloor m/2 \rfloor, \lceil n/2 \rceil) + A(\lceil m/2 \rceil, \lfloor n/2 \rfloor) + \lceil m/2 \rceil + \lceil n/2 \rceil - 1,$$

when $A(0, n) = A(m, 0) = 0$, is more difficult.

A bitonic merge makes $B(m, n) = C'(m + n)$ comparisons; see (15). Therefore we can use the fact that $\{\lfloor m/2 \rfloor + \lceil n/2 \rceil, \lceil m/2 \rceil + \lfloor n/2 \rfloor\} = \{\lfloor (m + n)/2 \rfloor, \lceil (m + n)/2 \rceil\}$ to show that $B(m, n) = B(\lfloor m/2 \rfloor, \lceil n/2 \rceil) + B(\lceil m/2 \rceil, \lfloor n/2 \rfloor) + \lfloor (m + n)/2 \rfloor$. Then $A(m, n) \le B(m, n)$ by induction.

Let $D(m, n) = C(m + 1, n + 1) + C(m, n) - C(m + 1, n) - C(m, n + 1)$. We have $D(0, n) = D(m, 0) = 1$, and $D(m, n) = 1$ when $m + n$ is odd. Otherwise $m + n$ is even and $mn \ge 1$, and we have $D(m, n) = D(\lfloor m/2 \rfloor, \lfloor n/2 \rfloor) - 1$. Consequently $D(m, n) \le 1$ for all $m, n \ge 0$.

The recurrence for A is equivalent to the recurrence for C except when m and n are both odd. And in that case we have $A(m, n) \ge C(\lfloor m/2 \rfloor, \lceil n/2 \rceil) + C(\lceil m/2 \rceil, \lfloor n/2 \rfloor) + \lceil m/2 \rceil + \lceil n/2 \rceil - 1 = C(m, n) + 1 - D(\lfloor m/2 \rfloor, \lfloor n/2 \rfloor) \ge C(m, n)$ by induction.

Let $l = \lceil \lg \min(m, n) \rceil$. On level k of the even-odd recursion, for $0 \le k < l$, we perform 2^k merges of the respective sizes $(m_{jk}, n_{jk}) = (\lfloor (m + j)/2^k \rfloor, \lfloor (n + 2^k - 1 - j)/2^k \rfloor)$ for $0 \le j < 2^k$. The cost of recursion, $\sum_j (\lceil m_{jk}/2 \rceil + \lceil n_{jk}/2 \rceil - 1)$, is $f_k(m) + f_k(n) - 2^k$; we can write $f_k(n) = \max(n'_k, n - n'_k)$, where $n'_k = 2^k \lfloor n/2^{k+1} + 1/2 \rfloor$ is the multiple of 2^k that is nearest to $n/2$. Since $0 \le f_k(n) - n/2 \le 2^{k-1}$, the total cost of recursion for levels 0 to $l - 1$ lies between $\frac{1}{2}(m + n)l - 2^l$ and $\frac{1}{2}(m + n)l$.

Finally, if $m \le n$, the 2^l merges (m_{jl}, n_{jl}) on level l have $m_{jl} = 0$ for $0 \le j < 2^l - m$, and $m_{jl} = 1$ for the other m values of j. Since $A(1, n) = n$, the total cost of level l is $\sum_{k=n}^{m+n-1} \lfloor k/2^l \rfloor \le \sum_{k=n}^{m+n-1} k/m = \frac{m-1}{2} + n$.

Thus even-odd merging, unlike bitonic merging, is within $O(m + n)$ of the optimum number of comparisons $\hat{M}(m, n)$. Our derivation shows in fact that $A(m, n) = \sum_{k=0}^{l-1}(f_k(m) + f_k(n) - 2^k) + g_l(m + n) - g_l(\max(m, n))$, where $g_l(n)$ can be expressed in the form $\sum_{k=0}^{n-1} \lfloor k/2^l \rfloor = \lfloor n/2^l \rfloor (n - 2^{l-1}(\lfloor n/2^l \rfloor + 1))$.

58. If $h[k + 1] = h[k] + 1$ and the file is not in order, something must happen to it on the next pass; this decreases the number of inversions, by exercise 5.2.2–1, hence the file will eventually become sorted. But if $h[k + 1] \ge h[k] + 2$ for $1 \le k < m$, the smallest key will never move into its proper place if it is initially in R_2.

59. We use the hint, and also regard $K_{N+1} = K_{N+2} = \cdots = 1$. If $K_{h[1]+j} = \cdots = K_{h[m]+j} = 1$ at step j, and if $K_i = 0$ for some $i > h[1] + j$, we must have $i < h[m] + j$ since there are fewer than n 1s. Suppose k and i are minimal such that $h[k] + j < i < h[k + 1] + j$ and $K_i = 0$. Let $s = h[k + 1] + j - i$; we have $s < h[k + 1] - h[k] \le k$. At step $j - s$, at least $k + 1$ 0s must have been under the heads, since $K_i = K_{h[k+1]+j-s}$ was set to zero at that step; s steps later, there are at least $k + 1 - s \ge 2$ 0s remaining between $K_{h[1]+j}$ and K_i, inclusive, contradicting the minimality of i.

The second pass gets the next $n - 1$ elements into place, etc. If we start with the permutation $N \; N{-}1 \; \ldots \; 2 \; 1$, the first pass changes it to

$$N{+}1{-}n \; N{-}n \; \ldots \; 1 \; N{+}2{-}n \; \ldots \; N{-}1 \; N,$$

since $K_{h[1]+j} > K_{h[m]+j}$ whenever $1 \le h[1] + j$ and $h[m] + j \le N$; therefore the bound is best possible.

60. Suppose that $h[k+1] - s > h[k]$ and $h[k] \le s$; the smallest key ends in position R_i for $i > 1$ if it starts in R_{n-s}. Therefore $h[k+1] \le 2h[k]$ is necessary; it is also sufficient, by the special case $t = 0$ of the following result:

Theorem. *If $n = N$ and if $K_1 \ldots K_N$ is a permutation of $\{1, 2, \ldots, n\}$, a single sorting pass will set $K_i = i$ for $1 \le i \le t+1$, if $h[k+1] \le h[k] + h[k-i] + i$ for $1 \le k < m$ and $0 \le i \le t$.* (By convention, let $h[k] = k$ when $k \le 0$.)

Proof. By induction on t; if step t does not find the key $t+1$ under the heads, we may assume that it appears in position $R_{h[k+1]+t-s}$ for some $s > 0$, where $h[k+1] - s < h[k]$; hence $h[k-t] + t - s > 0$. But this is impossible if we consider step $t - s$, which presumably placed the element $t+1$ into position $R_{h[k+1]+t-s}$ although there were at least $t+1$ lower heads active. ∎

(The condition is necessary for $t = 0, 1$, but not for $t = 2$.)

61. If the numbers $\{1, \ldots, 23\}$ are being sorted, the theorem in the previous exercise shows that $\{1, 2, 3, 4\}$ find their true destination. When 0s and 1s are being sorted one can verify that it is impossible to have all heads reading 0 while all positions not under the heads contain 1s, at steps -2, -1, and 0; hence the proof in the previous exercise can be extended to show that $\{5, 6, 7\}$ find their true destination. Finally $\{8, \ldots, 23\}$ must be sorted, by the argument in exercise 59.

63. When $r \le m-2$, the heads take the string $0^p 1^1 0 1^3 0 1^7 0 \ldots 01^{2^r-1} 0 1^q$ into the string $0^{p+1} 1^1 0 1^3 0 1^7 0 \ldots 01^{2^{r-1}-1} 0 1^{2^r-1+q}$; hence $m-2$ passes are necessary. [When the heads are at positions $1, 2, 3, 5, \ldots, 1+2^{m-2}$, Pratt has discovered a similar result: The string $0^p 1^a 0 1^{2^b-1} 0 1^{2^{b+1}-1} 0 \ldots 0 1^{2^r-1} 0 1^q$, $1 \le a \le 2^{b-1}$, goes into $0^{p+1} 1^{a-1} 0 1^{2^b-1} 0 1^{2^{b+1}-1} 0$ $\ldots 0 1^{2^{r-1}-1} 0 1^{2^r+q}$, hence at least $m - \lceil \log_2 m \rceil - 1$ passes are necessary in the worst case for this sequence of heads. The latter head sequence is of special interest since it has been used as the basis of a very ingenious sorting device invented by P. N. Armstrong [see *U.S. Patent 3399383* (1965)]. Pratt conjectures that these input sequences provide the true worst case, over all inputs.]

64. During quicksort, each key $K_2, \ldots, K_N$ is compared with K_1; let $A = \{i \mid K_i < K_1\}$, $B = \{j \mid K_j > K_1\}$. Subsequent operations quicksort A and B independently; all comparisons $K_i : K_j$ for i in A and j in B are suppressed, by both quicksort and the restricted uniform algorithm, and no other comparisons are suppressed by the unrestricted uniform algorithm.

In this case we could restrict the algorithm even further, omitting Cases 1 and 2 so that arcs are added to G only when comparisons are explicitly made, yet considering only paths of length 2 when testing for redundancy. Another way to solve this problem is to consider the equivalent tree insertion sorting algorithm of Section 6.2.2, which makes precisely the same comparisons as the uniform algorithm in the same order.

65. (a) The probability that K_{a_i} is compared with K_{b_i} is the probability that c_i other specified keys do not lie between K_{a_i} and K_{b_i}; this is the probability that two numbers chosen at random from $\{1, 2, \ldots, c_i+2\}$ are consecutive, namely

$$(c_i + 1) \bigg/ \binom{c_i + 2}{2}.$$

(b) The first $n - 1$ values of c_i are zero, then come $(n - 2)$ 1s, $(n - 3)$ 2s, etc.; hence the average is $2\sum_{k=1}^{n}(n - k)/(k + 1) = 2\sum_{k=1}^{n}((n + 1)/(k + 1) - 1) = 2(n + 1)(H_{n+1} - 1) - 2n$.

(c) The "bipartite" nature of merging shows that the restricted uniform algorithm is the same as the uniform algorithm for this sequence. The pairs involving vertex N have c's equal to $0, 1, \ldots, N-2$, respectively; so the average number of comparisons is exactly the same as quicksort.

66. No; when $N = 5$ no pair sequence ending in $(1, 5)(1, 2)(2, 3)(3, 4)(4, 5)$ will require 10 comparisons. [An interesting research problem: For all N, find a (restricted) uniform sorting method whose worst case is as good as possible.]

67. (Gil Kalai has informally announced a proof of minimality for the restricted case, using methods related to his article in *Graphs and Combinatorics* **1** (1985), 65–79; however, his proof has not been published.)

68. An item can lose at most one inversion per pass, so the minimum number of passes is at least the maximum number of inversions of any item in the input permutation. The bubble sort strategy achieves this bound, since each pass decreases the inversion count of every inverted item by one (see exercise 5.2.2–1). An additional pass may be needed to determine whether or not sorting is complete, but the wording of this exercise allows us to overlook such considerations.

It is perhaps unfortunate that the first theorem in the study of computational complexity via automata established the "optimality" of a sorting method that is so poor from a programming standpoint! The situation is analogous to the history of random number generation, which took several backward steps when generators that are "optimum" from one particular point of view were recommended for general use. (See the comments following Eq. 3.3.3–(39).) The moral is that optimality results are often heavily dependent on the abstract model; the results are quite interesting, but they must be applied wisely in practice.

[Demuth went on to consider a generalization to an r-register machine (saving a factor of r), and to a Turing-like machine in which the direction of scan could oscillate between left-right and right-left at will. He observed that the latter type of machine can do the straight insertion and the cocktail-shaker sorts; but any such 1-register machine must go through at least $\frac{1}{4}(N^2 - N)$ steps on the average, since each step reduces the total number of inversions by at most one. Finally he considered r-register random-access machines and the question of minimum-comparison sorting. These portions of his thesis have been reprinted in *IEEE Transactions* **C-34** (1985), 296–310.]

SECTION 5.4

1. We could omit the internal sorting phase, but that would generally be much slower since it would increase the number of times each piece of data is read and written on the external memory.

2. The runs are distributed as in (1), then Tape 3 is set to $R_1 \ldots R_{2000000}$; $R_{2000001} \ldots R_{4000000}$; $R_{4000001} \ldots R_{5000000}$. After all tapes are rewound, a "one-way merge" sets T_1 and T_2 to the respective contents of T_3 and T_4 in (2). Then T_1 and T_2 are merged to T_3, and the information is copied back and merged once again, for a total of five passes. In general, the procedure is like the four-tape balanced merge, but with copy passes between each of the merge passes, so one less than twice as many passes are performed.

3. (a) $\lceil \log_P S \rceil$. (b) $\log_B S$, where $B = \sqrt{P(T - P)}$ is called the "effective power of the merge." When $T = 2P$ the effective power is P; when $T = 2P - 1$ the effective power is $\sqrt{P(P - 1)} = P - \frac{1}{2} - \frac{1}{8}P^{-1} + O(P^{-2})$, slightly less than $\frac{1}{2}T$.

4. $\frac{1}{2}T$. If T is odd and P must be an integer, both $\lceil T/2 \rceil$ and $\lfloor T/2 \rfloor$ give the same maximum value. It is best to have $P \geq T - P$, according to exercise 3, so we should choose $P = \lceil T/2 \rceil$ for balanced merging.

SECTION 5.4.1

1. 087 154 170 426 $\begin{cases} 503 \begin{cases} 503 & \infty \\ 908 & \infty \end{cases} \\ 426 \begin{cases} 426 & 653 & \infty \\ 612 & \infty \end{cases} \end{cases}$

2. The path $\boxed{061}$—$\boxed{512}$—$\boxed{087}$—$\boxed{154}$—$\boxed{061}$ would be changed to $\boxed{612}$—$\boxed{612}$—$\boxed{512}$—$\boxed{154}$—$\boxed{087}$. (We are essentially doing a "bubble sort" along the path!)

3. and fourscore our seven years/ ago brought fathers forth on this/
a conceived continent in liberty nation new the to/ and dedicated men
proposition that/ all are created equal.

4. (The problem is slightly ambiguous; in this interpretation we do not clear the internal memory until the reservoir is about to overflow.)

and fourscore on our seven this years/ ago brought continent fathers
forth in liberty nation new to/ a and conceived dedicated men
proposition that the/ all are created equal.

5. False; the complete binary tree with P external nodes is defined for all $P \geq 1$.

6. Insert "If $\mathtt{T} = \mathtt{LOC}(X[0])$ then go to R2, otherwise" at the beginning of step R6, and delete the similar clause from step R7.

7. There is no output, and $\mathtt{RMAX}$ stays equal to 0.

8. If any of the first P actual keys were ∞, their records would be lost. To avoid ∞, we can make two almost-identical copies of the program; the first copy omits the test involving $\mathtt{LASTKEY}$ in step R4, and it jumps to the second copy when $\mathtt{RQ} \neq 0$ in step R3 for the first time. The second copy needs no step R1, and it never needs to test $\mathtt{RQ}$ in step R3.

9. Assume, for example, that the current run is ascending, while the next should be descending. Then the steps of Algorithm R will work properly except for one change: In step R6, if $\mathtt{RN(T)} = \mathtt{RQ} > \mathtt{RC}$, reverse the test on $\mathtt{KEY(LOSER(T))}$ versus $\mathtt{KEY(Q)}$.

When $\mathtt{RC}$ changes, the key tests of steps R4 and R6 should change appropriately.

10. Let $\cdot j \equiv \mathtt{LOC}(X[j])$. The mechanism of Algorithm R ensures that the following conditions are true whenever we reach step R3, if we set first $\mathtt{LOSER}(\cdot 0) \leftarrow \mathtt{Q}$ and $\mathtt{RN}(\cdot 0) \leftarrow \mathtt{RQ}$: The values of $\mathtt{LOSER}(\cdot 0)$, ..., $\mathtt{LOSER}(\cdot(P-1))$ are a permutation of $\{\cdot 0, \cdot 1, \ldots, \cdot(P-1)\}$; and there exists a permutation of the pointers $\{\mathtt{LOSER}(\cdot j) \mid \mathtt{RN}(\cdot j) = 0\}$ that corresponds to an actual tournament. In other words, when $\mathtt{RN}(\cdot j)$ is zero, the value of $\mathtt{KEY(LOSER}(\cdot j))$ is irrelevant; we may permute such "losers" among themselves. After P steps all $\mathtt{RN}(\cdot j)$ will be nonzero, so the entire tree will be consistent. (The answer to the hint is "yes.")

Purists might complain that the algorithm compares $\mathtt{KEY}$ values that haven't been initialized. If such behavior is too shocking, it can be avoided by setting all $\mathtt{KEY}$s to 0, say, in step R1.

11. True. (Both keys are from the same subsequence in the proof of Theorem K.)

13. The keys left in memory when the first run has ended tend to be smaller than average, since they didn't make it into the first run. Thus the second run can output more of the smaller keys.

14. Assume that the snow suddenly stops when the snowplow is at a random point u, $0 \le u < 1$, after it has reached its steady state. Then the next-to-last run contains $(1 + 2u - u^2)P$ records, and the last run contains $u^2 P$. Integrating this times du yields an average time of $(2 - \frac{1}{3})P$ records in the penultimate run, $\frac{1}{3}P$ in the last.

15. False; the last run can be arbitrarily long, but only in the comparatively rare circumstance that all records in memory belong to the same run when the input is exhausted.

16. If and only if each element has fewer than P inversions. (See Sections 5.1.1, 5.4.8.) The probability is 1 when $N \le P$, $P^{N-P}P!/N!$ when $N \ge P$, by considering inversion tables. (In actual practice, however, a one-pass sort is not too uncommon, since people tend to sort a file even when they suspect it might be in order, as a precautionary measure.)

17. Exactly $\lceil N/P \rceil$ runs, all but the last having length P. (The "worst case.")

18. Nothing changes on the second pass, since it is possible to show that the kth record of a run is less than at least $P + 1 - k$ records of the preceding run, for $1 \le k \le P$. (However, there seems to be no simple way to characterize the result of P-way replacement selection followed by P'-way replacement selection when $P' > P$.)

19. Argue as in the derivation of (2) that $h(x, t)\,dx = KL\,dt$, where this time $h(x, t) = I + Kt$ for all x, and $P = LI$. This implies $x(t) = L\ln((I + Kt)/I)$, so that when $x(T) = L$ we have $KT = (e - 1)I$. The amount of snowfall since $t = 0$ is therefore $(e - 1)LI = (e - 1)P$.

20. As in exercise 19, we have $(I + Kt)\,dx = K(L - x)\,dt$; hence $x(t) = LKt/(I + Kt)$. The snow in the reservoir is $LI = P = P' = \int_0^T x(t)K\,dt = L\big(KT - I\ln((I + KT)/I)\big)$; hence $KT = \alpha I$, where $\alpha \approx 2.14619$ is the root of $1 + \alpha = e^{\alpha - 1}$. The run length is the total amount of snowfall during $0 \le t \le T$, namely $LKT = \alpha P$.

21. Proceed as in the text, but after each run wait for $P - P'$ snowflakes to fall before the plow starts out again. This means that $h(x(t), t)$ is now KT_1, instead of KT, where $T_1 - T$ is the amount of time taken by the extra snowfall. The run length is LKT_1, $x(t) = L(1 - e^{-t/T_1})$, $P = LKT_1 e^{-T/T_1}$, and $P' = \int_0^T x(t)K\,dt = P + LK(T - T_1)$. In other words, a run length of $e^\theta P$ is obtained when $P' = \big(1 - (1 - \theta)e^\theta\big)P$, for $0 \le \theta \le 1$.

22. For $0 \le t \le (\kappa - 1)T$, $dx \cdot h = K\,dt\,(x(t + T) - x(t))$, and for $(\kappa - 1)T \le t \le T$, $dx \cdot h = K\,dt\,(L - x(t))$, where h is seen to be constantly equal to KT at the position of the plows. It follows that for $0 \le j \le k$, $0 \le u \le 1$, and $t = (\kappa - j - u)T$, we have $x(t) = L(1 - e^{u-\theta}F_j(u)/F(\kappa))$. The run length is LKT, the amount of snowfall between the times that consecutive snowplows leave point 0 in the steady state; P is the amount cleared during each snowplow's last burst of speed, namely $KT(L - x(\kappa T)) = LKTe^{-\theta}/F(\kappa)$; and $P' = \int_0^{\kappa T} x(t)K\,dt$ can be shown to have the stated form.

Notes: It turns out that the stated formulas are valid also for $k = 0$. When $k \ge 1$ the number of elements per run that go into the reservoir *twice* is $P'' = \int_0^{(\kappa-1)T} x(t)K\,dt$, and it is easy to show that (run length) $- P' + P'' = (e - 1)P$, a phenomenon noticed by Frazer and Wong. Is it a coincidence that the generating function for $F_k(\theta)$ is so similar to the generating function in exercise 5.1.3–11?

23. Let $P = pP'$ and $q = 1 - p$. For the first T_1 units of time the snowfall comes from the qP' elements remaining in the reservoir after the first pP' have been initially removed in random order; and when the old reservoir is empty, uniform snow begins to fall again. We choose T_1 so that $LKT_1 = qP'$. For $0 \le t \le T_1$, $h(x, t) = (p + qt/T_1)g(x)$, where $g(x)$ is the height of snow put into the reservoir from position x; for $T_1 \le t \le T$, $h(x, t) = g(x) + (t - T_1)K$. For $0 \le t \le T_1$, $g(x(t))$ is $(q(T_1 - t)/T_1)g(x(t)) + (T - T_1)K$; and for $T_1 \le t \le T$, $g(x(t)) = (T - t)K$. Hence $h(x(t), t) = (T - T_1)K$ for $0 \le t \le T$, and $x(t) = L(1 - \exp(-t/(T - T_1)))$. The total run length is $LK(T - T_1)$; the total amount "recycled" from the reservoir back again (see exercise 22) is LKT_1; and the total amount cleared after time T is $P = KT(L - x(T))$.

So the assumptions of this exercise give runs of length $(e^s/s)P$ when the reservoir size is $(1 + (s - 1)e^s/s)P$. This is considerably worse than the results of exercise 22, since the reservoir contents are being used in a more advantageous order in that case.

(The fact that $h(x(t), t)$ is constant in so many of these problems is not surprising, since it is equivalent to saying that the elements of each run obtained during a steady state of the system are uniformly distributed.)

24. (a) Essentially the same proof works; each of the subsequences has runs in the same direction as the output runs. (b) The stated probability is the probability that the run has length $n + 1$ and is followed by y; it equals $(1 - x)^n/n!$ when $x > y$, and it is $(1 - x)^n/n! - (y - x)^n/n!$ when $x \le y$. (c) Induction. For example, if the nth run is ascending, the $(n - 1)$st was descending with probability p, so the first integral applies. (d) We find that $f'(x) = f(x) - c - pf(1 - x) - qf(x)$, then $f''(x) = -2pc$, which ultimately leads to $f(x) = c(1 - qx - px^2)$, $c = 6/(3 + p)$. (e) If $p > eq$ then $pe^x + qe^{1-x}$ is monotone increasing for $0 \le x \le 1$, and $\int_0^1 |pe^x + qe^{1-x} - e^{1/2}| \, dx = (p - q)(e^{1/2} - 1)^2 < 0.43$. If $q \le p < eq$ then $pe^x + qe^{1-x}$ lies between $2\sqrt{pqe}$ and $p + qe$, so $\int_0^1 |pe^x + qe^{1-x} - \frac{1}{2}(p + qe + 2\sqrt{pqe})| \, dx \le \frac{1}{2}(\sqrt{p} - \sqrt{qe})^2 < 0.4$; and if $p < q$ we may use a symmetrical argument. Thus for all p and q there is a constant C such that $\int_0^1 |pe^x + qe^{1-x} - C| \, dx < 0.43$. Let $\delta_n(x) = f_n(x) - f(x)$. Then $\delta_{n+1}(y) = (1 - e^{y-1}) \int_0^1 (pe^x + qe^{1-x} - C)\delta_n(x) \, dx + p \int_0^{1-y} e^{y-1+x}\delta_n(x) \, dx + q \int_y^1 e^{y-x}\delta_n(x) \, dx$; hence if $\delta_n(y) \le \alpha_n$, $|\delta_{n+1}(y)| \le (1 - e^{y-1}) \cdot 1.43\alpha_n < 0.91\alpha_n$. (f) For all $n \ge 0$, $(1-x)^n/n!$ is the probability that the run length exceeds n. (g) $\int_0^1 (pe^x + qe^{1-x})f(x) \, dx = 6/(3 + p)$.

26. (a) Consider the number of permutations with $n + r + 1$ elements and n left-to-right minima, where the rightmost element is not the smallest. (b) Use the fact that

$$\sum_{1 \le k < n} \left[{k \atop k - r} \right] k = \left[{n \atop n - r - 1} \right],$$

by the definition of Stirling numbers in Appendix B. (c) Add $r + 1$ to the mean, using the fact that $\sum_{n \ge 0} [{n+r \atop n}](n + r)/(n + r + 1)! = 1$, to get $\sum_{n \ge 0} [{n+r \atop n}]/(n + r - 1)!$.

The formula in (b) is due to P. Appell, *Archiv der Math. und Physik* **65** (1880), 171–175. We have, incidentally, $[[{r \atop k}]] = (r + k)! [x^k z^r] e^{z f(z)}$, where $f(z) = z/2 + z^2/3 + \cdots = -z^{-1} \ln(1 - z) - 1$; hence $c_r = [z^r](r + 1 + f(z))e^{f(z)}$. The number of derangements of n objects having k cycles, sometimes denoted by $[{n \atop k}]_{\ge 2}$, is $[[{n-k \atop k}]]$; see J. Riordan, *An Introduction to Combinatorial Analysis* (Wiley, 1958), §4.4.

27. When $P'/P = 2(e^{-\theta} - 1 + \theta)/(1 - 2\theta + \theta^2 + 2\theta e^{-\theta})$, for $0 \le \theta \le 1$, the steady-state average run length will be $2P/(1 - 2\theta + \theta^2 + 2\theta e^{-\theta})$. [See *Information Processing Letters* **21** (1985), 239–243.]

Dobosiewicz has also observed that we can continue the replacement selection mechanism even longer, because we can be inputting from the front of the reservoir queue while outputting to its rear. For example, if $P' = .5P$ and we continue replacement selection until the current run contains $.209P$ records, the average run length increases from about $2.55P$ to about $2.61P$ with this modification. If $P' = P$ and we continue replacement selection until only $.314P$ records remain in the current run, the average run length increases from eP to about $3.034P$. [See *Comp. J.* **27** (1984), 334–339, where an even more efficient method called "merge replacement" is also presented.]

28. For multiway merging there is comparatively little problem, since P stays constant and records are processed sequentially on each file; but when forming initial runs, we would like to vary the number of records in memory depending on their lengths. We could keep a heap of as many records as will fit in memory, using dynamic storage allocation as described in Section 2.5. M. A. Goetz [*Proc. AFIPS Joint Computer Conf.* **25** (1964), 602–604] has suggested another approach, breaking each record into fixed-size parts that are linked together; they occupy space at the leaves of the tree, but only the leading part participates in the tournament.

29. The top 2^k loser nodes go into the corresponding host positions. The remaining loser nodes consist of 2^k subtrees of $2^n - 1$ nodes each; they are assigned to host nodes in symmetric order — the leftmost subtree into the leftmost host node, etc. [See K. Efe and N. Eleser, *Acta Informatica* **34** (1997), 429–447.]

30. Suppose t of the host nodes hold a *connected* 2^n-node subgraph of the complete 2^{n+k}-node loser tree. That tree has one node at level 0 and 2^{l-1} nodes at level l for $1 \le l \le n + k$. A subtree rooted at level $l \ge 1$ has $2^{n+k+1-l} - 1$ nodes; therefore the roots of t disjoint 2^n-node subtrees must all be on levels $\le k$. And each of these subtrees must contain at least one node on level k, because there are only $2^{k-1} < 2^n$ nodes on levels $< k$. It follows that $t \le 2^{k-1}$. But the number of edges in the host graph is at least $t + 2(2^k - t) - 1$, by (ii) and (iii), since there are at least this many loser nodes whose parent has a different image in the host.

[The hypothesis $n \ge k$ is necessary: When $n = k - 1$ there is a suitable host graph with $2^k + 2^{k-1} - 2$ edges.]

SECTION 5.4.2

1.

2. After the first merge phase, all remaining dummies are on tape T, and there are at most $a_n - a_{n-1} \le a_{n-1}$ of them. Therefore they all disappear during the second merge phase.

3. We have $(\texttt{D[1]},\texttt{D[2]},\ldots,\texttt{D[T]}) = (a_n-a_{n-P},a_n-a_{n-P+1},\ldots,a_n-a_n)$, so the condition follows from the fact that the a's are nondecreasing. The condition is important to the validity of the algorithm, since steps D2 and D3 never decrease $\texttt{D}[j+1]$ more often than $\texttt{D}[j]$.

4. $(1-z-\cdots-z^5)a(z) = 1$ because of (3). And $t(z) = \sum_{n\ge1}(a_n+b_n+c_n+d_n+e_n)z^n = (z+\cdots+z^5)a(z)+(z+\cdots+z^4)a(z)+\cdots+za(z) = (5z+4z^2+3z^3+2z^4+z^5)a(z)$.

5. Let $g_p(z) = (z-1)f_p(z) = z^{p+1}-2z^p+1$, and let $h_p(z) = z^{p+1}-2z^p$. Rouché's theorem [*J. École Polytechnique* **21**, 37 (1858), 1–34] tells us that $h_p(z)$ and $g_p(z)$ have the same number of roots inside the circle $|z| = 1+\epsilon$, provided $|h_p(z)| > |h_p(z)-g_p(z)| = 1$ on the circle. If $\phi^{-1} > \epsilon > 0$ we have $|h_p(z)| \ge (1+\epsilon)^p(1-\epsilon) > (1+\phi^{-1})^2(1-\phi^{-1}) = 1$. Hence g_p has p roots of magnitude ≤ 1. They are distinct, since $\gcd(g_p(z),g_p'(z)) = \gcd(g_p(z),(p+1)z-2p) = 1$. [*AMM* **67** (1960), 745–752.]

6. Let $c_0 = -\alpha p(\alpha^{-1})/q'(\alpha^{-1})$. Then $p(z)/q(z)-c_0/(1-\alpha z)$ is analytic in $|z| \le R$ for some $R > |\alpha|^{-1}$; hence $[z^n]\,p(z)/q(z) = c_0\alpha^n + O(R^{-n})$. Thus, $\ln S = n\ln\alpha + \ln c_0 + O((\alpha R)^{-n})$; and $n = (\ln S/\ln\alpha) + O(1)$ implies that $O((\alpha R)^{-n}) = O(S^{-\epsilon})$. Similarly, let $c_1 = \alpha^2 p(\alpha^{-1})/q'(\alpha^{-1})^2$ and $c_2 = -\alpha p'(\alpha^{-1})/q'(\alpha^{-1})^2 + \alpha p(\alpha^{-1}q''(\alpha^{-1})/q'(\alpha^{-1})^3$, and consider $p(z)/q(z)^2 - c_1/(1-\alpha z)^2 - c_2/(1-\alpha z)$.

7. Let $\alpha_p = 2x$ and $z = -1/2^{p+1}$. Then $x^{p+1} = x^p + z$, so we have the convergent series $\alpha_p = 2\sum_{k\ge0}\binom{1-kp}{k}z^k/(1-kp) = 2-2^{-P}-p2^{-2p-1}+O(p^2 2^{-3p})$ by Eq. 1.2.6–(25).

Note: It follows that the quantity ρ in exercise 6 becomes approximately $\log_4 S$ as p increases. Similarly, for both Table 5 and Table 6, the coefficient c approaches $1/((\phi+2)\ln\phi)$ on a large number of tapes.

8. Evidently $N_0^{(p)} = 1$, $N_m^{(p)} = 0$ for $m < 0$, and by considering the different possibilities for the first summand we have $N_m^{(p)} = N_{m-1}^{(p)} + \cdots + N_{m-p}^{(p)}$ when $m > 0$. Hence $N_m^{(p)} = F_{m+p-1}^{(p)}$. [*Lehrbuch der Combinatorik* (Leipzig: Teubner, 1901), 136–137.]

9. Consider the position of the leftmost 0, if there is one; we find $K_m^{(p)} = F_{m+p}^{(p)}$. *Note:* There is a simple one-to-one correspondence between such sequences of 0s and 1s and the representations of $m+1$ considered in exercise 8: Place a 0 at the right end of the sequence, and look at the positions of all the 0s.

10. *Lemma:* If $n = F_{j_1}^{(p)} + \cdots + F_{j_m}^{(p)}$ is such a representation, with $j_1 > \cdots > j_m \ge p$, we have $n < F_{j_1+1}^{(p)}$. *Proof:* The result is obvious if $m < p$; otherwise let k be minimal with $j_k > j_{k+1}+1$; we have $k < p$, and by induction $F_{j_{k+1}}^{(p)} + \cdots + F_{j_m}^{(p)} < F_{j_k-1}^{(p)}$, hence $n < F_{j_1}^{(p)} + \cdots + F_{j_1-k-1}^{(p)} \le F_{j_1+1}^{(p)}$.

The stated result can now be proved, by induction on n. If $n > 0$ let j be maximal such that $F_j^{(p)} \le n$. The lemma shows that each representation of n must consist of $F_j^{(p)}$ plus a representation of $n - F_j^{(p)}$. By induction, $n - F_j^{(p)}$ has a unique representation of the desired form, and this representation does not include all of the numbers $F_{j-1}^{(p)},\ldots,F_{j-p+1}^{(p)}$ because j is maximal.

Notes: The case $p = 2$, which is due to E. Zeckendorf [*Simon Stevin* **29** (1952), 190–195], has been considered in exercise 1.2.8–34. There is a simple algorithm to go from the representation of n to that of $n+1$, working on the sequence $c_j \ldots c_1 c_0$ of

0s and 1s such that $n = \sum c_j F_{j+p}^{(p)}$: For example, if $p = 3$, we look at the rightmost digits, changing $\ldots 0$ to $\ldots 1$, $\ldots 01$ to $\ldots 10$, $\ldots 011$ to $\ldots 100$; then we "carry" to the left if necessary, replacing $\ldots 0111 \ldots$ by $\ldots 1000 \ldots$. (See the sequences of 0s and 1s in exercise 9, in the order listed.) A similar number system has been studied by W. C. Lynch [*Fibonacci Quarterly* **8** (1970), 6–22], who found a very interesting way to make it govern both the distribution and merge phases of a polyphase sort.

12. The kth power contains the perfect distributions for levels $k - 4$ through k, on successive rows, with the largest elements to the right.

13. By induction on the level.

14. (a) $n(1) = 1$, so assume that $k > 1$. The law $T_{nk} = T_{(n-1)(k-1)} + \cdots + T_{(n-P)(k-1)}$ shows that $T_{nk} \le T_{(n+1)k}$ if and only if $T_{(n-P)(k-1)} \le T_{n(k-1)}$. Let r be any positive integer, and let n' be minimal such that $T_{(n'-r)(k-1)} > T_{n'(k-1)}$; then $T_{(n-r)(k-1)} \ge T_{n(k-1)}$ for all $n \ge n'$, since this relation is trivial for $n \ge n(k-1) + r$ and otherwise $T_{(n-r)(k-1)} \ge T_{(n'-r)(k-1)} \ge T_{n'(k-1)} \ge T_{n(k-1)}$. (b) The same argument with $r = n - n'$ shows that $T_{n'k'} < T_{nk'}$ implies $T_{(n'-j)k'} \le T_{(n-j)k'}$ for all $j \ge 0$; hence the recurrence implies that $T_{(n'-j)k} \le T_{(n-j)k}$ for all $j \ge 0$ and $k \ge k'$. (c) Let $\ell(S)$ be the least n such that $\Sigma_n(S)$ assumes its minimum value. The sequence M_n exists as desired if and only if $\ell(S) \le \ell(S+1)$ for all S. Suppose $n = \ell(S) > \ell(S+1) = n'$, so that $\Sigma_n(S) < \Sigma_{n'}(S)$ and $\Sigma_n(S+1) \ge \Sigma_{n'}(S+1)$. There is some smallest S' such that $\Sigma_n(S') < \Sigma_{n'}(S')$, and we have $m = \Sigma_n(S') - \Sigma_n(S'-1) < \Sigma_{n'}(S') - \Sigma_{n'}(S'-1) = m'$. Then $\sum_{k=1}^{m} T_{n'k} < S' \le \sum_{k=1}^{m} T_{nk}$; hence there is some $k' \le m$ such that $T_{n'k'} < T_{nk'}$. Similarly we have $l = \Sigma_n(S+1) - \Sigma_n(S) > \Sigma_{n'}(S+1) - \Sigma_{n'}(S) = l'$; hence $\sum_{k=1}^{l'} T_{n'k} \ge S+1 > \sum_{k=1}^{l'} T_{nk}$. Since $l' \ge m' > m$, there is some $k > m$ such that $T_{n'k} > T_{nk}$. But this contradicts part (b).

15. This theorem has been proved by D. A. Zave, whose article was cited in the text.

16. D. A. Zave has shown that the number of records input (and output) is $S \log_{T-1} S + \frac{1}{2} S \log_{T-1} \log_{T-1} S + O(S)$.

17. Let $T = 3$; $A_{11}(x) = 6x^6 + 35x^7 + 56x^8 + \cdots$, $B_{11}(x) = x^6 + 15x^7 + 35x^8 + \cdots$, $T_{11}(x) = 7x^6 + 50x^7 + 91x^8 + 64x^9 + 19x^{10} + 2x^{11}$. The optimum distribution for $S = 144$ requires 55 runs on T2, and this forces a nonoptimum distribution for $S = 145$. D. A. Zave has studied near-optimum procedures of this kind.

18. Let $S = 9$, $T = 3$, and consider the following two patterns.

Optimum Polyphase:					Alternative:			
T1	T2	T3	Cost		T1	T2	T3	Cost
$0^2 1^6$	$0^2 1^3$	—			$0^1 1^6$	$0^1 1^3$	—	
1^3	—	$0^2 2^3$	6		1^3	—	$0^1 2^3$	6
—	$1^2 3^1$	2^2	5		—	$1^1 3^2$	2^1	7
3^2	3^1	—	6		3^1	3^2	—	3
3^1	—	6^1	6		—	3^1	6^1	6
—	9^1	—	9		9^1	—	—	9
			32					31

(Still another way to improve on "optimum" polyphase is to reconsider where dummy runs appear on the output tape of every merge phase. For example, the result of merging $0^2 1^3$ with $0^2 1^3$ might be regarded as $2^1 0^1 2^1 0^1 2^1$ instead of $0^2 2^3$. Thus, many unresolved questions of optimality remain.)

19.

Level	T1	T2	T3	T4	Total	Final output on
0	1	0	0	0	1	T1
1	0	1	1	1	3	T6
2	1	1	1	0	3	T5
3	1	2	1	1	5	T4
4	2	2	2	1	7	T3
5	2	4	3	2	11	T2
6	4	5	4	2	15	T1
7	5	8	6	4	23	T6

n	a_n	b_n	c_n	d_n	t_n	$T(k)$
$n+1$	b_n	$c_n + a_n$	$d_n + a_n$	a_n	$t_n + 2a_n$	$T(k-1)$

20. $a(z) = 1/(1 - z^2 - z^3 - z^4)$, $t(z) = (3z + 3z^2 + 2z^3 + z^4)/(1 - z^2 - z^3 - z^4)$, $\sum_{n\geq 1} T_n(x) z^n = x(3z + 3z^2 + 2z^3 + z^4)/(1 - x(z^2 + z^3 + z^4))$. $D_n = A_{n-1} + 1$, $C_n = A_{n-1} A_{n-2} + 1$, $B_n = A_{n-1} A_{n-2} A_{n-3} + 1$, $A_n = A_{n-2} A_{n-3} A_{n-4} + 1$.

21. 333343333332322 3333433333323 33334333333 3333433 333323 T5

22. $t_n - t_{n-1} - t_{n-2} = -1 + 3[n \bmod 3 = 1]$. (This Fibonacci-like relation follows from the fact that $1 - z^2 - 2z^3 - z^4 = (1 - \phi z)(1 - \hat{\phi} z)(1 - \omega z)(1 - \bar{\omega} z)$, where $\omega^3 = 1$.)

23. In place of (25), the run lengths during the first half of the nth merge phase are s_n, and on the second half they are t_n, where

$$s_n = t_{n-2} + t_{n-3} + s_{n-3} + s_{n-4}, \qquad t_n = t_{n-2} + s_{n-2} + s_{n-3} + s_{n-4}.$$

Here we regard $s_n = t_n = 1$ for $n \leq 0$. [In general, if v_{n+1} is the sum of the first $2r$ terms of $u_{n-1} + \cdots + v_{n-P}$, we have $s_n = t_n = t_{n-2} + \cdots + t_{n-r} + 2t_{n-r-1} + t_{n-r-2} + \cdots + t_{n-P}$; if v_{n+1} is the sum of the first $2r-1$ terms, we have $s_n = t_{n-2} + \cdots + t_{n-r-1} + s_{n-r-1} + \cdots + s_{n-P}$, $t_n = t_{n-2} + \cdots + t_{n-r} + s_{n-r} + \cdots + s_{n-P}$.]

In place of (27) and (28), $A_n = (U_{n-1} V_{n-1} U_{n-2} V_{n-2} V_{n-3} U_{n-3} U_{n-4} V_{n-4}) + 1$, $\ldots, D_n = (U_{n-1} V_{n-1}) + 1$, $E_n = (U_{n-2} V_{n-2} U_{n-3}) + 1$; $V_{n+1} = (U_{n-1} V_{n-1} U_{n-2}) + 1$, $U_n = (V_{n-2} U_{n-3} V_{n-3} U_{n-4} V_{n-4}) + 1$.

25.

1^{16}	1^8	—	1^8
1^{12}	1^4	R	$1^8 2^4$
1^8	—	2^4	R

R	$8^1 16^1$	8^1	8^0
16^0	R	8^1	—
16^1	16^1	8^0	R
R	16^1	—	24^0
16^1	16^1	R	$24^0 32^0$
16^0	16^0	32^1	(R)

26. When 2^n are sorted, $n \cdot 2^n$ initial runs are processed while merging; each half phase (with a few exceptions) merges 2^{n-2} and rewinds 2^{n-1}. When $2^n + 2^{n-1}$ are sorted, $n \cdot 2^n + (n-1) \cdot 2^{n-1}$ initial runs are processed while merging; each half phase (with a few exceptions) merges 2^{n-2} or 2^{n-1} and rewinds $2^{n-1} + 2^{n-2}$.

27. It works if and only if the gcd of the distribution numbers is 1. For example, let there be six tapes; if we distribute (a, b, c, d, e) to T1 through T5, where $a \geq b \geq c \geq d \geq e > 0$, the first phase leaves a distribution $(a-e, b-e, c-e, d-e, e)$, and

$\gcd(a-e, b-e, c-e, d-e, e) = \gcd(a, b, c, d, e)$, since any common divisor of one set of numbers divides the others too. The process decreases the number of runs at each phase until $\gcd(a, b, c, d, e)$ runs are left on a single tape.

[Nonpolyphase distributions sometimes turn out to be superior to polyphase under certain configurations of dummy runs, as shown in exercise 18. This phenomenon was first observed by B. Sackman about 1963.]

28. We get any such (a, b, c, d, e) by starting with $(1, 0, 0, 0, 0)$ and doing the following operation exactly n times: Choose x in $\{a, b, c, d, e\}$, and add x to each of the other four elements of (a, b, c, d, e).

To show that $a+b+c+d+e \le t_n$, we shall prove that if $a \ge b \ge c \ge d \ge e$ on level n, we always have $a \le a_n$, $b \le b_n$, $c \le c_n$, $d \le d_n$, $e \le e_n$. The proof follows by induction, since the level $n+1$ distributions are $(b+a, c+a, d+a, e+a, a)$, $(a+b, c+b, d+b, e+b, b)$, $(a+c, b+c, d+c, e+c, c)$, $(a+d, b+d, c+d, e+d, d)$, $(a+e, b+e, c+e, d+e, e)$.

30. The following table has been computed by J. A. Mortenson.

Level	$T = 5$	$T = 6$	$T = 7$	$T = 8$	$T = 9$	$T = 10$	
1	2	2	2	2	2	2	M_1
2	4	5	6	7	8	9	M_2
3	4	5	6	7	8	9	M_3
4	8	8	10	12	14	16	M_4
5	10	14	18	17	20	23	M_5
6	18	20	26	27	32	31	M_6
7	26	32	46	47	56	42	M_7
8	44	53	74	82	92	92	M_8
9	68	83	122	111	138	139	M_9
10	112	134	206	140	177	196	M_{10}
11	178	197	317	324	208	241	M_{11}
12	290	350	401	488	595	288	M_{12}
13	466	566	933	640	838	860	M_{13}
14	756	917	1371	769	1064	1177	M_{14}
15	1220	1481	1762	2078	1258	1520	M_{15}
16	1976	2313	4060	2907	3839	1821	M_{16}

31. [*Random Structures & Algorithms* **5** (1994), 102–104.] $K_d(n) = F_{n-2}^{(d)} = N_{n-d-1}^{(d)}$. We have $n - d - 1 = a_1 + \cdots + a_r$ if the tree has $r + 1$ leaves and the $(k+1)$st leaf has $a_k - 1$ ancestors distinct from the ancestors of the first k leaves. (The seven example trees correspond respectively to $1 + 1 + 1 + 1$, $1 + 1 + 2$, $1 + 2 + 1$, $1 + 3$, $2 + 1 + 1$, $2 + 2$, and $3 + 1$.)

SECTION 5.4.3

1. The tape-splitting polyphase is superior with respect to the average number of times each record is processed (Table 5.4.2–6), when there are 6, 7, or 8 tapes.

2. The methods are essentially identical when the number of initial runs is a Fibonacci number; but the manner of distributing dummy runs in other cases is better with polyphase. The cascade algorithm puts 1 on T1, then 1 on T2, 1 on T1, 2 on T2, 3 on T1, 5 on T2, etc., and step C8 never finds $D[p-1] = M[p-1]$ when $p = 2$. In effect, all dummies are on one tape, and this is less efficient than the method of Algorithm 5.4.2D.

3. (Distribution stops after putting 12 runs on T3 during Step $(3,3)$.)

T1	T2	T3	T4	T5	T6
1^{26}	1^{21}	1^{24}	1^{14}	1^{15}	—
1^5	—	1^{12}	$1^2 2^7$	1^{15}	$2^4 12$
8^4	$6^2 9^3$	5^2	6^3	1^1	—
—	9^1	23^1	17^1	25^1	26^1
100^1	—	—	—	—	—

4. Induction. (See exercise 5.4.2–28.)

5. When there are a_n initial runs, the k pass outputs a_{n-k} runs of length a_k, then b_{n-k} of length b_k, etc.

6.

$$\begin{pmatrix} 1 & 1 & 1 & 1 & 1 \\ 1 & 1 & 1 & 1 & 0 \\ 1 & 1 & 1 & 0 & 0 \\ 1 & 1 & 0 & 0 & 0 \\ 1 & 0 & 0 & 0 & 0 \end{pmatrix}.$$

7. We save $e_2 e_{n-2} + e_3 e_{n-3} + \cdots + e_n e_0$ initial run lengths (see exercise 5), which may also be written $a_1 a_{n-3} + a_2 a_{n-4} + \cdots + a_{n-2} a_0$; it is $[z^{n-2}] (A(z)^2 - A(z))$.

8. The denominator of $A(z)$ has distinct roots and greater degree than the numerator, hence $A(z) = \sum q_3(\rho)/(1 - \rho z)\rho(1 - q_4'(\rho))$ summed over all roots ρ of $q_4(\rho) = \rho$. The special form of ρ is helpful in evaluating $q_3(\rho)$ and $q_4'(\rho)$.

9. The formulas hold for all *large* n, by (8) and (12), in view of the value of $q_m(2 \sin \theta_k)$. To show that they hold for all n we need to know that $q_{m-1}(z)$ is the quotient when $q_{r-1}(z)q_m(z)$ is divided by $q_r(z) - z$, for $0 \le m < r$. This can be proved either by using (10) and noting that cancellations bring down the degree of the polynomial $q_{r-1}(z)q_m(z) - q_r(z)q_{m-1}(z)$, or by noting that $A(z)^2 + B(z)^2 + \cdots + E(z)^2 \to 0$ as $z \to \infty$ (see exercise 5), or by finding explicit formulas for the numerators of $B(z)$, $C(z)$, etc.

10. $E(z) = r_1(z)A(z)$; $D(z) = r_2(z)A(z) - r_1(z)$; $C(z) = r_3(z)A(z) - r_2(z)$; $B(z) = r_4(z)A(z) - r_3(z)$; $A(z) = r_5(z)A(z) + 1 - r_4(z)$. Thus $A(z) = (1 - r_4(z))/(1 - r_5(z))$. [Notice that $r_m(2 \sin \theta) = \sin(2m\theta)/\cos \theta$; hence $r_m(z)$ is the Chebyshev polynomial $(-1)^{m+1} U_{2m-1}(z/2)$.]

11. Prove that $f_m(z) = q_{\lfloor m/2 \rfloor}(z) - r_{\lceil m/2 \rceil}(z)$ and that $f_m(z)f_{m-1}(z) = 1 - r_m(z)$. Then use the result of exercise 10. (This explicit form for the denominator was first discovered by David E. Ferguson.)

13. See exercise 5.4.6–6.

SECTION 5.4.4

1. When writing an ascending run, *first* write a sentinel record containing $-\infty$ before outputting the run. (And a $+\infty$ sentinel should be written at the end of the run as well, if the output is ever going to be read forward, as on the final pass.) For descending runs, interchange the roles of $-\infty$ and $+\infty$.

2. The smallest number on level $n + 1$ is equal to the largest on level n; hence the columns are nondecreasing, regardless of the way we permute the numbers in any particular row.

3. In fact, during the merge process the first run on T2–T6 will always be descending, and the first on T1 will always be ascending. (By induction.)

4. It requires several "copy" operations on the second and third phases; the approximate extra cost is $(\log 2)/(\log \rho)$ passes, where ρ is the "growth ratio" in Table 5.4.2–1.

5. If α is a string, let α^R denote its left-right reversal.

Level	T1	T2	T3	T4	T5					
						2				
						3	2			
0	0	—	—	—	—	4	3	2		
						3	4	3		
1	1	1	1	1	1	4	3	4	2	
						5	4	3	3	
2	12	12	12	12	2	4	5	4	4	
						3	4	5	3	
3	1232	1232	1232	232	32	2	3	4	4	2
						3	2	3	5	3
4	12323432	12323432	2323432	323432	3432	4	3	2	4	4
						3	4	3	3	3
· · · · · · ·	· · · · ·	· · · · ·	· · · · ·	· · · · ·	· · ·	2	3	4	2	4
n	A_n	B_n	C_n	D_n	E_n	3	2	3	3	5
						2	3	2	4	4
$n+1$	$B_n(A_n^R+1)$	$C_n(A_n^R+1)$	$D_n(A_n^R+1)$	$E_n(A_n^R+1)$	A_n^R+1	1	2	3	3	3

We have

$$E_n = A_{n-1}^R + 1,$$
$$D_n = A_{n-2}^R A_{n-1}^R + 1,$$
$$C_n = A_{n-3}^R A_{n-2}^R A_{n-1}^R + 1,$$
$$B_n = A_{n-4}^R A_{n-3}^R A_{n-2}^R A_{n-1}^R + 1, \quad \text{and}$$
$$A_n = A_{n-5}^R A_{n-4}^R A_{n-3}^R A_{n-2}^R A_{n-1}^R + 1$$
$$= n - Q_n,$$

where

$$Q_n^R = Q_{n-1}(Q_{n-2}+1)(Q_{n-3}+2)(Q_{n-4}+3)(Q_{n-5}+4), \qquad n \geq 1,$$

$Q_0 = 0$, and $Q_n = \epsilon$ for $n < 0$.

These strings $A_n, B_n, \ldots$ contain the same entries as the corresponding strings in Section 5.4.2, but in another order. Note that adjacent merge numbers always differ by 1. An initial run must be A if and only if its merge number is even, D if and only if odd. Simple distribution schemes such as Algorithm 5.4.2D are not quite as effective at placing dummies into high-merge-number positions; therefore it is probably advantageous to compute Q_n between phases 1 and 2, in order to help control dummy run placement.

6. $y^{(4)} = (+1, +1, -1, +1)$
$y^{(3)} = (+1, \quad 0, -1, \quad 0)$
$y^{(2)} = (+1, -1, +1, +1)$
$y^{(1)} = (-1, +1, +1, +1)$
$y^{(0)} = (\quad 1, \quad 0, \quad 0, \quad 0)$

7. (See exercise 15.)

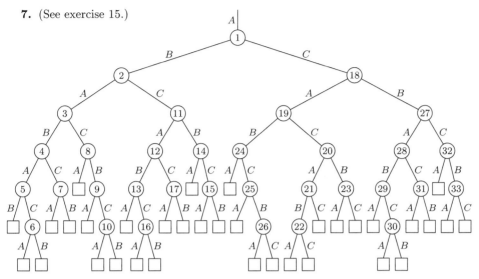

Incidentally, 34 is apparently the smallest Fibonacci number F_n for which polyphase doesn't produce the optimum read-backward merge for F_n initial runs on three tapes. This tree has external path length 178, which beats polyphase's 176.

8. For $T = 4$, the tree with external path length 13 is not T-lifo, and every tree with external path length 14 includes a one-way merge.

9. We may consider a complete $(T-1)$-ary tree, by the result of exercise 2.3.4.5–6; the degree of the "last" internal node is between 2 and $T-1$. When there are $(T-1)^q - m$ external nodes, $\lfloor m/(T-2) \rfloor$ of them are on level $q-1$, and the rest are on level q.

11. True by induction on the number of initial runs. If there is a valid distribution with S runs and two adjacent runs in the same direction, then there is one with fewer than S runs; but there is none when $S = 1$.

12. Conditions (a) and (b) are obvious. If either configuration in (4) is present, for some tape name A and some $i < j < k$, node j must be in a subtree below node i and to the left of node k, by the definition of preorder. Hence the "$j - l$" case can't be present, and A must be the "special" name since it appears on an external branch. But this contradicts the fact that the special name is supposed to be on the leftmost branch below node i.

13. Nodes now numbered 4, 7, 11, 13 could be external instead of one-way merges. (This gives an external path length one higher than the polyphase tree.)

15. Let the tape names be A, B, and C. We shall construct several species of trees, botanically identified by their root and leaf (external node) structure:

Type $r(A)$	Root A
Type $s(A,C)$	Root A, no C leaves
Type $t(A)$	Root A, no A leaves
Type $u(A,C)$	Root A, no C leaves, no compound B leaves
Type $v(A,C)$	Root A, no C leaves, no compound A leaves
Type $w(A,C)$	Root A, no A leaves, no compound C leaves

A "compound leaf" is a leaf whose sibling is not a leaf. We can grow a 3-lifo type $r(A)$ tree by first growing its left subtree as a type $s(B, C)$, then growing the right subtree as type $r(C)$. Similarly, type $s(A, C)$ comes from a type $s(B, C)$ then $t(C)$; type $u(A, C)$ from $v(B, C)$ and $w(C, B)$; type $v(A, C)$ from $u(B, C)$ and $w(C, A)$. We can grow a 3-lifo type $t(A)$ tree whose left subtree is type $u(B, A)$ and whose right subtree is type $s(C, A)$, by first letting the left subtree grow except for its (non-compound) C leaves and its right subtree; at this point the left subtree has only A and B leaves, so we can grow the right subtree of the whole tree, then grow off the A leaves of the left left subtree, and finally grow the left right subtree. Similarly, a type $w(A, C)$ tree can be fabricated from a $u(B, A)$ and a $v(C, A)$. [The tree of exercise 7 is an $r(A)$ tree constructed in this manner.]

Let $r(n), \ldots, w(n)$ denote the minimum external path length over all n-leaf trees of the relevant type, when they are constructed by such a procedure. We have $r(1) = s(1) = u(1) = 0$, $r(2) = t(2) = w(2) = 2$, $t(1) = v(1) = w(1) = s(2) = u(2) = v(2) = \infty$; and for $n \geq 3$,

$$
\begin{aligned}
r(n) &= n + \min_k\big(s(k) + r(n - k)\big), & u(n) &= n + \min_k\big(v(k) + w(n - k)\big), \\
s(n) &= n + \min_k\big(s(k) + t(n - k)\big), & v(n) &= n + \min_k\big(u(k) + w(n - k)\big), \\
t(n) &= n + \min_k\big(u(k) + s(n - k)\big), & w(n) &= n + \min_k\big(u(k) + v(n - k)\big).
\end{aligned}
$$

It follows that $r(n) \leq s(n) \leq u(n)$, $s(n) \leq v(n)$, and $r(n) \leq t(n) \leq w(n)$ for all n; furthermore $s(2n) = t(2n + 1) = \infty$. (The latter is evident *a priori*.)

Let $A(n)$ be the function defined by the laws $A(1) = 0$, $A(2n) = 2n + 2A(n)$, $A(2n+1) = 2n+1+A(n)+A(n+1)$; then $A(2n) = 2n+A(n-1)+A(n+1) - (0 \text{ or } 1)$ for all $n \geq 2$. Let C be a constant such that, for $4 \leq n \leq 8$,

i) n even implies that $w(n) \leq A(n) + Cn - 1$.

ii) n odd implies that $u(n)$ and $v(n)$ are $\leq A(n) + Cn - 1$.

(This actually works for all $C \geq \frac{5}{6}$.) Then an inductive argument, choosing k to be $\lfloor n/2 \rfloor \pm 1$ as appropriate, shows that the relations are valid for *all* $n \geq 4$. But $A(n)$ is the lower bound in (9) when $T = 3$, and $r(n) \leq \min(u(n), v(n), w(n))$, hence we have proved that $A(n) \leq \hat{K}_3(n) \leq r(n) \leq A(n) + \frac{5}{6}n - 1$. [The constant $\frac{5}{6}$ can be improved.]

17. [The following method was used in the UNIVAC III sort program, and presented at the 1962 ACM Sort Symposium.]

Level	T1	T2	T3	T4	T5
0	1	0	0	0	0
1	5	4	3	2	1
2	55	50	41	29	15

$$\cdots \cdots \cdots \cdots \cdots \cdots \cdots \cdots \cdots$$

n	a_n	b_n	c_n	d_n	e_n
$n+1$	$5a_n+4b_n+$	$4a_n+4b_n+$	$3a_n+3b_n+$	$2a_n+2b_n+$	a_n+b_n+
	$3c_n+2d_n+c_n$	$3c_n+2d_n+e_n$	$3c_n+2d_n+e_n$	$2c_n+2d_n+e_n$	$c_n+d_n+e_n$

To get from level n to level $n + 1$ during the initial distribution, insert k_1 "sublevels" with $(4, 4, 3, 2, 1)$ runs added respectively to tapes $(T1, T2, \ldots, T5)$, k_2 "sublevels" with $(4, 3, 3, 2, 1)$ runs added, k_3 with $(3, 3, 2, 2, 1)$, k_4 with $(2, 2, 2, 1, 1)$, k_5 with $(1, 1, 1, 1, 0)$, where $k_1 \leq a_n$, $k_2 \leq b_n$, $k_3 \leq c_n$, $k_4 \leq d_n$, $k_5 \leq e_n$. [If $(k_1, \ldots, k_5) = (a_n, \ldots, e_n)$ we have reached level $n + 1$.] Add dummy runs if necessary to fill out a sublevel. Then merge $k_1 + k_2 + k_3 + k_4 + k_5$ runs from $(T1, \ldots, T5)$ to T6, merge $k_1 + \cdots + k_4$ from $(T1, \ldots, T4)$ to T5, $\ldots$, merge k_1 from T1 to T2; and merge k_1 from $(T2, \ldots, T6)$ to T1, k_2 from $(T3, \ldots, T6)$ to T2, $\ldots$, k_5 from T6 to T5.

18. (Solution by M. S. Paterson.) Suppose record j is written on the sequence of tape numbers τ_j. At most $C|\tau|$ records can have a given sequence τ, where C depends on the internal memory size (see Section 5.4.8). Hence $|\tau_1| + \cdots + |\tau_N| = \Omega(N \log_T N)$.

19.

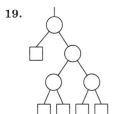

20. A strongly T-fifo tree has a T-fifo labeling in which there are no three branches having the respective forms

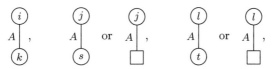

for some tape name A and some $i < j < k < l < s$. Informally, when we grow on an A, we must grow on all other A's before creating any new A's.

21. It is very weakly fifo:

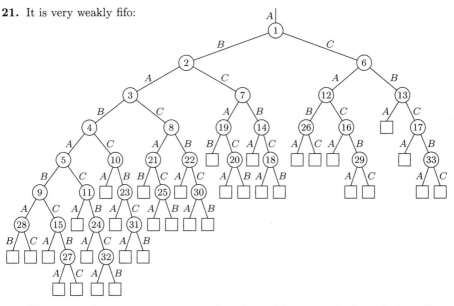

22. This occurs for any tree representations formed by successively replacing all occurrences of, for example,

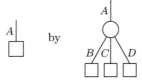

for some fixed tape names A, B, C, D. Since all occurrences are replaced by the same pattern, the lifo or fifo order makes no difference in the structure of the tree.

Stating the condition in terms of the vector model: Whenever $(y^{(k+1)} \neq y^{(k)}$ or $k = m)$ and $y_j^{(k)} = -1$, we have $y_j^{(k)} + \cdots + y_j^{(1)} + y_j^{(0)} = 0$.

23. (a) Assume that $v_1 \leq v_2 \leq \cdots \leq v_T$; the "cascade" stage

$$(1, \ldots, 1, -1)^{v_T} (1, \ldots, 1, -1, 0)^{v_T - 1} \ldots (1, -1, 0, \ldots, 0)^{v_2}$$

takes $C(v)$ into v. (b) Immediate, since $C(v)_k \leq C(w)_k$ for all k. (c) If v is obtained in q stages, we have $u \to u^{(1)} \to \cdots \to u^{(q)} = v$ for some unit vector u, and some other vectors $u^{(1)}, \ldots$. Hence $u^{(1)} \preceq C(u)$, $u^{(2)} \preceq C(C(u))$, $\ldots$, $v \preceq C^{[q]}(u)$. Hence $v_1 + \cdots + v_T$ is less than or equal to the sum of the elements of $C^{[q]}(u)$; and the latter is obtained in cascade merge. [This theorem generalizes the result of exercise 5.4.3–4. Unfortunately the concept of "stage" as defined here doesn't seem to have any practical significance.]

24. Let $y^{(m)} \ldots y^{(l+1)}$ be a stage that reduces w to v. If we have $y_j^{(i)} = -1$, $y_j^{(i-1)} = 0$, $\ldots$, $y_j^{(k+1)} = 0$, and $y_j^{(k)} = -1$, for some $k < i - 1$, we can insert $y^{(k)}$ between $y^{(i)}$ and $y^{(i-1)}$. Repeat this operation until all (-1)'s in each column are adjacent. Then if $y_j^{(i)} = 0$ and $y_j^{(i-1)} \neq 0$ it is possible to set $y_j^{(i)} \leftarrow 1$; ultimately each column consists of $+1$'s followed by -1's followed by 0s, and we have constructed a stage that reduces w' to v for some $w' \succeq w$. Permuting the columns, this stage takes the form $(1, \ldots, 1, -1)^{a_T} \ldots (1, -1, 0, \ldots, 0)^{a_2} (-1, 0, \ldots, 0)^{a_1}$. The sequence of $T - 1$ relations

$$(x_1, \ldots, x_T) \preceq (x_1 + x_T, \ldots, x_{T-1} + x_T, 0)$$
$$\preceq (x_1 + x_{T-1} + x_T, \ldots, x_{T-2} + x_{T-1} + x_T, x_T, 0)$$
$$\preceq (x_1 + x_{T-2} + x_{T-1} + x_T, \ldots, x_{T-3} + x_{T-2} + x_{T-1} + x_T, x_{T-1} + x_T, x_T, 0)$$
$$\preceq \cdots$$
$$\preceq (x_1 + x_2 + x_3 + \cdots + x_T, x_3 + \cdots + x_T, \ldots, x_{T-1} + x_T, x_T, 0)$$

now shows that the best choice of the a's is $a_T = v_T$, $a_{T-1} = v_{T-1}$, $\ldots$, $a_2 = v_2$, $a_1 = 0$. And the result is best if we permute columns so that $v_1 \leq \cdots \leq v_T$.

25. (a) Assume that $v_{T-k+1} \geq \cdots \geq v_T \geq v_1 \geq \cdots \geq v_{T-k}$ and use

$$(1, \ldots, 1, -1, 0, \ldots, 0)^{v_{T-k+1}} \ldots (1, \ldots, 1, 0, \ldots, 0, -1)^{v_T}.$$

(b) The sum of the l largest elements of $D_k(v)$ is $(l - 1)s_k + s_{k+l}$ for $1 \leq l \leq T - k$. (c) If $v \Rightarrow w$ in a phase that uses k output tapes, we may obviously assume that the phase has the form $(1, \ldots, 1, -1, 0, \ldots, 0)^{a_1} \ldots (1, \ldots, 1, 0, \ldots, 0, -1)^{a_k}$, with each of the other $T - k$ tapes used as input in each operation. Choosing $a_1 = v_{T-k+1}, \ldots$, $a_k = v_T$ is best. (d) See exercise 22(c). We always have $k_1 = 1$; and $k = T - 2$ always beats $k = T - 1$ since we assume that at least one component of v is zero. Hence for $T = 3$ we have $k_1 \ldots k_q = 1^q$ and the initial distribution $(F_{q+1}, F_q, 0)$. For $T = 4$ the undominated strategies and their corresponding distributions are found to be

$$
\begin{aligned}
q = 2 \quad & 12 \ (3, 2, 0, 0) \\
q = 3 \quad & 121 \ (5, 3, 3, 0); \ 122 \ (5, 5, 0, 0) \\
q = 4 \quad & 1211 \ (8, 8, 5, 0); \ 1222 \ (10, 10, 0, 0); \ 1212 \ (11, 8, 0, 0) \\
q = 5 \quad & 12121 \ (19, 11, 11, 0); \ 12222 \ (20, 20, 0, 0); \ 12112 \ (21, 16, 0, 0) \\
q = 6 \quad & 122222 \ (40, 40, 0, 0); \ 121212 \ (41, 30, 0, 0) \\
q \geq 7 \quad & 12^{q-1} \ (5 \cdot 2^{q-3}, 5 \cdot 2^{q-3}, 0, 0)
\end{aligned}
$$

So for $T = 4$ and $q \geq 6$, the minimum-phase merge is like balanced merge, with a slight twist at the very end (going from $(3, 2, 0, 0)$ to $(1, 0, 1, 1)$ instead of to $(0, 0, 2, 1)$).

When $T = 5$ the undominated strategies are $1(32)^{n-1}2$, $1(32)^{n-1}3$ for $q = 2n \geq 2$; $1(32)^{n-1}32$, $1(32)^{n-1}22$, $1(32)^{n-1}23$ for $q = 2n + 1 \geq 3$. (The first strategy listed has most runs in its distribution.) On six tapes they are 13 or 14, 142 or 132 or 133, 1333 or 1423, then 13^{q-1} for $q \geq 5$.

SECTION 5.4.5

1. The following algorithm is controlled by a table $A[L-1] \ldots A[1]A[0]$ that essentially represents a number in radix P notation. As we repeatedly add unity to this number, the carries tell us when to merge. Tapes are numbered from 0 to P.

> **O1.** [Initialize.] Set $(A[L-1], \ldots, A[0]) \leftarrow (0, \ldots, 0)$ and $q \leftarrow 0$. (During this algorithm, q will equal $(A[L-1] + \cdots + A[0]) \bmod T$.)
>
> **O2.** [Distribute.] Write an initial run on tape q, in ascending order. Set $l \leftarrow 0$.
>
> **O3.** [Add one.] If $l = L$, stop; the output is on tape $(-L) \bmod T$, in ascending order if and only if L is even. Otherwise set $A[l] \leftarrow A[l]+1$, $q \leftarrow (q+1) \bmod T$.
>
> **O4.** [Carry?] If $A[l] < P$, return to O2. Otherwise merge to tape $(q - l) \bmod T$, set $A[l] \leftarrow 0$ and $q \leftarrow (q + 1) \bmod T$, increase l by 1, and return to O3. ∎

2. Keep track of how many runs are on each tape. When the input is exhausted, add dummy runs if necessary and continue merging until reaching a situation with at most one run on each tape and at least one tape empty. Then finish the sort in one more merge, rewinding some tapes first if necessary. (It is possible to deduce the orientation of the runs from the A table.)

3.

Op	T0	T1	T2		Op	T0	T1	T2
Dist	—	A_1	$A_1 A_1$		Dist	$D_2 A_1$	A_1	A_4
Merge	D_2	—	A_1		Merge	D_2	—	$A_4 D_2$
Dist	$D_2 A_1$	—	A_1		Merge	—	A_4	A_4
Merge	D_2	D_2	—		Dist	—	A_4	$A_4 A_1$
Dist	D_2	$D_2 A_1$	A_1		Copy	—	$A_4 D_1$	A_4
Merge	$D_2 D_2$	D_2	—		Copy	—	A_4	$A_4 A_1$
Merge	D_2	—	A_4		Merge	D_5	—	A_4

At this point T2 would be rewound and a final merge would complete the sort.

To avoid useless copying in which runs are simply shifted back and forth, we can say "If the input is exhausted, go to B7" at the end of B3, and add the following new step:

> **B7.** [Do the endgame.] Set $s \leftarrow -1$, and go to B2 after repeating the following operations until $l = 0$: Set $s' \leftarrow A[l-1, q]$, and set q' and r' to the indices such that $A[l-1, q'] = -1$ and $A[l-1, r'] = -2$. (We will have $q' = r$, and $s' \leq A[l-1, j] \leq s' + 1$ for $j \neq q'$, $j \neq r'$.) If $s' - s$ is odd, promote level l, otherwise demote it (see below). Then merge to tape r, reading backwards; set $l \leftarrow l - 1$, $A[l, q] \leftarrow -1$, $A[l, r] \leftarrow s' + 1$, $r \leftarrow r'$, and repeat.

Here "promotion" means to repeat the following operation until $(q+(-1)^s) \bmod T = r$: Set $p \leftarrow (q+(-1)^s) \bmod T$ and copy one run from tape p to tape q, then set $A[l, q] \leftarrow s + 1$, $A[l, p] \leftarrow -1$, $q \leftarrow p$. And "demotion" means to repeat the following until $(q - (-1)^s) \bmod T = r$: Set $p \leftarrow (q - (-1)^s) \bmod T$ and copy one run from tape p to tape q, then set $A[l, q] \leftarrow s$, $A[l, p] \leftarrow -1$, $q \leftarrow p$. The copy operation reads backwards on tape p, hence it reverses the direction of the run being copied. If $D[p] > 0$ when copying from p to q, we simply decrease $D[p]$ and increase $D[q]$ instead of copying.

[The basic idea is that, once the input is exhausted, we want to reduce to at most one run on each tape. The parity of each nonnegative entry $A[l,j]$ tells us whether a run is ascending or descending. The smallest S for which this change makes any difference is $P^3 + 1$. When P is large, the change hardly ever makes much difference, but it does keep the computer from looking too foolish in some circumstances. The algorithm should also be changed to handle the case $S = 1$ more efficiently.]

4. We can, in fact, omit setting $A[0,0]$ in step B1, $A[l,q]$ in steps B3 and B5. [But $A[l,r]$ *must* be set in step B3.] The new step B7 in the previous answer does need the value of $A[l,q]$ (unless it explicitly uses the fact that $q' = r$, as noted there).

5. $P^{2k} - (P-1)P^{2k-2} < S \leq P^{2k}$ for some $k > 0$.

SECTION 5.4.6

1. $\lfloor 23000480/(n+480) \rfloor n$.

2. At the instant shown, all the records in that buffer have been moved to the output. Step F2 insists that the test "Is output buffer full?" precede the test "Is input buffer empty?" while merging, otherwise we would have trouble (unless the changes of exercise 4 were made).

3. No; for example, we might reach a state with P buffers $1/P$ full and $P-1$ buffers full, if file i contains the keys i, $i+P$, $i+2P$, $\ldots$, for $1 \leq i \leq P$. This example shows that $2P$ input buffers would be necessary for continuous output even if we allowed simultaneous reading, unless we reallocated memory for partial buffers. [Well, we don't really need $2P$ buffers if the blocks contain fewer than $P-1$ records; but that is unlikely.]

4. Set up S sooner (in steps F1 and F4 instead of F3).

5. If, for example, all keys of all files were equal, we couldn't simply make arbitrary decisions while forecasting; the forecast must be compatible with decisions made by the merging process. One safe way is to find the smallest possible m in steps F1 and F4, namely to consider a record from file $C[i]$ to be less than all records having the same key on file $C[j]$ whenever $i < j$. (In essence, the file number is appended to the key.)

6. In step C1 also set $\text{TAPE}[T+1] \leftarrow T+1$. In step C8 the merge should be to $\text{TAPE}[p+2]$ instead of $\text{TAPE}[p+1]$. In step C9, set $(\text{TAPE}[1], \ldots, \text{TAPE}[T+1]) \leftarrow (\text{TAPE}[T+1], \ldots, \text{TAPE}[1])$.

7. The method used in Chart A is $(A_1 D_1)^4 A_0 D_0 (A_1 D_1)^2 A_0 D_0 (A_1 D_1)^3 A_0$, $D_1 (A_1 D_1)^4$ $A_0 D_0 (A_1 D_1)^3 A_0 D_0 \alpha A_0 D_0 A_0$, $D_1 A_0 D_0 (A_1 D_1)^3 A_0 D_0 \alpha A_1 D_1 A_0$, $D_1 A_1 D_1 \alpha A_1 D_1 A_0$, where $\alpha = (A_0 D_0)^2 A_1 D_1 A_0 D_0 (A_1 D_1)^2 (A_0 D_0)^7 A_1 D_1 (A_0 D_0)^3 A_1 D_1 A_0 D_0$. The first merge phase writes $D_0 A_3 D_3 A_1 D_1 A_4 D_4 A_0 D_0 A_1 D_1 A_1 D_1 A_4 D_4 A_0 D_0 A_1 D_1 A_0 D_0 (A_1 D_1)^4$ on tape 5; the next writes $A_4 D_4 A_4 D_4 A_1 D_1 A_4 D_4 A_0 D_0 A_1 D_1 A_1 D_1 A_7$ on tape 1; the next, $D_{13} A_4 D_4 A_0 D_0 A_{10}$ on tape 4. The final phases are

$A_4 D_4 A_4$	—	$D_{19} A_3 D_3 A_{12}$	$D_{13} A_4 D_4 A_4$	$D_0 A_3$
A_4	$D_{23} A_{11}$	$D_{19} A_3$	$D_{13} A_4$	—
—	D_{23}	D_{19}	D_{13}	D_{22}
A_{77}	—	—	—	—

8. No, since at most S stop/starts are saved, and since the speed of the input tape (not the output tapes) tends to govern the initial distribution time anyway. The other advantages of the distribution schemes used in Chart A outweigh this minuscule disadvantage.

9. $P = 5$, $B = 8300$, $B' = 734$, $S = \lceil (3 + 1/P)N/(6P') \rceil + 1 = 74$, $\omega \approx 1.094$, $\alpha \approx 0.795$, $\beta \approx -1.136$, $\alpha' = \beta' = 0$; Eq. (9) ≈ 855 seconds, to which we add the time for initial rewind, for a total of 958 seconds. The savings of about one minute in the merging time does not compensate for the loss of time due to the initial rewinding and tape changing (unless perhaps we are in a multiprogramming environment).

10. The rewinds during standard polyphase merge involve about 54 percent of the file (the "pass/phase" column in Table 5.4.2–1), and the longest rewinds during standard cascade merge involve approximately $a_k a_{n-k}/a_n \approx (4/(2T-1))\cos^2(\pi/(4T-2)) < \frac{4}{11}$ of the file, by exercise 5.4.3–5 and Eq. 5.4.3–(13).

11. Only initial and final rewinds get to make use of the high-speed feature, since the reel is only a little more than 10/23 full when it contains the whole example file. Using $\pi = \lceil .946 \ln S - 1.204 \rceil$, $\pi' = 1/8$ in example 8, we get the following estimated totals for examples 1–9, respectively:

$$1115, \ 1296, \ 1241, \ 1008, \ 1014, \ 967, \ 891, \ 969, \ 856.$$

12. (a) An obvious solution with $4P+4$ buffers simply reads and writes simultaneously from paired tapes. But note that three output buffers are sufficient: At a given moment we can be performing the second half of a write from one, the first half of a write from another, and outputting into a third. This approach suggests a corresponding improvement in the input buffer situation. It turns out that $3P$ input buffers and 3 output buffers are necessary and sufficient, using a slightly weakened forecasting technique. A simpler and superior approach, suggested by J. Sue, adds a "lookahead key" to each block, specifying the final key of the subsequent block. Sue's method requires $2P+1$ input buffers and 4 output buffers, and it is a straightforward modification of Algorithm F. (See also Section 5.4.9.)

(b) In this case the high value of α means that we must do between five and six passes over the data, which wipes out the advantage of double-quick merging. The idea works out much better on eight or nine tapes.

13. No; consider, for example, the situation just before $A_{16}A_{16}A_{16}A_{16}$. But two reelfuls *can* be handled.

14. $\det \begin{pmatrix} 0 & -p_0 z & 0 & z-1 \\ 0 & 1 - p_1 z & -p_0 z & z-1 \\ 1 & 0 & 0 & 0 \\ 0 & 0 & 0 & 1 \end{pmatrix} \Big/ \det \begin{pmatrix} 1 - p_{\geq 1} z & -p_0 z & 0 & z-1 \\ -p_{\geq 2} z & 1 - p_1 z & -p_0 z & z-1 \\ 0 & -1 & 1 & 0 \\ 0 & 0 & 0 & 1 \end{pmatrix}.$

15. The A matrix has the form

$$A = \begin{pmatrix} B_{10} z & B_{11} z & \cdots & B_{1n} z & 1-z \\ \vdots & & & & \vdots \\ B_{n0} z & B_{n1} z & \cdots & B_{nn} z & 1-z \\ 0 & \cdots & 0 & 1 & 0 \\ 0 & \cdots & 0 & 0 & 0 \end{pmatrix},$$

$$\begin{aligned} B_{10} + B_{11} + \cdots + B_{1n} &= 1, \\ &\vdots \\ B_{n0} + B_{n1} + \cdots + B_{nn} &= 1. \end{aligned} \tag{11}$$

Therefore

$$\det(I - A) = \det \begin{pmatrix} 1 - B_{10} z & -B_{11} z & \cdots & -B_{1(n-1)} z & -B_{1n} z \\ \vdots & & & & \vdots \\ -B_{n0} z & -B_{n1} z & \cdots & 1 - B_{n(n-1)} z & -B_{nn} z \\ 0 & 0 & \cdots & -1 & 1 \end{pmatrix}$$

and we can add all columns to the first column, then factor out $(1 - z)$. Consequently $g_Q(z)$ has the form $h_Q(z)/(1 - z)$, and $\alpha^{(Q)} = h_Q(1)$ because we have $h_Q(1) \neq 0$ and $\det(I - A) \neq 0$ for $|z| < 1$.

SECTION 5.4.7

1. Sort from least significant digit to most significant digit in the number system whose radices are alternately P and $T - P$. (If pairs of digits are grouped, we have essentially the pure radix $P \cdot (T - P)$. Thus, if $P = 2$ and $T = 7$, the number system is "biquinary," related to decimal notation in a simple way.)

2. If K is a key between 0 and $F_n - 1$, let the Fibonacci representation of $F_n - 1 - K$ be $a_{n-2}F_{n-1} + \cdots + a_1 F_2$, where the a_j are 0 or 1, and no two consecutive 1s appear. After phase j, tape $(j + 1) \bmod 3$ contains the keys with $a_j = 0$, and tape $(j - 1) \bmod 3$ contains those with $a_j = 1$, in decreasing order of $a_{j-1} \ldots a_1$.

[Imagine a card sorter with two pockets, "0" and "1", and consider the procedure of sorting F_n cards that have been punched with the keys $a_{n-2} \ldots a_1$ in $n - 2$ columns. The conventional procedure for sorting these into decreasing order, starting at the least significant digit, can be simplified since we know that everything in the "1" pocket at the end of one pass will go into the "0" pocket on the following pass.]

4. If there were an external node on level 2 we could not construct such a good tree. Otherwise there are at most three external nodes on level 3, and six on level 4, since each external node is supposed to appear on the same tape.

5.

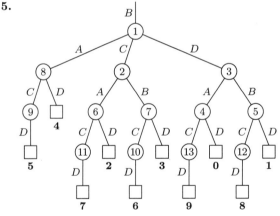

6. 09, 08, ..., 00, 19, ..., 10, 29, ..., 20, 39, ..., 30, 40, 41, ..., 49, 59, ..., 50, 60, 61, ..., 99.

7. Yes; first distribute the records into smaller and smaller subfiles until obtaining one-reel files that can be sorted individually. This is dual to the process of sorting one-reel files and then merging them into larger and larger multireel files.

SECTION 5.4.8

1. Yes. If we alternately use ascending and descending order in the selection tree, we have in effect an order-P cocktail-shaker sort. (See exercise 9.)

2. Let $Z_N = Y_N - X_N$, and solve the recurrence for Z_N by noting that

$$(N + 1)N Z_{N+1} = N(N - 1)Z_N + N^2 + N;$$

hence

$$Z_N = \tfrac{1}{3}(N+1) + \binom{M+2}{3} \Big/ N(N-1), \qquad \text{for } N > M.$$

Now eliminate Y_N and obtain

$$\frac{X_N}{N+1} = \frac{20}{3}(H_{N+1} - H_{M+2}) + 2\left(\frac{1}{N+1} - \frac{1}{M+2}\right)$$

$$- \frac{2}{3}\binom{M+2}{3}\left(\frac{1}{(N+1)N(N-1)} - \frac{1}{(M+2)(M+1)M}\right) + \frac{3M+4}{M+2}, \quad N > M.$$

3. Yes; find a median element in $O(N)$ steps, using a construction like that of Theorem 5.3.3L, and use it to partition the file. Another interesting approach, due to R. W. Floyd and A. J. Smith, is to merge two runs of N items in $O(N)$ units of time as follows: Spread the items out on the tapes, with spaces between them, then successively fill each space with a number specifying the final position of the item just preceding that space.

4. It is possible to piece together a schedule for floors $\{1, \dots, p+1\}$ with a schedule for floors $\{q, \dots, n\}$: When the former schedule first reaches floor $p+1$, go up to floor q and carry out the latter schedule (using the current elevator contents as if they were the "extras" in the algorithm of Theorem K). After finishing that schedule, go back to floor $p+1$ and resume the previous schedule.

5. Consider $b = 2$, $m = 4$ and the following behavior of the algorithm:

```
Floor 7: — 47  ─────────────●─77────────────────
                          5667 4566
Floor 6: — 23  ──────────✓─23────●66─────────
                          5667      2345
Floor 5: — 14  ──────────●─14──────↘45──────▶
                          5667        1234 2345
Floor 4: — 71  ──────────●─15─────────↘11─────
                          5566
Floor 3: — 63  ──────────✓─23──────────────────
                          2556
Floor 2: — 62  ──────────●─00───────────────
                          0055
Floor 1: — 55  ──────────✓─00───────────────
                          0000
                          /
```

Now 2 (in the elevator) is less than 3 (on floor 3).

[After constructing an example such as this, the reader should be able to see how to demonstrate the weaker property required in the proof of Theorem K.]

6. Let i and j be minimal with $b_i < b_i'$ and $b_j > b_j'$. Introduce a new person who wants to go from i to j. This doesn't increase $\max(u_k, d_{k+1}, 1)$ or $\max(b_k, b_k')$ for any k. Continue this until $b_j = b_j'$ for all j. Now observe that the algorithm in the text works also with b replaced by b_k in steps K1 and K3.

8. Let the number be P_n, and let Q_n be the number of permutations such that $u_k = 1$ for $1 \le k < n$. Then $P_n = Q_1 P_{n-1} + Q_2 P_{n-2} + \cdots + Q_n P_0$, $P_0 = 1$. It can be shown that $Q_n = 3^{n-2}$ for $n \ge 2$ (see below), hence a generating function argument yields

$$\sum P_n z^n = (1 - 3z)/(1 - 4z + 2z^2) = 1 + z + 2z^2 + 6z^3 + 20z^4 + 68z^5 + \cdots;$$

$$2P_n = (2 + \sqrt{2})^{n-1} + (2 - \sqrt{2})^{n-1}.$$

To prove that $Q_n = 3^{n-2}$, consider a ternary sequence $x_1 x_2 \ldots x_n$ such that $x_1 = 2$, $x_n = 0$, and $0 \le x_k \le 2$ for $1 < k < n$. The following rule defines a one-to-one correspondence between such sequences and the desired permutations $a_1 a_2 \ldots a_n$:

$$a_k = \begin{cases} \max\{j \mid (j < k \text{ and } x_j = 0) \text{ or } j = 1\}, & \text{if } x_k = 0; \\ k, & \text{if } x_k = 1; \\ \min\{j \mid (j > k \text{ and } x_j = 2) \text{ or } j = n\}, & \text{if } x_k = 2. \end{cases}$$

(This correspondence was obtained by the author jointly with E. A. Bender.)

9. The number of passes of the cocktail-shaker sort is $2\max(u_1, \ldots, u_n) - (0 \text{ or } 1)$, since each pair of passes (left-right-left) reduces each of the nonzero u's by 1.

10. Begin with a distribution method (quicksort or radix exchange) until one-reel files are obtained. And be patient.

SECTION 5.4.9

1. $\frac{1}{4} - \left(x \bmod \frac{1}{2}\right)^2$ revolutions.

2. The probability that $k = a_{iq}$ and $k + 1 = a_{i'r}$ for fixed k, q, r, and $i \ne i'$ is $f(q, r, k) L! L! (PL - 2L)! / (PL)!$, where

$$f(q, r, k) = \binom{k-1}{q-1}\binom{k-q}{r-1}\binom{PL-k-1}{L-q}\binom{PL-k-1-L+q}{L-r}$$
$$= \binom{k-1}{q+r-2}\binom{q+r-2}{q-1}\binom{PL-k-1}{2L-q-r}\binom{2L-q-r}{L-q};$$

and

$$\sum_{\substack{1 \le k < PL \\ 1 \le q, r \le L}} |q-r| f(q, r, k) = \sum_{1 \le q, r \le L} |q-r| \binom{PL-1}{2L-1}\binom{q+r-2}{q-1}\binom{2L-q-r}{L-q} = \binom{PL-1}{2L-1} A_{2L-1}.$$

The probability that $k = a_{iq}$ and $k + 1 = q_{i(q+1)}$ for fixed k, q, and i is

$$g(k, q) \bigg/ \binom{PL}{L}, \quad \text{where} \quad g(k, q) = \binom{k-1}{q-1}\binom{PL-k-1}{L-q-1};$$

and

$$\sum_{\substack{1 \le k < PL \\ 1 \le q < L}} g(k, q) = \sum_{1 \le q < L} \binom{PL-1}{L-1} = (L-1)\binom{PL-1}{L-1}.$$

[*SICOMP* **1** (1972), 161–166.]

3. Take the minimum in (5) over the range $2 \le m \le \min(9, n)$.

4. (a) $\left(0.000725(\sqrt{P} + 1)^2 + 0.014\right)L$. (b) Change "$amn + \beta n$" in formula (5) to "$(0.000725(\sqrt{m} + 1)^2 + 0.014)n$." [Computer experiments show that the optimal trees defined by this new recurrence are very similar to those defined by Theorem K with $\alpha = 0.00145$, $\beta = 0.01545$; in fact, trees exist that are optimal for both recurrences, when $30 \le n \le 100$. The change suggested in this exercise saves about 10 percent of the merging time, when $n = 64$ or 100 as in the text's example. This style of buffer allocation was considered already in 1954 by H. Seward, who found that four-way merging minimizes the seek time.]

5. Let $A_m(n)$ and $B_m(n)$ be the cost of optimum sets of m trees whose n leaves are all at (even, odd) levels, respectively. Then $A_1(1) = 0$, $B_1(1) = \alpha + \beta$; $A_m(n)$ and $B_m(n)$ are defined as in (4) when $m \geq 2$; $A_1(n) = \min_{1 \leq m \leq n}(\alpha mn + \beta n + B_m(n))$, $B_1(n) = \min_{1 \leq m \leq n}(\alpha mn + \beta n + A_m(n))$. The latter equations are well-defined in spite of the fact that $A_1(n)$ and $B_1(n)$ are defined in terms of each other!

6.

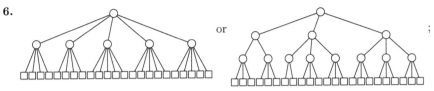

$A_1(23) = B_1(23) = 268$. [Curiously, $n = 23$ is the only value ≤ 50 for which no equal-parity tree with n leaves is optimal in the unrestricted-parity case. Perhaps it is the *only* such value, when $\alpha = \beta$.]

7. Consider the quantities $\alpha d_1 + \beta e_1$, ..., $\alpha d_n + \beta e_n$ in any tree, where d_j is the degree sum and e_j is the path length for the jth leaf. An optimum tree for weights $w_1 \leq \cdots \leq w_n$ will have $\alpha d_1 + \beta e_1 \geq \cdots \geq \alpha d_n + \beta e_n$. It is always possible to reorder the indices so that $\alpha d_1 + \beta e_1 = \cdots = \alpha d_k + \beta e_k$ where the first k leaves are merged together.

9. Let d minimize $(\alpha m + \beta)/\ln m$. A simple induction using convexity shows that $A_1(n) \geq (\alpha d + \beta)n \log_d n$, with equality when $n = d^t$. A suitable upper bound comes from complete d-ary trees, since these have $D(\tau) = dE(\tau)$, $E(\tau) = tn + dr$ for $n = d^t + (d-1)r$, $0 \leq r \leq d^t$.

10. See *STOC* **6** (1974), 216–229.

11. Using exercise 1.2.4–38, $f_m(n) = 3qn + 2(n - 3^q m)$, when $2 \cdot 3^{q-1} \leq n/m \leq 3^q$; $f_m(n) = 3qn + 4(n - 3^q m)$, when $3^q \leq n/m \leq 2 \cdot 3^q$. Thus $f_2(n) + 2n \geq f(n)$, with equality if and only if $4 \cdot 3^{q-1} \leq n \leq 2 \cdot 3^q$; $f_3(n) + 3n = f(n)$; $f_4(n) + 4n \geq f(n)$, with equality if and only if $n = 4 \cdot 3^q$; and $f_m(n) + mn > f(n)$ for all $m \geq 5$.

12. Use the specifications $-$, 1:1, 1:1:1, 1:1:1:1 or 2:2, 2:3, 2:2:2, ..., $\lfloor n/3 \rfloor : \lfloor (n+1)/3 \rfloor$: $\lfloor (n+2)/3 \rfloor$, ...; this gives trees with all leaves at level $q + 2$, for $4 \cdot 3^q \leq n \leq 4 \cdot 3^{q+1}$. (When $n = 4 \cdot 3^q$, two such trees are formed.)

14. The following tree specifications were found for $n = 1, 2, 3, \ldots$ by exhaustively examining all partitions of n: $-$, 1:1, 1:1:1, 1:1:1:1, 1:1:1:1:1, 1:1:1:1:1:1, 1:1:1:1:3, 1:1:3:3, 3:3:3, 1:3:3:3, 3:4:4, 3:3:3:3, 3:3:3:4, 3:3:4:4, 3:4:4:4, 4:4:4:4, ..., 5:6:6:6:12, 6:6:6:6:12, 6:6:6:6:13, ... (The degrees seem to be always ≤ 6, but such a result appears to be quite difficult to prove.)

15. If a people initially got on the elevator, the togetherness rating increases by at most $a + b$ at the first stop. When it next stops at the initial floor, the rating increases by at most $b + m - a$. Hence the rating increases at most $kb + (k - 1)m$ after k stops.

16. Eleven stops: 123456 to floor 2, 334466 to 3, 444666 to 4, 256666 to 5, 466666 to 6, 123445 to 4, 112335 to 5, 222333 to 3, 122225 to 2, 111555 to 5, 111111 to 1. [This is minimal, for a 10-stop solution with any elevator capacity can, by symmetry, be arranged to stop on floors 2, 3, 4, 5, 6, p_2, p_3, p_4, p_5, 1 in that order, where $p_2 p_3 p_4 p_5$ is a permutation of $\{2, 3, 4, 5\}$; such schedules are possible only when $b \geq 8$. See Martin Gardner, *Knotted Doughnuts* (New York: Freeman, 1986), Chapter 10.]

17. There are at least $(bn)!/b!^n$ configurations; and the number that can be obtained from a given one after s stops is at most $\left((n-1)\binom{b+m}{b}\right)^{s-1}$, which is less than $\left(n((b+m)e/b)^b\right)^s$ by exercise 1.2.6–67. Hence some configuration requires

$$s\left(\ln n + b\left(1 + \ln(1 + m/b)\right)\right) > \ln(bn)! - n\ln b! > bn\ln bn - bn - n\left((b+1)\ln b - b + 1\right)$$

by exercise 1.2.5–24.

Notes: Using the fact that $1/(x+y) \geq \frac{1}{2}\min(1/x, 1/y)$ when x and y are positive, we can express this lower bound in the convenient form

$$\Omega\left(\min\left(nb, \frac{n\log(1+n)}{\log(1+m/b)}\right)\right).$$

Related results have been obtained by A. Aggarwal and J. S. Vitter, *CACM* **31** (1988), 1116–1127, who also established the matching upper bound

$$O\left(\min\left(nb, \frac{n\log(1+n)}{\log(1+m/b)}\right)\right).$$

See also M. H. Nodine and J. S. Vitter, *ACM Symposium on Parallel Algorithms and Architectures* **5** (1993), 120–129, for extensions to several disks.

18. The expected number of stops is $\sum_{s\geq 1} p_s$, where p_s is the probability that at least s stops are needed. Let $q_s = 1 - p_{s+1}$ be the probability that at most s stops are needed. Then exercise 17 shows that $q_s \leq f(s - 1 + [s=0])$, where $f(s) = b!^n\alpha^s/(bn)!$ and $\alpha = n((b+m)e/b)^b$. If $f(t-1) < 1 \leq f(t)$ then $\sum_{s\geq 1} p_s \geq p_1 + \cdots + p_t = t - (q_0 + \cdots + q_{t-1}) \geq t - (f(0) + f(0) + \cdots + f(t-2)) \geq t - (\alpha^{1-t} + \alpha^{1-t} + \cdots + \alpha^{-1}) \geq t - 1 \geq L - 1$.

19. Consider doing step (vii) backwards, distributing the records into bin 1, then bin 2. This operation is precisely what step (iv) is simulating on the key file. [*Princeton Conference on Information Sciences and Systems* **6** (1972), 140–144.]

20. The internal sort must be carefully chosen, with paging in mind; methods such as shellsort, address calculation, heapsort, and list sorting can be disastrous if the actual internal memory is small, since they require a large "working set" of pages. Quicksort, radix exchange, and sequentially allocated merge or radix sorting are much better suited to a paging environment.

Some things the designer of an external sort can do that are virtually impossible to include in an automatically paged method are: (i) Forecasting the input file that should be read next, so that the data is available when it is required; (ii) choosing the buffer sizes and the order of merge according to hardware and data characteristics.

On the other hand a virtual machine is considerably easier to program, and it can give results that aren't bad, if the programmer is careful and knows the properties of the underlying actual machine. The first substantial study of this question was made by Brawn, Gustavson, and Mankin [*CACM* **13** (1970), 483–494.]

21. $\lceil(L-j)/D\rceil$; see *CMath*, Eq. (3.24).

22. After reading a group of D blocks that contains a_j, we might need to know α_{j+D-1} before reading the next group of D blocks. And if we store α_{j+D-1} with a_j, we also need the values $\alpha_0, \ldots, \alpha_{D-2}$ in some sort of file header to get the process started.

But with this scheme we cannot write blocks $a_0 \ldots a_{D-1}$ until we have computed $a_D \ldots a_{2D-2}$, so we will need $3D - 1$ output buffers instead of $2D$ to keep writing continuously. It is therefore better to put the α's in a separate (short) file. [The same analysis applies to randomized striping.]

23. (a) Algorithm 5.4.6F needs 4 input buffers, each of superblock size DB. (If we count output buffers as well, we have a total of $6DB$ buffer records in memory with Algorithm 5.4.6F and $5DB$ with SyncSort.)

(b) While we are reading a group of D blocks we need buffer space for the previous D blocks and one unfinished block, for a total of $(2D+1)B$ records. (Output requires another $2DB$. But many data processing operations that do 2-way merging on input actually produce comparatively little output.)

24. Let the lth block in chronological order be block j_l of run k_l; in particular, $j_l = 0$ and $k_l = l$ for $1 \leq l \leq P$. We will read that block at time $t_l = \sum_{k=1}^{P} t_{lkd}$, where

$$t_{lkd} = |\{r \mid 1 \leq r \leq l \text{ and } k_r = k \text{ and } (x_k + j_r) \bmod D = d\}|$$

is the number of blocks of run k on disk d that are chronologically $\leq l$, and $d = (x_{k_l} + j_l) \bmod D$. Let $u_{lk} = |\{r \mid 1 \leq r \leq l \text{ and } k_r = k\}|$; then

$$t_{lkd} = \left\lceil \frac{u_{lk} - (d - x_k) \bmod D}{D} \right\rceil,$$

because j_r runs through the values $0, 1, \ldots, u_{lk} - 1$ when $1 \leq r \leq l$ and $k_r = k$. The sequence t_l for the example of (19), (20), and (21) is

$$11111\ 22223\ 43456\ 34567\ 82345\ 67893\ \ldots.$$

If $l > P$, the number of buffer blocks we need as we begin to merge from the lth block in chronological order is $I_l + D + P$, where I_l is the number of "inversions-with-equality" of t_l, namely $|\{r \mid r > l \text{ and } t_r \leq t_l\}|$, the number of bufferfuls that we've read but aren't ready to use; D represents the buffers into which the next input is going, and P represents the partially full buffers from which we are currently merging. (With special care, using links as in SyncSort, we could reduce the latter requirement from P to $P - 1$, but the extra complication is probably not worthwhile.)

So the problem boils down to getting an upper bound on I_l. We may assume that the input runs are infinitely long. Suppose s of the elements $\{t_1, \ldots, t_l\}$ are greater than t_l; then t_l has $t_l D - l + s$ inversions-with-equality, because exactly $t_l D$ elements are $\leq t_l$. It follows that the maximum I_l occurs when $s = 0$ and t_l is a left-to-right maximum. We have $\sum_{k=1}^{P} u_{lk} = l$; hence by the formulas for t_l above,

$$I_l \leq \max_{l>P}(t_l D - l) \leq \sum_{k=1}^{P}(u_{lk} - (d - x_k) \bmod D + D - 1 - u_{lk})$$

$$= P(D-1) - \sum_{k=1}^{P}(d - x_k) \bmod D$$

$$\leq P(D-1) - \min_{0 \leq d < D}\sum_{k=1}^{P}(d - x_k) \bmod D,$$

and there exist chronological orders for which this upper bound is attained.

Suppose r_t of the x_k are equal to t. We want to choose the x_k so that $\min_{0 \leq d < D} s_d$ is maximized, where $s_d = \sum_{k=1}^{P}(d - x_k) \bmod D = \sum_{t=0}^{D-1}((d-t) \bmod D)r_t$. We can assume that the minimum occurs at $d = 0$. Then $s_1 = s_0 + P - r_1 D$, $s_2 = s_1 + P - r_2 D$, $\ldots$, hence we have $r_1 \leq \lfloor P/D \rfloor$, $r_1 + r_2 \leq \lfloor 2P/D \rfloor$, $\ldots$; it follows that the minimum is

$$s_0 = (D-1)r_1 + (D-2)r_2 + \cdots + r_{D-1} \leq \sum_{k=1}^{D-1}\lfloor kP/D \rfloor = \frac{1}{2}((P-1)(D-1) + \gcd(P,D) - 1),$$

by exercise 1.2.4–37. This bound is achieved when $x_j = \lceil jD/P \rceil - 1$ for $1 \le j \le P$.

With such x_j we can handle every chronological sequence at full speed if we have $I_{\max} + D + P = \frac{1}{2}PD + \frac{3}{2}D + \frac{1}{2}P + \frac{1}{2}\gcd(P,D) - 1$ input buffers containing B records each. (This is pretty good when $D = 2$ or 3.)

25. Notice that at Time 4, we go back to reading f_1 on disk 0:

	Active reading	Active merging	Scratch	Waiting for
Time 1	$e_0 b_0 g_0 a_0 c_0$	$-\,-\,-\,-\,-\,-\,-\,-$	$(-\,-\,-\,-\,-\,-\,-)$	a_0
Time 2	$f_1 d_0 d_1 d_2 f_0$	$a_0\,-\,-\,-\,-\,-\,-$	$b_0\,c_0\,(e_0\,g_0\,-\,-\,-)$	d_0
Time 3	$a_2 h_0 e_2 g_1 d_3$	$a_0 b_0\,c_0\,d_0\,-\,-\,-$	$e_0\,f_0 g_0\,(d_1 d_2 f_1 -)$	h_0
Time 4	$f_1 e_1 b_1 g_1 a_1$	$a_0 b_0\,c_0\,d_0 e_0\,f_0 g_0 h_0$	$d_1\,(d_2 e_2 d_3 f_1 g_1 a_2)$	e_1
Time 5	$a_2 f_2 h_1 e_3 g_2$	$a_0 b_0\,c_0\,d_1 e_1\,f_0 g_0 h_0$	$d_2 e_2 d_3 a_1 f_1 b_1 g_1 ()$	a_2
Time 6	$d_4 a_3 f_3 b_2 e_4$	$a_2 b_1\,c_0\,d_3 e_2 f_1 g_1 h_0$	$f_2 e_3 (h_1 g_2\,-\,-\,-)$	d_4
Time 7	$c_1 a_3 f_3\,?\,e_4$	$a_2 b_1\,c_0\,d_4 e_3\,f_2 g_1 h_0$	$(h_1 b_2 g_2 a_3 f_3 e_4 -)$	c_1
Time 8	$?\,d_5 d_6\,?\,?$	$a_2 b_1\,c_1\,d_4 e_3\,f_2 g_1 h_0$	$h_1 b_2 g_2 a_3 f_3 e_4\,(\,?\,)$	d_5

26. While D blocks are being read and D are being written, the merging procedure might generate up to $P + Q - 1$ blocks of output, under the assumptions of (24). (Not $P + Q$, since only one merge buffer becomes totally empty.) Reading is as fast as writing, so $D + P + Q - 1$ output buffers are necessary and sufficient to prevent output hangup.

However, at most D blocks are output for every D blocks of input, on the average, so about $3D$ output buffers should be adequate in practice.

27. (a) $E_n(m_1, \ldots, m_p) = \sum_{t=1}^{m} q_t$, where q_t is the probability that some urn contains at least t balls. Clearly $q_t \le 1$ and

$$q_t \le \sum_{k=0}^{n-1} \Pr(\text{urn } k \text{ contains at least } t \text{ balls}) = n \Pr(S_n(m_1, \ldots, m_p) \ge t).$$

(b) The probability generating function of $S_n(m_1, \ldots, m_p)$ is

$$p(z) = \prod_{k=1}^{p} z^{q_k}(1 + (z-1)r_k/n),$$

where $q_k = \lfloor m_k/n \rfloor$ and $r_k = m_k \bmod n$. Now $1 + \alpha \le (1 + \alpha/n)^n$ and $1 + \alpha r/n \le (1 + \alpha/n)^r$ when $\alpha \ge 0$; hence we have $\Pr(S_n(m_1, \ldots, m_p) \ge t) \le (1+\alpha)^{-t}p(1+\alpha) \le (1+\alpha)^{-t}\prod_{k=1}^{p}(1+\alpha/n)^{m_k} = (1+\alpha)^{-t}(1+\alpha/n)^m$.

If $t \le m/n$, we use the "1" term in the stated minimum. If $t > m/n$, the quantity $(1+\alpha)^{-t}(1+\alpha/n)^m$ takes its minimum value $(n-1)^{m-t}m^m/(n^m t^t(m-t)^{m-t})$ when $\alpha = (nt - m)/(m - t)$.

28. Numerical evidence seems to support this natural conjecture. For example, we have

$E_{10}(1,1,1,1,1,1,1,1) = 2.3993180,$	$E_{10}(2,2,2,2) = 2.178,$	$E_{10}(4,3,1) = 2.00,$
$E_{10}(2,1,1,1,1,1,1) = 2.364540,$	$E_{10}(3,2,2,1) = 2.166,$	$E_{10}(5,2,1) = 1.98,$
$E_{10}(2,2,1,1,1,1) = 2.32076,$	$E_{10}(3,3,1,1) = 2.152,$	$E_{10}(6,1,1) = 1.94,$
$E_{10}(3,1,1,1,1,1) = 2.29958,$	$E_{10}(4,2,1,1) = 2.138,$	$E_{10}(4,4) = 1.7,$
$E_{10}(2,2,2,1,1) = 2.2628,$	$E_{10}(5,1,1,1) = 2.090,$	$E_{10}(5,3) = 1.7,$
$E_{10}(3,2,1,1,1) = 2.2460,$	$E_{10}(3,3,2) = 2.02,$	$E_{10}(6,2) = 1.7,$
$E_{10}(4,1,1,1,1) = 2.2076,$	$E_{10}(4,2,2) = 2.01,$	$E_{10}(7,1) = 1.7.$

29. (a) At time t, all disks are reading blocks that occur no earlier than the block marked at time t. The next Q blocks are never removed from the scratch buffers once they have been read. Thus the relevant blocks on disk j all are read by time $\leq t + N_j$; they must all participate in the merge by time $t + \max(N_0, \ldots, N_{D-1})$.

(b) If the $(Q+1)$st block after a marked block is not removed, the same argument applies. Otherwise the previous Q are not marked, and the $Q+2$ blocks cannot all be on different disks.

(c) Divide the chronological order of blocks into groups of size $Q+2$, and consider any particular group. If there are M_k blocks from run k, then the numbers N_j are equivalent to the number of balls in the jth urn, in a cyclic occupancy problem with $n = D$ and $m = Q + 2$. Thus the expected number of marked cells in any group is at most the upper bound in exercise 27(b). Calling that upper bound $e_n(m)$, we may take $r(d, m) = (d/m)e_d(m)$.

[Actually this function $r(2, m)$ is not monotonic in m when m is small. Therefore the entries listed for $r(2, 4)$ and $r(2, 12)$ in Table 2 are actually the values of $r(2, 3)$ and $r(2, 11)$; additional buffers cannot increase the number of marked blocks.]

30. Let $l = \lceil (s + \sqrt{2s}) \ln d \rceil$, $\alpha = \sqrt{2/s}$. Then

$$e_d(sd \ln d) < l + \sum_{t>l} d(1 + \alpha/d)^{sd \ln d}/(1 + \alpha)^t$$

$$= l + d(1 + \alpha/d)^{sd \ln d}/\alpha(1 + \alpha)^l$$

$$\leq l + \alpha^{-1} \exp((\ln d)(1 + s\alpha - (s + \sqrt{2s}) \ln(1 + \alpha))),$$

and $(s + \sqrt{2s}) \ln(1 + \alpha) > s\alpha + 1 - \alpha/3$. Therefore

$$1 \leq r(d, sd \ln d) = \frac{e_d(sd \ln d)}{s \ln d} < 1 + \sqrt{\frac{2}{s}} + \frac{1}{\sqrt{2s} \ln d}\left(1 + \sqrt{\frac{2}{9s}} \ln d + O(s^{-1}(\log d)^2)\right),$$

if $s/(\log d)^2 \to \infty$. Convergence to this asymptotic behavior is rather slow (see Table 2).

31. (When $Q = 0$, we mark the first block and then repeatedly mark the next block that shares a disk with one of the blocks in the group starting with the previously marked block. For example, if the chronological order of disk accesses is 112020121210122, the marking would be $\bar{1}\bar{1}2020\bar{1}21\bar{2}10\bar{1}2\bar{2}$. Therefore as $P \to \infty$, we read an average of $Q(D)n$ blocks during n units of time, where Q is Ramanujan's function, defined in Eq. 1.2.11.3–(2). By contrast, $r(d, 2) = (d + 1)/2$ gives a much more pessimistic estimate.)

SECTION 5.5

1. It is difficult to decide which sorting algorithm is best in a given situation. ▌

2. For small N, list insertion; for medium N, say $N = 64$, list merge; for large N, radix list sort.

3. (Solution by V. Pratt.) Given two nondecreasing runs α and β to be merged, determine in a straightforward way the subruns $\alpha_1\alpha_2\alpha_3\beta_1\beta_2\beta_3$ such that α_2 and β_2 contain precisely the keys of α and β having the median value of the entire file. By successive "reversals," first forming $\alpha_1\alpha_2\beta_1^R\alpha_3^R\beta_2\beta_3$, then $\alpha_1\beta_1\alpha_2^R\beta_2^R\alpha_3\beta_3$, then $\alpha_1\beta_1\alpha_2\beta_2\alpha_3\beta_3$, we can reduce the problem to the merging of subfiles $\alpha_1\beta_1$ and $\alpha_3\beta_3$ that are of length $\leq N/2$.

A considerably more complicated algorithm due to L. Trabb Pardo provides the best possible asymptotic answer to this problem: We can do stable merging in $O(N)$ time and stable sorting in $O(N \log N)$ time, using only $O(\log N)$ bits of auxiliary memory for a fixed number of index variables, without transforming the records being sorted in any way [*SICOMP* **6** (1977), 351–372]. The same time and space bounds have been achieved with much smaller constant factors by B.-C. Huang and M. A. Langston, *Comp. J.* **35** (1992), 643–650. See also A. Symvonis, *Comp. J.* **38** (1995), 681–690, for stable merging of M items with N when M is much smaller than N.

4. Only straight insertion, list insertion, and list merge. The variants of quicksort could be made parsimonious, but only at the expense of extra work in the inner loops (see exercise 5.2.2–24).

Parsimonious methods are especially useful when the result of a comparison is not 100% reliable; see D. E. Knuth, *Lecture Notes in Comp. Sci.* **606** (1992), 61–67.

SECTION 6.1

1. $\sqrt{(N^2 - 1)/12}$; see Eq. 1.2.10–(22).

2. **S1′.** [Initialize.] Set P ← FIRST.

 S2′. [Compare.] If $K = $ KEY(P), the algorithm terminates successfully.

 S3′. [Advance.] Set P ← LINK(P).

 S4′. [End of file?] If P ≠ Λ, go back to S2′. Otherwise the algorithm terminates unsuccessfully. ∎

3.

```
   KEY       EQU   3:5
   LINK      EQU   1:2
   START     LDA   K                1
             LD1   FIRST            1
   2H        CMPA  0,1(KEY)         C
             JE    SUCCESS          C
             LD1   0,1(LINK)        C - S
             J1NZ  2B               C - S
   FAILURE   EQU   *                1 - S  ∎
```

The running time is $(6C - 3S + 4)u$.

4. Yes, if we have a way to set "KEY(Λ)" equal to K. [But the technique of loop duplication used in Program Q′ has no effect in this case.]

5. No; Program Q always does at least as many operations as Program Q′.

6. Replace line 08 by JE *+4; CMPA KEY+N+2,1; JNE 3B; INC1 1; and change lines 03–04 to ENT1 -2-N; 3H INC1 3.

7. Note that $\bar{C}_N = \frac{1}{2}\bar{C}_{N-1} + 1$.

8. Euler's summation formula gives

$$H_n^{(x)} = \zeta(x) + \frac{n^{1-x}}{(1-x)} + \frac{1}{2}n^{-x} - \frac{B_2 x}{2!}n^{-1-x} + \frac{B_3 x(x+1)}{3!}n^{-2-x} - O(n^{-3-x}).$$

[Complex variable theory tells us that

$$\zeta(x) = 2^x \pi^{x-1} \sin(\tfrac{1}{2}\pi x)\Gamma(1-x)\zeta(1-x),$$

a formula that is particularly useful when $x < 0$.]

9. (a) Yes: $\bar{C}_N = N - N^{-\theta}H_{N-1}^{(-\theta)} = N + 1 - N^{-\theta}H_N^{(-\theta)} = \frac{\theta}{1+\theta}N + \frac{1}{2} + O(N^{-\theta})$.

(b) $\bar{C}_N = \frac{\theta}{1+\theta}\left(1 + N/\left(1 - \binom{N-\theta}{N}\right)\right) = \frac{\theta}{1+\theta}(N + N^{1-\theta}/\Gamma(1-\theta) + 1) + O(N^{1-2\theta})$.

(c) When $\theta < 0$, (11) is not a probability distribution; (16) gives the estimate $\bar{C}_N = -\frac{\theta}{1+\theta}\Gamma(1-\theta)N^{1+\theta} + O(N^{1+2\theta}) + O(1)$ instead of (15).

10. $p_1 \leq \cdots \leq p_N$; (maximum $\bar{C}_N$) = $(N+1)$ − (minimum $\bar{C}_N$). [Similarly in the unequal-length case, the maximum average search time is $L_1(1+p_1) + \cdots + L_N(1+p_N)$ minus the minimum average search time.]

11. (a) The terms of $f_{m-1}(x_{i_1}, \ldots, x_{i_{m-1}})p_i$ are just the probabilities of the possible sequences of requests that could have preceded, leaving R_i in position m. (b) The second identity comes from summing $\binom{n}{m}$ cases of the first, on the different m-subsets of X, noting the number of times each P_{nk} occurs. The third identity is a consequence of the second, by inversion. [Alternatively, the principle of inclusion and exclusion could be used.] (c) $\sum_{m\geq 0} mP_{nm} = nQ_{nn} - Q_{n(n-1)}$; hence

$$d_i = 1 + (N-1) - p_i\sum_{j\neq i}\frac{1}{p_i + p_j};$$

$$\sum_i p_i d_i = N - \sum_{i<j}\frac{p_i^2 + p_j^2}{p_i + p_j} = N - \sum_{i<j}\left(p_i + p_j - \frac{2p_i p_j}{p_i + p_j}\right) = \text{Eq. (17)}.$$

Notes: W. J. Hendricks [*J. Applied Probability* **9** (1972), 231–233] found a simple formula for the steady-state probability of each permutation of the records. For example, when $N = 4$ the sequence will be $R_3\, R_1\, R_4\, R_2$ with limiting probability

$$\frac{p_3}{p_3 + p_1 + p_4 + p_2}\frac{p_1}{p_1 + p_4 + p_2}\frac{p_4}{p_4 + p_2}\frac{p_2}{p_2}.$$

James Bitner [*SICOMP* **8** (1979), 82–85] proved that, if the list is originally in random order, the expected search time after t random requests exceeds $\tilde{C}_N$ by the quantity $\frac{1}{4}\sum_{i,j}(p_i - p_j)^2(1 - p_i - p_j)^t/(p_i + p_j)$. Thus, t searches require fewer than $t\tilde{C}_N + \frac{1}{4}\sum_{i,j}(p_i - p_j)^2/(p_i + p_j)^2 < t\tilde{C}_N + \frac{1}{2}\binom{N}{2}$ comparisons altogether, on the average. See P. Flajolet, D. Gardy, and L. Thimonier, *Discrete Applied Math.* **39** (1992), 207–229, §6, for instructive proofs via generating functions.

12. $\tilde{C}_N = 2^{1-N} + 2\sum_{n=0}^{N-2}1/(2^n + 1)$, which converges rapidly to $2\alpha' \approx 2.5290$; exercise 5.2.4–13 gives the value of α' to 40 decimal places.

13. After evaluating the rather tedious sum

$$\sum_{k=1}^{n}k^2 H_{n+k} = \frac{n(n+1)(2n+1)}{6}(2H_{2n} - H_n) - \frac{n(n+1)(10n-1)}{36},$$

we obtain the answer

$$\tilde{C}_N = \frac{4}{3}N - \frac{2}{3}(2N+1)(H_{2n} - H_n) + \frac{5}{6} - \frac{1}{3}(N+1)^{-1} \approx .409N.$$

14. We may assume that $x_1 \leq x_2 \leq \cdots \leq x_n$; then the maximum value occurs when $y_{a_1} \leq y_{a_2} \leq \cdots \leq y_{a_n}$, and the minimum when $y_{a_1} \geq \cdots \geq y_{a_n}$, by an argument like that of Theorem S.

15. Arguing as in Theorem S, the arrangement $R_1 R_2 \ldots R_N$ is optimum if and only if

$$P_1/L_1(1 - P_1) \geq \cdots \geq P_N/L_N(1 - P_N).$$

16. The expected time $T_1 + p_1 T_2 + p_1 p_2 T_3 + \cdots + p_1 p_2 \cdots p_{N-1} T_N$ is minimized if and only if $T_1/(1 - p_1) \le \cdots \le T_N/(1 - p_N)$. [*BIT* **3** (1963), 255–256; some interesting extensions have been obtained by James R. Slagle, *JACM* **11** (1964), 253–264.]

17. Do the jobs in order of increasing deadlines, independent of the respective times T_j! [Of course in practice some jobs are more important than others, and we may want to minimize the maximum *weighted* tardiness. Or we may wish to minimize the sum $\sum_{i=1}^{n} \max(T_{a_1} + \cdots + T_{a_i} - D_{a_i}, 0)$. Neither of these problems appears to have a simple solution.]

18. Let $h = [s$ is present$]$. Let $A = \{j \mid q_j < r_1\}$, $B = \{j \mid q_j = r_j\}$, $C = \{j \mid q_j > r_j\}$, $D = \{j \mid t_j > 0\}$; then the sum $\sum_{i,j} p_i p_j d_{|i-j|}$ for the (q, r) arrangement minus the corresponding sum for the (q', r') arrangement is equal to

$$2 \sum_{i \in A,\, j \in C} (q_i - r_i)(q_j - r_j)(d_{|i-j|} - d_{h+1+2k-i-j}) + 2 \sum_{i \in C,\, j \in D} (q_i - r_i)t_j(d_{h+2k-i+j} - d_{i-1+j}).$$

This is positive unless $C = \emptyset$ or $A \cup D = \emptyset$. The desired result now follows because the organ pipe arrangements are the only permutations that are not improved by this construction and its left-right dual when $m = 0, 1$.

[This result is essentially due to G. H. Hardy, J. E. Littlewood, and G. Pólya, *Proc. London Math. Soc.* (2), **25** (1926), 265–282, who showed, in fact, that the minimum of $\sum_{i,j} p_i q_j d_{|i-j|}$ is achieved, under all independent arrangements of the p's and q's, when both p's and q's are in a consistent organ-pipe order. For further commentary and generalizations, see their book *Inequalities* (Cambridge University Press, 1934), Chapter 10).]

19. All arrangements are equally good. Assuming that $d(j, j) = 0$, we have

$$\sum_{i,j} p_i p_j \, d(i, j) = \tfrac{1}{2} \sum_{i,j} p_i p_j \big(d(i, j) + d(j, i) \big) = \tfrac{1}{2} c.$$

[The special case $d(i, j) = 1 + (j - i) \bmod N$ for $i \ne j$ is due to K. E. Iverson, *A Programming Language* (New York: Wiley, 1962), 138. R. L. Baber, *JACM* **10** (1963), 478–486, has studied some other problems associated with tape searching when a tape can read forward, rewind, or backspace k blocks without reading. W. D. Frazer observes that it is possible to make significant reductions in the search time if we are allowed to *replicate* some of the information in the file; see E. B. Eichelberger, W. C. Rodgers, and E. W. Stacy, *IBM J. Research & Development* **12** (1968), 130–139, for an empirical solution to a similar problem.]

20. Going from (q, r) to (q', r') as in exercise 18, with $m = 0$ or $m = h = 1$, gives a net change of

$$\sum_{i \in A,\, j \in C} (q_i - r_i)(q_j - r_j)\big(d_{|i-j|} - \min(d_{h+1+2k-i-j}, d_{i+j-1})\big),$$

which is positive unless A or C is $\emptyset$. By circular symmetry it follows that the only optimal arrangements are cyclic shifts of the organ pipe configurations. [For a different class of problems with the same answer, see T. S. Motzkin and E. G. Straus, *Proc. Amer. Math. Soc.* **7** (1956), 1014–1021.]

21. This problem was essentially first solved by L. H. Harper, *SIAM J. Appl. Math.* **12** (1964), 131–135. For generalizations and references to other work, see *J. Applied Probability* **4** (1967), 397–401.

22. A priority queue of size 1000 (represented as, say, a heap, see Section 5.2.3). Insert the first 1000 records into this queue, with the element of *greatest* $d(K_j, K)$ at the front. For each subsequent K_j with $d(K_j, K) < d(\text{front of queue}, K)$, replace the front element by R_j and readjust the queue.

SECTION 6.2.1

1. Prove inductively that $K_{l-1} < K < K_{u+1}$ whenever we reach step B2; and that $l \le i \le u$ whenever we reach B3.

2. (a, c) No; it loops if $l = u - 1$ and $K > K_u$. (b) Yes, it does work. But when K is absent, there will often be a loop with $l = u$ and $K < K_u$.

3. This is Algorithm 6.1T with $N = 3$. In a successful search, that algorithm makes $(N + 1)/2$ comparisons, on the average; in an unsuccessful search it makes $N/2 + 1 - 1/(N+1)$.

4. It must be an unsuccessful search with $N = 127$; hence by Theorem B the answer is $138u$.

5. Program 6.1Q' has an average running time of $1.75N + 8.5 - (N \bmod 2)/4N$; this beats Program B if and only if $N \le 44$. [It beats Program C only for $N \le 11$.]

7. (a) Certainly not. (b) The parenthesized remarks in Algorithm U will hold true, so it will work, but only if $K_0 = -\infty$ and $K_{N+1} = +\infty$ are both present when N is odd.

8. (a) N. It is interesting to prove this by induction, observing that exactly one of the δ's increases if we replace N by $N+1$. [See *AMM* **77** (1970), 884 for a generalization.] (b) Maximum $= \sum_j \delta_j = N$; minimum $= 2\delta_1 - \sum_j \delta_j = N \bmod 2$.

9. If and only if $N = 2^k - 1$.

10. Use a "macro-expanded" program with the DELTA's included; thus, for $N = 10$:

```
        START   ENT1    5
                LDA     K
                CMPA    KEY,1
                JL      C3A
        C4A     JE      SUCCESS         C3A     EQU     *
                INC1    3                       DEC1    3
                CMPA    KEY,1                   CMPA    KEY,1
                JL      C3B                     JGE     C4B
        C4B     JE      SUCCESS         C3B     EQU     *
                INC1    1                       DEC1    1
                CMPA    KEY,1                   CMPA    KEY,1
                JL      C3C                     JGE     C4C
        C4C     JE      SUCCESS         C3C     EQU     *
                INC1    1                       DEC1    1
                CMPA    KEY,1                   CMPA    KEY,1
                JE      SUCCESS                 JE      SUCCESS
                JMP     FAILURE                 JMP     FAILURE    ▮
```

[Exercise 23 shows that most of the "JE" instructions may be eliminated, yielding a program about $6 \lg N$ lines long that takes only about $4 \lg N$ units of time; but that program will be faster only for $N \ge 1000$ (approximately).]

11. Consider the corresponding tree, such as Fig. 6: When N is odd, the left subtree of the root is a mirror image of the right subtree, so $K < K_i$ occurs just as often as $K > K_i$; on the average $C1 = \frac{1}{2}(C + S)$ and $C2 = \frac{1}{2}(C - S)$, $A = \frac{1}{2}(1 - S)$. When N is even, the tree is the same as the tree for $N + 1$ with all labels decreased by 1, except that $\textcircled{0}$ becomes redundant; on the average, letting $k = \lfloor \lg N \rfloor$, we have

$$C1 = \frac{C+1}{2} - \frac{k}{2N}, \qquad C2 = \frac{C-1}{2} + \frac{k}{2N}, \qquad A = 0, \qquad \text{if } S = 1;$$

$$C1 = \frac{(k+1)N}{2(N+1)}, \qquad C2 = \frac{(k+1)(N+2)}{2(N+1)}, \qquad A = \frac{N}{2(N+1)}, \qquad \text{if } S = 0.$$

(The average value of C is stated in the text.)

12.

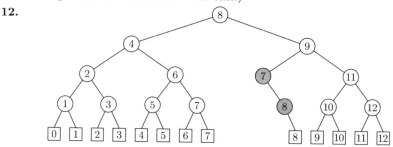

13.

$N =$	1	2	3	4	5	6	7	8	9	10	11	12	13	14	15	16
$C_N =$	1	$1\frac{1}{2}$	$1\frac{2}{3}$	$2\frac{1}{4}$	$2\frac{1}{5}$	$2\frac{2}{6}$	$2\frac{3}{7}$	$3\frac{1}{8}$	3	3	3	$3\frac{2}{12}$	$3\frac{3}{13}$	$3\frac{3}{14}$	$3\frac{4}{15}$	$4\frac{1}{16}$
$C'_N =$	1	$1\frac{2}{3}$	2	$2\frac{3}{5}$	$2\frac{4}{6}$	3	3	$3\frac{6}{9}$	$3\frac{8}{10}$	$3\frac{8}{11}$	$3\frac{8}{12}$	4	4	4	4	$4\frac{13}{17}$

14. One idea is to find the least $M \geq 0$ such that $N + M$ has the form $F_{k+1} - 1$, then to start with $i \leftarrow F_k - M$ in step F1, and to insert "If $i \leq 0$, go to F4" at the beginning of F2. A better solution would be to adapt Shar's idea to the Fibonaccian case: If the result of the very first comparison is $K > K_{F_k}$, set $i \leftarrow i - M$ and go to F4 (proceeding normally from then on). This avoids extra time in the inner loop.

15. The external nodes appear on levels $\lfloor k/2 \rfloor$ through $k - 1$; the difference between these levels is greater than unity except when $k = 0, 1, 2, 3, 4$.

16. The Fibonacci tree of order k, with left and right reversed, is the binary tree corresponding to the lineal chart up to the kth month, under the "natural correspondence" of Section 2.3.2, if we remove the topmost node of the lineal chart.

17. Let the path length be $k - A(n)$; then $A(F_j) = j$ and $A(F_j + m) = 1 + A(m)$ when $0 < m < F_{j-1}$.

18. Successful search: $A_k = 0$, $C_k = \big(3kF_{k+1} + (k - 4)F_k\big)/5(F_{k+1} - 1) - 1$, $C1_k = C_{k-1}(F_k - 1)/(F_{k+1} - 1)$. Unsuccessful search: $A'_k = F_k/F_{k+1}$, $C'_k = (3kF_{k+1} + (k - 4)F_k)/5F_{k+1}$, $C1'_k = C'_{k-1}F_k/F_{k+1} + F_{k-1}/F_{k+1}$. $C2 = C - C1$. (See exercise 1.2.8–12 for the solution to related recurrences.)

20. (a) $b = p^{-p}q^{-q}$. (b) There are at least *two* errors. The first blunder is that division is not a linear function, so it can't be simply "averaged over." Actually with probability p we get pN elements remaining, and with probability q we get qN, so we can expect to get $(p^2 + q^2)N$; thus the average reduction factor is really $1/(p^2 + q^2)$. Now the reduction factor after k iterations is $1/(p^2 + q^2)^k$, but we cannot conclude that $b = 1/(p^2 + q^2)$ since the number of iterations needed to locate some of the items is much more than to locate others. This is a second fallacy. [It is very easy to make plausible but fallacious probability arguments, and we must always be on our guard against such pitfalls!]

21. It's impossible, since the method depends on the key values.

22. *FOCS* **17** (1976), 173–177. See also Y. Perl, A. Itai, and H. Avni, *CACM* **21** (1978), 550–554; G. H. Gonnet, L. D. Rogers, and J. A. George, *Acta Informatica* **13** (1980), 39–52; G. Louchard, *RAIRO Inform. Théor.* **17** (1983), 365–385; *Computing* **46** (1991), 193–222. The variance is $O(\log\log N)$. Extensive empirical tests by G. Marsaglia and B. Narasimhan, *Computers and Math.* **26**, 8 (1993), 31–42, show that the average number of table accesses is very close to $\lg\lg N$, plus about 0.7 if the search is unsuccessful. When $N = 2^{20}$, for example, a random successful search in a random table takes about 4.29 accesses, while a random unsuccessful search takes about 5.05.

23. Go to the right on $\geq$, to the left on $<$; when reaching node $\boxed{i}$ it follows from (1) that $K_i \leq K < K_{i+1}$, so a final test for equality will distinguish between success or failure. (The key $K_0 = -\infty$ should always be present.)

     Algorithm C would be changed to go to C4 if $K = K_i$ in step C2. In C3 if `DELTA[j]` $= 0$, set $i \leftarrow i - 1$ and go to C5. In C4 if `DELTA[j]` $= 0$, go directly to C5. Add a new step C5: "If $K = K_i$, the algorithm terminates successfully, otherwise it terminates unsuccessfully." [This would not speed up Program C unless $N > 2^{26}$; the average successful search time changes from $(8.5\lg N - 6)u$ to $(8\lg N + 7)u$.]

24. The keys can be arranged so that we first set $i \leftarrow 1$, then $i \leftarrow 2i$ or $2i + 1$ according as $K < K_i$ or $K > K_i$; the search is unsuccessful when $i > N$. For example when $N = 12$ the necessary key arrangement is

$$K_8 < K_4 < K_9 < K_2 < K_{10} < K_5 < K_{11} < K_1 < K_{12} < K_6 < K_3 < K_7.$$

When programmed for **MIX** this method will take only about $6\lg N$ units of time, so it is faster than Program C. The only disadvantage is that it is a little tricky to set up the table in the first place.

25. (a) Since $a_0 = 1 - b_0$, $a_1 = 2a_0 - b_1$, $a_2 = 2a_1 - b_2$, etc., we have $A(z) + B(z) = 1 + 2zA(z)$. Several of the formulas derived in Section 2.3.4.5 follow immediately from this relation by considering $A(1)$, $B(1)$, $B(\frac{1}{2})$, $A'(1)$, and $B'(1)$. If we use two variables to distinguish left and right steps of a path we obtain the more general result $A(x, y) + B(x, y) = 1 + (x + y)A(x, y)$, a special case of a formula that holds in t-ary trees [see R. M. Karp, *IRE Transactions* **IT-7** (1961), 27–38].

     (b) $\operatorname{var}(g) = ((N + 1)/N)\operatorname{var}(h) - ((N + 1)/N^2)\operatorname{mean}(h)^2 + 2$.

26. The merge tree for the three-tape polyphase merge with a perfect level k distribution is the Fibonacci tree of order $k + 1$ if we permute left and right appropriately. (Redraw the polyphase tree of Fig. 76 in Section 5.4.4, with the left and right subtrees of A and C reversed, obtaining Fig. 8.)

27. At most $k + 1$ of the 2^k outcomes will ever occur, since we may order the indices in such a way that $K_{i_1} < K_{i_2} < \cdots < K_{i_k}$. Thus the search can be described by a tree with at most $(k + 1)$-way branching at each node. The number of items that can be found on the mth step is at most $k(k + 1)^{m-1}$; hence the average number of comparisons is at least N^{-1} times the sum of the smallest N elements of the multiset $\{k\cdot 1, k(k + 1)\cdot 2, k(k + 1)^2\cdot 3, \ldots\}$. When $N \geq (k + 1)^n - 1$, the average number of comparisons is $\geq ((k + 1)^n - 1)^{-1}\sum_{m=1}^{n} k(k + 1)^{m-1}m > n - 1/k$.

28. [*Skrifter udgivne af Videnskabs-Selskabet i Christiania*, Mathematisk-Naturviden-skabelig Klasse (1910), No. 8; reprinted in Thue's *Selected Mathematical Papers* (Oslo: Universitetsforlaget, 1977), 273–310.] (a) T_n has $F_{n+1}+F_{n-1} = F_{2n}/F_n$ leaves. (This is the so-called Lucas number $L_n = \phi^n + \hat{\phi}^n$.) (b) The axiom says that $T_0(T_2(x)) = T_1(x)$, and we obviously have $T_m(T_n(x)) = T_{m+n-1}(x)$ when $m = 1$ or $n = 1$. By induction on n, the result holds when $m = 0$; for example, $T_0(T_3(x)) = T_0(T_2(x) * T_1(x)) = T_0(T_1(T_2(x)) * T_0(T_2(x))) = T_0(T_2(T_2(x))) = T_2(x)$. Finally we can use induction on m.

29. Assume that $K_0 = -\infty$ and $K_{N+1} = K_{N+2} = \infty$. First do a binary search on $K_2 < K_4 < \cdots$; this takes at most $\lfloor \lg N \rfloor$ comparisons. If unsuccessful, it determines an interval with $K_{2j-2} < K < K_{2j}$; and K is not present if $2j = N + 2$. Otherwise, a binary search for K_{2j-1} will determine i such that $K_{2i-2} < K_{2j-1} < K_{2i}$. Then either $K = K_{2i-1}$ or K is not present. [See *Theor. Comp. Sci.* **58** (1988), 67.]

30. Let $n = \lfloor N/4 \rfloor$. Starting with $K_1 < K_2 < \cdots < K_N$, we can put K_1, K_3, $\ldots$, K_{2n-1} into any desired order by swapping them with a permutation of K_{2n+1}, K_{2n+3}, $\ldots$, K_{4n-1}; this arrangement satisfies the conditions of the previous exercise. Now we let $K_1 < K_3 < \cdots < K_{2^{t+1}-3}$ represent the boundaries between all possible t-bit numbers, and we insert $K_{2^{t+1}-1}$, $K_{2^{t+1}+1}$, $\ldots$, $K_{2^{t+1}+2m-3}$ between these "fence-posts" according to the values of x_1, x_2, $\ldots$, x_m. For example, if $m = 4$, $t = 3$, $x_1 = (001)_2$, $x_2 = (111)_2$, and $x_3 = x_4 = (100)_2$, the desired order is

$$K_1 < K_{15} < K_3 < K_5 < K_7 < K_{19} < K_{21} < K_9 < K_{11} < K_{13} < K_{17}.$$

(We could also let K_{21} precede K_{19}.) A binary search for $K_{2^{t+1}+2j-3}$ in the subarray $K_1 < K_3 < \cdots < K_{2^{t+1}-3}$ will now find the bits of x_j from left to right. [See Fiat, Munro, Naor, Schäffer, Schmidt, and Siegel, *J. Comp. Syst. Sci.* **43** (1991), 406–424.]

SECTION 6.2.2

1. Use a header node, with say $\text{ROOT} \equiv \text{RLINK(HEAD)}$; start the algorithm at step T4 with $\text{P} \leftarrow \text{HEAD}$. Step T5 should act as if $K > \text{KEY(HEAD)}$. [Thus, change lines 04 and 05 of Program T to "ENT1 ROOT; CMPA K".]

2. In step T5, set $\text{RTAG(Q)} \leftarrow 1$. Also, when inserting to the left, set $\text{RLINK(Q)} \leftarrow \text{P}$; when inserting to the right, set $\text{RLINK(Q)} \leftarrow \text{RLINK(P)}$ and $\text{RTAG(P)} \leftarrow 0$. In step T4, change the test "RLINK(P) $\neq \Lambda$" to "RTAG(P) $\neq 0$". [If nodes are inserted into successively increasing locations Q, and if all deletions are last-in-first-out, the RTAG fields can be eliminated since RTAG(P) will be 1 if and only if $\text{RLINK(P)} < \text{P}$. Similar remarks apply with simultaneous left and right threading.]

3. We could replace Λ by a valid address, and set $\text{KEY}(\Lambda) \leftarrow K$ at the beginning of the algorithm; then the tests for LLINK or RLINK $= \Lambda$ could be removed from the inner loop. However, in order to do a proper insertion we need to introduce another pointer variable that follows P; this can be done without losing the stated speed advantage, by duplicating the code as in Program 6.2.1F. Thus the MIX time would be reduced to about $5.5C$ units.

4. $C_N = 1 + (0 \cdot 1 + 1 \cdot 2 + \cdots + (n-1)2^{n-1} + C'_{2^n-1} + \cdots + C'_{N-1})/N = (1+1/N)C'_N - 1$, for $N \geq 2^n - 1$. The solution to these equations is $C'_N = 2(H_{N+1} - H_{2^n}) + n$ for $N \geq 2^n - 1$, a savings of $2H_{2^n} - n - 2 \approx n(\ln 4 - 1)$ comparisons. The actual improvement for $n = 1, 2, 3, 4$ is, respectively $0, \frac{1}{6}, \frac{61}{140}, \frac{274399}{360360}$; thus comparatively little is gained for small fixed n. [See Frazer and McKellar, *JACM* **17** (1970), 502, for a more detailed derivation related to an equivalent sorting problem.]

5. (a) The first element must be `CAPRICORN`; then we multiply the number of ways to produce the left subtree by the number of ways to produce the right subtree, times $\binom{10}{3}$, the number of ways to shuffle those two sequences together. Thus the answer comes to

$$\binom{10}{3}\binom{2}{0}\binom{1}{0}\binom{0}{0}\binom{6}{3}\binom{2}{0}\binom{1}{0}\binom{0}{0}\binom{2}{1}\binom{0}{0}\binom{0}{0} = 4800.$$

[In general, the answer is the product, over all nodes, of $\binom{l+r}{r}$, where l and r stand for the sizes of the left and right subtrees of the node. This is equal to $N!$ divided by the product of the subtree sizes. It is the same formula as in exercise 5.1.4–20; indeed, there is an obvious one-to-one correspondence between the permutations that yield a particular search tree and the "topological" permutations counted in that exercise, if we replace a_k in the search tree by k (using the notation of exercise 6).] (b) $2^{N-1} = 1024$; at each step but the last, insert either the smallest or largest remaining key.

6. (a) For each of the P_{nk} permutations $a_1 \ldots a_{n-1}a_n$ whose cost is k, construct $n+1$ permutations $a'_1 \ldots a'_{n-1} m\, a'_n$, where $a'_j = a_j$ or $a_j + 1$, according as $a_j < m$ or $a_j \geq m$. [See Section 1.2.5, Method 2.] If $m = a_n$ or $a_n + 1$, this permutation has a cost of $k+1$, otherwise it has a cost of k. (b) $G_n(z) = (2z + n - 2)(2z + n - 3)\ldots(2z)$. Hence

$$P_{nk} = \begin{bmatrix} n-1 \\ k \end{bmatrix} 2^k.$$

This generating function was, in essence, obtained by W. C. Lynch, *Comp. J.* **7** (1965), 299–302. (c) The generating function for probabilities is $g_n(z) = G_n(z)/n!$. This is a product of simple probability generating functions, so the variance of C'_{n-1} is

$$\operatorname{var}(g_n) = \sum_{k=0}^{n-2} \operatorname{var}\left(\frac{2z+k}{2+k}\right) = \sum_{k=0}^{n-2}\left(\frac{2}{k+2} - \frac{4}{(k+2)^2}\right) = 2H_n - 4H_n^{(2)} + 2.$$

[By exercise 6.2.1–25(b) we can use the mean and variance of C'_n to compute the variance of C_n, which is $(2 + 10/n)H_n - 4(1 + 1/n)(H_n^{(2)} + H_n^2/n) + 4$; this formula is due to G. D. Knott.]

7. A comparison with the kth largest element will be made if and only if that element occurs before the mth and before all those between the kth and mth; this happens with probability $1/(|m-k|+1)$. Summing over k gives the answer $H_m + H_{n+1-m} - 1$. [*CACM* **12** (1969), 77–80; see also L. Guibas, *Acta Informatica* **4** (1975), 293–298.]

8. (a) $g_n(z) = z^{n-1} \sum_{k=1}^{n} g_{k-1}(z)g_{n-k}(z)/n$, $g_0(z) = 1$.

(b) $7n^2 - 4(n+1)^2 H_n^{(2)} - 2(n+1)H_n + 13n$. [P. F. Windley, *Comp. J.* **3** (1960), 86, gave recurrence relations from which this variance could be computed numerically, but he did not obtain the solution. Notice that this result is *not* simply related to the variance of C_n stated in the answer to exercise 6.]

10. For example, each word x of the key could be replaced by $ax \bmod m$, where m is the computer word size and a is a random multiplier relatively prime to m. A value near to $(\phi - 1)m$ can be recommended (see Section 6.4). The flexible storage allocation of a tree method may make it more attractive than a hash coding scheme.

11. $N - 2$; but this occurs with probability $1/(N\,N!)$, only in the deletion

$$\textcircled{1}\; N\; N{-}1\; \ldots\; 2.$$

12. $\frac{1}{2}(n+1)(n+2)$ of the deletions in the proof of Theorem H belong to Case 1, so the answer is $(N+1)/2N$.

13. Yes. In fact, the proof of Theorem H shows that if we delete the kth element inserted, for any fixed k, the result is random. (G. D. Knott [Ph.D. thesis, Stanford, 1975] showed that the result is random after an arbitrary sequence of random insertions followed by successive deletion of the $(k_1, \ldots, k_d)$th elements inserted, for any fixed sequence $k_1, \ldots, k_d$.)

14. Let NODE(T) be on level k, and let LLINK(T) = Λ, RLINK(T) = R_1, LLINK(R_1) = R_2, $\ldots$, LLINK(R_d) = Λ, where $R_d \ne \Lambda$ and $d \ge 1$. Let NODE(R_i) have n_i internal nodes in its right subtree, for $1 \le i \le d$. With step D1$\frac{1}{2}$ the internal path length decreases by $k + d + n_1 + \cdots + n_d$; without that step it decreases by $k + d + n_d$.

15. 11, 13, 25, 11, 12. [If a_j is the (smallest, middle, largest) of $\{a_1, a_2, a_3\}$, the tree is obtained $(4, 2, 3) \times 4$ times after the deletion.]

16. Yes; even the deletion operation on permutations, as defined in the proof of Theorem H, is commutative (if we omit the renumbering aspect). If there is an element between X and Y, deletion is obviously commutative since the operation is affected only by the relative positions of X, Y, and their successors and there is no interaction between the deletion of X and the deletion of Y. On the other hand, if Y is the successor of X, and Y is the largest element, both orders of deletion have the effect of simply removing X and Y. If Y is the successor of X and Z the successor of Y, both orders of deletion have the effect of replacing the *first* occurrence of X, Y, or Z by Z and deleting the second and third occurrences of these elements within the permutation.

18. Use exercise 1.2.7–14.

19. $2H_N - 1 - 2\sum_{k=1}^{N}(k-1)^{\theta}/kN^{\theta} = 2H_N - 1 - 2/\theta + O(N^{-\theta})$. [The Pareto distribution 6.1–(13) also gives the same asymptotic result, to within $O(n^{-\theta} \log n)$.]

20. Yes indeed. Assume that $K_1 < \cdots < K_N$, so that the tree built by Algorithm T is degenerate; if, say, $p_k = (1 + ((N+1)/2 - k)\epsilon)/N$, the average number of comparisons is $(N + 1)/2 - (N^2 - 1)\epsilon/12$, while the optimum tree requires fewer than $\lceil \lg N \rceil$ comparisons.

21. $\frac{1}{8}, \frac{3}{20}, \frac{9}{20}, \frac{3}{20}, \frac{1}{8}$. (Most of the angles are 30°, 60°, or 90°.)

22. This is obvious when $d = 2$, and for $d > 2$ we had $r[i, j-1] \le r[i+1, j-1] \le r[i+1, j]$.

23.

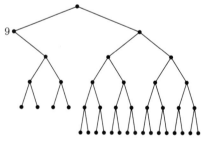

[Increasing the weight of the first node will eventually make it move to the root position; this suggests that dynamically maintaining a perfectly optimum tree is hard.]

24. Let c be the cost of a tree obtained by deleting the nth node of an optimum tree. Then $c(0, n-1) \le c \le c(0, n) - q_{n-1}$, since the deletion operation always moves $\boxed{n-1}$ up one level. Also $c(0, n) \le c(0, n-1) + q_{n-1}$, since the stated replacement yields a tree of the latter cost. It follows that $c(0, n-1) = c = c(0, n) - q_{n-1}$.

25. (a) Assume that $A \le B$ and $B \le C$, and let $a \in A$, $b \in B$, $c \in C$, $c < a$. If $c \le b$ then $c \in B$; hence $c \in A$ and $a \in B$; hence $a \in C$. If $c > b$, then $a \in B$; hence $a \in C$ and $c \in B$; hence $c \in A$. (b) Not hard to prove.

26. The cost of every tree has the form $y + lx$ for some real $y \ge 0$ and integer $l > 0$. The minimum of a finite number of such functions (taken over all trees) always has the form described.

27. (a) The answer to exercise 24 (especially the fact that $c = c(0, n{-}1)$) implies that $R(0, n{-}1) = R(0, n) \setminus \{n\}$.

     (b) If $l = l'$, the result in the hint is trivial. Otherwise let the paths to $\boxed{n}$ be

$$\boxed{r_0}, \boxed{r_1}, \ldots, \boxed{r_l} \qquad \text{and} \qquad \boxed{s_0}, \boxed{s_1}, \ldots, \boxed{s_{l'}} .$$

Since $r = r_0 > s_0 = s$ and $r_{l'} < s_{l'} = n$, we can find a level $k \ge 0$ such that $r_k > s_k$ and $r_{k+1} \le s_{k+1}$. We have $r_{k+1} \in R(r_k, n)$, $s_{k+1} \in R(s_k, n)$, and $R(s_k, n) \le R(r_k, n)$ by induction, hence $r_{k+1} \in R(s_k, n)$ and $s_{k+1} \in R(r_k, n)$; the result in the hint follows.

     Now to prove that $R'_h \le R_h$, let $r \in R'_h$, $s \in R_h$, $s < r$, and consider the optimum trees shown when $x = x_h$; we must have $l \ge l_h$ and we may assume that $l' = l_h$. To prove that $R_h \le R'_{h+1}$, let $r \in R_h$, $s \in R'_{h+1}$, $s < r$, and consider the optimum trees shown when $x = x_{h+1}$; we must have $l' \le l_h$ and we may assume that $l = l_h$.

29. It is a degenerate tree (see exercise 5) with YOU at the top, THE at the bottom, needing 19.158 comparisons on the average.

     Douglas A. Hamilton has proved that some degenerate tree is always worst. Therefore an $O(n^2)$ algorithm exists to find pessimal binary search trees.

30. See R. L. Wessner, *Information Processing Letters* **4** (1976), 90–94; F. F. Yao, *SIAM J. Algebraic and Discrete Methods* **3** (1982), 532–540.

31. See *Acta Informatica* **1** (1972), 307–310.

32. When M is large enough, the optimum tree must have the stated form and the minimum cost must be M times the minimum external path length plus the solution to the stated problem.

     [*Notes:* The paper by Wessner cited in answer 30 explains how to find optimum binary search trees of height $\le L$. In the special case $p_1 = \cdots = p_n = 0$, the stated result is due to T. C. Hu and K. C. Tan, MRC Report 1111 (Univ. of Wisconsin, 1970). A. M. Garsia and M. L. Wachs proved that in this case all external nodes will appear on at most two levels if $\min_{k=1}^{n}(q_{k-1} + q_k) \ge \max \sum_{k=0}^{n} q_k$, and they presented an algorithm that needs only $O(n)$ steps to find an optimum two-level tree.]

33. For the stated problem, see A. Itai, *SICOMP* **5** (1976), 9–18. For the alternatives, see D. Spuler, *Acta Informatica* **31** (1994), 729–740.

34. It equals $2^{H(p_1,\ldots,p_n)N}(2\pi N)^{(1-n)/2}(p_1 \ldots p_n)^{-1/2}(1 + O(1/N))$, if $p_1 \ldots p_n \ne 0$, by Stirling's approximation.

35. The minimum value of the right-hand side occurs when $2x = (1 - p)/p$, and it equals $1 - p + H(p, 1 - p)$. But $H(p, q, r) \le 1 - p + H(p, 1 - p)$, by (20) with $k = 2$.

36. First we prove the hint, which is due to Jensen [*Acta Math.* **30** (1906), 175–193]. If f is concave, the function $g(p) = f(px + (1 - p)y) - pf(x) - (1 - p)f(y)$ is concave and satisfies $g(0) = g(1) = 0$. If $g(p) < 0$ and $0 < p < 1$ there must be a value $p_0 < p$ with $g'(p_0) < 0$ and a value $p_1 > p$ with $g'(p_1) > 0$, by the mean value theorem; but this contradicts concavity. Therefore $f(px + (1 - p)y) \ge pf(x) + (1 - p)f(y)$ for $0 \le p \le 1$, a fact that is also geometrically obvious. Now we can prove by induction that $f(p_1x_1 + \cdots + p_nx_n) \geq p_1f(x_1) + \cdots + p_nf(x_n)$, since $f(p_1x_1 + \cdots + p_nx_n) \geq p_1f(x_1) + \cdots + p_{n-2}f(x_{n-2}) + (p_{n-1} + p_n)f((p_{n-1}x_{n-1} + p_nx_n)/(p_{n-1} + p_n))$ if $n > 2$.

By Lemma E we have

$$H(XY) = H(X) + \sum_{i=1}^{m} p_iH(r_{i1}/p_i, \ldots, r_{in}/p_i);$$

and the latter sum is $\sum_{j=1}^{n}\sum_{i=1}^{m} p_if(r_{ij}/p_i) \leq \sum_{j=1}^{n} f(\sum_{i=1}^{m} r_{ij}) = H(Y)$, where $f(x) = x\lg(1/x)$ is concave.

37. By part (a) of exercise 3.3.2–26, we have $\Pr(P_1 \geq s) = (1 - s)^{n-1}$. Therefore $E\,H(P_1, \ldots, P_n) = n\,E\,P_1\lg(1/P_1) = n\int_0^1 (1 - s)^{n-1}\,d(s\lg(1/s)) = -(A + B)/\ln 2$, where $A = n\int_0^1 (1 - s)^{n-1}\,ds = 1$ and

$$B = n\int_0^1 (1 - s)^{n-1}\ln s\,ds = \sum_{k=1}^{n}\binom{n}{k}(-1)^k s^k\left(\frac{1}{k} - \ln s\right)\Big|_0^1 = -H_n$$

by exercise 1.2.7–13. Thus the answer is $(H_n - 1)/\ln 2$. (This is $\lg n + (\gamma - 1)/\ln 2 + O(n^{-1})$, very near the maximum entropy $H(\frac{1}{n}, \ldots, \frac{1}{n}) = \lg n$. Therefore $H(p_1, \ldots, p_n)$ is $\Omega(\log n)$ with high probability.)

38. If $s_{k-1} = s_k$ we have $q_{k-1} = p_k = q_k = 0$; see (26). Construct a tree for the $n - 1$ probabilities $(p_1, \ldots, p_{k-1}, p_{k+1}, \ldots, p_n; q_0, \ldots, q_{k-1}, q_{k+1}, \ldots, q_n)$, and replace leaf $\boxed{k-1}$ by a 2-leaf subtree.

39. We can argue as in Theorem M, if $0 < w_1 \leq w_2 \leq \cdots \leq w_n$ and $s_k = w_1 + \cdots + w_k$, because $w_k \geq 2^{-t}$ implies that $s_{k-1} + 2^{-t} \leq s_k \leq s_{k+1} - 2^{-t}$ when the weights are ordered; hence we have $|\sigma_k| < 1 + \lg(1/w_k)$. [This result, together with the matching lower bound $H(w_1, \ldots, w_n)$, was Theorem 9 in Shannon's original paper of 1948.]

40. If $k = s+3$, the stated rearrangement changes the cost from $q_{k-1}l + q_kl + q_{k-2}l_{k-2}$ to $q_{k-2}l + q_{k-1}l + q_kl_{k-2}$, so the net change is $(q_{k-2} - q_k)(l - l_{k-2})$; this is negative if $l < l_{k-2}$, because $q_{k-2} > q_k$.

Similarly, if $k \geq s + 4$ the rearrangement changes the cost by

$$\delta = q_{s+1}(l - l_{s+1}) + q_{s+2}(l - l_{s+2}) + q_{s+3}(l_{s+1} - l_{s+3}) + \cdots + q_{k-2}(l_{k-2} - l_{k-4})$$
$$+ q_{k-1}(l_{k-3} - l) + q_k(l_{k-2} - l).$$

We have $q_{s+1} > q_{s+3}$, $q_{s+2} > q_{s+4}$, $\ldots$, $q_{k-2} > q_k$. Therefore we find

$$\delta \leq (q_{k-2} - q_k)(l - l_{k-2}) + (q_{k-3} - q_{k-1})(l - l_{k-3}) \leq 0;$$

for example, when $k - s$ is even we have

$$\delta \leq q_{k-3}(l - l_{s+1}) + q_{k-2}(l - l_{s+2}) + q_{k-3}(l_{s+1} - l_{s+3}) + \cdots + q_{k-2}(l_{k-2} - l_{k-4})$$
$$+ q_{k-1}(l_{k-3} - l) + q_k(l_{k-2} - l)$$

and a similar derivation works when $k - s$ is odd. It follows that δ is negative unless $l_{k-2} = l$.

41. E F G H T U X Y Z V W B C D A P Q R J K L M I N O S ␣.

42. Let $q_j = \text{WT}(P_j)$. The key point is that the actions of steps C2–C6 make *all* the q's greater than or equal to the initial value of $q_{k-1} + q_k$.

43. Invoke the recursive procedure $mark(\mathrm{P}_1, 0)$, where $mark(\mathrm{P}, l)$ means the following:

> LEVEL(P) $\leftarrow l$;
> if LLINK(P) $\neq \Lambda$ then $mark(\mathrm{LLINK(P)}, l+1)$;
> if RLINK(P) $\neq \Lambda$ then $mark(\mathrm{RLINK(P)}, l+1)$.

44. Set the global variables $t \leftarrow 0$, $m \leftarrow 2n$, and invoke the recursive subroutine $build(1)$, where $build(l)$ means the following:

> Set $j \leftarrow m$;
> if LEVEL(X_t) $= l$ then set LLINK(X_j) $\leftarrow t$ and $t \leftarrow t+1$,
>   otherwise set $m \leftarrow m-1$, LLINK(X_j) $\leftarrow \mathrm{X}_m$, and $build(l+1)$;
> if LEVEL(X_t) $= l$ then set RLINK(X_j) $\leftarrow t$ and $t \leftarrow t+1$,
>   otherwise set $m \leftarrow m-1$, RLINK(X_j) $\leftarrow \mathrm{X}_m$, and $build(l+1)$.

The variable j is local to the $build$ routine. [This elegant solution is due to R. E. Tarjan, *SICOMP* **6** (1977), 639.] Caution: If the numbers $l_0, \ldots, l_n$ do not correspond to any binary tree, the algorithm will loop forever.

45. Maintain the working array $\mathrm{P}_0, \ldots, \mathrm{P}_t$ as a doubly linked list that also has the links of a balanced tree (see Section 6.2.3). If the 2-descending weights are $q_0, \ldots, q_t$, with q_j at the root of the tree, we can decide whether to proceed left or right in the tree based on the values of q_j and q_{j+1}; the double linking provides instant access to q_{j+1}. (No RANK fields are needed; rotation preserves symmetric order, so it does not require any changes to the double links.)

Several families of weights for which the problem can be solved in $O(n)$ time have been presented by Hu and Morgenthaler, *Lecture Notes in Comp. Sci.* **1120** (1996), 234–243; it is unknown whether $O(n)$ steps are sufficient in general.

46. See *IEEE Trans.* **C-23** (1974), 268–271; see also exercise 6.2.3–21.

47. See Altenkamp and Mehlhorn, *JACM* **27** (1980), 412–427.

48. Don't let the complicated analyses of the cases $N = 3$ [Jonassen and Knuth, *J. Comp. Syst. Sci.* **16** (1978), 301–322] or $N = 4$ [Baeza-Yates, *BIT* **29** (1989), 378–394] scare you; think big! Some progress has been reported by Louchard, Randrianari-manana, and Schott, *Theor. Comp. Sci.* **93** (1992), 201–225.

49. This question was first investigated by J. M. Robson [*Australian Comp. J.* **11** (1979), 151–153], B. Pittel [*J. Math. Anal. Applic.* **103** (1984), 461–480], and Luc Devroye [*JACM* **33** (1986), 489–498; *Acta Inf.* **24** (1987), 277–298], who obtained limit formulas that hold with probability $\to 1$ as $n \to \infty$; see the exposition by H. M. Mahmoud, *Evolution of Random Search Trees* (Wiley, 1992), Chapter 2. Sharper results were subsequently found by Luc Devroye and Bruce Reed, *SICOMP* **24** (1995), 1157–1162, who proved that the average height is $\alpha \ln n + O(\log \log n)$ and the variance is $O(\log \log n)^2$, where

$$\alpha = 1/T(1/2e) \approx 4.31107\,04070\,01005\,03504\,70760\,96446\,89027\,83916-$$

and $T(z) = \sum_{n=1}^{\infty} n^{n-1}z^n/n!$ is the tree function.

SECTION 6.2.3

1. The symmetric order of nodes must be preserved by the transformation, otherwise we wouldn't have a binary search tree.

2. $B(S) = 0$ can happen only when S points to the root of the tree (it has never been changed in steps A3 or A4), and all nodes from S to the point of insertion were balanced.

3. Let ρ_h be the largest possible ratio of unbalanced nodes in balanced trees of height h. Thus $\rho_1 = 0$, $\rho_2 = \frac{1}{2}$, $\rho_3 = \frac{1}{2}$. We will prove that $\rho_h = (F_{h+1} - 1)/(F_{h+2} - 1)$. Let T_h be a tree that maximizes ρ_h; then we may assume that its left subtree has height $h - 1$ and its right subtree has height $h - 2$, for if both subtrees had height $h - 1$ the ratio would be less than ρ_{h-1}. Thus the ratio for T_h is at most $(\rho_{h-1}N_l + \rho_{h-2}N_r + 1)/(N_l + N_r + 1)$, where there are (N_l, N_r) nodes in the (left, right) subtree. This formula takes its maximum value when (N_l, N_r) take their minimum values; hence we may assume that T_h is a Fibonacci tree. And $\rho_h < \phi - 1$ by exercise 1.2.8–28.

4. When $h = 7$,

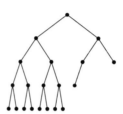

has greater path length. [*Note:* C. C. Foster, *Proc. ACM Nat. Conf.* **20** (1965), 197–198, gave an incorrect procedure for constructing N-node balanced trees of maximum path length; Edward Logg has observed that Foster's Fig. 3 gives a nonoptimal result after 24 steps (node number 22 can be removed in favor of number 25).]

The Fibonacci tree of order h does, however, minimize the value of $(h + a)N -$ (external path length(T)) over all balanced trees T of height $h - 1$, when a is any nonnegative constant; this is readily proved by induction on h. Its external path length is $\frac{3}{5}hF_{h-1} + \frac{4}{5}(h - 1)F_h = (\phi/\sqrt{5})hF_{h+1} + O(F_{h+1}) = \Theta(h\phi^h)$. Consequently the path length of any N-node balanced tree is at most

$$\min_h (hN - \Theta(h\phi^h) + O(N)) \leq N\log_\phi N - N\log_\phi\log_\phi N + O(N).$$

Moreover, if N is large and $k = \lceil \lg N \rceil$, $h = \lfloor k/\lg\phi - \log_\phi k \rfloor = \log_\phi N - \log_\phi\log_\phi N + O(1)$, we can construct a balanced tree of path length $hN + O(N)$ as follows: Write $N + 1 = F_h + F_{h-1} + \cdots + F_{k+1} + N' = F_{h+2} - F_{k+2} + N'$, and construct a complete binary tree on N' nodes; then successively join it with Fibonacci trees of orders k, $k+1$, $\ldots$, $h - 1$. [See R. Klein and D. Wood, *Theoretical Comp. Sci.* **72** (1990), 251–264.]

5. This can be proved by induction; if T_N denotes the tree constructed, we have

$$T_N = \begin{cases} \begin{array}{c} \\ T_{2^{n-1}-1} \quad T_{N-2^{n-1}} \end{array} & \text{if } 2^n \leq N < 2^n + 2^{n-1}; \\[2em] \begin{array}{c} \\ T_{2^n-1} \quad T_{N-2^n} \end{array} & \text{if } 2^n + 2^{n-1} \leq N < 2^{n+1}. \end{cases}$$

6. The coefficient of z^n in $zB_j(z)B_k(z)$ is the number of n-node binary trees whose left subtree is a balanced binary tree of height j and whose right subtree is a balanced binary tree of height k.

7. $C_{n+1} = C_n^2 + 2B_{n-1}B_{n-2}$; hence if we let $\alpha_0 = \ln 2$, $\alpha_1 = 0$, and $\alpha_{n+2} = \ln(1 + 2B_{n+1}B_n/C_{n+2}^2) = O(1/B_nC_{n+2})$, and $\theta = \exp(\alpha_0/2 + \alpha_1/4 + \alpha_2/8 + \cdots)$, we find that $0 \le \theta^{2^n} - C_n = C_n(\exp(\alpha_n/2 + \alpha_{n+1}/4 + \cdots) - 1) < 1$; thus $C_n = \lfloor \theta^{2^n} \rfloor$. For general results on doubly exponential sequences, see *Fibonacci Quarterly* **11** (1973), 429–437. The expression for θ converges rapidly to the value

$$\theta = 1.43687\,28483\,94461\,87580\,04279\,84335\,54862\,92481+.$$

8. Let $b_h = B_h'(1)/B_h(1) + 1$, and let $\epsilon_h = 2B_hB_{h-1}(b_h - b_{h-1})/B_{h+1}$. Then $b_1 = 2$, $b_{h+1} = 2b_h - \epsilon_h$, and $\epsilon_h = O(b_h/B_{h-1})$; hence $b_h = 2^h\beta + r_h$, where

$$\beta = 1 - \tfrac{1}{4}\epsilon_1 - \tfrac{1}{8}\epsilon_2 - \cdots = 0.70117\,98151\,02026\,33972\,44868\,92779\,46053\,74616+$$

and $r_h = \epsilon_h/2 + \epsilon_{h+1}/4 + \cdots$ is extremely small for large h. [*Zhurnal Vychisl. Matem. i Matem. Fiziki* **6**, 2 (1966), 389–394. Analogous results for 2-3 trees were obtained by E. M. Reingold, *Fib. Quart.* **17** (1979), 151–157.]

9. Andrew Odlyzko has shown that the number of balanced trees is asymptotically

$$c^n f\big(\log_{(\sqrt{10}+2)/3} n\big)/n,$$

where $c \approx 1.916067$ and $f(x) = f(x + 1)$. His techniques will also yield the average height. [See *Congressus Numerantium* **42** (1984), 27–52, a paper in which he also discusses the enumeration of 2-3 trees.]

10. [*Inf. Proc. Letters* **17** (1983), 17–20.] Let $X_1, \ldots, X_N$ be nodes whose balance factors $B(X_k)$ are given. To construct the tree, set $k \leftarrow 0$ and compute $\texttt{TREE}(\infty)$, where $\texttt{TREE}(hmax)$ is the following recursive procedure with local variables h, h', and Q: Set $h \leftarrow 0$, $Q \leftarrow \Lambda$; then while $h < hmax$ and $k < N$ set $k \leftarrow k + 1$, $h' \leftarrow h + B(X_k)$, $\texttt{LEFT}(X_k) \leftarrow Q$, $\texttt{RIGHT}(X_k) \leftarrow \texttt{TREE}(h')$, $h \leftarrow \max(h, h') + 1$, $Q \leftarrow X_k$; return Q. (Tree Q has height h and corresponds to the balance factors that have been read since entry to the procedure.) The algorithm works even if $|B(X_k)| > 1$.

11. Clearly there are as many $\texttt{+A}$'s as $\texttt{--B}$'s and $\texttt{+-B}$'s, when $n \ge 2$, and there is symmetry between $\texttt{+}$ and $\texttt{-}$. If there are M nodes of types $\texttt{+A}$ or $\texttt{-A}$, consideration of all possible cases when $n \ge 1$ shows that the next random insertion results in $M - 1$ such nodes with probability $3M/(n+1)$, otherwise it results in $M + 1$ such nodes. The result follows. [*SICOMP* **8** (1979), 33–41; Kurt Mehlhorn extended the analysis to deletions in *SICOMP* **11** (1982), 748–780. See R. A. Baeza-Yates, *Computing Surveys* **27** (1995), 109–119, for a summary of later developments in such "fringe analyses," which typically use the methods illustrated in exercise 6.2.4–8.

12. The maximum occurs when inserting into the second external node of (12); $C = 4$, $C1 = 3$, $D = 3$, $A = C2 = F = G1 = H1 = U1 = 1$, for a total time of $132u$. The minimum occurs when inserting into the third-last external node of (13); $C = 2$, $C1 = C2 = 1$, $D = 2$, for a total time of $61u$. [The corresponding figures for Program 6.2.2T are $74u$ and $26u$.]

13. When the tree changes, only $O(\log N)$ RANK values need to be updated; the "simple" system might require very extensive changes.

14. Yes. (But typical operations on lists are sufficiently nonrandom that degenerate trees would probably occur.)

15. Use Algorithm 6.2.2T with m set to zero in step T1, and $m \leftarrow m + \texttt{RANK(P)}$ whenever $K \ge \texttt{KEY(P)}$ in step T2.

16. Delete E; do Case 3 rebalancing at D. Delete G; replace F by G; do Case 2 rebalancing at H; adjust balance factor at K.

17. (a)

(b)

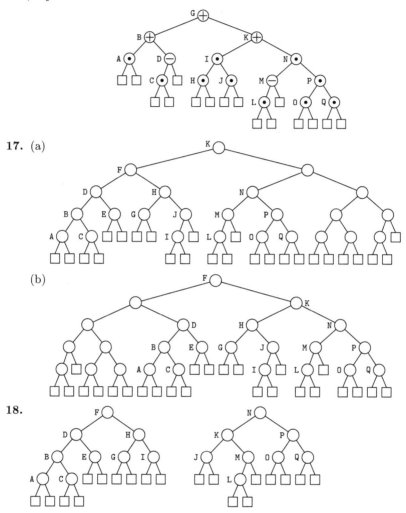

18.

19. (Solution by Clark Crane.) There is one case that can't be handled by a single or double rotation at the root, namely

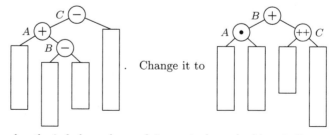

Change it to

and then resolve the imbalance by applying a single or double rotation at C.

20. It is difficult to insert a new node at the extreme left of the tree

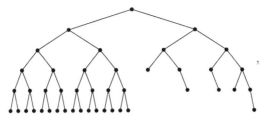

but K.-J. Räihä and S. H. Zweben have devised a general insertion algorithm that takes $O(\log N)$ steps. [*CACM* **22** (1979), 508–512.]

21. Algorithm A does the job in order $N \log N$ steps (see exercise 5); the following algorithm creates the same trees in $O(N)$ steps, using an interesting iterative rendition of a recursive method. We use three auxiliary lists:

$\quad$ $D_1, \ldots, D_l$ (a binary counter that essentially controls the recursion);

$\quad$ $J_1, \ldots, J_l$ (a list of pointers to juncture nodes);

$\quad$ $T_1, \ldots, T_l$ (a list of pointers to trees).

Here $l = \lceil \lg(N+1) \rceil$. For convenience the algorithm also sets $D_0 \leftarrow 1$, $J_0 \leftarrow J_{l+1} \leftarrow \Lambda$.

$\quad$ **G1.** [Initialize.] Set $l \leftarrow 0$, $J_0 \leftarrow J_1 \leftarrow \Lambda$, $D_0 \leftarrow 1$.

$\quad$ **G2.** [Get next item.] Let P point to the next input node. (We may invoke another coroutine in order to obtain P.) If there is no more input, go to G5. Otherwise, set $k \leftarrow 1$, $Q \leftarrow \Lambda$, and interchange $P \leftrightarrow J_1$.

$\quad$ **G3.** [Carry.] If $k > l$ (or, equivalently, if $P = \Lambda$), set $l \leftarrow l + 1$, $D_k \leftarrow 1$, $T_k \leftarrow Q$, $J_{k+1} \leftarrow \Lambda$, and return to G2. Otherwise set $D_k \leftarrow 1 - D_k$, interchange $Q \leftrightarrow T_k$, $P \leftrightarrow J_{k+1}$, and increase k by 1. If now $D_{k-1} = 0$, repeat this step.

$\quad$ **G4.** [Concatenate.] Set $\text{LLINK}(P) \leftarrow T_k$, $\text{RLINK}(P) \leftarrow Q$, $B(P) \leftarrow 0$, $T_k \leftarrow P$, and return to G2.

$\quad$ **G5.** [Finish up.] Set $\text{LLINK}(J_k) \leftarrow T_k$, $\text{RLINK}(J_k) \leftarrow J_{k-1}$, $B(J_k) \leftarrow 1 - D_{k-1}$, for $1 \le k \le l$. Then terminate the algorithm; J_l points to the root of the desired tree. $\blacksquare$

Step G3 is executed $2N - \nu(N)$ times, where $\nu(N)$ is the number of 1s in the binary representation of N.

22. The height of a weight-balanced tree with N internal nodes always lies between $\lg(N+1)$ and $2\lg(N+1)$. To get this upper bound, note that the heavier subtree of the root has at most $(N+1)/\sqrt{2}$ external nodes.

23. (a) Form a tree whose right subtree is a complete binary tree with $2^n - 1$ nodes, and whose left subtree is a Fibonacci tree with $F_{n+1} - 1$ nodes. (b) Form a weight-balanced tree whose right subtree is about $2 \lg N$ levels high and whose left subtree is about $\lg N$ levels high (see exercise 22).

24. Consider a smallest tree that satisfies the condition but is not perfectly balanced. Then its left and right subtrees are perfectly balanced, so they have 2^l and 2^r external nodes, respectively, where $l \ne r$. But this contradicts the stated condition.

25. After inserting a node at the bottom of the tree, we work up from the bottom to check the weight balance at each node on the search path. Suppose imbalance occurs at node A in (1), after we have inserted a new node in the right subtree, where B and its subtrees are weight-balanced. Then a single rotation will restore the balance unless $(|\alpha| + |\beta|)/|\gamma| > \sqrt{2} + 1$, where $|x|$ denotes the number of external nodes in a tree x. But in this case it can be shown that a double rotation will suffice. [See *SICOMP* **2** (1973), 33–43.]

27. It is sometimes necessary to make two comparisons in nodes that contain two keys. The worst case occurs in a tree like the following, which sometimes needs $2\lg(N+2)-2$ comparisons:

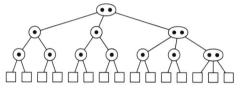

29. Partial solution by A. Yao: With $N \geq 6$ keys the lowest level will contain an average of $\frac{2}{7}(N+1)$ one-key nodes and $\frac{1}{7}(N+1)$ two-key nodes. The average total number of nodes lies between $0.70N$ and $0.79N$, for large N. [*Acta Informatica* **9** (1978), 159–170.]

30. For best-fit, arrange the records in order of size, with an arbitrary rule to break ties in case of equality. (See exercise 2.5–9.) For first fit, arrange the records in order of location, with an extra field in each node telling the size of the largest area in the subtree rooted at that node. This extra field can be maintained under insertions and deletions. (Although the running time is $O(\log n)$, it probably still doesn't beat the "ROVER" method of exercise 2.5–6 in practice; but the memory distribution may be better without ROVER, since there will usually be a nice large empty region for emergencies.)

An improved method has been developed by R. P. Brent, *ACM Trans. Prog. Languages and Systems* **11** (1989), 388–403.

31. Use a nearly balanced tree, with additional upward links for the leftmost part, plus a stack of postponed balance factor adjustments along this path. (Each insertion does a bounded number of these adjustments.)

This problem can be generalized to require $O(\log m)$ steps to find, insert, and/or delete items that are m steps away from any given "finger," where any key once located can serve as a finger in later operations. [See S. Huddleston and K. Mehlhorn, *Acta Inf.* **17** (1982), 157–184.]

32. Each right rotation increases one of the r's and leaves the others unchanged; hence $r_k \leq r_k'$ is necessary. To show that it is sufficient, suppose $r_j = r_j'$ for $1 \leq j < k$ but $r_k < r_k'$. Then there is a right rotation that increases r_k to a value $\leq r_k'$, because the numbers $r_1 r_2 \ldots r_n$ satisfy the condition of exercise 2.3.3–19(a).

Notes: This partial ordering, first introduced by D. Tamari in 1951, has many interesting properties. Any two trees have a greatest lower bound $T \wedge T'$, determined by the right-subtree sizes $\min(r_1, r_1') \min(r_2, r_2') \ldots \min(r_n, r_n')$, as well as a least upper bound $T \vee T'$ determined by the left-subtree sizes $\min(l_1, l_1') \min(l_2, l_2') \ldots \min(l_n, l_n')$. The left-subtree sizes are, of course, one less than the RANK fields of Algorithms B and C. For further information, see H. Friedman and D. Tamari, *J. Combinatorial Theory* **2** (1967), 215–242, **4** (1968), 201; C. Greene, *Europ. J. Combinatorics* **9** (1988), 225–240; D. D. Sleator, R. E. Tarjan, and W. P. Thurston, *J. Amer. Math. Soc.* **1** (1988), 647–681; J. M. Pallo, *Theoretical Informatics and Applic.* **27** (1993), 341–348; M. K.

Bennett and G. Birkhoff, *Algebra Universalis* **32** (1994), 115–144; P. H. Edelman and V. Reiner, *Mathematika* **43** (1996), 127–154.

33. First, we can reduce the storage to one bit A(P) in each node P, so that B(P) = A(RLINK(P)) − A(LLINK(P)) whenever LLINK(P) and RLINK(P) are both nonnull; otherwise B(P) is known already. Moreover, we can assume that A(P) = 0 whenever LLINK(P) and RLINK(P) are both null. Then A(P) can be eliminated in all other nodes by swapping LLINK(P) with RLINK(P) whenever A(P) = 1; a comparison of KEY(P) with KEY(LLINK(P)) or KEY(RLINK(P)) will determine A(P).

Of course, on machines for which pointers are always even, two unused bits are present already in every node. Further economies are possible as in exercise 2.3.1–37.

SECTION 6.2.4

1. Two nodes split:

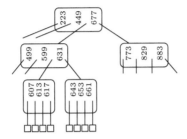

2. Altered nodes:

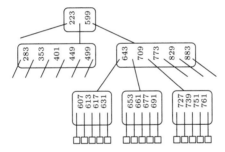

(Of course a B^*-tree would have no nonroot 3-key nodes, although Fig. 30 does.)

3. (a) $1 + 2 \cdot 50 + 2 \cdot 51 \cdot 50 + 2 \cdot 51 \cdot 51 \cdot 50 = 2 \cdot 51^3 - 1 = 265301$.
(b) $1 + 2 \cdot 50 + (2 \cdot 51 \cdot 100 - 100) + ((2 \cdot 51 \cdot 101 - 100) \cdot 100 - 100) = 101^3 = 1030301$.
(c) $1 + 2 \cdot 66 + (2 \cdot 67 \cdot 66 + 2) + (2 \cdot 67 \cdot 67 \cdot 66 + 2 \cdot 67) = 601661$. (Less than (b)!)

4. Before splitting a nonroot node, make sure that it has two full siblings, then split these three nodes into four. The root should split only when it has more than $3 \lfloor (3m - 3)/4 \rfloor$ keys.

5. Interpretation 1, trying to maximize the stated minimum: 450. (The worst case occurs if we have 1005 characters and the key to be passed to the parent must be 50 characters long: 445 chars + ptr + 50-char key + ptr + 50-char key + ptr + 445 chars.)

Interpretation 2, trying to equalize the number of keys after splitting, in order to keep branching factors high: 155 (15 short keys followed by 16 long ones).

See E. M. McCreight, *CACM* **20** (1977), 670–674, for further comments.

6. If the key to be deleted is not on level $l - 1$, replace it by its successor and delete the successor. To delete a key on level $l - 1$, we simply erase it; if this makes the node too empty, we look at its right (or left) sibling, and "underflow," that is, move keys in from the sibling so that both nodes have approximately the same amount of data. This underflow operation will fail only if the sibling was minimally full, but in that case the two nodes can be collapsed into one (together with one key from their parent); such collapsing may cause the parent in turn to underflow, etc. With variable-length keys as in exercise 5, a parent node may need to split when one of its keys becomes longer.

8. Given a tree $\mathcal{T}$ with N internal nodes, let there be $a_k^{(j)}$ external nodes that require k accesses and whose parent node belongs to a page containing j keys; and let $A^{(j)}(z)$ be the corresponding generating function. Thus $A^{(1)}(1) + \cdots + A^{(M)}(1) = N + 1$. (Note that $a_k^{(j)}$ is a multiple of $j + 1$, for $1 \le j < M$.) The next random insertion leads to $N + 1$ equally probable trees, whose generating functions are obtained by decreasing some coefficient $a_k^{(j)}$ by $j + 1$ and adding $j + 2$ to $a_k^{(j+1)}$; or (if $j = M$) by decreasing some $a_k^{(M)}$ by 1 and adding 2 to $a_{k+1}^{(1)}$. Now $B_N^{(j)}(z)$ is $(N+1)^{-1}$ times the sum, over all trees $\mathcal{T}$, of the generating function $A^{(j)}(z)$ for $\mathcal{T}$ times the probability that $\mathcal{T}$ occurs; the stated recurrence relations follow.

The recurrence has the form

$$\left(B_N^{(1)}(z),\ldots,B_N^{(M)}(z)\right)^T = \left(I + (N+1)^{-1}W(z)\right)\left(B_{N-1}^{(1)}(z),\ldots,B_{N-1}^{(M)}(z)\right)^T$$
$$= \cdots = g_N(W(z))(0,\ldots,0,1)^T,$$

where

$$g_n(x) = \left(1 + \frac{x}{n+1}\right)\cdots\left(1 + \frac{x}{2}\right) = \frac{1}{x+1}\binom{x+n+1}{n+1}.$$

It follows that $C_N' = (1,\ldots,1)(B_N^{(1)\prime}(1),\ldots,B_N^{(M)\prime}(1))^T = 2B_{N-1}^{(M)}(1)/(N+1)+C_{N-1}' = 2f_N(W)_{MM}$, where $f_n(x) = g_{n-1}(x)/(n+1) + \cdots + g_0(x)/2 = (g_n(x) - 1)/x$, and $W = W(1)$. (The subscript MM denotes the lower right corner element of the matrix.) Now $W = S^{-1}\operatorname{diag}(\lambda_1,\ldots,\lambda_M)S$, for some matrix S, where $\operatorname{diag}(\lambda_1,\ldots,\lambda_M)$ denotes the diagonal matrix whose entries are the roots of $\chi(\lambda) = (\lambda+2)\ldots(\lambda+M+1)-(M+1)!$. (The roots are distinct, since $\chi(\lambda) = \chi'(\lambda) = 0$ implies $1/(\lambda+2)+\cdots+1/(\lambda+M+1) = 0$; the latter can hold only when λ is real, and $-M - 1 < \lambda < -2$, which implies that $|\lambda + 2|\ldots|\lambda + M + 1| < (M + 1)!$, a contradiction.) If $p(x)$ is any polynomial, $p(W) = p(S^{-1}\operatorname{diag}(\lambda_1,\ldots,\lambda_M)S) = S^{-1}\operatorname{diag}(p(\lambda_1),\ldots,p(\lambda_M))S$; hence the lower right corner element of $p(W)$ has the form $c_1p(\lambda_1)+\cdots+c_Mp(\lambda_M)$ for some constants $c_1,\ldots,c_M$ independent of p. These constants may be evaluated by setting $p(\lambda) = \chi(\lambda)/(\lambda-\lambda_j)$; since $(W^k)_{MM} = (-2)^k$ for $0 \le k \le M-1$, we have $p(W)_{MM} = p(-2) = (M+1)!/(\lambda_j+2) = c_jp(\lambda_j) = c_j\chi'(\lambda_j) = c_j(M+1)!\left(1/(\lambda_j+2)+\cdots+1/(\lambda_j+M+1)\right)$; hence $c_j = (\lambda_j + 2)^{-1}\left(1/(\lambda_j + 2) + \cdots + 1/(\lambda_j + M + 1)\right)^{-1}$. This yields an "explicit" formula $C_N' = \sum_{j=1}^M 2c_jf_N(\lambda_j)$; and it remains to study the roots λ_j. Note that $|\lambda_j+M+1| \le M+1$ for all j, otherwise we would have $|\lambda_j+2|\ldots|\lambda_j+M+1| > (M+1)!$. Taking $\lambda_1 = 0$, this implies that $\Re(\lambda_j) < 0$ for $2 \le j \le M$. By Eq. 1.2.5-(15), $g_n(x) \sim (n+1)^x/\Gamma(x+2)$ as $n \to \infty$; hence $g_n(\lambda_j) \to 0$ for $2 \le j \le M$. Consequently $C_N' = 2c_1f_N(0) + O(1) = H_N/(H_{M+1} - 1) + O(1)$.

Notes: The analysis above is relevant also to the "samplesort" algorithm discussed briefly in Section 5.2.2. The calculations may readily be extended to show that $B_N^{(j)}(1) \sim (H_{M+1} - 1)^{-1}/(j+2)$ for $1 \le j < M$, $B_N^{(M)}(1) \sim (H_{M+1} - 1)^{-1}/2$. Hence the total number of interior nodes on unfilled pages is approximately

$$\left(\frac{1}{3 \times 2} + \frac{2}{4 \times 3} + \cdots + \frac{M - 1}{(M + 1) \times M}\right)\frac{N}{H_{M+1} - 1} = \left(1 - \frac{M}{(M + 1)(H_{M+1} - 1)}\right)N;$$

and the total number of pages used is approximately

$$\left(\frac{1}{3\times 2}+\frac{1}{4\times 3}+\cdots+\frac{1}{(M+1)\times M}+\frac{1}{M+1}\right)\frac{N}{H_{M+1}-1}=\frac{N}{2(H_{M+1}-1)},$$

yielding an asymptotic storage utilization of $2(H_{M+1}-1)/M$.

This analysis has been extended by Mahmoud and Pittel [*J. Algorithms* **10** (1989), 52–75], who discovered that the variance of the storage utilization undergoes a surprising phase transition: When $M \le 25$, the variance is $\Theta(N)$; but when $M \ge 26$ it is asymptotically $f(N)N^{1+2\alpha}$ where $f(e^{\pi/\beta}N)=f(N)$, if $-\frac{1}{2}+\alpha+\beta i$ and $-\frac{1}{2}+\alpha-\beta i$ are the nonzero roots λ_j with largest real part.

The height of such trees has been analyzed by L. Devroye [*Random Structures and Algorithms* **1** (1990), 191–203]; see also B. Pittel, *Random Structures and Algorithms* **5** (1994), 337–347.

9. Yes; for example we could replace each K_i in (1) by i plus the number of keys in subtrees $P_0, \ldots, P_{i-1}$. The search, insertion, and deletion algorithms can be modified appropriately.

10. Brief sketch: Extend the paging scheme so that exclusive access to buffers is given to one user at a time; the search, insertion, and deletion algorithms must be carefully modified so that such exclusive access is granted only for a limited time when absolutely necessary, and in such a way that no deadlocks can occur. For details, see B. Samadi, *Inf. Proc. Letters* **5** (1976), 107–112; R. Bayer and M. Schkolnick, *Acta Inf.* **9** (1977), 1–21; Y. Sagiv, *J. Comp. Syst. Sci.* **33** (1986), 275–296.

SECTION 6.3

1. Lieves (the plural of "lief").

2. Perform Algorithm T using the new key as argument; it will terminate unsuccessfully in either step T3 or T4. If in T3, simply set table entry k of NODE(P) to K and terminate the insertion algorithm. Otherwise set this table entry to the address of a new node Q $\Leftarrow$ AVAIL, containing only null links, then set P $\leftarrow$ Q. Now set k and k' to the respective next characters of K and X; if $k \ne k'$, store K in position k of NODE(P) and store X in position k', but if $k = k'$ again make the k position point to a new node Q $\Leftarrow$ AVAIL, set P $\leftarrow$ Q, and repeat the process until eventually $k \ne k'$. (We must assume that no key is a prefix of another.)

3. Replace the key by a null link, in the node where it appears. If this node is now useless because all its entries are null except one that is a key X, delete the node and replace the corresponding pointer in its parent by X. If the parent node is now useless, delete it in the same way.

4. Successful searches take place exactly as with the full table, but unsuccessful searches in the compressed table may go through several additional iterations. For example, an input argument such as TRASH will make Program T take *six* iterations (more than five!); this is the worst case. It is necessary to verify that no infinite looping on blank sequences is possible. (This remarkable 49-place packing is due to J. Scot Fishburn, who also showed that 48 places do not suffice.)

A slower but more versatile way to economize on trie storage has been proposed by Kurt Maly, *CACM* **19** (1976), 409–415.

In general, if we want to compress n sparse tables containing respectively x_1, ..., x_n nonzero entries, a first-fit method that offsets the jth table by the minimum amount r_j that will not conflict with the previously placed tables will have $r_j \leq (x_1 + \cdots + x_{j-1})x_j$, since each previous nonzero entry can block at most x_j offsets. This worst-case estimate gives $r_j \leq 93$ for the data in Table 1, guaranteeing that any twelve tables of length 30 containing respectively 10, 5, 4, 3, 3, 3, 3, 3, 2, 2, 2, 2 nonzero entries can be packed into $93 + 30$ consecutive locations regardless of the pattern of the nonzeros. Further refinements of this method have been developed by R. E. Tarjan and A. C. Yao, *CACM* **22** (1979), 606–611. A dynamic implementation of compressed tries, due to F. M. Liang, is used for hyphenation tables in the TEX typesetting system; see D. E. Knuth, *CACM* **29** (1986), 471–478; *Literate Programming* (1991), 206–233.

5. In each family, test for the most probable outcome first, by arranging the letters from left to right in decreasing order of probability. The optimality of this arrangement can be proved as in Theorem 6.1S. [See *CACM* **12** (1969), 72–76.]

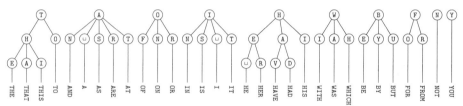

6.

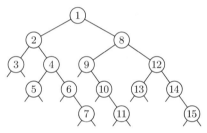

7. For example, 8, 4, 1, 2, 3, 5, 6, 7, 12, 9, 10, 11, 13, 14, 15. (No matter what sequence is used, the left subtree cannot contain more than two nodes on level 4, nor can the right subtree.) Even this "worst" tree is within 4 of the best possible tree, so we see that digital search trees aren't very sensitive to the order of insertion.

8. Yes. The KEY fields now contain only a truncated key; leading bits implied by the node position are chopped off. (A similar modification of Algorithm T is possible.)

```
9. START LDX   K              1      D1. Initialize. (rX ≡ K)
         LD1   ROOT           1      P ← ROOT.      (rI1 ≡ P)
         JMP   2F             1
   4H    LD2   0,1(RLINK)     C2     D4. Move right. Q ← RLINK(P).
         J2Z   5F             C2     To D5 if Q = Λ.
   1H    ENT1  0,2            C − 1  P ← Q.
   2H    CMPX  1,1            C      D2. Compare.
         JE    SUCCESS        C      Exit if K = KEY(P).
         SLB   1              C − S  Shift K left one bit.
         JAO   4B             C − S  To D4 if the detached bit was 1.
         LD2   0,1(LLINK)     C1     D3. Move left. Q ← LLINK(P).
         J2NZ  1B             C1     To D2 with P ← Q if Q ≠ Λ.
   5H    Continue as in Program 6.2.2T, interchanging the roles of rA and rX.
```

The running time for the searching phase of this program is $(10C - 3S + 4)u$, where $C - S$ is the number of bit inspections. For random data, the approximate average running times are therefore:

	Successful	Unsuccessful
Program 6.2.2T	$15 \ln N - 12.34$	$15 \ln N - 2.34$
This program	$14.4 \ln N - 6.17$	$14.4 \ln N + 1.26$

(Consequently Program 6.2.2T is a shade faster unless N is very large.)

10. Let $\oplus$ denote the exclusive or operation on n-bit numbers, and let $f(x) = n - \lceil \lg(x + 1) \rceil$ be the number of leading zero bits of x. One solution: (b) If a search via Algorithm T ends unsuccessfully in step T3, K is one less than the number of bit inspections made so far; otherwise if the search ends in step T4, $k = f(K \oplus X)$. (a, c) Do a regular search, but also keep track of the minimum value, x, of $K \oplus \texttt{KEY(P)}$ over all $\texttt{KEY(P)}$ compared with K during the search. Then $k = f(x)$. (Prove that no other key can have more bits in common with K than those compared to K. In case (a), the maximum k occurs for either the largest key $\leq K$ or the smallest key $> K$.)

11. No; eliminating a node with only one empty subtree will "forget" one bit in the keys of the nonempty subtree. To delete a node, we should replace it by one of its *terminal* descendants, for example by searching to the right whenever possible.

12. Insert three random numbers α, β, γ between 0 and 1 into an initially empty tree; then delete α with probability p, β with probability q, γ with probability r, using the algorithm suggested in the previous exercise. The tree

is obtained with probability $\frac{1}{4}p + \frac{1}{2}q + \frac{1}{2}r$, and this is $\frac{1}{2}$ only if $p = 0$.

13. Add a KEY field to each node, and compare K with this key before looking at the vector element in step T2. Table 1 would change as follows: Nodes (1), ..., (12) would contain the respective keys THE, AND, BE, FOR, HIS, IN, OF, TO, WITH, HAVE, HE, THAT (if we inserted them in order of decreasing frequency), and these keys would be deleted from their previous positions. [The corresponding program would be slower and more complicated than Program T, in this case. A more direct M-ary generalization of Algorithm D would create a tree with N nodes, having one key and M links per node.]

14. If $j \leq n$, there is only one place, namely KEY(P). But if $j > n$, the set of all occurrences is found by traversing the subtree of node P: If there are r occurrences, this subtree contains $r - 1$ nodes (including node P), and so it has r link fields with TAG = 1; these link fields point to all the nodes that reference TEXT positions matching K. (It isn't necessary to check the TEXT again at all.)

15. To begin forming the tree, set KEY(HEAD) to the first TEXT reference, and set LLINK(HEAD) ← HEAD, LTAG(HEAD) ← 1. Further TEXT references can be entered into the tree using the following insertion algorithm:

Set K to the new key that we wish to enter. (This is the first reference the insertion algorithm makes to the TEXT array.) Perform Algorithm P; it must terminate unsuccessfully, since no key is allowed to be a prefix of another. (Step P6 makes the second reference to the TEXT; no more references will be needed!) Now suppose that the key located in step P6 agrees with the argument K in the first l bits, but differs from it in position $l+1$, where K has the digit b and the key has $1-b$. (Even though the search in Algorithm P might have let j get much greater than l, it is possible to prove that the procedure specified here will find the longest match between K and *any* existing key. Thus, *all* keys of the text that start with the first l bits of K have $1-b$ as their $(l+1)$st bit.) Now repeat Algorithm P with K replaced by these leading l bits (thus, $n \leftarrow l$). This time the search will be successful, so we needn't perform step P6. Now set R $\Leftarrow$ AVAIL, KEY(R) $\leftarrow$ position of the new key in TEXT. If LLINK(Q) $=$ P, set LLINK(Q) $\leftarrow$ R, $t \leftarrow$ LTAG(Q), LTAG(Q) $\leftarrow 0$; otherwise set RLINK(Q) $\leftarrow$ R, $t \leftarrow$ RTAG(Q), RTAG(Q) $\leftarrow 0$. If $b=0$, set LTAG(R) $\leftarrow 1$, LLINK(R) $\leftarrow$ R, RTAG(R) $\leftarrow t$, RLINK(R) $\leftarrow$ P; otherwise set RTAG(R) $\leftarrow 1$, RLINK(R) $\leftarrow$ R, LTAG(R) $\leftarrow t$, LLINK(R) $\leftarrow$ P. If $t=1$, set SKIP(R) $\leftarrow 1+l-j$; otherwise set SKIP(R) $\leftarrow 1+l-j+$SKIP(P) and SKIP(P) $\leftarrow j-l-1$.

16. The tree setup requires precisely one dotted link coming from below a node to that node; it comes from that part of the tree where this key first differs from all others. If there is no such part of the tree, the algorithms break down. We could simply drop keys that are prefixes of others, but then the algorithm of exercise 14 wouldn't have enough data to find *all* occurrences of the argument.

17. If we define $a_0 = a_1 = 0$, then

$$x_n = a_n + \sum_{k \geq 2} \binom{n}{k}(-1)^k \hat{a}_k/(m^{k-1}-1) = \sum_{k \geq 2} \binom{n}{k}(-1)^k \hat{a}_k m^{k-1}/(m^{k-1}-1).$$

18. To solve (4) we need the transform of $a_n = [n>1]$, namely $\hat{a}_n = [n=0]-1+n$; hence for $N \geq 2$ we obtain $A_N = 1 - U_N + V_N$, where $U_N = K(N,0,M)$ and $V_N = K(N,1,M)$ in the notation of exercise 19. Similarly, to solve (5), take $a_n = n-[n=1] = \hat{a}_n$ and obtain $C_N = N + V_N$ for $N \geq 2$.

19. For $s = 1$, we have $V_n = K(n,1,m) = n((\ln n + \gamma)/\ln m - \frac{1}{2} - \delta_0(n-1)) + O(1)$, and for $s \geq 2$ we have $K(n,s,m) = (-1)^s n(1/\ln m + \delta_{s-1}(n-s))/s(s-1) + O(1)$, where

$$\delta_s(n) = \frac{2}{\ln m} \sum_{k \geq 1} \Re(\Gamma(s-2\pi ik/\ln m)\exp(2\pi ik \log_m n))$$

is a periodic function of $\log n$. [In this derivation we have

$$K(n+s,s,m)/(-1)^s \binom{n+s}{s} = \frac{n^{-s+1}}{2\pi i}\int_{1/2-i\infty}^{1/2+i\infty} \frac{\Gamma(z)n^{s-1-z}\,dz}{m^{s-1-z}-1} + O(n^{-s}).$$

For small m and s, the δ's will be negligibly small; see exercise 5.2.2–46. Note that $\delta_s(n-a) = \delta_s(n) + O(n^{-1})$ for fixed a.]

20. For (a), let $a_n = [n>s] = 1 - \sum_{k=0}^{s}[n=k]$; for (b), let $a_n = n - \sum_{k=0}^{s} k[n=k]$; and for (c), we want to solve the recurrence

$$y_n = \begin{cases} m^{1-n}\sum_k \binom{n}{k}(m-1)^{n-k}y_k & \text{for } n > s, \\ \binom{n+1}{2} & \text{for } n \leq s. \end{cases}$$

Setting $x_n = y_n - n$ yields a recurrence of the form of exercise 17, with

$$a_n = (1-M^{-1})\sum_{k=0}^{s} \binom{k}{2}[n=k].$$

Therefore, in the notation of previous exercises, the answers are (a) $1 - K(N,0,M) + K(N,1,M) - \cdots + (-1)^{s-1}K(N,s,M) = N/(s\ln M) - N(\delta_{-1}(N) + \delta_0(N-1) +$

$\delta_1(N-2)/2\cdot 1 + \cdots + \delta_{s-1}(N-s)/s(s-1)) + O(1)$; (b) $N^{-1}(N + K(N,1,M) - 2K(N,2,M) + \cdots + (-1)^{s-1}sK(N,s,M)) = (\ln N + \gamma - H_{s-1})/\ln M + 1/2 - (\delta_0(N-1)+\delta_1(N-2)/1+\cdots+\delta_{s-1}(N-s)/(s-1))+O(N^{-1})$; (c) $N^{-1}(N+(1-M^{-1}) \times \sum_{k=2}^{s}(-1)^k \binom{k}{2}K(N,k,M)) = 1 + \frac{1}{2}(1-M^{-1})((s-1)/\ln M + \delta_1(N-2) + \cdots + \delta_{s-1}(N-s)) + O(N^{-1})$.

21. Let there be A_N nodes in all. The number of nonnull pointers is $A_N - 1$, and the number of nonpointers is N, so the total number of null pointers is $MA_N - A_N + 1 - N$. To get the average number of null pointers in any fixed position, divide by M. [The average value of A_N appears in exercise 20(a).]

22. There is a node for each of the M^l sequences of leading bits such that at least two keys have this bit pattern. The probability that exactly k keys have a particular bit pattern is

$$\binom{N}{k}M^{-lk}(1-M^{-l})^{N-k},$$

so the average number of trie nodes on level l is $M^l(1-(1-M^{-l})^N) - N(1-M^{-l})^{N-1}$.

23. More generally, consider the case of arbitrary s as in exercise 20. If there are a_l nodes on level l, they contain a_{l+1} links and $Ma_l - a_{l+1}$ places where the search might be unsuccessful. The average number of digit inspections will therefore be $\sum_{l\geq 0}(l+1)M^{-l-1}(Ma_l - a_{l+1}) = \sum_{l\geq 0}M^{-l}a_l$. Using the formula for a_l in a random trie, this equals

$$1 + \frac{K(N+1,1,M) - 2K(N+1,2,M) + \cdots + (-1)^s(s+1)K(N+1,s+1,M)}{N+1}$$

$$= \frac{\ln N + \gamma - H_s}{\ln M} + \frac{1}{2} - \delta_0(N) - \frac{\delta_1(N-1)}{1} - \cdots - \frac{\delta_s(N-s)}{s} + O(N^{-1}).$$

24. We must solve the recurrences $x_0 = x_1 = y_0 = y_1 = 0$,

$$x_n = m^{-n}\sum_{n_1+\cdots+n_m=n}\binom{n}{n_1,\ldots,n_m}\left(x_{n_1}+\cdots+x_{n_m} + \sum_{1\leq j\leq m}[n_j\neq 0]\right)$$

$$= a_n + m^{1-n}\sum_{k}\binom{n}{k}x_k,$$

$$y_n = m^{-n}\sum_{n_1+\cdots+n_m=n}\binom{n}{n_1,\ldots,n_m}\left(y_{n_1}+\cdots+y_{n_m} + \sum_{1\leq i<j\leq m}[n_i\neq 0]n_j\right)$$

$$= b_n + m^{1-n}\sum_{k}\binom{n}{k}y_k,$$

for $n \geq 2$, where $a_n = m(1-(1-1/m)^n)$ and $b_n = \frac{1}{2}(m-1)n(1-(1-1/m)^{n-1})$. By exercises 17 and 18 the answers are (a) $x_N = N + V_N - U_N - [N=1] = A_N + N - 1$ (a result that could have been obtained directly, since the number of nodes in the forest is always $N-1$ more than the number in the corresponding trie!); and (b) $y_N/N = \frac{1}{2}(M-1)V_N/N = \frac{1}{2}(M-1)((\ln N + \gamma)/\ln M - \frac{1}{2} - \delta_0(N-1)) + O(N^{-1})$.

25. (a) Let $A_N = M(N-1)/(M-1) - E_N$; then for $N \geq 2$, we have $(1-M^{1-N})E_N = M - 1 - M(1-1/M)^{N-1} + M^{1-N}\sum_{0<k<N}\binom{N}{k}(M-1)^{N-k}E_k$. Since $M - 1 \geq M(1-1/M)^{N-1}$, we have $E_N \geq 0$ by induction. (b) By Theorem 1.2.7A with $x = 1/(M-1)$ and $n = N - 1$, we find $D_N = a_N + M^{1-N}\sum_{k}\binom{N}{k}(M-1)^{N-k}D_k$,

where $a_1 = 0$ and $0 < a_N < M(1-1/M)^N/\ln M \le (M-1)^2/M \ln M$ for $N \ge 2$. Hence $0 \le D_N \le (M-1)^2 A_N/M \ln M \le (M-1)(N-1)/\ln M$.

26. Taking $q = \frac{1}{2}$, $z = -\frac{1}{2}$ in the second identity of exercise 5.1.1–16, we get $1/3 - 1/(3 \cdot 7) + 1/(3 \cdot 7 \cdot 15) - \cdots = 0.28879$; it's slightly faster to use $z = -\frac{1}{4}$ and take half of the result. Alternatively, Euler's formula from exercise 5.1.1–14 can be used, involving only negative powers of 2. (John Wrench has computed the value to 40 decimal digits, namely $0.28878\ 80950\ 86602\ 42127\ 88997\ 21929\ 23078\ 00889+$.)

27. (For fun, the following derivation goes to $O(N^{-1})$.) In the notation of exercises 5.2.2–38 and 5.2.2–48, we have

$$\bar{C}_N = U_N + N - 1 + \frac{V_{N+1}}{N+1} - \alpha N - \beta + \sum_{n \ge 2}(-1)^n 2^{-n(n+1)/2}\frac{\sum_{m \ge 0}(2^{1-n})^m(1 - 2^{-m})^N}{\prod_{r=1}^n(1 - 2^{-r})},$$

where

$$\alpha = 2/(1 \cdot 1) - 4/(3 \cdot 3 \cdot 1) + 8/(7 \cdot 7 \cdot 3 \cdot 1) - 16/(15 \cdot 15 \cdot 7 \cdot 3 \cdot 1) + \cdots$$
$$\approx 1.60669\ 51524\ 15291\ 76378\ 33015\ 23190\ 92458\ 04806-$$

and $\beta = 2/(1 \cdot 3 \cdot 1) - 4/(3 \cdot 7 \cdot 3 \cdot 1) + 8/(7 \cdot 15 \cdot 7 \cdot 3 \cdot 1) - \cdots \approx 0.60670$. This numerical evaluation suggests that $\alpha = \beta + 1$, a fact that is not hard to prove. The value of $\sum_{m \ge 0}(2^{1-n})^m(1 - 2^{-m})^N$ is $O(N^{1-n})$, by exercise 5.2.2–46; and $V_{N+1}/(N+1) = U_{N+1} - U_N$. Hence $\bar{C}_N = U_{N+1} - (\alpha - 1)N - \alpha + O(N^{-1}) = (N+1)\lg(N+1) + N((\gamma - 1)/\ln 2 + \frac{1}{2} - \alpha + \delta_{-1}(N)) + \frac{1}{2} - 1/\ln 4 - \alpha - \frac{1}{2}\delta_1(N) + O(N^{-1})$, by exercise 5.2.2–50.

The variance of the internal path length of a digital search tree has been computed by Kirschenhofer, Prodinger, and Szpankowski, *SICOMP* **23** (1994), 598–616.

28. The derivations in the text and exercise 27 apply to general $M \ge 2$, if we substitute M for 2 in the obvious places. Hence the average number of digit inspections in a random successful search is $\bar{C}_N/N = U_{N+1} - \alpha_M + 1 + O(N^{-1}) = \log_M N + (\gamma - 1)/\ln M + \frac{1}{2} - \alpha_M + \delta_{-1}(N) + (\log_M N)/N + O(N^{-1})$; and for the unsuccessful case it is $\bar{C}_{N+1} - \bar{C}_N = V_{N+2}/(N+2) - \alpha_M + 1 + O(N^{-1}) = \log_M N + \gamma/\ln M + \frac{1}{2} - \alpha_M - \delta_0(N+1) + O(N^{-1})$. Here $\delta_s(n)$ is defined in exercise 19, and

$$\alpha_M = \sum_{j \ge 0}(-1)^j M^{j+1}/(M^{j+1} - 1)^2(M^j - 1)\ldots(M - 1).$$

29. Flajolet and Sedgewick [*SICOMP* **15** (1986), 748–767] have shown that the approximate average number of such nodes is $.372N$ when $M = 2$ and $.689N$ when $M = 16$. See also the generalization by Flajolet and Richmond, *Random Structures and Algorithms* **3** (1992), 305–320.

30. By iterating the recurrence, $h_n(z)$ is the sum of all possible terms of the form

$$\binom{n}{p_1}\frac{z}{2^{p_1} - 1}\binom{p_1}{p_2}\frac{z}{2^{p_2} - 1}\cdots\frac{z}{2^{p_m} - 1}\binom{p_m}{1}, \qquad \text{for } n > p_1 > \cdots > p_m > 1.$$

31. $h'_n(1) = V_n$; see exercise 5.2.2–36(b). [For the variance and limiting distributions of M-ary generalizations of Patricia trees, see P. Kirschenhofer and W. Prodinger, *Lecture Notes in Comp. Sci.* **226** (1986), 177–185; W. Szpankowski, *JACM* **37** (1990), 691–711; B. Rais, P. Jacquet, and W. Szpankowski, *SIAM J. Discrete Math.* **6** (1993), 197–213.]

32. The sum of the SKIP fields is the number of nodes in the corresponding binary trie, so the answer is A_N (see exercise 20).

33. Here's how (18) was discovered: $A(2z) - 2A(z) = e^{2z} - 2e^z + 1 + A(z)(e^z - 1)$ can be transformed into $A(2z)/(e^{2z} - 1) = (e^z - 1)/(e^z + 1) + A(z)/(e^z - 1)$. Hence $A(z) = (e^z - 1) \sum_{j \geq 1} (e^{z/2^j} - 1)/(e^{z/2^j} + 1)$. Now if $f(z) = \sum c_n z^n$, $\sum_{j \geq 1} f(z/2^j) = \sum c_n z^n/(2^n - 1)$. In this case $f(z) = (e^z - 1)/(e^z + 1) = \tanh(z/2)$, which equals $1 - 2z^{-1}(z/(e^z - 1) - 2z/(e^{2z} - 1)) = \sum_{n \geq 1} B_{n+1} z^n (2^{n+1} - 1)/(n + 1)!$. From this formula the route is apparent.

34. (a) Consider $\sum_{j \geq 1} \sum_{k=2}^{n-1} \binom{n}{k} B_k / 2^{j(k-1)}$; $1^{n-1} + \cdots + (m-1)^{n-1} = (B_n(m) - B_n)/n$ by exercise 1.2.11.2–4. (b) Let $S_n(m) = \sum_{k=1}^{m-1} (1 - k/m)^n$ and $T_n(m) = 1/(e^{n/m} - 1)$. If $k \leq m/2$ we have $e^{-kn/m} > \exp(n \ln(1 - k/m)) > \exp(-kn/m - k^2 n/m^2) > e^{-kn/m}(1 - k^2/m^2)$, hence $(1 - k/m)^n = e^{-kn/m} + O(e^{-kn/m} k^2 n/m^2)$. Since $S_n(m) = \sum_{k=1}^{m/2} (1 - k/m)^n + O(2^{-n})$ and $T_n(m) = \sum_{k=1}^{m/2} e^{-kn/m} + O(e^{-n/2})$, we have $S_n(m) = T_n(m) + O(e^{-n/m} n/m^2)$. The sum of $O(\exp(-n/2^j)n/2^{2j})$ is $O(n^{-1})$, because the sum for $j \leq \lg n$ is of order $n^{-1}(1 + 2/e + (2/e)^2 + \cdots$ and the sum for $j \geq \lg n$ is of order $n^{-1}(1 + 1/4 + (1/4)^2 + \cdots$. (c) Argue as in Section 5.2.2 when $|x| < 2\pi$, then use analytic continuation. (d) $\frac{1}{2} \lg(n/\pi) + \gamma/(2 \ln 2) - \frac{3}{4} + \delta(n) + 2/n$, where

$$\delta(n) = (2/\ln 2) \sum_{k \geq 1} \Re(\zeta(-2\pi i k/\ln 2)\Gamma(-2\pi i k/\ln 2) \exp(2\pi i k \lg n))$$
$$= (1/\ln 2) \sum_{k \geq 1} \Re(\zeta(1 + 2\pi i k/\ln 2) \exp(2\pi i k \lg(n/\pi)))/\cosh(\pi^2 k/\ln 2).$$

The variance and higher moments have been calculated by W. Szpankowski, *JACM* **37** (1990), 691–711.

35. The keys must be $\{\alpha 0 \beta 0 \omega_1, \alpha 0 \beta 1 \omega_2, \alpha 1 \gamma 0 \omega_3, \alpha 1 \gamma 1 \delta 0 \omega_4, \alpha 1 \gamma 1 \delta 1 \omega_5\}$, where $\alpha, \beta, \ldots$ are strings of 0s and 1s with $|\alpha| = a - 1$, $|\beta| = b - 1$, etc. The probability that five random keys have this form is $5! \, 2^{a-1+b-1+c-1+d-1}/2^{a+b+a+b+a+c+a+c+d+a+c+d} = 5!/2^{4a+b+2c+d+4}$.

36. Let there be n internal nodes. (a) $(n!/2^I) \prod(1/s(x)) = n! \prod(1/2^{s(x)-1} s(x))$, where I is the internal path length of the tree. (b) $((n + 1)!/2^n) \prod(1/(2^{s(x)} - 1))$. (Consider summing the answer of exercise 35 over all a, b, c, $d \geq 1$.)

37. The smallest modified external path length is actually $2 - 1/2^{N-2}$, and it occurs only in a degenerate tree (whose external path length is *maximal*). [One can prove that the *largest* modified external path length occurs if and only if the external nodes appear on at most two adjacent levels! But it is not always true that a tree whose external path length is smaller than another has a larger modified external path length.]

38. Consider as subproblems the finding of k-node trees with parameters $(\alpha, \beta), (\alpha, \frac{1}{2}\beta), \ldots, (\alpha, 2^{k-n}\beta)$.

39. See Miyakawa, Yuba, Sugito, and Hoshi, *SICOMP* **6** (1977), 201–234.

40. Let N/r be the true period length of the sequence. Form a Patricia-like tree, with $a_0 a_1 \ldots$ as the TEXT and with N/r keys starting at positions $0, 1, \ldots, N/r - 1$. (No key is a prefix of another, because of our choice of r.) Also include in each node a SIZE field, containing the number of tagged link fields in the subtree below that node. To do the specified operation, use Algorithm P; if the search is unsuccessful, the answer is 0, but if it is successful and $j \leq n$ the answer is r. Finally if it is successful and $j > n$, the answer is $r \cdot$ SIZE(P).

43. The expected height is asymptotic to $(1 + 1/s) \log_M N$, and the variance is $O(1)$. See H. Mendelson, *IEEE Transactions* **SE-8** (1982), 611–619; P. Flajolet, *Acta Informatica* **20** (1983), 345–369; L. Devroye, *Acta Informatica* **21** (1984), 229–237; B. Pittel, *Advances in Applied Probability* **18** (1986), 139–155; W. Szpankowski, *Algorithmica* **6** (1991), 256–277.

The average height of a random digital search tree with $M = 2$ is asymptotically $\lg n + \sqrt{2 \lg n}$ [Aldous and Shields, *Probability Theory and Related Fields* **79** (1988), 509–542], and the same is true for a random Patricia tree [Pittel and Rubin, *Journal of Combinatorial Theory* **A55** (1990), 292–312].

44. See *SODA* **8** (1997), 360–369; this search structure is closely related to the multikey quicksort algorithm discussed in the answer to exercise 5.2.2–30. J. Clément, P. Flajolet, and B. Vallée have shown that the ternary representation makes trie searching about three times faster than the binary representation of (2), with respect to nodes accessed [see *SODA* **9** (1998), 531–539].

SECTION 6.4

1. $-37 \le \text{rI1} \le 46$. Therefore the locations preceding and following **TABLE** must be guaranteed to contain no data that matches any given argument; for example, their first byte could be zero. It would certainly be bad to store K in this range! [Thus we might say that the method in exercise 6.3–4 uses less space, since the boundaries of that table are never exceeded.]

2. **TOW**. [Can the reader find ten common words of at most 5 letters that fill all the remaining gaps between -10 and 30?]

3. The alphabetic codes satisfy $\text{A} + \text{T} = \text{I} + \text{N}$ and $\text{B} - \text{E} = \text{O} - \text{R}$, so we would have either $f(\text{AT}) = f(\text{IN})$ or $f(\text{BE}) = f(\text{OR})$. Notice that instructions 4 and 5 of Table 1 resolve this dilemma rather well, while keeping rI1 from having too wide a range.

4. Consider cases with k pairs. The smallest n such that

$$ m^{-n} n! \sum_k \binom{m}{n-k} \binom{n-k}{k} 2^{-k} < \frac{1}{2}, \qquad \text{for } m = 365, $$

is 88. If you invite 88 people (including yourself), the chance of a birthday trio is .511065, but if only 87 people come it is lowered to .499455. See C. F. Pinzka, *AMM* **67** (1960), 830.

5. The hash function is bad since it assumes at most 26 different values, and some of them occur much more often than the others. Even with double hashing (letting $h_2(K) = 1$ plus the second byte of K, say, and $M = 101$) the search will be slowed down more than the time saved by faster hashing. Also $M = 100$ is too small, since FORTRAN programs often have more than 100 distinct variables.

6. Not on **MIX**, since arithmetic overflow will almost always occur (dividend too large). [It would be nice to be able to compute $(wK) \bmod M$, especially if linear probing were being used with $c = 1$, but unfortunately most computers disallow this since the quotient overflows.]

7. If $R(x)$ is a multiple of $P(x)$, then $R(\alpha^j) = 0$ in $\text{GF}(2^k)$ for all $j \in S$. Let $R(x) = x^{a_1} + \cdots + x^{a_s}$, where $a_1 > \cdots > a_s \ge 0$ and $s \le t$, and select $t - s$ further values $a_{s+1}, \ldots, a_t$ such that $a_1, \ldots, a_t$ are distinct nonnegative integers less than n.

The Vandermonde matrix

$$\begin{pmatrix} \alpha^{a_1} & \cdots & \alpha^{a_t} \\ \alpha^{2a_1} & \cdots & \alpha^{2a_t} \\ \vdots & & \vdots \\ \alpha^{ta_1} & \cdots & \alpha^{ta_t} \end{pmatrix}$$

is singular, since the sum of its first s columns is zero. But this contradicts the fact that $\alpha^{a_1}, \ldots, \alpha^{a_t}$ are distinct elements of $GF(2^k)$. (See exercise 1.2.3–37.)

[The idea of polynomial hashing originated with M. Hanan, S. Muroga, F. P. Palermo, N. Raver, and G. Schay; see *IBM J. Research & Development* **7** (1963), 121–129; *U.S. Patent 3311888* (1967).]

8. By induction. The strong induction hypotheses can be supplemented by the fact that $\{(-1)^k(rq_k + q_{k-1})\theta\} = (-1)^k\big(r(q_k\theta - p_k) + (q_{k-1}\theta - p_{k-1})\big)$ for $0 \le r \le a_k$. The "record low" values of $\{n\theta\}$ occur for $n = q_1, q_2 + q_1, 2q_2 + q_1, \ldots, a_2 q_2 + q_1 = 0 q_4 + q_3$, $q_4 + q_3, \ldots, a_4 q_4 + q_3 = 0 q_6 + q_5, \ldots$; the "record high" values occur for $n = q_0$, $q_1 + q_0, \ldots, a_1 q_1 + q_0 = 0 q_3 + q_2, \ldots$. These are the steps when interval number 0 of a new length is formed. [Further structure can be deduced by generalizing the Fibonacci number system of exercise 1.2.8–34; see L. H. Ramshaw, *J. Number Theory* **13** (1981), 138–175.]

9. We have $\phi^{-1} = /\!/1, 1, 1, \ldots /\!/$ and $\phi^{-2} = /\!/2, 1, 1, \ldots /\!/$. Let $\theta = /\!/a_1, a_2, \ldots /\!/$ and $\theta_k = /\!/a_{k+1}, a_{k+2}, \ldots /\!/$, and let $Q_k = q_k + q_{k-1}\theta_{k-2}$ in the notation of exercise 8. If $a_1 > 2$, the very first break is bad. The three sizes of intervals in exercise 8 are, respectively, $(1 - r\theta_{k-1})/Q_k$, θ_{k-1}/Q_k, and $\big(1 - (r-1)\theta_{k-1}\big)/Q_k$, so the ratio of the first length to the second is $(a_k - r) + \theta_k$. This will be less than $\frac{1}{2}$ when $r = a_k$ and $a_{k+1} \ge 2$; hence $\{a_2, a_3, \ldots\}$ must all equal 1 if there are to be no bad breaks. [For related theorems, see R. L. Graham and J. H. van Lint, *Canadian J. Math.* **20** (1968), 1020–1024, and the references cited there.]

10. See F. M. Liang's elegant proof in *Discrete Math.* **28** (1979), 325–326.

11. There would be a problem if $K = 0$. If keys were required to be nonzero as in Program L, this change would be worthwhile, and we could also represent empty positions by 0.

12. We can store K in KEY[0], replacing lines 14–19 by

```
      STA   TABLE(KEY)        A − S1
      CMPA  TABLE,2(KEY)      A − S1
      JE    3F                A − S1
   2H ENT1  0,2               C − 1 − S2
      LD2   TABLE,1(LINK)     C − 1 − S2
      CMPA  TABLE,2(KEY)      C − 1 − S2
      JNE   2B                C − 1 − S2
   3H J2Z   5F                A − S1
      ENT1  0,2               S2
      JMP   SUCCESS           S2   ∎
```

The time "saved" is $C - 1 - 5A + S + 4S1$ units, which is actually a net *loss* because C is rarely more than 5. (An inner loop shouldn't always be optimized!)

13. Let the table entries be of two distinguishable types, as in Algorithm C, with an additional one-bit TAG[i] field in each entry. This solution uses circular lists, following a suggestion of Allen Newell, with TAG[i] $= 1$ in the first word of each list.

A1. [Initialize.] Set $i \leftarrow j \leftarrow h(K) + 1$, $Q \leftarrow q(K)$.

A2. [Is there a list?] If TABLE$[i]$ is empty, set TAG$[i] \leftarrow 1$ and go to A8. Otherwise if TAG$[i] = 0$, go to A7.

A3. [Compare.] If $Q =$ KEY$[i]$, the algorithm terminates successfully.

A4. [Advance to next.] If LINK$[i] \neq j$, set $i \leftarrow$ LINK$[i]$ and go back to A3.

A5. [Find empty node.] Decrease R one or more times until finding a value such that TABLE$[R]$ is empty. If $R = 0$, the algorithm terminates with overflow; otherwise set LINK$[i] \leftarrow R$.

A6. [Prepare to insert.] Set $i \leftarrow R$, TAG$[R] \leftarrow 0$, and go to A8.

A7. [Displace a record.] Repeatedly set $i \leftarrow$ LINK$[i]$ one or more times until LINK$[i] = j$. Then do step A5. Then set TABLE$[R] \leftarrow$ TABLE$[i]$, $i \leftarrow j$, TAG$[j] \leftarrow 1$.

A8. [Insert new key.] Mark TABLE$[i]$ as an occupied node, with KEY$[i] \leftarrow Q$, LINK$[i] \leftarrow j$. ▌

(Note that if TABLE$[i]$ is occupied it is possible to determine the corresponding full key K, given only the value of i. We have $q(K) =$ KEY$[i]$, and then if we set $i \leftarrow$ LINK$[i]$ zero or more times until TAG$[i] = 1$ we will have $h(K) = i - 1$.)

14. According to the stated conventions, the notation "X $\Leftarrow$ AVAIL" of 2.2.3–(6) now stands for the following operations: "Set X $\leftarrow$ AVAIL; then set X $\leftarrow$ LINK(X) zero or more times until either X $= \Lambda$ (an OVERFLOW error) or TAG(X) $= 0$; finally set AVAIL $\leftarrow$ LINK(X)."

To insert a new key K: Set Q $\Leftarrow$ AVAIL, TAG(Q) $\leftarrow 1$, and store K in this word. [Alternatively, if all keys are short, omit this and substitute K for Q in what follows.] Then set R $\Leftarrow$ AVAIL, TAG(R) $\leftarrow 1$, AUX(R) $\leftarrow$ Q, LINK(R) $\leftarrow \Lambda$. Set P $\leftarrow h(K)$, and

if TAG(P) $= 0$, set TAG(P) $\leftarrow 2$, AUX(P) $\leftarrow$ R;

if TAG(P) $= 1$, set S $\Leftarrow$ AVAIL, CONTENTS(S) $\leftarrow$ CONTENTS(P), TAG(P) $\leftarrow 2$, AUX(P) $\leftarrow$ R, LINK(P) $\leftarrow$ S;

if TAG(P) $= 2$, set LINK(R) $\leftarrow$ AUX(P), AUX(P) $\leftarrow$ R.

To retrieve a key K: Set P $\leftarrow h(K)$, and

if TAG(P) $\neq 2$, K is not present;

if TAG(P) $= 2$, set P $\leftarrow$ AUX(P); then set P $\leftarrow$ LINK(P) zero or more times until either P $= \Lambda$, or TAG(P) $= 1$ and either AUX(P) $= K$ (if all keys are short) or AUX(P) points to a word containing K (perhaps indirectly through words with TAG $= 2$).

Elcock's original scheme [*Comp. J.* **8** (1965), 242–243] actually used TAG $= 2$ and TAG $= 3$ to distinguish between lists of length one (when we can save one word of space) and longer lists. This is a worthwhile improvement, since we presumably have such a large hash table that almost all lists have length one.

Another way to place a hash table "on top of" a large linked memory, using coalescing lists instead of separate chaining, has been suggested by J. S. Vitter [*Inf. Proc. Letters* **13** (1981), 77–79].

15. Knowing that there is always an empty node makes the inner search loop faster, since we need not maintain a counter to determine how many times step L2 is performed. The shorter program amply compensates for this one wasted cell. [On the other hand, there is a neat way to avoid the variable N and to allow the table to become completely full, in Algorithm L, without slowing down the method appreciably except when the table actually does overflow: Simply check whether $i < 0$ happens twice! This trick does not apply to Algorithm D.]

16. No: 0 always leads to SUCCESS, whether it has been inserted or not, and SUCCESS occurs with different values of i at different times.

17. The second probe would then always be to position 0.

18. The code in (31) costs about $3(A - S1)$ units more than (30), and it saves $4u$ times the difference between (26), (27), and (28), (29). For a successful search, (31) is advantageous only when the table is more than about 94 percent full, and it never saves more than about $\frac{1}{2}u$ of time. For an unsuccessful search, (31) is advantageous when the table is more than about 71 percent full.

20. We want to show that

$$\binom{j}{2} \equiv \binom{k}{2} \pmod{2^m} \qquad \text{and} \qquad 1 \le j \le k \le 2^m$$

implies $j = k$. Observe that the congruence $j(j-1) \equiv k(k-1) \pmod{2^{m+1}}$ implies $(k - j)(k + j - 1) \equiv 0$. If $k - j$ is odd, $k + j - 1$ must be a multiple of 2^{m+1}, but that's impossible since $2 \le k + j - 1 \le 2^{m+1} - 2$. Hence $k - j$ is even, so $k + j - 1$ is odd, so $k - j$ is a multiple of 2^{m+1}, so $k = j$. [Conversely, if M is not a power of 2, this probe sequence does not work.]

The probe sequence has secondary clustering, and it increases the running time of Program D (as modified in (30)) by about $\frac{1}{2}(C-1)-(A-S1)$ units since $B \approx \binom{C+1}{3}/M$ will now be negligible. This is a small improvement, until the table gets about 60 percent full.

21. If N is decreased, Algorithm D can fail since it might reach a state with no empty spaces and loop indefinitely. On the other hand, if N isn't decreased, Algorithm D might signal overflow when there still is room. The latter alternative is the lesser of the two evils, because rehashing can be used to get rid of deleted cells. (In the latter case Algorithm D should increase N and test for overflow only when inserting an item into a previously *empty* position, since N represents the number of nonempty positions.) We could also maintain two counters.

22. Suppose that positions $j - 1$, $j - 2$, $\ldots$, $j - k$ are occupied and $j - k - 1$ is empty (modulo M). The keys that probe position j and find it occupied before being inserted are precisely those keys in positions $j - 1$ through $j - k$ whose hash address does not lie between $j - 1$ and $j - k$; such problematical keys appear in the order of insertion. Algorithm R moves the first such key into position j, and repeats the process on a smaller range of problematical positions until no problematical keys remain.

23. A deletion scheme for coalesced chaining devised by J. S. Vitter [*J. Algorithms* **3** (1982), 261–275] preserves the distribution of search times.

24. We have $P(P - 1)(P - 2)P(P - 1)P(P - 1)/(MP(MP - 1)\ldots(MP - 6)) = M^{-7}(1 - (5 - 21/M)P^{-1} + O(P^{-2}))$. In general, the probability of a hash sequence $a_1 \ldots a_N$ is $(\prod_{j=0}^{M-1} P^{\underline{b_j}})/(MP)^{\underline{N}} = M^{-N} + O(P^{-1})$, where b_j is the number of a_i that equal j.

25. Let the $(N + 1)$st key hash to location a; P_k is M^{-N} times the number of hash sequences that leave the k locations a, $a - 1$, $\ldots$, $a - k + 1$ (modulo M) occupied and

$a - k$ empty. The number of such sequences with $a+1, \ldots, a+t$ occupied and $a+t+1$ empty is $g(M, N, t+k)$, by circular symmetry of the algorithm.

26. $\dfrac{9!}{2!\,2!\,4!\,1!}\,f(3, 2)\,f(3, 2)\,f(5, 4)\,f(2, 1) = 2^2 3^5 5^4 7 = 4252500.$

27. Following the hint,

$$s(n, x, y) = \sum_k \binom{n}{k} x(x+k)^k (y-k)^{n-k-1}(y-n) + n \sum_k \binom{n-1}{k-1}(x+k)^k(y-k)^{n-k-1}(y-n).$$

In the first sum, replace k by $n - k$ and apply Abel's formula; in the second, replace k by $k + 1$. Now

$$g(M, N, k) = \binom{N}{k}(k + 1)^{k-1}(M - k - 1)^{N-k-1}(M - N - 1),$$

with $0/0 = 1$ when $k = N = M - 1$, and

$$M^N \sum_{k \geq 0} (k + 1)P_k = \sum_{k \geq 0} \binom{k + 2}{2} g(M, N, k)$$

$$= \frac{1}{2}\left(\sum_{k \geq 0}(k + 1)g(M, N, k) + \sum_{k \geq 0}(k + 1)^2 g(M, N, k)\right).$$

The first sum is $M^N \sum P_k = M^N$, and the second is $s(N, 1, M-1) = M^N + 2N M^{N-1} + 3N(N - 1)M^{N-2} + \cdots = M^N Q_1(M, N)$. [See J. Riordan, *Combinatorial Identities* (New York: Wiley, 1968), 18–23, for further study of sums like $s(n, x, y)$.]

28. Let $t(n, x, y) = \sum_{k \geq 0}\binom{n}{k}(x + k)^{k+2}(y - k)^{n-k-1}(y - n)$; then as in exercise 27 we find $t(n, x, y) = xs(n, x, y) + nt(n-1, x+1, y-1)$, $t(N, 1, M-1) = M^N(3Q_3(M, N) - 2Q_2(M, N))$. Thus $\sum(k+1)^2 P_k = M^{-N}\sum(\frac{1}{3}(k+1)^3 + \frac{1}{2}(k+1)^2 + \frac{1}{6}(k+1))g(M, N, k) = Q_3(M, N) - \frac{2}{3}Q_2(M, N) + \frac{1}{2}Q_1(M, N) + \frac{1}{6}$. Subtracting $(C'_N)^2$ gives the variance, which is approximately $\frac{3}{4}(1 - \alpha)^{-4} - \frac{2}{3}(1 - \alpha)^{-3} - \frac{1}{12}$. The standard deviation is often larger than the mean; for example, when $\alpha = .9$ the mean is 50.5 and the standard deviation is $\frac{1}{2}\sqrt{27333} \approx 82.7$.

29. Let $M = m+1$, $N = n$; the safe parking sequences are precisely those in which location 0 is empty when Algorithm L is applied to the hash sequence $(M - a_1)\ldots(M - a_n)$. Hence the answer is $f(m+1, n) = (m + 1)^n - n(m + 1)^{n-1}$. [This problem originated with A. G. Konheim and B. Weiss, *SIAM J. Applied Math.* **14** (1966), 1266–1274.]

30. Obviously if the cars get parked they define such a permutation. Conversely, if $p_1 p_2 \ldots p_n$ exists, let $q_1 q_2 \ldots q_n$ be the inverse permutation ($q_i = j$ if and only if $p_j = i$), and let b_i be the number of a_j that equal i. Every car will be parked if we can prove that $b_n \leq 1$, $b_{n-1} + b_n \leq 2$, etc.; equivalently $b_1 \geq 1$, $b_1 + b_2 \geq 2$, etc. But this is clearly true, since the k elements $a_{q_1}, \ldots, a_{q_k}$ are all $\leq k$.

[Let r_j be the "left influence" of q_j, namely $r_j = k$ if and only if $q_{j-1} < q_j, \ldots$, $q_{j-k-1} < q_j$ and either $j = k$ or $q_{j-k} > q_j$. Of all permutations $p_1 \ldots p_n$ that dominate a given wakeup sequence $a_1 \ldots a_n$, the "park immediately" algorithm finds the smallest one (in lexicographic order). Konheim and Weiss observed that the number of wakeup sequences leading to a given permutation $p_1 \ldots p_n$ is $\prod_{j=1}^{n} r_j$; it is remarkable that the sum of these products, taken over all permutations $q_1 \ldots q_n$, is $(n + 1)^{n-1}$.]

31. Many interesting connections are possible, and the following three are the author's favorites [see also Foata and Riordan, *Æquat. Math.* **10** (1974), 10–22]:

a) In the notation of the previous answer, the counts $b_1, b_2, \ldots, b_n$ correspond to a full parking sequence if and only if $(b_1, b_2, \ldots, b_n, 0)$ is a valid sequence of *degrees* of tree nodes in preorder. (Compare with 2.3.3–(9), which illustrates postorder.) Every such tree corresponds to $n!/b_1! \ldots b_n!$ distinct labeled free trees on $\{0, \ldots, n\}$, since we can let 0 be the label of the root, and for $k = 1, 2, \ldots, n$ we can successively choose the labels of the children of the kth node in preorder in $(b_k + \cdots + b_n)!/b_k! \, (b_{k+1} + \cdots + b_n)!$ ways from the remaining unused labels, attaching labels from left to right in increasing order. And every such sequence of counts corresponds to $n!/b_1! \ldots b_n!$ wakeup sequences.

b) Dominique Foata has given the following pretty one-to-one correspondence: Let $a_1 \ldots a_n$ be a safe parking sequence, which leaves car q_j parked in space j. A labeled free tree on $\{0, 1, \ldots, n\}$ is constructed by drawing a line from j to 0 when $a_j = 1$, and from j to $q_{a_j - 1}$ otherwise, for $1 \le j \le n$. (Think of the tree nodes as cars; car j is connected to the car that eventually winds up parked just before where wife j woke up.) For example, the wakeup times 3 1 4 1 5 9 2 6 5 lead to the free tree

by Foata's rule. Conversely, The sequence of parked cars may be obtained from the tree by topological sorting, assuming that arrows emanate from the root 0 and choosing the smallest "source" at each step. From this sequence, $a_1 \ldots a_n$ can be reconstructed.

c) First construct an auxiliary tree by letting the parent of node k be the first element $> k$ that follows k in the permutation $q_1 \ldots q_n$; if there's no such element, let the parent be 0. Then make a copy of the auxiliary tree and relabel the nonzero nodes of the new tree by proceeding as follows, in preorder: If the label of the current node was k in the auxiliary tree, swap its current label with the label that is currently $(1 + p_k - a_k)$th smallest in its subtree. For example,

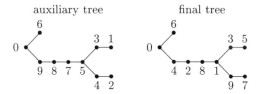

To reverse the procedure, we can reconstruct the auxiliary tree by proceeding in preorder to swap the label of each node with the largest label currently in its subtree.

Constructions (a) and (b) are strongly related, but construction (c) is quite different. It has the interesting property that the sum of displacements of cars from their preferred locations is equal to the number of *inversions* in the tree — the number of pairs of labels $a > b$ where a is an ancestor of b. This relation between parking sequences and tree inversions was first discovered by G. Kreweras [*Periodica Math. Hung.* **11** (1980), 309–320]. The fact that tree inversions are intimately related to connected graphs [Mallows and Riordan, *Bull. Amer. Math. Soc.* **74** (1968), 92–94] now makes it possible to deduce that the sum of $\binom{D(p)}{k}$ taken over all parking sequences, where $D(p) = (p_1 - a_1) + \cdots + (p_n - a_n)$, is equal to the total number of connected graphs with $n + k$ edges on the labeled vertices $\{0, 1, \ldots, n\}$. [See equations (2.11), (3.5), and

(8.13) in the paper by Janson, Łuczak, Knuth, and Pittel, *Random Struct. & Alg.* **4** (1993), 233–358.]

32. Let subscripts be treated cyclically, so that $c_M = c_0$, $c_{M+1} = c_1$, etc. There is no solution with $c_j = b_j + c_{j+1} - 1$ for all j, since the sum over all j would give $\sum c_j = \sum b_j + \sum c_j - M < \sum c_j$. Hence every solution has $M - \sum b_j$ values of j such that $b_j = c_{j+1} = 0$. If $(c'_0, \ldots, c'_{M-1})$ is a different solution we must have $c'_{j+1} > 0$ for at least one such j; but this implies $c'_{j+2} > c_{j+2}$, $c'_{j+3} > c_{j+3}, \ldots$, a contradiction. The solution can be found by defining c_{M-1}, c_{M-2}, $\ldots$ on the assumption that $c_0 = 0$; then if c_0 turns out to be greater than 0, it suffices to redefine c_{M-1}, c_{M-2}, $\ldots$ until no more changes are made.

33. The individual probabilities are not independent, since the condition $b_0 + b_1 + \cdots + b_{M-1} = N$ was not taken into account; the derivation allows a nonzero probability that $\sum b_j$ has any given nonnegative value. Equations (46) are not strictly correct; they imply, for example, that q_k is positive for all k, contradicting the fact that c_j can never exceed $N - 1$.

Gaston Gonnet and Ian Munro [*J. Algorithms* **5** (1984), 451–470] have found an interesting way to derive the exact result from the argument leading up to (51) by introducing a useful operation called the *Poisson transform* of a sequence $\langle A_{mn} \rangle$: We have $e^{-mz} \sum_n A_{mn}(mz)^n/n! = \sum_k a_k z^k$ if and only if $A_{mn} = \sum_k a_k n^k/m^k$.

34. (a) There are $\binom{N}{k}$ ways to choose the set of j such that a_j has a particular value, and $(M-1)^{N-k}$ ways to assign values to the other a's. Therefore

$$P_{Nk} = \binom{N}{k}(M-1)^{N-k}/M^N.$$

(b) $P_N(z) = B(z)$ in (50). (c) Consider the total number of probes to find all keys, not counting the fetching of the pointer in the list head table of Fig. 38 if such a table is used. A list of length k contributes $\binom{k+1}{2}$ to the total; hence

$$C_N = M \sum \binom{k+1}{2} P_{Nk}/N = (M/N)(\tfrac{1}{2}P''_N(1) + P'_N(1)).$$

(d) In case (i) a list of length k requires k probes (not counting the list-head fetch), while in case (ii) it requires $k + \delta_{k0}$. Thus in case (ii) we get $C'_N = \sum (k + \delta_{k0})P_{Nk} = P'_N(1) + P_N(0) = N/M + (1 - 1/M)^N \approx \alpha + e^{-\alpha}$, while case (i) has simply $C'_N = N/M = \alpha$. The formula $MC'_N = M - N + NC_N$ applies in case (iii), since $M - N$ hash addresses will discover an empty table position while N will cause searching to the end of some list from a point within it; this yields (18).

35. (i) $\sum (1 + \tfrac{1}{2}k - (k+1)^{-1})P_{Nk} = 1 + N/(2M) - M(1 - (1 - 1/M)^{N+1})/(N+1) \approx 1 + \tfrac{1}{2}\alpha - (1 - e^{-\alpha})/\alpha$. (ii) Add $\sum \delta_{k0}P_{Nk} = (1 - 1/M)^N \approx e^{-\alpha}$ to the result of (i). (iii) Assume that when an unsuccessful search begins at the jth element of a list of length k, the given key has random order with respect to the other k elements, so the expected length of search is $(j \cdot 1 + 2 + \cdots + (k + 1 - j) + (k + 1 - j))/(k + 1)$. Summing on j now gives $MC'_N = M - N + M \sum (k^3 + 9k^2 + 2k)P_{Nk}/(6k+6) = M - N + M(\tfrac{1}{6}N(N-1)/M^2 + \tfrac{3}{2}N/M - 1 + (M/(N+1))(1 - (1 - 1/M)^{N+1}))$; hence $C'_N \approx \tfrac{1}{2}\alpha + \tfrac{1}{6}\alpha^2 + (1 - e^{-\alpha})/\alpha$.

36. (i) $N/M - N/M^2$. (ii) $\sum (\delta_{k0} + k)^2 P_{Nk} = \sum (\delta_{k0} + k^2)P_{Nk} = P_N(0) + P''_N(1) + P'_N(1)$. Subtracting $(C'_N)^2$ gives the answer, $(M-1)N/M^2 + (1 - 1/M)^N(1 - 2N/M - (1 - 1/M)^N) \approx \alpha + e^{-\alpha}(1 - 2\alpha - e^{-\alpha}) \leq 1 - e^{-1} - e^{-2} = 0.4968$. [For data structure (iii), a more complicated analysis like that in exercise 37 would be necessary.]

37. Let S_N be the average value of $(C - 1)^2$, considering all $M^N N$ choices of hash sequences and keys to be equally likely. Then

$$M^N N S_N = \frac{1}{3} \sum \binom{N}{k_1, \ldots, k_M} \left(k_1(k_1 - \tfrac{1}{2})(k_1 - 1) + \cdots + k_M(k_M - \tfrac{1}{2})(k_M - 1) \right)$$

$$= \frac{1}{3} M \sum_k \binom{N}{k} (M - 1)^{N-k} k(k - \tfrac{1}{2})(k - 1)$$

$$= \frac{1}{3} M N(N - 1)(N - 2) \sum_k \binom{N - 3}{k - 3} (M - 1)^{N-k}$$

$$+ \frac{1}{2} M N(N - 1) \sum_k \binom{N - 2}{k - 2} (M - 1)^{N-k}$$

$$= \frac{1}{3} M N(N - 1)(N - 2) M^{N-3} + \frac{1}{2} M N(N - 1) M^{N-2}.$$

The variance is $S_N - ((N - 1)/2M)^2 = (N - 1)(N + 6M - 5)/12M^2 \approx \frac{1}{2}\alpha + \frac{1}{12}\alpha^2$.

See *CMath* §8.5 for interesting connections between the total variance calculated here and two other notions of variance: the variance (over random hash tables) of the average number of probes (over all items present), and the average (over random hash tables) of the variance of the number of probes (over all items present). The total variance is always the sum of the other two; and in this case the variance of the average number of probes is $(M - 1)(N - 1)/(2M^2 N)$.

38. The average number of probes is $\sum P_{Nk}(2H_{k+1} - 2 + \delta_{k0})$ in the unsuccessful case, $(M/N) \sum P_{Nk} k(2(1 + 1/k)H_k - 3)$ in the successful case, by Eqs. 6.2.2–(5) and 6.2.2–(6). These sums are $2f(N) + 2M(1 - (1 - 1/M)^{N+1})/(N + 1) + (1 - 1/M)^N - 2$ and $2(M/N)f(N) + 2f(N - 1) + 2M(1 - (1 - 1/M)^N)/N - 3$, respectively, where $f(N) = \sum P_{Nk} H_k$. Exercise 5.2.1–40 tells us that $f(N) = \ln \alpha + \gamma + E_1(\alpha) + O(M^{-1})$ when $N = \alpha M$, $M \to \infty$.

[Tree hashing was first proposed by P. F. Windley, *Comp. J.* **3** (1960), 84–88. The analysis in the previous paragraph shows that tree hashing is not enough better than simple chaining to justify the extra link fields; the lists are short anyway. Moreover, when M is small, tree hashing is not enough better than pure tree search to justify the hashing time.]

39. (This approach to the analysis of Algorithm C was suggested by J. S. Vitter.) We have $c_{N+1}(k) = (M - k)c_N(k) + (k - 1)c_N(k - 1)$ for $k \geq 2$, and furthermore $\sum k c_N(k) = N M^N$. Hence

$$S_{N+1} = \sum_{k \geq 2} \binom{k}{2} c_{N+1}(k) = \sum_{k \geq 2} \binom{k}{2} \left((M - k)c_N(k) + (k - 1)c_N(k - 1) \right)$$

$$= \sum_{k \geq 1} \left((M + 2)\binom{k}{2} + k \right) c_N(k) = (M + 2)S_N + N M^N.$$

Consequently $S_N = (N - 1)M^{N-1} + (N - 2)M^{N-2}(M + 2) + \cdots + M(M + 2)^{N-2} = \frac{1}{4}(M(M + 2)^N - M^{N+1} - 2N M^N)$.

Consider the total number of probes in unsuccessful searches, summed over all M values of $h(K)$; each list of length k contributes $k + \delta_{k0} + \binom{k}{2}$ to the total, hence $M^{N+1} C'_N = M^{N+1} + S_N$.

40. Define U_N to be like S_N in exercise 39, but with $\binom{k}{2}$ replaced by $\binom{k+1}{3}$. We find $U_{N+1} = (M+3)U_N + S_N + NM^N$, hence

$$U_N = \tfrac{1}{36}\big(M^N(M-6N) - 9M(M+2)^N + 8M(M+3)^N\big).$$

The variance is $2U_N/M^{N+1} + C'_N - (C'_N)^2$, which approaches

$$\tfrac{35}{144} - \tfrac{1}{12}\alpha - \tfrac14\alpha^2 + (\tfrac14\alpha - \tfrac58)e^{2\alpha} + \tfrac49 e^{3\alpha} - \tfrac{1}{16}e^{4\alpha}$$

for $N = \alpha M$, $M \to \infty$. When $\alpha = 1$ this is about 4.50, so the standard deviation is bounded by 2.12.

41. Let V_N be the average length of the block of occupied cells at the "high" end of the table. The probability that this block has length k is $A_{Nk}(M-1-k)^{\underline{N-k}}/M^N$, where A_{Nk} is the number of hash sequences (35) such that Algorithm C leaves the first $N-k$ and the last k cells occupied and such that the subsequence $1\,2\,\ldots\,N{-}k$ appears in increasing order. Therefore

$$M^N V_N = \sum_k k A_{Nk}(M-1-k)^{\underline{N-k}} = M^{N+1} - \sum_k(M-k)A_{Nk}(M-1-k)^{\underline{N-k}}$$
$$= M^{N+1} - (M-N)\sum_k A_{Nk}(M-k)^{\underline{N-k}} = M^{N+1} - (M-N)(M+1)^N.$$

Now $T_N = (N/M)(1+V_N-T_0-\cdots-T_{N-1})$, since $T_0+\cdots+T_{N-1}$ is the average number of times R has previously decreased and N/M is the probability that it decreases on the current step. The solution to this recurrence is $T_N = (N/M)(1+1/M)^N$. (Such a simple formula deserves a simpler proof!)

42. $S1_N$ is the number of items that were inserted with $A = 0$, divided by N.

43. Let $N = \alpha M'$ and $M = \beta M'$, and let $e^{-\lambda} + \lambda = 1/\beta$, $\rho = \alpha/\beta$. Then $C_N \approx 1 + \tfrac12\rho$ and $C'_N \approx \rho + e^{-\rho}$, if $\rho \le \lambda$; $C_N \approx \tfrac{1}{8\rho}(e^{2\rho-2\lambda}-1-2\rho+2\lambda)(3-2/\beta+2\lambda) + \tfrac14(\rho+2\lambda-\lambda^2/\rho)$ and $C'_N \approx 1/\beta + \tfrac14(e^{2\rho-2\lambda}-1)(3-2/\beta+2\lambda) - \tfrac12(\rho-\lambda)$, if $\rho \ge \lambda$. For $\alpha = 1$ we get the smallest $C_N \approx 1.69$ when $\beta \approx .853$; the smallest $C'_N \approx 1.79$ occurs when $\beta \approx .782$. The setting $\beta = .86$ gives near-optimal search performance for a wide range of α. So it pays to put the first collisions into an area that doesn't conflict with hash addresses, even though a smaller range of hash addresses will cause more collisions to occur. These results are due to Jeffrey S. Vitter, *JACM* **30** (1983), 231–258.

44. (The following brute-force approach was the solution found by the author in 1972; a much more elegant solution by M. S. Paterson is explained in *Mathematics for the Analysis of Algorithms* by Greene and Knuth (Birkhäuser Boston, 1980), §3.4. Paterson also found significant ways to simplify several other analyses in this section.)

Number the positions of the array from 1 to m, left to right. Considering the set of all $\binom{n}{k}$ sequences of operations with k "p steps" and $n-k$ "q steps" to be equally likely, let $g(m, n+1, k, r)$ be $\binom{n}{k}$ times the probability that the first $r-1$ positions become occupied and the rth remains empty. Thus $g(m, l, k, r)$ is $(m-1)^{-(l-1-k)}$ times the sum, over all configurations

$$1 \le a_1 < \cdots < a_k < l, \qquad (c_1, \ldots, c_{l-1-k}), \qquad 2 \le c_i \le m,$$

of the probability that the first empty location is r, when the a_jth operation is a p step and the remaining $l-1-k$ operations are q steps that begin by selecting positions $c_1, \ldots, c_{l-1-k}$, respectively. By summing over all configurations subject to the further condition that the a_jth operation occupies position b_j, given $1 \le b_1 < \cdots < b_k < r$, we obtain the recurrence

$$g(m, l, k+1, r) = \sum_{\substack{a<l \\ b<r \\ 1\le b\le a}} \frac{(l-b-1)!}{(l-r)!} \frac{(m-r)!}{(m-b)!}(m-l+1)g(m,a,k,b);$$

$$g(m,l,0,r) = \frac{(l-1)!}{(l-r)!} \frac{(m-r)!}{m!}(m-l+1)\left(P_l + [r\ne 1]\frac{m}{l-1}(1-P_l)\right),$$

where $P_l = (m/(m-1))^{l-1}$. Letting $G(m,l,k) = \sum_{r=1}^{l}(m+1-r)g(m,l,k,r)$, it follows that

$$G(m,l,k+1) = \frac{m-l+1}{m-l+2}\sum_{a=1}^{l-1}G(m,a,k); \qquad G(m,l,0) = \frac{m-l+1}{m-l+2}(m+P_l).$$

The answer to the stated problem is $m - \sum_{k=0}^{n} p^k q^{n-k} G(m, n+1, k)$, which (after some maneuvering) equals $m - ((m-n)/(m-n+1))(Q_n + mR + pSR)$, where

$$Q_j = P_{j+1}q^j,$$

$$R = \left(1 - \frac{p}{m+1}\right)\left(1 - \frac{p}{m}\right)\cdots\left(1 - \frac{p}{m-n+2}\right) = \prod_{j=0}^{n-1}\left(1 - \frac{p}{m+1-j}\right),$$

$$S = \frac{\left(1 - \frac{1}{m+1}\right)Q_0}{\left(1 - \frac{p}{m+1}\right)} + \frac{\left(1 - \frac{1}{m}\right)Q_1}{\left(1 - \frac{p}{m+1}\right)\left(1 - \frac{p}{m}\right)} + \cdots + \frac{1 - \left(\frac{1}{m-n+2}\right)Q_{n-1}}{R}$$

$$= \sum_{k=0}^{n-1} \frac{(1 - 1/(m+1-k))Q_k}{\prod_{j=0}^{k}(1-p/(m+1-j))}.$$

When $p = 1/m$, $Q_j = 1$ for all j. Letting $w = m+1$, $n = \alpha w$, $w \to \infty$, we find $\ln R = -(H_w - H_{w(1-\alpha)})p + O(p^2)$; hence $R = 1 + w^{-1}\ln(1-\alpha) + O(w^{-2})$; and similarly $S = \alpha w + O(1)$. Thus the answer is $(1-\alpha)^{-1} - 1 - \alpha - \ln(1-\alpha) + O(w^{-1})$.

Notes: The simpler problem "with probability p occupy the leftmost, otherwise occupy any randomly chosen empty position" is solved by taking $P_j = 1$ in the formulas above, and the answer is $m - (m+1)(m-n)R/(m-n+1)$. To get C'_N for random probing with secondary clustering, set $n = N$, $m = M$ and add 1 to the answer above.

45. Yes. See L. Guibas, *JACM* **25** (1978), 544–555.

46. Define the numbers $[[\begin{smallmatrix}n\\k\end{smallmatrix}]]$ for $k \ge 0$ by the rule

$$\sum_k \binom{x+k}{k}\left[\!\left[\begin{matrix}n\\k\end{matrix}\right]\!\right] = (x+n+1)^n$$

for all x and all nonnegative integers n. Setting $x = -1, -2, \ldots, -n-1$ implies that

$$\left[\!\left[\begin{matrix}n\\k\end{matrix}\right]\!\right] = \sum_j \binom{k}{j}(-1)^j(n-j)^n \qquad \text{for } 0 \le k \le n;$$

then setting $x = 0$ implies that we may take $[[\begin{smallmatrix}n\\k\end{smallmatrix}]] = 0$ for all $k > n$, so the two sides of the defining equation are polynomials in x of degree n that agree on $n+1$ points. It follows that the numbers $[[\begin{smallmatrix}n\\k\end{smallmatrix}]]$ have the stated property.

Let $f(N,r)$ be the number of hash sequences $a_1 \ldots a_N$ that leave the first r locations occupied and the next one empty. There are $\binom{M-r-1}{N-r}$ possible patterns of occupied cells, and each pattern occurs as many times as there are sequences $a_1' \ldots a_N'$, $1 \le a_i' \le N$, that contain each of the numbers $r+1$, $r+2$, $\ldots$, N at least once. By inclusion-exclusion, there are $\left[\left[\begin{smallmatrix} N \\ N-r \end{smallmatrix}\right]\right]$ such sequences; hence

$$f(N,r) = \binom{M-r-1}{N-r}\left[\left[\begin{matrix} N \\ N-r \end{matrix}\right]\right].$$

Now

$$C_N' = 1 + M^{-N-1} \sum_{r=0}^{N} f(N,r)\left(\sum_{a=0}^{r-1} r + \sum_{a=r+1}^{M-1} \frac{N-r}{M-r-1}(r+1)\right)$$

$$= 1 + M^{-N-1} \sum_{r=0}^{N} f(N,r)\big(N + (N-1)r\big).$$

Let $S_n(x) = \sum_k k\binom{x+k}{k}\left[\left[\begin{smallmatrix} n \\ k \end{smallmatrix}\right]\right]$; we have

$$(x+1)^{-1}S_n(x) + \sum_k \binom{x+k}{k}\left[\left[\begin{matrix} n \\ k \end{matrix}\right]\right] = \sum_k \binom{x+1+k}{k}\left[\left[\begin{matrix} n \\ k \end{matrix}\right]\right];$$

hence $S_n(x) = (x+1)\big((x+n+2)^n - (x+n+1)^n\big)$. It follows that $C_N' = N(1+1/M) - (N-1)(1-N/M)(1+1/M)^N \approx N(1-(1-\alpha)e^\alpha)$; and $C_N = (N-1)\big((1+1/M)/2 + (1+1/M)^N\big) + (3M^2 + 6M + 2)\big((1+1/M)^N - 1\big)/N - (3M+2)(1+1/M)^N$, which is $(e-2.5)M + O(1)$ when $N = M - 1$.

For further properties of the numbers $\left[\left[\begin{smallmatrix} n \\ k \end{smallmatrix}\right]\right]$, see John Riordan, *Combinatorial Identities* (New York: Wiley, 1968), 228–229.

47. The analysis of Algorithm L applies, almost word for word! Any probe sequence with cyclic symmetry, and which explores only positions adjacent to those previously examined, will have the same behavior.

48. $C_N' = 1 + p + p^2 + \cdots$, where $p = N/M$ is the probability that a random location is filled; hence $C_N' = M/(M-N)$, and $C_N = N^{-1}\sum_{k=0}^{N-1} C_k' = N^{-1}M(H_M - H_{M-N})$. These values are approximately equal to those for uniform probing, but slightly higher because of the chance of repeated probes in the same place. Indeed, for $4 = N < M \le 16$, linear probing is better!

In practice we wouldn't use infinitely many hash functions; some other scheme like linear probing would ultimately be used as a last resort. This method is inferior to those described in the text, but it is of historical importance because it suggested Morris's method, which led to Algorithm D. See *CACM* **6** (1963), 101, where M. D. McIlroy credits the idea to V. A. Vyssotsky; the same technique had been discovered as early as 1956 by A. W. Holt, who used it successfully in the GPX system for the UNIVAC.

49. $C_N' - 1 = \sum_{k>b}(k-b)P_{Nk} \approx \sum_{k>b}(k-b)e^{-\alpha b}(\alpha b)^k/k! = \alpha b t_b(\alpha)$. [*Note:* We have

$$\sum_{b\ge 0}\left(\sum_{k>b}(k-b)P_k\right)z^b = \frac{P'(1)}{1-z} + \frac{z(P(z)-1)}{(1-z)^2}$$

in general, if $P(z) = P_0 + P_1 z + \cdots$ is any probability generating function.] And

$$C_N - 1 = \frac{M}{N} \sum_{k>b} \binom{k-b+1}{2} P_{Nk}$$

$$= \frac{M}{2N} \sum_{k>b} (k(k-1) - 2k(b-1) + b(b-1)) P_{Nk}$$

$$= \tfrac{1}{2} e^{-b\alpha} (b\alpha)^b b!^{-1} (b + b\alpha - 2b + 2 + (b\alpha^2 - 2\alpha(b-1) + b - 1) R(\alpha, b)).$$

[The analysis of successful search with chaining was first carried out by W. P. Heising in 1957. The simple expressions in (57) and (58) were found by J. A. van der Pool in 1971; he also considered how to minimize a function that represents the combined cost of storage space and number of accesses. We can determine the variance of C_N' and of the number of overflows per bucket, since $\sum_{k>b}(k-b)^2 P_{Nk} = (2N/M)(C_N - 1) - (C_N' - 1)$. The variance of the total number of overflows may be approximated by M times the variance in a single bucket, but this is actually too high because the total number of records is constrained to be N. The true variance can be found as in exercise 37. See also the derivation of the chi-square test in Section 3.3.1C.]

50. And next that $Q_0(M, N-1) = (M/N)(Q_0(M, N) - 1)$. In general, $rQ_r(M, N) = MQ_{r-2}(M, N) - (M - N - r)Q_{r-1}(M, N) = M(Q_{r-1}(M, N+1) - Q_{r-1}(M, N))$; $Q_r(M, N-1) = (M/N)(Q_r(M, N) - Q_{r-1}(M, N))$.

51. $R(\alpha, n) = \alpha^{-1}(n! e^{\alpha n}(\alpha n)^{-n} - Q_0(\alpha n, n))$.

52. See Eq. 1.2.11.3–(9) and exercise 3.1–14.

53. By Eq. 1.2.11.3–(8), $\alpha(\alpha n)^n R(\alpha, n) = e^{\alpha n}\gamma(n+1, \alpha n)$; hence by the suggested exercise $R(\alpha, n) = (1-\alpha)^{-1} - (1-\alpha)^{-3}n^{-1} + O(n^{-2})$. [This asymptotic formula can be obtained more directly by the method of (43), if we note that the coefficient of α^k in $R(\alpha, n)$ is

$$1 - \binom{k+2}{2} n^{-1} + O(k^4 n^{-2}).$$

In fact, the coefficient of α^k is

$$\sum_{r\geq 0}(-1)^r n^{-r} \left\{ \begin{matrix} r+k+1 \\ k+1 \end{matrix} \right\}$$

by Eq. 1.2.9–(28).]

54. Using the hint together with Eqs. 1.2.6–(53) and 1.2.6–(49), we have

$$\sum_{b\geq 1} t_b(\alpha) = \sum_{m\geq 1} \frac{\alpha^m}{(m+1)(m)m!} \sum_k \binom{m}{k}(-1)^{m-k}k^{m+1} = \sum_{m\geq 1} \alpha^m/2.$$

The hint follows from Kummer's well-known hypergeometric identity $e^{-z}F(a; b; z) = F(b-a; b; -z)$, since $(n+1)! t_n(\alpha) = e^{-n\alpha}(\alpha n)^n F(2; n+2; \alpha n)$; see *Crelle* **15** (1836), 39–83, 127–172, Eq. 26.4.

55. If $B(z)C(z) = \sum s_i z^i$, we have $c_0 = s_0 + \cdots + s_b$, $c_1 = s_{b+1}$, $c_2 = s_{b+2}$, ...; hence $B(z)C(z) = z^b C(z) + Q(z)$. Now $P(z) = z^b$ has $b-1$ roots q_j with $|q_j| < 1$, determined as the solutions to $e^{\alpha(q_j-1)} = \omega^{-j}q_j$, $\omega = e^{2\pi i/b}$. To solve $e^{\alpha(q-1)} = \omega^{-1}q$, let $t = \alpha q$

and $z = \alpha\omega e^{-\alpha}$ so that $t = ze^t$. By Lagrange's formula we get

$$\frac{1}{1-q} = 1 + \sum_{r\geq 0} r \sum_{n\geq r} \frac{n^{n-r-1}\omega^n\alpha^{n-r}e^{-n\alpha}}{(n-r)!}$$

$$= 1 + \sum_{r\geq 1} r \sum_{m\geq 0} \frac{\alpha^m}{m!}(-1)^m \sum_{n\geq r} \binom{m}{n-r}(-1)^{n-r}\omega^n n^{m-1}.$$

By Abel's limit theorem, letting $|\omega| \to 1$ from inside the unit circle, this can be rearranged to equal

$$\frac{1-\alpha\omega}{1-\omega} + \sum_{m\geq 2} \frac{\alpha^m}{m!}(-1)^m \sum_{n\geq 0} \binom{m-2}{n}(-1)^n\omega^{n+1}(n+1)^{m-1}.$$

Now replacing ω by ω^j and summing for $1 \leq j < b$ yields

$$\frac{b-1}{2} + \alpha\frac{b-1}{2} + \sum_{m\geq 2} \alpha^m\left(-\frac{1}{2} + \frac{(-1)^m}{m!}b\sum_{n\geq 1}\binom{m-2}{nb-1}(-1)^{nb-1}(nb)^{m-1}\right)$$

and the desired result follows after some more juggling using the hint of exercise 54.

This analysis, applied to a variety of problems, was begun by N. T. J. Bailey, *J. Roy. Stat. Soc.* **B16** (1954), 80–87; M. Tainiter, *JACM* **10** (1963), 307–315; A. G. Konheim and B. Meister, *JACM* **19** (1972), 92–108.

56. See Blake and Konheim, *JACM* **24** (1977), 591–606. Alfredo Viola and Patricio Poblete [*Algorithmica* **21** (1998), to appear] have shown that

$$C_{Mb} = 1 + \frac{M-1}{2Mb} + \frac{1}{b}\sum_{j\geq 2}\binom{bm-1}{j}m^{-j}\sum_{k\geq 1}\binom{j-2}{bk-1}(-1)^{j+bk-1}k^{j-1}$$

$$= \sqrt{\frac{\pi M}{8b}} + \frac{1}{3b} + \frac{1}{b}\sum_{j=1}^{b-1}\frac{1}{(1-T(e^{2\pi ij/b-1}))} + \frac{1}{24}\sqrt{\frac{\pi}{2b^3 M}} + O(b^{-2}M^{-1}),$$

where T is the tree function of Eq. 2.3.4.4–(30).

58. 0 1 2 3 4 and 0 2 4 1 3, plus additive shifts of 1 1 1 1 1 mod 5, each with probability $\frac{1}{10}$. Similarly, for $M = 6$ we need 30 permutations, and a solution exists starting with

$$\tfrac{1}{20} \times 0\,1\,2\,3\,4\,5, \quad \tfrac{1}{60} \times 0\,1\,3\,2\,5\,4, \quad \tfrac{1}{60} \times 0\,2\,4\,3\,1\,5, \quad \tfrac{1}{20} \times 0\,2\,3\,4\,5\,1, \quad \tfrac{1}{30} \times 0\,3\,4\,1\,2\,5.$$

For $M = 7$ we need 49, and a solution is generated by

$$\tfrac{1}{35} \times 0\,1\,2\,3\,4\,5\,6, \quad \tfrac{2}{105} \times 0\,1\,5\,3\,2\,4\,6, \quad \tfrac{1}{35} \times 0\,2\,4\,3\,5\,1\,6, \quad \tfrac{2}{105} \times 0\,2\,6\,3\,1\,4\,5,$$

$$\tfrac{1}{35} \times 0\,3\,6\,1\,4\,2\,5, \quad \tfrac{1}{105} \times 0\,3\,2\,6\,4\,1\,5, \quad \tfrac{1}{105} \times 0\,3\,1\,5\,4\,2\,6.$$

59. No permutation can have a probability larger than $1/\binom{M}{\lfloor M/2\rfloor}$, so there must be at least $\binom{M}{\lfloor M/2\rfloor} = \exp(M\ln 2 + O(\log M))$ permutations with nonzero probability.

60. Preliminary results have been obtained by Ajtai, Komlós, and Szemerédi, *Information Processing Letters* **7** (1978), 270–273.

62. See the discussion in *AMM* **81** (1974), 323–343, where the best cyclic hashing sequences are exhibited for $M \leq 9$.

63. MH_M, by exercise 3.3.2–8; the standard deviation is $\approx \pi M/\sqrt{6}$.

64. The average number of moves is equal to $\frac{1}{2}(N-1)/M + \frac{2}{3}(N-1)(N-2)/M^2 + \frac{3}{4}(N-1)(N-2)(N-3)/M^3 + \cdots \approx \frac{1}{1-\alpha} - \frac{1}{\alpha}\ln\frac{1}{1-\alpha}$. [An equivalent problem is solved in *Comp. J.* **17** (1974), 139–140.]

65. The keys can be stored in a separate table, allocated sequentially (assuming that deletions, if any, are LIFO). The hash table entries point to this "names table"; for example, TABLE[i] might have the form

$$\boxed{}\ \boxed{}\ \boxed{}\ \boxed{\text{L}_i}\ \boxed{\text{KEY}[i]}\,,$$

where L$_i$ is the number of words in the key stored at locations KEY[i], KEY[i]$+1,\ldots$.

The rest of the hash table entry might be used in any of several ways: (i) as a link for Algorithm C; (ii) as part of the information associated with the key; or (iii) as a "secondary hash code." The latter idea, suggested by Robert Morris, sometimes speeds up a search [we take a careful look at the key in KEY[i] only if $h_2(K)$ matches its secondary hash code, for some function $h_2(K)$].

66. Yes; and the arrangement of the records is unique. The average number of probes per unsuccessful search is reduced to C_{N-1}', although it remains C_N' when the Nth term is inserted. This important technique is called *ordered hashing*. See *Comp. J.* **17** (1974), 135–142; D. E. Knuth, *Literate Programming* (1992), 144–149, 216–217.

67. (a) If $c_j = 0$ in (44), an optimum arrangement is obtained by sorting the a's into nonincreasing "cyclic order," assuming that $j - 1 > \cdots > 0 > M - 1 > \cdots > j$. (b) Between steps L2 and L3, exchange the record-in-hand with TABLE[i] if the latter is closer to home than the former. [This algorithm, called "Robin Hood hashing" by Celis, Larson, and Munro in *FOCS* **26** (1985), 281–288, is equivalent to a variant of ordered hashing.] (c) Let $h(m,n,d)$ be the number of hash sequences that make $c_0 \le d$. It can be shown [*Comp. J.* **17** (1974), 141] that $(h(m,n,d) - h(m,n,d-1))M$ is the total number of occurrences of displacement $d > 0$ among all M^N hash sequences, and that we can write $h(M,N,d) = a(M,N,d+1) - Na(M,N-1,d+1)$ where $a(m,n,d) = \sum_{k=0}^{d}\binom{n}{k}(m+d-k)^{n-k}(k-d)^k$. An elaborate calculation using the methods of exercises 28 and 50 now shows that the average value of $\sum d_j^2$ is

$$M^{1-N}\sum_{d=1}^{N} d^2\big(h(M,N,d) - h(M,N,d-1)\big)$$

$$= \frac{M^2}{2} + \frac{2M}{3} + \frac{N}{6} + \frac{N^2}{6M} - \frac{N}{6M} - M\left(\frac{M}{2} - \frac{N}{2} + \frac{2}{3}\right)Q_0(M,N)$$

$$= M\left(\frac{1}{2(1-\alpha)^2} - \frac{7}{6(1-\alpha)} + \frac{2}{3} + \frac{\alpha}{6} + \frac{\alpha^2}{6}\right) + O(1)$$

when $N = \alpha M$. Without the modification (see exercise 28), $\mathrm{E}\sum d_j^2$ comes to

$$\frac{M}{3}(Q_2(M,N) - Q_1(M,N)) - \frac{M}{2}(Q_0(M,N) - 1) + \frac{N}{6}$$

$$= M\left(\frac{1}{3(1-\alpha)^3} - \frac{1}{3(1-\alpha)^2} - \frac{1}{2(1-\alpha)} + \frac{1}{2} + \frac{\alpha}{6}\right) + O(1).$$

If the records all have approximately the same displacement d, and if successful searches are significantly more common than unsuccessful ones, it is advantageous to start at position $h' = h(K) + d$ and then to probe $h' - 1$, $h' + 1$, $h' - 2$, etc. P. V. Poblete, A. Viola, and J. I. Munro have shown [*Random Structures and Algorithms*

10 (1997), 221–255] that $\sum d_j^2$ can be made almost as small as in the Robin Hood method by using a much simpler approach called "last-come-first-served" hashing, in which every newly inserted key is placed in its home position; all other keys move one step away until an empty slot is found. The Robin Hood and last-come-first-served techniques apply to double hashing as well as to linear probing, but the reduction in probes does not compensate for the increased time per probe with respect to double hashing unless the table is extremely full. (See Poblete and Munro, *J. Algorithms* **10** (1989), 228–248.)

68. The average value of $(d_1 + \cdots + d_N)^2$ can be shown to equal

$$\frac{N}{12}\big((M-N)^3 + (N+3)(M-N)^2 + (8N+1)(M-N) + 5N^2 + 4N - 1$$

$$- \big((M-N)^3 + 4(M-N)^2 + (6N+3)(M-N) + 8N\big)Q_0(M,N-1)\big)$$

using the connection between the parking problem and connected graphs mentioned in the answer to exercise 31. To get the variance of the average number of probes in a successful search, divide by N^2 and subtract $\frac{1}{4}(Q_0(M,N-1)-1)^2$; this is asymptotically $\frac{1}{12}\big((1+2\alpha)/(1-\alpha)^4 - 1\big)/N + O(N^{-2})$. (See D. E. Knuth, P. Flajolet, P. V. Poblete, and A. Viola, *Algorithmica* (1998), to appear. The variance calculated here should be distinguished from the total variance, which is $\mathrm{E}\sum d_j^2/N - \frac{1}{4}(Q_0(M,N-1)-1)^2$; see the answers to exercises 37 and 67.)

69. Let $q_k = p_k + p_{k+1} + \cdots$; then the inequality $q_k \geq \max(0, 1-(k-1)(M-n)/M)$ gives a lower bound on $C'_N = \sum_{k\geq 1} q_k$.

70. A remarkably simple proof by Lueker and Molodowitch [*Combinatorica* **13** (1993), 83–96] establishes a similar result but with an extra factor $(\log M)^2$ in the O bound; the stated result follows in the same way by using sharper probability estimates. A. Siegel and J. P. Schmidt have shown, in fact, that the expected number of probes in double hashing is $1/(1-\alpha) + O(1/M)$ for fixed $\alpha = N/M$. [Computer Science Tech. Report 687 (New York: Courant Institute, 1995).]

72. [*J. Comp. Syst. Sci.* **18** (1979), 143–154.] (a) Given keys $K_1, \ldots, K_N$ and K, the probability that K_j is in the same list as K is $\leq 1/M$ if $K \neq K_j$. Hence the expected list size is $\leq 1 + (N-1)/M$.

(b) Suppose there are Q possible characters; then there are M^Q possible choices for each h_j. Choosing each h_j at random is equivalent to choosing a random row from a matrix H of M^{Ql} rows and Q^l columns, with the entry $h(x_1 \ldots x_l) = (h_1(x_1) + \cdots + h_l(x_l)) \bmod M$ in column $x_1 \ldots x_l$. In columns $K = x_1 \ldots x_l$ and $K' = x'_1 \ldots x'_l$ with $x_j \neq x'_j$ for some j, we have $h(K) = (s + h_j(x_j)) \bmod M$ and $h(K') = (s' + h_j(x'_j)) \bmod M$, where $s = \sum_{i\neq j} h_i(x_i)$ and $s' = \sum_{i\neq j} h_i(x'_i)$ are independent of h_j. The value of $h_j(x_j) - h_j(x'_j)$ is uniformly distributed modulo M; hence we have $h(K) = h(K')$ with probability $1/M$, regardless of the values of s and s'.

(c) Yes; adding any constant to $h_j(x_j)$ changes $h(x)$ by a constant, modulo M.

73. (i) This is the special case of exercise 72(c) when each key is regarded as a sequence of bits, not characters. (ii) The proof of (b) shows that it suffices to show that $h_j(x_j) - h_j(x'_j)$ is uniform modulo M when $x_j \neq x'_j$. And in fact, the probability that $h_j(x_j) = y$ and $h_j(x'_j) = y'$ is $1/M^2$, for any given y and y', because the congruences $a_j x_j + b_j \equiv y$ and $a_j x'_j + b_j \equiv y'$ have a unique solution (a_j, b_j) for any given (y, y'), modulo the prime M.

When M is not prime and p is a prime $> M$, a similar result holds if we let $h_j(x_j) = ((a_j x_j + b_j) \bmod p) \bmod M$, where a_j and b_j are chosen randomly mod p.

In this case the family is not quite universal, but it comes close enough for practical purposes: The probability that different keys collide is at most $1/M + r(M-r)/Mp^2 \leq 1/M + M/4p^2$, where $r = p \bmod M$.

74. The statement is false in general. For example, suppose $M = N = n^2$, and consider the matrix H with $\binom{N}{n}$ rows, one for every way to put n zeros in different columns; the nonzero entries are $1, 2, \ldots, N - n$ from left to right in each row. This matrix is universal because there are $\binom{N-2}{n-2} = \binom{N}{n}\frac{n}{N}\frac{n-1}{N-1} < \binom{N}{n}\left(\frac{n}{N}\right)^2 = R/M$ matches in every pair of columns. But the number of zeros in every row is $\sqrt{N} \neq O(1) + O(N/M)$.

Notes: This exercise points out that expected list size is quite different from the expected number of collisions when a new key is inserted. Consider letting $h(x_1 \ldots x_l) = h_1(x_1)$, where h_1 is chosen at random. This family of hash functions makes the expected size of every list N/M; yet it is certainly not universal, because a set of N keys that have the same first character x_1 will lead to one list of size N and all other lists empty. The expected number of collisions will be $N(N-1)/2$, but with a universal hash family this number is at most $N(N-1)/2M$, regardless of the set of keys.

On the other hand we *can* show that the expected size of every list is $O(1) + O(N/\sqrt{M})$ in a universal family. Suppose there are z_h zeros in row h. Then that row contains at least $\binom{z_h}{2}$ pairs of equal elements. The maximum of $\sum_{h=1}^{R} x_h$ subject to $\sum_{h=1}^{R}\binom{z_h}{2} \leq \binom{N}{2}R/M$ occurs when each z_h is equal to z where $\binom{z}{2} = \binom{N}{2}/M$, namely

$$z = \frac{1}{2} + \sqrt{\frac{1}{4} + \frac{N(N-1)}{M}} < 1 + \sqrt{\frac{N(N-1)}{M}}.$$

75. (a) Obviously true, even if $h_2, \ldots, h_l$ are identically zero. (b) True, by the answer to 72(b). (c) True. The result is clear if K, K', and K'' all differ in some character position. Otherwise, say $x_j = x'_j \neq x''_j$ and $x_k \neq x'_k = x''_k$. Then the quantities $h_j(x_j) + h_k(x_k)$, $h_j(x_j) + h_k(x'_k)$, and $h_j(x''_j) + h_k(x'_k)$ are independent of each other, uniformly distributed, and independent of the other $l - 2$ characters of the keys. (d) False. Consider, for example, the case $M = l = 2$ with 1-bit characters. Then all four keys hash to the same location with probability $1/4$.

76. Use $h(K) = \bigl(h_0(l) + h_1(x_1) + \cdots + h_l(x_l)\bigr) \bmod M$, where each h_j is chosen as in exercise 73. Generate the random coefficients for h_j (and, if desired, precompute its array of values) when a key of length $\geq j$ occurs for the first time. Since l is unbounded, the matrix H is infinite; but only a finite portion is relevant in any particular run of the program.

77. Let $p \leq 2^{-16}$ be the probability that two 32-bit keys have the same image under H. The worst case occurs when two given keys agree in seven of their eight 32-bit subkeys; then the probability of collision is $1 - (1-p)^4 < 4p$. [See Wegman and Carter, *J. Comp. Syst. Sci.* **22** (1981), 265–279.]

SECTION 6.5

1. The path described in the hint can be converted by changing each downward step that runs from $(i-1, j)$ to a "new record low" value $(i, j-1)$ into an upward step. If c such changes are made, the path ends at $(m, n - 2t + 2c)$, where $c \geq 0$ and $c \geq 2t - n$; hence $n - 2t + 2c \geq n - 2k$. In the permutation corresponding to the changed path, the smallest c elements of list B correspond to the downward steps that changed, and list A contains the $t - c$ elements corresponding to downward steps that didn't change.

When $t = k$ it is not difficult to see that the construction is reversible; hence exactly $\binom{n}{k}$ permutations are constructed. Incidentally, according to this proof, the contents of lists A and C may appear in arbitrary order.

Notes: We have counted these paths in another way in exercise 2.2.1–4. When $k = \lfloor n/2 \rfloor$ this construction proves *Sperner's Lemma*, which states that it is impossible to have more than $\binom{n}{\lfloor n/2 \rfloor}$ subsets of $\{1, 2, \ldots, n\}$ with no subset contained in another. [Emanuel Sperner, *Math. Zeitschrift* **27** (1928), 544–548.] For if we have such a collection of subsets, each of the $\binom{n}{k}$ permutations can have at most one of the subsets appearing in the initial positions, yet each subset appears in some permutation. The construction used here is a disguised form of a more general construction by which N. G. de Bruijn, C. van Ebbenhorst Tengbergen, and D. Kruyswijk [*Nieuw Archief voor Wiskunde* (2) **23** (1951), 191–193] proved the multiset generalization of Sperner's Lemma: "Let M be a multiset containing n elements (counting multiplicities). The collection of all $\lfloor n/2 \rfloor$-element submultisets of M is the largest possible collection such that no submultiset is contained in another." For example, the largest such collection when $M = \{a, a, b, b, c, c\}$ consists of the seven submultisets $\{a, a, b\}$, $\{a, a, c\}$, $\{a, b, b\}$, $\{a, b, c\}$, $\{a, c, c\}$, $\{b, b, c\}$, $\{b, c, c\}$. This would correspond to seven permutations of six attributes A_1, B_1, A_2, B_2, A_3, B_3 in which all queries involving A_i also involve B_i. Further comments appear in a paper by C. Greene and D. J. Kleitman, *J. Combinatorial Theory* **A20** (1976), 80–88.

2. Let a_{ijk} be a list of all references to records having (i, j, k) as the respective values of the three attributes, and assume that a_{011} is the shortest of the three lists $a_{011}, a_{101}, a_{110}$. Then a minimum-length list is $a_{001}a_{011}a_{111}a_{101}a_{100}a_{110}a_{111}a_{011}a_{010}$. However, if a_{011} is empty and so is either of a_{001}, a_{010}, or a_{100}, the length can be shortened by deleting one of the two occurrences of a_{111} [*CACM* **15** (1972), 802–808].

3. (a) Anise seed and/or honey, possibly in combination with nutmeg and/or vanilla extract. (b) None.

4. Let p_t be the probability that the query involves exactly t bit positions, and let P_t be the probability that t given positions are all 1 in a random record. Then the answer is $\sum_t p_t P_t$, minus the probability that a particular record is a "true drop"; the latter probability is $\binom{N-q}{r-q} / \binom{N}{r}$, where $N = \binom{n}{k}$. By the principle of inclusion and exclusion,

$$P_t = \sum_{j \geq 0} (-1)^j \binom{t}{j} f(n-j, k, r)/f(n, k, r),$$

where $f(n, k, r)$ is the number of possible choices of r distinct k-bit attribute codes in an n-bit field, namely

$$f(n, k, r) = \binom{\binom{n}{k}}{r}.$$

And If $q = r$ we have, by exercise 1.3.3–26,

$$p_t = \sum_{l \geq 0} (-1)^l \binom{t+l}{t} \binom{n}{t+l} P_{t+l} = \binom{n}{t} \sum_{j \geq 0} (-1)^j \binom{t}{j} f(t-j, k, q)/f(n, k, q).$$

Notes: The calculations above were first carried out, in more general form, by G. Orosz and L. Takács, *J. of Documentation* **12** (1956), 231–234. The mean $\sum tp_t$ is easily shown to be $n(1 - f(n-1, k, q)/f(n, k, q))$. Another assumption, that the random attribute codes in records and queries are not necessarily distinct, as in the techniques of Harrison and Bloom, can be analyzed by the same method, setting $f(n, k, r) = \binom{n}{k}^r$.

When the parameters are in appropriate ranges, we have $P_t \approx (1 - e^{-kr/n})^t$ and $\sum p_t P_t \approx P_{n(1-\exp(-kq/n))}$.

6. $L(t) = \sum_j \binom{m_1}{j}\binom{m_2}{t-j} L_1(j) L_2(t-j) / \binom{m_1+m_2}{t}$. [Hence if $L_1(t) \approx N_1 \alpha^{-t}$ and $L_2(t) \approx N_2 \alpha^{-t}$, then $L(t) \approx N_1 N_2 \alpha^{-t}$.]

7. (a) $L(1) = 3$, $L(2) = 1\frac{3}{4}$. (b) $L(1) = 3\frac{3}{4}$, $L(2) = 2\frac{1}{3}$, $L(3) = 1\frac{9}{16}$. [*Note:* A trivial projection mapping such as $00** \to 0$, $01** \to 1$, $10** \to 2$, $11** \to 3$, has a worse worst-case behavior; but it has a better average case, because of the exercise that follows: $L(1) = 3$, $L(2) = 2\frac{1}{6}$, $L(3) = 1\frac{1}{2}$.]

8. (a) When $S = S_0 0 \cup S_1 1$, we have $f_t(S) = f_t(S_0 \cup S_1) + f_{t-1}(S_0) + f_{t-1}(S_1)$. Therefore $f_t(s, m)$ is the minimum of $f_t(s_0, m-1) + f_{t-1}(s_0, m-1) + f_{t-1}(s_1, m-1)$ over all s_0 and s_1 such that $2^{m-1} \geq s_0 \geq s_1 \geq 0$ and $s_0 + s_1 = s$. To prove that the minimum occurs for $s_0 = \lceil s/2 \rceil$ and $s_1 = \lfloor s/2 \rfloor$, we can use induction on m, the result being clear for $m = 1$: Given $m \geq 2$, let $g_t(s) = f_t(s, m-1)$ and $h_t(s) = f_t(s, m-2)$. Then, by induction, $g_t(s_0) + g_{t-1}(s_0) + g_{t-1}(s_1) = h_t(\lceil s_0/2 \rceil) + h_{t-1}(\lceil s_0/2 \rceil) + h_{t-1}(\lfloor s_0/2 \rfloor) + h_{t-1}(\lceil s_0/2 \rceil) + h_{t-2}(\lceil s_0/2 \rceil) + h_{t-2}(\lfloor s_0/2 \rfloor) + h_{t-1}(\lceil s_1/2 \rceil) + h_{t-2}(\lceil s_1/2 \rceil) + h_{t-2}(\lfloor s_1/2 \rfloor)$, which is $\geq g_t(\lceil s_0/2 \rceil + \lceil s_1/2 \rceil) + g_{t-1}(\lceil s_0/2 \rceil + \lceil s_1/2 \rceil) + g_{t-1}(\lfloor s_0/2 \rfloor + \lfloor s_1/2 \rfloor)$. And if $s_0 > s_1 + 1$, we have $\lceil s_0/2 \rceil + \lceil s_1/2 \rceil < s_0$, except in the case $s_0 = 2k+1$ and $s_1 = 2k-1$. In the latter case, however, $g_t(s_0) + g_{t-1}(s_0) + g_{t-1}(s_1) \geq h_t(2k+1) + 2h_{t-1}(2k) \geq h_t(2k) + 2h_{t-1}(2k)$.

(b) Observe that the set S containing the numbers $0, 1, \ldots, s-1$ in binary notation has the property that $S_0 \cup S_1 = S_0$, and S_0 contains $\lceil s_0/2 \rceil$ elements. It follows, incidentally, that $f_t(2^{m-n}, m) = [z^t] (1+z)^n (1+2z)^{m-n}$.

10. (a) There must be $\frac{1}{6}v(v-1)$ triples, and x_v must occur in $\frac{1}{2}v$ of them. (b) Since v is odd, there is a unique triple $\{x_i, y_j, z\}$ for each i, and so S' is readily shown to be a Steiner triple system. The pairs missing in K' are $\{z, x_2\}$, $\{x_2, y_2\}$, $\{y_2, x_3\}$, $\{x_3, y_3\}$, $\ldots$, $\{x_{v-1}, y_{v-1}\}$, $\{y_{v-1}, x_v\}$, $\{x_v, z\}$. (d) Starting with the case $v = 1$ and applying the operations $v \to 2v - 2$, $v \to 2v + 1$ yields all nonnegative numbers not of the form $3k + 2$, because the cases $6k + (0, 1, 3, 4)$ come respectively from the smaller cases $3k + (1, 0, 1, 3)$.

Incidentally, "Steiner triple systems" should not have been named after Steiner, although that name has become deeply entrenched in the literature. Steiner's publication [*Crelle* **45** (1853), 181–182] came several years after Kirkman's, and Felix Klein has noted [*Vorlesungen über die Entwicklung der Math. im 19. Jahrhundert* **1** (Springer, 1926), 128] that Steiner quoted English authors without giving them credit, during the later years of his life. Moreover, the concept had appeared already in two well-known books of J. Plücker [*System der analytischen Geometrie* (1835), 283–284; *Theorie der algebraischen Curven* (1839), 245–247].

11. Take a Steiner triple system on $2v+1$ objects. Call one of the objects z and name the other objects in such a way that the triples containing z are $\{z, x_i, \bar{x}_i\}$; delete these triples.

12. $\{k, (k+1) \bmod 14, (k+4) \bmod 14, (k+6) \bmod 14\}$, for $0 \leq k < 14$, where $(k+7) \bmod 14$ is the complement of k. [Complemented systems are a special case of *group divisible block designs*; see Bose, Shrikhande, and Bhattacharya, *Ann. Math. Statistics* **24** (1953), 167–195.]

14. Deletion is easiest in k-d trees (a replacement for the root can be found in about $O(N^{1-1/k})$ steps). In quadtrees, deletion seems to require rebuilding the entire subtree rooted at the node being removed (but this subtree contains only about $\log N$ nodes on the average). In post-office trees, deletion is almost hopeless.

16. Let each triple correspond to a codeword, where each codeword has exactly three 1 bits, identifying the elements of the corresponding triple. If u, v, w are distinct codewords, u has at most two 1 bits in common with the superposition of v and w, since it had at most one in common with v or w alone. [Similarly, from quadruple systems of order v we can construct $v(v-1)/12$ codewords, none of which is contained in the superposition of any three others, etc.]

17. (a) Let $c_0 = b_0$ and, for $1 \le k \le n$, let $c_k = $ (if $b_{k-1} = 0$ then $*$ else b_k), $c_{-k} = $ (if $b_{k-1} = 1$ then $*$ else b_k). Then the basic query $c_{-n} \ldots c_0 \ldots c_n$ describes the contents of bucket $b_0 \ldots b_n$. [Consequently this scheme is a special case of combinatorial hashing, and its average query time matches the lower bound in exercise 8(b).]

(b) Let $d_k = $ [bit k is specified], for $-n \le k \le n$. We can assume that $d_{-k} \le d_k$ for $1 \le k \le n$. Then the maximum number of buckets examined occurs when the specified bits are all 0, and it may be computed as follows: Set $x \leftarrow y \leftarrow 1$. Then for $k = n, n-1, \ldots, 0$, set $(x, y) \leftarrow (x, y) M_{d_{-k}+d_k}$, where

$$ M_0 = \begin{pmatrix} 1 & 1 \\ 1 & 1 \end{pmatrix}, \qquad M_1 = \begin{pmatrix} 1 & 1 \\ 1 & 0 \end{pmatrix}, \qquad M_2 = \begin{pmatrix} 1 & 1 \\ 0 & 0 \end{pmatrix}. $$

Finally, output x (which also happens to equal y, after $k = 0$).

Say that $(x, y) \succeq (x', y')$ if $x \ge x'$ and $x + y \ge x' + y'$. Then if $(x, y) \succeq (x', y')$ we have $(x, y) M_d \succeq (x', y') M_d$ for $d = 0, 1, 2$. Now

$$ (x, y) M_2 M_1^j M_0 = (F_{j+3} x, F_{j+3} x), $$
$$ (x, y) M_1 M_1^j M_1 = (F_{j+3} x + F_{j+2} y, F_{j+2} x + F_{j+1} y), $$
$$ (x, y) M_0 M_1^j M_2 = (F_{j+2} x + F_{j+2} y, F_{j+2} x + F_{j+2} y); $$

therefore we have $(x, y) M_1 M_1^j M_1 \succeq (x, y) M_2 M_1^j M_0$, because $2y \ge x$; and similarly $(x, y) M_1 M_1^j M_1 \succeq (x, y) M_0 M_1^j M_2$, because $x \ge y$. It follows that the worst case occurs when either $d_{-k} + d_k \le 1$ for $1 \le k \le n$ or $d_{-k} + d_k \ge 1$ for $1 \le k \le n$. We also have

$$ (x, y) M_0 M_1^j = (F_{j+2} x + F_{j+2} y, F_{j+1} x + F_{j+1} y), $$
$$ (x, y) M_1^j M_0 = (F_{j+2} x + F_{j+1} y, F_{j+2} x + F_{j+1} y); $$
$$ (x, y) M_2 M_1^j = (F_{j+2} x, F_{j+1} x), $$
$$ (x, y) M_1^j M_2 = (F_{j+1} x + F_j y, F_{j+1} x + F_j y). $$

Consequently the worst case requires the following number of buckets:

$$ 2^{n-t} F_{t+3}, \qquad \text{if } 0 \le t \le n \qquad \text{[from } M_1^t M_0^{n+1-t}\text{]}; $$
$$ 2^{t-n} F_{3n-2t+3}, \ \text{if } n \le t \le \lceil 3n/2 \rceil \quad \text{[from } M_1^{3n-2t} (M_1 M_2)^{t-n} M_0\text{]}; $$
$$ 2^{2n+1-t}, \qquad \text{if } \lceil 3n/2 \rceil \le t \le 2n \quad \text{[from } M_2^{2t-3n} (M_1 M_2)^{2n-t} M_0\text{]}. $$

[These results are essentially due to W. A. Burkhard, *BIT* **16** (1976), 13–31, generalized in *J. Comp. Syst. Sci.* **15** (1977), 280–299; but Burkhard's more complicated mapping from $a_0 \ldots a_{2n}$ to $b_0 \ldots b_n$ has been simplified here as suggested by P. Dubost and J.-M. Trousse, Report STAN-CS-75-511 (Stanford Univ., 1975).]

18. (a) There are $2^n (m-n)$ $*$'s altogether, hence $2^n n$ digits, with $2^n n/m$ digits in each column. Half of the digits in each column must be 0. Hence $2^{n-1} n/m$ is an integer, and each column contains $(2^{n-1}n/m)^2$ mismatches. Since each pair of rows has at least one mismatch, we must have $2^n(2^n - 1)/2 \le (2^{n-1}n/m)^2 m$.

(b) Consider the 2^n m-bit numbers that are 0 in $m - n$ specified columns. Half of these have odd parity. A row with $*$ in any of the unspecified columns covers as many evens as odds.

(c) $*000$, $*111$, $0*10$, $1*10$, $00*1$, $10*1$, $010*$, $110*$. This one isn't as uniform as (13), because a query like $*01*$ hits four rows while $*10*$ hits only two. Notice that (13) has cyclic symmetry.

(d) Generate 4^3 rows from each row of (13) by replacing each $*$ by $****$, each 0 by any one of the first four rows, and each 1 by any one of the last four rows. (A similar construction makes an $\mathrm{ABD}(mm', nn')$ from any $\mathrm{ABD}(m,n)$ and $\mathrm{ABD}(m',n')$.)

(e) Given an $\mathrm{ABD}(16,9)$, we can encircle one $*$ in each row in such a way that there are equally many circles in each column. Then we can split each row into two rows, with the circled element replaced by 0 and 1. To show that such encirclement is possible, note that the asterisks of each column can be arbitrarily divided into 32 groups of 7 each; then the 512 rows each contain asterisks of 7 different groups, and the $32 \times 8 = 512$ groups each appear in 7 different rows. Theorem 7.5.1E (the "marriage theorem") now guarantees the existence of a perfect matching with exactly one circled element in each row and each group.

References: R. L. Rivest, *SICOMP* **5** (1976), 19–50; A. E. Brouwer, *Combinatorics*, edited by Hajnal and Sós, *Colloq. Math. Soc. János Bolyai* **18** (1978), 173–184. Brouwer went on to prove that an $\mathrm{ABD}(2n,n)$ exists for all $n \ge 32$. The method of part (d) also yields on $\mathrm{ABD}(32,15)$ when (13) is combined with (15).

19. By exercise 8, the average number with $8 - k$ specified bits is $2^{k-3}f_{8-k}(8,8)/\binom{8}{k}$, which has the respective values $(32, 22, \frac{104}{7}, \frac{69}{7}, \frac{45}{7}, \frac{33}{8}, \frac{73}{28}, \frac{13}{8}, 1) \approx (32, 22, 14.9, 9.9, 6.4, 4.1, 2.6, 1.6, 1)$ for $8 \ge k \ge 0$. These are only slightly higher than the values of $32^{k/8} \approx (32, 20.7, 13.5, 8.7, 5.7, 3.7, 2.4, 1.5, 1)$. The worst-case numbers are $(32, 22, 18, 15, 11, 8, 4, 2, 1)$.

20. J. A. La Poutré [*Disc. Math.* **58** (1986), 205–208] showed that an $\mathrm{ABD}(m,n)$ cannot exist when $m > \binom{n}{2}$ and $n > 3$; therefore no $\mathrm{ABD}(16,6)$ exists. La Poutré and van Lint [*Util. Math.* **31** (1987), 219–225] proved that there is no $\mathrm{ABD}(10,5)$. We get an $\mathrm{ABD}(8,6)$ from an $\mathrm{ABD}(8,5)$ or $\mathrm{ABD}(4,3)$ using the methods of exercise 18; this produces several nonisomorphic solutions, and additional examples of $\mathrm{ABD}(8,6)$ might also exist. The only remaining possibilities (besides the trivial $\mathrm{ABD}(5,5)$ and $\mathrm{ABD}(6,6)$) are $\mathrm{ABD}(8,5)$ distinct from (15), and perhaps one or more $\mathrm{ABD}(12,6)$.

> *All right—I'm glad we found it out detective fashion;*
> *I wouldn't give shucks for any other way.*
> — TOM SAWYER (1884)

APPENDIX A

TABLES OF NUMERICAL QUANTITIES

Table 1
QUANTITIES THAT ARE FREQUENTLY USED IN STANDARD SUBROUTINES
AND IN ANALYSIS OF COMPUTER PROGRAMS (40 DECIMAL PLACES)

$$\sqrt{2} = 1.41421\ 35623\ 73095\ 04880\ 16887\ 24209\ 69807\ 85697-$$
$$\sqrt{3} = 1.73205\ 08075\ 68877\ 29352\ 74463\ 41505\ 87236\ 69428+$$
$$\sqrt{5} = 2.23606\ 79774\ 99789\ 69640\ 91736\ 68731\ 27623\ 54406+$$
$$\sqrt{10} = 3.16227\ 76601\ 68379\ 33199\ 88935\ 44432\ 71853\ 37196-$$
$$\sqrt[3]{2} = 1.25992\ 10498\ 94873\ 16476\ 72106\ 07278\ 22835\ 05703-$$
$$\sqrt[3]{3} = 1.44224\ 95703\ 07408\ 38232\ 16383\ 10780\ 10958\ 83919-$$
$$\sqrt[4]{2} = 1.18920\ 71150\ 02721\ 06671\ 74999\ 70560\ 47591\ 52930-$$
$$\ln 2 = 0.69314\ 71805\ 59945\ 30941\ 72321\ 21458\ 17656\ 80755+$$
$$\ln 3 = 1.09861\ 22886\ 68109\ 69139\ 52452\ 36922\ 52570\ 46475-$$
$$\ln 10 = 2.30258\ 50929\ 94045\ 68401\ 79914\ 54684\ 36420\ 76011+$$
$$1/\ln 2 = 1.44269\ 50408\ 88963\ 40735\ 99246\ 81001\ 89213\ 74266+$$
$$1/\ln 10 = 0.43429\ 44819\ 03251\ 82765\ 11289\ 18916\ 60508\ 22944-$$
$$\pi = 3.14159\ 26535\ 89793\ 23846\ 26433\ 83279\ 50288\ 41972-$$
$$1° = \pi/180 = 0.01745\ 32925\ 19943\ 29576\ 92369\ 07684\ 88612\ 71344+$$
$$1/\pi = 0.31830\ 98861\ 83790\ 67153\ 77675\ 26745\ 02872\ 40689+$$
$$\pi^2 = 9.86960\ 44010\ 89358\ 61883\ 44909\ 99876\ 15113\ 53137-$$
$$\sqrt{\pi} = \Gamma(1/2) = 1.77245\ 38509\ 05516\ 02729\ 81674\ 83341\ 14518\ 27975+$$
$$\Gamma(1/3) = 2.67893\ 85347\ 07747\ 63365\ 56929\ 40974\ 67764\ 41287-$$
$$\Gamma(2/3) = 1.35411\ 79394\ 26400\ 41694\ 52880\ 28154\ 51378\ 55193+$$
$$e = 2.71828\ 18284\ 59045\ 23536\ 02874\ 71352\ 66249\ 77572+$$
$$1/e = 0.36787\ 94411\ 71442\ 32159\ 55237\ 70161\ 46086\ 74458+$$
$$e^2 = 7.38905\ 60989\ 30650\ 22723\ 04274\ 60575\ 00781\ 31803+$$
$$\gamma = 0.57721\ 56649\ 01532\ 86060\ 65120\ 90082\ 40243\ 10422-$$
$$\ln \pi = 1.14472\ 98858\ 49400\ 17414\ 34273\ 51353\ 05871\ 16473-$$
$$\phi = 1.61803\ 39887\ 49894\ 84820\ 45868\ 34365\ 63811\ 77203+$$
$$e^\gamma = 1.78107\ 24179\ 90197\ 98523\ 65041\ 03107\ 17954\ 91696+$$
$$e^{\pi/4} = 2.19328\ 00507\ 38015\ 45655\ 97696\ 59278\ 73822\ 34616+$$
$$\sin 1 = 0.84147\ 09848\ 07896\ 50665\ 25023\ 21630\ 29899\ 96226-$$
$$\cos 1 = 0.54030\ 23058\ 68139\ 71740\ 09366\ 07442\ 97660\ 37323+$$
$$-\zeta'(2) = 0.93754\ 82543\ 15843\ 75370\ 25740\ 94567\ 86497\ 78979-$$
$$\zeta(3) = 1.20205\ 69031\ 59594\ 28539\ 97381\ 61511\ 44999\ 07650-$$
$$\ln \phi = 0.48121\ 18250\ 59603\ 44749\ 77589\ 13424\ 36842\ 31352-$$
$$1/\ln \phi = 2.07808\ 69212\ 35027\ 53760\ 13226\ 06117\ 79576\ 77422-$$
$$-\ln \ln 2 = 0.36651\ 29205\ 81664\ 32701\ 24391\ 58232\ 66946\ 94543-$$

Table 2

QUANTITIES THAT ARE FREQUENTLY USED IN STANDARD SUBROUTINES
AND IN ANALYSIS OF COMPUTER PROGRAMS (45 OCTAL PLACES)

The names at the left of the "=" signs are given in decimal notation.

$0.1 =$	$0.06314\ 63146\ 31463\ 14631\ 46314\ 63146\ 31463\ 14631\ 46315-$
$0.01 =$	$0.00507\ 53412\ 17270\ 24365\ 60507\ 53412\ 17270\ 24365\ 60510-$
$0.001 =$	$0.00040\ 61115\ 64570\ 65176\ 76355\ 44264\ 16254\ 02030\ 44672+$
$0.0001 =$	$0.00003\ 21556\ 13530\ 70414\ 54512\ 75170\ 33021\ 15002\ 35223-$
$0.00001 =$	$0.00000\ 24761\ 32610\ 70664\ 36041\ 06077\ 17401\ 56063\ 34417-$
$0.000001 =$	$0.00000\ 02061\ 57364\ 05536\ 66151\ 55323\ 07746\ 44470\ 26033+$
$0.0000001 =$	$0.00000\ 00153\ 27745\ 15274\ 53644\ 12741\ 72312\ 20354\ 02151+$
$0.00000001 =$	$0.00000\ 00012\ 57143\ 56106\ 04303\ 47374\ 77341\ 01512\ 63327+$
$0.000000001 =$	$0.00000\ 00001\ 04560\ 27640\ 46655\ 12262\ 71426\ 40124\ 21742+$
$0.0000000001 =$	$0.00000\ 00000\ 06676\ 33766\ 35367\ 55653\ 37265\ 34642\ 01627-$
$\sqrt{2} =$	$1.32404\ 74631\ 77167\ 46220\ 42627\ 66115\ 46725\ 12575\ 17435+$
$\sqrt{3} =$	$1.56663\ 65641\ 30231\ 25163\ 54453\ 50265\ 60361\ 34073\ 42223-$
$\sqrt{5} =$	$2.17067\ 36334\ 57722\ 47602\ 57471\ 63003\ 00563\ 55620\ 32021-$
$\sqrt{10} =$	$3.12305\ 40726\ 64555\ 22444\ 02242\ 57101\ 41466\ 33775\ 22532+$
$\sqrt[3]{2} =$	$1.20505\ 05746\ 15345\ 05342\ 10756\ 65334\ 25574\ 22415\ 03024+$
$\sqrt[3]{3} =$	$1.34233\ 50444\ 22175\ 73134\ 67363\ 76133\ 05334\ 31147\ 60121-$
$\sqrt[4]{2} =$	$1.14067\ 74050\ 61556\ 12455\ 72152\ 64430\ 60271\ 02755\ 73136+$
$\ln 2 =$	$0.54271\ 02775\ 75071\ 73632\ 57117\ 07316\ 30007\ 71366\ 53640+$
$\ln 3 =$	$1.06237\ 24752\ 55006\ 05227\ 32440\ 63065\ 25012\ 35574\ 55337+$
$\ln 10 =$	$2.23273\ 06735\ 52524\ 25405\ 56512\ 66542\ 56026\ 46050\ 50705+$
$1/\ln 2 =$	$1.34252\ 16624\ 53405\ 77027\ 35750\ 37766\ 40644\ 35175\ 04353+$
$1/\ln 10 =$	$0.33626\ 75425\ 11562\ 41614\ 52325\ 33525\ 27655\ 14756\ 06220-$
$\pi =$	$3.11037\ 55242\ 10264\ 30215\ 14230\ 63050\ 56006\ 70163\ 21122+$
$1° = \pi/180 =$	$0.01073\ 72152\ 11224\ 72344\ 25603\ 54276\ 63351\ 22056\ 11544+$
$1/\pi =$	$0.24276\ 30155\ 62344\ 20251\ 23760\ 47257\ 50765\ 15156\ 70067-$
$\pi^2 =$	$11.67517\ 14467\ 62135\ 71322\ 25561\ 15466\ 30021\ 40654\ 34103-$
$\sqrt{\pi} = \Gamma(1/2) =$	$1.61337\ 61106\ 64736\ 65247\ 47035\ 40510\ 15273\ 34470\ 17762-$
$\Gamma(1/3) =$	$2.53347\ 35234\ 51013\ 61316\ 73106\ 47644\ 54653\ 00106\ 66046-$
$\Gamma(2/3) =$	$1.26523\ 57112\ 14154\ 74312\ 54572\ 37655\ 60126\ 23231\ 02452+$
$e =$	$2.55760\ 52130\ 50535\ 51246\ 52773\ 42542\ 00471\ 72363\ 61661+$
$1/e =$	$0.27426\ 53066\ 13167\ 46761\ 52726\ 75436\ 02440\ 52371\ 03355+$
$e^2 =$	$7.30714\ 45615\ 23355\ 33460\ 63507\ 35040\ 32664\ 25356\ 50217+$
$\gamma =$	$0.44742\ 14770\ 67666\ 06172\ 23215\ 74376\ 01002\ 51313\ 25521-$
$\ln \pi =$	$1.11206\ 40443\ 47503\ 36413\ 65374\ 52661\ 52410\ 37511\ 46057+$
$\phi =$	$1.47433\ 57156\ 27751\ 23701\ 27634\ 71401\ 40271\ 66710\ 15010+$
$e^\gamma =$	$1.61772\ 13452\ 61152\ 65761\ 22477\ 36553\ 53327\ 17554\ 21260+$
$e^{\pi/4} =$	$2.14275\ 31512\ 16162\ 52370\ 35530\ 11342\ 53525\ 44307\ 02171-$
$\sin 1 =$	$0.65665\ 24436\ 04414\ 73402\ 03067\ 23644\ 11612\ 07474\ 14505-$
$\cos 1 =$	$0.42450\ 50037\ 32406\ 42711\ 07022\ 14666\ 27320\ 70675\ 12321+$
$-\zeta'(2) =$	$0.74001\ 45144\ 53253\ 42362\ 42107\ 23350\ 50074\ 46100\ 27706+$
$\zeta(3) =$	$1.14735\ 00023\ 60014\ 20470\ 15613\ 42561\ 31715\ 10177\ 06614+$
$\ln \phi =$	$0.36630\ 26256\ 61213\ 01145\ 13700\ 41004\ 52264\ 30700\ 40646+$
$1/\ln \phi =$	$2.04776\ 60111\ 17144\ 41512\ 11436\ 16575\ 00355\ 43630\ 40651+$
$-\ln\ln 2 =$	$0.27351\ 71233\ 67265\ 63650\ 17401\ 56637\ 26334\ 31455\ 57005-$

Several interesting constants without common names have arisen in connection with the analyses of sorting and searching algorithms. These constants have been evaluated to 40 decimal places in Eqs. 5.2.3–(19) and 6.5–(6), and in the answers to exercises 5.2.3–27, 5.2.4–13, 5.2.4–23, 6.2.2–49, 6.2.3–7, 6.2.3–8, 6.3–26, and 6.3–27.

Table 3

VALUES OF HARMONIC NUMBERS, BERNOULLI NUMBERS,
AND FIBONACCI NUMBERS, FOR SMALL VALUES OF n

n	H_n	B_n	F_n	n
0	0	1	0	0
1	1	$-1/2$	1	1
2	3/2	1/6	1	2
3	11/6	0	2	3
4	25/12	$-1/30$	3	4
5	137/60	0	5	5
6	49/20	1/42	8	6
7	363/140	0	13	7
8	761/280	$-1/30$	21	8
9	7129/2520	0	34	9
10	7381/2520	5/66	55	10
11	83711/27720	0	89	11
12	86021/27720	$-691/2730$	144	12
13	1145993/360360	0	233	13
14	1171733/360360	7/6	377	14
15	1195757/360360	0	610	15
16	2436559/720720	$-3617/510$	987	16
17	42142223/12252240	0	1597	17
18	14274301/4084080	43867/798	2584	18
19	275295799/77597520	0	4181	19
20	55835135/15519504	$-174611/330$	6765	20
21	18858053/5173168	0	10946	21
22	19093197/5173168	854513/138	17711	22
23	444316699/118982864	0	28657	23
24	1347822955/356948592	$-236364091/2730$	46368	24
25	34052522467/8923714800	0	75025	25
26	34439742267/8923714800	8553103/6	121393	26
27	312536252003/80313433200	0	196418	27
28	315404588903/80313433200	$-23749461029/870$	317811	28
29	9227046511387/2329089562800	0	514229	29
30	9304682830147/2329089562800	8615841276005/14322	832040	30

For any x, let $H_x = \sum_{n \geq 1} \left(\dfrac{1}{n} - \dfrac{1}{n+x} \right)$. Then

$$H_{1/2} = 2 - 2\ln 2,$$

$$H_{1/3} = 3 - \tfrac{1}{2}\pi/\sqrt{3} - \tfrac{3}{2}\ln 3,$$

$$H_{2/3} = \tfrac{3}{2} + \tfrac{1}{2}\pi/\sqrt{3} - \tfrac{3}{2}\ln 3,$$

$$H_{1/4} = 4 - \tfrac{1}{2}\pi - 3\ln 2,$$

$$H_{3/4} = \tfrac{4}{3} + \tfrac{1}{2}\pi - 3\ln 2,$$

$$H_{1/5} = 5 - \tfrac{1}{2}\pi\phi^{3/2}5^{-1/4} - \tfrac{5}{4}\ln 5 - \tfrac{1}{2}\sqrt{5}\ln\phi,$$

$$H_{2/5} = \tfrac{5}{2} - \tfrac{1}{2}\pi\phi^{-3/2}5^{-1/4} - \tfrac{5}{4}\ln 5 + \tfrac{1}{2}\sqrt{5}\ln\phi,$$

$$H_{3/5} = \tfrac{5}{3} + \tfrac{1}{2}\pi\phi^{-3/2}5^{-1/4} - \tfrac{5}{4}\ln 5 + \tfrac{1}{2}\sqrt{5}\ln\phi,$$

$$H_{4/5} = \tfrac{5}{4} + \tfrac{1}{2}\pi\phi^{3/2}5^{-1/4} - \tfrac{5}{4}\ln 5 - \tfrac{1}{2}\sqrt{5}\ln\phi,$$

$$H_{1/6} = 6 - \tfrac{1}{2}\pi\sqrt{3} - 2\ln 2 - \tfrac{3}{2}\ln 3,$$

$$H_{5/6} = \tfrac{6}{5} + \tfrac{1}{2}\pi\sqrt{3} - 2\ln 2 - \tfrac{3}{2}\ln 3,$$

and, in general, when $0 < p < q$ (see exercise 1.2.9–19),

$$H_{p/q} = \frac{q}{p} - \frac{\pi}{2}\cot\frac{p}{q}\pi - \ln 2q + 2 \sum_{1 \leq n < q/2} \cos\frac{2pn}{q}\pi \cdot \ln\sin\frac{n}{q}\pi.$$

INDEX TO NOTATIONS

In the following formulas, letters that are not further qualified have the following significance:

j, k	integer-valued arithmetic expression
m, n	nonnegative integer-valued arithmetic expression
x, y	real-valued arithmetic expression
z	complex-valued arithmetic expression
f	real-valued or complex-valued function
P	pointer-valued expression (either Λ or a computer address)
S, T	set or multiset
α, β	strings of symbols

Formal symbolism	Meaning	Where defined
$V \leftarrow E$	give variable V the value of expression E	1.1
$U \leftrightarrow V$	interchange the values of variables U and V	1.1
A_n or $A[n]$	the nth element of linear array A	1.1
A_{mn} or $A[m, n]$	the element in row m and column n of rectangular array A	1.1
NODE(P)	the node (group of variables that are individually distinguished by their field names) whose address is P, assuming that $P \neq \Lambda$	2.1
F(P)	the variable in NODE(P) whose field name is F	2.1
CONTENTS(P)	contents of computer word whose address is P	2.1
LOC(V)	address of variable V within a computer	2.1
P $\Leftarrow$ AVAIL	set the value of pointer variable P to the address of a new node	2.2.3
AVAIL $\Leftarrow$ P	return NODE(P) to free storage; all its fields lose their identity	2.2.3
top(S)	node at the top of a nonempty stack S	2.2.1
$X \Leftarrow S$	pop up S to X: set $X \leftarrow$ top(S); then delete top(S) from nonempty stack S	2.2.1
$S \Leftarrow X$	push down X onto S: insert the value X as a new entry on top of stack S	2.2.1

Formal symbolism	Meaning	Where defined
$(B \Rightarrow E;\ E')$	conditional expression: denotes E if B is true, E' if B is false	
$[B]$	characteristic function of condition B: $$(B \Rightarrow 1;\ 0)$$	1.2.3
δ_{kj}	Kronecker delta: $[j = k]$	1.2.6
$[z^n]\, g(z)$	coefficient of z^n in power series $g(z)$	1.2.9
$\displaystyle\sum_{R(k)} f(k)$	sum of all $f(k)$ such that the variable k is an integer and relation $R(k)$ is true	1.2.3
$\displaystyle\prod_{R(k)} f(k)$	product of all $f(k)$ such that the variable k is an integer and relation $R(k)$ is true	1.2.3
$\displaystyle\min_{R(k)} f(k)$	minimum value of all $f(k)$ such that the variable k is an integer and relation $R(k)$ is true	1.2.3
$\displaystyle\max_{R(k)} f(k)$	maximum value of all $f(k)$ such that the variable k is an integer and relation $R(k)$ is true	1.2.3
$j \backslash k$	j divides k: $k \bmod j = 0$ and $j > 0$	1.2.4
$S \setminus T$	set difference: $\{a \mid a$ in S and a not in $T\}$	
$\gcd(j, k)$	greatest common divisor of j and k: $$\left(j = k = 0 \Rightarrow 0;\ \max_{d \backslash j,\, d \backslash k} d\right)$$	1.1
$j \perp k$	j is relatively prime to k: $\gcd(j, k) = 1$	1.2.4
A^T	transpose of rectangular array A: $$A^T[j, k] = A[k, j]$$	1.2.3
α^R	left-right reversal of α	
x^y	x to the y power (when x is positive)	1.2.2
x^k	x to the kth power: $$\left(k \geq 0 \Rightarrow \prod_{0 \leq j < k} x;\ 1/x^{-k}\right)$$	1.2.2
$x^{\bar{k}}$	x to the k rising: $\Gamma(x + k)/\Gamma(x) =$ $$\left(k \geq 0 \Rightarrow \prod_{0 \leq j < k} (x + j);\ 1/(x + k)^{\overline{-k}}\right)$$	1.2.5
$x^{\underline{k}}$	x to the k falling: $x!/(x - k)! =$ $$\left(k \geq 0 \Rightarrow \prod_{0 \leq j < k} (x - j);\ 1/(x - k)^{\underline{-k}}\right)$$	1.2.5

Formal symbolism	Meaning	Where defined
$n!$	n factorial: $\Gamma(n+1) = n^{\underline{n}}$	1.2.5
$\binom{x}{k}$	binomial coefficient: $(k < 0 \Rightarrow 0;\ x^{\underline{k}}/k!)$	1.2.6
$\binom{n}{n_1, n_2, \ldots, n_m}$	multinomial coefficient (defined only when $n = n_1 + n_2 + \cdots + n_m$)	1.2.6
$\left[\begin{matrix} n \\ m \end{matrix}\right]$	Stirling number of the first kind: $$\sum_{0 < k_1 < k_2 < \cdots < k_{n-m} < n} k_1 k_2 \ldots k_{n-m}$$	1.2.6
$\left\{\begin{matrix} n \\ m \end{matrix}\right\}$	Stirling number of the second kind: $$\sum_{1 \le k_1 \le k_2 \le \cdots \le k_{n-m} \le m} k_1 k_2 \ldots k_{n-m}$$	1.2.6
$\{a \mid R(a)\}$	set of all a such that the relation $R(a)$ is true	
$\{a_1, \ldots, a_n\}$	the set or multiset $\{a_k \mid 1 \le k \le n\}$	
$\{x\}$	fractional part (used in contexts where a real value, not a set, is implied): $x - \lfloor x \rfloor$	1.2.11,2
$[a \mathrel{..} b]$	closed interval: $\{x \mid a \le x \le b\}$	1.2.2
$(a \mathrel{..} b)$	open interval: $\{x \mid a < x < b\}$	1.2.2
$[a \mathrel{..} b)$	half-open interval: $\{x \mid a \le x < b\}$	1.2.2
$(a \mathrel{..} b]$	half-closed interval: $\{x \mid a < x \le b\}$	1.2.2
$|S|$	cardinality: the number of elements in set S	
$|x|$	absolute value of x: $(x \ge 0 \Rightarrow x;\ -x)$	
$|\alpha|$	length of α	
$\lfloor x \rfloor$	floor of x, greatest integer function: $\max_{k \le x} k$	1.2.4
$\lceil x \rceil$	ceiling of x, least integer function: $\min_{k \ge x} k$	1.2.4
$x \bmod y$	mod function: $\left(y = 0 \Rightarrow x;\ x - y\lfloor x/y \rfloor\right)$	1.2.4
$x \equiv x' \pmod{y}$	relation of congruence: $x \bmod y = x' \bmod y$	1.2.4
$O\bigl(f(n)\bigr)$	big-oh of $f(n)$, as the variable $n \to \infty$	1.2.11.1
$O\bigl(f(z)\bigr)$	big-oh of $f(z)$, as the variable $z \to 0$	1.2.11.1
$\Omega\bigl(f(n)\bigr)$	big-omega of $f(n)$, as the variable $n \to \infty$	1.2.11.1
$\Theta\bigl(f(n)\bigr)$	big-theta of $f(n)$, as the variable $n \to \infty$	1.2.11.1

Formal symbolism	Meaning	Where defined
$\log_b x$	logarithm, base b, of x (when $x > 0$, $b > 0$, and $b \neq 1$): the y such that $x = b^y$	1.2.2
$\ln x$	natural logarithm: $\log_e x$	1.2.2
$\lg x$	binary logarithm: $\log_2 x$	1.2.2
$\exp x$	exponential of x: e^x	1.2.2
$\langle X_n \rangle$	the infinite sequence $X_0, X_1, X_2, \ldots$ (here the letter n is part of the symbolism)	1.2.9
$f'(x)$	derivative of f at x	1.2.9
$f''(x)$	second derivative of f at x	1.2.10
$f^{(n)}(x)$	nth derivative: $\big(n = 0 \Rightarrow f(x); \ g'(x)\big)$, where $g(x) = f^{(n-1)}(x)$	1.2.11.2
$H_n^{(x)}$	harmonic number of order x: $\sum_{1 \leq k \leq n} 1/k^x$	1.2.7
H_n	harmonic number: $H_n^{(1)}$	1.2.7
F_n	Fibonacci number: $(n \leq 1 \Rightarrow n; \ F_{n-1} + F_{n-2})$	1.2.8
B_n	Bernoulli number: $n! \, [z^n] \, z/(e^z - 1)$	1.2.11.2
$\det(A)$	determinant of square matrix A	1.2.3
$\operatorname{sign}(x)$	sign of x: $[x > 0] - [x < 0]$	
$\zeta(x)$	zeta function: $\lim_{n \to \infty} H_n^{(x)}$ (when $x > 1$)	1.2.7
$\Gamma(x)$	gamma function: $(x - 1)! = \gamma(x, \infty)$	1.2.5
$\gamma(x, y)$	incomplete gamma function: $\int_0^y e^{-t} t^{x-1} \, dt$	1.2.11.3
γ	Euler's constant: $\lim_{n \to \infty}(H_n - \ln n)$	1.2.7
e	base of natural logarithms: $\sum_{n \geq 0} 1/n!$	1.2.2
π	circle ratio: $4 \sum_{n \geq 0} (-1)^n/(2n + 1)$	
∞	infinity: larger than any number	
Λ	null link (pointer to no address)	2.1
ϵ	empty string (string of length zero)	
$\emptyset$	empty set (set with no elements)	
ϕ	golden ratio: $\frac{1}{2}\big(1 + \sqrt{5}\big)$	1.2.8
$\varphi(n)$	Euler's totient function: $\sum_{0 \leq k < n} [k \perp n]$	1.2.4
$x \approx y$	x is approximately equal to y	1.2.5

Formal symbolism	Meaning	Where defined
$\Pr\big(S(X)\big)$	probability that statement $S(X)$ is true, for random values of X	1.2.10
$\mathrm{E}\,X$	expected value of X: $\sum_x x \Pr(X = x)$	1.2.10
$\mathrm{mean}(g)$	mean value of the probability distribution represented by generating function g: $g'(1)$	1.2.10
$\mathrm{var}(g)$	variance of the probability distribution represented by generating function g: $g''(1) + g'(1) - g'(1)^2$	1.2.10
$(\min x_1, \text{ave } x_2, \max x_3, \text{dev } x_4)$	a random variable having minimum value x_1, average (expected) value x_2, maximum value x_3, standard deviation x_4	1.2.10
$\Re z$	real part of z	1.2.2
$\Im z$	imaginary part z	1.2.2
$\overline{z}$	complex conjugate: $\Re z - i \Im z$	1.2.2
$(\ldots a_1 a_0 . a_{-1} \ldots)_b$	radix-b positional notation: $\sum_k a_k b^k$	4.1
$/\!/x_1, x_2, \ldots, x_n/\!/$	continued fraction: $1/\big(x_1 + 1/(x_2 + 1/(\cdots + 1/(x_n)\ldots))\big)$	4.5.3
$\alpha \top \beta$	intercalation product	5.1.2
$S \uplus T$	multiset sum; e.g., $\{a, b\} \uplus \{a, c\} = \{a, a, b, c\}$	4.6.3
$f(x)\big|_a^b$	function growth: $f(b) - f(a)$	
▮	end of algorithm, program, or proof	1.1
␣	one blank space	1.3.1
rA	register A (accumulator) of MIX	1.3.1
rX	register X (extension) of MIX	1.3.1
rI1, ..., rI6	(index) registers I1, ..., I6 of MIX	1.3.1
rJ	(jump) register J of MIX	1.3.1
(L:R)	partial field of MIX word, $0 \le \text{L} \le \text{R} \le 5$	1.3.1
OP ADDRESS,I(F)	notation for MIX instruction	1.3.1, 1.3.2
u	unit of time in MIX	1.3.1
*	"self" in MIXAL	1.3.2
0F, 1F, 2F, ..., 9F	"forward" local symbol in MIXAL	1.3.2
0B, 1B, 2B, ..., 9B	"backward" local symbol in MIXAL	1.3.2
0H, 1H, 2H, ..., 9H	"here" local symbol in MIXAL	1.3.2

INDEX AND GLOSSARY

If you don't find it in the Index,
look very carefully through the entire catalogue.
— SEARS, ROEBUCK AND CO., *Consumers Guide* (1897)

When an index entry refers to a page containing a relevant exercise, see also the *answer* to that exercise for further information. An answer page is not indexed here unless it refers to a topic not included in the statement of the exercise.

757

Prediction, *see* Forecasting.
Preferential arrangements, 194.
Prefetching, 369–373.
Prefix, 492.
Prefix code, 452–453.
  for all nonnegative integers, 6.
Prefix search, *see* Trie search.
Preorder merge, 307–309.
Prestet, Jean, 24.
Prime numbers, 156, 516, 529, 557, 627.
Primitive comparator networks, 240, 668.
Principle of optimality, 363, 438.
Pring, Edward John, 564.
Prins, Jan Fokko, 618.
Priority deques, 157.
Priority queues, 148–152, 156–158,
    253, 646, 705.
  merging, 150, 157.
Priority search trees, 578.
Probability density functions, 177.
Probability distributions, 105, 399–401.
  beta, 586.
  binomial, 100–101, 341, 539, 555.
  fractal, 400.
  normal, 45, 69, 650.
  Pareto, 401, 405, 710.
  Poisson, 555.
  random, 458.
  uniform, 6, 16, 20, 47, 127, 606.
  Yule, 401, 405.
  Zipf, 400, 402, 435, 455.
Probability generating functions, 15–16,
    102, 104, 135, 177, 425, 490, 539,
    553, 555, 739.
Prodinger, Helmut, 576, 634, 644,
    648, 726, 726.
Product of consecutive binomial
    coefficients, 612.
Proof of algorithms, 49–51, 112–113,
    315, 323, 355, 677.
Prusker, Francis, 377.
Prywes, Noah Shmarya, 578.
Pseudolines, 670.
Psi function $\psi(z)$, 637, 751.
Puech, Claude Henri Clair Marie Jules,
    565, 566, 576.
Pugh, William Worthington, Jr., 213, 478.
Punched cards, 169–170, 175, 383–385.

q-multinomial coefficients, 32.
q-nomial coefficients, 32, 594, 595.
q-series, 20, 32, 594–596, 644.
Quadrangle inequality, 457.
Quadratic probing, 551.
Quadratic selection, 141.
Quadruple systems, 581, 746.
Quadtrees, 565–566, 581, 745–746.
Queries, 559–582.
Questionnaires, 183.

Queues, 135, 148–149, 156, 171, 299,
    310, 322–323.
Quickfind, 136.
  median-of-three, 634.
Quicksort, 113–122, 135–138, 148, 159,
    246, 349–351, 356, 381, 382, 389,
    389, 431, 698.
  binary, *see* Radix exchange.
  median-of-three, 122, 136, 138, 381, 382.
  multikey, 389, 633, 728.
  with equal keys, 136, 635–636.

Rabbits, 424.
Rabin, Michael Oser (מיכאל עוזר רבין), 242.
Radix-2 sorting, 387.
Radix exchange sort, 122–128, 130–133,
    136–138, 159, 177, 351, 382, 389,
    500–501, 509, 698.
  with equal keys, 127–128, 137.
Radix insertion sort, 176–177.
Radix list sort, 171–175, 382.
Radix sorting, 5, 169–179, 180–181,
    343–348, 351, 359, 374, 381, 385,
    389, 421, 502, 698.
  dual to merge sorting, 345–348, 359.
Radke, Charles Edwin, 297.
Räihä, Kari-Jouko, 717.
Railway switching, 168.
Rains, Eric Michael, 611.
Rais, Bonita Marie, 726.
Raman Rajeev, 634.
Raman, Venkatesh (வெங்கடேஷ்
    ராமன்), 655.
Ramanan, Prakash Viriyur (பிரகாஷ்
    விரியூர் ரமணன்), 218.
Ramanujan Iyengar, Srinivasa
    (ஸ்ரீனிவாஸ ராமானுஜன் ஐயங்கார்),
    function $Q(n)$, 701.
Ramshaw, Lyle Harold, 729.
Random data for sorting, 20, 47, 76,
    383, 391.
Random probability distribution, 458.
Random probing, independent, 548, 555.
  with secondary clustering, 548, 554.
Randomized adversary: An adversary
    that flips coins, 219.
Randomized algorithms, 121–122, 351,
    455, 517, 519, 557–558.
Randomized binary search trees, 478.
Randomized data structures, 478.
Randomized striping, 371–373, 379, 698.
Randrianarimanana, Bruno, 713.
Raney, George Neal, 297, 298.
Range queries, 559, 578.
RANK field, 471, 476, 479, 713, 718.
Ranking, 181, *see* Sorting.
Raver, Norman, 729.
Ravikumar, Balasubramanian
    (பாலசுப்ரமணியன் ரவிகுமார்), 673.
Rawlings, Don Paul, 595.

Although you may pass for an artist, computist, or analyst, yet you may not be justly esteemed a man of science.

— GEORGE BERKELEY, *The Analyst* (1734)

THIS BOOK was composed on a Sun SPARCstation with Computer Modern typefaces, using the TEX and METAFONT software as described in the author's books *Computers & Typesetting* (Reading, Mass.: Addison–Wesley, 1986), Volumes A–E. The illustrations were produced with John Hobby's METAPOST system. Some names in the index were typeset with additional fonts developed by Yannis Haralambous (Greek, Hebrew, Arabic), Olga G. Lapko (Cyrillic), Frans J. Velthuis (Devanagari), Masatoshi Watanabe (Japanese), and Linbo Zhang (Chinese).